# ABOUT THE AUTHOR

Dr. Carl Midkiff Wheeless, professor emeritus, High Point University, has devoted the past ten years to a study of the American presidents. For more than twenty-five years he served as professor of history and political science at High Point University and East Tennessee State University and as professor and academic dean at Forman Government College (Pakistan). During his early career he served as an archivist, intelligence specialist, and foreign affairs analyst for the United States government.

He received his education at Cornell College (BA), University of Tennessee (MA), and Georgetown University (PhD). He has been awarded numerous study grants, including a Fulbright fellowship for a two-year study in Turkey. His travel interest has taken him to all fifty states on multiple visits and to more than ninety foreign countries. While teaching, he conducted a series of annual academic study tours as lecturer and guide to historical sites.

For Mary and my three children
Letha, Richard, and Ann

# LANDMARKS
## *of* AMERICAN
## PRESIDENTS

*A Traveler's Guide*

# LANDMARKS
## *of* AMERICAN
## PRESIDENTS

*A Traveler's Guide*

Carl Wheeless

*Foreword by*
James R. Garfield, II

 **Gale Research**

*An ITP Information/Reference Group Company*

**Changing the Way the World Learns**

NEW YORK • LONDON • BONN • BOSTON • DETROIT
MADRID • MELBOURNE • MEXICO CITY • PARIS
SINGAPORE • TOKYO • TORONTO • WASHINGTON
ALBANY NY • BELMONT CA • CINCINNATI OH

**Gale Research Inc. Staff**

Lawrence W. Baker, *Managing Editor*
Kenneth Estell, *Developmental Editor*
Jolen Gedridge and Camille Killens, *Associate Editors*
Andrea Kovacs and Jessica Proctor, *Assistant Editors*


Mary Beth Trimper, *Production Director*
Evi Seoud, *Assistant Production Manager*


Cynthia Baldwin, *Product Design Manager*
Barbara J. Yarrow, *Graphic Services Supervisor*
Pamela A. E. Galbreath, *Cover and Page Designer*
Randy Bassett, *Image Database Supervisor*
Robert Duncan, *Scanner Operator*
Sherrell Hobbs, *Map Designer*


Benita Spight, *Data Entry Services Manager*
Gwendolyn Tucker, *Data Entry Supervisor*
Nancy Sheridan, *Data Entry Associate*

Front cover photograph: Mount Rushmore, *courtesy of Susan Edgar.* Back cover photographs: Pierce Gravesite and Lincoln Home, *courtesy of L* Baker; John F. Kennedy, *courtesy of Library of Congress.*

**Library of Congress Cataloging-in-Publication Data**

Wheeless, Carl
      Landmarks of American presidents: a traveler's guide / Carl
Wheeless.
      p. cm.
      Includes bibliographical references and index.
      ISBN 0-8103-8301-2
      1. Presidents—Homes and haunts—United States—Guidebooks.
2. United States—Guidebooks. 3. Historic sites—United States—
Guidebooks. I. Title.
E176.1.W56 1995          95-32146
973'.099—dc20    CIP

Printed in the United States of America by Gale Research Inc.
I(T)P™
The trademark ITP is used under license.

# CONTENTS

## GEOGRAPHIC GUIDE TO PRESIDENTIAL LANDMARKS

# FOREWORD

When Dr. Carl Wheeless sent to me the segment of his book *Landmarks of American Presidents: A Travelers Guide* relating to my great grandfather, my first thought was, what a wonderful idea, a non-political chronological and geographic history of those who have served in the highest office in our land.

Since retiring in 1990, I have been involved with Lawnfield, President Garfield's home in Mentor, Ohio. In addition to cutting grass, washing windows, and catching mice, I have conducted tours for young and old. To my surprise, the many questions asked of me are not about Garfield's political life but rather where he was born, how many children did he have, where he went to school, whether he liked horses, when he served as president, whether

he always lived in this house, whether he served in the Civil War, etc.

Having been born and raised on the farm where Lawnfield is located, I look forward to meeting and talking to many folks in the future, from busloads of school children to individual visitors, as Dr. Wheeless has given me material that not even I was aware of.

I know of no other publication like this, and I commend Dr. Wheeless for this incredibly accurate "from the cradle to the grave" account of our first forty-one presidents. The book will not only be interesting to the public but an invaluable resource for many years to come.

*My Heartiest Congratulations!*

*James R. Garfield, II*

# PREFACE

Since early childhood, any book, magazine, news photo, or article relative to the presidents has been like a magnet to me. The election of Herbert Hoover in 1928, whose birthplace was within an hour's drive of my home, only increased an avaricious appetite for scrapbook material and books on the presidents. From the time of my visit to Hoover's birthplace, as a nine-year-old boy in 1929, to my visit to the site of Clinton's birthplace in 1993, I have followed the presidents, spending days in libraries and archives, travelling over 40,000 miles of road, and snapping more than 4,000 photographs.

Although there are hundreds of books written about the American presidents and on the presidency, geographical information on presidential sites had not been organized into a complete and readily available source. Given this, I have spent the past ten years researching and composing this book.

Following the presidents has been a study, a hobby, a pastime, and more than anything fascinating. Far from being a tiresome exercise, finding sites connected to the presidents has been like putting together pieces of a gigantic jigsaw puzzle. Many times, after being hundreds of miles from home, it has been a disappointment to find, upon returning home, that if I had only known at the time of the existence of another presidential site in the vicinity I could have enjoyed another interesting site. On other occasions, I was particularly impressed by the reaction of local residents when I pointed out a presidential site in their vicinity and heard the response, "Well, I never knew that!"

Coverage of these forty-one chiefs of state and their combined 2,987 years spent on this earth has been a monumental task. Add to this the approximately 230 years of movement following their deaths when at least eight of the deceased were ceremoniously moved from their original resting place to a more imposing site. The number of miles covered by the presidents is in the millions.

Like others, the presidents too had their particular interests, whether historic, nature loving, or professional, and where they lived reflects this. Following the travels of a president or presidents to hundreds of geographic locations in the fifty states, the District of Columbia, and overseas can give structure to any tour of the United States or around the world; it can give an added dimension to the scenic, scientific, or cultural attractions. It is a great way to learn about American history. For me, a site comes to life when I know that a particular president sat in a particular chair at his home, in church, or in an old schoolroom.

Obviously it would be impossible to follow the movement of a president from cradle to gravefrom every lodging, visit to a friend or relative, a trip to church, or to every place of work, be it peanut hawker, newspaper carrier, and temporary clerk's job to the holding of the presidential office. There is limited coverage of the four living former presidents since they left office, most entries follow the president from birth to the day he left the White House.

Even with great effort to give accurate data, contradictory records, including accounts given by the president himself, and in other cases sketchy materials, make it highly possible that some sites may be geographically and chronologically misplaced; others may be lost forever. Buildings have been burned or demolished, street names and numbers or even town names have been changed, and some towns have disappeared altogether. Many who use this reference work may have access to details of sites and locations not known to the author. I will be grateful to receive additional information, which might be used in a revised edition.

These forty-one people became for me people I feel I have known all my life; I hope they will become the same for you. I hope the user will begin to think of each as a friend in the same way I think of Max Miller next door as a neighbor and friend. Although these men are members of an exclusive club, paradoxically one can come to know them as well as a neighbor, since one can follow them from home

to school and church, on picnics and honeymoons, and even on trips around the world.

## ARRANGEMENT

This reference work is organized into two major sections.

The first section provides access to sites by president, beginning with Washington and ending with Clinton. Within each chapter, sites are arranged by the following topics: birthplace, baptism, church, education, marriage and honeymoon, homes and lodgings, work, travel, and (where appropriate) death, funeral, and burial. With the exception of travel, the coverage of each of these topics is complete.

The second section provides access to sites by states. Within each state, sites are arranged by city; sites in the District of Columbia and New York City are arranged by location.

## ACKNOWLEDGEMENTS

The author is greatly indebted to the librarians across the country and to friends and relatives who have been ever on the lookout for facts they thought would be helpful to this book. Local people, in chance meetings, also have been invaluable in giving detailed information. Most of all, I am indebted to my wife, Mary, who spent countless hours with me on the road, going through the trials of navigation, keeping a log of photograph subjects and locations, and above all, constantly encouraging me to the completion of the study.

*Carl Midkiff Wheeless*
*October 1995*

# THE PRESIDENTS

# GEORGE WASHINGTON

1732–1799
1ST PRESIDENT 1789–1797: FEDERALIST PARTY

George Washington, "Father of His Country," was born February 22, 1732, to Augustine and Mary Ball Washington. He was the first of seven presidents to be born in Virginia. Through common ancestry he would be related to Elizabeth II, queen of England, and according to one source his lineage goes back to Henry I, king of France. He was half-first-cousin twice removed of President James Madison. However, in a time when primogeniture ruled, his future was unpromising as the third son born of a second wife.

*"Liberty, when it begins to take root, is a plant of rapid growth."*

*—Letter to James Madison, March 2, 1788*

## CHARACTERISTICS

Washington was well-built, with broad shoulders, a narrow waist, and long arms and legs. He wore a size 13 shoe. When he became president at age 57 he weighed almost 200 pounds. According to contemporaries, when measured for his coffin he was 6′3½″, making him one of the tallest U.S. presidents. He had pale skin which burned with the sun, light blue-gray eyes with heavy eyebrows, and powdered reddish-brown hair that he wore in a queue when he was young. He never wore a wig. He had a rather large mouth that he usually kept firmly closed to hide ugly teeth. Although he never had wooden false teeth, he had only one of

# A Life in Review

**Birth:** February 22, 1732; Wakefield, VA

**Died:** December 14, 1799; Mount Vernon, VA

**Married:** Martha Dandridge Custis; January 6, 1759; No children

## Career

**1748–1752** Surveyor

**1754–1763** Military service French and Indian War

**1759–1774** Member Virginia House of Burgesses

**1774–1775** Member Continental Congress

**1775–1783** Commander-in-Chief Continental Army

**1783–1789** Landlord at Mount Vernon

## Administration Events

**1789** First inaugural ball

**1790** First Federal census

**1791** Established Cabinet system

**1792** Cornerstone White House laid

**1793** Cornerstone Capitol laid

**1794** Whiskey Rebellion

**1797** Two term tradition established

tries for 1768 show he hunted foxes on 49 days and went to church only 15 times. Thomas Jefferson, among others, regarded Washington as the best horseman of the age.

He kept copy books from childhood till the end of his life. Much of his diary records the weather from day to day and is boring to read.

Washington often played the flute with his adopted daughter, Nellie, who accompanied him on the harpsichord. He loved dancing and could and sometimes did go on for hours.

## Birthplace

Washington was born February 22, 1732 at 10:00 A.M. in Pope's Creek (Wakefield), in Westmoreland County, Virginia. Pope's Creek is located 38 miles east of Fredericksburg via Virginia 3 and Route 204. The original house burned in 1799, but a memorial house was built in 1930–31 on a site nearby.

## Baptism

Washington was christened on April 5, 1732, at Yeocomico Church in Westmoreland County, Virginia, near Wakefield, when he was six weeks old. It is likely that Yeocomico Church, his mother's church, was the site of his baptism, however, there is a possibility he was baptized at Pope's Creek Episcopal Church in Oak Grove, Virginia.

## Church

On Sundays, Washington was more likely to be riding or hunting, or writing letters than attending church. However, he supported the moral positions of the church, and when he did attend, after listening to a sermon, he enjoyed talking with fellow churchgoers.

Writing in 1793, he summed up his religious philosophy by saying how events in life would terminate "is known only to the great

his own teeth left when he became president. He often complained of being, "indisposed with an aching tooth, and swelled and inflamed gum."

He was fond of playing cards and occasionally gambled both at cards and at cockfights. He often went fox hunting, and his diary en-

ruler of events and confiding in his wisdom and goodness, we may safely trust the issue to him, without perplexing ourselves to seek for that which is beyond human ken, only taking care to perform our parts assigned to us in a way that reason and our own consciences approve of." He was not a fundamentalist in his thinking but, like Thomas Jefferson, a deist and humanist.

In the early days of his marriage, when he went to the church with Martha, he stood while she knelt for Communion. When the pastor spoke to him about standing, he did not respond but from then on left the church at Communion time and waited for Martha outside.

**1732–** *Westmoreland County, Virginia.* Yeocomico Church, a frame building on the northwest side of Yeocomico River, was likely the site of Washington's baptism. The same baptismal font is used today. All members of the Washington family regularly attended services here.

**1732–1745** *Fairfax County, Virginia.* The Old Pohick Church, no longer standing, stood a few miles southwest of where the New Pohick church was built across Pohick Creek. *Pohick* is Indian for "hickory." Probably one of the first churches ever attended by Washington, it was used for regular worship services until February 15, 1745, when the vestry officially accepted the new church for the use of the parish.

**1732–1745** *Falmouth, Virginia.* Brunswick Parish Church, near Ferry Farm, northeast of Fredericksburg in Falmouth near junction of U.S. 17 and U.S. 1. He probably attended here until the ferry was made free in 1745. Only the ruins of one wall remain but there are some plans for restoration.

**1744–** *Oak Grove, Virginia.* Popes Creek Episcopal Church on SR 3, east of Oak Grove where the Washington and Lee families sometimes worshipped after the church was built 1744. Possibly the site of his baptism.

**1745–1773** *Fairfax County, Virginia.* The New Pohick Church, 9301 Richmond Highway, is on U.S. 1, 10 miles south of Alexandria. Washington was a vestryman here. He owned pew 28, located just before the Communion table on the north side and currently marked with a red cord.

**1745–1773** *Falls Church, Virginia.* Falls Church is located at the corner of South Washington and Fairfax Streets. This church became a recruiting station during the Revolutionary War. Washington was a vestryman, was on the building committee, and was one of its earliest members.

**1745–1773** *Westmoreland County, Virginia.* Cople Parish, Nominy Church. SR 3, 3.7 miles east of Templemans Cross Roads. Building was burned in 1814 by the British; present building dates to 1852.

**1745–1773** *Fredericksburg, Virginia.* St. George Episcopal Church, George Street. Washington's family probably attended here after the ferry across the Rappahannock River was made free in 1745.

**1754–** *Williamsburg, Virginia.* Bruton Parish Church, located at the corner of Duke of Gloucester Street and the Palace Green. Martha was attending at the time of their marriage. Washington attended when visiting the capital city for meetings of the Virginia Assembly.

**1770s** *Boston, Massachusetts.* Trinity Church on Summer Street. Washington attended Trinity Church during the War days when his military headquarters were in Boston.

**1773–1799** *Alexandria, Virginia.* Christ Church at 118 N. Washington Street. On June 12, 1773, Washington attended worship services at the new church for the first time. His pew is still preserved at this church. The chandelier is from England and was purchased at his expense.

**1774** *Richmond, Virginia.* St. John's Church, 24th and Broad. Washington was here on the occasion of Patrick Henry's historic speech.

**1775** *Cambridge, Massachusetts.* Christ Church at Farwell Place on Garden Street.

**1789–1790** *New York City, New York.* St. Paul's Chapel, on Broadway at Fulton, opened in 1766. The very fashionable attended this church, which held property extending from Broadway to the Hudson River. Washington was here for the first service after his inauguration and worshipped here while the capital was in New York City and he lived in the Franklin House.

**1789** *Boston, Massachusetts.* King's Chapel at the corner of School and Tremont Streets. On the south side of the church is the large canopied pew used by the governors of Massachusetts. Washington sat in this pew with Governor Shirley in February of 1776 and again on October 27, 1789. The church was Anglican but became the first church of the Unitarian denomination after the Revolution.

**1790–** *New York City, New York.* Trinity Church, Broadway and Wall Street (built in 1696, rebuilt after being burned in 1788). Washington went to the consecration of this church on March 25, 1790, in which a pew was reserved for him.

**1790–1797** *Philadelphia, Pennsylvania.* St. Peter's Episcopal Church at 3rd and Pine Streets. Washington attended St. Peter's while president when the capital was in Philadelphia. He sat in pew number 41.

**1790–1797** *Philadelphia, Pennsylvania.* Christ Church on Second Street above Market Street. Washington attended Christ Church from time to time.

**1791** *York, Pennsylvania.* First Reformed Church on West Market Street. There was no Episcopal church in York so Washington attended here. The service was in German and he did not understand a word.

**1794** *Carlisle, Pennsylvania.* First Presbyterian Church, northwest corner of Public

*George Washington attended this log structure at Falmouth called Mr. Hobby's school.*

Square at intersection of Hanover and High Streets.

**1799** *Philadelphia, Pennsylvania.* Zion German Lutheran Church which until 1870 was located at 4th and Cherry Streets. A memorial service for Washington was held here on December 26, 1799.

# EDUCATION

Of the first six presidents, George Washington was the only one without a college education. There is no authentic record whatever of his instructors. His early education was principally by private tutors; his later education, experience and self-instruction. Possibly he had early instruction from a convict servant and attended a school across the river from Ferry Farm opened by Reverend James Marye in 1740. The school might have been on land owned by Marye that is now the northwest corner of Princess Anne and Charlotte Streets, in Fredericksburg, Virginia. Reference is also made to a log structure at Falmouth called Mr. Hobby's school. By the age of 16 years anything resembling formal education was finished. In 1748 he attended a short course for surveyors at Williamsburg in the Wren Building at the College.

**1739–1744**   *Falmouth, Virginia.* Mr. Hobby's School, located beside the ruins of the Brunswick Church at U.S. 17 and U.S. 1 on the road to Fredericksburg, was kept by William Grove. Local tradition holds Washington attended here. The log building still exists on the edge of Falmouth.

**1744–1746**   *Oak Grove, Virginia.* Virginia 3 and 205 junction south of Colonial Beach. A marker indicates that Washington, while living at Wakefield with a brother, went to school here.

## MARRIAGE AND HONEYMOON

On January 6, 1759 Washington married Martha Dandridge Custis, a very wealthy widow of New Kent County and probably one of the richest unmarried ladies in all Virginia. Martha had dark hair, hazel eyes, and beautiful teeth. When her husband became president, her function continued to be more that of wife than First Lady. They had no children, but Washington adopted the two Martha had by her previous marriage. Modern physicians speculate Washington's apparent sterility might have stemmed from malaria (suffered by most Virginians) or from a chromosomal defect.

**1759**   *New Kent County, Virginia.* Martha's home, called White House, was situated on what is now Virginia 614 off Virginia 608 on the Pamunkey River. There is no proven record of whether the ceremony took place at Martha's home or in church. The official Virginia Travel Guide claims the site of the wedding was St. Peter's Parish Church which is southwest of the New Kent Court House. However, references reveal it was celebrated "at candlelight." At that time home weddings were common because a colonial law prohibited meetings of any kind at churches after sunset. No church was ever lighted at night and no church had provision for heating in the winter. In addition, it was not the custom for widows to marry in the church.

In the confusion of the Civil War the "White House" was burned June 1862. There have been three houses on the site with some excavation since 1935.

No formal honeymoon is mentioned, but the Washingtons did spend the winter in Williamsburg at Martha's "six-chimney house," at the corner of Francis and Nassau Streets (now Custis Square). In the spring Washington brought Martha and her two children to Mount Vernon. Some sources say they spent their honeymoon and their first home at Martha's house in New Kent County. One source indicates Martha and George stayed at a cottage in Rockahock (near the Custis White House) which belonged to Martha's brother.

## HOMES

George Washington lived in several different homes but Mount Vernon was his most famous and is the best known of all the homes of the presidents. Almost nothing is known of the origins of the house on Little Hunting Creek, at first called Epsewasson and later renamed Mount Vernon for Admiral Edward Vernon, under whom Lawrence, elder brother of George, served in British battles with Spain. Some of the dates given here overlap as he shifted between staying with a brother and living at home with his mother.

**1732–1745**   *Pope's Creek (Wakefield), Westmoreland County, Virginia.* Pope's Creek was Washington's birthplace and early home. The house was a large U-shaped building of at least nine rooms. The original house burned Christmas Day, 1779. Oyster shells now outline the site of the original home.

*Mount Vernon, home of George Washington.*

**1735–1738** *Mount Vernon, Alexandria, Virginia.* Southern terminus of the Mount Vernon Memorial Highway 8 miles south of Alexandria. Washington went back and forth between his home on Pope's Creek and his brother's home here, at this time called Little Hunting Creek and later renamed Mount Vernon.

**1738–1748** *Fredericksburg, Virginia.* Little Ferry Farm on the Rappahannock River at 712 Kings Highway 1, 1 mile east of Fredericksburg on Virginia 3. It is the traditional site of the mythic cherry tree story, but the house has long since disappeared. There is a marker on site. Plans are in the making for replicating the original Washington farmhouse and reestablishing ferry service to Fredericksburg. In Fredericksburg there is a spot along the Rappahannock River, a short distance south of the corner of Sophia and Hanover Streets, that is the traditional site of his throwing a silver dollar across the river.

**1748–1799** *Mount Vernon, Alexandria, Virginia.* Although he was often away from home in military and government service, his permanent home was here from 1748 until the end of his life. To accommodate the requirements of the family and the constant stream of guests, changes were made in the house. In 1774 both ends of the house were extended. In 1775 Washington had four small octagonal buildings incorporated. He purchased Mount Vernon in 1754, which was his first full year here.

**1771–1789** *Alexandria, Virginia.* Townhouse at the corner of Pitt and Cameron Streets. Washington spent little time here, and after the War of Independence he usually lent it to relatives or rented it.

**1776** *New York City.* The Morris-Jumel Mansion at Edgecombe Avenue and 160th Street in Manhattan. This mansion was Washington's headquarters until his defeat at Fort Washington and the Laurel Hill redoubt, September 14 to October 18, after which he retreated to Harlem Heights. Washington reportedly courted Roger Morris's wife before her marriage, when she was Mary Philipse, twenty years earlier.

**1781**  *New York City.* The Van Courtlandt House at North Broadway and 242nd Street. Washington occupied this house for a short time after the Revolution.

**1789–1790**  *New York City.* The Franklin House at the corner of Pearl and Cherry Streets. Washington's residence was number 3. Marker on site. An architectural masterpiece for the time, the home was owned by Samuel Osgood, who rented it to Washington for $2,500 a year. Washington lived here from April 1789 to February 1790. He moved because the house was too far from the city center and also because Osgood wanted it back.

**1790**  *New York City.* The McComb Mansion at 39-41 Broadway, just below Trinity Churchyard. Washington was here five months. The house was called the Mansion House while he lived there; later it was known as Bunker's Hotel. Marker on site.

**1790–1797**  *Philadelphia.* The President's home on High Street was one door east from the southeast corner of 6th Street. Marker on site.

**1793**  *Philadelphia.* The Deshler-Morris House at 5441 Germantown Avenue. Washington used this house as the presidential residence very briefly when the government moved to escape the yellow fever epidemic. Meetings of Cabinet were held here, and for a brief time it was the seat of the United States Government. While here he attended services in the Market Square Church directly across the Square from the house.

**1793**  *Washington, D.C.* A stone outside the Capitol to the north between the Capitol and Union Station shows the location of lots Washington owned and the site of two

three-story brick houses which he built just before he died.

# WORK

Much of Washington's work, including his years in military service, is intermingled with his travel and visits, and listings in these categories reflect this aspect. Most entries for the Revolutionary War period 1775–83 have been listed under the heading Travel/Visits.

**1748–1752**  *Winchester, Virginia.* Washington worked as a surveyor principally in the Winchester area of the Shenandoah Valley.

**1752–1758**  *Virginia.* As a colonel with the Virginia Militia on the frontier between British and French, Washington had the responsibility of protecting Virginia's frontiers from the French and Indians. Washington was in command or built the following forts during the French and Indian War: Fort Ashby, in present West Virginia, near intersection of WV 28 and WV 46; Fort Blackwater (Terry's Fort), northwest of U.S. 220 near Rocky Mount, Franklin County, Virginia; Fort Breckenridge, 16 miles from Fort Dickinson in Bath County, Virginia; Christy's Fort, 15 miles from Fort Dinwiddie, Bath County; Fort Frederick on west bank of New River at Ingles Ferry in Montgomery County, Virginia; Harper's Fort on Bullpasture River in present Highland County, Virginia; Fort Mayo on Mayo River in Patrick County, just above the North Carolina line in Virginia, marker on U.S. 58.

**1753**  *Pennsylvania.* See Washington Crossing Bridge at 40th St. over the Allegheny River which was used during French and Indian Wars. In Franklin, See also French Fort Machault at Sixth and Elk and Fort Venango at Eigth and Elk, which he reconnoitered. At Fort LeBoeuf, (near Waterford), he was sent to the Ohio Valley by colonial Governor Dinwiddie to deliver an ultimatum to the French at this fort. He was known by the Indians as Caunotaucarius, "the town-taker." In the area there is the George Washington Monument which is the only memorial where he is wearing a British uniform. At Meadville, see George Washington Bicentennial Oak, 263 Randolph Street. A plaque marks the spot where he may have stopped on his trip to Fort LeBoeuf. At Waterford, see Washington Sentinel Tree which legend claims he climbed to reconnoiter Fort LeBoeuf.

**1754** *Fort Necessity, Pennsylvania.* On the level area of the Youghiogheny River about 10 miles east of present Uniontown in SW Pennsylvania. It was a small fortification erected by him in Great Meadows. Attacked by French and Indians he was forced to surrender 7-3-1754. This was a prelude to the opening of the French and Indian War. Off U.S. 40. Later he bought the Great Meadows natural clearing. See the Mount Washington Tavern Museum. The Tavern was built on a 234-acre piece of land which he owned from 1769 to 1799 and was a stagecoach stop during the time.

**1754** *Jumonville, Pennsylvania.* Jumonville's Rocks is the site of his first combat in which one of his Indian allies killed the French commander Jumonville. Now a camp owned by the United Methodist Church. Half King's Rock is the spot where Tenacharison, Delaware Indian chief and friend of the English, met with Washington at the Jumonville victory.

**1754–1758** *Fort Duquesne, Pennsylvania.* A French fort on the site of modern Pittsburgh where he was engaged in fighting. It was captured by the British in 1758 and renamed Fort Pitt. See Fort Pitt Museum and Block House in Point State Park at 25 Penn Avenue, Pittsburgh. Site of Washington visits in 1753 and 1758.

**1755–1757** *Winchester, Virginia.* A small log cabin at the corner of Braddock and Cork Streets is alleged to have served as his

military in office Winchester. In December 1756 he moved his office from the log cabin to the highest hill in Winchester (Fort Loudon). He spent a substantial part of ten years in Winchester. Site between Clark and Peyton Streets. Part of SW bastion is all that is left of the redoubt built in 1756–1757.

**1758–** *Alexandria, Virginia.* City Hall, Cameron Street between Royal and Fairfax Streets where he often conducted business.

**1758–1774** *Williamsburg, Virginia.* Member of House of Burgesses of Virginia.

**1774–1775** *Philadelphia, Pennsylvania.* Member of First Continental Congress. Carpenter's Hall, between 3rd and 4th Streets.

**1775** *Philadelphia, Pennsylvania.* Member of Second Continental Congress, Independence Hall in the Assembly Room.

**1775–1783** *Pennsylvania.* Commander-in-Chief of the Continental Army. During the early part of the War the Colonists maintained they were not rebelling against the King but against the tyranny of the Parliament. By 1775 they were still flying a flag with 13 red and white stripes but, in the canton, where the stars are now was a Union Jack and each night Washington and his officers toasted the king's health.

**1783–1789** *Mount Vernon, Virginia.* Farming.

**1787** *Philadelphia, Pennsylvania.* Presided over the Constitutional Convention in Independence Hall in the Assembly Room.

**1788** *Richmond, Virginia.* Quesnay Academy on Academy Square, attending Virginia Convention meetings.

**1789–1790** *New York City and Philadelphia.* As first president of the United States. Corner of Wall and Broad Streets in Federal Hall in the Senate chamber on a balcony overlooking a crowd of spectators, he took the oath of office April 30, 1789. In eight years as president he vetoed only two bills. He declined his salary as president. What is now known as Federal Hall was at the time the City Hall and a two-story building with a cupola. The House of Representatives met on the first floor and the Senate on the second.

**1790–1797**  *Philadelphia, Pennsylvania.* In the second inaugural he appeared at the senate chamber and delivered the shortest inaugural address in U.S. history on March 4, 1990. Held in Congress Hall at Sixth and Chestnut Streets. Even great presidents with devotion to duty sometimes explode. Jefferson describes one Cabinet meeting when Washington said in a rage because of some unfair criticism, "by god he had rather be on his farm than to be made emperor of the world."

**1794**  *Trenton, New Jersey.* State House located on West State Street where the Federal Government met to escape the yellow fever epidemic in Philadelphia.

# TRAVEL/VISITS

Although he often expressed the wish to go to England, Washington's only foreign travel was to Barbados with his ailing brother. Washington traveled in every one of the original thirteen states—Connecticut, Delaware, Georgia, Maryland, Massachusetts, New Hampshire, New Jersey, New York, North Carolina, Pennsylvania, Rhode Island, South Carolina, and Virginia—and into frontier lands that are now in West Virginia and Ohio. Many of his travels are covered extensively in his personal diaries as well as in historical accounts of the French and Indian Wars and the War of Independence.

George Washington's first surveying job away from home occurred in 1748 when he was hired by Lord Fairfax to lay out lands in the Shenandoah Valley in farm-sized lots. Further travel for surveying and service in the French and Indian Wars marked the beginning of many nights away from home during his

lifetime. "Washington slept here" is true much more often than people might think. Obviously it is not possible to know every place where he lodged, but the following list of places is authenticated and, in general, felt to be interesting historical spots. Specific years are mentioned to give some structure to his movements, although he may have stayed at the same place on several occasions. Readers wishing to learn more about travel lodgings may wish to refer to his diaries, edited by Donald Jackson and Dorothy Twohig, which give considerable detail.

**1740–**  *Arlington, Virginia.* Abingdon, north of Four Mile Run fronting the Potomac River and opposite mouth of the Anacostia River, was the home of his stepson, John Parke Custis where he often came to visit and also to spend the night. The house burned March 4, 1930 and only the chimney remains at the edge of the Washington National Airport.

**1740–**  *Belvoir, Fairfax County, Virginia.* An estate owned by the wealthy Lord Fairfax located west of Mount Vernon on the grounds of Fort Belvoir south of Alexandria on US 1 towards Gunston Hall. The family was special friends of the Washingtons. The Belvoir mansion overlooked the Potomac within sight of distant Mount Vernon. Sally, the romantic love of Washington's early days, lived at Belvoir with her husband, George William Fairfax. Demolished by the British 1814. Site of ruins on the grounds of the present military base with markers.

**1740–**  *Pope's Creek (Wakefield) Westmoreland County, Virginia.* Blenheim on the original Pope Creek property of the Washington family became the principal home of the Washington family (1780–1787) after Wakefield burned in 1779. The house was renovated in the late 1970s and is on the National Register of historic places.

**1740–**  *New Kent County, Virginia.* Eltham Mansion, on the Pamunkey River opposite

*Wakefield, Washington family home.*

the mouth of the Mattapony River, was the home of his intimate friend, Colonel Bassett and his wife, who was a sister of Martha. He probably spent more time here than at any private home in America outside of Mount Vernon. He often stopped here to and from his meetings at Williamsburg and to check on his property in the area. His stepson is buried in the Eltham Garden. There is no marker. Nothing remains of the house, which was destroyed by fire in 1875. The bricks of the old house were sold to Colonial Williamsburg.

**1740–** *Fredericksburg, Virginia.* Mary Washington lived at 1200 Charles Street her last 17 years. Washington frequently visited her there 1772–1789.

**1740–** *Fredericksburg, Virginia.* Kenmore, 1201 Washington Avenue between Lewis and Fauquier Streets. This was the eighteenth century house built by Fielding and Betty Washington Lewis, Washington's only sister. This elegant house is near his mother's home. Although Washington stopped to visit and eat with his mother, he most often stayed overnight with the Lewises.

**1740–** *Westmoreland County, Virginia.* The Glebe, near Bushfield and St. Peter's Church, where he was entertained by the rector who had married his parents in 1731. It was damaged by fire and demolished. The Glebe house faced the New Kent Stage Road and was later the site of the New Kent Charity School property. Marker.

**1740–** *Near Lorton, Virginia.* Gunston Hall, eighteen miles south of Washington, D.C. via I-95. Home of George Mason, who is sometimes called the "Pen of the Revolution."

**1740–** *Alexandria, Virginia.* Lee-Fendall House, 614 Oronoco Street. Washington often visited members of the Lee family here.

**1740–** *Shirley Plantation.* West of Berkeley Plantation on Virginia 5. Belonged to the Carter family. Anne Carter Lee was the mother of Robert E. Lee. Washington was a regular visitor here.

**1740–** *Near Richmond, Virginia.* Wilton House, six miles below Richmond on the banks of the James River, at the south end of Wilton Road off Cary Street Road. Washington was entertained here by William Randolph.

**1740–** *Near Mount Vernon, Virginia.* Woodlawn Plantation was once part of Washington's farm. He gave the estate to his adopted daughter.

**1749** *Washington, Virginia.* Ninety miles west of Washington, D.C., via U.S. 211. This is the first place (of 121) in the United States named for Washington and was laid out by young George in 1749. A white frame building once visited by Washington still stands. The current First Presbyterian Church stands on one of the two lots presented to him.

**1750–** *Near Richmond, Virginia.* Halfway House, between Richmond and Petersburg, is a famous old inn where he was a guest. Today it is still operated as an inn.

**1750–** *Natural Bridge near Lexington, Virginia.* Washington, while surveying the bridge, climbed 23 feet up and carved his initials, which can still be seen today. It is related that Washington, standing at the bottom of the Natural Bridge, could throw a stone to the top.

**1750–** *Fairfield, Virginia.* Albright Tavern where he lodged. On one occasion the rain leaked through the roof and ruined a painting he had just purchased, much to his annoyance.

**1750–** *New Kent County, Virginia.* Claremont across the James River from the Green Springs estate of the Harrisons was

the home of the Allen family where he visited.

**1752–** *Fredericksburg, Virginia.* Masonic Lodge, at Princess Anne and Hanover Streets, where he became a Master Mason.

**1754–** *Williamsburg, Virginia.* While at the Assembly sessions he stayed at Finnie's Ordinary and boarded at Mrs. Coulthard's. Finnie's is probably the same as Raleigh Tavern, located on Duke of Gloucester Street. Researchers have been unable to locate the site of Mrs. Coulthard's.

**1755–1757** *Winchester, Virginia.* While building Fort Loudon he had his quarters in a log building at 204 S. Loudon St. Site only.

**1755** *Alexandria, Virginia.* Carlyle Mansion, 121 N. Fairfax Street. Here Washington received a commission as aide-de-camp from General Braddock. Later in 1785 met here in conference to settle the dispute between Maryland and Virginia. The meeting adjourned to Mount Vernon and initiated the call for an assembly of delegates from all the commonwealth and led to the Congress in Philadelphia and ultimately the Constitution.

**1756** *Cumberland, Maryland.* In Riverside Park at Greene St. is a log cabin, extensively restored, that was moved to the park in 1921. This was his headquarters when he commanded the Virginia militia stationed here during the French and Indian War. The cabin was originally built within the walls of Fort Cumberland on the hill above the park. (The Allegheny County Court House now stands on the approximate site.) The last military function of the Fort was held in 1794 when he reviewed troops summoned here to suppress the Whiskey rebellion.

**1758–** *New Kent County, Virginia.* Chestnut Grove Plantation. This was the house of Frances Jones Dandridge, Martha's mother, and where Martha was born and grew up. The house burned in 1926 and a new house is on site. Stone with tablet on the grounds.

**1758–** Poplar Grove Mansion on the Pamunkey River, near the landing of the Williams Ferry was the home of Colonel Chamberlayne where Washington first met Martha Custis. No marker and exact site undetermined.

**1758–** *Alexandria, Virginia.* Gadsby's Tavern (in Washington's day called Wise's Fountain Tavern). 134 North Royal Street. It was a favorite haunt of Washington.

**1758–** *Annapolis, Maryland.* He frequently stayed in the rectory of St. Anne's Church on School Street. 162 Duke of Gloucester Street. House where he was entertained December 20, 1783. Marker. Church Circle and Franklin Street, Reynolds Tavern. Washington, Jefferson, Madison, Monroe frequented this place.

**1758** *Rock Hall, Maryland.* On the shore of Chesapeake Bay. See historical marker where he crossed many times.

**1758–** *New Kent County, Virginia.* Courthouse at Old Tavern, where Washington and friends gathered. Site and markers.

**1774** *Philadelphia, Pennsylvania.* Second Street above Walnut, where he probably stayed with Dr. William Shippen, Jr., and often ate at the New Tavern (or City Tavern).

**1774** *Philadelphia, Pennsylvania.* Washington's lodgings during his attendance at the First Continental Congress are uncertain, but he probably stayed at William Carson's tavern called the Harp and Crown, on North Third Street just below Arch Street.

**1775** *Philadelphia, Pennsylvania.* Washington lodged at Mrs. Randolph's who lived on Chestnut Street between Third and Fourth Streets, while he was attending the meetings of the Second Continental Congress held in the State House.

**1775** *Richmond, Virginia.* Ampthill Plantation home, while attending Virginia Ratification Convention. Restored.

**1775** *Cambridge, Massachusetts.* Craigie House, 105 Brattle Street. Washington received his commission here.

**1775–1776** *Cambridge, Massachusetts.* Vassal-Wadsworth House, Harvard Yard opposite Holyoke Street. Washington moved into the Wadsworth House, residence of the president of Harvard, but then moved to Vassal-Wadsworth House.

**1776** *Trenton, New Jersey.* Washington's Crossing State Park, northwest of NJ 29 at intersection with Route 546. This park is dedicated in memory of Washington and his 2,400 soldiers who crossed the Delaware River here on December 25, 1776. Near the site is McKonkey Ferry (also known as Johnson House) where Washington is said to have stopped Christmas night before going on to Trenton. Washington had previously crossed the Delaware into Pennsylvania on December 11. At Barrack Street is the site of the Battle of Trenton, where Washington captured the Hessian garrison in a surprise attack.

**1776** *Baltimore, Maryland.* Congress Hall, corner of Liberty and Baltimore Streets. Here he was voted full military command. Site only.

**1776** *Princeton, New Jersey.* Thomas Olden House, 344 Stocton Street. Washington reviewed his troops and was here again in 1791.

**1776** *New York City, New York (Brooklyn Heights).* Here he was defeated in the Battle of Long Island, August 27, by Lord Howe. The site of the battle is across the East River from Manhattan.

**1776** *New York City, New York.* Site of the Battle of Harlem Heights in upper Manhattan, September 16th in which the Americans were unsuccessful. Plaque on the east side of Broadway between 116th and 117th Street.

**1776** *Fort Lee, New York.* Fort Lee Historic Park, New York 9. Washington selected this site at the crest of the Palisades from which he watched the attack and surrender of his garrison at Fort Washington across the Hudson River, October 5th. Fort Washington was located in the vicinity of present West 183rd Street in Manhattan. It was captured by the British November 1776.

**1776** *White Plains, New York.* Virginia Road in North White Plains northeast of Yonkers. Site of the Battle of White Plains, scene of Washington's retreat from the British attack under General Howe, October 28th. Trenton, New Jersey. Washington's Crossing State Park, northwest of New Jersey 29 at intersection with New Jersey County 546. This park is dedicated in memory of Washington and his 2,400 soldiers who crossed the Delaware River here December 25, 1776. Near the site is McKonkey Ferry (also known as Johnson House) where Washington is said to have stopped Christmas night before going on to Trenton. Washington had previously crossed the Delaware into Pennsylvania December 11. Trenton, New Jersey. Barrack Street. Site of Battle of Trenton where Washington captured the Hessian garrison in a surprise attack.

**1777** *Madison, New Jersey.* 31 Ridgedale Road. The dwelling he visited has been restored.

**1777** *Princeton, New Jersey.* Nasau Hall on Princeton University campus where the Battle of Princeton ended and the British defeated, January 2–3.

**1777** *Lambertsville, New Jersey.* John Holcombe house, north end of Main Street on the right, where he stayed before the Battles of Germantown and of Monmouth. Marker on the roadside. July 1777. He was also here June 1778.

**1777** *Wilmington, Delaware.* 303 West Street. Washington had his headquarters August–September. The rear section is the only part of the original remaining.

**1777** *Chadds Ford, Pennsylvania.* Site of the Battle of Brandywine where General Howe defeated Washington September 11 is now private property. At Chadds Ford, is the Benjamin Ring home used by Washington as headquarters.

**1777** *Philadelphia, Pennsylvania.* Germantown Battlefield, Germantown Road in morthwestern Philadelphia. In the Battle of Germantown, October 4, Washington tried unsuccessfully to dislodge the British troops. The Peter Wentz Homestead, Valley Forge, served as headquarters for Washington before and after this battle.

**1777–1778** *Valley Forge, Chester County, Pennsylvania.* This was Washington's winter headquarters. The site now consists of reconstructed buildings on a 2,500 acre park. Washington said of his men, "naked and starving as they are we cannot enough admire the incomparable patience and fidelity of the soldiery."

**1778** *Englishtown, New Jersey.* Hulse Memorial Home, Main Street. (Today a funeral home). Plaque on front door. This was his headquarters the night before the Battle of Monmouth, June 27–28. The Village Inn on Main Street is where he held meetings and also drew up charges against General Charles Lee leading to his court martial.

**1778–1779** *Middlebrook, New Jersey.* On U.S. 22, near Plainfield. This was the winter headquarters of Washington.

**1779** *Jersey City, New Jersey.* Van Wagener House, 298 Academy Street. It was part of the Apple Tree house. Washington dined here under an apple tree in 1779. The tree fell in 1821.

**1779–1780** *Morristown, New Jersey.* 230 Morris Street. This was the winter headquarters of Washington's soldiers. They spent two severe winters here beginning October 17th. This was also the site of a mutiny on May 4, 1780. Washington's headquarters may be seen at the Ford Mansion at Washington Place in Morristown National Historical Park (south of Morristown). The park contains a great storehouse of Washington relics. See also the Washington statue across the street from the Ford Mansion. Morristown is also the site of Arnold Tavern, on the town square.

**1779** *Pompton Lake, New Jersey.* Located near New Jersey 208 and Pompton Lake. This small house with marker is where Washington stopped.

**1779** *Somerville, New Jersey.* Old Dutch Parsonage & Wallace House, 38 & 65 Washington Place, near I-287. These two houses are located across the street from each other. The parsonage evolved into Rutgers University and faces the Wallace House, which was used by Washington as a headquarter.

**1779** *Wayne, New Jersey.* Dey Mansion, 199 Totowa Road, This was one of Washington's many headquarters. Washington stayed here in July, October, and November.

**1780** *West Point, New York.* Beverly House, south of Garrison, near the foot of Sugar Loaf Hill. He visited here at the time Benedict Arnold's treason was uncovered. West Point was indicated by Washington as an eligible place for a military academy as early as 1783 and was definitely recommended by him in 1793.

**1780** *Tappan, New York.* Rockland County on the New York/New Jersey border, off New York 505. This was his headquarters during trial of Major Andre in September. He was here again 1783.

**1780–** *Bladensburg, Maryland.* The Indian Queen Tavern (also known as the George Washington House). Located at the intersection of Baltimore Avenue and Upshur Street. This narrow, two-story brick house was used as both store and tavern at the time Washington visited. Now restored.

**1780–** *Perryville, Maryland.* Rodgers Tavern. He stopped here many times during the 1780s and 1790s.

**1780–** *Red Lion, Delaware.* Red Lion Tavern, southwest of New Castle. He often stopped here. It is now a private residence.

**1780–** *Ephrata, Pennsylvania.* The Cloisters on the western edge of town where he visited in the 1780s at the home of Johann Peter Miller. Exact house of Miller undetermined. 1780s.

**1780** *Montclair, New Jersey.* Valley Road and Claremont Avenue. Washington had headquarters here in 1780 and stayed overnight in a house the site of which is marked by a boulder.

**1780–** *South Orange, New Jersey.* Timothy Ball House, 425 Ridgewood Avenue. He was also here during the 1770s. Nearby in the South Mountain Reservation is the Washington Rock where he observed American troops intercepting British efforts to reach Morristown and destroy his supplies.

**1780–1781** *New Windsor, New York.* Washington's headquarters June 24 to July 21, 1779 and Dec. 6, 1780 to June 25, 1781.

**1781** *New York City (Bronx), New York.* Van Cortlandt House. This is where he had lodgings 1781 and 1783. Open for tours.

**1781** *Dobbs Ferry, New York.* Livingston House, at corner of Broadway and Livingston Avenues. This site served as headquarters in 1781 and 1783. Washington met here with George Clinton to discuss evacuation of New York City by the British. See Marker.

**1781** *Fishkill, New York.* Van Wyck Homestead Museum. This site was used as officer's headquarters for Washington's forces.

**1781** *(near) Erskine, New Jersey.* Ringwood Manor. This is where he was a frequent visitor with the Erskine family.

**1781** *Wethersfield, Connecticut.* Webb House, 211 Main Street. Washington met with Rochambeau to plot the final moves of the war.

**1781**  *Silas Deane House, 203 Main Street.* Washington lodged with this American patriot.

**1781**  *Princeton, New Jersey.* Nassau Street. See stone marker on grounds of Trinity Church for Washington-Rochambeau route to Yorktown. See also monument honoring Washington in front of the police station on Nassau Street.

**1781**  *Williamsburg, Virginia.* Wythe House, corner of Prince George Street and the Palace Green. He used the Wythe House as headquarters before the siege of Yorktown.

**1781**  *Yorktown, Virginia.* Moore House. Here General Cornwallis surrendered to Washington and while the formal end came here there were still some clean-up operations. The Moore House was the scene of the British surrender. See also battlefield markers on the banks of the York River on Virginia 238.

**1781**  *Yorktown, Virginia.* Shield House (also known as the Thomas Sessions House), Nelson Street. This is where Washington stayed while in Yorktown. At least five presidents have been guests here. See also site of old courthouse and across the street the reconstructed Swan Tavern on the corner of Main and Ballard Streets, which was visited by Washington. There is a statue of Washington at the junction of Main Street and Zweybrucken Road. See also the National Park Center and the tent used by Washington during his campaigns. The Victory Center has a film showing and artifacts of the Revolutionary War.

**1781–1782**  *Newburgh, New York.* Hasbrouck House, Liberty Street. This was Washington's headquarters April 16, 1782 to August 18, 1783.

**1782**  *Verplanck's Point, New York.* Located across the river from the Stony Point lighthouse. This is where he had his headquarters for some time in 1782.

**1782**  *Kutztown, Pennsylvania.* Old Kemp House, U.S. 222. This is where he watered his horse; now called Whispering Springs.

**1782**  *Bethlehem, Pennsylvania.* Sun Inn, 560- 564 Main Street. Washington stopped here on July 25.

**1782**  *Newton, New Jersey.* The old Cochran House (now greatly altered), near Court House Square.

**1782**  *Fredon, New Jersey.* The White House Inn. This is where he took dinner July 1782.

**1782**  *Annapolis, Maryland.* Lloyd Dulany House, 162 Conduit Street. In 1783 Dulany's house was sold to George Mann, an innkeeper. Later it became the City Hotel. Washington stayed at Mann's when he came to Annapolis in 1783 to resign his commission and again in 1791. It is now used as a temple by the Freemasons. It was one of the largest homes built in Annapolis before the Revolution.

**1782**  *Princeton, New Jersey.* Morven. While the Continental Congress met in Princeton, Washington, who was residing in nearby Rocky Hill, visited. It is now the official residence of the governor.

**1782**  *Rockingham, New Jersey.* The Berien House, on New Jersey 518. This site was leased for Washington and his wife while the Continental Congress met in Princeton at Nassau Hall from late August until mid-November 1783. Washington wrote his "Farewell Orders to the Armies" here in the Blue Room and delivered this famous speech from the second-story porch.

**1782**  *Albany, New York.* Schuyler Mansion, 32 Catherine Street at the southeast corner of Clinton and Catherine Streets. Washington visited several times.

**1782**  *Albany, New York.* Pruyn House, 19 Elk Street. Washington was a guest here.

**1782**  *Albany, New York.* Whitehall Mansion on Second Street (was White Hall Road). Site of Washington's visits.

**1782**  *New York City, New York.* Fraunces' Tavern, 54 Pearl Street, southeast corner

Pearl and Broad Streets. This is where he took leave of his officers.

**1782** *Annapolis, Maryland.* Old Senate Chamber in the State House, State Circle. He resigned his Commission before Congress.

**1784** *New Castle, Delaware.* Amstel House, north corner of Fourth and Delaware Streets. Washington attended a wedding here April 30, 1784.

**1784** *Richmond, Virginia.* Bell Tavern, East Main Street in Shockoe district. Washington visited friends and members of the state legislature.

**1785** *Great Falls Park, Virginia.* Patowmack Company. This was a canal company organized by Washington to connect coastal Virginia with the interior West. It was a failure. Remnants of the canal can still be seen.

**1789** *Elizabeth, New Jersey.* Boxwell Hall, 1073 East Jersey Street. Washington was entertained here April 23, 1789 on his way to his first inaugural.

**1789** *Chestertown, Maryland.* Washington College, Washington Avenue. Washington received the Doctor of Laws degree here 1789. He was a member of the first board of directors.

**1789** *New Haven, Connecticut.* Hubbard House, at junction of Church, George, and Meadow Streets. Washington lodging. He was also entertained at Beers House where New Haven House now stands. October.

**1789** *Providence, Rhode Island.* Governor Stephen's House. 260 Benefit and Hopkins Streets. Washington entertained twice here.

**1789** *Boston, Massachusetts.* Ingersol Inn. The inn was directly across the street from the Sears block. Site now occupied by State Street Bank. In the Revolutionary period it was a large four-story building owned by Joseph Ingersol. Washington stayed here during his six-day visit October 1789. No marker on site.

**1789** *Boston, Massachusetts.* James Bowdoin Mansion, 10 1/2 Beacon Street. The Bellevue Hotel now stands on the site. Washington was twice a guest here in 1789.

**1789** *Boston, Massachusetts.* Cromwell's Head, at 19 School Street. This was a famous inn where Washington was a guest. It is in the historical area but there is no marker.

**1789** *Boston, Massachusetts.* Soldier's Monument on Dorchester Heights. Washington visited here.

**1789** *Boston, Massachusetts.* Faneuil Hall, Merchants Row. Washington visited in 1789.

**1789** *Springfield, Massachusetts.* Zenas Parson Tavern, southeast corner of Court Street (now Court Square), near Water Street. He arrived in October in a chariot drawn by four horses, attended by his own servants and several government officials. Later Monroe stayed here.

**1789** *Palmer, Massachusetts.* Scott Tavern (now site of a K-Mart store at the edge of town). There is a prominent marker.

**1789** *Lexington, Massachusetts.* Munroe Tavern, 1332 Massachusetts Avenue. Washington entertained here. See hat rack where he hung his hat.

**1789** *Salem, Massachusetts.* Court House on Federal Street. Washington delivered an address and was honored at a reception.

**1789** *Salem, Massachusetts.* Joshua Ward home, 148 Washington Street. Today the home where he visited is called the Hotel Washington.

**1789** *West Brookfield, Massachusetts.* Hitchcock's Tavern, near the center of the village. Washington dined here.

**1789** *Portsmouth, New Hampshire.* Governor Langdon House, 143 Pleasant Street. He stayed here several times. Washington called this home "the handsomest in Portsmouth."

**1789** *Portsmouth, New Hampshire.* Stephen Chase home, Court Street. Washington visited this merchant.

**1789** *Exeter, New Hampshire.* Washington had a meal at Colonel Samuel Folsom's public house.

**1789** *Newport, Rhode Island.* Old Colony House, Washington Square. Washington was entertained here in the nation's second oldest capitol building.

**1789** *Windsor, Connecticut.* David Ellsworth home, 778 Palisado Avenue. Both Washington and John Adams were guests here. House is open for tours.

**1789** *Norwich, Connecticut.* Teel House, on the Parade. This is where he once stopped. He also visited at the Samuel Huntington House on Huntington Lane.

**1789** *Durham, Connecticut.* Swathiel House.

**1789** *Lebanon, Connecticut.* He was a guest of Jonathan Trumbull, on the Green, as was Jefferson who was his Secretary of State at the time. Trumbull had provided food for Washington's army troops at a particularly difficult time during the war.

**1789** *New London, Connecticut.* While staying at the Shaw House, 11 Blinham Street, President Washington slept in the four-poster still canopied in white. On another occasion he spent a night at the Red Lion Inn on Main Street going and coming from Boston.

**1790** *Providence, Rhode Island.* Golden Ball Inn (opposite the Old State House). The same room he occupied August 1790 was later used by Presidents Monroe and John Quincy Adams. The name was changed to Roger Williams House, later the City Mansion House. He had refreshments and reception at the governor's residence, a banquet in the Courthouse (the Old State House), and at night went to the Rhode Island College grounds at the invitation of the students.

**1790** *Williamsport, Maryland.* Spring House, Springfield Lane. This is where he discussed Williamsport as a possible site for the new United States capital. Near the home of General Williams, founder of the town. General Holland Williams home, Springfield Lane off U.S. 11. Here Washington dined over discussion of the possible site of new capital.

**1790** *Washington, D.C.* Rosedale, 3501 Newark Street, NW. Washington dined several times with his friend, General Uriah Forrest in 1790s. The house is owned privately and is well-maintained.

**1790** *Washington, D.C.* Varnum Hotel, New Jersey Avenue and C Street, SE. Here he dined with his friend, Thomas Law. Later Jefferson resided here at the time of his inauguration. Site now occupied by House Office Building.

**1791** *York, Pennsylvania.* Washington lodged at the Baltzer Spangler Tavern, on the north side of East Market Street. Later the name was changed to Sign of General Washington, and finally Washington House, which was demolished 1885. He was only the first of many important figures who stayed at the Washington House. While in York he attended a reception honoring him at the Courthouse on South George Street; historical markers are in the vicinity.

**1791** *Richmond, Virginia.* Eagle Tavern, south side of Main Street, between Twelfth and Thirteenth Streets. Honored at a dinner. He also visited Masonic Lodge and lodged at the Swan Inn on Broad St. between Eighth and Ninth Streets.

**1791** *Petersburg, Virginia.* Golden Ball Tavern, southeast corner of Grove Avenue and North Market Street. He was entertained here. It is an unpainted frame building with brick ends and dormers.

**1791** *Alexandria, Virginia.* South corner stone for the District of Columbia. He laid the first corner stone. A lighthouse was built over the stone but a cross on the steps marks the spot beneath which the corner stone lies.

**1791** *Savannah, Georgia.* McIntosh House, 110 East Oglethorpe Avenue. This site is generally acknowledged to be the oldest brick house in Savannah. He took lodging in the house at the northwest corner of Barnard and State Streets, on St. James Square (now Telfair Square) and where the Odd Fellows Hall now stands. Plaque on side of the building.

**1791** *Mulberry, Georgia.* Washington lodged at General Greene's house, ten miles northwest of Savannah on the Savannah River and Black Creek. On the highway there is a sign near Monteith. The old plantation stretched from the main highway eastward to the Savannah River and the mansion was situated on the bank across the river from Isla Island. Only foundations remain. This is the same place where Eli Whitney invented the cotton gin.

**1791** *Ebenezer, Georgia.* Marker at Georgia 275 and Ebenezer Road.

**1791** *Augusta, Georgia.* Washington visited the Richmond Academy on Bay Street May 1791. Marker.

**1791** *Wilmington, North Carolina.* Burgwin-Wright House, 224 Market Street. Now restored. Cornwallis also stopped here.

**1791** *New Bern, North Carolina.* Tryon Palace, tour entrance on Pollock Street, where he dined and danced on his southern tour. While in New Bern he spent two nights at the home of Revolutionary War patriot John Wright Stanly, 307 George Street.

**1791** *Charleston, South Carolina.* Thomas Heyward, Jr. House, Church Street. Washington lodged here.

**1791** *Georgetown, South Carolina.* Hampton Plantation, U.S. 17, 12 miles south of Georgetown on the road to Charleston. Washington was a guest here. Later, in Georgetown, Washington lodged at the Py-

att House on Front Street, between Wood and King Streets. He also visited the Winyah Indigo Society Hall, 632 Prince Street, where he addressed the Masons.

**1791** *Arcadia, South Carolina (near Georgetown).* Clifton Plantation, off U.S. 17. He stayed overnight on April 29, 1791, with Benjamin Alston.

**1791** *Heath Springs, South Carolina.* James Ingram home (destroyed by Sherman's army in 1865). The site is located approximately three miles south of Heath Springs. Marker designates where Washington lodged. His return trip through South Carolina followed roughly the course of U.S. 1 and U.S. 521, by way of Columbia, Camden, and Lancaster.

**1791** *Lancaster, South Carolina.* Barr's Tavern, east of U.S. 521 at northern city limits. Washington had breakfast here on May 27, 1791, see roadside marker.

**1791** *Camden, South Carolina.* Adam Brisbane home, southeast corner Fair and York Streets. Washington was a guest here. Burned down years ago. A reception was held in the Washington House, now standing at 1413 Mill Street, having been moved here from the northwest corner of King and Fair Streets. At that time, it was the home of Colonel John Chestnut.

**1791** *Columbia, South Carolina.* A reception was held for him in the unfinished State House, Main and Gervais Streets. See also Washington statue in front of the State House.

**1791** *Salisbury, North Carolina.* The steps from which he spoke are preserved at the library.

**1791** *Salem, North Carolina.* Washington stayed at the Salem Tavern, 800 South Main Street and attended the Salem Church.

**1791** *Princeton, New Jersey.* Thomas Olden House, 344 Stocton Street.

**1791** *Rahway, New Jersey.* Merchants and Drovers Tavern, at the junction of Westfield and Grand Avenues. Restored.

**1791** *Uxbridge, Massachusetts.* Taft Tavern, corner of Sutton and Sylvan Streets.

**1791** *Watertown, Massachusetts.* Marshall Fowle House, 28 Marshall Street.

**1791** *Haverhill, Massachusetts.* Mason's Arms Tavern. Now the site of the town hall.

**1792** *Washington, D.C.* He laid the cornerstone of the White House on October 13. (Then referred to as President's Palace).

**1793** *Washington, D.C.* He laid the cornerstone of the Capitol on September 18. (Then referred to as Congress House).

**1793** *Philadelphia, Pennsylvania.* Watson House, 5275-5277 Germantown Avenue. He spent several nights here.

**1793** *Womelsdorf, Pennsylvania.* Seltzer House, Tulpehocken Road. Washington stayed here when escaping the yellow fever plague in Philadelphia.

**1794** *Carlisle, Pennsylvania.* Blaine House, 4 North Hanover Street. He stayed here during the Whisky Rebellion.

**1794** *Bedford Springs, Pennsylvania.* Epsy House, 123 East Pitt Street. This site was used as headquarters during Whiskey Rebellion.

**1794** *Pottsgrove, Pennsylvania.* The Trappe, about nine miles from Pottsgrove on Pennsylvania 113, off U.S.422. Here he had his headquarters from September 21 to 26, 1794.

**1795** *Charlestown, Maryland.* Maryland 267, off Maryland 7. The gambrel-roofed frame house, next door to the Indian Queen, is thought to be where he stopped.

**1796–** *Philadelphia, Pennsylvania.* Gilbert Stuart Studio, 5140 Germantown Avenue. Martha pushed her reluctant husband to sit for a portrait here. Today this is the portrait which appears on the one dollar bill.

**1798** *Philadelphia, Pennsylvania.* Mrs. Rosannah White's Boarding House, 9 North Eighth Street. Washington lodged here for a month.

**1798** *Philadelphia, Pennsylvania.* Powell House, 244 South 3rd Street. Here he was a frequent guest of the mayor, Samuel Powell.

**1790s** *New York City, New York.* Gracie Mansion, East End Avenue and 88th Street. Now used as official residence for the mayor.

**1790s** *New York City, New York.* Laurel Hill Mansion, 192nd Street and Audubon Avenue.

# DEATH

Washington died December 14, 1799, at Mount Vernon in his second-floor bedroom. Washington had been out more than five hours on horseback in rain and hail, when he caught cold. His cold and sore throat turned to pneumonia. He bore the pain stoically, but at the end he began to worry about being buried alive. "I am just going. Have me decently buried, and do not let my body be put in the vault in less than three days after I am dead." His wishes were followed; four days after his death, he was placed in the vault.

# FUNERAL

Washington's funeral was held at the Old Presbyterian Meeting House, 321 South Fairfax Street in Alexandria, Virginia. Memorial services were held throughout the country and his death observed in both England and France. Almost 33,000 veterans of the American Revolution accompanied his coffin to the grave at Mount Vernon.

# BURIAL

Washington's body was placed in a mahogany casket and originally buried in the old family vault on the grounds of the estate, a short distance from the site of the present tomb.

In 1831 the present vault was constructed. Washington and his wife, Martha, are buried here.

## SPECIAL SITES

*Alexandria, Virginia.* George Washington Masonic National Memorial on Shooter's Hill. Contains Washington's family bible and also bronze medallions of U.S. Presidents who have been Freemasons.

*Baltimore, Maryland.* Mount Vernon and Washington Place is the site of the first monument begun in the United States to honor Washington.

*Washington, D.C.* Washington Monument.

## BIBLIOGRAPHY

Bellamy, Francis Rufus. *The Private Life of George Washington.* New York: Thomas Y. Crowell Company, 1951.

Flexner, James T. *George Washington: A Biography.* 4 vols. Boston: Little, Brown, 1965–1972.

Jackson, Donald, and Dorothy Twohig, eds. *The Diaries of George Washington.* Charlottesville: University Press of Virginia, 1979.

# JOHN ADAMS

## 1735–1826
### 2ND PRESIDENT 1797–1801: FEDERALIST PARTY

John Adams, "the Patriot," from Massachusetts is considered by some historians to be among the ten greatest presidents. He was born October 30, 1735 to farmer John and Susanna Bolston Adams.

*"Independence forever!"*

## CHARACTERISTICS

John Adams was not a tall man, standing about 5′6″, but he was well-built. Later in life, as he gained weight, he was jokingly called "His Rotundity." He had a light complexion and turned a fiery red when he became angry. He had blue eyes and fine light brown hair, which he tied at the back with a black string. He was short-tempered, stubborn, head strong, and sometimes openly arrogant. He was conscious of his superior education, and when he compared himself with Washington, who had limited formal education, he believed himself to be far more qualified to be president.

His home was near the seaside where he enjoyed playing. As a small boy, Adams enjoyed playing in the ruins of an old fort near his home, playing marbles, and climbing trees. As a youth, he was popular among his associates. He enjoyed wrestling and shooting. He

## A LIFE IN REVIEW

**Birth:** October 30, 1735; Braintree (Quincy), MA

**Died:** July 4, 1826; Quincy, MA

**Married:** Abigail Smith; October 25, 1764; 3 sons, 2 daughters

### CAREER

**1755–1758** Teacher

**1758–1768** Lawyer

**1768–1774** Member state legislature

**1774–1777** Member Continental Congress

**1777–1788** Foreign Diplomat

**1789–1797** U.S. Vice President

### ADMINISTRATION EVENTS

**1797** Constitution "Old Ironsides" launched

**1798** XYZ Affair, strained relations with France

**1798** Alien and Sedition Act

**1800** Washington, D.C. becomes capital

begin smoking at age of eight and throughout his life made many unsuccessful efforts to quit. As an adult, he was known to drink hard cider.

Many remarks he made throughout his life showed his love for and close association with the farm. When his future mother-in-law showed him a waistcoat she made for his wedding embroidered with a pattern of sprays of wheat and asked him what he thought, the whole family laughed when he said, "I wish to God that all my wheat were equally free of the epidemic rust."

## BIRTHPLACE

Adams was born October 30, 1735 in Braintree (now Quincy), Massachusetts at 133 Franklin Street. His birthplace was typical of farm houses in Braintree. It was a plain two-story clapboard house with a large fireplace and chimney in the center that was used to heat the building's four rooms—two downstairs and two up. There were hidden stairs around the chimney that could be used as a place of refuge from possible Indian attacks.

## BAPTISM

Adams was baptized at the (Puritan) Congregational Meeting House, 1266 Hancock Street, Braintree, Massachusetts, on November 6, 1735 by the modern calendar (October 26, 1735, by the old style calendar). He was baptized by the Reverend John Hancock, father of the patriot, John Hancock. The church is now known as First Parish Church.

## CHURCH

Although Adams attended many different churches, including Baptist, Presbyterian, Catholic, and the Friends Meeting House, his diaries specify no particular church home. Entries listed here are for those he attended on numerous occasions or for special events.

Adams considered Jesus to be the ideal example but did not believe in the Trinity nor that Jesus was the Son of God.

**1735–1826** *Braintree, Massachusetts.* The First Congregational Meeting House, 1266 Hancock Street. This was the parish church he attended most of his life. The meeting house of the Puritan descendants was built in 1732. The church also is known as the Stone Temple and Church of the Presidents, since John Adams and John Quincy Adams are buried in the church's starkly austere crypt.

**1751–1755**  *Cambridge, Massachusetts.* Like his fellow students at Harvard, Adams attended services at the First Church of Cambridge. This church was built in 1796 and was referred to as the Third Meeting House. It faced south and stood on Watch House Hill southwest of the present Lehman Hall. He usually took notes in church, and in his diary Adams often wrote critiques of sermon and notes on Scripture. The church was replaced in 1756. He also regularly attended morning prayers in Holden Chapel in the Harvard Yard and the First Parish Church (Unitarian) on Massachusetts Avenue.

**1751–1756**  *Boston, Massachusetts.* King's Chapel (Unitarian) at the corner of School Street. It was built in 1749 and was the first Episcopal church in New England. It later became the first Unitarian church in America.

**1756–1758**  *Worcester, Massachusetts.* First Parish Church of Worcester, or the Congregational Meeting House, on the Green. The pastor here was the Reverend McCarty. While Adams was teaching and studying here, he attended McCarty's long Sunday sermons. It was called Old South Church. The City Hall now stands on the site.

**1758–**  *Arlington, Massachusetts.* Unitarian Church, on Pleasant Street. He attended services here when he was in the area for one of his law cases.

**1763–**  *Weymouth, Massachusetts.* Weymouth Meeting House, 17 Church Street. He attended here while courting Abigail and after marriage while in Weymouth. Abigail's father was the pastor here. The church also was known as First Church, and sometimes the North Parish.

**1768–**  *Philadelphia, Pennsylvania.* St. Peter's Episcopal Church, at Third and Pine Streets. Adams preferred the Episcopal Church to others available in Philadelphia. Washington also attended this church.

**1768–**  *Philadelphia, Pennsylvania.* Christ Episcopal Church, between Fifth and Sixth Streets on the south side of Chestnut Street. Adams often sat in the president's pew.

**1768–**  *Philadelphia, Pennsylvania.* Second Presbyterian Church, at the northwest corner of Third and Arch Streets. (Since 1872 at Twenty-Second and Walnut Streets.) Adams often attended while in Philadelphia for the Continental Congresses. The church purchased a glass chandelier from Washington that was used in his Philadelphia home. For many years when it held candles it was difficult to prevent visitors from extracting drops from the chandelier.

**1777**  *Baltimore, Maryland.* Presbyterian Church. The site of the old church is now the property of the United States Post Office. The successor church is located at the northwest corner of Fayette and North Streets. When the British occupied Philadelphia, Adams attended this church while Congress was in session in Baltimore. The pastor also served as the chaplain to the Continental Congress. The original church was a plain brick building built in 1766 and enlarged in 1772.

**1789–**  *New York City, New York.* St. Paul's Chapel, at Broadway and Fulton Street. He attended following Washington's inauguration and on other occasions.

**1799**  *Philadelphia, Pennsylvania.* Zion German Lutheran Church, at Fourth and Cherry Streets. He attended a memorial funeral service for Washington who for the first time was characterized as "First in war, first in peace, and first in the hearts of his countrymen."

**1801–1826**  *See above under entry 1735–1826*

## EDUCATION

Adams began his schooling at a private school near his home, which he enjoyed. However, later when he was transferred to the

Latin School, he began to dislike school, as well as the teacher. By the time he was fifteen he wanted to leave school altogether. Like other young men who grew up on farms, Adams wanted to be a farmer, but his parents wanted none of this. They had planned, from the beginning, that he would study at Harvard College and follow in the steps of his grandfather, who was a Congregational minister. His father in an attempt to bring him "back to his senses" took him to the fields and piled on the work—making him shovel tons of manure, dig water channels, and clear dead trees. When his father asked, "Are you satisfied with being a farmer?" Adams replied, "I like it very well, sir." After that, with the family completely ignoring him, it was more than he could bear, and Adams made the decision to return to school and went on to complete a bachelor's degree at Harvard College. He received his bachelor's degree in 1755 and his master's in 1758.

**1735–1741** *Braintree, Massachusetts.* Adams's early childhood education began at home with his mother as his tutor.

**1741–1743** *Braintree, Massachusetts.* Dame Belcher's School. Dame Belcher conducted a primary school in her home which was across Coast Road from Adams's home. The specific location is not known.

**1743–1750** *Braintree, Massachusetts.* Free Latin School, near the Meeting House. Classes here were taught by a Mr. Cleverly. At this time Adams became more interested in learning arithmetic than Latin, and his top priority was to get away from Mr.Cleverly.

**1750–1751** *Braintree, Massachusetts.* Reverend Dr. Marsh's School, which was two doors from the Adams house. Here he prepared for the Harvard entrance examination.

**1751** *Cambridge, Massachusetts.* Mrs. Hill's on Charlestown Road (present Kirkland Street) near Cambridge Square. Adams studied here while appearing for the entrance examination. The definite location is unknown.

**1751–1755** *Cambridge, Massachusetts.* Harvard College. He was ranked fourteenth in a class of twenty-five. He received a bachelor's degree in 1755. At Harvard College he lived at 19 Massachusetts Hall. At the time, Harvard had three buildings: Harvard Hall, Stoughton Hall, and Massachusetts Hall. Winthrop's classes were held in the western room of the second floor of Old Harvard Hall. Old Harvard Hall burned in 1764. His greatest influence was Professor John Winthrop. The Winthrop home was located at the northwest corner of present Boylston and Mount Auburn Streets. During his last three years he lived in the lowermost northwest chamber of Massachusetts Hall, then designated as Number 3 and subsequently Number 19.

**1756–1758** *Worcester, Massachusetts.* In August 1756, Adams started law study with the only trained lawyer in Worcester, James Putnam—at the same time, Adams was preparing a dissertation for his master's degree at Harvard. Putnam's office was located in a little one-room building on the town Green. Adams boarded with the Putnams who lived three doors from Judge Chandler off the Green. He was admitted to the Massachusetts bar in November 1758.

# MARRIAGE AND HONEYMOON

Adams married Abigail Smith at her home at the corner of North and East Streets, in Weymouth, Massachusetts. The house is now at the corner of North and Norton Streets (in an area known as Weymouth Heights). There are no details of the wedding. As a young man, Adams fell in and out of love, and is said to have gallanted the girls "from Friday to Monday." However, he held to his father's admonition, marriage or nothing. Finally, at the age

*John Adams's birthplace*

of twenty-six, he was captivated by Abigail Smith, the daughter of the Weymouth Congregational pastor. After an engagement of more than two years, they were married.

Abigail was an attractive young woman, who throughout her life showed great diplomatic skill in managing her husband. Abigail, with little formal education, was self-educated, having read the great books which she would discuss with her husband. She had the advantage of being related to one of the first families of Boston—the Quincy family. She was an advocate of equal rights for women, and writing to her husband said, "Remember the ladies" and "if particular care and attention is not paid to the ladies, we are determined to foment a rebellion and will not hold ourselves bound by any laws in which we have no voice, or representation."

After the ceremony in Weymouth, the groom mounted his horse, leaned down and swung his bride up behind him, and off they rode for Braintree and their home at 141 Franklin Street.

## HOMES/LODGINGS

John Adams's true home, from birth to death, was always in Braintree (later renamed Quincy), Massachusetts. Three famous homes still stand in Quincy: 133 Franklin Street, 141 Franklin Street, and 135 Adams Street.

In his diary, Adams gives an almost day to day account of his dining and lodging, with many entries involving trips to Philadelphia, New York, and his home in Braintree (Quincy). As a result his lodgings are too numerous to mention individually.

**1735–1764** *Braintree (Quincy), Massachusetts.* 133 Franklin Street. See description of birthplace. Early in 1774 he purchased this family homestead from his brother, Peter, and the large farm that went with it.

**1755** *Worcester, Massachusetts.* Home of Major Nathaniel Green, about midway between Walnut and Sudbury Streets on the site of the present Day Building. For six months he boarded here while teaching. The house burned.

**1755–1756** *Worcester, Massachusetts.* Home of Dr. Nahum Willard, on the Green across the street from Franklin (originally South Street) on Main Street. The site is now occupied by the Boston Store and was on the same spot where he studied law. Adams boarded here while he was teaching; the cost of boarding was paid by the town.

**1756–1758** *Worcester, Massachusetts.* Home of James Putnam, just off the Green. Adams lived here, where the Park Building now stands, while studying law.

**1758–** *Arlington, Massachusetts.* Pleasant Street and Massachusetts Avenue. A marker on the Green marks the site of his dwelling.

**1764–1768** *Braintree (Quincy), Massachusetts.* 141 Franklin Street. Just before his marriage, this house next door to his birthplace was made ready for him and his new bride. The house was bought by his father in 1744, when Adams was nine. It is similar in structure to his birthplace.

**1764** *Weymouth, Massachusetts.* Corner of North and East Streets. This was the home of his wife's parents. Part of the original house was moved to the corner of North and Norton Streets. The lumber part of the original house was used to construct a new parsonage at 8 East Street (now a private residence).

**1764** *Boston, Massachusetts.* Washington Street. This was the home of his uncle, James Cunningham. Adams was here to get an inoculation for the smallpox epidemic.

**1768–1769** *Boston, Massachusetts.* Brattle Street on the corner across from the Brattle Square Church and the house of William Cooper and about two blocks from the Town Hall. Also called "the White House," this residence was a three-story building belonging to a Mr. Bollan. Adams lived here when the state legislature was in session and while he practiced law. The building has been demolished.

**1769–1770** *Boston, Massachusetts.* Cold (Cole) Lane by the Mill Pond. Adams moved here in order to get away from the noise of downtown. This street ran northward from Hanover Street to Mill Pond and was indiscriminately called Cold or Cole Lane. This is where the Adams's son, Charles, was born in 1770. No marker.

**1770–1771** *Boston, Massachusetts.* Brattle Street. Adams returned to this location to a rented house across the street from the Meeting House. He had his study on King Street. Now the site of office buildings.

**1771–** *Braintree (Quincy), Massachusetts.* 141 Franklin Street. The family returned to live in their own home between May and November of 1771.

**1771–1775** *Boston, Massachusetts.* Queen Street (Court Street), near the Court House and the Old State House. The street was originally known as Prison Lane; the name was changed in 1784, after a new courthouse was built at the site of the old prison. As a lawyer, it was convenient for Adams to be near the courthouse. Adams purchased this house in 1771. "I made it answer both for a dwelling and an office." Adams remained here until just before the war commenced in April 1775, when he moved his family back to 141 Franklin Street, in Braintree, while maintaining an office in Boston. Adams found the commute too much and moved back to Boston after almost nineteen months in Braintree. Adams returned to Braintree whenever he was home from his public service.

**1774–1777** *Philadelphia, Pennsylvania.* Stone House, on Arch Street opposite the City Tavern. This was a boarding house run by a Mrs. Yard. He stayed here while in the city for meetings of the Continental Congress. He stayed briefly at Jane Port's boarding house, on Arch Street about halfway between Front and Second Streets, from August 31 to September 3 but then returned to Mrs. Yard's. The City Tavern, where he often ate, stood on the west side of Second Street between Walnut and Chestnut Streets.

**1777** *Baltimore, Maryland.* Mrs. Ross's boarding house, a few doors below Fountain Inn on East Redwood Street. Adams stayed here during February. He also mentions a public house kept by a Mr. Johnson, which he appraised as the best inn he had ever seen.

**1777** *Philadelphia, Pennsylvania.* Mr. Duncan's house, south side of Walnut Street, between Second and Third Streets. He resided here from March 14 to September 12.

**1777** *Philadelphia, Pennsylvania.* Third Street, a few doors from the Meeting House. Between September 12 and 15, he had a short stay with Reverend Sprouts before escaping from the British. On September 18, he was in Fishkill, where he stayed at the Loudon home. He arrived in Braintree on November 27, 1777.

**1777** *York, Pennsylvania.* The Globe Inn, rented by General Daniel Roberdeau. Adams and many delegates to the Continental Congress stayed here. The Globe Inn was one of the most conspicuous buildings in York. The oldest surviving structure in York today is the Golden Plow Tavern, located on West Market Street. It was frequented by Adams during this period.

**1777** *Kutztown, Pennsylvania.* Kemp's Inn (now Whispering Springs), on U.S. 222. Adams was a lodger here.

**1778–1779** *Passy (near Paris), France.* Hotel de Valentinois, corner of Rue Reynouard and Rue Singer. Benjamin Franklin was living here in a separate building. The hotel

was close to the Bois de Boulogne, overlooking the Seine and Paris to the east. A tablet marks its site. Entries in his diary show a stream of dinner invitations and attendance to operas and museums. He often dined with LaFrete at Mont Calvaire, also called Mont Valerien, which rises above the village of Suresnes, west of the Seine and across from the Bois de Boulogne. Adams returned here February 9 to July 27, 1780.

**1780–1782** *Amsterdam, The Netherlands.* Keysersbragt near the Spiegel Straat. From August 1780 to January 1781, Adams lived here while in the diplomatic service. His son, John Quincy, was with him. Later he moved to Agterburg-Walby de Hoogstraat, behind the city wall near High Street and Oude Kerk and on the edge of area reserved for licensed prostitutes.

**1782–1783** *Paris.* The Hotel du Roi, Place du Carrousel between the Palais Royal and the Quai du Louvre. He lodged here from October 1782 until September 1783.

**1782–1784** *The Hague, The Netherlands.* On the Fluwelen Burgwal at Hotel des Etats Unis (the first American owned legation building in Europe). Fluwelen Burgwal— the Street of the "Velvet Makers".

**1783–1785** *Paris, France.* Auteuil 43–47 Rue d'Auteuil at the Hotel de Roualt near the Bois de Boulogne. He had a short period back in the Netherlands in 1784 and then returned to Paris.

**1784** *Paris.* Again at Hotel du Roi, Place du Carrousel.

**1785–1788** *London, England.* 9 Grosvenor Square at the northwest angle of the Square in the Parish of St. George, Hanover Square. This was the first United State legation in London and is at the junction of Duke and Brook Streets.

**1788–1826** *Braintree (Quincy), Massachusetts.* 135 Adams Street. In June 1788 Adams returned to the former John Borland house, which he purchased for 600 pounds on September 26, 1787. It was called "Peacefield" by Adams and by later generations as "Old House." When he returned here in 1801 he called it "Stony Field." In 1812 he adopted the name "Montezillo" and sometimes the English "Little Hill." The weather vane which is seen on the mound in front of the house was placed there by Adams a few years before his death. It had been on one of the old churches of the Congregational Society with which he worshipped until the church was struck by lightning. He was here whenever home in Quincy until his death. This was the family home of the Adams from 1788–1927. The house has been on fire twice: 1805 and 1821, when it narrowly escaped complete destruction.

**1789–1790**  *New York City, New York.* Richmond Hill, at the intersection of Charlton and Varick Streets, a mile outside the city. This had been Washington's headquarters. He lived here while vice-president during the year the capital was in New York. It was a high-columned house with eleven-foot ceilings and a view of the Hudson River. In 1817 the property was sold to John Jacob Astor, who cut down the hill and rolled the mansion down to the southwest corner of Charlton and Varick Streets. The house became a theater, menagerie, and tavern, and was demolished in 1849.

**1790–1791**  *Philadelphia, Pennsylvania.* Bush Hill, Vine Street on the Schuykill River about two miles out of town at the Hamilton estate. The property belonged to Governor Hamilton.

**1791–1794**  *Philadelphia, Pennsylvania.* He took a house in the heart of town, between Sixth and Market Streets. For a time during his first term as vice president, he lived at Francis' Hotel, 11–13 South Fourth Street.

**1797–1800**  *Philadelphia, Pennsylvania.* The "President's Residence" at Sixth and Market Streets (old address listed as 190 High Street). Adams stayed here while he served as president. Previously this house had served as Washington's dwelling. He preferred to stay in the house between Fifth and Sixth on Market.

**1797**  *New York City, New York.* Vincent-Halsey House, 3701 Provost Avenue at 233rd Street, the Bronx. This place served for two months as the nation's executive mansion, when Adams left Philadelphia to escape the yellow fever epidemic. The house has been altered and is no longer impressive. While living here, one of his sons drowned while swimming in nearby Eastchester Creek.

**1800–1801**  *Washington, D.C.* The White House, called the President's House at that time. Mrs. Adams hung her washing in the East Room.

# WORK

As a boy, Adams helped on his father's farm. While receiving his legal education he taught in order to help with his expenses. He was admitted to the bar on November 6, 1758. He was a political activist during and after the Revolutionary War, and most of his adult life was spent either in diplomatic service or with the federal government.

**1755–1758**  *Worchester, Massachusetts.* Worcester Center Grammar School, 50 miles west of Boston. Adams worked as a teacher in the one-room log house, while at the same time studying law. There is a plaque on the wall of the City Hall.

**1758–1768**  *Braintree, Massachusetts.* Law office at home at 141 Franklin Street.

**1766**  *Braintree, Massachusetts.* He was elected selectman for Braintree. Meetings were held in the Town Hall.

**1768–1774**  *Boston, Massachusetts.* Law office in his home at Brattle Square,

**1770**  *Boston, Massachusetts.* King Street. Adams worked as a lawyer in offices located here.

**1770** *Boston, Massachusetts.* He served as Clerk of the Suffolk bar association in the County Courthouse.

**1770–1774** *Boston, Massachusetts.* He was elected as representative to the General Court (lower house) from Boston. Meetings were held in the State House.

**1771–1774** *Boston, Massachusetts.* Queen Street. Adams worked as a lawyer in offices here.

**1774–1777** *Philadelphia, Pennsylvania.* Independence Hall. He was a member of both the First and Second Continental Congress and a member of the committee to draft the Declaration of Independence. The first session of the Continental Congress met in September 1774 and was held in Carpenter's Hall. On May 10, 1775 the Second Continental Congress convened in the State House, on Chestnut between Fifth and Sixth Streets. He, like others, became frustrated during the session and notes in his diary October 24, 1777, "In Congress, nibbling and quibbling—as usual."

**1775** *Boston, Massachusetts.* He was appointed Chief Justice of Massachusetts, meeting in Old State House on Beacon Hill. He resigned in 1777.

**1776** *Philadelphia, Pennsylvania.* He was appointed to a committee to draft a declaration of independence. Congress adjourned at Philadelphia December 12, 1776 and convened at Baltimore December 20. Adams arrived at Baltimore on February 1, 1777. He left Baltimore March 2 and arrived in Philadelphia March 6.

**1777** *Baltimore, Maryland.* Congress met in a house at the corner of Liberty and Baltimore. A memorial tablet marks the site of this building (Congress Hall). December 20, 1776 to February 27, 1777.

**1777** *York, Pennsylvania.* James Smith law office, corner of South George Street and Mason Alley, which was used as a meeting place of the Board of War over which he presided.

**1777** *York, Pennsylvania.* Courthouse with main entrance on South George Street where he met with other members of the Continental Congress on the second floor.

**1777–1788** Diplomat in England, France, and the Netherlands. Office at the Hotel des Etats Unis at the Hague.

**1788–1797** *New York City, New York and Philadelphia, Pennsylvania.* Adams was elected to the first Congress under the new Constitution on June 6, 1788. Vice president of the United States and presiding over the Senate meeting in Federal Hall. The capitol was in New York City from 1789 until December 6, 1790, when Congress moved to Philadelphia. The Senate chamber in Philadelphia was on the second floor of Congress Hall.

**1797–1801** *Philadelphia, Pennsylvania and Washington, D.C.* President of the United States. Adams was inaugurated as president in the House of Representatives on the second floor of Congress Hall, on March 4, 1797, in Philadelphia. In 1800 the capital was moved to Washington. He was absent from the capital in Philadelphia from March 11, 1798 to October 10, 1799, spending the time at his home in Quincy. He spent July through October 1800 in Braintree. On March 4, 1801 he refused to attend Jefferson's inauguration and left early that morning for Braintree. However, by 1812 he resumed a long, friendly correspondence with Jefferson.

# TRAVEL/VISITS

Like some modern day Americans, Adams travelled more in Europe than he did in his own country. In the United States, his travel was confined to states north of Washington, D.C. Prior to 1774, he remained in central and eastern Massachusetts, with the exception of a trip to Stafford Springs, Connecticut for health reasons.

**1769–** *Boston, Massachusetts.* Faneuil Hall, Merchants Row. He often attended banquets, receptions, and town hall meetings.

**1769–** *Boston, Massachusetts.* Green Dragon Tavern on Union Street was a frequent stopping place. The site is marked by a tablet.

**1770s–** *Springfield, Massachusetts.* Parsons Tavern which stood at the west end of Court Street was a favorite stopping place.

**1770s–** *West Brookfield, Massachusetts.* Hitchcock Tavern is still standing near the center of the village and still used.

**1770s–** *York, Maine.* He was here a number of times while on the Provincial Circuit. In 1770 he stayed at the Woodbridge Tavern the name of which had been changed to Ritchie's Tavern when he stayed there in 1771. He made an excursion to Agamenticus Mountain. When in town on Sunday he attended the Meeting House which was built on site of the old Meeting House in 1774 and renovated and greatly changed in 1882.

**1771** *Stafford Springs, Connecticut.* The site of the spring is between the library and the Episcopal Church in Hyde Park on Spring Street. He stayed at the Spring House Tavern while here bathing for his health. Visitors are welcome and can still drink the "iron water" today from the spring from which he drank.

**1771–** *Boston, Massachusetts.* American Coffee House (Previously known as British Coffee House).

**1774** *New York City, New York.* Tobias Stoutenburgh House, corner of Nassau Street near the City Hall, He was here on business and sightseeing for a week. Site only.

**1776** *Tottenville, New York.* Christopher Billopp House, Hyland Boulevard at the extreme southwest point of the island. Here Adams, in company with Benjamin Franklin and Edward Rutledge, met with the British Vice Admiral Lord Richard Howe seeking a peaceful settlement of the war that had started with Lexington and Concord. Adams wrote that Howe's preparations were wholesome and romantically elegant and the food and wine excellent.

**1788** *Boston, Massachusetts.* John and John Quincy stayed with John Hancock, the governor, upon their return from Europe. The house was demolished in 1863. Site is currently the statehouse grounds. Attempts by the state to acquire it as a governor's mansion failed but many relics were preserved.

**1789** *New York City, New York.* John Jay House, 133 Broadway. He stayed here after arriving April 20. The house has been demolished.

**1789** *Boston, Massachusetts.* Ingersoll Inn, directly across the street from Sears Block. He attended dinner here with Washington.

**1790** *Philadelphia, Pennsylvania.* The Indian Queen, an inn of the late eighteenth century, on the east side of Fourth Street below Market. Later site of modern business. He was also here in 1774.

**1800–** *Washington, D.C.* Duddington House, on the square between First and Second Streets on Capitol Hill. It was the first real mansion on the Hill and belonged to Daniel Carroll. It was a two-story, 60 foot long brick house with a white colonial style porch. It was a popular center for social affairs. Besides Adams, Jefferson, Madison, Monroe, and Jackson attended affairs here at one time or another.

**1800–** *Washington, D.C.* Rosedale. 3501 Newark Street, NW. Adams stayed here when coming to view the new capital.

**1800–** *Washington, D.C.* Suter's Tavern (also named Fountain Inn). High Street (now Wisconsin Avenue), between Bridge (M Street) and Water Streets.

**1800–** *Washington, D.C.* Union Tavern, at northeast corner of Bridge and Washington

Streets (now M and Thirtieth Streets). Modern building on site.

**1800–** *New Brunswick, New Jersey.* White Hart Tavern, northeast corner of Albany and Peace Streets. Marker on site.

# DEATH

Adams died July 4, 1826, at the age of ninety, in Quincy, Massachusetts, at 135 Adams Street, at 6:00 P.M. in an upstairs bedroom. He slipped quietly away. It is said his last words were "Thomas Jefferson still lives," although Jefferson had passed away a few hours earlier. In answer to a letter from Jefferson asking "Is death an evil?" he answered, "It is not an evil. It is a blessing to the individual and to the world. Yet we ought not to wish for it till life becomes insupportable; we must wait the pleasure and convenience of this great teacher. Winter is as terrible to me, as to you, I am almost reduced in it to the life of a Bear or torpid swallow." He left an estate of about $42,000.

# FUNERAL

Services were held July 7, 1826, in Quincy, Massachusetts, at the Congregational Church (the same church where he had been baptized), 1266 Hancock Street. The body was taken to Stone Temple, where another sermon was preached to a crowd of more than 2,000. Afterwards neighbors carried the coffin to the churchyard grave. John Quincy did not get there in time to attend the funeral.

# BURIAL

Adams's gravesite was located in Quincy, Massachusetts, in the Hancock Cemetery, across the street from the church. Later he was moved to the crypt in the First Parish Church (Unitarian) 1266 Hancock St where his wife and son, John Quincy Adams, are also buried.

# BIBLIOGRAPHY

Bowen, Catherine Drinker. *John Adams and the American Revolution Little.* Boston: Brown and Company, 1950.

Butterfield, L.H. ed. *John Adams: Diary and Autobiography,* 4 vols. Cambridge, Mass: Harvard University Press, 1961.

Levin, Phyllis Lee. *Abigail Adams.* New York: St. Martin's Press, 1987.

# THOMAS JEFFERSON

### 1743–1826
### 3RD PRESIDENT 1801–1809: DEMOCRATIC-REPUBLICAN PARTY

*"A little rebellion, now and then, is a good thing, and as necessary in the political world as storms in the physical.... It is a medicine necessary for the sound health of government."*

*Letter to James Madison, January 30, 1787*

Thomas Jefferson, the "Sage of Monticello," was born April 13, 1743, to Peter Jefferson, a Virginia planter, and Jane Randolph Jefferson, a member of one of Virginia's leading families. One source traces Jefferson's lineage back to David I, King of Scotland, through Sir Henry de Greene, who was beheaded in the fourteenth century.

## CHARACTERISTICS

Standing over 6′2″, Jefferson was one of the tallest presidents. He probably never weighed more than 175 pounds. His eyes were bluish green or hazel color; his hair a reddish hue. He had a light complexion that freckled easily. His most attractive feature was his even, nice looking teeth, which remained attractive as he got older. He could have profited from the use of a microphone, since his voice, like Madison's, could scarcely be heard ten feet away. As he spoke, he usually kept his arms folded. He did not drink, except for wine with dinner, and, unlike Washington and Adams, he did not smoke. Throughout his life he was a good dancer and violin player. He was known as an inventor—both of things mechanical and in customs. He was an outstanding architect and designed

# A LIFE IN REVIEW

**Birth:** April 13, 1743; Shadwell, VA

**Died:** July 4, 1826; Monticello, VA

**Married:** Martha Wayles Skelton; January 1, 1772; 1 son, 5 daughters (2 daughters lived to maturity)

## CAREER

**1767–1769** Lawyer

**1769–1774** Member Virginia House of Burgesses

**1774–1776** Member Continental Congress; Declaration of Independence, 1776

**1776–1779** Member Virginia House of Burgesses

**1779–1781** Governor of Virginia

**1783–1784** Member of Continental Congress

**1785–1789** Foreign Diplomat

**1789–1793** U.S. Secretary of State

**1797–1801** U.S. Vice President

## ADMINISTRATION EVENTS

**1801–1805** War with Tripoli

**1803** Marbury vs Madison

**1803** Louisiana Purchase

**1804–1806** Lewis and Clark Expedition

**1807** Fulton's steamboat Clermont voyage

**1807** Slave trade abolished

buildings throughout the state of Virginia. At times he gave architectural plans for a new house as wedding presents to new couples. On one occasion he told a visitor, "Architecture is my delight and putting up and pulling down, one of my favorite amusements." One custom he introduced was that of shaking hands in place of bowing. A Frenchman described him "as one who is at once a musician, skilled in drawing, a geometrician, an astronomer, a natural philosopher, legislator, and statesman."

## BIRTHPLACE

Jefferson was born in Shadwell in Goochland County (now Albemarle County), Virginia. Peter Jefferson had acquired the land in 1735 and built the house around 1737, six years before the birth of Thomas. The house burned in 1770; there is an historical marker at the site.

## BAPTISM

Jefferson was most likely baptized at St. Paul's Episcopal Church, in Shadwell, not far from the birthplace. Since the Jeffersons were regular communicants here, it is a fair assumption that Thomas was baptized here as an infant. There are no church remains, and there is no marker.

## CHURCH

Jefferson was a Deist with a belief in God. He admired the teachings of Jesus, calling them the "most perfect and sublime that has ever been taught by man," but he did not believe in the divinity of Christ. Throughout his life he regularly attended churches in Virginia, New York, and Pennsylvania. He might have put many pious churchgoers to shame by comparing their own giving with his generous voluntary support. From the time he entered political life he was in the forefront in the fight against religious tyranny. He stated, "I have sworn upon the altar of God, eternal hostility against every form of tyranny over the mind of man." In keeping with this thinking he founded the University of Virginia in 1819. For the first time in America, with Jefferson's innovation, higher education was independent of a church.

**1743–1752** *Shadwell, Virginia.* St. Paul's Episcopal Church. It was located between Shadwell and Charlottesville. Nothing remains.

**1752–1757** *Manikan, Virginia.* Dover Church in St. James Parish, Northam, River Road just east of Manikan. Exact site disputed. At the time he was attending a school run by the Reverend William Douglas who was pastor of the Dover Church.

**1757–1759** *Albemarle County, Virginia.* Fredericksville Parish Church, in the part of Albemarle County lying north and west of the Rivanna River. He attended while he was attending the Reverend James Maury School.

**1760–1767** *Williamsburg, Virginia.* Bruton Church. He attended while at William and Mary College. He sat near the pulpit in the half of the south gallery, which was assigned to the college students. Later, while practicing law in Williamsburg, he attended here and was a vestryman.

**1770–1826** *Charlottesville, Virginia.* Albemarle County courthouse, northwest corner of Jefferson and Park Streets. The northwest wing was used at first as a church. Jefferson referred to it as "the common temple." He attended here while living at Monticello, serving for a time as vestryman.

**1775–1781** *Richmond, Virginia.* St. John's Church, East Broad Street between North 24th and 25th Streets. Jefferson was present in the audience when Patrick Henry gave his famous speech in 1775. Later, when he lived in Richmond, he worshiped here.

**1790–1793** *Philadelphia, Pennsylvania.* St. Peter's Church, Third and Pine Streets.

**1801–1807** *Washington, D.C.* Christ Church, located at the foot of Capitol Hill near the intersection of New Jersey Avenue and D Streets, SE. The parishioners left for him the seat he had chosen on the first Sunday he attended. Christ Church was the first place of worship in the Washington area and occupied a building which had first been used as a tobacco warehouse. It had been "fitted up as a church in the plainest and crudest manner."

# EDUCATION

**1745–1752** *Tuckahoe, Virginia.* West of Richmond on Virginia 649 and River Road. Near his home is a small frame house where he attended school with his brothers, sisters, and cousins. He was not happy with school and often skipped out. In his early years he also received instruction from private tutors, in addition to studies in the regular classroom.

**1752–1757** *Northam, Virginia.* Dover Church in St. James Parish. Here he was taught by the Reverend William Douglas while boarding with him. Dover was five miles from Tuckahoe and a long way from his family in Shadwell, so that he stayed with Douglas eight or nine months of the year for five years, going back to Shadwell only during the summers. The exact site is disputed.

**1757–1759** *Fredericksburg Parish, Virginia.* Maury School, between Shadwell and Gordonsville to the east in a small log house. Here he was given a good foundation in Greek and Latin by the Reverend James Maury. Although he was close enough to Shadwell to go home on weekends, he boarded during the week with the Maury family. James Madison, who later became the president of William and Mary College and was a second cousin of the future president was one of his classmates. There is a Virginia marker JE-6 on the Shadwell-Gordonsville highway.

**1760–1762**  *Williamsburg, Virginia.* William and Mary College. After two years in the school of philosophy, he received a bachelor's degree in 1762. By this time he was used to lodging away from home. As a "paying scholar" at the college he was not compelled to eat and sleep there. However, he did not choose to stay outside and the records show he began to pay board on March 25, 1760 and continued to do so for two years. He lodged in the main building. Several of the old buildings remain that were there during his time. The central building, even then more than sixty years old, was generally called the College. In addition there was Brafferton Hall where a small number of Indian students stayed and directly opposite, a twin structure known as the President's house.

**1762–1767**  *Williamsburg, Virginia.* During these years Jefferson studied law under the direction of George Wythe. The Wythe House is at the corner of Prince George Street and the Palace Green. Lodging during this period was possibly on Duke of Gloucester Street, although there is no record of a definite site. As a law student he had lodgings in town—these could have been on either of the two narrower streets that parallel Duke of Gloucester Street. He probably stayed at several different places during this period. For a time he studied in the same room as John Tyler, father of the future president. He often dined with Governor Francis Fauquier at the Palace.

## MARRIAGE AND HONEYMOON

Jefferson was married on January 1, 1772, at "The Forest" in Charles City County, Virginia, about two miles southeast of Malvern Hill and two miles northwest of Shirley Plantation. This was the home of Martha Wayles Skelton, his bride. The site is now an empty lot of tangled weeds and bushes covering the ruined substructure which was destroyed years ago by fire. A marker V-15 indicates the nearby site. Like John Adams, Jefferson was married shortly before his twenty-ninth birthday. His bride Martha Wayles Skelton was the daughter of John Wayles, a wealthy lawyer of Charles City County. She was the widow of Bathwest Skelton, who died before Martha was twenty. The Jefferson's honeymoon took place at Blenheim and Monticello, Virginia. On the first night of their marriage, as they made their way to Monticello, there was a heavy snowfall. While eight miles from Monticello they were forced to spend the night at Blenheim, now called the Honeymoon Lodge. According to another account, the homeward trip was delayed by a stay of more than two weeks at the Forest; in mid-January they set out for Monticello and this may be the time they had to stop in Blenheim. The site is located off Virginia County Route 708.

During their ten years of married life they made a good couple, since she was an accomplished musician with the harpsichord and the pianoforte and he played the violin and cello. Martha died nineteen years before he became president and he never remarried. Lacking a first lady while in the White House, he did very little formal entertaining. For these functions he depended upon his eldest daughter, Martha Jefferson Randolph, to serve as hostess and to manage the household.

## HOMES/LODGINGS

**1743–1745**  *Shadwell, Virginia.* On U.S. 250, east of Charlottesville. At Shadwell he lived in a simple wooden house. A marker on the highway indicates the site of this house. At the site there is a small stone monument marking the actual site.

*Thomas Jefferson birthplace marker*

**1745–1752** *Tuckahoe, Virginia.* West of Richmond, on Virginia 649 on River Road. This was an older and better house than Shadwell. His boyhood home was a large H-shaped building with two wings connected by a large room, making it adaptable to the two-family living which it had to accommodate. His earliest recollection was of being carried on a pillow by a mounted slave on the journey from Shadwell to Tuckahoe. Members of the Randolph family still live on the grounds.

**1768–** *Williamsburg, Virginia.* He lodged at Charlton's on the Duke of Gloucester and had his meals at Raleigh Tavern, while serving with the General Court of Virginia and pursuing his law practice.

**1770–1826** *Monticello, Virginia.* On Virginia 53, three miles south of Charlottesville. Next to George Washington's Mount Vernon home, Jefferson's home at Monticello, where he lived most of his life, is possibly the most famous presidential home in the United States. Jefferson began construction in 1769 and continued for more than forty years, as he designed and redesigned this architectural masterpiece.

**1774** *Elkhill and Elk Island, Goochland County, Virginia.* The site is located at the junction of Virginia 6 and County Route 608, near Columbia. The site was added to his possessions through his wife's inheritance. It has some historical significance, since the family stayed here at times during the war.

**1774** *Edgehill, Virginia.* About a mile east of Shadwell on Virginia 22 is a two-story brick house covered with clapboarding, which was a home belonging to Jefferson. It became the residence of his daughter Martha after her marriage.

**1774–** *Poplar Forest, Bedford County, Virginia.* Off U.S. 221, near Lynchburg. This site was also acquired by inheritance. In 1806, while he was president, he assisted the masons in laying the foundation for the dwelling that is considered as one of his most creative and original architectural designs. Here he often enjoyed the company of his grandchildren. Pressed by debt, he was forced to sell this charming house several years before his death. Currently excavation is being done.

**1775** *Philadelphia, Pennsylvania.* He stayed at the home of Mr. Benjamin Randolph on Chestnut Street, between Third and Fourth Streets. He usually took his dinner and supper at the City Tavern on Second Street. He was here for the Continental Congress of 1775.

**1775–** *Philadelphia, Pennsylvania.* He also frequented the Indian Queen Hotel, 15 South Fourth Street at the southeast corner of High and Fourth Streets. Jefferson also visited Dunwoody's Tavern, known as the Spread Eagle Inn at 715 Market Street, between Seventh and Eighth Streets.

**1776** *Philadelphia, Pennsylvania.* He stayed in a new, three-story brick house, on the southwest corner of Market and Seventh

*Boyhood home of Thomas Jefferson.*

Streets, belonging to a Mr. Graaf. Here he wrote the Declaration of Independence.

**1779–1780**  *Williamsburg, Virginia.* As Governor he resided at the Governor's Palace until the capital was moved to Richmond. This building has been reconstructed.

**1780**  *Richmond, Virginia.* In 1779, Richmond was made the capital of Virginia; in 1780 Jefferson moved into a rented house belonging to his uncle by marriage, Thomas Turpin. The location has not been confirmed, but was possibly at the southeast corner of Broad and Governor Streets, where the Memorial Hospital now stands. Although an inscription on the present governor's mansion lists Jefferson among the governors having lived on that spot, it is not likely Jefferson was ever an occupant of the old Palace.

**1780–1783**  *Philadelphia, Pennsylvania.* Off and on during these years, Jefferson stayed

at the home of Mrs. Mary House and her daughter, Mrs. Trist, at 368 Chestnut Street, while visiting the national capitol.

**1784–1789**  *Paris, France.* Hotel d'Orleans, on Rue de Richelieu near the King's Library and a few yards from the birthplace of Voltaire. Four days later in August 1784, he moved to a hotel of the same name on present day Rue Bonaparte on the Left Bank. He was a short walk away from the quayside chateau of Chastellux, who lived at Rue de Bac. From October 16, 1784 to October 17, 1785, Jefferson lived in Hotel Landron in the Cul-de-sac Taitbout, which branched off from the Rue Taitbout toward the Rue de la Chaissee d'Antin (later the street was lengthened southward to the Boulevard des Italiens and renamed Rue du Helder). The site of his home is on the northern segment of the Rue du Helder in the vicinity of the Opera. From October 17, 1785 to September 26, 1789, Jefferson stayed at the Hotel de Langeac, near the Grille de Chaillot, at the corner of the Grande Route des Champs Elysees and Rue Neuve de Berri. The current structure stands at the northeast corner of the Rue de Berri and the Champs Elysees. The site is marked by a plaque. He also kept rooms at the Carthusian Monastery on Mount Calvary.

**1789–** *Germantown, Pennsylvania.* 18th and Courtland Streets. He stayed here while serving as Secretary of State.

**1790–** *New York City, New York.* 57 Maiden Lane. He stayed here while serving as Secretary of State.

**1791–1793** *Philadelphia, Pennsylvania.* 806 Market Street (274 High Street). His large four story house was on the south side of Market Street, the fourth house west of Eighth Street. It was razed in 1900 to make room for a building erected by Gimbel Brothers.

**1793–1794** *Philadelphia, Pennsylvania.* He had a house located near Gray's Ferry on the Schuylkill River while Secretary of State. It was a simple three-room cottage located on the east side of the Schuylkill River at a point between 36th and 37th Streets and Reed and Dickinson Streets. He rented the house from April 1793 to January 2, 1794

**1794** *Philadelphia.* Clarkson-Watson House, 5275 Germantown Avenue. He moved here from the house near Gray's Ferry during the yellow fever epidemic. The house is now a Costume Museum.

**1794–1797** *Monticello, Virginia.*

**1797–1800** *Philadelphia, Pennsylvania.* Francis Hotel, 11-13 South Fourth Street. While vice president, he maintained no independent place of residence, staying at the hotel of John Francis and spending as much time as he could back home in Monticello.

**1800–1801** *Washington, D.C.* Thomas Conrad and McMun Boarding House (later Var-

num Hotel), on the south side of the Potomac on New Jersey Avenue. He stayed here during his last few months as vice president.

**1801–1809** *Washington, D.C.* The White House.

**1806–1819** *Poplar Forest, near Lynchburg, Virginia.* This site was a part-time home he used when he wanted to get away from Monticello.

# WORK

Jefferson grew up as part of an aristocratic landowning family in Virginia. Like the other early presidents from Virginia, he claimed farming as a profession. Although he practiced law briefly, for most of his life he worked in public service, including a short period in France in the diplomatic service.

**1767–1774** *Williamsburg, Virginia.* He began his legal career in the General Court of colonial Virginia. See the reconstructed buildings in Old Williamsburg. The site of his law practice has not been determined.

**1775–1776** *Philadelphia, Pennsylvania.* Jefferson was a delegate to the Continental Congresses—at the age of thirty-two, he was one of the youngest delegates. The Congress met in what was then the Pennsylvania State House and is now known as Independence Hall.

**1776–1779** *Williamsburg, Virginia.* The legislature convened in the Wren Building until the capitol was built.

**1779–1781** *Williamsburg and Richmond, Virginia.* As governor of Virginia, he lived in Richmond until the Capitol was built. The Assembly met in a building known as the Cuninghame Ware House, located on the northwest corner of Cary and 14th (then Pearl) Streets.

**1783–1784** *Pennsylvania, New Jersey, and New York.* In Philadelphia the House of

Representatives met downstairs in Congress Hall. In Annapolis they met in the Old State House. On June 24, 1783 the Congress moved to Princeton, New Jersey, using Nassau Hall. Congress met in Trenton, New Jersey on November 1, 1784, and in New York City from January 11, 1785. See plaque on State Street in Trenton.

**1785–1789** *Paris France.* Minister to France.

**1790–1793** *Philadelphia, Pennsylvania.* As secretary of state, Jefferson worked in Philadelphia in a private house at 307 High Street, on the northwest corner of Eighth and Market Streets. Later the state department moved to Arch Street, two doors east of Sixth Street. He left the office of secretary of state in December 1793.

**1797–1801** *Philadelphia, Pennsylvania.* As vice president, Jefferson presided over the Senate in the Senate Chamber on the second floor of Congress Hall in Philadelphia.

**1801–1809** *Washington, D.C.* "Being President," he said, "is a splendid misery." His inauguration was simple and as president he walked back to the tavern where he had been living. His second inaugural was even more simple.

**1819** *Charlottesville, Virginia.* The University of Virginia at West and Main Street was founded by Jefferson.

# TRAVEL/VISITS

**1760s** *Gordonsville, Virginia.* Exchange Hotel, on U.S. 33 at the eastern edge of the downtown area. Jefferson often lodged and dined here.

**1760s** *Charlottesville, Virginia.* Eagle Tavern, on Court Square. Now the site of the Monticello Hotel, which kept the old Eagle register including the names of Jefferson, Madison, Monroe, T. Roosevelt, and Wilson.

**1770s** *Gloucester County, Virginia.* Rosewell, located near Carter's Creek on the east bank of the York River, north of Yorktown. He visited one of his best friends here, John Page, who was later governor of Virginia. The mansion is now in ruins, following a fire in 1916.

**1770s** *Wilmington, Delaware.* Sign of the Ship Tavern, southeast corner Third and Market Streets (now a retail shop). This was a stopping off place between Virginia and Philadelphia. Plaque at the site.

**1770s** *Richmond, Virginia.* Hogg's Tavern, southwest corner of Fifteenth and Main Streets.

**1770–** *Richmond, Virginia.* 818 East Marshall Street. This was the home of his cousin, John Marshall, who later became Chief Justice of the Supreme Court.

**1774–** *Near Lorton, Virginia.* Gunston Hall. Off I-95, eighteen miles south of Washington. This was the home of George Mason. Jefferson often attended political meetings here.

**1777** *Fredericksburg, Virginia.* Rising Sun Tavern, Caroline Street, between Fauquier and Hawke Streets. Jefferson met here with others when he outlined the Virginia religious liberty bill. This bill was passed in 1779.

**1779** *Lovingston, Virginia.* Union Hill, on County Road 647, about two miles from Lovingston. This was the home of William Cabell. Jefferson stopped here when in flight from the British. There is a new house on site. In the old cemetery near the site of the old house are buried two of Patrick Henry's sons.

**1780s** *Ephrata, Pennsylvania.* Home of Johann Peter Miller, the Cloisters, on the western edge of town. This was a restful retreat of a religious order popular with many statesmen of the time. The exact location of Miller house is unknown.

**1783** *Annapolis, Maryland.* Ghiselin Boarding House, 28-30 West Street, on north side

*Thomas Jefferson's home at Monticello*

just below Frances Bryce Boarding House at 18 West Street. Now the site of the Telephone Building. Jefferson took lodging here until February 1784, while attending the Continental Congress. On February 25, 1784, he moved to Dulany's house on the east side of Conduit Street, between Southeast Street (now Duke of Glouchester Street) and Church Street (now Main Street), now used as a Masonic lodge. James Monroe shared his quarters here.

**1786**   *London, England.* While in London, he lodged at Number 14, Golden Square. This was his first and only visit to London. He met with John Adams here. He visited Twickenham and Hampton Court and, then together with John Adams, went to Woburn Farm, Caversham, Wotton, Stowe, Edgehill, Stratford-upon-Avon, Birmingham, the Leasowes, Hagley, Stourbridge, Worcester, Woodstock, Blenheim, Oxford,

High Wycomb, and back to Grosvenor Square in London.

**1786–1787**   *France.* While stationed in France he visited Dijon, Lyons, Pont St. Esprit, Nimes—seeing his model for the capitol in Richmond,—Arles, St. Remis, Aix, Marseilles, Toulon, Hieres, Freju Antibes, Nice, and on to Italy and Col de Tende, Coni, Turin, Vercelli, Milan, Pavia, Tortona, Novi, Genoa, Albenga, and back to Monaco and to France, Nice, Brignolles, Avignon, Pont du Gard, Montpelier, Narbonne, Toulouse, Bordeaux, Rochefort, Rochelle, Nantes, Lorient, Nantes, Tours, Orleans and finally Paris.

**1790–1793**   *Philadelphia, Pennslyvania.* Home of Benjamin Franklin in Franklin Court. An underground museum is built where Franklin's house once stood. Nearby is the private house where Jefferson stayed.

**1801–1809**   *Philadelphia, Pennsylvania.* American Philosophical Society, 104 South

Fifth Street. Jefferson was the president of the society.

**1800–1809** *Washington, D.C.* Duddington House and the Griffith Coombe House, at the corner of Third Street and Georgia Avenue, SE.

**1809** *Richmond, Virginia.* Swan Inn, northwest corner Broad and Ninth Streets. No markers.

**1818** *Waynesboro, Virginia.* On the grounds of the site of the Old Mountain Top Tavern, he met with Madison, Monroe, and others to decide the location of the University of Virginia.

# DEATH

Jefferson died on July 4, 1826 at Monticello, Virginia. He passed away in his bedroom. His friends, Garrett and Carr placed his body in a simple shroud. He died without leaving an estate, and his years in public service and his generous hospitality left him heavily in debt.

# FUNERAL

His funeral was held at Monticello. It was a simple ceremony at the grave site.

# BURIAL

Jefferson's grave site is located at Monticello, in an enclosed plot next to his wife, Martha's. He sketched the plan for his own tombstone and left instructions that it be carved of coarse stone to discourage vandals and with an inscription listing his proudest achievements: Author of the Declaration of Independence, Statute of Virginia Religious Freedom, and Father of the University of Virginia with no mention of being President of the United States. A grand memorial stands in the nation's capital.

# SPECIAL SITES

Black Hills, South Dakota. Mount Rushmore.

Washington, D.C. Jefferson Memorial, on the banks of the Tidal Basin off the Potomac River.

# BIBLIOGRAPHY

Dumbauld, Edward. *Thomas Jefferson American Tourist.* Norman: University of Oklahoma Press, 1946.

Malone, Dumas. *Jefferson and His Time.* 6 vols. Boston: Little, Brown and Company, 1948–1981.

THE PRESIDENTS

# JAMES MADISON

## 1751–1836
### 4TH PRESIDENT 1809–1817: DEMOCRATIC-REPUBLICAN PARTY

*"If there be a principle that ought not to be questioned within the United States, it is that every nation has a right to abolish an old government and establish a new one."*

— *To "Pacificus," April 22, 1793*

James Madison, "Father of the Constitution," was born March 16, 1751, at midnight, to James and Eleanor Conway Madison.

## CHARACTERISTICS

Although he was impressive in his writings, he was not impressive in size. He was hardly 5′4″ tall and weighed approximately 100 pounds. He was a pleasant-looking man with blue eyes, brown hair, and a somewhat sallow complexion. At the time he became president, he had hair at the sides of his head but was bald on top. He had regular features, although his nose was scarred from once having been frostbitten. Notes from youth to old age indicate constant health problems. He usually wore dark colored clothes, which never fully fit. Although he never went out without his high conical hat, he remained obviously short in stature. He had a slight speech defect and a very low voice; people had to strain to hear him. An associate described him as a gentleman of great modesty with a remarkably sweet temper. He was fond of reading and chess, and for exercise he enjoyed walking and horseback riding. Jefferson called him "the best farmer in the world."

## A LIFE IN REVIEW

**Birth:** March 16, 1751; Port Conway, VA

**Died:** June 28, 1836; Montpelier, VA

**Married:** Dolley Payne Todd; September 15, 1794; No children

### CAREER

**1776–1777** Member Virginia House of Burgesses

**1778–1779** Member Virginia Council of State

**1780–1783** Member Continental Congress

**1784–1786** Member Virginia House of Burgesses; again 1799–1800

**1786** Delegate to Annapolis Convention

**1789–1797** Member U.S. Congress

**1801–1809** U.S. Secretary of State

### ADMINISTRATION EVENTS

**1812–1814** War of 1812

**1813** First White House wedding

**1813** Admiral Perry's victory on Lake Erie

**1813** Creek War

**1816** Chartered 2nd Bank of United States

## BIRTHPLACE

Madison was born in Port Conway, King George County, Virginia, at the Belle Grove plantation on the Rappahannock River. This was the home of his maternal grandmother, Catlett Moore. The site is located on Virginia 207. The house is no longer standing, only a marker designates the spot.

## BAPTISM

Madison was baptized on March 31, 1751, in King George County, Virginia, at Strother's Church (named for the family on whose land it had been erected). It was replaced some years later by a second building on the same location, which was destroyed soon after the Revolution. Here he was baptized by the Reverend William Davis. The approximate site is on Millbank land, about a mile upstream northeast of the birthplace, Belle Grove, and the current Emmanuel Church.

## CHURCH

Madison was a strong supporter of the principle of separation of church and state. He opposed the concept of an "established" church. He supported his position citing the example of President Jefferson, "During the administration of Mr. Jefferson no religious proclamation was issued." In the legislature Madison sponsored a measure decriminalizing heresy and abolishing the religious test for public office.

As a boy, and for most people of his community, the big event of the week was the six or seven mile ride over rough roads to the Brick Church. However, between the time he left college and his marriage to Dolley, there is almost no mention made of his church attendance in his diaries or in other writings. Despite their regular attendance at the old Brick Church and in Washington churches, after his marriage, neither he nor Dolley ever joined a church. During his early years in government service and while residing in New York City, evidence shows that he spent more time writing letters than attending church on Sunday.

**1751** *King George County, Virginia.* Hanover Parish Church, off U.S. 301 at 9415 King's Highway. Here Madison would have been taken as a baby when he and his mother were staying with his maternal grandparents.

**1751–** *Orange, Virginia.* Old Brick Church (Anglican), St. Thomas Parish, off County Road 639, three miles southeast of the courthouse and a few miles from Montpelier. The church was built during the 1750s on the land owned by his great uncle, James Taylor, whose plantation, Meadow Farm, stretched along the old road toward Fredericksburg.

**1776–1779** *Williamsburg, Virginia.* Bruton Parish Church on the Palace Green. Madison would attend services here whenever he was in Williamsburg for legislative sessions or visiting his cousin who was president of William and Mary.

**1780–1783** *Philadelphia, Pennsylvania.* St. Peter's Episcopal Church, Third and Pine Streets. He worshipped here while in the city, particularly after his marriage to Dolley. From 1790 to 1797 he attended while serving in Congress.

**1789–1790** *New York City, New York.* Trinity Episcopal Church, Wall Street. Madison accompanied others following Washington's inaugural for the special service.

**1799–1800** *Richmond, Virginia.* St. John's Episcopal, East Broad Street between North 24th and North 25th Streets, In this old white frame historic building, he attended while serving as a member of the Virginia legislature.

**1801–1817** *Washington, D.C.* Christ Church, Sixth and G Streets, SE. He first attended services here upon arrival in Washington. After his death, Dolley came back to Washington and continued her regular attendance here.

# EDUCATION

**1751–1762** *Montpelier, Orange County, Virginia.* Madison had his early education at home, probably with his mother, grandmother, or a local Anglican clergyman.

**1762–1767** *Newton, King and Queen County, Virginia.* Donald Robertson School, in the Drysdale Parish, on the plantation of the Reverend Robert Innis. It was north of the Mattapony River, near the junction of County Roads 625 and 618. Madison boarded with the Innis family and stayed with his grandparents from time to time. This school was considered unequalled for that time. The site is now a meadowland with no markers.

**1767–1769** *Montpelier, Orange County, Virginia.* He studied at home, tutored by Reverend Thomas Martin, a teacher and Episcopal clergyman. Under Martin's tutelage, he was introduced to Hebrew, Greek, and Latin.

**1769–1772** *Princeton, New Jersey.* College of New Jersey (now Princeton University). Here he enrolled as a sophomore. He had a close association with his Presbyterian tutor, Samuel Smith. He graduated in the Fall of 1771 with a bachelor's degree. He remained at Princeton until April 1772, due to poor health; he studied Hebrew during this period. A restored Nassau Hall is the only building remaining from his time. He lodged in Nassau Hall. He was an early member of the newly formed Whig Literary Society.

# MARRIAGE AND HONEYMOON

Madison was married on September 15, 1794, in Berkeley Springs, Virginia, at the Harewood estate, off Virginia 51. He was married to the widow Dolley Payne Todd at the home of George Steptoe Washington in the Blue Ridge foothills. None of his family was present. The site is now the private residence Dr. and Mrs. John Washington.

The honeymoon took place in Winchester, Virginia, at the Belle Grove plantation, five miles south of Middletown on U.S. 11. Later this was the site of the Civil War Battle of

*James and Dolley Madison's honey-moon site.*

Cedar Creek. The couple had planned to go on from here to Montpelier, but Dolley became ill and they went north instead and spent two weeks with his sister, Nelly Hite, (beginning four days after the wedding) while Dolley recovered. Communications were limited and his father and mother were not told of the wedding until about three weeks later, when he sent his servant to give the news and it was many more months before they first saw their new daughter-in-law. The honeymoon site is but a short distance from Harewood, where the couple was married. The Hite home, Long Meadows Farm, was near Strasburg.

While at the White House Mrs. Madison loved parties and entertained extravagantly. It is said that some of the more conservative people of Washington said that when the British burned part of the White House in 1814 it was punishment from heaven for all the goings on there. Dolley Madison became the model for the First Lady for years to come. Her dress designs and hairstyles were copied by women in the United States and all over the world.

# HOMES/LODGINGS

**1751–** *Orange, Virginia.* Meadow Farm, plantation of his uncle on the highway between Orange and Fredericksburg.

**1751–1836** *Montpelier, Orange County, Virginia.* Four miles southeast of Orange on Virginia 20. Montpelier was Madison's lifelong home and was to him what Mount Vernon and Monticello were to Washington and Jefferson. The site of the earlier plantation wooden house to which he first came is not known, but local tradition places it on a knoll near the Madison family graveyard and about one-half mile south of the present mansion. The current house was probably built around 1760. The home was not called Montpelier until around 1780. Madison added one story wings to either side of the house in 1809. Many changes have been made to the old plantation home. Limestone plaster was added to the brick exterior and wings added, among other changes. Later, when the house belonged to the DuPont family (1901–1983), a second story was added to the wings on either side. A number of other changes were made, however, an effort has been made to restore the mansion.

**1778–1779** *Williamsburg, Virginia.* President's House, on the campus of William and Mary. He lived with his second cousin, Reverend James Madison, who was president of the college. The house stands today much as it was then.

**1780–1793** *Philadelphia, Pennsylvania.* Boarding house of Mrs. Mary House, Fifth and Market Streets, a block from the Pennsylvania State house (now Independence Hall). He always stayed here when in Philadelphia until Mrs. House died in 1793. Sometimes it is known as House-Trist home.

**1783–1784** *Philadelphia, Pennsylvania.* Todd House, Fourth and Walnut Streets. This was the home of Dolley's mother.

**1786–1787** *Annapolis, Maryland.* George Mann's Tavern, 162 Conduit Street. He stayed here during the Constitutional Convention. He frequented other inns for meals and gatherings, including the Donald-Stewart House, 10 Francis Street, one of the oldest. This house is sometimes listed as "Sign of the Indian King." He also visited the Maryland Inn, Church Circle and Main Street (has been restored) and Reynolds Tavern, Church Circle and Franklin Street.

**1787–1790** *New York City, New York.* Mrs. Dorothy Elsworth Boarding House. 19 Maiden Lane. He stayed here while serving in Congress.

**1793–1794** *Philadelphia, Pennsylvania.* He lived in a house belonging to James Monroe on Spruce Street.

**1794–1797** *Philadelphia, Pennsylvania.* After marriage, he lived in a large fashionable house on Spruce Street.

**1797–1801** *Montpelier, Orange County, Virginia.*

**1801–** *Washington, D.C.* "Six Buildings" on Pennsylvania Avenue between 21st and 22nd Streets. The Madisons moved from the White House, where they were staying with Jefferson in the unfinished President's House to "Six Buildings" and remained in this row house for two months. It was located among other fashionable dwellings on the road to Georgetown.

**1801–1809** *Washington, D.C.* 1333 F Street, NW, two blocks east of the White House. They lived here for eight years. Later this house was occupied by John Quincy Adams. It was a three-story brick building with a cupola. There were four dormer bedrooms on the third floor, wine and coal rooms in the cellar, a coach house, and stables for four horses in the rear.

**1809–1814** *Washington, D.C.* The White House (President's House). Fire, set by the British in the War of 1812, gutted the house forcing him to flee and arrange living quarters elsewhere for the rest of his term of office.

**1814–1816** *Washington, D.C.* Tayloe Mansion (generally called The Octagon House), 1799 New York Avenue, NW.

**1816–1817** *Washington, D.C.* He lived in the two houses forming the corner of the "Seven Buildings" on Pennsylvania Avenue for a brief time. He entertained General Andrew Jackson and his wife here. On Lafayette Square, northeast corner, stands the square solid mansion, now owned by the Cosmos Club but pointed out as "Dolley Madison's House." It was built by Dolley's sister, Anna, and brother-in-law, Richard Cutts. Anna occupied it for many years. It ended up in Madison's hands and became Dolley's residence when she returned to Washington after Madison's death in 1836.

# WORK

While Madison pursued his studies, he considered pursuing law but disliked the dull reading. He also considered the clergy, but his liberal views probably discouraged him from following the career path. At a time when others were entering military service, he finally opted for a life-long career in the public service.

**1776–1777** *Williamsburg, Virginia.* Council Room in the Capitol. Here he helped write the Virginia state constitution.

**1780–1783** *Philadelphia, Pennsylvania.* He served as a delegate to the Continental Congress. The Congress met in the Pennsylvania State House (now Independence Hall) on Chestnut Street. The Congress met in Princeton on June 23, 1783 and on November 26 reconvened in Annapolis.

**1784–1786** *Richmond, Virginia.* He served as a member of Virginia legislature. The assembly met in a building known then as the Cuningham Warehouse.

**1786** *Annapolis, Maryland.* The Constitutional Convention met in the Old State House on State Circle.

**1787–1788** *Philadelphia, Pennsylvania.* Members of Congress met in the Assembly Room of Independence Hall to draw up a new constitution. Members of the House of Representatives met downstairs in the Congress Hall. During this period Madison wrote many of the *Federalist Papers.* During this period he earned the title "Father of the Constitution."

**1789–1797** *New York City, New York and Philadelphia, Pennsylvania.* Members of the House of Representatives met in New York in Federal Hall and in Philadelphia in Congress Hall. Congress Hall was constructed as the Philadelphia County Court House.

**1799–1800** *Richmond, Virginia.* The Virginia legislature met on Capitol Square. The Assembly met in the old Hall of Delegates, on the first floor off the Rotunda and opposite the portico entrance.

**1801–1809** *Washington, D.C.* The State Department Building, on 17th Street, NW. The building is no longer extant.

**1809–1817** *Washington, D.C.* The White House. His inauguration was the first to be marked by pomp and festivity.

**1826** *Charlottesville, Virginia.* He succeeded Jefferson as rector of the University of Virginia.

**1829–1830** *Richmond, Virginia.* First African Baptist Church, College and East Broad Streets. He served as co-chairman of the Virginia State Constitutional Convention. At first they met in the Hall of Delegates (now a museum) on the first floor of the Capitol.

# TRAVEL/VISITS

Madison had no travel outside the United States. He is one of the least travelled of the presidents. Outside his native Virginia he visited Connecticut, Delaware, Kentucky, Maryland, New Jersey, New York, Pennsylvania, Vermont, and (what is now) West Virginia. Most of his travel was limited to journeys between home and Princeton and between his home and public service in the capitals of New York City, Philadelphia, and Washington, D.C. On the trips to the capitals he often stopped with Monroe in Fredericksburg or with Washington at Mount Vernon.

**1769** *Philadelphia, Pennsylvania.* On his way to Princeton he stopped in Philadelphia for the first time and stopped at the London Coffee House.

**1772** *Warm Springs (Berkeley), in what is now Morgan County, West Virginia.* He stayed here during the summer of 1772. None of the original resort hotels remain.

**1776–** *Richmond, Virginia.* George Wythe House, 503 East Grace Street.

**1784–** *Richmond, Virginia.* John Marshall House, 818 East Marshall.

**1784–** *Mount Vernon, Virginia.* He often stopped here to see Washington.

**1788–** *Richmond, Virginia.* Quesnay Academy, on Academy Square. He attended Convention meetings here.

**1800s** *Monticello, Virginia.* He often visited Jefferson here.

**1801–** *Fountain Rock, Maryland.* The Ringgold House, College Road, off Maryland 68.

**1812–** *Brookville, Maryland.* Caleb Bentley House, Maryland 97 and Brookville Road. He stayed here after escaping from the British in 1812. It is a two-story white brick house. Marker on the side of the house.

**1814** *Salona, Virginia.* Smoot House, 1214 Buchanan Street, off Virginia 9, near Falls Church. It is a large red brick structure which sheltered the Madisons when Washington, D.C. was occupied by the British in 1814.

**1820–** *Washington, D.C.* Van Ness Mansion, 17th Street, NW. It was completed in

*Montpelier was James Madison's life-long home.*

1820. It was one of the first residences to have hot and cold water in all the bed chambers. He was a visitor here. The Pan American Union now occupies the site.

## DEATH

Madison died June 28, 1836, at Montpelier. Madison was the last survivor of the Constitutional Convention. It is said that when asked if he wished to extend his life a few days so he could die on July 4th, the 60th anniversary of the signing of the Declaration of Independence, he rejected the idea. He was shaved, had his breakfast, and while visiting with his niece, Nelly Willis, "ceased breathing as quietly as the snuff of a candle goes out." It was just after 6:00 A.M. when he died. The value of the estate he left is unknown. Although he was comfortably fixed, his stepson had drained a considerable portion of the estate.

## FUNERAL

The funeral service was held on June 29. He was carried to his grave in the family plot half a mile south of his house by his neighbors. Family and friends from all parts of Orange County and one hundred Montpelier slaves attended the short Episcopal service at the grave site.

## BURIAL

The grave site is located in the Madison Cemetery in Orange County near Montpelier, off County 639. An unimposing monolith marks the grave of James Madison and a small stone for Dolley, whose body was moved here in 1858. The monolith was erected in 1856.

## SPECIAL SITES

*Orange, Virginia.* Madison Museum, 129 Caroline Street. The Museum displays such ar-

*Grave of James Madison.*

tifacts as Madison's favorite chair and Dolley's black shawl and snuff box.

## BIBLIOGRAPHY

Ketcham, Ralph. *James Madison: A biography.* New York: The Macmillan Company, 1971.

Rutland, Robert A. *James Madison: The Founding Fathers.* New York: MacMillian Company, 1987.

THE PRESIDENTS

# JAMES MONROE

## 1758–1831
### 5TH PRESIDENT 1817–1825: DEMOCRATIC-REPUBLICAN PARTY

*"If a system of universal and permanent peace would be established, or if in war the belligerent parties would respect the rights of neutral powers, we should have no occasion for a navy or an army. . . ."*

*—Speech, House of Representatives, January 30, 1824*

James Monroe, whose administration was called "Era of Good Feeling" and the only president other than Washington who was elected unopposed, was born April 28, 1758 to Spence Monroe and Elizabeth Jones Monroe and is descended from King Edward III of England. His family was respected but not in the class of the larger landowners like Washington, Madison, and Jefferson.

## CHARACTERISTICS

Monroe was a tall, distinguished-looking man, a bit over six feet tall and weighing less than 200 pounds; although he seemed larger because of a large frame and broad shoulders. The first things people noticed about him were his broad forehead and wide-set blue gray eyes. To complete the plain-looking face he had a large, regular nose, a large mouth, and a dimple in his chin. His hair was almost completely gray by the time he entered the White House. He combed his hair straight back from his forehead and kept it slicked down with a coating of hair oil. He did not set any fashions while president. He continued to wear the dress common in Washington's time, silk hose, low cut shoes fastened with silver buckles, knee breeches, a sash with brass buttons, flare coat, and a

## A LIFE IN REVIEW

**Birth:** April 28, 1758; Colonial Beach (near), VA

**Died:** July 4, 1831; New York City

**Married:** Elizabeth Kortright; February 16, 1786; 2 daughters

### CAREER

**1776–1779** Officer in the Continental Army

**1782–1783** Member state legislature; also 1786–1790

**1783–1786** Member U.S. Congress

**1786–1789** Private law practice

**1790–1794** Member U.S. Senate

**1799–1802** Governor of Virginia

**1803–1807** Foreign Diplomat

**1811–1817** U.S. Secretary of State

### ADMINISTRATION EVENTS

**1817** Erie Canal begun

**1817–1818** First Seminole War

**1820** Missouri Compromise

**1823** Monroe Doctrine proclaimed

buff vest with a frilled ruffle of his shirt fluttering in the breeze. Among his favorite pastimes were hunting and horseback riding. He was shy, ambitious and hypersensitive to criticism. On one occasion, when he was seated at the foot of the table between the representatives of two principalities no bigger than his farm (as he put it), his irritation led to momentary awkwardness from which he was rescued by the Russian Ambassador. After the first toast had been drunk Monroe inadvertently put his wine glass in the finger bowl, but the Russian Ambassador came to his rescue, proposing a toast welcoming the new Minister and honoring the future president.

## BIRTHPLACE

Monroe was born in Colonial Beach (Monrovia), Westmoreland County, Virginia. The site is located between Oak Grove and Colonial Beach, on Virginia 205, and is occupied by a clump of locust trees with only a historical marker to indicate the site of the birthplace.

## BAPTISM

Monroe was baptized in Washington Parish, Westmoreland County, possibly at Round Hill (Episcopal) Church, located southwest of Alexandria, Virginia. There is no church record.

## CHURCH

Monroe, like all his predecessors in the White House from Virginia, was baptized in and attended the Episcopal Church. During his years in public life he attended church regularly and on occasion was a vestryman. All of the family activities: worship, marriage, funerals, were conducted within the walls of this denomination. A search of his papers and his biographies reveals almost nothing on his religious beliefs. There are no expressions of profound religious philosophy or public speeches including Biblical quotes.

**1758–1786** *Westmoreland County in Washington Parish, Virginia.* He possibly attended Round Hill Church, southwest of Alexandria. No records exist.

**1770s** *Williamsburg, Virginia.* Bruton Parish Church on the Palace Green. He worshipped here while attending William and Mary and when in Williamsburg on business.

**1782–** *Richmond, Virginia.* St. John's Church, 24th and East Broad Street. He attended while serving as a member of the House of Delegates.

**1786–1788** *Fredericksburg, Virginia.* St. George's Episcopal Church, northeast corner of Princess Anne and George Streets. Here he was a vestryman.

**1786–1790** *Richmond, Virginia.* He attended services held in the old Hall of Delegates on the first floor of the Capitol where services were held on alternate Sundays by the Episcopal and Presbyterian churches. He also attended here from 1799 to 1802 and in 1811, while he was governor.

**1790–1799** *Charlottesville, Virginia.* Albemarle Court House, northwest corner of Jefferson and Park Streets. He attended services here while living in the Charlottesville area.

**1799–1811** *Richmond, Virginia.* St John's Church, 24th and East Broad Streets. He attended here while serving as governor and while practicing law.

**1811–** *Washington, D.C.* Christ Church at Sixth and G Streets, SE.

**1817–1825** *Washington, D.C.* St. John's Episcopal Church on Lafayette Square, near the White House.

**1817** *Boston, Massachusetts.* Christ Episcopal (Old North Church) 193 State Street. He attended here while on his tour of New England.

**1817** *Boston, Massachusetts.* Federal Street Church (Unitarian) on Federal Street.

**1819** *Savannah, Georgia.* Independent Presbyterian Church, southwest corner Oglethorpe and Bull Streets. Present church building is a copy of the original.

**1825–1830** *Leesburg, Virginia.* St. James Episcopal Church, 14 Cornwall Street, NW.

**1830–1831** *New York City, New York.* Trinity Church on Broadway at the head of Wall St.

**1858** *New York City, New York.* Church of the Annunciation, West 14th Street. Memorial service before removing his body from New York City to Richmond, Virginia.

# EDUCATION

**1758–1769** *Colonial Beach (Monrovia) Westmoreland County, Virginia.* He was taught at home. Nothing remains of the home.

**1769–1774** *Washington Parish, Virginia.* The Campbelltown Academy. By some accounts the academy was at Johnsville (formerly) in what was Westmoreland County and is now King George County. The exact location is undetermined. He was here as a day student. John Marshall, later Chief Justice, was at the school during the same period. The school was operated by the Reverend Archibald Campbell. He received the classic instruction in Latin and mathematics. His education at the school was brought to a halt when his father died when James was age fourteen.

**1774–1775** *Williamsburg, Virginia.* College of William and Mary. With his excellent background from Campbell's school he was admitted to the upper division. Either his patriotic fervor or his desire for a relief from study encouraged him to drop out of college when the Revolutionary War broke out and he joined up as a cadet in the Third Virginia Regiment. Although he returned to William and Mary later he did not receive a degree. While he was a student at William and Mary College he stayed in the large brick building housing the college. In 1780, he reentered William and Mary and also started reading law. Jefferson took a special interest in Monroe and when Richmond became the capital, he encouraged Monroe to go with him and pursue his law studies there. Exact location of lodging not determined.

## MARRIAGE AND HONEYMOON

Monroe was married on February 16, 1786, in New York City, at Trinity Church, on Broadway at the head of Wall Street. He married Elizabeth Kortright, whose father was a New York businessman. Elizabeth was a very beautiful woman, whose background gave her an aptness for taste in dress; she wore dresses of the latest style and her wardrobe was copied by fashionable women around the country. The honeymoon took place on Long Island, after which the newlyweds returned to New York City to live at the home of the bride's father, Lawrence Kortwright, at 90 Broadway, until Congress adjourned. The details and exact location of the honeymoon site are unknown.

*Home of James Monroe, Fredericksburg, Virginia.*

## HOMES/LODGINGS

**1758–1780** *Colonial Beach, Westmoreland County, Virginia.* Nothing remains. (See birthplace). Although he owned this property until 1780, this was not his primary residence. After 1774, he went away to college and subsequently joined the military service. Monroe owned land in Westmoreland County, on Monroe's Creek (named for his great great grandfather) within one and a half miles of the Potomac River. Monroe sold the land and the house in 1783 to Gawen Corbin. It was later sold and subdivided in 1870. The birthplace site is now under control of Westmoreland Preservation Corporation. For some time the site was marked by a locust tree, but this has disappeared. The Monroes were not of the wealthy land-owning class and the house, where he was born, was not a house which would have been preserved.

**1780** *Richmond, Virginia.* During this time he was sent by Jefferson as a special military agent through the southern states of North and South Carolina.

**1780–1781** *King George County, Virginia.* Here he settled down on a small estate he owned to complete his law studies.

**1782–1783** *Richmond, Virginia.* He boarded at a private house or stayed at Formicola's Tavern between 15th and 17th on the south side of Main Street spending his evenings playing cards or going to the theater.

**1783–1784** *Annapolis, Maryland.* Ghiselin Boarding House on West Street. Here he shared lodgings with Jefferson. When Jefferson left for France the spring of 1784 Monroe purchased many of his books and inherited his French cook.

**1784** *Trenton, New Jersey.* He was here for the session of Congress. Location of lodging not determined, possibly at Rising Sun Hotel. He was also here in 1794. Exact location of Rising Sun not determined.

**1785–1786** *New York City, New York.* He rented a house with two other members of the Congressional delegation, William Grayson and Samuel Hardy. Location not confirmed. Some Congressmen boarded at the home of Mrs. Daubigny at No. 15 Wall Street and it is possible Monroe was here.

**1786** *New York City, New York.* This was the home of his father-in-law, Lawrence

Kortwright, at No. 90 Broadway between the time of his honeymoon and the adjournment of Congress.

**1786–1789** *Fredericksburg, Virginia.* 301 Caroline Street. He lived in a simple, but comfortable, two-story house owned by Joseph Jones just a few squares from his law office. Privately owned now.

**1789–1790** *Charlottesville, Virginia.* Northeast corner Fifth and Market Streets. Marker on site.

**1790–1794** *Charlottesville, Virginia.* In 1788 he acquired 800 acres of land (present site of the University of Virginia) and a house in Charlottesville from George Nicholas. The Monroe House on the crest of Monroe Hill is a brick residence painted white. Monroe remodeled the house when he first came to Albemarle County in 1790 and lived here until he moved to Ashlawn. The house is now a part of the University. In this old house he was so cramped that the best accommodations he could offer Madison and his wife (1797) was a room in a building formerly used as an office.

**1794–1795** *Paris, France.* Rue de la Roi (now 101 rue de Richelieu).

**1795–1796** *Paris, France.* Folie de la Bouexiere on the rue de clithy. At this time he purchased the Louis XVI pieces now at the Monroe Museum in Fredericksburg.

**1799–1819** *(near) Charlottesville, Virginia.* Ashlawn (then called "lower plantation" and later referred to as the "Highlands"), Virginia, five miles southeast of Charlottesville via Virginia 53 and County 795. He built a one-story frame structure of about six rooms into which he moved December 1799. It was intended as a temporary dwelling but it remained his home for the next twenty years. This is his most famous home and is open to the public.

**1799–1802** *Richmond, Virginia.* He lived at the "Palace" or governor's residence while he was governor. This was in such a state of disrepair that it could not be occupied until

*Ashlawn, home of James Monroe.*

renovated, so the Monroes did not move into the official residence until the fall of 1800. Temporary residence not determined.

**1803–1807** *London, England.* Embassy residence, Portland Place in the Marlebone area. The first winter was far from agreeable with difficulty in adjusting to the damp and smoky London climate and the fantastically high cost of living.

**1808–1830** *Loudon County, Virginia.* Oak Hill, on US 15 about a mile north of the junction with U.S. 50 south of Leesburg. It was less than 30 miles from Washington making it possible for him to come to enjoy this country home from time to time and to pursue a favorite pastime of horseback riding. Before building the large mansion in 1819, that one can see when approaching from the south, the Monroes lived in a modest 6-room frame cottage (1808–1819) located at a site nearby the present mansion. The current approach to the mansion from the highway is through an impressive avenue of trees. His daughter, Eliza Hays, usually lived with them at Oak Hill and his son-in-law George Hays said Monroe reported she was so busy she lost 30 or 40 pounds of flesh and "had increased in value as she has diminished in size." Elizabeth Monroe died in 1830 and was buried in a vault at Oak Hill. Later the body was transferred to Richmond at the time her husband's body was removed from New York City in 1858. After retirement in 1825 Monroe lived at Oak Hill until after his wife's death when, broken in spirit and in ill health, his daughter took him to New York City to live with her.

**1811** *Richmond, Virginia.* Governor's Mansion. Monroe lived here for a brief time as governor.

**1811–1817** *Washington, D.C.* 2017 I Street, NW. He lived here while serving as Cabinet Secretary.

**1817** *Washington, D.C.* 2017 I Street, NW. Monroe lived here as president from March to September because repairs to the White House following its burning in the War of 1812 had not been completed.

**1817–1825** *Washington, D.C.* at the White House as President. The front portico was not built until 1824 and the East Room remained unfinished until the Jackson administration. The term "White House" first came into use when the scars on the stone facing left by the fire were covered with a gleaming coat of white paint. During their first few years in the White House the Monroes used their own furniture which they brought from Paris. Some of this furniture and other items are considered among the greatest White House treasures.

**1830–1831** *New York City, New York.* No. 63 Prince Street at the Samuel L. Gouverneur home (daughter and son-in-law). Damaged by fire in 1905.

# WORK

Like Washington, even while deeply involved in politics, Monroe regarded himself as a farmer by profession.

**1776–1779** Military service during the Revolution. He joined Washington's troops in New York and fought in the Battles of Harlem, White Plains, Trenton (where he was wounded), Brandywine, Germantown, and Monmouth. Also visited with Washington at Middlebrook. He was one of those who survived the winter at Valley Forge. See Monument north of the Courthouse in Freehold. He declined all recompense for his services in the Revolution. From 1794 to 1797, he served in Paris, France as the U.S. Minister to France. In 1803 he returned to France as Negotiator for the Louisiana Purchase.

**1780** *Richmond, Virginia.* He was sent by Jefferson as a special military agent through southern states of North and South Carolina.

**1780–1781** *King George County, Virginia.* He completed his law studies while staying on a small estate he owned in this county.

**1782–1783** *Richmond, Virginia.* As a member of House of Delegates and the Governor's Council, Monroe met in a building, then known as the Cuningham Warehouse, located on the northwest corner of Cary and 14th (then Pearl) Streets.

**1783–1784** *Annapolis, Maryland.* As a member of House of Representatives from Virginia he worked here. Congress located here after delegates fled from Philadelphia earlier in the year in face of a possible mutiny among unpaid troops. They settled here after a brief sojourn in Princeton where accommodations were inadequate. Monroe was also on the committee for selection of site for the capital. Continental Congress met in the Old State House.

**1784–1786** *Trenton, New Jersey and New York City, New York.* As a member of the House of Representatives, he met in old City Hall (Federal Hall), New York City. Congress first met in Trenton on November 1, 1784, and later in New York City, beginning January 11, 1785.

**1786–1789** *Fredericksburg, Virginia.* He established a private law practice with law office at 908 Charles Street between George and William Streets. Now a museum open to the public.

**1786–1790** *Richmond, Virginia.* As a member of the House of Delegates, he attended the first meeting in the Cuningham Warehouse (mentioned above, 1782–1783). In October 1788, the assembly met for the first time in the new Capitol. The House of Delegates was on the first floor.

**1788** *Richmond, Virginia.* As a delegate to the ratifying convention, he met in the newly constructed academy on Shockoe Hill (now an historic district).

**1790–** *Charlottesville, Virginia.* His law office was in the outbuildings of Monroe House, now a part of the University of Virginia.

**1790–1794** *Philadelphia, Pennsylvania.* As a U.S. Senator from Virginia, he met in Congress Hall at Sixth and Chestnut Streets in a chamber on the south end of the second floor.

**1794–1797** *Paris, France.* U.S. Minister to France.

**1797–1799** *Charlottesville, Virginia.* Farming and practicing law. His house and law office are now part of the University of Virginia.

**1799–1802** *Richmond, Virginia.* Governor of Virginia. Richmond at this time had a population of 5,000. Office in the present state capitol building.

**1802–1803** *Richmond, Virginia.* Practicing law after completing term as Governor. Location not determined.

**1803–1807** *London, England.* As U.S. Minister to England he worked here. The Legation was located at Great Cumberland Place near present Marble Arch.

**1807–1811** *Richmond and Charlottesville, Virginia.* Private law practice.

**1811** *Richmond, Virginia.* As governor for second time, his office was located in the

present state capitol building on the second floor.

**1811–1817** *Washington, D.C.* As secretary of state, he worked at 17th Street NW.

**1817–1825** *Washington, D.C.* He was inaugurated in the Old Brick Capitol at First and A Streets, NW which was the temporary home for Congress while the Capitol building was being rebuilt. It was used from 1815 to 1819. The Supreme Court stands on this site today.

**1826–** *Charlottesville, Virginia.* Co-Chancellor of the University with James Madison.

**1829** *Richmond, Virginia.* Hall of Delegates to attend the state constitutional convention. Later meetings shifted to First African Baptist Church.

# TRAVEL/VISITS

In 1785, he took a tour via Pittsburgh into the Ohio country, then south through the Cumberland Gap, and through Tennessee to Lexington, Kentucky. He was also in Indiana and Illinois on this trip. In 1794 he sailed from Baltimore to LeHavre and from there travelled overland to Paris. In 1796 he took leave and went with his family to vacation in Amsterdam and other cities in Holland. In 1803 he again sailed for England to take up his post at London. From 1804 to 1805, he travelled from London to Madrid, returning to London via Paris after six months in Spain. He left London on New Year's Day 1805 and returned to London on July 23. In 1805 he visited Madrid, Spain. He lived on the Calle de Alcala en Frente de la Aduana from January to June. In 1807 he sailed from London back to the United States, landing in Norfolk, Virginia.

**1769s** *Charlottesville, Virginia.* Eagle Tavern on the Court Square. He also stayed in the Colonial Hotel in the 1820s.

**1778** *Elizabethtown, New Jersey.* Stirling's country residence, Basking Ridge. Exit 26 off I-287, County 525 spur, 527 spur to 96 Lord Stirling Road. Only two small brick slave quarters remain. He enjoyed the luxury of his friend's house interspersed with weeks of stark living under war conditions.

**1784**   *Richmond, Virginia.* 818 E. Marshall Street. Monroe made a short visit with John Marshall.

**1784**   *(near) Charlottesville, Virginia.* Castle Hill, on Virginia 231. Other presidents who were guests here were Jefferson, Madison, Jackson, Van Buren, Tyler, and Buchanan.

**1815**   *Brookeville, Maryland.* The Caleb Bentley Home, where he met with Madison after he left the burning Washington and drove back with Madison to Washington. (See under Madison).

**1815**   *White Sulphur Springs, West Virginia.* Green Brier Hotel. A stone marker commemorates the site of the old hotel.

**1817**   *Belmont, Loudon County, Virginia.* Ludwell Lee's home, between Dranesville and Leesburg. JQ Adams and Monroe were quartered in the same bed chamber. Private home now.

**1817–**   *Norfolk, Virginia.* Moses Myers House, on the corner of Bank and Freemason Streets. He often dined here with Myers, a merchant prince, in a dramatically decorated room.

**1817**   *Trenton, New Jersey.* Stayed at the Rising Sun Hotel.

**1817**   *Bristol, Rhode Island.* He stopped at Linden Place, 500 Hope Street.

**1817**   *Providence, Rhode Island.* He stayed at Golden Ball Inn, opposite the Old State House.

**1817**   *York, Maine.* Had a meal at the home of Judge David Sewall while on his New England tour.

**1817**   *Middlebury, Vermont.* He received an honorary degree at Middlebury College. The surrey he used can be seen near the Sheldon Art Museum.

**1817**   *West Point, New York.* He visited the Military Academy. Almost every president since has visited the Academy.

**1817**   *Boston, Massachusetts.* Monroe attended church services at Christ Episcopal Church and the Federal Street Church (Unitarian). A reception was held at 45 Beacon Street at Harrison Gray House. He lodged at Exchange Tavern on King Street, located at what is now the northwest corner of State and Congress Streets. He also visited Faneuil Hall on Merchants Row on July 4, 1817.

**1817**   *Quincy, Massachusetts.* 135 Adams Street. He dined here with John Adams. Later a reception was held at 20 Muirhead Street, the home of Josiah Quincy.

**1817**   *Springfield, Massachusetts.* He stopped at Zenas Parson's Tavern, on southeast corner of Court Square, near Water Street.

**1817**   *Salem, Massachusetts.* Nathaniel Silsbee House, 94 Washington Square East (now a Knights of Columbus hall). He was entertained here. He also visited Almshouse on the Neck from lower Essex Street. This building was used by the large number of drifting seamen. The new Town Hall was opened to the public on the day of his visit.

**1817**   *Concord, New Hampshire.* Barker's Tavern. He attended a concert at the Meeting House. On the 19th he attended a party at the home of Colonel William A. Kent on Pleasant Street.

**1817**   *Dover, New Hampshire.* William Hale House, 5 Hale Street (now 192 Central Street and site of an Episcopal Church).

**1817–**   *Monticello, Virginia.* He often went here to see Jefferson and was here for the last time in 1825, the year before Jefferson died.

**1817**   *Detroit, Michigan.* He arrived at Government Wharf at the foot of Randolph Street, where his arrival was announced by the firing of a cannon from Fort Shelby Hotel, followed by a triumphal procession through the crowd-lined streets to the hotel. He was received at Governor Cass's residence. He also lodged at Woodward's Steamboat Hotel; the site is at the northwest corner of Randolph and Woodbridge Streets. On Sunday he attended church in the Indian council house, which was later occupied by Fireman's Hall.

**1818** *Somerfield, Pennsylvania.* Great Crossings Bridge, which he dedicated July 4th. Now visible only during dry season.

**1818** *Washington, Pennsylvania.* Sign of General Jackson Tavern, corner of South Main and West Strawberry Streets.

**1819** *Huntsville, Alabama.* Convention Building, northwest corner of Franklin and Gates Streets in Constitution Hall Park where he was entertained at an elaborate banquet. Since torn down with site marked by a gray stone boulder.

**1819** *Savannah, Georgia.* Scarbrough House, West Broad Street, which was the focal point of his entertainment when he visited. While in Savannah he attended the dedication of the Independent Presbyterian Church.

Lodging at 111 West Broad Street which later became a public school building for Blacks. West Broad Street is now Martin Luther King Boulevard.

**1819** *Lexington, Georgia.* Woodlawn, home of cabinet secretary and Senator Crawford. Burned 1936. Site only. US 78 southeast of Athens, between Lexington and Crawford. He also visited Gainesville on this tour.

**1819** *Arcadia, South Carolina.* Waccamaw River at Prospect Hill mansion, April 21, 1819.

**1819** *Edenton, North Carolina.* Chowan County Courthouse, East King Street, where he was entertained.

**1819** *New Bern, North Carolina.* Lodging at Coor-Bishop House, 501 East Front Street.

**1819** *Louisville, Kentucky.* Locust Grove, 561 Blankenberger Lane, as a guest while president. He also visited Harrodsburg and Lexington on this tour.

**1819** *Frankfort, Kentucky.* Liberty Hall, guest of John Brown.

**1819** *Nashville, Tennessee.* Nashville Inn, corner of the Public Square and Market Street (Second Street) on the north side of the Square. He was also a guest of Andrew Jackson at the Hermitage June 9–11. He attended a dinner and ball at Nashville Inn and was a guest of Nashville Female Academy on his second day. He went from Nashville to Louisville (Locust Grove), Frankfort, Lexington, and Harrodsburg, Kentucky, and Knoxville and Rogersville, Tennessee.

**1819** *Adena, Ohio.* visiting Governor Worthington at his mansion on Adena Road, off Pleasant Valley Road.

**1819** *Cincinnati, Ohio.* Middle of Pearl Street between Broadway and Sycamore Street at the Pearl Street Grower's market. He was fascinated by the color and variety.

**1824** *Washington, D.C.* Williamson's Hotel where he attended a dinner which honored Lafayette.

**1825** *Warrenton, Virginia.* Old Warren Green Hotel. He was served here together with Lafayette.

**1835** *Fountain Rock, Maryland.* Ringgold home on College Road off Maryland 68 where he was a guest in the Ringgold home.

**1835** *Piney Point, Maryland.* On Maryland 249. This resort served as a summer social center. Monroe stayed here first in the hotel and later in a cottage that became in effect the Summer White House. Pierce and Theodore Roosevelt also visited here.

# DEATH

Monroe died July 4, 1831, shortly after 3:00 P.M., in New York City, New York, at the Gouverneur home, 63 Prince Street. He lived at the home of his daughter, Maria Gouverneur, at the end of his life. The exact amount of his estate is unknown, but was relatively small.

# FUNERAL

The funeral was held in New York City, at St. Paul's Episcopal Church, between Fulton, Church, and Vessey Streets. The casket was taken by a guard of honor from the Gouverneur's residence to City Hall to lay in state. After services at St. Paul's, the procession accompanied the cortege up Broadway to the Second Avenue Cemetery.

# BURIAL

Monroe's body was temporarily placed in the Gouverneur family vault, in the Second Avenue Cemetery, New York City. The remains were moved to Richmond, Virginia in 1858. He now rests at the Hollywood Cemetery, in area G 7, near the site of President Tyler's grave. The original coffin was taken to the Church of the Annunciation on 14th Street, New York City. A new coffin with silver handles was used. Hollywood Cemetery is located at 412 South Cherry Street, at south end of Laurel Street. His wife's body was removed from Oak Hill and placed beside his in the Hollywood Cemetery.

*Grave of James Monore.*

# BIBLIOGRAPHY

Ammon, Harry. *James Monroe: The Quest for National Identity.* New York: McGraw-Hill, 1971.

Wetzel, Charles. *James Monroe.* New York: Chelsea House Publishers, 1989.

# JOHN QUINCY ADAMS

## 1767–1848
### 6TH PRESIDENT 1825–1829:DEMOCRATIC-REPUBLICAN PARTY

*"Individual liberty is individual power, and as the power of a community is a mass compounded of individual powers, the nation which enjoys the most freedom must necessarily be in proportion to its numbers the most powerful nation."*

*—Letter to James Lloyd*

John Quincy Adams, sometimes called "Old Man Eloquent," was born July 11, 1767 to John and Abigail Adams and upon becoming president in 1825 became the only father-son combination in our history to serve as president of the United States. On his father's side were found some of the most substantial farmers in Braintree. His mother's family was one of the most respected in Massachusetts claiming as an ancestor King Edward III of England.

## CHARACTERISTICS

John Quincy Adams at maturity was only 5′7″ in height and weighed 177 pounds. He gained this excessive weight early in life which he said was due to over-indulgence in drinking wine plus overeating because of frustration. He had dark eyes in a smooth round-shaped face and while a boy he had light colored hair but by the time he became president he was almost completely bald. Like many other New Englanders he was reserved. On occasion he was short-tempered and almost without a sense of humor. When a sculptor was commissioned to make a bust when he was ex-

# A LIFE IN REVIEW

**Birth:** July 11, 1767; Braintree (Quincy), MA

**Died:** February 23, 1848; Washington, D.C.

**Married:** Louisa Catherine Johnson; July 26, 1797; 3 sons, 1 daughter

## CAREER

**1790–1795** Lawyer

**1795–1801** Foreign Diplomat

**1802–1803** Member state legislature

**1803–1808** Member U.S. Senate

**1809–1816** Foreign Diplomat

**1817–1825** U.S. Secretary of State

## ADMINISTRATION EVENTS

**1826** Pan-American cooperation

**1828** Protective Tariff Act

# BIRTHPLACE

John Quincy Adams was born in Braintree (now Quincy), Massachusetts, at 141 Franklin Street, next door to his father's birthplace. He was born in the upstairs bedroom of this modest "salt box" New England farmhouse.

# BAPTISM

Adams was baptized on July 12 1767, in Braintree (Quincy), Massachusetts, in the Congregational Meeting House (built in 1732) now called First Parish Church, 1266 Hancock Street.

# CHURCH

John Quincy Adams grew up as an independent Congregationalist with a belief in the Christian faith. He had a tolerance for the religious beliefs of others. Like his father before him he attended many churches and did not hold a strong denominational commitment. He and his father were as familiar with the Bible as any American president. He did not support a fundamental or literal interpretation of the Bible. However, he made great use of the Bible and it was his practice to read the Bible through each year. He attended church regularly both as president and otherwise and often made comments on the sermons. He was concerned over the lack of attendance at public worship in Washington. With this strong background, it is interesting to note that it was only after the death of his father that he became a professed Christian and joined the Unitarian Church in Quincy on October 1, 1826.

**1767–1828** *Braintree, Massachusetts.* First Congregational Church, 1266 Hancock Street which was the church of his father and the Adams family. Replaced in 1828.

**1767–** *Weymouth, Massachusetts.* First Church, 17 Church Street where he at-

president, he was told he was forbidden to smile, for that was not presidential. He said that consequently he was possessed with "an irresistible propensity to laugh."

In sports he was good at shooting billiards, horseback riding, and swimming. He engaged in skinny-dipping and swam in the Potomac River until he was an old man. He rose between 5 and 6, making his own fire, reading three chapters of the Bible, and retiring between eleven and twelve. Many believe no man has ever been better fitted as a professional servant for the office of the president but few have had less aptitude or inclination as a politician.

tended when visiting his maternal grandfather, Smith, who was pastor of the church.

**1778–1779** *Paris, France.* Church of the Minimes. While at LaCoeur School he followed the French custom and went to mass there near the school.

**1780–1782** *Amsterdam, Netherlands.* He attended the English Presbyterian Church. His diary often mentions attendance at this church.

**1782** *Rotterdam, Netherlands.* He attended the English speaking Protestant Church.

**1785–1786** *Haverhill, Massachusetts.* First Parish Church, Main Street, where his uncle John Shaw was the minister. Church demolished in 1908.

**1786–1787** *Cambridge, Massachusetts.* Harvard. First Congregational Church, located on Watch House Hill southwest of present Lehman Hill. The structure where his father attended was built 1706 and was known as the Third Meeting House. It was replaced on the same site in 1756. Attendance was compulsory for students and faculty.

**1786–** *Boston, Massachusetts.* Old South Church, Copley Square. He occasionally attended. On July 4, 1809 he received his commission as Minister Plenipotentiary to Russia while attending an oration here. Until 1782 it was located at 310 Washington Street at Downtown Crossing when it was moved to its present site.

**1790–** *New York City, New York.* St. Paul's Church, facing Broadway between Fulton, Church and Vesey Streets. On one occasion he writes about a gentleman preaching from a text: "He spoke well, but was so slow that the first part of a phrase was lost before he finished the last."

**1815** *Paris, France.* The Chapel of the Tuileries was where he attended Mass on April 23, 1815 and noted like any good tourist, "I had a full and steady view of the Emperor's (Napoleon) countenance."

**1821–1848** *Washington, D.C.* All Souls' Church (Unitarian). Sixth and D Streets, NW. Adams was associated with this congregation and was one of twenty-seven men who in 1821 signed the constitution formally organizing the First Unitarian Church of Washington. The first building for the church was dedicated 1822. When he was president this was his principal church. Often he would go to church twice on Sunday—in the morning to the Unitarian and in the evening to the Second Presbyterian Church.

**1821–** *Washington, D.C.* Second Presbyterian Church, in the triangle of H Street and New York Avenue, NW, was where he was a trustee.

**1822** *Washington, D.C.* Foundry Methodist Church. 14th and G Streets, NW. He attended on occasion. Building no longer exists. Marker on site.

**1825–** *Washington, D.C.* Christ Church, Sixth and G Streets, SW—the church of Madison and Monroe. When he attended here he sat in the carpeted pew which was reserved for the president.

**1825** *Washington, D.C.* St. Patrick's Church, 609 10th Street, NW. He attended the first Christmas during his presidency. On one occasion he went unannounced and found it hard to get a seat.

**1828–1848** *Braintree, Massachusetts.* First Unitarian Church (the Temple) which was built on the site of the old church at 1266 Hancock Street. It was built shortly after his father died using funds donated by the former president for a church and a school. When he returned to Quincy in 1829 he choked in tears when he took his place in the family pew in the new Temple.

**1843** *Cincinnati, Ohio.* Wesley Chapel, Methodist Church, 322 East Fifth Street, north side between Sycamore and Broadway. He addressed a meeting here.

# EDUCATION

A combination of circumstances gave John Quincy Adams the opportunity for one of the most complete educational backgrounds a young man could have. While getting a formal education he was mixing on a daily basis with leaders of the world. At eleven years of age he was speaking with Thomas Jefferson and Benjamin Franklin and mingling with the royal families and intellectuals of Europe. He was travelling across Europe when only the very wealthy had such an opportunity. From the early age of eight when the Declaration was signed he had a daily diet of politics and serious subjects being discussed in his presence.

**1767–1774** *Braintree, Massachusetts.* 141 Franklin Street. His early education was directed almost entirely by his mother. The town grammar school was closed to save money for the war and teachers had joined the army. By the time he was ten he was reading Shakespeare and attempting to read Milton's *Paradise Lost.*

**1774–1778** *Braintree.* 141 Franklin Street and Boston at Brattle Street. Being taught by his mother privately and by his father's law clerks, John Thaxter and Nathan Rice.

**1778–1779** *Paris, France.* The suburban boarding school, Passy Academy of M. LeCoeur which was situated on the Montagne de Creve Coeur.

**1779** *LaCoruna, Spain.* The Grand Amiral (Spanish Grante Amirante). While waiting the month of December to go on to France he started to learn Spanish.

**1780** *Paris, France.* He again joined the pension Academy at Passy run by M. Pechigny. He was there half a year. See above under 1778–1779.

**1780** *Amsterdam, The Netherlands.* On the Singel, a canal in the heart of Amsterdam on the moat by the Muntplein (Mint Square), between the street called Heiligaen-wed and the Money Tower—formerly

a charity house. This was a well-known Latin School which dated back to 1343. John Quincy Adams stayed here four months and hated it, the course of study, the master, and perhaps most of all the difficulty he had with the Dutch language. Today the building is occupied by the Amsterdam police.

**1780** *Fall Leyden, Netherlands.* On the Langeburg, not far from Kloksteeg, the site of the church where in 1620 John Robinson preached to the English separatists before they sailed to Plymouth Rock. This was the home of Benjamin Waterhouse, a medical student who was studying in Leyden. John Adams arranged for John Quincy to stay with his friend, John Thaxter, and to make arrangements for his son to study Latin and Greek under good masters.

**1781** *Leyden, Netherlands at Leyden University (at age 13).* He still lived on the Langeburg. (See above entry.) John Quincy was here five months before he joined Francis Dana to act as his secretary and interpreter in Russia.

**1781–1782** *St. Petersburg, Russia.* Hotel de Paris and later at the home of a Mr. Artaud's. Because tutors were so scarce and expensive Adams continued independent study including a number of books on British history written by Hume and Macaulay. He was also observant of the weather and kept a daily record noting in his diary many readings of freezing temperatures until, he notes in his diary one morning that the thermometer was stolen. His knowledge of foreign languages increased and his father, writing from the Hague, said it was mortifying to find that John Quincy wrote better in a foreign language than he did in his mother tongue.

**1783–1785** *The Hague, Netherlands.* Hotel des Etats Unis on the Fluwelen Burgwal. From April to August he was tutored by Charles William Frederick Dumas, continuing with his classical studies, including translations. With his father's help he further studied Latin and Mathematics.

**1785–1786** *Haverhill, Massachusetts.* He stayed at the parsonage of the First Parish Church. Here he was tutored by his Uncle John Shaw, being prepared for the examination required for admission to Harvard. Site of the parsonage is on Main Street adjacent to the city library.

**1786–1787** *Cambridge, Massachusetts.* Harvard College, where he lodged in Hollis Hall. He graduated second out of fifty-one in August 1787 with a B.A. degree and as a member of Phi Beta Kappa. Massachusetts Hall is the only surviving building from pre-1726. Wadsworth Hall was erected in 1726 and is Harvard's second oldest surviving building and is located in Harvard Square on Massachusetts Avenue. Harvard Hall III was erected in 1764. He lived at the Wigglesworth home on the campus from mid-December to mid-February. Because of heavy snows and a shortage of wood the college was closed and the students given an eight-week vacation. The site of the Wigglesworth home is behind Widener Hall. Hollis Hall, in which he also lived, contained 32 rooms, each with two small studies or a study and a sleeping closet. During the next year he shared a corner room on the third floor on the southeastern side with Henry Ware. The following year he was less fortunate. Because he lived with his brother, Charles, a sophomore, he was assigned a room of much inferior living on the second floor, room number 6.

**1787–1790** *Newburyport, Massachusetts.* He studied law in the office of Theophilus Parsons. Parsons was so popular and outstanding that limitations were put on the number of people he could tutor because the young flocked to him and left other would-be tutors out in the cold. He had a room at Mrs. Martha Leather's located on State Street just a block from Parsons' law office where he read law with Parsons. Of Mrs. Leathers, Adams wrote, "what is very much in her favor, uncommonly silent so that if I am deprived of the charms, I am also free from the impertinence of conversation." He was in Newburyport in 1789 when Washington visited and rode in the welcoming procession.

**1790** *Cambridge, Massachusetts.* He received his Masters of Arts degree from Harvard University and soon after was admitted to practice law at the bar in Essex County.

# MARRIAGE AND HONEYMOON

Adams married on July 26, 1797, in London, England, in the church of the parish of All Hallows Barking, east end of Byward Street toward Tower Hill—William Penn was baptized in this church. He was married to Louisa Catherine Johnson. Adams first met Louisa Johnson in Nantes, France, when she was four years old and he twelve. It was not a passionate romance, but it lasted over fifty years until Adams's death in 1848. Louisa survived him by four years. Adams wrote "Our union has not been without its trials, nor invariably without dissensions between us.... But she has always been a faithful and affectionate wife...a full conviction that my lot in marriage has been highly favored."

Adams had an earlier romance with Mary Frazier, the daughter of a highly respected citizen of Newburyport, but it was not an auspicious time to pursue affairs of the heart and the two went their own ways. As a young man looking over the field Adams wrote in his diary: "It is strange how some girls, without either fortune, beauty, or any amiable qualities, have a talent at engaging a man's affections, so as to escape, the name of old maid, which next to death is most dreaded by a female; but there is no accounting for the opinions and caprices of mankind; they must be taken as they are; for better, for worse."

*Birthplace of John Quincy Adams, Quincy, Massachusetts.*

The honeymoon took place in London, England. Immediately after the wedding ceremony the newlyweds went to see Tilney House which was one of the great country seats of England and the next two months were spent in England before leaving for Berlin where Adams took up duties as Minister to the Prussian Court. The Tilney House was demolished for building materials in 1824. The site of the house is now part of the Wanstead Golf Club and is off Barking Relief Road north of City of London Cemetery.

## HOMES/LODGINGS

His homes between 1767 and 1782 parallel those of his father (John Adams, second president of the United States), both in America and in Europe.

**1767–1768** *Braintree, Massachusetts.* 141 Franklin Street (See also birthplace).

**1767** *Weymouth, Massachusetts.* He often stayed with his Smith grandparents at the Unitarian parsonage here. On the corner of North and East Streets. Part of the original house has been moved to North and Norton.

**1768–1769** *Boston, Massachusetts.* Brattle Street in a place called The White House which was located about two blocks from the old Town Hall. It was conveniently placed for his father to pursue his legal work.

**1769–1770** *Boston, Massachusetts.* He moved to Cold Lane by the Mill Pond.

**1770–1771** *Boston, Massachusetts.* He moved back to Brattle Square in a house across the street from the Meeting House.

**1771** *Braintree, Massachusetts.* 141 Franklin Street between May and November.

**1771–1774** *Boston, Massachusetts.* Queen Street (now Court Street), near the courthouse.

**1774–1778** *Braintree, Massachusetts.* 141 Franklin Street. During the period 1778–1780 he was staying with his father who was American diplomat to several European capitals.

**1778** *Paris, France.* Hotel de Valois, Rue de Richelieu.

**1778** *Paris, France.* Suburb of Passy, at the Hotel de Valentinois where Benjamin Franklin was also living.

**1778–1780** *Paris, France.* Hotel de Valois, rue de Richelieu. His father did not think the active lifestyle of Benjamin Franklin was the best influence for his son and did not renew his stay at the same residence.

**1780–1782** *Amsterdam, The Netherlands.* Keysersbragt, near the Spiegel Straat where he lived with his father.

**1782** *The Hague, The Netherlands.* Hotel des Etats Unis, on the Fluwelen Burgwal.

**1782–1783** *St. Petersburg, Russia.* Hotel de Paris, in the heart of the Russian capital, not far from the Imperial Winter Palace. Later he changed lodgings to a Mr. Autaud's. No address found.

**1783–1785** *Paris, France.* Hotel de Rouault, Auteuil, near the Bois de Boulogne.

**1790–1795** *Boston, Massachusetts.* He moved into the family house on Court Street (formerly called South Queen Street) opposite the courthouse. He had his law office in the front room of his home in the same building.

**1795** *London, England.* He was briefly at the Virginia Coffee House and then at Osborne's Hotel for about ten days.

**1795–1796** *The Hague, The Netherlands.* Heeren Legement. He took up his diplomatic assignment here.

**1796–1797** *London, England.* Osborne's Hotel and then again to the Heeren in The Hague for two months.

**1797** *Berlin, Prussia.* Soleil d'Or, otherwise as known as the Hotel de Sussie, at Brandenburg Gate.

**1797–1801** *Berlin, Prussia.* An apartment on Bearen Strasse. He first had a place at Captain Stanck's house at the Brandenburg Gate and then moved to the house on the Friedrichstrasse, May 1798 at the corner of Friedrichstrasse and Behrenstrasse.

**1801–1803** *Boston, Massachusetts.* 39 Hanover Square, in a house which he bought. In 1801 Adams owned two houses in Boston. In 1803 he had to sell the house on Hanover to satisfy debts.

**1803–1807** *Washington, D.C.* The Hellen home. 2618–2620 K Street, NW, about two and one-half miles from the capitol. It was the home of Mrs. Adam's sister—Mrs. Walter Hellen. He moved here in the autumn of 1803 taking up his duties as U.S. Senator. The senate did not meet until November 16 because it was unable to achieve a quorum until the horse-racing season was over on this date.

**1803–1809** *Quincy, Massachusetts.* 141 Franklin Street. John Quincy bought from John Adams the old Penn's Farm where he was born and afterwards spent recesses of Congress and many summers.

**1806–1809** *Boston, Massachusetts.* Corner of Nassau Street (now Tremont) and Frog Lande (now Boylston Street). The elegant building just across the street from the Masonic building on the opposite side of Boylston Street is the former Hotel Touraine. On this site was the mansion house of John Quincy Adams. His son Charles was born here in 1807.

**1809** *St. Petersburg, Russia.* Hotel de Londres.

**1809–1811** *St. Petersburg, Russia.* He rented a house in the Novy Pereulok (New Place) where it met at the Moika Canal but had to move when the landlord sold this house.

**1811**  *St. Petersburg, Russia.* Apothecaries' Island.

**1811–1814**  *St. Petersburg, Russia.* Vosnesensky Prospekt and Ofitserskaia Street at the close of the summer 1811, living here until he left for Goteborg, Sweden on April 28, 1814.

**1814**  *Ghent (now in Belgium).* Hotel Lovendeghem, on the Rue des Champs in bachelor apartments while he served as chairman of the American delegation negotiating the Treaty of Ghent.

**1814–1815**  *Ghent.* Later he took lodgings at the Hotel des Pays-Bas on the Place D'Armes until January 26, 1815.

**1815**  *Paris, France.* Hotel du Nord, Rue de Richelieu, where he had a second floor apartment with two small rooms directly on the street. He often attended the theater at the Opera, the Theater Francais, and the Odeon.

**1815**  *London, England.* 67 Harley Street, Cavendish Square, from May to November in a house which had been rented for them prior to their arrival in England.

**1815–1817**  *London, England.* A suburb of Ealing, roughly eight miles from Hyde Park Corner in a house rented from a Mrs. Clitherow called appropriately "Little Boston House."

**1815–1817**  *London, England.* The Office of the American legation maintained a chancery first at 25 Charles Street and later at 13 Craven Street, the Strand, a narrow street which ran from 10 the Strand to the Thames Embankment, and still later at 28 Craven Street. These quarters also served as Adam's London residence when he was unable to make the trip to Ealing.

**1818–1820**  *Washington, D.C.* Northeast corner of 4 1/2 and F Street, NE and later John Marshall Place where the Municipal Center Building now stands. He rented the houses here from his chief clerk, Daniel Brent. It was about a mile and a quarter from his office. Adams made the walk daily to his office in precisely twenty-two minutes.

**1820–1848**  *Washington, D.C.* 1333–1335 F Street, NW. April 1820 he bought the house on F Street, lots 8 and 16, square 253. The original house remained in the possession of the Adams family until 1884. He lived here while serving as Secretary of State and when he was elected President. On the morning of his inauguration he left the house at half past seven and proceeded to the Capitol for the ceremonies. After leaving the White House this was his principal residence until the end of his life. The site of the house is now occupied by a clothing store. (See *A History of the City of Washington, Its Men and Institutions* by Allen B. Saluson, ed. Washington, D.C., Washington Post, 1903).

**1825–1829**  *Washington, D.C.* The White House.

**1829**  *Washington, D.C.* Porter Mansion on Meridian. Leaving the presidential office he rented the home of Commodore David Porter in the country (then) about a mile and a half from the White House. This house sat astride the original center line of D.C. The "meridian line" of 76 degrees 53 minutes W. longitude ran due north and south through both the portals of the White House and the entrance to the Porter Mansion. It was here the retiring president joined his family the evening of March 3 after walking back to the White House from the Capitol. Porter sold this house and in December Adams moved to Sixteenth Street. Nothing remains of the Porter Mansion but the wall and iron mermaids.

**1829–1834**  *Washington, D.C.* 2400 16th Street, NW, the northwest corner of 16th Street and Crescent Place, between I and K Streets and less than two blocks north of the President's Square. Adams moved in with his son, John, whose house had been built with his help. When John died in 1834 John Quincy took the remaining family and moved back to the house at 1333–1335 F

St. NW where he had resided as Secretary of State.

**1843–1848** *Washington, D.C.* 1333–1335 F Street, NW. (see entry above 1829–1834).

**1842** *Boston, Massachusetts.* 57 Mount Vernon Street which he had bought in 1842 and used as a winter residence and where his son, Charles Francis Adams, lived.

# WORK

**1781–1782** *St. Petersburg, Russia.* Interpreter and secretary to Charles Dana of the American legation.

**1790–1795** *Boston, Massachusetts.* He was a lawyer with office in the front room of his house on Court Street.

**1795–1797** *The Hague, The Netherlands.* He served as U.S. Minister Resident.

**1797–1801** *Berlin, Prussia.* As Minister to Prussia, he came back to the United States on the "George Washington," docking in Philadelphia after a seven-year absence from the United States. His father had him recalled by the Secretary of State before he could be dismissed by the new incoming President Jefferson.

**1801–1802** *Boston, Massachusetts.* He resumed his law practice with law office on State Street under the Centinel printing shop.

**1802–1803** *Boston, Massachusetts.* He was senator from Suffolk County to the General Court of Massachusetts. Meeting in the State House. After 1795 the State House was on Beacon Hill. Before this the Old State House was at Washington and State Streets.

**1803–1808** *Washington, D.C.* He served as a U.S. Senator from Massachusetts. The Senate met in the north wing of the old Capitol, second floor. He resigned in 1808.

**1805–** *Cambridge, Massachusetts.* Harvard, where he was the Nicholas Boylston Professor of Oratory and Rhetoric when not attending session in the U.S. Congress.

**1809–1814** *St. Petersburg, Russia.* He served as Minister to Russia. He was 79 days aboard the "Horace," past Newfoundland, Norway, Denmark, and from Kronstadt into St. Petersburg. He engaged five chambers at the Hotel de Londres. Louisa described her room as a stone hole entered by a stone passage full of rats.

**1814–1815** *Ghent, Belgium.* He was head of the American Mission to negotiate the peace treaty at the end of the War of 1812.

**1817** *Boston, Massachusetts.* He was nominated for president at Faneuil Hall.

**1817–1825** *Washington, D.C.* He served as Secretary of State under Monroe. The Department of State was located in a large brick building on 17th Street opposite G Street, NW on the site of the later State, War and Navy Building. In January 1829 it moved to the corner of Fifteenth Street and Pennsylvania Avenue, where the north wing of the Treasury Building now stands. The Department remained there until October 1866 when it moved out to Fourteenth St., near S Street, where it leased the premises later occupied by the Washington Orphan Asylum. In 1875 it moved into the State War and Navy Building immediately west of the White House where it remained until 1947. It was in the old brick building that Adams took up his duties. The entire staff consisted of a chief clerk and translator, and seven assistant clerks.

**1825–1829** *Washington, D.C.* He took the oath of the office of president in the Hall of the House of Representatives that is today the Statuary Hall.

**1831–1848** *Washington, D.C.* He served as U.S. Representative (Whig) from Massachusetts serving until death. For more than ten years in Congress he served as chairman of the special Smithsonian Committee. He was the most active and effective in his post-presidential career of any until his fellow Unitarian, many years later, William Howard Taft. As a member of House of

Representatives he sat in the part of the Capitol in what is known today as "Statuary Hall." See bronze disk in the floor for site of his desk.

# TRAVEL/VISITS

John Quincy Adams was one of the most widely travelled presidents, until modern times—even compared with young people of the current times, he had travelled many more miles in European countries before he reached the age of eighteen than most dream about.

In 1778 he left the United States for Europe for the first time. From France he wrote his mother of seeing Versailles, Invalides, Notre Dame and Montmarte. In 1779 he made a second trip to Europe. He went first to Spain and on the way to Paris visited Burgos, Bordeau, Poitiers, Tours, and Orleans. In 1780 he travelled through Belgium to the Netherlands. In The Netherlands he stopped at Leyden at La Cour D'Hollande on the Langebrug not far from the Kloksteeg where John Robinson had ministered to English Separatists before they sailed for America in 1620. In The Hague he lodged at Hotel du Marechal de Turenne and in Amsterdam at Hotel des Armes d'Amsterdam.

He began a trip to Russia in 1781 from Utrecht, The Netherlands. In Prussia he stopped in Dusseldorf, Cologne, Leipzig, Frankfort, and Berlin. He continued through Poland and the current Baltic states stopping in the cities of Memel, Riga, and Tallin and finally arriving in Russia at St. Petersburg. At the end of 1782 and beginning of 1783, he made the return trip from Russia to The Netherlands going through Finland, Sweden and Denmark. He visited numerous places including Helsinki and Stockholm with an extended stay in Stockholm, Sweden for five weeks. In January 1783 he had to stay at Norrkioping, Sweden for two weeks because of a heavy fall of snow. He was in Goteborg for a couple of weeks. After Goteborg he travelled to Helsingor and to Copenhagen, Denmark

where he stayed about two weeks. He travelled from Copenhagen to Hamburg where he stayed nearly a month. He arrived back to Amsterdam on April 15, 1783. On August 6 he left with his father from The Hague to Rotterdam and Antwerp where he mentions seeing the Cathedral, and returned to Paris. In 1784 he made a trip from The Hague to London with the idea of meeting his mother and sister who failed to arrive and he returned to The Hague. He made another trip to London in July at which time he met his mother and returned to Paris in August. In London he stayed at the Bath Hotel in Picadilly. In Dover he stayed at the Royal Hotel Inn. In 1785 he made his return trip to the United States starting from Paris to Locmine, where he lodged at Hotel de la Marine (near L'Orient). He boarded the French *Courier de l'Amerique* and arrived at New York City, New York on July 17–20. The diaries and writings of John Quincy Adams can give a fuller account of his travels and be interesting for anyone wishing to make a comparable trip.

**1785** *Palmer, Massachusetts.* He dined at Scott's Tavern.

**1788** *Boston, Massachusetts.* Brackett's Tavern (Cromwell's Head), 19 School Street.

**1801** *Philadelphia, Pennsylvania.* This was probably his first visit to the city.

**1817** *Belmont, Loudon County, Virginia.* Ludwell Lee's home, where he was quartered in the same room with James Monroe.

**1820s** *Washington, D.C.* Henry Foxhall home, 2908 N Street, NW, where, like presidents before him, he was a frequent guest.

**1820** *New York City, New York.* Gracie Mansion, East End Avenue and 88th Street. Entertained as a guest.

**1825** *Salem, Massachusetts.* He dedicated the East India Marine Hall, 173 Essex Street.

**1825–** *Baltimore, Maryland.* Barnum Hotel. Site southwest corner Fayette and Calvert Streets.

**1825** *Leesburg, Virginia.* Oak Hill to visit James Monroe. He travelled by carriage from Washington.

**1825–1829** *Washington, D.C.* Van Ness Mansion, 18th and C Streets NW where he was a frequent guest.

    *Providence, Rhode Island.* John Brown House, 52 Power Street. which he described as "the most magnificent and elegant mansion that I have seen on this continent."

**1830s** *Lowell, Massachusetts.* Shattuck and Merrimac Streets speaking at the Old Town Hall.

**1837** *Newburyport, Massachusetts.* Entertained at the Cushing House on the corner of Fruint Street.

**1843** *Cincinnati, Ohio.* Mt. Ida, renamed Mt. Adams in his honor. He came to speak at the laying of the cornerstone of the first professional observatory in America. At 76 he made the long trip by train and canal boat to dedicate this project. He also spoke at Wesley Chapel Methodist Church, 322 E. Fifth Street.

*John Quincy Adams' grave site.*

# DEATH

Adams died on February 23, 1848, in Washington, D.C., in the Hall of the House of Representatives in the Capitol (now Statuary Hall). Here he had a stroke and was carried first to the Rotunda, then to the East Portico, and finally into the Speaker's room. He died at 7:20 P.M. He left an estate valued at $60,000.

# FUNERAL

The funeral was held on February 25, in Washington, D.C. They laid his body in a committee room of the House of Representatives. During the next two days thousands of people filed past the open coffin which was silver mounted. The Scripture from Job 21: 17–18 was read, the chaplain delivered a funeral discourse, and the choir sang a dirge. After the funeral the cortege moved out through the east front of the Capitol and to the Congressional Cemetery. President Polk and, then Secretary of State, James Buchanan attended. It is probable that Lincoln and Andrew Johnson who were members of Congress also attended. Later the body lay in state in the rotunda of the Exchange in Baltimore, Maryland.

# BURIAL

The body rested temporarily in the Public Vault in the Congressional Cemetery at 1801 E Street, SE, in Washintong D.C. There is also a cenotaph bearing his name in the cemetery. A week later the corpse was taken to Fanueil Hall in Boston by train. It remained there until the following day when it was taken to Quincy. After a brief repose at the Adams Mansion the mourners followed the remains to the Stone Temple where another funeral sermon was preached and then his remains were placed in the family tomb that he himself had prepared in the churchyard. Later the body was moved to the granite crypt beneath the church portal at 1266 Hancock Street.

## BIBLIOGRAPHY

Bemis, Samuel Flagg. *John Quincy Adams and the Union.* New York: Knopf, 1956.

Falkner, Leonard. *The President Who Wouldn't Retire: John Quincy Adams, Congressman from Massachusetts.* New York: Coward-McCann, 1967.

Hecht, Marie B. *John Quincy Adams, A Personal History of an Independent Man.* New York: Macmillan, 1972.

THE PRESIDENTS

# A N D R E W   J A C K S O N

## 1767–1845
### 7TH PRESIDENT 1829–1837: DEMOCRATIC PARTY

*"As long as our Government is administered for the good of the people, and is regulated by their will. . ."*

—*First inaugural address, March 4, 1829*

Andrew Jackson, known as "Old Hickory" and the first "log cabin" president, was born March 15, 1767 to Andrew (who died before his son was born) and Elizabeth Hutchinson Jackson.

## CHARACTERISTICS

Jackson was a tall, thin man who as an adult was six feet, one inch tall and weighed 145 pounds. He was a freckled-faced man with bright blue eyes and red hair which had become pure white by the time he became president. By 1833 he had lost all his front teeth. According to one author he had one of the biggest and handsomest noses of all and was one of two presidents who had their noses pulled while they were in Washington. He was on a boat when a man rushed up to him, grabbed his nose, and gave it a terrific yank. This fellow was a lieutenant who had been dismissed from the navy and who blamed President Jackson for his trouble. Jackson's face was scarred resulting from the saber lashing of a British officer who tried to force him to polish his shoes and the aftermath of smallpox he contracted while in prison. He had a fiery temper and would fight at the least provocation. He was a

74

# A LIFE IN REVIEW

**Birth:** March 15, 1767; Waxhaws, SC

**Died:** June 8, 1845; The Hermitage, TN

**Married:** Rachel Donelson Robards;
August 1, 1794 (Legal); No children;
1 adopted son

## CAREER

**1785–1796** Lawyer and District Attorney

**1796–1797** Member U.S. Congress

**1797–1798** Member U.S. Senate; also
1823–1825

**1798–1804** Lawyer and Judge

**1804–1813** Landlord of the Hermitage

**1812** Officer in War of 1812 at New
Orleans

**1813–1818** Military Officer Seminole War

**1821** Governor of Florida Territory

## ADMINISTRATION EVENTS

**1829–** Spoils system

**1832** Nullification Question

**1832** Black Hawk War (Sac and Fox
Indians)

**1832** Opposed Bank of the United States

**1835** Second Seminole War

# BIRTHPLACE

Jackson was born near Waxhaw, South Carolina. The site is located off U.S. 521, approximately eight miles north of Lancaster. Jackson says he was born on his uncle's (James Crawford) plantation about one mile from the Carolina road crossing of Waxhaw Creek. At that time the Crawford house was on the soil of South Carolina. By the time Jackson was fourteen, he was alone as his mother and brothers had died, and he went to live with uncles. North Carolina disputes the South Carolina claim and has placed a marker near the old Charlotte Road north of Waxhaw.

# BAPTISM

Jackson was baptized in 1767, in Waxhaw, South Carolina, at the Presbyterian Church off U.S. 521, six miles north of Lancaster.

# CHURCH

Under the influence of his mother who had been a Presbyterian and his wife, who was a devout Presbyterian, he attended the Presbyterian Church regularly. From a young age he was an avid reader of the Bible and believed that God had a hand in the outcome of battles and in the events of daily life. Even so, he had never made a public confession of faith or joined a church formally until he was a few days away from the age of 70 and long after Rachel had died.

**1767–1781** *Waxhaw, South Carolina.* Waxhaw Presbyterian Church. See location under Baptism above. It is a white frame building with gable roof and is the latest of several which replaced the log cabin erected in 1755. His father lies in the churchyard and a monument was erected there in honor of his mother although she died of fever in Charleston and, despite a diligent search, Jackson was never able to find the place of burial.

daring horseman and could beat almost anyone in a foot race or broad jump. Few men have been more popular among the common people than Jackson. There was such a demand for a lock of his hair that he had the habit of carefully saving the trimmings whenever he had his hair cut and he used these for the souvenirs which he sent to correspondents and to admiring visitors.

**1781–** *(near) Salisbury, North Carolina.* Third Presbyterian Church, between Iredell and Thyatira. He had mixed feelings about this church since it was here that his rival, Joseph Kilpatrick, for the hand of Margaret Dilley crowned his success by his marriage to Margaret in 1786.

**1788–** *Jonesborough, Tennessee.* Presbyterian Church, Main Street. He attended while on circuit.

**1791–1823** *Nashville, Tennessee.* Downtown Presbyterian Church. (Was formerly First Presbyterian Church), Fifth Avenue and Church Street. Rachel Jackson was a member. The present structure was built 1849–1851 and is the third to be built on this site.

**1823–1845** *Lebanon, Tennessee.* The Presbyterian Hermitage Church, originally built in 1823, is a plain and simple brick church. Jackson's pew is marked with a silver plate. The church burned in 1965 and an identical building to replace it was built in 1967.

**1829–1837** *Washington, D.C.* National Presbyterian Church. This church was born in the one-time carpenter shop on what is now the White House grounds. It later came to be known as St. Andrew's Presbyterian Church and still later was known as the First Presbyterian Church. The ledger book shows Jackson's rent for pew number 6 for the years 1829–1837. The church was later located on Connecticut Avenue at 18th and N Streets, NW.

## EDUCATION

**1772–1778** *Waxhaw, South Carolina.* Academy at the Waxhaw Church. See site off US 521. Replica of school at the time can be found in Jackson State Park. The Academy was run by William Humphries and later by James Stephenson.

**1778–1780** *New Acquisition, South Carolina.* Francis Cummins's "classical school" in the territory across the Catawba River which South Carolina received from North Carolina. Nothing remains and no definite location can be determined.

**1783–1784** *Charlotte, North Carolina.* Queen's Museum. Also called Queen's College (Colonial) and Liberty Hall Academy. The site is commemorated by a stone marker at the southeast corner of Third and South Tryon Streets. Now occupied by First Union Bank.

**1784–1786** *Salisbury, North Carolina.* 200 West Fisher Street. He studied at the law office of Spruce McKay and Colonel John Stokes. Replica of a law office of the time stands on the grounds of the Salisbury Public Library.

## MARRIAGE AND HONEYMOON

Jackson was married on August 1, 1791, near Natchez, Mississippi. The site is located off U.S. 61, south of Fayette and 23 miles north of Natchez, where Mississippi 553 crosses the Trace. A side trip past Springhill comes to the site of the marriage. Springfield was the stately brick mansion of Thomas Green where wedding vows were exchanged in its tall parlor between Andrew Jackson and Rachel Donelson Robards. The honeymoon took place in the same area, near the ruins of Windsor, twelve miles southwest of Port Gibson on Mississippi 552. A historical marker for the Bruinsburg Road relates Jackson had a trading post here and also honeymooned here. It is difficult to reach during the wet season.

## HOMES/LODGINGS

**1767–1782** *Waxhaw, South Carolina.* He was reared at the home of James Crawford. There is a marker on the site of the Crawford homestead. He joined the military (1780–1782) at age 13. See location of home under birthplace. See also marker in the Jackson State Park off South Carolina 521.

**1782–1784**  *Waxhaw, North Carolina.* He made his home at George McCamie's (or McKemey's) whose house was on the east side of the road which put it in North Carolina while Crawford's home, near South Carolina 521, was on the west side in South Carolina.

**1784**  *Salisbury, North Carolina.* Rowan House, 201 S. Main Street while studying law.

**1786**  *Wadesboro, North Carolina.* He stayed at the Ingram House, eleven miles from Lilesville at the site of Old Wadesboro while practicing law. There is a marker, almost hidden, deep in the woods indicating the former location of the house in the nearby field.

**1786**  *Summerfield, North Carolina.* He lived near the old McNairy House, near Lake Brandt.

**1787**  *Martinsville, (also known as Guilford Courthouse), North Carolina.* Place of lodging not determined.

**1787**  *Morganton, North Carolina.* Old Courthouse on City Square, while on circuit. The courthouse where he met has been replaced by another courthouse built in 1837 on the same site.

**1788–**  *Jonesborough, Tennessee.* Christopher Taylor's home one mile west of town where he roomed and boarded. House was built in 1777. Marker near the original site. The original house has been moved to 124 North Main Street. The Chester Inn (or Jonesborough Inn) was at the corner of Main and Cherokee Streets, 106 West Main Street. Jackson, Polk, and Andrew Johnson stopped here on the Great State Route from Washington, D.C. Jackson is credited with saving the Inn from fire in 1832.

**1788–**  *Nashville, Tennessee.* Fort Nashboro. 170 First Avenue North at Church Street. Reproduction of original stockade. It was

the center of activity when Jackson first arrived in Nashville. City Hall, on the public square, was the site of his shooting match.

**1789–1792**  *Clover Bottom, near Lebanon, Tennessee.* Donelson home. Jackson and a fellow lawyer, John Overton, boarded here and it was here he met Rachel Donelson, his future wife. After the marriage in 1791 the couple continued to live here until in 1792 they acquired their own home located across the Cumberland River in the curve of Stone's River called Clover Bottom. Clover Mansion, off Stewart's Ferry Pike near the Tennessee School for the Blind (a former 1,500 acre plantation), was the site of Jackson's race track and gambling activities. His general store, in Clover Bottom, was four miles from the Hermitage. The Donelson house was a log house and nothing remains and no marker indicates the site. To reach the Widow Donelson's blockhouse it was necessary to ferry the river and take the Kentucky Road northward six to seven miles, then branch off on a poor trail for three or four miles more. He shared a bed in a cabin away from the main house. It is difficult to locate the exact site since the area is completely built up with subdivisions.

**1790–**  *Nashville, Tennessee.* Nashville Inn, on the north side of the public square. It became Winn's Inn in 1806 and the Nashville Inn a few years later. No other comparable inn was closer than New Orleans, St. Louis, or Lexington. President Monroe stayed here in 1819 and Andrew Johnson was living here while governor when it was destroyed by fire in 1856. When in town Andrew Jackson often stayed here. Site now occupied by a business building.

**1790–**  *Donelson, near Lebanon, Tennessee.* Mud Tavern on Elm Hill Road where he sometimes spent the night. The old road, which Jackson travelled, came out from Nashville somewhat as the present Murfreesboro Road does, into Elm Hill Road (or Chicken Pike) and went on over to

*The Hermitage, home of Andrew Jackson.*

Merritt's Lane or McGavocks Lane. Nothing remains. No marker.

**1790–1791**  *(near) Lebanon, Tennessee.* Casper Mansker Blockhouse, near Mrs. Donelson's place. No markers and exact location not determined.

**1791**  *Bayou Pierre, Mississippi.* A log house about thirty miles above Natchez, near Port Gibson. Exact location undetermined.

**1791–1796**  *Poplar Grove Plantation, Tennessee.* In October, Jackson brought Rachel to the Cumberland and bought Donelson's plantation. It stood roughly in the center of the hairpin of the Cumberland River just across the river from Mrs. Donelson's on the Gallatin Road. Later he called it Poplar Flat. It was swallowed up in 1917 in the United States government powder manufacturing plant known as the Old Hickory Powder Plant and the town is called Old Hickory.

**1796–1804**  *Hunter's Hill, near Lebanon, Tennessee.* The site which he bought from John Shannon to set up his new home is further up in the bend of the river. This house no longer exists, having burned, but at the time was a notable house being built of wood rather than of logs as most houses were of the frontier days. Mid-century it was still in the hands of the Donelson branch of the family. The property was owned recently by Aubrey Maxwell. Located on present Saundersville Road, Old Hickory. Marker on Tennessee 70 on the Lebanon Road off Shute Lane.

**1804–1819**  *(near) Lebanon, Tennessee.* Hermitage, off I-70, Hickory exit, seven miles from Nashville. Here he established a group of log houses with a large central building which provided the principal living area. The family lived here for fifteen years. The main building was 24′ x 26′ and on the first floor had only one large room with a huge fireplace. One of the small log cabins is still standing of the original group. The larger house was built using logs taken from the original house and is built on the original site.

**1819–1829** *(near) Lebanon, Tennessee.* Hermitage. The first big house on the site was begun in 1818 and occupied in 1819. In 1831 it was extensively remodelled along the lines of the present structure which was erected in 1834 after a fire destroyed almost everything but the walls of the original building. The Hermitage of the present is located on a site selected by Rachel and is identical to what it was when Jackson died. The two-story house faced south with an 85-foot front. An imposing set of six modified Corinthian columns creates an impressive view at the main front. Jackson returned to the Hermitage to live from 1837 to 1845.

**1829–1837** *Washington, D.C.* The White House.

**1836–** *(near) Lebanon, Tennessee.* Tulip Grove was the residence of his stepson, Andrew Jackson Donelson. It was originally called Poplar Grove but Van Buren on his visit suggested the name change.

# WORK

Jackson's places of work in the area of Waxhaw, South Carolina while he was still a boy (1782–1786) were roughly constructed buildings and nothing remains nor are there markers indicating the sites. After completing his law studies and being admitted to the bar his practice took him on the circuit where, for the most part, he lodged in different homes (1786–1796). Many of these are no longer exsiting and no markers indicate the definite location.

**1780–1782** *Camden, Fishing Creek, and Hanging Rock, South Carolina.* He served

as messenger and orderly in the Revolutionary War. See the marker at 600 block of Broad Street on the site of the prison where he was held. The remains of the old Revolutionary War stockade have been rebuilt into a church. See Hanging Rock Battlefield on South Carolina 58 south of Heath Springs where he also served.

**1783** *Waxhaw, South Carolina.* He worked in saddler shop of relative, Joseph White.

**1784** *Waxhaw, South Carolina.* He taught in a country school in this community.

**1785–1786** *Salisbury, North Carolina.* Law office, 200 West Fisher Street. Similar building found on corner of the public library grounds.

**1786** *Wadesboro, North Carolina.* He was admitted to the bar. See above under Homes 1786. The courthouse and the town of Old Wadesboro where he practiced have disappeared.

*Rockford, Surry County.* North Carolina practicing law on circuit.

**1787** *Martinsville, (also known as Guilford Courthouse), North Carolina.* He was helping in friend's store and practicing law.

**1787** *Morganton, Burke County, North Carolina.* Courthouse practicing law on circuit.

**1787** *Johnsonville, Harnett County, North Carolina.* Practicing law on circuit.

**1787** *McLeansville, Guilford County, North Carolina.* Practicing law on circuit.

**1787–1788** *Jonesborough, Tennessee.* Courthouse, Main and Cherokee Streets. Present Courthouse is the fifth on the same site. He was practicing law on circuit.

**1788–1796** *Nashville, Tennessee.* Law office site 333 Union Street. Site now occupied by a drug store.

**1791–1796** *Nashville, Tennessee.* He served as Tennessee District Attorney. At this time the capital was in Knoxville. Much of his activity in town was centered around the site of Fort Nashboro or his office site at 333 Union Street.

**1792–** *Clover Bottom, Tennessee.* He owned a store with tavern and boatyard, located on Nashville-Lebanon Road. This was Stone's River bottom land where Donelson (early settler of Nashville) landed and built cabins. It included the area in front of the present bridge. Donelson's widow was the future mother-in-law of Jackson and his landlady in the early days of his life in Tennessee. He built boats at Burr's Landing where Lebanon Road crosses the bridge at Stone's Landing. 1791 ff.

**1792–1845** *(near) Lebanon, Tennessee.* He was a plantation owner and manager of the Hermitage from 1792 until his death.

**1796** *Knoxville, Tennessee.* He was a member of the first constitutional convention for Tennessee. The governor's office, located behind Blount Mansion, 200 West Hill, served as the capitol of the Southwest Territory from 1792–1796 and was the site where the Tennessee State Constitution was drafted.

**1796–1797** *Philadelphia, Pennsylvania.* He was the first member from Tennessee in the United States House of Representatives, which met downstairs in Congress Hall north wing at Chestnut and Sixth Streets.

**1797–1798** *Philadelphia, Pennsylvania.* He was appointed United States Senator from Tennessee. He resigned in 1798. The Senate met on second floor of Congress Hall in the north wing.

**1798–1804** *Nashville, Tennessee.* He was a member of Tennessee Superior Court. During this period he was elected Major General of Tennessee Militia in 1802. See above entry 1791–1796 for office locations.

**1821** *Pensacola, Florida.* He was governor of the Florida Territory. Plaza Ferdinand VII, South Palafox Street between East Government and East Zarragossa Streets, site of the original Spanish Square. A granite marker commemorates the cession of Florida from Spain to the United States.

**1823–1825** *Washington, D.C.* He was appointed United States Senator and resigned in 1825. The Senate met in the Old Senate Chamber of the Capitol.

**1829–1837** *Washington, D.C.* The White House. He was the first president to be inaugurated on the east front steps. In 1835 he was the first president to have an assassination attempt on his life.

**1829–** *Washington, DC.* Adams Mill Road, Ontario Place. He took vacations here.

# TRAVEL/VISITS

Jackson travelled widely within the United States which included military excursions and his time in government service. He did not travel outside the continental United States. He visited twenty-two states including: Alabama, Connecticut, Delaware, Florida, Georgia, Kentucky, Louisiana, Maine, Maryland, Massachusetts, Mississippi, New Hampshire, New Jersey, New York, North Carolina, Ohio, Pennsylvania, Rhode Island, South Carolina, Tennessee, Virginia, and West Virginia.

Military service travel is included in this section. More specific details of location are included in the geographic section.

**1783** *Waxhaw to Charleston, South Carolina.* His first trip to a city was Charleston. He visited Quarter House Tavern at the fork of the Broad Path about six miles north of the city. He was in Charleston to claim a legacy from his Irish grandfather. He stayed at McCrady's Tavern on Meeting Street, on Unity Alley, off East Bay Street, the site of present Restaurant Million.

**1790–** *Greeneville, Tennessee.* Dickson-Williams Mansion, Church and Irish Streets, where he was a guest.

**1790–** *Dandridge, Tennessee.* Shepard's Inn, 136 E Main Street where he was a guest.

**1791**  *Rogersville, Tennessee.* Hale Springs Inn (known previously as Rogers Inn and also McKinney Tavern) on Main Street. He stayed here several times. Part of the original building still stands.

**1791**  *Natchez, (23 miles north), Mississippi.* Abner Green mansion which was once the country seat of Don Manuel Gayoso de Lemos, Spanish commandant of Natchez. Jackson took Rachel here to reside prior to their wedding.

**1794–**  *Knoxville, Tennessee.* Blount Mansion, 200 West Hill Avenue. He was often a guest here in this oldest frame house west of the Allegheny Mountains.

**1795**  *Nashville, Tennessee to Philadelphia, Pennsylvania.* His first visit to a center of culture since his visit to Charleston.

**1800–**  *Washington, D.C.* Conrad's Boarding House at the foot of a grassy hill leading to the Capitol, 219 New Jersey Avenue, SE. Stayed here when in Washington on business.

**1800–**  *Williamson County, Tennessee.* Riverside, near Franklin where Jackson often visited his friends. He brought the saplings of the cedar trees growing there today.

*Carnton Mansion, near Franklin, Tennessee.* He often visited here. Off US 431 one mile southeast of Franklin.

**1800–**  *Nashville, Tennessee.* Traveller's Rest, 636 Farwell Parkway. He often came to see his friend, Judge Overton, his first roommate when he came to Tennessee.

**1800–**  *Nashville, Tennessee.* Belle Meade Mansion, 110 Leake Avenue at Harding Road off US 70-S. Home of a close friend.

**1800–**  *Murfreesboro, Tennessee.* Oakland, 900 North Maney Avenue where Jackson often visited this home of his physician, Dr. Mentlo. See the little medical office adjacent. He spent time and money at the race track on Major Bradley's farm, Hurricane Hill.

**1800–**  *Gallatin, Tennessee.* Castalian Springs, Cragfont, seven miles east of Gallatin on Tennessee 25. Home of General James Winchester, friend of Andrew Jackson, where he was often a guest in the elegant dining room.

**1804–1811**  *Jefferson, Tennessee.* He also conducted legal business here in the brick courthouse in the middle of the public square before the country seat was moved to Murfreesboro.

**1813–1814**  *Fort Bowyer, Alabama.* Jackson headquarters. It was a United States outpost at the entrance to Mobile Bay.

**1813**  *Fayetteville, Alabama.* He took command of Infantry here. Markers in the town square.

**1813**  *Ditto's Landing on Tennessee River.* Ten miles below Huntsville, (now Alabama). Jackson joined cavalry here.

**1813**  *Fort Deposit, Marshall County, Alabama* at southernmost dip of Tennessee River. Moving through enemy territory he threw up defenses here.

**1813**  Early victories in November 1813 at Tallussachatchee and Talledega but after encounters at Emuckfau and Enitachopco (Horseshoe Bend in Alabama) Jackson was again forced to withdraw to Fort Strother. (See below under 1814).

**1814**  *Huntsville, Alabama.* Pope home, 403 Echols Street. It is the oldest documented mansion in Alabama. May 1814 Jackson and his company who were passing through on their return from the Battle of Horseshoe Bend were hosted at a dinner.

**1814–1815**  *New Orleans, Louisiana.* Jackson headquarters, Number 106 Royal Street and Macarte House on Rodriques Canal where it joins with the Mississippi River south of New Orleans.

**1814–1815**  *New Orleans.* He defeated the British January 1, 1815. Chalmette National Historical Park at 8606 West Saint

Bernard Highway in the final battle of the War of 1812. Old Mint, 400 Esplanade Avenue. Site on which the Mint now stands was the scene of his review of the troops before battle.

**1815**  *Hickory, Mississippi.* He camped just south of town on the banks of Pottoxchitto Creek.

**1815**  *New Orleans, Louisiana.* Home of Colonel Livingston, 417 Royal Street. Patio Royal. He was here for five months.

**1815–1816**  *Nashville to Washington by way of Lynchburg, Virginia and return to Tennessee.*

**1818**  *Gainesville, Georgia.* O. Young's Tavern. Here while fighting the Indians.

**1818**  *Hoschton (near), Georgia.* Georgia 124. Lodging in this log house during Seminole Wars. Site of Jackson headquarters. Jackson trail is marked in the nearby vicinity.

**1818**  *Bainbridge, Georgia.* See marker for Camp Recovery on the corner of Shotwell and Broad detailing location of hospital camp.

**1818**  *Herod, Georgia.* Site of Jackson's march through one of the last Indian villages to remain. Marker.

**1818**  *Fort Marks, Florida.* San Marcos Fort. Here he lowered the Spanish colors. See the bastion wall which defended the soldiers from the cannons or gun shot from the river. This strategic area controlled access to the St. Marks River. On May 7 he left Fort Gadsden for Pensacola and marched northward and across the Apalachicola River at Ocheesse Bluff near present-day Torreya State Park near Rock Block on Florida 271. He proceeded to present-day Blue Spring (six miles north of Marianna on Florida 164). He marched across the natural bridge of the Chipola River near Marianna. His next stop was at Rockarch Spring (site of San Carlos, a Spanish Mission), then crossing the Okchi-

ahatchee Creek (now Holmes Creek) six miles southwest of today's Graceville off Florida 277. Follow Florida 2 across Wright's Creek and Ten-mile Creek. He swam his horses across the Choctawhatchee River at a point near the present State Road 2 bridge. The travel was at an average rate of 14 miles per day. Jackson marched with his army northwest, camping at Lake Jackson (was called David's Lake) and just south of Florala, Alabama. The route goes on Florida 2 to just south of Laurel Hill and the Yellow River near present day Oak Grove and to Blackman. They crossed the Blackwater River and reached the northern shore of Escambia Bay at what is now Mulat and Floridatown. The army marched up the eastern side of the Escambia River and crossed at Parker Island near Molino before reaching the Fort Montgomery-Pensacola road near present-day Cantonment before marching south to Pensacola. On June 17 he entered West Florida. He lodged at the home of Manuel Gonzales, Vacaria Baja, about fifteen miles north of Pensacola. He was a guest for three weeks. Here again 1821.

**1819**  *Negro Fort* (now named Fort Gadsden), on Gulf of Mexico.

**1819**  *Franklin, Tennessee.* Masonic Hall, Second Avenue North. See under 1830.

**1819**  *Franklin.* Eaton House, 125 North Third Avenue where he was often a guest at a time when he was prosecuting attorney in this district.

**1819**  *York, Pennsylvania.* Hammersly Inn, later renamed Sign of General Jackson and still later was site of Hartman Building, southeast corner of Centre Square and George Street. He arrived in York by sled after his sleigh drawn by four large horses broke down. He was angry about the matter and refused to pay the sleigh man but later did. He also spent four days in the city during this year and was again here in 1833 on a presidential tour.

**1819–** *Kingsport, Tennessee.* Netherland Inn, 2144 Netherland Inn Road just west of downtown Kingsport while traveling the Great Stage Road to and from Washington, D.C.

**1819** *Washington, D.C.* Strothers Hotel, 14th Street and Pennsylvania Avenue NW.

**1821** *Galves Springs, just west of Pensacola.* Cantonment Clinch, down the hill from present-day Jackson Street near the end of Zaragoza Street at the head of Bayou Chico. Jackson camped here in 1814 before attacking the city and slept here the night before the changing of the flags in 1821. Pensacola surrendered to him May 28 and the exchange of flags took place on July 17, 1821 in the old Spanish Government House on Plaza Ferdinand VII. The two-story wooden building near the bay on the old common (Plaza Ferdinand VII) later became the courthouse. The site is now occupied by the Chipley Monument.

**1821** *Pensacola.* He and Rachel attended the Tivoli Theater on the southwest corner of Zaragoza and Barracks Streets.

**1823–1824** *Washington, D.C.* O'Neal's Tavern, north side of Pennsylvania Avenue between 20th and 21st Streets, NW.

**1824–1825** *Washington, D.C.* Gadsby's Tavern, northeast corner Pennsylvania Avenue and Sixth Street NW. Staying in Washington as U.S. Senator. Also at New Capital Hotel (was St. Charles Hotel), Third Street and Pennsylvania Avenue, NW.

**1825** *Scenery Hill, Pennsylvania.* Century Inn near the center of town. Was a guest here with Lafayette.

**1828** *Jackson, Mississippi.* There was a heroes welcome at the state capitol, corner of President and Capitol Streets. Building gone but tablet on site on side of the Baptist book store.

New Orleans, Louisiana. Patio Royal, 417 Royal Street. He was a guest in Col. Livingston's home here.

**1828–** *Gallatin, Tennessee.* Castalian Springs, at Wynnewood Tavern, 8 and 1/2 miles east of Gallatin, Tennessee 25, where he was often a guest.

**1829–** *Crab Orchard, Tennessee.* He often made stops at the Crab Orchard Inn (owned by Burke) on the Great Stage Road. However, making the trip on horseback he usually camped on his way between Tennessee and Washington.

**1829–** *Readyville, Tennessee.* He frequently spent a night at the Charles Ready home, The Corners, on his way from Tennessee to Washington while he was president. The line separating Cannon and Rutherford Counties is drawn through the center of the Ready house.

**1829** *Washington, D.C.* Gadby's Hotel, northwest corner Pennsylvania Avenue and Fifth Street, NW, where he spent the week before and night after inauguration.

**1829** *Portsmouth, Virginia.* Visiting in home of John W. Murbaugh, northwest corner Crawford and London Streets.

**1829–** *Ballston Spa, New York.* Sans Souci Hotel on Broadway.

**1829** *Charleston, West Virginia.* Hollygrove, 1710 Kanawha Boulevard. He was a guest here. Now private home.

**1829** *Frankfort, Kentucky.* Liberty Hall, 202 Wilkinson Street, where he visited the home of John Brown.

**1829** *Louisville, Kentucky.* Locust Grove, 561 Blankenbaker Lane, where he visited.

**1829** *Cincinnati, Ohio.* Yeatman's Tavern, northeast corner of Front and Sycamore Streets. Site became a vacant lot.

**1830** *Franklin, Tennessee.* Hiram Masonic Lodge, Second Avenue South. On the grounds President Jackson negotiated the Chickasaw Treaty of 1830.

**1830** *Franklin, Tennessee.* Carnton Mansion built by ex-mayor Randall McGavock. Mrs. Jackson helped Mrs. McGavock plan her

*Andrew Jackson's grave site.*

flower garden here. Jackson, and later Polk, were visitors here.

**1830s** *Washington, D.C.* Summer home, Adams Mill Road at Ontario Place, NW. Now part of National Zoo.

**1833** *Hampton Roads, Virginia.* He visited Dry Dock Company on Washington Avenue between 35th and 49th Streets. He was here again 1835 for 41 days vacation.

**1836** *Columbia, Tennessee.* He visited James K Polk at his home, 305 East Seventh Street.

    *Jonesborough, Tennessee.* Broyles home, 119 West Main Street. Entertained by friend.

**1840** *Natchez, Mississippi.* Mercer House near corner of South Wall and State Streets.

# DEATH

Jackson died June 8, 1845, at the Hermitage. Perhaps the most interesting room in the Hermitage is the front bedroom, Jackson's bedroom. It is today as it was when he died. In the center is the high, old four-poster bed in which he died, with its heavy canopy and with the little steps at its side and nearby the couch where he spent much of his time during the latter part of his life.

On the last morning he was lifted from his bed and placed in his big chair by the window surrounded by his weeping family and servants. His last words were: "Do not cry. Be good children, and we shall all meet in heaven."

The value of the estate he left is unknown. A substantial amount was pilfered away by his adopted son.

# FUNERAL

The funeral was held June 10. Despite his expressed wish that his funeral be simple a military company marched out from Nashville to attend the funeral and march with the body to the grave along with a multitude of people estimated at 3,000. Because of the large crowd services had to be conducted outside on the porch instead of inside the house. One disturbing note during the service was when Jackson's old parrot, Polly, had an outburst of profanity and was removed to the back of the house. The Scripture reading was from Ecclesiastes 1:8, Vanity of vanities; all is vanity. What profit hath a man of all his labour which he taketh under the sun? His favorite hymns were played and a final gun salute fired.

# BURIAL

Jackson is buried in the Hermitage garden. Following the services the casket was carried to the garden tomb and placed beside Rachel's. The site is marked with a simple obelisk surmounted by a small cupola resting on eight columns.

# BIBLIOGRAPHY

Davis, Burke. *Old Hickory, A Life of Andrew Jackson.* Pittsburg: The Dial Press, 1977

James, Marquis. *Andrew Jackson: The Border Captain.* Magnolia, Massachusetts: Peter Smith 1977.

James, Marquis. *The Life of Andrew Jackson.* New York: Garden City Publishing Co., Inc., 1940.

# MARTIN VAN BUREN

## 1782–1862
### 8TH PRESIDENT 1837–1841: DEMOCRATIC PARTY

*"The people under our system, like the king in a monarchy, never dies."*

*—Inquiry into the Origin and Course of Political Parties, 1867*

Martin Van Buren was born on December 5, 1782 to Captain Abraham and Maria Hoes Van Alen Van Buren with Dutch background on both sides. He was the first president not born as a British subject but as a citizen of the United States.

## CHARACTERISTICS

He had blond hair, a fair complexion, and blue eyes. He was slightly under 5′6″ tall, but he held his shoulders back and always stood up straight, and therefore seemed taller. As president, he was fat and balding. He was self-conscious about his lack of education and cultural background and tried to make up for it with an emphasis on the clothes he wore. One report describes his dress of a "snuf-colored broadcloth coat with velvet collar; cravat orange with modest lace tips; vest of pearl hue; trousers of white duck, silk hose corresponding with vest; shoes morocco, gloves yellow kid and long furred beaver hat with broad brim of Quaker color." Aside from law books, he was practically ignorant of literature, and throughout his life he was embarrassed at his lack of general knowledge. He had the nicknames: Little Van, Flying Dutchman, Red Fox of Kinderhook, and Little Magician. He had a merry disposition and an in-

# A LIFE IN REVIEW

**Birth:** December 5, 1782; Kinderhook, NY

**Died:** July 24, 1862; Kinderhook, NY

**Married:** Hannah Hoes; February 21, 1807; 4 sons

## CAREER

**1803–1812** Lawyer

**1812–1820** Member state legislature

**1821–1828** Member U.S. Senate

**1829** Governor of New York

**1829–1831** U.S. Secretary of State

**1831–1832** Minister to England

**1837–1841** U.S. President

## ADMINISTRATION EVENTS

**1837** Depression of 1837

**1838** Caroline Affairs straining U.S.-Anglo relations

**1838** Texas Question

**1838–1839** "Trail of Tears," Cherokee Indian removal

---

fectious smile. As a young man he was a very successful lawyer and by age 26 had the reputation of being the best lawyer on the Democratic-Republican Party side in Columbia County, New York.

# BIRTHPLACE

Van Buren was born in Kinderhook, New York, in what was the Kinderhook Tavern on Hudson Street, about three miles from the town center. A marker indicates the site.

# BAPTISM

He was baptized on December 15, 1782, in Kinderhook, New York, at the Dutch Reformed Church, Main Street. A new church is located on the same site.

# CHURCH

He had the reputation of being a faithful churchman, but his writings and speeches show little interest in deep theological matters. Every Sunday, from the time he was growing up and into retirement, he was in his usual high-backed pew in the Dutch Reformed Church where he was baptized.

**1782–1862** *Kinderhook, New York.* Dutch Reformed Church, Main Street, which is still on the same site but in a newer building.

**1813–1821** *Albany, New York.* Dutch Reformed Church, North Pearl Street at Clinton Square.

**1821–1841** *Washington, D.C.* St. John's Episcopal Church on Lafayette Square. There was no Dutch Reformed church in Washington. During his years in the capital he attended and held a pew at St. John's.

**1858** *New York City, New York.* Dutch Reformed Church, an old Middle Dutch Church, on William Street, where he attended while visiting New York City. His friends and relatives also attended this charming old church.

# EDUCATION

His early education was sketchy. At age eight, he went up the road to the common village school near the tavern where he lived. According to one source, this little frame schoolhouse was afterwards made famous by Washington Irving through his character Ichabod Crane of Sleepy Hollow.

**1794–1796** *Kinderhook, New York.* Kinderhook Academy which, in his day, was a run-down, one-room wooden building. Marker on Main Street.

**1796–1802** *Kinderhook, New York.* He studied in the law office of Francis Sylvester in the town center. He was admitted to the New York bar in 1802.

## MARRIAGE

Van Buren was married on February 21, 1807, in Catskill, New York. The house where he married Hannah Hoes, a distant cousin on his mother's side, is located on West Main Street off West Bridge Street. It was the home of Hannah's older sister, Christina Cantine. Hannah was also Van Buren's classmate at school in Kinderhook. The house where they married, built in 1797, now called "the wedding house" is now a lawyer's office. There is a marker outside the house.

There is no record of a honeymoon, but it probably took place at the house where he was married, since he had come here to avoid the noisy celebration of the old-fashioned Dutch wedding. Within a few days after the wedding he was back at work.

## HOMES/LODGINGS

**1782–1796** *Kinderhook, New York.* Hudson Street, where his father kept an inn or tavern some three miles from his retirement home at Lindenwald. It stood at the bottom of a hill on a slight knoll on the present Hudson Street, opposite Williams street. A marker is on the site near 46 Hudson Street. Same house as birthplace.

**1796–** *Kinderhook, New York.* After he left home, his entire life, other than his years in the White House, was spent in temporary quarters, boarding houses, hotels, and rented houses in Albany and in Washington.

He spent many nights in dirty, disorderly taverns where he had the choice of sleeping in a chair in front of the fire or crowded in with two or three fully clothed, usually dirty, bedmates. There are no details in his writings which provide the names of the many taverns where he stayed in his early years.

**1802–1803** *New York City, New York.* Catherine Lane in an inexpensive boarding house near the foot of Manhattan Island.

**1808–1815** *Hudson, New York.* 309 Warren Street, where he also had his law practice. The building is standing but not marked in any way.

**1813** *New York City, New York.* 1 Wall Street, at the fashionable boarding house kept by Mrs. Rosa Keese across the corner of Broadway from Trinity Church.

**1815–1827** *Albany, New York.* State Street. When he became attorney general, he rented a house on State Street large enough for him to maintain his law offices in one of the parlors off the spacious entryway. He purchased the house later and sold it in 1827. No marker and business buildings now occupy the site.

**1821** *Washington, D.C.* Strother's Hotel, Fourteenth Street and Pennsylvania Avenue. He settled here in temporary quarters but later moved out to stay with Rufus King. He was a United States senator during this period.

**1822** *Washington, D.C.* Rooming with Rufus King in Georgetown. Location unknown.

**1822** *New York City, New York.* City Hall Park, 237 Broadway, at the corner of Park Place and Broadway at Mechanics Hall, where he took quarters for the November session of the New York Supreme Court.

**1823–1828** *Washington, D.C.* United States senator during this period. Location of lodging not determined.

**1828–1829** *Albany, New York.* 92 State Street, where he rented a three-story brick

*Van Buren purchased the Van Ness mansion in 1839 and renamed it Lindenwald.*

structure in the Georgian style, known as the Stevenson House, a few blocks from the capitol. The site is now occupied by the National Savings Bank.

**1829–1831** *Washington, D.C.* 748 Jackson Place on LaFayette Square in the Decatur House which the Clay family had recently vacated. He also rented rooms elsewhere at times. He was Secretary of State during this period.

**1831** *Albany, New York.* Congress Hall "on the Hill." Site between the Capitol and Washington Avenue. Hotel demolished.

**1831** *London, England.* Thomas Hotel, 25 Berkeley Square. He was here for a few days in September before moving to Stratford Place.

**1831–1832** *London, England.* No. 7 Stratford Place, a five-story townhouse. He was very friendly with Washington Irving in London and toured the English countryside

with him, including a stay at Marlborough Hall, a rambling Tudor vicarage in Derbyshire. December 1831. He was a guest of the King and Queen for two days at Windsor Castle. He was in London as Minister to the Court of St. James.

**1833** *Washington, D.C.* "Seven Buildings" on the corner of Pennsylvania Avenue and 19th Street. He rented one of these houses from James Kirk Paulding. It was within walking distance of the White House and had at one time housed the State Department.

**1833–1837** *Washington, D.C.* Gadsby's Tavern, northeast corner of Pennsylvania Avenue and Sixth Street, NW, while serving as vice president (what he called "his stuffy quarters").

**1837–1841** *Washington, D.C.* The White House. He was the third widower to enter the White House. His wife had died in 1819, and his eldest son Abraham's wife—

Angelica Singleton of South Carolina and a cousin of Dolley Madison—served as mistress of the White House during his term.

**1841–1862** *Kinderhook, New York.* Lindenwald, two miles south of Kinderhook. He purchased the Van Ness mansion in 1839 for his retirement and renamed it Lindenwald. He had never had a permanent home during his busy career, though he owned several farm houses in Kinderhook and surrounding towns. In 1841, he redid the mansion with expensive French wallpaper in the downstairs rooms and the finest Brussels carpets obtainable in New York covered the floors. When the work began on Lindenwald, he moved to Kinderhook where he engaged rooms for two months.

# WORK

**1796–** *Kinderhook, New York.* He worked in Cornelius Sylvester's store.

**1796–1800** *Kinderhook, New York.* During this period, he was also studying law.

**1798–1801** *Valatie, New York.* He made his first official court appearance in the tavern in Valatie before he became a practicing lawyer.

**1801–1803** *New York City, New York.* William Van Ness' law office, 30 Broad Street.

**1803–1808** *Kinderhook, New York.* He practiced law with his half brother, James Van Allen, in the town center.

**1808–1813** *Hudson, New York.* Law office at (now) 309 Warren Street. Appointed to his first public office, Surrogate of Columbia County. His home and office were at the same address.

**1812–1821** *Albany, New York.* Office in his home. See under home for location. Practicing law. At the same time he served in the state senate.

**1813–1820** *Albany, New York.* As a state senator in the first capitol, located just east

of the present building. Part of his new job was to sit as a member of the Court for the Correction of Errors which required him to spend some time in New York City.

**1821–1828** *Washington, D.C.* United States senator. Those who have stage fright may take some comfort from what happened to Senator Van Buren; he was so nervous during his maiden speech that he suddenly froze and fell back to his seat, thoroughly embarrassed and unable to continue.

**1829** *Albany, New York.* Governor. Office in the old state capitol located at the head of State Street in a square bounded by Washington Avenue, Park Place, Congress Street and Hawk Street. He was governor for only 64 days when he resigned to become Secretary of State under Jackson.

**1829–1831** *Washington, D.C.* Secretary of State. Office, corner of Fifteenth Street and Pennsylvania Avenue, where the north wing of the Treasury Building now stands.

**1831–1832** *London, England.* Minister to the Court of St. James. The Senate rejected his nomination, and he returned to the United States. Actually, this refusal gained him sympathy when he ran for president in 1836.

**1832–1833** *Kinderhook, New York.* He spent time with his family, travelled in the Catskill Mountains with Washington Irving, and did some political campaigning.

**1833–1837** *Washington, D.C.* Vice President of the United States. Because of bad weather, he took the oath of office in the Hall of the House of Representatives.

**1837–1841** *Washington, D.C.* President of the United States.

# TRAVEL/VISITS

In addition to his two trips to Europe, Van Buren visited Alabama, Connecticut, Delaware, Georgia, Illinois, Indiana, Kentucky, Maine, Maryland, Massachusetts. Michigan, Missouri, New Hampshire, New

Jersey, New York, North Carolina, Ohio, Pennsylvania, Rhode Island, South Carolina, Tennessee, Virginia, and West Virginia.

**1822** *Virginia.* He travelled throughout the state, including Richmond.

**1823** *Charlottesville, Virginia.* Monticello, to visit Jefferson.

**1828** *Owasco, New York.* Enos Throp house on Willow Brook, Lake Owasco, at the foot of the Owasco River.

**1829** *New York City, New York.* City Hotel, 115 Broadway, where he often stayed when in New York.

**1830** *Washington, D.C.* Jesse Brown's Indian Queen Hotel, north side of Pennsylvania Avenue between Sixth and Seventh Streets, NW.

**1831–** *Saratoga, New York.* United States Hotel, Broadway and Division, and Congress Hotel at Broadway and Spring and Sans Souci. He vacationed here. Both hotels are gone, but Congress Hall Park and the upper end of the main street are well worth a visit.

**1831** *London, England.* He travelled to Europe after his appointment as Minister by Jackson. In 1832, he made a trip to France, including a tour of Paris, and returned in early Spring 1832 to the United States.

**1832** *Lebanon Springs, New York.* In mid-August, he stayed at the Columbia Hotel on the stage road between Albany and Buffalo, one mile north of the village.

**1833** *Albany, New York.* He rented the ladies' parlor at Bement's on State Street. It is no longer standing.

**1833** *Decatur, Alabama.* Old State Bank, 925 Bank Street, NW, where he attended the opening of the bank while Vice President. He later visited Mobile.

**1833** *Lowell, Massachusetts.* Merrimack House, 310 Merrimack Street. He accompanied Jackson on his New England tour.

See under Jackson for Boston, Massachusetts, and Concord, New Hampshire entries.

**1833** *New York.* Catskills with Washington Irving in the summer.

**1834** *Washington. D.C.* He stayed at the White House with Jackson while the Paulding House in the "Seven Buildings" was being renovated.

**1836** *Jonesborough, Tennessee.* He visited in the home of Nathan Gammon. He also lodged in the Chester Inn.

**1837–** *White Sulphur Springs, West Virginia.* While he was president, he spent the summers in the president's Cottage at the Greenbrier Hotel.

**1837** *Caldwell, West Virginia.* Greenbrier River Inn on West Virginia 60. A reception was held here in his honor.

**1837** *Union, West Virginia.* South on West Virginia 219, Salt Sulphur Springs, south on west Virginia 219, where he was a guest. It is now private.

**1837–1841** *New York City, New York.* When president, he often stayed at the Washington Hotel, corner of Broadway and Chambers.

**1837** *Murfreesboro, Tennessee.* Colonel Charles Ready, Jr., house located on the east corner of the public square on the site of the present-day Commerce Union Bank park area. He was entertained here while president.

**1837** *Washington, D.C.* He spent the night before his inauguration in the White House with President Jackson.

**1837** *York, Pennsylvania.* White Hall, a three-story hotel, northeast corner of Market and Beaver Streets, where the National Hotel stood later. Here he was provided with entertainment hosted by Peter Dinkle, a leading citizen of York. He arrived in York in a carriage.

**1839** *Philadelphia, Pennsylvania.* Washington Hotel (later Merchants' Hotel). He was entertained with an elaborate banquet while lodging here in 1839.

**1839** *Saratoga, New York.* United States Hotel on Broadway. He often stayed here. The old hotel burned in 1865, and the new hotel, opened in 1874, was razed in 1946.

**1839** *Washington, D.C.* Bodisco House, 3322 O Street, NW. He attended a wedding here.

**1841** *New York City, New York.* Benjamin Butler house, Gramercy on Greene Street and Waverly Place near Gramercy Park, when he left for home as ex-president.

**1842** *(near) Georgetown, South Carolina.* Greenfield Plantation, at the "White House," home of Robert Poinsett, on the Black River east of Georgetown on the Conway–Georgetown Road.

**1842** *Columbia, Tennessee.* Visiting the home of James K. Polk.

**1842** *Detroit, Michigan.* Staying at American House, south side of Jefferson Avenue, east of Randolph Street, where he received a great welcome as ex-president. While in Detroit, he attended services at the Methodist Church on Woodward Avenue and Congress Street in the morning; in the afternoon he went to St. Paul's Episcopal Church at Shelby and Congress Streets and then to a Roman Catholic Church.

**1842** *Jacksonville, Illinois.* Governor Duncan's house. 4 Duncan Place at Duncan Park.

**1842** *Lexington, Kentucky.* Ashland, 1400 block of Richmond Road (East Main Street), visiting the home of Henry Clay.

**1842** *Mobile, Alabama.* Lodging at the Mansion House. He attended a play at the Corinthian Theater.

**1842** *Nashville, Tennessee.* The Hermitage for a visit with Andrew Jackson. He spent the first night at the Nashville Inn. He visited Nashville Female Academy and dined with George W. Campbell, who lived where Capitol Boulevard joins Cedar Street.

**1842** *Plainfield, Indiana.* On the grounds of the Friends Meeting House, 205 S. East Street is a tablet marking the site of the "Van Buren Elm." The plaque reads, "tree that spilled a President." As he arrived, his coach struck the roots of the old elm tree, overturned and spilled him into the mud. It is reported that the accident was planned to make a protest of Van Buren's road construction policies.

**1848** *New York City.* City Hotel, 115 Broadway. He stayed here during the coldest months of the year after his retirement.

**1848** *New York City, New York.* Julian's Hotel, overlooking New York's Washington Square, while working on a manuscript.

**1854** *Buren, Province of Gelderland, Holland, to visit the Buren Castle of his forebears.*

**1855** *Nice, France.* the Hotel Grand Bretagne.

**1857–** *New York City.* 152 East Thirtyeighth Street. The Gatehouse of an estate which belonged to a member of his family remains.

**1855** *Sorrento, Italy.* At the Villa Farangola, high above the bay while working on his memoirs. He was there for several months.

# DEATH

Van Buren died on July 24, 1862, in Kinderhook, New York, at Lindenwald. He suffered from arteriosclerosis and from congestive heart failure. He died at 2:00 A.M., in his room on the second floor. He left an estate valued at about $225,000 to his three surviving sons.

# FUNERAL

It was a very simple service in the Dutch Reformed Church, in Kinderhook. There were no bells, and the only music was the hymn "Oh God, Our Help in Ages Past." The rosewood

*Grave of Martin Van Buren.*

coffin was open for viewing during the service. President Lincoln did not attend and there were no living ex-presidents.

## BURIAL

The funeral procession of some 80 carriages made its way to the village cemetery where the rosewood coffin was placed in a protective wooden container and lowered into a grave beside that of his wife in the family plot. The tomb stone is a simple obelisk.

## BIBLIOGRAPHY

Curtis, James C. *The Fox at Bay: Martin Van Buren and the Presidency 1837–1841.* 1970.

Lynch, Denis Tilden. *An Epoch and a Man: Martin Van Buren and His Times.* 1961 (originally published 1929).

Niven, John. *Martin Van Buren: The Romantic Age of American Politics.* New York, 1983.

# WILLIAM HENRY HARRISON

1773–1841
9TH PRESIDENT 1841: WHIG PARTY

*"But I contend that the strongest of all governments is that which is most free."*

—*Letter, Simon Bolivar, September 27, 1829*

William Henry Harrison, nicknamed "Tippecanoe" from his famous victory, was the last president born a British subject. He was born February 9, 1773 to a wealthy planter and governor of Virginia, Benjamin Harrison V, and Elizabeth Bassett Harrison. On his paternal grandmother's side he was descended from King Henry III of England.

## CHARACTERISTICS

Harrison was about average height, estimated at 5′9″ but looking taller since he probably never weighed more than 145 pounds. His sparse brown hair turned gray by the time he occupied the White House. He was fair in complexion and had blue eyes. His photographs show a man with a long face, thin lips, and firm jaw. According to one visitor at his home, "He is a small and rather sallow looking man but he grows upon the eye and upon more intimate acquaintance."

# A LIFE IN REVIEW

**Birth:** February 9, 1773; Berkeley Plantation, Charles City County, VA

**Died:** April 4, 1841; Washington, D.C.

**Married:** Anna Tuthill Symmes; November 25, 1795; 6 sons, 4 daughters

## CAREER

**1793–1798** U.S. Military officer; Again 1812–1816 War of 1812

**1798–1800** Administration of Northwest Territory

**1800–1812** Governor of Indiana Territory

**1816–1819** Member U.S. Congress

**1825–1828** Member U.S. Senate

**1828–1830** Minister to Columbia

## ADMINISTRATION EVENTS

**1841** Died one month after taking office. No major events.

# BIRTHPLACE

Harrison was born in Charles City County, Virginia, on the Berkeley plantation. It is one of the beautiful plantations along the James River Virginia 5 between Williamsburg and Richmond.

# BAPTISM

He was probably baptized in 1773, in Charles City County, at Westover Episcopal Church. No actual records have been found, but this was the family church.

# CHURCH

His family background was traditionally Episcopal. As a child he attended the family church and when at school attended compulsory chapel. After his inauguration he had purchased a new Bible and had announced his intention of becoming a communicant of the Episcopal church when he caught a severe cold and died within a month of becoming president. In his long inaugural address he included a paragraph expressing his reverence for the Christian religion saying it was "the foundation of the welfare of the republic." Because of the military nature of his work he was often on the march or in areas where there was no formal church building so the list of churches associated with his name is necessarily short. Once seen reading a Bible in his hotel room, he said he had this practice of reading for twenty years—"at first it was a duty but now it has become a pleasure."

**1773–1791**  *Charles City County, Virginia.* Westover Episcopal Church near Berkeley Plantation on Virginia 5. The old church was on the banks of the river when he attended. Ruins remain.

**1787–1790**  *Hampden-Sydney College, Hampden-Sydney, Virginia.* During his time there was a little wooden chapel at which attendance was compulsory for the students. Nothing remains of the building. No marker.

**1791–1798**  *Fort Washington (near Cincinnati), Ohio.* Worship services were held in homes. Memorial stone for the Fort is on the corner of Third Street. At 429 East Third Street was a building which was once the home of Dr. Daniel Drake, earlier used as a church and where Harrison attended. Site is now occupied by the St. Anthony Syrian Maronite Church. The church organized at the home of Daniel Drake became the First Protestant Episcopal Church.

**1799–1801**  *North Bend, Ohio.* Services were held in his home, situated on the banks of the Ohio River. He often encouraged the use of his home for religious meetings. See location under home 1796–1801.

**1801–1812** *Vincennes, Indiana.* 3 West Scott Street off Harrison Street where services were held at his home, Grouseland. At the opening service for Methodists he held the candle while the minister read the text. The Methodist minister lodged with him at Grouseland.

**1812–1817** *North Bend, Indiana.* His home was used for public worship.

**1817–1841** *Cincinnati, Ohio.* Christ Church (Episcopal), 318 East Fourth Street. He was one of the sponsors and was named vestryman at the founding. The church was built in 1835 and is still standing.

**1817–1819** *Washington, D.C.* St. John's Episcopal Church, Lafayette Square where he occasionally worshipped. Also again in 1841 when he became president when he occupied pew number 45.

**1831–** *Cleves, Ohio.* Cleves Presbyterian Church. Site donated by Harrison and his wife. His grandson and future president, Benjamin Harrison, was baptized here.

**1836** *York, Pennsylvania.* First Presbyterian Church, north side of East Market Street and east side of Queen Street. This building, put up in 1789, was demolished in 1860. A new church is on site. He attended on his way to Washington.

# EDUCATION

**1773–1786** *Charles City County, Virginia.* Young William Henry Harrison was tutored in an outbuilding on the Berkeley Plantation in his early years. On either side of the main house there was a small building. The one to the south known as the "Bachelor House" was where he and his siblings went to school. He was also educated in "Mr. Burgess's school."

**1786–1787** *Lower Brandon, Virginia.* Brandon School. Lower Brandon was the home of Nathaniel Harrison and one of the finest houses in Prince George County on the lower side of the James River and where Harrison often spent Sundays. The school was an adjunct of the estate. See location under Homes/Lodgings—Brandon 1786.

**1787–1790** *Hampden-Sydney, Virginia.* He attended Hampden-Sydney College for pre-medical instruction. This was a small "log college" founded by the Presbyterians. He was listed as a member of the class of 1791 and as an attendant from 1787–1790. The only building remaining from the time of Harrison is the "Birthplace" which was built in the 1750's as a law office on the Slate Hill Plantation of Nathaniel Venable, one of the founders. The "Birthplace" was moved to the campus in 1944. See this historic building on the Via Sacra. He lodged in the college building on the main campus while in school here. Demolished.

**1790** *Richmond, Virginia.* Dr. Andrew Leiper, physician at 18th and Franklin Streets. Harrison served as an apprentice.

**1791** *Philadelphia, Pennsylvania.* University of Pennsylvania Medical School, studying under Benjamin Rush. He attended a few classes for only 16 weeks in Anatomical Hall, a square brick building on Fifth Street. Financial problems after his father died made it difficult to continue and in August he left to join the army as an Ensign in the First U.S. Infantry Regiment. Later he was in Philadelphia as a recruiting officer.

# MARRIAGE AND HONEYMOON

Harrison was married on November 25, 1795, in North Bend, Ohio. He married Anna Tuthill Symmes at the home of Doctor Stephenson, 116 Mt. Nebo Street, who was Treasurer of the Northwest Territory and Jus-

*William Harrison family home at Grouseland*

tice of the Peace. Dr. Stephenson performed the ceremony in the parlor of his log house where he was a tenant of the bride's father. Anna was considered a well-educated woman for the time. The Harrisons had ten children of whom only four were alive at the time he became president and only one was still alive at the time Anna died. Anna did not go with him to Washington for the inauguration but remained at home making preparation to go later in the spring. Because of his sudden death she never occupied the White House. She was the first president's widow to receive a pension. During the years 1838–1842, there was a death in the immediate family every year. Like other families they also had their worries with their children. Their son, Henry, was a youth of great popularity but occasionally erratic, bringing on warnings from his father against the perils of fast living. The embarrassing escapades of Van Buren's son, John, had also become noted in the press media of the time.

During the summer of 1833 his son, John Scott and wife, Elizabeth, had a new child. Since John Scott's house was under construction, Elizabeth was staying at General Harrison's home and consequently this was the birthplace of Benjamin Harrison. They spent their honeymoon at Fort Washington (now Cincinnati) as Harrison was still on duty. A stone on the corner of East Third in downtown Cincinnati marks the site of the Fort.

## HOMES/LODGINGS

**1773–1795** *Charles City County, Virginia.* Berkeley Plantation, eight miles west of Charles City on Virginia 5. It is a pleasant, rather plain red brick house, two stories high with gable roof and dormer windows in the midst of poplar trees.

**1773–** *New Kent County, Virginia.* Eltham Plantation, on the Pamunkey River, Virginia

249 west of New Kent Courthouse and north on County 30 where his mother was born and where he often visited.

**1786–** *Burrowsville, Prince George County, Virginia.* Brandon estate on County 611. Visiting relatives of the Harrisons.

**1786** *Richmond, Virginia.* Governor's executive mansion while his father, Benjamin Harrison, was governor. Site of this old mansion noted in listing under Richmond, Virginia.

**1791–** *Charles City, Virginia.* Berkeley Plantation. He often visited the Harrison family home after moving to the Northwest Territory.

**1796–1801** *North Bend, Ohio.* By 1795 the town of Cincinnati had been growing from the cluster of 20-30 log cabins which he saw there in 1791 to a village of 400. In 1796 he purchased 160 acres of land at North Bend together with a four-room cabin on the property. This house and its improvements were destroyed by fire in 1858. In March 1793 he had transferred his inheritance of 3000 acres in Virginia to his brother, Benjamin, and in exchange received a tract of land in Kentucky. Most of his life Harrison lived by a river. The house at North Bend, facing south, stood about 300 yards back from the Ohio River. Many years the house was open for public worship. He was generous and kept an open table, to which every visitor was welcomed.

**1799–** *Cleves, Ohio.* 116 Mt. Nebo Street was Symmes home (his father-in-law). Wedding near by in the residence of Dr. Stephenson who was a tenant of Symmes.

**1801–1812** *Vincennes, Indiana.* Beginning in January 1801 he lodged with a friend until he had cleared a 300-acre farm he had purchased and built his home, Grouseland, (now 3 West Scott Street at Park) where he lived while Territorial Governor. It is a two-and-a-half-story brick Georgian house containing 26 rooms and 13 fireplaces. It was built on a slight elevation in the midst of a walnut grove and was the first brick mansion in that region. On the first floor were two very large rooms, one used for council meetings and entertainment and the other as the family living room which was illuminated by firelight and candles. Living in a time when there was danger from Indian attacks he paid particular attention to details of defense. The outer walls were 18 inches thick and of solid brick and were slit for portholes and the broad-silled attic windows were designed for sharpshooters. The restored mansion is still standing. A year or two following the completion of Grouseland he purchased a few hundred acres on Blue River, near Corydon in southern Indiana where he erected a grist and sawmill.

**1812–1814** *Cincinnati, Ohio.* He lived with his family in a rented house, a comfortable house on Broadway just below Fourth Street, during the time he was engaged in the War of 1812.

**1814–1817** *North Bend, Ohio.* His home in Virginia had been a plantation but the home in the West could never be dignified by any other name than that of a farm. One wing of the house at North Bend had been originally a log cabin. It is sometimes referred to as the "Big House." This remained his major home until his death in 1841.

**1817–1819** *Washington, D.C.* He took living quarters at Mrs. Clarke's on F Street NW while a member of the U.S. Congress.

**1819–1825** *North Bend, Ohio.* See entry North Bend above 1814–1817.

**1825–1828** *Washington, D.C.* Gadsby's, Pennsylvania Avenue and Sixth Street NW while serving in the United States Senate. He was here again 1836.

**1828–1830** *Bogota, Columbia.* "Garden of James" (Huerto Jayme), a large house which he purchased for the United States Legation.

**1841** *Washington, D.C.* White House.

# WORK

**1791–1798**  *Fort Washington, (Cincinnati), Ohio.* United States Army, rising to rank of captain and in command of Fort Washington.

**1791**  *Philadelphia, Pennsylvania.* He obtained a commission as Ensign in the First Regiment of the United States Army.

**1791–**  *Fort Hamilton, Ohio.*

**1791–1792**  *Fort Jefferson, Ohio.* Marched from Fort Washington to Miami River towns in the vicinity of present-day Fort Wayne, Indiana.

**1791–1792**  *Fort St. Clair,* (near the present site of Eaton), *Ohio.* Here he encamped.

**1791–1792**  *Fort Fayette, Ohio.* Here he encamped before moving with army to Legionville.

**1793**  *Fort Greenville, Ohio.*

**1793**  *Fort Recovery, Ohio.* He was here with General Wayne when this permanent stockade was built. Located in western Ohio in Mercer County, on Ohio 119 near town of Fort Recovery.

**1798**  *Cincinnati, Ohio.* His resignation from the army was accepted. In the spring he was appointed Land Officer Register.

**1798–1799**  *Cincinnati.* He served as Secretary of the Northwest Territory. He held this office for little more than a year. When the governor was absent or incapacitated he acted as governor. Since custom had fixed the seat of government in the territory at Cincinnati he continued his residence here with meetings in the First Territorial House.

**1799**  *Philadelphia, Pennsylvania.* He served as the first delegate from Northwest Territory to Congress. Met in Congress Hall.

**1800**  *Corydon, Indiana.* This town was founded by Harrison in 1800. See the Corydon Historic District which preserves original grid plan around the public square, including the Branham Tavern at North Capitol Avenue which was put up by Harri-son. The capitol area on the public square on the north side of Walnut Street was a tract of land purchased in 1804 by Harrison and sold by him in 1807. The capitol was begun in 1814 and completed 1816 and served as capitol until 1825.

**1800–1812**  *Vincennes, Indiana.* Governor of the territory. He arrived early January 1801 and began his duties in the little two story capitol. He also used as his office the great parlor in the home of Colonel Vigo which was located off Harrison Street near "Grouseland." See the Indiana Territory State Historic Site at First and Harrison Streets. The original site was 217 Main Street. It was moved to the east side of Park Street in 1949. Now a museum. It contains a table used by him.

**1803**  *Fort Wayne, Indiana.* Meetings in council with the Indians.

**1803**  *Gosport, Indiana.* North of town on Indiana 67 is a marker commemorating the Fort Wayne treaty negotiations between Harrison and Chief Little Turtle.

**1811**  *Graysville, Indiana.* Fort Turman, off Indiana 154. It was used by Harrison during the War of 1812. He was here September 1811.

**1811**  *Perrysville, Indiana.* Harrison's Crossing, Indiana 63, is where he crossed the Big Vermillian River on the march preceding the Battle of Tippecanoe. This battle was later used to bolster his presidential campaign on the one side and by his enemies to vilify him. See Fort Knox II on Fort Knox Road, Indiana 41 from where he marched with troops for the Battle. The Tippecanoe Battlefield is on Railroad Street, West Lafayette and Harrison's camp site is marked with a large obelisk.

**1812**  *Fort Amanda, Ohio.* Nine miles northwest of Wapakoneta is the site of a fort used in 1812. August 22 he received word he had been made a brigadier general in the regular army by President Madison.

**1812** *Fort Wayne, Indiana.* In operation against the Indians. He rescued the Fort in 1812 which was replaced with a stronger one in 1815.

**1812** *Delaware, Ohio.* 24 miles north of Franklinton, Ohio (now west side of Columbus) where going via the Sanduskys, he took up his headquarters.

**1813** *Cincinnati, Ohio.* After a 10-day stay here he started for the Rapids by way of Piqua and St. Marys (Auglaize County). At Fort Amanda in Allen County, he climbed into the boats with the men. The guns of Fort Meigs saluted his arrival just south of Toledo.

**1813** *Fort Meigs, Ohio.* Fort Meigs was under siege for nine days and nights but under Harrison the fort twice held the British. In May he retraced the route across Black Swamp to Lower Sandusky. Fallen Timbers, just south of Toledo, Ohio marks the site where Indians relinquished the Firelands Territory to the white settlers. In June. Returned to headquarters at Franklinton where he banned the sale of liquor at the various army posts, and issued strict orders against duelling. One man of his army said he "resembled more a father than a military commander in care of his troops. His disposition was such a mixture of sympathy, kindness and humanity that he was like my uncle Toby—he would not hurt even a fly."

**1813** *Middle Bass Island, Ohio.* Here he met with Commodore Perry. A 352-foot high monument can be seen from the shoreline.

**1817–1819** *Washington, D.C.* Member of U.S. House of Representatives from Ohio. Immediately active in legislative matters. The first session of the Fourteenth Congress raised its own pay from six dollars a day (about $900 annually) to $1,500 a year, taking care to make the provision retroactive. It was denounced in most homes west of the Alleghenies. Harrison disagreed with the new raise saying the essential dignity of Congress had been compromised by an over hasty move to increase its own pay without first consulting the people. The Fourteenth Congress met in the structure known as the "Brick Capitol," erected by public subscription on the site of the present Supreme Court building.

**1819–1821** *Columbus, Ohio.* Member of the Ohio state senate. During his two years in the state senate he was an outstanding and active figure being on many committees and chairman of two. Since 1817 the Ohio legislature had been meeting in the borough of Columbus near Franklinton, the new and permanent capital.

**1825–1828** *Washington, D.C.* U.S. Senator from Ohio. May 26, 1828 when the Senate held its last meeting of the session he left Washington and returned to North Bend to prepare for his departure for Columbia.

**1828–1829** *Bogota, Columbia.* U.S. Minister to Columbia. Appointed by President John Quincy Adams. Legation at "Garden of James."

**1834–1840** *North Bend, Ohio.* As Clerk of the Court of Common Pleas of Hamilton County. Necessarily, as part of the court, he did not take a very active part in politics during the early thirties. Resigned his office Dec. 10, 1840.

**1841** *Washington, D.C.* The White House. Dying in office a month later, he had the shortest term as president.

# TRAVEL/VISITS

**1792** *Pittsburgh, Pennsylvania.* Tannehill's tavern on Water Street. He was here at the time he joined the U.S. infantry.

**1800** *Lexington, Kentucky.* Home of Major Short a close friend.

**1801–** *Vincennes, Indiana.* Colonel Francis Vigo home, off Harrison Street. He was friend and political associate.

**1804**   *St. Louis, Missouri.* Auguste Chouteau home, fronted on Main Street and occupied the whole square bounded by Market, Main Walnut and Second Streets. Auguste Chouteau was a rich land owner who, with his brother, owned a large part of St. Louis. The house had been used as government headquarters. Harrison was here on business. The house was razed in 1841.

**1804**   *St. Genevieve, Missouri.* Francois Valle House, 167 South Gabouri Street. He visited here while on a visit to Missouri.

**1804**   *St. Louis, Missouri.* He was here to organize the District of Upper Louisiana which had been attached to Indiana. October to December.

**1806**   *Wyandotte, Indiana.* Wyandotte Caves, four miles east of new Leavenworth. He was probably investigating the mineral content.

**1812–**   *Cincinnati, Ohio.* General James Findlay home, 30 North Front Street which was near his office.

**1832–**   *Albany, New York.* Van Rensselaer home, Cherry Hill between McCarty and First Avenues.

**1832–1833**   *Indianapolis, Indiana at the new capital.* Since the statehouse was then under construction, the legislature met in the court house where Harrison was greeted as a friend home from the wars.

**1835–1840**   *Cincinnati, Ohio.* Boarded at Main Street Hotel while Clerk of Court.

**1836**   *White Sulphur Springs, West Virginia.* Greenbrier Hotel on vacation during the summer.

**1836**   *Baltimore, Maryland.* Eutaw House, northwest corner of Eutaw and West Baltimore Streets.

**1836**   *Hot Springs, Virginia.* None of the old hotels remain. It was five miles southwest of Warm Springs.

**1836**   *Richmond, Virginia.* Powhatan House, southeast corner of Broad and Eleventh Streets.

**1836**   *Warm Springs, Bath County, Virginia.* Homestead Hotel, off Virginia 501.

**1840**   *Jeffersonville, Indiana.* Grisamore House, 111–113 West Chestnut Street where he visited and delivered a speech from the front porch in the 1840 political campaign.

**1840**   *Lebanon, Ohio.* Golden Lamb, 27 South Broadway. Others who were guests at some time included Hayes, McKinley, and several others who were president.

**1840**   *York, Pennsylvania.* Washington House. East Market and Centre Square.

**1840**   *Indianapolis, Indiana.* Lodging at Aquilla Parker's Tavern a few miles east of town.

**1841**   *Cincinnati, Ohio.* Henri House, West Main between Court and Canal on the way to Washington for his inaugural. See next three entries as part of the inaugural tour.

**1841**   *Concord, New Hampshire.* The Eagle Hotel, Eagle Square.

**1841**   *Frederick, Maryland.* Dorsey's City Hotel on north side of West Patrick between Market Street and Public Street (now Court Street).

**1841**   *Hagerstown, Maryland.* McIlhenny's Tavern, North Potomac Street.

**1841**   *New York City, New York.* The American House, 135 Fulton Street.

**1841**   *Richmond, Virginia.* Merchant's Coffee House.

# DEATH

Harrison died April 4, 1841, in Washington, D.C., at the White House, at 12:30 P.M., after catching cold on Inauguration Day, a month earlier. On his death bed he asked that Psalm 103 be read to him. His last words: "Sir, I wish you to understand the true principles of government. I wish them carried out. I ask nothing more."

## FUNERAL

The funeral was held on April 7, in the East Room of the White House. Services were conducted by the rector of St. John's Episcopal Church. President John Tyler and ex-President John Quincy Adams attended. He was the first to lay in state in the White House as well as later in the Capitol Rotunda. The casket was open for viewing. In Cincinnati, Ohio, memorial services were held at 322 East Fifth Street, at Wesley Chapel.

## BURIAL

He was buried in Washington, D.C. His body was accompanied by 26 pall bearers and 10,000 mourners, and was buried temporarily in Washington in the old Congressional Cemetery. In June of the same year, he was taken to North Bend for permanent burial. He was buried in five coffins, one inside the other, to discourage grave robbers, because of the experience with grave robbers who violated the grave of his son, John.

The final burial took place at the William Henry Harrison Memorial State Park on the summit of Mount Nebo.

## BIBLIOGRAPHY

Cleaves, Freeman. *Old Tippecanoe: William Henry Harrison and His Time.* Port Washington, NY: Kennikat Press, 1939.

Goebel, Dorothy Burne. *William Henry Harrison: A Political Biography.* Philadelphia: Porcupine Press, 1926.

*William Harrison grave site.*

# JOHN TYLER

1790–1862
10TH PRESIDENT 1841–1845: WHIG PARTY

John Tyler, the first vice president to become president upon the death of his predecessor, was born on March 29, 1790, to John Tyler, who served as governor of Virginia, and Mary Armistead Tyler. He was sometimes called "Old Veto" because of his extensive use of this executive power.

## CHARACTERISTICS

Tyler was a distinguished-looking man with all the charm and grace of the well-bred southerner. Throughout his life, he put on very little weight, and his slimness accentuated his height of just over six feet. He had blue eyes and wavy brown hair. His face was long and thin with high cheek bones, and a large Roman nose and cartoonish large ears. He liked all the activities of the southern country gentleman. One of his favorite pastimes was playing the violin, and he did it very well.

## BIRTHPLACE

Tyler was born in Greenway, Charles City County, Virginia, between Richmond and Williamsburg on the James River. A marker

*"The practical statesman . . . has to look at things as they are, to take things as he finds them, to supply deficiencies and to prune excesses as far as in him lies."*

—First annual message, Congress, December 7, 1841

# A LIFE IN REVIEW

**Birth:** March 29, 1790; Greenway, Charles City County, VA

**Died:** January 18, 1862; Richmond, VA

**Married:** Letitia Christian; March 29, 1813; 3 sons, 4 daughters
Julia Gardiner; June 26, 1844; 5 sons, 2 daughters

## CAREER

**1811–1816** Member Virginia House of Delegates

**1816–1821** Member U.S. Congress

**1823–1825** Member Virginia House of Delegates

**1825–1827** Governor of Virginia

**1827–1836** Member U.S. Senate

**1838–1840** Member Virginia House of Delegates

**1841** U.S. Vice President

## ADMINISTRATION EVENTS

**1841** Established right of presidential succession

**1842** Webster-Ashburton Treaty with Great Britain

**1842** Mount Saint Helens erupted

**1843** Mount Rainier erupted

**1844** Married while in office

**1845** Annexation of Texas

# BAPTISM

He was probably baptized at Westover Episcopal Church near Greenway on Virginia 5, east of Berkeley Plantation. All records of the church prior to 1833 were either destroyed in the Civil War or during the time the church was closed from 1805 to 1833. There is no extant record of his baptism, but this was the family church for the Tyler family.

# CHURCH

The Episcopal Church was part of his traditional heritage. There is nothing in his own writings about his religious views, and a diligent search reveals practically nothing definite on his attitudes. From what is available, he could properly be called a Deist. He had a broad-ranging knowledge of the Bible. Like most of his predecessors of the Episcopal faith, he was tolerant of all faiths and a firm believer in the doctrine of the separation of church and state.

**1790–1862** *Charles City County, Virginia.* Westover Episcopal Church near the family home which he attended from birth to the end of his life. He usually went to the chapel of the parish called St. Thomas Chapel; after it was burned and rebuilt in the 1840s, it was called Mapsico Church.

**1802–** *Williamsburg, Virginia.* Bruton Parish Church, corner of the Palace Green and Duke of Gloucester Street, which he attended while he was at the College of William and Mary and later when he practiced law in Williamsburg.

**1809–1811** *Richmond, Virginia.* St. John's Episcopal Church. East Broad Street, attended while living with his father, the Governor, in Richmond.

**1811–1816** *Richmond, Virginia.* The State Capitol, in the old Hall of the House of Delegates located off the Rotunda; Episcopal and Presbyterian services were held on alternate Sundays.

at the side of the road one mile south of Charles City on Virginia 5 indicates the site of his birth. Most of his life was lived within a short distance of this site.

**1816–** *Washington, D.C.* St. John's Episcopal Church, attended when he was in Washington as a member of Congress and later as vice president and president.

**1845–1862** *Richmond, Virginia.* St. Paul's Episcopal, corner of Grace and Ninth Streets.

## EDUCATION

**1795–1802** *Charles City County, Virginia.* He started school at the little school on the River Road near Greenway. He attended this "old field school" until 1802. The school is at the back of Greenway Plantation and can still be seen.

**1802–1805** *Williamsburg, Virginia.* In the secondary division of the College of William and Mary. Board and lodging with his brother-in-law, Judge James Semple, on Francis Street, near the intersection with Waller Street.

**1805–1807** *Williamsburg, Virginia.* College of William and Mary. He graduated at age seventeen, having joined the college at age fifteen.

**1807–1809** *Charles City County, Virginia.* He returned to study law under his father and a cousin, Samuel Tyler. Samuel Tyler's house was West Berry on the west side of Virginia 156 (not far from the Benjamin Harrison Memorial Bridge on Virginia 5).

**1809–1811** *Richmond, Virginia.* 1002 Capitol Street, where he studied law under the great Edmund Randolph.

## MARRIAGE AND HONEYMOON

Tyler was married on March 29, 1813, at the Cedar Grove Plantation, in New Kent County, Virginia, on the west side of Virginia 609 and on Virginia 106. His bride was Letitia Christian of Cedar Grove Plantation. Their

*Cedar Grove, home of Letitia Christian Tyler.*

honeymoon was spent in a small cottage, now vandalized and in ruins, but still visible, in the north section of the family plantation at Greenway.

All descriptions of Letitia emphasize her domestic virtues, sweetness of manner, devout religious life, and selflessness. She stayed in the background and much preferred her successive homes at Woodburn, Greenway, Gloucester, and Williamsburg to the life in Washington. She died within the year after her husband became president.

Tyler's second marriage took place on June 26, 1844, in New York City the Church of the Ascension, on Fifth Avenue at Tenth Street. His second wife, who was thirty years younger than he, Julia Gardiner was very pretty and had raven-black hair, a light complexion and dark eyes. She was only five feet three inches in height and tended to plumpness. Her pleasing manner and extroverted personality brought gaiety to the White House. The Gardiner residence on LaFayette Square, East Hampton (New York City), was the site of the wedding reception.

*John Tyler's honeymoon cottage.*

After a light wedding breakfast, the guests went to the foot of Cortland Street where they boarded the ferry boat *Essex* for a turn around the harbor. The newlyweds got off at Jersey City and took a train to Philadelphia to begin the wedding trip to Washington, D.C. The wedding night was spent in Philadelphia, and the following night they were in the White House. They later travelled to White Sulphur Springs, West Virginia, and stayed in the president's cottage and then to Sherwood Forest in Charles City County, Virginia, before returning to the White House. Tyler wrote a honeymoon ballad for the occasion, and it remains the only known musical collaboration of a president and his first lady.

# HOME/LODGING

**1790–1813**  *Greenway, Charles City County, Virginia.* He was born on the 1200-acre family estate on the James River. The two-story clapboard house was built before 1700 and is the second oldest house in Charles City. It is now privately owned.

**1809–1811**  *Richmond, Virginia.* With his father in the governor's mansion at the corner of Capitol and Governor Streets.

**1813–1815**  *Greenway, Charles City County, Virginia.* Mons-Sacer, a beautiful 500-acre section of the Greenway estate he had inherited from his father. It can only be reached after driving over an unfinished road. The house is in ruins, but there are some plans for restoration.

**1823–1825**  *Richmond, Virginia.* Capitol on Capitol Square bounded by Bank, North Ninth, Capitol and Governor Streets. Lodging not determined.

**1825–1827**  *Richmond, Virginia.* Governor's Mansion, on Capitol Square at the side of the State Capitol. He was governor.

**1827–1836**  *Washington, D.C.* In various hotels and rooming houses while serving in Congress. Tyler House, on Fourth Street between Madison and Constitution Avenue, NW, disappeared long ago.

**1829–1844**  *Gloucester County, Virginia.* His 630-acre farm on the north side of the York River. The farm was sold in 1844.

**1836–1838**  *Williamsburg, Virginia.* Corner of Francis and South England Streets. He shifted between the farm in Gloucester County and the law practice in Williamsburg.

**1838–1841**  *Williamsburg, Virginia.* In Bassett Hall in the southeast section of the old town off Francis Street, near the intersection with Walter Street. He was here off and on in law practice.

**1840s**  *White Springs, Virginia.* Here for many vacation trips. White Sulphur Springs, West Virginia. President's Cottage (Greenbrier Hotel) used as a summer home while he was president.

**1841**  *Washington, D.C.* As vice president of the United States, he stayed at Brown's Hotel, north side of Pennsylvania Avenue between Sixth and Seventh Streets, NW. He

*John Tyler home, Sherwood Forest, said to be the longest frame house in the United States.*

took the oath of office here. He also stayed at 3000 Cathedral.

**1841–1845**  *Washington, D.C.* The White House.

**1842–1862**  *Charles City County, Virginia.* Sherwood Forest (previously known as Walnut Grove), about two miles from Greenway. It is said to be the longest frame house in the United States and is about the length of a football field. Harrison R. Tyler, grandson of the president and his wife, live in the house, which has been continuously occupied by President Tyler's direct descendants.

**1858–**  *Hampton, Virginia.* Villa Margaret, near Old Point Comfort. The site on Queen Street was later occupied by the former Dixie/Bayberry Hospital. This was a summer place bought by Julia Tyler and the Tylers summered here during the last years before the Civil War. Nothing remains.

# WORK

**1811–**  *Charles City County, Virginia.* The little building beside the house was used as a law office by Governor John Tyler, Sr., and afterwards by his son who became president.

**1811–1816**  *Richmond, Virginia.* Member of Virginia House of Delegates. State Capitol on Capitol Square.

**1813**  *Sioux City, Iowa.* Brief career in the military in which he was commissioned captain. Although he laughed over the ludicrousness of this career, he received a quarter section in what is now Sioux City, Iowa, for his contribution to the defense of Williamsburg.

**1816–1821**  *Washington, D.C.* Member of the House of Representatives. The House met in the "Brick Capitol" where the Supreme Court now stands, First Street and A Street, NE (now Maryland Avenue). It also met in Statuary Hall of the present Capitol.

**1821–1823** *Charles City, Virginia.* Sherwood Forest on Virginia 5. Law practice and overseeing lands.

**1823–1825** *Richmond, Virginia.* Member of the Virginia House of Delegates. State Capitol. The old House of Delegates is now a museum, located just north of the rotunda on the first floor.

**1825–1827** *Richmond.* Governor of Virginia. State Capitol. Governor's office on the second floor.

**1827–1836** *Washington, D.C.* U.S. Senator from Virginia. Serving in the north wing of the Capitol in a room which later became the Supreme Court Chamber.

**1829** *Richmond, Virginia.* Hall of Delegates in the State Capitol for state constitutional convention. Then shifted to First African Baptist Church on College and East Broad Streets.

**1836–1838** *Williamsburg, Virginia.* Home and law office, corner of Francis and South England Streets, where he began practicing law again. No marker.

**1838–1840** *Richmond, Virginia.* Member of Virginia legislature (speaker of the lower house). Old Hall of Delegates on the first floor of the Capitol.

**1839** *Harrisburg, Pennsylvania.* Delegate to Whig National Convention, Zion Lutheran Church, where he was nominated vice president.

**1841** *Washington, D.C.* Vice president of the United States. U.S. Capitol.

**1841–1845** *Washington, D.C.* President of the United States.

**1861** *Washington, D.C.* President of Peace Conference.

**1862** *Richmond, Virginia.* Member of the Congress of the Confederate States, which met in the State Capitol in the old Hall of Delegates.

# TRAVEL/VISITS

Tyler is one of the few presidents who never travelled outside of the United States. Even within the United States, his travel was limited to places within Virginia (including what is now West Virginia) and the eastern states lying between Virginia and southern New England.

In Virginia, he made many vacation trips to Old Point Comfort, White Springs, and Sweet Springs. In New York the Tylers went to places each summer, including East Hampton, Pittsfield, Saratoga or Newport. He tried to avoid the posh hotels. For instance, he stayed at Mrs. Sylvia S. Rogers' home in Saratoga and similar accommodations between 1848 and 1851.

**1790s–** *Charles City County, Virginia.* Historic County Courthouse building. Marker V-11 about one half mile from Greenway.

**1841–** *Baltimore, Maryland.* Barnum Hotel, southwest corner of Fayette and Calvert Streets, for speaking engagements and visits.

**1842–** *New York City, New York.* On the west side of 428-434 Lafayette Street are the remains of Colonnade Row, a house belonging to David Gardiner, whose daughter, Julia, married Tyler and where he first courted her.

**1842** *New Kent County, Virginia.* Cedar Grove Cemetery, off Virginia 609, where his first wife is buried.

**1843** *Boston, Massachusetts.* Bunker Hill Monument, 43 Monument Square. Dedication.

**1843** *Lowell, Massachusetts.* He spoke at Merrimack House, 310 Merrimack.

**1845** *Washington, D.C.* Fuller's Hotel, Pennsylvania Avenue and Fourteenth Street, NW, where he stayed upon leaving the White House.

**1845** *Richmond, Virginia.* Powhattan House, southeast corner of Broad and Eleventh

Streets. He often stayed here while in Richmond on business.

**1846** *Washington, D.C.* Dinner with President Polk at the White House.

**1850** *Richmond, Virginia.* He attended the laying of the cornerstone of the Washington Monument on the State Capitol grounds.

**1850** *Richmond, Virginia.* Union Hotel, southwest corner of Nineteenth and Main Streets.

**1851** *Niagara Falls, New York.* On a visit here, Tyler refused to set so much as a foot on British soil.

**1852–** *Staten Island, New York.* What is now West New Brighton, at Castleton Hill, 27 Tyler Street, a short street between Broadway and North Burgher (Clove Road). They often visited and in the summer of 1857 vacationed here. After Tyler died in 1862, Mrs. Tyler stayed from 1862 to 1868 on Colonnade Row and from 1868 to 1874 here on Staten Island.

**1861–1862** *Richmond.* When in the city, he stayed at the Exchange Hotel, Franklin at Fourteenth Street. Demolished in 1900.

**1861** *Richmond, Virginia.* Ballard House, across from the Exchange Hotel, Franklin at Fourteenth Street. Demolished in 1920.

**1861** *Washington, D.C.* Brown's Hotel, north side of Pennsylvania Avenue, between Sixth and Seventh Streets, NW, while attending the Peace Conference which came to naught.

# DEATH

Tyler died on January 18, 1862, in Richmond, Virginia, at the Exchange Hotel, at 12:15 A.M. His wife died in the same hotel 20 years later, in room 27, a few doors down the hall from where Tyler died. Having died in disgrace, as a supporter of the southern Confederacy, there was no official proclamation by President Lincoln or lowering of the flag over the national capitol.

The *New York Times* of January 22, 1862 printed a highly uncomplimentary obituary saying he retired "the most unpopular man that had ever held any public office in the United States." This was from a northern point of view after Tyler had thrown in his lot with the southern Confederacy and been elected a member of the Confederate government.

# FUNERAL

Tyler's body lay in state at the Confederate Congress in the State Capitol of Virginia in the chamber of the House of Delegates, off the Rotunda, opposite the portico entrance. His open coffin was draped in the Confederate flag.

Services were held in Richmond, at St. Paul's Episcopal Church, southwest corner of Grace and Ninth Streets. Following the Episcopal funeral rites a 150-carriage cortege proceeded amid light rain to the nearby cemetery.

# BURIAL

Tyler is buried in Richmond, in Hollywood Cemetery, next to the tomb of President Monroe. Later, his second wife was buried beside him. His first wife was buried at Cedar Grove.

# BIBLIOGRAPHY

Seager, Robert. *And Tyler Too*. New York: McGraw-Hill Book Company, Inc., 1963.

# JAMES KNOX POLK

### 1795–1849
### 11TH PRESIDENT 1845–1849: DEMOCRATIC PARTY

*"I must have shook hands with several thousands persons. . . . Some gentlemen asked me if my arm was not sore. . . . I told them that I had found that there was a great art in shaking hands."*

*— The diary of James K. Polk*

James K. Polk, called by some "Young Hickory" because of his association with Andrew Jackson, "Old Hickory," was born to well-to-do Scotch-Irish farmers, Samuel and Jane Knox Polk, at about noon on November 2, 1795.

## CHARACTERISTICS

James Knox Polk was about 5′8″ tall with a solid build, weighing between 160 and 175 pounds. His height gave him the nickname "Napoleon of the Stump." He had gray eyes and in his youth black hair, which he wore long and combed straight back, but it was usually messed. His hair turned white during his time in the White House. He had a high prominent forehead, high cheek bones, thin lips, and a rather large nose. He had the dubious distinction of having his nose pulled when he was Speaker of the House. In spite of his public success, he was by nature an introvert. He and his wife were strict about temperance observance, and, long before Lucy Hayes was first lady, they abolished wine and dancing at White House receptions.

# A LIFE IN REVIEW

**Birth:** November 2, 1795; Pineville, Mecklenberg County, NC

**Died:** June 15, 1849; Nashville, TN

**Married:** Sarah Childress; January 1, 1824; No children

## CAREER

**1819–1823** Lawyer

**1823–1825** Member state legislature

**1825–1839** Member U.S. Congress

**1835–1839** Speaker of the House

**1839–1841** Governor of Tennessee

## ADMINISTRATION EVENTS

**1845** U.S. Naval Academy opened

**1846** Settlement of Oregon boundary with Canada

**1846–1848** War with Mexico

**1848** Cornerstone Washington Monument laid

# BIRTHPLACE

Polk was born near Pineville, Mecklenburg County, North Carolina. A restoration of the two-story log house is on the site, off US 521, a few miles south of Charlotte.

# BAPTISM

As a baby, he was taken to Providence Meeting House (Presbyterian), seven miles from home, but his father, angered by the requirement for a profession of faith by the par-

ents, quarreled with the parson and took the baby home unbaptized. On his death bed, he was baptized a Methodist on June 9, 1849 by the Reverend McFerren of Nashville, Tennessee. In his diary, he writes that having thus formally embraced Christianity, he felt prepared "to meet the great event." See location under church listing.

# CHURCH

Polk was a straight-laced follower of the Methodist Church, and his wife was a serious Presbyterian. They acted on their principles and forbade drinking, dancing, and card playing in the White House. Sam Houston said the only thing wrong with Polk was that he drank too much water!

In 1833, he attended a religious camp meeting outside Columbia, Tennessee and was greatly moved by the evangelist. After that, he was actually a Methodist, but, out of respect for his mother and wife, he continued to attend Presbyterian services except when his wife was unable to go, at which time he would generally go to a Methodist church.

**1795–1806** *(near) Pineville, North Carolina.* Providence Presbyterian Church (Meeting House), on North Carolina 16 south of Charlotte toward Waxhaw. The church was established in 1767. The present sanctuary was built in 1858 by slaves. The family attended here after the marriage of his mother and father. Members of the family are buried in the nearby cemetery.

**1795–1806** *Pineville, North Carolina.* Hopewell Presbyterian Church in the northern end of Mecklenberg Country where his mother was a member. The church was organized in 1762 and the first building was put up in 1765. The present church was built on the same site in 1831.

**1806–1816** *Columbia, Tennessee.* Zion Church, which also figured in his education. Three miles past Ashwood, and six and three tenth miles west of Columbia.

**1816–1818**   *Chapel Hill, North Carolina.* While at the University, he received a rigorous Presbyterian indoctrination and regularly attended chapel in the "Old Chapel," or Person Hall, on the campus.

**1816–1825**   *Columbia, Tennessee.* At first, the Presbyterians worshipped in the courthouse, but by 1823 they had a church of their own, located on the corner of North Garden and West Sixth Streets. After his marriage, he purchased a pew in the new church and was there every Sunday when in town. It was destroyed by fire in 1847.

**1816–1825**   *Columbia, Tennessee.* First Methodist Church on West Seventh is on the site of the old church where Polk attended. It has a memorial stained-glass window for President Polk.

**1825–1839**   *Washington, D.C.* First Presbyterian Church on Four-and-one-half Street, where he purchased a pew and attended regularly.

**1825–1839**   *Washington, D.C.* Methodist church called the Foundry Methodist today. He attended when it was located at Fourteenth and G Streets, NW. He also attended here while serving as president of the United States.

**1839–**   *Nashville, Tennessee.* First Presbyterian Church (now Downtown Presbyterian Church), Fifth Avenue North and Church Street, where Mrs. Polk, like Mrs. Andrew Jackson, was a member. The first structure was built in 1814 and the present (third) from 1849 to 1851. It has fascinating Egyptian revival architecture.

**1849**   *Savannah, Georgia.* Independent Presbyterian, Bull Street and Oglethorpe Avenue. Burned in 1889. There is now a copy of the original on the site.

**1849**   *Nashville, Tennessee.* At times, he at-tended McKendree Methodist Church, 523 Church Street.

# EDUCATION

Polk received informal basic instruction in Pineville, North Carolina. A neighbor recalled years later that "Little Jimmy Polk used to pass along this road often to the 'old field school' bare-footed with his breeches rolled up to his knees. He was a mighty bashful little fellow." There is no marker; the exact location is unknown.

**1813–1814**   *(near) Columbia, Tennessee.* Zion Church Academy. It is located three miles past Ashwood at the Zion Church in Maury County, one mile south of Tennessee 99, 6.3 miles west of Columbia at the Zion Church which is on the site of a log cabin school where he is said to have had his early education.

**1814–1816**   *Murfreesboro, Tennessee.* He attended the Academy of Samuel P. Black. The site is northeast of the 1918 Bradley School building on South Academy Street. Shortly after he arrived, the school moved to a large log building in the town, and he boarded with a nearby family, William Lytle. There is a marker near the Coca Cola plant on South Broad Street.

**1816–1818**   *Chapel Hill, North Carolina.* University of North Carolina, which he entered as a sophomore. He received a classical education and graduated with honors in 1818. At the University, the recently completed New College (later called South Building), a three-story structure surmounted by a cupola, contained dormitory rooms. It faced northward on the "Grand Avenue." Old East was the original college building. He roomed on the third floor of the New College Hall (South Hall) in the southwest corner with William D. Moseley (later governor of Florida). He also boarded at the Yeargin farm about a mile from the University buildings near Bowlin's Creek in the northern part of land owned by Oregon Tenney. In 1845, the degree of Doctor of Laws was conferred on him by the University. In 1847, he was an honored guest at the commencement with a special reception at Gerrard Hall on the University campus.

**1818–1820** *Nashville, Tennessee.* He studied law in the office of Judge Felix Grundy. He was admitted to the bar in 1820. Grundy's house was on the southwest corner of Union and Vine at Seventh Avenue.

## MARRIAGE AND HONEYMOOON

Polk was married on January 1, 1824, in Murfreesboro, Tennessee, at the Childress house on East Main Street, three blocks away from the red brick house of his bride's brother, John W. Childress, on Lytle and Academy Streets. Sarah Childress, the bride, was a decided beauty of the Spanish type. She was well-educated for a woman of her time and place at a Moravian school. She was lively, charming, intelligent, and a good conversationalist. The large country wedding was held on a Thursday. Mrs. Polk hosted the first Thanksgiving, also on a Thursday, at the White House. His father-in-law was a well-established merchant and tavern keeper in Murfreesboro, who also owned land on the Bradyville Pike near the Black Fox Springs area.

The honeymoon took place in Murfreesboro, at the plantation home where parties continued through the Monday following the ceremony; it was nearly a week when they finally reached Columbia. The home was located on the edge of town.

## HOMES/LODGINGS

**1795–1806** *Pineville, Mecklenburg County, North Carolina.* Reconstructed log house at the site. Museum nearby. U.S. 521 south of Pineville. The house was a saddle bag type—actually two houses connected by a central passage.

**1806–1816** *Duck River Valley (southwest of Nashville), Maury County, Tennessee.* Marker on the side of the road. His grandfather had a house ten miles north of the westward flowing Duck River in the valley of Carter's Creek. James' father, Sam, had a tract on his grandfather's (Ezekiel's) place to the south on what would shortly be the main road from the Duck River to the nearest town, Franklin, and on to Nashville. It was probably along present-day Tennessee 31 just north of Columbia, with the likely site marked by a Tennessee Historical Commission sign.

**1812** *Columbia, Tennessee.* Rattle and Snap, home of his cousin, on a hilltop 7.5 miles west of Columbia on the Tennessee River. Referred to as "the most monumental house in Tennessee." It still exists. Hamilton Place is on the same tract of land as Rattle and Snap and is also in the Polk family. It still exists.

**1812** *Columbia, Tennessee.* Rally Hill, home of his brother-in-law, James Walker, and his sister, Jane Marie. It no longer exists. Columbia. Athenaeum Rectory on Athenaeum Street, where he often visited the home of his nephew, Samuel Polk Walker.

**1812** *Columbia, Tennessee.* 301 West Seventh Street, home of his uncle, James Walker.

**1816–1824** *Columbia, Tennessee.* 301 West Seventh Street. Two-story brick building on the best street in Columbia (population then 300). His uncle James Walker lived next door. He was living with his parents while practicing law. See also the site of the house (only the steps remain) on West Seventh Street near 301 West Seventh Street, where the couple also lived briefly. See also the Samuel Polk (family) vault, Greenwood Cemetery in Columbia.

**1822** *Murfreesboro, Tennessee.* He visited Sarah Childress, daughter of Major Joel

*James Polk home, Columbia, Tennessee.*

Childress. The major, by the time Murfrees-boro became the state capital, had moved his family to a plantation several miles out of town. Examination of land tracts in the county office failed to turn up the exact location.

**1824** *Columbia, Tennessee.* Right after the wedding he rented a cottage for a year. One of the wedding presents from Polk's father was a water cart, complete with barrel and driver, since the townspeople had to haul water from the spring. His father also gave them a young servant boy who was with them for many years. Their cottage was a two-room log house across the street from the present-day Polk house.

**1825** *Columbia, Tennessee.* They moved into a house of their own across the street from Sam Polk's. It was a modest structure with an unfinished second floor and a separate kitchen and smokehouse standing in the backyard.

**1825–1839** *Washington, D.C.* When Polk went to serve in Congress, it was customary for two or more families to rent a single house for the season and eat together. None of these places remain.

**1825** *Washington, D.C.* He lodged with the five members from middle Tennessee at Captain Benjamin Burch's house on Capitol Hill.

**1826** *Washington, D.C.* Williamson's Hotel. Pennsylvania Avenue, between Fourteenth and Fifteenth Streets, NW.

**1826** *Washington, D.C.* Quarters in a house on Pennsylvania Avenue, NW., near the Capitol. Number not identified.

**1827–1834** *Washington, D.C.* 4½ Pennsylvania Avenue, NW, at the boarding house of Mrs. Ann Peyton. Also at Brown's Hotel, Pennsylvania Avenue, NW, between Sixth and Seventh Streets. The hotel was razed in the 1930s.

**1834–1837** *Washington, D.C.* Clements' Boarding House, New Jersey Avenue, NW, between D and E Streets. In 1835, to maintain his new dignity as Speaker of the House, Polk ordered a luxurious coach, with glass windows, venetian blinds, and curtains of claret-colored silk.

**1837–1839** *Washington, D.C.* He moved to Jonathan Elliott's fashionable house on Pennsylvania Avenue on the north side between Third and Four and one half Streets, NW, where they had their own parlor and dining room for meals and entertaining.

**1839–1841** *Nashville, Tennessee.* As the state had no executive mansion, as governor, he and Sarah rented a spacious brick house, with kitchen, stables, and a pleasant garden in the rear, on one of Nashville's better streets. Exact location not determined.

**1845** *Washington, D.C.* Coleman's Hotel, corner of Pennsylvania Avenue and Sixth Street, NW, in a four-room suite, staying for two weeks before inauguration.

**1845–1849** *Washington, D.C.* The White House as eleventh president. A great event during his tenure was the introduction of gas for illumination in the White House in 1848.

**1849** *Nashville, Tennessee.* Polk Place. For his retirement, he purchased the home of Senator Felix Grundy, which he renamed Polk Place. The house has been demolished, and a motel occupies the site. A marker on the side of the motel commemorates the spot at the southwest corner of Union Street and North Seventh Avenue. In his will, Polk had specified that the house and lot should become the property of the State of Tennessee, but the heirs broke the will, and this beautiful house and historic spot were lost. At the time, the property extended in one direction to Vine and Union Streets and on the other to Polk Avenue. The house was a large two-story mansion with columns in front extending the full height of the building. Mrs. Polk lived here for forty-two years after his death and kept it much the way it was when President Polk was alive.

## WORK

**1812** *Columbia, Tennessee.* He clerked briefly in a store in order to learn merchandising, but he disliked it and quit after a few weeks. While his exact store location has not been determined, see store fronts of the period on the town square which existed at the time he worked here.

**1819** *Murfreesborough, Tennessee.* Clerk of the state senate. He was reelected for 1821 and for the special sessions that met in 1820 and 1822. It rarely met for more than a month, so he spent most of the year building up his law practice in Maury County. The senate met in the courthouse on the town square before 1823.

**1820–1825** *Columbia, Tennessee.* Law practice. He had a little one-room law office on the south side of the public square. A few months after he began to practice he formed a partnership with Madison L. Caruthers. It was dissolved in 1822, and he formed a new partnership with Aaron V. Brown. Office at northwest corner of Seventh Street and Gordon Street (present day names) and the site of today's Sovran Bank. Marker.

**1820–1825** *Columbia, Tennessee.* Maury County Courthouse at center of the Public Square. A more recent courthouse has been built on the site of the courthouse where Polk argued cases.

**1823–1825** *Murfreesboro, Tennessee.* Member of state legislature. Since the courthouse had burned the year before, the legislature was meeting in the Presbyterian church with the senate sitting in the gallery, 300 block of East Vine Street. A stone monument in the midst of the cemetery marks the spot where the old church was located.

**1825–1839** *Washington, D.C.* Member from Tennessee of the U.S. House of Representatives. The showplace of the Capitol was the Hall of the House of Representatives (now Statuary Hall) which took up nearly the whole southern wing. His first session began on December 5, 1825.

**1835–1839** *Washington, D.C.* Speaker of the House of Representatives. He was the only Speaker ever to become president. He had a private office tucked into a corner off the House chamber.

**1839–1841** *Nashville, Tennessee.* Campaigning for governor, he travelled 1,300 miles on horseback in little more than two months through 37 of the state's 66 counties, and made 43 scheduled and numerous impromptu addresses. On Monday, October 14, 1839, the two houses of the legislature assembled in their meeting rooms at the county courthouse and moved in procession to the Presbyterian Church, Fifth Avenue and Church Street, for the inaugural ceremonies. Andrew Jackson was there in a place of honor as Polk was sworn in as Governor. Later, he visited Jackson at the Hermitage.

**1841–1845** *Columbia, Tennessee.* Practicing law, campaigning and unsuccessfully running for governor. Law office, northwest corner of Seventh and Garden Streets.

**1844** *Baltimore, Maryland.* Odd Fellows Hall. He was nominated for president at the Democratic National Convention held at the end of May.

**1845–1849** *Washington, D.C.* President of the United States—the first so-called "dark horse" candidate. At 49 years of age, he was the youngest president up to that time.

# TRAVEL/VISITS

**1812–** *Franklin, Tennessee.* Carnton, off Tennessee 431 southeast of town where he visited Mayor Randal McGavock at his country mansion.

**1825–** *Greeneville, Tennessee.* Dickson-Williams Mansion, Church and Irish Streets, visiting friends.

**1825–** *Kingsport, Tennessee.* Netherland Inn, 2144 Netherland Inn Road just west of downtown Kingsport while travelling the Great State Road to and from Washington, D.C.

**1841** *Jonesborough, Tennessee.* Visit and campaign speech near the Presbyterian Church. He was here again in 1843.

**1845–** *Prince George County, Virginia.* Brandon House, where he was entertained by a member of the Harrison family while he was president. It is on County 611 south of the James River and southeast of Berkeley.

**1847** *Chapel Hill, North Carolina, while visiting the University of North Carolina.* He stayed at Hilliard's Hotel fronting on Franklin Street. It was afterwards known as the Eagle and then Chapel Hill Hotel.

**1847** *Lowell, Massachusetts.* Merrimack House, 310 Merrimack Street. He spent two days here. His speech at the railway depot could not be heard due to the constant cannon salutes honoring his visit.

**1847** *Maine.* He was received in Representatives Hall of the State House. He attended a reception at Augusta House at the junction of Green, Water, and Gage Streets. He was accompanied by Secretary of State James Buchanan, who later became president.

**1847**   *Richmond, Virginia.* Reception at the Capitol, Capitol Square.

**1847**   *Salem, Massachusetts.* There was a pouring rain so he was unable to stop much to the disappointment of the town's people who had gathered at the railway station.

**1848**   *Washington, D.C.* He laid the cornerstone of the Washington Monument.

**1849**   *Washington, D.C.* Irving Hotel, Pennsylvania Avenue, NW. He stayed here as outgoing president and rode to the Capitol from here with Zachary Taylor. Following the inauguration of Taylor, he went on a month-long southern tour along the Atlantic seaboard, west along the gulf states, and up the Mississippi to Tennessee. The trip included Richmond, Virginia, with a reception at the Capitol, Wilmington, North Carolina, Charleston, South Carolina, Savannah, Pulaski House, 203 West Charlton Street, and Columbus (lodging at St. Elmo Mansion, 2810 Elmo Drive), Georgia. Montgomery and Mobile (arriving by boat), Alabama, New Orleans and Baton Rogue, Louisiana, Vicksburg, Mississippi, Memphis, Tennessee, Paducah and Smithland (where he stayed for several days at Gower House recovering from an illness), Kentucky. He was welcomed home with a tremendous reception in Nashville, Tennessee.

# DEATH

Polk died on June 15, 1849, in Nashville, Tennessee, at Polk Place, near the Capitol. A motel now occupies the site. There is a marker on the southwest corner of Union Street at Seventh Avenue North. He died only three months after leaving office.

# FUNERAL

The funeral took place in Nashville, Tennessee, at McKendree Methodist Church, 523 Church Street, between Fifth and Sixth Avenues. Funeral services were held in the sanctuary. Thousands joined the procession at Broad Street bringing the coffin to Polk Place, where a prayer was said, an ode to the dead sung, and Bishop James H. Otey, who had been a college classmate of Polk, gave an address.

# BURIAL

Polk was buried at Old City Cemetery, near South Fourth Avenue, in Nashville. When Polk died on June 15, his tomb at Polk Place was not yet ready and he was temporarily entombed here. On May 22, 1850, his walnut coffin was lifted from a vault in the old City Cemetery, put in a black walnut shell, and placed on a hearse "drawn by four Greys with grooms." The cortege moved from the City Cemetery to Polk Place, accompanied by a military band, the elite, his Masonic Fraternity, and most of the citizens of Nashville. The coffin was placed in the marble sarcophagus in the new tomb on the eastern lawn where he had designated it should remain forever.

His heirs had his will overturned in the courts and against his wishes sold his home. In 1893 his tomb along with that of Mrs. Polk, was removed to the grounds of the State Capitol, and so for the third time he was buried. There is a monument on the grounds to commemorate the site. Within the Capitol, there is a statue of Polk on the executive level and a bust of him on the legislative level.

# BIBLIOGRAPHY

McCormac, Eugene Irving. *James K. Polk: A Political Biography.* New York: Russell & Russell, 1922.

Sellers, Charles Grier, Jr. *James K. Polk, Continentalist 1843–1846.* Princeton: Princeton University Press. 1966.

———. *James K. Polk, Jacksonian.* Princeton: Princeton University Press, 1957.

# ZACHARY TAYLOR

1784–1850
12TH PRESIDENT 1849–1850: WHIG PARTY

Zachary Taylor "Old Rough and Ready" was born November 24, 1784 to Lieutenant Colonel Richard and Sarah Dabney Strother Taylor. He was a relative of future president James Madison and of the famous Lee family. Franklin Delano Roosevelt was a fourth cousin three times removed.

## CHARACTERISTICS

Taylor was 5'8" tall. He was heavy set and short-legged with the bowlegs of a horseman. He weighed about 170 pounds as a young man and 200 as president. He had brown hair and hazel eyes, a lined and weathered face, a large nose, thin lips, and a high forehead. He made no pretense at fashion; he usually appeared in a straw hat and shabby clothing and often sat with his feet propped up. As he stood or walked, he kept one hand behind him. He did not smoke or drink, but he was a tobacco chewer and known as a dead-shot spitter. He went to bed at nine o'clock and got up before six. The man on the street and behind the plow admired his victories. Many infants were named in his honor, including one who was named Rough and Ready.

# A LIFE IN REVIEW

**Birth:** November 24, 1784; Montebello, Orange County, VA

**Died:** July 9, 1850; Washington, D.C.

**Married:** Margaret "Peggy" Mackall Smith; June 21, 1810; 1 son, 3 daughters

## CAREER

**1808–1848** Military officer

## ADMINISTRATION

**1850** Clayton-Bulwer Treaty

**1850** Galphin scandal

**1850** Opposed slavery

# BIRTHPLACE

Taylor was born in Montebello, near Barboursville, Orange County, Virginia. At the time of his birth, his mother was living with a relative, Colonel Valentine Johnstone. There is some evidence he may have been born at Hare Forest in Orange County. The mansion at Montebello no longer stands, but a newer house stands on the original foundation. A marker on the road in front of the house describes the site as Taylor's birthplace. Since the main house was not large, his mother was sleeping in one of the outlying log cabins where Taylor was born according to one report.

In Rhoadesville, Virginia, there is a long, white painted, brick two-story house, which is one of three places in Virginia said to be his birthplace.

# BAPTISM

No record of a baptism exists. He was possibly baptized at St. Thomas Episcopal Church, 119 Caroline Street, Orange, Virginia. This was the church of his grandfather, Zachary Taylor.

# CHURCH

Usually, Taylor has been listed as an Episcopalian, but he belonged to no church and never made any recorded profession of faith. He followed his wife's religion throughout his entire married life. She was a devout Episcopalian, and, whenever she was with him at forts and other military establishments, she organized religious services. Travellers in the Northwest often stayed several days at Fort Crawford residing with Colonel Taylor. Taylor's daughter reports that her father was a constant reader of the Bible. He obviously had strong religious sentiments since he postponed taking his oath of office as president for one day because the official inauguration day fell on Sunday.

His advice to his children included the instruction "to read aloud after tea in the history of England or Shakespeare's plays, till near bedtime, and to conclude with a chapter in the Bible."

**1850–** *Orange, Virginia.* St. Thomas' Episcopal Church, 119 Caroline Street, near Orange Courthouse about four miles from his grandfather's mansion, Meadow Farm, was the traditional family worship center and probably attended by Taylor when he visited his Virginia relatives.

**1785–1803** *Louisville, Kentucky.* There was no church edifice until 1803, and it is assumed services were held in various homes by itinerant preachers.

**1803–** *Louisville, Kentucky.* Episcopal services were held in a small house on Second Street.

**1832–1836**  *Fort Crawford, Wisconsin.* (Located in present day Prairie du Chien.) The Reverend Richard F. Cadle held regular services on Sunday at the Fort. Fort Crawford Medical Museum on the site at 717 South Beaumont Road.

**1841–1845**  *Fort Smith, Arkansas.* At first, army chaplains held services in one of the government buildings. Later, Methodist circuit riders came to the Fort and preached to all denominations. A Methodist Sunday School was organized in a small log house between Green and Howard Avenue (now Fourth and Fifth Streets).

**1845–1849**  *Baton Rouge, Louisiana.* Episcopal Church. Services held in the Pentagon Barracks.

**1847**  *New Orleans, Louisiana.* St. Louis Cathedral. Jackson Square.

**1849–1850**  *Washington, D.C.* St. John's Episcopal Church on Lafayette Square.

# EDUCATION

With only the most basic education, he was one of the least formally educated of all the presidents. For a while he attended a school in Louisville, run by travelling schoolmaster Elisha Ayer. Other teachers known listed are Lewis Wetzel and his last instructor, Kean O'Hara. He was also taught by his mother and father. He was very poor in English grammar and wrote badly all his life. His chief education came from the army.

# MARRIAGE AND HONEYMOON

Taylor was married on June 21, 1810, in Jefferson County, Kentucky, in a double log cabin on what came to be known as Wolf Pen Road, two miles from Harrod's Creek Station, at the home of the bride's sister, Mary Chew. No details of the wedding or of the honeymoon are known. As a wedding present, his father gave Taylor 324 acres of farmland at the mouth of the Beargrass Creek. This land is today in downtown Louisville, Kentucky. His bride was Margaret (Peggy) Mackall Smith from Calvert County, Maryland. Peggy Taylor was slender, about average in height, and quite personable. She was a semi-invalid and remained in seclusion on the second floor of the White House when the family came to Washington. Her daughter, Elizabeth Taylor Bliss, acted as hostess for her father in the White House.

# HOMES/LODGING

**1784–1785**  *Montebello (near Barbourville), Orange County, Virginia.* He spent his first seven months here.

**1784–**  *Bloomsbury, Virginia.* Meadow Farm, several miles from Bloomsbury off County 612 is the site of his grandfather's home.

**1784–**  *Louisville, Kentucky.* Locust Grove, 561 Blankenbaker Lane. This is a country home adjoining Springfield and home of his childhood friend, George Croghan.

**1784–**  *Louisville.* Soldier's Retreat, three miles east of Springfield, was the home of Richard Anderson whose children were Taylor's childhood playmates.

**1785–1786**  *Louisville, Kentucky.* A log house about five miles east of Louisville, on the muddy fork of Beargrass Creek. The family was here temporarily until the main house could be built. The log house had glassless holes for windows and, when the new brick building with high ceilings and thick walls was fitted with glass, it was such a new feature that one young lad reported to his mother, "that new house down the street is wearing specs."

**1786–1810**  *Louisville, Kentucky.* Springfields, 5608 Apache Road, seven miles east

*Zachary Taylor home, Louisville, Kentucky.*

on Kentucky 42. Taylor was eight months old when the family settled just east of Louisville and here he grew up. At 17, he swam the breadth of the Ohio River to Indiana and back again in the cold of early spring. Springfields is a substantial two-story house. It is still standing. Although he went to the army in 1806, he continued to call Springfields home, and, after marriage, he left his family here from time to time. Taylor stayed in a room on the second floor across the hall from his parents.

**1810–1822** *Louisville, Kentucky.* A log cabin he had built on his land at Beargrass Creek east of Louisville.

**1820** *Bay St. Louis, Hancock County, Mississippi.* Army barracks.

**1822–** *St. Francisville (about forty miles north of Baton Rouge), near Feliciana Parish, Louisiana.* In Locust Grove Cemetery, about four miles east of this home is the burial place of Sarah Knox Taylor Davis, his daughter, and first wife of Jefferson Davis. On January 27, 1823, he purchased from Byrd Buford 380 acres in West Feliciana Parish, near the Mississippi border not far from the Deer Range Plantation.

**1828–1829** *Fort Snelling, Minnesota.* South of the center of Minneapolis. He lived in the commandant's quarters inside the fortress which contained four rooms on the main floor with kitchen and pantries in the basement.

**1829** *Jefferson County, Kentucky.* He inherited Charles Farm from his father. He sold this soon after he inherited it and bought 137 acres in Wilkinson County, Mississippi, called the Sligo Tract on March 6, 1831. This Sligo Tract was adjacent to his West Feliciana property. In 1838, he added a third plantation when he bought 163 acres in West Feliciana Parish.

**1830** *Louisville, Kentucky.* On an extended furlough, he occupied a house on the east side of First Street, near Jefferson Street.

**1832–1837** *Prairie du Chien, (now) Wisconsin.* 717 South Beaumont Road. A large house provided by the government just outside Fort Crawford.

**1837–1840** *Tampa Bay, Florida.* House on the southwest corner of Platt and Franklin Streets. His wife and family were living here while he was engaged in the Seminole War. Marker.

**1840–** *Baton Rouge, Louisiana.* The old Spanish commandant's cottage near the barracks. The site is now known as the "old Campus" of Louisiana State University. The house was a raised cottage overlooking the Mississippi River.

**1841–1849** *Cypress Grove Plantation, Jefferson County, Mississippi.* On the bank of the river near Rodney, between Natchez and Vicksburg. It was a 2,500 acre place which he purchased for $95,000. One visitor described the house as an unpretentious wooden building with a large library and a colonnaded veranda. Exact site undetermined. He also bought for his son a 1,000 acre plantation, about twenty miles above New Orleans in St. Charles Parish.

**1847–1849** *Baton Rouge, Louisiana.* A boulder and plaque on a corner of the grounds of the State Capitol commemorate his residence in Baton Rouge. 727 Lafayette Street is the actual original site of the residence.

**1849–1850** *Washington. D.C.* The White House.

# WORK

Taylor fought in the Black Hawk War and in the Mexican War in which he overthrew Santa Ana at Buena Vista. His army career lasted from 1808 to 1849. In 1849, he was

elected president as the candidate of the Whig Party. His premature death, 16 months after his inauguration, was part of the downfall of the Whig Party.

**1849–1850** *Washington, D.C.* He was the first president elected who had had no previous political experience. At the time of his nomination he was staying in Baton Rogue. The notification was delayed because he had decided to stop accepting letters if the postage had not been pre-paid as was the case with this notification. He lived to see California admitted as a free state in the struggle over slavery.

# TRAVEL/VISITS

**1808–1809** *Maysville, Kentucky.* Quarters in a boarding house. Recruiting officer. Exact site not determined.

**1808** *Washington, Kentucky.* Inducted in the army and commissioned first lieutenant. No marker.

**1809** *Fort Pickering (site of modern city of Memphis), Tennessee.*

**1809** *New Orleans and Terre Aux Boeufs, Louisiana.* Thirteen miles south of the city.

**1809** *Washington village (near Natchez), Mississippi Territory.* From here he returned to Springfield and Louisville to await further orders.

**1811** *Fort Knox (Vincennes), Indiana.* As a captain, Taylor met with then governor and future president, William Henry Harrison, who sent a glowing report of Taylor to Washington.

**1812** *Louisville, Kentucky.* As a recruiting officer, he arrived at Fort Harrison, on the banks of Wabash River, Indiana (three miles above Terre Haute). Here he assumed command of the Seventh Infantry. On October 31, he received the brevet rank of major—the first brevet of any kind ever awarded by the government of the

United States. In one encounter with the Indians, Taylor reported, "And from the raging of the fire, the yelling and howling of several hundred Indians, the cries of nine women and children, I can assure you my feelings were unpleasant." The Fort was about 150 feet square. At each corner there was a two-story blockhouse, with log barracks between where Taylor stayed with his men.

**1813–1814**   *Fort Knox, Vincennes, Indiana.*

**1814**   *Credit Island, near Davenport, Iowa.* At the end of Schmidt Street, a boulder at the entrance to the park gives an account of the battle. Taylor led men from here up the Mississippi River against the Indians in the battle of Credit Island, Illinois Territory.

**1814**   *Fort Howard, Green Bay, Wisconsin.* Here he added material comforts to his military quarters with fine old china sent from Louisville and his huge sideboard and mahogany tables replaced the rough benches of Green Bay. Site of Fort Howard is at the foot of Dousman Street Bridge near Chicago and Northwestern Railway Depot. A white flagpole marks the site. He left Green Bay in late summer 1818 for Louisville.

**1814**   *St. Louis, Missouri.* He was here to assume command of all the troops in the Missouri Territory on temporary assignment.

**1814**   *Warsaw, Illinois.* He built Fort Johnson on the Des Moines River, on the site of what is now Warsaw, Illinois. In late October, he was forced to burn the fort.

**1818–1819**   *Louisville, Kentucky.* He spent most of the time superintending recruitment. He was promoted to rank of lieutenant colonel. In the early summer of 1819 President Monroe, accompanied by Andrew Jackson, coming from Knoxville and Nashville, visited Louisville. They were fellow guests at Liberty Hall, the residence of ex-Senator John Brown, in Frankfort, Kentucky.

**1819**   *Fort Mackinac, Michigan.* Here he was stationed on the Straits connecting Lake Huron and Lake Michigan.

**1820–1822**   *Natchitoches, Louisiana.* Here he established Fort Selden overlooking Bayou Pierre upstream from the junction of the bayou with the Red River and twelve miles from Natchitoches.

**1820**   *Baton Rogue, Louisiana.* The Cottage (Kleinpeter House, also referred to as Conrad Plantation), River Road Louisiana 327, 18666 Perkins Road about ten miles south of Baton Rogue, visiting Almon Duncan. Also here 1826.

**1820**   *Bayou Sara, Louisiana.* His wife and two youngest daughters, Octavia and Margaret died of fever here within four months of each other. Nothing remains of Bayou Sara, across from Francisville, just north of Mobile.

**1822–1824**   *Baton Rouge, Louisiana.* Commanding officer of the post.

**1822**   *Shield's Spring, Louisiana.* He built Fort Jesup.

**1822–1823**   *Sabine Parish, Louisiana.* One block from the highway, in the eastern part of Sabine Parish Historical Park, is a marker marking the entrance to the old fort. All that remains of the original fort is one of the log buildings, recently restored and several stone pillars nearby. About twenty-two miles southwest of Nachitoches and east of the present town of Many, Louisiana. He divided his time between Jesup and Fort Smith.

**1827–1828**   *New Orleans, Louisiana.* Army headquarters, in City Hall, 545 St. Charles Avenue. He was stationed thirteen miles south of New Orleans.

**1828–1829**   *Fort Snelling, Minnesota.* The junction of the Mississippi and St. Peter's Rivers (South Minneapolis). As commander, he prevented the Indians from renewing their attacks on the whites.

**1829–1830**   *Prairie du Chien, Wisconsin.* Fort Crawford, Beaumont Road and Dunn Street. He built a new fort at this site. The site is now occupied by St. Mary's College.

**1832–1836**   *Fort Crawford, Prairie du Chien, Wisconsin.* Black Hawk War was over, and Colonel Taylor and his family lived outside the fort in a large house provided by the government. He had his headquarters here as commander.

**1832–1836**   *Fort Crawford, Wisconsin.* Colonel Taylor was here almost continuously during this period.

**1832**   *Fort Armstrong, Illinois.* Leaving his family at Galena, Illinois he assumed command of the First Infantry here.

**1835**   *Fort Winnebago, Wisconsin.* He supervised the building of the road between Fort Crawford and Fort Winnebago. In 1836 he led three companies here to ward off possible Indian attacks. Currently this is the town of Portage and on the site the only remains is a rough log building of the Surgeon's quarters.

**1836**   *Jefferson Barracks, Missouri.* Here he assumed command in November. Located in the southern part of St. Louis.

**1837–**   *Florida.* His first stop was Fort Brooke, at the southwest corner Platt and Franklin Streets. Marked by a bronze plaque. Taylor visited Fort Fraser, on Pease Creek 50 miles, east of Tampa Bay, near Plant City. In late November, he visited Bartow; see marker block west of the courthouse where Taylor took command. There is also a marker at Fort Gatlin, Summerlin Street and Gatlin Avenue, in the Edgewood area of Orlando. At Fort Shannon, Palatka, at State Roads 100 and 20, he was also stationed here; there is a marker on Reid Street (U.S. 17) between Second and Third Streets. At the head of Kissimmee Lake, east of Lake Wales, he built Fort Gardiner and remained for two weeks in December. Fort Basinger, where Carpon Trail crosses

Kissimmee River, just north of Lake Okeechobee, was the site of the Second Seminole War. In northern Florida he constructed a line of forts from Tampa Bay to New Smyrna on the Atlantic Coast.

**1838–**   *Middleburg, Florida.* Clark-Chalker House, 3889 Main Street, was built circa 1835 as an officer headquarters. In Middleburg, Florida, there is also a marker for Fort Heileman, at Wharf and Main Street, in front of an elementary school on Florida 21.

**1838–**   *Ocala, Florida.* Fort King, Southeast 39th Avenue, Fort King Road. Marker.

**1840–1841**   *Baton Rouge, Louisiana.* Here he assumed command of Baton Rouge post. See marker on Pentagon Buildings, which were used as a garrison from 1822 to 1877, now the site of Louisiana State University. Many famous people have been connected with these buildings and either stayed or visited including: Lincoln, Grant, Taft and Harding.

**1841–**   *Fort Gibson, Oklahoma.* On the Grand River, in what is now eastern Oklahoma, he became commander of the Second Military Department. While en route he received a rousing reception by the people of Little Rock on June 27.

**1841–1845**   *Camp Belknap, Arkansas.* He established his departmental headquarters at Camp Belknap, one mile from Fort Smith. He was in command of the army of observation for the annexation of Texas. He lived in a one-story log house on the north side of Garrison Avenue, where the Sisters of Mercy Convent now stands. The chimney of his house still stands on the convent grounds.

**1842**   *Fort Scott, Kansas.* When Fort Wayne was abandoned, he established this post on the military road to Fort Leavenworth.

**1842**   *Fort Washita, Oklahoma.* This fort was constructed under his command.

**1845**   *New Orleans.* Arrived at Jackson Barracks.

**1845–1846**  *Corpus Christi, Texas.* Artesian Park, 800 Chaparral Street. Marker on site of his headquarters.

**1845**  *St. Joseph Island, Texas.* He landed with troops and established temporary camp on way to Corpus Christi, Texas.

**1846**  *Laredo, Texas.* His headquarters were on the main square.

**1846**  *Fort Texas, opposite Matamoros, Mexico.* Site marked by an upright cannon.

**1846**  *Palo Alto, Texas.* Site of the first battle of the Mexican War. He defeated a force three times the size of his own.

**1846**  *Resaca de la Palma, Texas.* Site of the second of the two battles fought within the United States.

**1846**  *La Angostura.* Site of the Battle of Buena Vista. His victory over Santa Anna made him a national hero.

**1847–1848**  *Baton Rouge, Louisiana.* The old "Spanish cottage" on the military reservation, just outside the city limits and a few yards from the Barracks for the next thirteen months.

**1849**  *Northern trip to Washington for his inauguration from Louisiana to Washington included: Memphis and Nashville, Tennessee, Louisville, Frankfort and Carrollton, Kentucky.* In Frankfort he visited the Governor's Mansion, 420 High Street a reception at First Presbyterian Church on West Main Street and lodged at home of John J. Crittenden, Main and Franklin Streets. He continued through Indiana to Cincinnati, lodging at Pearl Street House and Pomeroy, Ohio; Parkersburg and Wheeling, and lodging at United States Hotel, West Virginia; Moundsville, and Lancaster with lodging at White Swan Hotel on Center Square; Washington, where he stayed at the famous Old Globe Inn, west corner of Main Street and Strawberry Alley; and Waterford at the Eagle Hotel on corner of High and First Streets, Uniontown.

*Zachary Taylor's cemetery monument.*

**1850**  *Richmond, Virginia.* Union Hotel, southwest corner 19th and Main Streets. While in Richmond, he laid the cornerstone to the Washington Monument, in the State Capitol area.

## DEATH

Taylor died on July 9, 1850, at the White House. Shortly after dinner that evening he became violently ill; he died just after 10:00 P.M. The First Lady refused to permit the mortician to embalm the body or allow a death mask to be taken.

## FUNERAL

The body was moved to the East Room of the White House and the public admitted for viewing. The body lay in a leaden coffin, enclosed in one of mahogany with silver decorations. Just after noon the choir sang the anthem "I heard a voice from Heaven saying." The Episcopal service was read, after which the Marines carried the coffin from the White House.

## Burial

Taylor was buried in Washington, D.C., in Congressional Cemetery. The catafalque was drawn by eight white horses, with more than 100 carriages following. In October, the body was removed from Washington and taken to Louisville, Kentucky for burial at the Taylor family cemetery, at 4701 Brownsboro Road.

## Bibliography

Dyer, Brainerd. *Zachary Taylor*. New York: Barnes and Noble Inc., 1946.

Hamilton, Holman. *Zachary Taylor: Soldier in the White House*. Indianapolis: The Bobbs-Merrill Company, Inc., 1951

McKinley, Silas Bent. *Old Rough and Ready: The Life and Times of Zachary Taylor*. New York: Vanguard Press, 1946.

# MILLARD FILLMORE

### 1800–1874
### 13TH PRESIDENT 1850–1853: WHIG PARTY

Millard Fillmore was born on the morning of January 7, 1800 to farmer Nathaniel and Phoebe Millard Fillmore, a pioneer school teacher. He was the first president to be born in the 19th century.

## CHARACTERISTICS

In his youth, he was very handsome and was one of the best looking presidents this nation has had. He was six feet tall and probably weighed about 170 pounds as an adult, although by the time he became president he had become quite heavy. He had blue eyes and wavy brown hair which turned white before he was fifty. He dressed well and was a good mixer. From his youth he did not smoke, drink, or gamble. He was a great reader and as president, with the extra encouragement of his wife, established the first permanent White House library.

## BIRTHPLACE

Fillmore was born near Locke, now called Summerhill, in Cayuga County, New York, in a log cabin. The site is located on

*"It is a national disgrace that our Presidents, after having occupied the highest position in the country, should be cast adrift, and, perhaps, be compelled to keep a corner grocery for subsistence."*

*—Inaugural address*

# A LIFE IN REVIEW

---

**Birth** January 7, 1800; Locke, Cayuga County, NY

**Died** March 8, 1874; Buffalo, NY

**Married:** Abigail Powers; February 5, 1826; 1 son, 1 daughter
Caroline Carmichael McIntosh; February 10, 1858; No children

## CAREER

**1814–1819** Apprentice to clothmaker

**1819–1822** Teacher

**1823–1848** Lawyer. Practiced law when not in public office

**1829–1831** Member state legislature

**1833–1835** Member U.S. Congress; also 1837–1843

**1848** New York state comptroller

**1849–1850** U.S. Vice President

## ADMINISTRATION EVENTS

**1850** New Fugitive Slave Law

**1852** Matthew Perry expedition to Japan

Skinner Hill Road, southeast of Moravia. The site is indicated by a marker in a picnic area. In Moravia, New York, a replica of the log cabin in which he was born has been constructed in the Fillmore Glen State Park.

## BAPTISM

A baptism was unlikely, since the family was not by habit churchgoing.

## CHURCH

There is little information about his religious beliefs although there are indications the family had some ties with the Methodist Church but churchgoing and Bible reading were not the usual practice in his home. Unlike many other presidents he rarely quoted the Bible. It is interesting that in his boyhood home his father's "library" consisted of only two books—a King James version of the Bible and a collection of hymns. Most of his adult life he was a Unitarian and before 1831 he had been without a church. Throughout his life he observed Sunday inviolate as a day of rest.

**1826** *Moravia, New York.* St. Matthew's Episcopal Church on Church Street. The original church burned May 14, 1842.

**1831–1865** *Buffalo, New York.* Unitarian Church, 695 Elmwood, near the Erie County Courthouse. The church has been turned into an office building. A bronze plaque on the side of the building notes that Lincoln as president-elect attended church with Fillmore. Fillmore and his wife were charter members at a time soon after their marriage and he remained a life-long supporter. The church was a few hundred feet down the street from their front door. Lincoln visited February 16–17, 1861.

**1833–1853** *Washington, D.C.* All Soul's Church (Unitarian) now at 16th and Harvard Streets, NW. During his time the church was located at Sixth and D Streets, NW. Present church was dedicated 1924.

**1854** *Savannah, Georgia.* Independent Presbyterian Church southwest corner Bull Street and West Oglethorpe Avenue. Church is a replica of the one that burned 1889. He visited Augusta on this trip after leaving the White House.

**1865–1874** *Buffalo, New York.* Baptist Church, 965 Delaware Avenue. Soon after 1865 he was rebuffed by the members of the Unitarian church and attended this church with his wife. Occasionally they went to Episcopal services.

## EDUCATION

His schooling was limited to primitive schools that existed in that region, and which he attended less than three months of each year. When he was fifteen, with his first wages as a wool carder, he purchased a small English dictionary, which he studied while attending the carding machines. Until age seventeen he received only basic instruction in reading, writing, and math. Reports have it that he never saw a history of the United States nor a map of his own country until he was nineteen years old! Fillmore, who never attended a college, became the first Chancellor of the University of Buffalo.

**1819** *New Hope, New York.* New Hope Academy. He enrolled at this recently erected academy where his teacher was his future wife. No exact location determined and no marker.

**1819–1821** *Montville, New York.* He studied law with Judge Wood. Nothing remains of the law office. Marker on site along Main Street.

**1821–1823** *Buffalo, New York.* He studied law in the office of Asa Rice and Joseph Clary on Main Street.

## MARRIAGE AND HONEYMOON

Fillmore was married on February 5, 1826, in Moravia, New York, at the home of the bride's brother, Judge Powers, on Church Street. This home has been moved to a site on Smith Street, two blocks away, and a beautiful Victorian-style home is now on the site. The house is privately owned and not open for tours; a marker is located at the front of the house. A tablet in St. Matthew's Episcopal Church on Church Street commemorates the

marriage of the Fillmores. One report claims that the wedding was held in the church and the reception was held in the home. The church and home are within a short distance of each other. The honeymoon took place in New York. After the ceremony, they left by sled, probably to Auburn and west to East Aurora with stops along the way. Nothing in his correspondence about the honeymoon. Unfortunately there are few details of this or his career because all his private papers were burned by his son.

His wife, Abigail, was the daughter of Lemuel Powers, a Baptist preacher. She was a school teacher both before and after her marriage. When Fillmore became president she was an invalid and her daughter, Abigail, presided at White House functions. Abigail died on March 30, 1853.

Fillmore married again on February 18, 1858, in Albany, New York. The site is located at Schuyler Street, on the southwest corner of Clinton and Catherine Streets. The wedding took place in the same room of the Schuyler mansion that Alexander Hamilton was married in 75 years before. His bride, Caroline, was the widow of Ezekiel McIntosh, a merchant of Albany, and a daughter of Charles Carmichael of Morristown, New Jersey. The honeymoon took place in Albany, New York, at the home of the bride, while their Buffalo home was being readied for their move-in. There is no account in the newspapers of the time of their going anywhere on a honeymoon.

## HOMES/LODGINGS

**1800–1802** *Locke (now Summerhill), Cayuga County, New York.* He was born and started life in a small log cabin on this site. A replica of the cabin now stands in a park near Moravia. There is a marker and small park at the site of the birthplace itself.

**1802–1819** *New Hope (near), Niles Township, New York.* Located a mile west of Lake Skaneateles of the Finger Lakes district where he grew up on a farm before moving southwest to Montville, New York. The house where he lived was in ruins and was torn down in 1936. There is no marker although some of the foundation can still be seen. Located on Carver Road, turning north off Route 66 A, east of New Hope.

**1819–1821** *Montville, New York.* He boarded with Judge Wood while he studied law under him. Judge Wood's home still exists and has a historical marker. Home is now the residence of Lloyd Quick.

**1821–1826** *East Aurora, New York.* His parents moved here. Both of the homes of his father, Nathaniel Fillmore, are still standing. See also graves of his parents in the Uptown Cemetery on Temple Place.

**1826–1830** *East Aurora, New York.* 24 Shearer Avenue. The house has been moved from the original site to a place about a mile away. It is now open to the public June 1 to October 15, Wednesday to Saturday and 2–4 on Sunday.

**1829–1831** *Albany, New York.* Delvan House, corner of Broadway and Steuben while serving as member of state legislature.

**1830–1848** *Buffalo, New York.* 114 (now 180) Franklin Street which was a six-room frame house two blocks from the main street and three-eighths of a mile north of the village's physical center. A simple two-story clapboard house with five bays and a center hall designed in the Federal style. Rented furnished when he went to Albany in 1848 to become Comptroller.

**1833–1835** *Washington, D.C.* Gadsbys Tavern, northeast corner Pennsylvania and 6th Street NW while serving in U.S. House of Representatives.

**1835–1837** *Buffalo, New York.* See above Buffalo 1830–1848.

**1837–1843** *Washington, D.C.* Willard's Hotel, 14th Street and Pennsylvania Avenue NW while serving in the House of Representatives. He also lived at 226 Third Street but dates are uncertain.

**1848–1849** *Albany, New York.* This is where he rented apartments for himself and his family while he held the comptroller's office. He moved to Albany the last week of December.

**1849–1850** *Washington, D.C.* Willard's Hotel. His first wife died here March 30, 1853. He was notified here that President Taylor had passed away and reported that he did not sleep a wink that night.

**1850–1853** *Washington, DC.* The White House. The Fillmores were the first occupants of the White House to have a stationary bathtub with hot and cold running water. They also brought in the first cook stove. Before they came all food had been prepared in open fireplaces. Abigail Powers Fillmore was shocked to discover there was not a book in the mansion, not even a Bible. She started the White House library.

**1853–1858** *Buffalo, New York.* 114 (now 180) Franklin Street, the old home he lived in 1830–1848.

**1858–1874** *Buffalo, New York.* Home at West Genesee Street and Delaware Avenue. Site of the Fillmore house is marked by a bronze tablet on the wall of the Statler Hotel now occupying the site on Niagara Square. With his second wife he purchased the huge John Hollister mansion on Niagara Square, which with its gothic style, with parapets, balustrades, and simulated towers was a sharp contrast to the plain house on Franklin Street that had been his home for 26 years. Presidents Lincoln and Johnson were entertained here. Before being demolished to make way for the Statler Hotel, it was the Castle Inn.

# WORK

**1814** *Sparta or West Sparta (near Dansville), New York.* This was where he was apprenticed to a clothmaker, Benjamin

Hungerford. He quit after four months. Robert J. Scarry, an expert on the life of Fillmore, states other authors have Fillmore working at numerous mills in the area.

**1815–1819**   *New Hope, New York.* Old Salt Road, at Kellogsville. He worked here with clothmakers Zaccheus Cheney and Alvan Kellogg where he remained for several years.

**1819–1821**   *Montville, New York.* He worked as clerk in the law office of Judge Walter Wood. See entry under education above.

**1819–**   *Scott (Sempronius), New York.* He obtained a job teaching school. No definite location established.

**1821**   *East Aurora, New York.* He taught school briefly.

**1822**   *Buffalo, New York.* He taught school and in spare time studied law with Rice and Clary on Main Street between Eagle and Court.

**1823**   He was admitted to the bar to practice law in New York.

**1823–1829**   *East Aurora, New York.* He opened his law office 686 Main Street located a few yards from his home in a remodeled out-building. The old building burned. Now the site of Vidler's Variety Store.

**1829–1831**   *Albany, New York.* He was a member of New York State Legislature. He failed reelection and moved back to Buffalo. The old Capitol was at this time at the head of State Street.

**1830–1832**   *Buffalo, New York in a law partnership with Joseph Clary, his former teacher.* With Clary and also afterwards on Main Street between Eagle and Court he always maintained his place of business. For most of his career the firm occupied a suite of rooms on the second floor of the American Block attained by climbing steep wooden steps.

**1832–1847**   *Buffalo, New York.* In a law partnership with Nathan K. Hall, his former law student. Later Solomon G. Haven joined

them. One of the students of the firm was future president Grover Cleveland. See location of office in entry above.

**1833–1835**   *Washington, D.C.* He served as U.S. Representative from New York, meeting in the Capitol, in what is today called Statuary Hall.

**1837–1843**   *Washington, D.C.* U.S. Representative from New York.

**1843–1848**   *Buffalo, New York.* Main Street, between Eagle and Court. Here he devoted time to his law practice. He continued to be prominent in public life. Extended official welcome when John Quincy Adams visited the city in the summer of 1843. He closed out all his law matters in 1848.

**1848**   *Albany, New York.* Comptroller of the state of New York. Offices in the Old Capitol at the head of State Street.

**1849–1850**   *Washington, D.C.* Vice president of the United States. Inaugurated in the Senate chamber, in the right wing of the Capitol. Here he also presided over the Senate from his raised dais.

**1850–1853**   *Washington, D.C.* President of the United States. He was sworn in before joint session of Congress in the House of Representatives in "Statuary Hall," following the death of Zachary Taylor. During his term of office he laid the cornerstone of the new wings of the Capitol July 4, 1851.

**1853–1874**   *Retired to Buffalo and his law practice.* The propriety of what to do after the presidency worried him. All other presidents before him had either returned to gentlemen's estates or to the protection of family patrimonies. He had to earn money but he insisted that it be made in a genteel manner. He had also wanted a suitable house that would reflect on an ex-president. When Mrs. Fillmore died shortly after he left office he no longer felt the necessity to leave the modest house on Franklin Street and he did not feel pressed into social activities and the requisite salary for this purpose. His total retirement was short lived as he began to tour the country in the spring of 1854. He wrote, "It is a national disgrace that our Presidents...should be cast adrift, and perhaps compelled to keep a corner grocery for subsistence." He thought the solution would have been a pension of about $12,000 annually. He spent much time in committees desiring to improve the city of Buffalo, including libraries, business groups, fine arts, Y.M.C.A., and as the University of Buffalo Chancellor 1856 till his death. He was also expected to welcome all important visitors and delegations, including President Andrew Johnson when he came through the summer of 1866 on his trip West. In 1862 he became captain of the Union Continentals in Buffalo.

He had been criticized for seeing slavery as a political question rather than moral as president but during the last twenty years of his life he was withdrawn from active participation in public life and enjoyed during his retirement the respect of the nation.

**1856**  *Buffalo, New York.* University of Buffalo as first chancellor.

# TRAVEL/VISITS

**1839**  *Washington, D.C.* Willard's Hotel at 14th and Pennsylvania Avenue, NW. He remained here during the Whig convention.

**1848–**  *New York City, New York.* The Astor House, west side of Broadway, between Vesey and Barclay Streets. Here he met with fellow politicians of his party.

**1850–**  *Boston, Massachusetts.* Revere House at mid-block on the Cambridge Street side of the Saltonstall Building. He stayed here as a guest during his term of office. Pierce and Grant were guests here later during their terms of office.

**1850**  *Richmond, Virginia.* Union Hotel, southwest corner 19th and Main Streets for dedication of Washington Monument.

**1850s**  *White Sulphur Springs, West Virginia.* He stayed at President's Cottage, Greenbrier Hotel, which he used as a summer White House while president.

**1851**  *Richmond, Virginia.* Powhattan House, southeast corner of Broad and 11th Street. June 26–27.

**1854**  *Atlanta, Georgia.* Arriving from Augusta in a private car of the Georgia Railroad. Dinner and ball at the Atlanta Hotel, southwest corner of Decatur and Pryor Streets.

**1854**  *Augusta, Georgia.* St. Elmo Mansion, 2810 St. Elmo Drive (18th Street). Received at City Hall and reception at Augusta Hotel with lodging at St. Elmo.

**1854**  *Columbus, Ohio.* Received at the State Capitol for a reception.

**1854**  *Lexington, Kentucky.* He visited Ashland, the home of Henry Clay, and his tomb.

**1854**  *Macon, Georgia.* Lanier Hotel, southeast corner of Second and Mulberry Streets. Site is now occupied by Charter Medical Center. Fillmore entertained at a ball on his southern tour. Reception held at Macon City Hall on southwest corner of Poplar Street and Cotton Avenue at intersection with Cotton Avenue and First Street. Hall used as Capitol in 1864.

**1854**  *Mobile. Alabama.* Visited the mayor at his home "Stone Quary" at Glenmore. Called at Josephine Bunker's home. Went to the South Mobile Theater at Royal and St. Michael Streets.

**1854**  *Nashville, Tennessee.* He attended a reception with lodging at the Nashville Inn. Later he visited The Hermitage.

**1854**  *New Orleans, Louisiana.* Stayed at St. Charles Hotel, 211 St. Charles Avenue and visited City Hall (Cabildo, now known as Gallier Hall). 545 St. Charles Avenue April 6.

**1854**  *New York City, New York.* St. Nicholas Hotel, 521–523 Broadway. Also visited

Greenwood Cemetery and the Crystal Palace.

**1854** *Oxford (near Covington), Georgia.* Orna Villa, 1008 Emory Street on Georgia 81 North, home of his friend Alexander Means. The house, now privately owned, was built 1797. He lodged here with his friend while touring the south.

**1854** *Savannah, Georgia.* Pulaski House, 4 Bryan Street, northwest corner of Bull Street on Johnson Square. Site only.

**1869** *Saratoga, New York.* Congress Hall (Hotel) on Broadway for vacation during the summer. New Congress opened 1868 after old one burned 1866. Torn down 1913.

**1872** *Letchworth State Park, Wyoming County, New York.* He attended a historical council meeting with Seneca Indians in October. See museum and Senecan longhouse.

**1849** *Detroit, Michigan.* Guest of Mayor Howard.

**1849** *Fairview, (near Asheville), North Carolina.* See marker on US 74 east from Asheville, 3.1 miles east of Fairview post office. House restored and privately owned. He was an overnight visitor. Still in the family of James McClure and Clarkes. September visit to New England taking part in the opening of new railroad lines connecting Boston with Canada and the West.

*Millard Fillmore's grave site.*

# DEATH

Fillmore died March 8, 1874, in Buffalo, New York, at his home at West Genesee Street and Delaware. He suffered strokes February 13 and 26 and fell unconscious the evening of March 8 dying peacefully a couple of hours later at 11:10 P.M. Estate estimated at a minimum of $102,000 and a maximum of $174,000. The home is gone and the site marked by a bronze tablet.

# FUNERAL

Funeral was held on March 10, in the mansion on Niagara Square, in Buffalo. No Unitarian took part in his funeral. A Baptist, an Episcopalian, and a Presbyterian shared the ceremonies. The procession went out Delaware Avenue to Forest Lawn Cemetery.

## BURIAL

Fillmore was buried at 1411 Delaware Avenue, in Forest Lawn Cemetery, in Buffalo. The entrance is at Delaware and Delavan Avenues. His two wives are buried on either side of him in the Fillmore family plot. His monument is a reddish brown, polished obelisk, on a dark gray granite pedestal and base. The plot is surrounded by a green-painted iron picket fence.

## SPECIAL SITES

A statue has been erected in front of the City Hall on Niagara Square in Buffalo, New York.

## BIBLIOGRAPHY

Rayback, Robert J. *Millard Fillmore: Biography of a President.* Buffalo: Stewart. 1959.

# FRANKLIN PIERCE

---

### 1804–1869
#### 14TH PRESIDENT 1853–1857: DEMOCRATIC PARTY

Franklin Pierce was born in Hillsboro County, New Hampshire, on November 23, 1804, to Benjamin and Anna Kendrick Pierce. His father was a future governor of New Hampshire.

## CHARACTERISTICS

Pierce was a handsome man who carried himself well. He weighed approximately 145 pounds and stood 5'10" tall. He had thick curly black hair, which often hung down over his forehead, and gray eyes. He was an avid fisherman. He was a master at getting along with people. He was active in the temperance movement because alcohol was a life-long temptation to him. After Mrs. Pierce died, he often drowned his sorrows in drinking, and his health declined rapidly before his death in 1865. Although he drank heavily most of his life, he often spoke against drinking. A report in a Concord newspaper in 1843 says, "He delivered a most eloquent and powerful address upon the subject of temperance at the Old North Church Concord. He held his audience in breathless attention for one hour and a half." One of his characteristics, shared with many of the presidents, was that he never forgot names.

*"No citizen of our country should permit himself to forget that he is a part of its Government and entitled to be heard. ..."*

*—Special message, Congress, January 24, 1856*

## A LIFE IN REVIEW

**Birth:** November 23, 1804; Hillsboro, NH

**Died:** October 8, 1869; Concord, NH

**Married:** Jane Means Appleton; November 19, 1834; 3 sons

### CAREER

**1823–1824** Teacher

**1827–1853** Lawyer

**1829–1833** Member state legislature

**1833–1837** Member U.S. Congress

**1837–1842** Member U.S. Senate

**1846** Military service Mexican War

### ADMINISTRATION

**1853** Gadsden Purchase; Trade with Japan opens

**1854** Ostend Manifesto

**1857** Financial Panic

## BIRTHPLACE

Pierce was born in Hillsboro, New Hampshire, in a log house on the Branch of the Contoocook River. The house has long since disappeared, and its exact location is uncertain. It is believed to be under man-made Lake Franklin Pierce.

## BAPTISM

Pierce was baptized on December 3, 1865, in Concord, New Hampshire, at St. Paul's Episcopal Church, 18 Park Street. He was 61 years old at the time. In the following spring of 1866, he was confirmed.

## CHURCH

Pierce was brought up in a religious home and thought much about religious themes. In the White House, he would not even read the mail on Sunday, and family prayers were held every morning with the servants present. His wife was the daughter of a Congregational minister, and he attended church with her. After she died, the slavery question became such an obsession of the Congregational Church in Concord that he turned to the Episcopal Church, where the minister did not preach on politics. Following his son's tragic death, he had the feeling this loss was punishment for his sins.

**1804–1829** *Hillsboro, New Hampshire.* Smith Congregational Church, town center.

**1818–1820** *Hancock, New Hampshire.* Meeting House near Main Street on Route 123. It was built in 1820 and remodeled and moved in 1851. He attended while in school in Hancock.

**1820** *Francestown, New Hampshire.* Old Meeting House on the village common. It was built in 1801, and he attended while in school.

**1820–1824** *Brunswick, Maine, at the unpainted wooden chapel of Bowdoin College (also used as the library).* He was once fined fifty cents for "sitting in an improper posture in chapel."

**1820–1824** *Brunswick, Maine.* The First Parish Church at Nine Cleveland Street. Church attendance was compulsory for Bowdoin students, and reports were sent home to parents.

**1827–** *Amherst, New Hampshire.* Methodist Chapel on Middle Street. See also the original Amherst Congregational Church, where he sometimes attended.

**1829–** *Concord, New Hampshire.* South Congregational Church, 27 Pleasant Street. He attended this church most of his life.

**1833–1842** *Washington, D.C.* Fourth and one half Street Presbyterian Church during the period he was in Congress.

**1843** *Concord, New Hampshire.* He spoke on temperance at the Old North Church, Main Street.

**1853–1857** *Washington, D.C.* Fourth-and-one-half Street Presbyterian Church. He worshipped here at times while President.

**1853–1857** *Washington.* Presbyterian Church, Ninth Street, NW. On Sundays when Mrs. Pierce did not go, he walked from 1600 Pennsylvania Avenue to church.

**1860s–** *Little Boar's Head, New Hampshire.* Where Locke Road runs into Chapel Road, was the site of outdoor services. Nothing remains. He attended here while on summer vacations.

**1863–1869** *Concord, New Hampshire.* St. Paul's Episcopal Church, 18 Park Street.

# EDUCATION

**1807–1818** *Hillsborough Center, New Hampshire.* One and a half mile away from his home, he attended a brick schoolhouse. There is no indication of the exact site.

**1818–1820** *Hancock, New Hampshire.* Hancock Academy, second floor of the vestry in the first building east of the present location of the church on Route 123. While attending this private school, he stayed at the Hancock Academy boarding house across the street from the bandstand.

**1820** *Francestown, New Hampshire.* Francestown Academy for final preparation for college entrance. Located on the Commons, it is the building surmounted by a golden eagle; it is now the town hall. He was a mischievous fun-loving boy who would frequently get into friendly squabbles with his fellow students and leave their rooms with upset tables, chairs, and even beds. Marker on Francestown turnpike. He may have lodged in the Academy Boarding

House, a three-decker building, east across the street.

**1820–1824** *Brunswick, Maine.* Bowdoin College, with classes in Massachusetts Hall. He graduated with a B.A. on August 31, 1824. He ranked third in the class. While in Brunswick, he boarded at Mrs. Grows' boarding house on Cross (now Cleveland) Street. He also boarded at the home of Mr. Benjamin Orr on Park Row; this house no longer exists. For a time, he roomed at Bowdoin College, Main Hall, Room 26 (in 1823) and Room 13 (in 1824).

**1824** *Hillsborough, New Hampshire.* He studied law under John Burnham at his home on Main Street.

**1825** *Portsmouth, New Hampshire.* He studied in the law office of Levi Woodbury.

**1826–1827** *Northampton, Massachusetts.* He studied law with Samuel Howe. He roomed with a friend, also named Pierce. The location is undetermined.

**1827** *Amherst, New Hampshire.* He studied law with Edmund Parker at 12 Main Street at the Parker home. In September he was admitted to the bar to practice law.

# MARRIAGE AND HONEYMOON

Pierce was married on November 19, 1834, in Amherst, New Hampshire, at what is now 1 Pierce Lane. The marriage took place in the parlor of the bride's wealthy grandparents, Colonel and Mrs. Robert Means. The bride's brother-in-law, Silas Aiken, presided. Jane Means Appleton was a petite, frail, shy, melancholy figure. Following the death of their third and last son just two months before they entered the White House, she never recovered and wore black during the whole of her stay in the White House.

Shortly after the ceremony, the couple set out. Three days later, they arrived somewhere

*The Appleton home, site of Franklin and Jane Pierce's wedding.*

in the vicinity of Washington (perhaps Baltimore), and stayed for six days at the boarding house of Sophia Southurt. No exact location has been determined.

## HOMES/LODGINGS

**1804**   *Hillsboro, New Hampshire.* Log cabin and early childhood home. Nothing remains as the site is now under Lake Franklin Pierce.

**1804–1833**   *Hillsboro, New Hampshire.* At the junction of New Hampshire 9 and 31 was the Pierce family home. (Lower village.) It was built in 1804.

**1820**   *Francestown, New Hampshire.* Peter Woodbury's house, an imposing yellow-painted colonial across from the town hall on the village common, near the Francestown Academy marker. He stayed with Woodbury to study law.

**1823**   *Hebron, Maine.* Stayed with Zenas Caldwell during the summer while teaching in the area. The location has not been found.

**1824**   *Castine, Maine.* Stayed the month of August with friends Little and Mason. No location has been determined.

**1829**   *Concord, New Hampshire.* John George's house near the North Church.

**1830s**   *Concord.* He lived at the Eagle Hotel, Eagle Square, while a member of the New Hampshire legislature.

**1831**   *Andover, Massachusetts.* Mary and Silas Aiken house. (Mary was related to Pierce's wife.) They usually spent several weeks with them every year. They were on a train about a mile from here going towards Concord in 1852 when their son was killed. The location has not been determined.

**1833**   *Washington, D.C.* Gadsby's, northeast corner of Pennsylvania Avenue and

Sixth Street, NW. He stayed here before shifting to cheaper quarters. At the time, he was a member of the U.S. House of Representatives.

**1833** *Washington, D.C.* Mrs. A. Hill's, "on the south side of the Avenue (Pennsylvania)" and just west of Third Street. Here he said, "the location is convenient, rooms pleasant and company agreeable." Mrs. Hill's four-story brick house was one of the many Congressional "messes."

**1834** *Washington, D.C.* As a newlywed, he registered at Brown's Indian Queen Inn on the north side of Pennsylvania Avenue, between Sixth and Seventh Streets, NW.

**1834** *Washington, D.C.* Birth's, Third Street north of Pennsylvania Avenue, where they settled for the winter. They paid $10 a week plus $1.50 per session for the luxury of a rocking chair. He also stayed here in 1837 and in 1841.

**1834–1842** *Hillsborough, New Hampshire.* He moved into General McNeil's house, which his father had enlarged for him, as his first home after marriage. The site is on New Hampshire 31 and the Old Turnpike.

**1835** *Washington, D.C.* Dowson's at No. 1 Capitol Hill, "right under the eaves of the Capitol building itself." He was here again in 1841.

**1837** *Washington, D.C.* Mrs. C. A. Pittman's boarding house, at Third Street on the northwest side between Pennsylvania Avenue and C Street. He was serving as U.S. Senator.

**1842–1848** *Concord, New Hampshire.* Montgomery Street, not far from the law office and court. The building was sold in 1847–1848. It was reconstructed and moved to the present site at 14 Penacook Street.

**1849–1853** *Concord, New Hampshire.* 52 South Main Street at the corner of Thorndike. Willard Williams was living in the same pleasant white cottage house. The

Williams provided the meals. Pierce was living here when his wife died in 1863.

**1853–1857** *Washington, D.C.* The White House. Following his inauguration, he was escorted by Fillmore back to the White House. In the evening, when he and his secretary decided to retire, they found that no preparations had been made. The servants were not within call, and Pierce had not yet had a moment to look at his new quarters. After a little search, they found a candle and went upstairs. In the private apartments, all was confusion, and nothing was ready. After inspecting these deserted disorderly rooms, so dreary in the light of the flickering candle, Pierce pointed to one and said to Sidney, "You had better turn in here and I will find a bed across the hall." At the formal dinners he said grace before the meal was served.

**1859** *Concord, New Hampshire.* He bought 60 acres on Pleasant Street on the fringe of Concord.

**1865–1869** *Rye Beach, New Hampshire.* Little Boar's Head by the sea. In 1865, he purchased the 84 acre Brown Farm on the coast not far from the hotels on Rye Beach. His vacation cottage, built in 1866, was a small two-storied building on high ground. The present Union Chapel, near where the present Locke Road runs into Chapel Road, was built in 1877; before that time, services were held here outdoors. The lot on which the Chapel was built was formerly part of the Franklin Pierce property. It is now built up, and it is impossible to identify the site.

# WORK

**1823–1824** *Hebron, Maine.* He taught at a little rural schoolhouse in the Maine woods. The location has not been determined.

**1824** *Hillsboro, New Hampshire.* He was briefly the postmaster in Hillsboro in 1824.

**1827–1829** *Hillsboro, New Hampshire, practicing law.* His father built an office for him just across the road from his mansion.

**1829–1833** *Concord, New Hampshire.* He was a member of the New Hampshire state legislature. The legislature still occupies the original chambers. This was his first elected office. He was never defeated for office, but he was not nominated for a second term as president.

**1833–1837** *Washington, D.C.* He was a U.S. Representative from New Hampshire. He became good friends with future President Polk. Jackson was president. Pierce served on a committee with John Quincy Adams. From 1837 to 1842, he served as U.S. Senator from New Hampshire. One of his colleagues was future President Buchanan. Pierce was the youngest Senator.

**1838–1845** *Concord, New Hampshire.* Law partnership with Asa Fowler. Offices in the Merrimack Bank Building, Main Street. Also many activities at Merrimack County Court House and in the brick "blocks", such as Low's, Stickney's, and Hill's, and the hotels.

**1845–1857** *Concord, New Hampshire.* Law partnership with Josiah Minot with offices in Ayre's Block (once Hill's) over the Franklin Bookshop, right on Main Street near the Capitol.

**1848–1853** *Concord, New Hampshire.* Law practice, Merrimack Bank Building.

**1850** *Concord, New Hampshire.* President of state constitutional convention. See marker on Main Street.

**1853–1857** *Washington, D.C.* President of the United States.

# Travel/Visits

Pierce travelled through the following states: Connecticut, Delaware, Kentucky, Louisiana, Maine, Maryland, Massachusetts, Michigan, Mississippi, New Hampshire, New Jersey, New York, Ohio, Pennsylvania, Rhode Island, Tennessee, Texas, Virginia, and West Virginia.

**1834–** *Boston, Massachusetts.* Tremont House, 275 Tremont Street, was often used as his political headquarters and hotel when in Boston.

**1834** *Baltimore, Maryland.* Barnum Hotel, corner of Calvert and Fayette Streets. He often stayed at this hotel on his way to and from home and also when in Baltimore on special occasions. It was the most prestigious in Baltimore.

**1836** *Baltimore, Maryland.* Eutaw House on Baltimore Street.

**1852** *Cambridge, Massachusetts.* Brattle House, 105 Brattle Street, for a weekend just after his nomination for the presidency.

**1852** *Newport, Rhode Island.* Bellevue House and at Fort Adams on Harrison Avenue, visiting friends.

**1852** *Providence, Rhode Island.* City Hotel.

**1852** *Rye Beach, New Hampshire.* Ocean House and Isles of Shoals. Hotels from this period have been demolished.

**1853–1857** *New York City, New York.* Astor House, Broadway.

**1853–** *Irvington, near Tarrytown,* New York, visiting his friend, Washington Irving, at his home Sunnyside.

**1853** *Ballston Spa, New York.* Sans Souci Hotel on Broadway. It was a popular place for vacations.

**1853** *New York City, New York.* On the site of what is now Bryant Park, fronting on Sixth Avenue.

**1853** *Philadelphia, Pennsylvania.* 40–48 North Fourth Street, below Arch, staying at McKibbens' (Merchants Hotel) on the way to his inaugural.

**1853** *Salem, Massachusetts.* Stayed several times at the home of George P. Loring, 328 Essex Street.

**1853** *Washington, D.C.* He stayed at the Willard Hotel, Fourteenth Street and

Pennsylvania Avenue, NW, prior to his inauguration.

**1854** *Cape May, New Jersey.* Congress Hall, Ocean Avenue. He was here for a ten-day vacation. He was here again in July 1855. The hotel has burned.

**1854** *Staunton, Virginia.* Virginia Hotel, South New Street. This was the first stop on the way to his vacation in White Sulphur Springs, West Virginia. He was also here in 1855.

**1854** *White Sulphur Springs, West Virginia.* He was here for a week with ex-President John Tyler. He stayed at Paradise Row in President's Cottage and also at the White Sulphur Springs Hotel (known as Old White, and torn down in 1913). He also stopped briefly at the resort hotel in Bedford Springs, Virginia.

**1856** *Warrenton Springs, Virginia.* He was here for week end vacation at the Old Warren Green Hotel.

**1857** *Washington, D.C.* When he left the White House he stayed with Secretary William L. Marcy, 736 Jackson Place, NW.

**1858** *Concord, New Hampshire.* He stayed at the Eagle Hotel, on Eagle Square, and at his old boarding house with Mr. Williams.

**1859–1860** *New York City, New York.* Clarendon Hotel, 137 Riverside Drive, at Eighty-sixth Street. He was here several weeks.

**1860** *Nassau, Bahamas, staying at the home of Miss Vandervort for a five-month winter vacation.*

**1861** *Detroit, Michigan.* He stayed at the home of Robert McClelland, congressman, governor, and former cabinet secretary under Pierce. He had travelled to Saginaw to visit his niece, Fanny McNeil Potter, and her husband, but they were not at home, so he returned to Detroit. He travelled from here to Louisville, Kentucky.

**1853** *Capon Springs, West Virginia.* Hotel Mountain House, built in 1849 and burned

*Grave site of Franklin Pierce*

in 1911. He was here again in September 1854.

## DEATH

Pierce died on October 8, 1868, in Concord, New Hampshire, at 52 South Main Street. Early in September, he became confined to his room in the southeast corner of the house. He died there just before dawn, at 4:40 A.M. He left an estate of approximately $90,000.

## Funeral

The funeral was held on October 11, in Concord, New Hampshire, at St. Paul's Episcopal Church, 18 Park Street. His body lay in state in the State Capitol, North State Street. On the day of the funeral, the coffin was borne to St. Paul's and then to the grave site on North State Street.

## Burial

Pierce was buried in Concord, in the Minot family enclosure at the Old North Cemetery.

He is buried beside his wife and three children. There is a granite memorial at his grave. The cemetery is on North State Street near downtown.

## Bibliography

Nichols, Roy Franklin. *Franklin Pierce*. Philadelphia: University of Pennsylvania, 1931; completely revised, 1969.

# JAMES BUCHANAN

## 1791–1868
### 15TH PRESIDENT 1857–1861: DEMOCRATIC PARTY

James Buchanan was born to James and Elizabeth Speer Buchanan on April 23, 1791. He was the last president to be born in the eighteenth century. According to one source, Buchanan could trace his ancestry back to Robert the Bruce, King of Scotland.

## CHARACTERISTICS

Buchanan was a handsome, distinguished looking man, just over 6 feet tall. He probably weighed about 200 pounds when he became president, and his black suit covered a paunch. His wavy hair had turned silvery gray and complimented his large blue eyes and extremely fair complexion.

As a young man he seemed vain, arrogant and somewhat rebellious. His drinking resulted in his being expelled from college, but later he was reinstated. He enjoyed reading and entertaining friends and playing cards at home. One writer says that his greatest joy seemed to be in balancing his accounts, and that no man could have been more precise about a penny. Although judged by some to be a dandy, he was a skillful diplomat, a gifted orator, and respected for his tact, discretion, and moderation.

*"Be firm in politics, but avoid giving personal offense."*

—*Letter, Maria Yates, January 3, 1831*

# A LIFE IN REVIEW

**Birth:** April 23, 1791; Cove Gap, PA

**Died:** June 1, 1868; Lancaster, PA

**Married:** Remained bachelor

## CAREER

**1812** Began law practice

**1814–1816** Member state legislature

**1821–1831** Member U.S. Congress

**1832–1833** U.S. Minister to Russia

**1834–1845** Member U.S. Senate

**1845–1849** Secretary of State

## ADMINISTRATION EVENTS

**1857** Dred Scott decision

**1858** Lincoln-Douglas debates; Atlantic cable completed

**1859** John Brown's raid

**1860** Pony Express Service began

He had a defect in one eye, and, to compensate for it, he tilted his head slightly forward and sideways in a perpetual attitude of courteous deference and attentive interest. One of his quotes: "It is better to bear the ills we have than to fly to others we know not of."

# BIRTHPLACE

Buchanan was born in Cove Gap, Pennsylvania, a few miles outside Mercersburg in a log cabin. This cabin, while crude and rustic by our later standards, was quite comfortable for the time. The cabin has been moved to Mercersburg, but the original site is marked by a stone pyramid in the James Buchanan State Forest Monument in a beautiful natural setting four miles north of Mercersburg on Route 16.

# BAPTISM

Buchanan was probably baptized in Church Hill, northwest of Mercersburg, Pennsylvania, at the Presbyterian Church of the Upper West Conococheaque. This was the church attended by the family at the time of Buchanan's birth. The date is unknown.

# CHURCH

James Buchanan regularly attended the Presbyterian Church all his life, but he did not unite with it formally until late in life. An account of his meeting with the Reverend William M. Paxton of the First Presbyterian Church of New York City tells something of his feeling. Buchanan, who was president at the time, questioned the minister closely on regeneration, atonement, repentance, and faith. At the end of the talk, Buchanan said, "Well, sir ... I hope I am a Christian. I think I have much of the experience which you describe, and as soon as I retire, I will unite with the Presbyterian Church." When asked why he delayed, he said, "I must delay for the honor of religion. If I were to unite with the church now, they would say 'hypocrite' from Maine to Georgia." Later, he was refused membership in the Presbyterian Church apparently because of the dominant abolitionist sentiment in the northern Presbyterian Church. In 1865, when he was 74, he was admitted to Communion and upon his death provided generously for the church in his will. He had been an active Christian all his life. He scrupulously observed the Sabbath. While he was minister to Russia, he refused to dance at the official court balls held on Sunday in St. Petersburg.

**1791–1796** *Church Hill, Pennsylvania.* The Presbyterian Church of the Upper West

Conococheaque served the whole area. It is northeast of Mercersburg on County 3009.

**1796–1809** *Mercersburg, Pennsylvania.* Presbyterian Church, corner of Seminar and Park Streets. Here the Buchanan family was linked to one of the oldest Presbyterian churches in western Pennsylvania.

**1812–** *Lancaster, Pennsylvania.* English Presbyterian Church, 140 East Orange Street, where he rented pew no. 35. Soon after stepping down as president, he joined here.

**1814–1816** *Harrisburg, Pennsylvania.* Presbyterian Church.

**1821–** *Washington, D.C.* First Presbyterian Church, Marshall Place (formerly Four and one half Street, NW). The area now is occupied by public buildings. He attended here while serving in the U.S. House of Representatives.

**1856–** *New York City, New York.* First Presbyterian Church, Forty-eighth and Fifth Avenue.

*Birthplace of James Buchanan.*

multaneously as the State Capitol and the county seat.

# EDUCATION

**1797–1807** *Mercersburg, Pennsylvania.* He attended the Old Stone Academy. It stood on the grounds of the Presbyterian Church, where the parsonage now stands in Old Mercersburg on West California Street.

**1807–1809** *Carlisle, Pennsylvania.* West High Street, at Dickinson College, from which he was expelled in 1808 for disorderly conduct, but he was readmitted and received his B.A. degree in 1809. At Dickinson College he may have stayed with Professor James McCormick.

**1809–1812** *Lancaster, Pennsylvania.* He studied law under James Hopkins. When he arrived in Lancaster, the courthouse, a small two-story building, occupied the square at the intersection of two main streets, on corner of East King and Duke Streets. It was crowded since it served si-

# MARRIAGE

He is the only bachelor president. In 1819, he was engaged to Ann Coleman, whose father, Robert, was one of the country's first millionaires and the most powerful man in Lancaster. She wrote a letter ending the engagement, and then on December 9, 1819, she died. Perhaps because of this romantic association, he later bought the Coleman family house.

# HOMES/LODGINGS

**1791–1794** *Cove Gap, Pennsylvania.* The log cabin in which he was born has been moved to Mercersburg and is situated in a glen at Mercersburg Academy in Mercersburg at the end of a impressive archway of trees.

**1794–1796** *Dunwoodie Farm, Pennsylvania.* The farm is located about five miles east of the Gap, along the West Conococheague Creek, and two miles east of

Mercersburg. Buchanan spent summers on the Dunwoodie Farm, which is sometimes called Bridge Farm. It is off County 3009.

**1796–1809** *Mercersburg, Pennsylvania.* North Main Street, in the center of town in a two-story brick house. Currently, part of the house is a hotel. He spent his childhood here after the age of five. The Harriet Lane house, directly across the street, is the birthplace and home of his niece, Harriet Lane, who served as mistress of the White House while he was president. There are markers.

**1809–** *Lancaster, Pennsylvania.* Widow Dutchman's Inn, East King Street, a block and a half from the courthouse and across the street from Hopkin's mansion at the corner of East King and Duke Streets. He kept this place as he came back to Lancaster from time to time.

**1809–** *Lancaster, Pennsylvania.* White Swan Hotel on town square, where he took meals. It has been torn down, and department store now occupies the site.

**1813–1821** *Lancaster, Pennsylvania.* 42 East King Street. He purchased a small tavern here for living quarters. In 1814, he bought several buildings on the southwest corner of the square as an investment.

**1814** *Harrisburg, Pennsylvania.* He stayed at the Golden Eagle on Market Square while at the State Assembly. There is a marker on the site.

**1816–** *Bedford Springs, Pennsylvania.* He went here for vacations throughout his life. He enjoyed walks up Constitution Hill and Federal Hill to the magnificent Bedford Springs Hotel. During his presidency, it served as the summer White House. It is now on the National Register of Historic Places. It is located about a mile and a half south of the town of Bedford. He received the first trans-Atlantic cable here on August 17, 1858, from Queen Victoria, "Come let us talk together."

**1821–** *Washington, D.C.* Mrs. Peyton's establishment, Four-and-one-half Street, NW, between Pennsylvania Avenue, and C Street, NW.

**1821–1829** *Washington, D.C.* Buchanan stayed in rooming houses between 1821 and 1829, and there is scant information as to definite locations and dates.

**1829** *Washington, D.C.* Mrs. Cottinger's, west side of Thirteenth Street, NW, between E and F Streets, with Senator Barnard, with whom he had been rooming for the past year.

**1832–1833** *St. Petersburg, Russia.* For Legation headquarters, he rented the Ville Dame Brockhauser at Wassilioshoff on the Grand Neva, No. 66, with a good view of the river.

**1833–1848** *Lancaster, Pennsylvania.* 52 East King Street. In 1833, Buchanan bought the former home of Robert Coleman. By 1848, he had decided it was time to have the house fully furnished, as he had only used a few rooms up till then. Seven bedrooms got new furniture, and he bought a piano for which he paid all of $17.50.

**1834–** *Washington, D.C.* He lodged with Senator William R. King from Alabama. The location has not been determined. It was possibly at Rock Creek Church Road and Upshur Street, NW.

**1845–1849** *Washington, D.C.* He rented a house at 1331 F Street, between Thirteenth and Fourteenth Streets, NW, next to the residence of John Quincy Adams and just a block from the State Department building. He paid $2,000 a year for the elegantly furnished house which had nearly enough chinaware for state occasions. He sent to Paris for an ornamental centerpiece for the table because, as the ladies informed him, "you cannot set a handsome dinner without one and they are not to be had in this country." He arranged a grand ball and "served venison, hams, beef, turkey, pheasant, chicken, oysters, lobster, ice cream, water ice, charlotte russe, punch, fruit and cake pyramids, blanc mange, apple toddy, kisses, chocolate, coffee, 300 bottles of wines, 150 bottles of champagne, and harder beverages for harder drinkers."

**1849–1857** *Lancaster, Pennsylvania.* Wheatland, 1120 Marietta Avenue, a lovely country estate, a mile west of Lancaster, where he took up residence the Spring of 1849.

**1852–1854** *London, England.* August. London. He stayed at Clarendon House. He moved from Clarendon House to a place at 56 Harley Street, which became the U.S. Legation during his ministry to the Court of St. James.

**1857–1861** *Washington, D.C.* The White House.

**1857–1860** *Washington, D.C.* During the summer months he stayed at the Soldier's Home, a stone cottage, on Pershing Drive, NW, in the 3700 block of North Capitol Street, NW. It was opened in 1853.

**1861–1868** *Lancaster, Pennsylvania.* At Wheatland, he spent his retirement.

# WORK

**1812** *Pennsylvania.* On November 17, he was admitted to the Pennsylvania bar.

**1812** *Elizabethtown, Kentucky.* He worked on a law case, involving his father's property, at Hardin County Courthouse on the City Square, and made side trips to Bowling Green and Russellville. He stayed only a short time before returning to Lancaster. He may have lodged at Eagle House (Smith Hotel).

**1812–1814** *Lancaster, Pennsylvania.* He had his law office and quarters in a small tavern, two doors above Dutchman's Inn. He was also appointed prosecutor for Lebanon County. See also James Hopkins law office under Education above.

**1814–1816** *Harrisburg, Pennsylvania.* He served as State Assemblyman. The Courthouse, which also served as the State Capitol, stood at the head of the Square about three blocks from the river. The temporary Capitol, a brick structure, two stories high, had two small wings and on the roof a cone of copper gilt. The Dauphin County Courtroom on the first floor served as the chamber of the Assembly and that of the Senate on the second floor.

**1814** *Baltimore, Maryland.* He was a volunteer in the Lancaster County Dragoons in the War of 1812.

**1821–1831** *Washington, D.C.* Member of the U.S. House of Representatives from Pennsylvania. The gallery of the House was simply a platform raised a foot or two above the floor. It was in the part of the Capitol known today as Statuary Hall. From 1821 to 1828, he served with the Federalist Party. In 1828, he ran for the first time as a Democrat. On December 7, 1833, he was defeated in the Pennsylvania State Legislature election for U.S. Senator. On December 15, 1834, he took a seat in the Senate, filling a vacant seat.

**1832–1833** *St. Petersburg, Russia.* U.S. Minister to Russia. He had good relations with the Emperor and the Empress. He praised the Empress as a fine dancer who often took him as a partner at court balls. He took leave of the Emperor at Peterhof August 5, 1833.

**1834–1845** *Washington, D.C.* U.S. Senator from Pennsylvania. During his years in the Senate, he had been in daily contact with outstanding people, including five future presidents: Van Buren, Tyler, Polk, Fillmore, and Pierce.

**1845–1849** *Washington, D.C.* Secretary of State. His office was in the building at the corner of Pennsylvania Avenue and Fifteenth Street, NW, where the north wing of the Treasury Building now stands.

**1853–1856** *London, England.* U.S. Minister to Great Britain. In 1861, the Legation moved to Portland Place at 5 Mansfield Street from Cadogan House, Piccadilly. The United States was still a struggling nation, and the English attitude towards Americans was arrogant and condescending. Of Buchanan, Nathaniel Hawthorne wrote: "We were shown into a stately dining room, the furniture of which was sufficiently splendid, but rather the worse for wear—being hired furniture, no doubt..." When Hawthorne's wife, Sophia, asked about getting admission into sessions of the Houses of Parliament, "He drew from his pocket a coloured silk handkerchief (which ought to have gone into the week's wash) and made a knot in it to remind himself to ask the Lord Chamberlain."

**1857–1861** *Washington, D.C.* President of the United States.

# Travel/Visits

Buchanan travelled very little in the United States. He saw more of the continent of Europe during his assignment to the Russian Mission than he saw of the United States during his whole lifetime. Up to 1848, except for his quick trip to Kentucky, his travel was in an area circumscribed by Philadelphia, Boston, Buffalo, Pittsburgh, Richmond, and back to Philadelphia. He was in the following states: Connecticut, Delaware, Kentucky, Maryland, Massachusetts, Michigan, New Jersey, New York, North Carolina, Ohio, Pennsylvania, Virginia, and West Virginia. In 1833, he travelled by steamboat from St. Petersburg to Lubeck, then to Hamburg, Amsterdam, the Hague, Brussels, Paris, London, Edinburgh, Glasgow, Belfast, Dublin, and to Liverpool for passage to Philadelphia. From Hamburg, he toured the Low Countries and enjoyed a trip down the Rhine Valley. In Ireland, he visited the home of his ancestors at Ramelton. On this tour, he had mixed with emperors and empresses, dukes and counts, and chancellors and ministers who wore medals and ribbons, and it seemed to him that they were not much better informed than he was. For the first time in his life, he began to think seriously about the presidency; he could measure up to many others who were interested.

**1823** *Lancaster, Pennsylvania.* Heritage Center. Masonic Lodge 43. He was worshipful master in 1823. He had joined in 1816.

**1832** *New York City, New York.* He boarded the *Silas Richards* and arrived in Liverpool twenty-five days later. After five days in Liverpool, he went to Manchester on the railroad—his first ride by this new mode of travel. On the way to London, he made stops at Birmingham, Kenilworth Castle, Warwick Castle, Stratford-upon-Avon, Blenheim, and Oxford, and on to London for several weeks. He went from London to Hamburg and on May 24 to Lubeck and St. Petersburg, which he reached on June 2.

**1834–** *Philadelphia, Pennsylvania, 518 Walnut Street.* He often visited friends here and possibly courted a woman.

**1834** *Mercersburg, Pennsylvania,* to visit the grave site of his family at the Spring Grove Cemetery.

**1840** *York, Pennsylvania.* Golden Horse Inn, corner of Market and Water Streets. He gave campaign speeches from the balcony to the crowd in the rear yard.

**1843** *Smithland, Pennsylvania.* Smithland Hotel, south of Pennsylvania 0861. He stopped at this inn in June 1843.

**1847** *Lowell, Massachusetts.* Merrimac House, 310 Merrimack Street. He accompanied President Polk on a tour in New England.

**1847** *Augusta, Maine.* As Secretary of State, he was with President Polk as he was received in the

**1848** *York, Pennsylvania.* From the Courthouse on Center Square, he addressed the returning veterans of the Mexican War.

*Grave of James Buchanan.*

**1849**  *Washington, D.C.* Walter Reed Hospital, 6825 Sixteenth Street, NW, to have a tumor removed from his nose.

**1856**  *New York City, New York.* He stayed at the Astor House, on Broadway (former site of the old Drover's Inn). The old address was 1 Great George Street, an extension of Broadway between St. Paul's Chapel and Broome Street.

**1857–**  *White Sulphur Springs, West Virginia.* Greenbrier Hotel.

**1857**  *Washington, D.C.* Before his inauguration, he stayed at the National Hotel, northeast corner Sixth Street and Pennsylvania Avenue, NW.

**1860**  *Baltimore, Maryland.* Barnum's Hotel, southwest corner of Fayette and Calvert Streets. This leading hotel was a regular stopping place for him when he was travelling between Washington and his home. His southern tour included Norfolk, Virginia, Raleigh and Chapel Hill, North Carolina.

**1860s**  *Ephrata, Pennsylvania.* Mountain Spring Hotel (Camp Silver Bell), Main and Garden Streets.

**1861**  *Washington, D.C.* Stayed at the home of Robert Ould after Lincoln's inauguration and with Zenos Barnum in Baltimore.

**1861**  *York, Pennsylvania.* Henry Welsh house, West Market Street. He stopped here for a visit after retiring from the White House. Representatives Hall of the State House and later at a reception in the Augusta House. He went from here to Gardiner and spent a short time at the mansion of Robert H. Gardiner. From there, he went on board the Huntress to sail to Portland.

# DEATH

Buchanan died on June 1, 1868, in Lancaster, Pennsylvania, at Wheatland. In May 1868, he became seriously ill from a cold and the complications of old age. He was aware that the end was coming as he lay in his upstairs bedroom. He left instructions to be buried in Woodward Hill Cemetery, Lancaster, and also prescribed a plain white marble tombstone. At about 8:30 A.M, he died. He left an estate worth about $300,000.

# FUNERAL

The funeral was held in Lancaster, Pennsylvania. A public meeting was held in his honor on June 2, and later in the day thousands of country folk came to Wheatland to file past the coffin. More than 20,000 people attended the funeral on June 4, including official delegations from all over the nation. The simple funeral was conducted by the Reverend John W. Nevin. Only a small item on the funeral appeared in the *New York Times*.

# BURIAL

Buchanan was buried in Lancaster, Pennsylvania, at the Woodward Hill Cemetery, 511 South Queen Street.

# BIBLIOGRAPHY

Curtis, George Ticknor. *Life of James Buchanan: Fifteenth President of the United States*. New York: Harper & Bros., 1883.

Klein, Philip S. *President James Buchanan*. University Park, Pa.: Pennsylvania State University Press, 1962.

# ABRAHAM LINCOLN

## 1809–1865
### 16TH PRESIDENT 1861–1865: REPUBLICAN PARTY

Abraham Lincoln, "Honest Abe," was born on February 12, 1809, to Thomas and Nancy Hanks Lincoln. His mother died when he was nine, and his stepmother, Sarah Bush Johnston Lincoln, raised him.

## CHARACTERISTICS

At 6′4″ tall, he was the tallest of the presidents. He was well built, with coarse black hair and black bushy eyebrows over gray eyes. His adam's apple stood out on a scrawny neck. He had a dimple on the chin and a large nose. Clothes hung on him as if they were on a rack to dry. Joking, people would say, "You are a man to look up to." His trademarks in photos and in reality were the umbrella and stovepipe hat. He was serious in study from the beginning, but he was also well-known for his wit and sense of humor, and he had a national reputation as a story-teller. When he came to Washington in 1847, he was recognized as the champion story-teller and often used his stories to make a point or relieve tension. He was a down-to-earth man who persisted in using his own knife in the butter, instead of the silver-handled one intended for that purpose. He would often lie on the front room carpet to read. One day he answered the door to two very fine ladies who

*"My paramount object in this strruggle is to save the Union . . . ."*

—*Letter to Horace Greeley, August 22, 1862*

# A LIFE IN REVIEW

**Birth:** February 12, 1809; Hodgenville, KY

**Died:** April 9, 1865; Washington, D.C.

**Married:** Mary Todd; November 4, 1842; 4 sons

## CAREER

**1827–1828** Ferry hand

**1833** Saloon keeper

**1833** Postmaster

**1835–1837** Member state legislature

**1837–** Lawyer

**1847–1849** Member U.S. Congress

## ADMINISTRATION EVENTS

**1861–1865** Civil War

**1862** Emancipation Proclamation

**1863** Delivered Gettysburg Address

wanted Mrs. Lincoln; he looked the house over and came back to tell the women, "She'll be down soon as she gets her trotting harness on." He drank little or no wine and never used tobacco.

The whiskers almost always seen in photos were grown only after his election as president. On the way to Washington for the inaugural, his train stopped in Westfield, New York. Here Lincoln called for a little girl named Grace Bedell saying, "She wrote me that she thought I would be better looking if I wore whiskers." He looked down at little Grace, "You see, I let these whiskers grow for you."

One town in America was named for him with his consent—Lincoln, Illinois—and he helped christen it with watermelon juice. Alto-

gether, there are fifteen towns in the United States named Lincoln. About Lincoln, Grant said, "He was incontestably the greatest man I ever knew."

# BIRTHPLACE

Lincoln was born in Sinking Spring Creek, near Hodgenville, Kentucky, in a log cabin, located on U.S. 31E and Kentucky 61. The cabin, tradition says is the birthplace is inside a granite and marble memorial building close to a spring which flows near by. There are 56 steps leading up to the shrine, one for each year of his life. In 1905, the birthplace (110 acres) was sold for $3,600. The logs of the house were put in storage on Long Island and later reconstructed and placed in the memorial building.

# BAPTISM

Abraham Lincoln's father and mother were married by a Methodist circuit rider, but, after moving to Kentucky, they attended Baptist services. Lincoln's parents were active churchgoers all their lives, and his father often served as moderator at church meetings. But since Baptists do not practice infant baptism, he was probably not baptized, and there is no information as to an actual baptism.

# CHURCH

It is certain that Abraham Lincoln was a deeply religious man. His speeches and conversation are filled with Biblical quotations and religious sentiments. On membership, he said "that I am not a member of any Christian Church, is true; but I have never denied the truth of the Scriptures; and I have never spoken with intentional disrespect of religion in general, or of any denomination in particular."

Lincoln was well acquainted with the Bible. On one occasion, a man complained to him that Secretary Stanton had refused to release a

*The cabin that tradition says is the birthplace of Abraham Lincoln.*

friend of his from prison although the release had been ordered by Lincoln himself. The man attempted to cast the blame on Stanton when Lincoln said, "My friend you should remember the passage of Scripture which says, 'Accuse not a servant unto his master.'" The visitor remarked that he had been an attentive reader of the Bible, but he could not recollect such a passage in it. "Oh, you'll find it in the thirtieth or thirty-first chapter of Proverbs," said Lincoln. And the gentleman went home and read Proverbs 30:10: "Accuse not a ser-

vant unto his master, lest he curse thee and thou be found guilty!"

His boyhood was saturated by a primitive evangelistic theology, but he never deviated from his conviction that God intended the ultimate salvation of all men—a heresy to the orthodox.

**1809–1812**    *Hodgenville, Kentucky.* Sinking Spring Church. Severn Valley Baptist Church, oldest Baptist organization west of the Alleghenys. Later Lincoln's parents

*Marble memorial building housing the birthplace of Abraham Lincoln.*

joined the Little Mount Separate Baptist Church.

**1812–1816** *Hodgenville, Kentucky.* Little Mount Separate Baptist Church was situated about five miles north of their cabin. It was at the Little Mount log meeting house where he heard his first sermon.

**1816–1830** *Lincoln City, Indiana.* Little Pigeon Baptist Church, which was a mile across the field from the Lincoln home. It was a log-built meeting house put up in 1822 with the help of Abraham and his father. Lincoln State Park near Gentryville, Indiana, on Indiana 62.

**1831–1837** *New Salem, Illinois.* The reconstructed New Salem does not contain a church. However, as many as fifty men, women, and children were baptized in the nearby Sangamon River on one Sunday. At first members of the faith met in a dwelling house, then at camp-meetings, and, as they

grew in number, they built churches. In its time, New Salem had fifteen houses, a church, a school, and a saloon.

**1837–1861** *Springfield, Illinois.* The Lincolns attended the First Presbyterian Church, Seventh and Capitol Avenue. It has the pew once occupied by the Lincolns. On the day their four-year-old son, Eddie was buried, the service was conducted by the Reverend James Smith of the church, and a friendship developed between the Lincolns and the minister. The Lincolns rented a pew in the church, and Mrs. Lincoln took the sacrament and joined the church. Abe attended revival meetings held in the church and said he was interested, but, when asked to join, he said he "couldn't quite see it."

**1842–** *Springfield, Illinois.* St. Paul's Episcopal Church (now Cathedral), 815 South Second Street. Mary was an Episcopalian, and they were married by a clergyman of that church. A record of the marriage is in the church books. She first attended this church in Springfield, and Lincoln often went with her.

**1860** *Chicago, Illinois.* St. James Episcopal Church, Huron Street and Wabash Avenue. Lincoln attended with Isaac Arnold.

**1861–** *Washington, D.C.* St. John's Episcopal Church on Lafayette Square. The Sunday before inauguration and on other occasions, the Lincolns and their three boys attended services in this church.

**1861–1865** *Washington, D.C.* New York Avenue Presbyterian Church, New York Avenue and H Street, NW. He sat in pew number 14, seven rows from the front on the center aisle. Reliable sources hold that Lincoln had definitely planned to become an official member of this church on Easter Sunday morning in 1865. The present church was dedicated in 1951, but Lincoln's pew is located in approximately the same place in the new building as in the old. The church is on the same spot as the old "Lincoln church." Outside on New York Avenue can be found the hitching post where the Lincoln carriage was tied. Whenever a president of the United States is present for services, he is seated in the Lincoln pew. Lincoln often went to Wednesday night prayer meeting, and the minister put him out of sight in the pastor's room to avoid publicity and distraction.

**1861–** *Washington, D.C.* Dumbarton Methodist Church, 3133 Dumbarton Avenue, has a Lincoln pew with an engraved plaque, third row from the front on the right.

**1861–** *Washington, D.C.* Foundry Methodist Church, 1500 Sixteenth Street, NW. He attended at the old site. A Lincoln window commemorates his association.

**1861–** *Georgetown, D.C.* Holy Trinity, 3513 N Street, NW. He attended a funeral service here.

# EDUCATION

**1809–1816** *Hodgenville, Kentucky.* When he was five years old, his mother was teaching him his letters at home and it is claimed that by the time he was seven he was able to take his turn in the family's daily Bible reading. At seven Abe and his sister walked four miles a day—two miles north of their Knob Creek home on the same road on which they lived. The school was a log cabin with a dirt floor, no windows, and one door. It was a "blab" school where the children learned to recite in unison. His father paid $2.00 per child for the session.

**1816–1819** *Lincoln, Indiana.* During this period, there was no school available, and he was mostly self-taught. At a young age, he learned by writing letters for his elders in the community. He not only improved his English and writing skills, but also gained a knowledge of character from being privy to the most confidential aspects of his neighbors' lives from the private information in the letters they asked him to write.

**1819–1820** *Lincoln, Indiana, at Little Pigeon Creek.* He went to three different schools in Indiana and two in Kentucky. Altogether, he had about four months of formal schooling. Lincoln said it was by "littles" and that the "aggregate of all his schooling did not amount to one year." However, he read everything he could get his hands on. In addition to the Bible, his childhood reading included *Aesop's Fables, Robinson Crusoe, Pilgrim's Progress, A History of the United States, Weem's Life of Washington,* and the *Statutes of Indiana.* At Little Pigeon Creek, he and his sister walked eighteen miles to school, nine miles to and from. The school at Pigeon Creek was kept when a schoolmaster happened to drift in, and school was out when he drifted away. It was located about 200 yards east of Little Pigeon Church. His formal education was over by the age of sixteen.

**1819–1820** *Lincoln, Indiana, at Little Pigeon Creek.* He attended Andrew Crawford's school, which stressed reading aloud from the Bible. It was a one-room log cabin built on the farm of Noah Gordon about one and one half miles south of the Lincoln Cabin in Hurricane township in Perry County.

**1821–1822** *Little Pigeon Creek.* James Swaney was his teacher in a school standing on the Hoskins farm, Jackson township in Spencer County, four and one half miles southwest of the Lincoln farm.

**1824–1825** *Little Pigeon Creek.* Azel W. Dorsey taught in the new schoolhouse near the Pigeon Creek Baptist Church, which was a little over a mile southwest of Lincoln's farm and very close to the site of the present Little Pigeon Creek cemetery.

**1831** *New Salem, Illinois.* New Salem State Park, twenty miles northwest of Springfield on Illinois 97. He began studying law on his own, reading from documents of the state of Indiana.

## MARRIAGE AND HONEYMOON

While living at New Salem, he courted Ann Rutledge whose family had moved from New Salem, where they ran the tavern, to a farm near Sand Ridge. In the fall of 1835, Ann Rutledge died, and Lincoln was present at the burial in the Concord burying ground. See the reconstructed tavern in New Salem State Park.

Mary Owens of Green County, Kentucky, who stood five feet and five inches tall and weighed 150 pounds, said of him, "he was deficient in those little links which make up a woman's happiness." Previously, he had agreed to marry her sight unseen and he said of her, "I knew she was oversize, but . . . when I beheld her I could not for my life help thinking of my mother; and this, not from her withered features, for her skin was too full of fat to permit of its contracting into wrinkles, but

from her want of teeth . . . In short I was not at all pleased with her."

Lincoln was married on November 4, 1842, in Springfield, Illinois, at the Ninian W. Edwards home, 700 North Fourth Street. He married Mary Todd, in the evening with the ring ceremony of the Episcopal Church. (Mrs. Lincoln died in this house in 1882.) A replica of the house is at 406 South Eighth Street. There is a record of the marriage in the books at St. Paul's Episcopal Church, 815 South Second Street. Lincoln and Mary Todd were first engaged to be married in 1840. They fell out, made up, fell out, and made up again. The wedding was set for January 1, 1841, and Lincoln did not show. On November 4, 1842, he said to a friend, "I am going to be married today." On the street that day he told Ninian Edwards, Mary's guardian, that he and Mary were going to be married. With that short notice things were rushed, the house was readied, the cake baked, and Abraham and Mary were married that evening.

With such minimal planning for the wedding and Lincoln's short money supply, it is doubtful that there was any special honeymoon.

Abraham Lincoln and his wife had good times together. Although tales spread of Lincoln's being a hen-pecked husband, he rose above such remarks and handled difficult occasions philosophically. In his own words, "Quarrel not at all. No man resolved to make the most of himself can spare time for personal contention."

## HOMES/LODGINGS

**1809–1812** *Hodgenville, Kentucky.* He was born at Sinking Spring Creek (sometimes called Rock Spring Farm) in a one-room log cabin with a packed down dirt floor, one window, and one door on the Big South Fork of Nolin's Creek. It is two and one-half miles south of Hodgenville on US 31E and Kentucky 61.

**1812–1816** *Hodgenville, Kentucky.* Knob Creek Farm, eight miles northeast of Hodgenville on Kentucky 31E. When he was three years old, the family moved here to another one-room log cabin near the "ole swimming hole" Lincoln enjoyed as a boy. This boyhood cabin was used for firewood, but a replica has been built on the side of the main highway from Louisville to Nashville. There is a marker on the highway. Pleasant Grove Baptist Church, on Kentucky 84, has the grave of Austin Gollaher, who was his schoolmate and playmate when the Lincoln family lived in this area. Gollaher is credited with saving Lincoln from drowning in Knob Creek.

**1816** *Vine Grove, Kentucky.* The Lincoln family travelled along the old pioneer trail through here on their way to Spencer County, Indiana.

**1816–1830** *Lincoln City, Indiana.* Most of his boyhood was spent at the Little Pigeon site. The Lincolns lived for a year in a pole shed before the log cabin was built forty yards away. Here his mother, Nancy Hanks Lincoln, died and was buried. The hearth and sill logs are still shown at the traditional site. In addition, the village has replicas of the Old Pigeon Baptist Church to which the Lincolns belonged, the pioneer schoolhouse with dirt floor–Abe's school, the Jones store which was near Gentryville, where Abe clerked and John Pitcher's law office, to which he often walked seventeen miles to borrow books. The cabin was a one-room house eighteen feet square with a loft. He worked out of Crawford House near Gentryville and also operated the ferry boat from the mouth of Anderson Creek across the Ohio River. In Rockport, Indiana, see replicas of the Lincoln home.

**1830** *Lawrenceville, Illinois.* The Lincoln Trail Monument on U.S. 50 east of town marks the site where the Lincoln family entered Illinois from Indiana. They turned northeastward towards Palestine, where the land office was located.

**1830** *Lovingston, Illinois.* The Lincoln family camped two and one half miles south of town, on Illinois 32 where it intercepts the Paris to Springfield road.

**1830–1831** *Decatur, Illinois.* The Lincolns went by covered wagon to Macon County on the north bank of the Sangamon River, where they built their first log cabin in Illinois. A terrible winter encouraged them to move on the following spring. It is located ten miles west of Decatur, south on US 36 (Lincoln Homestead State Park).

**1831–** *Charleston, Coles County, Illinois.* The family lived at Goose Nest Prairie in the southern part of the county, beginning in 1831. It is now in Lincoln Log Cabin State Park.

Abe may have lived with them for a short time, and he visited numerous times afterwards. However, shortly after they moved, he took a job ferrying a load to New Orleans, and, when he returned, he settled in New Salem, eight miles south of Charleston. This was the last home of his parents. See also Shiloh Cemetery northwest of the Park where Thomas and Sarah Lincoln are buried, about one and one half miles south of Campbell.

**1831–1837** *New Salem, Illinois.* New Salem State Park. Lincoln's home was in what was a new log-cabin village when he first came; before he left, it had grown to twenty-five cabins. He lodged here and ate in different homes and other buildings. At first, while working in Offut's store, he slept together with young Bill Green on a narrow cot in the back of the store: "when one turned over, the other had to." He also boarded at the home of the Reverend John Cameron and later at the tavern of James Rutledge, father of Ann Rutledge. Onstat Cooper Shop is the only original building in the park but nearby Sand Ridge Farm was the home of Ann Rutledge, Lincoln's early romantic friend. She

*Home of Abraham Lincoln, Springfield, Illinois.*

also lived at Petersburg, Illinois. Ann Rutledge's grave is in the Oakwood Cemetery in the southwest section of Petersburg.

**1834–1837** *Vandalia, Illinois.* He took a room during legislative sessions in the Vandalia Hotel and shared a room with John T. Steward and others. He lodged at 615 West Johnson Street where according to local tradition he rented a room during a legislative session.

**1837–1842** *Springfield, Illinois.* 105 South Fifth Street. He was greatly appreciated by the people of New Salem. In one election out of the 284 votes cast, he got 277. Following a successful start in the state legislature at Vandalia and having received his license to practice law, he moved to Springfield. He was unable to afford the price of bedding for a single bedstead so took up Joshua Speed's offer to share his own double bed upstairs over the general store. The site of the store is on the south-

west corner of Fifth and Washington Streets. Later, Lincoln moved in with Bill Butler's family until his marriage in 1842. This was also the site of the last Lincoln-Herndon law office.

**1842–1843** *Springfield, Illinois.* Globe Tavern, 315 East Adams Street. Here the couple boarded and bedded immediately following their wedding. They paid $4.00 a week for room and board.

**1843** *Springfield, Illinois.* 214 South Fourth Street in a small one-story house.

**1843–1847** *Springfield, Illinois.* Eighth and Jackson Streets. They moved to this house, which was the only house he ever owned, a few blocks from the public square. At first, it was a story-and-a-half frame house, later enlarged to two stories. The framework and floors were oak; doors, door frames, and weather boarding were black walnut. The house was painted a "Quaker tint of light brown." In the back lot were a cistern, a well and pump, a barn thirty feet by thirteen feet, and a carriage house eighteen feet by twenty feet. When he went to Washington in 1847, it was leased as it also was when he went for his inaugural in 1861.

**1847** *Washington, D.C.* Brown's Hotel, Pennsylvania Avenue, north side between Sixth and Seventh Streets, NW. He stayed here upon his arrival to serve in the House of Representatives.

**1847–1849** *Washington, D.C.* Mrs. Sprigg's boarding house, Carol Row on Capitol Hill. When ground was being condemned for the first House Office Building, a historian wrote that in a single square slated for oblivion were houses where Abraham Lincoln had lived.

**1849–1861** *Springfield, Illinois.* House at Eighth and Jackson Streets.

**1861–1865** *Washington, D.C.* The White House. The main executive office was on the second floor. In the room, twenty-five by forty feet, was a large white marble fireplace with brass andirons and a high brass fender, a few chairs, two hair-covered sofas, and a large oak table. Lincoln was often at his desk before seven in the morning. His White House bed, nine feet long and nearly nine feet high at the headboard, had bunches of grapes and flying birds carved into its black walnut.

**1861–1865** *Washington, D.C.* Soldier's Home, Pershing Drive, NW, at the 3700 block of North Capitol Street. The cottage he used during the summer and as a getaway place during the year is just beyond the flagpole.

# WORK

**1809–1820** *Hodgenville, Kentucky.* At home with his father.

**1820s** *Grandview, Indiana.* Downtown in front of the library on Indiana 66 is a Lincoln marker indicating where he travelled hauling hoop poles (wood stock for barrel hoops) with an ox team to the river for shipment.

**1820s** *Ferry Park, (near Troy) Indiana.* On Indiana 66 just west of the Anderson River, there is a small roadside memorial park at a site where Lincoln worked as a ferryman.

**1826–1830** *Lincoln City and Gentryville, Indiana.* He worked on the farm of James Taylor at the mouth of Anderson Creek near the Ohio River. Besides plowing and doing barn and field work, he ran the ferryboat across the Ohio River near Gentryville.

**1827** *Hawesville, Kentucky.* Samuel Pate house on Kentucky 334, three miles west of town. He won his first law case: pleading his own case when he was charged with operating a ferry without license. Marker 667.

**1828** *Rockport, Indiana.* At the lower end of Main Street is a marker that commemorates his first trip on a flatboat down the Ohio and Mississippi Rivers to Baton Rogue and back to Pigeon Creek.

**1831–1837** *New Salem, Illinois.* Replicas are close together in the Lincoln theme park. See the replica of Offut's store, where he worked as a clerk and where he roomed in the back.

**1831** *New Salem, Illinois.* He clerked in the store of Denton Offut.

**1832** *New Salem, Illinois.* He jointly owned a store with friend Berry. He had a license to keep a tavern, but he failed disastrously.

**1832** *Beardstown, Illinois.* At the north end of Wall Street (now a recreation park) was the muster point at which he joined as a volunteer soldier for the Black Hawk War. Zachary Taylor was a colonel in this engagement in Illinois-Wisconsin at Beardstown, Yellow Banks, and Dixon.

**1832** *Dixon, Illinois.* The Lincoln Monument State Memorial on the west bank of the Rock River marks the site where Jefferson Davis, Zachary Taylor, and Lincoln met during the Black Hawk War. A bronze statue depicts Lincoln as a young captain of volunteers.

**1832** *Ottawa, Illinois.* The Lincoln Sun Dial at the Ottawa Boat Club by the bridge shows the spot where Lincoln was mustered out following the end of the Black Hawk War in 1833.

**1833–1834** *New Salem, Illinois.* He was postmaster, did odd jobs, and surveyed in the area.

**1834–1842** *Vandalia, Illinois.* Vandalia State House, 315 West Gallatin, where Lincoln served as a member of the House of Representatives. He continued as a state legislator in Springfield until 1842. He supported and voted for the move of the capital to Springfield. The Capitol where the legislature met in his time became the Sangamon County Courthouse and is now a Lincoln shrine.

**1835–1837** *New Salem, Illinois.* He surveyed, read law, and followed political activities.

**1837–1841** *Springfield, Illinois.* No. 4 Hoffman's Row (upstairs), 109 North Fifth Street. He went into law practice with J.T. Stuart. The building has been remodeled.

**1837–1861** *Charleston, Illinois.* Courthouse on the town square where he practiced law. Building remodeled.

**1837–1861** *Danville, Illinois.* Lincoln-Lamon law office site, northwest corner of Redden Square, Main and Vermilion Streets.

**1837–1861** *Decatur, Illinois.* Lincoln Square. Site where Lincoln practiced law and made his first political speech. A bronze tablet on the building on the southeast corner commemorates the arrival of the Lincoln family by oxcart in 1830. See also old Macon House where he helped unload and screw into place the first piano to arrive in central Illinois.

**1837–1861** *Lincoln, Illinois.* Logan County Courthouse, 914 Fifth Street, midtown, site

of building where Lincoln practiced law for almost 25 years. Here he received his nickname, "Honest Abe."

**1837–1861** *Metamora, Illinois.* Metamora Courthouse, 113 East Partridge Street.

**1837–1861** *Mount Pulaski, Illinois.* The Courthouse on the Town Square is the original building where he practiced law on the Eighth Circuit.

**1840s** *Springfield, Illinois.* State Representative. While the Capitol was being built, the legislature met in the Second Presbyterian Church. It later moved into the Capitol in the square bounded by Fifth, Sixth, Washington, and Adams Streets. This was not a full-time job, and he carried on his law practice at the same time.

**1841–1844** *Springfield, Illinois.* He went into law practice with Stephen T. Logan. The third-floor office was on the southwest corner of Sixth and Adams Streets.

**1844–1847** *Springfield, Illinois.* He had a law practice with Herndon, on the southwest corner of Fifth and Washington Streets at 109 North Fifth Street.

**1847–1849** *Washington, D.C.* U.S. Congressman from Illinois, meeting in that part of the Capitol known today as Statuary Hall.

**1849–1861** *Springfield, Illinois.* Back with his law practice.

**1861–1865** *Washington, D.C.* President of the United States. His inauguration took place on the East Terrace of the Capitol. The same site has been used by succeeding presidents ever since. He arrived at the Capitol by carriage. Shortly before the Civil War broke out, he declared in his inaugural address, "The Union of these States is perpetual." In 1863, he issued the Emancipation Proclamation. Just before Lincoln's death in 1865, Lee surrendered to Grant on April 9, 1865.

**1861–** *Washington, D.C.* Jackson Hall, 339 Pennsylvania Avenue, NW. This site of Lincoln's inaugural ball was torn down in 1949.

**1861–** *Washington, D.C.* Patent Office between F and G Streets, NW, on the west side of Seventh Street NW. The third-floor rooms were the site of Lincoln's second inaugural ball on March 5. It now houses the National Collection of Fine Arts.

# TRAVEL/VISITS

**1830** *Vincennes, Indiana.* Lincoln Memorial Bridge on Vigo Street. Lincoln and his family crossed the Wabash River by ferry near this location. There is a monument on the Illinois side of the river.

**1835** *Jacksonville, Illinois.* Governor Duncan house, Duncan Park, 4 Duncan Place.

**1837–** *Danville, Illinois.* McCormick Hotel, 103 West Main Street, where he lodged while on circuit. The Grier-Lincoln Hotel is now on the site.

**1837–** *Hillsboro, Illinois.* Blockburger Inn, Main and Tilson Streets. He often stayed here overnight on trips to Vandalia, then the capital. He also stayed at the Eccles house, corner of Berry and Water Streets. The Hillsboro Courthouse, on the town square, is where Lincoln spoke in July 1844.

**1837–** *Lincoln, Illinois.* Old Postville Hotel (formerly Duskin's Inn), Fifth and Madison Streets. Lincoln often stayed here overnight during court sessions.

**1837–** *Pleasant Plains, Illinois.* Clayville Tavern, on the highway, twelve miles west of Springfield. The stagecoach stop where Lincoln frequently stayed has been restored. Clayville was once a rallying spot for members of Lincoln's Whig political party.

**1837–** *Salem, Illinois.* Houses at 321 South Franklin and 304 West Schwartz. Lincoln made an important speech here that helped bring about the election of William Henry Harrison in 1840. The houses in which he stayed are open to the public.

**1837** *Lewiston, Illinois.* Newton Walker House (private), 1127 North Main Street.

**1840** *Philadelphia, Pennsylvania.* Delegate to the national convention of the Whig Party, which nominated Zachary Taylor.

**1841** *Louisville, Kentucky.* Farmington, 3033 Bardstown Road. Lincoln visited in 1841. He spent two months here recuperating from a "melancholic depression," caused by a broken engagement with his future wife. The house was built from a design by Jefferson.

**1842–** *Springfield, Illinois.* Vachel Lindsay House, 603 South Fifth Street, home of his sister-in-law, Ann Todd Smith.

**1844** *Rockford, Illinois.* Courthouse in the block bounded by Walnut, Main, Second, and Third Streets. This is the fifth courthouse on site. Lincoln spoke in the third debate on this site in October 1844. While in Rockford, he stayed in the Rockford Tavern, the site of which is on the northeast corner of Main and Second Streets. A small stone marker indicates the site.

**1847–** *Lexington, Kentucky.* Mary Todd Lincoln's girlhood home, 573 West Main Street. She was born at 501 West Short.

**1847** *Lowell, Massachusetts.* He spoke at the old City Hall, Shattuck and Merrimac Streets, and stayed at the home of Linus Child or Homer Barlett (the two houses were connected) on Kirk Street.

**1847** *Beardstown, Illinois.* Hunter House, which is still standing.

**1847** *Chicago, Illinois.* Tremont House, southeast corner of Lake and Dearborn Streets, where he spoke and where politicians slept during the 1860 convention.

**1847** *Clinton, Illinois.* Barnett Hotel, 738 North Grant, is now a private residence and has been moved from its original site. A statue of Lincoln at the courthouse commemorates his speech here of 1848.

**1847** *Springfield, Illinois.* Executive Mansion at Fourth and Fifth and Jackson and Edwards. He was the Governor's guest here.

**1847** *St. Louis, Missouri.* Scott's Hotel, southwest corner Third and Market Streets, where the Lincoln family stayed. They travelled by boat to Frankfort, Kentucky, and from there to Lexington and on to Washington, D.C. Another entry mentions the Old National Hotel at the southeast corner of Third and Market Streets where Lincoln once registered. There is a marker on the site.

**1847** *Worcester, Massachusetts.* Lincoln Mansion, 49 Elm Street, where he dined.

**1848–** *Philadelphia, Pennsylvania.* Delegate to the National Convention of the Whig Party, which met in the elegant hall of the Chinese Museum. Later, he stumped the New England states for the National Whig Party ticket and went to Boston and New York.

**1850s** *Vincennes, Indiana.* Ellis Mansion, 111 North Second Street. Lincoln provided legal service for Abner T. Ellis.

**1855–** *Danville, Illinois.* The William Fithian house, 116 North Gilbert Street, is now the Vermillion County Museum Society.

**1856** *Chicago, Illinois.* Wigwam Convention Hall. Here he made himself famous by his speech at the Republican National Convention.

**1856** *Dixon, Illinois.* Courthouse at Second and Ottaway Avenues where he gave a two-hour speech on July 17. He lodged at the Nachusa Hotel, 215 South Galena Avenue. The hotel is now dilapidated and needs repair. He also visited Hazelwood, the great estate three miles outside Dixon.

**1856** *Galena, Illinois.* Main and Green Streets at DeSoto House, where he spoke.

**1858** *Bloomington, Illinois.* Majors Hall. There is a monument commemorating the site where Lincoln made his "Lost Speech" against slavery. The speech is lost because

reporters were so engrossed, that they forgot to take notes.

**1858** *Bloomington.* Miller-Davis House, 101 North Main Street, which he used as a temporary office.

**1858** *Burlington, Iowa.* Hudson House, northwest corner of Columbia and Fifth Streets, on a visit. He gave a speech at the Grimes Opera House, which stood on the northeast corner of Valley and Main Streets.

**1858** *Carthage, Illinois.* The site of the Lincoln speech is south of the courthouse entrance on the square, on October 22. There is a stone marker on the site.

**1858** *Chicago, Illinois.* Sherman House, Clark and Randolph Streets, where he usually stayed while in Chicago.

**1858** *Edwardsville, Illinois.* Wabash Hotel (now made into apartments). Stephen Douglas also lodged here.

**1858** *Farmington, Illinois.* Capp's house, southwest corner of Fort and Main Streets. He spoke on a platform erected here. He lodged at the home of his friend, the Reverend Wilkenson, on East Fort Street.

**1858** *Lewiston, Illinois.* He gave his classic eulogy of the Declaration of Independence between the central pillars of the old Court House.

**1858** *Springfield.* State Capitol, Fifth and Adams Streets, where he gave his famous "house divided" speech in 1858.

**1859** *Atchison, Kansas.* Massasoit House, 201 Main Street is on the site of a hotel where Lincoln stayed. A plaque in the Courthouse square commemorates a speech Lincoln made here.

**1859** *Council Bluffs, Iowa.* A Lincoln Monument, Oakland Drive and Lafayette Avenue, commemorates his visit here on August 12–14.

**1859** *Elwood, Kansas.* On US 36, was his

first stop in Kansas while on a political speaking tour.

**1859** *Janesville, Wisconsin.* Tallman Mansion, 440 North Jackson Street, where he was a guest.

**1859** *Leavenworth, Kansas.* Planters' House, northeast corner of Shawnee and Main Streets (now an empty lot). Stockton Hall site, 401 Delaware Street, where he gave a campaign speech. The site is now occupied by the Leavenworth National Bank.

**1859** *St. Joseph, Missouri.* Edgar House, 101 Francis Street, is now occupied by the Paper Box Company.

**1860** *Bardstown, Kentucky.* Old Talbott Tavern, 107 West Stephen Foster Avenue. He and his family stayed here.

**1860** *Chicago, Illinois.* The Wigwam, southeast corner of Lake Street and Wacker Drive, was the site of the Republican National Convention that nominated Lincoln for president. The land was then and is still owned by the Garrett Biblical Institute of Evanston.

**1860** *Dover, New Hampshire.* The Lincoln House, 107 Locust Street, is a frame cottage where Lincoln stayed after making a political speech at the old city hall on Central Street.

**1860** *Evanston, Illinois.* White House, 2009 Dodge. Only a part of the house remains. Lincoln stayed overnight with Julius White.

**1860** *New York City, New York.* The Cooper Union, Lower East Side of Manhattan, in the Astor Place district, across Lafayette Street and slightly to the south, is where Lincoln made the speech that is credited with winning him the nomination for the presidency.

**1860** *Providence, Rhode Island.* The Federal Building, east end of Exchange Place, has a plaque commemorating Lincoln's speech on February 28, 1860.

**1860** *Woonsocket, Rhode Island.* City Hall, 169 Main, has a plaque commemorating the speech Lincoln made on March 8.

**1860** *Springfield, Illinois.* Benjamin Edwards house, 700 North Fourth Street (now the Springfield Art Association). Lincoln, Grant, and other notables stayed here. At 116 North Sixth Street is a second-floor room where Lincoln received notice of his nomination to the presidency.

**1861** *Albany, New York.* Delwan House, corner of Broadway and Steuben. He spoke at the Old State Capitol. Both houses have commemorative tablets. Lincoln stayed here for three weeks in 1847. (Site of cotton mills of Oldham, Todd & Company.) The house has been restored.

**1861** *Philadelphia, Pennsylvania.* He arrived at Kensington Depot, on February 21, and went to the Continental Hotel, Ninth and Chestnut Streets, for a reception and lodging.

**1861–** *Washington, D.C.* 3238 R Street, NW, often visited friends here.

**1861–** *Washington, D.C.* Baltimore and Ohio Railway Station, New Jersey Avenue and C Street, NW, which he used at times.

**1861–1865** *Washington, D.C.* Winder Building, 604 Seventeenth Street, NW, where he often visited officials.

**1861** *Baltimore, Maryland.* 702 Cathedral Street, where he stayed overnight.

**1861** *Chicago, Illinois.* Julian S. Rumsey residence, 40 East Huron Street.

**1861** *Cincinnati, Ohio.* Burnett House, once the city's leading hotel, on the northwest corner of Third and Vine Streets. Lincoln stopped en route to his inauguration. The building was razed in 1926.

**1861** *Cleveland, Ohio.* Weddell House, southwest corner of West Sixth Street and Superior Avenue. From the second-floor balcony, Lincoln addressed the street crowd on February 13. A plaque is at the site now occupied by the Rockefeller Building.

**1861** *Fort Wool, Virginia, in the middle of Hampton Roads channel.* This abandoned army base is often called "Rip Raps" after the shoal on which it rests. Lincoln watched an artillery barrage from its ramparts. At present, it is not open to the public.

**1861** *Sharpsburg, Maryland.* Mount Airy, a plain brick mansion on Maryland 34. Two weeks after the Battle of Antietam, Lincoln visited the wounded who were being cared for in the building.

**1861** *Springfield, Illinois.* The Smith Store, 528 East Adams Street, is the building in which Lincoln wrote his first inaugural address. He often visited the Chenery House while in Springfield. The Lincoln Depot Museum, at Tenth and Monroe Streets, is the site of his farewell speech to Springfield on February 11.

**1861** *Washington, D.C.* Willard's Hotel, Fourteenth Street and Pennsylvania Avenue, NW. Having his mind on the coming inauguration, he left without paying his bill. He sent a note of apology promising payment. This letter is on display. The current Willard's stands on the same corner. More than the Capitol itself, Willard's was the heart of the Union, for it was here that Northern leaders gathered throughout the War. From the balcony on the second floor, Lincoln and General Burnside watched the Ninth Union Corps march down Fourteenth Street past Willard's into Virginia to join Grant's Army for its attack into the Wilderness. Look directly across Pennsylvania Avenue from the north front of the Treasury Building. This elegant building stood on the northwest corner of Fifteenth Street and Pennsylvania Avenue from 1824 to 1904. It was used as a branch bank of the U.S. government and later became Riggs Bank. President Lincoln deposited his salary in a checking account at Riggs throughout the war.

**1862** *Fort Monroe, Virginia.* Quarters Number One. He stayed here in May, 1862, planning operations that led to the fall of Norfolk. Lincoln and Grant were both guests here.

**1863–** *Manchester, Vermont.* Hildene, Lincoln's summer home. Here, Mrs. Lincoln and Mrs. Grant spent their summers. Robert Todd Lincoln, the president's favorite son and one time president of the Pullman Car Company, died here. A VHS marker is located in front of the estate. Presidents Taft and Theodore Roosevelt were also visitors at Hildene.

**1863** *Chancellorsville, Virginia.* He visited the battlefield.

**1863** *Chatham Manor, Virginia.* He came here to confer with his military commanders who had headquarters here.

**1863** *Gettysburg, Pennsylvania.* Wills residence on Center Square. He was here to deliver the famous Gettysburg Address. The room where he wrote it has been preserved. Gettysburg National Military Park is located off U.S. 15, 30. The site where Lincoln delivered the Gettysburg Address is marked by the Lincoln Address Memorial, near the west entrance to the cemetery. Here he also dedicated a National Soldiers' Cemetery.

**1863** *Harrogate, Tennessee on US 25.* The Abraham Lincoln Museum on the Lincoln Memorial University campus is considered to have the largest collection of Lincoln and Civil War materials in the world.

**1864** *Baltimore, Maryland.* He spoke at the American Institute.

**1865** *Charles City County, Virginia.* Berkeley Plantation. He met here with General McClellan during the War.

**1865** *Hopewell, Virginia.* Appomatox Manor, end of Cedar Lane. Lincoln met with Grant here. He spent two of the last three weeks of his life here.

**1865** *Petersburg, Virginia.* Center Hill, on a court off the north side of Franklin Street between Jefferson and Adam Streets, was the residence of the Bolling family and where Lincoln visited Grant. Lincoln made the quip while visiting here, "General Grant seems to have attended sufficiently to the matter of rent." It is now the headquarters of the National Park Service.

**1865** *Petersburg, Virginia.* Wallace-Seward House, 204 South Market Street, which was occupied as headquarters by Grant. On the porch, Grant discussed with Lincoln the terms of the expected surrender of General Robert E. Lee.

**1865** *Point Comfort, Virginia.* Lincoln came for an informal peace conference with Confederate commissioners.

**1865** *Richmond, Virginia.* The White House of the Confederacy, 1201 East Clay Street, where Jefferson Davis lived, was visited by Lincoln at the end of the War.

# DEATH

Lincoln died on April 15, 1865, at 7:22 A.M., at 453 Tenth Street, NW, in Washington, D.C. He was shot while seated in Ford's Theatre, 511 Tenth Street, NW, watching *Our American Cousin.* He died from a lead ball that crashed into the left side of his head. Within half an hour, he was taken to the house of William Peterson across the street. The president was laid on his back in a humble walnut bed, on white sheets under which was a cornhusk mattress resting on rope lacings. The back room where he died is so small that the bed was angled across the room, and Lincoln had to be angled on the bed.

Surratt's Boarding House, 604 H Street, NW, is the site where the assassination plot was planned.

# FUNERAL

Before embalming, his scalp and brain were removed. He was dressed in a black suit

*Abraham Lincoln was shot while seated in the Presidential Box at Ford's Theatre watching* Our American Cousin.

and placed in a mahogany coffin, lined with lead, covered with black broadcloth, and adorned with silver handles. Roses, magnolias, and lilies surrounded the catafalque. Reports from those who viewed the dead president said that he had an expression of happiness and repose.

The body of Abraham Lincoln lay in state in the East Room of the White House. On April 19 prayers and words were said by Presbyterian, Methodist, and Baptist clergyman. The Bible reading was from I Corinthians 15.

The body was moved in a procession to a place of honor in the Capitol Rotunda. He was the first to lie on the catafalque in the Capitol Crypt. President Johnson and future president Grant attended the ceremonies at the White House and at the Capitol. On Friday, April 21, they went with others to escort the body to the railway station where the coffin was placed aboard a special funeral car which moved out of Washington to Baltimore. In Baltimore, the coffin was taken up Conway and Eutaw Streets to the Exchange Building, where the body lay in state for public viewing. In Philadelphia, the coffin stood in Independence Hall. In New York in City Hall a large catafalque was built at the top of the grand staircase. (Later Grant lay in state here.) Eighteen hundred people per hour filed past the coffin hour after hour.

In Harrisburg, Pennsylvania, there was a military escort to the State House (the State House of that time burned in 1897) where throngs of people came for the viewing. In Lancaster, Pennsylvania, there were perhaps thirty to forty thousand people awaiting the arrival of the train.

Ex-President Fillmore attended the funeral in Buffalo, which was also witnessed by the youthful Grover Cleveland, who became president in 1885. At Cleveland, the Episcopal service was read, and the body lay in state in the rotunda of the capitol at Columbus. The coffin was borne into the Statehouse at Indianapolis, the Courthouse in Chicago, and finally at home in Springfield. The casket stood in the state capitol and 75,000 people passed by the bier. In Springfield, the remains arrived at the Chicago and Alton Railroad Station.

## BURIAL

A procession moved with the hearse from the State Capitol to Oak Ridge Cemetery, in Springfield, Illinois. There thousands of peo-

*Tomb of Abraham Lincoln.*

ple heard prayers and sang hymns, and his Second Inaugural speech was read.

In 1876, thieves broke into the tomb, forced open the sarcophagus, and pulled Lincoln's coffin partially out, with the idea of demanding $200,000 in ransom, but they were apprehended and sentenced to one year in prison.

In 1900, his remains were transferred to a vault just north of the monument during the reconstruction of the tomb. The coffin was in a bad state of decay. On April 24, 1901, the remains of Lincoln and the members of his family who had been entombed in the national Lincoln Monument were removed to the crypt. They were secured against desecration at the insistence of Robert Lincoln. Lincoln's body was placed thirteen feet in the ground and surrounded by more than six feet of solid cement.

## SPECIAL SITES

*Elizabethtown, Kentucky.* Lincoln-Haycraft Memorial Bridge, where as a boy, Lincoln crossed the Severn Valley Creek going through Elizabethtown on the way to Indiana.

*Ottawa, Illinois.* Washington Park, Columbus and LaFayette Streets, has a boulder marking the site of the first debate between Lincoln and Douglas. Mrs. William Cratty of Seneca said, "I felt so sorry for Lincoln while Douglas was speaking, and then to my surprise I felt so sorry for Douglas when Lincoln replied."

*Peoria, Illinois.* Courthouse Square, Main and Adams Streets. There is a tablet on the south portico of the courthouse commemorating the site of Lincoln's speech.

*Pittsfield, Illinois.* Central Park has a boulder marking the site of the Lincoln speech of October 1, 1858. He stayed at Worthington House, 626 West Washington.

*Freeport, Illinois.* The site of the second Lincoln-Douglas debate, North State Avenue and East Douglas Street, is marked by a memorial boulder.

*Jonesboro, Illinois.* The Fair Grounds, North Main Street, is the site of the third debate on September 15, 1858. There is a marker near the town square.

*Charleston, Illinois.* A stone at the eastern end of Charleston fairgrounds marks the site of the fourth debate.

*Galesburg, Illinois.* The site of the October 7, 1858, debating platform is on the present day Knox College campus, East South between Cherry and Cedar. The speakers entered the front door of "Old Main" and stepped out on the platform through a window.

*Quincy, Illinois.* Debate on the east side of Washington Park. The site of the sixth debate is marked by a bronze plaque. It is the only commemorative marker of the seven debates that depicts Douglas as a participant.

*Alton, Illinois.* Broadway at end of Market Street. The last of the great debates took place October 15, 1858 on a platform erected at the east side of the old City Hall.

*Beardtown, Illinois.* City Hall, West Third and State Street has original courtroom where Lincoln defended "Duff" Armstrong in a murder trial. Known as "Almanac Trial." At City Square, granite memorials mark sites where Lincoln and Douglas spoke from opposite ends of the square.

*Bement, Illinois.* Bryant House, across railroad tracks from business section. In this house July 29, 1858 Lincoln and Douglas made arrangements for their debates. There is a marker on Illinois 105. Now a state memorial.

*Washington, D.C.* Lincoln Memorial.

# BIBLIOGRAPHY

Brooks, Noah. *Washington in Lincoln's Time.* New York: Rinehart & Company, 1958.

Fuller, Edmund, and Green, David E. *God in the White House.* New York: Crown Publishers, 1968.

Sandburg, Carl. *Abraham Lincoln: The Prairie Years and the War Years*, 6 vols. New York: Harcourt, Brace, and World, 1926–1939.

# ANDREW JOHNSON

## 1808–1875
### 17TH PRESIDENT 1865–1869: DEMOCRATIC PARTY

*"I have returned to the South and to the place of my boyhood, to try, if possible, to heal the breaches made by war."*

Andrew (Andy) Johnson was born on December 29, 1908, to Jacob and Mary McDonough Johnson. His father was a laborer, and his mother worked as a seamstress and washerwoman. Of all the presidents, he was probably born in the lowest level of poverty. As a boy, he was called A.J. by the family—a style common in the South even today.

## CHARACTERISTICS

He was of medium height, standing about 5'10" tall, and weighed about 175 pounds. He had broad shoulders and was muscular with a short thick neck. He had deep-set dark piercing eyes under a mass of straight black hair, a massive head, cleft chin, and a large nose. When he smiled, his face lit up and he became attractive. One person in 1865 wrote, "I have heard ladies name him the handsomest of all our national dignitaries, and should you ever meet him in the social circle and converse with him, you will doubtless indorse their opinion." His voice was particularly adapted to speaking in the open air and in ordinary conversation was "soft and low." On occasion, he liked playing checkers, but he had no social life and did not appear to want any. When he was

168

## A LIFE IN REVIEW

**Birth:** December 29, 1808; Raleigh, NC

**Died:** July 31, 1875; Carter's Station, TN

**Married:** Eliza McCardle; May 17, 1827;
3 sons, 2 daughters

### CAREER

**1822–1839** Tailor

**1830–1833** Mayor

**1835–1837** Member state legislature

**1841–1843** Member state Senate

**1843–1853** Member U.S. Senate

**1853–1857** Governor of Tennessee

**1857–1862** Member U.S. Senate

**1862–1865** Military Governor of
Tennessee

**1865** U.S. Vice President

### ADMINISTRATION EVENTS

**1865** Slavery abolished by 13th
Amendment

**1867** Reconstruction Acts

**1867** Tenure of Office Act

**1868** Impeachment trial and acquittal

**1868** Fourteenth Amendment ratified

a lawyer. An article in the *New York Times* on February 24, 1907, calls him the "greatest patriot" of the Civil War.

## BIRTHPLACE

Johnson was born in Raleigh, North Carolina, at 123 Fayetteville Street, in a cabin house a few yards away from Casso's Tavern. There is a marker at the site of his birthplace in downtown Raleigh at the corner of Fayetteville and Morgan Streets, but the small house has been moved to 1 Minosa Street. Another source (Hans L. Trefousse) establishes his birthplace as a two-and-a-half-story log house on Carrabus Street, adding that it was dismantled for souvenir seekers.

## BAPTISM

Johnson was baptized in 1808, in Raleigh, North Carolina, by a minister of the Presbyterian Church. No church had been built in Raleigh prior to 1816, and the members met in a room in the State House, located on Union Square. Although there is no extant record, his baptism was probably in the State House, which was used at the time for worship services by travelling preachers of all denominations in Raleigh until the building burned in 1810. Johnson's father was a sexton of the church, and it is probable that he was baptized. In 1808, the State House was located on the site of the present capitol.

## CHURCH

He was suspected of being a nonconformist. His wife was a devout Methodist, but she was unable to convince Johnson to attend church regularly in Greeneville. Members of his family had been Baptist and he had been exposed to their teachings, but he never became a member of any church although he described himself as a church member. He appeared to have a natural

not working, he was studying and busy in self-improvement. Until he went to Washington, he made his own suits and was one of the best dressed Congressmen. At his boardinghouse, he was considered a nuisance because of his habit of taking a bath every day; once a week was the rule, and, if a week should be skipped, it was all to the good. He was the first president who had not been either a military man or

*Birthplace of Andrew Johnson.*

leaning towards the Methodist Episcopal Church. His attitude toward religion and the Bible was something like that of Abraham Lincoln. He had a feeling of broad tolerance toward all churches of the Christian faith but without personal allegiance. He had a sincere respect for the religious beliefs of others, but he was uncertain as to the reality of heaven. He was familiar with the Bible, read it on a regular basis, and owned a fine edition which he carried with him when he travelled. Johnson often expressed himself in religious terms, and his speeches are filled with Biblical quotes and references. His stated creed was "the doctrines of the Bible, as taught and practiced by Jesus Christ."

**1808–1810** *Raleigh, North Carolina.* The State House on Union Square was used as a church by the Presbyterians and others. His father was the custodian and a much loved man by those who knew him.

**1810–1824** *Raleigh, North Carolina.* There are no details on his church attendance in these years.

**1824–1825** *Carthage, North Carolina.* He was in Carthage only briefly, and no church is mentioned in his writings.

**1825** *Laurens, South Carolina.* Old Methodist Church. He was particularly interested in Sarah Word, who attended here.

**1825** *Mooresville, Alabama.* There are two churches in this small town, and he attended both: Old Brick Church and the Church of Christ near Bibb's Spring.

**1826** *Greeneville, Tennessee.* Asbury Methodist Church, corner of Main and Summer Streets.

**1826–1827** *Rutledge, Tennessee.* There is no mention of church attendance here in his writings.

**1827–1875** *Greeneville, Tennessee.* He attended the Asbury Methodist Church, corner of Main and Summer Streets, with his wife, Eliza.

**1827–1875** *Greeneville, Tennessee.* Cumberland Presbyterian Church, Church and Main Streets, where he attended from time to time.

**1827–1875** *Greeneville.* First Presbyterian Church, 100 West Main, first organized 1789.

**1843–** *Washington, D.C.* Foundry Methodist Church, Fourteenth and G Streets, NW, which he sometimes attended during his years as a member of Congress.

**1853–** *Nashville, Tennessee.* McKendree Methodist Church, 523 Church Street. This was the church where he was sworn in as Governor and where he attended while with the government in Nashville. This was near his lodging place, and he walked to the church on the day of his inauguration as Governor.

**1865–1869** *Washington, D.C.* New York Avenue Presbyterian Church, New York Avenue and H Street, NW, which he most often attended while president.

**1865–** *Washington, D.C.* St. Patrick's Roman Catholic Church, 609 Tenth Street, NW, where he often chose to worship.

**1867** *Richmond, Virginia.* St. Paul's Church, southwest corner of Grace and Ninth Streets.

# EDUCATION

He never attended a day of school in his life. His father died while he was still a small boy, and his mother was unable to afford schooling for her children. He was willing and got his start on education when a public spirited gentleman from town read the classics to a group of young apprentices as they worked in the tailor shop.

Greeneville College had a debating society, and he obtained permission to join the debates and walked from home to the college, a distance of eight miles, each Friday. When Greeneville College no longer had its debating society, he walked four miles out the other side of town to attend the debates at Tusculum Academy. The Greeneville College site is marked and is four miles out of town on the old road to Asheville, North Carolina.

Tusculum Academy (now Tusculum College) is three miles east of Greeneville on Tennessee 107. Tusculum College has recognized his association through the establishment of a library for his works. Young Andrew Johnson participated in Literary Society debates and activities—the Philamatheon Society dates to 1839 and its rival, Philogian, to 1847 or 1848 on campus.

When his daughter, Martha, went to school and started bringing home her lessons and textbooks, he studied alongside her, not a bit concerned to "go to school" with his own daughter. He was also helped along by his wife, who was a school teacher at the time of their marriage.

# MARRIAGE AND HONEYMOON

Johnson was married on May 17, 1827, in Warrensburg, Tennessee, by Justice of the Peace Mordecai Lincoln, in his office. His bride Eliza McArdle, was an attractive and graceful woman. After the wedding, they returned to the McCardle home. The exact location of the McCardle house is unknown, but according to tradition it was on Main Street near the present Greene County Court House. At the time she met Johnson, she was teaching school in a mountain village in Tennessee. She was in poor health while living in the White House and her daughter, Martha (Johnson) Patterson, acted as hostess at White House social events. Nothing remains of Mordecai Lincoln's home or office. There is no marker to indicate that this momentous event in Johnson's life took place in this vicinity. There is no mention of a honeymoon, and they probably had none since they saved the cost of a church wedding and Andrew was still struggling.

# HOMES/LODGING

**1808–1824** *Raleigh, North Carolina.* 123 Fayetteville Street. See birthplace. It is a little frame house two stories high with a room on each floor. It has been moved and can be seen in Mordecai Historic Park at 1 Minosa Street. There is a marker on Fayetteville Street.

**1824–1825** *Carthage, North Carolina.* 50 miles southwest of Raleigh, he obtained the use of a shack to live in and pursue his tailoring. There is a marker on the lawn of the courthouse.

**1825** *Laurens, South Carolina.* He set up shop in an empty cabin on the north side of the town square. He reputedly had a romance with Sarah Word while making a quilt with her.

**1825** *Mooresville, Alabama.* McNiell House, which is the last house down from the church. He was here while tailoring in a small shop on the same lot as the house. The churches and the stagecoach stop and inn nearby were the social centers. The buildings are still there.

**1825–1826** *Columbia, Tennessee.* 207 West Sixth Street. He resided here while working with tailor James Shelton for about six months before returning to Raleigh to pick up his mother. He loaded up her few possessions and took her and his stepfather, Turner Doughtry, to Tennessee, arriving at Greeneville in September.

**1826–1827** *Greeneville, Tennessee.* He camped near the "Gum Spring" during the autumn. He started work in George Boyle's tailor shop and rented the back room of the Russell House. One source says he lived in a "small frame house" on the site of present-day 207 West Sixth Street.

**1827–1830** *Greeneville, Tennessee.* Main Street. After marriage, they moved into a two-room frame and puncheon-board house on Greeneville's Main Street. The front room was the shop; the back room was the couple's home–their kitchen, bedroom, and parlor all rolled into one.

**1830–1851** *Greeneville, Tennessee.* Water Street. He acquired a real home for his family, a house they owned. He bought it at an auction sale–a small brick building on Water Street with a "smith's shop" in the yard—for less than $1,000   for the property. Then he bought a whitewashed clapboard building containing a single room lighted by a door and two shuttered windows and rolled it two and one half blocks to his own lot, where he fitted it up as a shop at Depot and College Streets.

**1835** *Nashville, Tennessee.* He took rooms with John Netherland when he arrived to serve as state representative.

**1836** *He bought a small farm outside Greeneville where he established his mother and stepfather.* His mother and stepfather both died in 1856 and were laid to rest in the Baptist churchyard. The location is not definite, but some say it was on the White House Road near the present airport.

**1843–1853** *Washington, D.C.* Mrs. Russell's on North Capitol Street, an inexpensive boarding house close to the Capitol.

The buildings in the row have been demolished. The site is in the vicinity of the Library of Congress.

**1852–1875** *Greeneville, Tennessee.* An unfinished brick house on South Main Street in a good residential part of town came on the market when the owner was unable to complete it. Johnson bought the house and lot for $950, plus the deed to his old house on Water Street. Not by coincidence, behind the house was "Gum Spring" where Andy and his family had camped on their first night in Greeneville. The Johnson family moved in January 1852. His daughter, Mary (married to William R. Brown), moved into a house across the street. There is a marker in front which refers to it as the Valentine Sevier house.

**1853–1857** *Nashville, Tennessee.* While Governor, he lived in a hotel, the Nashville Inn on the north side of the town square, Market Street (2nd Avenue) and Public Square, northeast corner. When the Nashville Inn burned in 1856, he moved to the Verandah Hotel nearby.

**1857** *Washington, D.C.* Willard Hotel, Fourteenth Street and Pennsylvania Avenue, NW, where he first stayed while serving as a U.S. Senator from Tennessee.

**1857–1862** *Washington, D.C.* St. Charles Hotel, northwest corner of Third Street and Constitution Avenue, NW. He stayed here while serving in the U.S. Senate.

**1860s** *Carter County, Tennessee.* He often stayed with his daughter, Mrs. Mary Stover. The house has been moved intact to Elizabethton, Tennessee.

**1862–1865** *Nashville, Tennessee.* St. Cloud Hotel, corner of Spring and Summer (now Church and Fifth) Streets, while military governor of Tennessee. From May to September, he boarded with Mrs. Anna M. Roach (later Mrs. Edward P. Cone). See also the house of Neill S. Brown, where Eliza Johnson visited him in October.

*Home of Andrew Johnson, Greeneville, Tennessee.*

**1862–1864**　*Nashville, Tennessee.* As a wartime governor he commandeered the home of Mrs. Lizinka Campbell Brown which stood directly in front of the State Capitol building on Charlotte Avenue.

**1865**　*Washington, D.C.* Kirkwood House, where he lived as vice president. This hotel once stood on the northeast corner of Twelfth Street and Pennsylvania Avenue. It was torn down after the Civil War and replaced by the Raleigh Hotel, one of the city's finest. It, too, is now gone, and a nondescript office building has taken its place. Here on April 15, 1865, in his third floor suite, he was told he was now president of the United States. Lincoln died at about 7:30 A.M., and Johnson took the oath of office at 10:00 A.M.

**1865**　*Washington, D.C.* Lee House, 1653 Pennsylvania Avenue. He rented this house for a short time near the end of his vice presidency and waited here during his first days as president for Mary Lincoln to leave the White House. Pending Mrs. Lincoln's removal from the White House, he used Representative Samuel Hooper's vacant residence, 334 H Street, NW, and moved to the White House directly after Mrs. Lincoln left it on May 23.

**1865–1869**　*Washington, D.C.* The White House. The mansion was in woeful condition when he moved in. For weeks the doors had been left unguarded, and strangers had wandered in and carried off pictures, silverware, ornaments, even heavy pieces of furniture. The wallpaper was in tatters, pieces had been snipped out of the lace curtains, the carpets were slashed, and the upholstery soiled and torn. His daughter, Martha, did much to restore the beauty of the interior of the White House.

# WORK

**1822–1824** *Raleigh, North Carolina.* Tailor's apprentice to James I. Selby, on Fayetteville Street, a few doors below the market. When Andrew ran away in 1824, Selby advertised and offered a $10 reward for his return.

**1824–1825** *Carthage, North Carolina.* He obtained the use of a shack and opened a tailoring business of his own. There is a marker on the Courthouse lawn.

**1825** *Laurens, South Carolina.* On the north side of the town square stood his little tailor shop. Here, between sessions with his needle and tailor's goose, he poured over his books. Some of the coverlets he designed are still valued heirlooms in the family of the girl whom he wooed in Laurens.

**1825** *Mooresville, Alabama.* He worked under a tailor, Sloss, whose shop was at the southwest corner of Piney and Market Streets. The shop and street names no longer exist. The McNeill house stands on the corner of the lot where he was lodging at the time.

**1825–1826** *Columbia, Tennessee.* He was hired by Columbia's leading tailor, James Shelton, northeast corner of the Public Square. He stayed six months.

**1826–1827** *Rutledge, Tennessee.* A lawyer who had been elected to Congress was leaving for Washington, and the little brick building he had used as an office was vacant. Johnson rented it for a tailor shop and worked here for six months. News came to him that the tailor in Greeneville had closed his shop and moved on. With this news and the memory of Eliza in his mind, he went back in 1827 and opened a business in his own name. There is a marker at southwest corner of the courthouse. Johnson had his first establishment here in what was also the sheriff's office. There is a replica of his first tailor shop at the corner of Court Street.

**1827–1843** *Greeneville, Tennessee.* Tailor shop, northwest corner of Depot and College Streets. The frame structure is now enclosed in a brick building. From 1829 to 1831 he served as an alderman on the Town Council. No particular building served as town hall, and meetings often took place in his shop.

**1831–1835** *Greeneville, Tennessee.* He was elected Mayor three times. He had his office in his tailor shop.

**1835–1837** *Nashville, Tennessee.* He was a member of the lower house of the Tennessee Legislature, and again in 1839–1841. The capitol was in the Masonic Hall (1826–1853). The First Masonic Hall was on Church Street between Fourth and Fifth Avenues. Hume Fogg High School is now on the site. From 1841 to 1843, he served as a member of the State Senate.

**1843–1853** *Washington, D.C.* U.S. House of Representatives from the First District, Tennessee. Meetings of the Congress were held in the Capitol in the chamber now known as Statuary Hall.

**1853–1857** *Nashville, Tennessee.* Governor of Tennessee. He was sworn in at McKendree Church. The cornerstone of the new Capitol on Charlotte Avenue was laid in 1843, and the building was completed 1855.

**1857–1862** *Washington, D.C.* U.S. Senator from Tennessee. He was very colorful in his speech and could be extreme when exasperated. For example, annoyed with Southern extremists and Northern abolitionists, he said he would chastise both, "I would chain Massachusetts and South Carolina together, and I would transport them to some island in the Arctic Ocean, the colder the better, till they cool off and come to their senses." On January 4, 1859, the Senate moved from the historic chamber where Jackson, Calhoun, Webster, and others had served into more spacious quarters in the Capitol.

**1862–1864** *Nashville, Tennessee.* He was Military Governor of Tennessee with the rank of Brigadier General. He moved into the still unfinished state capitol at its present site.

**1865** *Washington, D.C.* Vice president of the United States.

**1865–1869** *Washington, D.C.* President of the United States.

**1870s** *Greeneville, Tennessee* Tusculum College. As ex-President, he was a trustee of Tusculum.

**1875** *Washington, D.C.* U.S. Senator from Tennessee.

# TRAVEL/VISITS

**1843–** *Kingsport, Tennessee.* Netherland Inn, 2144 Netherland Inn Road, just west of downtown Kingsport, while travelling the Great State Road, to and from Washington, D.C.

**1860s** *Jonesborough, Tennessee.* The Chester Inn, Main Street, was a popular stopping place. The Mansion House (May House) was also a stopover when he travelled on the Great Stage Road. See also the Washington House (Hotel) site near the Railway Station.

**1860s** *Buckhorn House at 613 East Main.* He visited here many times with a close friend. He also visited Blair House and the Gosnell House.

**1860s** *Leesburg, Tennessee.* DeVault Tavern on the old Great Stage Road was another stopover. It is off Tennessee 81 northeast of Jonesborough.

**1861** *Cincinnati, Ohio.* Burnett House, northwest corner of Third and Vine Streets, now the site of Union Central annex. He stopped here as a fugitive from the angry secessionists of Kentucky and his home state, on his way to Washington as the only senator from a seceding state who remained loyal to the Union. He was here again on February 27, 1863.

**1863** *Indianapolis, Indiana.* Speech at the State House, corner of Senate and Capitol Streets. (The Old capitol was on this site.)

**1864** *Baltimore, Maryland.* Front Street Theater, where he was nominated for vice president. He won the election on November 8.

**1865** *Philadelphia, Pennsylvania.* Continental Hotel, southeast corner of Ninth and Chestnut Streets.

**1865** *Richmond, Virginia.* Spottswoode House, Tanyard area, Main and Eighth Streets, was one of the few hotels open at the close of the Civil War. He was here again in 1867.

**1866** *Baltimore, Maryland.* Reception at Eutaw House.

**1866** *Cincinnati, Ohio.* Spencer House, northwest corner of Front and Broadway for a lavish reception.

**1866** *Cleveland, Ohio.* Stadium Hotel, southeast corner of West Sixteenth Street and South Clair Avenue, which opened on April 17, 1854, as the Angier House and later became the Kennard House. The old iron balcony facing west on the second floor was the scene of many political speeches. Johnson made a plea for leniency toward the south and was hissed by an antagonistic crowd on the street. Grant was on the balcony with Johnson at the time.

**1866** *Columbus, Ohio.* Visit and reception at the State House. He spent the night at Neil House.

**1866** *Columbus, Ohio.* Speech at the State Capitol, Broad and High Streets.

**1866** *Detroit, Michigan.* He arrived at the Michigan Central Railway Station, southeast corner of Michigan Avenue and Griswold Streets. He stayed at the Biddle House Hotel on Woodbridge Street.

**1866** *Harrisburg, Pennsylvania.* Banquet and lodging at Bolton House.

**1866** *Illinois.* In Chicago, he stayed at the Sherman Hotel and dedicated the Douglas Monument. He took the Chicago-Alton Railroad to Springfield. In Springfield, he visited Lincoln's tomb and spent the night at the St. Nicholas Hotel.

**1866** *Indianapolis, Indiana.* The disgraceful reception by citizens here made it impossible for him to give his speech. He spent the night at Bates House.

**1866** *Louisville, Kentucky.* Reception at Louisville Hotel.

**1866** *New York.* In New York City, he reviewed a parade at the Park, corner of Fourteenth Street and Fifth Avenue. He spent the night at the Delmonico Hotel, at Fourteenth Street and Fifth Avenue. In Albany, he visited the capitol and was received in the Executive Chamber. He dined and spent the night at Delwan House. In Niagara Falls, he visited and spent the night at the International Hotel of Mr. Fulton. In Buffalo, he spoke at Niagara Square after being introduced by ex-President Fillmore.

**1866** *Pittsburgh, Pennsylvania.* Banquet and evening at St. Charles Hotel.

**1866** *St. Louis, Missouri.* Banquet at Southern Hotel. Night at Lindell Hotel on Washington Avenue.

**1867** *Raleigh, North Carolina.* He visited his father's grave in City Cemetery, at the corner of South East and East Hargett Streets. There is a simple flat stone, just inside the gate, marked only with J.J. On May 24 and 30, he made a visit to Chapel Hill.

**1867** *Richmond, Virginia.* He visited the city and was honored at City Hall. City Hall was demolished in 1874.

**1875** *Nashville, Tennessee.* Maxwell House, where he stayed while in Nashville to follow the balloting for the senate seat which he ultimately won.

**1875** *Washington, D.C.* Imperial Hotel, E Street, between Thirteenth and Fourteenth Streets, NW, where he stayed during the special session of Congress after he had been elected to the Senate.

# DEATH

Johnson died on July 31, 1875, at Stover Farm, Carter's Station, Carter County, Tennessee, where his daughter lived near the Isaac Lincoln house on the Watauga River. On July 30, Johnson suffered a stroke. He refused to let the family send for a doctor. The next afternoon, a second stroke left him unconscious, and although the doctors were called, he died. He left no will, although his estate was valued at more than $100,000.

The house has been moved to Elizabethton (Fudd Town) and is located on West Elk Avenue.

# FUNERAL

The funeral was held on August 3, in Greeneville, Tennessee. The body was taken from Stover Farm to Greeneville, where it reposed in a beautiful, large, metal casket with silver mountings. His wish, expressed years before, to "let the Stars and Stripes be my winding sheet, and pillow my head with the Constitution of the United States" was carried out. An American flag was wrapped around his body, and his head was rested on his copy of the Constitution. The funeral was conducted by Masonic Mother Lodge 119, of which he and Andrew Jackson had been members. Dignitaries from throughout Tennessee and from Washington attended the funeral held at the courthouse. The courthouse was located on the site of the present courthouse, on the corner of Main and Depot Streets.

# BURIAL

The grave site is located in Greeneville, in the Andrew Johnson Cemetery, on Monument

Avenue, in the southern part of the city. Memphis, Nashville, and Knoxville each wanted the privilege of providing the grave site. For several years, his grave remained unmarked. Then the family, at their own expense, erected an impressive monument—a shaft of marble, draped with the Stars and Stripes, and on its crest an American eagle. The burial spot had been marked by a willow tree, grown from a shoot, he had planted years before; it in turn was from one grown at Napoleon's tomb at St. Helena. More than 5,000 people attended the burial.

## SPECIAL SITES

*Tusculum, Tennessee.* Tusculum College. Andrew Johnson Collection.

## BIBLIOGRAPHY

Graf, Leroy P. et al, eds. *The Papers of Andrew Johnson, Vol. 1.* Knoxville: University of Tennessee Press, 1967.

Thomas, Lately. *The First President Johnson.* New York, William Morrow & Company, 1968.

Trefousse, Hans L. *Andrew Johnson: A Biography.* New York, W. W. Norton and Company, 1989.

# ULYSSES SIMPSON GRANT

### 1822–1885
### 18TH PRESIDENT 1869–1877; REPUBLICAN PARTY

*"I will not hire a house at the capital and direct the war from an armchair in Washington."*

—*New York Tribune, March 10, 1864*

Ulysses S. Grant was born on April 27, 1822, to Jesse Root and Hannah Simpson Grant. Grant was fourth cousin once removed of Franklin Delano Roosevelt and sixth cousin once removed of Grover Cleveland. In his book, *Your Family Tree*, David Starr Jordan traces Grant's ancestry back to William the Conqueror.

## CHARACTERISTICS

As a boy of seventeen Grant weighed 117 pounds and stood 5′1″ tall, but grew to be almost 5′8″ tall and weighed more than 150 pounds. He was a good-looking man, with blue eyes and wavy brown hair, which was nearly always a bit mussed. His thin lips and false teeth were hidden by a full beard and mustache.

He enjoyed playing cards. He loved horses and was able to do anything with them. At West Point, he spoke of wasting his time reading novels, "although not of the cheap kind." His paintings show talent. He had little patience for sitting still and, if not doodling, he would whittle a small stick into nothing, making nothing.

He enjoyed smoking. He began by smoking a pipe and later switched to cigars, which he smoked at the rate of 20 a day. This

# A LIFE IN REVIEW

**Birth:** April 27, 1822; Point Pleasant, OH

**Died:** July 23, 1885; Mount McGregor, NY

**Married:** Julia Boggs Dent; August 22, 1848; 3 sons, 1 daughter

## CAREER

**1843–1854** Military Service

**1854** Farming and real estate

**1860** Working in father's store

**1861–1865** Military Service

**1867–1868** Secretary of War

## ADMINISTRATION EVENTS

**1869** Transcontinental rail service began

**1869** Black Friday financial panic

**1870** Fifteenth Amendment ratified

**1872** Credit Mobilier stock scandal

**1876** Custer's Last Stand at Little Big Horn

# BIRTHPLACE

Grant was born in Point Pleasant, in Claremont County, about 25 miles east of Cincinnati, Ohio. He was born at about 5:00 A.M., in a small one-story house, which has been restored, at the corner of Routes 232 and 52, at the Ohio State Memorial.

# BAPTISM

There is no record of an early baptism. His mother was a pious Methodist who saw to it that her husband and five other children were baptized but somehow Grant was not. Towards the end of his life, when Grant was almost in a coma and without his consent, it is said that the Reverend John P. Newman sprinkled him with water and baptized him, in the cottage at Mount McGregor, New York, on May 28, 1885.

He was named Hiram Ulysses and at home was called "Lys." When he arrived at West Point with the initials H.U.G. showing on his trunk, he was so embarrassed that he began signing his name, Ulysses H. Grant. Later, an administrator at West Point misread the U. H. and made it U.S. Grant on the records, and this designation stayed with him for the rest of his life. Further, his nickname at West Point was "Sam," which followed from U.S. Grant. In a letter to his future wife, Julia, he asked her to suggest a name beginning with S which he might use.

may have contributed to the mouth cancer he suffered in later years. Rare steak made him sick. He wanted his meat charred to a crisp. He did not hunt. He was prudish, and in the army he always bathed alone in a closed tent.

He wrote of an experience in Mexico in 1848. "Every Sunday there was a bull fight for the amusement of those who pay their fifty cents. I attended one of them—just one—not wishing to leave the country without having witnessed the national sport. The sight to me was sickening. I could not see how human beings could enjoy the suffering of beasts, and often of men, as they seemed to do on these occasions."

# CHURCH

His mother Hannah led the family along religious paths. She was a firm Methodist and strove to live "unspotted from the world." While still at home, Grant attended church regularly, and, like other children of the time, observed the Sabbath.

Attending church was not his favorite pastime, and he probably attended because it was

*Point Pleasant, Ulysses S. Grant birthplace.*

the thing to do; after marriage it may have been because his wife Julia wanted him to. One writer, describing his attitude towards the ceremonies of the church, says the last thing that would have brought him near to God was music. There is no mention of religion in his memoirs.

**1822–1823** *Point Pleasant, Ohio.* Methodist Church. Grant Memorial Church, now occupying the site, was built in 1868. It stands near the Grant house at the corner of Ohio 232 and US 52.

**1823–1839** *Georgetown, Ohio.* Methodist Church directly across the street from his house, now the corner of Grant and North Water Streets. The first church building in Georgetown had two front doors, one for the men and the other for the women. The site is an empty lot now.

**1839–1843** *West Point.* Attendance at Episcopal chapel was required. See the old chapel near the West Point Cemetery.

In a letter, he wrote, "We are not only obliged to go to church but must march there by companys."

**1843–1849** *Sackets Harbor, New York.* Presbyterian Church.

**1848–** *St. Louis, Missouri.* After marriage, he attended the First Methodist Church with Julia regularly. She became a member, but he never did.

**1849–** *Detroit, Michigan.* St. Paul's Church, Shelby and Congress Streets. He also attended the Methodist Church, which was at Gratiot Avenue and Library Avenue.

**1851–1852** *Sackets Harbor, New York.* Presbyterian Church.

**1860–** *Galena, Illinois.* Methodist Church, 125 South Bench Street. There is a plaque marking Grant's pew in the First Methodist Church.

*Grant Memorial Church.*

were already in progress and the church crowded. The president started down the center aisle to the front pew which he understood was reserved for him. Embarrassed to find it occupied and following an exchange of stares, the first family turned, left the church, and went to occupy their rented pew in the First Presbyterian Church.

**1865–1877** *Washington, D.C.* First Presbyterian Church, Marshall Place at four and one half Street. A ledger entry shows he held pew number 69.

**1865–1877** *Washington, D.C.* Old Adas Israel Synagogue, G Street at Third, originally at Sixth and G Streets, NW. It is no longer a synagogue.

*Long Branch, New Jersey.* St. James Episcopal Chapel, known as the Church of the Presidents, Ocean Boulevard near Takanasses Bridge. It is now the museum and headquarters of the Long Branch Historical Society.

**1873** *Covington, Kentucky.* Union Methodist Episcopal Church (now First Methodist), corner of Fifth and Greenup Streets, where his father was a member and where his father's funeral was held in 1873. See also Spring Grove Cemetery where his father is buried.

**1865–1877** *Washington, D.C.* Metropolitan Memorial Methodist Church, now at Nebraska and New Mexico Avenues, NW. The building where he attended at John Marshall Place and C Streets, NW, is no longer standing, and a building serving the District of Columbia is there. He occupied a pew at this church a great part of the time, but he is recorded as having paid pew rent for a time at least in one other Washington church. On the Sunday after his inauguration, the Grant family arrived at the church where services

## EDUCATION

**1827–1839** *Georgetown, Ohio.* The old Grant schoolhouse has been preserved at Second and South Water Streets. Grant learned the fundamentals at subscription schools when he started school in 1827 and later at the brick school on Dutch Hill. He also attended the little brick building on Grant Avenue which was built as a schoolhouse but later became a house belonging to Mrs. Charles Thompson, at the corner of North Apple and East Grant Avenue, where he began to attend in 1829.

**1836–1837** *Maysville, Kentucky.* Richardson and Rand's subscription school (also called Maysville Academy), West Fourth Street. He lived with an aunt at the time.

**1838–1839** *Ripley, Ohio.* He attended Ripley College, a Presbyterian academy run by John Rankin, Third and Mulberry Streets.

**1839–1843** *West Point, New York.* West Point Military Academy. He graduated twenty-first out of 39 cadets in 1843. He was most outstanding in his handling of horses. He did not like West Point and was happy when he left.

## MARRIAGE AND HONEYMOON

Grant was married on August 22, 1848, in St. Louis, Missouri. He married Julia Dent at the home of her parents, Colonel and Mrs. Dent, at Fourth and Cerre Streets—a modest two-story, four-chimneyed, brick structure. Grant's proposal to Julia was romantic. The story is that as they were driving in a buggy across a flooded bridge, she cried, "I'm going to cling to you no matter what happens." Safely over, he asked, "How would you like to cling to me for the rest of your life?" He first proposed marriage May 1844.

They spent the first night at Julia's home in St. Louis. After a long boat ride on the Mississippi, they visited Grant's parents and relations in Ohio. At the end of his leave, he reported to his post at Sacket's Harbor, New York. Julia wrote, "The day following our wedding, Mr. Grant and I started on a visit to his friends in Ohio by boat to Louisville." In Louisville, they visited some of Grant's cousins and sailed up the Ohio from Louisville to Cincinnati and took the stage to Bethel, home of Grant's parents. They visited Grant's friends in Cincinnati, Georgetown, Maysville, and Bethel and returned home to St. Louis about the middle of October. He left St. Louis late in November to join the Fourth Infantry in Detroit, Michigan.

## HOMES

**1822–1823** *Point Pleasant, Clermont County, Ohio.* Corner of Ohio 232 and Ohio 52, where he was born. It is a one-story saltbox house with two rooms. Before it became a national historical site, Michael Hirsh, the owner, stated that if a sufficient sum were offered, he would sell the house and that he could sell it piecemeal; he did sell a window catch for $5 and many splinters.

**1823–1840** *Georgetown, Brown County, Ohio.* 219 Grant Avenue (northwest corner of Main Cross and Water Streets) in a two-story brick house. A veranda and a concrete wall were added in 1909.

**1840–1843** *Bethel, Ohio.* Corner of West Plane and North Charity, now the site of a laundromat. His father and family moved here while he was away at West Point. Grant writes, "Opposite our house in Bethel stood the old stage tavern." Grant spent his vacations away from West Point here. He and his bride visited his parents here in 1848 while on their honeymoon. His father and mother lived here from 1840 to 1854. During most of the time from 1839 to 1843, he was studying at West Point and only spent vacations in Bethel.

**1843–1849** *Sackets Harbor, New York.* Madison Barracks, Pike Street. Despite popular legend about Grant's fondness for liquor, he is reported to have organized the Sons of Temperance in Sackets Harbor. While in Sackets Harbor, he often stayed at the Union Hotel, now a visitor center with orientation show.

## LODGINGS

**1848–1854** *St. Louis, Missouri.* Southwest corner, Fourth and Cerre Streets, just after marriage. One source says the Grants lived with Julia's parents at White Haven, on Gravois Road, until they completed their

*Detroit home of Julia and Ulysses Grant.*

own log house called Hardscrabble. He often lodged here after 1854.

**1848–1849** *Detroit, Michigan.* National Hotel, corner of Woodward Avenue and Cadillac Square. After a few weeks, he moved to a small frame house at 253 Fort Street East.

**1848–** *Detroit, Michigan.* Exchange Hotel, southwest corner of Jefferson Avenue and Shelby, where he attended weekly balls. He did not dance but stood around looking bored.

**1849–1850** *Detroit, Michigan.* East Fort Street. Julia writes, "Ulys secured a sweet, pretty home which had been occupied by Quartermaster E.S. Sibley for several years. Next winter we messed with Major John H. Gore. This arrangement was much more economical as there was but one house and one set of servants to be kept." This house has been moved to the State Fair Grounds.

**1850–1851** *Detroit, Michigan.* He rented a house on the northeast corner of Jefferson Avenue and Russell Street from W. A. Bacon and shared it with Captain J.H. Gore to cut expenses for both his family and the Gores.

**1854–1855** *White Haven, outside St. Louis,*

*Missouri.* The home of Julia's father, on Gravois Road.

**1855–** *St. Louis, Missouri.* The farm of Lewis Dent, on the Dent estate, White Haven. It was about a mile and a half south of the White Haven house.

**1854–** *Covington, Kentucky.* 520 Greenup Street, where he visited his parents. In January, 1862, Grant sent his wife and children here to live while he was on active duty. His father had a leather goods store on Madison Avenue.

**1856–1857** *St. Louis, Missouri.* Hardscrabble was completed in the summer of 1856. The current location is 10581 Gravois Road. It was built on 60 acres of land southwest of St. Louis, given to him by his father-in-law. It is now known as the Grant log cabin. It is on the Anheuser-Busch estate and open to the public. Julia wrote, "I cannot imagine why he ever built it, as we were then occupying Wish-ton-Wish (Whitehaven)." They lived in it scarcely three months before her mother died, and her father insisted they come to him at White Haven, where they lived for about a year and a half. Later, he traded the Hardscrabble farm for a house and lot at Ninth and Barton Streets in St. Louis, but the new owner could not fulfill the agreement, and the farm came back to him in 1867.

**1858–1860** *St. Louis, Missouri.* Seventh and Lynch Streets. He took a small frame house by the river. Julia Grant wrote, "The Captain (Grant) went up to St. Louis early in March and secured a neat little house for us which was simple but comfortably furnished."

**1858–1859** *St. Louis, Missouri.* 209 South Fifteenth Street, where he stayed with Harry and Louisa Boggs while working in the real estate business, but he went home every weekend to White Haven.

**1859–1860** *St. Louis.* Ninth and Barton Streets.

*Now called the General Grant House, a two-story shuttered house, where his family stayed during part of the Civil War in Burlington, New Jersey.*

**1860–1861**   *Galena, Illinois.* 121 High Street. This was Grant's first house in Galena. He lived here with his family in 1861. The family remained here throughout most of the war. There is a D.A.R. marker. The area is called Cemetery Hill. There were 200 steps up from Main Street to the house.

**1862–1865**   *Burlington, New Jersey.* 309 Wood Street, now called the General Grant House, is a graceful two-story shuttered house, where his family stayed during part of the Civil War. He is said to have been in residence here the night Lincoln was assassinated.

**1865–**   *Galena, Illinois.* Grant Memorial Home, 510 Bouthillier Street which was presented to Grant on August 19, 1865, by grateful townspeople. The china and silver used by the Grants in the White House are displayed in the dining room. Later, in 1880, Grant retired here but left for New York City a year later.

**1865–**   *Philadelphia, Pennsylvania.* 2009 Chestnut Street. A four-story brick house, brownstone trimming, eighteen-room, was given to him by admirers. He visited but never lived here, preferring to live in Burlington, New Jersey. The house was rented after he became president.

**1865–1869**   *Washington, DC.* 205 I Street, NW, which he sold when he became president, is a large two-story double house with extensive grounds for which he paid $30,000.

**1869–1877**   *Washington, D.C.* The White House.

**1875**   *Long Branch, New Jersey.* 991 Ocean Avenue was bought by friends and given to President Grant, who came here every sum-

*Grant Cottage, where he and his family stayed while he wrote his memoirs and where he died.*

mer of his two terms as president and many times during the rest of his life. It was a 3-story structure with seven dormers and twenty-eight rooms. He was the first president to have a summer White House.

**1880**  *Galena, Illinois.* 510 Bouthillier Street.

**1880–1885**  *New York City, New York.* 3 East Sixty-sixth Street was a reddish brown limestone house, four stories high.

**1885**  *Wilton, New York.* Grant Cottage, off Route 9, eight miles north of Saratoga Springs, where he and his family stayed while he wrote his memoirs and where he died. The living room, dining room, and office contain the furniture used by the Grants. The house sits in the midst of a correctional institution and is not always open to the public. The front porch, where he sat with his hat on, the view he saw of the Hudson River, the distant mountains of Vermont, and the valley to Albany are all rewarding aspects of a visit to Grant's cottage.

# WORK

**1835–1839**  *Georgetown, Ohio.* As a boy he worked in his father's tannery across Main Cross Street from his home. Later it was the site of Single's grist mill and is now an empty lot. At the age of eight, he was driving the draft horses, and, by the time he was eleven, he was plowing and sawing firewood.

**1839–1843**  *West Point, New York.* West Point Military Academy.

**1854–1858**  *St. Louis, Missouri.* Farming at Hardscrabble.

**1858–1859**  *St. Louis, Missouri.* Real estate agency business in partnership with Julia's cousin Harry Boggs. The business office was located in a room with the law firm of McClellan, Hillyer and Moody in an old French mansion on Pine Street.

**1859**  *St. Louis, Missouri.* He worked for a few months at the United States Customs House, southeast corner of Third and Olive Streets. It was demolished in 1941.

**1860–1861**  *Galena, Illinois.* 120 South Main. See the marker showing the site where Grant worked in his father's store. There is a reconstructed Grant Leather Store at 211 South Main.

**1860–1861**  *Lafayette, Indiana.* Reynolds House, 622 Main Street, where Grant visited his West Point classmate, General Joseph Reynolds, when he learned he had been offered the commission of colonel of the 21st Illinois Regiment.

**1865–**  *Washington, D.C.* Winder Building, F Street, NW. The Winder Building was used as Union Army Headquarters U.S. ("Unconditional Surrender") Grant had offices here. Grant's headquarters, 604 Seventeenth Street, NW, at the corner of F Street, across from the Winder Building on the southwest corner. This building was the first to have central heating in Washington. Lincoln often came here to see people. It was demolished in the 1940s.

**1865–1868**   *Washington, D.C.* Secretary of War *ad interim.*

**1869–1877**   *Washington, D.C.* President of the United States.

**1881–1884**   *New York City, New York.* 2 Wall Street, at the corner of Wall Street, where he had his office as president of the Mexican Southern Railroad.

## MILITARY SERVICE

**1844**   *St. Louis, Missouri.* He was stationed at Jefferson Barracks, alternate 67 and Bypass 50, southeast of Kirkwood.

**1844–1845**   *Camp Salubrity, near Nachitoches, Louisiana.* He lived in a tent. In August, he was at Camp Necessity, five miles northwest of Nachitoches.

**1845–1846**   *Corpus Christi, Texas.*

**1846**   *Palo Alto, northeast of Brownsville, Texas.* See the Palo Alto Battlefield National Historical Site. Resaca de la Palma, Texas.

**1848**   *Detroit, Michigan.* Fort Wayne, at 6325 West Jefferson Street, at Livernois Avenue.

**1848**   *Sackets Harbor, New York.* Madison Barracks. See Sacket Mansion on Main Street for pamphlet guide.

**1849–1851**   *Detroit, Michigan.* Fort Wayne. House at 253 East Fort Street. The house was moved to the Michigan State Fair Grounds, Woodward Avenue and Eight Mile Road, in 1937. Barracks were located on the south side of Gratiot Avenue, centering about Russell Street.

**1852**   *Governor's Island, New York.*

**1852–1853**   *Fort Vancouver, Washington.* He was transferred here and travelled via Panama-Aspinwall, Cruces to San Francisco and to Fort Vancouver (previously called Columbia Barracks and located about eight miles north of Portland). He shared a house with several officers. It is

now maintained as the Ulysses S. Grant Museum, 1106 East Evergreen Boulevard.

**1853–1854**   *Bucksport, near Eureka, California.* 3431 Fort Avenue, Fort Humboldt State Historic Park, where he was stationed and resigned from the army in 1854, going from here to New York to Bethel, Ohio, and then to White Haven in St. Louis. Briefly, in 1853 he was stationed at Fort Gaston near Hoopa, California.

**1861**   *Galena, Illinois.* Jo Daviess County Courthouse, 312 North Bench Street, where Captain Grant volunteered for duty at a mass meeting in April. He organized the Galena volunteers.

**1861**   *Matoon, Illinois.* He mustered the 21st Illinois infantry in June 1861. There is a marker on the Illinois Central Depot.

**1861**   *Springfield, Illinois.* Camp Yates on the outskirts, on the old Jacksonville road west of Springfield. There is a campsite marker here. He was at the State Capitol part of the time serving as an aide to the Governor for the first few days of May. He stayed at the Principle Hotel and boarded at Chenery House.

**1861**   *Anna, Illinois.* He camped here in May 1861.

**1861**   *St. Louis, Missouri.* Jefferson Barracks, Telegraph Road south of US 67 on the Mississippi River.

**1861**   *Cape Girardeau, Missouri.* He was in command of the district of southwest Missouri.

**1861**   *Perry, Illinois.* Grant's campsite was on the Perry-Naples road, north of Valley City and east of Perry. There is a marker on the site where Grant camped with the 21st Regiment on July 8.

**1861**   *Cairo, Illinois.* 609 Ohio Street. Grant's headquarters. During part of his stay, his family lived in rooms opposite his office. In Cairo, his Civil War command truly began. St. Charles Hotel at Ohio and

Second Streets, which was later known as the Halliday Hotel, burned in 1943. One wing of the hotel remains.

**1861** *Louisville, Kentucky.* Galt House, Second and Main Streets. There is a marker at the site of the hotel where Grant was a guest.

**1861** *Paducah, Kentucky.* Grant Landing, First and Broadway on the wharf. There is a marker on the site where Grant arrived in the fall of 1861, proclaimed martial law, and stated that the Union Army was taking possession of Paducah "to defend you" against Confederate attack. Paducah was taken without a battle in September. There is a marker at North Eighth and Julia Streets. Wallace headquarters, northwest corner Sixth and Clark Streets, was where Grant was a guest of General Lew Wallace. Fort Anderson, at Trimble Street, between Fourth and Fifth, is the site of fortifications built by Grant.

**1861** *Smithland, Kentucky.* This was the staging area for his campaign against Fort Donelson at the junction of the Ohio and Cumberland Rivers.

**1862** *Fort Jefferson, Kentucky.*

**1862** *St. Francisville, Louisiana.* Fairview Plantation, which Grant used for a time, and which was also a hospital.

**1862** *Monroe City, Missouri.* Monroe Seminary Building, Third Street. Grant routed the Confederates at Monroe City.

**1862** *Fort Henry, Tennessee.* This fort on the east bank of the Tennessee River was captured by Grant.

**1862** *Fort Donelson, Tennessee.* Captured by Grant. Here he won national prominence. See the Fort Donelson National Battlefield, Route 79, west of Dover, on the west bank of the Cumberland River. The Dover Hotel, Petty Street, is the site of the formal unconditional surrender to Grant. This was the first important victory of the

Civil War and started Grant on the way to the White House.

**1862** *Bolivar, Tennessee.* Magnolia Manor, 418 North Main Street, served as his headquarters.

**1862** *Jackson, Tennessee.* Grant's Command Post. There is a marker on the building, 512 East Main Street. He occupied the house of James Lyon at this site before the Battle of Shiloh.

**1862** *Savannah, Tennessee.* Cherry Mansion at the west edge of town where the road branches north. Grant's headquarters. He was breakfasting here when the cannon began to fire at Pittsburg landing. See also Pittsburg Landing.

**1862** *Shiloh (Pittsburg Landing), Tennessee.* On the west bank of the Tennessee River, on the ridge dividing the waters of the Snake and Lick Creeks, Grant compelled a Confederate withdrawal. See the Shiloh National Park on Tennessee 22. Grant's army was camped around Shiloh Methodist Church. More people died in two days here than had in the Revolutionary War, the War of 1812, and the Mexican War combined.

**1862** *Memphis, Tennessee.* The Gayoso House. He was here for several weeks with his family. He had headquarters at Milliken's Bend, Hunt-Phelan House, 533 Beale Street.

**1862** *Corinth, Mississippi.* Grant's Headquarters. Fred Elgin House (private), 615 Jackson Street. There is a marker on US 45.

**1862** *Holly Springs, Mississippi.* Coxe-Dean house, 330 Salem Avenue. Grant occupied a house designed like a Swiss chalet. There is a marker on Salem Avenue. He also had headquarters at Airliewood, which was built in 1858. At Walter Place, 331 West Chulahoma Avenue, Mrs. Grant waited for General Grant when Van Dorn captured the city.

**1862** *Iuka, Mississippi.* Headquarters, Brinley home, Eastport Street.

**1863**   *Newellton, Louisiana.* Near here are Grant's winter headquarters at the time of his Vicksburg campaign. The house used was said to be the oldest house in the parish. The house of Dr. Haller Nutt, on the road between Milliken's Bend and Hard Times Landing, was spared when Julia Nutt begged Grant to spare the house in exchange for feeding and quartering the troops.

**1863**   *Port Gibson, Mississippi.* L.P. Williams House, northwest corner Church and Walnut Streets. Standing on the porch here, Grant is reported to have said, "Port Gibson is too beautiful to burn." The Port Gibson Battlefield is on US route 61. The victory here secured his Mississippi bridgehead.

**1863**   *Champion's Hill, Mississippi, on the old Edwards-Bolton highway, twenty miles east of Vicksburg on I- 20.* Grant's headquarters were at the Champion house. The Union victory was decisive. The battlefield is not open to the public.

**1863**   *Grand Gulf Military Park, Mississippi.* Located eight miles west of Highway 61 on Grand Gulf Road.

**1863**   *Natchez, Mississippi.* Rosalie, at the foot of South Broadway. He and his family lodged here for some time.

**1863**   *Vicksburg, Mississippi.* Grant captured the fortress and the town following a siege. Headquarters were located on the heights of Vicksburg in a large white colonial house. Vicksburg National Military Park, entrance east end of Clay Street at Memorial Arch. During the forty-seven-day siege which began in May, his headquarters were to the northeast of Vicksburg. The surrender which was received at Pemberton's headquarters, the Stone House, sealed the fate of the Confederacy. The Union Army raised the Stars and Stripes over the Warren County Courthouse. Balfour House, 1002 Crawford Street, was Union headquarters after Vicksburg fell. It is a bed and breakfast

now. Court House, 1008 Cherry Street hosted Grant in 1863.

**1863**   *Decatur, Alabama.* Burleson-Hinds Mansion (McEntire House). Grant was here for a war conference in 1863.

**1863**   *Chattanooga, Tennessee.* Brown's Ferry. When he first arrived, he used Brown's Ferry as the site of the first series of operations to relieve the Union troops who were under siege in Chattanooga. Brown's Ferry is on Brown's Ferry Road south of Chattanooga. Chattanooga Battlefields, between McCallie Avenue and East Third Street, is a seven-acre reservation on the site where Grant had his field headquarters. He observed the attack on Missionary Ridge from Orchard Knob Ridge (named for the fruit trees it bore). The battlefield is at the intersection of I- 59 and I-75.

**1863**   *Chattanooga, Tennessee.* Brabson House, 407 East Fifth Street, was headquarters for Union officers. It was later used as a hospital. At Lookout Mountain, see Point Park. This was called the Battle Above the Clouds, 1100 Brow Road. By his victory, Grant secured the railway center of Chattanooga. One of the historic sites on Lookout Mountain is Cravens House, halfway up the slope. Cravens House changed hands several times and served as headquarters for both sides during the fighting. The writing desk used by Grant can be seen here.

**1863**   *Missionary Ridge (west of Chattanooga), Tennessee.* This was the site of Confederate General Bragg's headquarters. Grant succeeded in pushing the Confederates off the ridge, which secured the Union's hold on Chattanooga.

**1863–**   *Fort Monroe, Virginia.* Lincoln and Grant were both guests here. From 1-64 take either Virginia 143 or 169 and follow signs to Fort Monroe.

**1864**   *Cincinnati, Ohio.* Grant headquarters, 739 West Eighth Street. He stayed here in

March 1864. However his table here was too small for maps and he adjourned to the Burnett House to work out strategy.

**1864**  *Washington, D.C.* Willard's Hotel. Here he met Lincoln for the first time. On March 8, he walked into the hotel and asked for a room. The clerk said he had only a top floor room. Grant said that would do and signed the register. When the clerk took a look at the name he jumped fast to assign Grant the best room in the house.

**1864**  *Culpeper, Virginia.* He commandeered the Virginia Hotel, corner of North Main and West Cameron, for his headquarters before the 1864 campaign. The Massaponax Church, built in 1859, was a rendezvous point in a number of troop movements, especially in Grant's 1864 Wilderness-to-Cold Harbor campaign. The building is best remembered because of a series of photographs taken of Grant and the ranking generals in the Army of the Potomac, all seated in the yard on church pews.

**1864**  *North Anna Battlefield, Virginia.* Grant launched a series of assaults. None of the battlefield is preserved today. Five miles south of Carmel Church, U.S. 1 crosses the North Anna virtually in the center of the battle area. Carmel Church, US 1. Long Creek about two and one-half miles south, where Grant's troops took Confederate earthworks. Mount Carmel Church was Grant's headquarters in May 1864.

**1864**  *Spottsylvania Battlefield, Virginia.* Virginia 613, southwest of Fredericksburg.

**1864**  *Charles City County, Virginia.* His army passed the Charles City Court House on the way to the James River. See Marker V-12. He crossed the James River with his army at Flower de Hundred just east of Maycocks.

**1864**  *Cold Harbor, Virginia.* He suffered his greatest repulse here. See the visitor center in Richmond at 3215 East Broad Street. His headquarters here were in a tent, southeast of Richmond, on Virginia 156.

**1864–1865**  *Petersburg, Virginia.* Wallace-Seward House, 204 South Market Street, was occupied as headquarters and is where he discussed the terms of the surrender with Lincoln.

**1865**  *Hopewell, Virginia.* Located near Appomattox Manor (also known as Eppes House). General Grant used this as his headquarters during the siege of Petersburg. Lincoln stayed here for several weeks while waiting for Richmond to fall.

**1865**  *Nottaway, Virginia.* He occupied the courthouse (built 1839–1843) on April 5.

**1865**  *Appomattox, Virginia.* Appomattox Court House, National Historical Park on Virginia State 24, three miles northeast of Appomattox. There are a number of markers along State 24 indicating Grant and Lee headquarters. See McLean's House where the Confederate surrender took place. "In a naked little parlor, containing a table and two or three chairs." The chair in which he sat to arrange Lee's surrender was given to the United States government in 1905.

**1865**  *Chicago, Illinois.* Chicago Historical Society, Clark Street at North Avenue, has the table on which the Grant-Lee surrender terms were signed.

**1865**  *Washington, D.C.* Final review of the Army of the Republic. In 1866, Congress bestowed on him the rank of full general, which had been held by no other American since Washington.

# TRAVEL/VISITS

**1859**  *St. Louis, Missouri.* Old Courthouse Fourth Street to Broadway and Market to Chestnut Street, where Grant freed his only slave.

**1861**  *Springfield, Illinois.* He took command of his regiment at the Fair Grounds, and went from here to Mexico, Missouri, and finally to his headquarters in Cairo, Illinois.

**1863–** *Summer Hill, Virginia.* Off County Route 605, a sign points to Summer Hill. At various times, Grant occupied the house here. The modest frame house still belongs to the Newton family, but visitors are welcomed.

**1864–1865** *Washington, D.C.* Decatur Mansion, corner of Lafayette Square and H Street, NW. A three-story house with a parlor that was one of the largest in Washington, was Grant's headquarters. In April, he stayed in Willard's Hotel but left the day before the assassination and returned afterwards.

**1864** *St. Louis, Missouri.* He visited Washington University.

**1865** *Albany, New York.* He attended a military review at the state capitol where an overloaded grandstand collapsed.

**1865** *Atlanta, Georgia.* He stayed in the building now known as Ivy Street Hospital, formerly a large boarding house. This was just after the end of the Civil War, and it was his only visit to Atlanta.

**1865** *Boston, Massachusetts.* Faneuil Hall.

**1865** *Detroit, Michigan.* Biddle House on Woodbridge Street. He was also entertained at the home of Senator Zacharia Chandler at Second and Fort Streets.

**1865** *Galena, Illinois.* There was a parade on Main Street for his triumphal return, and he lodged at DeSoto House. He had his presidential campaign headquarters here in 1868 and 1872.

**1865** *New York City, New York.* Lodged in Astor House.

**1865** *Richmond, Virginia.* He was on a fact finding trip for President Johnson, and he stayed with Julia's sister and her husband. He also visited Raleigh, North Carolina, Charlestown, South Carolina, and Savannah and Augusta, Georgia.

**1865** *Saratoga Springs, New York.* Grand Union Hotel on Broadway. On July 4 a grand ball was held in his honor while he was staying there. The hotel was demolished in 1952.

**1865** *Schenectady, New York.* He received an honorary degree from Union College.

**1865** *York, Pennsylvania.* He was accompanying President Andrew Johnson. He lodged in the Washington House, which hosted many important people. While in York, he went to the home of Erastus Weiser to see some fine horses.

**1866** *Cincinnati, Ohio.* Spencer House, Front and Broadway, where he was entertained lavishly.

**1868** *Chicago, Illinois.* John L. Wilson house, 1145 South Wabash Avenue.

**1868** *Greensboro, Pennsylvania.* Monongahela House, north side of County Street, near the river.

**1868** *Hollywood, Pennsylvania.* Tyler Hotel on Pennsylvania 255 near the Elk County line.

**1868** *Upland, Pennsylvania.* Old Wilcox-Kane-Clay house, north of Wilcox on Wilcox-Clermont Road, near the McKean County line.

**1868** *Washington, Pennsylvania.* Washington Town Hall. He laid the cornerstone. At the time, he and Mrs. Grant were visiting friends, Mr. and Mrs. William W. Smith.

**1869–** *Baltimore, Maryland.* George Small house on Mount Vernon Place, where he was entertained several times.

**1869–** *Boston, Massachusetts.* Hotel Vendome on Commonwealth Avenue. The hotel originally had its long side and main entrance on Dartmouth Street, but much of that part of the structure was destroyed by a fire in 1975. Benjamin Harrison, Cleveland, and McKinley also stayed here.

**1869–** *Deer Park Hotel, off Maryland 135, as a favorite resort for the wealthy of Baltimore* *and Washington.* Grant, Benjamin Harrison, Cleveland and McKinley stayed here.

**1869–**    *Garrison, New York.* Hamilton Fish Hudson River estate, Glenclyffe. The Grant family often stayed here.

**1869**    *Boston.* St. James Hotel, West Newton Street. When this was first built, it was considered to be one of the most luxurious hotels in the South End.

**1869**    *Groton, Massachusetts.* Governor Boutwell House, opposite Town Hall, 279 Main Street.

**1869**    *Lakewood (then Bricksburg), New Jersey.* Bricksburg House (now Laurel House), north side of Main Street, west of Lexington Avenue.

**1869**    *New York City, New York.* On the northeast corner of Beekman and Gold Streets is the Old Beekman, a tavern and coffee house, where Grant is said to have imbibed his favorite Peoria whiskey.

**1869**    *Worcester, Massachusetts.* Bay Street Hotel on Bay Street, where he was honored at a dinner.

**1870**    *San Antonio, Texas.* He was a guest at the Menger Hotel on Alamo Plaza in its early rough and tumble years.

**1870s**    *Philadelphia, Pennsylvania.* George W. Childs house, Twenty-Second and Walnut. He was here again in 1877, the week before he left on his around-the-world tour.

**1873**    *Augusta, Maine.* Blaine House, across from the State Capitol.

**1873**    *Brunswick, Maine.* From Bowdoin College, he received an honorary degree. The ceremony was held at the First Parish Church, 9 Cleaveland Street. The reception was at the Chamberlain house, 226 Main Street, which is now a museum.

**1874**    *Springfield, Illinois.* He attended the dedication of the Lincoln National Monument at the tomb.

**1876**    *Salt Lake City, Utah.* He was the first president to visit while in office. The capi-

tol at the time was the Old Council House, which has burned.

**1876**    *Washington, D.C.* Grant unveiled the statue at the Freedman's Monument of Lincoln.

**1877–**    *Des Moines, Iowa.* Hoyt Sherman house, Woodland Avenue at Fifteenth Street. Hoyt was the brother of General Sherman who lived here in the 1870s, when Presidents Grant and McKinley were visitors.

**1879**    *Central City, Colorado.* Eureka Street. Teller House. Ex-president Grant walked along a path of solid silver bricks from his stagecoach to the hotel door.

**1879**    *Chicago, Illinois.* Palmer House, 17 East Monroe. He was in Chicago to attend a reunion of the Army of Tennessee.

**1879**    *Hartford, Connecticut.* He visited Mark Twain's home, 351 Farmington Avenue.

**1879**    *Little Rock, Arkansas.* Markham Hotel, 5170 West Markham, where he was entertained and also at the Capitol. The hotel has been restored.

**1879**    *Murphys, California.* He stayed at the famous Murphys Hotel.

**1879**    *Salt Lake City, Utah.* He lodged in the Walker House.

**1879**    *San Francisco, California.* He stayed at the Palace Hotel, Market and New Montgomery Streets.

**1880**    *Chicago.* Potter Palmer Mansion, Castle on the Drive, 1350 Lake Shore Drive.

**1880**    *Cumberland Island (near St. Mary's), Georgia.* He visited the ruins of Dungeness.

**1880**    *DeBary, Florida.* DeBary House, Sunrise Boulevard off US 17-92 and Mansion Road. Cleveland also visited here later. It is now being restored.

**1880**    *Enterprise, Florida.* Brock House, about three miles from De Bary Mansion, was razed in the 1930s. The United Methodist Children's Home now occupies the site.

**1880** *Green Cove Springs, Florida.* He stayed at the Old Magnolia Hotel. There is a new hotel on the site.

**1880** *Jacksonville, Florida.* He stayed at the St. James Hotel, west side of Laura Street between Duval and Church Streets, facing Henning Park. It was an elegant 500-room hotel, which burned in 1901, and is now the site of the May-Cohen Department store.

**1880** *Little Rock, Arkansas.* He attended a banquet for 250 in Concordia Hall.

**1880** *Mentor, Ohio.* He visited Garfield at his home.

**1880** *Mobile, Alabama.* He was a guest of the Cotton Exchange. There was an enthusiastic welcome and reception at the Custom House with a banquet and lodging at Battle House.

**1880** *Orange Park, Florida.* Park View Hotel, Kingsley Avenue on the river front. The hotel has been destroyed.

**1880** *Palatka, Florida.* Putnam House (Hotel), southwest corner of Reid and Second Streets. It burned in 1884. See the beautiful entry to Palatka along the St. Johns River.

**1880** *Sanford, Florida.* He inaugurated the South Florida Railroad while he was making a tour of Florida. The shovel he used is on display in the Henry Shelton Sanford Library and Museum on First Street. He stayed at Sanford House, located between Commercial and First Streets, which is now the site of the library.

**1880** *Savannah, Georgia.* Screven House, southeast corner of Bull and Congress Streets, is now the site of a bank building.

**1880s** *Chicago, Illinois.* Charles Farwell home, 120 East Pearson Street.

**1881** *Cairo, Illinois.* David Davis house, 1000 E. Monroe, "Clover Lane."

**1881** *New York City, New York.* Fifth Avenue Hotel before moving to 3 East Sixty-sixth Street.

**1877** He left May 17, 1877, for a "dream trip" around the world, where he was entertained by royalty and government leaders everywhere. The trip took two years and four months and is described in John Russell Young's *Around the World with General Grant (1879).* One author writes, "Grant's limited background and intellect left him almost completely unaffected by the educational opportunities of his trip around the world. In Berne he refused to be dragged to yet another cathedral. The narrow phlegmatic army officer who left the White House to see the world returned unimpaired by the experience." However, the account by Young shows a man who continued in his desire to see everything long after most of those in his party were ready to call it quits. He valued some sites more than others. In Naples, he made a tour of the city with a guide who said, "This is the picture of Mr. So and So who generously gave this museum to Naples." "Well," said Grant in an aside, "if I had a museum like this I would give it to Naples or whoever would take it." However, when he visited Pompeii, he said that Pompeii was one of the few things which had not disappointed his expectations, that the truth was more striking than imagination had painted, and that it was worth a journey over the sea to see and study its stately columns. Grant was very methodical in his arrangements. He mapped out his route for days ahead from maps and time tables, arranged the hour of his arrival and departure, and never varied from it.

# DEATH

Grant died on July 23, 1885, in Mount McGregor, New York, at about 8:00 A.M. In the spring of 1884, Grant noted pain in his throat. He went from 200 pounds in weight to 130. In June 1885, he moved to Mount McGregor, ten miles from Saratoga Springs, for rest and cure of the cancer and to work on his Memoirs. Those present reported that "He simply closed his eyes and it was over." It is on US 9 north of Saratoga Springs.

# FUNERAL

Grant's body was dressed in a Prince Albert black broadcloth suit and placed in a polished oak coffin with copper interior covered with dark purple velvet and fitted with solid silver handles. The military stood guard around the house as protection against relic hunters.

Mrs. Grant sat with her family in the parlor of Mount McGregor cottage and heard Methodist Bishop John P. Newman deliver a funeral sermon to a large crowd on the front lawn. After the funeral, the body was taken to Albany, where it lay in state in the state capitol on August 4, and was then removed to New York City, where it lay in state in City Hall between Broadway and Park Row. On August 8, an estimated one million people turned out for the funeral procession to the temporary burial site near the current Grant Tomb. President Cleveland and ex-presidents Hayes and Arthur attended at Riverside Drive.

# BURIAL

The line of march was up Broadway from City Hall to Fourteenth Street, west to Fifth Avenue, north to 57th Street, and again west to Broadway, which traverses Manhattan at an angle, north again to 72nd Street, then west to Riverside Drive, to the vault at One- hundred and 22nd Street. Gilmore's great band of 500 pieces played Miss Fanny Crosby's hymn "Safe in the Arms of Jesus" as the body of Grant was lowered into the vault. There was a military service at the tomb. Twice as many bricks were required for the tomb because of souvenir hunters.

President William McKinley formally dedicated Grant's Tomb, in New York City, where he was finally laid to rest in 1897. Benjamin Harrison had laid the cornerstone.

# SPECIAL SITES

*Washington, D.C.* The Grant Memorial on the Mall at First Street, SW, is one of the largest equestrian statues in the world. The monument has twelve horses, eleven soldiers, and four lions. It took the sculptor twenty-two years to complete. It was dedicated on April 27, 1922, on the 100th anniversary of Grant's birth.

# BIBLIOGRAPHY

Grant, Julia Dent. *The Personal Memoirs of Julia Dent Grant.* New York, G. F. Putnam's Sons, 1975.

Goldhurst, Richard. *Many are the Hearts: The Agony and Triumph of Ulysses S. Grant.* New York, Reader's Digest Press, distributed by Thomas Y. Crowell Co., 1975.

McFeeley, William S. *Grant: A Biography.* New York, W. W. Norton & Company, 1982.

Woodward, W.E. *Meet General Grant.* New York, Liveright, 1928.

# RUTHERFORD BIRCHARD HAYES

## 1822–1893
### 19TH PRESIDENT 1877–1881: REPUBLICAN PARTY

*"Politics and law are (or rather, should be) merely results, merely the expression of what the people wish."*

—*Letter, November 25, 1885*

Rutherford B. Hayes was born on October 4, 1822, at 9:30 P.M., in a west room of the family home of Rutherford (who died shortly before his son was born) and Sophia Birchard Hayes. His Uncle Sardis served as a father for him. Upon the birth of the future president, Uncle Sardis said, "I paid Dr. Lamb $3.50 for the job."

## CHARACTERISTICS

Hayes was a well-built, healthy-looking, handsome man. His average weight was 175 pounds. His height of 5′8″ puts him slightly below the average height for presidents. He had an intelligent look with a high forehead. He had blue eyes and dark brown hair, which turned white when he was president. He wore the full beard common to the era. His portraits show a straight nose, firm lips, and even teeth. He did not use tobacco but sometimes drank table wine. He enjoyed hunting and fishing, as well as swimming and ice skating and he liked to play chess at home.

# A LIFE IN REVIEW

**Birth:** October 4, 1822; Delaware, OH

**Died:** January 17, 1893; Fremont, OH

**Married:** Lucy Ware Webb; December 30, 1852; 7 sons, 1 daughter

## CAREER

**1845–1860** Lawyer

**1857–1861** Cincinnati city solicitor

**1861–1865** Military Service Civil War

**1865–1867** Member U.S. Congress

**1868** Governor of Ohio

**1876–1877** Governor of Ohio

## ADMINISTRATION EVENTS

**1877** First significant nationwide strike

**1879** Sex discrimination in law practice before Supreme Court abolished

**1880** First president to visit west coast while in office

# BIRTHPLACE

Hayes was born in Delaware, Ohio, at 51 East William Street, between Sandusky and Union Streets. The house is gone, but there is a small stone monument to mark the site. A service station now stands on the nearly unnoticed site.

# BAPTISM

Hayes was baptized on June 15, 1823, in Delaware, Ohio, at the Presbyterian Meeting House, which probably met in the Courthouse or in a private house, since the first church building was constructed in 1825. See the old Courthouse in the city center.

# CHURCH

He attended a number of different churches, including the Episcopalian, Presbyterian, Unitarian, and the Methodist to which he had the closest ties. After his marriage to Lucy at the end of 1852, he switched from the Episcopal church which he had been attending to Lucy's Methodist Church. In the White House, after breakfast, family and guests gathered in the library to listen to a chapter from the Bible and to repeat the Lord's Prayer.

During the Civil War, he came to admit for the first time a belief in God. He wrote in his diary, "But will I not take refuge in the faith of my fathers at last? Are we not all impelled to this? The great abyss, the unknown future— are we not happier if we give ourselves up to some settled faith? Am I not more and more carried along, drifted, towards surrendering to the best religion that the world has yet produced? It seems so."

**1822–1843** *Delaware, Ohio.* The Presbyterian Meeting House. At the time of his birth, people met in the courthouse or a private house. The original brick Courthouse was destroyed by fire in 1908. From 1825 to 1843, he attended the stone Presbyterian Church at 73 West Winter Street. The present First Presbyterian Church is built on the same site.

**1843–1845** *Boston, Massachusetts.* While attending Harvard Law School, he attended some church every Sunday, including Dr. Walker's, Parker's, and Dr. Kirk's.

**1845–1849** *Lower Sandusky (Fremont), Ohio.* He attended church regularly, usually the Episcopalian. St. Paul's Episcopal Church, northwest corner of Park and Court Streets. It still exists.

**1849–1852** *Cincinnati, Ohio.* He made it a point to appear on alternate Sundays at two leading churches—the Episcopalian and the Presbyterian (to show himself to the right people). The Presbyterian Church is on the north side of East Fourth Street, near Main Street. St. John's Episcopal Church, southeast corner Seventh and Plum Streets. The site is now a parking lot.

**1852–**   *Cincinnati, Ohio.* St. Paul's Methodist, southwest corner of Seventh and Smith, was torn down in 1937. See also Wesley Chapel, north side of Fifth Street between Sycamore and Broadway, 322 to 328 East Fifth. A note from an official of the church, responding to criticism of Hayes, said that Hayes did not join but that "he is a member in good and regular standing in the Methodist Episcopal Church here."

**1865–1867**   *Washington, D.C.* Foundry Methodist, Sixteenth and Church Streets, NW. See below 1877–1881.

**1867–1872**   *Columbus, Ohio.* First Methodist Church.

**1872–**   *Fremont (formerly Lower Sandusky), Ohio.* Methodist Episcopal Church (Hayes Memorial Methodist Church), northeast corner of Park and Birchard Avenues; now occupied by First Brethren Church. From 1881 to 1898, he was a trustee of the church and vice president of the county Bible Society.

**1877–1881**   *Washington, D.C.* Foundry Methodist Church, Sixteenth and Church Streets, NW. He was never officially a member, but he attended regularly and supported it generously. Washington society, aware that the Hayes regularly attended Methodist services, waited to see whether they would go to the fashionable Metropolitan Church (which the Grants frequented). On his first Sunday in Washington, he walked to the less pretentious Foundry Methodist Church and continued to worship there. The original Foundry was located at Fourteenth and G Streets, NW, and was disposed of in 1902. The proceeds were used to purchase the present site, and

the new building was dedicated in 1904. Foundry Church had a president's pew but one president, John Quincy Adams, came late and the pew was filled so he sat in a chair placed in the aisle.

**1880–**   *Cleveland, Ohio.* First Methodist Church, southwest corner of Erie and Euclid.

# EDUCATION

**1827–1833**   *Delaware, Ohio.* His mother taught him to read, spell, and write; later he learned from Daniel Granger, a traditional strict schoolmaster.

**1833–1835**   *Delaware, Ohio.* Corner of Franklin and Winter Streets in a stone building. His teacher was Miss Eliza Thompson, later Mrs. William Carson.

**1835–1836**   *Delaware, Ohio.* At a private grade school, operated by Dr. Hill's daughter, Mrs. Murray. He was chosen as the outstanding boy scholar. The private house at 15 North Franklin was built in 1821 and is a two-story brick house with hand-hewn timbers.

**1836–1837**   *Norwalk, Ohio.* Norwalk Academy, a Methodist school run by Jonah Chaplin, near 80 East Main Street, and now the site of Norwalk High School. Temporary classrooms were in the basement of the Methodist Church on East Seminary Street and in the Baptist Church at 67 East Main Street. While in school here, he attended the chapel at Norwalk Academy (Methodist) on East Seminary Street. He boarded in a house near 80 East Main.

**1837–1838**   *Middleton, Connecticut.* College preparatory at the academy of Isaac Webb. This was later absorbed into Wesleyan University. It was located on Wyllys Street to Lawn Avenue. The oldest building (1831), South Hall is on High Street. It was a dormitory when Hayes lodged there.

**1838–1842**   *Gambier, Ohio.* Kenyon College. He graduated as class valedictorian.

This Episcopalian school failed to make him a professed Christian, and, although he considered himself a Christian, he kept from professing Christ. The present Rosse Hall and Old Kenyon existed at the time he was a student. Rosse Hall on the college campus was built originally as the college chapel and used as such when Hayes was there. He lived in Old Kenyon, which was completely destroyed by fire in 1949, but the exterior of the current building is an exact replica of the original with the same stones in their original positions. There is a plaque at the entrance to the East Wing, where he lived during his four years at Kenyon.

**1842–1843** *Columbus, Ohio.* He studied law in the office of Thomas Sparrow and boarded with Dr. Peleg Sisson on the east side of High Street near Rich Street.

**1843–1845** *Cambridge, Massachusetts.* Harvard Law School, where he spent three semesters before returning to Ohio. He roomed and boarded at Mrs. Ford's, not far from the Dane Law School, where his classrooms were.

## MARRIAGE AND HONEYMOON

Hayes first met Lucy Webb in 1847, on the campus of the Ohio Wesleyan University, in Delaware, which she attended. On the campus there was a large beautiful park and in the center an immense sulphur spring where the ladies gathered in the evening and where the young men of the town made a point to come at the same time. It was here, while visiting his mother at his birthplace, that young Rutherford met the laughing and poplar Lucy Webb. The park is still there.

He courted Lucy at Cincinnati Wesleyan Female Academy. At the time, she had long flowing black hair, dark eyebrows, and beautiful eyes. Although still charming, she was a short chubby woman by the time she reached

*Birthplace of Lucy Webb Hayes, the first wife of a United States president to have earned a college degree.*

the White House. The Hayes celebrated their twenty-fifth wedding anniversary in the White House. Mrs. Hayes wore her wedding dress, which had been let out.

In Cincinnati, at the home of Dr. C. C. Comegys, he proposed. As he wrote in his diary, "On a sudden the impulse seized me ... I grasped her hand hastily in my own and with a smile. . .said I love you."

Hayes was married December 30, 1852, in Cincinnati, at 141 Sixth Street, the home of the bride. It was demolished and later became the site of the Clarion Hotel. The honeymoon took place in Columbus, Ohio, where they stayed with his sister, Fanny, and brother-in-law on High Street, near Spring. They took a second honeymoon in 1860 and went to Niagara Falls for three days and to Montreal, Quebec, Boston, and Vermont.

Lucy was the first wife of a United States president to have earned a college degree. A reference to Lucy Hayes as "first lady" is the first known appearance of the term in print. Of a large family, several of the children were

*Spiegel Grove is arranged and furnished with original pieces much as it was in the time of Hayes.*

youngsters during Hayes' administration, and news reports of the day describe family life in the White House as delightful.

## HOMES/LODGING

**1822–1842**   *Delaware, Ohio.* 51 Williams Street; there is a tablet at the spot. The site is now the location of a Standard Oil Company station.

**1842–1843**   *Columbus, Ohio.* High Street, near Spring, with his sister Fanny and her husband, William Platt. His mother's home in Delaware had been sold.

**1845–1849**   *Fremont, Ohio.* Thompson House, a little hotel located south of the junction of East State Street and Ohio Avenue and now the location of a tire store or muffler shop. He stayed here during his early years in law practice and before his

marriage. He also lodged with his uncle at 1829 Buckland Avenue (Vallett house) before 1852.

**1849–1852**   *Cincinnati, Ohio.* Room number 6 in the new law building on Third Street between Main and Sycamore. He also used the twelve-square-foot office for living quarters. He took his meals at a boarding house three squares off at Fourth and Vine Streets, operated by a Mrs. Fulton.

**1852–1853**   *Cincinnati, Ohio.* 141 West Sixth Street, the first home of the Hayes after marriage, has been demolished.

**1852–**   *Kingston, Ohio.* Elmwood, home of Lucy's Aunts Margaret Wood and Lucy Cook, for occasional visits.

**1852**   *Circleville, Ohio.* Boggs Farm, north of Chillicothe, 5769 Street, Route 361. He visited relatives. It is now the home of Charles Rittinger.

**1853–1872**    *Cincinnati.* 383 Sixth Street was a three-story, narrow red brick house with all the marks of middle-class respectability. It has been demolished. See Spring Grove Cemetery, where their son Joseph (18 months) was buried in 1863.

**1854–**    *Cincinnati, Ohio.* John Herron house. He often lodged here when visiting the city for social or political purposes.

After the fall campaign of 1876, he was a guest here and was serenaded during his visit on December 12.

**1868–1869**    *Columbus, Ohio.* 51 East State.

**1869–1870**    *Columbus.* 96 South Grant.

**1870**    *Columbus.* Seventh Street near the Capitol while serving as governor.

**1872–1873**    *Cincinnati, Ohio.* Carlisle House, northwest corner of Sixth and Mound Streets. He had temporary lodgings at $50 a week.

**1873–**    *Fremont, Ohio.* Spiegel Grove, at the junction of Hayes and Buckland Avenues, in Spiegel Grove State Park. It is open to the public. An impressive museum and bookstore are located nearby. The beautiful house is arranged and furnished with original pieces much as it was in the time of Hayes.

**1876–1877**    *Columbus, Ohio.* 60 East Broad Street. He rented a two-story duplex, only two rooms deep, which was across the street from the State House.

**1877–1881**    *Washington, D.C.* The White House.

**1881–1893**    *Catawba Island, Ohio.* Off shore, a short distance to the northeast, is Mouse Island, once the summer home of President Hayes and until recently still used by his relatives.

# WORK

**1845–1849**    *Fremont, Ohio.* Second story of the M. and J.S. Tyler's Building, where he started his law practice, northwest corner of Front and Croghan Streets. It was torn down in the late 1970s and an S & L building is now on the site.

**1849–1861**    *Cincinnati, Ohio.* Law practice in the new Law Building, 127 East Third Street, between Main and Sycamore—a short distance from the Ohio River. Later he moved to Hayes & Corwine, at 8 Selves' Building, Sixth and Walnut (demolished).

**1858–1861**    *Cincinnati, Ohio.* City Solicitor. City Hall, Eighth Street between Plum and West Row. At the same time, he carried on his law practice.

**1861**    *Camp Chase, near Columbus, Ohio.* He lived under tents as an officer of the Twenty-third Regiment of Ohio Volunteers. (McKinley was also with the same regiment.) It is located about four miles west of Columbus, Ohio.

**1861**    *Weston, West Virginia.* Near Gauley Bridge, twenty-three miles south of Clarksburg and twenty miles from Walkersville. He was stationed here in July and August, 1861.

**1861**    *Camp Tompkins, near Gauley Bridge, West Virginia.* Gauley Mount, house of Christopher Tompkins, where Hayes held courtmartial sessions in one of the parlors. It was looted and later burned. The house stood on the present site of the Hawk's Nest Golf Club.

**1861**    *Gauley Bridge, West Virginia.* Miller Tavern, Main Street, northeast of the railway overhead crossing, was headquarters for Union army officers. Among them were the future presidents Hayes and McKinley.

**1861–1862**    *Fayetteville, West Virginia.* Sixteen miles from Gauley Bridge. Winter quarters. He shared a deserted cottage with two other officers.

**1862**    *Raleigh (now Beckley), West Virginia.* He maintained a command location here with headquarters in a house belonging to a Mrs. Martha Davis.

**1863**  *Camp Reynolds, West Virginia.* Nicholas County in the Gauley River Valley. He lived in a double log cabin for the winter of 1863. He wrote that he needed to sit with an upraised umbrella because of "snow coming in clouds" through the shingles.

**1863**  *Parkersburg, West Virginia.* Swan House Hotel. After returning to the Kanawha Valley, he went to the Shenandoah Valley and the area of Winchester.

**1863–1864**  *Kanawha Valley, West Virginia.*

**1865–1867**  *Washington, D.C.* U.S. Representative from Ohio. The House of Representatives met in the south wing of the Capitol, as it does now. As a Congressman he lodged at 452 Thirteenth Street, NW. He had two rooms on the first floor of a widow's home. It has since been torn down.

**1868–1872**  *Columbus, Ohio.* Governor. State Capitol at Broad and High Streets in the Governor's office. There was a house, 51 East State Street, near the capitol, which he rented while governor. On November 29, 1869, he moved to 96 South Grant.

**1870**  *Columbus, Ohio.* Residence on Seventh Street, fairly close to the Capitol—a neoclassic brick house. Nothing remains.

**1876**  *Cincinnati, Ohio.* National Convention, Exposition Hall, Elm Street between Twelfth and Fourteenth Streets, where he was nominated for president at the Republican National Convention.

**1877–1881**  *Washington, D.C.* President of the United States. Although he won the electoral vote, his opponent had won the popular vote. By his bitter opponents, he was called "His Fraudulency" and "Rutherfraud B. Hayes."

# Travel/Visits

He visited the states of Alabama, Arizona, California, Connecticut, Delaware, Georgia, Illinois, Indiana, Kentucky, Maryland, Massa-chusetts, Michigan, Minnesota, Missouri, New Hampshire, New Mexico, New Jersey, New York, North Carolina, North Dakota, Ohio, Pennsylvania, Rhode Island, Tennessee, Texas, Vermont, Virginia, and Wisconsin.

**1871**  *Cincinnati, Ohio.* Fountain Square, Fifth Street, between Vine and Walnut. He spoke at the unveiling of the fountain.

**1876**  *Philadelphia, Pennsylvania.* He attended the Centennial Exhibition in Fairmont Park and stayed at the Continental Hotel, southeast corner of Ninth and Chestnut Streets. He was here again on May 10, 1877.

**1877**  *Bennington, Vermont.* He attended a celebration and mixed with thousands at a banquet in a tent pavilion.

**1877**  *Brattleboro, Vermont.* Hotel Brooks on Main Street.

**1877**  *Chattanooga, Tennessee.* He visited Civil War sites, lodged and attended a banquet at Stanton House.

**1877**  *Concord, New Hampshire.* He lodged at the Eagle Hotel, was received at the State House, and made a speech on the Capitol steps. He visited St. Paul's School, had dinner at the home of ex-governor Stearns, and attended a reception at White's Opera House.

**1877**  *Long Branch, New Jersey.* He owned a summer cottage at Elberon. He also stayed at the old Elberon Hotel on Ocean Avenue, which, like the cottage, no longer stands. This area was a favorite vacation site of presidents in the last half of the nineteenth century and the first quarter of the twentieth.

**1877**  *Middle Bass Island, near Sandusky, Ohio.* Retreat where Hayes, Cleveland, Harrison, and Taft were entertained.

**1877**  *Nashville, Tennessee.* He came in at the Louisville railway depot. There was a reception and speech late at night outside the Capitol. He lodged at Hotel Hermitage. At the Customs House, corner of Broadway and Eighth Avenue, he laid the cornerstone—this impressive building is still standing. He visited Mrs. Polk, widow of President Polk, at her home on Union and Seventh Street.

**1877** *New York City, New York.* Fifth Avenue Hotel, second floor suite. He had dinner at Delmonico's. He also visited ex-governor E.D. Morgan's home, at 411 Fifth Avenue, and J.J. Astor's home, 338 Fifth Avenue, at which Theodore Roosevelt was also a guest. At Central Park, he unveiled the statue of Halleck. At City Hall, he attended a reception in the Governor's Room. Here he saw the writing desk used by Washington in his first inauguration.

**1877** *Providence, Rhode Island.* He was entertained at the Executive Mansion, 83 John Street.

**1877** *Richmond, Virginia.* Reception at the Capitol. He lodged at the Exchange Hotel, corner of Fourteenth Street and Franklin. The Exchange was demolished in 1900.

**1877** *Rutland, Vermont.* Sycamore Lodge, Main Street near Park. He was guest in the home of Gov. John Page. (It is now a private house).

**1877** *Washington, D.C.* He stayed at Senator Sherman's house just before his inauguration. 1323 K Street, NW.

**1878** *Chicago, Illinois.* Stockyard Inn, 4178 South Halstead.

**1878** *Madison, Wisconsin.* He attended the State Fair, Camp Randall. He was the first sitting president to visit Madison.

**1878** *Montpelier, Virginia.* He visited the home of Madison and made a speech at Madison's tomb.

**1878** *Pasadena, California.* He was the first president in office to visit Pasadena. He made public appearances in the city and visited the Green Home on Columbia Street.

**1878** *Philadelphia, Pennsylvania.* He lodged at the Continental Hotel, visited the Mint, and watched the coining of money. He later attended a reception in his honor at Independence Hall.

**1878** *Washington, D.C.* He spoke at Howard University on Georgia Avenue, NW.

**1879** *Detroit, Michigan.* Reception at the residence of ex-Governor Baldwin, 110 West Fort Street.

**1880** *Los Angeles, California.* Dinner at the then elegant Cosmopolitan Hotel (now the St. Elmo), Main Street.

**1880** *New York City, New York.* He was at the Metropolitan Museum on Central Park for the opening ceremonies.

**1880** *Portland, Oregon.* Esmond Hotel, Front and Morrison Streets.

**1880** *Salt Lake City, Utah.* He lodged in the Walker House.

**1881** *Cleveland, Ohio.* He attended Garfield's funeral.

**1885** *New York City, New York.* He attended Grant's funeral and stayed at the Fifth Avenue Hotel.

**1886** *Albany, New York.* He attended Arthur's funeral.

**1889** *Brattleboro, Vermont.* The former Hayes Tavern, restored by Mrs. Bigelow as a summer residence. Hayes' father was a native of Brattleboro, and his grandfather had been the saloon keeper of Hayes Tavern. Dummerston Center is a small community of less than a dozen houses including the Knight homestead. President Hayes' ancestral family lived there, off U.S. 5 or Vermont 30.

**1889** *Lake Mohon, New York.* He attended a conference and visited family graveyards.

**1891** *Augusta, Georgia.* He visited the exposition.

**1892** *Cleveland, Ohio.* He visited the Linus Austin home, 3625 Prospect Street, where his son lived.

*Hayes family grave site.*

# DEATH

Hayes died on January 17, 1893, in Fremont, Ohio, at Spiegel Grove. He had been visiting his son, who was staying at Mrs. L. C. Austin's home in Cleveland, and was on his way home when he suffered a heart attack in the Cleveland railroad station on January 14, 1893. He died at home three days later at 11:00 P.M. The value of his estate is unknown.

# FUNERAL

Hayes lay in state in an open cedar coffin with black cloth in the dining room at Spiegel Grove. Psalm 23 was read and a choir sang, "It is well with my soul." The Reverend J. L. Albritton of the Methodist Church conducted the services in the front hall of the house, but there was no sermon. Because of the extreme cold (five degrees below zero), ceremonies were held at home before going to the cemetery. President-elect Cleveland attended as well as future President McKinley (then governor of Ohio), but Benjamin Harrison, the current president, was on the verge of being ill and did not.

# BURIAL

He was buried in Oakwood Cemetery, 1225 Oakwood Road, one half mile south of Fremont, on January 20. In 1915 he was reinterred at Spiegel Grove, at the south side of the estate, beside Mrs. Hayes.

# SPECIAL SITES

*Columbus, Ohio.* My Jewels Monument, near the northwest corner of the Capitol, honors Grant, Hayes, and Garfield.

# BIBLIOGRAPHY

Barnard, Harry. *Rutherford B. Hayes and His America.* New York, Russell & Russell, 1954, reissued 1967.

Geer, Emily Apt. *First Lady: the Life of Lucy Webb Hayes.* Kent University Press, 1984.

# JAMES ABRAM GARFIELD

## 1831–1881
### 20TH PRESIDENT 1881: REPUBLICAN PARTY

James A. Garfield was born on November 19, 1831, to Abram and Eliza Ballou Garfield. He was the last president to be born in a log cabin and the first and last to have been a preacher. Despite his lowly birth one researcher traces his ancestry back to William the Conqueror.

*"Equality — the informing soul of Freedom!"*

*—Maxims, 1880*

## CHARACTERISTICS

Garfield was impressive in appearance. He was well-built, 6' tall, and weighed about 185 pounds. He had blue eyes, and his unusually large head was covered with light-brown hair. His hair, beard, and mustache had touches of gray by the time he became president. He was left handed. He enjoyed hunting and fishing and played chess, euchre, and whist. He was a moderate social drinker. He had little association with things outside his immediate area. He was nineteen before he heard a piano and twenty-three before he ate his first banana. As the youngest child, and a son without a father, he was spoiled and petted; he hated work. He was touchy and responded to imagined or real taunts with his fists.

# A LIFE IN REVIEW

**Birth:** November 19, 1831; Orange, OH

**Died:** September 19, 1881; Elberon, NJ

**Married:** Lucretia Rudolph; November 11, 1858; 5 sons, 2 daughters

## CAREER

**1849** Teacher

**1849–** Preacher

**1857–1861** College President

**1859** Member state legislature

**1861–1863** Military Service Civil War

**1863–1880** Member U.S. Congress

## ADMINISTRATION EVENTS

**1881** American Red Cross organized

# BIRTHPLACE

Garfield was born in Orange Township (now Moreland Hills), a suburb of Cleveland, Ohio. He was born about a mile and a half south of Orange Center, next to the farm of Amos Boynton, near the village of Chagrin Falls, three miles from the present town of Chagrin Falls and four miles from the village of Solon, neither of which existed then. The spot is marked by a ring of wooden benches.

# BAPTISM

Garfield was baptized on March 3, 1850, in Chagrin River, Ohio. He recorded his conversion and baptism as a member of the Disciples of Christ (Campbell's Movement). Disciples shared with Baptists a belief in adult baptism. Garfield said he opened his soul and allowed the light of the Lord to come in. He renounced his sinful past. He put the vice of swearing aside and never swore again—not even when he was in the army. The tumult of a Methodist camp meeting left him grieved and disgusted with the shameful proceedings. "This religion is only adapted to the coarser order of mind and has more of the animal than spiritual in it." The errors of the Presbyterians left him in dismay.

# CHURCH

At the age of three, he was reading from the Bible but had periods when he tired of the pressures of strict religion. One year, he rebelled against the weekly three-mile tramp through the woods to attend church and refused to go. His mother agreed that he could stay home on Sunday on the condition that he not leave the house. A year of this weekly house arrest was more than enough for his restless nature, and he meekly returned to church.

He believed in a literal interpretation of the Scriptures and in life after death. He was a lay preacher for a time. Like many others who found the joy of a personal spiritual experience, he was something of a zealot in his early days.

**1831–1856** *Orange Township, Moreland Hills (Chagrin Falls), southeast of Cleveland, Ohio.* At first, the church met in various places but most often in its original location, Griffith School House, near the junction of the two branches of the Chagrin River, one mile west of what is now Chagrin Falls. Later, the church moved into Chagrin Falls and from 1843 to 1851 worshipped wherever the congregation could be accommodated. 24 Walnut Street is the site of the Disciple Church on which Garfield worked. It was torn down in 1932. For a time following December 1858, he was minister of the congregation and gained experience as an orator which contributed towards his being elected president. While working on the church, he stayed in the house at 23 Water

Street. The front part of the house is original with later additions at the back.

Cleveland area. The 18th Ward Disciples Church was established in 1842 at Circle and Franklin Streets. Garfield served here in the later part of 1857 to 1858. In 1858, he participated in lectures at the Disciples Church, Chagrin Falls, and was a minister at Solon Disciples Church.

**1848–1850**  *Chesterland, Ohio.* Freewill Baptist Church. Originally, it was on the east side of Chillicothe, south of Sherman Road. His family was associated with the church located at the southwest corner of Sherman and Chillicothe–site of the Presbyterian church organized on November 12, 1819, built around 1830, and dedicated in 1830. It faced the road on the drive off Sherman Road. The Disciples Church was built on Township Park about 250 feet north of Mayfield Road, facing Chillicothe Road. It was dedicated in 1853. On the platform, there was a low marble- topped table for communion. Garfield used it when he travelled to different Disciple churches, including Chester, as lay minister. He received the Certificate of Ordination on September 18, 1858. Garfield Memorial United Methodist Church on Lander Circle, Pepper Pike (near Cleveland), was one of his churches. Garfield Chapel, on Bainbridge Road, Ohio 91, Solon, Ohio, is now the Historical Society Building.

**1851–1861**  *Hiram, Ohio.* He is listed on the rolls of Hiram Christian Church, 6868 Wakefield Road.

**1854–1856**  *Poestenkill, New York.* He preached at the Disciples of Christ Church.

**1863**  *Mooresville, Alabama.* There is a white frame church where he spoke several times in 1863. It is interesting because all the furnishings are those that were there in his time. See also the old Stage Coach Inn (1825) and the Brick Church which existed while he was in Mooresville.

*James Garfield church in Mooresville, Alabama, he spoke here several times in 1863.*

**1861–**  *Murfreesboro, Tennessee.* East Main Street Church of Christ where he conducted worship services during the Civil War. He used to enter the church, throw off his gun belt, enter the pulpit, and begin preaching. The church was torn down in 1900 and replaced on site.

**1863–1881**  *Washington, D.C.* National City Christian Church (Disciples of Christ), Thomas Circle, NW. In his time, services were held in another building. At the entrance of the present building is the old-fashioned pew that came from the congregation's former church building on Vermont Avenue. This was Garfield's pew and bears his name and the dates of his birth and death. He preached many sermons for this congregation. The present building was dedicated in 1930.

**1880–1881**  *Long Branch, New Jersey.* He attended St. James Episcopal Chapel, known as the Church of the Presidents, on the corner of Ocean and Lincoln Avenues. There is a plaque on south side of the chancel and a stained glass memorial.

# EDUCATION

**1847–** *Orange Township, Chagrin Falls, Ohio.* He first attended in the Boynton district in a crude one-room log cabin school. The family later bought the school building and added it to their house, which was across the brook. It is also possible that he attended the River Road School at River Road and Miles corner on SOM Center Road between Solon and Moreland Hills.

**1848–1850** *Chesterland, Geuga County, Ohio.* Geuga Academy, a three-story wooden structure. The chapel occupied one room of the Academy. A few years later, the Academy was closed. The site is now occupied by the old high school building. He roomed in an upstairs room of an old unpainted frame house just across the road from the Seminary and boarded downstairs with the landlady, Mrs. Reed. The second year, he rented a room in a farmhouse, where he slept and cooked his own meals. The house he lived in in 1848 was built in 1835 by Herman Woodworth and still exists at 12570 Chillicothe. It is now the Remembrance Shop.

**1851–1854** *Hiram, Portage County, Ohio.* Hiram Eclectic Institute (now Hiram College). He roomed in the basement of the original college building. This building, among other buildings of the Institute, was demolished in 1969.

**1854–1856** *Williamstown, Massachusetts.* Williams College. He graduated with honors in the class of 1856. There is no record of his rooming place.

**1858–1860** *Hiram, Ohio.* He studied law on his own and was admitted to the bar in 1860.

# MARRIAGE AND HONEYMOON

Garfield was married on November 11, 1858, in Hiram, Ohio. It was a quiet solemn ceremony, held in the home of Lucretia Rudolph, the bride. They were married by a Presbyterian minister, Henry Hitchcock. Later, it became the home of Zeb Rudolph, located on the north side of Ohio 305, east of Hiram Center. It has been demolished.

There was no honeymoon. In Garfield's diary, the entry consists of a curt statement that he was married, and there is no further detail.

# HOMES/LODGINGS

**1831–1842** *Moreland Hills, Ohio.* His birthplace was a log cabin in Orange Township, on the edge of a ravine sloping down to the Chagrin River. The area is now the plush community of Moreland Hills. The property now belongs to the Chagrin Valley Country Club. The long side of the Garfield farm ran east and west along the present Jackson road, to the corner of the SOM center road.

**1842–1843** *Bedford, Ohio.* He lived here briefly when his mother moved here after her marriage to Warren (Alfred) Belden. Little is said in any of his writings about this failed marriage.

**1843–1856** *Moreland Hills, Ohio.* He returned from Bedford, and the family built a frame house in 1846. It was destroyed by fire after he left home.

**1851** *Muskingum County, Ohio.* He taught here in the spring. It is near Duncan's Falls, southwest of Zanesville, off highway 60 on Black Run. Later the log school house was enclosed with weatherboards and rooms added to make a house, but by 1990 it had sadly deteriorated although local efforts were made to preserve it. He stayed with his mother's brother, Henry Ballou, in Brush Creek township. He arrived here by stagecoach, since no train served the area until 1852.

**1856–1859** *Hiram, Ohio.* While at Western Reserve Eclectic Institute and following his marriage in 1858, they probably lived part

*Hiram Ohio, home James Garfield bought during the Civil War.*

of this time with the Rudolph family (bride's family) in their house on the north side of Ohio 305. It is now demolished. See also the cemetery at Hiram Hill where his last born son was buried next to his first born. Fairview Cemetery, corner of Ohio 82 and Ryder Road, west of Hiram.

**1859–1861**   *Hiram, Ohio.* He and his wife roomed and boarded at the boarding house of Eunice C. Northrup, now situated at 11221 Ohio 700. He was on the faculty and later president of Hiram College at the time.

**1859–1861**   *Columbus, Ohio.* While a member of the legislature, he stayed at 193 South Third Street.

**1861–1872**   *Hiram, Ohio.* 6825 Hinsdale Street (owned by Mr. and Mrs. John Zimmerman). This house, which he had bought during the Civil War, was sold in 1872. During much of this time, he was in war service or in the United States Congress.

**1862**   *Washington, D.C.* He stayed with Chase on C Street, near the corner of Four and one half Street, NW.

**1863**   *Washington, D.C.* C Street, near the corner of Four and one half Street, rooming with Schenck. Nearly five years later, when Garfield returned to Washington for a second session, he moved out of Schenck's bachelor quarters and rented rooms for his family. From then on, his wife always lived with him while he was in Washington

**1869–1881**   *Washington, D.C.* Corner of Thirteenth and I Street, NW, with a fine view of Franklin Square across the street. It was a plain 3-story brick house, which he bought for just over $13,000. The site is 901 Thirteenth Street.

**1876–1881**   *Mentor, Ohio.* Lawnfield, 1059 Mentor Avenue, was the last home of Garfield prior to his occupancy of the White House. In 1876 he bought almost

120 acres of land in Mentor to which he added 40 acres at a total cost of almost $17,500. It is now the Garfield National Historic Site in northeast Ohio. He won his famous "front porch" campaign from the mansion. The house includes his library and is a good example of late nineteenth-century interior design. The rooms of the first two floors are filled with furniture and other possessions of the Garfield family.

**1881**    *Washington, D.C.* The White House as twentieth president of the United States. He lived here for only about 2 months before he was shot by an assassin.

# WORK

The dates and places of his work—particularly in the early years—are estimates. The buildings where he worked and lodged during these early years were nearly all poorly constructed and have collapsed or been demolished with little or no trace to show where they once stood. However, to provide continuity, each is listed and its general location indicated. Like many young people who try to better themselves, Garfield frequently changed jobs between 1845 and 1856.

**1845–1847**    *Orange, Ohio.* He worked in the ashery of Perry Mapes, a few miles from the Garfield home. During this period, he boarded at home.

**1847**    *Solon, Ohio.* He worked in the ashery of Daniel Morse. He quit in a huff when Mrs. Morse addressed him as a servant. He boarded at the Morse home, which is located near a spring on the south side of Mayfield Road, just west of Heath Road.

**1848**    *Independence, Ohio.* He had land clearing and planting jobs while boarding either with a farmer named Watts or with his sister, Mary, and her husband, Marenus Larabee.

**1848**    *Cleveland, Ohio.* He first worked on a freighter on the Great Lakes and then as a "tow boy," driving horses and mules pulling boats on the Ohio Canal. His experience is often compared to that of an Horatio Alger hero. In six weeks he fell overboard fourteen times but never learned to swim. He slept and ate on the barge.

**1849–1850**    *Solon, Ohio.* He taught in District Two School, two miles from his home, just off the Center Road, and did carpentry work. He boarded around as was the custom.

**1850**    *Warrensville Township, Cuyahoga County, Ohio.* He taught school here and also at Blue Rock, where he served as both janitor and teacher.

**1851**    *Muskingum County, Ohio.* He taught in a "miserable old log schoolhouse." His purpose in teaching was to earn money to go back to school himself.

**1851–1854**    *Hiram, Ohio.* While going to school here, he paid his expenses by tutoring other students, including his wife. In 1853, he began preaching at neighboring churches.

**1854–1855**    *North Pownal, Vermont.* He taught school for one winter in Old Oak Seminary. Chester Arthur, who was later his vice president, also taught at this school at a different time.

**1856–1857**    *Hiram, Ohio.* At Hiram Eclectic (later Hiram College) he was Professor of Latin and Greek.

**1857–1861**    *Hiram, Ohio.* Hiram Eclectic. President of the college.

**1858–**    *Chagrin Falls, Ohio.* He preached at Disciples Churches in the area.

**1859–1861**    *Columbus, Ohio.* He was a member of the state senate, which met in temporary quarters until the new capitol at Broad and High Streets was completed in 1861.

**1859–1861**    *Cincinnati, Ohio.* Garfield Place, between Vine and Elm Streets. As a young attorney, he maintained an office here for several years.

**1861–1863** *Military service.* He went from Lieutenant Colonel to Major General. Garfield's Ohio soldiers were appalled by the squalor and ignorance they found in the Ohio valley. In isolated cabins, they encountered families that had never seen a church, never heard of railroads, and who stared in open-mouthed amazement at a common jackknife. He served in Indiana, Illinois, Kentucky, Tennessee, Mississippi, Georgia, and Virginia. Pikesville, Kentucky. In City Park, there is a plaque commemorating the spot where he was sworn in as a Union brigadier general in January 1862. Prestonsburg, Kentucky. His headquarters were off Main Street. There is a marker at the site. Catlettsburg, Kentucky. The Civil War Army Base, US 23 and 60 at Twenty-sixth and Louisa, was a supply base and communication center for Union forces in the Big Sandy region (to protect Ohio River traffic). In the winter of 1861–1862, troops under Garfield drove the enemy from the area in a victory at Middle Creek. Murfreesboro, Tennessee. His headquarters were in the Robert Wendell home on East College Street. Chattanooga, Tennessee. His headquarters were on the northeast corner of Fourth and Walnut Street. Chickamauga Battlefield, on US 27, was the site of two of the bloodiest battles of the Civil War in an effort to gain control of Lafayette Road. Garfield was serving with General Rosencranz on September 19 and 20, 1863. Chickamauga, 217 Cove Road. Gordon-Lee Mansion. Garfield was here with Rosencranz for three days of conference. It is the only structure to survive the battle. Lynchburg, Virginia. He was quartered here in 1864 at Sandusky in a two-story L-shaped house.

**1863–1880** *Washington, D.C.* U.S. Congressman from Ohio. As early as 1872, he urged that the nation's ties with its southern neighbors be strengthened. In 1876, about

abolishing the number of diplomatic posts in Latin America, he replied: "I would rather blot out five or six European missions than these South American ones. They are our neighbors and friends." He struggled against the idea of senatorial courtesy. On another issue, he said, "Further our Educational System and you strike a blow at ignorance and crime which will greatly reduce our jail and prison expenses." When he started serving in the House of Representatives, this body had moved from their old quarters in what is now Statuary Hall to the south wing extension of the Capitol where the House has met from 1857 to the present.

**1880** *Chagrin Falls, Ohio.* Town Hall on Main Street where he spoke when running for president. Part of the original burned but has been partially restored.

**1881** *Washington, D.C.* President of the United States.

# TRAVEL/VISITS

Aside from travel to and from Washington and his military service, he visited relatives in Massachusetts. In nearby Vermont and New York, he found colonies of Disciples and preached actively among them. While he did a bit of travel during political campaigns, this was a far cry from the extensive travelling done in twentieth century campaigns. He travelled in: Alabama, Delaware, Georgia, Illinois, Indiana, Kentucky, Maryland, Massachusetts, New Hampshire, New Jersey, New York, Ohio, Pennsylvania, Tennessee, Vermont, Virginia, West Virginia, and Wisconsin.

**1871** *Keene, New Hampshire.* He participating in the dedication of the Soldier's Monument. He had dinner at Cheshire House, southeast corner of Central Square between Roxbury and Church Streets. While in the area, he went with his mother to visit her birthplace in Richmond, New Hampshire.

**1873** *Zanesville, Ohio.* Black's Music Hall for a campaign speech. It is now on the second floor of the Eckerd Drug Store building in the town center.

**1877** *Mobile, Alabama.* He lodged at Oakleigh, 350 Oakleigh Place, at the head of Savannah Street, where he is said to have drunk his first mint julep.

**1880** *Chicago, Illinois.* Exposition Building, which was on the future site of the Art Institute, Jackson and LaSalle Streets. An immense flag draped the auditorium which was as wide as a city block and twice as long. The delegates to the Republican National Convention stayed at the Grand Pacific Hotel, which was second to the Palace in San Francisco as the most luxurious in the United States.

**1880s** *York, Pennsylvania.* He was a frequent visitor to the large mansion, Brockie, house of his close and intimate friend Jeremiah Black. It is about two miles southwest of York.

**1881** *Deer Park, Maryland.* He was entertained in one of the cottages here while on vacation.

**1881** *Long Branch, New Jersey.* A cottage on the grounds of the old Elberon Hotel, Ocean Avenue opposite Lincoln Avenue. Both hotel and cottage have been demolished. At Broadway is a life-sized statue of Garfield, who died in Long Branch several weeks after being shot. An emergency raillway track was laid within hours from the mainline to the cottage to carry the wounded man.

*The James A. Garfield Monument is a circular tower 50 feet in diameter and 180 feet high.*

# DEATH

On July 2, 1881, Garfield was shot while at the old Sixth Street depot (Baltimore and Potomac), near Capitol Hill, in Washington, D.C. He died on September 19, in Elberon, New Jersey, of blood poisoning. To move Garfield from the White House to the Charles Franck-

lyn cottage on the grounds of the Elberon Hotel in Long Branch, 2,000 men worked round the clock to lay a railway spur five-eighth-mile in twenty-four hours.

# FUNERAL

The viewing was in the Elberon Francklyn Cottage, and there was a short funeral service

Washington, D.C. His body lay in state in the Capitol Rotunda for two days, and religious ceremonies were held there. The hymns, "To Thee, Oh Lord, I Yield My Spirit," "Jesus, Lover of My Soul" and "Asleep in Jesus" were sung. President Arthur and ex-presidents Hayes and Grant attended the Rotunda service.

A funeral train took the body and mourners from Washington to Ohio. In Cleveland, he lay in state in Monumental Park. By this time, after many days of viewing, the body was beginning to decompose and a disagreeable odor started coming from the coffin. There was a funeral service at the Pavilion in the Public Square of Cleveland. Ex-president Hayes attended.

# BURIAL

At first, his body was placed temporarily in the public vault but was later moved to the Garfield Memorial, Lake View Cemetery, 12316 Euclid Avenue and East 123rd Street, Cleveland, Ohio.

The James A. Garfield Monument is a circular tower 50 feet in diameter and 180 feet high. On the exterior wall, a paneled frieze depicts highlights in Garfield's career: as country school teacher, soldier, statesman, and president. Inside the chapel, in the base of the monument, stands the marble statue of Garfield. Stairs lead below to where the Garfield casket is on view. President Harrison dedicated the tomb in 1890, and then Congressman McKinley attended.

# BIBLIOGRAPHY

Peskin, Allan. *The Graphic Story of the American Presidents. Garfield*. Kent, Ohio, Kent State University Press, 1978.

Leech, Margaret and Brown, Jarry J. *The Garfield Orbit: The Life of President James A. Garfield*. New York, Harper & Row, 1978.

# CHESTER ALAN ARTHUR

**1829–1886**
**21st President 1881–1885: Republican Party**

Chester (Chet) Alan Arthur was born to the Reverend William (Irish born) and Malvina Stone Arthur (English descent).

## CHARACTERISTICS

Arthur was well–built and handsome. He was six feet two inches tall; as a young man he weighed about 180 pounds, but in middle age he went up to nearly 225. He had a full face with a high forehead, extremely dark eyes, and wavy brown hair, which he wore long. During most of his career, he wore side whiskers and a mustache. He was fond of the latest clothes and was a careful dresser. He liked dress pants and is said to have had a wardrobe which included 80 pairs of pants. He liked to fish and hunt and was an accomplished angler. His great enjoyment of long evenings of conversation with "the boys," smoking cigars and telling humorous stories, probably threatened his marriage. He could be found on his front doorstep with a willing listener until 3:00 A.M. and showed an inclination to be a night person rather than an early riser.

## A LIFE IN REVIEW

**Birth:** October 5, 1829; Fairfield, VT

**Died:** November 18, 1886; New York City

**Married:** Ellen Lewis Herndon; October 25, 1859; 2 sons, 1 daughter

### CAREER

**1848–1853** Teacher

**1854–1881** Lawyer

**1861–1863** State militia

**1871–1878** Collector for Port of New York

**1881** U.S. Vice President

### ADMINISTRATION EVENTS

**1882** Chinese immigration exclusion act

**1883** Civil Service Commission organized

**1885** Washington Monument dedicated

## BIRTHPLACE

Arthur was born October 5, 1829, in Fairfield, Vermont, three and a half miles east of the Fairfield Station, off Vermont 108. He was born in a small log cabin which was the temporary parsonage while the parsonage was being built on a piece of land about a half mile from his father's church in rural Fairfield. On his records, Arthur changed the date from 1829 to 1830—possibly out of simple vanity.

## BAPTISM

No records of a baptism have been located. It seems unlikely that he was never baptized since his father was a Baptist minister and he attended his father's church regularly during the years he was growing up.

## CHURCH

Although he was the eldest son of a Baptist minister and had a Baptist upbringing under a firm father and later had the habit of attending Episcopal churches, much to the disappointment of his parents, he never formally joined any church by confession of faith. He attended his father's churches while growing up, and these are listed below. There is no record to show that he had strong religious interests. The addresses of the churches in the smaller towns are not given, since there is little problem in locating the church which is, in almost every case, the only Baptist church in the town.

**1829–1832** *North Fairfield, Vermont.* Baptist Church.

**1832–1834** *Williston (near Burlington), Vermont.* Baptist Church.

**1834–1835** *Hinesburgh, Vermont.* Baptist Church.

**1835–1837** *Perry, Wyoming County, New York.* Baptist Church.

**1837–1839** *York, Livington County, New York.* Baptist Church.

**1839–1844** *Union Village (now Greenwich), New York.* Bottskill Baptist Church, 32 Church Street.

**1844–1846** *Watervliet, New York.* First Particular Baptist Church and Society of Gibbonsville and West Troy. Three churches were built beginning in 1828. The first two were built facing Sixteenth Street. The first burned and the second was torn down in 1869.

**1845–1848** *Schenectady, New York.* He entered Union College in 1845 and attended chapel, which was compulsory.

**1846–1849** *Lansingburgh, New York.* Baptist Church.

**1849–1853** *Hoosick, New York.* Baptist Church.

**1853–1855** *West Troy (now Watervliet), New York.* First Baptist Church, corner of Canal and Ohio. It united with North Reformed Dutch Church to form Christ Church in 1968.

**1855–1864** *Albany, New York.* Calvary Baptist Church. His father was pastor of a large number of churches. and it is likely he visited these even after he was no longer under parental supervision when he came home.

**1859–1880** *New York City, New York.* Cavalry Episcopal Church, Fourth Avenue and Twenty–first Street, was his wife's home church.

**1880–1886** *New York City, New York.* Church of the Heavenly Rest, Fifth Avenue near Forty–fifth Street, now on the southwest corner of Fifth Avenue and East Ninetieth Street. The funerals of both Arthur and his wife were here.

**1881–1885** *Washington, D.C.* LaFayette Square. St. John's Episcopal Church, where his wife sang in the choir before they were married. He attended this church during his presidency but never formally joined. He donated a window to the church in memory of his wife. This was on the south side of the church so he could see it from his windows at the White House. He went to church on foot and unattended.

**1881** *Washington, D.C.* On his first day as president, he worshipped at the Metropolitan A.M.E. Church, 1518 M Street, NW. He returned on Thanksgiving Day.

**1881–** *Long Branch, New Jersey.* He attended St. James Episcopal Chapel.

**1883** *St. Augustine, Florida.* Trinity Episcopal Church, 215 St. George Street. In the afternoon, he attended the Negro church. Trinity was almost completely rebuilt in the early 1900s, with the exception of the north transept and the baptistery.

**1883** *Sanford, Florida.* Episcopal Church of the Holy Cross, 410 South Magnolia Avenue.

**1884** *Kingston, New York.* First Reformed Church on Main Street between Wall and Fair Streets.

# EDUCATION

**1829–1839** *He was taught by his father at home.*

**1839–1844** *Union Village (now Greenwich), New York.* Greenwich Academy is where Arthur first attended school. Originally, the site was on Academy Street where the present Greenwich town offices are located. In 1849 it moved into a new brick building on the corner of Academy and Bleecher Streets.

**1844–1845** *Schenectady, New York.* Lyceum, Union, and Yale Streets.

**1845–1848** *Schenectady, New York.* Union College on Union Street (see North and South College Halls). He entered as a sophomore and graduated three years later near the top of his class. He won a Phi Beta Kappa key. Lincoln's secretary, William H. Steward, had studied here and just outside the window of his college room was a broad stone sill in which he had carved his name. Years later, Arthur occupied the room directly above and carved his autograph in the wood of the window frame. This wood was later used in fencing but an enterprising souvenir hunter found and preserved this piece of frame.

**1849–1851** *Ballston Spa, New York.* State and National Law School, which was newly opened. He was here for several months and was also studying law privately. He returned to the family home at Hoosick and continued his studies there. The school only lasted three years and occupied the Sans Souci Hotel on Main Street. Van Buren attended the final examinations in 1849, and Tyler was present at the commencement of 1850.

**1851–1852** *New York City, New York.* Erastus D. Culver law office, 289 Broadway.

*A replica, based on photographs of the original Arthur family home in North Fairfield, Vermont.*

## MARRIAGE AND HONEYMOON

Arthur was married on October 10, 1859, in New York City, New York, at Calvary Episcopal Church, Fourth Avenue and Twenty–first Street, near the home of his bride, Ellen Lewis Herndon. Arthur first met his future wife at Bancroft House, at 904 Broadway in 1856. Later, at Saratoga Springs, New York, he proposed to her on the porch of the United States Hotel which has since been torn down. Two weeks following the wedding, they were at home to friends at the bride's mother's house, 34 West Twenty-first Street, New York City. There is no account of the honeymoon.

Mrs. Arthur died before President Arthur entered the White House. It is said that he appeared to be looking for a permanent hostess and courted a number of ladies, including Frances Willard, the temperance advocate. Reports are that he proposed to at least two of them, but he never remarried.

## HOMES/LODGINGS

**1829–1830** *Fairfield, Vermont.* He started life in a small log cabin, three and four tenth miles east of Fairview Station leading off Vermont 108.

**1830–1832** *North Fairfield, Vermont.* Within a year of his birth, the family moved to a small one–story house. A replica, based on photographs of the original house, stands on the site. The Vermont legislature authorized the purchase of a shaft of Barre granite to be erected on the site. The site is in a meadow on a dirt side road, miles from any population center, and it looks much the same today.

**1832–1834** *Willston, Vermont.* Baptist parsonage.

**1834–1835** *Hinesburgh, Vermont.* Baptist parsonage, Main Street on route 116 two doors from the public library. Private.

**1835–1837**  *Perry, New York.* Parsonage on Elm Street, which no longer exists.

**1837–1839**  *York, New York.* Baptist parsonage.

**1839–1844**  *Union Village (now Greenwich), not far from Sarasota, New York.* The parsonage where the Arthurs lived has been removed twice and now stands at 24 Woodlawn Avenue. The parsonage was on Church Street in the lot next to the Bottskill Baptist Church.

**1846–1849**  *Lansingburgh, New York.* Baptist parsonage.

**1848–1855**  *West Troy, New York.* Parsonage on Canal Street between Erie and Ohio.

**1849–1853**  *Hoosick, New York.* This was his parents' home and near North Pownal, Vermont, where he was teaching.

**1851–1852**  *North Pownal, Vermont.* He had a room at the Academy.

**1852–1853**  *Cohoes, New York.* He stayed at the Cohoes Academy.

**1853–1855**  *New York City, New York.* Forty–second Street at the Continental Hotel, where Arthur lived during his bachelor days. Between Twenty–third and Twenty–fourth Streets was the Fifth Avenue Hotel, perhaps the most famous of the many hotels in the city. It was the New York headquarters of the Republican Party in Arthur's day.

**1855–1859**  *New York City.* 904 Broadway at Bancroft House, a family hotel. He was rooming at the Bancroft when he met his future wife who was visiting relatives there.

**1859–1861**  *New York City.* 34 West Twenty–first Street, where he lived until the outbreak of the Civil War.

**1861–1865**  *New York City.* Near Twenty–second and Broadway in a two–story plushly furnished family hotel, while serving with the militia as quartermaster.

**1865–1886**  *New York City.* 124 Lexington Avenue on Grammercy Park, which was a much better house than the previous one. He also had an office in the front basement of this dwelling. This was his home until his death.

**1881–1885**  *Washington, D.C.* The White House. People in his day could easily enter the front door of the White House. During his administration, a number of visitors said they had come because they "were willing to marry the President." He enjoyed mixing with the upper class and gave elegant dinner parties at the White House. In his entertaining, he followed examples of generous hospitality set by Washington, Jefferson, both Adamses, Buchanan, and Grant.

**1883–1885**  *Washington, D.C.* Soldier's Home. Summer White House, Pershing Drive, NW.

# WORK

**1846–1851**  *Schaghticoke, New York.* District School No. 14. Here and elsewhere during long winter vacation time from college and after his graduation, he taught school in towns near Schenectady including this one. See also Hoosick. This was a one–room school which was still standing 123 years later in 1975.

**1851–1852**  *North Pownal, Vermont.* He was principal of North Pownal Academy, sometimes called Old Oak Seminary. The academy met in the Baptist Church basement. Three years after he left, future president Garfield taught a writing class in the same room. Together, they headed the Republican ticket in 1880.

**1852–1853**  *Cohoes, New York.* Went from North Pownal to Cohoes beginning November 8 to become principal of the academy called High Department of District School in Cohoes.

**1852–1856**  *New York City, New York.* Culver, Partsen and Arthur law firm, 289 Broadway.

**1856**  *New York City, New York.* 117 Nassau Street, where he had a law partnership with Henry D. Gardiner.

**1856**  *Kansas City, Kansas.* With Gardiner, he spent three months looking to set up offices here, but gave it up and returned to New York City.

**1857–1865**  *New York City, New York.* Law practice with Henry D. Gardiner. See 1856 above.

**1858–1862**  *New York City, New York.* He was a member of the New York State Militia.

**1861**  *New York City, New York.* Elm Street office, where he was assistant quartermaster general.

**1862–1863**  *New York City, New York.* 51 Walker Street. He was promoted to Quartermaster General.

**1863–1871**  *New York City, New York.* He returned to his law practice, and, at the same time, he acted as a claims agent. He had an office in the front basement of his house at 123 Lexington Avenue.

**1869–1870**  *New York City, New York.* Along with his law practice, he was also counsel to the New York Tax Commission.

**1871**  *New York City, New York.* He formed a law partnership with Ransom and later with Phelps, 82 Nassau Street.

**1871–1878**  *New York City, New York.* Wall Street, in the old Merchant's Exchange Building of dark granite with Ionic columns (present site of the National City Bank Building). He was collector of the Port of New York in the Customs House.

**1878–1880**  *New York City, New York.* 155 Broadway. He resumed his law practice while engaging in national politics as his primary concern.

**1880**  *Chicago, Illinois.* Exposition Hall. He was nominated for vice president by the Republican party on June 10.

**1880–1881**  *New York City, New York.* 155 Broadway. He became senior member of the firm, Arthur, Phelps, Knevals, and Ransom.

**1881**  *Washington, D.C.* Vice President of the United States, with his office in the Capitol, near the Senate Chamber.

**1881–1885**  *Washington, D.C.* President of the United States. He first took the oath of office at his home at 23 Lexington Avenue, New York City, and again in Washington at the U.S. Capitol in the room reserved for the Vice President, near the Senate Chamber.

**1885–1886**  *New York City, New York.* He resumed the practice of law with his old firm, with a plush office on the fourth floor of the Mutual Life Building, Nassau Street at Cedar and Liberty Streets.

# TRAVEL/VISITS

His travel between 1829 and 1856 was limited to times when his father moved from pulpit to pulpit from Vermont to New York and later to when he was teaching and studying in New York and Vermont. His first long trip was in 1856 to Kansas City, Kansas. During his lifetime he travelled in the following states: Connecticut, Delaware, Florida, Georgia, Illinois, Indiana, Iowa, Kansas, Kentucky, Maine, Maryland, Massachusetts, Minnesota, Mississippi, Montana, Nebraska, New Hampshire, New Jersey, New York, North Carolina, Ohio, Pennsylvania, Rhode Island, South Carolina, South Dakota, Virginia, Vermont, Wisconsin, and Wyoming. When he became president, he took several long trips that were planned to give him rest and build up his health, but, in a number of cases, they seemed to have the opposite effect. On his southern trip in March and April 1883, the journey turned out to be hot and dusty and marked by many discomforts. An over–zealous conductor, for example, insisted on trying to collect fares. Arrangements had been made to welcome the president in Orlando, Florida, but Arthur, ill and irritable, had seen enough of crowds and agreed only to appear on the platform. When the train stopped instead of slowing down, Arthur quickly reentered his car with a look of "intense anger."

**1831–** *Saratoga Springs, New York.* United States Hotel, since torn down, but see Congress Hall Park and the row of elegant houses which were there in Arthur's day. A pizza parlor is at the site of the old United States Hotel on Broadway and Division.

**1856** *Lecompton, Kansas.* He visited the old Capitol and lodged at the Rowena Hotel at the south end of Main Street. The hotel became dormitories for Lane University.

**1858–** *Fredericksburg, Virginia.* He visited relatives of his wife in the Dr. Brodie Herndon house and in the Hansbrough family home, The Chimneys, 623 Caroline Street.

**1863** *Englewood, New Jersey.* While staying here for a few weeks, their first son died.

**1864** *Baltimore, Maryland.* He attended the Republican National Convention at the Front Street Theater.

**1865** *Washington, D.C.* He attended Lincoln's inauguration on the East Portico of the Capitol.

**1873** *New Brunswick, Canada.* He vacationed here, and, with friends, caught almost a ton of salmon.

**1876** *Cincinnati, Ohio.* Exposition Hall, Elm Street, for the Republican National Convention. He stayed at the Grand Hotel, southwest corner of Fourth and Central. Theodore Roosevelt was also there.

**1877** *Washington, D.C.* He attended Hayes' inauguration on the East end of the Capitol.

**1880–** *New York City, New York.* Fifth Avenue Hotel, 810 Sixty–second and Fifth Avenue.

**1880** *Chicago, Illinois.* Republican National Convention at Exposition Hall. He stayed at the Grand Pacifica Hotel, Jackson and LaSalle Streets. He was nominated for vice president.

**1880s** *Little Boar's Head, New Hampshire.* Bachelder's Hotel. The hotel was torn down 1928.

**1881–** *Saranac Lake, New York.* He stayed at the Saranac Inn.

**1881–** *Saratoga Springs, New York.* Moon's Lake House, with George Crum, the creator of the potato chip.

**1881** *Elberon, New Jersey.* Francklyn Cottage. He visited after Garfield's death. Arthur was also in residence in Long Branch when Garfield died and returned each summer for the rest of his term. It is on Ocean Avenue on the grounds of the old Elberon Hotel.

**1881** *Washington, D.C.* New Jersey Avenue and B Streets. Gray House in a block here. The house belonged to Senator John P. Jones of Nevada. Arthur stayed here until December 7, as the temporary White House, after Garfield died.

**1882** *Salem, Massachusetts.* He visited Essex Institute and Peabody Museum, 132 Essex Street.

**1883** *Bristol, Rhode Island.* Linden Place at 500 Hope Street. He came to dedicate the new Town Hall.

**1883** *Cape May, New Jersey.* Stockton Hotel in Rooms 21–23 on the first floor (south) ocean wing of the hotel, elaborately prepared for the president's occupancy. The reception included two or three hours for handshaking. New lace curtains had been hung and new carpet laid.

**1883** *Louisville, Kentucky.* Southern Exposition was housed in a large building near the river. He was here for the opening.

**1883** *Maitland, Florida.* He lodged at the Park House, located at the corner of Cotton Tail Lane and Lake Avenue between Lake Catherine and Lake Park, which was the center of social life in the 1880s.

**1883** *New York City, New York.* He unveiled a statue of Washington at the site where

Washington took his first oath of office on Wall Street. The same sculptor made Arthur's statue at Madison Square.

**1883** *New York City, New York.* Arthur dedicated the Brooklyn Bridge, Manhattan to Brooklyn over the East River.

**1883** *Savannah Southern Tour.* Georgia. He visited his relative, Henry Botts, at 125 West Gordon Street, on the southwest corner of Bull and Gordon. He also visited 126 Liberty Street, which is now the site of the Liberty Inn. He was accompanied by Secretary Chandler, Charles E. Miller, and several others. The train stopped first at Savannah, Georgia, and then at the following places in Florida: Jacksonville (boat ride up the St. Johns River to Sanford), Green Cove Springs, Palatka and to Sanford to a hotel for the night. They took the train to Kissimmee. Near Maitland, they stopped to visit some orange groves; after all other means of getting the ripe fruit had failed, Secretary Chandler scaled the tree to pick some. They stayed at Sanford House in Sanford. From there they went to Winter Park on Lake Osceola. It was intensely hot and the road was sandy. Secretary Chandler, who was riding on a buckboard, met with an accident. Lt. Dyer was driving, and Mrs. Dyer and the secretary were riding in the backseat, which gave way in a dip in the road; the secretary and Mrs. Dyer were both thrown out backwards. The president and his party stopped briefly at Rogers House, on Lake Osceola, and from there they went into Orlando and on to Kissimmee. From Kissimmee, Arthur's party went by boat up the Florida Improvements Canal. Here, the mosquitoes made them miserable, and they retreated hurriedly to St. Augustine, where Arthur spent four days (his most delightful). On the way from Washington to Florida, the train had to stop at Wilmington, North Carolina, to change trucks for the gauge difference. The president stepped out on the observation platform at the end of the car and sat on a camp stool to smoke a cigar. The night was dark, but clear. Just in front of the president stood an engine, and he sat full in the glare of its headlight. If he could have seen across this stream of light he would have been interested in a throng of black men who stood like statues, with their eyes fixed upon the president. Later, the coupling attaching the president's car to the train ahead of it snapped suddenly, the tail rope broke without alarming the engineer, and, before the engineer found out that he had lost anything, the president's car was left standing in a wood two miles behind. Later, early in the morning, there were only a few people at the Savannah station, and, when the president's car was run off on a siding, they gathered about and inspected the resident with as little apparent concern for the president's feelings as though he had been made of wood. St. Augustine, Florida. He spent four days at the Magnolia Hotel, corner of St. George and Hypolita Streets. It burned in 1927. St. Francis Barracks/State Arsenal on Marine Street at the corner of St. Francis Street. It is now the headquarters for the Department of Military Affairs.

**1883** *Winter Park, Florida.* Railway station visit. The site is across the street from the present railway station.

**1883** *Winter Park, Florida.* Seminole Hotel. The site is on the corner of Chase and Osceola Avenue on Lake Osceola. The hotel burned in 1902.

**1883** *Winter Park, Florida.* Lewis Lawrence house, corner of Park Avenue and Summerland, at 1300 Summerland Avenue on the southwest shore of Lake Maitland.

**1884** *New York.* Vacation in the Catskill Mountains. Hotel Kaaterskill (railroad station Pheonicia). At the end of the vacation, he went to Lake Mohonk and to Kingston, where he stayed with General Sharpe on Albany Avenue at the corner of Clinton Avenue. In Kingston, he attended services at

*Tomb of Chester Arthur.*

the First Reformed Church with Sharpe. One of the engines of the train burned soft coal, an unusual circumstance, and the passengers were "sadly begrimed."

**1884** *Washington, D.C.* Arthur dedicated the statue of Admiral Dupont at Dupont Circle.

**1885** *New York City, New York.* Grant's funeral.

**1885** *Washington, D.C.* Arthur dedicated the Washington Monument.

**1886** *New London, Connecticut.* Pequot House, where he stayed in a cottage for quiet relaxation, as an invalid, shortly before his death.

## DEATH

Arthur died November 18, 1886, in New York City, New York, at 123 Lexington Avenue, at 5:10 A.M. It was recognized that he had Bright's disease (a kidney disease) and that he had had it for some time could account for his irritability and his short hours of work in office. He did not speak following his attack on the last day as he did not have the power of

speech even though he was still rational. His sisters and son were with him at the time of his death. He left an estate of approximately $200,000.

## FUNERAL

The funeral took place on November 22, in New York City, New York, at the Church of the Heavenly Rest, Fifth Avenue and Forty–fifth Street. There was no embalming. He was dressed in a black suit and placed in an oak coffin covered with plain black cloth. There was a procession of more than a hundred carriages between the Arthur home and the church; 1,200 policemen and six companies of the United States artillery kept back the crowd. A choir of 30 men and boys sang "Asleep in Jesus," "Abide with Me," and "Nearer My God to Thee." President Cleveland and his cabinet and former President Hayes attended. After the chief mourners had left the church, the crowds slipped in and stripped the baptismal fount of its floral decorations. The body did not lay in state but was readied for viewing at home before the church service.

# BURIAL

The oak coffin was accompanied by the family and bearers in a special train from Grand Central Station in New York to Albany, where, after receiving the formal attentions of the governor and the New York legislature, it was taken to the Rural Cemetery, in Albany. New York, for graveside services. He was buried in the family plot. His wife's funeral had been in the same New York City church six years before, and she had also been buried in the Rural Cemetery. In 1889, a massive black monument surmounted by a bronze angel was erected to mark the grave site.

# BIBLIOGRAPHY

Bronner, Frederick L. *Chester Alan Arthur: His College Years*. (Bronner was in Chester Alan Arthur's class of 1848.) Schenectady, New York: 1848.

Reeves, Thomas. *Gentleman Boss: The Life of Chester A. Arthur.* New York, Alfred A. Knopf: 1975.

THE PRESIDENTS

# GROVER CLEVELAND

## 1837–1908
### 22ND PRESIDENT 1885–1889 / 24TH PRESIDENT 1893–1897: DEMOCRATIC PARTY

Stephen Grover Cleveland was born on March 18, 1837, to the Reverend Richard and Ann Neal Cleveland. He later dropped the first name. He was the sixth cousin once removed of U. S. Grant.

## CHARACTERISTICS

Cleveland was appropriately called "Big Steve" as a boy. As president, he was a big man, weighing more than 250 pounds and standing five feet and eleven inches tall. Photos taken during his presidency show his hair gray and receding in contrast to the brown hair of his boyhood. He had blue eyes, a fair complexion, and from young adulthood, a ragged bushy mustache. One description of his size reads, "a line drawn through the center of his stomach to the small of his back would measure at least two feet." While he was on a trip south, one curious old fellow stared long and hard at the president, and, as Cleveland passed through the crowd, he grabbed his hand. "Well, so you're the president," he said looking him up and down. "Yes, I'm the president, my friend." "Well," the old man exclaimed, "I've voted for lots of presidents in my time but I ain't never seen one before." He

# A LIFE IN REVIEW

**Birth:** March 18, 1837; Caldwell, NJ

**Died:** June 24, 1908; Princeton, NJ

**Married:** Frances Folsom; June 2, 1886;
2 sons, 3 daughters

## CAREER

**1852–1853** Store clerk

**1853–1855** Teacher

**1855–1859** Clerk and law study

**1859–** Lawyer

**1862–1865** Assistant District Attorney

**1871–1873** County Sheriff

**1882** Mayor of Buffalo

**1883–1884** Governor of New York

## ADMINISTRATION EVENTS

**1886** Presidential Succession Act

**1893** Financial Panic

**1893** World's Columbian Exposition

**1894** Pullman Company Strike

paused, then he laughed and slapped his side, "Well, you're a whopper."

S. C. Nevins, in his book *Grover Cleveland*, states Cleveland's greatness lies in typical rather than unusual qualities. He was honest, courageous, firm, independent and had common sense. On the human side, he smoked cigars, drank liquor, had a quick temper, and would at times swear violently. His favorite recreation was fishing, which he did as a boy in the canal and Green Lake of Fayetteville and later in the Adirondacks.

# BIRTHPLACE

Cleveland was born in Caldwell, New Jersey, at 207 Bloomfield Avenue, in the manse of the First Presbyterian Church.

# BAPTISM

He was baptized on July 1, 1837, in Caldwell, New Jersey, at the First Presbyterian Church, 814 Madison Street, which was his father's church.

# CHURCH

He first joined the church while his father was pastor of the First Presbyterian Church in Fayetteville, New York. The family met for worship every evening, and all the children were required to memorize the Westminster Catechism and to become familiar with the Bible. On Sundays, Cleveland attended two long church services and could not play or read secular books on the Lord's Day. He retained his simple religious convictions, but, in a possible reaction against the incessant observances of a minister's home, he never went to church in Buffalo (except when he was at his uncle's place at Black Rock). On his visits back home in Holland Patent, he always did and seemed to enjoy it.

**1837–1841** *Caldwell, New Jersey.* First Presbyterian Church, 814 Madison Street. There is a new church on the site.

**1841–1850** *Fayetteville, New York.* First Presbyterian Church (now the United Church), Genessee Street. He joined the church here during his father's pastorate.

**1850–1852** *Clinton, New York.* First Presbyterian Church, South Park Row. The original church was destroyed by fire in 1876, and a new church was built in 1878 on the same site.

**1852–** *Holland Patent, New York.* First Presbyterian Church. Attended in 1852 and thereafter when on trips to visit his mother.

*Birthplace of Grover Cleveland.*

**1853–1854** *New York City, New York.* Plymouth Congregational Church (now Our Lady of Lebanon) of Henry Ward Beecher, Orange and Cranberry Streets in Brooklyn Heights.

**1855–1873** *Buffalo, New York.* Breckenridge Street Church, corner of Breckenridge and Mason is a brick structure where he attended whenever visiting with his uncle Lewis F. Allen.

**1885–1889** *Washington, D.C.* First Presbyterian Church, later called National Presbyterian Church, Four and one-half Street, NW. As president he rented and occupied pew 132. He also attended here from 1893 to 1897.

**1887** *St. Louis, Missouri.* Washington Avenue Presbyterian Church, southwest corner of Washington and Compton Avenues. He sat in the ninth pew left center. The announcement that the Clevelands would attend that church brought an immense crowd of people. When they arrived and walked forward to the pew reserved for them, those occupying seats in the rear stood up and stared at them.

**1897–1908** *Princeton, New Jersey.* First Presbyterian Church, 61 Nassau Street. His pew is marked by a small brass plate.

# EDUCATION

Young Grover Cleveland began his schooling in Fayetteville. He was four when his family first came to Fayetteville, and he went to private homes (home schools) and to the Academy.

**1845–1848** *Fayetteville, New York.* District School. His schooling began in the little red frame district schoolhouse.

**1848–1850** *Fayetteville, New York.* Fayetteville Academy, a wooden edifice just across the road from the manse, now the site of the Twitchell house, 402 Elm Street. At the age of 11 he entered the Academy. The Fayetteville historian tells of some of his childhood escapades. On one occasion he climbed into the Academy belfry late at night and set the bell to ringing to wake the village.

**1850–1851** *Clinton, New York.* Clinton Grammar School, down College Street beyond the Chenago Canal. Here, he studied Math and Latin.

**1851–1852** *Fayetteville, New York.* He returned to Fayetteville academy. He had to give up the idea of higher education because of the family financial situation.

**1855** *Buffalo, New York.* Spaulding's Exchange, training at the law firm of Rogers, Bowen and Sherman.

# MARRIAGE AND HONEYMOON

Cleveland was married on June 2, 1886, in Washington, DC. He was married at the White House to Frances Folsom. The newspapers were full of rumors of the wedding long before the event. Miss Folsom's trousseau was purchased in Paris. The wedding took place in the Blue Room, which was decorated with pansies and roses. The reception and supper were held in the state dining room. The honeymoon took place at Mountain Lake Park Village, in Deer Park, Maryland, on Maryland 135. The couple left after nine o'clock in the evening on a special train of two cars and reached Deer Park in western Maryland the next morning in drizzling rain. Behind Deer Park Hotel is the Grover Cleveland Cottage. There is a marker which describes the public details of Cleveland's honeymoon. The cottage is a gray-shingled frame building two and one-half stories high. Grant and Garfield had also been entertained at one of the cottages. *The New York Times* has a running account of the honeymoon from June 4 to 9, when it ended. While there, they attended services at Oakland Presbyterian Memorial Chapel.

# HOMES

During his adolescent years Cleveland lived in a number of houses in small towns as his father moved to different Presbyterian churches. However, after leaving his birthplace in New Jersey, he never returned to visit Caldwell, and, until his retirement in Princeton, his legal residence was in New York State.

**1837–1841** *Caldwell, New Jersey.* 207 Bloomfield Avenue, where he was born in the rear room of the first floor.

**1841–1850** *Fayetteville, New York.* 109 Academy Street. The big room at the top of the stairs was used as a nursery, where all the younger children slept. He enjoyed his boyhood here going swimming in Limestone Creek and Chittenango River and fishing in Green Lake.

**1850–1852** *Clinton, New York.* 26 Utica Street. During this time, Cleveland was absent for more than a year in Fayetteville.

**1852** *Fayetteville, New York.* He returned to work in McViccar's store. He slept on a

*Grover Cleveland family home in Holland Patent, New York.*

corded bed in a bare unfurnished room without heat, light, or water. He ate at a nearby boarding house on Mill Street. McViccar's store is located on Genesee Street.

**1853–** *Holland Patent, New York.* Main and Elm Streets. He was here periodically in 1854, 1855, and thereafter to see his mother after his father died in 1853.

**1853–1854** *New York City, New York.* New York Institute for the Blind, Thirty-third and Thirty-fourth Streets and Eighth and Ninth Avenues. He roomed and worked here.

**1855** *Buffalo (Black Rock), New York.* Lewis F. Allen house on Niagara Street (originally the house of General Porter). The business center of Buffalo was two miles distant. The house was on a broad tract between Niagara Street and the Niagara River. Uncle Lewis Allen also had a large farm on Grand Island in the Niagara River.

**1855–1873** *Buffalo, New York.* He lived in various rooming houses. He stayed with the family of a fellow student in 1856 and then took rooms with a Fayetteville friend in the cockloft of the old Southern Hotel at the corner of Seneca and Michigan Streets (now an empty field).

**1873–1883** *Buffalo, New York.* Swan Street. In 1873, he moved to a small suite, called Room F, in the Weed Block. He ate for several years in a popular boarding house kept by a Mrs. A. B. Ganson. On the third floor of a brick addition at the rear of the Weed Block, Cleveland lived in a small apartment with southerly windows opening on Swan Street. At one time, he took his meals at Gerot's French restaurant, a block east of his office, in some saloon, or later at the City Club. Ex-President Fillmore's nephew, who had an apartment on the same floor, called Cleveland "Uncle Jumbo." A bronze wall plaque at 284 Main and Swan Streets marks the location.

**1883–1885** *Albany, New York.* The Governor's Mansion, 138 Eagle Street, about a mile south of the capitol.

**1885** *Albany, New York.* "The Towers." After his election as president, he moved out of the governor's mansion to this small house near the mansion.

**1885–1889** *Washington, D.C.* The White House. In Cleveland's time, it was easy for the ordinary man to see the president, and any one could enter the front door of the White House without being questioned.

**1886–1890** *Georgetown, D.C.* 3542 Newark Street, NW. He purchased a small house in what was then farming country, two miles north of Georgetown on Tenallytown Road (now Wisconsin Avenue), about three miles from the White House, and near the Woodley property. Frances called it Oak View but the newspaper men called it Red Top. The property included about twenty-seven acres plus the house. It was used as the summer White House, and they spent many summer weekends here. The area was later called Cleveland Park in honor of his living here. It has been torn down.

**1888–** *Marion, Massachusetts.* Sippican Harbor on Buzzard Bay. They rented a house with the Gilders for the summer. Again in 1889, they occupied a small cottage near the Gilders, the Reverend Percy Browne's cottage on the main road from the railroad station to Sippican Point.

**1888** *Marion.* Heller House, 182 Front Street, next to the Percy Brown House.

**1889–1892** *New York City, New York.* 816 Madison Avenue near Sixty-eighth Street, a dignified four-story residence of red brick and brownstone.

**1890** *Marion, Massachusetts.* Kelly house on Water Street. He wanted to buy the house but was unable to arrange the purchase.

**1891–1904** *Monument Point, Massachusetts.* Gray Gables, a cottage located between Cedar Pond Lake and Uncle Bill's Cove. He bought it in 1891. It had vistas over the Monument River and the Cohasset Narrows. After 1904 he leased the property and went to the hills of New Hampshire for the summer.

**1892–1893** *New York City, New York.* 12 West Fifty-first Street.

**1893–1897** *The White House.* During his first term the White House had been lighted by gas, but it was now lighted by electricity. In 1885 there had been but one telephone which Cleveland often answered himself, now there was a telephone operator. Cleveland spent long hours in the office, sometimes until two or three in the morning. The Clevelands' second child, Esther, was the first child of a president ever born in the White House. His daughter, Ruth, was so popular that a candy bar, Baby Ruth, was named after her.

**1893–1908** *Lakewood, New Jersey.* Little White House, Forest Avenue near Third Street. He often used this as his retreat out of Washington. In March 1908, he went to Lakewood to recuperate, and, in the suite of the hotel, he celebrated his last birthday.

**1893** *Washington, D.C.* Woodley Estate, 3000 Cathedral Avenue, is now owned by Maret School.

**1896–1908** *Princeton, New Jersey.* Westland, 58 Bayard Lane, is a large three-story colonial mansion built of stone and covered with stucco. When the Clevelands moved to Princeton, they made a number of changes in the colonial style house. Because of persistent callers they had to have the doorbell removed. He also purchased a rocky little farm about three miles away as a convenient stopping place when out for a day's hunting. While at Princeton he had many associations with Woodrow Wilson. He usually spent nine months in Princeton and three months in the summer at Gray Gables.

**1904–1908** *Tamworth, New Hampshire.* Intermont, Grover Cleveland Memorial Road, in sight of Mount Chocorua and Mount Passonconway and not far from Lakes Ossipee and Winnipesaukee. In the summer of 1990, his grandson Grover and his family were living here. Francis, his only living child, lived in town.

# WORK

**1852–1853** *Fayetteville, New York.* Genessee Street (near Limestone Creek), in the general store of John McViccar. It is a big brick building which still exists and one can point out where he lived in a bare room without heat on the third floor. The McViccar house has become the Fayetteville Library and is located at 111 Genessee Street.

**1853–1855** *New York City, New York.* New York Institute for the Blind, where he assisted his brother in teaching.

**1855–1862** *Buffalo, New York.* In 1855, he went to Buffalo to visit his uncle, Lewis F. Allen, and stayed there six months straightening out his uncle's cattle breeding records. At the same time he started studying law. At the end of the year he moved to a room in downtown Buffalo and began his apprenticeship in the firm of Rogers, Bower and Rogers. The firm occupied quarters in Spaulding's Exchange. On his first day in the law office, all the partners and clerks forgot he was in a corner of the library and locked him in during the dinner hour; he merely said to himself, "Some day I will be better remembered."

**1858** *Buffalo, New York.* He began to do political work with the Democratic Party.

**1859** *Buffalo, New York.* He was admitted to the bar to practice law.

**1862–1865** *Buffalo, New York.* He was appointed assistant district attorney with offices in the old courthouse of Erie County.

Lafayette Square. The library is on the site now.

**1865** *Buffalo, New York.* He was nominated for district attorney but was defeated in the election and returned to private law practice.

**1865–1871** *Buffalo, New York.* He formed law partnerships, first with Vandefpoel and then with Laning and Folsom, on the corner of West Seneca and Pearl Streets.

**1868** *Buffalo, New York.* In the old Post Office Building at the corner of Pearl and Swan, as a lawyer.

**1870** *Buffalo, New York.* He moved into a suite of rooms in the Weed Block, 284 Main and Swan Streets, to practice law.

**1871–1873** *Buffalo, New York.* County Courthouse. Sheriff of Erie County. As sheriff, he was also public executioner which was used against him when he ran for president.

**1872–1881** *Buffalo, New York.* During these years, he became a prominent attorney and partner in three successive firms: Bissell, Cleveland, and Bissell; Cleveland and Bissell; and Cleveland, Bissell and Sicard. His offices were in the same building as his apartment at Main and Swan. The name is still on the door at 284 Main Street, not far from where he had always lived since moving to town. The offices of the firm were on the second floor.

**1882** *Buffalo, New York.* Mayor of Buffalo, with offices in the City Hall. He still lived in Room F of the Weed Block. City Hall was on the site of the old Erie County Hall, Church and Franklin Streets.

**1883–1884** *Albany, New York.* Governor of New York, in the executive office of the governor in the State Capitol.

**1884** *Chicago, Illinois.* Exposition Hall was the site of the Democratic nomination for president.

**1885–1889** *Washington, D.C.* The White House as twenty-second President. The Inauguration was held at the east front of the

Capitol. The mass audience was concentrated around the large statue of Washington.

**1889–1893**  *New York City, New York.* At first his office was at 15 Broad Street and later at 45 William Street, as an associate in the law firm of Bangs, Stetson, Tracy and MacVeagh.

**1893–1897**  *Washington D.C.* The White House. Thousands were eager for the magnetic touch of the president. On one occasion, he shook hands with eight thousand people in thirty-three   minutes an average of one hundred and eleven per minute. He delivered his second inaugural address to a shivering audience standing on ground white with snow.

**1897–1908**  *Princeton, New Jersey.* After leaving the White House, he would not "sell" his name for use by a corporation.

# TRAVEL/VISITS

Cleveland was provincial and had no desire to travel abroad; only in later life did he see the Mississippi River and venture south of the Potomac. He never travelled much farther west than Chicago. He visited and made stops in the following states: Alabama, Connecticut, Delaware, Florida, Georgia, Illinois, Indiana, Iowa, Louisiana, Maryland, Massachusetts, Michigan, Minnesota, Mississippi, Missouri, Nebraska, New Hampshire, New Jersey, New York, North Carolina, Ohio, Pennsylvania, Rhode Island, South Carolina, Tennessee, Virginia, and Wisconsin.

**1880s**  *Saratoga Springs, New York.* Moon's Lake House on the western side of Lake Saratoga. He was entertained here by George Crum, the potato chip creator.

**1880–**  *DeBary, Florida.* DeBary house, Sunrise Boulevard, where he was entertained by millionaire DeBary.

**1880–**  *Green Cove Springs, Florida.* Here he went to visit the spa and stayed at the Union Hotel. He also stayed at the Magnolia Springs Hotel, two miles north of town, which is now the site of the Magnolia Springs Apartments.

**1880–**  *Maitland, Florida.* Park House, located at the corner of Cotton Tail Lane and Lake Avenue, was destroyed in 1916.

*Winter Park, Florida.* He stayed at the Seminole Hotel, corner of Chase and Osceola Avenues on Lake Osceola. The Orlando Ice Works honored him by sending a wreath frozen in the center of a cake of ice.

**1880**  *Sanford, Florida.* Sanford House, between Commercial and First Streets, where the library is now.

**1880**  *Key West, Florida.* Russell House. He also visited Tampa.

**1883**  *Albany, New York.* Pruyn house on Elk Street.

**1884**  *Upper Saranac, New York.* Adirondacks, at Derby's Prospect House. He was again on Saranac Lake in 1885. He often stayed at Saranac Inn at the northern end of Upper Saranac Lake on Route 30. The Inn burned some years ago, but some of the cottages are still standing. He also stayed in the former Blagden Cottage, also called Camp Alpha or Camp Sunrise.

**1885**  *New York City, New York.* Hotel Victoria, 4 West Twenty-seventh Street. He stayed in a richly furnished suite on the second floor while holding conferences with members of his new Cabinet. He often stayed here between 1885 and 1889 and again in 1889 at the end of his first term.

**1885**  *Washington, D.C.* Arlington Hotel, H Street and Vermont Avenue, NW, a block from the White House grounds, where he stayed just before his inaugural.

**1885**  *New York City, New York.* Fifth Avenue Hotel, where he stayed while in New York for Grant's funeral.

**1885**  *DeBary, Florida.* DeBary house, Sunrise Boulevard off US 17-92 and Mansion Road. It is being restored.

**1885** *Green Cove Springs, Florida.* Union Hotel and spa.

**1885** *Maitland, Florida.* Park House, site on the corner of Cotton Tail Lane and Lake Avenue.

**1885–1886** *Folsomdale, (near Cowlesville), New York.* The Folsom house, off New York 239, is where he courted Frances Folsom. It is now occupied by a member of the Folsom family.

**1886** *Cambridge, Massachusetts.* Harvard president's house, north of Dana Palmer, facing on Quincy Street. The current president's house which is on the same site as was Eliot's house in 1886 when he hosted President Cleveland.

**1886** *New York.* Adirondacks vacation at Prospect House (adjoining cottage), now called Saranac Inn. He went to Lake Placid to attend church at Stevens House. Rain interrupted some of the events, and they stayed in playing cribbage. He was here again in May 1887 and 1889.

**1887** *Clinton, New York.* He visited the home of Mrs. O. S. Williams on West Park Row, now Clinton House Inn and Restaurant. He returned to celebrate the Clinton Centennial with a banquet at the O & W Railroad freight house, which today is a garage for residents of the Clinton House apartments but was then the largest and newest building in town. Security for the president was the one-man police department, but others suffered from the skill of professional pickpockets.

**1888** *Florida.* In Jacksonville they stayed in the St. James Hotel (suite at southwest corner), on the west side of Laura Street. It was the most elegant hotel in the south and had 500 rooms. This was his first trip to Florida. Like other presidents of the time, he was accompanied by other Washington dignitaries on his tour of the country. St. Augus-

tine, Florida. Hotel Ponce de Leon in the pink bridal suite. They visited Palatka, Sanford, and Winter Park briefly and thought Winter Park the prettiest.

**1889** *Newport, Rhode Island.* C.C. Baldwin home, Chateau Nooga, corner of Bellevue and Narragansett.

**1889–90** *Lakewood, New Jersey.* Laurel House, formerly the Bricksburg House, north side of Main Street, west of Lexington Avenue.

**1890–** *New York City, New York.* The Players, 16 Gramercy Park, where he frequently lunched in later life.

**1891** *Buffalo, New York.* Iroquois Hotel, One M & T Plaza and now the site of the new M & T Bank and Tower, making a return trip to Buffalo.

**1891** *New York City, New York.* St. Vincent's Hospital on Seventh Avenue as a patient.

**1891–1892** *Lakewood, New Jersey.* Straus cottage for six weeks in the winter. This was a three-story building, a short distance north of the Lakewood Hotel. He sometimes visited friends at Edgemere, the Freeman Cottage. During bad weather, he played billiards. He was also here in the winter of 1892–1893. He commuted from here to his business in New York and was here until just before his inauguration in 1893.

**1893** *Washington, D.C.* Arlington Hotel, in Pomercy Annex, Vermont and I, NW, where he had a suite of rooms on the second floor before moving into the White House.

**1893** *Chicago, Illinois.* He visited the World's Fair and the Joy Morton home, 638 Groveland Park.

**1894** *Fredericksburg, Virginia.* Dedication of Mary Washington Monument, Washington Avenue and Pitt Street.

**1903** *St. Louis, Missouri.* He helped dedicate the Exposition. President Theodore Roosevelt was there.

**1906** *Greensboro, Pennsylvania.* Mononga-hela House, north side of County Street near the river.

# DEATH

Cleveland died on June 24, 1908 in Princeton, New Jersey, at Westland, 58 Bayard Street, in a large room on the second floor. He left an estate of approximately $250,000.

# FUNERAL

Simple funeral services were held in his home, at Westland, to which a select few were invited. President Theodore Roosevelt was there. The funeral was in the large library on the ground floor. There was no eulogy, sermon, or music. He was placed in a simple oak coffin with silver handles. The "Happy Warrior" of Wordsworth was read: "Who is the happy warrior? Who is he That every man in arms should wish to be?"

# BURIAL

Cleveland was buried June 26, in Princeton, New Jersey, at the Princeton Cemetery, 28 Greenview Avenue, near Witherspoon and

*Grave of Grover Cleveland.*

Wiggins Streets. The grave was guarded for some time.

# BIBLIOGRAPHY

Tugwell, Rexford G. *Grover Cleveland.* New York: Macmillan, 1968.

Welch, Richard E. Jr. *The Presidencies of Grover Cleveland.* Lawrence, University of Kansas: 1988.

# BENJAMIN HARRISON

1833–1901
23RD PRESIDENT 1889–1893: REPUBLICAN PARTY

*"Unlike many other people less happy, we give our devotion to a Government, to its Constitution, to its flag, and not to men."*

*—Speech, Monterey, California, April 30, 1891*

Benjamin Harrison was born on August 20, 1833, in the home of future president William Henry Harrison, who was his grandfather. His parents, John Scott and Elizabeth Irwin Harrison, were from good families, but not well off. Benjamin was eight years old when his grandfather, William Henry Harrison, died.

## CHARACTERISTICS

Harrison could never claim to be a well-built athletic figure. He had short stubby legs to go with a short stocky frame rounded out with a paunch. He was about 5′6″ tall. He had blue-gray eyes, light brown hair, and a fair complexion. He had a great talent for public speaking and spoke in a high soft voice. He was known to some as the "human iceberg." One observer said, "He can make a speech to ten thousand men, and every man of them will go away his friend. Let him meet the same ten thousand men in private and every one will go away his enemy." From his youth, Harrison smoked cigars.

After his nomination, people came to his house and ended up taking the picket fence surrounding the house. He came out on the

232

## A LIFE IN REVIEW

**Birth:** August 20, 1833; North Bend, OH

**Died:** March 13, 1901; Indianapolis, IN

**Married:** Caroline Lavinia Scott; October 20, 1853; 1 son, 1 daughter    Mary Scott Lord Dimmick; April 6, 1896; 1 daughter

### CAREER

**1852–1862** Lawyer; 1887–1889

**1862–1865** Military Service Civil War

**1865–1881** Reporter Indiana Supreme Court

**1881–1887** Member U.S. Senate

### ADMINISTRATION EVENTS

**1889** Johnstown Flood

**1889** Pan American Conference

**1890** Sherman Anti-trust Act

front porch and began speaking and that initiated his front porch campaign. He started the custom of flying the flag from public buildings. He recalled having seen it "wave over every schoolhouse" on one of his tours. He enjoyed hunting and at times went duck hunting away from Washington.

## BIRTHPLACE

Harrison was born in North Bend, Ohio, at the southwest corner of Symmes Avenue and Washington Avenue. The house, which was a red brick 13-room house, was torn down in 1859. There is a marker.

## BAPTISM

He was baptized in 1833 in Cleves, Ohio, at Cleves Presbyterian Church.

## CHURCH

He was a strong supporter of the Presbyterian Church. When he was president, every member of his Cabinet was Presbyterian. When travelling, he made an effort to stop over on Sunday and usually attended a Presbyterian church in the vicinity.

As a leader of his church, be became a deacon of the church in Indianapolis and was for almost 40 years an elder. He was a Sunday School teacher of young men and at home the family activities centered around their church and his law practice.

**1833–1850** *Cleves, Ohio.* Cleves Presbyterian Church. There is a marker to the right of the front entrance to the church.

**1850–1852** *Oxford, Ohio.* Miami University, High Street. A strenuous revival was conducted in that Presbyterian-dominated institution, and here, in the enthusiasm of youth, he made his formal religious commitment. The original "Old Main," where the chapel was located, was replaced in the early 1960s by a new Harrison Hall.

**1851–** *Cincinnati, Ohio.* First Presbyterian Church, between Fourth and Fifth and Walnut and Main. It was demolished in 1936.

**1854–1901** *Indianapolis, Indiana.* Second Presbyterian Church, Pennsylvania and Vermont Streets (now at 7700 North Meridian). He joined in 1854, became a deacon in 1837, and in 1861 an elder.

**1881–1893** *Washington, D.C.* National Presbyterian Church, which was new when he and his wife first attended services here in 1889 (in those days it was known as the Church of the Covenant). Its members had been meeting for some time before 1889 in what is now the Church Hall, awaiting final completion of the main building. The Harrisons' pew, No. 43, bears a plate with this inscription, "Benjamin Harrison, President of the United States occupied this pew 1889–1893."

**1888** *Glenwood Springs, Colorado.* First Presbyterian Church. He was brought from his train by a hired hack whose driver did not know the location of the church and went two blocks out of the way. Then, not knowing the ways of the church, he knocked on the door and said that the President of the United States desired to attend. From then on, it is reported that he received more attention than the minister. He was embarrassed and angry, and on returning to his train, ordered all curtains pulled and would see no one.

**1890–** *Cape May, New Jersey.* Presbyterian Church. He sometimes attended at Cold Spring.

**1890–** *Cresson Springs, Pennsylvania.* He attended services at the Mountain House.

**1896** *New York City, New York.* St. Thomas Protestant Episcopal Church, Fifth Avenue at Fifty-third Street. It was destroyed by fire 1907.

# EDUCATION

He learned the basics from tutors at home at the Point, five miles below North Bend on the Ohio River, at its intersection with the Miami River, and in a one-room log cabin school nearby.

**1847–1850** *Cincinnati, Ohio.* Farmers' College, 5553 Belmont Avenue, was a preparatory school near Cincinnati in the Pleasant Hill section.

**1850–1852** *Oxford, Ohio.* Oxford College, now Miami University, where he was admitted as a junior and graduated in 1852. At the west end of High Street is the attractive faded brick building which for 79 years

housed Oxford College. It is now a women's dormitory. The newer Harrison Hall is the site of Old Main, where Harrison held debates. Two dormitories remain that were there when he was a student. He graduated fourth in his class. The chapel, literary society meeting halls, and the library were all located in Old Main.

**1852–1854** *Cincinnati, Ohio.* Hart's Building, East Fourth Street. He studied law at the law office of Storer and Gwynne. He was admitted to the bar in 1854.

# MARRIAGE AND HONEYMOON

Harrison was married on October 20, 1853 in Oxford, Ohio, at the Reverend John W. Scott's house, corner of West High and South College, 121 High Street. Scott was a Presbyterian minister and the father of the bride, Caroline Scott. The wedding was small and simple. The house was a cream-colored two-story frame house built in about 1827. It had been the Temperance Tavern. The house was torn down and currently a British Petroleum service station on the site.

Caroline wore a gray travelling dress for her wedding, for they were travelling immediately after the wedding breakfast to The Point, in North Bend, seventy miles away, on the coach by way of Hamilton. In North Bend, they stayed with Benjamin's family.

Carrie Lavinia Scott Harrison died on October 5, 1892.

Harrison's second marrage took place on April 6, 1896, in New York City, at St. Thomas Episcopal Church, Fifth Avenue at Fifty-third Street. His bride was the widowed niece of the first Mrs. Harrison, Mary Scott Lord Dimmick. The wedding reception was held at 2 Grammercy Park. They left on the train for his home in Indianapolis, Indiana, for a few days and then on to a cottage in the Adirondacks at First Lake in the Fulton chain.

*Benjamin Harrison home, in Indianapolis, Indiana.*

Harrison's second wife did not receive a pension as his widow since she was not the wife of a president when he was serving.

## HOMES/LODGINGS

**1833–1853**  *The Point, near North Bend, Ohio.* The house on Brower Road was given to his father, John Scott Harrison, by his grandfather, William Henry Harrison. Benjamin and his new bride were here in 1853–1854. The house was a two-story brick structure with a small two-pillar portico, near the site of Fort Finney.

**1833–**  *North Bend, Ohio.* 116 Mount Nebo Street, at the Symmes home (his maternal grandparents).

**1850–1852**  *Oxford, Ohio.* Mansion House, southwest corner of Main and High Streets, in a two-story gray brick house that was built as a tavern in 1830. Caroline Scott Harrison's birthplace is on the southwest corner of Campus and High Streets. A marker states that Caroline Scott was born here in 1832. He courted Caroline here while attending the College.

**1853–1854** *Cincinnati, Ohio.* 323 West Third Street, where he stayed with his married sister, Betsy Eaton, while a law apprentice.

**1854** *Indianapolis, Indiana.* Apartment in 600 Block of North Pennsylvania, where they rented the ground floor of a two-story flat. A fire forced them to move.

**1854–1862** *Indianapolis, Indiana.* At the corner of Vermont and New Jersey, they rented a three-room house.

**1865–1875** *Indianapolis, Indiana.* 299 North Alabama. This is now the site of the fire department headquarters.

**1875–1901** *Indianapolis, Indiana.* 1230 North Delaware Avenue. He bought two lots together and built a spacious mansion. It was of red brick, in somber Victorian style, with its interior suggesting the old Harrison mansion, Berkeley. It is now open as a museum.

**1881–1887** *Washington, D.C.* While in the Senate, he had a house at 1013 Fifteenth Street, NW. Iowa Circle (now Logan), the Woodmont apartment building. Nothing remains. He also stayed at the Riggs House (Hotel), Fifteenth and G Streets, NW.

**1889–1893** *Washington, D.C.* The White House. In 1891, electricity was installed in the White House, but Mrs. Harrison was so frightened of it that she refused to handle the switches and left the lights on all night until the engineer came to turn them off in the morning.

**1890–** *Cape May Point, New Jersey.* A new cottage was built especially for Mrs. Harrison with 20 rooms and large porches.

**1890** *Cresson Springs, Pennsylvania.* In September, since the remodeling at the White House was not completed, they

resided in a Queen Anne cottage here in the mountains west of Altoona.

**1892** *Loon Lake, New York.* They leased a cottage in the Adirondacks from July to September before returning to Washington with the dying first lady. After his wife's burial in October, there were no further out-of-town expeditions during the remainder of his administration.

**1895–1909** *New York.* He had a summer camp on Second Lake near Old Forge in the Adirondacks in Herkimer County, New York. Berkeley Lodge on the second Lake Fulton chain was planned and built by President Harrison and used till his death. The log construction with two towers and an outstanding view is one of the finest cottages in the Adirondacks.

# WORK

**1852–1854** *Cincinnati, Ohio.* Storer and Gwynne Law Office in Hart's Building on East Fourth Street.

**1854–1857** *Indianapolis, Indiana.* Law practice. Office on Washington between Meridian and Illinois Streets.

**1857–1860** *Indianapolis, Indiana.* Law partnership with William Wallace, 30 1/2 West Washington.

**1860–1862** *Indianapolis, Indiana.* He was elected reporter of the Supreme Court of Indiana, which met in the Old Capitol, located on the same site as the present State House, at the corner of Senate and Capitol.

**1862–1865** Military service in the Civil War. He was the last Civil War general to serve as president. He advanced from colonel to brigadier general. He was present for the Resaca Battle, May 15, 1864, at Peach Tree Creek, Georgia. On July 20, 1864, at Durham Station, North Carolina, he was present for the surrender of General Johnson's Confederate troops.

**1865–1881** *Indianapolis, Indiana.* He resumed his post as Supreme Court Reporter of Indiana and practiced law in the firm of Albert G. Porter, Harrison and William P. Fishback. The Supreme Court offices were in the first state house, corner of Senate and Capitol, on the site where the present state house is located.

**1881–1887** *Washington, D.C.* U.S. Senator from Indiana, U.S. Capitol, Senate Chamber in the north wing of the Capitol, where the Senate presently meets.

**1887–1889** *Indianapolis, Indiana.* He practiced law in the firm of Harrison, Hines and Miller, Wright's Market Street Block, which refers to a piece of property at 120 East Market.

**1889–1893** *Washington, D.C.* The White House.

**1894** *Palo Alto, California.* Stanford University, where he delivered a series of lectures on constitutional law. Palm Drive (University Avenue).

**1899** *Paris, France.* He served as counsel for Venezuela in its boundary dispute with British Guiana before an international arbitration panel.

# TRAVEL/VISITS

**1880s** *Rockport, Indiana.* Brown-Kercheval house, 315 South Second Street.

**1888–** *Indianapolis, Indiana.* Union Station, 39 Jackson Place. He often came in here when it first opened on 1888.

**1888** *Chicago, Illinois.* Auditorium, Michigan Avenue and Parkway. He was nominated for president at the Republican National Convention.

**1889–** *Long Branch, New Jersey.* He stayed at the old Elberon Hotel on Ocean Avenue. It has been demolished.

**1889** *Woodstock, Connecticut.* He made several trips to the Henry Bower Roseland Park Estate, on the west side of the Green.

**1889** *Augusta, Maine.* Blaine House, across the street from the Capitol.

**1889** *Chicago, Illinois.* Ferdinand Peck house, 1826 South Michigan Avenue.

**1889** *Deer Park, Maryland.* He stayed in a cottage with Senator Davis and Stephen Elkins and also at the Deer Park Hotel, off Maryland 135.

**1889** *New York City, New York.* He followed Washington's movements of 1789 to St. Paul's, Federal Hall, and the original Senate chamber.

**1889** *Connersville, Indiana.* Elmhurst Mansion, just opposite the railway station, was the home of his campaign manager and U.S Treasurer, James N. Huston, and he often visited here.

**1889** *Washington, D.C.* Arlington Hotel, Vermont Avenue. Before his inauguration, he had a suite of rooms in the hotel's Johnson House annex.

**1890** *Decatur, Alabama.* He lodged in the elegant Tavern Hotel, corner of Grant Street and Sixth Avenue.

**1890** *Cleveland, Ohio.* He participated in dedication of the Garfield Memorial in Lake View Cemetery and lodged at the Stillman Hotel, Euclid Avenue.

**1890** *Ottumwa, Iowa.* He visited the Coal Palace.

**1891** *San Antonio, Texas.* He arrived during a heavy rain storm and attended a reception at the Grand Opera House. He also visited the regiment at Fort Sam Houston, and in Houston he stayed at the Menger Hotel.

**1891** *Bennington, Vermont, to unveil a monument.* August tour of Vermont. Montpelier, with visit to the Capitol.

**1891** *Boise, Idaho.* He spoke and planted a water oak on the Capitol grounds.

**1891** *El Paso, Texas.* He arrived at the railway station from San Antonio. There was a grand reception, and he spoke at the courthouse.

**1891** *Monterey, California.* Hotel del Monte on California 1.

**1891** *Pasadena, California.* Hotel Green (then called Hotel Webster). He came in at the railroad station and went for a two-hour drive through the main streets.

**1891** *San Francisco, California.* Palace Hotel, southwest corner of Market and New Montgomery Streets. There was a reception in the Mechanics Pavilion. He reviewed the troops at the Presidio, and visited the Golden Gate Park. He lunched at the home of Adolphus Sutro on the Heights. He attended the First Presbyterian Church on Sunday.

**1891** *Saratoga, New York.* Grand Union Hotel, Broadway Street.

**1891** *Tulare, California.* Here he gave the "Biggest stump" speech on a gigantic Sequoia stump.

**1892** *Loon Lake (near Plattsburg), New York.* In the Adironacks, he took a cottage for the summer White House. President's Cottage is still standing. It was part of Loon Lake Hotel.

**1892** *New York City, New York.* He laid the corner stone for Grant's Tomb on Riverside Drive.

**1892** *Virginia Beach, Virginia.* Princess Anne Hotel, Sixteenth Street and Oceanfront for a week's vacation, including a couple of days at Ragged Island Club House near Norfolk.

**1893** *Chicago, Illinois.* He dedicated a statue commemorating the Fort Dearborn Massacre at Eighteenth Street and Prairie Avenue. The statue is now in the lobby of Chicago Historical Society.

**1895** *New York City, New York.* Fifth Avenue Hotel. He was scarcely noticed in the hotel.

*Benjamin Harrison's tomb at Crown Hill Cemetery.*

# DEATH

Harrison died on March 13, 1901, at 4:45 P.M. in Indianapolis, Indiana, at his home on 1230 Delaware Street. None of his children were present, but Mrs. Harrison and other relatives were at the bedside as he quietly passed away having been unconscious for several hours before his death. He left an estate of approximately $400,000. The estate included the North Delaware Street homestead in Indianapolis and six lots in Herkimer County, New York.

# FUNERAL

There was a brief funeral service on March 17, at the home and at the Second Presbyterian Church, on Pennsylvania Avenue and Vermont Streets. James Whitcomb Riley delivered the eulogy. His body lay in state at the Indiana State House. His favorite hymn, "Rock of Ages," and "Hark, Hark, My Soul" were sung. More than 50,000 people came to view the body at the state Capitol where he lay in state. The railway company had made arrangements for a round-trip journey at the price of a one-way ticket. President McKinley came for the funeral but ex-president Cleveland did not.

# BURIAL

He is buried in Indianapolis at Crown Hill Cemetery, 700 West Thirty-eighth Street, beside his first wife. On the coffin was placed a

heavy walnut cover and then the granite roof. The tomb, 5' deep, was encased in granite four inches thick.

# BIBLIOGRAPHY

Sievers, Harry J. *Benjamin Harrison, Hoosier President: The White House and After*. Indianapolis: Bobbs-Merrill Co., 1968.

Socolofsky, Homer E. and Spetter, Allan B. *The Presidency of Benjamin Harrison*. Lawrence: University Press of Kansas, 1987.

# WILLIAM McKINLEY

**1843–1901**
**25TH PRESIDENT 1897–1901: REPUBLICAN PARTY**

*"Peace is preferable to war in almost every contingency."*

—*Inaugural address, March 4, 1897*

William McKinley was born on January 29, 1843 to William and Nancy Allison McKinley of Scotch-Irish and English background.

## CHARACTERISTICS

McKinley was 5'7" tall, had a paunch by the time he entered the White House, and was overweight at 200 pounds. He had a pleasant-looking face with blue-gray eyes, bushy eyebrows, a fair complexion, a cleft chin, and a rather large nose. He did not like to be told that it looked like Napoleon's nose, which was broad at the top. For work, he wore reading glasses. He particularly enjoyed opera and the theater. Ten to twenty cigars a day were a habit with him, and he drank an occasional glass of wine or scotch. He was not to be outdone in politeness; he would doff his hat to an ambassador or to a bootblack. He was the first of the presidents to take an active interest in golf.

## BIRTHPLACE

McKinley was born in Niles, Ohio, at 36 South Main Street, in the two-story family home. A country store occupied part of the

# A LIFE IN REVIEW

**Birth:** January 29, 1843; Niles, OH

**Died:** September 14, 1901; Buffalo, NY

**Married:** Ida Saxton; January 25, 1871; 2 daughters

## CAREER

**1859–1860** Teacher

**1860** Post Office clerk

**1861–1865** Military Service Civil War

**1867** Law practice

**1869–1871** County prosecutor

**1877–1891** Member U.S. Congress

**1892–1896** Governor of Ohio

## ADMINISTRATION EVENTS

**1897** Klondike gold rush

**1898** U.S.S. Main blown up in Havana

**1898** Spanish-American War

**1899** Philippines, Puerto Rico, and Guam acquired

**1900** Gold Standard Act

**1900** First automobile show

*Statue of William McKinley at the McKinley Birthplace Memorial and Museum in Niles, Ohio.*

## BAPTISM

The Methodist Church attended by his parents in Niles, Ohio from 1843 to 1851 burned, and no records remain of the actual place and date of his baptism. While a boy, he became a member of the Methodist Church in Poland, Ohio, on June 1858.

## CHURCH

He was brought up in a devout Methodist home; at ten, he publicly professed his faith at a revival meeting in Poland, Ohio; at sixteen, he became a communicant. Throughout his life, he was an active Methodist and a regular churchgoer. His favorite hymns were "Nearer My God to Thee," "Lead, Kindly Light," "Jesus, Lover of My Soul," and "There's A Wideness in God's Mercy." During his administration, churches of every denomination entered new fields of missionary endeavor, and there was popular enthusiasm for colonial dependencies.

first floor of the house. The house was later cut in two, and the section with the room of his birth was moved a mile away to Riverside Park (McKinley Heights), where it was raided by relic hunters. It was operated as a private museum until it burned, around 1935. Currently, the Dollar Bank occupies the site where he was born. A plaque is located on the left side of the building.

**1843–1852** *Niles, Ohio.* Methodist Episcopal Church. The church he knew burned down.

**1852–1867** *Poland, Ohio.* Methodist Episcopal Church. It was built on land later occupied by the Poland Branch of the Union National Bank. McKinley united with the church in June 1858, was an active member, and sang in the choir. The site of the current church is 1940 Boardman-Poland Road.

**1867–1877** *Canton, Ohio.* First Methodist Church, southwest corner of West Tuscarawas Street and Cleveland Avenue, 120 Cleveland Avenue southwest. He became superintendent of its Sunday School and also worked for the Y.M.C.A. A silver plate marks the McKinley pew. The church is now called Church of the Savior United Methodist.

**1867–1877** *Mooresville, Alabama.* He attended the same church in which future President Garfield had preached during Civil War days.

**1877–1901** *Washington, D.C.* During the White House years, he attended the Metropolitan Methodist Church, which is now at Nebraska and New Mexico Avenues, NW. The church of McKinley and Grant was located at John Marshall Place and C Streets, NW, where today the old edifice with its high spire no longer stands. In the current church, on the arm of a pew, midway between and in direct line with two large tablets on the side walls, is a silver plate with the word President engraved marking the pew occupied by the two presidents.

**1877–** *Washington, D.C.* National Presbyterian Church. Connecticut Avenue, Eighteenth and N Streets, NW. He purchased a pew here.

**1897** *Plattsburg, New York.* Methodist Episcopal Church, 19 Oak Street. This church burned in 1956 and the site is now occupied by a senior citizens apartment building.

**1897** *Plattsburg, New York.* First Presbyterian Church, 34 Brickerhoff Street.

**1897** *Plattsburg, New York.* Bluff Point Trinity Episcopal Church, Trinity Square.

**1899** *Holyoke, Maine.* Second Congregational Church, 395 High Street. He also attended the Baccalaureate at the Chapel of Holyoke College on Homestead Avenue.

**1899** *Pittsburgh, Pennsylvania.* Christ Methodist Episcopal Church, which he attended while on tour.

**1899** *Sioux City, Iowa.* First Methodist Church.

# EDUCATION

**1848–1852** *Niles, Ohio.* He got his fundamentals at the public school. Years ago a local guide said, "There," pointing to a red-colored building, "is the old school in which Bill (McKinley) and I learned our A.B.C.s." The building was later occupied by a marble and granite company and is situated on the main street of town. On Church Street, the same guide pointed out the high school which they had attended.

**1852–1855** *Poland, Ohio.* At first, he enrolled in the local public school in Poland, possibly in the schoolhouse on Poland Village Green. The building was later moved to Main Street, north of the Withers Apartment. See Poland Common by the Town Hall where he played ball. The swimming hole on Yellow Creek is identified by a black oak just beyond the business center.

**1855–1860** *Poland, Ohio.* Lee's New Academy, 47 South College Street, later became the site of Poland Junior High School. It was also known as Poland Academy.

**1860–1861** *Meadville, Pennsylvania.* Allegheny College. He entered as a junior but was forced by illness to drop out. Bentley Hall between Park Avenue and North Main

Street was there during his time. While at Allegheny College, he had a room in a house north of the college campus. It is now the home for orphans of the Odd Fellows, 400 North Main Street.

**1865–1866**  *Youngstown, Ohio.* Here, he studied law in the office of Judge Charles E. Glidden, near the junction of Boardman and Youngstown Streets. Later, this was the home of J.J. Johnston. He lived at 210 Main Street, south on Ohio 616.

**1866–1867**  *Albany, New York.* Albany Law School, southeast corner New Scotland and Holland Avenues. He dropped out before graduation. No rooming place has been located. He was admitted to the Ohio bar in March 1867.

# MARRIAGE AND HONEYMOON

McKinley was married on January 25, 1871, in Canton, Ohio, at the. First Presbyterian Church, 530 Tuscara was Street West (southwest corner of Tuscarawas and McKinley Avenue). The church is now known as Christ Presbyterian Church. Here he married Ida Saxton. He had met Ida at Meyer's Lake picnic two miles out of Canton. Serious relations began when their paths crossed while she was a cashier in the First National Bank of Canton. After their marriage, Ida joined McKinley's church. The minister, Dr. Buckingham, having become a little absent-minded, forgot about the wedding. The guests and bridal party had all arrived but not Dr. Buckingham. Messengers were sent for him and arrangements made for a fill-in when he finally arrived.

They visited several eastern cities on their wedding trip in New York and then returned to Canton to live. Their silver wedding anniversary was celebrated in 1896 in the same house in which they had begun their homemaking at 331 North Market Street.

# HOMES

**1843–1853**  *Niles, Ohio.* 36 South Main Street. At one time one part of the house was used as a storehouse and could be seen near the fire engine house.

**1843–**  *Lisbon, Ohio.* He visited his grandfather. His home is now the main office of the Columbiana Council of Boy Scouts. See Columbiana, Camp McKinley, just west of the village.

**1853–1855**  *Poland, Ohio.* 214 South Main Street. The site is now a parking lot.

**1855–1867**  *Poland, Ohio.* 111 South Main. The site is now a parking lot.

**1867**  *Poland, Ohio.* 21 Riverside Drive is still standing.

**1867–1871**  *Canton, Ohio.* 101 Tuscarawas Street West at the corner of Shorb and Tuscarawas Streets in a small frame house about a half mile away from where his parents lived. In 1870, the city directory lists McKinley Senior as living at 131 Tuscarawas Street West. The Saxton homestead where he and his wife lived for some time is 331 South Market Avenue.

**1871–1901**  *Canton, Ohio.* Ninth and North Market Street. The house was given to Ida as a wedding present. It was at the corner of North Market Street and Louis Avenue and was also their residence during the campaign of 1896. He purchased the white frame house, set in a neatly fenced lawn, in 1899 for $14,500. During the White House years, a miniature executive office was installed in the library. After the death of Mrs. McKinley's mother, they took up residence in the Saxton homestead and were there during his fourteen years in Congress and stayed here whenever they were home. See also the McKinley Farm on Lincoln Highway, two miles east of Minerva.

**1877–1891**  *Washington, D.C.* They lived quietly in the Ebbit House, suite 332, fronting on Fourteenth Street, NW. There was an extra room across the hall from his living quarters which he used as an office.

**1892–1894** *Columbus, Ohio.* As governor, he lived at the Chittenden Hotel, on the northwest corner of Highland and Spring Streets, across from the State Capitol. After it burned, he moved into a large apartment in nearby Neil House.

**1894–1896** *Columbus, Ohio.* Neil House, west side of High between Broad and State.

**1897–1901** *Washington, D.C.* White House as twenty-fifth president. Provisions were made for the first time in its history for sightly and convenient cloakroom areas for about 1500 people.

# WORK

**1859–1860** *Poland, Ohio.* He taught school for a term at Kerr District School about four miles from Poland in Poland Township. The exact location is unknown.

**1860** *Poland, Ohio.* He clerked at the town post office. The post office was located on South Main Street in the same building as the Case tailor shop.

**1861** *Columbus, Ohio.* Camp Chase, where he joined the regiment, four miles west of Columbus.

**1861** *Conrad Station, West Virginia.* He served with the Union forces near here.

**1861** *Clifftop, West Virginia.* Old Stone House (Tyree Tavern), two miles south of junction US 60 and West Virginia 41. Andrew Jackson, Rutherford Hayes, and he were all guests here at one time.

**1862** *West Virginia.* He saw his first action at Carnifex Ferry.

**1862** *Sharpsburg, Maryland.* He was present for the Battle of Antietam, on September 17. He served with future President Hayes. He was then lieutenant colonel. See the McKinley Monument near Burnside Bridge. More men were killed or wounded at Antietam than on any other single day of the Civil War. This battle also gave Abraham Lincoln the opportunity to issue the Emancipation Proclamation.

**1862** *Gauley Bridge, West Virginia.* Headquarters in Miller Tavern.

**1863** *Buffington's Island, Ohio.* Clash with Morgan's Raiders.

**1864** *Winchester, Virginia.* Battle of Kernstown.

**1864** *Strasburg, Virginia.* Fisher's Hill Battle.

**1864** *Battle of Cedar Creek, West Virginia.*

**1864** *Lynchburg, Virginia.* Sandusky, where he roomed with Hayes.

**1865–1867** *Albany, New York.* Law College, southwest corner of New Scotland and Holland Avenues.

**1867** *Navarre, Ohio.* He tried his first law case in the old brick store building at the northeast corner of Market and Canal Streets.

**1867–** *Canton, Ohio.* First National Bank Building, Second floor, southwest corner of the Public Square. Law practice.

**1869–1871** *Canton, Ohio.* County courthouse. He was elected Stark County prosecutor.

**1871–1877** *Canton, Ohio.* Practicing lawyer. See location above 1867–.

**1871–** *Canton, Ohio.* Harter Bank, 7 East Tuscarawas. He was an organizer and director.

**1877–1891** *Washington, D.C.* U.S. Congressman from Ohio (with the exception of 1883–1885).

**1892–1896** *Columbus, Ohio.* Governor. Executive office, Broad and High Streets. The governor's office was in the northwest corner of the Capitol.

**1897–1901** *Washington, D.C.* Twenty-fifth president. His campaign was famous as the "front porch" campaign. For his inauguration, he wore a suit of American wool.

The gifts received after the election included three eagles, four racoons, two roosters, one rabbit and one lamb. White House policy was total abstinence from wine. The Inauguration was held on the east side of the Capitol.

# TRAVEL/VISITS

Under no circumstances would McKinley travel on Sunday.

**1861** *Youngstown, Ohio.* Sparrow or Stone Tavern, 121 South Main Street, where he enlisted in the Union Army in April 1861. It is now the site of Stone Tavern Antiques.

**1877–** *Des Moines, Iowa.* Hoyt Sherman Place, Woodlawn Avenue at Fifteenth Street, as guest of the Sherman family.

**1880–** *Chicago, Illinois.* Potter Palmer Mansion, Castle on the Drive, 1350 Lake Shore Drive.

**1887** *Poland, Ohio.* He dedicated the Soldiers Monument at Riverside Cemetery.

**1890–** *Long Branch, New Jersey.* Normanhurst house, Monmouth College. The Guggenheim Library is on the site. He rode up and down Ocean Avenue in electric cars.

**1890** *Chicago, Illinois.* Grand Pacifica Hotel, Jackson and LaSalle, on a vacation.

**1890** *Savannah, Georgia.* W.W. Gordon House, northeast corner of Bull Street and Oglethorpe Avenue, is a stuccoed brick dwelling with a small Ionic portico. He visited the Green-Meldrim House on Macon Street, now the parish house of St. John's Episcopal Church.

**1892** *Minneapolis, Minnesota.* Chairman, Republican National Convention. Campaigning for Benjamin Harrison, his route went through seventeen midwest and southern states and covered more than 10,000 miles.

**1895** *Thomasville, Georgia.* Hanna House, 830 North Dawson Street. He stayed for three weeks with politician Hanna in his rented house.

**1895** *Washington, D.C.* He called on Cleveland at the White House.

**1896** *Chicago, Illinois.* At the home of his wife's cousin Lafayette McWilliams, on the south side. He spent one night at the Charles H. Dawes residence at Evanston. He attended Southside Presbyterian Church. He also visited the Peck home, 1826 South Michigan Avenue, in 1897 and 1900. John Borden Mansion, 3949 Lake Park Avenue in old Oakland.

**1897** *Asheville, North Carolina.* Glen Rock Hotel. The site is at 400 Depot Street, across from the Southern Railway Station. He was received here and addressed the crowd.

**1897** *Ausable Chasm, New York.* New York 373, south of Plattsburgh; Lake Placid, off New York 86. He spent one night with Senator Redfield Proctor in Proctor, Vermont (just north of Rutland), and returned to Plattsburg. Later, he was at the Niagara Hotel in Buffalo.

**1897** *Bluff Point on Lake Champlain, New York.* Vacation and summer White House for month of August at the Champlain Hotel, three miles from Plattsburg. He had a suite of seven rooms on the second floor in the southwest corner of the hotel annex. Clinton Community College is on the site. The hotel golf course was famous and is the subject of a recent book. President McKinley spent time sitting under the "McKinley Pine" watching the golf players. A monument was erected at the site on the access road to the clubhouse where the tree stood before it was destroyed by lightning in 1902.

**1897** *New York City, New York.* He attended the removal of the remains of Grant to his tomb on Morningside Heights. He stayed at the Windsor Hotel.

**1897** *Washington, D.C.* 1500 Rhode Island Avenue, NW, was the home of Count Cassini of the Imperial Russian Embassy who entertained lavishly. It is now the National Paint and Coatings Association.

**1898** *Chicago, Illinois.* University of Chicago, Kent Chemical Laboratory Theatre, to receive honorary doctorate.

**1899** *Atlanta, Georgia.* Kimball House, Decatur Street at the corner of Pryor. He made a visit to the Agricultural Building at Piedmont Park. He had been in Atlanta in 1895.

**1899** *Galena, Illinois.* He spoke at Grant Monument.

**1899** *Galesburg, Illinois.* Knox College. Site of Lincoln debates. He visited a home at 560 North Prairie.

**1899** *Hot Springs, Virginia.* Homestead Hotel for 10-day vacation.

**1899** *Jekyll Island, Georgia.* Cornelius Bliss estate.

**1899** *Milwaukee, Wisconsin.* Hotel Pfister, lodging and banquet. He visited the National Home (veterans).

**1899** *Minneapolis, Minnesota.* He visited the Thomas Lawry house for lunch and dinner and the Exposition Building for a speech where he had nominated Benjamin Harrison for president 1892.

**1899** *Peoria, Illinois.* Courthouse Square dedication Monument. Dinner at residence of J. B. Greenhut.

**1899** *Philadelphia, Pennsylvania.* Hotel Walton at Broad and Locust Streets, with front rooms of the entire floor. He was there to honor veterans.

**1899** *Richmond, Virginia.* Jefferson Hotel, West Franklin, Jefferson and West Main Street.

**1899** *St. Paul, Minnesota.* He gave a speech and spent the evening at the J. S. Hill home.

**1899** *Tallahassee, Florida.* State Capitol, South Monroe Street, for reception. The crush was so great that Mrs. McKinley fainted.

**1899** *Washington, D.C.* He unveiled the Washington Monument.

**1901** *Austin, Texas.* State Capitol for speech. Reception in the Senate Chamber. Governor's Mansion for dinner.

**1901** *Buffalo, New York.* Pan-American Exposition. The site is on Fordham Drive between Elmwood Avenue and Lincoln Parkway. It is now a residential area. He stayed at the John C. Milburn house, 1168 Delaware Avenue, which no longer stands.

**1901** *El Paso, Texas.* Station Street Methodist Church, Station Street. He spoke in the Plaza and visited the Texas end of the International Bridge.

**1901** *Los Angeles, California.* Vannuyea Hotel for reception and reviewing stand for Floral Parade. General Harrison Gray Otis house for dinner and the night.

**1901** *Phoenix, Arizona.* Lunch and reception at Adams Hotel.

**1901** *Redlands, California.* Casa Loma Hotel for speech and reception.

**1901** *Prairie View, Texas.* Speech to students from the State Normal School, which is now Prairie View A & M University.

**1901** *San Antonio, Texas.* Trevis Square, opposite the Alamo, speaking from a platform here.

**1901** *San Francisco, California.* Henry T. Scott house, located on the crest of the hill overlooking Lafayette Square. He visited the Presidio, where he saw companies of soldiers going to and coming from the Philippines. He was at the Palace Hotel and at Market Street Ferry Depot for receptions.

**1901** *Santa Barbara, California.* Speech and visit to old Spanish Mission.

# DEATH

On September 10, 1901, while visiting the Temple of Music Building at Pan-American

Exposition in Buffalo, New York, he was shot by an assassin. He was taken to the Exposition Medical Center and later to the Milburn home. The assassin, Leon Czolgosz, was caught, tried, and later executed. There is a bronze tablet, set in a rock in the parkway of Fordham Drive, which marks the site where McKinley was shot.

He died on September 14, in the house of John G. Milburn on Delaware Avenue. His last illness and burial were paid for at public expense for a total of $43,000. He left an estate of more than $215,000.

# FUNERAL

The funeral at the Milburn House, in Buffalo, on September 15, was attended by his embole and personal friends. The funeral cortege from there to city hall passed 50,000 people. President Roosevelt's carriage was the first in line. The coffin was of Santo Domingo mahogany, six feet and three inches long, and hand carved. The body lay in state at the City Hall until the following morning when it was taken to the funeral train at the Buffalo Union Station and transported to Washington via Williamsport, Harrisburg and Baltimore. A star in the middle of the floor in City Hall marks the spot where he lay in state.

The body was taken from Pennsylvania Station, in Washington, D.C., to lie in state in the East Room of the White House. A Methodist service took place here.

On September 17, the coffin was moved from the White House to the Capitol and placed in the Rotunda. President Roosevelt and ex-President Cleveland were there. Following services, the Rotunda was opened for the public viewing. A terrible crush, accompanied by a panic, occurred in front of the Capitol as thousands of people struggled to get a look at the dead president. Many people were injured, and one man lost his life. Hats, coats, umbrellas, neckties, women's silk waists and

*Temporary tomb of William McKinley.*

summer gowns were torn and scattered in every direction. Later in the evening, the body was taken to the depot and the funeral train departed for Canton.

On September 19, his mortal remains were taken to the First Methodist Episcopal Church on Cleveland Avenue, Canton, where a brief service was held. President Roosevelt was present. See the church memorial which includes the American flag which draped the casket.

# BURIAL

He was buried on September 19, in Canton, Ohio, at the Westlawn Cemetery. This was just twenty years to the day since President Garfield had died from the hand of another assassin. Just inside the entrance to the cemetery, the coffin was put in a gray stone receiving vault temporarily.

In 1907 the body was interred in a final resting spot at the McKinley National Memorial, Seventh Street, NW. Theodore Roosevelt dedicated the monument on September 30, 1907. The body was placed in a new casket. The tomb is a large granite structure, in part resembling in its lines and setting the Taj Mahal of India and to a lesser extent the tomb of Hadrian. In the foreground is a lagoon, built in four sections, each one a few feet higher than the one below, and flanked on both sides by tree-shaded walks and driveways. The building is in the form of a large cylinder topped by a simple Roman dome and relieved by the projecting entrance way. Less than halfway up the steps is the bronze standing figure of McKinley, one hand in his trousers pocket, the other holding a sheaf of papers. The bodies of McKinley, his wife, and two infant daughters rest within.

## SPECIAL SITES

*Niles, Ohio.* McKinley Birthplace Memorial and Museum, 40 East Main Street. A statue of President McKinley stands in the courtyard of the Memorial.

## BIBLIOGRAPHY

Leech, Margaret. *In the Days of McKinley*, New York: Harper and Brothers, 1959.

Olcott, Charles S. *The Life of William McKinley*, 2 volumes. Boston, Houghton: Mifflin, 1916.

# THEODORE ROOSEVELT

---

## 1858–1919
### 26TH PRESIDENT 1901–1909: REPUBLICAN PARTY

Theodore (Teddy) Roosevelt was born on October 27, 1858, at 7:45 P.M. in New York City to Theodore Senior and Martha Bulloch Roosevelt. He was third cousin twice removed of President Van Buren, fifth cousin of Franklin Delano Roosevelt, and uncle to Eleanor Roosevelt.

*"If elected, I shall see to it that every man has a square deal, no less and no more."*

*—Speech, November 4, 1904*

## CHARACTERISTICS

Teddy Roosevelt stood five feet and eight inches tall and weighed about two hundred pounds. He had a great barrel chest, bull neck, cleft chin, closely cropped brown hair, wide set blue eyes, a drooping bushy mustache, a rather large nose, small ears and feet, and a foot-wide toothy grin. He loved to be the center of attention and, as someone said, he set out to be "the bride at every wedding and the corpse at every funeral." He was rather strait-laced at times and detested dirty jokes. He boxed, wrestled, and learned the art of jujitsu. He did not smoke and drank very little. His prominent teeth and his spectacles made him a cartoonist's delight. With his ability to relate to everyone in one way or another, he was called "Old 57 Varieties." He was a great talker and as one associate said he could talk for two hours, allowing four and one-half minutes to a companion.

---

# A LIFE IN REVIEW

**Birth:** October 27, 1858; New York City

**Died:** January 6, 1919; Oyster Bay, NY

**Married:** Alice Hathaway Lee; October 27, 1880; 1 daughter    Edith Kermit Carow; December 2, 1886; 4 sons, 1 daughter

## CAREER

**1882–1884** Member state legislature

**1884–1886** Cattle rancher

**1886–1889** Writer

**1889–1895** U.S. Civil Service Commissioner

**1895–1897** Police Commissioner

**1897–1898** Assistant Secretary of Navy

**1898** Military Service, Spanish American War

**1898–1900** Governor of New York

**1901** U.S. Vice President

## ADMINISTRATION EVENTS

**1903** Panama Canal Zone leased

**1903** Wright brother's airplane flight

**1904** St. Louis, MO, Louisiana Purchase Exposition

**1905** Portsmouth, NH, Russo-Japanese peace treaty

**1906** San Francisco earthquake

# BIRTHPLACE

Roosevelt was born in New York City, at 28 East Twentieth Street.

# BAPTISM

He was baptized at 432 Third Avenue, at Madison Square Presbyterian Church, in New York City. There is a plaque on the baptismal font relating to Theodore Roosevelt.

# CHURCH

His family background was Dutch Reformed, and he himself joined the church at age sixteen and became a church leader. As a boy in his middle teens, before he went to Harvard he had conducted a "Mission class" in New York. In 1880, he started work at a Mission School in East Cambridge. While at Harvard University, he taught a Sunday School class at Christ Church for three and one half years. Politically, he was a firm believer in the idea of the separation of church and state. His favorite hymns were "How Firm a Foundation," "A Mighty Fortress Is Our God," and "Jerusalem the Golden."

**1858–** *New York City, New York.* Manhattan (Middle and Upper East Side Fifth Avenue Shopping District). The Collegiate Church of St. Nicholas, at the northwest corner of Forty-eighth Street, is the oldest congregation in Manhattan, dating from 1628. He was a member of this church, and his pew is marked by a tablet.

**1858–** *New York City, New York.* Madison Square Presbyterian Church, 432 Third Avenue, northwest corner of East Thirtieth Street, where he attended Sunday School and church as a boy, since there was no Reformed Church nearby. It has been torn down for apartments.

*New York City.* Fifth Avenue Presbyterian Church, 705 Fifth Avenue, northwest corner West Fifty-fifth Street. Funeral services were held here for his wife and mother who both died on February 14, 1884. The Roosevelts were members here.

**1876–** *Cambridge, Massachusetts.* Christ Church, Cambridge, on Farwell Place (Garden Street). Although Christ Church was Episcopalian, he served as a teacher in the Sunday School while he was a student at Harvard.

**1878–** *Island Falls, Maine.* From 1878 on, he formed the habit of reading his Bible a mile downstream from Lake Mattawamkeay at a spot which has for this reason become known as Bible Point. The Theodore Roosevelt Association has erected a plaque here.

**1882–** *Albany, New York.* First Dutch Reformed Church, southwest corner of North Pearl and Orange Streets. The box pew used by Roosevelt is marked with a bronze tablet.

**1882–** *Washington, D.C.* Grace Reformed Church, Fifteenth and O Streets, NW, which he attended while vice president and president. He usually walked to and from the church. A new building has been erected in front of the old chapel. Roosevelt's pew No. 5 is on the third row of the chancel in the middle aisle.

**1884–1919** *Sagamore Hill, Oyster Bay, New York.* Christ Episcopal Church, 61 East Main. His mother and his second wife were Episcopalian, and when the family was at Oyster Bay, they went here.

**1903** *Harrisburg, Pennsylvania.* Zion Lutheran Church, which was also the place where William Henry Harrison had been nominated for president.

**1903** *Seattle, Washington.* Church services held at the Grand Opera House, Seattle Center.

**1903** *Cheyenne, Wyoming.* First Methodist Church, Eighteenth and Central Avenue.

**1903** *Sioux Falls, South Dakota.* German Lutheran Church, 214 South Walts Street. The organizers mistakenly thought he was a member, and he sat through a service all in German. When the mistake was discovered, arrangements were made for him to attend another service in the evening at Livingston Reformed Church, Sixth and Fairfax Avenue, which is now East Side Presbyterian and located at 1001 East Sixth Street.

**1905** *Silt, near Glenwood Springs, Colorado.* On Divide Creek near his camp at the Old Blue Hen School House. The "Roosevelt Window" in the Rifle Public Library commemorates his visit to the area.

**1905–** *Scottsville (Pine Knot), Virginia.* Christ Church.

**1907** *St. Augustine, Florida.* Presbyterian Memorial Church, northwest corner of Valencia and Sevilla Streets.

**1910** *Cheyenne, Wyoming.* First Congregational Church, 3501 Forest Drive.

# EDUCATION

As a boy, he went to school very little; most of the time, he had tutors after he passed from the earlier instruction of his aunt, Anna Bulloch. Much of his education was received in the course of travelling.

**1872** *Dresden, Germany.* Here, he was placed in the home of the family of Dr, Minkwitz, city counselor, where he was to be saturated in the German atmosphere as much as possible in five months.

**1873–1875** *New York.* Arthur Hamilton Cutler was engaged as a tutor for his entrance examinations for Harvard.

**1876–1880** *Cambridge, Massachusetts.* Harvard University. He graduated magna cum laude, with Phi Beta Kappa key, twenty-first out of one hundred and seventy-seven. While at Harvard he roomed on the second floor of a boarding house at 16 Winthrop Street on the southwest corner of Holyoke two blocks below Harvard Square near Harvard's Indoor Athletic Building. Graduation was held in Sanders Theater in 1880. He was a member of the Hasty Pudding Club at the corner of Massachusetts Avenue and Holmes Place.

**1880–1881** *New York City, New York.* Columbia Law School. He dropped out to run for the State Assembly and never sought admission to the bar. The main campus was at Forty-ninth and Madison, but the law school was located downtown at 8 Great Jones Street on the northwest corner of Lafayette Place. It was a three-mile walk from his home down Fifth Avenue to Great Jones Street.

## MARRIAGE AND HONEYMOON

Roosevelt was married on October 27, 1880, in Brookline, Massachusetts, at First Parish (Unitarian) Church, 382 Walnut Street. His bride was Alice Hathaway Lee. According to one account, "They drove out into the country to the church. It was the dearest little wedding." When Alice married in 1905, she received, among other things, a carload of coal as a wedding present. The honeymoon took place in Springfield, Massachusetts, at the Massasoit House, at Main and Lyman Streets. From there they went to Oyster Bay, New York, where they stayed for two weeks before going on to New York.

Alice Hathoway died on February 14, 1884.

Roosevelt's second marrage took place on December 2, 1886, in London, England, at St. George's Church, Hanover Square. The bride was Edith Kermit Carow. They had a four-month honeymoon in England, France, and Italy, including a weekend at Wroxton Abbey in Warwickshire where they slept in the Duke of Clarence's bed. Before the wedding, he had stayed at Brown's Hotel at Dover Street 21, London. See the marriage certificate on display there.

## HOMES/LODGINGS

**1858–1873** *New York City, New York.* 28 East Twentieth Street. Birthplace and home. On the first floor was a parlor and a library, both

*Birthplace of Theodore Roosevelt.*

opening from the hall, with a dining room running across the full width of the house at the rear. The formal parlor was open for general use only on Sunday evening.

**1858–** *Staten Island, New York.* Left side of Signs Road, not far from Richmond Avenue, New Springville. The house and property belonged to his grandfather, and he visited as a boy. The house is gone, and it is now the site of New Springville Park.

**1863–1866** *Madison, New Jersey.* The Loantaka, the Roosevelt place where he spent four summer seasons, was on the western side of Kitchell Road (directly across from Fairleigh Dickinson University—(formerly the Twombly estate) south to Woodland Avenue. Sometimes Teddy, then quite little, would follow the tally-ho into town on a pony and was the center of attention for the children of the town.

**1867** *Barrytown-on-Hudson, New York.* John Aspinwall place in Duchess County, which they rented for the summers 1867 and 1868.

**1871** *Dobbs Ferry, New York.* Their summer residence in 1871 and 1872.

**1872** *Moosehead Lake, Somerset County, Maine.* Camping. He was sent by his father for a change of air and to improve his health.

**1873–1882** *New York City.* 6 West Fifty-seventh Street, close to Central Park. He spent the first winter after his marriage here. In April 1884, he dismantled and sold the family home. Both his wife and mother died here on February 14, 1884.

**1874–** *Oyster Bay, Cove Neck, New York.* Here they established a summer residence called Tranquility (now demolished.)

**1882–1883** *New York City.* 55 West Forty-fifth Street, in a small brownstone where he and Alice first set up housekeeping by themselves.

**1882–1884** *Albany, New York.* Delwan House, at the corner of Broadway and Steuben, while serving in the state legislature.

**1883–1884** *Albany, New York.* While Alice was with him, they stayed in a residential hotel, corner of Eagle and State Streets.

**1883–1887** *Medora, North Dakota.* In his Maltese Cross Cabin, he raised cattle and began to regain his health and recover from the grief of losing his parents and his first wife. The cabin has been moved to the state capitol grounds in Bismarck. Maltese Cross, or Chimney Butte, was eight miles from Medora, and had a one-story three-room house. Thirty miles down the river was the Elkhorn Ranch. See Theodore Roosevelt National Park, South Unit, on US Highway 10. There is little to see except the site of the former buildings.

**1883–** *Elkhorn Ranch, North Dakota.* The site is marked by only a few foundation stones. See location above.

**1884–1919** *Oyster Bay, New York.* The house, whose name by 1885 had changed from Leeholm to Sagamore, was located on the hill at Cove Neck, east and north of Oyster Bay. It was a 23-room Victorian structure of frame and brick with eight fireplaces.

**1886–1897** *New York City, New York.* 422 Madison Avenue. Following Alice's death, he stayed here with Bamie (his sister) when he was East. Bamie also cared for his infant daughter, Alice.

**1886–** *New York City.* 689 Madison Avenue. He first stayed here in April and May, 1886, when he took over his sister's new house before moving to Sagamore at the end of May.

**1889–1901** *Washington, D.C.* 1733 N Street, NW. He often stayed at this home of his sister, Bamie (now Mrs. Sheffield Cowes). He was here the night of McKinley's funeral. He also waited here for Mrs. McKinley to vacate the White House. The house has been described as a typical turn of the century middle-class house.

**1889–1891** *Washington, D.C.* 1820 Jefferson Place, off Connecticut Avenue, where he rented a house about one-tenth the size of his Sagamore Hill house. He entertained many guests here, and a comment reads, "He considered himself nobly sacrificing for essential economy by not serving champagne at his dinners in this small house."

**1891–1895** *Washington, D.C.* 1215 Nineteenth Street, NW, where he rented a house larger than 1820 Jefferson Place.

**1895–1897** *New York City, New York.* 422 Madison Avenue, while working as New York City Police Commissioner.

**1897–1899** *Washington, D.C.* 1810 N Street, NW, a house just opposite the British Embassy.

**1899–1901** *Albany, New York.* Executive Mansion, 138 Eagle Street.

**1901–1909** *Washington, D.C.* The White House as twenty-sixth president. While the new West Wing, then called the Executive Office Building, was being built, he

*Pine Knot, Virginia, Theodore Roosevelt retreat.*

and his family went to live in a house on Lafayette Park, 736 Jackson Place, NW. While they were in the White House, they had more pets than any other First Family, before or since. These pets had complete freedom of the house and included dogs, puppies, cats, kittens, rabbits, guinea pigs, snakes, a badger, a macaw, and other birds. Outside were a bear cub, ponies, horses, and more dogs.

**1905–** *Pine Knot, Virginia.* His wife bought a small tract of mountain land south of Culpeper, overlooking the Rapidan River for a summer retreat, Plain Dealing. In 1908 they discovered that a hobo had been using it in their absence. It is now in ruins.

**1909–1919** *Oyster Bay, New York.* Sagamore Hill on Cove Neck Road, in retirement. The house is now open for tours.

# WORK

**1882–1884** *Albany, New York.* New York State assemblyman. At age twenty-four, he was the minority speaker. Member of Judiciary Committee which held Friday and Saturday sessions in the old St. James Hotel.

**1884–1886** *Dakota Territory (now North Dakota).* He worked as a cattle rancher and for a time deputy sheriff of Billings County.

**1886–1889** *Sagamore Hill, Oyster Bay, New York.* He concentrated on writing.

**1889–1895** *Washington, D.C.* Member and commissioner of the U.S. Civil Service Commission. His office was located in the west wing of City Hall at the south end of Judiciary Square. It was a large building with Ionic columns with a flight of seventeen stone steps leading up to it.

*Sagamore Hill in Oyster Bay, New York.*

**1895–1897**   *New York City, New York.* President of the New York City Police Board. Police commissioner. Headquarters were at 300 Mulberry Street in a squat square building with a stained marble facade.

**1897–1898**   *Washington, D.C.* Assistant secretary of the Navy, with an annual salary of $4,500. From his office on Pennsylvania Avenue, he could look through the window at the lawns and gardens of the White House.

**1898**   *Cuba.* Spanish-American War. He first saw action at the Battle of Las Guasimas on June 24. He was present at San Juan and Kettle Hill on July 1 and at the occupation of Santiago Harbor on August 8. He mustered out at Camp Wickoff, Mantauk, Long Island, New York.

**1898–1900**   *Albany, New York.* Governor. He was the first governor to occupy the new Capitol. On its completion, it was said to be the most magnificent legislative hall in the world.

**1901**   *Washington, D.C.* Vice President of the United States.

**1901** *Newcomb, Essex County, New York.* Route 28N (Roosevelt-Marcy Memorial Highway). A bronze marker reads, "Near this point, while driving hastily from Tahawus Club to North Creek at 2:15 A.M. September 14, 1901, Theodore Roosevelt became President of the United States".

**1901–1909** *Washington, D.C.* President of the United States.

**1909–1919** *New York City, New York.* 44 Wall Street. Roosevelt and Kobbe law firm. He had an office but did not practice law.

**1909–1919** *Sagamore Hill, Oyster Bay, New York.* Retirement.

# TRAVEL/VISITS

**1871** *New York.* The family took a trip via Lake George and Plattsburg to Paul Smith's in the Adirondacks and spent nine days camping "in the bush."

**1878–** *Island Falls, Aroostook County, Maine.* On camping trips in 1878 and 1879. He made several trips to Island Falls.

**1878–1880** *Boston, Massachusetts.* He visited Alice (daughter of George Cabot Lee), his future first wife, who lived next door to the Leverett Saltonstalls on Chestnut Hill with whom he stayed.

**1880** *Desert Island, Maine.* He was here with Alice on vacation near Bar Harbor, Hancock County. At first, he stayed with Jack Tebbetts at Schooner Head, three miles from Bar Harbor, but later with Christopher Minot Weld at Bar Harbor.

**1880** *Huntley, Illinois.* He stayed on the farm of a man named Wilcox. On September 3, he went to Carroll, Iowa, where he remained a week, and then he visited his cousin Jack Elliott at Moorhead, Minnesota.

**1880** *Marmarth, North Dakota.* Slightly north of town on the Little Missouri River, off US 12. He shot his first buffalo.

**1880** *Medora, North Dakota.* De Mores Chateau in De Mores State Park, about one mile from Medora. He often visited here.

**1884** *Chicago, Illinois.* The Grand Pacific Hotel, Jackson and LaSalle, for the Republican National Convention, which was held in the Exposition Hall on the lake side of Michigan Avenue.

**1884** *Nahant, Massachusetts.* Henry Cabot Lodge summer home.

**1884** *Utica, New York.* Bagg's Hotel, across Lake Erie from the Opera House, where he attended the Republican convention which propelled him into a leadership position.

**1885** *New York City, New York.* He marched in Grant's funeral parade.

**1886–1903** *North Dakota.* His cattle-raising operations at Maltese Cross and Elkhorn were a loss, and by 1899 his Dakota business affairs had been practically liquidated. After 1886, his primary interest in the site was as a base for autumn hunting trips. The Elkhorn house was closed as a residence by 1891, but it was used by Roosevelt on the brief fall visits which he made each year from 1886 through 1896, except 1895.

**1889–** *Washington, D.C.* 1603 H Street, NW, where he often visited in the home of Henry Adams. (Now Hay-Adams Hotel).

**1893** *Madison, Wisconsin.* He visited here first in 1893 when he addressed the State Historical Society. In 1911, he addressed the State Legislature in the State Capitol and in 1918 visited the Executive Mansion, 130 East Gilman Street. He was houseguest of Robert M. LaFollette, Sr. at 314 South Broom Street.

**1897** *Washington, D.C.* 1500 Rhode Island Avenue, NW. Home of Count Cassini of the Imperial Russian Embassy, where he visited frequently.

**1897** *Washington, D.C.* Henry Cabot Lodge home, 1765 Massachusetts Avenue, NW.

**1898** *San Antonio, Texas.* He went to Camp Wood to join his Rough Riders during the Spanish-American War. Roosevelt Park, off Mission Road at the old fairgrounds, is where he joined the Rough Riders. In San Antonio he stayed at the Menger Hotel, 204 Alamo Plaza, northeast corner of Alamo Plaza and Blum Street. He recruited his Rough Riders here. He also visited the Alamo.

**1898** *Fort Worth, Texas.* White Elephant Saloon, 106 East Exchange Avenue.

**1898** *Pensacola, Florida.* Wright Street and Tarragona Street, where he and his Rough Riders were welcomed before leaving for Tampa and Cuba.

**1898** *Tampa, Florida.* He stayed at the Tampa Bay Hotel between Lafayette and Casa Streets. It is now occupied by University of Tampa.

**1900–** *New York City, New York.* National Arts Club at 15 Gramercy Park South (formerly Governor Tilden's residence), which he used for daily luncheon conferences.

**1900** *Galena, Illinois.* He visited Grant's home on Bouthillier Street.

**1900** *Philadelphia, Pennsylvania.* Hotel Walton, Broad and Locust Streets, for the Republican National Convention. The convention was held in Exposition Hall. His campaign tour began on August 29, and he went as far west as Helena, Montana, and he stopped in (partial listing) Chicago, Illinois; Detroit, Michigan; Denver, Colorado (at the Capitol); St. Louis, Missouri; Indianapolis, Indiana; Louisville, Kentucky; Columbus, Ohio; and Charleston, West Virginia (at the old Capitol). On the tour he made 673 speeches in 567 towns in twenty-four states and travelled 21,209 miles.

**1901** Isle La Motte, Vermont. He was attending a meeting of the Vermont Fish and Game League when he was told that McKinley had been shot in Buffalo. On

*Site where on September 14, 1900 on the death of William McKinley, Roosevelt took the oath of office as President.*

September 11, he was at Camp Tahawus, New York, on the slopes of Mount Marcy and on the twelfth at Lake Golden. He was near Tear-in-the-Cloud when he received the telegram reporting McKinley's death at approximately 1:25 P.M.

**1901** *Buffalo, New York.* The Wilcox House, 641 Delaware Avenue, where on September 14, on the death of McKinley, he took the oath of office as President at 3:32 P.M. on Saturday afternoon.

**1901** *Canton, Ohio.* Mrs. George H. Harter House, 933 North Market Street, while in Canton for the funeral of McKinley.

**1901** *Weverton, New York.* From Weverton to Blue Mountain Lake, New York 28, through North Creek and Minerva to Boreas Bridge State Campsite. On the ridge above the Boreas Valley, a bronze plaque on a granite boulder marks the approximate spot where Roosevelt was when he automatically became the twenty-sixth president.

**1902** *Mobile, Alabama.* He dedicated the

Masonic Temple, St. Joseph Street. His first visit to Mobile was on June 1, 1898.

**1902**  *Newport, Rhode Island.* Cliff Lawn, corner of Cliff Walk and Bath Road. He came for the christening of his godson, Theodore Chandler.

**1903**  *Bismarck, North Dakota.* He visited the State Capitol. The old Capitol burned in 1930. He was a guest at the Governor's mansion (since 1893), 320 Avenue B.

**1903**  *Boise, Idaho.* Idanha Hotel, northeast corner of Main and Tenth Streets. He visited the old Capitol Building. The present one was constructed 1905–1912.

**1903**  *Helena, Montana.* He visited the State Capitol, Sixth Avenue.

**1903**  *Indianapolis, Indiana.* He visited the State Capitol, State House Square and Governor's Circle.

**1903**  *Lincoln, Nebraska.* State Capitol, Fifteenth and K Streets. The Governor's mansion (1901–1956) was across from the Capitol to the south. It was razed in 1956.

**1903**  *Los Angeles, California.* Westminster Hotel, 342-350 South Main Street. Reception.

**1903**  *Madison, Wisconsin.* He visited the Capitol and Executive Mansion, 130 East Gilman Street.

**1903**  *Milwaukee, Wisconsin.* Banquet at Plankinton House, southeast corner of Second and Wisconsin. It is now the site of Plankinton Arcade.

**1903**  *Monterey, California.* Hotel del Monte, on California 1. The present hotel is on the same site. While here, he attended St. John's Chapel on the hotel grounds.

**1903**  *Portland, Oregon.* Hotel Portland, southwest Sixth Street.

**1903**  *Redlands, California.* Hotel Casaloma. Razed in the 1960s.

**1903**  *San Bernardino, California.* Mission Inn Hotel, 3649 Seventh Street.

**1903**  *San Francisco, California.* Palace Hotel, southwest corner Market and New Montgomery Streets.

**1903**  *Sioux Falls, South Dakota.* Cataract Hotel, Ninth Street side, commencing at the corner of Phillips Avenue on the second floor. The landlord made special preparations in his suite of rooms. "The suite was papered in imported chambray. The furniture was solid mahogany, upholstered in green with drapery and carpet to match. The room was illuminated with bargee lamps of stensland brass with opalescent glass globes. On the sideboard was an English water pitcher of cut glass and glasses to match."

**1903**  *South Pasadena, California.* Mrs. James Garfield, 1001 Buena Vista Street, and a reception at the Raymond Hotel on Raymond Street. The modern address is 150 South Orange Grove.

**1903**  *Springfield, Illinois.* He visited the Capitol, had lunch at the Executive Mansion, and visited the Lincoln Monument.

**1903**  *St. Paul, Minnesota.* He visited the Capitol, 700 Wabasha Street. He stayed at the Nicollet Hotel, Washington Avenue between Hennepin and Nicollet Avenue. The site is now occupied by the modern Nicollet Hotel.

**1903**  *St. Louis, Missouri.* David R. Francis home, while there to open the St. Louis Exposition. Ex-president Cleveland was also there for the Exposition.

**1903**  *Topeka, Kansas.* State Capitol, Capitol Square, Jackson and Harrison Streets. He visited the governor at the Governor's mansion.

**1903**  *Yellowstone National Park, Wyoming.* Mammoth Hot Springs Hotel. He laid the cornerstone of Roosevelt Arch on the northern (Wyoming-Montana) boundary to the park.

**1903**  *Yosemite National Park, California.* He visited Camp Bridal Falls and lodged at the Glacier Point Hotel, south entrance gate at Chinquapin Junction.

**1905**   *Cambridge, Massachusetts.* Lawrence house, 101 Brattle Street, where he stayed with the Lawrences who were friends.

**1905**   *Charleston, South Carolina.* Mills House Hotel, corner of Meeting and Queen Streets.

**1905**   *Glenwood Springs, Colorado.* Hotel Colorado, before and after going to a camp on Divide Creek near Rifle.

**1905**   *Little Rock, Arkansas.* Capitol, 300 West Markham. He visited Fort Roots in North Little Rock and spoke in City Park (now MacArthur Park) and at Albert Pike Consistory building.

**1905**   *Montgomery, Alabama.* State Capitol on Goat Hill at the east end of Dexter Avenue.

**1905**   *New Orleans, Louisiana.* St. Charles Hotel (Fairmont now), 100 Block University Place.

**1905**   *Roswell, Georgia.* He visited Bulloch, the home of his maternal grandparents and spoke in Roswell Town Square.

**1905**   *St. Augustine, Florida.* Ponce de Leon Hotel, King Street.

**1905**   *Tuskegee, Alabama.* Varner-Alexander House, Montgomery Street(Also called Grey Columns). He also stayed at The Oaks, the home of Booker T. Washington, on the edge of Tuskegee College campus.

**1905**   *Worchester, Massachusetts.* Rockwood Hoar house, 16 Hammond Street.

**1906**   *Harrisburg, Pennsylvania.* He dedicated new Capitol, Capitol Hill at Third and State Streets.

**1906**   *St. Louis, Missouri.* Planter's Hotel, 410 Pine, Fourth Street, Chestnut to Pine. He stayed here again in 1916.

**1907**   *Canton, Ohio.* Westlawn Cemetery, Seventh Street, Northwest. He attended Mrs. McKinley's funeral.

**1907**   *Jamestown, Virginia.* He opened the Jamestown Tercentennial celebration at Sewall Point. Today the grounds are occupied by the Naval Training Station.

**1907**   *Lake Providence, Louisiana.* Twelve miles from Stamboul, on a camping trip. He was greatly annoyed when his boat was bumped.

**1907**   *Montpelier, Virginia.* He visited the Madison home and tomb and remained in meditation near the tomb for some time.

**1907**   *Nashville, Tennessee.* The Hermitage. He came in at Union Station, gave a speech at Ryman Auditorium, a brief talk outside Peabody College, and later a speech at the Hermitage.

**1907**   *Newport, Rhode Island.* Alfred Vanderbilt mansion, Beaulieu, between Marble House and Clarendon Court.

**1908**   *Princeton, New Jersey.* 58 Bayard Lane. He attended private funeral services for ex-president Cleveland.

**1909–1910**   *Africa and Europe.* African hunt and tour of Europe. On his African trip, he showed great interest in missionary activities. He sailed on the Nile and visited Khartoum, where he stayed at the Palace. He placed the keystone of the new Cathedral of Khartoum and visited Omdurman. Further down the Nile he visited Luxor, Karnak, Aswan, and the Valley of the Kings, and spent four days in Cairo, where he stayed at the Shepheard's Hotel. He spent time at the pyramids, sphinx, and Sakkara, and, on March 30, 1910 he left for Naples. After landing in Naples, he went to Rome for an official dinner with the king at the Quirinal Palace. In Vienna, he inspected the Spanish Riding School and had dinner at Schonbrunn Palace. Two days later, he was at the Royal Palace in Budapest. In Paris, he had dinner with the French president at the Elysee Palace. In Brussels he had dinner with the king and queen of the Belgians in Laeken Palace. In

Amsterdam he had lunch with Queen Wilhelmina at Hetloo Palace.

**1910**   *Cheyenne, Wyoming.* He attended the Frontier Celebration. On his western journey, he traveled 5,000 miles through fourteen states. It was on this trip that he objected strongly to being photographed by news photographers as he stood on the railroad platform in pajamas and raincoat speaking to early morning crowds.

**1910**   *Rome, Georgia.* Martha Berry School for Girls. He stayed in the special cabin on the campus built for him. He also visited Louisa Hall, one of the old log cabin buildings on campus.

**1910**   *Atlanta, Georgia.* State Capitol. He visited again on March 10, 1911.

**1911**   *Newark, New Jersey.* He dedicated the Lincoln statue at the Essex County Courthouse.

**1911**   *Phoenix, Arizona.* He visited the Capitol, 1700 West Washington.

**1912**   *Chicago, Illinois.* Congress Hotel, on the third floor during the Republican National Convention. The Convention opened on June 18 at the Chicago Coliseum, which had also been used for the 1904 and 1908 conventions.

**1912**   *Columbus, Ohio.* State Capitol, bounded by High, Broad, State and Third Streets.

**1912**   *Manchester, Vermont.* He lodged at Equinox House, Main Street.

**1912**   *Roosevelt, Louisiana.* He stopped at a hunting lodge which had been set up on Tensas Bayou near the present village. This expedition is said to have inspired the popular toy, the "Teddy bear."

**1912**   *Saginaw, Michigan.* Hotel Vincent. Campaigning for the "Bull Moose" party, he spoke at the auditorium October 14.

**1912**   *Chicago, Illinois.* Mercy Hospital, Stevenson Expressway at King Drive, following an assassination attempt in Milwaukee.

*Grave of Theodore Roosevelt.*

**1913–1914**   *Brazil.* On a seven-month 1,500 mile expedition through Brazil up the River of Doubt since renamed Rio Roosevelt. He also visited Argentina and Chile.

**Europe.**   He was a dinner guest at the Christian VII Palace in Copenhagen and visited Elsinore on May 3. At an official dinner given for him by the King and Queen of Denmark at the Royal Palace, he romped with the young Prince Olaf. He visited Stockholm next and from there went to

Berlin and on to London and Windsor Castle where he lunched. For more details see Letters Volume 8 Chronology.

# DEATH

Roosevelt died on January 6, 1919, in Oyster Bay, New York, at Sagamore Estate. On January 5, 1919, he told his valet, "Please put out the light." In his sleep he suffered a coronary embolism and died. He left an estate valued at $500,000.

# FUNERAL

At his request, a simple funeral service, without music, was held at at Christ Episcopal Church, in Oyster Bay, New York.

# BURIAL

Roosevelt is buried in Oyster Bay, New York, at Young Memorial Cemetery, one mile east on Main Street. His first wife is buried in Cambridge and his second next to him in Oyster Bay.

After his burial in a simple grass plot, there were thousands of visitors, including at first many in the military service—more than 5,000 per day. By the first of September, several hundred thousand had made the pilgrimage. On one occasion, five Italians visited and before leaving dug up handfuls of dirt at the site to take back to Italy. An iron fence, eight feet high, was set in concrete to enclose the plot with a locked gate, and a flat granite stone was placed over the grave.

# BIBLIOGRAPHY

Morris, Edmund. *The Rise of Theodore Roosevelt*. New York: Coward, McCann & Geoghegan, 1979.

Putnam, Carleton. *Theodore Roosevelt, Vol. 1 The Formative Years 1858–1886*. New York: Charles Scribner's Sons, 1958.

# WILLIAM HOWARD TAFT

1857–1930
27TH PRESIDENT 1909–1913: REPUBLICAN PARTY

*"We have passed
beyond the times of . . .
the laissez-faire
school which believes
that the government
ought to do nothing
but run a police
force."*

—*Speech, Milwaukee, WI,
September 17, 1909*

William Howard Taft was born on September 15, 1857, on Mt. Auburn in Cincinnati, Ohio, to Alphonso and Louisa Maria Torrey Taft. He was the seventh cousin twice removed of Richard Nixon. According to one source, in common with Thomas Jefferson, he could trace his ancestry back to David I, King of Scotland.

## CHARACTERISTICS

He was the biggest of our presidents, at 6'2" tall and weighed three hundred and thirty-two pounds. In his youth, he was called "Big Lub." He had smooth delicate skin, blue eyes, and light brown hair. He wore handlebar mustaches, which were light colored in his youth and turned tawny grey as he aged.

He looked a genial man with his spreading smile, his redundant chins, his winged collar and bowler hat. His famous infectious chuckle was a lifelong characteristic. He followed his father's quote, "He whose plate is always right side up, is sure to catch the porridge." While generous with his chuckles, he was more careful with his spending and was anti-tipping. He shaved himself in a day when being shaved at the barber shop was common. His barber re-

# A LIFE IN REVIEW

**Birth:** September 15, 1857; Cincinnati, OH

**Died:** March 8, 1930; Washington, D.C.

**Married:** Helen Herron; June 19, 1886; 2 sons, 1 daughter

## CAREER

**1880** Newspaper reporter

**1880–1882** Assistant County prosecutor

**1882–1883** Collector Internal Revenue

**1883–1887** Law practice

**1887–1890** Superior Court judge

**1890–1892** U.S. Solicitor general

**1892–1900** U.S. circuit judge

**1896** Law professor

**1900–1903** President of Philippine Commission and Governor of Philippines

**1904–1908** Secretary of War

## ADMINISTRATION EVENTS

**1909** Admiral Peary discovers North Pole

**1909** "Dollar Diplomacy" instituted

**1910** Boy Scouts of America formed

ported that he carefully counted out thirty-five cents for a haircut and left. He was a temperate man who seldom drank. He was the second president (after McKinley) to take up golf and the first to own an automobile. He often played on the links of the Chevy Chase Club. In addition to golf and driving as pastimes, he was an avid reader of detective stories.

He had a remarkable memory for names and faces. At an arms conference in Washing-ton, he called a foreign newspaper correspondent by name saying, "I haven't seen you since we met in Rome twenty years ago." He loved to mix with people and talk with others while walking. On one occasion, as he was passing a ladder on which a painter was perched, the painter dropped his brush. "Hey, you," said the workman, "hand me that brush, will you?" The Chief Justice stopped, picked up the brush, handed it to the painter, and continued on his way.

## BIRTHPLACE

Taft was born in Cincinnati, Ohio, at 2038 Auburn Avenue. The house and grounds have been restored.

## BAPTISM

There is no record of any baptism and as Taft was a lifelong Unitarian it is doubtful there was one.

## CHURCH

Unitarianism was part of his family background. As a youth, he went to the Sunday School of the Unitarian Church. He wrote, "I do not believe in the Divinity of Christ. I am a Unitarian. I believe in God." He was regular in attending church and urged others to go to church. After he became president, he made the statement that he did not believe in making speeches on Sundays. Taft and his wife often attended different churches.

**1857–1900** *Cincinnati, Ohio.* First Congregational Unitarian Church, southeast corner of Fourth and Race Streets. He was a member here from his youth. After his marriage, he sometimes attended Christ Episcopal, 318 East Fourth Street. See also St. John's Unitarian Church at the northwest corner of West Twelfth and Elm Streets, which he attended on occasion.

*Birthplace of William Taft.*

**1864** *Millbury, Massachusetts.* Congregational Church, Main and Church Streets. He went here with his grandfather, Samuel Torrey.

**1874–1878** *New Haven, Connecticut.* Yale Chapel, where he found the seats unduly hard and the sermons dull. Later, when he was at Yale as a professor, he also attended services here from time to time since there was no Unitarian church in New Haven. He sat in a front pew.

**1890–1930** *Washington, D.C.* He attended All Souls' Church when it was located at Fourteenth and L Streets, NW, and the present building at Sixteenth and Harvard Streets, NW, from its dedication in 1924 until his death; he sat in the front row pew.

**1908** *Hot Springs, Virginia.* St. Luke's Episcopal during July, August and November 1908.

**1908** *Augusta, Georgia.* St. Paul's Episcopal, 605 Reynolds Street.

**1909** *Augusta, Georgia.* St. James Methodist Episcopal Church (now St. James United Methodist Church), 439 Greene Street.

**1909–1913** *Lynn, Massachusetts.* First Unitarian Church while vacationing.

**1909** *Augusta, Georgia.* He spoke at the Negro Great Bethel Church (now Bethel African Methodist), 839 Ninth Street.

**1909** *Charleston, South Carolina.* Unitarian Church, 4 Archdale Street. March 14.

**1909** *Washington, D.C.* New York Avenue Presbyterian Church to which he walked from the White House.

**1909** *Minneapolis, Minnesota.* Westminster Presbyterian Church, Nicollet Mall at Twelfth Street.

**1909–** *Beverly, Massachusetts.* Unitarian Church, 225 Cabot between Hale and Essex during the summers.

**1910–** *Augusta, Georgia.* Tabernacle Baptist Church, 1223 Laney-Walker Boulevard.

**1913–1920** *New Haven, Connecticut.* Yale University Battell Chapel, where he sat in the front pew, northeast corner to the left of the choir.

# EDUCATION

**1862–1870** *Cincinnati, Ohio.* Sixteenth District School in the Mount Auburn section of Cincinnati, where he learned the fundamentals. William Howard Taft School on Southern Avenue facing Young Street has a bronze marker on the building which says he attended school in a four-room brick structure on this site from 1862 to 1870.

**1864** *Millbury, Massachusetts.* The village school.

**1870–1874** *Cincinnati, Ohio.* Woodward High School, Woodward Street. A report says he spent hours at the home of a friend reading *Harper's Weekly.*

**1874–1878** *New Haven, Connecticut.* Yale University. He placed second out of one hundred and thirty-two in the class of 1878. He received the B.A. degree. At Yale, during his freshman year, he roomed with George Edwards of Kentucky in Farnham Hall. During 1874–1875, he stayed at 64 High Street. Later, he shared a room with his younger brother, Harry, who entered Yale in the fall of 1876. In his senior year, he lived in Old South College.

**1878–1880** *Cincinnati, Ohio.* University of Cincinnati Law School, 414 Walnut Street, housed in the old Mercantile Library Building in the heart of the city. Lectures for first year students were held on the third floor. He did not wait for his degree from the Cincinnati Law School, but went to Columbus for the Ohio bar examination.

# MARRIAGE AND HONEYMOON

Taft was married on June 29, 1886, in Cincinnati, Ohio. The bride was Helen (Nellie) Herron. The wedding was held at the Herron House, at 69 Pike Street, at 5:00 P.M. They first met at a coasting party on Mount Auburn in 1874 when Nellie was 18. The Herron home and the Taft home were close together on Pike Street. Nothing remains, and the house has been replaced by a freeway. There is a picture of the old three-story brick Herron House, where they were married, in the *New York Times* on the occasion of their twenty-fifth wedding anniversary, for which 5,000 invitations were sent to all blood relatives of former presidents.

For their honeymoon, the Tafts spent one night in New York City at the Albemarle Hotel on Madison Avenue. From there they spent four days at Sea Bright, New Jersey, and a side trip to Elberon to see the cottage where President Garfield died. They spent three months in Europe touring France, England, and Scotland during the summer. By fall they were back in Cincinnati and living in their new house. They visited Addison's Walk at Magdalene College and all the sights of London, including the Tower, where they had their first quarrel (over a visit to relatives). In London, they stayed at the Royal Hotel, Blackfriars and visited Hampton Court and Richmond. They then went to the Lake Country to see Wordsworth and Coleridge landmarks, Lincoln and York Cathedrals, and Holyrood and the Castle in Edinburgh. In Paris they saw all the sights, with extra time for walking in the Luxembourg Gardens, attended services at the Madeleine, and visited the Bastille. They travelled to Holland and returned to the United States.

# HOMES

**1857–1886** *Cincinnati, Ohio.* At 2030 Auburn Avenue is the two-story house where he was born and spent his boyhood.

**1864–** *Saratoga Springs, New York.* Congress Hall, Broadway and Spring Streets. He stayed here on vacations.

**1871–** *Cincinnati, Ohio.* Stinton House, 316 Pike Street, which eventually became the Taft Museum.

**1876–** *Washington, D.C.* Ebbitt House, Fourteenth Street, NW, where his parents lived when his father was first secretary of war under U.S. Grant and later Attorney General. It has been torn down and the paneling and decoration moved to a building at 1427 F Street, NW.

**1884–** *Little Boar's Head, New Hampshire.* He visited Nellie Herron at her family's summer house on the beach. Nothing remains.

**1884** *New York City, New York.* He lodged with his brother Horace on the west side of Broadway between Fourth and Fifth Streets.

**1886–1890** *Cincinnati, Ohio.* The Tafts lived in their own Victorian house in East Walnut Hills on McMillan Street near Forest Avenue on their return home from their honeymoon. The lot overlooking the river had been given to Nellie by her father. The house was not quite finished, so they stayed with Taft's parents for a month at 60 Auburn Avenue.

**1890** *Washington, D.C.* They stayed first at Ebbitt House on Fourteenth Street and later moved to 5 Dupont Circle.

**1890–1892** *Washington, D.C.* 5 Dupont Circle is a small house with which they rented for $100 a month. A library had been established on the second floor. Nothing remains, and there is no marker.

**1892–** *Quebec, Canada.* Murray Bay on the St. Lawrence River. They rented a cottage here first in 1892 and returned almost every summer. Except for the years he was president, he usually summered here. At first, they stayed at Chamard's Lorne House, that stood where the Manoir Richelieu was later

built. They were staying here when the First World War broke out. Sassifern was the name of the cottage they owned and where the family usually congregated. It was near Pointe au Pic. It was a large ten-bedroom house with three large open fireplaces. The house burned in 1952.

**1892–1898** *Cincinnati, Ohio.* 118 East Third Street at the northeast corner of Third and Lawrence. Much of this time, he was on the circuit court in an area from Michigan to Tennessee.

**1898–1900** *Cincinnati, Ohio.* Madison Road, east of Annwood Avenue in East Walnut Hills and near their old house on McMillan. He was still travelling on the law circuit.

**1901–1904** *Manila, Philippines.* He became governor on July 4 and moved into the Malacanan Palace.

**1904** *Washington, D.C.* Arlington Hotel, H Street and Vermont Avenue, NW, where he took rooms pending the arrival of his family.

**1904–1909** *Washington, D.C.* 1603 K Street, while he was secretary of war. He often dined at the White House.

**1904** *Murray Bay, Canada.* He rented the Buchanan cottage during the summer.

**1909–1913** *Washington, D.C.* The White House. They celebrated their twenty-fifth wedding anniversary here with a grand reception.

**1909–1913** *Beverly, Massachusetts.* Parramatta cottage, Main Street, was the place where he took summer vacations while he was in the White House. In 1909, he leased the R. D. Evans cottage at Beverly for a summer house. There was a realty boon in Beverly and rents rose because so many wanted to be near the president. The Evans house was on Beverly Cove at Woodberry Point, and he had offices in the Chamber of Commerce rooms at Beverly. Ex-President Benjamin Harrison liked the sea breezes of

Beverly. Taft also had a summer home at Burgess Point in the Green Cottage. Both houses were in the same area, but they are no longer standing. The site is now the Lynch Park at 55 Ober Street.

**1913–1917** *New Haven, Connecticut.* 367 Prospect Street, York Square, in a Victorian house named Hillcrest. This was the first of four houses they lived in, in New Haven.

**1917–1918** *Washington, D.C.* 2029 Connecticut Avenue, NW, southeast corner of Connecticut and Wyoming Avenues. He lived here while serving as co-chairman of the National War Labor Board.

**1918–1919** *New Haven, Connecticut.* 70 Grove Street. Demolished.

**1919–1920** *Washington, D.C.* 2029 Connecticut Avenue, NW.

**1920–1921** *New Haven, Connecticut.* 113 Whitney Avenue.

**1921** *New Haven, Connecticut.* 60 York Square.

**1921–1930** *Washington, D.C.* 2215 Wyoming Avenue (and Twenty-third Street), where he lived as Chief Justice. The Georgian house was the first of their many homes that they actually owned except for the Sassifern cottage at Murray Bay. It was three miles from the Capitol, to which he walked.

# WORK

**1878–1880** *Cincinnati, Ohio.* Johnston Buildings, Rooms 55-57. He worked part time in his father's firm of Taft and Lloyd while studying at the Law School.

**1880** *Cincinnati, Ohio.* Halstead's newspaper as a reporter. He was also the court reporter. Later, he worked for the *Cincinnati Commercial News*, with offices on the northeast corner Fourth and Race.

**1880–1882** *Cincinnati, Ohio.* He was appointed assistant prosecutor of Hamilton County and took office on January 3, 1881.

The present Hamilton County Courthouse was completed in 1919 and is the fourth courthouse on the site, bounded by East Central Parkway, Main, East Court, and Sycamore Streets.

**1882–1883** *Cincinnati, Ohio.* He became collector of internal revenue for the first district with headquarters in Cincinnati. William Henry Harrison had once been collector for the same district.

**1883–1887** *Cincinnati, Ohio.* He was in partnership with Major Harlan Page Lloyd, who was the only law partner with whom Taft ever associated. He had the same office as his father in rooms 55-57 Johnston Building.

**1887–1890** *Cincinnati, Ohio.* In 1887, he was appointed to the Superior Court of Cincinnati and in 1888 elected for a full term on the Superior Court. The site of old city hall is West Eighth Street and Plum. The present city hall is on the site of his former office.

**1890–1892** *Washington, D.C.* He was sworn in as Solicitor General of the United States. At first, he stayed at the Ebbitt House. His legal quarters amounted to a single shabby room, three flights up in the Department of Justice, Fourteenth Street, NW.

**1892–1900** *Cincinnati, Ohio.* He resigned as Solicitor General to become U.S. circuit Judge for the Sixth Judicial Circuit. In 1896, he also became dean and professor of property at the Cincinnati Law School. As a circuit judge, his offices were on the third floor of the U.S. Customs House and Post Office.

**1896** *Cincinnati, Ohio.* Cincinnati Law School, 414 Walnut Street, where he was dean and professor.

**1900–1903** *Manila, the Philippines.* He was president of the Philippine Commission. The commission worked in the Ayuntamiento (General MacArthur's headquarters), where they were squeezed into one small room.

**1901–1903** *Manila, the Philippines.* On July 4, he was inaugurated as colonial governor of the Philippines. On one of his journeys into the hills above Baguio, he was considerably surprised to have the Igorot children bow very low as he approached and say, "Good morning, Mrs. Kelly." Taft was puzzled, as well as amused, at the greeting. The explanation was simple. Some years before, a Mrs. Alice Kelly had started a school among the children. She taught them to greet her in English. So now seeing another white face they called cheerily, "Good morning, Mrs. Kelly."

**1904–1908** *Washington, D.C.* Secretary of War, War Department.

**1909–1913** *Washington, D.C.* President of the United States.

**1909–1913** *Beverly, Massachusetts.* Summer offices in the Board of Trade Building at 224 Cabot Street on the corner of Federal Street. The site is now occupied by Beverly National Bank.

**1913–1921** *New Haven, Connecticut.* Yale University professor. When he arrived, the students met him on College Street and marched in procession to Memorial Hall, where he made a speech. His special lectures were given in Lampson Lyceum, and his regular lectures were in A 1 Osborne Hall.

**1921–1930** *Washington, D.C.* Chief Justice of the U.S. Supreme Court. He presided in the Senate's old home in the Capitol.

# Travel/Visits

Taft loved to travel. No previous president had left the United States during his presidency with the exception of Theodore Roosevelt, who was on an American warship and away from American waters for only a few hours. While he was one of the most widely travelled men of his time, there was one means of transportation he never used. He never used

an airplane. He said jokingly that aircraft were not adapted to his use because of his "style of architecture," adding it would capsize the stablest of them.

**1879** *Cincinnati, Ohio.* Grand Hotel, site southwest corner of Fourth Street and Central Avenue for the welcome to ex-president Grant upon his return from his two-year around the world tour.

**1885** *(near) Lowville, New York.* Fenton's, which was a small rustic resort in the Adirondacks and where the Collins side of Nellie's family had lived for years. It was the site of much of Taft's courting of Nellie that summer.

**1901** *Manila, The Philippines.* He left on Christmas Eve for Washington, D.C. for several weeks.

**1903** *Baguio, in the province of Benguet, the Philippines.* As a health measure for the family.

**1904** *Panama City, Panama.* He was sent by President Roosevelt on the first of many visits to Panama.

**1905** *Tokyo, Japan.* Secretary of War. He sailed across the Pacific on the *Manchuria* to Japan via Honolulu and to the Philippines. In Tokyo, he stayed at the Shiba Palace, which had been built originally for General Grant's reception on his world tour. In Manila, he was back at Malacanan Palace.

**1906** *Havana, Cuba.* On an official mission. Here, he stayed in the historic old government palace.

**1907** *Pointe-au-Pic, Quebec.* His summer lodge.

**1907** *Yellowstone National Park, Wyoming.* He stayed at Old Faithful Inn for three days.

**1908–** *Augusta, Georgia.* Winter home, end of Cumming Road at Milledge Road.

**1908** *Jackson, Michigan.* Memorial Rocks under the Jackson Oaks, Second and West Franklin Streets. He dedicated the tablet here as the birthplace of the Republican Party. (Preliminary meetings had been held in a small school house in the Ripon College Campus in 1854.)

**1908** *Hot Springs, Virginia.* Homestead Hotel, just east of US 220 in town. He rested here before his inauguration. He occupied a suite of rooms once used by former president McKinley.

**1908** *Madison, Wisconsin.* For campaign address. He returned to Madison in 1915 to lecture at the Union. In 1916, a newspaper reporter spotted him eating at the luncheon counter at the North Western depot, where he was changing trains. No one else had noticed him.

**1908** *Middle Bass Island, Ohio.* The island is in Lake Erie twenty miles from Toledo. He stayed at the Middle Bass Club. Hayes, Garfield, and McKinley had been members. He did some fishing but could not get away from photographers and other fishing boats.

**1909–** *Saratoga Springs, New York.* He often lodged in the Congress Hotel.

**1909** *Atlanta, Georgia.* Piedmont Hotel, Forsythe Street. He arrived on a special train at the old Union Depot. He was honored at the Governor's office in the State Capitol. He made a speech at the City Auditorium and attended a banquet at the Capital City Club, where he was served possum and could only swallow one bite.

**1909** *Burlington, Vermont.* Celebration of Hudson-Fulton and commemoration of the tercentenary of the discovery of Lake Champlain.

**1909** *Butte, Montana.* He visited the old Leonard Copper Mine and Spoke at the court house, corner of Montana and Broadway.

**1909** *Helena, Montana.* He laid the cornerstone of the Roman Catholic Church and visited the State Capitol.

**1909** *Charleston, South Carolina.* Charleston Hotel, Meeting Street. The building was razed in 1960.

**1909** *Chicago, Illinois.* Congress Hotel, 520 South Michigan lodging. West Side Baseball Park, Lincoln Street, where he attended a Giants-Cubs baseball game.

**1909** *Cincinnati, Ohio.* Burnett House at Third and Lawrence Streets with Mary Hann (relative) just before he left for the White House.

**1909** *Columbia, South Carolina.* He addressed the students from the portico of the president's house at DeDaussure College on Sumter Street. The house was demolished in 1939.

**1909** *Corpus Christi, Texas.* He visited Mrs. H. M. King of the famous King ranch (1,300,000 acres) and went to the ranch at Kingsville.

**1909** *Dallas, Texas.* Oriental Hotel.

**1909** *Denver, Colorado.* He gave a speech on the steps of the State Capitol, Colorado Springs, Colorado. Visit to nearby "Garden of the Gods," on Ridge Road off US 24.

**1909** *El Paso, Texas.* He met Mexican President Diaz at the Chamber of Commerce building.

**1909** *Grand Canyon, Arizona.* He lunched at the Hotel El Tovar.

**1909** *Santa Fe, New Mexico.* He visited the State Capitol.

**1909** *LaCrosse, Wisconsin.* He dedicated the new YMCA building.

**1909** *Little Boar's Head, New Hampshire.* Summer home of Judge Hollister of Cincinnati. Second house north of Atlantic Avenue on Ocean Boulevard. Vacation.

**1909** *Merced, California.* He attended services at the Presbyterian Church.

**1909** *Minneapolis, Minneapolis.* He lodged at the Minneapolis Club. Fort Snelling, I-494 (SR 5) at East Seventy- eighth Street for review of troops and reception.

**1909**  *Montrose, Colorado.* He opened Gunnison Tunnel.

**1909**  *Nashville, Tennessee.* Belle Meade Mansion.

**1909**  *New Orleans, Louisiana.* St. Charles Hotel (Fairmont), 100 Block University Place, where he lodged and had an alligator dinner.

**1909**  *New York City, New York.* 36 West Forty- Eighth Street with his brother, Henry. He was here again in 1912. The auto taking him from the railway station to his brother's house ran out of gas.

**1909**  *Newbury, Massachusetts.* His chauffeur- driven car was caught in a speed trap. As president, he took a 13,000-mile swing through the country from Springfield, Massachusetts, westward to the Pacific and return.

**1909**  *Portland, Oregon.* Hotel Portland. He attended services at the First Unitarian Church and laid the cornerstone of the First Universalist Church (East Portland).

**1909**  *Riverside, California.* He dedicated the tablet on Rubidoux Mountain honoring Fra Junipera Serra.

**1909**  *Sacramento, California.* He made an address on the State Capitol grounds.

**1909**  *Salem, Oregon.* He was present for the laying of the cornerstone of Carroll College on Benton Avenue.

**1909**  *Salt Lake City, Utah.* Knutsford Hotel overnight. He attended Church services Unitarian Church, went to the Mormon Tabernacle on Temple Square for an organ recital, and also gave a "Sermon" at the Mormon Tabernacle.

**1909**  *San Antonio, Texas.* Menger Hotel, 204 Alamo Plaza. He laid the cornerstone of the Chapel at Fort Sam Houston.

**1909**  *San Antonio, Texas.* St. Anthony Hotel, 300 East Travis.

**1909**  *San Francisco, California.* He attended a banquet at the Fairmont Hotel and spent the night at the St. Francis Hotel. The

next day, he laid the cornerstone of new Y.M.C.A. building.

**1909**  *Savannah, Georgia.* W.W. Gordon House, northeast corner of Bull Street and Oglethorpe Avenue. It was a stuccoed brick dwelling with a small Ionic portico. McKinley had also lodged here.

**1909**  *St. Paul, Minnesota.* Reception, State Capitol, 700 Wabasha Street.

**1909**  *Washington, D.C.* Dupont Circle at the Boardman House before his inauguration.

**1909**  *Yosemite, California.* He spent the night at El Portal, at the foot of the Sierras, near the gateway to Yosemite Valley, in one of the cottages of the Wanona Hotel—about eight miles from the entrance to Mariposa Grove. His park visit included Grouse Creek Forest near Chinquapin, where luncheon was served at the foot of pines. Photographs were taken at "Grizzly Bear" (a tree). One night was spent in a little hotel at Glacier Point and then another night in El Portal. While in Yosemite, he had to go to bed in the Sentinel Hotel while his clothes, wet from perspiration, dried in the sun. He had only one outfit with him.

**1910**  *Augusta, Georgia.* Bon Air Hotel. Not everyone bows to a president. Rockefeller refused to give up a suite in the Augusta Hotel to accommodate the Taft party.

**1911**  *El Paso, Texas.* La Aduana Fronteriza (Custom House), southeast corner of Calle 16 de Septembre and Ave Juarez for a state dinner served on the gold plates of Emperor Maximilian, with President Diaz of Mexico.

**1911**  *Indianapolis, Indiana.* He visited the State Capitol.

**1911**  *Nashville, Tennessee.* He visited the Capitol and the Hermitage near Lebanon. He arrived at the Union Station on Broadway, gave a public speech at the Ryman Auditorium on Fifth Avenue, and lodged at the Hermitage Hotel.

**1911**  *Saginaw, Michigan.* He was the first

sitting president to visit. He spoke at the City Auditorium. For his visit, there were not enough hitching posts for all the horses. He stayed at the Bancroft Hotel.

**1911**  *Springfield, Illinois.* He visited the Capitol, Governor's Mansion, and the Lincoln home and tomb.

**1911**  *Washington, D.C.* He went to the top of the Washington Monument for the first time, using the elevator. He later visited the Capitol and the Senate area, remarking that the Senators did not lack for convenience.

**1912**  *Burlington, Vermont.* He celebrated the tercentenary of discovery of Lake Champlain.

**1912**  *Manchester, Vermont.* He spoke at Music Hall (still standing), town center, and was an overnight guest of Robert Lincoln at Hildene—a bedroom there is known as the "Taft bedroom." He visited here on a number of occasions and played golf with Robert.

**1912**  *Montpelier, Vermont.* State Capitol, where he made an address to the legislature.

**1912**  *Salem, Massachusetts.* He unveiled a bronze tablet at Essex Institute, 132 Essex Street, in honor of the men who had served in the Civil War.

**1913–**  *New York City, New York.* Garden City Hotel, 45 Seventh Street, where he visited his brother, Harry.

**1913**  *Clinton, New York.* Hamilton College, where he received an honorary degree.

**1913**  *New Haven, Connecticut.* After leaving the White House, until the commencement at Yale, he took quarters at the Hotel Taft, which is now the Taft apartments.

**1915**  *Pocatello, Idaho.* He dedicated the Oregon Short Line depot and also visited Boise.

**1916**  *Chicago, Illinois.* He said that he walked for at least four blocks in downtown Chicago and made a purchase in one store without being recognized.

**1917**  *Concord, New Hampshire.* He spoke to the legislature at the Capitol.

**1917**  *Madison, Wisconsin.* Governor's Mansion, 130 East Gilman, as guest of Governor Phillips for three days.

**1917**  *Niles, Ohio.* He dedicated the McKinley Memorial, 40 North Main Street.

**1919**  *Detroit, Michigan.* He arrived in Detroit "broke" and walked a mile and a half to City Hall where the mayor cashed a check for him. He explained to reporters, "I just ran out of change."

**1919**  *Lansing, Michigan.* State Capitol on Capitol Avenue, for a speech.

**1919**  *Oyster Bay, New York.* He attended the funeral of Theodore Roosevelt at Christ Episcopal Church on Main Street.

**1920**  *Marion, Ohio.* He had a breakfast meeting with President-elect Harding at 380 Mount Vernon Avenue.

**1922**  *Washington, D.C.* He presented the Lincoln Memorial to President Harding.

**1923**  *Marion, Ohio.* To attend funeral of President Harding.

**1924**  *Washington, D.C.* He called on Coolidge at the White House.

**1930**  *Asheville, North Carolina.* Grove Park Inn, with a room looking toward the Smoky Mountains.

**1930**  *Washington, D.C.* Garfield Hospital for treatment in his final illness.

# DEATH

Taft died on March 8, 1930, in Washington, D.C. at 2215 Wyoming Avenue, NW. He died in a coma at 5:15 P.M. Earlier, he had gone to the mountains of North Carolina for a rest, but he grew worse and desired to come home to Washington, where he lingered but a few weeks. He left an estate of almost $300,000.

*Graves of Helen and William Taft at Arlington National Cemetery.*

## FUNERAL

Simple services were held in Washington, at All Soul's Church at Sixteenth and Harvard Streets, NW. He lay in state at the U.S. Capitol building, where services included his favorite hymns: "Lead Kindly Light" and "Abide With Me." For the first time in history, the radio broadcast the entire ceremony of a presidential funeral.

## BURIAL

Taft was buried at Arlington National Cemetery, Virginia, near the grave of Robert Todd Lincoln. His wife, Helen, is also buried here. The grave is marked by a simple marble stone.

## SPECIAL SITES

*Cincinnati, Ohio.* The Taft Museum is located in the former home of his brother, Charles Taft, on Pike Street.

## BIBLIOGRAPHY

Anderson, Judith Icke. *William Howard Taft: An Intimate History.* New York: Norton, 1981.

Pringle, Henry F. *The Life and Times of William Howard Taft*, Volumes I and II. Hamden, Connecticut: Archon Books, 1964.

Ross, Ishbel. *An American Family: The Tafts 1678–1964.* Cleveland: The World Publishing Company, 1964

# WOODROW WILSON

## 1856–1924
### 28TH PRESIDENT 1913–1921: DEMOCRATIC PARTY

Thomas Woodrow Wilson was born on December 28 or 29, 1856, to Joseph Ruggles and Janet Woodrow Wilson in the Presbyterian manse at Staunton, Virginia. To his parents and to his boyhood friends, he was "Tommy." By 1883, he had dropped the first name and used T. Woodrow Wilson; later he dropped the "T."

## CHARACTERISTICS

His wife, Ellen, wrote: "Governor Wilson is 5'10½" in height, chest measurement 39, collar 16, size of hat 7 3/8, weight 170 pounds. His weight has been practically the same for 10 or 15 years. He has good shoulders, the neck round, strong and very young looking. He has no accumulation of flesh around the waist. He has an excellent constitution—very elastic—steel rather than iron. He is a splendid sleeper—can go to sleep at any moment that he makes up his mind to do so. He decides beforehand just when he will wake up and always does it to the moment, with his mind perfectly clear. He is in much better physical condition than when he was a young man. Then, owing to bad food at colleges, etc. he suffered from chronic indigestion, but, living since under more

*"America is not a mere body of traders; it is a body of free men. Our greatness is built upon our freedom—is moral, not material. We have a great ardor for gain; but we have a deep passion for the rights of man."*

—*Speech, New York, New York, January 29, 1911*

# A Life in Review

**Birth:** December 29, 1856; Staunton, VA

**Died:** February 3, 1924; Washington, D.C.

**Married:** Ellen Louise Axson; June 24, 1885; 3 daughters    Edith Bolling Galt; December 18, 1915; No children

## CAREER

**1882–1883** Law practice

**1883–1902** Professor

**1902–1910** University President

**1911–1913** Governor of New Jersey

## ADMINISTRATION EVENTS

**1913** Federal Reserve Act

**1914** Clayton Anti-trust Act

**1915** San Francisco, Panama-Pacific Exposition

**1916** Virgin Islands purchased

**1917–1919** World War I

**1918** Issued Fourteen Points for Peace

wholesome conditions, he has entirely outgrown all tendency to trouble of that sort. He has dark brown hair, now turning iron-gray, a rather dark and somewhat ruddy complexion and very large, dark gray eyes, with dark eyebrows and very long dark lashes." Another report says that he had a long, drawn face, strong, memorable, but not handsome, with a sallow and blotchy complexion, high forehead, and oversized ears.

His sense of humor was extremely limited, and he could be chillingly cold. He had an explosive temper. He had a sympathetic nature and showed consideration for people of every rank. One houseguest left his shoes outside his door to be polished, but Wilson, feeling this was not a proper job for their female servants, did the job himself. He took pride in being a Virginian, and he remained a southerner at heart with little to say on the rights of African Americans. Neither was he a great advocate of women's rights, saying on one occasion, "Why is it cleverness is so apt to unsettle a woman's brains?" Wilson was human in his daily habits. One friend wrote to him, "Do not leave your spoon in your cup when you drink your tea." He was much opposed to alcohol, and all liquor was banned from the White House during his administration. Although he loved vacations and hiking in the mountains, he was not an avid outdoorsman or sportsman. He was more interested in lectures, literature, and theater. He was a talented mimic and liked to tell humorous stories. He tells one on the man who played golf and always said, "Aswan" when he missed the ball. When asked why, he replied that Aswan was the biggest dam in the world.

## BIRTHPLACE

Wilson was born in Staunton, Virginia, at 24 North Coalter Street, in a ground floor room. The Greek Revival house is a beautiful and well-preserved building. He was born about midnight, so there is some question as to whether it was December 28 or 29.

## BAPTISM

Wilson was baptized in April 1857, in Staunton, Virginia, at First Presbyterian Church, Coalter and Frederick Streets, by the Reverend J. H. Smith of Charlottesville. Mary Baldwin College has plans to restore the chapel where the president was baptized to its original design. The old edifice where he was christened is used as the chapel of that school.

THE PRESIDENTS

*Birthplace of Woodrow Wilson.*

# CHURCH

The Wilson home had daily devotions, Bible reading and prayers. Wilson never showed signs of religious doubt and prayed on his knees morning and night. On Sundays, he was always there to hear his father, Dr. Wilson, preach. In his diaries he spoke of the excellent sermons of his father and most often characterized sermons given by other pastors as poor or dull or described them as good as usual—that is poor. He was fond of hymn-singing, and some hymns moved him to tears. He read the Bible every day and viewed it as the most perfect rule of life. After he married for the second time, he and his wife usually attended different churches—she the Episcopal and he the Presbyterian. In order to avoid crowds when he was president, he often disappointed those who had gathered at the church where he was expected by chosing another church.

**1858**  *Staunton, Virginia.* First Presbyterian Church at Coalter and Frederick Streets.

**1858–1870**  *Augusta, Georgia.* First Presbyterian Church, 642 Telfair Street. It was used as a military hospital during the Civil War. The family sat in the fourth pew directly in front of the pulpit. While here, he attended Sunday School regularly.

**1858–1870**  *Augusta, Georgia.* Greene Street Baptist Church. Sometimes he attended here during the period the First Presbyterian Church was being used as a military hospital.

**1860s**  *Washington, Georgia.* Washington Presbyterian Church, 312 East Toombs Avenue, where his father often preached.

**1865**  *Chillicothe, Ohio.* First Presbyterian Church, attending with relatives.

**1870–1874**  *Columbia, South Carolina.* First Presbyterian Church, 1324 Marion Street. Here he joined the church on July 5, 1873.

**1870–1874**  *Columbia, South Carolina.* Columbia Theological Seminary (Chapel), corner of Pickens and Blanding Streets, nearly opposite the family home on Pryor Street, where his father led services from time to time.

**1873–1874**  *Davidson, North Carolina.* The old chapel where he sometimes attended compulsory chapel was located in one part of the building which is now the site of the Fine Arts Building on the Davidson College campus.

**1874–1885**  *Wilmington, North Carolina.* First Presbyterian Church, corner of Third and Orange Streets. The original church which he attended burned in 1925. The current church is built on the same site. He sometimes went to hear the minister at Second Presbyterian Church, particularly on Sunday evenings.

**1875–1879**  *Princeton, New Jersey.* He regularly attended the Seminary Chapel of Princeton on the campus. First Presbyterian Church, 61 Nassau Street. Trinity Episcopal Church, on occasion, but he was very critical of the service and approach.

**1883–**  *Rome, Georgia.* First Presbyterian Church, 101 East Third Avenue, where he saw his future bride for the first time while he was visiting his uncle, James W. Bones. Her father, Samuel E. Axson, was the local pastor. The church burned but was rebuilt in perfect replica. The funeral of his first wife was held in this church.

**1880s**  *Savannah, Georgia.* Anderson Street Presbyterian Church, northeast corner of Anderson and Barnard Streets, now Hull Memorial Presbyterian Church, Bull and Thirty-seventh Streets.

**1880s**  *Savannah, Georgia.* Independent Presbyterian Church, Bull Street and Oglethorpe Avenue.

**1882–1883**  *Atlanta, Georgia.* First Presbyterian Church on Marietta Street. There is a new house of worship on the same site.

**1884–**  *Baltimore, Maryland.* Independent Presbyterian Church, which later became the First Unitarian Church, Charles and Franklin Streets. Here he sang in the church choir. He wrote, "I was invited a short time since to join the finest choir in town, but it was a Methodist choir and I declined."

**1884–**  *Baltimore, Maryland.* Scotch Presbyterian Church, 53 West Fourteenth Street, which he attended while at Johns Hopkins from time to time, especially evenings.

**1884–**  *New York City, New York.* Madison Square Presbyterian Church, 432 Third Avenue, where Dr. Charles H. Parkhurst was preaching in the 1880s. It has been torn down for apartments.

**1884–**  *New York City, New York.* Church of the Heavenly Rest (Protestant Episcopal), 551 Fifth Avenue. He sometimes attended here and also Henry Ward Beecher's Plymouth Congregational Church in Brooklyn.

**1885–1888**  *Bryn Mawr, Pennsylvania.* He joined the Bryn Mawr Presbyterian Church, 625 Montgomery Avenue. According to sources in Bryn Mawr, he attended the old Baptist Church (still extant) on Gulph Road near the manse where he lived.

**1888–1890**  *Middletown, Connecticut.* First Congregational Church, Pleasant and Crescent Street. He had been asked to teach Sunday School in the Second Congregational Church, but, in November, Wilson and his wife chose to join the First.

**1890–1897**  *Princeton, New Jersey.* The Wilsons were dissatisfied with both the First and Second Presbyterian Churches during their early years in Princeton. They first joined the smaller church but later became members of the First Presbyterian Church, 61 Nassau Street. Pew number 57 is marked with a small brass plate.

**1891–**  *Princeton, New Jersey.* Marquand Chapel on the Princeton University Campus, where he gave talks in chapel on occasion.

**1897–1913** *Princeton, New Jersey.* Wilson and his family joined the Second Presbyterian Church, 26 Nassau Street. The Second Presbyterian merged with First and the building at 26 Nassau is now the Nassau Christian Center.

**1910** *Old Lyme, Connecticut.* Congregational Church, southwest corner of Ferry Road and Lyme Street. The old Church burned, and Wilson dedicated the new one.

**1911** *Spring Lake, New Jersey.* East Orange Presbyterian Church, during vacation.

**1913–1924** *Washington, D.C.* Central Presbyterian Church, Third and Irving Streets, NW, sitting in the third row at the north end of the middle section. President Wilson laid the cornerstone of this church on December 19, 1913, and worshipped there until his death.

**1913–** *Washington, D.C.* He sometimes attended the First Presbyterian Church on Marshall Place (formerly known as Four and one half Street). It has been demolished.

**1913–1916** *Cornish, New Hampshire.* South Congregational Church on Center Road. On July 6, 1913, it merged with the Baptist church and is now the United Church of Cornish.

    *Gulfport, Mississippi.* Gulfport Presbyterian Church, Thirty-first Avenue facing Thirteenth Street. It is now a Lutheran Church. A bronze plate marks the pew where he sat.

**1915–** *New York City, New York.* Fifth Avenue Presbyterian Church, 705 Fifth Avenue, northwest corner West Fifty-fifth Street.

**1916–** *Long Branch, New Jersey.* St. James Chapel, known as the Church of the Presidents, when vacationing there during the summers.

**1918** *New York City, New York.* Brick Presbyterian Church, Fifth Avenue and Thirty-ninth Street.

**1919** *Des Moines, Iowa.* Central Presbyterian Church.

**1919** *Seattle, Washington.* First Presbyterian Church.

# EDUCATION

**1858–1870** *Augusta, Georgia.* For his early education, his father was his chief teacher, continuing until he left for college. He did not learn his letters until he was nine and the fundamentals of reading when he was 11. This may have been occasioned by the Civil War when no schools were open in Augusta. In Augusta, he briefly attended the school run by Joseph T. Derry. The school called Houghton Institute, was on the corner of Bay and McIntosh Streets, on the Savannah River bank, not far from St. Paul's Episcopal Church.

**1870** *Columbia, South Carolina.* Charles H. Barnwell school, to the rear of his house, corner of Hampton and Henderson Streets, and directly across the street from the Pryor house, where the Wilsons were living. He was one of only three students to begin with.

**1870–1873** *Columbia, South Carolina.* Columbia Theological Seminary, corner of Pickens and Blanding Streets. He often listened to the lectures his father gave here.

**1873–1874** *Davidson, North Carolina.* Davidson College. He dropped out at the end of his freshman year. There is a plaque commemorating his attendance on the college campus. There was one main building, Chambers Hall, where he roomed at 9 ground floor, north wing, and had his classes. Like others who stayed here, he cleaned and filled his own lamps and carried in firewood. He boarded at Mrs. Mary Scofield's boarding house next to the Carolina Inn across the street from the campus at Main and Depot Streets. At the time, there were one hundred and five other boys. He was a member of the Eumenean Literary Society. The original Chambers Hall burned, but the Eumenean building is still standing. He was a good debater and, among other topics, supported republicanism versus monarchy and, on one occasion, spoke in favor of compulsory education. While president, he made a quick surprise visit to the campus and visited his old room in Chambers Hall.

**1874–1875** *Wilmington, North Carolina.* Fourth and Orange Streets. He remained at home because of ill health and studied under his father.

**1875–1879** *Princeton, New Jersey.* Princeton University, graduating in 1879. His knowledge of shorthand helped him greatly in taking notes. Mrs. Josiah Wright's boarding house, southeastern corner Washington Road and Nassau Street, front room, second floor. The first year he had a room and boarded here since there was no room in the dormitories. In February 1877, in his sophomore year, he had a corner room in Witherspoon Hall. His cronies were known as the Witherspoon Gang or as his fellow "Alligators" and were part of a rather well-to-do eating club with a house on Nassau Street. After eating, they would meet for prayer meetings in No. 9 East Witherspoon. He was an active member of the "Whig Society," as was James Madison before him, and attended meetings in Whig Hall.

**1876** *Princeton, New Jersey.* University Hotel, where he lodged with his father when he rejoined Princeton in September.

**1879–1880** *Charlottesville, Virginia.* University of Virginia, as a law student. He left the University of Virginia at the end of his first year in ill health but recovered sufficiently to reenter in the autumn of 1880. Again, he became ill and withdrew from the university in December and returned home to Wilmington. While here, he was active in the Jefferson Literary Society, including debates, and also sang as first tenor in the chapel choir. In his first year he lodged at

Dawson Row, a row of six brick buildings now torn down. He occupied room 158, House F, at the west end of the lawns. In his second year, until December, he stayed in room 31 in West Range. There is a marker above the door. He joined the Phi Kappa Psi fraternity.

**1880–1882** *Wilmington, North Carolina.* Fourth and Orange Streets. Here he studied law on his own and was admitted to the bar in October 1882.

**1883–1886** *Baltimore, Maryland.* Johns Hopkins University, Charles and Thirty-fourth Streets. He took special exams and submitted "Congressional Government" as his dissertation and was awarded the Ph.D. degree in May 1886. He studied in the department of history and political science. He is the only president to have earned a doctorate. At the university, he helped to organize and was an active member in the Johns Hopkins House of Commons. From 1883 to 1884, he lodged in a house at 146 Charles Street, across from the Peabody Institute, and ate at a boarding house run by Jane and Hannah Ashton. From 1884 to 1885, he roomed at 8 McCulloh Street, near the university.

## MARRIAGE AND HONEYMOON

Wilson was married on June 24, 1885, in Savannah, Georgia. He was married in the evening in the parlor of the manse, next door to the Independent Church, Bull Street and Oglethorpe Avenue, the home of the bride's paternal grandfather. There was one disturbing incident. The bride's brother, nine-year-old Edward, and the groom's small nephew, Wilson Howe, meeting for the first time, became enemies at sight. Immediately after the ceremony, the boys engaged in a knock-down-drag-out battle on the parlor floor. The bride was shocked, but Wilson enjoyed the spectacle.

The honeymoon took place in Columbia, South Carolina. They spent the first week at the home of his sister, Annie Howe, at the old manse, 1531 Blanding Street. Then they went to Arden Park, in the North Carolina Hills, a small summer resort in a pine forest in a tiny vine-covered cottage on the grounds of the Arden Park Hotel, near Skyland, on US 25. The site has become an industrial park, and, without markers, it is difficult to locate the exact site. After two weeks here, they went to stay for a week with friends of Mrs. Wilson at Maplewood on North Carolina 18/US 64, north of Morganton, North Carolina. The private house is just north of Piedmont Road on the east side. There are two brick columns at the entrance, and the white brick house is past a pond. It is a beautiful house somewhat altered from the time when Wilson was here. After the honeymoon, they spent the rest of the summer with other relatives and friends. In September they moved into their home in Bryn Mawr, Pennsylvania.

Ellen Wilson died on August 6, 1914, at the White House.

Wilson's second marrage took place on December 18, 1915, in Washington, D.C. to Edith Bolling Galt, a widow, at her home, 1308 Twentieth Street, NW. It was a small affair attended by about forty guests.

The honeymoon took place in Hot Springs, Virginia, at the Homestead Hotel in suites 1, 2, 3 in the new wing for two weeks. An account of his arrival at the Hot Springs station belies the usual picture of Wilson as a stern person.

Edith Galt Wilson had no children, by her first or second marriage. She is buried next to the president in Washington Cathedral.

# HOMES

**1858–1859** *Staunton, Virginia.* The manse, 24 North Coalter Street, is a square house of gray-painted brick. A flat-roofed portico, somewhat altered and now at the rear, was originally the main entrance. Its two-story columns face the garden, which is landscaped to conform to the old pattern. When he was less than a year old, the family moved to Augusta, Georgia.

**1859–1870** *Augusta, Georgia.* 624 Telfair Street, where the family resided in a large comfortable manse, with slaves to help Dr. Wilson and his family.

**1870** *Columbia, South Carolina.* Pryor House, corner of Pickens and Blanding Streets, opposite the theological seminary. The family stayed here temporarily while the manse was being readied.

**1870–1872** *Columbia, South Carolina.* Presbyterian Manse, 1531 Blanding Street. He often visited there after the family moved. He and his new bride spent the first week following their wedding (June 24 to July 1, 1885) with his sister, who lived here.

**1870–** *Columbia, South Carolina.* 1301 Washington Street visiting his aunt, Mrs. James Woodrow.

**1872–1874** *Columbia, South Carolina.* 1705 Hampton Street. Dr. Wilson purchased a lot and built a home here in 1872. It is a two-story white frame house and was Wilson's boyhood home. On the lawn, surrounded by a green wooden fence, four magnolia trees and a giant sweet olive remain from Mrs. Wilson's garden. Among the Wilson mementoes displayed is the bed in which the president was born.

**1874** *Wilmington, North Carolina.* C. H. Robinson house, Front and Nun Street, where the Wilson family lived until the manse was ready.

**1875–1885** *Wilmington, North Carolina.* Presbyterian Manse, corner of Fourth and Orange Streets. His father was pastor of the First Presbyterian Church. The manse is no longer standing, and the site is a church playground. While living in Wilmington, Woodrow owned one of the first bicycles in the city.

**1875–** *Rome, Georgia.* 709 Broad Street (Featherston Place) visiting Mr. and Mrs. James W. Bones (Marion Woodrow, aunt). Bones house, (Oakdene), 205 East Tenth Street. Wilson was a guest here in the spring of 1883. 304 East Fourth was the manse where Ellen Axon Wilson lived 1867 to 1869. It is now the home of J. Bailey Gordon.

**1881** *Chillicothe, Ohio.* (Uncle) Thomas Woodrow house, 62 South Paint Street. He spent several months with his uncle and saw much of his cousin, Hattie Woodrow. After Hattie's rejection of his marriage proposal, he went to the local hotel for one night and left the next day for home. He told his new wife the whole story.

**1882** Ellen Axson was living in the Presbyterian parsonage at 402 East Third Avenue. It was torn down in 1970 and there is a modern house now on the spot.

**1882** *Atlanta, Georgia.* The Mrs. J. Reid Boylston House, 344 Peachtree Street, was a big private house in the best residential section of town, where he and his law partner found rooms together. Later, he and Edward Rennick moved to Mrs. James S. Turpin's boarding house.

**1885–1887** *Bryn Mawr, Pennsylvania.* The Wilsons lived in a house on the edge of Bryn Mawr's campus, facing Taylor Hall of the college. It was one of three small frame houses built by the college authorities and rented for a reasonable price to members of the faculty. One was known as Danery, another Scenery, and the third, between the other two, was "Betweenery," which is where the Wilsons lived in two rooms. (Also called Yarrow Hall). The site is now a small park.

**1887–1888** *Bryn Mawr, Pennsylvania.* 905 Old Gulph Road, a house in a ravine in back of the college. It was a small Baptist parsonage, just off the campus. This rented cottage was their first true home. It is now a private home.

**1888–1890** *Middletown, Connecticut.* 106 High Street, just a step from the Wesleyan campus, was a roomy Greek revival house, which they rented.

**1890–1896** *Princeton, New Jersey.* 48 Steadman Street, now 72 Library Place, was a house large enough to accommodate the relatives who lived with them comfortably.

**1891–** *Savannah, Georgia.* 166 Hall Street, the home of Ellen's uncle, Randolph Axson.

**1896–1902** *Princeton, New Jersey.* 82 Library Place. In 1896, they bought a lot on Library Place, adjoining the house in which they had lived, and moved into their own house which they had planned and built.

**1902–1911** *Princeton, New Jersey.* Prospect, the president's house on the campus, was built of yellow stone. There were more than 20 rooms, most of them large and high-ceilinged. The entrance is paved with marble under a large rotunda. There was a gloomy stained glass window at the top of an impressive stairway. The house had been redecorated when they moved in. It is now used as a reception place with a fancy restaurant.

**1911–1913** *Princeton, New Jersey.* Princeton Inn, opposite Trinity Church, on Stockton Street, next to the current police station. While he was governor, the Wilsons had four rooms at the Princeton Inn, which they called home. New Jersey did not provide a home for governors in Trenton, and Wilson preferred to travel twenty miles each day to his office and come back to Princeton at night.

**1911–1913** *Sea Girt, New Jersey.* There was a "summer mansion" near the ocean, where they went in June. The first summer at Sea Girt was far from restful. The governor's home is on the edge of New Jersey's national guard campground, and, in July, the annual training period began. He learned of his nomination for president here in 1912.

**1913** *Princeton, New Jersey.* 25 Cleveland Lane. In the fall, the Wilsons rented this small house and moved from the Princeton

*Washington, D.C., Woodrow Wilson lived here until his death in 1924.*

Inn. During the presidential campaign, reporters and the general public occupied the area around the house on Cleveland Lane day and night. This house was just behind Grover Cleveland's house and garden.

**1916** *Long Branch, New Jersey.* Shadow Lawn, intersection of Cedar and Norwood Avenues in West Long Branch. Woodrow Wilson Hall of Monmouth College is now on the site. Wilson used it for vacation and as a summer White House. There is a marker at Cedar Gate. Wilson was notified of the Democratic Party nomination for president here on September 1, 1916. He made many speeches from the front porch.

**1913–1921** *Washington, D.C.* The White House.

**1921–1924** *Washington, D.C.* 2340 S Street, NW, which his friends helped to purchase and where he lived until his death in 1924.

# WORK

**1881** *Chillicothe, Ohio.* Henry Woodrow law office, 4 Carlisle Block (corner of Paint

and Main Streets), where he served as an apprentice clerk in his uncle's firm.

**1881–1882** *Wilmington, North Carolina.* House, Fourth and Orange. During his convalescence at home he worked hard at perfecting his writing and speaking, delivering orations on political subjects to the empty pews in his father's church, and composing essays on various subjects.

**1882–1883** *Atlanta, Georgia.* First, he had an office in the Central Building, southwest corner of East Alabama and South Pryor Street. Later, he was at 48 Marietta Street, Room 10, near the southeast corner of North Forsyth. His law office with Edward I. Renick was on the second floor. However, by February 1883, he had decided to make teaching and writing his profession and went home to spend the summer with his family in Wilmington, North Carolina.

**1883–1885** *Baltimore, Maryland.* Johns Hopkins University. In the fall of 1885, he left Johns Hopkins for a post at Bryn Mawr and began a 17-year career as a professor and scholar by joining the faculty of the newly established college.

**1885–1888** *Bryn Mawr, Pennsylvania.* Bryn Mawr College, where for three years he was the sole professor of history. When he arrived, the college had two stone buildings: Taylor and Merion Halls. Taylor Hall contained all the classrooms, while Merion was a dormitory.

**1888–1890** *Middletown, Connecticut.* Wesleyan University, where he was professor of history. At the same time, he was lecturing at Johns Hopkins University in Baltimore. At Wesleyan, his classroom was in Memorial Chapel, lower level, as was his office. There is a plaque on the wall. He was also a football coach at Wesleyan, and he is the only president who served officially as a college football coach. His teams did well.

**1890–1902** *Princeton, New Jersey.* Princeton University, where he was professor of jurisprudence and political economy.

**1891–** *Baltimore, Maryland.* Johns Hopkins University. He delivered his lectures in a room in Hopkins Hall.

**1891** *Princeton, New Jersey.* Study-office, 12 West Witherspoon Hall.

**1902–1910** *Princeton, New Jersey.* Princeton University, as president of the university. Office Room 1, Nassau Hall.

**1911–1913** *Trenton, New Jersey.* State Capitol, 121 West State Street, as governor of New Jersey. His office was on the first floor, the first office on the right.

**1913–1921** *Washington, D.C.* President of the United States.

# TRAVEL/VISITS

**1860s** *Washington, Georgia.* 47 Spring Street, Barnett-Edwards House, near the city limits. He visited here as a boy when his father preached.

**1879** *North and South Carolina.* In the Blue Ridge Mountains with his mother and brother during the summer. August. Horse Cove, Macon County, North Carolina, in the Blue Ridge Mountains at the western most corner of North Carolina. Here he stayed in one of the frame houses belonging to a Mr. Thompson. They were here for a short time before moving to Walhalla for the rest of the family vacation.

**1880** *Fort Lewis, Green Valley, Bath County, Virginia.* For vacation and staying in the Lewis house.

**1880** *Asheville, North Carolina.* Eagle Hotel, South Main Street (now Biltmore Avenue) and a couple of blocks from the Square at Eagle Street and Biltmore. He also stayed at the Swannanoa Hotel, South Main Street at Willow, now 49 Biltmore Avenue, which is now a parking lot.

**1883** *Flat Rock, North Carolina.* Farmer's Hotel on US 25, south entry to Flat Rock,

for vacation. It has been restored and is now called Woodfield Inn.

**1884** *Baltimore, Maryland.* 257 Madison Avenue, for frequent visits at the Robert C. Hall home during the years he was attending Johns Hopkins University.

**1885–** *Gainesville, Georgia.* Broad Street (renamed Jesse Jewell and now the site of the Holiday Inn). Home of Louisa Cunningham (Wade) Hoyt Brown (Mrs. Warren A.), aunt of Wilson's first wife, Ellen. Ellen went here to stay during her pregnancy with the two older daughters.

**1885–** *Savannah, Georgia.* Screven Hotel, which was the hotel nearest the church the night before his wedding.

**1885–** *Savannah, Georgia.* 143 South Broad Street where he visited Ellen's grandparents at the Presbyterian manse. See also the site of Randolph Axon home, 164 Hall Street, which is now an empty lot.

**1885–1893** *Clarksville, Tennessee.* 304 South Second Street, visiting his father, who had a teaching position at the Southwestern Presbyterian University. The house was razed, and the offices of the Tennessee Employment Bureau now occupy the site. His father also lived at 211 Second Street in the Burney House (1885).

**1886** *Boston, Massachusetts.* United States Hotel. He visited here to see about publication of his book. While in Boston, he attended the Central Congregational Church. August.

**1886** *Little Rock, Arkansas.* Anderson Ross Kennedy home, 506 West Third Street, with his sister, Marion while on a lecture tour. House gone. Marion's husband was pastor at the Second Presbyterian Church, corner of 4th and State.

**1886** *New York City, New York.* Astor House, 225 Broadway, for a meeting of the Princeton Alumni Association.

**1887** *Gainesville, Georgia.* For a short time, the Wilsons roomed and boarded with Mrs.

S.A. Langston and then at the Piedmont Hotel, where their second daughter was born.

**1890–** *Princeton, New Jersey.* While Ellen visited family and their house was being readied, Wilson stayed at the Nassau Hotel, Palmer Square. Only the site remains.

**1891–** *Baltimore, Maryland.* 906 and 909 North McCulloh Street, while giving lectures at Johns Hopkins.

**1893** *Chicago, Illinois.* World's Columbian Exposition, Jackson Park, on the south side. He visited the Midway Plaisance, which included the world's first ferris wheel. He stayed at the home of Cyrus McCormick, 321 Huron Street.

**1894** *Colorado Springs, Colorado.* 1109 North Weber Street. He stayed here with a cousin while giving lectures at Colorado College. He saw the Rocky Mountains for the first time. He was here again in 1911.

**1894** *Saratoga Springs, New York.* Congress Hall Hotel. Site on Broadway.

**1896** *East Gloucester, Massachusetts.* The Flying Jib cottage for six weeks'summer vacation.

**1896** *England.* In May he suffered what was apparently a small stroke and, in June, went abroad for a change. He left the United States for the first time and spent two and one-half months in England and Scotland. Most of his travelling was done by bicycle. Glasgow, The Grand Hotel at Charing Cross. He visited University of Glasgow. Edinburgh, The Clarendon Hotel. He visited the Castle, Holyrood Palace, St. Giles, and Canongate Church to see Adam Smith's tomb. (He sent grass home from the grave.) From here, he visited Robert Burns country, the Lake District, and Burn's birthplace. Carlisle, Great Central Hotel. He was especially interested in Carlisle as the birthplace of his mother and in the Annetwell Street Congregational Church, where his grandfather had been pastor from 1820 to 1835. He also visited Grasmere and Stratford-on-Avon. Rydal Mount, where he plucked a flower to send home from the Wordsworth place. He visited England again in 1899, 1904, and 1908.

**1897** *Markham, near Front Royal, Virginia.* Mountain View, home of Robert M. Stribling, in the Blue Ridge Mountains. He stayed in a room on the second floor. He was met at the Markham railway station by Mr. Stribling.

**1898** *Washington, D.C.* He visited the U.S. Congress for the first time.

**1900–** *Judd Haven, Ontario, Canada.* Bluff Hotel in the Muskoka Lake District on Lake Rosseau. Summer vacation.

**1900–** *Palm Beach, Florida.* Flagler house, Whitehall, Coconut Row and Whitehall Way.

**1903** *London, England.* Buckingham Palace Hotel, later Brown's Hotel. Vacation with Ellen.

**1905** *Lyme, Connecticut.* Miss Thibet's boarding house. Summer vacation with the family.

**1907–** *Glen Cove, Padget West, Bermuda.* Again in 1908 and 1910.

**1907** *St. Hubert's, New York.* Cottage on the Au Sable River in the Adirondack Mountains for vacation.

**1912** *Nashville, Tennessee.* He attended a banquet and gave a speech at the Y.M.C.A. He also visited his brother Joseph R. Wilson, who lived at 1012 Fifteenth Avenue South.

**1913–1914** *Pass Christian, Mississippi.* Dixie White House, 767 East Beach Boulevard, fronting on the Gulf of Mexico for a three-week vacation.

**1913** *Bermuda.* Ten days after the election Wilson took his family for vacation and stayed at the Peck (Hulbert) house, overlooking the sea. Like Roosevelt and Taft before him he used the presidential yacht *Mayflower* for cruises while he was in the White House.

**1913** *Washington, D.C.* Before his inauguration, he stayed at the Shoreham Hotel, 2500 Calvert Street, NW.

**1914** *White Sulphur Springs, West Virginia.* Greenbrier Hotel, on vacation.

**1915–** *Washington, D.C.* St. Regis, 2219 California Street, NW, between Phelps Place and Twenty-third Street. Wilson's second wife's brother lived here, and she played bridge here with her sister for more than thirty years.

**1915** *New York City.* 115 East Fifty-third Street, with Colonel E.M. House.

**1915–** *Washington, D.C.* 1308 Twentieth Street, NW, Edith Galt's (his future bride) house.

**1916** *St. Louis, Missouri.* He was renominated for president at the Democratic National Convention at the Coliseum.

**1916** *Lakewood, New Jersey.* Seton Inn, Hope Road, on the south branch of the Meteconk. He stayed over night.

**1916** *Long Branch, New Jersey.* Shadow Lawn. The Shadow Lawn campus of Monmouth takes its name from the ornate Victorian seaside mansion once occupied by Wilson as a summer White House. Here, Wilson retired to sleep in 1916, believing he had lost the election, only to be awakened at dawn with the word from California that he had won. There is a marker at Cedar Avenue Gate at the intersection of Cedar and Norwood Avenue in West Long Branch.

**1916** *Asbury Park, New Jersey.* 601 Mattison Avenue, entire fifth floor of Midlantic National Bank Building. His political campaign was conducted from the presidential executive offices here.

**1918** *Magnolia, Massachusetts.* He rented a colonial mansion next to Colonel House on the North Shore (near Manchester). While there he spent one day sightseeing in Boston on the downtown streets and among thousands of people went unrecognized.

**1919** *Bismarck, North Dakota.* State Capitol.

**1919** *Des Moines, Iowa.* Fort Des Moines Hotel, Tenth and Walnut Streets. He gave a speech at the Coliseum.

**1919** *Helena, Montana.* Speech in City Auditorium.

**1919** *Los Angeles, California.* Hotel Alexandria, 501 South Spring Street at the corner of Fifth Street, which is still in use.

**1919** *Oakland, California.* Hotel Oakland.

**1919** *Portland, Oregon.* He had lunch at the Portland Hotel and gave a speech at the Auditorium.

**1919** *Rome, Italy.* He stayed at the Quirinal Palace, the royal residence. He had an audience with the Pope and visited the Methodist College in Rome.

**1919** *San Diego, California.* Dinner at the U.S. Grant Hotel, 326 Broadway (now renovated).

**1919** *San Francisco, California.* St. Francis Hotel, the Presidential Suite, 450 Powell Street. He attended a meeting and lunch at the Palace Hotel, southwest corner Market and New Montgomery Streets.

**1919** *Seattle, Washington.* Hotel Washington and dinner at the Hippodrome in Pasco, Washington.

**1919** *St. Paul, Minnesota.* City Auditorium and state legislature at the Capitol.

**1921** *Arlington National Cemetery, Virginia.* Tomb of Unknown Soldier final services.

**1923** *Washington, D.C.* He attended the funeral of President Harding at the White House.

*Bolivar, near Harpers Ferry, West Virginia.* Hilltop House on Ridge Road, which was once his retreat.

# DEATH

Wilson died on February 3, 1924, at 11:00 A.M. in Washington, D.C., at his home at 2340

S Street, NW. His bed was a replica of the Lincoln bed in the White House and is on view in this house. His bedroom furnishings were moved from the White House and set up in the Wilson House on S Street just as they had been in the White House, all within a four-hour period following Harding's inauguration. His last word was "Edith" and his last sentence was "I am ready." Wilson left an estate of $250,000.

## FUNERAL

There was no state funeral. The Reverend James Taylor of Central Presbyterian Church, Reverend Sylvester Beach of Princeton, and Bishop James Freeman of the Washington Cathedral conducted simple services without music at the home. Later there were services in the Bethlehem Chapel of the Washington Cathedral. Calvin Coolidge attended the services in the home. Taft was to have been a pall bearer at Wilson's funeral but was unable to attend at all because of a severe heart attack. Wilson's favorite hymns were sung: "How

Firm a Foundation" and "Day is Dying on the West."

## BURIAL

Until the tomb was ready, the body was in the crypt in the Bethlehem Chapel before being moved to the tomb on the south aisle of Washington Cathedral. His second wife is buried beside him.

## SPECIAL SITE

*Alexandria, Maryland.* Route 495, midway on the bridge are two aluminum medallions honoring Wilson.

## BIBLIOGRAPHY

Baker, Ray Stannard. *Woodrow Wilson: Life and Letters*, 8 volumes New York: Doubleday, Doran & Co., 1927–1939.

Link, Arthur S. *The Papers of Woodrow Wilson*. Princeton: Princeton University Press, 1966.

Mulder, John M. *Woodrow Wilson: Years of Preparation*. Princeton: Princeton University Press, 1978.

# WARREN GAMALIEL HARDING

1865–1923
29TH PRESIDENT 1921–1923: REPUBLICAN PARTY

*"I am a man of limited talents, from a small town. I do not seem to grasp that I am President."*

—*Cited in Vic Fredericks, The Wit and Wisdom of the Presidents*

Warren Harding was born on the morning of November 1, 1865, at the family farmhouse, north of Mount Gilead, at Corsica (now Blooming Grove), Ohio, to George Tryon and Phoebe Elizabeth Dickerson Harding. He was named Warren Gamaliel for a Methodist clergyman whom his father admired. His mother's pet name for him was "Winnie."

## CHARACTERISTICS

Harding was six feet tall and weighed about one hundred and seventy-five pounds. He was well built, with broad shoulders. In his youth, he had thick black hair which turned white and contrasted beautifully with his dark complexion and soft gray eyes. His dress, good looks, and manners set him apart, and he looked the part of the distinguished statesman.

As a boy, he ran with the gang of boys his own age, went swimming in Whetstone Creek, and played scrub baseball in the Rice

# A LIFE IN REVIEW

**Birth:** November 2, 1865; Blooming Grove, OH

**Died:** August 2, 1923; San Francisco, CA

**Married:** Florence Kling DeWolfe; July 8, 1891; No children

## CAREER

**1882** Teacher

**1882–1900** Newspaper reporter, editor, publisher

**1901–1904** Member state legislature

**1904–1906** Lt. Governor of Ohio

**1906–1915** Newspaper manager and owner

**1915–1921** Member U.S. Senate

## ADMINISTRATION EVENTS

**1921** Immigration quota act passed

**1921** Dedication Tomb of Unknown Soldier

**1921** Arms limitation conference

**1923** Teapot dome scandals

**1923** Motion picture sound film

corn flakes. Following that, he returned from time to time to Battle Creek for rest. According to one reporter, he was a regular "he man." He attended baseball games regularly, played golf and poker twice a week, and was not at all averse to putting a foot on the brass rail. He kept the White House stocked with bootleg liquor. When he felt the need for a chew of tobacco, he had to dodge upstairs because the Duchess (Mrs. Harding) disapproved. He, made many speeches on patriotism, saying, "It is the soul of nationality and the energy of civilization." Both in the state and in the U.S. Senate, he was always the harmonizer. He liked to feel close to people and wanted to be called Warren.

## BIRTHPLACE

Harding was born in Corsica (now Blooming Grove), Ohio, at the Harding homestead. There is a marker at the site near highway 97 and highway 298.

## BAPTISM

At ten days of age he was taken to a Methodist preacher to be blest. His mother said then, and often repeated, that he might grow up to be President of the United States. See Blooming Grove Methodist Church on the edge of town.

Bottom. When he was almost ten, his father brought home a B-flat cornet which he learned to play and joined a band. All of his life, he loved debating and public speaking. He liked people and got along with them. It was against his easygoing ways to hurt anyone except when he was sharply challenged. He would even walk carefully to avoid treading on ants. At twenty-four he suffered a nervous breakdown and spent several weeks in a sanitarium in Battle Creek, Michigan, run by Dr. J. P. Kellogg, the inventor of peanut butter and Kellogg

## CHURCH

Religion was for Harding like the Constitution, something to be honored and let alone. As a member of the First Baptist Church in Marion, he attended as often as a politician should. His mother had been a Methodist, who became a Seventh-Day Adventist when she came to Marion. His sister went to India as a missionary, but, for the most part, his religion was taken lightly. For a time, he was a religious skeptic, but, as his paper grew and he became

*Birthplace marker for Warren Harding.*

an important figure in the community, he joined Trinity Baptist Church. In 1912 he made the statement, "No nation can survive if it ever forgets Almighty God."

His grandfather, Salmon Harding, organized the Bloomfield Baptist Church and built the first church building, a small frame structure some two miles beyond the village crossroads.

**1865–1873** *Blooming Grove, Ohio.* Methodist Church. During his childhood,

he attended the Methodist Sunday School here as well as church. It stands at the edge of town. See also the cemetery for family members.

**1873–1880** *Caledonia, Ohio.* Caledonia Methodist Church, on the 200 block of Main Street, near the Harding house. Here the Hardings attended all church services, suppers, and entertainments.

**1880–1882** *Iberia, Ohio.* The Iberia Methodist Church, 3607 County Road 30, while attending Iberia College. He earned some extra money by helping paint the church and by his skill in graining the pews. It became the Iberia United Presbyterian church, and the church now stands where the college was.

**1882** *Marion, Ohio.* Seventh-Day Adventist, southwest corner of Center and Mill Streets, after meeting at one time temporarily in city hall. Shortly after his mother arrived in Marion, she converted to this church and harried her children and relations into the new faith. Most of the Harding descendants remained communicants of this church. However, Warren became Baptist and his future wife was also Baptist. The current address of the church is 550 Windsor Avenue.

**1882–1923** *Marion, Ohio.* Trinity Baptist Church, 220 South Main, between Prospect and Pleasant. After going to Washington, the Hardings remained members of their home church. Before 1901, it was located at 1330 North Main Street.

**1915–1923** *Washington, D.C.* Calvary Baptist Church, Eighth and H Streets, NW. On his first Sunday in the White House, he skipped church to play golf, and the newspapers noted it.

**1920** *Raritan (near Bound Brook), New Jersey.* Third Dutch Reformed Church, 10 West Somerset Street.

**1920** *Jamestown, Virginia.* The Billy Sunday Tabernacle.

**1923**   *Palm Beach, Florida, near Fort Worth.* The Royal Poinciana Chapel (nonsectarian).

**1923**   *Sitka, Alaska.* The brown wooden mission church. A plate marks the pew where he sat.

## EDUCATION

**1865–1873**   *Blooming Grove, Ohio.* He attended at a one-room schoolhouse. He was taught by his mother to recite poetry even before being sent off to school. At four years of age, he made his first declamation at a country school entertainment in the Buckhorn Tavern School. Before he left Blooming Grove, he spent several terms in the village school his grandfather had built.

**1873–1880**   *Caledonia, Ohio.* He attended the school across from the Methodist Church on Main Street and used McGuffey Readers.

**1880–1882**   *Iberia College (Ohio Central College), Ohio.* Seven miles east of Blooming Grove and near Caledonia. He was one of three graduates in 1882, graduating with a B.S. degree. This college later became a school for the blind, and, in 1885, the building burned down and was not rebuilt. A bronze marker marks the site of Ohio Central College and also gives the information that Harding and a friend founded the paper *The Iberia Spectator.* While at Iberia, he boarded with other students at Professor A. C. Crist's.

## MARRIAGE AND HONEYMOON

Harding was married on July 8, 1891, at 8:30 P.M., in Marion, Ohio, at his home at 380 Mount Vernon, in the front hall to Florence Mabel Kling DeWolfe (a divorcee with one son). His name for her was "the Duchess."

The Hardings left just after the wedding for Chicago, St. Paul, and the Northwest, including Yellowstone National Park. They were at home to their friends after August 3.

## HOME

**1865–1867**   *Blooming Grove, Ohio.* The Harding Homestead. Later in life, Harding bought the old homestead and 266 acres and engaged a Columbus architect to restore it. During the first years of his life, he lived here with his parents in the grandparents' home. There is a marker near highway 88 and 297.

**1867–1873**   *Blooming Grove, Ohio.* The Harding family moved into their own clapboard house near the homestead. There is a marker next to the Harding homestead.

**1873–1880**   *Caledonia, Ohio.* 139 Main Street, fourteen miles from Blooming Grove and a few doors from the town square is a small yellow-brown frame structure with gingerbread trimming.

**1880–1882**   *Caledonia, Ohio.* His father lost the house in town and moved to a 40-acre farm three miles to the east, just over the county line, measuring from the city limit sign. The house is set back from the road just behind and to the right of another house.

**1882–1891**   *Marion, Ohio.* His father moved to a shabby house that he bought on North East Street (now North Prospect Street), opposite the old interurban station and the second door south of the county jail. It has been demolished, and there are no markers.

**1889–**   *Marion, Ohio.* 498 East Center Street. His father had built a stark little Victorian utility house for himself and his family. It was here, while Florence Kling was giving piano lessons to Warren's sister, Chat, that Warren first met his future wife. This is also the place where he stayed on his return visits from Washington and where his body was brought before being taken to the Marion Cemetery.

*Harding family home in Marion, Ohio.*

**1891–1923** *Marion, Ohio.* 380 Mount Vernon Avenue, in a house that Warren and his future wife had planned and had built. It was a large styless two-story frame structure with wooden scalloped shingles and inserts of garish stained glass. Originally, the house number was 284, but, with the building of new houses in the area, the number has been changed to 380.

**1900–1904** *Columbus, Ohio.* Great Southern Hotel, 310 South High Street. He lived here as state senator.

**1904–1906** *Columbus, Ohio.* Great Southern Hotel, 310 South High Street. He lived here as lieutenant governor.

**1915–1921** *Washington, D.C.* 2314 Wyoming Avenue, NW, is a neo-Georgian style house which was later sold for $60,000 and is now used by the Burmese embassy. It was separated from the street by a terrace.

**1921–1923** *Washington, D.C.* The White House.

## WORK

**1875** *Caledonia, Ohio.* When his father became owner of the *Argus* newspaper, Warren was taken on as a printer's devil. He also learned to set type.

**1882** *Crestline, Ohio.* For a short time he served customers in a hardware store here.

**1882** *Marion, Ohio.* He taught for one term at the White Schoolhouse outside Marion. He took the examination required by the county school board for a district teacher's job. The school was only two miles from Marion, so he was able to stay at home. WMRN Radio Station, 1330 North Main, is on the site. There is no marker or building left.

**1882–1883**   *Marion, Ohio.* The second school term found Warren idle at home. At this time, he helped organize a band, in which he played the cornet and served as manager.

**1882–1884**   *Marion, Ohio.* He studied law briefly, was an insurance salesman for a brief time, and then took a job as a reporter and all-around-man at the *Marion Mirror*, 131– 134 East Center Street.

**1884**   *Chicago, Illinois.* He attended the Republican National Convention and watched the nomination of James G. Blaine at the Exposition Building in the park opposite Adams Street.

**1884–1900**   *Marion, Ohio.* Owner, editor, and publisher of the daily *Marion Star*. The printing office was on the second floor of the Miller Block. In the beginning, he often slept at the office. In 1885, the office was moved from the Miller Block to larger quarters on the second floor of the Fite Block at the corner of East and Center Streets, opposite the Methodist Church, 195 East Center. In 1890, the *Star* made the final move from the Fite Block to the lower half of a much more substantial building on the south side of East Center Street next to the Episcopal Church and almost opposite the county jail, 229 East Center. What was once the Star Building has been masked by a veneer of artificial stone and has become the central office of the Marion Water Company. The new *Star* offices were around the corner near the jail.

**1901–1904**   *Columbus, Ohio.* Ohio state senator. On January 1, he was one of twenty-three new senators to take his place in the ornate senate chamber of the gray limestone Capitol.

**1904–1906**   *Columbus.* Lieutenant-Governor. Office in the Capitol.

**1906–1915**   *Marion, Ohio.* Manager and owner of the Star, 229 East Center Street and, while not holding office, active in politics.

**1912**   *Chicago, Illinois.* Coliseum for the Republican National Convention, where he put William Howard Taft's name in nomination for president.

**1915–1921**   *Washington, D.C.* U.S. senator from Ohio. He was a likeable and harmonious member, with complete loyalty to the Republican Party, but not a leader in pressing any important bills.

**1916**   *Chicago, Illinois.* Coliseum for Republican National Convention.

**1920**   *Chicago, Illinois.* Coliseum, 1513 South Wabash Avenue. He attended the Republican National Convention, where he was nominated for the presidency.

**1921–1923**   *Washington, D.C.* President.

## TRAVEL/VISITS

In the United States, he visited most of the states, including the future states of Alaska and Hawaii.

**1875**   *Chicago, Illinois.* When his band went on a free trip to Chicago for the opening of the Erie Railroad, it was his first journey outside Ohio.

**1884**   *Chicago, Illinois.* Exposition Building in the park opposite Adams Street for the Republican National Convention.

**1889–**   *Battle Creek, Michigan.* The Battle Creek Sanitarium, North Washington Avenue and Champion Street. This was the first of five visits he made during the next twelve years.

**1892**   *Washington, D.C.* His first trip to the Capital. He visited the capitol and talked with Ohio senators and members of Congress.

**1893**   *Chicago, Illinois.* World's Columbian Exposition, Jackson Park on the South side.

**1895**   *Florida.* With Mrs Harding, this was his first of many trips to various parts of the United States.

**1899** *Richwood, Ohio.* The Globe Hotel, on Main Street, was a ramshackle two-story frame structure. Here, he had his first encounter with Harry Daugherty, a leading politician of the time.

**1900** *Daytona Beach, Florida.* J. G. Brown's boarding house. He stayed here in a four-dollar-a week room with the Duchess. They took their meals down the street at the Parkinson House on the corner of Ridgewood and Magnolia. It was at this time that he took up golf.

**1903** *Columbus, Ohio.* Neil House, 41 South High Street. He was here for the Republican convention.

**1904** *St. Louis, Missouri.* He visited the World's Fair, went on from here to Yellowstone Park, and ended his summer travels with a steamer trip on the Great Lakes.

**1905** *Marion, Ohio.* Carrie Fulton Phillips house, 417 South Main Street, on a rise of land known as Gospel Hill, is a gracious house with wide windows and small columns to its porch, where Harding visited Carrie, who had been the love of his life for fifteen years which ended when he became a candidate for president in 1920.

**1905** *Marion, Ohio.* Ann Britton house, 733 East Center Street. Ann Britton was another close friend.

**1915–** *Washington, D.C.* 2020 Massachusetts Avenue, NW, visiting Tom Walsh in his exposition-like palace.

**1915** *Honolulu, Hawaii.* Beach Hotel.

**1917** *Connersville, Indiana.* McFarlan Hotel, southeast corner of Sixth and Central, where the Central State Bank is now, to meet Nan Britton.

**1917** *Indianapolis, Indiana.* Claypool Hotel, 8 North Illinois Street (formerly Bates House), to meet Nan Britton.

**1917** *New York City, New York.* Manhattan Hotel, Forty-third Street entrance, where he met Nan Britton.

**1917** *New York City, New York.* Imperial Hotel, Broadway and Thirty-second Street, on lower Broadway, to meet Nan Britton.

**1917** *Plattsburg, New York.* New Witherill Hotel, 25 Margaret Street, to meet Nan Britton. The site is now occupied by a bank building.

**1918** *Augusta, Georgia.* Bon-Air-Vanderbilt Hotel, corner of Walton Way and Hickman Road.

**1918** *Washington, D.C.* New Willard Hotel, Fourteenth Street and Pennsylvania Avenue, NW, to meet Nan Britton.

**1919** *Oyster Bay, New York.* Christ Episcopal Church. He attended the funeral of Theodore Roosevelt.

**1920** *Chattanooga, Tennessee.* He toured the battlegrounds, including Missionary Ridge, Lookout Mountain, and Chickamauga Battlefield. There was a reception at the Patten Hotel, and he spoke at the Billy Sunday Tabernacle.

**1920** *Chicago, Illinois.* LaSalle Hotel, 720 North LaSalle, where he had a personal suite, some distance from the Coliseum, where the Republican Convention was held. He also visited the Scott Willits House, 6103 Woodlawn Avenue, corner of Sixty-first Street where he arranged for Nan Britton and her child, Elizabeth Ann, to stay with Nan's sister, Elizabeth, and her brother-in-law, Scott Willits, in a small four-room apartment.

**1920** *Cleveland, Ohio.* There was a dinner at the Hotel Hollenden, and he spoke at Gray's Armory.

**1920** *Des Moines, Iowa.* Hotel Fort Des Moines, Tenth and Walnut Streets, lodging and speaking.

**1920** *Fort Worth, Texas.* Chamber of Commerce. He was the first Republican presidential candidate ever to speak in Texas. He left here for Dallas, San Antonio, Denver, and then back to Indiana and Ohio.

**1920**  *Fremont, Ohio.* Spiegel Grove. He visited the Hayes Memorial Library, 1337 Hayes Avenue.

**1920**  *Indianapolis, Indiana.* Hotel Severin. He spoke at Monument Circle.

**1920**  *Louisville, Kentucky.* Seelbach Hotel.

**1920**  *Oklahoma City, Oklahoma.* He spoke at the State Fair Grounds stock pavilion, northwest, Tenth Street and May Avenue.

**1920**  *Omaha, Nebraska.* He lodged at Fontanelle Hotel and spoke in the Auditorium.

**1920**  *St. Louis, Missouri.* He came in at Union Station, south side of Market Street between Eighteenth and Twentieth Streets and was honored at a reception in the Union Station Plaza.

**1920**  *St. Paul, Minnesota.* State Capitol, Wabash and Tenth. Reception. Dinner at the home of Senator Kellogg.

**1920**  *Texas and Mexico.* On a vacation trip going to Point Isabel, Texas, he got away from the campaign pressures, but his fishing was limited because of the cold weather. He stayed in a small cottage owned by R. B. Creager on a sandy bluff jutting into the bay. In Brownsville, he played golf at the Brownsville Country Club. While in Brownsville, he visited the battlefields of the Mexican War era and went across the Rio Grande River to visit Matamoras in Mexico. On November 18, he left for Panama.

**1921–**  *Bethesda, Maryland.* He played on Burning Tree Golf Course.

**1921–1924**  *Merritt Island, Florida.* Indianola House, 50 miles south of Daytona Beach, where he spent vacations.

**1921**  *(near) Fredericksburg, Virginia.* Camp for reenactment of the Battle of Chancellorsville on US 3 off US 20.

**1921**  *Elsmore, near Valley Forge, Pennsylvania.* He spent one weekend with Harry Daugherty at Philander Knox's farm.

**1921**  *Marion, Ohio.* 498 East Center Street, with his father, since the Mount Vernon street house had been rented.

**1921**  *St. Augustine, Florida.* Ponce de Leon Hotel, Cordova Street between King and Valencia Streets, extending to Sevilla Streets. It is now part of Flagler College.

**1921**  *Washington, D.C.* New Willard Hotel, just before his inauguration.

**1922**  *Lancaster, New Hampshire.* Home of John W. Weeks, Secretary of War, Mt. Prospect. He stayed here while on vacation.

**1922**  *Palm Beach, Florida.* James Clark King house on Clarke Avenue, where he was a frequent guest. He stayed at the Edward McLean villa in St. Augustine with reception at Ponce de Leon Hotel, where he later stayed.

**1922**  *Point Pleasant, Ohio.* He attended the Grant celebration at Point Pleasant and other ceremonies at Bethel and Georgetown.

**1922**  *Washington, D.C.* He dedicated the Lincoln Memorial.

**1923**  *Anchorage, Alaska.* On the way to Anchorage, he stayed at the Curry Hotel, which is almost equidistant between Seward and Fairbanks. In Anchorage, he viewed Mount McKinley. He also visited Prince Edward Sound, Sitka, and Juneau.

**1923**  *Fairbanks, Alaska.* Hotel Norvale, 511 Second Avenue. The temperature while he was there was 96 degrees. Harding Gateway, which was renamed for him when he visited, is between the Rugged and Cheval Islands.

**1923**  *Portland, Oregon.* Multnomah Hotel, 319 Southwest Pine (now an office building).

**1923**  *San Francisco, California.* Palace Hotel, Room 8064, on the eighth floor overlooking Market Street.

**1923**  *Washington to San Francisco.* For his last trip, he left Union Station on June 20 for St. Louis on the first lap of his trip riding in the last car of the train, called the Su-perb. At Kansas City he stayed at the Muehlbach Hotel. He was in Denver for a weekend. Tuesday, he arrived at Salt Lake City. He moved on to Zion National Park and crossed from Utah into Idaho at Cache Junction. After Helena, Montana, he visited a mine at Butte and then spent a weekend holiday exploring Yellowstone National Park. Saturday morning, he arrived at Gardiner, Montana, with breakfast at the Mammoth Hot Springs Hotel and left for Old Faithful Inn, 50 miles away.

# DEATH

Harding died on August 2, 1923, in San Francisco, California, at the Palace Hotel, Room 8064. As his nurse was returning with a glass of water for him to take his night medicine, she saw him in a half-sitting position resting on pillows, his face twitched sharply, his mouth dropped open, and his body slumped. He was dead at 7:32 P.M. Later, two undertakers and an embalmer arrived from N. Gray and Company with a brown metal coffin. The body, dressed in a cutaway with black trousers, was placed in the coffin and moved to the adjoining drawing room, where it was placed against the wall between two windows. He left an estate of more than $700,000.

# FUNERAL

A simple prayer was said over the body, at the Palace Hotel, on August 3. The coffin was closed and moved to a train. At 7:15 P.M., the funeral train moved out of the Southern Pacific Railway station. Two hymns were sung and played: "Lead Kindly Light" and "Nearer My God to Thee," which had been favorites of President McKinley. On August 4, the coffin was placed on a bier in the East Room of the White House under the massive central chandelier where Lincoln had lain in state in 1865.

After a brief private service in the East Room, his body was carried to the caisson under the front portico. Those in the procession included President Coolidge and ex-Presidents Taft and Wilson.

In the Capitol Rotunda, the coffin was placed on the black catafalque which had originally been built for Lincoln and borne the bodies of Garfield, McKinley, and the Unknown Soldier. The minister of the Washington Calvary Baptist Church conducted the brief service. Following this, thousands passed by four abreast. Then the coffin was closed and taken to Union station for the overnight journey and final funeral in Marion.

In Marion, Ohio, at 498 East Center Street, the body lay in state at the home of his father, Dr. George Harding. Thousands filed by. President Coolidge and ex-president Taft were there and accompanied the procession to the cemetery, a mile and a half from the house. At the grave site there was a fourth and final brief funeral service when the coffin was carried through the ivy-grown gateway into the interior. Following the service, the Duchess went into the crypt alone and remained for several minutes.

# BURIAL

The body was left temporarily in the Marion Memorial Cemetery's receiving vault, an arched Victorian-Gothic stone building set into the hillside. This vault is in the section across Vernon Heights Boulevard from the present Memorial. In October 1923, the Marion vault was opened and Harding's coffin was placed in a 2,600 pound asphalt sarcophagus.

In 1927, the marble cylinder of the Harding memorial was completed, and, four days before Christmas, at a private service, the bodies of Harding and the Duchess were interred in the central grass plot, each under a two-ton slab of Labrador granite. Marion Memorial Cemetery is located at Vernon Heights Boulevard, Marion, Ohio.

*Warren Harding's body was left temporarily in this receiving vault at Marion Memorial Cemetery.*

On June 16, 1931, President Hoover dedicated the tomb and former President Coolidge, as honorary president of the association, accepted the monument for the Harding Memorial Association. Harding's grave is marked by a bronze palm wreath and the Duchess's by a bronze wreath of roses.

See also, the cemetery at Blooming Grove for family members.

## BIBLIOGRAPHY

Russell, Francis. *The Shadow of Blooming Grove*. New York: McGraw Hill Book Company, 1968.

Sinclair, Andrew. *The Available Man: The Life Behind the Mask of Warren Gamaliel Harding*. New York: Macmillan, 1965.

THE PRESIDENTS

# CALVIN COOLIDGE

1872–1933
30TH PRESIDENT 1923–1929: REPUBLICAN PARTY

*"It has been my observation in life that, if one will only exercise the patience to wait, his wants are likely to be filled."*

— *The Autobiography of Calvin Coolidge, 1929*

Calvin Coolidge, "Silent Cal," was born on July 4, 1872, to John Calvin and Victoria Josephine Moor Coolidge. Most of the Coolidge family remained in Vermont although his great grandparents, Sally and Israel Brewster, moved to Hampden (near Portage), Wisconsin, and while Coolidge was President he ordered a stone for their grave. According to one source, the Coolidge ancestry can be traced to Charlemagne.

## CHARACTERISTICS

Coolidge stood about five feet and nine inches tall and weighed about one hundred and forty-five pounds. He had sandy red hair and blue eyes, a narrow pointed nose, cleft chin, and rather thin lips. It was a great matter of pride to him that he had Indian as well as Yankee blood.

He smoked cigars regularly, seldom drank, and, as president during Prohibition, he abstained completely. He had remained an outsider during his college days, but, in his senior year, he was pledged by a fraternity. He seemed to have much more influence on university students when he was president than when he him-

# A LIFE IN REVIEW

**Birth:** July 4, 1872; Plymouth, VT
**Died:** January 5, 1933; Northampton, MA
**Married:** Grace Anna Goodhue; October 4, 1905; 2 sons

## CAREER

**1898–1933** Law practice
**1898** City councilman
**1900–1902** City solicitor
**1903** Clerk of Courts
**1907–1908** Member state legislature
**1910–1912** Mayor, Northampton, MA
**1912–1915** Member state legislature
**1916–1918** Lt. Governor of Massachusetts
**1919–1920** Governor of Massachusetts
**1921–1923** U.S. Vice President

## ADMINISTRATION EVENTS

**1924** U.S. Foreign Service created
**1925** Scopes trial
**1927** Lindberg transatlantic solo flight
**1929** Kellogg-Briand peace pact ratified

self was a student: the increase in the use of cigars at Yale University during his presidency was said to be due to his example, as had been the switch among the students from belts to suspenders earlier. Once, whoever packed for him for a train trip forgot to put in his sleeping clothes; when he got to New Orleans and spent a sleepless night in the hotel using the pajamas provided, he sent out the next day for an old-fashioned nightshirt. It is not known what influence this had on the sale of nightshirts.

He was the first president to speak on the radio, but he did not have the persuasive voice of Franklin Roosevelt. He has been characterized as serious, unsmiling, penurious, and without humor. He was always extremely quiet, and on being told Coolidge was dead, someone asked, "How can you tell?" Asked on one occasion what his hobby was, he said, "Holding office."

He was not an outdoorsman or avid sportsman; however, he usually took a walk twice a day and took up fishing while he was president. Both the Coolidges enjoyed putting together jigsaw puzzles and were experts at it. Often, after dinner, when Will Rogers was a guest at the White House, they would spend the evening over a jigsaw puzzle.

## BIRTHPLACE

Coolidge was born in Plymouth Notch, Vermont, in a small drab room in the family quarters that adjoined his father's store. The house is said by some to be the most authentic and well-preserved presidential birthplace in the nation.

## BAPTISM

He was baptized in Plymouth Notch, Vermont, at the Congregational Church. He was named for his father, John Calvin, but he was later known simply as Calvin Coolidge. Actually, it is not known when he was christened or where the ceremony took place or, even if there was a ceremony. Coolidge himself writes, "I have always attended church regularly when I could but there being no organized church in our town when I was a boy I did not join a church." The church is located across the street from his boyhood home in Plymouth Notch.

*Birthplace of Calvin Coolidge.*

# CHURCH

In his youth he attended the Sunday School of the local church. The Bible was the basis for instruction both at church and at home. Plymouth was so small that much of the time its church life depended on visiting preachers. Rumors that seances were held at the White House were officially denied. In a speech given in Washington in October 1924 while unveiling an equestrian statue of Francis Asbury, he called religion the nation's foundation. Churches attended by Coolidge:

**1872–1933** *Plymouth Notch, Vermont.* The congregational Church (also called Union Church) was the Coolidge family church and where he attended whenever home in Plymouth Notch. He always sat three rows from the front. It is a small, white frame building just across the street from his boyhood home. After he became president, the

church suffered greatly from tourists taking hymnals and prayer books from the church.

**1886–1891** *Ludlow, Vermont.* He attended the chapel of Black River Academy while a student there.

**1891** *St. Johnsbury, Vermont.* North Congregational Church, corner of Main and Church Streets.

**1891–1895** *Amherst, Massachusetts.* Amherst College in Johnson Chapel on the main campus. Attendance at two church services on Sunday was compulsory for all students.

**1905–1933** *Northampton, Massachusetts.* The church, South and Main Streets. The Edwards Church he attended has been replaced by a modern structure on the same site. Grace Coolidge was a member, but he was neither a member nor a leader. After their marriage, this was their regular church, and they returned to it after leaving the

*Union Christian Church, the Coolidge family church.*

White House. He occupied pew 10 about half-way down the church. In retirement, he attended almost every Sunday. It was said that he spent as much time in church figuring out who was absent as in listening to the sermons. When a Baptist preacher dined at their house before a revival meeting and scarcely touched his food, saying abstinence improved his preaching, Calvin reported back to Grace after listening to him, "Might as well have et."

**1921–1929** *Washington, D.C.* First Congregational Church, Tenth and G Streets, NW. A new building dedicated in 1961 replaced the old church. While closed for repairs during his presidency, the church met on Sunday mornings at Loews Palace Theater and evenings at the Eighth Street Synagogue. The First Congregational Church where he worshipped is marked with a name plate at the east end of the third row in the middle section of benches. On August 23, 1923, he was met by the pastor, and on the following Sunday he joined a church for the first time in his life.

**1924** *Alexandria, Virginia.* Christ Church,

Cameron and Columbia Streets, where George Washington once worshipped.

**1925** *Salem, Massachusetts.* Congregational Tabernacle, corner of Washington and Federal Streets, while they were at the Swampscott summer White House.

**1926** *Saranac Lake, New York.* First Presbyterian Church, 23 Church Street, in White Pines Camp. It was a small chapel with hardly enough room for the regular parishioners and with no room for the many visitors while the president was there during the summer—and particularly on the weekend when Governor and Mrs. Al Smith came to visit and went to church with Coolidge.

**1927** *Hermosa, South Dakota.* Congregational Mission Church, nineteen miles from Rapid City, served by a 19-year old student pastor. The church was a small box-like frame building with a steeple. It had no pews, and chairs were brought in from houses around for the presidential party. He worshipped here regularly during the summer of 1927.

**1928** *Brule, Wisconsin.* Brule Presbyterian Church. Turn right from Brule on County Road H about 0.2 mile and five miles from Cedar Island. They drove here each Sunday and listened to a blind lay preacher. After church, there were usually photo opportunities, showing the President wearing the heavy overcoat which he had worn all through the service. At a church which could hold 100, there were 3,000 to 4,000 on each of the Sundays Coolidge attended.

**1928** *Staunton, Virginia.* First Presbyterian Church, Coalter and Frederick Streets, where Woodrow Wilson's father had been minister when Wilson was born.

# EDUCATION

**1877–1886** *Plymouth Notch, Vermont.* District Number 9, in an ungraded school. It was a small stone building just a few steps away from his home. He began school in December 1877.

**1886–1890** *Ludlow, Vermont.* Black River Academy. The sole building of the academy was a towered red brick building, standing on a low hill above the village. This was a Baptist-sponsored "finishing school." In his final year, classes were held in Whitcomb and Atherton Halls. After he graduated in May 1890, he returned to Ludlow in the winter for postgraduate study. There were no dormitories, so he was obliged to take room and board in town while attending the Academy. He lodged on Main Street at the home of Charles Parker and later at Mrs. Sherwin's.

**1890–1891** *St. Johnsbury, Vermont.* St. Johnsbury Academy, southern end of Main Street for a preparatory course for an examination which would win him admission to Amherst. He attended for two months. In 1894, two elm trees from the Coolidge home in Plymouth were planted and a bronze tablet was placed on a small boulder to commemorate his presence. On one occasion, he wrote from St. Johnsbury to his father, "I have met with a misfortune, someone has taken my pocketbook. I had eleven dollars in it, it was taken last night while I was in bathing I suppose ... I shall need seven dollars to settle up and get home on." He stayed at the home of L. W. Rothwell, 4 Main Street.

**1891–1895** *Amherst, Massachusetts.* Amherst College. He graduated cum laude in 1895. During his final year, he was pledged and initiated into the Phi Gamma Delta Fraternity.

**1891–1893** *Amherst, Massachusetts.* The Trott House, 27 South Pleasant Street, where he roomed during his first and second years, is still standing a little back from the street and can be identified by its peculiar pointed windows. He had a small cheap bedroom here. His boarding places changed many times.

**1893–1894** *Amherst, Massachusetts.* Avery house on Prospect Street.

**1894–1895** *Amherst, Massachusetts.* Dr. Henry E. Paige house, Prospect Street, next door to Mrs. Avery's. He and his roommate occupied the two rooms to the right on the second floor.

**1895–1897** *Northampton, Massachusetts.* John C. Hammond and Henry P. Field law office, corner of Main and King Streets. He studied law here and was admitted to the bar in 1897.

## MARRIAGE AND HONEYMOON

Coolidge was married on October 4, 1905, in Burlington, Vermont, at the Goodhue House, Maple Street. The bride was Grace Anna Goodhue. It was a small wedding with fifteen guests. He drove up to the house with his own pair of horses, arriving just a moment before the ceremony was scheduled to begin. When Grace first saw him in 1903, he was near a window shaving, in his underwear and wearing a hat. He explained to her after they met that he had an undisciplined lock of hair that got in the way while he washed and shaved. To solve the problem he had to anchor the lock with his hat.

On their honeymoon they went to Montreal, Canada for one week. They had planned for more, but Grace was bored with Montreal, and Calvin wanted to get back home for political activities.

## HOMES/LODGINGS

Except for the brief time Coolidge was in Washington, D.C., he lived his whole life in New England.

**1872–1898** *Plymouth Notch, Vermont.* This house was associated with him throughout his life from birth to death. The house in which he was born, extended in 1876, had in the parlor and sitting room pieces of black walnut furniture brought all the way from Boston. A piazza, very unusual for the time, was added to the house later. It was a five-room cottage attached to the post office and his father's general store. Like other boys of his time, he was up before daylight, putting on his clothes in a cold room and washing with cold water in the kitchen. There was only an outside privy until 1932. Calvin worked on the farm until he was twenty-six.

**1895** *Northampton, Massachusetts.* Lyman House, 63 Center Street, in an upstairs room when he first came to Northampton. It is no longer standing.

**1895–1898** *Northampton, Massachusetts.* Robert Weir house, 40 Round Hill, northeast from Elm Street. He took his meals at Rahar's Inn, a three-story brick building on a side street. Calvin and Grace sometimes went here for Sunday supper. It is now the site of La Cazuela restaurant.

**1898–1905** *Northampton, Massachusetts.* Charles Lavake house, 162 King Street.

**1905** *Northampton, Massachusetts.* Norwood Hotel, corner of Bridge Street and Market, for three weeks after the honeymoon.

**1905–1906** *Northampton, Massachusetts.* 5 Crescent Street at the corner of Prospect.

**1906–1930** *Northampton, Massachsetts.* 21 Massasoit Street. This was their home for many years and the birthplace of their two sons and the place to which they returned from the White House. The house was a simple frame dwelling, with three bedrooms and bath, a parlor, dining room, kitchen and attic. As a duplex, a Mr. Plummer shared one wall of the house with the Coolidges. The porch was Coolidge's favorite sitting place in good weather. After his presidency, it was almost impossible to get any privacy, and he had to give up using the porch.

**1907–1921** *Boston, Massachusetts.* Adams House, 553 Washington Street, in a fourth

floor suite. While serving in the legislature, he stayed in a dollar-a-day room at the Adams House. He went home every weekend on the day train. While governor, he took a second room at the Adams House. Massachusetts does not provide a mansion for its governor. While in the legislature he also used his room as his office.

**1921–1923** *Washington, D.C.* Willard Hotel, Fourteenth Street and Pennsylvania Avenue, NW. As vice president, he took over the eight-dollar-a-day suite of the retiring vice president, Suite 328-332, with two bedrooms, a dining room, and a reception room.

**1923–1929** *Washington, D.C.* The White House.

**1925** *Swampscott (near Lynn), Massachusetts.* White Court, on Little's Point, was used as the summer White House. It is now Marian Court Junior College at 35 Little's Point. It is a twenty-six-room white pillared mansion with a breathtaking view of the Atlantic Ocean. While others enjoyed the fishing he preferred walking and horseback riding. At one time, he said that fishing was for the young and that he had enjoyed it during his own boyhood. While in Swampscott for rest, he was persuaded to have the Harper hair treatment for his thinning hair.

**1925** *Lynn, Massachusetts.* Summer executive office, Security Trust Company Building, Central Square, about three miles from White Court.

**1926** *Saranac Lake, New York.* White Pines Camp is in an estate close to Saranac Lake owned by Kirkwood, a Kansas City publisher. The camp, with a group of detached houses built of split logs, was situated on a low bluff overlooking Lake Osgood. For entertainment, they spent a lot of time putting together jigsaw puzzles. They were here for two months. He was the first president since Theodore Roosevelt to have a summer White House in New York State. The site is fourteen miles from Saranac.

*Calvin Coolidge summer home in Wisconsin.*

**1927** *Black Hills, South Dakota.* Located thirty-two miles from Rapid City at the South Dakota State Game Lodge. He arrived here by special train. It was the furthermost west seat of government up to this time, 1,800 miles from Washington, D.C. Some wished to set up a permanent summer White House, but Coolidge disagreed, saying it would limit others who did not wish to stay in that place. While here, he visited Armore and the Sioux Indian tribe, who considered that an appropriate name for him might be "Still Waters." They also visited Yellowstone National Park.

**1927** *Rapid City, South Dakota.* Rapid City High School, where he had his summer office. Here he made his announcement, "I do not choose to run for president in 1928."

**1927** *Washington, D.C.* Eleanor Patterson Mansion, 15 Dupont Circle, while the White House was being renovated. The Coolidges were there most of the year.

**1928** *Brule, Wisconsin.* Cedar Island Lodge, on a 5,000 acre Pierce estate on the Bois Brule River on US 2 west of Iron River. The lodge was an eleven-room one story birch log dwelling on the island. He was the first president to have vacationed here although Cleveland stayed and fished at a camp here in 1883 before he was president. The camp has fallen into ruin. When Coolidge came, the rents in the village shot up 700 percent. Superior, Wisconsin. The central High School Library, 1015 Belknap Street, was the summer executive office.

**1929–1930** *Northampton, Massachusetts.* 21 Massasoit Street. Describing his retirement, a reporter wrote: "When he is riding, motorists often drive past his car, then slow down so he will pass them, and so get a second look. Maps are distributed by the hotels showing how to reach the Coolidge home. Often at night when Mr. and Mrs. Coolidge are sitting in their living room, they see faces peering in the windows at them." One reporter tried to get into Mr. Coolidge's bathroom while he was taking a shower.

**1930–1933** *Northampton, Massachusetts.* The Beeches on Munroe Street, after they found it difficult to have any privacy. The Beeches was an estate with nine acres. The sixteen-room shingled house was one of the finest houses in town with a good view of the river and the mountains. Coolidge paid $45,000 for it.

# WORK

**1895** *Plymouth Notch, Vermont.* He worked on the family farm.

**1895–1897** *Northampton, Massachusetts.* Hammond and Field law office, in the First National Bank Building, on the corner of Main and King Streets. He read law here.

**1898–1933** *Northampton, Massachusetts.* Law office, second floor of the new Masonic Building, 25 Main Street. It is still marked with his name on a second floor window.

**1898** *Northampton, Massachusetts.* City Hall, Main Street. City councilman—his first election to government office.

**1900–1902** *Northampton, Massachusetts.* City Hall, where he worked as city solicitor.

**1903** *Northampton, Massachusetts.* Courthouse, Main Street. He was appointed clerk of the courts for Hampshire County.

**1904** *Northampton, Massachusetts.* Chairman of the Republican city committee.

**1907–1908** *Boston, Massachusetts.* State House. He was elected a member of the general court.

**1910–1912** *Northampton, Massachusetts.* City Hall. He was elected mayor and had an office on the ground floor (now occupied by the tax commissioner).

**1912–1915** *Boston, Massachusetts.* State House. He was elected state senator and senate president.

**1916–1918** *Boston, Massachusetts.* State House. He was elected lieutenant governor.

**1919–1920** *Boston, Massachusetts.* State House. He was elected governor. See the old office of the governor.

**1921–1923** *Washington, D.C.* Vice president of the United States. He took the oath of office in the Senate Chamber with President-elect Harding looking on. His inaugural address was the shortest ever given.

**1923** *Plymouth Notch, Vermont.* He took the oath of office in his father's farm house by the light of an oil lamp, August 3, 2:47 A.M. The room was the sitting room; it later became known as the Oath of Office room.

**1923–1929** *Washington, D.C.* President of the United States. He was quietly sworn into office a second time at the Willard Hotel by a justice of the Supreme Court. Following his election in 1925, he was sworn in by ex-president Taft. For the first time, the inaugural message was broadcast. He did not run again in 1928.

# TRAVEL/VISITS

**1891** *Bennington, Vermont.* He attended the address given by President Benjamin Harrison and the dedication of the 300-foot high Battle Monument on Monument Avenue.

**1916** *Washington, D.C.* Shoreham Hotel, 2500 Calvert Street, NW.

**1920–1921** *Asheville, North Carolina.* Grove Park Inn, off Macon Avenue.

**1920** *Marion, Ohio.* 300 Mount Vernon Avenue, to visit the Hardings at their home.

**1921** *Arlington, Virginia.* National Cemetery. When the Unknown Soldier was laid to rest.

**1922**  *Minneapolis, Minnesota.* State Fair.

**1923**  *Marion, Ohio.* President Harding's funeral.

**1923**  *Tuskegee, Alabama.* Booker T. Washington home, The Oaks.

**1923**  *White Sulphur Springs, West Virginia.* Greenbrier Hotel. The old resort hotel has been turned into a museum.

**1924**  *Chicago, Illinois.* Drake Hotel, 140 East Walton Street.

**1924**  *Chicago.* Coliseum, 1513 South Wabash, where the Republican National Convention nominated him for president.

**1924**  *Chicago.* He took an ordinary Pullman car and saved the nation $1,700. The menu is listed, and Coolidge had a $1.25 dinner.

**1924**  *Plattsburg, New York.* Witherill Hotel.

**1924**  *Washington, D.C.* President Wilson's funeral at 2340 S Street, NW, and later the memorial service at Washington Cathedral at Massachusetts and Wisconsin Avenues. June.

**1924**  *Wakefield, Virginia.* Washington's Birthplace. There was only a marble shaft marker there at the time.

**1925**  *Sherman House, Clark and Randolph.*

**1926**  *Camden, New Jersey.* He dedicated what is now the Benjamin Franklin Bridge.

*Potomac Park.* The monument emphasizes friendship between Sweden and the United States.

**1926**  *Washington, D.C.* He unveiled the Ericsson Monument.

**1928–1929**  *Sapelo Island, Atlantic Ocean, off the mainland of McIntosh County, Georgia.* He visited the Coffin estate near Sea Island Beach, where he enjoyed the live oak trees draped with Spanish moss.

**1928**  *Annapolis, Maryland.* He visited the first capital of the United States and had lunch at the governor's executive mansion, northwest side of State Circle.

**1928**  *Fredricksburg, Virginia.* He visited Spottsylvania Battlefield Park and attended a reception at the nearby Country Club to honor the park.

**1928**  *Havana, Cuba.* He stayed at the Palace.

**1928**  *Waynesboro, Virginia.* Swananoa Country Club, junction of Blue Ridge Parkway and US 250, for a five-day holiday. The building is constructed of Italian marble and is an impressive site today.

**1929**  *Mount Dora, Florida.* Lakeside Inn near town center.

**1929**  *Mountain Lake (Lake Wales), Florida.* He dedicated the Bok Memorial (Singing Tower).

**1929**  *Orlando, Florida.* Frederick E. Godfrey House, 335 Ponce de Leon Place, as a dinner guest before returning to Mount Dora where he was vacationing. On February 1, he passed through Orlando on the train and more than 1,000 people came to see him, but he did not appear until the train had passed the depot; then he came to the platform and waved to the crowd.

**1930**  *Los Angeles, California.* He visited the Warner Brother Studio as well as MGM and United Artists. Although an ex-president, a small incident reveals the importance in which holders of the office are held. When he threw away a half-smoked cigar, a crowd of souvenir hunters immediately started a fight for the butt. A woman who refused to give her name won the stub, put it in her purse, and disappeared.

**1930**  *New Orleans, Louisiana.* Roosevelt Hotel (now Fairmont Hotel) 100 Block of University Place.

**1930**  *Petersburg, Florida.* Vinoy Hotel (now Stouffer-Vinoy) on the waterfront.

**1930**  *San Simeon, California.* Hearst Mansion. He was here for a week and occupied the Doric suite in the front on the third floor.

*Calvin Coolidge's gravesite.*

**1931** *Marion, Ohio.* Harding Memorial, Vernon Heights Boulevard. Dedication.

**1932** *New York City, New York.* Vanderbilt Hotel, 4 Park Avenue between East Thirty-third and East Thirty-fourth Streets.

## DEATH

Coolidge died on January 5, 1933, in Northampton, Massachusetts, at the Beeches in his dressing room; he had a heart attack as he was shaving. He left an estate of more than $700,000.

## FUNERAL

The funeral was held in Northampton, Massachusetts, at Edwards Congregational Church. President Hoover attended the funeral. He was laid to rest in a bronze casket.

## BURIAL

Coolidge was buried in Plymouth Notch, Vermont, in the family plot. The grave is marked by a simple slab of Vermont granite. The cemetery is about one mile southwest of Plymouth Notch, off Vermont 100A.

## BIBLIOGRAPHY

McCoy, Donald R. *Calvin Coolidge: The Quiet President.* New York: The Macmillan Company, 1967.

Ross, Ishbel. *Grace Coolidge and her Era.* New York: Dodd, Mead & Company, 1962.

White, William Allen. *A Puritan in Babylon: The Story of Calvin Coolidge.* Gloucester, MA: Peter Smith, 1973.

# HERBERT HOOVER

1874–1964
31ST PRESIDENT 1929–1933: REPUBLICAN PARTY

*"The first requisites of a President of the United States are intellectual honesty and sincerity."*

—*Addresses on the American Road, 1933–1966*

Herbert Hoover was born on August 10, 1874, to Jesse and Hulda Randall Minthorn Hoover. He was eighth cousin once removed of Richard Nixon. According to one genealogical source, Hoover had 947,356 relatives in the United States, who were also descendants of Andrew Hoover, who came from Baden, Germany, in 1740.

## CHARACTERISTICS

When he was a boy, someone described him as "a funny looking little fellow, with a short neck, and a round head which was always surrounded with a funny little round hat." Later, when he was president, there were editorials and articles about his wearing a fedora to church with the complaint that millions would follow. He was five feet and eleven inches tall and of average weight. As he passed middle age, he became quite portly and weighed two hundred pounds. He had hazel eyes and straight brown hair. Although he dressed modestly, his trademark was the stiff white collar which he nearly always wore during his years in the government.

THE PRESIDENTS

## A Life in Review

**Birth:** August 10, 1874; West Branch, IA

**Died:** October 20, 1964; New York City

**Married:** Lou Henry; February 10, 1899; 2 sons

### Career

**1888–1891** Office work

**1892–1914** Mining engineer

**1914–1920** Relief and food administrator

**1921–1929** Secretary of Commerce

### Administration Events

**1929** Stock market crash

**1930** Hawley-Smoot Tariff bill passed

**1931** "Star Spangled Banner" became national anthem

**1932** Bonus army march on Washington

He had a peculiar habit of not looking at a person when he spoke. He did not engage in small talk and never wasted a word nor a moment. It was his habit to read detective stories in bed before going to sleep. Like Cleveland, he was an avid fisherman.

He drank moderately, and after prohibition enjoyed a martini in his own home. He smoked a pipe and owned more than thirty. One of his favorite pastimes, recalling his boyhood days in Iowa, was wading shoeless and sockless into a brook and proceeding methodically to alter its course. He told a friend that he wished to make enough money so that he could spend a sovereign and not count the change. By the time he was forty in 1914, he was worth well over a million dollars.

## Birthplace

Hoover was born in West Branch, Iowa, around midnight in a three-room cottage facing east on Downey Street. It is now part of the Hoover National Memorial.

## Baptism

Hoover was not baptized. He was received into membership in the Newburg Oregon Meeting of Friends on January 1, 1887.

## Church

There are few details known of Hoover's basic religious beliefs. During childhood, he attended the Friends Meeting with relatives and had read the entire Bible by the age of ten. However, there is no conclusive evidence that he attended a single church service from the time he left Stanford in 1895 until World War I. There is nothing to indicate the Hoovers ever attended a Quaker meeting while they lived their many years in London. In his autobiography, he wrote, "individual Bible-reading was part of the Quaker concept of education and before I left Iowa I had read the Bible in several stints from cover to cover."

Asked once whether he believed in God, heaven, and immortality, he said, "I try to." Once he remarked, "Well, I was raised as a Quaker, but I never worked very hard at it."

He was the first member of the Society of Friends to become president.

**1874–1884** *West Branch, Iowa.* Friends Meeting House, Downey Street. It can still be seen and is a plain white building divided by a low partition. On one side sat the women and on the other, the men.

**1885–1886** *Kingsley, Iowa.* Congregational Church, where he attended Sunday School. He went with his grandmother since there was no Quaker meeting in the village.

*Birthplace of Herbert Hoover.*

**1885–1888**  *Newburg, Oregon.* Meeting House, 414 North Meridian at the Friends Pacific Academy.

**1888–1891**  *Salem, Oregon.* Highland Avenue Friends Church, South Highland Avenue.

**1891–1895**  *Palo Alto, California.* Stanford University Memorial Chapel in the campus center.

**1921–1933**  *Washington, D.C.* Friends Meeting House, 2111 Florida Avenue, NW, just off Connecticut Avenue, while serving as U.S. secretary of commerce and president of the United States. No plate marks the plain bench where the Hoovers silently worshipped. They sat midway down the center aisle.

**1928**  *Sandy Springs, Maryland.* A small Eighteenth-century Friends Meeting House.

**1931**  *Washington, D.C.* New York Avenue Presbyterian Church where he sat in the Lincoln pew.

**1931**  *Alexandria, Virginia.* Christ Church, Washington's family church.

**1933**  *Palm Beach, Florida.* Royal Poinciana Community Chapel. See Royal Poinciana Hotel, listed below under travel.

**1933–1964**  *New York City, New York.* St. Bartholomew's Episcopal Church, east side of Park Avenue between Fiftieth and Fifty-first Streets.

# EDUCATION

**1879–1885**  *West Branch, Iowa.* West Branch Free School, Downey Street between Main and Wetherell Streets where he learned the fundamentals. The only part of school he liked was recess. The school has been moved to the Hoover National Historic Site, corner of Penn and Poplar Streets.

**1884**  *Lawrence, Kansas.* Quincy Street School, Eleventh and Vermont Streets. After his mother died in 1884, he may have attended here.

**1885**   *Kingsley, Iowa.* He attended the school on north Main Street at the top of the hill.

**1885–1887**   *Newberg, Oregon.* Friends Pacific Academy (now George Fox College), 414 North Meridian. At the time he was "an undersized, rosy cheeked boy," was the smallest student in the school, and was called "Bertie." In 1887, he graduated from the Grammar School Department. He shared a room with his brother in one of the newly completed buildings.

**1889–1890**   *Salem, Oregon.* Capitol Business College, Chemeketa, southwest corner of Commercial, where he learned more about mathematics.

**1891–1895**   *Palo Alto, California.* Stanford University. He received his A.B. in geology in 1895. In 1893, he listened to the lectures of ex-President Benjamin Harrison when he came to Stanford. While attending Stanford, he stayed in: Adelante Villa, from his arrival until October; Encina Hall, room 38, the men's dormitory, where he shared a room with Fred Williams; Romero Hall, an off-campus building, 1892–1894.

## MARRIAGE AND HONEYMOON

Hoover proposed to Lou Henry by telegram on his way from London to New York to China. He stopped off in Monterey for the wedding. They were married on February 10, 1899, in Monterey, California, by a Catholic priest, on a Friday at high noon in the home of the bride, at 302 Pacific Street.

On the day of their wedding, they boarded a train for San Francisco, and the next day they sailed for China. In China, they spent their first three and one-half weeks in Tientsin.

## HOMES/LODGINGS

**1874–1878**   *West Branch, Iowa.* Downey Street, corner of Penn and Downey Streets.

The cottage had a small bedroom, a combined living-dining area, and a room used variously for storage, summer cooking, and occasional guests. The house measured fourteen by twenty feet. In August 1928, Mrs. Hoover tried to buy the house to give to Hoover as a birthday present. Overnight, after his nomination to the presidency, West Branch became a magnet to thousands. To a place that had seldom been visited, more than 15,000 came in less than four months.

**1878–1879**   *West Branch, Iowa.* A block down and across Downey Street from the birthplace. The location is unclear.

**1879–1884**   *West Branch, Iowa.* Corner of Downey and Cedar Streets. In 1878, the Hoovers sold their cottage, blacksmith shop, and the adjoining property. It is uncertain where the family lived in town. They may have stayed with relatives or rented a house—perhaps even in the house they sold on Downey Street. Their new home was a spacious two-story structure fronted by maple trees, just across the street from the birthplace. It was later destroyed.

**1881**   *Sioux City, Iowa.* They stayed briefly with his uncle, Pennington Minthorn, in his pioneer sod house. No record remains of the location.

**1882**   *Pawhuska, Arkansas.* Osage Indian Reservation in Oklahoma territory, where he lived with his uncle Laban Miles and aunt Agnes for eight months. He also attended the Indian Sunday School there.

**1884–1885**   *West Branch, Iowa.* Farm of his Uncle Allan and Aunt Millie, a mile north of West Branch, while attending a school in which Millie Brown was the teacher.

**1885**   *Hubbard, Iowa.* He lived with an uncle near here. His grandfather is buried here.

**1885**   *Kingsley, Iowa.* He lived with his maternal grandmother Minthorn since both his mother and father had died. The house was small and located across the street south of the Methodist Church on the corner.

**1885–1888** *Newberg, Oregon.* 115 South River Street, twenty-two miles southwest of Portland, with his uncle Henry John Minthorn. He went from Council Bluffs, Iowa, over the Missouri River, the Great Plains, and the Rockies to Portland. In Newberg, his uncle had a white two-story wooden frame house built in 1881.

**1888–1891** *Salem, Oregon.* Uncle Henry's new house, Hazel and Highland Avenues. They lived in a barn until the house was ready.

**1895–1896** *Oakland, California.* 1077 Twelfth Street still exists and is a city landmark.

**1896–1897** *Oakland, California.* 2225 Ellsworth, where he registered to vote on his twenty-second birthday. Later, he and his two siblings lived in Berkeley for a few months. It was the first time they had been together for a long time.

**1897–1903** *Australia, New Zealand, and Burma.* He lived in company houses in Kalgoorlie and Coolgardie in Western Australia.

**1897–1898** *Coolgardie, Australia.* He lived in a company-owned bungalow, complete with cook and valet. The mining company was the Bewick, Moreing Co.

**1899–1901** *Tientsin, China.* He rented a spacious, two-story blue-brick house on Race Course Road. The house, Astor House, included the American Engineer's Club.

**1901–1902** *Monterey, California.* 600 Martin Street. He gave his father-in-law money to purchase land and build a cottage in Monterey.

**1902–1903** *London, England.* The Hoovers lived in a small home called the White House at Ashley Drive, Walton-on-Thames, a few miles southwest of London.

**1902–1907** *London, England.* Hyde Park Gate 39, Kensington.

**1907–** *Palo Alto, California.* He bought his first permanent family place—a six-room cottage on San Juan Hill. Later he acquired a more elaborate house on the Stanford University campus. Except for a few months living on Pacific Avenue in San Francisco, they kept this base.

**1907–1916** *London, England.* The Red House on Horton Street, Kensington, was a rambling, two-story villa built in the 1830s and set in a garden enclosed by a high brick wall. A country house in the city, it had the unusual features of steam heating and large bathrooms. While they were in England, the Hoovers entertained thousands of Americans at their successive homes in London. They held on to this house until 1914 although they took country cottages for a few weeks during the summers at Swanage, Dorsetshire, and Stratford-on-Avon. To get to the Kensington House, take the High Street and Horton Street to the Red House. Coming to High Street, direct the cabby to take the second turn to the left beyond the church (Camden Hill).

**1908–1909** *Palo Alto, California.* Dean Evelyn Allen's house, 611 Salvatierra, was half of a double house.

**1909–1911** *New York City, New York.* Apartment at 14 East Sixtieth Street.

**1912–1913** *San Francisco, California.* Wheeler House, 1901 Pacific Avenue.

**1913–1914** *Palo Alto, California.* Professor Howard's house at what is 774 Dolores (then No. 8) on campus.

**1914–1915** *Palo Alto, California.* Hempel House at 747 Santa Ynez.

**1914–1917** *New York City, New York.* Gotham Hotel, 2 West Fifty-fifth Street. He lived here off and on when he came to New York City.

**1915** *Palo Alto, California.* Professor Seward's house, 262 Kingsley (off campus).

**1916** *Palo Alto, California.* Mrs. Kimball's, (may be either Alice Kimball 530 Lincoln, or Mrs. Rufus Kimball, 1100 Bryant Street).

**1917** *Palo Alto, California.* Professor Gray's house was then 22 Alvarado (now 612).

**1917** *Washington, D.C.* 1628 Sixteenth Street, NW, where he lived for a few months.

**1917** *Washington, D.C.* Old Adams residence, 2221 Massachusetts Avenue, NW.

**1917–1918** *Washington, D.C.* 1701 Massachusetts Avenue.

**1917–1918** *Palo Alto, California.* Professor Houston's house is now 575 Salvatierra Street (then 21).

**1918–1919** *Washington, D.C.* 1720 Rhode Island Avenue was kept for the family during his stay in Paris.

**1918–1919** *Paris, France.* Hotel Crillon, Place de la Concorde. His offices were at 51 Avenue Montaigne. On Saturday, June 28, 1918, he went to the Hall of Mirrors at Versailles to witness the signing of the Peace Treaty.

**1919–1920** *Paris, France.* 19 Rue de Lubeck, in a large residence.

**1919–1920** *Palo Alto, California.* Whitaker's house, 746 Santa Ynez (then 7 Cabrillo), while their new house was planned and built.

**1920** *Palo Alto, California.* MacDowell House, 775 Santa Inez.

**1920** *Palo Alto, California.* Gregory House, 14 Cabrillo Road.

**1920–1934** *Palo Alto, California.* 612 Miranda, near the Stanford campus, is a western-style building on a hill, with a view of the mountains and the bay. After 1933, whenever the Hoovers were in California, this was their base. Later, this was the president of Stanford's house.

**1920** *New York City, New York.* Travelling back and forth between New York City and Palo Alto, they stayed in hotels at: 950 Park Avenue; 993 Park Avenue; 876 Park Avenue; and 55 East Seventy-seventh Street.

**1921–1929** *Washington, D.C.* 2300 S Street, NW. This was an old brick house. They re-stored the garden and added a rear porch for outdoor dining and entertaining. It is now occupied by the Burmese ambassador.

**1929–1933** *Washington, D.C.* The White House as thirty-first president.

**1929–1933** *Brightwood, Virginia, on the Rapidan River.* A summer camp about 100 miles from the White House. Mrs. Hoover supervised the building of a series of log cabins, and, at the end of his term, the Rapidan Camp was presented to the Shenandoah National Park. They vacationed here for two weeks in June 1931 and often stayed here as a getaway from Washington during his years in the White House. The Camp can be approached from Criglersville, Virginia.

**1933–1964** *New York City, New York.* Waldorf Towers, thirty-first floor on Park Avenue. Lou Henry Hoover died here in 1944.

# WORK

**1888–1891** *Salem, Oregon.* Oregon Land Company, 325 Commercial, where he learned to type and acquired some knowledge of accounting.

**1892** *Northern Arkansas and Pawhuska, Oklahoma.* Mining field work.

**1893** *Oregon.* Searching for fossils and working with engineers.

**1894** *California and Nevada.* In the Sierras and near Lake Tahoe with the U.S. Geological Survey for a starting salary of $1200 a year.

**1895** *Nevada City, California.* He stayed at the National Hotel, 211 Broad Street, and worked in the Grass Valley district for about 2 months, pushing ore carts seventy hours a week at a gold mine. Later, he had a modest office job in San Francisco.

**1895** *Nevada City.* The Reward Mine, near the southwest corner of the square which formed the boundary line of Nevada City and the Mayflower Mine, located on the Lava Cap Road, which is now the site of Mayflower estates.

**1896–1897**   *San Francisco.* He was sent to the Steeple Rock Mine in New Mexico with Louis Janin (mining engineer).

**1897–1899**   *Australia.* Coolgardie with Beswick, Moreing and Company.

**1899–1902**   *China.* He arrived in London in January 1899 from Australia to learn details of the China job.

**1899–1900**   *Tientsin, China.* Chief engineer of China's Bureau of Mines.

**1901**   *Tientsin, China.* General Manager of the Chinese Engineering and Mining Company.

**1908–1914**   *London, England.* Headquarters of his own engineering firm. He supervised projects in many countries. He opened an office at 62 London Wall on August 3, 1914.

**1909**   *New York City, New York.* 14 East Sixtieth Street.

**1910**   *New York City.* 5th Avenue between Fifty-ninth and Sixtieth Streets.

**1914–1920**   *London, England.* Administrator, Commission for Relief in Belgium. From 1914 on, Hoover never accepted a dollar in payment for any of his manifold public services, including for his own travel and out-of-pocket expenses. His salaries as Secretary of Commerce and as President went into a special fund for charitable causes.

**1917–1919**   *Washington, D.C., and Paris, France.* Administrator for the American Food Administration. He first set up office at the Willard Hotel, then had a few rooms in the Interior Department, then the complete occupancy of an old hotel, the Gordon. Later, a two-story temporary building was erected and was still in use 33 years later.

**1918–1920**   *Paris, France.* The Relief and Reconstruction of Europe. He had offices in

an apartment house (50 rooms) at 51 Avenue Montaigne. He travelled a great deal, including a trip to Poland via Switzerland and Czechoslovakia.

**1921–1929**   *Washington, D.C.* U.S. Secretary of Commerce. Department of Commerce, Fifteenth and Constitution Avenue.

**1929–1933**   *Washington, D.C.* President of the United States.

**1946–1947**   *Poland, Finland, and Belgium.* Coordinator of the Food Supply for World Famine and chairman of relief organization.

**1947–1953**   *Washington, D.C.* Commission on Organization of the Executive Branch (Hoover Commission), 441 G Street, NW. Appointed by President Truman.

**1952**   *Chicago, Illinois.* International Amphitheatre, Republican National Convention.

# TRAVEL/VISITS

Up to his time, he was the most travelled president, including President Theodore Roosevelt and President Taft. He had visited more than half the world's countries, including almost all of Europe and South America and most of the United States, including Alaska. In Asia, he visited most of southeast Asia including Burma and Ceylon and in the Far East, Korea and Manchuria, and he had lived in China. He was also in New Zealand, Australia, and South Africa. His first trip to South America was in 1929 as president-elect.

**1917–1920**   *Washington, D.C.* Shoreham Hotel, 2500 Calvert St. NW.

**1921–1928**   He travelled to Honduras, El Salvador, Nicaragua, Costa Rica, Ecuador, Argentina, Uruguay, and Brazil.

**1923**   He went on the western trip with President Harding to Alaska and was with him when he died at the Palace Hotel in San Francisco, southwest corner of Market and Montgomery Streets.

**1928**   *Brule, Wisconsin.* He visited Coolidge at his summer White House.

**1928** *Palo Alto, California.* Stanford University stadium. He accepted the Republican presidential nomination.

**1929** *Cincinnati, Ohio.* Eden Park Hill, dedication of monument celebrating completion of the Ohio River Improvement Project.

**1929** *Detroit, Michigan.* Detroit City Hall. "Golden Jubilee of Light," Fiftieth anniversary of Edison's invention of the light bulb. Dinner/speech at replica of Independence Hall in Greenfield Village.

**1929** *Fort Myers, Florida.* Edison's winter home, 2350 McGregor Boulevard, on the occasion of Edison's birthday. While on vacation, Hoover went fishing at several places including: Angel Creek in the Miami Keys, Key Largo, and Long Key. While at Long Key, he lived on the houseboat, "Saunterer."

**1929** *Belle Isle, Florida.* He took a month's vacation as a guest at J.C. Penney's estate, located off the causeway east of Miami. He attended the Community Church while staying here.

**1929** *Louisville, Kentucky.* Memorial Auditorium. Address celebrating completion of Ohio River Improvement Project.

**1929** *Washington, D.C.* National Academy of Sciences Building. Honoring Madame Marie Curie.

**1929** *Washington, D.C.* He gave a Memorial Day address at Arlington National Cemetery.

**1929** *Washington, D.C.* Department of Commerce Building, corner of Fourteenth Street and Constitution Avenue, NW. He laid the cornerstone.

**1929** *Washington, D.C.* He used rooms at the Mayflower Hotel as headquarters, 1127 Connecticut Avenue, NW.

**1930** *Washington, D.C.* Mayflower Hotel. Address on receiving the First Hoover Gold Medal.

**1930** *Washington, D.C.* American Red Cross Building. He dedicated Red Cross Chapter House.

**1930** *Washington, DC.* Meridian Hill Park, Sixteenth Street and Florida Avenue, NW. Dedication of Buchanan statue.

**1931** *Asheville, North Carolina.* Grove Park Inn, 290 Macon Avenue.

**1931** *Columbus, Ohio.* Reception at State Capitol.

**1931** *Marion, Ohio.* For dedication of Harding Memorial. Coolidge gave a speech accepting the memorial.

**1931** *San Juan, Puerto Rico.* Address at the Capitol. Visited Morro Castle.

**1931** *Springfield, Illinois.* Lincoln Tomb. Rededication of the Lincoln tomb. Address to the legislature in the State Capitol Assembly Chamber.

**1931** *Valley Forge Park, Pennsylvania.* Memorial Day address.

**1931** *Washington, D.C.* Dedication of District of Columbia War Memorial.

**1931** *Yorktown, Virginia.* Yorktown Battlefield, for speech.

**1932** *Des Moines, Iowa.* He made remarks at the State Capitol Plaza and lodged at the Fort Des Moines Hotel.

**1932** *Mount Vernon, Virginia.* Washington's home for a speech and laying a wreath at the tomb.

**1932** *New York City, New York.* Campaign address, Madison Square Gardens, and remarks at Carnegie Hall.

**1932** *Ossabaw Island, Georgia.* H.H. Torrey estate. Fishing and as a guest.

**1932** *Salt Lake City, Utah.* He spoke at the Tabernacle on Temple Square.

**1932** *Sapelo Island, Georgia.* Howard E. Coffin home. Christmas dinner guest.

**1932** *Washington, D.C.* Howard University. Commencement address on campus.

**1932** *Washington, D.C.* On August 14, he visited the James Cardinal Gibbons Memorial Statue, Sixteenth and Park Road, NW. Unveiling. On September 26, he laid the cornerstone for the Post Office Department Building.

**1932** *Washington, D.C.* Department of Labor and Interstate Commerce Commission Building, Fourteenth Street and Constitution Avenue, NW. He laid the cornerstone.

**1933** *Northampton, Massachusetts.* He attended Coolidge's funeral.

**1933** *Palm Beach, Florida.* He fished from the *Sequoia* and stayed in the Royal Poinciana Hotel. The site is South Lake Trail between Royal Poinciana Boulevard and Coconut Walk.

**1933** *Washington, D.C.* He laid the cornerstone for the National Archives, at Seventh and Constitution Avenue, NW, and the Department of Justice Building, at Tenth and Constitution Avenue, NW.

**1933** *West Branch, Iowa.* He visited his birthplace. He could not get accommodations in one of the leading hotels at Davenport on September 27. There was a large reception in West Branch on the 28th.

**1935** *Hannibal, Missouri.* He visited Mark Twain's boyhood home, 208 Hill Street.

**1935** *Nevada City County, California.* He visited his old mining site and was a guest at the Empire House (now called the Bourn Mansion).

**1935** *Vermont.* He visited the Coolidge homestead and grave site.

**1953–1964** *Key Largo, Florida.* He usually spent the winter at the Key Largo Angler's Club.

**1953–1964** *Palo Alto, California.* He usually spent a month or two in the summer here. He stayed in the house at Stanford which was used as a residence for Stanford presidents.

## DEATH

Hoover died on October 20, 1964, in New York City, at the Waldorf Towers apartment. In 1958, he had had his gall bladder removed. In 1963, he experienced massive gastrointestinal bleeding. At the end of his life, he was virtually deaf and blind.

## FUNERAL

The funeral was held in New York City, at St. Bartholomew's Episcopal Church, on the east side of Park Avenue between Fiftieth and Fifty-first Streets. Thousands filed past the closed casket in New York and then in the Capitol Rotunda during two days in Washington. All four of the candidates for president and vice president came to honor him at the simple funeral service which befitted his Quaker faith. The Scripture was taken from Romans, 8:14–39, John 14:1–6, and Psalms 23 and 124. There were organ anthems of "Come, Sweet Death," "Fight the Good Fight," "Now the Day Is Over," and "O Beautiful for Spacious Skies." An army band played the "Battle Hymn of the Republic," and Elton Trueblood gave a prayer and brief eulogy at the grave side. President Lyndon Johnson and future President Richard Nixon attended the funeral. Eisenhower was ill and Truman was suffering from a recent fall and did not attend.

## BURIAL

Hoover was buried in West Branch, Iowa, on a hillside about a quarter of a mile from his birthplace. Lou Henry Hoover was transferred from Palo Alto for reburial at his side.

## SPECIAL SITES

*West Branch, Iowa.* The Herbert Hoover Presidential Library and Museum.

*Palo Alto, California.* Stanford University. The 185-foot Hoover Tower is a landmark of Stanford University. Nearby is a museum housing many of his memorabilia.

## BIBLIOGRAPHY

Lyons, Eugene. *Herbert Hoover (A Biography)*. Garden City, New Jersey: Doubleday and Company, 1964.

Nash, George H. *The Life of Herbert Hoover: The Engineer*. New York: W.W. Norton & Company, 1983.

# FRANKLIN DELANO ROOSEVELT

### 1882–1945
#### 32ND PRESIDENT 1933–1945: DEMOCRATIC PARTY

Franklin Delano Roosevelt was born on January 30, 1882 at the Hudson River estate of Springwood in Hyde Park, New York at 8:45 P.M., to James and Sara Delano Roosevelt. He was the fourth cousin once removed of President U.S. Grant, fourth cousin three times removed of President Zachary Taylor, fifth cousin of President Theodore Roosevelt, and fifth cousin once removed of Winston Churchill.

*"It is common sense to take a method and try it. If it fails, admit it frankly and try another. But above all, try something."*

## CHARACTERISTICS

As an adult Roosevelt was 6'1" tall and weighed approximately one hundred and ninety pounds. He was a handsome man with dark brown wavy hair and blue eyes.

He was a moderate drinker and smoked more than a pack of cigarettes a day. In 1921, at the age of 39, he contracted polio and for the rest of his life had to use a wheelchair. He loved trees and would be a patron saint to today's environmentalists. Even as a boy, he

# A LIFE IN REVIEW

**Birth:** January 30, 1882; Hyde Park, NY

**Died:** April 12, 1945; Warm Springs, GA

**Married:** Anna Eleanor Roosevelt;
   March 17, 1905; 5 sons, 1 daughter

## CAREER

**1908–1911** Law practice

**1911–1913** Member state legislature

**1913–1921** Assistant Secretary of the
   Navy

**1924–1929** Law practice

**1929–1933** Governor of New York

## ADMINISTRATION EVENTS

**1933** New Deal Recovery Reforms

**1934** Gold Reserve Act

**1935** Civilian Conservation Corps created

**1935** Social Security Act passed

**1940** Selective Service Act

**1941–1945** World War II

**1941** Atlantic Charter

**1941** "Four Freedoms"

liked to give orders. On one occasion, his mother said to him, "Why don't you let someone else give the order?" He replied, "Because if I wait for that nothing will get done." He habitually left his spoon in his coffee cup. He also insisted on reading his own temperature and announcing the result. He related well to people.

## BIRTHPLACE

Roosevelt was born in Hyde Park, New York, at the family estate. He weighed ten pounds at birth. The big mahogany bed in the upstairs room in which he was born can still be seen.

## BAPTISM

Roosevelt was baptized at St. James Episcopal Chapel, in Hyde Park, on March 20, 1883. The Chapel is a frame building in downtown Hyde Park and not to be confused with St. James Episcopal Church.

## CHURCH

The religious tradition in the Roosevelt family was Episcopal. Roosevelt knew the Bible well and once said, "I feel that a comprehensive study of the Bible is a liberal education for anyone. Nearly all the great men of our country have been well versed in the teachings of the Bible."

**1882** *Hyde Park, New York.* St. James Episcopal Chapel, where he was baptized.

**1882–1945** *Hyde Park, New York.* St. James Episcopal Church. He was senior warden of this church. Hyde Park is about a mile away and another two miles is the Roosevelt estate where the president was born.

**1886–1921** *Weshpool, Campobello Island.* St. Anne's Church, when they were at their summer home.

**1891–1900** *Bad Nauheim, Germany.* The Roosevelts spent many summers here and attended the Anglo-American Church.

**1896–1900** *Groton, Massachusetts.* Chapel and church at the Groton Academy Chapel on the campus.

**1900–1904** *Cambridge, Massachusetts.* Harvard University, Holden Chapel, Peabody Street.

**1929–1933** *Albany, New York.* Episcopal Church.

**1929–1933** *Washington, D.C.* St. John's Episcopal Church. He attended on the morning of his first inauguration.

*Roosevelt family estate, Franklin was born here.*

**1929–1933** *Washington, D.C.* St. Thomas Episcopal Church, near Dupont Circle at Eighteenth and Church Streets, NW. He and his family attended this church regularly from 1913 to 1920 when he was assistant secretary of the navy. About midway down the center aisle were two pews—one behind the other—with red carpet on the floor under them, used by the president and his family. Only ruins remain.

**1929–1933** *Warm Springs, Georgia.* Chapel on the grounds of the Warm Springs Foundation, opposite Georgia Hall on Oak Road.

**1935–** *Washington, D.C.* Foundry Methodist Church. He attended with Prime Minister Churchill in 1941.

## EDUCATION

**1882–1896** *Hyde Park, New York.* He did not attend school until he was fourteen be-cause it was the custom of estate owners to have their children privately tutored and to learn through travelling. His first trip to Europe was just before he reached the age of three. While his mother gave him his first schooling, at the age of six he went to a kind of kindergarten under a German governess at the house of some family friends nearby.

**1891** *Bad Nauheim, near Frankfurt, Germany.* He went to a local school here for six weeks while abroad with his parents. This is the only public school he ever attended.

**1896–1900** *Groton, Massachusetts.* Groton Academy.

**1900–1904** *Cambridge, Massachusetts.* Harvard University. While at Harvard, he stayed on the "Gold Coast" (center for the wealthy), and ate at the Groton table in Westmorly Hall. He was a member of the Hasty Pudding Club which met at the corner of Massachusetts Avenue and Holmes Place.

**1904–1907**   *New York City, New York.* Columbia Law School, One hundred sixteenth Street and Broadway. He dropped out after passing the bar exam in 1907 and never graduated from law school. He had failed the exam twice before passing it.

## MARRIAGE AND HONEYMOON

Roosevelt was married on March 17, 1905, in New York City, at East Seventy-sixth Street, where the bride, Anna Eleanor Roosevelt, lived with her cousins, Mr. and Mrs. Henry Parish, Jr. In reality, the wedding took place in the home of Mrs. E. Livingston Ludlow, as the sliding doors between the two houses opened into one another. About sixty close friends and relatives attended and a few more were invited to the reception. President Theodore Roosevelt gave the bride away saying at the end, "Well, Franklin, there's nothing like keeping the name in the family."

They had a honeymoon of one week at Hyde Park, and then set up housekeeping at an apartment in New York. During the summer of 1905, they went on their formal honeymoon— a three-month tour of Europe. He had nightmares and occasions of sleepwalking during the trip. In London, they stayed in the royal suite at Brown's Hotel, 21 Dover Street, and lunched at the American Embassy. They crossed the Channel to Paris, France, where they dined and shopped. In Italy, they visited Rome and Venice, where they fed the pigeons on the Piazza San Marco and glided along the canals in a gondola, before going on to Florence and the Dolomites. They drove on to Germany, where they visited Augsburg and Ulm. In Switzerland, they spent time in Saint Moritz and then returned to Paris, where they stayed at the Imperial Hotel. In Scotland, they stayed with the Robert Fergusons at their family seat at Raith near Kirkcaldy, north of the Firth of Forth and at their country seat at No-

var. Upon returning to New York City, they had an apartment at 40 West Forty-fifth Street.

## HOMES/LODGINGS

**1882–1905**   *Hyde Park, New York.* On Route 9. This is now Franklin Delano Roosevelt National Historic Site, which is maintained as it was at the time of his death in 1945. This was his permanent home from 1882 to 1945.

**1883–**   *Campobello Island, Maine.* His father completed a house, known as Granny"s Cottage, in 1886. It no longer exists. It was next door to what was later the summer home of Roosevelt and his family.

**1883–1921**   *Campobello, Maine.* Summer vacation home. The 34-room summer "cottage" is a simple gamble- roofed maroon house and is the focal-point of Roosevelt International Park.

**1904**   *New York City, New York.* He lived at 200 Madison Avenue in a rented house with his mother at the time he entered Columbia Law School.

**1905**   *New York City, New York.* Apartment at 40 West Forty-fifth Street.

**1905–1907**   *New York City.* House at 125 East Thirty-sixth Street.

**1907–1910**   *New York City, New York.* 47 East Sixty-fifth Street. His mother had two adjoining houses prepared at 47 and 49 East 65th. Franklin and Eleanor moved into No. 47. The house was sold in 1936 to Hunter College and set up as the "Sara Delano Roosevelt Interfaith House." It was a 5-story building, with an American basement, between Madison and Park Avenue.

**1908**   *Sea Bright, New Jersey.* They rented a house on the boardwalk.

**1910–1912**   *Albany, New York.* H. King Sturdee house, 248 State Street. Eleanor reported, "The house seems palatial after New York and it is a comfort to have only three stories instead of six."

**1913** *Albany, New York.* Hotel Ten Eyck, northwest corner of State and Pearl Streets (now the site of the Albany Hilton). They had two rooms.

**1913** *Washington, D.C.* 1733 N Street, NW, about six blocks away from his office, which he reached by walking down Connecticut Avenue.

**1913–1920** *Washington, D.C.* 2131 R Street, NW, (now the Embassy of Mali), while working as assistant secretary of the navy.

**1920–1929** *Hyde Park, New York.* See above 1882–1905.

**1924–1945** *Warm Springs, Georgia.* They stayed in a cottage he had built in an area which he organized as the Georgia Warm Springs Foundation—the "Little White House." He often stayed here during the White House years. From 1925 on, it was his practice to come here annually for Thanksgiving. The Roosevelt Farm is four miles south of Warm Springs on Georgia 85. There is a marker at the entrance to Pine Mountain Trail.

**1929–1933** *Albany, New York.* Governor's Mansion, 138 Eagle Street.

**1933–1945** *Washington, D.C.* The White House as president.

**1938–** *East Park, New York.* Eleanor's Dream Cottage, south of East Park between the Hudson and Poughkeepsie State 9G, is a one story structure designed by Roosevelt and built as a retreat.

**1942–** *New York City, New York.* 29 Washington Square at the corner of Waverly Place. They had a 7- room suite in 16-story building, which they leased as a residence while staying in New York City.

# WORK

**1904** *New York City.* Basil O'Connor law firm, 120 Broadway.

**1907–1911** *New York City, New York.* Carter Ledyard and Milburn law firm, 54 Wall Street.

**1911–1913** *Albany, New York.* New York state senator. The legislature had to meet in Albany's City Hall on Eagle Street after a fire in the Capitol.

**1913–1921** *Washington, D.C.* Assistant secretary of the navy. His office was in what is now the Executive Office Building, which has been described as the huge pile of scrabbled architecture on Pennsylvania Avenue flanking the White House that the Navy shared with the Departments of State and War.

**1915–** *New York City, New York.* Marvin, Hooker and Roosevelt law firm, 52 Wall Street.

**1921–1924** *Campobello/Hyde Park, New York.* He was struck with polio and spent three years convalescing.

**1924** *New York City, New York.* Basil O'Connor law firm as a partner. 120 Broadway.

**1929–1933** *Albany, New York.* Governor of New York. Office in the Old Capitol at the head of State Street.

**1933–1945** *Washington, D.C.* President of the United States. The first three inaugurations were held at the traditional site, but the fourth inauguration ceremony was held on the south porch of the White House rather than on Capitol Hill. The war provided the excuse. It was a bleak ceremony on a day of driving rain and sleet.

# TRAVEL/VISITS

He was the first president to fly while in office, and the first to leave the United States in time of war. His trip to North Africa in 1943 made him the most travelled president in history, far surpassing Taft who had previously held the record. By August 1944, he had made seven foreign trips during wartime and travelled 306,265 miles. In travelling as president, he seldom lodged in hotels or private homes but was more likely to stay in his own railroad car or on board ship.

**1887** *Washington, D.C.* While Franklin Roosevelt was on a visit to the White House, Cleveland said to him, "My Little Man, I am making a strange wish for you. It is that you may never be president of the United States."

**1905** *Fairhaven, Massachusetts.* He took Eleanor to visit the Delano "clan."

**1911** *Colon, Panama.* On April 12, he boarded the United Fruit Company's *SS Carrillo* for Colon and Culebra, Panama.

**1912** *Baltimore, Maryland.* For the Democratic National Convention. Headquarters in Room 214, Munsey Building.

**1912** *Sea Girt, New Jersey.* He visited President Wilson at his summer home.

**1913** *Washington, D.C.* Powhatan Hotel, Pennsylvania Avenue at Eighteenth and H Streets NW.

**1917–** *Washington, D.C.* 2244 S Street (later Irish Embassy), NW, visiting his uncle.

**1917** *Haiti.* On an inspection tour.

**1920** *Chicago, Illinois.* Auditorium Theater, 70 East Congress Street. First speech in his campaign for vice president.

**1920** *San Francisco, California.* Civic Auditorium, where he was nominated as vice-presidential candidate by the Democratic National Convention.

**1920** *Salt Lake City, Utah.* He spoke in the Mormon Tabernacle.

**1921** *New York City, New York.* He was treated for polio at Presbyterian Hospital, 622 West One hundred sixty- eighth Street.

**1924–** *Warm Springs, Georgia.* The Old Depot (marker only) is the site where he came in and out of Warm Springs; finally his coffin left from this station, Georgia 85W at Alternate 27 intersection. The Outdoor Treatment Pool (original treatment center), south side of US 27 alternate, is currently being restored.

**1928** *Columbus, Georgia.* Springer Opera House, First Avenue and Tenth Street. He gave his "Happy Warrior" speech here in support of Al Smith.

**1928** *Houston, Texas.* Sam Houston Hall (now known as the Coliseum), 810 Bagby Street, for the Democratic Convention.

**1928** *New York City, New York.* Biltmore Hotel, campaign headquarters, Madison to Vanderbilt Avenues, East Forty-third to East Forty-fourth Streets.

**1931** *Hackensack, New Jersey.* The George Washington Bridge was opened in 1931 while he was Governor. It is on I-95.

**1932** *Chicago, Illinois.* Congress Hotel, 520 South Michigan, for the Democratic National Convention. He flew from Hyde Park in July to accept the nomination.

**1932** *Washington, D.C.* He visited President Hoover at the White House.

**1932** *Wrigley Field, Chicago.* He threw out the first pitch of the third game of the 1932 World Series between the Cubs and the Yankees when Babe Ruth pointed to right-center field and promptly hit a home run there.

**1933** *Annapolis, Maryland.* Commencement at the U.S. Naval Academy.

**1933** *Chicago, Illinois.* He visited the Century of Progress Administration Building on Columbus Drive. He also visited the grave of Mayor Cermak in the Bohemian Cemetery. Cermak had been shot at the time of the attempted assassination on him.

**1933** *Miami, Florida.* Amphitheater, Bayfront Park, Biscayne Boulevard between Southeast Second Street and Southeast Sixth Street and extending to Biscayne Bay. This was the scene of an assassination attempt.

**1933** *Fredericksburg, Virginia.* He visited James Monroe's office and other historic places.

**1933** *Washington, D.C.* He dedicated the Gompers Memorial Monument.

**1933** *Washington, D.C.* George Washington Memorial Bridge for Memorial Day celebration.

**1933** *Washington, DC.* Mayflower Hotel, 1127 Connecticut Avenue, NW, before his inauguration.

**1934** *Cap Hatien, Haiti.* He was received by President Vincent, and there was a reception at the Union Club.

**1934** *Cristobal, Panama.* Going through the Panama Canal to Balboa, he was the first president to travel through the Canal. In Panama City, he was entertained at a state dinner at the Presidential Palace.

**1934** *Gettysburg, Pennsylvania.* Memorial Day address on the battlefield.

**1934** *Glacier National Park, Montana.* He spoke at the Two Medicine Chalet lodge. He was the first president to visit the area since it opened in 1913.

**1934** *Harrodsburg, Kentucky.* Dedication of monument to commemorate George Rogers Clark and his frontiersmen, who founded the town.

**1934** *Honolulu, Hawaii.* He dedicated Ala Moana Park on Ala Moana Boulevard and planted a kukui tree at Iolani Palace on King Street. He viewed Pearl Harbor, had dinner with Governor Poindexter at Washington Place, and stayed at the Royal Hawaiian Hotel. In 1944, he met with MacArthur in Honolulu.

**1934** *Jacksonville, Florida.* He began a 15-day fishing cruise off the east coast of Florida on Vincent Astor's yacht, *Nourmahal.* He conducted Episcopal services aboard the yacht and was the first president to do so.

**1934** *Lebanon, Tennessee.* He visited the Hermitage where he had a Jacksonian breakfast, sitting at the head of Jackson's table. He was served sausage and fried apples, turkey hash, hominy croquettes, beaten biscuits, and old fashioned scrambled eggs prepared with brown meal and sprinkled with cinnamon.

**1934** *Nashville, Tennessee.* He visited the Capitol and President Polk's tomb on the Capitol grounds. The next day, on returning from the Hermitage, he visited the Andrew Jackson School, the Ward Belmont School for Girls, the George Peabody School, Vanderbilt University, and Fisk University, where he was serenaded by the school choir.

**1934** *New Haven, Connecticut.* Yale University. He received an honorary degree.

**1934** *Roanoke, Virginia.* He was the first president in office to visit Roanoke. He stopped at the Elks Lodge Home for the Elderly in Bedford. This home had been dedicated by President Harding.

**1934** *San Juan, Puerto Rico.* He visited La Fortelesa (Governor's Mansion), El Moro Fort, and lunched at Jajome Alto, the governor's summer place.

**1934** *St. Thomas, Virgin Islands.* He visited Government House, the Botanical Gardens, and Blue Beard's Castle.

**1934** *Washington, D.C.* He unveiled the statue of William Jennings Bryant near the Lincoln Memorial and the George Washington Memorial bridge.

**1934** *Washington, D.C.* American University. He received an honorary degree.

**1934** *Williamsburg, Virginia.* He dedicated Duke of Gloucester Street, toured the area, including the Governor's Palace, and received an honorary degree from William and Mary College in front of the Wren Building.

**1935** *Atlanta, Georgia.* He dedicated Techwood Public Housing, corner of North and Techwood, and addressed a crowd of more than 100,000.

**1935** *Charleston, South Carolina.* He spoke at the Citadel and took a city tour which included a stop at the Sergeant Jasper (Revolutionary War) Monument.

**1935**  *Los Angeles, California.* There was a crowd of more than one million people along the parade route. He spoke at the Memorial Coliseum and he spent the night at the Coronado Hotel.

**1935**  *New York.* White Face Mountain Highway in the Adirondacks. Between White Face Mountain and Saratoga Springs, for the first time in thousands of miles of travel he had a flat tire.

**1935**  *Washington, D.C.* He visited Washington National Cathedral.

**1935**  *West Point, New York.* Commencement at West Point Academy. He was the first president to attend since Wilson had in 1916.

**1936**  *Albany, New York.* Dinner at the Governor's Mansion.

**1936**  *Asheville, North Carolina.* He drove from Knoxville to Asheville and the Great Smoky Mountain National Park. He spent the night at Grove Park Inn and had lunch at Forney's Point on the side of Clingman's Dome.

**1936**  *Mount Rushmore, South Dakota.*

**1936**  *Big Meadows, Virginia.* He dedicated Shenandoah National Park.

**1936**  *Bismarck, North Dakota.* State capitol.

**1936**  *Buenos Aires, Argentina.* He spoke in the Chamber of Deputies and attended a banquet at Casa Rosada.

**1936**  *Buffalo, New York.* He visited the McKinley Monument on Niagara Square.

**1936**  *Cheyenne, Wyoming.* He gave a speech at Fort Francis Warren and attended services at St. Mark's Episcopal Church.

**1936**  *Chicago, Illinois.* He gave a speech in Chicago Stadium on the same platform where he had accepted the nomination in 1932.

**1936**  *Dallas, Texas.* He spoke at the Dallas Centennial Exposition. In the afternoon he dedicated the statue of Robert E. Lee in the Robert E. Lee Park, Hall Street and Turtle Creek Boulevard.

**1936**  *Denver, Colorado.* He spoke in front of the State Capitol and visited Fitzsimons Hospital.

**1936**  *Detroit, Michigan.* He spoke in Cadillac Square in front of (old) City Hall.

**1936**  *Hannibal, Missouri.* He dedicated Mark Twain Memorial Bridge.

**1936**  *Hot Springs, Arkansas.* This was the first visit of a president. He visited a bath house.

**1936**  *Lincoln, Nebraska.* He spoke in the plaza in front of the tall state capitol.

**1936**  *Montevideo, Uruguay.* He toured the city and lunched at the Presidential Palace.

**1936**  *Monticello, Virginia.* He gave an address on the lawn in front of Jefferson's mansion.

**1936**  *Montpelier, Vermont.* State Capitol for conferences with state governor and other officials.

**1936**  *New York City, New York.* Ground breaking ceremony for Queens midtown tunnel under the East River.

**1936**  *New York City, New York.* Bedloes Island for the fiftieth anniversary of dedication of the Statue of Liberty.

**1936**  *Harrisburg, Pennsylvania.* He gave a speech on the steps of the State Capitol.

**1936**  *New York City, New York.* He dedicated the Theodore Roosevelt Memorial at the American Museum of Natural History.

**1936**  *New York City, New York.* Dedication of Triborough Bridge.

**1936**  *Niagara Falls, New York.* He dedicated Niagara Falls station.

**1936**  *Orlando, Florida.* He rode down Orange Avenue on the way to Rollins College with a crowd of 75,000–100,000 people on the route to see him.

**1936**  *Philadelphia, Pennsylvania.* Temple University. He received honorary degree.

**1936**  *Philadelphia, Pennsylvania.* Franklin Field. He accepted the Democratic Party's renomination after the convention held in Convention Hall.

**1936** *Port-of-Spain, Trinidad.* He made a 25-mile motor trip around the island and paused at the Memorial Gateway, honoring Commodore Oliver Hazzard Perry, who died there of yellow fever in 1819.

**1936** *Providence, Rhode Island.* He spoke on the steps of the state capitol.

**1936** *Rio de Janeiro, Brazil.* He spoke at Congress Hall (the Legislative Palace) and attended a banquet at Itamaraty.

**1936** *Rockport, Arkansas, between Malvern and Hot Springs.* He went to celebrate the Arkansas centennial and had lunch on the back porch at Couchwood, home of his friend, Harvey Crouch, on Lake Catherine. He delivered a speech at Kentucky Baptist Church. There was a great reception, which included all the houses being freshly painted in his honor.

**1936** *Springfield, Illinois.* He visited Lincoln's Tomb and Lincoln's home and lunched at the Executive Mansion.

**1936** *St. Paul, Minnesota.* He spoke from the steps of the Capitol.

**1936** *St. Louis, Missouri.* He dedicated the unfinished Soldier's Monument in the plaza opposite City Hall.

**1936** *Vincennes, Indiana.* He dedicated the George Rogers Clark Memorial statue on Second Street. He made a side trip to Hodgenville, Kentucky, to see the log cabin birthplace of Lincoln.

**1936** *Virginia.* He cruised on the James River, lunched at Carter's Grove and visited Jamestown, with a short drive around the island and an inspection of the ruins of the old church. He also sailed to Yorktown. On Sunday, he attended services in the old Bruton Parish Church at Williamsburg. Most presidents have attended services here. Theodore Roosevelt presented the lectern used in the church, and Wilson the reading desk.

**1936** *Washington, D.C.* Dedication of the Grover Cleveland Monument.

**1936** *Washington, D.C.* Rock Creek Park, where he dedicated the Jean Jules Jusserand Memorial. This was the site where Ambassador Jusserand often met with Theodore Roosevelt. By the end of 1936, Roosevelt had visited at least 47 of the American states, excepting Louisiana and possibly Arizona and New Mexico.

**1936** *Washington, D.C.* He dedicated new Department of Interior Building.

**1936** *Winter Park, Florida.* Rollins College, Knowles Memorial Chapel, off Fairbanks, Avenue, to receive an honorary degree.

**1937** *Boise, Idaho.* He spoke in front of the state house.

**1937** *Chicago, Illinois.* Dedication of Outer Drive Bridge. Lunch with George Cardinal Mundelin at his residence, 1555 North State Parkway.

**1937** *Gainesville, Georgia.* Dedication of Roosevelt Monument in the public square, renamed Roosevelt Square. Bronze arm supports can be seen in the local Gainesville High School.

**1937** *Mount Vernon, Virginia.* He visited the tomb of George Washington.

**1937** *Washington, D.C.* Dedication of the new Federal Reserve Building.

**1937** *Washington, D.C.* He attended service at St. John's Episcopal Church before his second inauguration. Following the inauguration, he was complimented by fashion experts for setting a new style in wearing a cutaway. Mrs. Roosevelt said it was ironic since she never saw anyone who could care less about dress than her husband.

**1937** *Yellowstone National Park, Wyoming.* Mammoth Springs Hotel.

**1938** *Columbia, South Carolina.* Governor's Mansion on Richland Street. He had a breakfast which consisted entirely of South Carolina dishes.

**1938**  *Hyde Park, New York.* He laid the cornerstone of the library to house his public papers.

**1938**  *Mount Vernon, Virginia.* He made a speech from the front portico on the occasion of the one hundred and fiftieth anniversary of Washington's notification of election as first president.

**1938**  *New York City, New York.* Dedication and opening of the New York World's Fair. He spoke in front of the Federal Building.

**1938**  *Washington, D.C.* Jefferson Memorial, Tidal Basin. He laid the cornerstone, using a silver trowel which had belonged to George Washington, and tamped the stone with a gavel made from an elm tree planted by Jefferson at Monticello.

**1938**  *West Point, New York.* Military Academy, for commencement, which was held inside at the Field House (armory) for the first time in decades.

**1940**  *Chattanooga, Tennessee.* Dedication Chickamauga Dam. He went from here to Knoxville and Newfound Gap to dedicate the Smoky Mountain National Park.

**1940**  *Washington, D.C.* Dedication of Washington National Airport.

**1940**  *Ash Lawn, Virginia.* Home of Monroe. He inspected the house and grounds.

**1941**  *Bethesda, Maryland.* Dedication of Naval Medical Center.

**1941**  *Newfoundland, Canada.* He met with Churchill at Placentia Bay.

**1941**  *Staunton, Virginia.* He dedicated the memorial at Woodrow Wilson's birthplace.

**1942**  *Hyde Park, New York.* He dedicated the Roosevelt Library near the family home. This was the first time a president of the United States dedicated a library to house his own documents, standing on land he himself donated.

**1943**  *Cairo, Egypt.* Mena House Hotel. He was here for a wartime conference.

**1943**  *Casablanca, Morocco.* Conference at the resort town of Anfa, five miles from the city. Roosevelt stayed in a villa. During this trip, he set a travel record for a President with more than 200,000 miles and exceeded Taft's previous record. He was the first president since Lincoln to visit an actual theater of war.

**1943**  *Washington, D.C.* Dedication of Jefferson Memorial.

**1943**  *Catoctin Mountains, Maryland.* He visited the mountain retreat in a government reservation administered by the Interior Department. It is now named Camp David.

**1944**  *(north of) Charleston, South Carolina.* For four weeks at Bernard Baruch's 23,000 acre plantation, Hobcaw Barony.

**1944**  *Chicago, Illinois.* Blackstone Hotel, 636 South Michigan Avenue, for the Democratic National Convention.

**1944**  *Savannah, Georgia.* Two hundredth anniversary celebration. He rode down Broughton Street and gave an address at Grayson Stadium, 1401 Victory Drive.

**1944**  *Tehran, Iran.* Conference. He went via Tunis and Cairo.

**1945**  *Valetta, Malta.* On the way to the Yalta conference in the Crimea.

## DEATH

Roosevelt died on April 12, 1945, in Warm Springs, Georgia, at 3:35 P.M. He suffered a stroke while posing for a portrait. His body was taken back to Washington on a train in his special car "Ferdinand Magellan." He left an estate valued at more than 1.9 million dollars.

## FUNERAL

On the morning of April 13, a hearse, carrying the flag-draped bronze coffin, drove from the Little White House to the Warm Springs

*Grave of Franklin Roosevelt.*

## BURIAL

On the night of April 14, the presidential train pulled out of Union Station for Hyde Park. It passed through Maryland, Delaware, Pennsylvania, New Jersey, and into New York, where it reached Hyde Park on April 15. Mourners assembled in the rose garden and the Reverend Anthony of St. James Church read the committal words and the coffin was lowered into the ground on the anniversary of Lincoln's death. "The President was at rest, his grave a short distance from the room where his wicket basket had swung." Now a National Historic Site.

railroad station. The undertaker's bill in Warm Springs was $3,100. On the morning of April 15, the train crossed the Potomac and backed into Union Station, from which a small, black-draped caisson drawn by six white horses carried the coffin to the White House with full military honors.

In the East room of the White House, the coffin, kept closed because the cerebral hemorrhage had turned the president's face purple, lay between the tall portraits of George Washington and Martha Washington. At 4:00 P.M., there was a brief service led by Bishop Angus Dun of the Episcopal Diocese of Washington. The Scripture readings included Psalms 46 and 121, Romans 8:14, and John 14:1. The music was "Eternal Father, Strong to Save," and "Faith of Our Fathers."

## SPECIAL SITES

*Washington, D.C.* Roosevelt Memorial, West Potomac Park, near the Jefferson Memorial. It is to be completed by 1995.

*Washington, D.C.* Roosevelt Memorial there is a small monument in front of National Archives at Seventh and Pennsylvania Avenue, NW.

## BIBLIOGRAPHY

Burns, James MacGregor. *Roosevelt: The Lion and the Fox.* New York: Harcourt, Brace, and World, 1956.

Burns, James MacGregor. *Roosevelt: Soldier of Freedom.* New York: Harcourt, Brace, and Jovanovich, 1957.

Freidel, Frank. *Franklin D. Roosevelt* (4 volumes). Boston: Little, Brown, 1952–1973.

# HARRY S TRUMAN

1884–1972
33RD PRESIDENT 1945–1953: DEMOCRATIC PARTY

*"Being a President is like riding a tiger. A man has to keep on riding or be swallowed."*

—*Memoirs, 1948*

Harry Truman was born on May 8, 1884, at 4:00 P.M. to John Anderson and Martha Ellen Young Truman.

## CHARACTERISTICS

Truman was 5′9″ tall and weighed one hundred and eighty-five pounds when he became president in 1945. He had blue eyes and brown hair, which had turned gray by the time he entered the White House. He was near-sighted and had worn glasses since childhood.

He is often described as "down to earth" and friendly with people at all levels. It is reported that he always washed his own socks! He was a joiner, and on the top on his list was his membership in the Masonic Lodge. As an adult, he walked two miles every morning at a rapid clip of one hundred and thirty-eight steps per minute. He enjoyed small stakes poker and was a talented pianist. He did not smoke and drank only moderately.

He was very fond of reading history, ancient and modern. In his mind, the great men of the Roman Republic were not military. Truman's favorite was Marcus Aurelius, who always thought of the welfare of his people. Truman's statement, "If you can't stand the heat, stay out of the kitchen," is often quoted.

# A LIFE IN REVIEW

**Birth:** May 8, 1884; Lamar, MO

**Died:** December 26, 1972; Kansas City, MO

**Married:** Elizabeth "Bess" Virginia Wallace; June 28, 1919; 1 daughter

## CAREER

**1917–1919** Military Service World War I

**1919–1921** Haberdashery business

**1922–1934** County judge

**1935–1945** Member U.S. Senate

**1945** U.S. Vice President

## ADMINISTRATION EVENTS

**1945** German unconditional surrender

United Nations Charter signed

Potsdam Conference

Atomic bombs dropped on Japan

Japanese surrendered

**1946** Atomic Energy Commission created

**1947** Truman Doctrine-aid to Greece and Turkey

Taft-Hartley Act passed

**1948** Air lift to overcome Berlin blockade

**1949** North Atlantic Treaty signed

**1950** War with North Korea

Attempted assassination on Truman

# BIRTHPLACE

Truman was born in Lamar, Missouri, at (what is now) 1009 Truman Avenue, in the downstairs southwest bedroom.

# BAPTISM

One source reports that his baptism took place outside the Truman farmhouse at the gate by a Baptist circuit rider. It seems more likely that he was baptized at a later date in a church. In 1916, he joined the Grandview Baptist Church by letter and that indicates he had already been baptized somewhere else. One researcher writes, "Usually the church clerk would have noted what church Mr. Truman came from in the minutes of the September meeting (1916). Unfortunately September 1916 was unusual in that the church did not have a business meeting that month."

# CHURCH

The Trumans were active members of their church. When the family moved to Independence in 1890, Truman wrote, "my mother's first thought was to get us into a good Sunday School." He had a remarkably broad knowledge of the Bible and singled out the Sermon on the Mount as its greatest passage. He believed in the power of prayer.

Throughout his life, he retained his membership in Grandview Baptist Church. He liked his liturgy simple and informal. After he became president he only attended occasionally because his attendance attracted so much attention. He was little interested in theological issues, but he had great tolerance and supported the ecumenical movement among the churches. He was probably one of our more religious presidents. He said, "I'm a Baptist because I think that sect gives the common man the shortest and most direct approach to God."

**1884–1885** *Lamar, Missouri.* Baptist Church, 1108 Gulf Street. His name is on the cradle roll there, and his mother is listed as a member.

**1885–1887** *(near) Harrisonville and Peculiar, Missouri.* The family lived on the Dye farm, about five miles southeast of Belton, and his parents attended churches in the vicinity.

**1887–1972** *Grandview, Missouri.* 2400 Grandview Boulevard. In his autobiography, he notes, "my membership is now in the Grandview Baptist Church where it has been for forty years."

**1890–1896** *Independence, Missouri.* First Presbyterian Church, Lexington and Pleasant Streets, where he started Sunday School. This was the nearest Protestant church. He attended every Sunday, and this is where he first saw his future wife, Elizabeth Wallace.

**1896–1902** *Independence, Missouri.* First Baptist Church, 500 West Truman Road.

**1902–1904** *Kansas City, Missouri.* Benton Boulevard Baptist Church. At one time, he considered himself a Presbyterian but at the age of eighteen he joined this church and later changed his membership to Grandview. He was a member of the Baptist Church till the end of his life.

**1904–1906** *Clinton, Missouri.* Clinton Baptist Church.

**1906–1917** *Grandview, Missouri.* Grandview Baptist Church, 244 Grandview Boulevard.

**1919–1972** *Independence, Missouri.* Baptist Church, 500 West Truman Road (just around the corner from "Bess's" Episcopal Church at 409 North Liberty).

**1935–1953** *Washington, D.C.* First Baptist Church, Sixteenth and O Streets, NW. The building on the Sixteenth Street site, opened in 1890, has since been razed, and a new church, dedicated in 1956, has replaced the structure where Truman worshipped.

**1945–1953** *Key West, Florida.* The New Naval Chapel.

**1947** *Fairfax County, Virginia.* Pohick Episcopal Church. He and his family sat in George Washington's pew.

**1947** *Washington, D.C.* National Presbyterian Church, Connecticut Avenue. He was present at the ceremonies establishing it as the national church for all Presbyterians.

**1949** *Washington, D.C.* St. John's Episcopal Church, Lafayette Square. Pew 63 is reserved for the president. He attended on his inauguration day.

# EDUCATION

**1884–1890** *Lamar/Harrison, Missouri.* He was taught to read by his mother at age five. He did not start formal schooling until he was eight and one-half.

**1890–1893** *Independence, Missouri.* Noland School on South Liberty Street. (Named Southside first and later renamed Noland.)

**1893–1894** *Independence, Missouri.* He was ill and missed most of the year but was tutored some at home. He skipped the third grade.

**1894–1897** *Independence, Missouri.* Westside (renamed Columbian for the recent World's Fair). It has been torn down, and the site is now part of the parking lot of the Latter Day Saints Auditorium.

**1897–1901** *Independence, Missouri.* Ott High School, 624 North Liberty Street. He went to fifth and sixth grades here, but in seventh grade, he was back at Columbian. It is said that he read and read and read. Grammar schools in Missouri had seven grades and high schools three grades in his day. Independence High School, Maple and Pleasant; he graduated in May. He was in the first class to graduate from this school. The Palmer Junior High School is on the site of the old Central High School. The original building was destroyed by fire.

**1901–1902** *Kansas City, Missouri.* Spalding's Commercial College, New York Life Building (east wing), northeast corner of Ninth Street and Baltimore Avenue.

**1923–1925** *Kansas City, Missouri.* Kansas City Law School, Nonquitt Building (fifth floor), 1013–1015 Grand Avenue. The building is gone.

# MARRIAGE

Truman was married on June 28, 1919, in Independence, Missouri, at Trinity Episcopal Church, 409 North Liberty, to Elizabeth "Bess" Virginia Wallace. In his memoirs, Truman wrote, "We went to Sunday School and public school from the 5th through high school in the same class." When Truman first met her in childhood, she lived at 610 North Delaware. He first proposed by letter on June 22, 1911, and wrote, "Speaking of diamonds, would you wear a solitaire on your left hand should I get it? ... You may not have guessed it but I've been crazy about you ever since we went to Sunday School." She did not accept at that time but finally gave her word in a letter of November 1913.

The reception was held at the home of George Porterfield Gates, 219 North Delaware, at the corner of Blue Avenue. They had a brief honeymoon in Detroit, Michigan where they stayed with his cousin, Mary Colgan, then to Port Huron, to Chicago with a room in the Blackstone Hotel, and back to Independence to settle in the home of Bess's mother.

# HOMES/LODGINGS

**1884–1885** *Lamar, Missouri.* 1009 Truman Avenue.

**1885–** *Harrison, Missouri.* Twice in 1885, his family moved to different houses in Cass County.

**1885–1887** *(near) Peculiar, Missouri.* They lived five miles southeast of Belton on the Dye Farm. The house was on a hilltop facing south in Mount Pleasant Township. The house had two stories and nine rooms.

**1887–1890** *Grandview, Jackson County, Missouri.* They again removed themselves to the Young house, which was the old home of his mother's father, Solomon Young. In 1893, the Solomon Young family mansion burned and a temporary house (still standing nearly a century later) was built. It is sixteen miles south of Independence, near Hickman's Mills on Blue Ridge.

**1890–1896** *Independence, Missouri.* 619 South Crysler Street. The family moved here so that Harry could have a town schooling. His father bought two lots on this street, and, in mid-1892, he bought lots on Railroad Avenue.

**1896–1902** *Independence, Missouri.* 909 West Waldo Avenue and River Boulevard. At one point (dates confused), his father lost heavily in the stock market and was forced to sell; they moved to Kansas City.

**1902** *Independence, Missouri.* 902 North Liberty.

**1902–1905** *Kansas City, Missouri.* 2108 Park Avenue (sold in 1905).

**1904–1905** *Clinton, Missouri.* His father traded the house on Park Avenue for an equity in 80 acres in Henry County, on the Grand River, toward Lewis, Missouri. The Trumans lived about five miles southwest of the farm at 506 East Bodine Street, but Harry went back to Kansas City after three weeks and moved in with his Aunt Emma (Mrs. Rochester Colgan). There is a marker at the site in Clinton.

**1905** *Kansas City, Missouri.* 2650 East Twenty-ninth Street. He lived with his paternal aunt, Emma Colgan. The building has been razed.

**1905–1906** *Kansas City, Missouri.* He Boarded at 1314 Troost Avenue with some of the bank boys. "For lunch we paid ten cents to a box lunch place on East Eighth Street." For a time, Arthur Eisenhower, brother of the future president, was a fellow boarder.

**1906–1917** *Grandview, Missouri.* The homestead of his maternal grandfather. There is now a different house on the site, which is now in a suburb of Kansas City.

**1919–1935** *Independence, Missouri.* 219 North Delaware Street. Following their marriage in 1919, the Trumans moved in with Bess's mother in the house then known as the Gates House. It was an Independence showplace even before it became known as the Summer White House, and, when Truman retired, the President's House. It is a rambling three-story white frame structure with wide verandas, gingerbread gables, and stained- glass windows. It has fourteen large rooms, with a center hall and a dark walnut stairway. The hall is flanked on the right by an old-fashioned double parlor. On the left is the music room. Across the back of the house is a huge dining room, whose antique mahogany table can be extended to seat thirty guests.

**1921** *Kansas City, Missouri.* He owned a house at 3404 Karnes Boulevard but never lived there. In April 1921, he traded this house for one at 3932 Bell. In July, he bought a 160- acre farm in Johnson County, Kansas.

**1928 & 1935** *Washington, D.C.* Lafayette Hotel, Sixteenth and I Streets, NW. He stayed here when he was a Senator.

**1935** *Washington, D.C.* Hotel Continental, while serving in the Senate.

**1935–1936** *Washington, D.C.* 3016 Tilden Gardens, 3000 Tilden Street, NW, is a triangular block bounded by Connecticut Avenue and Tilden and Sedgwick Streets. They rented a four-room apartment.

**1936** *Washington, D.C.* Sedgwick Gardens, 3726 Connecticut Avenue, NW, southwest corner of Connecticut Avenue and Sedgwick Street.

**1937** *Washington, D.C.* Carroll Arms Apartments, 301 First Street, NE.

**1938** *Washington, D.C.* Warwick Apartments, 3051 Idaho Avenue, NW.

**1939** *Washington, D.C.* Tilden Gardens, again, 3000 Tilden Street, NW.

**1940** *Washington, D.C.* 3930 Connecticut Avenue, NW.

**1941–1945** *Washington, D.C.* 4701 Connecticut Avenue, NW, northeast corner of Connecticut Avenue and Chesapeake Street. Apartment 209 was a five-room apartment, nearly where nearly four years later, he slept his first night as President of the United States. He paid $120 a month rent.

**1945** *Washington D.C.* He moved into the Blair House temporarily while Mrs. Roosevelt was preparing to leave the White House.

**1945–1953** *Washington, D.C.* The White House. On May 6, 1945 (VE Day), the Trumans spent their first full day in the White House. He moved to Blair House again while the White House was being remodelled. Once the restoration was completed (after more than three years in Blair House, they moved back to the White House in the spring of 1952.

**1945–1953** *Maryland.* Shangri-La (now Camp David), for vacations away from the White House.

**1945–1953** *Independence, Missouri.* 219 North Delaware Street served as the Summer White House.

**1953–1972** *Independence, Missouri.* He lived at 219 North Delaware Street during his retirement years.

# WORK

**1895** *Independence, Missouri.* He had a job as a newsboy.

**1896** *Independence, Missouri.* He worked as a soda jerk at Jim Clinton's drug store on the town square, 101 West Walnut. It is now known as Clinton's Drugstore Gift Shop.

**1901–1902** *Kansas City, Missouri.* He was a timekeeper for a railroad construction outfit under L. J. Smith, building a double track for the Sante Fe RR from Eton to Sheffield, a suburb of Kansas City. While on this job, he lived in camps along the Missouri River.

**1902–1903** *Kansas City, Missouri.* He worked for the Kansas City Star, 1729 Grand, as a mailroom clerk.

**1903–1905** *Kansas City, Missouri.* He worked in the basement of the National Bank of Commerce at Tenth and Walnut as a clerk.

**1903** *Kansas City, Missouri.* He supplemented his income by working Saturday matinees as an usher at Kansas City's Grand Theater, 704 Walnut Street. The building was razed in 1926.

**1905–1906** *Kansas City, Missouri.* He went to work for the Union National Bank. At Ninth and Main and Delaware, just north of the C & A office, was the soda fountain and candy shop of Jesse James, Jr.

**1906–1917** *Grandview, Missouri.* He helped to run the family farm. His father died in 1914 and Truman was appointed road overseer in his place (1914–1916).

**1911–1916** *South Dakota, Montana, and Oklahoma.* He engaged in various activities, including land acquisition attempts, mining and oil in Gregory, South Dakota (October 1911), Harve, Montana (September 1913), and Commerce, Oklahoma (1916). He was a partner in the company called T.C.H. Mining Company.

**1914–1915** *Grandview, Missouri.* He was appointed as postmaster although he never occupied the office. The post office is on the grounds of the Grandview Truman farm home.

**1917–1919** *Oklahoma.* He arrived at Camp Doniphan in September 1917, located just west of and adjoining Fort Sill, where he was quartered in a tent. As first lieutenant he drilled his men inside the Convention Hall in Kansas City. He served in France during World War II.

**1919** *Kansas City, Missouri.* Ventures in oil. 703 Ridge Arcade was the address of Morgan and Company Oil Investments.

**1919–1922** *Kansas City, Missouri.* He opened his elite haberdashery at 104 West Twelfth on the ground floor of the Baltimore Hotel across the street from the Muehlebach Hotel. Later, the Phillips Hotel (now the Radisson Suite Hotel) was built on this site and opened in 1930. He worked in partnership with Jacobson.

**1921** *Kansas City, Missouri.* He dabbled in some real estate ventures.

**1922–1924** *Kansas City, Missouri.* Judge of Jackson County, Missouri. Courthouse, Twelfth to Thirteenth and Oak to Locust Streets.

**1924–1926** *Kansas City, Missouri.* He worked for a time selling memberships for the Kansas City Automobile Club, setting up shop at the Tenth and Central Club office in downtown Kansas City. At the same time, he worked for the Farm and Home Savings and Loan Association.

**1926–1934** *Kansas City, Missouri.* Presiding judge of Jackson County at the Jackson County Courthouse, Independence Square. The office he used has been restored to the period when he was on the Court.

**1935–1945** *Washington, D.C.* United States senator from Missouri. At first he occupied Room 238 in the Russell Office Building and later Suite No. 240. In the Senate Chamber, he was assigned seat number 94. At times, he sat in the vice president's chair as presiding officer.

**1945–** *Washington, D.C.* Vice president of the United States. He kept his same quarters in the Russell Senate Office Building, and used the vice president's office mainly to greet visitors.

**1945–1953** *Washington, D.C.* President of the United States. He was having a drink at the office of House Speaker Sam Rayburn when he was summoned to the White House and told of Roosevelt's death. On April 12 at 7:09 P.M., he took the oath of office in the White House Cabinet Room. In 1949, the weather was very cold but with bright sunlight in a clear blue sky when he was sworn in, in his own right, on the East Portico of the Capitol.

**1953–1957** *Kansas City, Missouri.* He had offices on the eleventh floor of the Federal Reserve Bank Building (1107) at Tenth and Grand.

**1957–1972** *Independence, Missouri.* He had offices in the Truman Library.

# TRAVEL/VISITS

As a senator, he rode 30,000 miles by auto on a tour of American defense installations. As a vice presidential candidate in 1944, he made a 10,000-mile swing around the country. Two years after becoming president, he had travelled 50,000 air miles, 5,000 rail miles, and an unestimated number of sea miles. He liked travelling and particularly enjoyed air travel. During his presidency, the Sacred Cow aircraft of Roosevelt was replaced. While he travelled many miles by plane, he still used the train on occasion. He went to the Democratic Party Conference in Chicago from Washington by train in 1953.

**1900** *Kansas City, Missouri.* He was present at the Democratic National Convention which nominated William Bryan. He worked as a page.

**1903** *Kansas City, Missouri.* He had his first sight of a president when Theodore Roosevelt appeared at the back of a railroad car.

**1909** *Belton, Missouri.* Masonic Lodge, 12101 East Bannister Road, where he was first initiated into the Masonic Lodge.

**1914–** *Kansas City, Missouri.* Union Station, 2400 Main Street, was dedicated in 1914 and Truman came in here many times.

**1915** *Dallas, Texas.* Adolphus Hotel, 1321 Commerce Street, southwest corner Commerce and Agard. He was here again in 1941.

**1917–1919** *France.* World War I.

**1917** *Fort Sill (near Lawton), Oklahoma.* Camp Doniphan with the U.S. Army, July through March 1918.

**1918** *Camp Merritt (near Cresskill), New Jersey.* His embarkation point for France. See the Soldiers Monument on Madison Avenue.

**1918** *France.* In Brest, he stayed at the Continental Hotel for six days before going to artillery school. When the war was over in November, he visited Paris, dined at Maxims, saw the Folies Bergeres and all the other major sites, including Notre Dame, Napoleon's Tomb, and the Arc de Triomphe. He went to Nice and the casino at Monte Carlo. In Nice, he stayed at the Hotel Mediterranee. From December 14, 1918 to January 21, 1919, he was at Camp La Baholle near Verdun. In January 22, in Rosieres, near Bar-le-Duc, he attended mass. In April, he returned to the United States and went to Camp Mills, Long Island.

**1918** *New York City, New York.* Hotel McAlpin. For first time, he went to Broadway, the top of the Woolworth Building, and Central Park.

**1923** *Fort Leavenworth, Kansas.* Summer camp.

**1925–** *Fort Riley (near Manhattan), Kansas.* Army camp between 1925 and 1938.

**1927** *Albuquerque, New Mexico.* Franciscan Hotel on business while Judge.

**1928** *Cumberland, Maryland.* Fort Cumberland Hotel en route to Washington.

**1930–** *Kansas City, Missouri.* He sometimes stayed at the Phillips Hotel, corner of Baltimore and Wyandotte.

**1930** *Independence.* The Missouri Pacific RR Station, Pacific at Grand Streets. Was the site of his return to Independence in 1948 after his famous Whistle Stop campaign.

**1934** *New York City, New York.* Hotel Governor Clinton, Thirty-first and Seventh Avenue, to visit the artist executing the figure of Jackson for the courthouse in Kansas City.

**1936** *Philadelphia, Pennsylvania.* Majestic Hotel. He attended the Democratic National Convention.

**1937–** *Hot Springs, Arkansas.* Park Hotel, One Convention Plaza, to visit the Army-Navy Hospital for a checkup.

**1937** *New York City, New York.* Hotel New Yorker. He stayed here on his way to West Point to see a ballgame.

**1939** *Battle Creek, Michigan.* Post Tavern on the return to Washington. There is a marker for the hotel location.

**1939** *Kansas City, Missouri.* The Muehlebach Hotel, Twelfth Street, SW, at corner of Baltimore Avenue, was one of the great hotels of the country, but it was slated to be demolished in 1993.

**1939** *San Antonio, Texas.* St. Anthony Hotel, on government business.

**1939** *San Francisco, California.* St. Francis Hotel, 450 Powell Street.

**1941** *Los Angeles, California.* Biltmore Hotel, 515 South Olive Street.

**1942** *Hot Springs, Virginia.* The Homestead.

**1944** *Boston, Massachusetts.* The Ritz-Carlton Hotel is where he met with Joseph Kennedy during the Democratic campaign and threatened to throw Kennedy out the window.

**1944** *Chicago, Illinois.* Stevens Hotel, where he stayed for the Democratic National Convention held at Chicago Stadium.

**1944** *New Orleans, Louisiana.* Roosevelt Hotel (now Fairmont), 100 block of University Place, for Democratic Party meetings.

**1944** *Uvalde, Texas.* Former vice president John Nance Garner's home, 333 North Park.

**1945** *Gilbertsville, Kentucky.* Dedication of Kentucky Dam.

**1945** *Key West, Florida.* Little Winter White House, 111 Front Street, in the two-story wooden house of the Navy Commandant. He enjoyed swimming. On one occasion, the choppy surf swept his glasses off his nose.

**1945** *Potsdam, Germany.* On the *U.S.S. Augusta* for Conference. He disembarked at Antwerp, and the Potsdam Conference began on July 17. Cecilienhof Castle, in which the Potsdam Agreement was negotiated, is now a museum. He lodged in Number 2 Kaiserstrasse, a three-story villa beside Lake Griebnitz in Babelsberg, a Berlin suburb, three miles from Potsdam. It was here on the morning of July 24 that he made the fateful decision to use the atomic bomb.

**1945** *Salt Lake City, Utah.* Hotel Utah. June 26. He was here again in 1944, 1948, and 1952.

**1945** *San Francisco, California.* Civic Center, Golden Gate Avenue, for the opening of the United Nations. He gave a speech at the Opera House, Van Ness Avenue, in 1945.

**1945** *Washington D.C. and Hyde Park, New York.* He attended the state funeral of President Roosevelt in the East Room of the White House and boarded the funeral train that took the body to its final resting place in Hyde Park.

**1946** *Fulton, Missouri.* Westminster College, in the gymnasium where Churchill made his famous speech, "An iron curtain has descended on Europe."

**1946** *Hamilton, Bermuda.* He attended services at Holy Trinity Cathedral.

**1946** *Hyde Park, New York.* He dedicated the Franklin Roosevelt home as a National Shrine.

**1946** *Key West, Florida.* He visited the Fort Jefferson National Monument.

**1946** *New York City, New York.* Fordham University, Keling Hall. He received an honorary degree.

**1946** *West Point, New York.* U.S. Military Academy. He made remarks in Washington Hall.

**1947** *Charlottesville, Virginia.* Stanley Woodward house, Colle, five miles from town on 210 acres which used to belong to Jefferson. He spoke at Monticello on July 4 and laid a wreath on Jefferson's tomb. He also visited Ash Lawn.

**1947** *Everglades City, Florida.* He dedicated the Everglades National Park.

**1947** *Independence, Missouri.* Dee and Butch Tavern, Main Street, where he had often been before the daughter of the owners refused to write up a bill for him, and he gave her a dollar bill which he autographed.

**1947** *Mexico City, Mexico.* He spoke at the Palacio Nacional. He made a special visit to Chapultepec Castle and the monument of the "child heroes."

**1947** *Ottawa, Canada.* He addressed Parliament in the House of Commons Chamber.

**1947** *Princeton, New Jersey.* Princeton University, Nassau Hall. He gave the commencement address and received an honorary degree.

**1947** *Rio de Janeiro, Brazil.* He addressed a joint session of Congress at Tiradentes Palace.

**1947** *Shangri-la (now Camp David), Maryland.* He was here many times during his term of office.

**1948** *Annapolis, Maryland.* While on vacation on the presidential yacht, he visited the Naval Academy and attended church there with the midshipmen.

**1948** *Berkeley, California.* University of California. He gave the commencement address in Memorial Stadium.

**1948** *Bolivar, Missouri.* He dedicated the Simon Bolivar Memorial Statue in town square.

**1948** *Bonham, Texas.* He was at the Bonham High School football stadium and a reception at the home of Speaker of the House Sam Rayburn on Highway 82 West. He was here again in November 1961 to attend Rayburn's funeral. Lyndon Johnson was on the train with him for the day through Texas.

**1948** *Cheyenne, Wyoming.* He was a guest at the Governor's Mansion.

**1948** *Denver, Colorado.* He gave an address at the State Capitol Grounds.

**1948** *Kansas City, Missouri.* Muehlebach Hotel, West Twelfth Street, at the time of his reelection to the presidency.

**1948** *Detroit, Michigan.* Cadillac Square, where he kicked off his reelection campaign on Labor Day with his "Give 'em Hell" speech and began his "Whistlestop Campaign" on board the Magellan. Starting out on September 17, he travelled almost 22,000 miles.

**1948** *Los Angeles, California.* Ambassador Hotel, 3400 Wilshire Boulevard.

**1948** *New Bern, North Carolina.* First Baptist Church, Middle Street between South Front and Pollock Streets. For the presidential campaign, he travelled for seven weeks on the train Ferdinand Magellan, a custom-built Pullman. He went 9,505 miles through 18 states and gave 73 speeches. The Magellan can still be seen in the Railroad Museum, south Miami.

**1948** *New York City, New York.* Dedication of Idlewild International Airport.

**1948** *Omaha, Nebraska.* He dedicated the War Memorial, spoke at 35th Division reunion in Ak-sar-ben Coliseum, and visited Boys Town.

**1948** *Philadelphia, Pennsylvania.* Convention Hall, Thirty-fourth and Civic Center Boulevard. He gave his acceptance speech.

**1948** *Quincy, Massachusetts.* He spoke at the First Parish Church, Quincy Square.

**1948** *Raleigh, North Carolina.* Dedication of monument to Jackson, Polk, and Andrew Johnson.

**1948** *San Antonio, Texas.* He spoke at the Alamo and had dinner at the Gunter Hotel, 205 East Houston Street.

**1948** *Williamsburg, Virginia.* At William and Mary College, in front of the Sir Christopher Wren Building, he received an honorary degree and sat in the chair used by Washington in the Masonic Lodge here in about 1760. He attended a reception and luncheon in the Williamsburg Lodge.

**1949** *Arlington National Cemetery, Virginia.* He unveiled the Memorial Carillon.

**1949** *Little Rock, Arkansas.* Hotel Marion. He visited the old State Capitol, dedicated the War Memorial Park, and also visited the widow of Senator Joe Robinson on South Broadway.

**1949** *New York City, New York.* He laid the cornerstone of the United Nations Building, Forty-second Street, and had lunch with the mayor at Gracie Mansion.

**1949** *Orlando, Florida.* He landed at the Air Force base and then went in a cavalcade from Orlando to Rollins College in Winter Park. He dedicated the causeway over Lake Estelle on Mills Street.

**1949** *Washington, D.C.* He had breakfast at the Mayflower Hotel on the morning of his inauguration. 1127 Connecticut Avenue, NW.

**1949** *Winter Park, Florida.* Rollins College, Knowles Memorial Chapel, to receive an honorary degree. He went to 208 North Interlachen for lunch at the home of Dr. Holt, president of Rollins College.

**1950** *Arlington National Cemetery, Virginia.* He unveiled the statue of Sir John Dill.

**1950** *Baltimore, Maryland.* He dedicated the Friendship Airport.

**1950** *Palm Beach, Florida.* He stayed at the Charles Wrightman house on Ocean Boulevard.

**1950** *Quantico, Virginia.* U.S. Marine Corps Base, Harry Lee Hall.

**1950** *San Francisco, California.* War Memorial Opera House.

**1950** *Wake Island.* He met General MacArthur in a quonset hut on the shore and continued a meeting in the Civil Aeronautics administration building.

**1951** *Gompers Square, Washington, D.C.* Tenth Street and Massachusetts Avenue, NW. Dedication of Square.

**1951** *Memorial Bridge, Washington, D.C.* Dedication of Italian gift horses.

**1951** *Philadelphia, Pennsylvania.* Chapel of the Four Chaplains, in Russell H. Conwell Memorial Church, Broad and Berks Streets.

**1951** *San Francisco, California.* Fairmont Hotel. War Memorial Opera House. Palace Hotel.

**1951** *Union Station.* Dedication of the Presidential Lounge, Union Station Plaza.

**1951** *Washington, D.C.* Rock Creek Park. Dedication of Carter Barron Amphitheater.

**1951** *Washington, D.C.* Washington Monument. One hundred seventy-fifth anniversary of the Declaration of Independence.

**1951** *Washington, D.C.* Dedication of the new General Accounting Office.

**1952** *Alexandria, Virginia.* Cornerstone laying of Westminster Presbyterian Church.

**1952** *Bull Shoals, Arkansas.* He dedicated the Bull Shoals Dam.

**1952** *Chicago, Illinois.* Chicago Stockyard Amphitheater for the Democratic National Convention. He had room 709 at the Blackstone.

**1952** *Washington, D.C.* National Archives. He dedicated the new shrine for the Declaration of Independence, the Constitution, and the Bill of Rights.

**1953–** *New York City, New York.* Carlyle Hotel, 35 East Seventy-sixth Street and northeast corner of Madison. He usually stayed here when visiting his daughter Margaret.

**1953** *Chicago, Illinois.* Democratic Party Conference. Conrad Hilton Hotel, 720 South Michigan Avenue.

**1953** *Washington, D.C.* After Eisenhower's inauguration ceremony, he had lunch at Dean Acheson's house in old Georgetown, 2805 P Street, NW. At 6:00 P.M. on the same day, the Trumans left Washington's Union Station for Independence.

**1954** *Kansas City, Missouri.* Research Hospital, 2316 East Meyer Boulevard, for gall bladder surgery. He was here again in 1963 for an operation for an intestinal hernia.

**1955** *San Francisco, California.* Tenth Anniversary of the United Nations. He stayed at the Fairmont Hotel, 950 Mason Street.

**1956** *Chicago, Illinois.* For the Democratic National Convention, staying at the Blackstone.

**1959** *Fort Myer, Virginia.* He was here for the funeral service of General Marshall, and sat beside President Eisenhower.

**1959** *New York City, New York.* He lectured at Columbia University.

**1960** *Washington, D.C.* Mayflower Hotel. He met with John Kennedy. About Kennedy, Truman said, "It's not the Pope I'm afraid of, it's the pop."

**1963** *Washington, D.C.* Blair House, where he stayed for the funeral of Kennedy.

**1964** *Washington, D.C.* He spoke in the Senate, who had gathered to celebrate his 80th birthday. He stayed in the presidential suite, the penthouse on the seventeenth floor.

# DEATH

Truman died on December 26, 1972, in Kansas City, Missouri. He died on the sixth floor of the Research Hospital. His estate was valued at about $600,000. Bess survived him until October 18, 1982, when she died at the age of 97.

# FUNERAL

Arrangements were made by the Carson Funeral home, Lexington Avenue and Fuller Street, and there was a ceremony here on December 27. Ex-President Johnson and President Nixon paid respects to the family at home and visited the bier, which was placed in the main lobby of the Truman Library. The rector of Trinity Episcopal Church of Independence, the Reverend John H. Lembcke, Jr., conducted the services held at the Truman Library and attended by 250 invited guests. The Bible readings were from Psalms 27 and 46 and I Corinthians 15:20. The Apostle's Creed was recited. There was no eulogy and no hymns were sung. At the library, an estimated 75,000 people passed by the closed casket.

# BURIAL

Truman was buried in Independence, Missouri, in the courtyard behind the library. A military band played "Ruffles and Flourishes," and there was a 21-gun salute. The library is located on Independence Avenue at Delaware Street.

# SPECIAL SITES

*Independence, Missouri.* Harry S Truman Library and Museum at Delaware Street and

*Harry S Truman Library and Museum.*

U.S. 24. President Hoover was there, among others, for the dedication on July 6, 1957.

*Kansas City, Missouri.* Young and Truman family plots in the Forest Hill Cemetery.

## BIBLIOGRAPHY

Lawrence, Richard Lawrence. *Truman: The Rise to Power.* New York: McGraw-Hill Book Company, 1986. (Excellent)

McCullough, David. *Truman.* New York: Simon and Schuster, 1992.

# Dwight David Eisenhower

## 1890–1969
### 34th President 1953–1961: Republican Party

Dwight David Eisenhower was born on the night of October 14, 1890, in a rented house near the railroad tracks in Denison, Texas, to David Jacob and Ida Elizabeth Stover Eisenhower. He was born David Dwight, but his mother reversed the names later.

## CHARACTERISTICS

Eisenhower was 5′10″ tall and weighed one hundred and seventy-eight when be became president. He had a fair complexion, blue eyes, and light brown hair. He was almost completely bald as president. At the office, he wore reading glasses. He had a pleasing personality, but, at times he became depressed or momentarily lost his temper. He was very fond of playing golf. He first enjoyed poker but later turned to bridge and canasta. He enjoyed reading westerns, including Zane Grey, and watching western movies. He also developed a talent for landscape painting. At West Point, he began smoking cigarettes and built up to a four-

## A LIFE IN REVIEW

**Birth:** October 14, 1890; Denison, TX

**Died:** March 28, 1969; Washington, D.C.

**Married:** Mamie (Marie) Geneva Doud;
July 1, 1916; 2 sons

### CAREER

**1915–1952** Military officer

**1948–1950** University president

### ADMINISTRATION EVENTS

**1953** Korean armistice

**1954** Supreme Court orders racial desegregation of schools

**1955** First presidential news conference televised

**1956** Suez crisis

**1957** Civil Rights Commission established

**1959** Fidel Castro rises to power in Cuba

THE PRESIDENTS

Both he and Mamie were frugal. Mamie, in order to save a few cents on the fare, would get out of the taxi at Florida Avenue and carry groceries up the hill to the Wyoming Apartments, a distance of more than a quarter of a mile. Eisenhower walked to his office several miles away.

## BIRTHPLACE

Eisenhower was born in Denison, Texas, at 208 East Day Street. The exterior of the house has been restored, including an upstairs porch which was part of the house at the time Eisenhower was born.

## BAPTISM

He was baptized on February 1, 1953, in Washington, D.C., at the National Presbyterian Church, Eighteenth and N Streets, NW. The church has been demolished.

## CHURCH

He grew up in a family that had strong religious traditions and belonged to the River Brethren, later called Brethren in Christ. For the Eisenhower boys, religious training was strict, fundamentalist, and somewhat puritanical. His father read from the Bible before meals, and then asked a blessing. After dinner, the Bible was read again. The boys took turns reading. None of the Eisenhower boys was a regular churchgoer as an adult except for Eisenhower, who after he became president, was persuaded to do so as a moral example for youth.

**1890–1911** *Abilene, Kansas.* Church of the River Brethren. He was not regular, and his parents did not insist on regular attendance. By 1896, his mother had become closely associated with the Jehovah's Witnesses and perhaps he may have sat in on meetings held in her parlor. Most of the time, the

pack-a-day habit, but he quit cold turkey in 1949. While he was at Key West, Ike had been told by his physician that he would have to cut down from four packs of cigarettes to one. After a few days of limiting his smoking, he decided that counting his cigarettes was worse than not smoking at all and he quit. He never had another cigarette in his life. He was frequently asked how he did it, and he replied that it was simple, all he did was put smoking out of his mind. It helped, he added, to develop a scornful attitude toward those weaklings who did not have the willpower to break their enslavement to nicotine. He told one friend, "I nursed to the utmost my ability to sneer."

*Birthplace of Dwight Eisenhower in Denison, Texas.*

group worshipped in members' houses or in a meeting house.

**1911–1915** *West Point, New York.* West Point Chapel. Attendance was compulsory. He also attended meetings of the Y.M.C.A. on Sunday evenings while at West Point.

**1916–1969** *Denver, Colorado.* Corona Presbyterian Church, Lafayette Street, about two blocks from the Doud house. This was Mamie's girlhood church and is where he attended with her when he was in Denver, particularly after he became president. See also the Central Presbyterian Church, which they sometimes attended.

**1917** *Fort Leavenworth, Kansas.* Memorial Chapel on Scott Avenue.

**1953–1961** *Washington, D.C.* The National Presbyterian Church, Connecticut at Eighteenth and N Streets, NW. He occupied pew number 41 and was officially a member.

The National Presbyterian Church is now at 4101 Nebraska Avenue, NW.

**1954** *Augusta, Georgia.* St. James Methodist Church, while vacationing in Augusta.

**1954** *Palm Springs, California.* Palm Springs Community Church, while on vacation.

**1954** *Washington, D.C.* New York Avenue Presbyterian Church where he sat in the Lincoln Pew. St. John's Episcopal Church, Lafayette Square. St. Matthew's Cathedral, Rhode Island Avenue. He attended the Red Mass for the legal profession. He was the first president to attend.

# EDUCATION

**1896–1902** *Abilene, Kansas.* Lincoln Elementary School, which went only to the sixth grade, 308 South Buckeye Street. It is now the site of the visitors center.

**1902–1904** *Abilene, Kansas.* Garfield School, 215 West North Seventh Street, for seventh and eighth grades.

**1904–1909** *Abilene, Kansas.* He graduated from Abilene High School. Injuring his left knee put him a year behind in school. During his first two years in high school, while a new high school was being built, classes were held in the old city hall on the southeast corner of Fifth and Broadway. The new Abilene High School, located on Seventh Street, which he began attending at the beginning of his junior year is now the Frontier Apartments.

**1911–1915** *West Point, New York.* U.S. Military Academy. He graduated 61 out of 164 and was a commissioned as second lieutenant. He roomed in Beast Barracks at the Military Academy with Paul A. Hodgson. They had a small efficient room with a cobblestone floor and a fireplace for heat.

**1929** *Washington, D.C.* He graduated from Fort McNair Army War College, P Street, SW, between Third and Fourth Streets.

# MARRIAGE AND HONEYMOON

Eisenhower met Mamie Doud for the first time on October 3, 1915, at the home of Major and Mrs. Hunter Davis, who had the house at Fort Sam Houston, San Antonio, next to the bachelor quarters where Ike lived.

They were married on July 1, 1916, in Denver, Colorado, at the home of the bride's parents, Mr. and Mrs. John Doud, 750 Lafayette Street. The ceremony was performed by the pastor of the Denver Central Presbyterian Church in front of the white-tiled fireplace. There were no outside guests.

The honeymoon took place in Eldorado Springs, Colorado, a resort north of Denver where they spent one night in a rustic cottage.

They took the electric trolley for the 32-mile trip to Eldorado Springs. They were greatly surprised when the bride's parents showed up the first morning of their honeymoon to take them back to Denver. They went back for a day or so at 750 Lafayette Street and then by Union Pacific railway to Abilene where they spent only eight hours. On their honeymoon in Abilene they had a first class quarrel when Ike missed the supper hour to play cards downtown with former high school buddies.

# HOMES/LODGINGS

**1890–1891** *Denison, Texas.* 208 East Day Street. See description under birthplace.

**1891–1898** *Abilene, Kansas.* 112 Southeast Second Street is south of the tracks where on three acres they raised vegetables and kept a horse and several cows.

**1898–1916** *Abilene, Kansas.* 201 Southeast Fourth Street is a two-story white frame house, which was occupied by his mother until she died in 1946.

**1915** *San Antonio, Texas.* The Doud winter home, 1216 McCullough Street, was a large white-shingled house with wide, curving verandas and tall Corinthian columns. It was here that Ike picked Mamie up for their first real date in November 1915. It was two miles from Fort Sam Houston, and Ike frequently walked back after taking Mamie home.

**1915–1916** *Fort Sam Houston, Houston, Texas.* The red-brick Bachelor Officers' Quarters. During their first thirty-five years of married life, Ike and Mamie moved thirty-five times.

**1916–1917** *Fort Sam Houston, Houston, Texas.* On Infantry Row, three rooms in the Bachelor Oficers' Quarters. The building is to the left of the entrance to the post, and his quarters were on the second stairway, first floor. The apartment has an historical marker over the entrance.

**1917–1918**  *Fort Oglethorpe, Georgia.* Near Chattanooga-Chickamauga National Military Park. Bachelor quarters, 14 Barnhardt Circle, a few houses up from what is now known as the Captain's Quarters.

**1918**  *Camp Colt, Gettysburg, Pennsylvania.* He rented a house for the family on Spring Avenue, near the campus of Gettysburg College. At one time the house was the Sigma Alpha Epsilon fraternity house, it is still standing.

**1918**  *Gettysburg, Pennsylvania.* They moved into the vacant Alpha Tau Omega fraternity house on North Washington Street across from the campus. With no kitchen, they used an electric hot plate and washed the dishes in the bathtub.

**1918**  *Fort Dix, New Jersey.*

**1919**  *Camp Meade, Maryland, where he stayed in bachelor quarters without Mamie.*

**1919**  *Laurel, Maryland.* He took a room in a rooming house several miles from the post for himself and Mamie. The only bathroom was down the hall, and they ate at a boarding house around the corner. Another source says the room was in Odentown and had only one unwashed window. Ike was back in his bachelor quarters from October till May 1920.

**1920–1922**  *Camp Meade, Maryland.* A duplex apartment on the post. Their first child died at Camp Meade on January 3, 1921.

**1922–1924**  *Camp Gaillard, the Panama Canal Zone.* "A double deck shanty," described as a two-story house on stilts above the canal with a roof of sheet iron. They had to keep the bed legs in pans of kerosene to keep off the invasion of bedbugs during the night.

**1924**  *Fort Logan, near Denver, Colorado.* They lived with the Douds at 750 Lafayette Street.

**1925–1926**  *Fort Leavenworth, Kansas.* A red-brick building with white trim called Otis Hall, 213 Kearney Avenue, while he

was at the Command and General Staff School. It is marked with a plaque.

**1926–1927**  *Fort Benning, Georgia.* 206 Austin Loop. There is a marker at the intersection of Vibbert Avenue and Austin Loop.

**1926–1935**  *Washington, D.C.* Wyoming Apartments, 2022 Columbia Road, NW, at the southeast corner of Columbia Road and Connecticut Avenue, near Rock Creek Park. He was here off and on between 1926 and 1935.

**1928**  *Paris, France, 110 Rue d'Auteuil on the right bank of the Seine in a ground floor apartment.*

**1928–1929**  *Paris, France.* He had a furnished apartment, 68 Quai d'Auteuil, near the Pont Mirabeau on the left bank of the Seine while he was at the Battle of Monuments Commission. It was known to his friends as "Chez Eisenhower."

**1929–1935**  *Washington, D.C.* They returned to the Wyoming Apartments.

**1935–1939**  *Manila, The Philippines.* He stayed in the Manila Hotel in a rent-free room furnished by the Philippine Government. When Mamie arrived with John in 1936, they continued to stay in a suite in the Manila Hotel. When he met Mamie at the gangplank and swept off his hat, he was completely bald. He explained that he had shaved his head to keep cool. Though the apartment was not air-conditioned, they had a full complement of servants. In 1938, they moved into the recently completed annex to the hotel.

**1940**  *San Francisco, California.* He had an apartment with Mamie near the Presidio for the month. He was on temporary duty at the Ninth Corps Area Headquarters. The Presidio is located in northwest San Francisco on US 1 off Park Presidio Boulevard.

**1940**  *Camp Ord (now Fort Ord), California.* Located on US 1 south of Santa Cruz.

**1940–1941**  *Fort Lewis, Washington.* They left Manila in December 1939 and were in

Hawaii for Christmas and in San Francisco for New Year's Eve. At Fort Lewis, they lived in a house on base.

**1941**   *Camp Polk, Texas.* Not far from the Gulf coast on the Texas border, in barracks.

**1941**   *Fort Sam Houston, Texas.* 177 Artillery Post Road. He found the house too small and remained here for only two months.

**1941–1942**   *Fort Sam Houston, Texas.* 179 Artillery Post Road in a 14-room red-brick house with five bedrooms. Eisenhower said it was a house as big as a stock barn. He left San Antonio for Washington on December 12.

**1942**   *Washington, D.C.* Wardman Park Hotel (now the Sheraton-Washington), 2660 Woodley Road, NW, in a three- room apartment.

**1942**   *Washington, D.C.* Fort Myer, in one of the houses reserved for senior staff. Jackson Avenue at the northwest corner of Arlington Cemetery off US 50.

**1942**   *London, England.* Suite 408 at Claridge's Hotel for two weeks before moving to the Dorchester.

**1942**   *London, England.* He moved to the Dorchester Hotel, where he had a three-room suite with a functional living room and two simple bedrooms. Brook Street across Park Lane from Hyde Park. Kingston, Surrey. He had a small seven-room house, called Telegraph Cottage, on Combe Hill, Kingston-on-Thames. It had five bedrooms and a single bath and was less than forty miles from 20 Grosvenor Square. He used it as his "hideout" for most of the War.

**1942–1943**   *Algiers, Algeria.* Hotel St. Georges, near the Boulevard de Telemny in the modern city center. The official headquarters was a modest suite with three bedrooms and a parlor. There was a small fireplace in the room he used as an office.

**1943–1944**   *Algiers, Algeria.* Villa dar el Ouad, fifteen miles outside Algiers, was large but had only two bedrooms and baths.

**1943**   *Naples, Italy.* Prince Umberto's hunting lodge (near Caserta Palace).

**1944**   *London, England.* Norfolk House, built on the site where George III was born, was the hub of preinvasion planning. It borders St. James Park.

**1944**   *London, England.* Hayes Lodge on Chesterfield Street (near Berkeley Square) served as his home and headquarters in London. In March, he settled in Telegraph Cottage again. June. Southwick House, which was an English country estate just north of Portsmouth. September. Versailles, in a handsome mansion at St. Germaine which had been occupied by Field Marshall Gert von Runstedt.

**1945**   *Rheims, France.* The chateau of a champagne baron. He also visited General Patton in Luxembourg.

**1945**   *Frankfurt, West Germany.* A small house in Bad Homburg.

**1945–1948**   *Washington, D.C.* Quarters No. 1 at Fort Myer were the best that they had ever had. The house in which Marshall and before him MacArthur had lived, was a large sprawling brick house with ample room to absorb all Mamie's furniture and the steady stream of house guests. They left here on May 2, 1948.

**1948–1951**   *New York City, New York.* Columbia University, the president's house at 60 Morningside Drive. They spent most of their time on the upper two floors as the house was too palatial for their tastes.

**1951–1952**   *Paris, France.* Mamie was with him at the elegant estate at Marnes-la-Coquette, called Villa St. Pierre by the French and Quarters 1 by the American officers.

**1952**   *New York City, New York.* 60 Morningside Drive until his election in November.

**1953–1961**   *Washington, D.C.* The White House.

*Gettysburg, Pennsylvania, home of Dwight Eisenhower until his death in 1969.*

**1961–1969** *Gettysburg, Pennsylvania.* Adjacent to the southwest boundary of Gettysburg National Military Park. He bought the 179-acre dairy farm and run-down farm house in 1950 as "an escape from concrete into the countryside." It is a 15-room modified Georgian farmhouse, including a part older than the United States itself. The marble fireplace in the living room was once in the White House (Pierce/Grant, 1854–1873) until sold in the 1870s. His desk is patterned after one used by Washington and was made from old White House floor boards.

## WORK

As a child, he peddled produce from the family garden 1909    Summer: he worked on the Bryan farm near Abilene and spent some time at the Rice-Johntz Lumber Company. He finished summer working at the Belle Springs Creamery, loading wagons and handling large chunks of ice.

**1911** *Jefferson Barracks, Missouri.* Just outside St. Louis is where he went to take his physical and academic examinations for West Point. At 400 miles from home, it was the farthest point he had ever been away from home.

**1915–1917** *Fort Sam Houston, San Antonio, Texas.* September 13 to May 28, 1917, except for a short period at Camp Wilson. He was engaged in drilling and training enlisted men.

**1917** *Camp Wilson, north of Fort Sam Houston, Texas.*

**1917** *Leon Springs, Texas.* About twenty miles out of San Antonio, ten miles northwest Loop 410, where he was regimental supply officer.

**1917** *Fort Oglethorpe, Georgia.* To teach officer candidates.

**1917** *Fort Leavenworth, Kansas.* To instruct provisional second lieutenants.

**1918** *Camp Meade, Maryland.* To join the 65th Engineers (tank unit).

**1918** *Camp Colt, Gettysburg, Pennsylvania.* Commander of tank training school.

**1918** *Camp Dix, New Jersey.* With tank unit.

**1918–1922** *Camp Meade, Maryland.* Commander of a tank battalion. He remained a major until July 1, 1936.

**1922–1924** *Camp Gaillard, Panama.* He sailed for Panama on *S.S. St.-Mihiel.* His job there was to reorganize and modernize the defense of the Canal Zone. He served under General Fox Conner.

**1924–1925** *Denver, Colorado.* Fort Logan, off US 285, on South Lowell Boulevard southwest of Denver center, as recruiting officer.

**1925–1926** *Leavenworth, Kansas.* Command and General Staff School.

**1926** *Fort Benning, Georgia.* Coaching the football team. Doughboy Athletic Field. Left on January 15, 1926.

**1926** *Washington, D.C.* Old State-War-Navy Building, Pennsylvania Avenue, just west of the White House. He wrote a guidebook on the battlefields in Europe on which American soldiers had fought.

**1927–1928** *Washington, D.C.* Army War College, later named Fort McNair, P Street between Third and Fourth Streets, SE.

**1928–1929** *Paris, France.* American Battle Monuments Commission to help revise the guidebook. He and the family sailed from New York on the *S.S. America* on July 31 to Southampton, across the Channel to Cherbourg, and by train to Paris. Paris. Paris Commission offices were at 20 Rue Molitor, a short walk from the apartment. During 1928, he travelled all over the battlefields of France. Of Verdun, the longest and bloodiest battle of the First World War, he wrote, "It proved nothing to take such a stronghold, just to prove you could do it." The family picnicked in the Argonne Forest and also visited Chateau-Thierry and St.-Mihiel. They sailed from Cherbourg to New York on September 17, 1929, on the *S.S. Leviathan.*

**1929–1933** *Washington, D.C.* State-War-Navy Building (Old Executive Office) at Seventeenth and Pennsylvania, NW. During September and October 1929, he was with the Monuments Commission to complete revision of the guidebook and worked with General Pershing. After this, he was charged with the development of a plan for mobilizing material and industrial organizations in the event of another war.

**1933–1935** *Washington, D.C.* State-War-Navy Building, Pennsylvania Avenue, working with General MacArthur.

**1935–1939** *Manila, the Philippines.* Senior aide to General Douglas MacArthur and military adviser to the Philippine Government. He travelled to Manila in October on the *S.S. Harding* with MacArthur. He left Manila on December 13, 1939, and arrived in San Francisco on January 16, 1940.

**1940** *San Francisco, California.* He was reassigned to detached service. February. Camp Ord, California, Executive Officer, 15th Infantry. March to November. Fort Lewis, Washington, with the 15th Infantry as Chief of Staff until November 30.

**1941** *July–Fort Sam Houston, Texas.* Duty with General Staff Corps. Chief of Staff of the Third Army. On August 11, he left Fort Sam Houston for Camp Polk.

**1941–1942** *Washington, D.C.* Old Munitions Building on Constitution Avenue in the War Plans Division. (The Pentagon was still being built.)

**1942** *London, England.* He was appointed commanding general of the U.S. forces in Europe and returned to England on June 23.

**1942–1943** *London, England.* Headquarters, 20 Grosvenor Square.

**1942**   *Gibraltar.* Headquarters were deep inside the Rock.

**1942–1943**   *Algiers, Algeria.* Hotel St. Georges, near the Boulevard de Telemny in the modern city center. February 11, 1943. Eisenhower was made a four-star general, the twelfth officer in the history of the United States Army to be so honored–the first was U.S. Grant.

**1943**   *Caserta, Italy.* Headquarters in the Caserta Palace north of Naples with a room large enough to serve as a railroad station. From 1943 to 1945, he served as Supreme Commander of Allied Expeditionary Forces in Europe.

**1944**   *Europe.* Back at 20 Grosvenor Square. In March, headquarters moved to a cantonment in Bushy Park, not far from Wimbledon and a short drive from London. June 2. Portsmouth, England. Headquarters moved about a mile from the British Naval War College at Southwick House. His office was in a two and one-half ton army truck. August 7. His advance command post moved from Portsmouth to an apple orchard near Tourniers, in Normandy, France. Here, his office was a tent with a board floor. September 1. Granville and Dieppe, France. He officially took over his Continental headquarters and met with Montgomery at his headquarters at Chartres.

**1944**   *Versailles, France.* He moved headquarters from Granville to Versailles, where he had his SHAEF office in an annex to the Hotel Trianon.

**1945**   *Europe.* Eisenhower and his staff moved from Versailles to an office in an old schoolhouse. May 7. Old schoolhouse. The surrender document was signed at a scarred oak table in the War Room. Previously, on May 2, in the palace of the Bourbon kings at Caserta, Italy, the unconditional surrender of the German forces in Italy took place. He also visited Patton headquarters in Marcy 1945. Frankfurt, Germany, with

headquarters in the I.G. Farben offices. He moved permanent headquarters here from Versailles on June 1.

**1948–1952**   *New York City, New York.* President of Columbia University.

**1951–1952**   *Paris, France.* Supreme Commander of NATO. He returned to Europe on January 27, 1951. On April 2, he took operational control of NATO forces. SHAPE headquarters was at first housed in a hotel near L'Etoile in Paris and then shifted to about twelve miles west of Paris near the village of Rocquencourt.

**1953–1961**   *Washington, D.C.* President of the United States. While in the White House, he was host to thirty-seven heads of state.

**1961–1969**   *Gettysburg, Pennsylvania.* He kept an office at 300 Carlisle Street on the Gettysburg College Campus.

# TRAVEL/VISITS

His travel from the beginning of World War II was generally by air. See military service, including Panama, the Philippine Islands, England, Algeria, Malta, Italy, Egypt, France, and Germany.

**1911**   *Abilene, Kansas.* 310 East Tenth Street, first street south of the Union Pacific tracks and north of the Santa Fe tracks is where he called on Gladys Harding.

**1915**   *Kansas City, Missouri.* The Baltimore Hotel where he was on holiday. Baltimore Avenue from Eleventh Street to Twelfth Street, was razed in 1939. The City Center Square office building now stands on the site.

**1916**   *Denver, Colorado.* The Brown Palace Hotel, 321 Seventeenth Street, is where he spent much time before, during, and after the presidency. He kept a suite here as office.

**1917**   *Fort Leavenworth, Kansas.* Union Pacific Depot, 123 South Esplanade. He went and came leaving from this station.

**1923**   *Denver (Aurora address), Colorado.*

Fitzsimmons General Hospital, for appendectomy.

**1926** *Kansas City, Missouri.* Muehlbach Hotel, to celebrate his first place finish at the Staff School.

**1942** *Falls Church, Virginia.* He stayed with his brother, Milton, at 708 East Broad Street. He was also here in 1934.

**1942** *Gibraltar.* He stayed in the governor's mansion.

**1942** *London, England.* He visited Buckingham Palace as a special tourist. He returned to England the following month as commanding general. On July 5, he was a guest of Churchill at Chequers, which he found to be a cold and drafty place.

**1943** *Malta, Algeria, and Egypt.* He stayed in the Verdala Palace, the summer residence of the governor. On November 15 met with Churchill. On November 20, he flew to Oran, Algeria to greet F.D. Roosevelt. Later he went with him to Amilcar, Tunis. On November 24, he flew to Cairo, Egypt, to meet Roosevelt at the Mena House. He flew to Luxor on the twenty-seventh and the next day visited the tombs and temples on both sides of the Nile. From here, he made a quick trip to Jerusalem, where he spent several days at the King David Hotel, and toured Bethlehem and Gethsemane. He returned to Cairo on the twenty-ninth and went on to Algiers. On December 8, he flew with Roosevelt to Malta and on the eighteenth to Casrta to establish an advance post there.

**1944** *Berlin, Germany.* Tempelhof airport, for the first meeting of Allied Control Council.

**1944** *Cannes, France.* For a rest at the villa, Sous le Vent.

**1944** *London, England.* Lunch at Mansion House with Queen Mary; tea at Buckingham Palace with King, Queen, and Princess Elizabeth. dinner with Churchill at Number 10 Downing Street.

**1944** *Paris, France.* State dinner at the Elysee Palace. He stayed at the Hotel Scribe and held numerous meetings here.

**1944** *Washington, D.C.* Wardman Park Hotel, 2660 Woodley Road, NW. January 6–7. White Sulphur Springs, West Virginia. Vacation with Mamie at the Greenbrier Hotel.

**1944** *London, England.* Buckingham Palace, for a private lunch with the King and Queen. White Sulphur Springs, West Virginia. Ashford General Hospital, with severe cold and bronchitis.

**1944** *Paris.* He visited Paris for the first time since 1928 on a triumphal tour.

**1945** *Hyde Park, New York.* He laid a wreath on the grave of Franklin Delano Roosevelt. August 14–19. He spent five days in Moscow, United Soviet Socialist Republic. September. Trip to Rome and Venice with a side trip to Sous le Vent, Cap d'Antibes.

**1946** *Denison, Texas.* Lamar Avenue, visiting his birthplace.

**1946** *Nanking, China.* Lunched with Madame and Generalissimo Chiang Kai Chek.

**1946** *Prestwick, Scotland.* He stayed at Culzean Castle, Ayrshire, for some days. October 3. He stayed the weekend at Balmoral Castle and attended church at Crathie, Scotland.

**1946** *Sea Island, Georgia.* Cloister Hotel, Sea Island Drive, on holiday.

**1946** *Tokyo, Japan.* With General MacArthur.

**1946** *Wake Island.* He stayed at Kilauea military camp, 31 miles from Hilo.

**1947** *Brule River, Wisconsin.* On the Bois Brule River off US 2 west of Iron River, Superior and at Cedar Island, for fishing. Coolidge and Hoover also fished here.

**1948–1967** *Augusta, Georgia.* Augusta National Golf Club, northwest Augusta on Berckmans Road, on vacation. At first, he stayed in a cottage belonging to Robert T.

Jones and later in what was called Mamie's cabin, near the tenth tee. He visited Augusta forty-five times. The last time was October in 1967.

**1951–** *Versailles, France.* He spent a few days in the Trianon Palace Hotel.

**1951–** *Washington, D.C.* Statler Hotel, Sixteenth and K Streets, NW.

**1952** *July Chicago, Illinois.* Blackstone Hotel, 636 South Michigan Avenue, for the Republican National Convention.

**1952** *U.S. Presidential campaign.* Whistle stop. The engineer on his special train started the train before he could finish his speech. New York City, New York. Hotel Commodore (now Grand Hyatt), 125 East Forty-second Street, northwest corner at Lexington Avenue. Campaign headquarters. In November, he listened to the election returns which gave him a landslide victory. Fraser (two miles west), Colorado at Aksel Nielsen's Byers Peaks Ranch, about 72 miles west of Denver, fishing for Colorado trout. He met Nixon here after the Republican National Convention. He stayed for seven days. September 20. St. Louis, Missouri. Hotel Statler. September. Cleveland, Ohio. Carter Hotel, Prospect Street near East Ninth Street, while listening to the Nixon "Checker's" speech. Wheeling, West Virginia. McLure Hotel, 1200 Market Street. He met Nixon after the "Checkers" speech.

**1953–1961** *Camp David, Maryland.* Catoctin Mountain National Park, Maryland 77. The Presidential retreat is in the middle of the park.

**1953–1961** *Milestone Plantation, near Thomasville, Georgia.* The George M. Humphrey estate was his favorite hunting retreat during his presidency, and he spent three to twelve days here every year hunting quail. It is 4.8 miles east of Thomasville on Metcalf Road.

**1953** *Annapolis, Maryland.* U.S. Naval Academy.

**1953** *Defiance, Ohio.* He laid the cornerstone for the library at Defiance College.

**1953** *Hanover, New Hampshire.* Dartmouth College Commencement.

**1953** *Mount Rushmore, South Dakota.*

**1953** *New Orleans, Louisiana.* Jackson Square address, celebrating the 150th anniversary of Louisiana Purchase.

**1953** *New York City.* He addressed the General Assembly of the United Nations.

**1953** *Ottawa, Canada.* He spoke to joint session of Parliament.

**1953** *Oyster Bay, New York.* Dedication of Theodore Roosevelt's Sagamore Hill as a national shrine.

**1953** *Rapid City, South Dakota.* Dedication of Ellsworth Air Force Base.

**1953** *Tucker's Town, Bermuda.* The Mid-Ocean Club for a weekend summit meeting.

**1953** *Washington, D.C.* Dedication of the American Red Cross Chapter House.

**1953** *Williamsburg, Virginia.* He made a speech at the historic House of Burgesses and also spoke at the College of William and Mary.

**1954** *Abilene, Kansas.* Ground breaking ceremony for Eisenhower Library followed by luncheon at Sunflower Hotel.

**1954** *Chestertown, Maryland.* Washington College Commencement.

**1954** *Hartford, Connecticut.* Convocation, Trinity College.

**1954** *Indianapolis, Indiana.* He gave an address at Butler University. The second half of October, he travelled more than ten thousand miles and made more than forty speeches, mostly in the eastern half of the United States.

**1954** *Lexington, Kentucky.* Transylvania College for a speech honoring the 175th anniversary of the college. He went to Ft. Knox nearby and watched a military display from a reviewing stand at Brooks

Field. Earlier he was in Hodgenville, Kentucky, speaking at the Lincoln Log Cabin Memorial.

**1954**    *New York City, New York.* He Addressed the Bicentennial dinner at Columbia University and stayed at the Waldorf-Astoria Hotel.

**1954**    *Palm Springs, California.* Brief vacation as a guest of P.G. Hoffman, but he stayed at Smoke Tree ranch of P. E. Helms, a block away, because of better security. He played golf at Tamarisk Country Club. While in Palm Springs, one of the porcelain caps on a front tooth chipped off and he had to see a dentist there.

**1954**    *Richmond, Virginia.* St. Paul's Episcopal Church, honoring Mother's Day. Later, at Fredericksburg, Virginia, he laid a wreath at the Mary Bell Washington Monument.

**1954**    *Springfield, Illinois.* He spoke at the State Fair Pavilion and later laid a wreath at the tomb of Abraham Lincoln. He was the second president to attend the fair. Hayes was the first (1879). He had lunch with Governor Stratton at the Governor's Mansion.

**1954**    *Walla Walla, Washington.* Dedication of McNary Dam.

**1954**    *Washington, D.C.* Capitol Rotunda, dedication of frieze.

**1954**    *Washington, D.C.* He laid a wreath at the Lincoln Memorial.

**1955**    *Concord, New Hampshire.* Remarks at State Capitol.

**1955**    *Denver, Colorado.* Fitzsimmons Army Medical Center. While on vacation at the home of his mother-in-law, he suffered a heart attack.

**1955**    *Franconia, New Hampshire.* Ceremony commemorating discovery of Old Man of the Mountain.

**1955**    *Geneva, Switzerland.* Summit meeting. He stayed at Creux de Genthod, a villa on Lake Geneva. The meetings were held in Palais des Nations and the Reactor Building.

**1955**    *San Francisco, California.* Opera House. Tenth Anniversary of the United Nations.

**1955**    *Washington, D.C.* Walter Reed Medical Center, dedication of Armed Forces Institute of Pathology.

**1955**    *West Point, New York.* Alumni luncheon at Washington Hall and speech at graduation ceremony.

**1955**    U*niversity Park, Pennsylvania.* Penn State University Centennial Commencement.

**1956**    *New York City, New York.* Address at Madison Square Garden.

**1956**    *San Francisco, California.* St. Francis Hotel for the Republican National Convention at the Cow Palace, where he accepted renomination for president.

**1956**    *Waco, Texas.* Commencement address, Baylor University.

**1956**    *Washington, D.C.* Dedication of the AFL- CIO Building.

**1957–1960**    *Washington, D.C.* National Airport. He welcomed: the King of Saudi Arabia, the President of Vietnam, Queen Elizabeth and Prince Philip, the King of Morocco, the Nixons home from South America, the President of Argentina, President of El Salvador, the President of Ireland, Winston Churchill, the King of Belgium, the President of Mexico, the President of Columbia, Charles DeGaulle, the King and Queen of Nepal, the King and Queen of Thailand, and the King and Queen of Denmark.

**1957**    *Providence, Rhode Island.* Old Colony House on Washington Square.

**1957**    *Washington, D.C.* American University Commencement and ground breaking ceremony for the School of International Service. June 28. Washington, D.C. He spoke at opening of the Islamic Center.

**1958**    *Baltimore, Maryland.* Commencement, Johns Hopkins. He was accompanied by British Prime Minister Macmillan.

**1958** *Emmitsburg, Maryland.* Sesquicentennial Commencement, Mount St. Mary's College. June 4. Annapolis, Maryland. Commencement, U.S. Naval Academy.

**1958** *New York City, New York.* Hotel Astor, for first Football Hall of Fame dinner.

**1958** *Newport, Rhode Island.* Summer White House, Fort Adams, Harrison Avenue at Commandant's Residence Quarters No. 1 where he lodged.

**1958** *Washington, D.C.* Dedication of the Edmund A. Walsh School of Foreign Service of Georgetown University.

**1959** *Ankara, Turkey.* He met with President Bayar at his Palace.

**1959** *Annapolis, Maryland.* Dedication, Francis Scott Key Memorial Auditorium, St. John's College.

**1959** *Athens, Greece.* He addressed the Greek Parliament and lunched at the Royal Palace.

**1959** *Casablanca, Morocco.* He lunched at the King's Palace.

**1959** *Gettysburg, Pennsylvania.* Temporary White House office in Hotel Gettysburg.

**1959** *Gettysburg, Pennsylvania.* Convocation, Gettysburg College.

**1959** *Kabul, Afghanistan.* Lunch at Chilstoon Palace with the King.

**1959** *Karachi, Pakistan.* He stayed at the residence of U.S. Ambassador Rountree and visited Peshawar.

**1959** *Langley, Virginia.* Cornerstone laying ceremony, CIA Building.

**1959** *London, England.* He met with Prime Minister Macmillan at No. 10, Downing Street.

**1959** *Madrid, Spain.* He dined at the Oriete Palace and breakfasted at the Pardo Palace.

**1959** *New Delhi, India.* Joint session of the Indian Parliament. He visited and dined at Rashtrapati Bhavan, the residence of President Prasad. He made a side trip to visit the Taj Mahal in Agra.

**1959** *Paris, France.* He spoke at the Hotel de Ville and the Palais de Chaillot and visited SHAPE headquarters. He was an overnight guest of General DeGaulle at Rambouillet.

**1959** *Rome, Italy.* Meetings with President Gronchi at Quirinal Palace.

**1959** *Tehran, Iran.* He lunched with the Shah at the Marble Palace where there was a presentation of gifts in the Crystal Room.

**1959** *Tunis, Tunisia.* He met with President Bourguiba at his palace, La Marsa, near Tunis.

**1959** *Washington, D.C.* Dedication, Robert A. Taft Memorial Bell Tower on the Capitol Grounds.

**1959** *Washington, D.C.* Simon Bolivar Plaza, Virginia Avenue and Eighteenth Street, NW. Dedication of Bolivar statue from Venezuela.

**1959** *Washington, D.C.* Cornerstone laying at east front of the Capitol for extension of the Capitol.

**1960** *Alaska.* He was the first president to visit Alaska following statehood. He spent the night in the Chateau, distinguished visitors quarters on Elmendorf Air Force Base, Anchorage.

**1960** *Buenos Aires, Argentina.* He addressed the National Congress and had dinner at the Plaza Hotel.

**1960** *Santiago, Chile.* He visited to President's residence, La Moneda Palace.

**1960** *Chicago, Illinois.* Union Stockyards Amphitheater, for the Republican National Convention.

**1960** *Huntsville, Alabama.* Dedication, George C. Marshall Space Flight Center, Huntsville Administration Bldg. October 18.

**1960** *Lisbon, Portugal.* He stayed at the

Queluz Palace and had dinner with President Salazar at the Ajuda Palace.

**1960** *Manila, the Philippines.* Dinner at Malacanang Palace.

**1960** *Montevideo, Uruguay.* He spoke at the obelisk, a memorial to constitutional government, and at the Legislative Palace. He was entertained at the Presidential residence.

**1960** *Red Wing, Minnesota.* Dedication, Hiawatha Bridge, intersection of Main and Broad Streets.

**1960** *Rio de Janeiro, Brazil.* He spoke to a joint session of the Brazilian Congress at Tiradentes Palace and to members of the Court in the Federal Room of the Supreme Court Building. In Sao Paulo, he made an address at Fasano Restaurant.

**1960** *Seoul, South Korea.* He addressed the National Assembly.

**1960** *Newport, Rhode Island.* Dedication of Eisenhower Park on Washington Square.

**1960** *Taipei, Taiwan.* He spoke at a mass rally.

**1960** *Washington, D.C.* Dedication, Veterans of Foreign Wars Memorial Building, Maryland Avenue, near the Capitol. February

**1960** *Washington, D.C.* Fort McNair. Dedication of a new building at the Industrial College of the Armed Forces.

**1964** *San Francisco, California.* Cow Palace, Geneva Avenue, the Republican National Convention and the nomination of Barry Goldwater. He stayed at the St. Francis Hotel.

*Dwight Eisenhower burial site.*

## DEATH

Eisenhower died on March 28, 1969, in Washington, D.C., at the Walter Reed Army Medical Center. He died a little after noon on Friday. The immediate family was at his bedside. He left an estate valued at nearly three million dollars.

## FUNDERAL

There was a 3-day state funeral with a cost to the Federal Government of $259,734. The army took over, and his body was dressed in the uniform jacket he had made famous. He was placed in an eighty dollar military coffin. He lay in state in the Bethlehem Chapel at the National Cathedral and then was taken to the Capitol Rotunda. He was the eighth president to lie in state there. Although the coffin remained closed, more than 100,000 people visited the Rotunda. Nixon delivered the eulogy—the first time a sitting president has done so for another president. The body was taken back to the National Cathedral for funeral services. President Nixon, ex-president Lyndon Johnson and future president Ford attended. Ex-president Truman was unable to come. Eighteen heads of state or government attended. The coffin was taken to Union Station and put on a special railway car to Abilene.

## BURIAL

He is buried in Abilene, Kansas, at 201 Southeast Fourth Street, east of Kansas High-way 15, and two miles south of Abilene exiting from I-70. Burial services were held in the Eisenhower Center Chapel. The Fifth Army Band provided the music at the grave side. President Nixon and ex-president Johnson attended.

## BIBLIOGRAPHY

Lyon, Peter. *Eisenhower, Portrait of the Hero*. Boston, Little, Brown and Company, 1974.

Miller, Merle. *Ike the Soldier: As They Knew Him*. New York, G. P. Putnam's Sons, 1987.

Neal, Steve. *The Eisenhowers: Reluctant Dynasty*. Garden City, NY, Doubleday, 1978.

# JOHN FITZGERALD KENNEDY

## 1917–1963
### 35TH PRESIDENT 1961–1963: DEMOCRATIC PARTY

John Fitzgerald Kennedy was on born May 29, 1917, to Joseph P. Kennedy and Rose Fitzgerald Kennedy, daughter of a Boston mayor. He was the first president to be born in the twentieth century.

*"The journey of a thousand miles begins with one step."*

## CHARACTERISTICS

Kennedy was an unusually handsome man at the time he became president. He was just over 6′ tall and weighing one hundred and seventy pounds. He had green eyes and thick reddish-brown hair. While he never wore glasses in public, he had worn reading glasses since the age of thirteen. His right leg was three-fourths inch longer than his left, and he wore corrective shoes to compensate. He made friends easily and had a great sense of humor. His time in the White House was often called the Age of Camelot because of the charm and grace of the Kennedy couple. He had an explosive temper, which he managed to keep under control in public. He liked golfing and swimming. He smoked cigars, was a light drinker, and liked beer. He liked ice cream with chocolate sauce and ate it by the gallon. His favorite songs included "Stardust" and "Stormy Weather."

## A Life in Review

**Birth:** May 29, 1917; Brookline, MA

**Died:** November 22, 1963; Dallas, TX

**Married:** Jacqueline Lee Bouvier; September 12, 1953; 2 sons, 1 daughter

### Career
**1941–1945** Served in U.S. Navy

**1945** Newspaper correspondent

**1946–1953** Member U.S. Congress

**1953–1961** Member U.S. Senate

### Administration Events
**1961** First live television press conference

    Peace Corps created

    Bay of Pigs failure

    Berlin Wall erected

**1962** John Glen orbited the earth

    Supreme Court declared school prayers unconstitutional

    Cuban missile crisis

## Birthplace

Kennedy was born in Brookline, Massachusetts, at 83 Beals Street, in an upstairs bedroom of a modest house.

## Baptism

He was baptized on June 19, 1917, in Brookline, at St. Aidan's Roman Catholic Church, 158 Pleasant Street. The font used at his baptism is still in the Church.

## Church

As a child, he faithfully attended mass every Sunday and was an altar boy at St. Aidan's Roman Catholic Church. He was the first Roman Catholic to become president. Quoting from an interview with a friend, "We were both Catholics and we talked about it a lot. I can clearly recall sitting in a jeep one night . . . having a long discussion. Jack had lost his religion . . . He said he'd work it out someday."

**1917–1927** *Brookline, Massachusetts.* St. Aidan's Roman Catholic Church, 158 Pleasant Street.

**1927–1930** *Riverdale, New York.* Local Roman Catholic Church.

**1929–1963** *Hyannis Port, Massachusetts.* Church of St. Francis Xavier, 347 South Street. Summer home.

**1930–1941** *Bronxville, New York.* St. Joseph's Roman Catholic Church.

**1930–1963** *Palm Beach, Florida.* St. Edward's Catholic Church, Sunrise Avenue and North County Road. He attended here when he was in Florida.

**1938–1940** *New York City, New York.* Brompton Oratory, Brompton Road.

**1942** *Charleston, South Carolina.* Catholic Cathedral, Broad Street, which he attended during his time with the navy.

**1947–1963** *Washington, D.C.* Holy Trinity, 3513 N Street, NW. John F. Kennedy sat in various pews, sometimes up front, sometimes in the gallery; no one pew was designated as the president's pew. (Lincoln and Hoover attended funeral services in this church, dedicated in 1851.)

**1953–** *New York City, New York.* St. Ignatius Loyola Roman Catholic Church, Eighty-fourth and Park Avenue. This was his wife's childhood church, and he attended with her from time to time. Her funeral was held here on May 23, 1994.

**1961–1963** *Washington, D.C.* St. Matthew's Church, 1725 Rhode Island Avenue, NW. His funeral was held here in 1963.

# EDUCATION

**1923–1924** *Brookline, Massachusetts.* Edward Devotion School, 347 Harvard Street, near the corner of Stedman Street. He attended his first year of elementary school here.

**1924–1927** *Brookline, Massachusetts.* Dexter School, on Freeman Street (which has now moved elsewhere). He attended until the family left Brookline. The Park Service brochure at the Kennedy National Historic Site, 83 Beals Street has a map of the local area. (It was called the Noble and Greenough School.)

**1927–1930** *Riverdale, New York.* Riverdale Country Day School on Fieldston Road, where he finished grades 4 through 6.

**1930–1931** *New Milford, Connecticut.* Canterbury (Catholic) School, until an attack of appendicitis forced his withdrawal in the spring of 1931. It is just above the town with a commanding view of the countryside and is now a coed school. He attended the Canterbury School Chapel where attendance was required every morning and evening. While at Canterbury, he roomed in North House.

**1931–1935** *Wallingford, Connecticut.* The Choate School (now Choate Rosemary Hall), a few miles north of New Haven and about sixty miles from the Kennedy mansion in Bronxville, New York. As a member of the Muckers Club, he was involved in several altercations with school authorities and narrowly missed being expelled. His father helped his standing somewhat by donating a swimming pool to the school. He finished Choate 65 out of 110. Chapel services were held each weekday at 7:20 P.M. in the Chapel, and attendance was required.

From 1931 to 1932, he stayed in Choate House (known as School House) on the first floor. From 1932 to 1933, he stayed in East Cottage on the second floor, southeast corner. During his year here, he wrote a letter to the authorities complaining about the path to East College. From 1933 to 1934, he stayed in the West Wing on the second floor, farthest west, south side. From 1934 to 1935, he stayed in the West Wing, in what is now part of a faculty apartment.

**1935** *London, England.* London School of Economics, with Harold Laski during the summer.

**1935** *Princeton, New Jersey.* Princeton University for a few months; a recurrence of jaundice forced his withdrawal. While at Princeton, he stayed in South Reunion Hall, next to Nassau Hall, on the fifth floor, and roomed with Lem Billings and Rip Horton. It was demolished in the 1960s. While at Princeton, he regularly attended mass at a Catholic church off campus.

**1936–1940** *Cambridge, Massachusetts.* Harvard University. He graduated cum laude with a major in political science. He toured Europe at the end of his sophomore year and spent the second semester of his junior year working as secretary to his father, who was the Ambassador to Great Britain. He had government class with Professor Hanford in Sever Hall. From 1936 to 1937, he roomed in 32 Weld Hall in the Yard, at the south boundary of the Old Yard. From 1937 to 1938, he roomed in 123 Winthrop House (Gore). As a member of the Spee Club he ate almost all his meals in their building on the corner of Mt. Auburn and Holyoke Streets. In 1938, he stayed in a larger room at F-14 in Winthrop House.

**1940–1941** *Stanford, California.* Stanford Business School. He studied briefly as a part-time student before touring South America. When he first arrived, he stayed at the President Hotel and then moved to The Cottage behind his landlady's, (Gertrude

*Birthplace of John Kennedy in Massachusetts.*

Gardiner), house at 624 Mayfield Road. He paid $60 a month. To eat he often went to L'Omlette, a French restaurant, and to Dinah's Shack. L'Omelette was relocated to 4170 El Camino Real from a site farther south on El Camino Real. He spent one weekend at Randolph Hearst's ranch at Wynton. When he came back he said that on the sumptuous, huge dinner table in the banquet hall, he saw a bottle of catsup!

**1942**   *Evanston, Illinois.* He was transferred to sea duty and went to Northwestern Uni-

versity to attend Midshipmen's School, which he completed on September 27, 1942. Classes were held in Tower Hall. He lived in Abbott Hall facing Lake Michigan.

## MARRIAGE AND HONEYMOON

Kennedy met Jacqueline Bouvier for the first time at the Charles and Martha Bartlett home, in Washington, D.C., on May 8, 1952. He proposed by telegram. They were married on September 12, 1953, in Newport, Rhode Island, at St. Mary's Church, Spring Street. The reception was held at the Hammersmith Farm.

The first night of the honeymoon was spent at the Waldorf-Astoria Hotel in New York City, followed by a few weeks in Acapulco, Mexico, where they stayed at the villa of the Mexican president, and a final few days in the home of his friend, Red Fay and his wife, in Monterey, California.

# HOMES/LODGINGS

**1917–** *Winthrop, Massachusetts.* His grandparents' house (P.J. Kennedy) at 165 Webster Street was a 3- story house with a front yard that faced the Boston city skyline.

**1917–1921** *Brookline, Massachusetts.* 83 Beals Street.

**1920s** *New York City, New York.* Gramercy Park Hotel, where he stayed at times with his father on the second floor.

**1921–1927** *Brookline, Massachusetts.* Northeast corner of Naples Road and Abbottsford Road. This was a gabled two-story colonial-style house.

**1927–1930** *Riverdale, New York.* 5040 Independence Avenue at West 252nd Street, on the southeast corner.

**1927–1963** *Hyannis Port, Massachusetts.* The home where the family spent their summers is on Cape Cod. It was a 15-room house, which his father bought for $25,000.

**1930–1941** *Bronxville, Westchester County, New York.* 294 Pondfield Road, in a very fashionable suburb of New York City, where they had a palatial house. It was a 20-room, red-brick colonial originally built for Anheuser Busch. It was sold and later torn down. Thereafter, when his father was in New York City, he took a suite at the Waldorf-Astoria.

**1933–1963** *Palm Beach, Florida.* 1095 North Ocean Drive (North County Road)

on the ocean at the north end of the island. He was here in the winter.

**1934–1935** *Marwood, was a Maryland estate with a 25-room house which his father rented.* It overlooked the Potomac. Kennedy spent occasional weekends.

**1938** *London, England.* 14 Princes Gate, Knightsbridge, when his father was U.S. Ambassador to England.

**1941–1942** *Washington, D.C.* Dorchester House 502, 2480 Sixteenth Street, NW, on the west side of Sixteenth Street between Kalorama Road and Euclid Street. Here he had his affair with the beautiful blonde Danish journalist, Inga Arvad, who lived at 1600 Sixteenth Street, NW.

**1942** *Charleston, South Carolina.* Mrs. G. A. Middleton, 48 Murray Road. He later rented a little house with some other officers on Sullivan's Island near the beach.

**1946** *Boston, Massachusetts.* Bellevue Hotel, 10-1/2 Beacon Street, near the State House. Jack's rooms were plain, but it constituted a legal residence within the district where he could begin his campaign.

**1946** *Boston, Massachusetts.* 122 Boudoin Street, apartment 36, near his office and which he maintained from the time he first ran for Congress.

**1947–1948** *Washington, D.C.* 1528 Thirty-first Street, NW. He rented and shared a three-story row house with his sister, Eunice.

**1949–1950** *Washington, D.C.* 1400 34th Street, NW.

**1951** *Washington, D.C.* 2808 P Street, NW.

**1951–1952** *Washington, D.C.* 3260 N Street, NW.

**1952–1953** *Washington, D.C.* 3271 P Street, NW.

**1953** *McLean, Virginia.* Following the honeymoon, the couple settled for several months at Merrywood, 700 Chain Bridge Road.

*Chain Bridge, home of John and Jacqueline Kennedy in McLean Virginia.*

---

**1953–1954** *Washington, D.C.* 3321 Dent Place, NW.

**1953–1956** *Hickory Hill, Virginia.* A three-story Georgian house at 1147 Chain Bridge Road, not far from Merrywood, and once owned by Supreme Court Justice Robert Jackson. Kennedy bought it for $125,000. After losing her baby in 1956, Jackie pushed to sell Hickory Hill to Robert Kennedy.

**1956** *Hyannis Port, Massachusetts.* Robert Kennedy bought a house next door to their parents', and Jack bought one next door to Bobby's.

**1957–1961** *Washington, D.C.* 3307 N Street, NW.

**1960–** *New York City, New York.* Hotel Carlyle, 35 East 76th Street and the northeast corner of Madison Avenue. He stayed here in his thirty-fifth floor suite when he was in New York City.

**1961–1963** *Washington, D.C.* The White House.

**1961–1963** *Camp David, Maryland.* The presidential retreat.

**1961–1963** *Palm Beach, Florida.* C. Michael Paul villa on North County Road, used as a holiday White House.

**1961–1962** *Glenora, Virginia.* Jackie took an estate as a family retreat from White House pressure, a week before the Bay of Pigs invasion of Cuba.

**1962** *Middleburg, Virginia.* They built a home of their own slightly south of the town center on Rattlesnake Mountain in 1963 (Atoka, near Wexford). While here, they attended mass in the Community Center in downtown Middleburg.

# WORK

**1938–1939** *London, England.* Junior diplomat (with his father, the Ambassador) and traveller.

**1941** *East Boston, Massachusetts.* Columbia Trust Company Bank.

**1941–1942** *Washington, D.C.* Office of Naval Intelligence, Constitution Avenue and Eighteenth Street, NW, beginning October 27.

**1942** *Charleston, South Carolina.* Office of Naval Intelligence at Sixth Naval District headquarters to lecture to workers in defense plants. He described his post as "Siberia."

**1942** *Melville, Rhode Island.* PT Training School. He graduated on December 12. After graduation, he was an instructor for a brief time at the Training School. While in Rhode Island, he often ate at the Lobster Pot in Newport and at the Bacardi Room in Providence. He stayed in a quonset hut.

**1943** *Tulagi near Guadacanal.* In command of PT 109. He lived in hut on Florida Island.

**1943** *Russell Islands.* He was quartered in an old farmhouse. He was in the Solomon Islands, including Blackett Strait, and had nine months in the Pacific.

**1943** *Blackett Strait.* Cruising back toward the base at Rendova.

**1945–1946** *San Francisco, California.* He was a journalist with the Hearst newspapers and stayed at the Palace Hotel. In 1945 he covered the parliamentary election and stayed at the Grosvenor House Hotel in London. On a side trip, he went to Ireland. He was in Potsdam with Truman and Eisenhower. He made a tour of Germany and visited Bremen, Bremerhaven, Kiel, Frankfurt, and Berchtesgaden, Hitler's Eagle's Nest.

**1947–1953** *Washington, D.C.* Member of Congress from Massachusetts. In his first term he was assigned a two-room suite in the Old House Office Building, Room 322.

**1953–1961** *Washington, D.C.* U.S. Senator from Massachusetts. Room 362, Senate Office Building.

**1961–1963** *Washington, D.C.* The White House.

# TRAVEL/VISITS

**1930** *Danbury, Connecticut.* Danbury Hospital, for appendectomy.

**1934–** *Boston, Massachusetts.* Peter Brent Brigham Hospital, 75 Francis Street, for a series of tests.

**1936** *Benson, Arizona.* Jay Six Ranch, owned by Jack Speiden, to regain his health.

**1937** *Europe.* He sailed on the George Washington with a friend to Le Havre. On the way to Paris, he visited Mont Saint Michel, Rouen, Beauvais (La Cotelette Inn), Soissons and Chemin des Dames, Rheims (Hotel Majesty), Pompernelle, Pompernay (visited champagne cellars), Chateau Thiery, and Paris. In Paris, he stayed at the Hotel Montana at the Gare du Nord. He visited all the major sites, including Notre Dame, the Louvre, Napoleon's Tomb, the top of the Eiffel Tower, Concierge, the Moulin Rogue, and the Cafe of Artists. He visited Ver-

sailles, the Trianon, and the cathedral at Chartres; driving south through the Loire Valley, he stopped at Orleans and attended mass at the cathedral. At Chambord, he swam in the Loire and went on to visit Bois, Amboise, Chenonceau, Angouleme, Tours, and Poitiers. He tried to enter Spain but was turned back by guards at the border. He attended a bull fight at Biarritz but did not like the cruelty. In Saint-Jean-de-Luz he stayed with Count Alexis de Pourtes for a week. He attended mass where Louis XIV married Marie Theresa. He visited Lourdes, Toulouse, Carcassonne, and Cannes. In Monte Carlo, he stayed in a double room in a seedy hotel for sixty cents a day. He entered Italy on August 1 and went to Genoa and Milan, where he saw da Vinci's *"Last Supper."* He climbed Mt. Vesuvius, visited Naples, Capri, Milan, Pisa, Florence, Venice, and Rome. According to his companion, he said prayers on his knees every night. At the Vatican, he had an audience with Pope Pius XI, attended a Mussolini rally, and visited all the major sites of Rome. He expressed some disappointment with Florence. In Venice, he stayed at the Excelsior Hotel. He crossed the Brenner Pass in their "old jalopy" and stayed at the Youth Hostel in Innsbruck. In Germany, he visited Garmisch, Obergammerau, Munich, Nuremburg, Wurtemburg, Frankfurt-on-Rhine, and attended mass at the cathedral in Cologne. After Germany he went to Utrecht, Doorn (the Kaiser's home in exile), Amsterdam and the Hague in Holland, Antwerp and Ostend in Belgium, Calais and Boulogne in France, and back to London.

**1937** *London, England.* He stayed at 17 Talbot Square.

**1937** *London, England.* U.S. Embassy, 9 Prince's Gate (a house J. P. Morgan had donated to the American people).

**1937** *Sussex, England.* Guest of Sir James Calder at Herstmonceux Castle at Kinrosshire.

**1937**    *Paris, France.* He stayed with Ambassador Bullitt and at Hotel Montana at Gare du Nord.

**1937**    *Venice, Italy.* Excelsior Hotel. Innsbruck, Austria. A Youth Hostel.

**1938**    *Europe.* In Paris, he stayed with Ambassador William C. Bullitt and had lunch with the Lindbergs, of whom he wrote, "the most attractive couple I've ever seen." From Paris he went to Germany and Poland, where he stayed for several weeks with Ambassador Biddle. He crossed into the Baltic states and on to Leningrad, Moscow, and the Crimea. He went by steamer from the Crimea to Istanbul and on to Palestine and Egypt. From the Middle East, he went to the Balkans, stopping in Bucharest and Belgrade, and returned to London. From Vienna, he went to Prague and Berlin, where he stayed at the Hotel Excelsior (August). At the end of summer 1939, his father sent him to Glasgow, Scotland, to help the American survivors of the Athenia.

**1938**    *London, England.* He met the King and Queen, Queen Mother Mary, and Princess Elizabeth. He thought Princess Elizabeth "had eyes for him." He visited Churchill's estate at Blenheim and attended a reception at 10 Downing Street in London.

**1938**    *Rome, Italy.* The whole Kennedy family went to the coronation of Pope Pius XII, who was a friend of the family, and afterwards they had a private audience.

**1939**    *London, England.* House of Commons. He witnessed the formal declaration of war against Germany.

**1940**    *Boston, Massachusetts.* Lahey Clinic, 41 Mall Road, Burlington.

**1940**    *San Simeon, California.* He visited the estate of newspaper magnate, Hearst.

**1941**    *Boston, Massachusetts.* New England Baptist Hospital, 125 Parker Hill Avenue. He also often visited the Parker House Hotel, 60 School Street, and the Union Oyster House, Union and Marshall Streets.

**1942**    *Aiken, South Carolina.* Canebrake, 531 Coker Springs Road (at Easy Street and Whiskey Road intersection). He came here to recuperate from his back problem. He attended a house party at the home of George Mead.

**1943**    *San Francisco, California.* Mark Hopkins Hotel, southeast corner of California and Mason Streets, Nob Hill, on the way to service in the Pacific.

**1944**    *Boston, Massachusetts.* Chelsea Naval Hospital, for out-patient treatment for his back.

**1944**    *Palm Beach, Florida.* He was hospitalized in St. Mary's Hospital for a high fever.

**1944**    *Phoenix, Arizona.* Dude Ranch outside Phoenix, to recuperate from illness.

**1944**    *Rochester, Minnesota.* Mayo Clinic, for physical examination.

**1945**    *Phoenix, Arizona.* Castle Hot Springs Hotel resort. Later, he rented a cottage nearby. He also stayed at the Arizona Biltmore and the Camelback Inn in Phoenix.

**1945–1946**    *San Francisco, California.* Palace Hotel, southwest corner of Market and New Montgomery Streets, while serving as a journalist with the Chicago Herald-American.

**1946**    *Boston, Massachusetts.* Ritz-Carlton Hotel, 15 Arlington Street. He stayed here during his political campaign. On July 4, he made an Independence Day speech in Faneuil Hall.

**1947**    *London, England.* Grosvenor House. Later at the Claridge Hotel. He also visited Potsdam on this trip. While in London, he became seriously ill and was put in London Clinic. Near Peterborough, England, he visited the Fitzwilliam ancestral estate, Milton. He visited Lismore, the Duke of Devonshire's magnificent estate in County Waterford, Ireland. He drove out to New Ross,

*Family home of Jacqueline Bouvier Kennedy in Newport, Rhode Island.*

Ireland, to find the "original Kennedys." The small village with the ancestral home with its whitewashed walls and thatched roof and all the barnyard animals clustered around the front door fascinated him.

**1947** *White Sulphur Springs, West Virginia.* Greenbrier Hotel, for a family gathering.

**1953–** *Newport, Rhode Island.* Hammersmith Farm (Auchincloss estate). He visited Jackie's family, where he was relegated to a tiny bedroom before his marriage.

**1956** *Chicago, Illinois.* Palmer House Hotel, 17 East Monroe, for the Democratic National Convention, International Amphitheatre.

**1960** *Anchorage, Alaska.* Westward Hotel. Reception at Edgewater Motel on Seward Highway.

**1960** *Charleston, West Virginia.* Kanawha Hotel, corner of Summers and Virginia Streets. Later, he spoke at the state Capitol.

**1960** *Houston, Texas.* Crystal Ballroom of the Rice Hotel. He met the question of his Catholic religion head on with a major speech on separation of church and state to the Greater Houston Ministerial Association. Lyndon Johnson also attended the speech. Kennedy was also at the Rice Hotel in November 1963.

**1960** *Independence, Missouri.* He visited President Truman at his home. In two months, he appeared and made campaign speeches in two hundred and thirty-seven cities. In one week alone, he visited twenty-seven states.

**1960** *Key Biscayne, Florida.* He met Nixon following the election.

**1960** *Los Angeles, California.* His headquarters were in the Biltmore Hotel, 506 West Grand. The Democratic National Convention, at which he received the Democratic nomination for president, was held in the Los Angeles Memorial Sports Arena, 3939 South Figueroa.

**1960**    *Stonewall, Texas.* He visited Lyndon Johnson.

**1960**    *Tampa, Florida.* There is a marker in front of the Courthouse at Madison and Pierce Streets, where he gave an address.

**1960**    *Warm Springs, Georgia.* He visited the home of Franklin D. Roosevelt.

**1961**    *Bogota, Columbia.* State dinner, San Carlos Palace.

**1961**    *London, England.* He attended the baptism of his niece at Westminster Cathedral, and a state dinner with Queen Elizabeth, at Buckingham Palace.

**1961**    *Mount Vernon, Virginia.* State dinner, given in honor of President Ayub Khan of Pakistan.

**1961**    *Big Cedar, Oklahoma.* Dedication of the Ouachita National Forest on Oklahoma 103.

**1961**    *New York City, New York.* He addressed the General Assembly of the United Nations.

**1961**    *Washington, D.C.* White House. He greeted Mrs. Jack Strawberry of Rome, Georgia, as the one millionth visitor in 1961.

**1962**    *Chantilly, Virginia.* Dedication of Dulles International Airport.

**1962**    *Miami Beach, Florida.* Fountainbleau Hotel.

**1962**    *New York City, New York.* Madison Square Garden, Marilyn Monroe sang "Happy Birthday" to him.

**1962**    *Newport, Rhode Island.* He met Pakistan President Ayub Khan at The Breakers.

**1962**    *Philadelphia, Pennsylvania.* He made an address at Independence Hall.

**1962**    *Pierre, South Dakota.* He dedicated the Oahe Dam on the Missouri River.

**1962**    *Washington, D.C.* Cornerstone laying, Rayburn House Office Building.

**1962**    *West Point, New York.* Field House, for graduation.

**1963–30**    *Birch Grove, Sussex.* Where he had meetings and stayed in the home of Prime Minister Macmillan.

**1963**    *Dublin, Ireland.* He visited New Ross and Redmond Place in Wexford.

**1963**    *Arlington National Cemetery, Virginia.* He dedicated Paderewski's grave marker.

**1963**    *Berlin, Germany.* On June 26, he spoke at the steps of the Schoneberger Rathaus, Rudolph Wilde Platz, and used the famous line "Ich bin ein Berliner."

**1963**    *Charleston, West Virginia.* He spoke at the State Capitol.

**1963**    *Chicago, Illinois.* He dedicated O'Hare International Airport.

**1963**    *Colorado Springs, Colorado.* Graduation, U.S. Air Force Academy, Falcon Stadium. He also visited the Missile Range at White Sands, New Mexico.

**1963**    *Fort Smith, Arkansas.* He visited old Fort Smith.

**1963**    *Fort Worth, Texas.* New Regency Hotel, Commerce and Eighth, where he spent his last night before going to Dallas. Rally in front of the Texas Hotel. Breakfast and talk at the hotel to the Chamber of Commerce.

**1963**    *Houston, Texas.* Dinner at the Coliseum, in honor of Representative Albert Thomas.

**1963**    *Maryland-Delaware border.* To dedicate the Delaware-Maryland Turnpike.

**1963**    *Milford, Pennsylvania.* He dedicated the Pinchot Institute.

**1963**    *New York City, New York.* He dedicated the East Coast Memorial in Battery Park.

**1963**    *Washington D.C.* Union Station, to welcome Haile Selassie of Ethiopia.

**1963**    *Washington, D.C.* American University. Commencement address, John M. Reeves Athletic Field.

*Grave of John Kennedy.*

**1963**  *San Diego, California.* San Diego State College, commencement. He received an honorary degree, the first given by San Diego State.

**1963**  *Dunganstown, Ireland.* Kennedy ancestral home site.

**1963**  *Honolulu, Hawaii.* He spoke in the Lawn House at the Hawaiian Village Hotel.

# DEATH

Kennedy was shot at 12:30 P.M., as his car passed by the Texas School Book Depository, in Dallas, Texas. He died at 1:00 P.M., at the Parkland Memorial Hospital, 5201 Harry Hines Boulevard, Trauma Room Number One. Although he always thought he would die young because of his severe back problem and Addison's disease, he was killed by an assassin, Lee Harvey Oswald. Vernon O'Neal's Funeral Home, Oak Lawn, Dallas, was called to provide a casket and to make the initial arrangements. O'Neal brought a solid bronze casket, but it was damaged in transit to Washington, and a second coffin was obtained. To prevent the original coffin from being placed on exhibition in the future, it was not returned to O'Neal.

After the flight on Airforce 1 to Andrews Airforce Base, he was taken by ambulance to the Bethesda Naval Hospital morgue where the autopsy and embalming took place. Washington, D.C. Gawler Funeral Home, Wisconsin Avenue. Gawler was requested to bring a replacement coffin which was solid African mahogany. Although he was cosmetically fixed for viewing, the family decided on a closed casket. He was dressed in a blue-gray suit with blue tie with white dots. At a last viewing by his widow, she removed a lock of his hair. Last letters, written by the children to their dead father, were placed in his coffin. He left an estate valued at millions of dollars.

# FUNERAL

After the body was flown from Dallas, he lay in state in the East Room of the White House, and a private mass was celebrated there. Later, he lay in state at the Rotunda at the Capitol. More than 250,000 mourners passed by the flag-draped coffin with the honor guard around it. Kennedy was the sixth to lie in state here. On Monday, November 25, the casket was taken from the Rotunda and went by caisson to St. Matthew's Cathedral for services led by the Cardinal. The funeral was attended by 11 heads of state and other royalty. President Johnson, ex-presidents Truman and Eisenhower and future president Nixon attended. Passages of the Bible were read and included Psalm 130 and a Kennedy favorite, Ecclesiastes, chapter 3. Many hymns were sung, including the Navy Hymn, "Eternal Father," "Abide with Me," and "Ave Maria."

# BURIAL

The Arlington National Cemetery lies west of Washington, D.C., across the Potomac River from the Lincoln Memorial. An eternal flame, lit by Mrs. Kennedy, marks the grave which lies just below the Lee Mansion. She was buried beside him and their two infant children in May 1994.

# BIBLIOGRAPHY

Blair, Joan and Clay Jr. *The Search for JFK.* New York, Berkley Publishing Corp., 1976.

Collier, Peter and Horowitz, David. *The Kennedys: An American Drama.* New York, Summit Books, 1984.

Manchester, William. *Portrait of a President: JFK in Profile.* Boston, Little, Brown, 1967.

Schlesinger, Arthur M. *A Thousand Days: John F. Kennedy in the White House.* Boston, Houghton, Mifflin, 1965.

# LYNDON BAINES JOHNSON

1908–1973
36TH PRESIDENT 1963–1969: DEMOCRATIC PARTY

Lyndon Johnson was born on the morning of August 27, 1908, in Stonewall, Texas, to Sam Ealy Johnson and Rebekah Baines Johnson.

## CHARACTERISTICS

He was one of the tallest presidents at 6'3", and he weighed 210 pounds. His black hair, which had become gray by the time he was president, was slicked down and combed straight back. He had brown eyes, prominent ears, a large nose, and a cleft chin. His chief relaxation was playing dominoes or a hand of poker with friends. He began smoking at an early age, and, at one time, he was a 3-pack-a-day smoker; he quit following a heart attack in 1955. He drank socially. He was a very outgoing person—almost embarrassingly so at times. Politicians and bureaucrats were called upon to swim naked with the president in the White House Pool, and members of the Cabinet and the White House staff were compelled to accompany their boss into the bathroom and continue their conversation.

*"In your time we have the opportunity to move not only toward the rich society and the powerful society, but upward to the Great Society."*

—*Speech at University of Michigan, May 22, 1964*

# A LIFE IN REVIEW

**Birth:** August 27, 1908; Stonewall, TX

**Died:** January 22, 1973; San Antonio, TX

**Married:** Claudia Alta (Lady Bird) Taylor; November 17, 1934; 2 daughters

## CAREER

**1928–1931** Teacher

**1932–1935** Secretary to U.S. Representative in Congress

**1935–1937** State director of National Youth Administration

**1937–1948** Member U.S. Congress

**1941–1942** Military Sevice U.S. Naval Reserve World War II

**1948–1961** Member U.S. Senate

**1961–1963** U.S. Vice President

## ADMINISTRATION EVENTS

**1964** New York City World's Fair opened

**1964** Civil Rights Act signed

**1965** "Great Society" program started

Beginning of American combat troops in Vietnam

First American to walk in space

**1966** U.S. bombs Hanoi

**1967** First human heart transplant

**1968** Martin Luther King, Jr. assassinated

Robert F. Kennedy assassinated

# BIRTHPLACE

Johnston was born in Stonewall, Texas, in Gillispie County, in a three-room house about a hundred yards from the Pedernales River.

# BAPTISM

In the summer of 1923, he was led with several others to Dallahite "baptizing hole" at Flat Creek. Outside Johnson City, where a highway bridge crosses the Pedernales River is where the Christian Church took converts for baptism.

# CHURCH

A great deal has been made of the fact that LBJ, who came from a long line of Baptists, joined the Christian Church (Disciples of Christ). His mother was a Baptist, but he had belonged to the International Convention of Christian Churches from his youth. This is the same group to which President Garfield belonged. His wife was Episcopalian, which is one reason Johnson so often worshiped in that church. During his years in public service, he made a practice of attending different Washington churches.

**1908–1973** *Johnson City, Texas.* First Christian Church, 401 East Sixth Street. This was his "home church" throughout his life.

**1908–** *Fredericksburg, Texas.* St. Barnabas Episcopal Church, 605 West Creek Street. This church is located within a few miles of the Stonewall ranch. He attended in both the old (still existing) and the new structures.

**1928–1929** *Cotulla, Texas.* Church of Christ, Medina and North Kerr.

**1930** *Pearsall, Texas.* Christian Church, 402 South Ash Street.

**1931–1969** *Washington, D.C.* National City Christian Church, Thomas Circle, Fourteenth Street at Massachusetts Avenue, NW.

**1935–1937** *Austin, Texas.* Central Christian Church, 1110 Guadalupe. This two-year period is the only break in his Washington service between 1931 and 1969.

**1937–1969**  *Washington, D.C.* St. John's Episcopal Church, Lafayette Square. Mrs. Johnson often attended here.

**1937–**  *Washington, D.C.* St. Mark's Episcopal Church, 301 A Street, NE. He often attended here while he was Vice President. The block on which it was located was slated for demolition. He attended a service here on the day of Kennedy's funeral.

**1937–**  *Washington, D.C.* St. Dominic's Catholic Church, 630 W Street, SW.

**1937–**  *Stonewall, Texas.* St. Francis Xavier Catholic Church, Ranch Road, where he was particularly close to the pastor.

# EDUCATION

**1908–1913**  *Stonewall, Texas.* From his mother, he learned the alphabet at two and learned to read at four.

**1913–1920**  *Stonewall, Texas.* Junction School, a little country schoolhouse where the teacher taught all eight grades in one room.

**1920–1921**  *Stonewall, Texas.* Stonewall and Albert Schools, about four miles from home. He rode a donkey to school and felt better about it when his mother told him Jesus rode into Jerusalem on an ass. He completed the eighth grade here.

**1921–1924**  *Johnson City, Texas.* Johnson City High School, Sixth Street and D Avenue. He graduated from high school at fifteen (the school only went to the eleventh grade). While in Johnson City in 1921, he boarded with his Uncle Tom and Aunt Kitty, who finally told his parents they "couldn't handle Lyndon." In 1922, his father sold their ranch, and the Johnsons moved back into Johnson City.

**1922**  *San Marcos, Texas.* He attended the private San Marcos Normal School to take make-up work. He returned to the Johnson City High School in the fall of 1922.

**1927–1930**  *San Marcos, Texas.* Southwest Texas State Teachers College, from which he graduated. Old Main, the heart of the college, is located off Austin Street and stands out with its four red spires. He took the year 1928–1929 to teach in Cotulla to earn money. The school had no dormitories so he stayed in the Pirtle House. There is a marker on the building. From 1928 to 1929, he roomed, rent free, with Alfred B. Johnson, in a room over Dr. Evan's (the college president's) garage. The house and garage have been demolished. To save money, he arranged a two-meal contract at Mrs. Gates' boarding house. In 1929, he roomed at Mrs. Miller's rooming house on North Comanche and had meals at Mrs. Gates'. From 1929 to 1930, he roomed at Mrs. Hooper's rooming house on West Hopkins, where his room was on a "big screen porch."

**1934–1935**  *Washington, D.C.* Georgetown University, 600 New Jersey Avenue, NW. He studied law for about two months. He said, "I earned only a B.A. degree—for Brief Attendance."

# MARRIAGE AND HONEYMOON

Claudia Alta (Lady Bird) Taylor and Johnson first met in the Texas Railroad Commission office at the instigation of a mutual friend. They were married on November 17, 1934, in San Antonio, Texas, at St. Mark's Episcopal Church, 315 Pecan Street, at the northwest corner of Jefferson. The reception supper was at St. Anthony's Hotel, across from the Plaza Hotel. They spent the wedding night in San Antonio, Texas, at the Plaza Hotel, 300 East Travis. The next day they continued to Mexico City but returned to Washington in time for the opening of Congress.

# HOMES/LODGINGS

**1908–1913**  *Stonewall, Texas.* The original three-room house was typical of early

*Birthplace of Lyndon Johnson.*

Texas farm houses. A breezeway separated the kitchen from the living and sleeping quarters. The house now on the site was built from the rough planking of the house in which Johnson was born. The house is unused today. The outdoor toilet was a flimsy, tilted two holer.

**1913–1924**   *Johnson City, Texas.* The house on Ninth Street is preserved as Johnson knew it. This was his boyhood home, with its Victorian gingerbread scrollwork on the gables and wisteria covered trellises.

**1921**   *Johnson City, Texas.* He stayed with his Aunt Kitty and Uncle Tom, at 507 East Seventh Street. See Education above.

**1924–1930**   *Johnson City, Texas.* During these years, he was intermittently at home on Ninth Street.

**1924**   *San Bernardino, California.* 376 F Street in an upstairs front room. The small two-story house is no longer standing.

**1925–1926**   *San Bernardino, Texas.* 1516 E Street.

**1928–1929**   *Cotulla, Texas.* 202 South Neal Street, a rather shabby house on stilts next to the railroad tracks. He boarded here with Sarah Tinsley Marshall while teaching, and shared the room with the high school football coach.

**1930**   *Pearsall, Texas.* 120 South Oak Street, while teaching in the high school.

**1931**   *Houston, Texas.* 435 Hawthorne Street, at the home of his Uncle George Desha Johnson in a two-story white frame house.

**1932**   *Washington, D.C.* Mayflower hotel, 1127 Connecticut Avenue, NW, with Congressman Richard Kleberg when he first came to Washington. He arrived here in December 1931 and stayed until January 1932.

**1932–1934**   *Washington, D.C.* Grace Dodge Hotel, 500 First Street, NW, one block

*Boyhood home of Lyndon Johnson in Johnson City, Texas.*

south of Union Station. He usually ate at the All States Restaurant, Massachusetts Avenue, across the Capitol Plaza from the hotel. He had a tiny cubicle in the basement where steam pipes ran across the ceiling. He and Lady Bird spent their first few days after their honeymoon in an upstairs room at the Grace Dodge Hotel, which has since been torn down.

**1934** *Washington, D.C.* 1910 Kalorama Road, in a one-bedroom apartment.

**1934–1935** *Washington, D.C.* 3133 Connecticut Avenue. He sublet an apartment from friends.

**1935** *Austin, Texas.* 4 Happy Hollow Lane, in half of a two-family frame house.

**1935–1937** *Austin.* Stephen F. Austin Hotel, 701 Congress Avenue. He maintained his headquarters here.

**1937–** *Culpepper, Virginia.* Longlea, estate of Charles Marsh. He also visited the Marsh home in Texas at 1309 Marshall Lane, Austin.

**1937**   *Washington, D.C.* Kennedy-Warren Apartment, 3133 Connecticut Avenue, NW, east side of Connecticut Avenue between the National Zoo and Klingle Road, from May to August 1937.

**1938**   *Washington, D.C.* The Chatham, 1707 Columbia Road (now a condo). He lived here briefly.

**1938–1940**   *Washington, D.C.* Kennedy-Warren Apartment, 3133 Connecticut Avenue, NW.

**1941–1942**   *Washington, D.C.* Woodley Park Towers, 2737 Devonshire Place, NW, northwest corner of Devonshire Place and Connecticut Avenue. For months in 1942 when LBJ was on active duty, it was sublet, and Mrs. Johnson moved in with Mrs. John Connally in the Buckingham Apartments, Arlington, Virginia, 222 North George Mason Drive.

**1942**   *Washington, D.C.* Wardman Park Tower, 2600 Woodley Road, NW, during World War II.

**1943–1961**   *Washington, D.C.* 4921 Thirtieth Place, NW.

**1943–**   *Austin, Texas.* 1901A Dillman Street. The Johnsons occupied one of three apartments.

**1950–**   *Middleburg, Virginia.* George Brown estate. Brown was a friend from Austin who was a financial adviser and backer of Johnson's campaigns. Johnson often spent time at his estate. Johnson suffered a heart attack while visiting here in 1955. He also visited Brown at his Texas home at 3363 Inwood Drive, Houston.

**1961–1963**   *Washington, D.C.* The Elms, 4040 52nd Street, NW, was Perle Mesta's lovely hilltop home and was modeled after a French chateau. Some of its walls and floors had been imported directly from ancient castles in France. The house is currently used by the Algerian Embassy.

**1963–1969**   *Washington, D.C.* The White House as thirty-sixth President.

**1969–1973**   *Stonewall, Texas.* A short distance from the site of his birthplace, is the LBJ ranch house to which LBJ and Lady Bird retired. He bought the ranch from his Aunt Frank in 1952.

# WORK

**1924**   *Johnson City and Austin, Texas.* He did road construction work on the highway between, because he refused to go to college. His father worried about his refusal to get up on time and his sneaking the family car out at night.

**1924**   *Robstown, Texas.* Roeder & Koether Gin Company, where he kept the boiler supplied with wood and water. He pretended he was having a good time and only agreed to come home with his father after his father promised not to punish him for the car he wrecked.

**1924–1926**   *Los Angeles, California.* After graduation from high school, he went off to California and led a vagabond life for nearly a year until his money dried up. He took many odd jobs—washing cars, hashing in a cafe, and worked and hitchhiked his way back to Texas.

**1926**   *San Bernardino, California.* He worked at 491 West Fifth Street as an elevator operator in the Platt Building and then as a clerk to attorney Tom Martin in the same building. A plaque was put at the side of the elevator but was later stolen. At last report the building was being considered for demolition.

**1926**   *Johnson City, Texas.* He spent several months doing odd jobs before getting a job on a road gang driving a gravel truck across the river from Johnson City. He lived at home.

**1928–1929**   *Cotulla, Texas.* Welhausen School, 804 Lane Street. He taught at this predominantly Mexican-American school.

**1930** *Pearsall, Texas.* Pearsall High School, as principal. The town had a single small "self-service" hotel, where one selected his own room and left the dollar payment in a slot. He later moved to a garage apartment.

**1930–1931** *Houston, Texas.* Sam Houston High School, 1304 Capitol. He taught public speaking. There is now a parking lot on the site.

**1931–1935** *Washington, D.C.* Secretary to Democratic Congressman Richard M. Klebert of Texas. Cannon Building, Room 258. The rooms have been renumbered and his office, now unnumbered, is next to the present Room 244. By 1932, his boss had a two-room suite, Office 1322, in the new Longworth Building. Johnson had his desk immediately inside the entrance, catching everyone who came in.

**1935–1937** *Austin, Texas.* Littlefield Building, sixth floor, Congress and Sixth Streets, as Director of the National Youth Administration in Texas, beginning on July 27, 1935.

**1937** *Austin, Texas.* The Stephen F. Austin Hotel, 701 Congress Avenue, was his campaign headquarters while he was running for Congress.

**1937–1949** *Washington, D.C.* U.S. Congressman from Texas. His office was in the Cannon Building, Room 118. He took leave of absence from Congress to serve briefly in the navy in 1942. Later, he moved to Room 544.

**1937 May 11** *College Station, Texas.* As a newly elected Congressman, he met with President Roosevelt at Texas A & M. He later went with the presidential party to Fort Worth.

**1940** *Washington, D.C.* Munsey Building, 1329 E Street, NW. He set up office here as congressional campaign manager for the House of Representatives.

**1941–1942** *The Pacific.* Navy Service. In May 1942, landed at Noumea on the island of Caledonia. He went to Auckland, New Zealand, and to Melbourne, Australia, where he checked into the Menzies Hotel. He travelled to Sydney, Brisbane, and Townsville, on Australia's northeastern tip, and to Port Moresby, where he spent the night on the porch of Government House. He was in Darwin and later in a family hotel at Winton. On June 22, he travelled to Sava, Fiji Island, where he stayed in the hospital for several days, followed by ten days at Pearl Harbor. He returned to resume his seat in Congress in mid-summer 1942. He received the Silver Star from General Douglas MacArthur for gallantry in action in New Guinea.

**1943–** *Austin, Texas.* KTCB office in the Brown Building, 119 East Tenth Street. This was the site of their radio business, which flourished under Lady Bird.

**1949–1961** *Washington, D.C.* U.S. Senator from Texas. In 1955, he became the youngest Majority Leader in Democratic party history. His office was 321 in the Senate Office Building.

**1961** *Washington, D.C.* He was sworn in for his third term as a senator and resigned three minutes later.

**1961–1963** *Washington, D.C.* Vice president of the United States. Executive Office Building, Room 274, corner of Seventeenth Street and Pennsylvania Avenue, NW.

**1963–1969** *Washington, D.C.* President of the United States. He took the oath of office on Air Force One, Federal Judge Sarah Hughes administered the oath while the plane still sat on the ground at Dallas' Love airport, seven miles southwest of downtown Dallas.

**1969–1973** *Stonewall, Texas.* Spent his in retirement at the LBJ Ranch.

# TRAVEL/VISITS

Johnson was the most travelled vice president in history up to this time. He visited thirty-three countries and made one hundred and eighty speeches.

**1924** *California.* Went with a group of friends, to seek their fortune.

**1924** *El Paso, Texas.* Group of friends went to El Paso, with a population of 74,000 thrilled them, as it was the first time any of them had been in a big city.

**1930** *Mexico.* Week-long holiday as a reward from Welly Hopkins for successfully managing his campaign for the Texas Lower House.

**1931** *Texas to Washington, D.C.* In early 1932, he heard President Hoover's address to a joint session of Congress, sitting on the top step in the gallery in the Capitol.

**1937** *Austin, Texas.* Seton Hospital, 1201 West 38th Street, for appendectomy.

**1948–** *Austin, Texas.* Driskill Hotel. In May, he announced his candidacy for the Senate. Later, he made his opening campaign speech at Wooldridge Park in downtown Austin.

**1948** *Fort Worth, Texas.* Blackstone Hotel. Johnson was here for the ruling of the State Democratic Executive Committee in a dispute to determine the Democratic nominee for the Senate race. The ruling was in his favor.

**1948** *Rochester, Minnesota.* Mayo Clinic, where he flew to have a kidney stone removed. The surgical instruments used are now displayed in the Mayo Museum. He was there again for similar treatment in January 1955.

**1952** *Chicago, Illinois.* He attended the Democratic National Convention, held in the International Amphitheatre.

**1952** *Uvalde, Texas.* He visited former Vice President Garner at his home. He was in Uvalde again along with Truman to celebrate Garner's ninety-second birthday.

**1955** *Bethesda, Maryland.* Naval Hospital, 8901 Wisconsin Avenue, following a heart attack. President Eisenhower and Vice President Nixon visited him here.

**1956** *Chicago, Illinois.* Democratic National Convention, held in the International Amphitheatre.

**1960** *Dallas, Texas.* Adolphus Hotel. He and Mrs. Johnson were verbally and physically assaulted—an incident he used to his advantage to give him a political advantage in Texas and the South.

**1960** *Hyannis Port, Massachusetts.* He visited Kennedy to discuss campaign strategy.

**1960** *Los Angeles, California.* Democratic National Convention. He stayed in a suite on the seventh floor of the Biltmore, 506 West Grand.

**1961–** *Kingsland, Llano County, Texas.* The Haywood Ranch and boat house was a vacation spot. It is located on the south branch of the Llano River an arm of Lake Lyndon B. Johnson.

**1961** *Kansas City, Missouri.* Muehlebach Hotel. While there, the hotel was evacuated because of a fire and his scheduled speech was cancelled.

**1963** *Austin, Texas.* Dedication of Agudas Achim Synagogue.

**1963** *Fort Worth, Texas.* Hotel Texas, 815 Main Street, where he was staying at the time of Kennedy's fatal trip to Texas.

**1963** *New York City, New York.* He addressed the General Assembly of the United Nations.

**1963** *St. Augustine, Florida.* St. Joseph Academy, corner St. George and Bridge Streets.

**1963** *Washington, D.C.* Lincoln Memorial, for Candlelight Memorial Service for John F. Kennedy.

**1964** *St. Louis, Missouri.* Celebration of the city's two hundredth anniversary. Bicentennial dinner at the Chase-Park Plaza Hotel.

**1964** *Atlantic City, New Jersey.* Convention

Hall on the Boardwalk from Mississippi to Florida Avenues, for the Democratic National Convention where he accepted the nomination for president on August 27.

**1964** *Texarkana, Arkansas.* He dedicated the J. F. Kennedy Memorial on State Line Avenue.

**1964** *Eufala, Oklahoma.* Dedication of Eufala Dam.

**1964** *New York City, New York.* Statue of Liberty, where he signed the first U.S. immigration laws in more than thirty years. Later, he met with the Pope at the Waldorf Towers.

**1964** *Orlando, Florida.* Cherry Plaza Hotel (now Lakeside), at the corner of East Central and Osceola. This was the first time a president ever slept in Orlando. There was a motorcade down Orange Avenue to Colonial Drive with 110,000 people along the parade route.

**1964** *Vancouver, Canada.* Attended for signing of the Columbia River Treaty at the International Peace Arch near Blaine, Washington, on the U.S.–Canadian border.

**1965** *Baltimore, Maryland.* Johns Hopkins University, Shriver Hall Auditorium, for speech "Peace Without Conquest."

**1965** *Washington, D.C.* Howard University, in the Main Quadrangle, commencement speech "To Fulfill These Rights."

**1965** *Independence, Missouri.* Truman Library, with ex-president Truman, to sign Medicare Bill.

**1965** *Washington, D.C.* He spoke at the National Cathedral School Commencement when his daughter, Lucie, graduated.

**1965** *Washington, D.C.* Capitol Rotunda, on the occasion of signing the Voting Rights Act.

**1966** *Campobello Island, New Brunswick.* At F. D. Roosevelt's summer cottage to meet Canadian Prime Minister Lester Pearson.

**1966** *Indianapolis.* Ceremony at the Sailors and Soldiers Monument on the one-hundred fiftieth anniversary of the State of Indiana.

**1966** *Mexico City, Mexico.* He dedicated the statue of Abraham Lincoln in Parque Polanco.

**1966** *Princeton, New Jersey.* Dedication of Woodrow Wilson Hall at the Woodrow Wilson School of Public and International Affairs. He received an honorary degree.

**1966** *San Antonio, Texas.* Ceremony signing Medicare Bill in Victory Plaza.

**1966** *Washington, D.C.* Georgetown University. He signed the Peace Corps Act in Walsh Hall.

**1966** *Denver, Colorado.* He received an honorary degree from the University of Denver in the Arena.

**1967** *Glassboro, New Jersey.* He had a conference with Alexsei Kosygin in Hollybusy, a house built in 1849 and later the home of the president of Glassboro State College.

**1967** *Hermitage, Tennessee.* Celebrating the two-hundredth anniversary of the birth of Andrew Jackson.

**1967** *Nashville, Tennessee.* He spoke to a joint session in the House Chamber in the State Capitol.

**1967** *Roosevelt Island, D.C.* Dedication of the Theodore Roosevelt Memorial.

**1968** *New York City.* St. Patrick's Cathedral, to attend the installation of Terence Cooke as Archbishop.

**1972** *Independence, Missouri.* He attended President Truman's funeral.

## DEATH

Johnson died on January 22, 1973 in Stonewall, Texas. He was stricken at home and died on the way to the hospital at 3:50 P.M. He left an estate estimated to be worth $20 million.

## FUNERAL

The day and night after his death he lay in state at the Ranch Library. People were still ar-

*Grave of Lyndon Johnson.*

riving the next morning when the body was removed and flown to Washington. It was taken from the airport to the Capitol Rotunda on a horse-drawn caisson. His body lay in state in the Capitol Rotunda. President Nixon accompanied Lady Bird Johnson to the Capitol. On January 25, the coffin was moved to the National City Christian Church at 8:00 A.M. Dr. G. R. Davis conducted the service. President Nixon led the official mourners. The body was returned to Austin late on the afternoon of the twenty-fifth and was taken in a motorcade to the ranch where Father Schneider, the priest at the little church in Stonewall, gave the eulogy—quoting from LBJ's favorite book in the Bible, Ecclesiastes, "Mourn but little for the dead for they are at rest."

## BURIAL

He was buried in Stonewall, Texas, at his ranch a few miles from Johnson City. Grave-

yard services were led by the Reverend Billy Graham, and Anita Bryant sang "The Battle Hymn of the Republic."

## SPECIAL SITES

*Austin, TX.* Lyndon Baines Johnson Library at the University of Texas campus. Nixon was there for the dedication on May 22, 1971.

*Washington, D.C.* Johnson Memorial Grove on the Potomac River near the Pentagon. There is a granite marker.

## BIBLIOGRAPHY

Caro, Robert A. *The Years of Lyndon Johnson: The Path to Power.* New York, Alfred A. Knopf, 1982.

Harwood, Richard, and Haynes Johnson. *Lyndon.* New York, Praeger, 1973.

Miller, Merle. *Lyndon: An Oral Biography.* New York, Ballantine Books, 1980.

Newlon, Clarke. *LBJ: The Man from Johnson City.* New York, Dodd, Mead & Company, 1976.

# RICHARD MILHOUS NIXON

1913–1994
37TH PRESIDENT 1969–1974: REPUBLICAN PARTY

Richard Milhous Nixon was born on January 9, 1913, at 9:30 P.M., to Francis "Frank" Anthony and Hannah Milhous Nixon. He was a seventh cousin twice removed of President Taft and an eighth cousin once removed of President Hoover. He is descended from King Edward III of England. His immediate family was lower middle class.

## CHARACTERISTICS

Nixon was just under 6' tall and weighed one hundred and seventy-five pounds. As a young man, he had wavy brown hair, dark brown eyes with heavy dark eyebrows, a ski jump nose, and drooping jowls. He had an attractive smile. He was known for his excellent memory, and he was a top debater. Surprisingly, this was his undoing when he faced John F. Kennedy in his campaign for president. He also liked playing golf and swimming. In moments of relaxation, he enjoyed playing the piano and the violin. He smoked a pipe occasionally. He was an excellent poker player. As a hobby, he collected gavels.

The tale of Nixon's early poverty is not supported by the evidence. From time to time, the Nixons had a hired girl who tucked the children in bed and read to them.

*"I discovered how isolated from the reality of American life a President can feel in the White House."*

*— The Memoirs of Richard Nixon, 1978*

# A LIFE IN REVIEW

**Birth:** January 9, 1913; Yorba Linda, CA
**Died:** April 22, 1994; New York, NY
**Married:** Patricia Ryan; June 21, 1940;
2 daughters

## CAREER

**1937–1942** Lawyer
**1942–1946** U.S. Navy
**1947–1950** Member U.S. Congress
**1950–1953** Member U.S. Senate
**1953–1961** U.S. Vice President

## ADMISTRATION EVENTS

**1969** Policy of gradual troop withdrawal
from Vietnam

First moon walk

**1971** Kent State University riots

**1972** Visit to Mao Tse-tunb in Peking,
China

Democratic National Committee
headquarters burglarized

**1973** Watergate affair prosecution

**1974** Impeachment proceedings. Nixon
resigned

# BIRTHPLACE

Nixon was born in Yorba Linda, California, at 18161 Yorba Linda Boulevard, in the small frame house his father had built in the middle of a lemon grove.

# BAPTISM

His family were members of a quaker group which did not follow the practice of baptism or communion. In September 1926, he made his personal commitment to Christian service.

# CHURCH

Nixon's father had been a Methodist prior to his marriage to Hannah when he became a Quaker. He attended many revival meetings including those of Aimee Semple McPherson. Following a Billy Graham rally, Nixon writes," We joined hundreds of others that night in making our personal commitments to Christ and to Christian service." In September 1926, on hearing evangelist Paul Rader, he had his public conversion. Later, he made the statement, "I believe that the modern world will find a real resurrection in the life and teachings of Jesus." In many ways, he may have been closer to the old religion of his father than to Quaker principles.

Throughout his first term in office he had services in the White House, inviting different ministers to lead interdenominational services on Sunday in the East Room. The first Sunday after his inauguration, Billy Graham was the speaker.

**1913–1922** *Yorba Linda, California.* Friends Meeting House, School Street.

**1922–** *Whittier, California.* Old Friends Meeting House. When the new Meeting House was built in 1922, his father bought the old one and moved it to his lot and used it as a general store. This was East Whittier Friends Church. See also First Friends Church, corner of Philadelphia Street and Washington Avenue.

**1922–1942** *Whittier, California.* Friends Meeting House of East Whittier, 15911 East Whittier Boulevard, near the Russell Street intersection. He played the piano and taught Sunday school.

**1926** *Los Angeles, California.* Angelus Temple of Aimee Semple McPherson, 1100 Glendale Boulevard.

*Birthplace of Richard Nixon.*

**1930–1934** *Whittier, California.* Whittier College. He attended compulsory chapel three times a week. During his college years, he continued to attend the East Whittier Friends Meeting four times each Sunday and on Wednesday evening.

**1934–1937** *Durham, North Carolina.* Friends Meeting House, 404 Alexander Avenue.

**1934–1937** *Durham, North Carolina.* Duke University Chapel on the West Campus.

**1939** *Whittier, California.* St. Mathias Episcopal Church, 7056 South Washington Avenue (146 Washington Avenue), is a church near the college where he first met his future wife in the Sunday school room where they had both gone to tryout for a play.

**1950s** *Washington, D.C.* Westmoreland Congregational Church, on Westmoreland Circle, NW. He attended here off and on.

Returning to Washington after Eisenhower's heart attack, he took the family to services here.

**1960** *New York City, New York.* Marble Collegiate Church, Fifth Avenue and West 29th Street. The church is called marble because the exterior is entirely of marble and collegiate because its ministers (usually three) serve on an equal basis and are called colleagues. Nixon attended here with some regularity while he was a New York lawyer. His daughter Julie's wedding was held here on December 22, 1968.

**1969–1980** *San Clemente, California.* San Clemente Presbyterian Church, 119 Estrella.

**1970s** *Key Biscayne, Florida.* Biscayne Presbyterian Church, located a short distance from the Nixon home at 160 Harbor Drive. He attended here when visiting Key Biscayne. At the Easter service in 1973, he and his family sat in the fourth row pew.

**1972** *Moscow, USSR*. He attended the All Union Council of Evangelical Christian Baptist Churches—Moscow's only Baptist Church.

# EDUCATION

**1918–1922** *Yorba Linda, California*. The public elementary school, at the corner of School Street and Lemon Drive, is where he began school. He skipped the second grade.

**1922–1926** *Whittier, California*. East Whittier Grammar School, 14421 East Whittier Boulevard, (1411 East Whittier). He entered the fifth grade here. He walked at first and later rode a bicycle to school, about two miles from home.

**1925** *Lindsay, California*. Sunnyside School, a rural school three and one-half miles south of Lindsay, northeast corner of Road 216 and Avenue 196. He stayed here for six months with his maternal aunt, Jane Beeson, who also gave him daily piano lessons. The Beeson ranch was two hundred miles north of Whittier. He attended the last half of the seventh grade here. The school which he attended burned just before World War II.

**1926–1928** *Fullerton, California*. Fullerton Union High School, 201 East Chapman Avenue. During his first year, he rode a school bus for an hour each way. In 1927–1928, he went to live in Fullerton with his Aunt Carrie Wildermuth during the week and spent the weekend working in his father's store at home.

**1928–1930** *Whittier, California*. Whittier Union High School, 12217 Philadelphia Street (725 West Philadelphia). He graduated first in his class and won a scholarship to Harvard which he was unable to accept because of his family's financial condition.

**1930–1934** *Whittier, California*. Whittier College on College Hill, Philadelphia Street

at Painter Avenue. He boarded at home and graduated second out of one hundred nine.

**1934–1937** *Durham, North Carolina*. Duke University Law School, Tower View Road, on West Campus. He was admitted to the California bar in November 1937. From 1934 to 1935, he lived at 814 Sixth Street (now Clarendon Street) in a small room in a boarding house because he found campus housing expensive; he changed houses and rented a room across town because he was disturbed by divinity students practicing their sermons. From 1935 to 1937, he rented a small house with three divinity students in Duke Forest. The shack was nicknamed "Whipporwhill Manor." It is now part of a golf course in the area of Duke University.

# MARRIAGE AND HONEYMOON

Nixon first called on Thelma Catherine (Pat) Ryan in 1939, in Los Angeles, California, at the apartment of her stepsister, Neva Bender. He proposed to Pat in March of 1940, in Dana Point, north of San Clemente, California. In Artesia, California, he often called on Pat at her apartment before their marriage.

They were married on June 21, 1940, in Riverside, California, 3649 Seventh Street at Mission Inn. The wedding was held in the Presidential Suite. The reception was held in the long Spanish art gallery. It was a private wedding, attended by less than twenty-five guests, and according to the Quaker service.

They started off on their honeymoon with no particular destination and spent the first night at the Westward Hotel, North Central Avenue at West Fillmore in Phoenix. From Phoenix, they took the new Pan-Am Highway to Mexico. In Mexico City, they lived it up and spent one night in its most famous hotel, the Reforma, on Paseo de la Reforma, and then moved to the Los Angeles Hotel. They made daily side trips to Taxco, Puebla, and Cuenavaca. To save money on hotel bills they drove back to Whittier non-stop. They spent $178 on the trip. They carried canned goods from his father's grocery store and found that all the labels had been removed, so they never knew beforehand whether they would have spaghetti or peaches for breakfast.

# HOMES/LODGINGS

**1913–1922** *Yorba Linda, California.* 18161 Yorba Linda Boulevard, where he was born.

**1922** *Whittier, California.* Whittier Boulevard, with his maternal grandparents while his father was building their house on Painter Street down the hill from the college. It was a two-story frame house with a balcony over the porch.

**1922–1924** *East Whittier, California.* 622 South Painter Street, in a frame clapboard house near Whittier Boulevard and Leffingwell Road (later called Santa Gertrudes). The numbering system changed in 1947, and it is now 7926. His father later abandoned the site and put up a small wooden house and garage behind his gas station three miles away on the boulevard with the house facing west onto Leffingwell Road.

**1924–1930** *Whittier, California.* East Whittier Boulevard, opposite Russell. It is now gone.

**1925** *Lindsay, California.* Corner of Avenue 200 and Road 100, with his Aunt Jane Milhous Beeson. He was here for six months during the second half of seventh grade.

**1926** *Fullerton, California.* He stayed here for a brief time with his Aunt Carrie Wildermuth.

**1928–1929** *Prescott, Arizona.* 937 West Apache Drive, where his mother had rented a house to be with his tubercular brother, Harold. There is a bronze plaque at the front entrance.

**1930–1942** *Whittier, California.* 1104 Santa Gertrudes Road. From 1939 on he had a

dinner meeting every Tuesday night with the Whittier 20–30 Club at the William Penn Hotel.

**1939–1940** *Whittier, California.* 731 North Beach Avenue, (now Scandia Gardens Smorgasbord).

**1940** *Long Beach and Whittier, California.* There is conflicting information. One account says the Nixons came home from their honeymoon to a one-bedroom furnished apartment in Long Beach. Another says they settled into an apartment over a garage in Whittier. According to the Long Beach account, they eventually moved twice more—once to a small apartment over a garage in La Habra and then to a small apartment on Whittier Boulevard which belonged to his father. His parents had a house at 731 North Beach Boulevard, La Habra, where he lived for a while.

**1942** *Whittier, California.* 1400 East Whittier Boulevard.

**1942** *Alexandria, Virginia.* Beverly Park Apartments, near Four-Mile Run in Alexandria, 3919 Old Dominion Road. The apartment where he lived has been demolished but there are similar apartments on the opposite side of the street.

**1942** *Quonset Point, Rhode Island.* He was here for naval training and lived in the barracks at the Naval Training School.

**1942–1943** *Ottumwa, Iowa.* 232 East Fourth, Apartment 9, Tisdale Apartments. He and Pat rented a small apartment on the top floor of a 3-story brick building on a hillside overlooking Ottumwa.

**1944** *Alameda, California.* Fleet Air Wing 8.

**1945** *Middle River, Maryland.* He was living here in a small apartment when he received word of his nomination as a Republican candidate from a California district for Congress. In December 1945, they set up a small apartment in Whittier.

**1946** *Whittier, California.* The Nixons lived with his parents, who still had the market in

*Forest Lane home of Richard Nixon in Washington, D.C.*

Whittier. Dick and Pat stayed in the southeast corner bedroom, next to the back door, in the house on Worsham Drive.

**1946** *Whittier, California.* 320 East Walnut (now 13221). The house was a small brick-trimmed, Spanish-style stucco house between the boulevard and the college.

**1947** *Washington, D.C.* Mayflower Hotel, 1127 Connecticut Avenue, while looking for an apartment.

**1947** *Washington, D.C.* Broadmoor Apartment, 3601 Connecticut Avenue, NW, northeast corner of Connecticut Avenue and Porter Street. He lived here temporarily from March to June while house hunting.

**1947–1951** *Alexandria (Parkfairfax), Virginia.* 3426 Gunston Road, where they lived in a two-bedroom unfurnished apartment for $80 a month. They also lived at 3538 Gunston Road for a longer period—probably from 1948 to 1951.

**1947** *South Whittier, California.* 14033 Honeysuckle Lane, adjacent to the Candlewood Country Club, where he bought a ranch-style house for $15,000. It was sold in May 1951.

**1951–1953** *Washington, D.C.* 4801 Tilden Street, NW, in a new section of Washington called Spring Valley. He paid $41,000 for a two-story white brick house with three bedrooms.

**1953–1954** *Whittier, California.* 15257 Anaconda.

**1953–1961** *Washington, D.C.* 4308 Forest Lane in Wesley Heights. In January, he bought this fieldstone English Tudor style house with a large backyard. Mrs. Nixon said that now, for the first time, they had more than one bath. He paid $75,000 for it and lived here during his vice-presidential years.

**1961** *Brentwood, California.* Walter Lang house on Bundy Avenue, which they rented while their house was being built.

**1961**  *Palm Springs, California.* He took a cottage near the Eisenhower's on the grounds of the Eldorado Country Club.

**1961–1963**  *Beverly Hills, California.* 410 Memory Lane (410 Martin Lane), in Trousdale Estates, near the Bel Air section of Los Angeles. Their house was a long, low, ranch with seven baths, four bedrooms, three fireplaces, a very large living room and a swimming pool. The cost was about $100,000. He sold the Wesley Heights house in Washington, D.C. for about $101,000. From February to June, he lived alone in a bachelor apartment on Wilshire Boulevard.

**1963**  *New York City, New York.* Waldorf Astoria, Park Avenue and Fiftieth Street, fifth floor, while they were looking for permanent quarters.

**1963–1969**  *New York City.* 810 Fifth Avenue, in an apartment on Manhattan's East Side—a ten-room cooperative at 62nd Street and 5th Avenue. The apartment had a view of Central Park and the Plaza Hotel, four bedrooms, a study, a large living room, and a dining room. Nelson Rockefeller lived in the same building.

**1968**  *Key Biscayne, Florida.* He bought two small houses on Biscayne Bay next to Bebe Rebozo on Bay Lane. This house was razed in 1982 and a 3-story mansion built on the site. Nothing remains of the Nixon occupancy except the helicopter pad.

**1969–1974**  *San Clemente, California.* Casa Pacifica, south of Los Angeles off I-5 and immediately north and west of Camp Pendleton, which adjoined his property. He used this as the Western White House while he was president. It was a white stucco house with red-tiled roof, built in 1926.

**1969–1974**  *Washington, D.C.* The White House.

**1974–1980**  *San Clemente, California.* See 1969–1974 above.

**1980–1981**  *New York City, New York.* 142 East 65th Street. They moved in February, to their new four-story East Side Manhattan townhouse, which cost $750,000 and sold for more than $2.9 million.

**1981–1990**  *Saddle River, New Jersey.* Here he had a 15-room house, which he later sold to a Japanese business man for $2.4 million.

**1990–1994**  *Park Ridge, Woodcliff Lake, New Jersey.* 239 Spring Valley Road, in a three-bedroom condominium in Bears Nest, Park Ridge, about a mile from his former house. He suffered a stroke here and was removed to the hospital where he died.

# WORK

**1920–1921**  *Whittier, California.* He worked as a produce picker in the bean fields and citrus groves.

**1922–1934**  *Whittier, California.* He worked at the Nixon Market, located on the southeast corner of Whittier Boulevard and Santa Gertrudes. It included a gas station. The family lived in a house behind. Richard helped out at home. Most of all, he hated washing dishes and while doing so would pull down the window shade lest some outsider see him doing women's work. A service station occupies the site today.

**1928–1929**  *Prescott, Arizona.* Frontier Days at Slippery Gulch. He worked here as a barker for the wheel of fortune.

**1934–1937**  *Durham, North Carolina.* Duke University Law School. He worked in the university library between classes.

**1937–1941**  *Whittier, California.* 111 East Philadelphia, southeast corner where Greenleaf and Philadelphia meet. He practiced law with the firm of Wingert and Bewley, 607 Bank of America Building, Room 193. He practiced law for four years before he entered politics.

**1939** *Whittier, California.* He became junior partner in the firm of Bewley, Knoop and Nixon.

**1939–1941** *LaHabra, California.* His firm opened a law office here in the rear of an abandoned hardware store (now a real-estate office) in a one-story building, Room 197-8, along LaHabra's only business street.

**1940–1942** *Whittier, California.* He joined in forming the Citra-Frost Company, which failed within two years.

**1942** *Washington, D.C.* Office of Price Administration, temporary building on Independence Avenue. He was in the tire rationing section. By the summer of 1942, he had a P-4 rating.

**1942** *Quonset Point, Rhode Island.* Basic training. He left Union Station in Washington on August 17, for Providence where he was at the Naval Officer Candidate School.

**1942–1943** *Ottumwa, Iowa.* Naval Air Station, five miles north of Ottumwa and now the Ottumwa Airport. He received orders to report to San Francisco and returned to Whittier to say his goodbyes. The family had breakfast at the Harvey House in Union Station, Whittier.

**1943–1944** *The Pacific.* He was assigned to the South Pacific Combat Air Transport. His orders were for Espiritu Santo in the New Hebrides. For the most part, he was at Noumea on the island of Caledonia, and afterwards Vella Lavella.

**1944** *Alameda, California.* Fleet Air Wing 8 (near San Francisco), after three weeks leave in Whittier.

**1944** *Washington, D.C.* Department of the Navy's Bureau of Aeronautics, Eighteenth and Constitution Avenue, NW, working with a navy legal unit.

**1945–1946** *Pennsylvania, Maryland, and New York.* He was ordered first to Philadelphia, then to New York City, and finally to Baltimore to settle navy war contracts. During this period, the Nixons lived in small apartments, first in Philadelphia and then four months in New York City. In New York City, he was with the navy legal unit in its twentieth floor office on Church Street, from which he watched the ticker tape parade for General Eisenhower.

**1945 Summer** *Middle River, Maryland.* A naval post on Chesapeake Bay just east of Baltimore.

**1946** *Whittier, California.* He left the navy and returned here to plunge full time into his political campaign for Congress.

**1947–1951** *Washington, D.C.* Congressman from California. He had an office in the back of the House Office Building, Suite 528, which was called "the attic."

**1951–1953** *Washington, D.C.* U.S. Senator from California. December 4, 1950, he took the Senate oath in the Capitol chamber once used by the Supreme Court. His office was in the Senate Office Building, Room 563.

**1953–1961** *Washington, D.C.* Vice President of the United States. His office was Room 363 in the Old Senate Office Building.

**1961–1963** *Los Angeles, California.* Adams, Duque, and Hazeltine law firm, 3950 Wilshire Boulevard, on the eleventh floor of the Pacific Mutual Insurance Company Building. This was also his headquarters during his campaign for governor of California in 1962.

**1963–1969** *New York City, New York.* Mudge, Stern, Baldwin and Todd law firm which became Nixon, Mudge, Rose, Guthrie, and Alexander, 20 Broad Street.

**1969–1974** *Washington, D.C.* President of the United States. He was the first president to resign office. Thursday, August 8, 1974, was the last full day he served as president. He handed his resignation letter to Secretary of State Henry Kissinger in the Lincoln sitting room.

# TRAVEL/VISITS

**1931**  *Pacific Northwest.* During his second year in college, he went with the debate team on a 3,500-mile tour which included San Francisco.

**1936**  *New York City, New York.* Sloan House YMCA during Christmas week.

**1941**  *Caribbean cruise on the United Fruit Company's ship* Ulua. He drove east to New Orleans where he and Pat embarked on a two-week cruise, going to the Panama Canal Zone.

**1942**  *Cape Porpoise, Maine.* Maine 9 north of Kennebunkport, for a long weekend before he entered the service.

**1946**  *Big Bridges, California.* Claremont College, for the third debate.

**1946**  *Monrovia, California.* Monrovia High School, for fourth debate.

**1946**  *San Gabriel, California.* Civic Auditorium, for a final debate with Voorhis.

**1946**  *South Pasadena, California.* San Marino Jr. High School, for first debate with Congressman Jerry Voorhis.

**1946**  *Whittier, California.* Patriotic Hall, for second debate with Voorhis.

**1947**  *Europe.* He sailed on the Queen Mary in late August and docked at Southampton. He had tea with Prime Minister Clement Atlee at 10 Downing Street. Later, he saw the ruins of the Reichs Chancellory in Berlin. He saw Mars Hill in Athens, and also visited Paris and Rome.

**1947**  *McKeesport, Pennsylvania.* Penn-Mc-Kee Hotel, for the first debate he had with J. F. Kennedy.

**1948**  *New York City, New York.* Commodore Hotel, 42nd Street, Suite 1400, for a meeting with Whittaker Chambers.

**1948**  *Philadelphia, Pennsylvania.* He attended the Republican National Convention in Convention Hall.

**1951**  *Vero Beach, Florida.* Driftwood Hotel, for a vacation and his first encounter with Charles "Bebe" Rebozo.

**1952–**  *Los Angeles, California.* Ambassador Hotel, 3400 Wilshire Boulevard, while on campaign tour. At the NBC studio, one block from the intersection of Hollywood and Vine, he gave the "Checkers" speech on September 23. He had the largest audience for a single event in the annals of American broadcasting. He was also at the Ambassador, Room 827, to receive election returns in November.

**1952**  *Honolulu.* Surfrider Hotel, for a 10-day vacation. July.

**1952**  *Chicago, Illinois.* Knickerbocker Hotel, 163 East Walton. He attended Republican National Convention. He was nominated for vice president in the International Amphitheater, 4220 Halstead Street. He moved from Knickerbocker to his own suite of rooms in the Stockyard Inn for the remainder of the Convention.

**1952**  *Portland, Oregon.* Benson Hotel, 309 Southwest Broadway, while on campaign tour.

**1952**  *Wheeling, West Virginia.* McClure House, with the Eisenhowers.

**1956**  *San Francisco, California.* For the Republican National Convention at Cow Palace. He stayed at the Mark Hopkins Hotel on Nob Hill, southwest corner of California and Mason Streets. During the campaign, he visited 32 states in 16 days. Speaking in Cheyenne, he was hit with a virus.

**1958**  *London, England.* The dedication of the American Memorial Chapel in St. Paul's Cathedral. He spoke at London's Guildhall.

**1958**  *White Sulphur Springs, West Virginia.* Greenbrier Hotel, for vacation.

**1959**  *Moscow, USSR.* He visited Krushchev's country dacha in Usovo, a half-hour drive from the Kremlin. He returned home via Poland. He made a five-day trip through the U.S.S.R. with stops in Leningrad, Novosibirsk, and Sverdlovsk.

He had his famous "Kitchen Debate" with Krushchev in Sokolniki Park, Moscow.

**1960** *Chicago, Illinois.* Blackstone Hotel, 636 South Michigan Avenue, for the Republican National Convention. He was nominated as Republican candidate for president.

**1960** *Los Angeles, California.* While house hunting, he first stayed at the Statler Hotel (now the Hilton), 930 Wilshire Boulevard, and then later to save money he moved to the Gaylord Hotel (now Gaylord Apartments), 3355 Wilshire Boulevard, across the street from the Ambassador.

**1963** *Washington, D.C.* St. Matthew's Cathedral for President Kennedy's funeral.

**1964** *San Francisco, California.* Cow Palace for the Republican National Convention. He introduced Barry Goldwater, the Republican nominee for president. Later, he undertook a five-week swing through 36 states on Goldwater's behalf. He stayed at the St. Francis Hotel during the Convention.

**1965** *Philadelphia, Pennsylvania.* Bellevue Stratford Hotel. He spoke at a fund raiser.

**1967** *Bel Air, Bohemian Grove, California.* This was where he first met Eisenhower in 1950.

**1967** *Gettysburg, Pennsylvania.* He met with Eisenhower at his home, hoping to get his endorsement for President.

**1967** *New York City, New York.* Waldorf Towers. He planned the 1968 campaign strategy in the suite where Herbert Hoover once lived.

**1968** *Atlanta, Georgia.* On April 9, he attended Martin Luther King, Jr.'s funeral.

**1968** *Key Biscayne, Florida.* November 6, the Nixon family began a brief vacation in a bungalow rented from Senator Smathers. The Nixons had been coming to Key Biscayne since 1953. He also spent time at Grand Cay, the Bahamas.

**1968** *Miami Beach, Florida.* Hilton-Plaza Hotel, 4441 Collins, Nixon headquarters

for the Republican National Convention. He stayed in the Penthouse. After his nomination, he refused to debate, and there were no presidential debates with Hubert Humphrey.

**1968** *New York City, New York.* Campaign headquarters at 521 Fifth Avenue.

**1968** *New York City, New York.* St. Patrick's Cathedral to attend Robert Kennedy's funeral.

**1969–** *San Juan Capistrano, Orange County, California.* El Adobe, a favorite restaurant of Nixon.

**1969** *Camp Pendleton, California.* He was a regular on the golf course here.

**1969** *Eureka, California.* He spoke on the occasion of the arrival of ex-president and Mrs. L.B. Johnson for the dedication of the Lady Bird Johnson Grove in Redwood National Park.

**1969** *Independence, Missouri.* On March 21, he met with ex-president Truman at the Truman Library.

**1969** *New York City, New York.* He addressed the General Assembly of the United Nations.

**1969** *Pacific Ocean.* July 24, aboard the USS Hornet, near the splashdown site of Apollo 11.

**1969** *Washington, D.C.* Capitol Rotunda. March 30, he delivered the eulogy for President Eisenhower at the state funeral.

**1970** *Honolulu, Hawaii.* Kawaiahao Church, for thanksgiving service for the safe return of astronauts.

**1970** *Columbus, Ohio.* He made remarks at the State House.

**1970** *Coronado, California.* Dinner honoring the Mexican president in the Crown Room, Hotel del Coronado. President Johnson and Governor Reagan were present. Presidents Benjamin Harrison, McKinley, Taft, and F. D. Roosevelt had spoken in this same room.

**1970** *San Clemente, California.* San Clemente Inn, where he announced the U.S. cease fire proposal for the Middle East.

**1970** *San Jose, California.* Municipal Airport. He had the experience of being the only president to have rocks thrown at him. Governor Reagan was also there.

**1970** *Washington, D.C.* Rib Room, Mayflower Hotel, where he ate his first meal in a Washington restaurant since becoming president.

**1971** *Anchorage, Alaska.* Elmendorf Air Force Base, to greet Japanese Emperor Hirohito.

**1971** *Austin, Texas.* He dedicated the Lyndon Johnson Library at the University of Texas.

**1971** *Caneel Bay, St. John, Virgin Islands.* He stayed in a white two-story bungalow frequently used by Laurence S. Rockefeller.

**1971** *Centerville, Iowa.* He dedicated Rathburn Dam.

**1971** *Dayton, Ohio.* He dedicated the Airforce Museum at Wright-Patterson Air Force Base.

**1971** *Des Moines, Iowa.* State Capitol, where he addressed a joint session. He stayed at the Fort Des Moines Hotel.

**1971** *Grand Teton National Park, Wyoming.* Visit.

**1971** *Springfield, Illinois.* He established the Lincoln House as a National Historical site, spoke at the Old Capitol, and visited Lincoln's tomb.

**1971** *Vernon, Indiana.* Courthouse. Nixon came to dedicate a plaque to his mother, Hannah, who had been born in a farmhouse south of Butlerville on Rush Branch Creek in 1885. The historical marker is located on the east side of Butlerville on the south side of U.S. 50.

**1971** *Washington, D.C.* Smithsonian Institution Great Hall, for the dedication of the Woodrow Wilson International Center for Scholars.

**1971** *Palm Desert, California.* Dedication of the Eisenhower Memorial Hospital.

**1972** *Independence, Missouri.* Wreath at Truman bier in the Truman Library.

**1972** *Miami Beach, Florida.* He accepted the Republican Party nomination for president at Convention Hall.

**1972** *Moscow, USSR.* May 22, he had dinner at Granovit Hall, Grand Kremlin Palace. In Moscow, he stayed in the Grand Palace inside the Kremlin and was given the entire floor of rooms in one wing. He held meetings in St. Valdimir Hall in the Grand Kremlin Palace. He visited Aleksandrov Gardens and laid a wreath at the Tomb of Unknown Soldier. He visited Chairman Leonid Brezhnev at his country residence and attended a performance of "Swan Lake" at the Bolshoi. He spent the night at Spasso House, the residence of the American Ambassador. On May 27, in Leningrad, he visited Piskaryev Cemetery and laid a wreath at the Tomb of the Unknown Soldier. He lunched at Mariinsky Palace and toured the ruins of the Imperial Palace. On May 28, in Moscow, he attended Sunday services at the Baptist Church. On May 29, in Kiev, he had dinner at the Presidium. May 30, at the Park of Eternal Glory, he laid a wreath at the tomb of the Unknown Soldier and visited St. Sophia's Cathedral and Museum.

**1972** *Peking, China.* February 21, at Capital Airport, he was met by Premier Chou En-lai. He stayed at Taio Yu Tai (Angling Terrace) Guest House, went to the residence of Mao tse-tung for a meeting and to the Great Hall of the People for a dinner. He visited the Great Wall of China at Ba Da Ling portion, visited the Ming Dynasty tombs, and toured the Forbidden City. On February 26, in Hangchow, He toured Flower Fort Park, West Lake, and Island of Three Towers Reflecting the Moon, and stayed at a guest house on West Lake (Chiang Kiang).

**1973 February 20**   *Columbia, South Carolina.* He spoke to a joint session at the State Capitol.

**1973**   *Orlando, Florida.* Contemporary Hotel at Walt Disney World for a speech to the Associated Press Editors Association.

**1974–**   *Bethesda, Maryland.* 7000 Armat Drive. He visited Julie and David's (his daughter and son-in-law) place at least twice a week.

**1974**   *Palm Springs, California.* Sunnylands, the home of Walter Annenberg.

**1974**   *Nashville, Tennessee.* He visited the Grand Ole Opry House and played "God Bless America" on the piano for the group.

**1976**   *China.* An eight-day private visit. He stayed in State Guest House No. 18 and was honored at a farewell banquet in the Great Hall of the People.

**1978**   *Hyden, Kentucky.* Dedication of new recreation center. This was his first major appearance before an American audience since leaving the White House.

**1993**   *Yorba Linda, California.* Richard M. Nixon Library. Funeral services were held for his wife, Pat Nixon, with the Reverend Dr. Billy Graham officiating.

   *Pocantico Hills, New York.* Overnight at the Nelson Rockefeller estate.

# DEATH

Nixon died in New York City, at New York Hospital. He suffered a major stroke on Monday, April 18, 1994 and died at 9:08 P.M., on April 22. His body was taken to a mortuary in Newark, New Jersey. On Tuesday, April 26, the body was driven north to Stewart Air National Guard Base at Newburgh, New York, a few miles north of West Point. At Stewart Air National Guard Base, a joint-service honor guard met the hearse and a 21-gun salute was fired.

*Grave of Richard Nixon.*

# FUNERAL

On April 22 the body was flown to the Marine Corps Air Station at El Toro, California, met by another honor guard and another 21-gun salute, and then taken to the Richard M. Nixon Library and birthplace in Yorba Linda. The body lay in state in the library's lobby from Tuesday afternoon until late Wednesday morning.

Funeral services were held at 7:00 P.M. on April 27. The Reverend Billy Graham officiated and eulogies were delivered by President Clinton, Governor Pete Wilson of California, Senator Bob Dole of Kansas, and Henry Kissinger, who served as Nixon's Secretary of State.

# BIBLIOGRAPHY

Kornitzer, Bela. *The Real Nixon: An Intimate Biography.* New York: Rand McNally, 1960.

Mazo, Earl. *Richard Nixon: A Political and Personal Portrait.* New York: Harper and Row, 1959.

Morris, Roger. *Richard Milhous Nixon.* New York: Henry Holt, 1990.

# GERALD RUDOLPH FORD

1913–
38TH PRESIDENT 1974–1977: REPUBLICAN PARTY

Ford was born on July 14, 1913, to Leslie L. King and Dorothy Gardner. He was christened Leslie L. King, Jr. His parents were divorced in 1915, and he left Omaha with his mother to live with his maternal grandparents, the Gardners. Later, when his mother married Gerald R. Ford, he was legally adopted by Ford and given his stepfather's name.

## CHARACTERISTICS

When he became president, he was six feet tall and weighed 195 pounds. He has blue eyes and thinning hair, which was originally blond, is combed straight back. Like Jimmy Carter and George Bush, he writes and eats with his left, hand but he is right-handed in sports activities. The first thing he reads in the newspaper is the sports page. He is an avid golfer and swimmer; before entering the White House, he swam twice daily. Although he is often described in the press as awkward and pictured falling down steps and hitting people with misguided golf balls, he has described himself in his book, *A Time to Heal,* as "the most athletic president to occupy the White House in years." His wife, being asked by a reporter if her husband was accident-prone, responded,

*"I am acutely aware that you have not elected me as your President by your ballots, and so I ask you to confirm me as your President with your prayers."*

—*Inaugural address, August 9, 1974*

387

## A LIFE IN REVIEW

**Birth:** July 14, 1913; Omaha, NE

**Married:** Elizabeth Bloomer Warren; October 15, 1948; 3 sons, 1 daughter

### CAREER

**1941–1949** Lawyer

**1942–1946** U.S. Navy

**1948–1973** Member U.S. Congress

**1973–1974** U.S. Vice President

### ADMINISTRATION EVENTS

**1974** Pardoned Richard Nixon

**1975** "Shuttle diplomacy era" of Henry Kissinger

**1976** First successful probe landing on Mars

"So what else is new?" He used to smoke a pipe but quit in the early 1980s. Most people who have worked around Betty and Gerald Ford say that they are "human" and that they are liked regardless of any political affiliation. During the days of his political life, he was often referred to as "Mr. Clean."

## BIRTHPLACE

Ford was born in Omaha, Nebraska, at 3202 Woolworth Avenue, in an ornate victorian house which was razed following a fire in 1917. A model is shown in the memorial park nearby.

## BAPTISM

There is no information on his baptism.

## CHURCH

While a Congressman, he attended a regular Wednesday prayer session at the Capitol. One of the members started out with a simple prayer and following this they went around the room. When the last person had finished, they said the Lord's Prayer in unison. He is the tenth Episcopalian to occupy the White House. He made it a rule to spend Sunday with his family. After going to church together, they would sit down for a huge brunch.

**1922–1948** *Grand Rapids, Michigan.* Grace Episcopal Church, 1815 Hall Street SE, corner of Plymouth and Hall.

**1948–1951** *Washington, D.C.* St. John's Episcopal Church, Lafayette Square, and other Episcopal Churches in Washington.

**1951–1974** *Alexandria, Virginia.* Immanuel- on-the-Hill (Episcopal), off Seminary Road. They attended regularly here for more than twenty years. When they moved to the White House, Mrs. Ford wrote, "There aren't going to be any more private services in the East Room for a select few."

**1974–1977** *Washington, D.C.* St. John's Episcopal Church, Lafayette Square, across from the White House.

**1975–** *Palm Desert, California.* St. Margaret's Episcopal Church.

## EDUCATION

**1919–1927** *East Grand Rapids, Michigan.* Madison Elementary School, northwest corner Madison Avenue and Franklin (now 747 Madison SE).

**1927–1931** *Grand Rapids, Michigan.* South High School, 421 Fountain Street NE. In January 1974, on a visit to his old school, his name was entered in the "Hall of Fame."

**1931–1935** *Ann Arbor, Michigan.* University of Michigan. The entrance to the University faces Regents Square. While there, he joined the Delta Epsilon Fraternity.

*Gerald Ford and Elizabeth (Betty) Warren were married here at the Grace Episcopal Church in Grand Rapids, Michigan.*

From 1932–1935, he lived in Deke House, known locally as the "Deke Shant," at 611 1/2 East Williams Street.

**1937**  *Ann Arbor, Michigan.* University of Michigan. He attended law classes.

**1937–1941**  *New Haven, Connecticut.* Yale University Law College, Sterling Law Building, 127 Wall Street. One of his former professors said he was an excellent student and received an A+ in legal ethics.

## MARRIAGE AND HONEYMOON

Ford was married on October 15, 1948, in Grand Rapids, Michigan, at Grace Episcopal Church, 1815 Southeast Hall Street, to Elizabeth Bloomer Warren. The rehearsal dinner was on the fifth floor of the Peninsula Club. The family story is that Jerry proposed to Betty while sitting with her on the couch in her apartment and that at the time he was wearing one black shoe and one brown. On their first date, they went to a place on the corner of Division and Hall Streets.

The honeymoon took place in Ann Arbor, Michigan, at the Allenel Hotel. They went to the Town Club for dinner and to the Allenel Hotel for the night. The next day, they attended a party in Ann Arbor and later went to the Michigan-Northwestern game (Betty came at half time). In the evening, they went to an outdoor rally for Thomas Dewey at Owosso and then headed for Detroit. On Monday, they attended meetings in Ann Arbor and returned to Grand Rapids late in the afternoon to attend another political meeting that night.

## HOMES

**1913–1914**  *Omaha, Nebraska.* 3203 Woolworth Avenue was a beautiful 14-room 3-story house and the home of his King grandparents, with whom his parents were living at the time of his birth. Currently, there is a memorial garden and kiosk at the birthsite.

**1914–1916**  *Grand Rapids, Michigan.* 457 Lafayette Avenue SE, near Garfield Park. Following his mother's divorce, they moved in with her parents.

*Boyhood home of Gerald Ford on Union Avenue SE in Grand Rapids, Michigan.*

**1917–1921**  *Grand Rapids, Michigan.* 716 Madison Avenue SE, where they lived in a rented two-family house for three years. It was an old building with a gravel playground in the back.

**1922–1923**  *East Grand Rapids, Michigan.* 630 Rosewood Avenue. The bank foreclosed on the mortgage, and the family moved to Union Avenue.

**1923–1929**  *Grand Rapids, Michigan.* 649 Union Avenue SE, where they rented a large house. It is now in a poor neighborhood.

**1930–1933**  *East Grand Rapids, Michigan.* 2163 Southeast Lake Drive. His parents bought an old house here.

**1933–1939**  *East Grand Rapids, Michigan.* 1011 Santa Cruz Drive. He lived here with his parents.

**1939–1940**  *New Haven, Connecticut.* 268 Dwight Street.

**1940–**  *Ottawa Beach, Michigan.* Located on Lake Michigan, thirty miles from Grand Rapids, where his stepfather along with three other men owned a cabin near Bitely, on the Little South Branch of the Pere Marquette River (near Holland).

**1940–1941**  *New Haven, Connecticut.* 100 Howe Street.

**1947–**  *Grand Rapids, Michigan.* 636 Fountain Street. Home of Betty's parents.

**1948**  *Grand Rapids, Michigan.* 330 Washington Street SE, on the ground floor in Betty's apartment right after their marriage.

**1948–1949**  *Alexandria, Virginia.* 3426 Gunston Road (Parkfairfax).

**1949–1951**  *Alexandria, Virginia.* 3538 Gunston Road (Parkfairfax).

**1951–1955**  *Alexandria, Virginia.* 1521 Mount Eagle Place (Parkfairfax).

**1955–1974**   *Alexandria, Virginia.* 514 Crown View Drive. The house was built in 1955 for $34,000 and sold in 1977 for $134,000.

**1967–**   *Vail, Colorado.* Vacation home. During the Christmas holidays, they went annually to their condominium where they skied together as a family. It was valued at $2.5 million in 1983.

**1974–1977**   *Washington, D.C.* The White House as president.

**1977–**   *Rancho Mirage, California.* 70612 Hwy 111, Thunderbird County Club, facing the thirteenth fairway. It was valued at $1 million in 1983.

# WORK

**1930–**   *Grand Rapids, Michigan.* Ford Paint and Varnish Co., 601 Crosby NW, where he worked in the family business.

**1935–1936**   *New Haven, Connecticut.* He was assistant line coach at Yale.

**1936**   *Yellowstone National Park, Wyoming.* Summer work as a seasonal ranger.

**1937–1941**   *New Haven, Connecticut.* He worked as a coach while attending law classes at Yale University Law School.

**1941–1942**   *Grand Rapids, Michigan.* He established the law firm of Ford and Buchen. 620 Michigan Trust Building (which was 40-50 Pearl Street. NW).

**1942**   *Annapolis, Maryland.* U.S. Naval Academy.

**1942**   *Chapel Hill, North Carolina.* V-5 pre-flight school.

**1945**   *Glenview, Illinois.* Naval Reserve Training Command. He was discharged from the Navy as a Lieutenant commander and returned to Michigan in 1946.

**1946–1948**   *Grand Rapids, Michigan.* Suite 500, Michigan Trust Building, 40-50 Pearl NW. He joined the law firm of Butterfield, Keeney & Amberg as a partner.

**1948–1973**   *Washington, D.C.* Member of the U.S. House of Representatives from Michigan. For his first term in Washington, he was assigned Room 321 in the old House Office Building.

**1973–1974**   *Washington, D.C.* Vice President of the United States. He took the oath of office in the Chamber of the House of Representatives on October 23, 1973. His office as Vice President was on the second floor of the Executive Office Building (Old State and War) at Seventeenth and Pennsylvania Avenue, NW.

**1974–1977**   *Washington, D.C.* President of the United States. He was sworn in at the East Room of the White House, August 9, 1974.

# TRAVEL/VISITS

**1948**   *Grand Rapids.* Peninsular Club, 120 Ottawa NW, corner of Fountain and Ottawa.

**1960**   *Chicago, Illinois.* Congress Hotel, Michigan Avenue for the Republican National Convention.

**1960s**   *White Sulphur Springs, West Virginia.* Greenbrier Hotel, for a weekend.

**1961**   *Mount Vernon, Virginia.* He attended a party given by the Kennedys. Vice President and Mrs Johnson were also there.

**1963**   *Washington, D.C.* The White House, East Room. The Fords called on the Kennedys. Both went to the Capitol, where Kennedy's body lay in state. On Monday November 25 they went to the Arlington National Cemetery. He attended the funeral mass at St. Matthew's Cathedral.

**1964**   *San Francisco, California.* Cow Palace for the Republican National Convention.

**1968**   *Miami Beach, Florida.* Convention Center for the Republican National Convention. He stayed at the Fountainbleau Hotel, 4441 Collins Avenue. He was Chairman of the Convention.

**1972** *Shanghai, China.* He arrived in Shanghai, China, and toured the city. In Peking, he attended a banquet at the Great Hall of the People. Later, he went to Manchuria.

**1974** *Washington, D.C.* He attended a dinner given by King Hussein at the Anderson House.

**1974** *Palm Springs, California.* He stayed at the 250-acre estate of Walter H. Annenberg, Ambassador to Great Britain and played golf at the La Quinta Country Club.

**1974** *Arlington, Virginia.* West bank of the Potomac River. Groundbreaking of the Lyndon Johnson Memorial Grove.

**1974** *Des Moines, Iowa.* Visit, Iowa State House. Luncheon, Hotel Fort Des Moines.

**1974** *Kansas City, Missouri.* Muehlebach Hotel.

**1974** *Long Beach, California.* He visited Nixon in Memorial Hospital Medical Center.

**1974** *New York City, New York.* He addressed the United Nations General Assembly.

**1974** *Philadelphia.* Independence Hall. Reconvening of the first Continental Congress.

**1974** *San Clemente, California.* He visited President Nixon.

**1974** *Tokyo, Japan.* Stayed at Geihinkan Palace (was called Akasaka), an eighteenth century baroque structure, near the Imperial Palace in downtown Tokyo. He met here with the Emperor in the Rising Sun Room. He was honored by the Emperor at a state banquet at Showa Palace and attended a reception by members of the Japanese Diet at the Hotel Okura. He went to Kyoto for a full round of sightseeing and visited the old Imperial Palace of Flowers, the Nijo Castle, a Buddhist pagoda called the Golden Pavilion, and had dinner at Tauruya Restaurant. The trip to Japan was his first trip abroad as president.

**1974** *Seoul, Korea.* He was the third American president to visit Korea. Eisenhower came in 1960 and Johnson in 1966. There was a dinner and speech in the Banquet Hall of the Capitol Building. He spent time with the American troops at Camp Casey, 15 miles from the demilitarized zone, where he took an outdoor lunch in Indianhead Field.

**1974** *Vladivostok, USSR.* He met with President Brezhnev. He went by train to the site—the small resort town of Okeansky, where they stayed at a dacha at the Okeansky Sanitorium, a health spa on the outskirts of Vladivostok.

**1974** *Fort de France, Martinique.* Meeting with French President Giscard d'Estaing. Dinner at the Governor's residence and stayed at the Meridien Hotel.

**1975** *Topeka, Kansas.* State Capitol joint session in the House Chamber. He met with former Governor Alf Landon.

**1975** *Baltimore, Maryland.* Ceremony at Fort McHenry National Monument.

**1975** *Belgrade, Yugoslavia.* He met Tito at the Federal Executive Council Building.

**1975** *Bonn, Germany.* He met with Helmut Schmidt at the Palais Schaumburg, went on a dinner cruise on the Rhine River, and had breakfast with Chancellor Schmidt at Schloss Gymnich.

**1975** *Boston, Massachusetts.* He made remarks at the Old North Church Lantern Service.

**1975** *Brussels, Belgium.* First trip to Europe as president.

**1975** *Bucharest, Rumania.* He was met by President Nicolae Ceausescu. There was a State dinner in the marble dining room of the Palace of the Republic and an excursion to Transylvania.

**1975** *Concord, Massachusetts.* Old North Bridge, for Patriot Day ceremony.

**1975** *Concord, New Hampshire.* He addressed the General Court in the House Chamber at the State Capitol.

**1975** *Des Moines, Iowa State Fair.* Hotel Fort Des Moines.

**1975** *Fort Smith, Arkansas.* He dedicated St. Edward Mercy Medical Center.

**1975** *Helsinki, Finland.* President's Palace. Meetings in the elegant Finlandia House. He also experienced a sauna bath during his stay.

**1975** *Krakow, Poland.* He helicoptered to Auschwitz. In Krakow, he had lunch at Wawel Castle.

**1975** *Lexington, Massachusetts.* Lexington Green, for Patriot Day ceremony.

**1975** *Libby, Montana.* He pulled the switch at the Libby Dam dedication.

**1975** *Madrid, Spain.* He received the key to the City of Madrid and spoke at Plaza Cibeles. He met with Franco at El Pardo Palace. State Dinner at the Royal Palace.

**1975** *Milwaukee, Wisconsin.* Phister Hotel, Room 621.

**1975** *Palm Springs, California.* Easter vacation home of his friend, Fred Wilson.

**1975** *Pearl Harbor, Hawaii.* He attended memorial Services at the *Arizona* at exactly 7:55 A.M., the moment of the Japanese attack in 1941. This was the end of his fourth overseas trip in 1975.

**1975** *Rome, Italy.* Palazzo Quirinale, the Villa Madama. He Met Pope Paul VI at the Library of the Papal Apartments in the Vatican.

**1975** *Sacramento, California.* Senator Hotel. He made a speech in the Assembly Chamber of the State Capitol. There was an assassination attempt outside the Senator Hotel on Union Square.

**1975** *Salzburg, Austria.* He was received by Chancellor Bruno Kreisky and had meetings at Schloss Klessheim. He also met with Egyptian President Anwar Sadat.

**1975** *San Francisco, California.* St. Francis Hotel.

**1975** *Seattle, Washington.* Olympic Hotel.

**1975** *Warsaw, Poland.* Dinner, Wilanow Palace.

**1976** *Arlington, Virginia.* He dedicated Lyndon Johnson Memorial Grove.

**1976** *Columbia, South Carolina.* Visit to Governor's Mansion.

**1976** *Columbus, Ohio.* Remarks at State Capitol.

**1976** *Kansas City, Missouri.* Republican Party National Convention headquarters, Crown Center Hotel. Kemper Arena, where he accepted the presidential nomination.

**1976** *Langley, Virginia.* He swore in George Bush as CIA director.

**1976** *Louisville, Kentucky.* Galt House Hotel, Fourth and River Street, for dinner and signing the Armed Forces Reserve Bill.

**1976** *Patterson, New Jersey.* Dedication of the Great Falls National Historic Site.

**1976** *Pocantico Hill, New York.* Union Church, with Nelson Rockefeller.

**1976** *Richmond, Virginia.* Remarks on State Capitol grounds.

**1976** *San Francisco, California.* Presidential debate with Jimmy Carter at Palace of Fine Arts Theater.

**1976** *San Francisco California.* Fairmont Hotel. Luncheon at Sheraton Palace Hotel.

**1976** *Springfield, Illinois.* Unveiling ceremony, Lincoln Home National Visitor Center.

**1976** *Valley Forge, Pennsylvania.* Valley Forge State Park.

**1976** *Williamsburg, Virginia.* Phi Beta Kappa Memorial Hall of William and Mary College for debate with Jimmy Carter.

**1976** *Williamsburg, Virginia.* Hall of House of Burgesses meeting and dinner at Williamsburg Lodge.

**1976** *Yellowstone, Wyoming.* Old Faithful Lodge. He gave a speech at Old Faithful Geyser proposing the extension of national park areas.

**1983** *Ann Arbor, Michigan.* University of Michigan, for the dedication of the Ford Memorial Library.

**1983** *New Brunswick, New Jersey.* Rutgers University. He delivered the Civics Lecture at the Eagleton Institute of Politics. He was appointed as the first holder of the Clifford Case Professorship of Public Affairs.

**1986** *Grand Rapids, Michigan.* Gerald R. Ford Museum, where he hosted a two day symposium on humor and the presidency.

**1992** *Houston, Texas.* Republican National Convention, Astrodome. He gave a speech to the delegates.

**1994** *Cambridge, Massachusetts.* St. John the Evangelist Church to attend the funeral of former Speaker of the House, Thomas P. "Tip" O'Neil.

**1994** *Yorba Linda, California.* He attended the funeral of former president Richard Nixon.

# BIBLIOGRAPHY

Ford, Gerald R. *A Time to Heal. Autobiography.* New York, Harper and Row, 1979.

Vestal, Bud. *Jerry Ford, Up Close.* New York, Coward, McCann & Geoghegan, 1974.

# JAMES EARL CARTER

## 1924–
### 39TH PRESIDENT 1977–1981: DEMOCRATIC PARTY

Jimmy Carter was born on October 1, 1924, at 7:00 A.M., to James Earl Carter and Lillian Gordy Carter at Wise Hospital in Plains, Georgia. From the beginning, he was called "Jimmy" and continued to use the diminutive when he became president. His ancestors came to Virginia about 1635 and later moved to Georgia.

## CHARACTERISTICS

Jimmy Carter is 5′9″ tall and weighed about 155 pounds as president. He has sandy hair and hazel eyes. When he entered the White House, he was parting his hair on the right; in 1979 he began parting it on the left, and this led to some discussion as to which way his political thought was taking him. His charming toothy grin was a favorite with cartoonists. The Fashion Foundation of America named him the "world's best dressed statesman" in 1978.

He is a soft-spoken man and makes people feel comfortable around him. He is generous with his time and effort to those who are less fortunate. In 1977 he was described as a 6-gallon donor to the Red Cross blood drive. Since leaving the White House, he does

*"Our American values are not luxuries but necessities—not the salt in our bread but the bread itself."*

*—Farewell address, January 14, 1981*

# A LIFE IN REVIEW

**Birth:** October 1, 1924; Plains, GA

**Married:** Rosalynn Smith; July 7, 1946;
3 sons, 1 daughter

## CAREER

**1946–1953** U.S. Navy

**1953–1977** Peanut farmer

**1963–1967** State senator Georgia
legislature

**1971–1977** Governor of Georgia

## ADMINISTRATION EVENTS

**1977** Pardon for most Vietnam draft
evaders

**1978** Panama Canal treaty

Camp David Talks with Egypt and
Israel

**1979** Diplomatic relations established
with China

Draft treaty with Soviet Union Salt II

U.S. personnel taken hostage in
Iran

*Wise Hospital in Plains, Georgia, birthplace of
Jimmy Carter, the first U.S. president to be born
in a hospital.*

## BIRTHPLACE

Carter was born in Plains, Georgia, at Wise
Hospital, Bond Street (now Plains Convalescent Home). He is the first U.S. president to be
born in a hospital. The wing of the hospital
where he was born is known but not the number of the room.

## BAPTISM

Carter was baptized in Plains, Georgia, at
Plains Baptist Church, North Bond Street. He
was baptized by immersion in 1935 at the age
of eleven.

## CHURCH

Of his religion Carter says, "I never doubt
my faith. I doubt what man does sometimes
with the power of free will, but I never doubt
my faith in God." People who know him well
say he lives his faith.

sit-ups every morning and plays tennis frequently. He has always been an avid fisherman
and occasionally hunts. At one time, he enjoyed stock car racing. In 1983, on a vacation
in Nepal, he went mountain climbing in the
Himalayas, and he kept on to the top while his
wife and others much younger than he had to
be returned to lower levels on stretchers. He is
almost a teetotaler and occasionally smokes a
cigar. Although not a vegetarian, he has had no
beef or pork since leaving the White House,
but he enjoys fish and game.

While on a visit to Orlando, Florida, in 1986 he participated in the kick-off for the annual fund-raising for the First United Methodist Church. He expressed close connections with the Methodist Church, saying that both his wife and his mother grew up as Methodists and only later joined the Baptist Church when they each married a Baptist.

Jimmy Carter had membership in three churches, two in Plains and one in Washington, D.C. He reads the Bible daily and is an Old Testament scholar.

**1924–1977** *Plains, Georgia.* Plains Baptist Church.

**1943–1946** *Annapolis, Maryland.* He attended the Naval Academy Chapel at Maryland Avenue as a midshipman. In addition to his required attendance, he taught a Sunday School class for officers' dependents; as a submarine officer, he sometimes conducted services.

**1951–1952** *Groton, Connecticut.* While in the Navy, he sometimes conducted services in the Chapel on the Thames, Shark Boulevard.

**1953–1971** *Plains, Georgia.* Plains Baptist Church.

**1971–1975** *Atlanta, Georgia.* Northside Drive Baptist Church, 311 Northside Drive, NW. He attended and sometimes taught a Sunday school class.

**1975–1977** *Plains, Georgia.* Plains Baptist Church.

**1977–1981** *Washington, D.C.* He attended the First Baptist Church of the City of Washington, 1328 Sixteenth Street, NW, where he also taught a Sunday school class every few weeks.

**1977–** *Sapelo Island, Georgia.* He attended the First African Baptist Church while on the island for vacation.

**1979** *Atlanta, Georgia.* Ebenezer Baptist Church. He spoke on the 50th anniversary of Martin Luther King, Jr.'s birth.

**1981–** *Woodstown, New Jersey.* First Baptist Church, 117 South Main Street, while in the area for Habitat for Humanity.

**1981–** *Plains, Georgia.* Marantha Baptist Church, Buena Vista Road. He changed his membership from the Plains Baptist Church when he refused to accept the segregationist policies of this church where he had had his membership since boyhood days. People travelling north and south often stop here on Sunday morning to attend his Sunday school class. As the finance officer of the church, he says their contributions are more than welcome. At times, he mows the church lawn, and Rosalynn vacuums the carpet and dusts the church pews.

**1992** *Washington, D.C.* First Rock Baptist Church in southeast Washington, where he spoke on the discrimination of rich people against the poor. Afterwards, he participated in the work on ten houses in the 4600 block of Benning Road.

# EDUCATION

**1930–1941** *Plains, Georgia.* Plains High School, Bond Street. It contained all grades one through eleven. There was no kindergarten and school finished at the eleventh grade. He was an almost straight A student.

**1941–1942** *Americus, Georgia.* Georgia Southwestern College, where his future wife, Rosalynn, also attended. He did not stay on campus but commuted back and forth from Plains.

**1942–1943** *Atlanta, Georgia.* Georgia Institute of Technology, where he took math courses in the D. M. Smith Building (now the Ivan Allen College of Management Policy & International Affairs), 225 North Avenue, NW. He stayed in Room 308 of Knowles Dormitory while attending the Institute. The site is now occupied by Bobby Dodd Stadium at Historic Grant Field, Techwood Drive and North Avenue.

*Jimmy Carter and Rosalynn Smith were married here at the Plains United Methodist Church.*

**1943–1946**  *Annapolis, Maryland.* U.S. Naval Academy, fulfillment of a dream he had since he was six years old. He graduated 60 in a class of more than 800. While at Annapolis, he lived in Bancroft Hall. Graduation exercises were in Dahlgren Hall.

**1946**  *Philadelphia, Pennsylvania.* He attended a radar school for three weeks.

**1951–1952**  *Groton, Connecticut.* He was stationed at the Naval Submarine Base and took classes in Cromwell Hall.

**1953**  *Schnectady, New York.* Union College. He took a non-credit one semester graduate course in the Physics Science building. He sometimes attended Union College Chapel.

**1953**  *Tifton, Georgia.* He enrolled in a crash course in scientific agriculture at the University of Georgia Experimental Station.

## MARRIAGE AND HONEYMOON

Carter was married on July 7, 1946, in Plains, Georgia, at Plains United Methodist Church, Church Street, to (Eleanor) Rosalynn Smith. Rosalynn was a home-town girl and was the best friend of his sister, Ruth. Rosalynn is about three years younger than Jimmy and they paid little attention to each other until the summer of 1945 when he was home from his second year at Annapolis. Toward the end of the summer, returning home from taking Rosalynn to a movie, Jimmy told his mother that he had found the girl he was going to marry.

They had a short honeymoon in the mountains at Chimney Rock, North Carolina, where they stayed in the home of an Annapolis friend. They began their life together in a small apartment in Norfolk, Virginia, a life of intermittent separations and reunions as Jimmy pursued his naval career.

*Boyhood home of Jimmy Carter in Archery, Georgia.*

# HOMES/LODGINGS

**1924**   *Plains, Georgia.* An upstairs apartment on Church Street, near the Carter store (now the Wellon home).

**1924–1927**   *Plains, Georgia.* A house on Bond Street; destroyed by fire.

**1927–1946**   *Archery, Georgia.* Three miles from Plains on the old Preston Road was a six-room farm house without electricity or indoor plumbing. Jimmy sold peanuts in nearby Plains. In a speech to a group of young people in 1977, he told of how excited he was when electricity was turned on for the first time in his boyhood home.

**1940**   *Roswell, Georgia.* Dolvin House, Bulloch Street, visiting his Aunt. He also visited her while he was president.

**1946–1948**   *Norfolk, Virginia.* Bolling Square Apartments, 1009 Buckingham Park, Apartment 236. They moved here four days after their marriage. It was a small apartment for which he paid $98 a month and where he stayed with Rosalynn when not on sea duty on the *Wyoming.*

**1948**   *New London, Connecticut.* He had quarters on the submarine base. Connecticut 12 north of Groton.

**1949–1950**   *Oahu, Hawaii.* 318 Sixth Street in Nimitz Naval Housing in a two-bedroom apartment.

**1950–**   *San Diego, California.* He lived in a neighborhood of Mexican immigrants for five months. The location is undetermined.

**1951–1952**   *Groton, Connecticut.* One fall they were in Provinceton, Massachusetts, where they rented an upstairs apartment. The location is not determined.

**1952–1953**   *Washington, D.C.* While working at the Atomic Energy Commission, he lived in an apartment. The location is not determined.

**1953**   *Plains, Georgia.* They lived on the south side of Church Street between Walters and Thomas Streets with his mother for two months. As his mother later said, "There's no house big enough for two women to live together." Plains on Paschal Street in a red brick public housing project in Apartment 9-A. He enjoyed living here

*Home of Jimmy Carter in Plains, Georgia.*

and was eligible to do so because their income was less than $250 per month. The next year, when the business began to flourish, their annual income exceeded $3,000, and they had to move out.

**1954–1956** *Plains, Georgia.* In the fall, they rented an old house on the outskirts of Plains. It stood high off the ground on brick pillars, was 104 years old, and had no central heat. It was antebellum plantation house and was a mile from his office. It was the old Montgomery House, sometimes called the Haunted House.

**1956–1961** *Archery, Georgia.* Dr. Thad Wise's house on Old Preston Road, Archery, located near the house where Jimmy grew up.

**1961–1971** *Plains, Georgia.* Woodland Drive which has been their permanent home since 1961. It is set back from the

road and surrounded by thick shade trees. Unseen guards with electronic voices keep uninvited visitors from trespassing.

**1971–1975** *Atlanta, Georgia.* Governor's Mansion, West Ferry Paces Road.

**1975–1977** *Plains, Georgia.* Woodland Drive. He returned in 1981.

**1977–1981** *Washington, D.C.* The White House as president.

**1982–** *Ellijay (near), Georgia.* In the Blue Ridge mountains of central Georgia is a vacation cabin built alongside Turnip Town Creek. It is constructed of hand-hewn yellow pine logs.

## WORK

**1946** *Pensacola, Florida.* Navy Boulevard (Florida 295) southwest of Pensacola was his first navy assignment.

**1946–1948** *Norfolk, Virginia.* The U.S. Navy Station is located off I-564, northwest Norfolk. He reported on August 6 as an electronics officer on experimental gunnery ships, first on the *Wyoming,* and then the *Mississippi.*

**1948–1950** *New London, Connecticut.* He attended the submarine school and started a five-year period with submarines.

**1950** *San Diego, California.* Broadway at Harbor Drive.

**1950–1953** *New London and Groton, Connecticut, and Schenectady, New York.* U.S. Navy Atlantic Submarine Base.

**1952–1953** *Washington, D.C.* He was on temporary duty with the Atomic Energy Commission, 1901 Constitution Avenue, NW.

**1953–1971** *Plains, Georgia.* Manager of a peanut farm and business. The Carter peanut warehouse is on Main Street.

**1963–1967** *Atlanta, Georgia.* He was a member of the State Senate. He was re-elected in 1964 unopposed.

**1963–1965** *Atlanta, Georgia.* He lodged in the Grady Hotel, 210 Peachtree Street, NW, while serving in the Georgia legislature.

**1965–1967** *Atlanta, Georgia.* Piedmont Hotel. 108 Peachtree Street, NW. A much quieter hotel than the Grady.

**1971–1977** *Atlanta, Georgia.* Governor. His office was on the second floor of the Capitol.

**1976–1877** *Plains, Georgia.* Campaigning for president. Carter Presidential Campaign Headquarters was in the old train station at Hudson and Main Streets.

**1977–1981** *Washington, D.C.* President of the United States.

**1981–** *Plains, Georgia.* He now writes and participates in Habitat for Humanity and other public service projects. He has set up office in his mother's old home.

**1982–** *Atlanta, Georgia.* Distinguished Professor at Emory University, 1380 S. Oxford Road, NE.

# TRAVEL/VISITS

**1946** *Richmond, Virginia.* He spent the night at the old Jefferson Hotel. It is now beautifully restored.

**1968** *Lock Haven, Pennsylvania.* Fallon Hotel, 131 East Water Street while doing mission work.

**1975** *Norfolk, Virginia.* Botanical Gardens, for the commissioning of the *Mississippi* at Pier 12.

**1975** *Philadelphia, Pennsylvania.* Walnut Street Theater, where he had his first debate with President Ford September 24.

**1975** *San Francisco, California.* Fine Arts Palace Theater, where he had the second debate with Ford on October 7.

**1975** *Williamsburg, Virginia.* William and Mary College, for a third and final debate with Ford.

**1976** *New York City, New York.* Americana Hotel, 801 Seventh Avenue, was his presidential campaign headquarters and is where he stayed during the Democratic National Convention held in July. During this week, an old-fashioned picnic was held for Democratic Party supporters at Pier 88. He was nominated for president at Madison Square Garden. After the Convention, he attended church services at the Fifth Avenue Presbyterian Church, 705 Fifth Avenue, on the northwest corner of West 55th Street.

**1976** *High Point, North Carolina.* High Point College Auditorium for a primary campaign speech.

**1977–1981** *Sapello Island, Georgia.* South End House, for vacations, and also at the Musgrove Plantation, home of Bagley Smith (tobacco heir), in a small cottage known as Grove House. He began annual visits here just after his election in 1976. From 1976 on, the area around St. Simon's Island was a favorite fishing spot. During the years 1977 to 1981, attending a "town meeting" and staying with a local family were popular with him.

**1977** *Arlington, Virginia.* He gave a speech at the Amphitheater and laid a wreath at the Tomb of the Unknown Soldier.

**1977** *Charleston, West Virginia.* 1716 Kanawha Boulevard. Guest at the Governor's Mansion.

**1977** *New York City, New York.* He addressed the United Nations in the General Assembly Hall.

**1977** *London, England.* He travelled to London for an economic summit meeting—his first trip abroad as president. He had dinner with Queen Elizabeth at Buckingham Palace and stayed at the Ambassador's residence, Winfred House. He had dinner with the Prime Minister at Number 10, Downing Street, lunch in Lancaster House, and attended meetings at the White Hall Banqueting House. During his five days in England, he also strolled in St. James Park, and worshipped in Westminster Abbey. Outside London, he visited Newcastle-on-Tyne and Washington, England, the area where George Washington's forebears lived from the twelfth to the seventeenth centuries. On this same trip, he went to Geneva, Switzerland, where he met with President Assad of Syria at the Hotel Intercontinental for a few hours before returning to London.

**1977** *St. Simons Island, Georgia.* Short vacation at Musgrove Plantation.

**1977** *Tehran, Iran.* He was received by the Shah at the Saadabad Palace and honored at a state dinner at the Niavaran Palace.

**1977** *Warsaw, Poland.* While in Warsaw, he stayed at the Wilanov Palace. He laid a wreath at the Unknown Soldier's Tomb, visited the Warsaw Ghetto Memorial, had lunch at the Parliament Building with First Secretary Edward Gierek, and attended a state dinner at the Palace of the Council of Ministers.

**1978** *New Delhi, India.* He attended a reception at Roosevelt House, residence of the American Ambassador, and laid a wreath at the Ghandhi Memorial. He lodged in the Rashtrapati Bhavan, the President's House. He visited Daulatpur, a small village in India which changed its name to Carterpoori to honor him.

**1978** *Asheville, North Carolina.* He visited and spoke at the Deer Park Pavilion, Biltmore Estate.

**1978** *Beaumont, Texas.* He dedicated the Jack Brooks Federal Building.

**1978** *Boise, Idaho.* He took a 3-day raft trip down the Middle Fork of the Salmon River. In Boise, he stayed at the Rodeway Inn, suite 400.

**1978** *Brussels, Belgium.* He was received by King Baudouin I and attended a state luncheon La Grande Galerie at the Royal Palace.

**1978** *Camp David, Maryland.* On August 5, he held meetings with Egyptian President Anwar al-Sadat and Israeli Prime Minister Menahem Begin which led to the Camp David Accord.

**1978** *Gettysburg, Pennsylvania.* He visited Gettysburg National Park and also visited Mrs. Eisenhower at her home. Mercersburg, Pennsylvania. He visited the birthplace of President Buchanan, the Antietam Battlefield site in Maryland, and Harpers' Ferry in West Virginia.

**1978** *Grand Teton National Park, Jackson Lake, Wyoming.* One week in Brinkerhoff Lodge.

**1978** *New York City, New York.* He spoke at City Hall, attended a reception in the Governor's Room, and spent the night at the mayor's home, Gracie Mansion.

**1978** *Normandy Beach, France, site of D-Day landings, visiting the American Ceme-*

*tery and Memorial.* He made remarks at the Hotel de Ville of Bayeux and returned to Paris, where he attended receptions at the Grand Trianon and at the Chateau de Versailles.

**1978**   *Panama Canal Zone.* He visited Fort Clayton and operated the controls at Miraflores Locks.

**1978**   *Paris, France.* He laid a wreath at the Tomb of the Unknown Soldier at the Arc de Triomphe. He was taken to the Palais Elysee Palace and charmed the French as he strolled down the Champs Elysees with French President Giscard. He was honored at a banquet at the Palace of Versailles.

**1978**   *Riyadh, Saudi Arabia.* He was guest of honor at a banquet in the royal palace and lodged in the Nasriyeh Guest Palace with its gold plated plumbing. Dinner at King Khalid's palace. He flew from here to Aswan for a meeting with President Anwar Sadat, and on the same day, continued to Paris, France.

**1978**   *Spokane, Washington.* He dedicated Riverfront Park.

**1978**   *St. Paul, Minnesota.* August 17, he boarded the *Delta Queen* at Lambert Landing for a cruise down the Mississippi.

**1979**   *Atlanta, Georgia.* State Capitol Senate Chamber. He unveiled his portrait as a former governor of Georgia.

**1979**   *Atlanta, Georgia.* He spoke of Martin Luther King at the Ebenezer Baptist Church.

**1979**   *Boston, Massachusetts.* October 20, he dedicated the John F. Kennedy Memorial Library.

**1979**   *Egypt.* From March 8 to 10, he stayed at the Qubba Palace, gave a luncheon for President Sadat at Mena House in Giza, and toured the Pyramids and Sphinx.

**1979**   *Hannibal, Missouri.* He toured Mark Twain's boyhood home, the Cave, and the Becky Thatcher Book Shop.

**1979**   *Israel.* From March 10 to 12, he visited Israel. He had dinner at Prime Minister Begin's residence. In Jerusalem, he stayed at the King David Hotel, visited Yad Vashem with its Hall of Names and Hall of Remembrance, and Mount Herzl.

**1979**   *Sapello Island, Georgia.* He vacationed here many times. He attended Easter services at the First African Baptist Church.

**1979**   *Springfield, Illinois.* He spoke to the State Legislature in the House Chamber in the State Capitol.

**1979**   *Tallahassee, Florida.* He spent the night at the Governor's Mansion, 700 North Adams Street and addressed a joint session in the House of Representatives Chamber in the State Capitol.

**1979**   *Washington, D.C.* National Cathedral. On November 15, he attended an interfaith service for the hostages held in Iran.

**1980**   *Hartford, Connecticut.* He spoke in front of Old State House.

**1980**   *Independence, Missouri.* He visited the Truman Library and the Truman grave site.

**1980**   *New York City, New York.* He spent the night at the Sheraton Centre Hotel, 811 Seventh Avenue at 52nd Street, and accepted the Democratic nomination at Madison Square Gardens.

**1980**   *St. Paul, Minnesota.* He attended the funeral of Senator Hubert H. Humphrey at the Church of Hope.

**1980**   *Cleveland, Ohio.* Presidential debate with Ronald Reagan at Cleveland Convention Center Music Hall on September 28.

**1980**   *Columbia, South Carolina.* He made remarks at the Governor's Mansion.

**1980**   *Jackson, Mississippi.* He made remarks at the Governor's Mansion.

**1980**   *Plains, Georgia.* November 4, he voted at Plains High School and made a speech at Plains Depot.

**1980**   *San Antonio, Texas.* Democratic rally at The Alamo.

**1981** *Buffalo, New York.* On January 7, he laid a wreath on former president Fillmore's grave in the Forest Lawn Cemetery.

**1981** *Egypt.* On October 9, he attended Anwar Sadat's funeral. He travelled with ex-presidents Nixon and Ford. The funeral was in a small mosque at Maadi Hospital, followed by burial near the Tomb of the Unknown Soldier. He saw Mrs. Anwar Sadat at her home in Giza and visited Mubarak at the Egyptian Parliament building.

**1981** *Hebgen Lake, Yellowstone National Park.* A family camping vacation.

**1981** *Wiesbaden, West Germany.* January 22, he greeted freed hostages at the American Hospital in Wiesbaden. He spent only a few hours before returning to the United States.

**1983** *Carter Center of Emory University inaugurated.* Conference on Mideast affairs.

**1985** *Atlanta, Georgia.* He was the first American to receive the World Methodist Peace Award for courage in confronting human rights violations.

**1985** *Orlando, Florida.* Fundraiser for First United Methodist Church and promoting Habitat for Humanity.

**1985** *Woodstown, New Jersey.* Habitat for Humanity project meetings. He attended the First Baptist Church, 117 South Main Street.

**1986** *Atlanta, Georgia.* The Carter Presidential Library Center opened. When at the Center, he sometimes eats at Manuel's Tavern on North Highland Avenue or Everybody's Pizza across from Emory University.

**1986** *Central America.* He went from San Jose, Costa Rica (talking with rebels), to Managua, Nicaragua, where he spoke with leaders of the government to bring about peace talks. The extreme rightists charged that he was an ally of communism. When asked to comment, he said, "Sometimes the greatest honor that can be paid to a person is the identity of his enemies."

**1986** *Dhaka, Bangladesh.* Talks on establishing a philanthropic center.

**1986** *Peshawar, Pakistan.* He stayed at the Afghan Refugee Camp near the border when visiting Pakistan as co-chairman of a group aiding health projects.

**1988** *Addis Ababa, Ethiopia.* For talks dealing with internal conflicts.

**1988** *Atlanta, Georgia.* He addressed the Democratic National Convention held at the Omni Hotel.

**1988** *Nairobi Kenya.* On December 2, he participated in mediation talks between the sides in the civil war in the Sudan.

**1988** *Private trip to Lhasa, Tibet.*

**1988** *San Diego, California.* For Habitat for Humanity project.

**1990** *Managua, Nicaragua.* As an observer in the election. He was here for three days and served as chairman of the Council of Freely Elected Heads of Government.

**1991** *Athens, Greece.* To receive the Onasis International Prize for Man and Society.

**1991** *Simi Valley, California.* He attended the dedication of the Reagan Presidential Library.

**1994** *Cambridge, Massachusetts.* St. John the Evangelist Church. He attended the funeral of former House Speaker Thomas P. "Tip" O'Neill.

**1994** *Port-au-Prince, Haiti.* He was a special envoy to negotiate the exit of the military leaders of Haiti and the return of President Aristide, with meetings at the Military Headquarters of General Cedras and in the Presidential Palace. This was his eighth trip to Haiti.

**1994** *Pyongyang, North Korea.* Talks with President Kim Il-Sung to diffuse the nuclear problem.

**1994** *Yorba Linda, California.* He attended the funeral of former president Richard Nixon.

# SPECIAL SITES

*Atlanta, Georgia.* The Carter Presidential Center, just off North Avenue in the Virginia Highlands neighborhood at One Copenhill Avenue. It was dedicated in President Reagan's presence on October 1, 1986.

*Atlanta, Georgia.* A statue of Carter in work clothes with his sleeves rolled up and his hands outstretched was unveiled on the lawn of the State Capitol in July 1994.

*Plains, Georgia.* The Jimmy Carter National Historical Site, which includes his birthplace, current Plains house, Plains High School, and the Plains railroad depot, which served as Carter's campaign headquarters. The Carter site is one of 30 historic areas in the National Park system that reflects the lives of former presidents.

*Plains, Georgia.* Carter Family Cemetery. Burial places of his ancestors, including his father and mother.

*Americus, Georgia.* James Earl Carter Library/Museum on the campus of Georgia Southwestern College.

# BIBLIOGRAPHY

Carter, Jimmy. *Keeping Faith: Memoirs of a President.* New York: Bantam Books, 1982.

Carter, Rosalynn. *First Lady From Plains.* New York: Fawcett Gold Medal, 1984.

Hyatt, Richard. *The Carters of Plains.* Huntsville: The Strode Publishers, Inc., 1977.

Wooten, James. *Dasher: The Roots and Rising of Jimmy Carter.* New York: Simon & Schuster, 1978.

THE PRESIDENTS

# RONALD WILSON REAGAN

1911–

40TH PRESIDENT 1981–1989: REPUBLICAN PARTY

*"If our Constitution means anything it means that we, the Federal Government, are entrusted with preserving life, liberty and the pursuit of happiness."*

—*Press conference on Supreme Court's abortion decision, June 11, 1986*

Ronald Reagan was born on February 6, 1911, to John Edward (Jack) and Nelle Wilson Reagan in the small town of Tampico, Illinois.

## CHARACTERISTICS

As president he was 6'1" tall and weighed 184 pounds. He had thick brown hair and blue eyes. Reagan has been severely near-sighted from childhood and wears contact lenses. About the horned rimmed spectacles he wore as a boy, he says, "I hate them to this day." In his autobiography, he relates that one of the doctors at the army physical examination told him after checking his eyes that if they sent him overseas, he'd shoot a general. The other doctor said, "Yes, and you'd miss him." He does not smoke and drinks very little other than an occasional glass of wine.

## BIRTHPLACE

Reagan was born in Tampico, Illinois, at 111 Main Street, above the H.C. Pitney General Store, where his father sold shoes.

# A LIFE IN REVIEW

**Birth:** February 6, 1911; Tampico, IL

**Married:** Jane Wyman; January 24, 1940; (Divorced) July 19, 1949; 1 son (adopted), 1 daughter     Nancy Davis; March 4, 1952; 1 son, 1 daughter

## CAREER

**1932–1937** Sports announcer

**1954–1965** Actor

**1967–1974** Governor of California

## ADMINISTRATION EVENTS

**1981** Assassination attempt

Air Traffic Controllers' strike

**1983** U.S. Marines killed in Beirut, Lebanon

Grenada invasion

**1986** U.S. air attack on Libya

Iran Contra scandal

# BAPTISM

Reagan was baptized in Dixon, Illinois at the Christian Church, 124 Hennepin Street, on June 21, 1922. Reagan remembers the minister saying, "Arise and walk in newness of faith."

# CHURCH

Reagan was reportedly deeply, though not ostentatiously, religious. In his childhood, the family attended the Disciples of Christ Church although he later often attended the Presbyterian Church. At age fifteen, he was teaching his own Sunday school class.

While he was in the White House much was made of the report that his wife, Nancy, depended on an astrologer and often consulted her horoscope. At the same time, there is much to support the description of the Reagans as deeply religious people. Reagan said, "Sometimes when I'm faced with an unbeliever, an atheist, I am tempted to invite him to the greatest gourmet dinner that one can ever serve and, when we finished eating that magnificent dinner, to ask him if he believes there's a cook."

**1913–1915** *Chicago, Illinois.* Hyde Park Church of Christ, corner of Fifty-seventh Street and Lexington Avenue.

**1915–1918** *Galesburg, Illinois.* Disciples (Christian) Church on Northwest Street.

**1918–1919** *Monmouth, Illinois.* Disciples Church. Location not determined

**1920–1933** *Dixon, Illinois.* Christian Church. At first, the church held meetings in the basement of the Y.M.C.A. before their own building was completed at 123 Hennepin in 1922.

**1932–1933** *Davenport, Iowa.* First Christian Church, 510 East Fifth Street.

**1933–1937** *Des Moines, Iowa.* Capitol Hill Christian Church, 3322 East Twenty-fifth Street.

**1937–1940** *Hollywood, California.* No records of attendance.

**1940–1989** *Hollywood, California.* On May 12, he joined the Hollywood Christian Church (Disciples of Christ Church), 1717 North Grammercy Place (Beverly Hills area).

**1981** *Los Angeles, California.* The Reagans also attended the Bel-Air Presbyterian Church, 16221 Mulholland Drive.

**1973–** *Phoenix, Arizona.* St. Thomas the Apostle Church, 2312 East Campbell Avenue, when visiting Mrs. Reagan's parents.

**1981** *Washington, D.C.* First Presbyterian Church. He attended church for the first time since assassination attempt.

**1981–** *Washington, D.C.* National Presbyterian Church. While president, Reagan rarely attended church in Washington, saying it interfered with the worship of others because of the security required when he was present.

**1982** *Huntsville, Tennessee.* First Presbyterian Church, in nearby Helenwood, with Howard Baker.

**1984** *Ballyporeen, Ireland.* Church of the Assumption.

**1986** *Solvang, California.* First Presbyterian Church, for Easter service. This was his first attendance at a regular worship service since Easter Sunday 1984 in Honolulu.

**1987** *Santa Barbara, California.* First Presbyterian Church, 21 East Constance, for Easter services.

# EDUCATION

**1911–1916** *Galesburg, Illinois.* His mother taught him to read at age five since there was no kindergarten available in Galesburg.

**1916–1918** *Galesburg, Illinois.* First grade at Silas Willard School, 495 East Fremont Street.

**1918–1919** *Monmouth, Illinois.* Central School.

**1919–1920** *Tampico, Illinois.* He entered the fifth grade in September at Tampico Grade School.

**1920–1923** *Dixon, Illinois.* He enrolled at South Central Grammar School, Fifth and Peoria, which was a five minute walk from home. The school had been built during the Civil War. Next to it was Northside High, a red-brick building with big bay windows, which Reagan entered a few years after coming to Dixon.

**1923–1925** *Dixon, Illinois.* He started high school at South Dixon but in his sophomore year transferred from the school at Fifth Street and Peoria Avenue.

**1925–1928** *Dixon, Illinois.* He graduated from North Dixon High School, Morgan and North Ottawa, in 1928. It no longer exists.

**1928–1932** *Eureka, Illinois.* He attended Eureka College, a Disciples of Christ School. He graduated with an economics and sociology major and received a B.A. degree. At Eureka College, his home was the Tau Kappa Epsilon Fraternity House, a buff-colored, brick, three-story building with a great front porch. Reagan lived on the third floor in the same dormer room overlooking the campus for the four years. To help with expenses, he washed dishes in a girl's dormitory.

# MARRIAGE AND HONEYMOON

Reagan was married January 24, 1940 in Glendale, California to actress Jane Wyman (Sara Jane Fulks) at 1712 South Glendale Avenue at the Wee Kirk O'Heather, a popular wedding chapel. The reception was held at the home of Louella Parsons, 612 North Maple Drive. They had a short honeymoon in Palm Springs, California, in their new car with rain falling much of the time. They stayed at the El Mirador Hotel on Indian Avenue. The Desert Hospital now occupies the site. The Tower of the El Mirador was rebuilt and stands on the grounds of the former hotel. The marriage ended in divorce in 1948.

Ciro's, a night club in Hollywood, California, which is now gone, is where Anne Frances "Nancy" Robbins Davis and Ronald had their first date. He first took her to dinner at LaRue's. He proposed to her at her apartment in Westwood. They were married on March 4, 1952, in North Hollywood, California, at the Little Brown Church in the San Fernando Valley. There were only five people there— Ronald and Nancy, Bill and Ardis Holden, and the minister. The reception was at William Holden's home at nearby Toluca Lake.

The Reagans went to Riverdale, California, for the first day of their honeymoon at the old

*Birthplace of Ronald Reagan.*

Mission Inn, 3649 Seventh Street and from there to Phoenix, Arizona, at the Biltmore Estates with Nancy's parents, Dr. and Mrs. Loyal Davis. They spent much of the time driving across the Mojave Desert, including a drive in a blinding sandstorm when the top of their convertible split in the wind and Nancy had to kneel in the front seat and hold the canvas top together to keep it from sailing off. Upon their return from the honeymoon, they moved into Nancy's apartment, but he also kept his because her place was small.

## HOMES/LODGINGS

**1911** *Tampico, Illinois.* 111 Main Street. A five-room flat above the general store where he was born and where the family remained for only a few months afterwards. The building was known as the Graham Building. There were no toilet facilities and they had to use an outside pump. There were two bedrooms which overlooked a back alley.

**1911–1913** *Tampico, Illinois.* The Burden House faced the grain elevator and was across from a park. Soon after Reagan was born, the family moved out of the flat and across the tracks. The boys played on a Civil War canon near by. Downstairs was a living room, a kitchen, a parlor, and a service porch. Upstairs was the luxury of three bedrooms. It had an indoor toilet and modern plumbing. It was a small white frame building.

**1913–1915**    *Chicago, Illinois.* A flat on Cottage Way, 832-834 East Fifty-seventh Street, which was on the south side of Chicago and near the Chicago State University campus in the Hyde Park area. The flat was lighted by a gas jet.

**1915**    *Galesburg, Illinois.* The family first lived in a rented bungalow on the edge of Galesburg at 1219 North Kellog Street.

**1915–1918**    *Galesburg, Illinois.* The family moved to a larger house a block away at 1260 North Kellog Street. It was their first house with hardwood floors. There were big lawns in front and back.

**1918–1919**    *Monmouth, Illinois.* 218 Seventh Avenue, in a two-story house.

**1919–1920**    *Tampico, Illinois.* His father returned to his old job, and they lived in a flat on Main Street above the Pitney store, across the street from the bakery.

**1920–1923**    *Dixon, Illinois.* Reagan lived in five different houses in this town from the time he was nine until he was twenty-one. On December 6, 1920 they moved to 816 South Hennepin Avenue, to a two-story white frame house on a tree-lined street. It had small rooms, including three bedrooms on the second floor, and an inside toilet.

**1923–1931**    *Dixon, Illinois.* 338 West Everett, in a smaller and less expensive house on the north side.

**1931–1932**    *Dixon, Illinois.* His parents moved into an apartment at 226 Lincolnway.

**1932**    *Dixon, Illinois.* 207 North Galena Avenue, in a two-room apartment.

*Reagan family home on Everett in Dixon, Illinois.*

**1932–1933**    *Davenport, Iowa.* He rented a room near the Palmer Chiropractic School for $8 a week and bought a weekly meal ticket at the Palmer Chiropractic School. The Perry Street Apartments (now the Vale Apartment Building) at 202-220 East Fourth Street are vacant and run down and being considered for demolition.

**1933–1934**    *Des Moines, Iowa.* He lived in an apartment near the nurses' quarters of Broadlawn General Hospital at 330 Center Street, in a rooming house belonging to a Miss Plummer.

**1934–1937**    *Des Moines, Iowa.* He later moved to a larger apartment at 400 Center Street. His apartment was on the ground floor and was originally the front and back sitting rooms.

**1937**    *Hollywood, California.* Hollywood Plaza Hotel, near the corner of Hollywood Boulevard and Vine Street.

**1937–1940**    *Hollywood, California.* Montecito Apartments, 1128 Cory Avenue, in a small cottage with an attractive yard on a corner above Sunset Boulevard.

**1940–1941** *Beverly Hills, California.* Apartment 5, 1326 Londonderry View, moving into Jane Wyman's apartment after their marriage. It was 3 blocks from his bachelor bungalow.

**1941** *Beverly Hills, California.* They added the adjoining Londonderry apartment to theirs to accommodate the arrival of Maureen.

**1941–1947** *Hollywood, California.* 9137 Cordell Drive, near the corner of Sunset Boulevard and Doheny. Here they built an eight-room house on a lot with a spectacular view—less than five minutes from their former apartment.

**1947–1948** *Hollywood, California.* On separating from Jane Wyman he moved into the Garden of Allah, an apartment hotel on Sunset Boulevard. He moved in and out of this hotel twice.

**1948–1952** *Beverly Hills, California.* 1326 Londonderry View, in his old apartment following his divorce.

**1940s** *San Fernando Valley, California.* He owned a small eight-acre ranch. When he knew that he and Nancy were going to be married, he bought a larger one. See also Yearling Row Ranch.

**1952** *Lake Malibu, California.* He bought a ranch here which he sold when he became governor. This 350-acre ranch was in the Santa Monica Mountains north of Los Angeles.

**1952** *Brentwood Park, California.* He moved into Nancy Davis's apartment following their marriage while they were looking for a suitable house.

**1952–1955** *Pacific Palisades, California.* 1258 Amalfi Drive, five miles west of Brentwood and a short drive from the Yearling Row Ranch where Reagan had his horse business, was a 7-room, two-story frame house with a living room 25' x 23', with three bedrooms and bath upstairs for which he paid approximately $23,000. It

overlooks the ocean on one side and the Santa Ynez Valley on the other.

**1955–1967** *Pacific Palisades, California.* 1669 Onofre Drive is a big house on the southern slope of the Santa Monica Mountains, high above the street and with an unlimited view of Los Angeles and the ocean.

**1967–1968** *Sacramento, California.* Governor's Mansion, Sixteenth and H Streets, from which they moved, claiming it was unsafe. It is a Victorian style mansion built in 1879 on a corner with two gas stations and a motel on the other corners. It is now a museum.

**1968–1975** *Sacramento, California.* He found a suitable house in a residential area away from the heart of town on Forty-fifth Street. In the meantime, funds were approved to build a governor's mansion in the suburbs overlooking the American River.

**1975–1989** *Santa Barbara, California.* Rancho del Cielo (Sky Ranch), Refugio Canyon. He bought 688 acres of rugged land in the Santa Ynez Mountains east of Santa Barbara in 1974 for $527,000. There, he built fences and remodelled the hundred-year-old two-bedroom adobe house on Refugio Beach Road (last gateway before the pass on the left) between the Santa Ynez township and Hwy 101 west of Goleta. From the street, one can see only the guardhouse.

**1989–** *Los Angeles, California.* 668 St. Cloud Drive, Bel Air. The number was changed from the original 666 at Nancy's request because 666 is associated with Satan in the book of Revelation.

# WORK

**1926–1932** *Dixon, Illinois.* During the summer, he worked as a life guard at Lowell Park on the Rock River. He was respected as a hero for having saved more than 70 people during his time on the job. His first summer job when he was fourteen (1926) was in construction when he helped dig the foundation for St. Anne's Catholic Church.

**1932–1933** *Davenport, Iowa.* As sports broadcaster for Radio WOC. The station occupied space on the top floor of the Palmer School of Chiropractic Medicine, 800-1100 Brady Street, between Eleventh and Eighth Streets.

**1933–1937** *Des Moines, Iowa.* As radio announcer for WHO, located in the Stoner Building at 914 Walnut Street. His office was at the back of the ground floor.

**1937–1965** *Hollywood, California.* As an actor. In June 1937, he walked through the gates of Warner Brothers in Burbank and started work. In 1949, he was in London working on the film, "The Hasty Heart." Warner Brothers Film Studio is at 4000 Warner Boulevard. His last movie was "The Killers." He made 53 films from 1937 to 1965. (The old address was given as 4000 W. Olive.)

**1937–** *Los Angeles, California.* He often came in on the train at Union Station, 800 North Alameda Street. It was years before he went by plane because he had a fear of flying.

**1942–1945** *California.* Military Service. On April 19, 1943 he said good-bye to his wife and their infant daughter, Maureen, and boarded a train at the Glendale station for San Francisco, Van Ness Avenue and Bay Street, for a month's duty as second lieutenant in the Cavalry Reserve, U.S. Army. He then shifted back to Hollywood, where he spent the rest of the war. For part of 1942 he was in Culver City, California, at the old Hal Roach Studios (newly called Fort Roach), where he was transferred to the Air Force. He was promoted to first lieutenant on October 1, 1942.

**1945–1947** *Hollywood, California.* He continued in his acting career.

**1947–1960** *Los Angeles, California.* President of the Screen Actors Guild. He first joined the guild in 1937. From 1947 to 1956, it was located at 7046 Hollywood Boulevard and from 1957 to 1960 at 7750 Sunset Boulevard.

**1952** *Las Vegas, Nevada.* Last Frontier Hotel. He stayed here while working as emcee for a nightclub show.

**1954–1962** *Los Angeles, California.* He went to work for General Electric on a one-half hour television series. His years with GE and the acquisition of valuable ranch land in the Malibu Hills north of Los Angeles made him a wealthy man.

**1964–1966** *Los Angeles, California.* He hosted the U.S. Borax Company show.

**1967–1975** *Sacramento, California.* Governor of California, with offices in the State Capitol.

**1975–1981** *Santa Barbara, California.* Working on his ranch.

**1981–1989** *Washington, D.C.* President of the United States. At the Old Executive Office Building, Room 450. He often spoke to groups here and made official announcements.

**1989–** *Los Angeles, California.* Speaking and writing. Office on the Thirty-fourth floor in the Fox Plaza Building—a tower that rises above the old Twentieth Century Fox in Century City. In retirement, he could expect $75,000 a week for a half hour show and up to $50,000 for an evening's oration, a fee which would make him the nation's highest paid speaker. His highest fee was in the millions for a trip to Japan in 1989.

# TRAVEL

While working for General Electric, the idea was for him to cover the 135 GE plants, beginning at Schenectady, New York.

**1940** *South Bend, Indiana.* Palace Theater (now Morris Civic Auditorium), 211 North Michigan Street, where he went for the premier of "Knute Rockne—All American."

**1941** *Dixon Illinois.* Nacusa House (hotel), 215 Galena Avenue where he stayed. There is an historic landmark; U.S. Grant had also stayed here.

**1941** *Dixon, Illinois.* At Hazelwood as guest of Myrtle Walgreen for a welcome home day to Louella Parsons and "Dutch" (his nickname) Reagan. It is located at the end of Brinton Avenue past the Correctional Center and is private.

**1948** *London, England.* Savoy Hotel. He was there for filming from November 1948 to March 1949.

**1968** *Miami Beach, Florida.* Deauville Hotel, Collins Avenue, for the Republican National Convention. After the Convention, he and Nancy went for a cruise through the Florida Keys.

**1969** *Houston, Texas.* While in Houston, Reagan stayed at the Shamrock Hilton Hotel, 6900 Main Street at Holcombe Boulevard.

**1976** *Kansas City, Missouri.* Alameda Plaza Hotel (now Ritz-Carlton), Wornall Road at Ward Parkway on the Tenth floor, for the Republican National Convention.

**1978** *Houston, Texas.* Hyatt Regency Hotel, 1200 Louisiana, for a Republican meeting.

**1979** *New York City, New York.* Hilton Hotel, 1335 Avenue of the Americas, where he announced his decision to run for president in a speech on November 13.

**1980** *Nashua, New Hampshire.* He had a debate with George Bush and other Republican contestants at the Nashua High School gymnasium. Here he felt that he had won the debate, the primary, and the nomination.

**1981** *Arlington, Virginia.* Pentagon. He dedicated the MacArthur Corridor.

**1981** *Grand Rapids, Michigan.* He dedicated the Ford Library.

**1981** *New York City, New York.* He stayed at the Waldorf-Astoria Hotel, where he most often stayed when in New York during his two terms as president, lunched at Angelo's, and dined at Le Cirque.

**1981** *New York City, New York.* Visit to Gracie Mansion.

**1981** *Palm Springs, California.* He was here for a few days vacation at the home of Walter Annenberg. He was often here from 1981 to 1989.

**1981** *Washington, D.C.* Dedication of the James Madison Memorial Building of the Library of Congress.

**1981** *Washington, D.C.* He visited the inaugural balls held at the Capital Hilton, Mayflower, Washington Hilton, Sheraton Washington, and Shoreham hotels, and the John F. Kennedy Center, Pension Building, National Air and Space Museum, Museum of Natural History, and Museum of American History.

**1981** *Washington, D.C.* He laid a wreath at the Lincoln Memorial.

**1981** *Williamsburg, Virginia.* He had dinner at the Williamsburg Lodge, stayed at Lightfoot House, and was with French President Francois Mitterand at the Royal Governor's Palace.

**1981** *Yorktown, Virginia.* Yorktown Battlefield, on the occasion of the bicentennial.

**1982** *Alexandria, Virginia.* February 21, he attended Christ Church.

**1982** *Arlington National Cemetery, Virginia.* He laid a wreath.

**1982** *Bridgetown, Barbados.* He stayed at the home of Paul H. Brandt, Casa de Pablo, and had dinner and Easter brunch at the home of Claudette Colbert. He attended Easter service at St. James Parish Church.

**1982** *Coronado, California.* Hotel del Coronade, to welcome the Mexican president.

**1982** *Des Moines, Iowa.* He addressed a joint legislative session in the State Capitol House Chamber. Marriott Hotel for the night.

**1982** *Dixon, Illinois, on a visit to his boyhood home.* Eureka, Illinois, at Eureka College Commencement in Reagan Physical Education Center.

**1982** *Indianapolis, Indiana.* He addressed a joint legislative session in the State Capitol House Chamber.

**1982** *Kingston, Jamaica, for conference and vacation.* He stayed overnight at the residence of the U.S. Ambassador, visited the Governor-General at his residence, King's House, and attended meetings in Jamaica House.

**1982** *Knoxville, Tennessee.* Opening of the International Energy Exposition (World's Fair).

**1982** *Montgomery, Alabama.* He spoke in the House Chamber of the State Capitol and later at the Civic Center.

**1982** *Mount Vernon, Virginia.* He laid a wreath at Washington's Tomb.

**1982** *Nashville, Tennessee.* He spoke in the House Chamber in the State Capitol and laid a wreath at Jackson's Tomb at the Hermitage.

**1982** *Oklahoma City, Oklahoma.* He spoke to a joint legislature session in the State Capitol. Overnight at the Shervin Plaza Hotel.

**1982** *Washington, D.C.* Decatur House. Formation of the James S. Brady Foundation.

**1983** *Anchorage, Alaska.* He arrived at Elmendorf Air Force Base en route to Japan and stayed at the Chateau.

**1983** *Carter's Grove Plantation, near Williamsburg, Virginia.* He hosted a dinner for the delegation heads.

**1983** *San Francisco, California.* There was a dinner in the Hearst Court of the M. H. de Young Memorial Museum, honoring Queen Elizabeth II. He and Mrs. Reagan spent the night at the St. Francis Hotel.

**1983** *Washington, D.C.* National Gallery of Art, West Building, to honor Andrew Mellon.

**1983** *Washington, D.C.* Anderson House. He was made an honorary member of the Society of the Cincinnati.

**1983** *Williamsburg, Virginia.* He spoke at the Economic Summit Conference. He stayed at Providence Hall from May 27 to May 30. Meetings were held in William and Mary Hall, College of William and Mary. There was a tent dinner at the Folk Art Center.

**1984** *Arlington National Cemetery, Virginia.* Ceremony at the Amphitheater.

**1984** *Ballyporeen, Ireland.* Village Square. He visited the Church of Assumption, O'Farrells Pub, and Ronald Reagan Lounge.

**1984** *Baltimore, Maryland.* Dedication of a statue of Christopher Columbus at President Street and Eastern Avenue.

**1984** *Beijing, China.* April 26, he was welcomed at the Great Hall of the People, stayed at Diaoyutai State Guest House, Villa 12, visited the Great Wall, and attended a reception in Beijing at the Great Wall Hotel. On April 29, he flew to Xi'an to see the terra cotta figures. On April 30, he visited Shanghai and attended a reception at Fudan University. He stayed at Jing Jang Hotel from April 30 to May 1.

**1984** *Dallas, Texas.* Convention Center. He accepted the Republican nomination for president. He spent the night at Loew's Anatole Hotel.

**1984** *Detroit, Michigan.* Cobo Hall, for Naturalization ceremonies.

**1984** *Dixon, Illinois.* Celebration of his birthday at Dixon High School gymnasium. He had lunch at his boyhood home and viewed a parade from Nachusa House Hotel.

**1984** *Dublin, Ireland.* Dublin Castle. He had dinner with Prime Minister FitzGerald, made a speech to the Irish National Parliament, Lancaster House (Dail House of Representatives), and visited Aras An Uachtarain (home of Irish President Patrick J. Hillery) for a tree planting ceremony. He stayed overnight at Deerfield, the home of the American Ambassador.

**1984** *Fairbanks, Alaska.* He visited the University of Alaska and had lunch at the Wood Student Center. He met Pope John Paul II at the airport.

**1984** *Galway, Ireland.* He spoke at University College in Quadrangle Square and received an honorary degree.

**1984** *Guam.* Overnight at Nimitz House, at the Naval Base.

**1984** *Honolulu, Hawaii.* He attended Easter Sunday services at St. Andrews Cathedral. Had tea at the Governor's Mansion, Washington House, and stayed at the Kahala Hilton Hotel.

**1984** *Kansas City, Missouri.* He spend the night at the Westin Crown Center Hotel. Convention Center, Music Hall, for presidential debate with Walter F. Mondale.

**1984** *London, England.* Economic Summit, Great Hall of Guild Hall and Lancaster House meetings, reception at St. James Palace. He visited the National Portrait Gallery, Tudor Room dinner. He stayed at Winfield House.

**1984** *Los Angeles, California.* Century Plaza Hotel, on a two-day visit. He was here on numerous occasions during his presidency.

**1984** *Los Angeles.* Hotel Bel-Air, for wedding of daughter Patti Davis to Paul Grilley. He also attended the rehearsal, the night before.

**1984** *Louisville, Kentucky.* Robert S. Whitney Hall, Kentucky Center for the Arts, for presidential debate with Walter F. Mondale. He spent the night at the Hyatt Regency.

**1984** *Monticello, Virginia.* March 25, he arrived by helicopter.

**1984** *Pointe du Hoc, France.* At the U.S. Ranger Monument on the Fortieth anniversary of the Normandy invasion. He visited the Omaha Beach Memorial, the Chapel

and Garden of the Missing, and Utah Beach.

**1984** *Sacramento, California.* Dedication ceremony State Capitol building. He spent the night at the Red Lion Motor Inn.

**1984** *Salt Lake City, Utah.* Little America Hotel overnight.

**1984** *Santa Barbara (near), California.* Rancho del Cielo, for a three-week vacation.

**1984** *Shannon, Ireland.* He arrived at Shannon International Airport, stayed several nights at Ashford Castle in Cong, County Mayo, and went to Ballyporeen to visit his family ancestral site.

**1984** *Springfield, Illinois.* Rally, State Capitol building.

**1984** *Little Rock, Arkansas.* Excelsior Hotel.

**1984** *Washington, D.C.* Dedication of the Vietnam Veterans Memorial Statue on the Mall, on November 11.

**1984** *Washington, D.C.* Dedication of new National Geographic Building.

**1984** *Winterset, Iowa.* Rally, Madison County Courthouse. He toured the boyhood home of John Wayne.

**1985** *Baltimore, Maryland.* Fort McHenry, Flag Day ceremony.

**1985** *Concord, New Hampshire.* He spoke outside the Statehouse.

**1985** *Fort Campbell, Kentucky.* Memorial Service, on December 16, for those killed in Airbourne crash at Gander, Newfoundland.

**1985** *Independence, Missouri.* Speech, Jackson County Court House.

**1985** *McLean, Virginia.* Edward M. Kennedy home fundraiser for Kennedy Library.

**1985** *Washington, D.C.* St. John's Episcopal Church, for service.

**1985** *Washington, D.C.* Washington Cathedral, for National Prayer Service.

**1986** *Atlanta, Georgia.* Dedication of Carter Presidential Library.

**1986** *Houston, Texas.* Avionics Building, Johnson Space Center. Memorial service for Challenger astronauts.

**1986** *Keflavik, Iceland.* October 12, he met with Soviet leader Mikhail Gorbachev at Hofdi House and stayed at the residence of the American Ambassador.

**1986** *New York City, New York.* Admiral House on Governor's Island, for a meeting with French President Mitterand.

**1986** *New York City, New York.* Governor's Island, at ceremony opening and lighting of the Torch of the Statue of Liberty.

**1986** *St. George's, Grenada.* He spoke to American students at St. George's University of Medicine.

**1986** *Tokyo.* Economic Summit. He stayed at the Hotel Okura, visited Prime Minister Yasuhiro Nakasone at his official residence, had meetings at the Akasaka Palace, and dinner at the Hotel New Otani, and a Banquet at the Imperial Palace.

**1987** *Jacksonville, Florida.* Mayport Naval Station, for Memorial Service for crew members of *USS Stark*, May 22.

**1987** *Miami, Florida.* September 10, he welcomed Pope John Paul II at Miami International Airport and went with him to the Vizcaya Museum.

**1987** *Phoenix, Arizona.* St. Thomas the Apostle Roman Catholic Church, for memorial service for mother-in-law Edith Davis.

**1987** *Topeka, Kansas.* Landon home, to celebrate Alfred Landon's one hundredth birthday.

**1987** *Venice, Italy.* During the economic summit conference, he stayed at Villa Condulmer in Mogliano. Meetings were held at the Hotel Cipriani and Palazzo Grassi. There was a reception at the Palazzo Ducale and a dinner at the Prefettura on the Grand Canal.

**1987** *West Point, New York.* U.S. Military Academy, Washington Hall.

**1988** *Alexandria, Virginia.* Ireland's Own Restaurant, for St. Patrick's Day luncheon.

**1988** *Brussels, Belgium.* NATO meetings. He lodged at the Chateau Stuyvenberg during his stay, had dinner at Val Duchesse, and met with King Baudouin I at the Laeken Palace.

**1988** *Moscow, Russia.* He arrived at Vnokovo II airport, held summit meetings in St. George's Hall at the Grand Kremlin Palace, and visited and spoke at Danislov Monastery. He lodged at Spaso House (residence of the American ambassador), where he had dinner in the Chandelier Room and a news conference in the ball room. He also had dinner at St. Vladimir's Hall at the Grand Kremlin Palace and made remarks at the Lecture Hall at Moscow State University.

**1988** *Simi Valley, California.* Ground breaking ceremony, for the Reagan Presidential Library.

**1989** *London, England.* On June 14, he was made an Honorary Knight Grand Cross of the Most Honorable Order of the Bath at Buckingham Palace. Eisenhower had received the same honor in 1943.

**1989** *Paris, France.* On June 15, he was honored by being inducted into the 200-year old Institut de France.

**1991** *Simi Valley, California.* Opening of the Reagan Presidential Library on November 4.

**1992** *Houston, Texas.* Republican National Convention held at the Astrodome. He gave a speech on August 17. Church of Jesus Christ of Latter-Day Saints.

**1992** *Pocantico Hills, New York.* Rockefeller Estate overnight.

**1994** *Yorba Linda, California.* He attended the funeral of former President Richard Nixon.

## SPECIAL SITES

*Simi Valley (near Thousand Oaks) near Tierra Rejada area, California, 45 miles northwest of Los Angeles.* Reagan Presidential Library. When completed, it will be 153,000 square feet and the largest of the Presidential museums. (Lyndon Johnson is second with 100,000 square feet.)

*Washington, D.C. Hilton Hotel.* Attempted assassination. March 30, 1981.

## BIBLIOGRAPHY

Boyarski, Bill. *Ronald Reagan: His Life and Rise to the Presidency.* New York, Random House, 1981.

Edwards, Anne. *Early Reagan: The Rise to Power.* New York, William Morrow and Company, Inc., 1987.

# GEORGE HERBERT WALKER BUSH

---

### 1924–
#### 41ST PRESIDENT 1989–1993: REPUBLICAN PARTY

*"A campaign is a disagreement, and disagreements divide. But an election is a decision, and decisions clear the way for harmony and peace."*

—*Campaign victory speech, November 8, 1988*

George Bush was on born June 12, 1924, to Prescott Bush of Columbus, Ohio and Dorothy Walker Bush from St. Louis. His father was a partner in the investment banking firm of Brown Brothers, Harriman and Company. He is a thirteenth cousin of Queen Elizabeth II, directly descended from King Henry VII, and related to all current European monarchs. In his younger days, he was often called by the nickname, "Poppy."

## CHARACTERISTICS

Bush is 6'2" tall and weighs approximately one hundred and ninety pounds. He keeps himself in good shape by daily exercise. He has light brown hair, blue eyes, a one-sided grin, and an engaging personality. Like President Clinton, he is left-handed. He is an all-around sportsman; tennis was his main interest in earlier times. In college, he was captain of the baseball and soccer teams and president of the senior class. As president, he played golf on a

# A LIFE IN REVIEW

**Birth:** June 12, 1924; Milton, MA

**Married:** Barbara Pierce; January 6, 1945; 4 sons, 2 daughters

## CAREER

**1945–1948** U.S. Navy pilot

**1963–1966** Executive with Petroleum Corporation

**1964, 1970** Member U.S. Senate

**1967–1970** Member U.S. Congress

**1971–1973** U.S. Permanent Representative to UN

**1974–1975** Chief, U.S. Liason Officer Peking, China

**1976–1977** Director C.I.A.

**1981–1989** U.S. Vice President

## ADMINISTRATION EVENTS

**1989** Invasion of Panama

Savings and Loan crisis

Ban on importation of assault weapons

Exxon Valdez oil spill off Alaska

**1991** Persian Gulf War

**1992** Tailhook scandal

*St. Ann's Church, Bush family church in Kennebunkport, Maine.*

Hutcheson Street, on the second floor of a Victorian mansion, in a make-shift delivery room.

# BAPTISM

Prescott and Dorothy Bush, George's parents, had their son baptized on September 7, 1924 at St. Ann's Church, Kennebunkport, Maine. The Bishop of North Dakota, J. P. Tyler, was visiting Kennebunkport and officiated at the ceremony.

# CHURCH

In Bush's words, "Religious teaching was also part of our home life. Each morning, as we gathered at the breakfast table, Mother or Dad read a Bible lesson to us. Our family is Episcopalian, and we regularly attended Sunday Services at Christ Church in Greenwich. Christmas was always important, the family usually spent it at the maternal grandparent's plantation in South Carolina.

regular basis and enjoyed throwing horse shoes on the White House lawn. During vacations in Maine, he goes out daily in his motor boat, and he is an avid deep-sea fisherman.

# BIRTHPLACE

Bush was born on June 12, 1924 in Milton, Massachusetts, 173 Adams Street, corner of

**1924–1994** *Kennebunkport, Maine.* St. Ann's, near Walker's Point. He was a vestryman.

**1924–** *Kennebunkport, Maine.* South Congregational Church, corner of Temple and North Streets.

**1924** *Milton, Massachusetts.* St. Michael's Episcopal Church, 112 Randolph Avenue, was his parent's church.

**1924** *Aiken, South Carolina.* St. Thaddeus Episcopal Church, Richland and Pendleton. Built in 1842, it is the oldest church in Aiken and was his grandparents' church, (Mr. and Mrs. George Herbert Walker).

**1925–** *Barnwell, South Carolina.* Church of the Holy Apostles, junction of Burr and Hagood, was also his grandparents' church.

**1925–1942** *Greenwich, Connecticut.* Christ Episcopal Church, 254 East Putnam Avenue.

**1945** *Trenton, Michigan.* St. Thomas Episcopal Church, Nichols Drive and Andover Road. A new church has replaced the church attended by Bush.

**1945** *Virginia Beach, Virginia.* Episcopal Church. On August 15, he went here to give thanks for the victory.

**1950–1960** *Midland, Texas.* First Presbyterian Church, 800 West Texas. Both George and Barbara Bush taught Sunday School here.

**1960–1967** *Houston, Texas.* St. Martin's Episcopal Church, 717 Sage Road. He was a vestryman.

**1967** *Washington, D.C.* Washington Cathedral, Wisconsin Avenue.

**1973–1975** *Beijing, China.* Beijing Diplomatic Community Church. His daughter, Dorothy, was christened here at age 16 by three Chinese Christian clergymen, an Episcopalian, a Presbyterian, and a Baptist. Bush attended regularly here while in China.

**1981–1993** *Washington, D.C.* St. John's Episcopal, Lafayette Square.

**1993–** *Houston, Texas.* St. Martin's Episcopal Church, 717 Sage Road.

# EDUCATION

**1929–1937** *Greenwich, Connecticut.* Greenwich Country Day School, Old Church Road, about a mile from his home.

**1937–1942** *Andover, Massachusetts.* Phillips Academy, Chapel Avenue, about twenty miles north of Boston off Massachusetts 28. He attended the Academy Chapel.

**1942** *Chapel Hill, North Carolina.* Preflight training for navy service.

**1942** *Charlestown, Rhode, Island.* Naval Air Station.

**1945–1948** *New Haven, Connecticut.* Yale University, B.A. in economics.

# MARRIAGE AND HONEYMOON

George Bush and Barbara Pierce were married January 6, 1945 at the First Presbyterian Church, on the Boston Post Road in Rye, New York. This was Barbara Pierce's, home church. Her father, Marvin Pierce, was the publisher of Redbook and McCall's magazines. The reception was held at the Apawamis Club in Rye. The Bushs honeymooned at Sea Island, Georgia, at a resort hotel, "The Cloister."

# HOMES/LODGINGS

George Bush moved thirty-three times and lived in twenty-one cities in several states.

**1924–1925** *Milton, Massachusetts.* 173 Adams Street.

**1924–1989** *Kennebunkport, Maine.* The family vacation home, Walker's Point, is a rambling nine-bedroom house, which was his grandfather Walker's summer cottage.

*George Bush home in Milton, Massachusetts.*

**1924–** *Barnwell, South Carolina.* His grandfather's plantation, Duncannon, was in the northwest part of the state.

**1924–** *Aiken, South Carolina.* At the end of Summerall Court on Magnolia Street, visiting his Walker grandparents. The house burned, and the site was later occupied by the Whitehall mansion.

**1925** *Milton, Massachusetts.* They lived briefly on Centre Street before the family moved to Connecticut.

**1925–1931** *Greenwich, Connecticut.* 11 Stanwich Road. From this five-bedroom house he walked a mile to school.

**1931–1942** *Greenwich, Connecticut.* 15 Grove Lane, in a section of the city called Deer Park, is a big nine-bedroom house, on a steep slope running down to a brook. It is now owned by another family. This was his primary boyhood home. The only memento left is a big mirror with a carved frame in the foyer. He played tennis at the Field Club on Lake Avenue.

**1942–1945** *Chapel Hill, North Carolina.* Navy service.

**1945** *Trenton, Michigan.* 2920 Parkwood. While he was still in the Navy, he and Barbara rented rooms from Grace Gargone.

**1945** *Virginia Beach, Virginia.* After Bush was reassigned to Norfolk, they moved to a house which they shared with three other young Navy couples. He was stationed at Oceana Naval Air Station when the Japanese sued for peace.

**1945** *New Haven, Connecticut.* The Bushes rented a small railroad flat next to a mortuary.

**1946** *New Haven, Connecticut.* They rented an upstairs flat on Whitney Avenue while Bush studied at Yale University.

**1946** *New Haven, Connecticut.* 37 Hillhouse Avenue, next door to the president of

Yale. While he was living here, on one occasion the university president was expecting important guests and came over to ask Bush to remove the baby diapers hanging on the clothesline.

**1945–**  *Rye, New York.* Marvin Pierce house, 25 Onondaga Street (Indian Village section). The two-story brick house is now privately owned.

**1947–1948**  *Odessa, Texas.* Their first Lone Star home was a duplex and is now a vacant lot. Bush describes it as a shotgun house on East Seventh Street with a shared bathroom. Their neighbors, a mother and daughter, entertained a long line of male guests every night.

**1948–1949**  *Huntington Park, California.* The exact location has not been determined.

**1949**  *Bakersfield, California.* They lived here about three months in an undetermined location.

**1949**  *Ventura, California.* Pierpont Inn Hotel, 500 Sanjon Road.

**1949**  *Ventura, California.* When Bush went west to sell oil drilling equipment, the family stayed in a number of places along the way. They lived at the Pierpont for several months.

**1949**  *Compton, California.* 624 B Santa Fe Avenue is now a rundown building and part of a complex called Santa Fe Gardens. Their first daughter, Robin, was born in Compton.

**1950–1953**  *Midland, Texas.* 405 East Maple Street in a neighborhood known as Easter Egg Row. This was the first house they bought.

**1953–1955**  *Midland, California.* 1412 West Ohio Avenue.

**1955–1960**  *Midland, California.* 2703 Sentinel Drive, in a house they built for themselves.

**1960–1967**  *Houston, Texas.* 5525 Briar Drive. Only the flag pole remains. The

*George Bush home on Hillbrook Lane in Washington, D.C.*

Bush house was removed to make room for five new houses.

**1967–1969**  *Washington, D.C.* 4910 Hillbrook Lane, NW, which they bought from former Senator Millard Simpson and sold after less than two years at a loss.

**1969–1977**  *Washington, D.C.* 5161 Palisade Lane NW (now home to Italian diplomats). Bush said, "a comfortable house and convenient to the kids' schools." During his two terms in Congress, he lived here not far from the National Cathedral. They bought it and kept it as their Washington base. It is a three-story brick town house with a small front lawn and a patio in back. They were here off and on between 1969 and 1976.

**1970–**  *Berclair, Texas.* He has hunted quail and vacationed at his friend William Farish's Lazy F Ranch for more than twenty years.

**1971–1973**  *New York City, New York.* The Waldorf-Astoria, the United Nations Ambassador's official residence, overlooking the East River.

**1973–1974**  *Washington, D.C.* 5161 Palisade Lane, NW.

**1974–1975** *Beijing, China.* They lived in the U.S. compound in the residence of the chief of the mission in a house which is open and well lighted. They travelled the area on bicycles. It is three miles from the commercial center and surrounded by a yellow brick wall.

**1975–1977** *Washington, D.C.* 5161 Palisade Lane, NW, while at the CIA.

**1977–1980** *Houston, Texas.* 5838 Indian Trail Street.

**1980–1981** *Houston, Texas.* 710 North Post Oak Road.

**1981–1989** *Washington D.C.* Observatory Circle, on Massachusetts Avenue at Thirty-fourth Street, NW, in the Vice President's House. It is a 12-room Victorian house built in 1893 and was designated the Admiral's House. It became the Vice Presidential residence in 1974. Ford was eligible to occupy it, but, with the Nixon resignation coming so quickly, the Fords moved directly from Alexandria to the White House. Bush is the first vice president who lived in both this house and later in the White House. The Bushes lived here for eight years—longer than anywhere else.

**1981–** *Houston, Texas.* The Houstonian, 111 North Post Oak Lane, where he had a hotel suite, Room 271, as his legal residence. He also owns a lot in the Tanglewood area.

**1989–1993** *Washington, D.C.* The White House as president.

**1993–1994** *Houston, Texas.* 11 SC Oak Street, while their permanent home was being built.

**1994–** *Houston, Texas.* 9 Southwest Oak Street. Permission was given to close off the street to the public.

# WORK

**1942** *Corpus Christi, Texas.* Bush began his military training at the naval station, Ocean Drive, Ward Island.

**1943** *Charlestown, Rhode Island.* In training at the Naval Air Station. He was commissioned ensign and was the youngest pilot in the United States Navy. He was assigned to the *USS San Jacinto.*

**1944** *Chi Chi Jima, north of Iwo Jima.* He was shot down.

**1944** *Pearl Harbor, Hawaii.* For rest and recreation.

**1945** *Michigan, Maine, and Virginia.* At military bases.

**1948–1950** *Odessa, Texas.* As an apprentice at Ideco, an oil company, sweeping floors and painting oil rigs. The company had offices in Huntington Beach, Bakersfield, Ventura, and Compton, California, and Midland, Texas.

**1949** *Ventura, California.* Security Engineering Company, 1622

**1949** *Ventura Avenue.* From here, he went to Huntington.

**1949** *Bakersfield, California.* Security Engineering Company, 1435 South Union Avenue.

**1951–1953** *Midland, Texas.* Partner in the Bush-Overbey Oil Development Company, 732 McClintic Building, 300 West Texas.

**1953–1960** *Midland, Texas.* Partner in Zapata Petroleum Company, offices in Midland National Bank Building, 401 West Texas.

**1960–1967** *Houston, Texas.* The headquarters of Zapata moved to the Houston Club Building in 1959.

**1967–1971** *Washington, D.C.* U.S. Representative from Texas. His office was in the Longworth Building.

**1971–1973** *New York City, New York.* U.S. Ambassador to the United Nations. He moved into an office in the State Department and then to the eleventh floor of the United States Mission directly across First Avenue from United Nations headquarters on Forty-fifth Street in Manhattan. He resigned in January 1973.

**1973–1974** *Washington, D.C.* Chairman of the Republican National Committee, 1625 I Street, NW, Room 201. The building was demolished in 1993.

**1974–1975** *Beijing, China.* Chief of the U.S. Liaison Office in China. He carried the title of Ambassador from his former post at the United Nations.

**1976–1977** *Langley, Virginia.* CIA Director, with offices on the seventh floor at CIA headquarters.

**1977–1981** *Houston, Texas.* Director, Eli Lilly, Texas Gulf Inc., 1079 Houston Club Building.

**1981–1989** *Washington, D.C.* Vice President of the United States. Office in the White House.

**1992–** *Houston, Texas.* Park Laureate Building, 1000 Memorial Drive has been used as an office since his retirement from the White House.

# TRAVEL/VISITS

From 1981 to 1987, he travelled to 73 foreign countries on presidential assignments. By January 1989, Barbara had accompanied him to 68 countries, for a total of 1,330,239 miles.

**1973–1975** *China.* He visited the Great Wall, the Ming Tombs, the Forbidden City, and the Summer Palace.

**1976** *Beijing, China.* He stayed at Guest House 18.

**1976** *Des Moines, Iowa.* The Fort Des Moines Hotel, Eighteenth and Walnut Streets.

**1980** *Detroit, Michigan.* Pontchartrain Hotel, 2 Washington Boulevard, while attending the Republican National Convention in the Joe Louis Arena, 600 Civic Center Drive. Here, he learned of his nomination as Vice President. He also visited the Reagans at the Renaissance Center Plaza Hotel (Westin Hotel). Gerald Ford was also staying here.

**1981** *Charlottesville, Virginia.* University of Virginia, where he gave the Commencement Address.

**1981** *Fort Worth, Texas.* New Hyatt Regency Hotel (formerly the Old Hotel Texas), 815 Main Street (March 30). This is where Kennedy spent the night of November 21, 1963, before his visit to Dallas.

**1981** *Grand Rapids, Michigan.* Dedication of the Ford Museum.

**1981** *Manila, The Philippines.* He attended the inauguration of President Ferdinand Marcos and a luncheon in the Presidential Palace.

**1981** *Tuskegee, Alabama.* Tuskegee Institute, where he spoke celebrating the one hundredth anniversary of the Institute.

**1982** *Moscow, USSR.* To attend Brezhnev's funeral.

**1982** *Peking, China.* He was greeted at the Great Hall of the People. He rested in Hawaii on the way home.

**1982** *Riyadh, Saudi Arabia.* He visited the Maather Palace to convey official condolences to King Fahd on the death of King Khalid.

**1982** *Seoul, Korea.* Celebrating 100 years of official contacts between the United States and Korea.

**1983** *Beirut, Lebanon.* He visited the site of Marine Headquarters to view the scene of the terrorist attack and visited President Gamayel at the Palace.

**1983** *Belgrade, Yugoslavia.* He attended a state dinner in his honor and laid a wreath at the tomb of Marshall Tito.

**1983** *Bonn, Germany.* On the first leg of a seven-nation West European tour regarding commitment to arms reduction.

**1983** *Europe.* He lodged at the Ambassador's residence at Villa Taverna, Rome, Italy, a seventeenth century building and met with Pope John Paul II. In Paris for one day. London. He spoke to the Royal Institute of International Affairs in the Guild Hall.

**1983**   *Kingston, Jamaica.* He spoke to Parliament and at Montego Bay and laid wreaths at the statues of Marcus Garvey and others.

**1983**   *Krefeld, West Germany.* Ceremony marking first emigration of Germans to America 300 years ago. Rocks and bottles were thrown at his motorcade.

**1983**   *London, England.* First stop on a two-week, eight-nation tour of Europe to discuss U.S. policy on Central America.

**1984**   *Agra, India.* He visited the Taj Mahal.

**1984**   *Conakry, Guinea.* He headed the delegation to the funeral of President Ahmed Toure; funeral eulogy in Sports Stadium; cortege to Grand Mosque (fourth largest in the world); the coffin to the Mausoleum of National Heroes.

**1984**   *Dallas, Texas.* Dallas Convention Center, 2101 Elm Street. He was renominated for vice president at the Republican National Convention.

**1984**   *London, England.* Stopover, with visit to Prime Minister Thatcher at Chequers (the prime minister's country house).

**1984**   *Moscow, Russia.* He attended the funeral of President Andropov, House of Unions, where he lay in state, the funeral in Red Square, and a reception in St. George's Hall.

**1984**   *New Delhi, India.* He attended a banquet at the Presidential Palace and met with Prime Minister Indira Ghandi.

**1984**   *Peshawar, Pakistan.* He inspected a refugee camp near the Afghanistan border and meet with President Zia-ul-Haq.

**1985**   *Africa.* 4,500-mile tour to see countries suffering from famine, including Niger and the Sudan. On March 11, he gave a speech in Geneva, Switzerland, to the U.N. conference on famine.

**1985**   *Beijing, China.* He stayed at the Guest House in the same suite used by President Reagan when he visited. He visited the Pepsi-Cola plant in Shanghai.

**1985**   *Frankfort, Germany.* He greeted hijacked TWA passengers.

**1985**   *Moscow, Russia.* He attended the funeral of former President Chernenko in Red Square.

**1986**   *New Orleans, Louisiana.* He received the Theodore Roosevelt Award of the National Collegiate Athletic Association, given to "a distinguished citizen of national reputation and outstanding accomplishment" who earned a varsity letter (his was baseball at Yale).

**1986**   *San Antonio, Texas.* He spoke in front of the Alamo and rode in a covered wagon in a parade celebrating the one-hundred and fiftieth anniversary of Texas independence.

**1988**   *New Orleans, Louisiana.* Republican National Convention, held in the Super Dome, where he was nominated for president.

**1988**   *West Point, New York.* He spoke at graduation. He was the first candidate for president to do so.

**1988**   *Winston-Salem, North Carolina.* Wait Chapel, Wake Forest University, for the first presidential debate with Michael Dukakis.

**1988**   *Los Angeles, California.* Pauley Pavilion (the sports arena), University of California at Los Angeles, for the second and final debate with Dukasis.

**1989**   *Anchorage, Alaska.* Elmendorf Air Force Base on the way to Japan.

**1989**   *Arlington, Virginia.* Iwo Jima Memorial, where he gave a speech supporting a proposed amendment against flag burning.

**1989**   *Austin, Texas.* He spoke at the State Capitol in the House Chamber.

**1989**   *Beijing, China.* He lodged at Diaoyutai State Guest House and attended Chong-menwen Christian Church on Sunday.

**1989** *Bismarck, North Dakota.* He dedicated the Centennial Grove at the State Capitol.

**1989** *Bonn, Germany.* He met with Chancellor Helmut Kohl in the Chancellery and dined at Redoute Castle. Together, they took a scenic boat trip on the Rhine.

**1989** *Brussels, Belgium.* He lodged at the Chateau Stuyvenberg, Val Duchesse, and lunched at the Brussels Palace.

**1989** *Brussels, Belgium.* He met with King Baudouin at the Laeken Palace and attended meetings at the Chateau Stuyvenberg.

**1989** *Budapest, Hungary.* He visited Kossuth Square, Karl Marx University Aula Hall, Old Prison on Castle Hill, and had dinner at the National Parliament Building. He stayed at the Hungarian Government Guest House.

**1989** *Columbia, South Carolina.* He spoke in the State Capitol House Chamber and had lunch at the Governor's Mansion.

**1989** *Helena, Montana.* Centennial celebration at the State Capitol grounds and speaking in the House Chamber of the Capitol.

**1989** *Leiden, the Netherlands, from where the Pilgrims left on the* Mayflower. He gave a speech at the site, Pieterskerk. This was the first visit of an American president to the Netherlands. In The Hague, he had tea with Queen Beatrix at Noordeinde Palace and lunch at the Cathuis, official residence of the Prime Minister.

**1989** *London, England.* He conferred with Prime Minister Margaret Thatcher at 10 Downing Street and lunched with Queen Elizabeth and Prince Phillip at Buckingham Palace.

**1989** *New York City, New York.* Federal Hall, speaking on the bicentennial of George Washington's inauguration.

**1989** *Paris, France, to attend his first Economic Summit Meeting as president—his second tour of Europe in six weeks.* Meetings were held at the Hotel de la Marine and the Louvre; lunches at the Hotel de Lassay, Arche de la Defense, Palais de l'Elysee, and dinner at Musee d'Orsay. He visited the Place du Trocadero celebration of the bicentennial French Revolution and attended church at the American Cathedral in Paris.

**1989** *Rome, Italy.* He held meetings in the Quirinale Palace, had dinner with Prime Minister Ciriaco de Mita at Villa Madam, and had an audience with Pope John Paul II in the Vatican Papal Library. He attended Mass on Sunday at the Church of Francesco. While in Italy, he visited the Anzio beaches and the American Cemetery at Nettuno.

**1989** *Seoul, Korea.* He was received at the Blue House, President Roh's official residence and addressed Parliament in the National Assembly Hall.

**1989** *Spokane, Washington.* Centennial celebration, Riverfront Park.

**1989** *St. Martin, French West Indies.* Meeting with French President Francois Mitterand at the Hotel L'Habitation de Lonvilliers.

**1989** *Tokyo, Japan.* He stayed at the Hotel Okura. He attended the funeral of Emperor Hirohito held at Shinjuka Imperial Gardens and a reception later at the Akasaka Palace.

**1989** *Valletta, Malta.* In Marsaxlokk Bay. Despite rough weather, this was the first super power summit ever held on a ship (first the *USS Belknap*, and then the Soviet vessel *Maxim Gorky*). He met with Gorbachev and with Maltese Prime Minister l'Auberge de Castille.

**1989** *Warsaw, Poland.* He lodged at Parkowa Guest House, spoke to the National Assembly in Parliament Building, and had dinner at Radziwil Palace. He visited the Tomb of the Unknown Soldier in the Warsaw Ghetto, Umschlag Platz. In Gdansk, he visited Lech Walesa at his residence, the Oliwa Cathedral, Westerplatte, and the Solidarity Worker's Monument. This was his first trip to Poland and Hungary as President.

**1989** *Washington, D.C.* Vietnam Veterans Memorial dedication.

**1990** *Cartegena, Columbia.* To sign a narcotics treaty with several South American presidents. He stayed at a guest house near Nacacacad.

**1990** *Cheyenne, Wyoming.* He spoke from the Capitol steps. Later, he went fishing in Middle Crow Creek.

**1990** *Dahran, Saudi Arabia.* He visited a marine tactical site in the desert. A major part of this overseas trip was his visit to the troops and military sites of the Gulf War and to eat Thanksgiving Day dinner with the troops.

**1990** *Des Moines, Iowa.* Fort Des Moines Hotel.

**1990** *Hamilton, Bermuda.* Talks with Prime Minister Margaret Thatcher. Overnight at the Governor-General's residence in Chelston.

**1990** *Helsinki, Finland.* Meetings with Gorbachev in the presidential palace.

**1990** *Jerusalem, Israel.* The King David Hotel. He visited the Pyramids in Cairo, Egypt.

**1990** *London, England.* He lodged at Winfield House, home of the U.S. Ambassador, met at Lancaster House, attended a reception at Bridgewater House, had dinner at Buckingham Palace, and breakfast at 10 Downing Street.

**1990** *Monterey, Mexico.* He visited Heroes Plaza and lunched at the Governor's Palace.

**1990** *Honolulu, Hawaii.* Dinner at the Hilton Hawaiian Village Hotel.

**1990** *Palm Springs, California.* Morningside Country Club. Guest of Walter Annenberg at "Sunnylands."

**1990** *Portland, Oregon.* Dedication of the Police Memorial Coliseum. He lodged at the Portland Hilton Hotel, 921 Southwest Sixth Avenue.

**1990** *Prague, Czechoslovakia.* He met President Vaclav Havel at his residence, Hradcany Castle, spoke to the Federal Assembly, visited the Archbishop's Palace, and laid a wreath at the St. Wenceslaus Memorial at Wenceslaus Square.

**1990** *Washington, D.C.* Soviet Embassy, Golden Dining Room, dinner with President Mikhail Gorbachev.

**1990** *Washington, D.C.* Dedication of the National Cathedral.

**1990** *Yorba Linda, California.* Dedication of the Nixon Presidential Library. Nixon, Ford, and Reagan spoke.

**1991** *Arlington National Cemetery Amphitheater.* Memorial Service for those lost in the Persian Gulf War.

**1991** *Athens, Greece.* Greek Parliament; tour of the Acropolis; dinner at the Presidential Palace.

**1991** *Hamilton, Bermuda.* Met with Prime Minister John Major of Great Britain at Government House.

**1991** *London, England.* Meeting at Lancaster House and 10 Downing Street; reception at the Tower of London; Lunch at Spencer House; dinner at Buckingham Palace; lodging at Winfield House.

**1991** *Montpelier, Virginia.* Dinner at the home of James Madison celebrating the Birth of Bill of Rights.

**1991** *Moscow, Russia.* He met with President Gorbachev. This was his first visit to Moscow as president. Meetings were held at the Kremlin in St. George's Hall and Vladimir's Hall, Grand Kremlin Palace, and the Radisson Hotel. He visited the Tomb of the Unknown Soldier and Novo Ogaryevo (President Gorbychev's suburban residence). He lodged at Spasso House, the residence of the U.S. Ambassador.

**1991** *Mount Rushmore, South Dakota.* He dedicated a National Monument.

**1991** *Pearl Harbor.* National Cemetery of the Pacific at the fiftieth anniversary of the *USS Arizona* disaster. He visited Kilo 8 Pier and the *USS Missouri.*

**1991** *Simi Valley, California.* Opening of the Reagan Presidential Library.

**1991** *Washington, D.C.* Khalil Gibran Memorial Garden dedication ceremony.

**1991** *Washington, D.C.* U.S. Capitol, unveiling a bust of himself.

**1992** *Tokyo, Japan.* State dinner at the home of Prime Minister Miyazwa. He lodged at the Asaka Palace.

**1992** *Arlington National Cemetery, Marine Corps War Memorial.* Speech on the fiftieth anniversary of the landing on Guadacanal.

**1992** *Atlanta, Georgia.* He visited the tomb of Martin Luther King, Jr., with Coretta Scott King.

**1992** *Concord, New Hampshire.* He visited the Legislature in the State Capitol.

**1992** *Grand Rapids, Michigan.* He spoke at the Gerald R. Ford Museum.

**1992** *Houston, Texas.* Renominated for president at the Republican National Convention in the Astrodome.

**1992** *Jackson, Mississippi.* Party rally at State Capitol Building.

**1992** *Lansing, Michigan.* Presidential debate with Bill Clinton at the Wharton Center for the Performing Arts at Michigan State University.

**1992** *Richmond, Virginia.* Debate with Bill Clinton at Robins Center, University of Richmond.

**1992** *St. Louis, Missouri.* Debate with Bill Clinton at Field House, Washington University.

**1992** *Warsaw, Poland.* He returned the remains of Ignace Jan Paderewski and attended a memorial service for Paderewski at St. John's Cathedral, visited the Royal Palace, and gave a speech at Castle Square.

**1992** *Washington, D.C.* Korean War Veterans Memorial ground breaking.

**1993** *Mogadishu and Baidoa, Somalia.* He visited on shore in the daytime and spent the nights on the helicopter carrier the *USS Tripoli.* He had lunch with Army and Marine troops at Baledogle. He was the second U.S. president to make an official visit to a sub-Saharan African nation; Carter had travelled to Nigeria for a three-day stop in 1978.

**1993** *Moscow, Russia.* He met with Yeltsin to sign the nuclear arms treaty at St. Vladimir Hall in the Grand Kremlin Palace and also had dinner at the Kremlin.

**1993** *Paris, France.* He met and dined with President Mitterand at the Elysee Palace. This trip was his twenty-fifth and final foreign trip of his presidency.

**1994** *Yorba Linda, California.* He attended the funeral of former President Richard Nixon.

## SPECIAL SITES

*College Station, Texas.* The Bush Presidential Library is to be established on the campus of A & M University.

## BIBLIOGRAPHY

Bush, George. *Looking Forward: An Autobiography.* New York, Doubleday, 1987.

# WILLIAM JEFFERSON CLINTON

1946–
42ND PRESIDENT 1993–: DEMOCRATIC PARTY

Bill Clinton was born in Hope, Arkansas, on August 19, 1946. His parents were Virginia Cassidy and William Blythe. William Blythe was killed in an auto accident four months before Bill was born. In 1950, his mother married Roger Clinton. In 1953, Clinton became known as Billy Clinton and legally changed his name in 1961. He has one half-brother, Roger, Jr., born in 1956. Roger Clinton, Sr., died in 1966, and in 1969, his mother married Jeff Dwire.

## CHARACTERISTICS

At the time he became president, Clinton was still boyish looking in spite of his prematurely gray hair, which he keeps cut fairly short. He stands 6′2″ tall and weighs about one hundred and seventy-five pounds. He has a fair complexion and blue eyes.

He is an outgoing, fun-loving person. It has been said he never saw a hand he did not want to shake. He has a contagious smile and is "a charming fellow."

*"America does not need a religious war. It needs reaffirmation of the values that for most of us are rooted in our religious faith."*

—*Address, Notre Dame University, September 11, 1992*

## A LIFE IN REVIEW

**Birth:** August 19, 1946; Hope, AR

**Married:** Hillary Rodham; October 11, 1975; 1 daughter

### CAREER

**1974–1976** Professor, University of Arkansas law school

**1977–1979** Attorney General state of Arkansas

**1979–1981** Governor of Arkansas

**1981–1983** Lawyer

**1983–1992** Governor of Arkansas

### ADMINISTRATION EVENTS

**1993** Family Leave Act

NAFTA treaty passed

Bombing World Trade Center

Brady Bill (gun control) passed

---

Over the years, he has played touch football and Monopoly and listened to Elvis Presely records. He likes singing at the piano, playing cards, doing crossword puzzles, reading, and eating mango ice cream, his favorite, at Cook's Ice Cream Parlor. He likes fast food and often lunches at McDonalds. He drinks decaffeinated coffee. Currently, his chief exercise is jogging, which he does on the White House grounds and in the vicinity of the White House. He also plays golf for relaxation when he is on tour around the country. In his school days, he was a band officer and was First Chair Tenor Saxophone in the All-State First Band. At times, when he is in the company of a band, he "borrows" the saxophone and joins in with

other members of the band in a display of unforgotten skill.

## BIRTHPLACE

Bill Clinton was on August 19, 1946 in Hope, Arkansas. The Julia Chester Hospital, where he was born, was located on Main Street about a mile from the center of town. He was born William Jefferson Blythe IV. A funeral home is now on this site.

## BAPTISM

Bill Clinton was baptized October 17, 1956 at Park Place Baptist Church, 721 Park Avenue, Hot Springs, Arkansas.

## CHURCH

Clinton is a regular attender and supporter of the Baptist Church.

**1946–1954** *Hope, Arkansas.* First Baptist Church, where he attended Sunday school and church.

**1954–1980** *Hot Springs, Arkansas.* Park Place Baptist Church, 721 Park Avenue. According to a letter from the church, he was an inactive member for many years until he transferred to the Immanuel Baptist Church in Little Rock.

**1964–1968** *Washington, D.C.* Georgetown Presbyterian Church, 3115 P Street, NW. He attended here because there was no Baptist church nearby.

**1973–1977** *Fayetteville, Arkansas.* First Baptist Church, 10 East Dickson.

**1977–1993** *Little Rock, Arkansas.* Immanuel Baptist Church, 1000 Bishop Street, where he was a regular member of the choir, singing tenor. He joined this church on July 27, 1980. On occasion, he attended the First Methodist Church,

*Birthplace of Bill Clinton.*

Eighth and Center in Little Rock, where his wife, Hillary, and daughter, Chelsea, are members.

**1993–** *Washington, D.C.* First Baptist Church of the City of Washington, D.C., 1328 Sixteenth Street, NW. He attended here the night before his inauguration, January 19.

**1993–** *Washington, D.C.* Foundry Methodist Church, 1500 Sixteenth Street, NW. He usually attends here with his wife.

**1993** *Washington, D.C.* African Methodist Episcopal Church, 1518 M Street, NW. He attended here on the day of his inauguration, January 20.

# EDUCATION

**1951–1952** *Hope, Arkansas.* Mary Perkins Kindergarten, 601 East Second Street, rear of the house. It is now a vacant lot.

**1952–1954** *Hope.* Brookwood Elementary (the Hope Public Elementary School), 500 South Spruce Street. Today, it is the Southwest Arkansas Teaching Cooperative.

**1954–1956** *Hot Springs, Arkansas.* St. John's Catholic School, 501 Grand.

**1956–1962** *Hot Springs, Arkansas.* Hot Springs Ramble Public School, 200 block of Ramble Street. It is now occupied by the First Apostolic Church and is a two-story red brick building with wooden floors.

**1962–1964** *Hot Springs, Arkansas.* Hot Springs High School, 215 Oak Street.

**1964–1968** *Washington, D.C.* Georgetown. Georgetown University School of Foreign Service, Walsh Building on Thirty-sixth Street, NW. He was elected president of his freshman and sophomore classes. For his first three years, he lived in the Loyola Hall dormitory on campus. In 1967–1968, he lived with four other students in a house at

4513 Potomac Avenue, NW. He joined the Alpha Phi Omega fraternity.

**1968–1970**  *Oxford, England.* On a Rhodes Scholarship. He studied at University College on High Street for a graduate degree in politics. From 1968 to 1969, he stayed in an almshouse facing Helen's Court in the right rear corner of Helen's Court. From 1969 to 1970, he roomed with Rick Stearns in a second floor room at Holywell Manor. Later, he moved in with Strobe Talbott in a flat at 46 Leckford Road. He often spent time at the Porter's Lodge of the College. His favorite pub was the Turf Tavern.

**1970–1973**  *New Haven, Connecticut.* Yale University Law School, where he met his future wife, Hillary Rodham, a fellow student. He was awarded a scholarship at Yale. In his first year, he lived in a beach house on Trumbull Beach in Milford, Connecticut. During his second year, his roommate was William Thaddeus Coleman, III, the son of President Nixon's Transportation Secretary. During his later years at Yale, he had a 3-room apartment, at 21 Edgewood, a short distance from the campus.

## MARRIAGE AND HONEYMOON

Clinton fell in love with Hillary Rodham when he saw her for the first time in the Yale University Library. They were married on October 11, 1975 in Fayetteville, Arkansas. They were married in a private family affair in their house at 930 California Boulevard and had large informal reception at a friend's home following the wedding.

There was no honeymoon. Some months later, they went to Acapulco, Mexico, for ten days together with Hillary's mother, father, and two brothers.

## HOMES/LODGINGS

From 1946–1950 Clinton lived at 117 South Hervey Street, Hope, Arkansas. He lived with his maternal grandparents, Edith and Eldridge Cassidy, after his mother left for New Orleans to study at Charity Hospital to become a nurse anesthetist. Eldridge Cassidy ran a small country store in a predominantly black neighborhood at 205 North Hazel Street.

**1950–1952**  *Hope, Arkansas.* 321 East Thirteenth Street. After his mother's marriage to Roger Clinton, Bill left his grandparents to live with his mother and stepfather.

**1952–1954**  *Hope, Arkansas.* He lived with his parents on a farm near the town.

**1954–1961**  *Hot Springs, Arkansas.* 1011 Park Avenue.

**1961–1964**  *Hot Springs, Arkansas.* 213 Scully Street.

**1973–**  *Chicago, Illinois.* 236 Wisner Avenue, Park Ridge area. Home of Hillary Rodham.

**1973–1975**  *Fayetteville, Arkansas.* He lived in an apartment off campus on East Highway 16.

**1975–1977**  *Fayetteville, Arkansas.* 930 California Boulevard was a house which he bought just before his marriage. It was a prairie-style house with beamed ceilings and a bay window.

**1977–1979**  *Little Rock, Arkansas.* 5419 L Street. Clinton bought this house for $35,000.

**1979–1981**  *Little Rock, Arkansas.* Governor's Mansion, West Eighteenth and Center Streets.

**1980**  *Little Rock, Arkansas.* Home of Hillary's parents, Dorothy and Hugh Rodham, 3501 Oakwood Road.

**1980**  *Little Rock, Arkansas.* Home of his mother, Dorothy, and her fourth husband Richard Kelley, 405 Bayside Drive.

**1981–1983**  *Little Rock, Arkansas.* 816 Midland. After losing his reelection bid for governor, Clinton bought this home for $112,000.

*Boyhood home of Bill Clinton in Hope, Arkansas.*

**1983–1993** *Little Rock, Arkansas.* Governor's Mansion.

# WORK

From 1964 to 1966 Clinton worked in the office of Senator J. William Fulbright as an administrative and research assistant for the Chairman of the Senate Foreign Relations Committee of Congress in Washington, D.C. at the Capitol.

**1970–1972** *New Haven, Connecticut.* He had a number of part-time jobs to cover his living expenses while he was on scholarship at Yale. They included teaching a law enforcement program at a local community college, working for a city councilman in Hartford, and assisting a lawyer in New Haven. During his first semester, he was busy with Joe Duffy's Senate campaign.

**1972** *Austin, Texas.* He managed George McGovern's campaign in Texas, working in the state campaign headquarters. While here, he shared an apartment with Taylor Branch.

**1973–1977** *Fayetteville, Arkansas.* He was on the Faculty of Law at the University of Arkansas in Waterman Hall, Maple Street and Garland Avenue.

**1974** *Fayetteville, Arkansas.* He ran for Congress and was defeated.

**1977–1979** *Little Rock, Arkansas.* He was elected and served as Attorney General. His office was in the Justice Building, 1500 West Seventh Street.

**1979–1981** *Little Rock, Arkansas.* Governor. He was the youngest governor in the United States. He was defeated in his bid for reelection. The governor's office is on the second floor of the Capitol. The Statehouse Convention Center, Markham and

Main Streets was the site of Clinton's gubernatorial inauguration balls.

**1981–1983** *Little Rock, Arkansas.* Wright Lindsey & Jennings, a law firm, 2200 Worthen Bank Building.

**1983–1992** *Little Rock, Arkansas.* Governor of Arkansas.

**1991–1992** *Little Rock, Arkansas.* Campaign headquarters, Gazette Building, 112 West Third Street, campaigning for the presidency of the United States. In November he made his victory speech at the Old State House, 300 West Markham, where he had declared his candidacy thirteen months earlier. The victory celebration was at the Camelot Hotel, Markham and Broadway.

**1993–** *Washington, D.C.* President of the United States.

# TRAVEL/VISITS

**1963** *Washington, D.C.* Clinton attended a Boys National American Legion Convention where he met President Kennedy in the Rose Garden of the White House and shook hands with him in July.

**1964** *Durham, North Carolina.* He visited his sick stepfather, Roger Clinton, at Duke University Medical Center on Easter weekend, they attended services at the Duke Chapel.

**1968–1970** *New York City, New York.* Manhattan's Forty-sixth Street dock, where he boarded the *S.S. United States* for England and study at Oxford.

**1979** *London, England.* Visited Oxford.

**1980** *Israel.* Visited major religious sites.

**1988** *Atlanta, Georgia.* He attended the Democratic National Convention held at the OMNI. He placed Governor Dukakis' name in nomination with a long speech. His remark at the end, "In conclusion," drew the biggest applause.

**1989** *Charlottesville, Virginia.* University of Virginia, Cabel Hall, University Hall and Rotunda for the Governor's Conference. President Bush was also there for the education summit.

**1992** *Arlington Cemetery, Virginia.* He laid a rose on John F. Kennedy's grave. Kennedy had been his hero since he met him when he was thirteen.

**1992** *Atlanta, Georgia.* He visited the Carter Museum Center with the other Democratic candidates.

**1992** *Austin, Texas.* He visited both the House and Senate Chambers in the State Capitol.

**1992** *Baltimore, Maryland.* He threw out the traditional first ball at the Baltimore Oriole's home opener.

**1992** *College Park, Maryland.* University of Maryland. He participated in a Democratic party primary debate.

**1992** *East Lansing, Michigan.* Michigan State University, for the third presidential debate.

**1992** *Fayetteville and Rogers (on Beaver Lake), Arkansas.* Three-day vacation.

**1992** *Goffstown, New Hampshire.* He participated in a Democratic primary debate.

**1992** *Hyde Park, New York.* He visited and laid a rose on the grave of Franklin D. Roosevelt, in the company of Roosevelt's grandson, James Roosevelt, Jr.

**1992** *Little Rock, Arkansas.* YWCA, 1200 South Cleveland. He attended a father-daughter banquet with his daughter, Chelsea.

**1992** *Manchester, New Hampshire.* At a local TV station, where he participated in the Democratic party primary debate.

**1992** *Martha's Vineyard, Massachusetts.* Nine-day vacation at the home of former Secretary of Defense, McNamara.

**1992** *New York City, New York.* Macy's Department Store, where he listened to the Democratic National Convention nominate him for president. He went from here to the convention at Madison Square Gardens.

**1992** *Orlando, Florida.* Picnic in Lock Haven Park. This was the culmination of a two-day bus tour of Florida.

**1992** *Richmond, Virginia.* University of Virginia, site of the second presidential debate in the "town hall" format.

**1992** *Sioux Falls, South Dakota.* Howard Johnson Hotel. He participated in the Democratic party primary debate.

**1992** *St. Louis, Missouri.* Washington University Gymnasium, where the first debate among President Bush, Clinton, and Ross Perot was held.

**1992** *Tampa, Florida.* Performing Arts Center, 1010 North MacInnes Place. He was here to start off the drive for support of his universal health plan.

**1993** *Scranton, Pennsylvania.* Court Street Methodist Church, for the funeral of Hillary's father, Hugh Rodham.

**1993** *Vail, Colorado.* On vacation here, he met and played a round of golf with ex-president Ford.

**1993** *Washington, D.C.* Blair House, Pennsylvania Avenue. He stayed here during the days preceding his inauguration.

**1993** *Washington, D.C.* Vietnam Memorial, for a major address.

**1993** *West Point, New York.* Addressed the graduating class of the Academy in the Stadium. He was the tenth president to do so.

**1994** *Brussels, Belgium, for NATO meetings.* This was his first trip to Europe as President.

**1994** *Kiev, Ukraine.*

**1994** *Los Angeles, California.* Riviera Country Club, for a game of golf while in California to promote his comprehensive health care reform.

**1994** *Moscow, Russia.* He met with President Boris Yeltsin. On the return, he stopped briefly in Minsk.

**1994** *Normandy, France.* Omaha and Utah Beaches.

**1994** *Oxford, England.* He received an honorary degree from the University and visited some of his old haunts.

**1994** *Paris, France.* He spoke to the French Parliament. He was the first U.S. president to so since President Wilson in 1918.

**1994** *Portsmouth, England.* D-Day observance on shore and later with Queen Elizabeth on the royal yacht.

**1994** *Prague, Slovakia.* He met with President Havel, toured the old city center, and mixed with the crowd in a popular beerhall, and visited an old Jewish cemetery.

**1994** *Rome, Italy.* He was received by the President of Italy and visited Pope John Paul II at the Vatican.

**1994** *Yorba Linda, California.* He attended funeral of President Nixon at the Nixon Presidential Library.

## BIBLIOGRAPHY

Levin, Robert E. *Bill Clinton: The Inside Story.* New York, S.P.I. Books. 1991.

Maraniss, David. *First in his Class: A Biography of Bill Clinton.* New York, Simon and Schuster. 1995.

# GEOGRAPHIC GUIDE TO PRESIDENTIAL LANDMARKS

1. Burleson House,
   *Decatur*
2. A. Johnson home,
   *Mooresville*

# ALABAMA

## BRIDGEPORT *(Jackson County)*

**Grant**
  *Work* • Visit to headquarters of General George Thomas off US 72 and AL 2. Late summer 1863.

## DADESVILLE *(Tallaposa County Peninsula, near Horseshoe Bend)*

**Jackson**
  *Travel* • Fought the Creek Indians. 1814. See also Horseshoe Bend, Horseshoe National Military Park.

## DECATUR *(Morgan County)*

**Grant**
  *Work* • Burleson House (later Hinds and now McEntire House) near the railroad bridge. Grant met here for war conference. 1863.

**Harrison, B**
  *Visit* • Lodged at Tavern Hotel, corner Grant Ave and Sixth St. Site burned. 1923.

**Johnson, A**
  *Travel* • Travelled by road as far as Knoxville, TN, then on a flat boat to Decatur and to Mooresville. Most of Decatur was destroyed by the end of the Civil War; few buildings other than the Old State Bank remain. 1825.

**Van Buren**
  *Visit* • Old State Bank, 925 Bank St NW. He attended the opening when he was vice president. He visited Mobile on this same trip. 1833.

## EMUCKFAW *(Tallapoosa County, west of Horsehoe Bend)*

**Jackson**
  *Travel* • Battle of Emuckfaw. On AL 49. 3–27–1814.

## ENITACHOPCO *(Tallapoosa County, west of Horsehoe Bend and north of Emuckfaw)*

**Jackson**
  *Travel* • Battle of Enitachopco. 1814.

## FAYETTEVILLE *(Talladega County)*

**Jackson**

> *Travel* • Battle with Creeks. Site on County Road 2. 1813.

## FORT BOWYER *(Mobile County, north of Mobile)*

**Jackson**

> *Travel* • Stationed at Mobile Point. 1813–1814.

## FORT STROTHER *(Calhoun County, on the Coosa River, four miles west of Ohatchee)*

**Jackson**

> *Travel* • Markers on highway and at original site on Coosa River. County Road 26. 1814.

## FORT TOHOPEKA *(See Horseshoe Bend)*

## FORT TOULOUSE (RENAMED FORT JACKSON) *(Elmore County, on US 231 in Wetumpka at the junction of the Coosa and Tallapoosa Rivers where they form the Alabama River)*

**Jackson**

> *Travel* • See reconstructed fort in Fort Toulouse Jackson Park 3 miles west of Wetumpka on US 231. 1814.

## FORT WILLIAM *(Tallapoosa County, north and west of Horseshoe Bend on the west side of the Coosa River)*

**Jackson**

> *Travel* • He left here March 14 on the way to the Battle of Horseshoe Bend. 1814.

## HORSESHOE BEND *(Tallapoosa County)*

**Jackson**

> *Travel* • National Military Park, AL 49. Replica of Fort Jackson at the confluence of the Coosa and Tallapoosa Rivers. Information on Emuckfaw, Enitachopco, and Fort Tohopeka here. 1814.

## HUNTSVILLE *(Madison County)*

**Eisenhower**

> *Visit* • Marshall Space Center. Dedication. 5 miles west of town. 9–8–1960.

**Garfield**

> *Work* • During Civil War he was the presiding officer at general court martial in Huntsville, probably near where Constitution Hall Park is now. Near 301 Madison Street. 1862.

**Jackson**

> *Visit* • Pope House, 403 Echols (the oldest documented house in Alabama). 1814.

> *Visit* • Town Square. Marker commemorating his organizing of troops here. Andrew Jackson Way follows US 72. 1814.

> *Travel* • Ditto's Landing on Tennessee River. From South Memorial Parkway, US 23, turn east on Hobbs Island Road and right on Ditto Landing Road. Tennessee River below Huntsville. Joined cavalry here. 1813.

**Monroe**

> *Visit* • Convention Building (since torn down). NW corner Franklin St and Gates Ave in Constitution Hall Park. 404 Madison Street. Marked by gray stone boulder. 1819.

> *Visit* • Oakland Plantation, 1620 Meridian Street. 1819.

## MOBILE *(Mobile County)*

**Fillmore**

> *Visit* • Glenmore, "Stone Quarry" home of the mayor. Visited home of Josephine Bunker. Attended Sixth Mobile Theater at Royal and St. Michael Sts. 4–8–1854.

**Garfield**

> *Visit* • 350 Oakleigh Place. Oakleigh is where he is said to have drunk his first mint julep. June 1877.

**Grant**

*Visit* • Battle House, corner of Royal and St. Francis Sts. Lodging and banquet. 4–9–1880.

*Visit* • Customs House for reception, N Royal St and St. Francis. Demolished. Guest of Cotton Exchange, NW corner Commerce and St. Francis Sts. Demolished. 4–9–1880.

**Harrison, WH**

*Visit* • 350 Oakleigh Place.

**Jackson**

*Visit* • SW corner Conti and Conception Sts opposite the India House. 1814. Headquarters destroyed in 1970s. Also stayed at the Battle House at Royal and St. Francis Sts. Another tradition says headquarters was a log cabin where the Battle House saloon long stood. See also Fort Condi, 150 S Royal St which was area headquarters of the military rule. 1815.

**Polk**

*Travel* • Arrived by boat 3–19–1849.

**Roosevelt, T**

*Visit* • Masonic Temple, St. Joseph St. Dedicated 1902. First visit to Mobile. 6–1–1898.

**Van Buren**

*Visit* • Lodged at Mansion House. Attended a play at Corinthian Theater. Location no longer exists. 4–6–1842.

## MONTGOMERY *(Montgomery County)*

**Cleveland**

*Visit* • Presidential visit to the city and the present State Capitol. Bainbridge St. October 1887.

**Jackson**

*Travel* • Fort Montgomery on the Alabama River readying for the attack on Pensacola. 11–1–1814.

**Reagan**

*Visit* • State Capitol on Goat Hill at east end of Dexter Ave. 3–15–1982.

**Roosevelt, T**

*Visit* • State Capitol. 1905.

## MOORESVILLE *(Limestone County, US Alt 72 east of Huntsville)*

**Garfield**

*Church* • Church of Christ. White frame church on Piney St where he preached. 1863.

*Church* • See also Brick Church existing while he was in Mooresville.

*Visit* • See Stage Coach Inn (1825) on the east edge of town. 1863.

**Johnson, A**

*Church* • Old Brick Church at the edge of town. 1825.

*Home* • McNiell House where he lodged. Last house on street down from the church. SW corner of Piney and Market Sts. 1825.

*Work* • Sloss Tailor Shop at SW corner of Piney and Market Sts. Nothing remains. The lot adjoins the McNiell House. 1825.

*Visit* • Stagecoach and Inn. Two blocks away from the old Brick Church. 1825.

*Travel* • Travelled by road to Knoxville then on a flatboat to Cotton Port, walking the rest of the way to Mooresville. Marker at entrance to town commemorating Johnson/Garfield visit. 1825.

**McKinley**

*Church* • Attended Church of Christ on Piney Street. 1863.

## PRATTVILLE *(Autauga County)*

**Jackson**

*Visit* • Major Montgomery House "Buena Vista," Reynolds Mill Rd. 1814.

## SNOWDOUN *(Montgomery County)*

**Bush**

*Visit* • Annual fishing trip to Pentala on US 231 near Snowdoun. 1980s.

## STEVENSON *(Jackson County)*

**Garfield**

*Work* • The "Little Brick House" where he plotted strategy during the Civil War (near town center). Now in ruins. 1864.

## TALLADEGA *(Talladega County, east of Birmingham)*

**Jackson**

*Travel* • Location of the conflict between the Creek Indians and army led by Jackson. See the Big Spring Monument, corner of Battle and Spring Sts. Also Marker. 1814.

## TUSKEGEE *(Macon County)*

**Bush**

*Visit* • Tuskegee Institute, Old Montgomery Rd. 4–13–1981.

**Coolidge**

*Visit* • Speaking tour. "The Oaks," Old Montgomery Rd. 2–13–1923.

**Roosevelt, FD**

*Visit* • George Washington Carver Museum on Tuskegee College grounds. Near entrance to the College on Old Montgomery Rd. 1938.

**Roosevelt, T**

*Visit* • Varner-Alexander House on Old Montgomery St (now called Grey Columns). 1905.

*Visit* • The Oaks, George Washington Carver's home. Located at edge of Tuskeegee College. 399 Old Montgomery Rd.

## WETUMPKA *(See Fort Toulouse)*

# ALASKA

## ANCHORAGE

### Presidents
*Visit* • The Chateau, Elmendorf AFB on the extention of North C Street. Almost every president since Eisenhower has visited.

### Ford
*Visit* • Westward Hotel (now Anchorage Hilton Hotel), 500 West Third Ave. 11-17-1975 and 11-29-1975.

### Johnson, LB
*Travel* • Westward Hotel. 11-1-1966.

### Kennedy
*Visit* • Westward Hotel. Reception, Edgewater Hotel (Idletime Inn). Site now occupied by Regal Alaskan Hotel, 4800 Spenard Road. 1960.

## CURRY *(Almost equidistant between Seward and Fairbanks)*

### Harding/Hoover
*Visit* • Curry Hotel (burned 1957) on the railroad right of way. Later McKinley Hotel built on site. Burned 1971 and new hotel built. 1923.

## FAIRBANKS

### Harding/Hoover
*Visit* • Hotel Norvale, 522 Second Ave. 1923.

## HARDING GATEWAY *(Between Rugged and Cheval Is. Gateway.) Named in honor of Harding's visit. 1923.*

## JUNEAU

### Harding
*Visit* • Capitol, Fourth Street between Main and Seward Streets. It was the Territorial Building and became the Capitol in 1959. Governor's Mansion, 716 Calhoun Ave. 1923.

## KETCHIKAN

### Harding
*Visit* • Laid the cornerstone of Masonic Temple. 1923.

## SITKA

### Harding
*Visit* • Church. Pew marked with plate.

Alaska

● Fairbanks

Anchorage ●①

● Juneau

1. Elmendorf Air Force
   Base, *Anchorage*

# ARIZONA

## BENSON *(Cochise County)*

**Kennedy**
*Visit* • Jay-6 Ranch of Jack Speiden. 1936.

## CASTLE HOT SPRINGS *(Yavapai County)*

**Kennedy**
*Visit* • Castle Hot Springs Hotel. 1945.

## GRAND CANYON *(Coconino County)*

**Bush**
*Visit* • Yavapai Point. 9–18–1991.

**Roosevelt, T**
*Visit* • 5–6–1903

**Taft**
*Visit* • Grand View. October 1909.

## PHOENIX *(Maricopa County)*

**Kennedy**
*Visit* • Arizona Biltmore, Twenty-fifth St and E Missouri Ave. January 1945

*Visit* • Camelback Inn, Lincoln Dr. January 1945.

*Visit* • Westward Ho Hotel, N Central Ave and W Fillmore St. 11–17–1962.

**McKinley**
*Visit* • Adams Hotel, Corner Adams and Central Ave for reception and speech. Demolished 1973. May 1901.

*Visit* • Territorial Capitol. Washington St and Seventeenth Ave. Also visited ancient Aztec irrigation system and the Indian Industrial School four miles out of Phoenix. 1901.

**Nixon**
*Honeymoon* • Westward Ho Motel, N Central Ave and W Fillmore St. 1940.

**Reagan**
*Church* • St. Thomas the Apostle, 2312 E Campbell Ave.1973–.

**Roosevelt, T**
*Visit* • Capitol, 1700 W Washington. March 1911.

## PRESCOTT *(Yavapai County)*

**Nixon**
*Home/Lodging* • 937 W Apache at a pri-

# Arizona

40    Flagstaff

1

17

10

10

Phoenix

Tucson

1. Nixon home, *Prescott*

vate TB sanitorium with mother and broth-ers. 1928 and 1929.

*Work* • Frontier Days at Slipper Gulch. Summers of 1928 and 1929.

**SCOTTSDALE** *(Maricopa County, suburb of Phoenix)*

**Reagan**

*Lodging* • Dr. Loyal Davis House (Nancy's parents), 24 Biltmore. 1952–.

# Arkansas

40

40

5
Little Rock

4

30

3

2

1

1. Clinton home, *Fayetteville*
2. Taylor home, *Fort Smith*
3. Clinton birthplace, *Hope*
4. Clinton home, *Hot Springs*
5. Clinton home, *Little Rock*

# ARKANSAS

## BULL SHOALS *(Marion County)*

**Truman**

*Visit* • Bull Shoals Dam at Bull Shoals State Park, off US 62. Dedication 7–3–1952.

## FAYETTEVILLE *(Washington County)*

**Clinton**

*Church* • First Baptist Church, 10 East Dickson. 1973–1977.

*Marriage* • 930 California Blvd. 1975.

*Honeymoon* • 930 California Blvd. 1975.

*Home* • Apartment on East AR 16. 1973–1975.

*Home* • 930 California Blvd. 1975–1977.

*Work* • Faculty of Law, University of Arkansas, Waterman Hall, Room 302 1973–1974; Room 206 1975–1977. Maple St and Garland Ave. 1973–1977.

## FORT SMITH *(Van Buren County, on I-40)*

**Ford**

*Travel* • Dedicated St. Edward School, Wildcat Mountain Rd at 7301 Rogers Ave. 8–10–1975.

**Kennedy**

*Visit* • Fort Smith, Garrison Ave. 9–29–1963.

**Taylor**

*Church* • Sunday school was held in a log house. Site between Green and Howard Aves (now Fourth and Fifth Aves). 1840s.

*Home* • A one-story log building on the north side of Garrison Ave just behind the present Catholic church where the Sisters of Mercy Convent is now. Marker. 1841–1845.

*Travel* • Post Commander. The old commissary building built in 1838 has been preserved and made into a museum on Garrison Ave near the present highway bridge. He was also at Camp Belknap about a mile from Fort Smith. 1841–1844.

## HEBER SPRINGS *(Cleburne County)*

**Kennedy**

*Visit* • Greers Ferry Dam and Reservoir 3,

*Hope's Centennial Marker.*

*The remains of Zachary Taylor's home in Fort Smith.*

1/2 mi NE on AR 25. Dedication. 10–3–1963.

# HOPE *(Hempstead County)*
## Clinton

*Birthplace* • Julia Chester Hospital on Main St between Ninth and Tenth. (Now site of Oakcrest Chapel Funeral Home). 1946.

*Church* • First Baptist Church, at East Fourth on South Main. 1946–1954.

*Education* • Mary Perkins Kindergarten, behind 509 Stores St. Vacant lot. 1949.

*Education* • Hope Public Elementary School (now SW Arkansas Teaching Cooperative), 500 S Spruce St. 1950.

*Home* • Eldridge grandparents' home, 117 North Hendrey St. Grandfather had Cassidy Country Store, 205 N Hazel St (now a warehouse). 1948–1950.

*Home* • 321 E Thirteenth St. 1950–1952.

*Home* • Roger Clinton farm. 1952–1954. Location not determined.

# HOT SPRINGS *(Garland County)*
## Clinton

*Church* • Park Place Baptist Church, 721 Park Ave. 1954–1973. Baptism. 10–17–1956.

*Education* • St. John's Catholic School, 581 Grand. 1954–1956.

*Education* • Ramble Public School, 200 block of Ramble St. Now First Apostolic Church. 1956–1962.

*Education* • Hot Springs High School, 125 Oak at the corner of Orange and Oak. Now unused. 1962–1964.

*Home* • 1011 Park Ave. 1954.

*Home* • 213 Scully St. 1954–1975.

*Visit* • 209 Bayside Drive, home of his mother Virginia (Mrs. Richard) Kelley.

*Site* • Clinton-Gore headquarters, corner Spring and Malvern. 1992.

### Kennedy

*Visit* • Arlington Hotel, Central Ave and Fountain St. Speech to American Bar Association. 9–29–1963.

*Visit* • St. Joseph's Hospital, Whittington Ave and Cliff Cedar St. to see Gov Faubus. 1963.

### Truman

*Visit* • Park Hotel, 211 Hot Springs Mountain Drive. 1941.

## LITTLE ROCK  *(Pulaski County)*

### Clinton

*Church* • Immanuel Baptist Church, 1000 Bishop St. 1975–1993.

*Home* • 5419 L St. 1977–1979.

*Home* • Governor's Mansion. West Eighteenth and Center Sts. (since 1950 and first official mansion). 1979–1981 and 1983–1993.

*Home* • 816 Midland. 1981–1983.

*Work* • Justice Building on Capitol grounds. Attorney General. 1977–1979.

*Work* • State Capitol, Capitol Ave and Woodlawn, west of downtown. Governor. 1979–1981 and 1983–1993.

*Work* • Law Firm of Wright Lindsey & Jennings, 2200 Worthen Bank Bldg, Corner of Capital and Center Sts. 1981–1983.

*Work* • Old State House, 300 West Markham. Victory Speech. Celebration at the Camelot Hotel, Markham and Broadway. November 1992.

*Visit* • Home of Virginia (mother) and Dick Kelley, 3300 Lorance Dr.

*Visit* • Home of Dorothy and Hugh Rodham (Hillary's parents), 3501 Oakwood Rd, Apt. 4.

### Grant

*Visit* • Capital Hotel. 111 West Markham. See restored 1877 hotel which stands opposite the former State Capitol. He was entertained here and at the Capitol. 1880.

*Visit* • Concordia Hall for reception. 305 1/2 W Markham. 1880.

### Reagan

*Visit* • Arkansas Excelsior Hotel, 3 State House Plaza. 11–2–1984. State House Convention Center, 1 State House Plaza. 11–3–1984.

### Roosevelt, FD

*Visit* • Centennial Stadium. Senator Joe Robinson home, 2122 S Broadway. 6–10–1936.

### Roosevelt, T

*Visit* • Capitol. 300 W Markham. 1905.

*Visit* • Fort Roots in North Little Rock. 10–25–1905.

*Visit* • Little Rock City Park. Speech. Also spoke in Albert Pike Consistory Building, E Eighth, NW corner. 1905.

### Taft

*Visit* • Capitol. 300 W Markham. 1909.

*Visit* • Union Station. N Victory and W Markham. Made remarks. 1909.

### Truman

*Visit* • Hotel Marion reception, 200 W Markham. 6–10–1949.

*Visit* • Bull Municipal Auditorium (Robinson Memorial), Markham and Broadway Sts. Speech. 1949.

*Visit* • Dedicated War Memorial Park, north side I-630 at Fair Park Blvd exit. 1949.

*Visit* • Joe T. Robinson (widow) home 2122 S Broadway. 6–10–1949.

### Wilson

*Visit* • Mrs. J. R. Kennedy (Marion, his

sister), 606 W Third Street. House gone, now a parking lot. 1886.

***Church*** • Second Presbyterian, W Third St, southeast corner at Gaines. Relocated. 1886.

## OZARKS *(Benton/Washington Counties)*

**Hoover**

***Work*** • North side of the Ozarks. Summer Work. 1892.

## ROCKPORT *(Hot Spring County, between Malvern and Little Rock)*

**Roosevelt, FD**

***Visit*** • Centennial celebration. Lunch at Couchwood on Lake Catherine. 6–10–1936.

***Visit*** • Kentucky Baptist Church. Speech and reception. 1936.

## TEXARKANA *(Miller County)*

**Johnson, LB**

***Visit*** • JF Kennedy Square dedication. 9–25–1964.

# CALIFORNIA

## ALAMEDA *(Alameda County, near Oakland)*
**Nixon**
> *Home* • Had quarters here with Pat near Fleet Air. August 1944.
>
> *Work* • Fleet Air Wing 8. 1944.

## BAKERSFIELD *(Kern County)*
**Bush**
> *Home* • Water Street near the Tam O'Shanter. 1949.
>
> *Work* • Dresser Industries, Security Engineering Company at 1435 S Union Ave. 1949.

## BERKELEY *(Alameda County)*
**Truman**
> *Visit* • Commencement speech, Memorial Stadium at the University. 6–12–1948.

## BEVERLY HILLS *(See Los Angeles)*

## BIG BRIDGES *(Los Angeles County)*
**Nixon**
> *Visit* • Claremont College. Debate with Vorhis. 1946.

## BRENTWOOD *(Park Los Angeles County)*
**Nixon**
> *Home* • Walter Lang House on Bundy Ave while his house was being built. 1961.

**Reagan**
> *Home* • Rockingham Ave.

## CAMP ORD *(Monterey County, north shore of Monterey Peninsula)*
**Eisenhower**
> *Work* • Executive officer with the infantry. Fort Ord is on CA 1 south of Santa Cruz. 1940.

## COMPTON *(Los Angeles County, south of Los Angeles center)*
**Bush**
> *Home* • 624 B Santa Fe Ave. Now a run down building. 1949.

## CORONADO *(San Diego County)*
**Presidents**
> *Visit* • Hotel del Coronado, 1500 Orange Ave: B Harrison, McKinley, Nixon, Reagan, FD Roosevelt, and Taft.

1. Eisenhower home, *San Francisco*
2. Hoover home, *Oakland*
3. Nixon home, *Alameda*
4. Bush home, *Bakersfield*
5. Hoover home, *Monterey*
6. Nixon home, *Lindsay*
7. Bush home, *Bakersfield*
8. Reagan home, *Santa Barbara*
9. Bush home, *Ventura*
10. L.B. Johnson home, *San Bernardino*
11. Ford home, *Los Angeles*
12. Bush home, *Whittier*
13. Nixon home, *Fullerton*
14. Nixon birthplace, *Yorba Linda*
15. Nixon home, *San Clemente*
16. Carter home, *San Diego*
17. Ford home, *Palm Springs*

## CULVER CITY *(Los Angeles County)*

**Reagan**
*Work* • Hal Roach Studios (Fort Roach). 1942.

## EL PORTAL *(Mariposa County)*

**Taft**
*Visit* • Wawona Hotel cottage on CA 41 at Yosemite National Park. 1909.

## EL TORO *(Orange County)*

**Nixon**
*Visit* • Marine Corps Air Station.

*Funeral* • Body flown here. Honor guard and 21-gun salute. 4–26–1994.

## EUREKA *(Humboldt County)*

**Grant**
*Work* • Resigned at Fort Humboldt and went from San Francisco to New York to Bethel, Ohio, then to White Haven in St. Louis. 1853–1854.

**Nixon**
*Visit* • Redwood National Park (near Eureka). 8–27–1969.

## FORT GASTON *(See Hoopa)*

## FORT MASON *(Near San Francisco, Buchanan St, and Marina Blvd)*

**Reagan**
*Work* • War service. 1942.

## FORT MONTEREY *(See Monterey)*

## FULLERTON *(Orange County, east of LongBeach/Anaheim)*

**Nixon**
*Education* • Fullerton High School, 201 E Chapman Ave. 1926–1928.

*Home* • Lived with his Aunt Carrie Wildermoth. House not found. 1926–1928.

## GLENDALE *(Los Angeles County, northeast of Los Angeles city center)*

**Reagan**
*Marriage* • Wee Kirk o' Heather Wedding Chapel, Forest Lawn Memorial Park, 1712 S Glendale Ave. Wedding reception at home of Louella Parsons, 612 N Maple Dr, Beverly Hills.

## HOLLYWOOD *(District of Los Angeles)*

**Coolidge**
*Visit* • Warner Brothers, 4000 Warner Blvd, MGM, and United Artists studios. 1930.

**Nixon**
*Home* • 410 Memory Lane (now Martin Lane). 1961–1963.

**Reagan**
*Church* • Hollywood-Beverly Christian Church. 1717 N Grammercy Pl. 1940–.

*Home* • Hollywood and Vine at the Hollywood Plaza Hotel. 1937.

*Home* • 1128 Cory Ave near Hollywood Blvd at Montecito Apartments. 1937–1941.

*Home* • 1326 Londonderry View, Apt 5. 1941–.

*Home* • 9137 Cordell Dr. 1941.

*Home* • Sunset Blvd at Garden of Allah Apartments. 1947.

*Home* • Londonderry View, following his divorce. 1948–1952.

*Home* • 668 St. Cloud Drive, Bel Air. West of Beverly Hills. 1989–present.

*Work* • Warner Brothers Film Studio. 4000 Warner Blvd. 1937–1965.

*Work* • President, Actors Screen Guild 1947–1960; 7046 Hollywood Blvd; 1947–1955; 7750 Sunset Blvd; 1957–1960.

## HOOPA *(Humboldt County)*

**Grant**
*Work* • Fort Gaston. See museum on CA 96, north of County Rd 299. 1853.

## IRVINE *(Orange County)*

**Johnson, LB**

  *Visit* • Dedicated University of California campus, upper end of Newport Bay. 6–20–1964.

## LAGUNA BEACH *(Orange County)*

**Nixon**

  *Visit* • Victor Hugo Inn, Cliff Drive.

## LaHABRA *(Orange County)*

**Nixon**

  *Work* • Law office on Main Street. Now a real estate office, room numbers 197–198. 1939–1941.

## LAKE MALIBU *(Los Angeles County)*

**Reagan**

  *Home* • Ranch, Canyon Rd. 1940s.

## LAKE TAHOE *(near California/Nevada border)*

**Hoover**

  *Work* • With the U.S. Geological Survey. Summer 1894.

## LA QUINTA *(Riverside County)*

**Eisenhower**

  *Visit* • 52827 Eisenhower Dr. 1954.

**Ford**

  *Visit* • Golf at La Quinta County Club. 77750 Ave 50. 1974 and 1975.

## LINDGREN

**Hoover**

  *Work* • In the mines. Summer 1895.

## LINDSAY *(Tulare County)*

**Nixon**

  *Education* • Sunnyside School NE corner of Rd 216 and Ave 196. Original building burned.

**Home** • Corner of Avenue 200 and Rd 208 with his aunt and uncle (Beeson). 1925.

## LONG BEACH *(Los Angeles County)*

**Presidents**

  *Visit* • Bush, Carter, Ford, LB Johnson, Reagan, T Roosevelt, Taft, and Truman.

**Ford**

  *Visit* • Memorial Hospital Medical Center, 2801 Atlantic Ave to see Nixon. November 1974.

**Roosevelt, FD**

  *Visit* • Douglas Aircraft plant. 9–25–1942.

## LOS ANGELES *(Los Angeles County)*

**Presidents**

  *Visit* • Biltmore Hotel, 505 S Olive St. LB Johnson, Kennedy, and Truman.

**Presidents**

  *Visit* • Century Plaza Hotel, 2025 Ave of the Stars. Bush, Carter, Ford, Nixon, and Reagan.

**Bush**

  *Travel* • Pauley Pavilion (sports arena) U of C. Figueroa St and Martin Luther King, Jr. Blvd. Second and final debate with Dukasis. 10–13–1988.

**Coolidge**

  *Visit* • Hotel on Fifth Street. Warner Brothers, MGM, 4000 Warner Blvd, United Artists Studios. 2–17–1920 to 2–20–1920.

**Ford**

  *Home* • Apartment in Los Angeles. 1977–.

  *Visit* • Sheraton Universal Hotel, 333 Universal Terrace Pkwy (Universal City). 10–7–1976.

**Hayes**

  *Visit* • Cosmopolitan Hotel on Main Street. Now St. Elmo. 1880.

**Johnson, L**

  *Visit* • Memorial Sports Arena, 3939 S Figueroa Street. Nominated by DNC for vice president. July 1960.

*Visit* • U of C Intermural Athletic Field 2–21–1964; Memorial Sports Arena, 3939 S Figueroa St. 2–22–1964.

### Kennedy

*Visit* • Hearst Estate. 1960.

*Visit* • DNC, New Sports Arena, 3939 S Figueroa Street. July 1960.

### McKinley

*Visit* • Bivouac, residence of Gen. Harrison Gray Otis. 1901.

### Nixon

*Church* • Angelus Temple to hear Aimee Semple McPherson. 1100 Glendale Blvd. 1926.

*Work* • 3950 Wilshire Blvd. With Adams, Duque and Hazeltine Law Firm. 1961–1963. Headquarters here during his losing campaign for governor of California. 1962.

*Visit* • Ambassador Hotel, 3400 Wilshire Blvd, on campaign tour. Also here RNC. 1952.

*Visit* • Statler Hotel (now Hilton), 930 Wilshire Blvd. 1960.

*Visit* • Gaylord Hotel (now Gaylord Apt), 3355 Wilshire Blvd. 1960.

### Reagan

*Church* • Bel Air Presbyterian Church, 16221 Mulholland Dr. 1989–.

*Work* • General Electric Television series. CBS Studios. 1954–1962.

*Work* • United States Borax Company Show. 1964–1966.

*Work* • Fox Plaza Building, 34th Floor (Century City). 1977–.

*Visit* • Hotel Bel Air, 11461 Sunset Blvd. Daughter's wedding. 8–14–1984.

### Roosevelt, FD

*Visit* • DNC in Convention Hall, 1201 S Figueroa; nominated for vice president. 1920.

*Travel* • Western tour. Memorial Coliseum and overnight Coronado Hotel

10–1–1935; RR Platform remarks. 7–16–1938.

### T Roosevelt

*Visit* • Westminster Hotel, 342–350 S Main. May 1903.

### Wilson

*Visit* • Hotel Alexandria, 501 S Spring St. 1919.

## MALIBU *(Los Angeles County)*

### Ford

*Visit* • Pepperdine U, 24255 W Pacific Coast Highway. Dedicated Firestone Fieldhouse. Spoke at Brock House. 9–20–1975.

## MERCED *(Merced County)*

### Taft

*Church* • Central Presbyterian Church, 520 W Twentieth. 1909.

## MONROVIA *(Los Angeles County)*

### Nixon

*Visit* • Monrovia High School for debate. 10–23–1946.

## MONTEREY *(Monterey County)*

### Presidents

*Visit* • Eisenhower, Ford, Hayes, McKinley, Nixon and Reagan.

### Harrison, B

*Visit* • Hotel del Monte on CA 1. Present hotel built 1924. 1891.

### Hoover

*Marriage* • 302 Pacific St at corner of Jackson and Pacific Sts. 1899.

*Home* • 600 Martin St. 1901–1902.

### Roosevelt, T

*Visit* • Hotel del Monte on CA 1. Present hotel built 1924. May 1903.

## MURPHYS *(Amador County)*

### Grant

*Visit* • Murphys Hotel, 457 Main St. 1879.

## NEVADA CITY   *(Nevada County)*

**Hoover**
> *Travel* • National Hotel, 211 Broad St. Also roomed with a classmate on Pioneer Hill. 1895.

## NORTH HOLLYWOOD   *(District of Los Angeles)*

**Reagan**
> *Marriage* • (Second) Little Brown Church in the San Fernando Valley, 4418 Coldwater Canyon Ave, Studio City. 1952.

## OAKLAND   *(Alameda County)*

**Presidents**
> *Visit* • Carter, Grant, B Harrison, Hayes, Hoover, McKinley, FD and T Roosevelt, Taft, Truman, and Wilson.

**Hoover**
> *Home* • 1077 Twelfth Street. Registered to vote here. 1895–1896.
>
> *Home* • 2225 Ellsworth. 1896–1897.

**Wilson**
> *Visit* • Hotel Oakland, 2333 Verna Court. 1919.

## ONTARIO   *(Los Angeles County)*

**Bush**
> *Visit* • Red Lion Hotel, 222 N Vineyard Ave. 12–6–1991.

## PACIFIC PALISADES   *(Los Angeles County)*

**Reagan**
> *Home* • 1258 Amalfi Dr. 1950–1955.
>
> *Home* • 1669 San Onofre Dr. 1955–1967.

## PALM DESERT   *(Riverside County)*

**Ford**
> *Church* • St. Margaret's Episcopal, 47535 CA 74. Easter 1975 and following.

> *Visit* • Bob Hope Cultural Center dedication, 73000 Fred Waring Dr. 1–1, 1988 to 1–2–.

## PALM SPRINGS   *(Riverside County)*

**Bush**
> *Visit* • Walter Annenberg home. Morningside Country Club, Frank Sinatra Dr. 3–3–1990.

**Eisenhower**
> *Church* • Palm Springs Community Church. 284 S Cahuilla Rd. 2–21–54 and following.
>
> *Visit* • Smoke Tree ranch, as guest of P.E. Helms. Vacation. February 1954.
>
> *Visit* • Played golf at Tamarisk Country Club, 70240 Frank Sinatra Dr. February 1954.
>
> *Visit* • Golf at La Quinta Country Club, Washington St. Easter 1974.
>
> *Visit* • Fred Wilson Home. 41001 Thunderbird Rd. Easter 1975, November 1976.

**Nixon**
> *Home* • Cottage near Eisenhower on the grounds of the Eldorado Country Club, Palm Desert. 1961

**Reagan**
> *Honeymoon* • El Mirado Hotel on Indian Ave. Now site of Desert Hospital. 1940.

## PALO ALTO   *(Santa Clara County)*

**Ford**
> *Visit* • Dedicated School of Law, Stanford University. 9–21–1975.

**Harrison, B**
> *Work* • Lectures at Stanford, Palm Dr, University Ave. 1894.

**Hoover**
> *Church* • Stanford University Memorial Church, Campus Center. 1891–1895.
>
> *Education* • Stanford University, a mile north of Palo Alto. 1891–1895. Attended

*Herbert Hoover's Palo Alto home.*

ex-president Harrison's lectures when he came. 1893.

***Lodging*** • Adelante Villa near campus. September–October 1891.

***Lodging*** • Room 38 Encina Hall, Sierra St. Stanford Campus. 1891–1892.

***Lodging*** • Romero Hall, 611 Waverly St. 1892–1894.

***Home*** • House on San Juan Hill. 1907.

***Home*** • Wright House. Not located. 1908–1909.

***Home*** • Allen House, 611 Salvatierra. 1912.

***Home*** • Howard House, 774 Dolores. 1913.

***Home*** • Hempel House, 747 Santa Ynez. 1914.

***Home*** • Seward House, 262 Kingsley. 1915–1916.

***Home*** • Kimball House, 530 Lincoln (Alice) or 1100 Bryant Street (Rufus). 1916.

***Home*** • Gray House, 612 Alvarado. 1917.

***Home*** • Houston House, 575 Salvatierra. 1917–1918.

***Home*** • Whitaker House, 747 Santa Ynez. 1918–1920.

***Home*** • MacDowell House, 775 Santa Inez.

***Home*** • Gregory House, 14 Cabrillo Rd. 1920.

***Home*** • Stanford University Campus, 623 Miranda. 1920–1934.

***Visit*** • Stanford University Stadium where he accepted Republican nomination for president. 8–11–1928.

***Visit*** • Stanford University Memorial Court at end of 1932 campaign.

***Site*** • 185-foot Hoover Tower which is a landmark on Stanford University campus.

***Site*** • Hoover Institution on War, Revolution, and Peace. Stanford University. Founded by Hoover. 1919.

**Kennedy**
*Education* • Stanford Business School. 1940–1941.

*Education* • The Cottage, 624 Mayfield Ave.

**Roosevelt, T**
*Visit* • Stanford University. 1903.

## PASADENA *(Los Angeles County)*

**Hayes**
*Visit* • Green House on Columbia Street. 1878.

**Harrison, B**
*Visit* • Green Hotel (then called Webster Hotel). April 1891.

**Nixon**
*Visit* • San Marino High School debate (South Pasadena). 9–13–1946.

**Roosevelt T**
*Visit* • Stopped to see President Garfield's widow, 1001 Buena Vista. Modern address is 150 S Orange Grove. Reception at Raymond Hotel. 1903.

## POMONA *(Los Angeles County)*

**Harrison, B**
*Visit* • Railroad station, 2701 N Garey Ave. 1891.

## RANCHO MIRAGE *(Suburb of Palm Springs, Riverside County.)*

**Eisenhower**
*Visit* • Eisenhower Medical Center, 3900 Bob Hope Dr. 11–27–1971.

*Visit* • Walter Annenberg Estate. Annenberg Ctr, 39000 Bob Hope Dr.

**Ford**
*Home* • Thunderbird Country Club, 70612 Hwy 111. 1977–present.

*Travel* • Annenberg Estate, Easter 1974. See Eisenhower for location.

*Visit* • Home of Fred Wilson, 41001 Thunderbird Rd. 1975.

*Visit* • Eisenhower Medical Center, 3900 Bob Hope Drive. 1981, 1983.

**Nixon**
*Visit* • Eisenhower Medical Center Dedication. 11–27–1971.

## REDLANDS *(San Bernardino County)*

**McKinley**
*Visit* • Hotel Casaloma reception and speech. 1901.

**Roosevelt, T**
*Visit* • Hotel Casaloma 1903. Razed 1960s. 1903.

## RIVERSIDE *(Riverside County)*

**Nixon**
*Marriage* • Old Mission Inn (Presidential Suite), 3649 Seventh Street. 1940.

**Reagan**
*Honeymoon* • (2nd) Old Mission Inn. On the first night. 3649 Seventh St.

**Taft**
*Visit* • Rubidoux Mountain top. 1909.

## SACRAMENTO *(Sacramento County)*

**Ford**
*Travel* • Senator Hotel, 1121 L St. Assassination attempt nearby. Community Convention Center, 1100 Fourteenth St. State Capitol Assemby Chambers. 9–5–1975.

**Harrison, B**
*Visit* • State Capitol. 1891.

**Johnson, L**
*Visit* • Steps State Capitol. 9–17–1964.

**Reagan**
*Home* • Sixteenth and H Sts, Governor's Mansion. 1967.

*Home* • Forty-fifth Street. 1968–1975.

*Work* • State Capitol, Governor's office. Capitol L Street between Tenth and Fifteenth Sts. 1967–1975.

*Visit* • State Capitol dedication. 11–5–1984.

**Taft**

*Visit* • State Capitol. 10–5–1909.

# SAN BERNARDINO  *(San Bernardino County)*

**Presidents**

*Visit* • Benjamin Harrison 1891, Taft 1909, and Reagan 1964.

**Johnson, LB**

*Home* • 376 F St. Destroyed. 1924–1926.

*Work* • Platt Building elevator operator, 491 W Fifth St. 1926.

*Visit* • 1516 E Street with his cousin Tom Martin. 1964.

**Roosevelt T**

*Visit* • Mission Inn Hotel, 3649 Seventh St, Riverside. 1903.

# SAN CLEMENTE  *(Orange County)*

**Ford**

*Visit* • Visited Nixon at La Casa Pacifica. July 1974.

**Nixon**

*Church* • San Clemente Presbyterian Church, 119 Estrella. 1969–1980.

*Home* • La Casa Pacifica, adjoining Camp Pendleton, 4100 Calla Isabella. Little White House. 1969–1974; home. 1974–1980.

*Visit* • Camp Pendleton golf course and Estrella Country Club. After 1969.

*Visit* • San Clemente Inn, 2600 Avenida del Presidente. 7–31–1970.

**Roosevelt, FD**

*Visit* • La Casa Pacifica, when it belonged to Hamilton Cotton. 1935.

# SAN DIEGO  *(San Diego County)*

**Bush**

*Visit* • U S Grant Hotel, 326 Broadway. 9–14–1992.

**Carter**

*Home* • Lived in a neighborhood of Mexican immigrants. Location not determined. 1950.

*Work* • U.S. Naval Base, Broadway and Harbor Dr. 1950.

*Visit* • Hotel del Coronado, 1500 Orange Ave. 11–1–1989.

*Visit* • Encanto project, 701 B St, Suite 205. 6–18–1990.

**Kennedy**

*Visit* • San Diego State College, Fairmont Ave and Montezuma Rd, and Hall Field Marine Corps Recruit Depot, Harbor Dr west of Lindberg Field. 6–6–1963.

**Wilson**

*Visit* • U S Grant Hotel, 326 Broadway for dinner. (Renovated.) 1919.

*Visit* • Balboa Stadium, Park Blvd and Russ Blvd for a speech. 1919.

# SAN FERNANDO  *(Los Angeles County)*

**Reagan**

*Home* • Owned a small ranch in the San Fernando Valley. 1940s.

# SAN FRANCISCO  *(San Francisco County)*

**Bush**

*Visit* • Cow Palace, Grand National Livestock Pavilion, 7–13–1964 to 7–16–1964.

**Carter**

*Travel* • Palace of Fine Arts Theater, Baker St and Marina Blvd, for second debate with Ford. 10–7–1976.

**Eisenhower**

*Home* • Apartment for a month. Location not determined. January 1940.

*Work* • Presidio Army Post, Lincoln Blvd and Funston Ave, in NW San Francisco on CA 1 off Park Presidio Blvd. 9th Army Corps. 1940.

*Visit* • Opera House, Grove St between Franklin and Van Ness. 6–20–1955.

*Visit* • Cow Palace for renomination for president. Stayed St. Francis Hotel. August 1956.

*Visit* • Cow Palace. Stayed St. Francis Hotel. July 1964.

**Ford**
*Visit* • Cow Palace. 1964.

*Visit* • St. Francis Hotel. 450 Powell St. Area of assassination attempt. 9–5–1975.

*Visit* • Fairmont Hotel, 950 Mason St. 3–26–1976.

*Visit* • Palace of Fine Arts Theater, 3301 Lyon. Second presidential debate with Carter. Spoke at St. Francis Hotel. 10–6–1976.

**Grant**
*Visit* • Palace Hotel. City Hall, S Van Ness Ave. 1879.

*Visit* • Millbrae, home of D.O. Mills Site CA 1. Burned. 1879.

*Site* • Grant Memorial at NE corner Music Concourse, Golden Gate Park.

**Harding**
*Death* • Palace Hotel Room 8064. 1923.

**Harrison, B**
*Visit* • Palace Hotel while visiting the Columbian Exposition. 1891.

*Home* • of Adolphus Sutro, Point Lobos and Forty-eighth Ave on the Heights. Ruins and now a park. 4–27–1891.

*Church* • First Presbyterian Church, Sacramento at Van Ness. 1891.

*Visit* • Presidio to review the troops. 1891.

*Visit* • Golden Gate Park, between Fulton and Lincoln. 1891.

**Hoover**
*Home* • Wheeler House, 1901 Pacific Ave. 1912–1913.

*Work* • Residence. Working out of here

and also in New Mexico with Louis Janin, mining engineer. 1896–1897.

*Visit* • Palace Hotel while travelling with Harding. 1923.

**Kennedy**
*Visit* • Mark Hopkins Hotel, 1 Nob Hill, corner California and Mason Sts. February 1943.

*Visit* • Palace Hotel. Attending opening sessions of the UN. 1945.

**McKinley**
*Visit* • Home of Henry T. Scott. Mansion located crest of high hill overlooking Lafayette Square. 1901.

*Visit* • Palace Hotel. Reception. 1901.

*Visit* • Market Street Ferry Depot for public reception.

*Visit* • Presidio. Reviewed troops, Parade Grounds. 1901.

**Nixon**
*Work* • State Supreme Court, 350 McAllister St. Admitted to the Bar. 1937.

*Visit* • Cow Palace. Nominated for vice president. Stayed Mark Hopkins Hotel, 1 Nob Hill. August 1956.

*Visit* • Cow Palace. 1964.

*Visit* • Sheraton Palace Hotel, 639 Market St. 1969–1974.

**Reagan**
*Visit* • Sheraton Palace Hotel, 639 Market St. 9–27–1972.

*Visit* • Hearst Court of M. H. de Young Memorial Museum, NE corner Music Concourse, S of Kennedy Drive near Eighth Ave. Stayed St. Francis Hotel. 3–3–1983 to 3–4–1983.

**Roosevelt, FD**
*Visit* • Civic Auditorium, 99 Grove St. DNC. Nominated for vice president. July 1920.

**Roosevelt T**
*Visit* • Palace Hotel. May 1903.

**Taft**
*Visit* • Fairmont Hotel, 950 Mason St. St.

Francis Hotel. YMCA, 220 Golden Gate Ave. Laid cornerstone. 1909.

*Visit* • Pan-Pacific International Exhibition. 1914.

**Truman**
*Visit* • St. Francis Hotel. 8–22–1941.

*Visit* • Civic Center, bounded by Market, Hayes, Franklin Sts and Golden Gate Ave. UN Conference held here. 1945.

*Visit* • Fairmont Hotel, 950 Mason St. 1948–1953.

*Visit* • Opera House, Grove St between Franklin and Van Ness. 1945. Again 10–17–1950.

*Visit* • War Memorial, Palace Hotel. 9–4–1951. Palace Hotel. 10–4–1952.

**Wilson**
*Visit* • St. Francis Hotel. 1919.

*Visit* • Meetings in Palace Hotel. 1919.

## SAN GABRIEL *(Los Angeles County)*

**Nixon**
*Visit* • Civic Auditorium, 320 S Mission Dr for debate. 1946.

## SAN JOSE *(Santa Clara County)*

**Nixon**
*Visit* • Civic Auditorium, 291 S Market. 10–29–1970.

## SAN JUAN CAPISTRANO *(Orange County)*

**Nixon**
*Visit* • 1969–.

## SAN SIMEON *(San Luis Obispo County)*

**Coolidge**
*Visit* • Hearst estate, off CA 1. 1929.

**Kennedy**
*Visit* • Visited San Simeon. 1940.

## SANTA BARBARA *(Santa Barbara County)*

**Reagan**
*Home* • Rancho del Cielo, Refugio Beach Rd between Santa Ynez township and US 101 miles to the west. 1975–1989.

*Church* • First Presbyterian at 21 E Constance. 1987.

## SIMI VALLEY *(Ventura County)*

**Reagan**
*Site* • Reagan Presidential Library, 40 Presidential Dr.

*Visit* • Library opening. Historic meeting of five living presidents: Bush, Carter, Ford, Nixon and Reagan. 11–4–1991.

## SOLVANG *(Santa Barbara County)*

**Reagan**
*Church* • First Presbyterian Church. 3–30–1986.

## SOUTH WHITTIER *(See Whittier)*

## TOLUCA LAKE *(Los Angeles County)*

**Reagan**
*Marriage* • Wedding reception at home of William Holden. 1952.

## TULARE *(Tulare County)*

**Harrison, B.**
*Visit* • Gave the "Biggest Stump" speech on a gigantic Sequoia stump. The tree was sawed off and brought in prompting Harrison to stop longer than anticipated and give a speech. April 25, 1891.

## VENTURA *(Ventura County)*

**Bush**
*Home* • Pierpont Inn Hotel at 500 Sanjon Rd. Stayed here while working in Ventura. 1949.

*Work* • Security Engineering Company, 1622 N Ventura Ave. Now occupied by R&R Tool and Machine Shop. Afterwards worked in Huntington Park and then Bakersfield, Whittier and Compton as a trainee and then selling oil drilling equipment.

# WHITTIER AND EAST WHITTIER
*(Los Angeles County)*

**Bush**
*Home* • Lived here for a time in 1949.

**Nixon**
*Church* • Old Friends Meeting House (became part of Nixon Market), corner Philadelphia St and Washington Ave.

*Church* • Friends Meeting House, 15911 E Whittier Blvd. near Russell St.

*Church* • Whittier College Chapel, College St. 1930–1934.

*Church* • St. Mathias, 7056 S Washington Ave where he first met Pat. 1939.

*Education* • East Whittier, Grammar School, 14421 E Whittier Blvd. 1922–1926.

*Education* • Whittier High School, 12217 Philadelphia St. 1928–1930.

*Education* • Whittier College, College St. 1930–1934.

*Home* • Whittier Blvd with maternal grandparents while his father built their house on Painter St. 1922.

*Home* • 622 South Painter St near Whittier Blvd and Leffingwell Rd in East Whittier. (622 is now number 7926.) 1922–1948.

*Home* • 2706 E Whittier. Gone. 1924–1930.

*Home* • 1104 Santa Gertrudes Rd. 1930–1942.

*Home* • 731 N Beach Blvd (now Scandia Gardens Smorgasbord). 1940.

*Home* • 1400 E Whittier Blvd. 1942.

*Home* • 320 E Walnut (now 13221). 1946.

*Home* • 14033 Honeysuckle Ln, adjacent to Candlewood Country Club. 1947.

*Home* • 15257 Anaconda. 1953–1954.

*Work* • Nixon Market, including a gas station, 2706 W Whittier Blvd. Gone. 1922–1934.

*Work* • Practiced law with firm of Wingert and Bewley. Office on second floor of the Bank of America Building in Suite 607. 111 E Philadelphia. 1937–1941.

*Work* • Junior partner in Bewley, Knoop and Nixon. Law office on second floor of the Bank of America Bldg. 1939. 1946.

*Work* • Joined in forming the Citra-Frost Co. which failed within two years. 1940–1942.

*Visit* • Maternal grandfather's house on south side of Whittier Blvd. 1911–.

*Visit* • Patriotic Hall for debate. 1946.

# WYNTON *(San Luis Obispo County)*
**Kennedy**
*Visit* • Guest at Hearst ranch. 11–14–1940.

# YEARLING ROW RANCH
**Reagan**
*Home* • Horse business.

# YORBA LINDA *(Orange County)*
**Nixon**
*Birthplace* • 18161 Yorba Linda Blvd. 1913.

*Church* • Friends Meeting House, School St. 1913–1922.

*Education* • Yorba Linda Elementary School, corner of School St and Lemon Dr. Torn down. 1918–1922.

*Home* • 18161 Yorba Linda Blvd. 1913–1922.

*Funeral* • Nixon Library, 18161 Yorba Linda Blvd. Presidents Carter, Clinton, Ford and Reagan attended. 4–27–1994.

*Burial* • Nixon Library grounds, next to his wife. 4–27–94.

*Site* • Nixon Presidential Library, 18161 Yorba Linda Blvd.

## YOSEMITE

### Roosevelt, FD
*Travel* • Western tour Yosemite, Tuolumne County. 1938.

### T Roosevelt
*Visit* • Bridal Veil Falls, Glacier Point Rd. Camp. May 1903.

*Visit* • Glacier Point Hotel. South entrance gate at Chinquapin Junction of Glacier Point Rd and CA 41. 1903.

### Taft
*Visit* • Wawona Hotel at south entrance gate, CA 41, 8 miles from Mariposa Grove. 1909.

*Visit* • Glacier Point Hotel. 1909. See location under T Roosevelt.

*Visit* • Sentinel Hotel. Site west of Southside Drive. 1909.

*Visit* • Union Point. Grouse Creek Forest. East and south of Southside Drive. 1909.

**Colorado**

70

2

1

Denver

76

● Colorado Springs

25

1. Eisenhower home, *Denver*
2. Ford home, *Vail*

# COLORADO

---

## BOULDER  *(Boulder County)*

**Eisenhower**
*Visit* • Dedication, National Bureau of Standards, 325 Broadway. 9–14–1954.

## CENTRAL CITY  *(Gilpin County)*

**Grant**
*Visit* • Eureka Street. Teller House where he walked along a path of solid silver bricks from his stagecoach to the hotel door. Teller House was the largest and finest hotel in the state outside of Denver. 1873.

## COLORADO SPRINGS  *(El Paso County)*

**Presidents**
*Site* • Hall of the Presidents Wax Museum, 1050 S Twenty–first St.

**Kennedy**
*Visit* • Air Force Academy, Falcon Stadium, Graduation. 6–5–1963.

**Nixon**
*Visit* • Air Force Academy, Falcon Stadium. 6–4–1969.

**Reagan**
*Visit* • Air Force Academy, Falcon Stadium. Broadmoor Hotel, Lake Ave. 5–29–1984.

**Taft**
*Visit* • Garden of the Gods NW of city off US 24. 1909.

**Wilson**
*Visit* • 1109 N Weber St. 1894.

## DENVER  *(Denver County)*

**Eisenhower**
*Church* • Corona Presbyterian Church, 1205 E Eighth Ave.

*Church* • Central Presbyterian Church, 1660 Sherman.

*Marriage* • 750 Lafayette St. 7–1–1916.

*Lodging* • 750 Lafayette St. 1916 –.

*Home* • Summer White House. 1953–1961.

*Work* • Summer office at USAF Lowry Base. E Alameda Ave Pkwy. 1954. Remarks to Olympic Committee. 10–8–1954.

*Visit* • Brown Palace Hotel, 321 Seventeenth St. 1916–.

---

*Visit* • Fitzsimons Army Medical Center in Aurora, E Colfax Ave, appendectomy. 1923. Following heart attack. 1955.

*Visit* • Cherry Hills Country Club, Cherry Hills Drive off University Blvd to play on the golf links. 1954 –.

**Harding**
*Travel* • Weekend stop on Western tour. 1923.

**Harrison, B**
*Visit* • State Capitol. 1891.

**Johnson, LB**
*Visit* • University of Denver Arena, E Jewell Ave and Race St. Remarks, Stapleton Airport. 8–26–1966.

**Roosevelt, FD**
*Visit* • State Capitol. Fitzsimons Hospital, E Colfax Ave. 10–12–1936.

**Roosevelt, T**
*Visit* • State Capitol. 1900; May 1903.

**Taft**
*Visit* • State Capitol. Speech. 1909.

*Visit* • Lunch at Welhurst, home of Thomas F. Walsh. 1909.

**Truman**
*Visit* • State Capitol grounds. Shirley-Savoy Hotel. 9–20–1948.

## ELDORADO SPRINGS *(Boulder County)*

**Eisenhower**
*Honeymoon* • One night in a resort cottage high on the hill above the railway station. 1916.

## FORT LOGAN *(Suburb of Denver)*

**Eisenhower**
*Work* • S Lowell Blvd off US 285. Recruiting officer. 1924–1925.

## FRASER *(Grand County, US 40, 72 miles NW of Denver)*

**Eisenhower**
*Visit* • Byers Peak Ranch of Aksel Nielsen

for trout fishing. On St. Louis Creek. August 1954.

**Hoover**
*Visit* • Accompanied President Eisenhower. September 1954.

## GLENWOOD SPRINGS *(Garfield County)*

**Harrison, B**
*Church* • First Presbyterian Church, 1016 Cooper Ave. 1888.

**Hayes**
*Visit* • 1881.

**Roosevelt, T**
*Visit* • Hotel Colorado, 526 Pine. 1905.

## MONTROSE *(Montrose County)*

**Taft**
*Visit* • Opened Gunnison Tunnel, 7 1/2 miles east off US 50. 1909.

## RIFLE *(See Silt)*

## SILT *(Garfield County)*

**Roosevelt, T**
*Visit* • Camped near here on Divide Creek east of Silt. 1905.

*Church* • Attended services at the Old Blue Hen Schoolhouse on the West Divide Creek. 1905.

## VAIL *(Eagle County, on US 6)*

**Clinton**
*Travel* • Vacation. Played round of golf with Ford. 1993.

**Ford**
*Home* • Vacations and almost every Christmas. 1960–.

# CONNECTICUT

**DANBURY** *(Fairfield County)*

**Kennedy**
*Visit* • Danbury Hospital for appendectomy, 24 Hospital Ave. 1930.

**EASTFORD** *(Eastford County)*

**Washington**
*Visit* • Eastford House (now called General Lyon Inn) on CT 198. Still has the desk on which he wrote his letters. 1789.

**FAIRFIELD** *(Fairfield County)*

**Washington**
*Visit* • The Sun Tavern (now Penfield's) on the Green. 1789.

**GLASTONBURY** *See Marborough*

**GREENWICH** *(Fairfield County)*

**Bush**
*Church* • Christ Episcopal, 254 E Putnam Ave. 1925–1937. Dorothy Bush (mother) funeral. 1993.

*Education* • Greenwich Country Day School, Old Church Rd (north end). 1928–1937.

*Home* • 11 Stanwich Rd. Private. 1925–1931.

*Home* • 15 Grove Ln (Deer Park). Private. 1931–1937.

*Home* • Field Club of Greenwich on Lake Ave for tennis. 1931–1937.

**GROTON** *(New London County)*

**Carter**
*Church* • Chapel on the Thames, Shark Blvd on the Naval Base. Sometimes conducted services. 1951–1952.

*Education* • Naval Base, Cromwell Hall on Growlee Ave. Also English and Fife Halls. 1951–1952.

*Home* • Provinceton, Massachusetts. 1951–1952.

*Home* • Quarters on Submarine Base, Thames St. 1948.

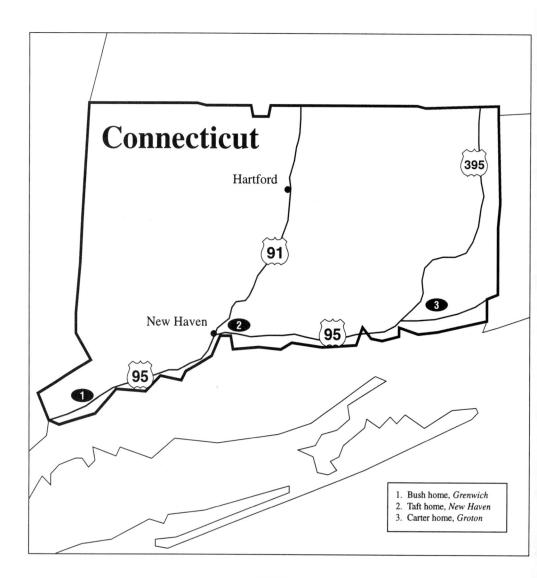

# Connecticut

Hartford

New Haven

1. Bush home, *Grenwich*
2. Taft home, *New Haven*
3. Carter home, *Groton*

**Jackson**

*Visit* • 108 Thames St, Mother Bailey House. 1833.

## HARTFORD  *(Hartford County)*

**Presidents**

*Visit* • Site of George Catlin House, 17 Hurlburt St, said to have been visited by every president from Adams to Lincoln, with the exception of Polk.

**Carter**

*Visit* • Old State House. 10–16–1980.

**Eisenhower**

*Visit* • Trinity College, Broad St. Convocation. 10–20–1954.

**Grant**

*Visit* • Mark Twain's house, 351 Farmington Ave. 1879.

## LEBANON  *(New London County)*

**Jefferson**

*Visit* • Homestead of Jonathan Trumbull, on the Green, open for tours. 1789.

**Washington**

*Visit* • Homestead of Jonathan Trumbull, on the Green. 1789.

## LITCHFIELD  *(Litchfield County)*

**Washington**

*Visit* • Elisha Sheldon House (Inn). CT 63 for a second visit. 1780.

## MARLBOROUGH  *(Near Glastonbury)*

**Monroe**

*Visit* • (Buell) Marlborough Tavern, junction of CT 2 and CT 66.

**Washington**

*Visit* • Marlborough Tavern. 1789.

## MIDDLETOWN  *(Middlesex County)*

**Hayes**

*Education* • Isaac Webb Academy later part of Wesleyan College. Wyllys St to Lawn Ave. He stayed in South College Hall on High St. 1837–1838.

**Washington**

*Visit* • Fuller's Tavern (later Amos Kirby Tavern), Berlin St. Breakfast. 1789.

**Wilson**

*Church* • First Congregational on Pleasant and Crescent. 1888–1890.

*Home* • 106 High St. 1888–1890.

*Work* • Wesleyan University Memorial Chapel, lower level, Church St. See plaque on wall. 1888–1890.

## MILFORD  *(New Haven County)*

**Clinton**

*Lodging* • He lived in a beach house on Trumbull beach while studying at Yale. 1970–1973.

**Washington**

*Visit* • Andrew Clark's Tavern. NF. 1789.

## NEW HAVEN  *(New Haven County)*

**Adams, J**

*Visit* • Beers House. It was on the lot where the New Haven House now stands. 1789.

**Bush**

*Church* • Trinity Church on edge of the Green.

*Education* • Yale University (Economics). See Harkness Hall. 1945–1948.

*Home* • Railroad Flat next to Mortuary. No longer exists. 1945.

*Home* • 37 Hillhouse in an upstairs flat. 1946.

*Work* • Yale Sterling Memorial Library, 120 High St between Elm and Wall. 1945–1948.

**Clinton**

*Education* • Yale University Law School, 127 Wall. He had an apartment at 21 Edgewood. 1970–1973.

*Marriage* • He met his future wife at the library of Yale University Law School, 120 High St. 1971.

**Ford**

*Education* • Yale Law School, at 127 Wall. 1937–1941.

*Home* • 268 Dwight St. 1939–1940.

*Home* • 100 Howe St. 1940–1941.

*Work* • York and Elm, College and Chapel Sts, Yale University at Payne Whit. Assistant line coach and coach. 1935–1941.

*Visit* • Yale University Law School, Woolsey Hall, convocation dinner. 4–25–1975.

**Kennedy**

*Visit* • Old Campus for commencement. 6–11–1962.

**Taft**

*Church* • Battel Chapel, Yale University campus. 1874–1878.

*Church* • The First Unitarian Universalist Society, 608 Whitney Ave. 1917–1921.

*Education* • Yale University, Connecticut Hall. College St at New Haven Green. 1874–1878.

*Education* • Farnam Hall. 1874–1878; 1876–1877.

*Lodging* • 64 High St. 1874–1875.

*Education* • Old South College. No longer standing. 1877–1878.

*Lodging* • Hotel Taft (now Taft apartments). 1913.

*Home* • 367 Prospect St, York Square. Plaque on site. 1913–1917.

*Home* • 70 Grove St. No longer existing. 1918–1919.

*Home* • 113 Whitney Ave. No longer existing. 1920–1921.

*Home* • 60 York Square. No longer existing. 1921.

*Work* • Lectured at Osborne Hall two days a week. Also at Hendrick Hall. Had an office in Hotel Taft. 1913–1921.

**Truman**

*Visit* • Yale University for three days. Lectures. College St at New Haven Green. 1958.

**Washington**

*Church* • Trinity Episcopal Church. Site east side of Church St.

*Church* • White Haven Congregational. Site later occupied by North Church. SE corner Elm and Church Sts. 1789.

*Visit* • Hubbard House at junction of Church, George and Meadow Sts. 1789.

*Visit* • Beers House. Was on the lot where the New Haven House now stands. 1789.

# NEW LONDON *(New London County)*

**Johnson, LB**

*Visit* • Coast Guard commencement at Jones Field, Mohegan Ave. 6–3–1964.

**Reagan**

*Visit* • U.S. Coast Guard Academy, Mohegan Ave. Nitchem Field. 5–18–1988.

**Washington**

*Visit* • Shaw Mansion, 11 Blinham St. 1789.

# NEW MILFORD *(Litchfield County)*

**Kennedy**

*Church* • Chapel, Canterbury School. 1930–1931.

*Education* • Canterbury School, located above the town. He stayed in North House Dormitory. 1930–1931.

# NORWICH *(New London County)*

**Jackson**

*Visit* • Unca Indian burial grounds, corner Washington and Sachem Sts. 1833.

**Washington**

*Visit* • Teel House on The Parade.

*Visit* • Samuel Huntington House, Huntington Ln. 1789.

*Visit* • Leffingwell Inn on CT 2 and CT 32, 348 Washington St.

## OLD LYME *(New London County)*

**Wilson**

*Church* • SW corner Ferry Rd and Lyme St at Congregational Church. He dedicated the new church as the old one had burned in 1907. 1910.

*Visit* • Vacation at Boxwood, boarding house of a Miss Thibetts. 1905.

*Visit* • Vacation. Florence Griswold's boarding house, 96 Lyme St. 1909.

## STAFFORD SPRINGS *(Tolland County)*

**Adams, J**

*Visit* • Now Hyde Park on Spring St at the rear of the public library. Here he took the waters on several occasions at the Spring House Tavern. Spring remains but not tavern. 1771.

## WALLINGFORD *(New Haven County)*

**Kennedy**

*Education* • Corner of Elm and Christian St, Choate School (Episcopalian), a few miles north of New Haven. 1931–1935. Merged with Rose-Mary Hall. 1975.

*Church* • Choate Chapel. 1931–1935.

*Lodging* • Choate House. 1931–1932.

**Washington**

*Visit* • Tea at Squire Stanley House on corner of Choate campus. 1789.

## WETHERSFIELD *(Hartford County)*

**Washington**

*Visit* • Webb house, 211 Main St, where he and Rochambeau made the plan that led to the British defeat at Yorktown. 1781.

*Visit* • Silas Deane House, 203 Main St. 1775. 1781.

## WINDSOR *(Hartford County)*

**Adams**

*Visit* • David Ellsworth House, 778 Palisado Ave. Open for tours. 1789.

**Washington**

*Visit* • David Ellsworth House. 1789.

## WOODSTOCK *(Windham County)*

**Presidents**

*Visit* • Roseland Cottage, estate of H. Bowen, west side of the Green on CT 169. Open for tours. Visited by Grant, Hayes, B Harrison, and McKinley.

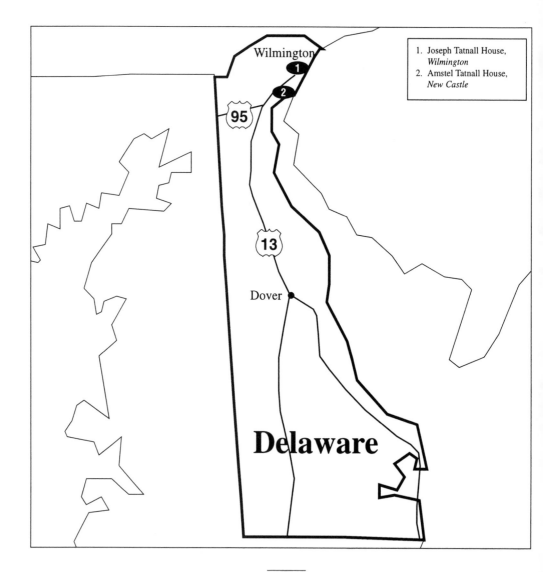

1. Joseph Tatnall House,
   *Wilmington*
2. Amstel Tatnall House,
   *New Castle*

Wilmington

**95**

**13**

Dover

**Delaware**

# DELAWARE

## DOVER *(Kent County)*

Old State House On The Green at the junction of State St and Bank Ln. Governor's Mansion, King St. In use since 1966.

## NEW CASTLE *(New Castle County)*

**Washington**

*Visit* • Gilpin House (Inn), 210 Delaware St. Now store and apartments. 1774.

*Visit* • Red Lion Tavern (see site of present Red Lion at the Post Office). (McCullough Tavern before 1800.) Now a private residence. He often stopped here. 1780–1790.

*Visit* • Amstel House, N corner Fourth and Delaware Sts. 1784.

## WILMINGTON *(New Castle County)*

**Jefferson**

*Visit* • Sign of the Ship Tavern (also known as Happy Patriot). Site on SE corner Market and Third Sts.

**Washington.**

*Travel* • Battle of Brandywine about 10 miles north on US 202 in Pennsylvania. 1777.

*Visit* • Military headquarters at 303 West St. 1777.

*Visit* • Joseph Tatnall House, 1803 N Market St. He often came here. 1777–1786.

*Visit* • John Dickinson House, corner Eighth and Market. 1786.

*Visit* • Sign of the Ship Tavern (also known as Happy Patriot). Site on SE corner Market and Third Sts. 1777–1786.

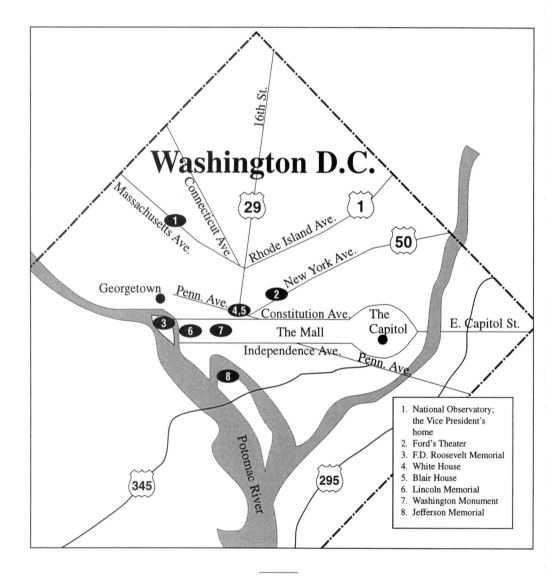

# Washington D.C.

16th St.

Connecticut Ave.

Massachusetts Ave.

29

1

Rhode Island Ave.

50

New York Ave.

Georgetown

Penn. Ave.

2

4,5

Constitution Ave.

The
Capitol

E. Capitol St.

3

6

7

The Mall

Independence Ave.

Penn. Ave.

8

Potomac River

345

295

1. National Observatory;
   the Vice President's
   home
2. Ford's Theater
3. F.D. Roosevelt Memorial
4. White House
5. Blair House
6. Lincoln Memorial
7. Washington Monument
8. Jefferson Memorial

# DISTRICT OF COLUMBIA

PRESIDENT • LANDMARK TYPE • DESCRIPTION • DATE

## ABC WASHINGTON BUREAU BLDG

**Reagan**
*Visit* • 1717 De Sales St. Dedication. 11–12–1981.

## ACHESON HOUSE

**Truman**
*Visit* • 2805 P St NW, Old Georgetown. Dean Acheson home. After Eisenhower inauguration he left from here going to Union Station and back to Missouri. 1953.

## ADAMS HOUSE

**Presidents**
*Visit* • 1603 H St N.W. across Lafayette Square from the White House. Destroyed in order to build the Hay-Adams Hotel. Visited by many Presidents between 1877 and 1918.

## ADAMS MILL RD

**Jackson**
*Lodging* • At Ontario Place, NW off Calvert St. Now part of National Zoo. Summer house. 1829.

## ADIRONDACKS ROOM

**Presidents**
*Visit* • Union Station, Massachusetts Ave between First and Second Sts, NE. Site of presidential suite.

## AFL-CIO NATIONAL HEADQUARTERS

**Eisenhower**
*Visit* • 815 Sixteenth St, NW. Cornerstone laid. 4–30–1955. Dedication 6–4–1956.

## ALL SOUL'S CHURCH

**Adams, JQ**
*Church* • Sixth and D Sts, NW. 1821–.

**Coolidge**
*Church* • Sixteenth and Harvard Sts, NW. Dedication. 1924.

**Fillmore**
*Church* • Sixth and D Sts, NW. 1833–.

**Taft**
*Church/Funeral* • Fourteenth and L Sts, NW. During 1920–1921 the church met in

the old Knickerboker Theater while a new church was being built at Sixteenth and Harvard Sts, NW. Taft attended until his death. 1890–1930.

## AMERICAN FOOD ADMINISTRATION

**Hoover**
    *Work* • O St between Eighteenth and Nineteenth Sts NW. Dupont Circle area and no building remains. 1917–1919.

## AMERICAN RED CROSS

**Eisenhower**
    *Visit* • 430 Seventeenth St, NW. Dedication of Chapter House. 10–1–1953.

**Hoover**
    *Visit* • Dedication. Red Cross Chapter House. 3–19–1930.

## AMERICAN UNIVERSITY

**Eisenhower**
    *Visit* • 4400 Massachusetts Ave. Groundbreaking, School International Service. 6–9–1957.

**Kennedy**
    *Visit* • Commencement Reeves Athletic Field. Nuclear test ban speech. 6–10–1963.

**Roosevelt, FD**
    *Visit* • Honorary degree. 3–3–1934.

## ANDERSON HOUSE

**Presidents**
    *Visit* • 2118 Massachusetts Ave, NW. Used for official entertainment by presidents and other officials. Now Cincinnatus Club.

## ARLINGTON HOTEL

**Presidents**
    *Visit* • H St and SW corner Vermont Ave, NW (a block from White House Grounds). Demolished in 1912. Site now occupied by Department of Veterans Affairs. Presidents Buchanan through Taft stayed here.

## ARLINGTON MEMORIAL BRIDGE

**Hoover**
    *Visit* • Between Lincoln Memorial and Arlington Cemetery. Opening ceremony. 1–18–1932.

**Truman**
    *Visit* • Dedication Equestrian Statues. 9–26–1951.

## ARTS AND INDUSTRIES BLDG

**Garfield**
    *Visit* • Smithsonian Institution at The Mall. Jefferson Drive at Ninth St, SW. Inaugural Ball. 1881.

## ASBURY STATUE

**Roosevelt, FD**
    *Visit* • Sixteenth and Mt. Pleasant Sts, NW. October 1924.

## ATOMIC ENERGY COMMISSION

**Carter**
    *Work* • 1901 Constitution Ave, NW. Other government offices in the building now. 1952–1953.

## AZTEC GARDENS

**Taft**
    *Visit* • Constitution Ave and Seventeenth St NW. Planted the "Peace Tree." 1910.

## BALTIMORE AND OHIO STATION

**Presidents**
    *Visit* • New Jersey Ave and C St NW. Last train pulled into this station in 1907 and the first train pulled into the brand new Union Station ending nearly 80 years of ugliness. Now site of Congressional offices. The old site is about where Louisiana and New Jersey Aves intersect. Presidents from Monroe to Theodore Roosevelt used this station.

## BALTIMORE AND POTOMAC STATION (SIXTH ST STATION)

**Presidents**

*Visit* • Sixth and B Sts, NW. Present site of the National Gallery of Art. Used beginning 1870.

**Garfield**

*Death* • Shot by assassin in this station. July 2, 1881.

## BARLOW HOUSE (ALSO KNOWN AS "KALORAMA")

**Presidents**

*Visit* • 2301 S St NW. Site of Joel Barlow's House. Demolished 1889. Jefferson, Madison, and Monroe were visitors here. Early 1800s.

## BARTLETT HOME

**Kennedy**

*Visit* • Home of Charles and Martha Bartlett apartment at 2237 48th. Where he first met Jackie. May 8, 1952.

## BELL–MORTON HOUSE

**McKinley**

*Visit* • 1500 Rhode Island Ave, NW. Now National Paint and Coatings Association. Home of Count Cassini of the Imperial Russian Embassy. 1897–1901.

**Roosevelt, T**

*Visit* • Same as above.

## BELMONT HOUSE

**Jefferson**

*Visit* • 144 Constitution Ave, NE. Home of Alva Belmont.

**Madison**

*Visit* • Same as above.

## BIRTH'S

**Pierce**

*Home* • Third St, NW, east side of Third St between B and C Sts, north of Pennsylvania Ave. 1834–.

## BLAIR HOUSE

**Presidents**

*Lodging* • 1651 Pennsylvania Ave, NW. Clinton stayed here prior to his inauguration, 1993, and during repairs to the White House, September 1994. Kennedy stayed here before his inauguration. January 1961. Reagan stayed here before his inauguration. January 1981. Truman used site as a temporary White House. 1948–1951.

## BODISCO HOUSE

**Van Buren**

*Visit* • 3322 O St, NW. Attended wedding here. 1839.

## BOLIVAR MONUMENT

**Eisenhower**

*Visit* • Front of Pan American Bldg, Virginia Ave and Eighteenth St, NW. Dedication Bolivar Plaza. 2–27–1959.

**Kennedy**

*Visit* • Dedication. 7–5–1961.

## BOWIE–SEVIER HOUSE

**Washington**

*Visit* • 3124 Q St, NW. On his way north to rejoin his troops. August 12, 1776.

## BRENT HOUSE

**Adams, JQ**

*Home* • 4 1/2 and F St, NE, at northeast corner. Rented this house from his chief clerk, Daniel Brent. 1818–1820.

## BROADMOOR HOTEL

**Nixon**

> *Home* • 3601 Connecticut Ave, NW, at the northwest corner of Connecticut and Porter St. 1947.

## BROWN'S HOTEL

**Presidents**

> *Lodging* • 601 Pennsylvania Ave, NE corner between Sixth and Seventh Sts, NW. Proprietor was Jesse Brown. Previously called Indian Queen Inn. After 1865 it was called Metropolitan Hotel. Much of the building was razed in 1935 and office complex now on site. Presidents from Polk to Andrew Johnson stayed here.

## BUCHANAN MEMORIAL

**Buchanan**

> *Site* • Meridian Hill Park. Statue of Buchanan. Sixteenth and Florida Ave NW.

**Hoover**

> *Visit* • Dedication. 1930.

## CAPTAIN BENJAMIN BURCH'S BOARDING HOUSE

**Polk**

> *Lodging* • East Capitol St between First and Second Sts. Now site of Supreme Court building. 1825.

## CALVARY BAPTIST CHURCH

**Harding**

> *Church* • Eighth and H Sts, NW. 1915–1923.

## CAPITAL HILTON HOTEL

**Presidents**

> *Visit* • Sixteenth and K Sts. NW. Originally Statler and then Statler Hilton. Speeches and dinners for all Presidents since Truman. Kennedy Inaugural ball held here. 1961.

## CAPITOL

**Washington**

> *Visit* • Capitol Hill (formerly Jenkins Hill). Laid cornerstone. 1793. Fillmore laid another cornerstone on July 4, 1851. See also marker north of Capitol for site of lots and buildings owned by Washington.

## CAPITOL ROTUNDA

**Eisenhower**

> *Funeral* • Lay in state. 1969.

**Garfield**

> *Funeral* • Lay in state. 1881.

**Harding**

> *Funeral* • Lay in state. 1923.

**Hoover**

> *Funeral* • Lay in state. 1964.

**Johnson, LB**

> *Funeral* • Lay in state. 1–23–1973.

**Kennedy**

> *Funeral* • Lay in state. 11–24–1963.

**Lincoln**

> *Funeral* • Lay in state. 1861.

**McKinley**

> *Funeral* • Lay in state. 1901.

**Taft**

> *Funeral* • Lay in state. 1930.

## HOUSE OF REPRESENTATIVES ("OLD CAPITOL")

**Harrison, WH**

> *Work* • First St and A St NE (Now Maryland Ave). Built in 1815. Demolished 1935. The site is now occupied by the Supreme Court Building. 1817–1819.

**Tyler**

> *Work* • 1816–1819.

**Monroe**

> *Visit* • Inaugurated here. 1819.

GEOGRAPHIC GUIDE TO LANDMARKS

## HOUSE OF REPRESENTATIVES (KNOWN TODAY AS "STATUARY HALL") 1807–1857

**Adams, JQ**
*Work* • Also took the oath of office as president and gave his inaugural address here. 1831–1848.

*Death* • Died in the House of Representatives. The funeral took place in the Capitol. 1848.

**Buchanan**
*Work* • 1821–1831.

**Fillmore**
*Work* • 1833–1835. 1837–1843.

**Johnson, A**
*Work* • 1843–1853.

**Lincoln**
*Work* • 1847–1849.

**Pierce**
*Work* • 1833–1837.

**Polk**
*Work* • 1825–1839.

**Tyler**
*Work* • 1819–1821.

**Van Buren**
*Visit* • Took oath of office as vice president.

## HOUSE OF REPRESENTATIVES (IN THE SOUTH WING EXTENSION OF THE CAPITOL) 1857–PRESENT

**Bush**
*Work* • 1967–1971.

**Ford**
*Work* • In 1974 he was sworn in as vice president in the House chamber. 1948–1974.

**Garfield**
*Work* • 1863–1880.

**Hayes**
*Work* • 1865–1867.

**Johnson, LB**
*Work* • 1937–1939.

**Kennedy**
*Work* • 1947–1953.

**McKinley**
*Work* • 1877–1891.

**Nixon**
*Work* • 1947–1951.

## SENATE (THE NORTH WING OF THE CAPITOL, LATER THE SUPREME COURT CHAMBER)

**Adams, JQ**
*Work* • 1803–1808.

## SENATE (THE NEW CHAMBER) 1819–1859

**Buchanan**
*Work* • 1834–1845.

**Harrison, WH**
*Work* • 1825–1828.

**Jackson**
*Work* • 1823–1825.

**Johnson, A**
*Work* • 1857–1859.

**Pierce**
*Work* • 1837–1842.

**Taft**
*Visit* • Sworn in as chief justice in the Senate's old home in the capitol.

**Tyler**
*Work* • 1827–1836.

**Van Buren**
*Work* • 1821–1828.

## SENATE (NORTH WING EXTENSION OF THE CAPITOL) 1859–PRESENT

**Arthur**
*Visit* • Took oath of office as vice president in the Senate chambers. 1881.

**Harding**
*Work* • 1915–1921.

**Harrison, B**
*Work* • 1881–1887.

**Johnson, A**
*Work* • 1859–1862. 1875.

**Johnson, LB**
*Work* • 1949–1961.

**Kennedy**
*Work* • 1953–1961.

**Nixon**
*Work* • 1951–1953.

**Truman**
*Work* • 1935–1945.

**Taft**
*Visit* • Took oath of office as President in Senate chamber. 1909.


## CARLTON (RITZ-CARLTON) HOTEL

**Truman**
*Visit* • 2100 Massachusetts Ave, NW. Often here for meetings and speeches.


## CARROLL ARMS APARTMENTS

**Truman**
*Home* • 301 First St, NE. 1937.


## CARROLL ROW

**Johnson, A**
*Lodging* • Probably in Carroll Row when he stayed in an inexpensive boarding house near the Capitol. 1843.

**Lincoln**
*Lodging* • Mrs. Sprigg's Boarding House, 100 Block First St, SE, corner First St at Pennsylvania Ave. Long's Hotel was also in Carroll Row. Torn down in 1886 to make way for Library of Congress. Jefferson Building on the site now. 1847–1849.


## CARUSI'S SALOON

**Presidents**
*Visit* • NE corner, 111 Constitution Ave,

NW. Now site of Internal Revenue Service. Inaugural balls held here for J Q Adams to Buchanan, except Tyler, Fillmore, and Pierce. Old Saloon was razed in 1930s.


## CATHOLIC UNIVERSITY

**Johnson, LB**
*Visit* • 620 Michigan Ave, NE. 6–6–1965.


## CBS STUDIO

**Eisenhower**
*Visit* • 2020 M St NW. 11–7–1960.


## CENTRAL PRESBYTERIAN CHURCH

**Cleveland**
*Church* • Fifteenth and Sixteenth Sts at Irving St. Attended this church when he was in the White House. Church was sold to another congregation. 1913–1924.

**Hoover**
*Visit* • Laid cornerstone for Sunday school building. Thanksgiving Day 1930.

**Wilson**
*Church* • Third row at the north end of the middle section.

*Visit* • Laid cornerstone of this church. 1913.


## CHRIST CHURCH

**Adams, J**
*Church* • New Jersey Ave and D Sts SE near the intersection. It was located at the foot of Capitol Hill and was the first church to be established within the city proper. 1800–1801.

**Adams, JQ**
*Church* • 620 G St, SE. The parish built its church here after moving from New Jersey and D St. 1825–1829.

**Jefferson**
*Church* • 1801–1809.

## Madison

*Church* • 620 G St, SE. Madison attended in a lined and carpeted pew reserved for him. 1809–1817.

## Monroe

*Church* • Used same pew as above. 1817–1825.

# CITY HALL (OLD)

**Garfield**

*Site* • Fourth and D Sts, NW. Trial of Charles Guiteau, his assassin. Now the D.C. Courthouse. 1881.

**Roosevelt, T**

*Work* • West wing of City Hall. 1889–1895.

# MRS. CLARK BOARDING HOUSE

**Harrison, WH**

*Lodging* • F St, NW. 1817–1819.

# HENRY CLAY HOME

**Van Buren**

*Lodging* • 1700 H St, NW. 1831; visit 1842.

# CLEMENT'S BOARDING HOUSE (MRS. CLEMENT'S "TEN BUILDINGS")

**Polk**

*Home* • New Jersey Ave NW between D and E Sts. Demolished. 1834–1837.

# COLUMBIA RD

**Eisenhower**

*Home* • 2022 Columbia Rd, NW, Apt. 302. Southeast corner of Columbia Rd and Connecticut Ave. 1926–1935.

**Johnson, LB**

*Home* • 1707 Columbia Rd NW. Now The Chatham. 1938.

# COLUMBUS MONUMENT

**Ford**

*Visit* • Union Station for Columbus Day ceremony. 10–11–1976.

# COMMANDANT HOUSE (MARINES)

**Jefferson**

*Visit* • Eighth and G Sts, SE, at Capitol Hill. He selected the site; it is the oldest government building in Washington continuously used for the purpose for which it was designed. 1801.

# CONGRESSIONAL BOARDING HOUSES

**Presidents**

*Lodging* • Numbers 20 and 22 Third St SE. Originally the boarding houses once covered much of the present area now occupied by Folger and Shakespeare Library and the Library of Congress.

# CONGRESSIONAL CEMETERY

**Adams, JQ**

*Burial* • 1801 E St, SE. In temporary public vault.

**Harrison, WH**

*Burial* • 1801 E St, SE. In temporary public vault. 1841.

**Taylor**

*Burial* • 1801 E St, SE. In temporary public vault. 1850.

# CONNECTICUT AVE

**Eisenhower**

*Home* • 1914 Connecticut Avenue NW. Pullman Highland now on site. 1929.

**Johnson, LB**

*Home* • 3133 Connecticut Ave, NW, at Kennedy–Warren Apartments. 1937. 1938–1940.

**Taft**

*Home* • 2029 Connecticut Ave NW. 1917–1918.

**Truman**

*Home* • 3930 Connecticut Ave, NW. 1940.

*Home* • 4701 Connecticut Ave NW. 1941–1945.

## CONRAD AND MCMUNN'S

**Jackson**

*Lodging* • 219 New Jersey Ave, SE, south side of Capitol Hill New Jersey and Sixth St, SE. Also called Varnum Hotel. Now Longworth office site. 1800–.

**Jefferson**

*Lodging* • Walked from here to capitol on inauguration day. 1800–1801.

## CONSTITUTION AVE

**Tyler**

*Lodging* • Constitution Ave and Fourth St, NW. Site of boarding house. Now site of the National Gallery of Art. 1841.

## CONSTITUTION HALL (DAUGTHERS OF THE AMERICAN REVOLUTION)

**Presidents**

*Visit* • Seventeenth and Eighteenth Sts, NW, between C and D Sts. Used by every president since Truman for speeches and meetings.

## CONTINENTAL HOTEL

**Truman**

*Lodging* • N Capitol between D and E Sts. 1935.

## CONVENTION CENTER (WASHINGTON)

**Presidents**

*Visit* • 900 Ninth St. NW. Presidents since 1983 have attended functions here.

## GRIFFITH COOMBE HOUSE

**Jefferson**

*Visit* • Third and Georgia Ave, SE. Madison and Washington were also frequent guests. 1800–1809.

## COSMOS CLUB (TOWNSHEND HOUSE)

**Roosevelt, FD**

*Home* • 2121 Massachusetts Ave, NW. 1920s.

## MRS. COTTNINGER'S BOARDING HOUSE

**Buchanan**

*Lodging* • Thirteenth St on west side between E and F Sts. Moved here with Senator Barnard. 1829.

## DECATUR MANSION (ALSO CALLED BEALE MANSION)

**Presidents**

*Visit* • 748 Jackson Place NW. Corner Lafayette Square and H St. Sometimes referred to as the lobby of the White House since it was the gathering place of those who sought an audience with the president. Grant habitually stayed here with his friend, General Beale, on his visits to Washington. Monroe visited in 1819 and following. Reagan visited for the formation of the James Brady Foundation, 7–20–1982. Van Buren used site as residence, 1828–1830.

## DELAWARE AVE

**Garfield**

*Lodging* • 307 Delaware Ave. Now Capitol Park area. 1868–1869.

## DENT PLACE NW

**Kennedy**

*Home* • 3321 Dent Place, NW. First house occupied by newlyweds. 1954.

## DEPARTMENT OF COMMERCE (OLD)

**Hoover**

*Work* • Pennsylvania Ave corner of Ninteenth St, NW. 1921–1929.

## DEPARTMENT OF COMMERCE (NEW)

**Hoover**

*Visit* • Pennsylvania Ave and Fourteenth, NW. Laid cornerstone. 6–10–1929.

## DEPARTMENT OF INTERIOR

**Roosevelt, FD**

*Visit* • 1849 C St NW. Dedication. 4–16–1936.

## DEPARTMENT OF JUSTICE

**Taft**

*Work* • Fourteenth St and Pennsylvania Ave. 1890–1892.

## DEPARTMENT OF JUSTICE (NEW)

**Hoover**

*Visit* • Tenth and Constitution, NW. Laid cornerstone. 2–23–1932.

## DEPARTMENT LABOR AND INTERSTATE COMMERCE

**Hoover**

*Visit* • 200 Constitution Ave, NW. Laid cornerstone. 12–15–1932.

## DEPARTMENT OF STATE (FIRST SITE)

**Madison**

*Work* • First Department of State Building was on SW corner Fifteenth St. and Pennsylvania Ave. It was burned by the British in 1814. (Present site of north wing of Treasury Building.) 1801–1809.

## DEPARTMENT OF STATE (1817 SITE)

**Adams, JQ**

*Work* • Seventeenth St, NW, in a large brick building immediately west of the White House. Later State, War, and Navy Building. Now site of Executive Office Building. 1817–1820.

**Eisenhower**

*Work* • At site of Executive Office Building. 1929–1933

## DEPARTMENT OF STATE (1820–1866 SITE)

**Adams, JQ**

*Work* • In January 1820, offices moved to old brick building on SW corner of Fifteenth and Pennsylvania NW, fronting on Fifteenth and Executive Way (earlier site of first State Department building) on site of north wing of Treasury Building. 1820–1825.

**Buchanan**

*Work* • 1845–1849.

**Van Buren**

*Work* • 1829–1831.

## DEPARTMENT OF STATE (1875–1947 SITE)

**Vice Presidents**

*Work* • Pennsylvania Ave and Seventeenth St in State, War, and Navy Building, immediately west of the White House. (Now Executive Office Building.) Every vice president since Lyndon Johnson has had an office here. Presidents after Hoover, when fire destroyed the White House offices, have used Room 450 for news conferences.

**Eisenhower**

*Work* • 1926. 1929–1933. 1933–1935.

**Ford**

*Work* • Vice president. 1973–1974 .

**Grant**

*Visit* • First inaugural ball was held in north section of State, War, and Navy Building. 1877.

**Taft**

*Work* • Secretary of War. 1904–1908.

## DEPARTMENT OF STATE (PRESENT SITE)

**Jefferson**

*Site* • 2201 C St, NW. See desk on which he wrote Declaration of Independence.

## DEVONSHIRE PLACE

**Johnson LB**

*Home* • 2737 Devonshire Place, NW, Apt. 224, northwest corner of Devonshire Place and Connecticut Ave. 1941–1942.

## DISTRICT OF COLUMBIA WAR MEMORIAL

**Hoover**

*Visit* • Independence Ave, west of Seventeenth St, SW. Dedicated. November 11, 1931.

## DOLLEY MADISON HOUSE (RICHARD CUTTS HOUSE)

**Madison**

*Visit* • 1520 H St, NW, Lafayette Square. Later became Dolley Madison home; restored 1967.

## DORCHESTER HOUSE

**Kennedy**

*Home* • 2480 Sixteenth St, NW, Apt 502. 1941–1942.

## ALFRED DOWSON'S BOARDING HOUSE

**Pierce**

*Lodging* • 1 Capitol Hill. A St, fronting Capitol Square, between North Capitol St and First St. Now part of Capitol Park area. 1835–.

## DUDDINGTON HOUSE

**Presidents**

*Visit* • Corner of Third and Georgia Ave, SE, at the square between First and Second Sts, SE. It was two–stories high with a white colonial style porch. It was the first real mansion on Capitol Hill. Five presidents often came here: Adams, Jefferson, Madison, Monroe, and Jackson. House belonged to Daniel Carroll and was built in 1794.

## DUMBARTON METHODIST CHURCH

**Lincoln**

*Church* • 3133 Dumbarton Ave, NW. See Lincoln pew with an engraved plaque, third row from the front on the right. 1861.

## DUPONT CIRCLE

**Arthur**

*Visit* • Dedication statue of Admiral Dupont. Statue since removed. 12–20–1884.

**Coolidge**

*Home* • 15 Dupont Circle, Eleanor Patterson's Mansion. Stayed here while White House was renovated. 1927.

**Taft**

*Home* • 5 Dupont Circle. Rented small house for $100 a month. Demolished. 1890. 1892. Also lodged on Dupont Circle for a few days just before his inauguration, possibly at Boardman House (1801 P St. NW). 1909.

## EBBITT HOUSE

**Presidents**

*Visit* • Northeast corner of Fourteenth and F Sts, NW. Later torn down in 1926 and paneling and decoration moved to building at 1427 F St. National Press Building now on site. The original Ebbitt House bar is in the Washington Post Bldg, 675 Fifteenth St. Grant, Cleveland, and T Roosevelt came to the Old Ebbitt Grill.

**McKinley**
*Lodging* • 1877–1891.

**Taft**
*Home* • Sworn in as solicitor general here. At first stayed here walking to and from work. His father lived here while serving in Grant's cabinet. 1876–.

## EIGHTH ST SYNAGOGUE (NOW GREATER NEW HOPE BAPTIST CHURCH)

**Coolidge**
*Church* • Eighth between H and I Sts NW. Attended while First Congregational was closed for repairs. 1921.

## ELEVENTH ST, NW

**Garfield**
*Lodging* • 435 Eleventh St, NW. Rooming with Schenck. 1863–1869.

## ELLIOTT HOUSE

**Polk**
*Lodging* • Pennsylvania Ave, NW, on north side between Third and 4 1/2 St NW. Home of Jonathan Elliott. Moved here when he became Speaker of the House. 1837–1845.

## ELMS, THE

**Johnson, L**
*Home* • 4040 Fifty–Second St, NW. He bought Perle Mesta's lovely hilltop home here June 1961. Now Embassy of Algiers. 1961–1963.

## ERICSSON MEMORIAL POTOMAC PARK

**Coolidge**
*Visit* • Unveiled this memorial.

## F SREET, NW

**Adams, JQ**
*Home* • 1333 F St, NW, north side of F St, between Thirteenth and Fourteenth Sts NW. Resided here when Secretary of State. In April 1820 he bought the house on F St., lots 8 and 16, Square 253, 1333–1335 F St, NW. This site now occupied by a clothing store. 1821–1825. Here off and on until 1848.

**Buchanan**
*Home* • 1331 F St, NW, between Thirteenth and Fourteenth Sts, NW, next to the residence of JQ Adams and just a block from the State Department Building. Now site of National Council of Senior Citizens. 1845–1849.

**Madison**
*Home* • 1333 F St, NW. 1809.

## FEDERAL RESERVE BUILDING

**Roosevelt, FD**
*Visit* • Constitution Ave and Twentieth Sts, NW. Dedication. 10–20–1937.

## FIFTEENTH ST, NW

**Harrison, B**
*Home* • 1013 Fifteenth St, NW. 1881–1885.

## FIRST BAPTIST CHURCH

**Carter**
*Church* • Randolph St, NW. July 1976.

## FIRST BAPTIST CHURCH OF THE CITY OF WASHINGTON

**Carter**
*Church* • 1328 Sixteenth St, NW. 1977–1981.

**Clinton**
> *Church* • First attended the night before his inauguration. 1993.

**Truman**
> *Church* • The Sixteenth St site, since razed for the new one, opened for worship 1890. New edifice dedicated 1956 replacing the old structure where he worshipped. 1935–1953.

## FIRST CONGREGATIONAL CHURCH

**Coolidge**
> *Church* • Tenth and G Sts, NW. 1868–1961. Replaced 1960s. Plate at the east end of the third row in the middle section of benches marks his pew. 1923–1929.

## FIRST PRESBYTERIAN CHURCH

**Buchanan**
> *Church* • Marshall Place (formerly 4 1/2 St). Paid pew rent. 1821–1831. 1834–1849. 1857–1861.

**Cleveland**
> *Church* • Attended while in the White House. 1885–1889.

**Grant**
> *Church* • Ledger entry shows he occupied pew 69. 1869–1877.

**Polk**
> *Church* • Purchased a pew and attended regularly. 1825–1839.

**Reagan**
> *Church* • After recovery from assassination attempt. 1981.

**Wilson**
> *Church* • Attended on occasion. 1913–1921.

## FIRST ROCK BAPTIST CHURCH

**Carter**
> *Church* • 4630 Alabama Ave, SE. May 1992.

## FLETCHER'S BOARDING HOUSE

**Fillmore**
> *Lodging* • E St, NW, near the Post Office. Between Sixth and Seventh. 1834.

## FORD'S THEATRE

**Lincoln**
> *Death* • 511 Tenth St, NW. Shot while watching performance of *Our American Cousin.* 1865.

## FOREST LANE

**Nixon**
> *Home* • 4308 Forest Lane, NW. 1953–1961.

## FOREST-MARBURY HOUSE

**Washington**
> *Visit* • 3350 M St, NW. Dealing for land for federal capital. 1791.

## FORT DE RUSSEY

**Lincoln**
> *Visit* • Oregon and Military Rds. 1864.

## FORT MCNAIR

**Eisenhower**
> *Work* • Army War College, P St between Third and Fourth Sts, SE. Stationed. 1928–1929.
>
> *Education* • 1929. Dedication of new bldg at Industrial College. 9–6–1960.

## FORT MYER

**Eisenhower**
> *Home* • Jackson Ave at NW corner of Arlington Cemetery off US Highway 50. On the base at Washington and Grant Sts in Quarters 1. 1945–1948.

## FOUNDRY METHODIST CHURCH (ORIGINAL SITE)

**Adams, JQ**
*Church* • Fourteenth and G Sts, NW.

**Grant**
*Church* • New church on the same site at Fourteenh and G Sts, NW. 1866–.

**Hayes**
*Church* • Attended regularly at the old site of Fourteenth and G Sts NW 1865–1867. 1877–1881.

**Jackson**
*Church* • Also boarded with a Foundry member. 1823–1825.

**Johnson, A**
*Church* • Often attended. Declared a life member in 1866. Marker. 1822–.

**Lincoln**
*Church* • 1861–.

**Madison**
*Church* • 1809–.

**Polk**
*Church* • 1825–1849.

## FOUNDRY METHODIST CHURCH (PRESENT SITE)

**Clinton**
*Church* • 1500 Sixteenth St, NW. Attended with Mrs. Clinton. Since January 1993.

**Coolidge**
*Church* • Attended. 1926.

**McKinley**
*Church* • 1897.

**Roosevelt, FD**
*Church* • See Sixth pew on the right. 1935 and with Churchill in 1941.

**Truman**
*Church* • 1945.

## FRANKLIN HOTEL

**Jackson**
*Lodging* • 2025 I St NW. Now site of Park Lane Apartments.

## FREEMASON'S HALL

**Harrison, WH**
*Visit* • SW corner John Marshall Place and D St, NW, opposite City Hall. Inaugural ball. Demolished 1930s. 1841.

**Jackson**
*Visit* • Inaugural ball. 1833.

## FREDERICK T. FRELINGHUYSEN HOUSE

**Arthur**
*Lodging* • 1013 Sixteenth St, NW (possible location). Stayed several days after Cleveland's inauguration. 1885.

## FRIEND'S MEETING HOUSE

**Hoover**
*Church* • 2111 Florida Ave, NW, just off Connecticut Ave. He usually sat midway down the center aisle. 1929–1933.

## FRIENDSHIP HOUSE

**Presidents**
*Visit* • 630 South Carolina Ave, SE. Until 1936 known as the Maples. Visited by several presidents.

## FULLER'S HOTEL

**Tyler**
*Lodging* • Pennsylvania Ave and Fourteenth St, NW. Renamed Kirkwood and later site of the Raleigh. Stayed here when leaving the White House. 1845.

## GADSBY'S TAVERN

**Fillmore**
*Lodging* • NE corner of Pennsylvania Ave and Sixth St NW. Now site of D.C. Employment Agency. John Gadsby was also proprietor of the National Hotel. 1833–1835.

**Harrison, WH**
  *Lodging* • Arrived 2–9–1841 to take up temporary residence before inauguration. Also lodged 1825–1828, when a U.S. Senator. 1836.

**Jackson**
  *Lodging* • 1824. February 1829.

**Pierce**
  *Lodging* • Took quarters here in 1833 until he moved to the other side of Pennsylvania Ave at Mr. Hill's (south side of the capital's main street just west of Third St).

**Tyler**
  *Lodging* • 1827–.

**Van Buren**
  *Lodging* • 1833.

## GARFIELD HOSPITAL

**Taft**
  *Visit* • Tenth St and Pennsylvania Ave, NW. January 1930.

## GARFIELD STATUE

**Garfield**
  *Site* • West side of Capitol.

## GAWLER FUNERAL HOME

**Presidents**
  *Funeral* • 5130 Wisconsin Ave. Until 1963 was at 1750–1758 Pennsylvania Ave, near the White House. Used for Taft, FD Roosevelt, and Kennedy.

## GENERAL ACCOUNTING OFFICE

**Truman**
  *Visit* • Fourth and G Sts, NW. Dedicated 9–11–1951.

## GEORGETOWN HEIGHTS

**Pierce**
  *Home* • Exact location unknown. Rented a house here called "English Cottage." 1853–.

**Van Buren**
  *Home* • Leased a house here. Summer and fall of 1841.

## GEORGETOWN PRESBYTERIAN CHURCH

**Clinton**
  *Church* • 3115 P St, NW. Attended while at Georgetown University. 1964–1968

## GEORGETOWN UNIVERSITY

**Clinton**
  *Education* • 37th and O Sts, NW. Foreign Service School. Classes in Walsh Bldg on 36th St, NW. Lodging in Loyola Hall 35th and P NW. 1964–1967.

**Eisenhower**
  *Visit* • Dedication. Edmund A. Walsh School of Foreign Service. 10–13–1958.

**Johnson, LB**
  *Visit* • Walsh Hall. 9–13–1966.

**Monroe**
  *Visit* • Attended first commencement. 1824.

## GEORGETOWN UNIVERSITY LAW SCHOOL

**Johnson, LB**
  *Education* • 600 New Jersey Ave, NW. 1934.

## GEORGE WASHINGTON HOSPITAL

**Reagan**
  *Lodging* • 901 Third St at Pennsylvania Ave, NW. Here after assassination attempt. 3–30–1981 to 4–11–1981.

## GEORGE WASHINGTON UNIVERSITY

**Kennedy**
  *Visit* • 2121 I St, NW. Honorary degree. 5–3–1961.

## JAMES CARDINAL GIBBONS STATUE

**Hoover**

*Visit* • Unveiled. Sixteenth. and Park Rd, NW. 8–14–1932.

## GOMPER'S SQUARE

**Roosevelt, FD**

*Visit* • Tenth St and Massachusetts Ave, NW. Dedication. Gomper's Memorial. 10–7–1933.

**Truman**

*Visit* • Dedication. 10–27–1951.

## GRACE DODGE HOTEL

**Johnson, LB**

*Lodging* • 500 First St, NW. Torn down. 1931. 1932–1934.

## GRACE REFORMED CHURCH

**Roosevelt, T**

*Church* • 1405 Fifteenth St, NW. Pew no. 5 at the third row of the chancel in the middle aisle. 1882–1903 meetings for worship were held in a brick chapel of Queen Anne style building located on the current site. Current building dedicated 1903. There is a Theodore Roosevelt Memorial Room in the building. Nixon and Eisenhower also visited here.

## GRANT BUILDING

**Grant**

*Work* • 532 Seventeenth St, NW. During the 1940s the house was demolished. 1865.

## GRANT MEMORIAL

**Grant**

*Site* • Union Square on the Mall at First St, SW. It is one of the largest equestrian statues in the world. 1922.

## GRAY HOUSE (ALSO KNOWN AS BUTLER HOUSE)

**Arthur**

*Home* • New Jersey Ave at 3 B St, SE, SW corner. Following the assassination of Garfield, 1881, it served as a temporary White House. Three houses built out of stone here. The Gray House was sold to Senator John P Jones (Nevada). 1881. Also known as Butler house. Was site of the Maltby Building and now site of Longworth House office building.

**Garfield**

*Lodging* • Stayed with Chase. 1862. Stayed with Schenck. 1863.

**Harding**

*Visit* • Attending Taft's 25th wedding anniversary. 1911.

## H ST, NW

**Cleveland**

*Home* • 1710 H St, NW. 1893.

**Wilson**

*Visit* • 1413 H St. NW. Called on second wife here before they were married. She was owner of this home (now City Center building). 1915.

## JOHN HAYES HAMMOND HOUSE (BARLOW HOUSE)

**Taft**

*Visit* • 2221 Kalorama Ave, NW. Later old French Embassy. 1909–1913.

## HARVEY'S

**Presidents**

*Visit* • SE corner Pennsylvania Ave and Eleventh St, NW. Removed 1930s. Grant through F D Roosevelt dined here.

## HELLEN HOME

**Adams, JQ**

*Lodging* • 2618–2620 K St, NW. Senator

and Mrs. J Q Adams boarded with the family of one of his wife's sisters, Mrs. Walter Hellen. Demolished. 1803–1807.

## HILLBROOK LANE, NW

**Bush**

*Home* • 4910 Hillbrook Lane NW in Spring Valley section. They bought the home from Senator Millard Simpson. 1967.

## HILTON (WASHINGTON) HOTEL

**Presidents**

*Visit* • 1919 Connecticut Ave. NW. Presidents since Truman have met and spoken here.

**Reagan**

*Visit* • Shot at T St level. 3–30–1981.

## HOLY TRINITY CHURCH

**Hoover**

*Visit* • 3513 N St, NW. Attended funeral service here.

**Kennedy**

*Church* • Sat in various pews, sometimes up front, sometimes in the gallery; no pew designated as his. Plaque on the side of the church. 1947–1963.

**Lincoln**

*Visit* • Attended a funeral service here. 1861.

## HOOVER COMMISSION OFFICE

**Hoover**

*Work* • 441 G St NW. Commission on Organization of Executive Branch of the Government in the General Accounting Building. 1947–1953.

## HOWARD UNIVERSITY

**Hayes**

*Visit* • Speech. 2–16–1878. Commencement. 6–10–1932.

**Hoover**

*Visit* • 2400 Sixth St, NW.

**Johnson, LB**

*Visit* • 6–4–1965.

**Truman**

*Visit* • Commencement. 6–13–1952.

## HYATT REGENCY HOTEL

**Presidents**

*Visit* • 400 New Jersey Ave, NW. All presidents since Kennedy met and spoke here.

## I ST, NW

**Garfield**

*Home* • 1227 I St, NW. Home with view of Franklin Square. Demolished in 1964. 1869–1881.

**Grant**

*Home* • 205/207 I St, NW near New Jersey Ave. Grant sold it when he became president. Also called Douglas Place. 1866–1869.

*Home* • 646 I St. NW. Grant bought a house here that was later sold to General Sherman. Possible discrepancy with previous entry. 1865–1869.

**Monroe**

*Home* • 2017 I St, NW. Living here as Secretary of State. 1811–1817.

*Home* • White House was being repaired following War of 1812. 1817.

## IDAHO AVE, NW

**Truman**

*Home* • 3051 Warwich Apartments. 1938.

## IMPERIAL HOTEL

**Johnson, A**

*Visit* • E St between Thirteenth and Fourteenth Sts, NW. While serving in special session of Senate. 1875.

## INDIAN QUEEN HOTEL

**Van Buren**

*Visit* • North side of Pennsylvania Ave, between Sixth and Seventh Sts, NW. Later known as Brown's Hotel and afterwards as Metropolitan Hotel. See also under Brown's. Attended Jefferson Dinner at Jesse Brown's Indian Queen Hotel. April 13, 1830.

## INGRAM MEMORIAL CONGREGATIONAL CHURCH

**Taft**

*Visit* • Tenth and A Sts, NE.

*Church* • built in 1907. (Now Seventh Day Adventist.) Spoke at the cornerstone laying and later at the dedication ceremonies.

## IOWA CIRCLE (NOW LOGAN CIRCLE)

**Harrison, B**

*Home* • At corner of Thirteenth St, NW. 1885.

## IRVING HOTEL

**Polk**

*Visit* • Pennsylvania Ave, NW. Here as out-going president. Rode to capitol from here with Taylor. 1849.

## ISLAMIC CENTER

**Eisenhower**

*Visit* • 2551 Massachusetts Ave, NW. Opening. 6–28–1957.

## JACKSON HALL

**Presidents**

*Visit* • 339 Pennsylvania Ave, NW. Torn down, 1949, to make room for the Federal Courthouse. Washington Assembly Rooms were located here where inaugural balls

*Jefferson Memorial*

took place. Inaugural balls for Lincoln, Taylor, and Fillmore.

## JACKSON PLACE

**Pierce**

*Visit* • 736 Jackson Place, NW. Leaving White House, he stayed with Secretary Marcy. 1857.

**Roosevelt, T**

*Home* • Lived here temporarily while White House was renovated. Fell on front step and fractured his leg while here. 1902.

**Van Buren**

*Home* • 748 Jackson Place NW. 1829–1830.

## JACKSON STATUE

**Jackson**

*Site* • Center of Lafayette Park, NW.

## JEFFERSON MEMORIAL

**Jefferson**

*Site* • South Basin Drive, SW.

*Granite marker for Lyndon Johnson.*

**Roosevelt, FD**
> *Visit* • Cornerstone laid 11–15–1939. Dedication 4–13–1943. See also statue in Capitol Rotunda.

## JEFFERSON PLACE, NW

**Roosevelt, T**
> *Home* • 1820 Jefferson Place, NW. 1889–1891.

## JOHN MARSHALL PLACE, NW

**Adams, JQ**
> *Home* • 4 1/2 and F Sts NW where the Municipal Center Building now stands. Lived here about a mile and a quarter from the Department of State. He made the walk daily to his office in 22 minutes. In April 1820 he bought the house on F St NW. 1820–.

## JOHNSON MEMORIAL GROVE

**Ford**
> *Visit* • Participated in ground breaking ceremony 9–27–1974. Dedication. 4–6–1976.

**Johnson, LB**
> *Site* • Columbia Island. Park and Granite Marker.

## JJ JUSSERAND MEMORIAL

**Roosevelt, FD**
> *Visit* • Rock Creek Park. Dedication. 11–7–1936.

## K ST, NW

**Harding**
> *Home* • 1625 K St, NW. Now site of Commonwealth Building.

**Taft**
> *Home* • 1603 K St, NW. Lived here while Secretary of War. Demolished. 1904–1909.

## KALORAMA RD

**Johnson, LB**
> *Home* • 1910 Kalorama Rd NW. First Washington apartment. 1934.

## JOHN F KENNEDY CENTER

**Presidents**
> *Visit* • North of Theodore Roosevelt Bridge. Since L B Johnson, all presidents have attended performances here. Inaugural balls held here.

## KIRKWOOD HOUSE

**Johnson, A**
> *Home* • 1111 Pennsylvania Ave and the NE corner of Twelfth St, NW. Here, in his third floor suite, he was told he was president and took the oath of office. Lived here as vice president. Torn down after the Civil War and replaced by the Raleigh Hotel which in turn has been removed. An office building is now on the site. April 16, 1865.

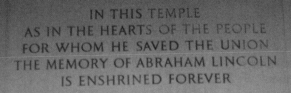

*Lincoln Memorial.*

## KOREAN WAR VETERANS MEMORIAL

**Bush**

*Visit* • Near Lincoln Memorial, Twenty-First St and Constitution Ave. Ground-breaking. 6–14–1992.

## LaFAYETTE HOTEL

**Truman**

*Home* • Sixteenth and I NW. 1928. 1935.

## THOMAS LAW HOUSE

**Washington**

*Visit* • New Jersey and C Sts, a block south of the Capitol. 1252 Sixth St, SW. Came to dine. Later converted to Varnum Hotel and now site of second House Office Building.

## LEE HOUSE

**Johnson, A**

*Lodging* • 1653 Pennsylvania Ave, NW. This house was joined to Blair. Johnson lived here until the Lincoln family left the White House. 1865.

## LIBRARY OF CONGRESS

**Presidents**

*Visit* • Across street from Capitol, off Independence Ave, SE. Dinners in Great Hall.

## LINCOLN MEMORIAL

**Harding**

*Visit* • Dedicated. 5–30–1922.

**Lincoln**

*Site* • West end of the Mall, West Potomac Park at the foot of Third St. See also: Lincoln Statue, East Capitol and Eleventh Sts NE in Lincoln Park; Lincoln Statue, D St between Fourth and Fifth Sts, NW; Lincoln Statue, Department of Interior Bldg, C St between Eighteenth and Nineteenth Sts, NW; Statue, Washington Cathedral.

## HENRY CABOT LODGE HOUSE

**Roosevelt, T**

*Visit* • 1765 Massachusetts Ave, NW. 1897–1909.

## MRS. McDANIEL'S BOARDING HOUSE

**Tyler**

*Lodging* • Pennsylvania Ave, between Third and 4 1/2 Sts. 1834.

## McLEAN'S GARDENS

**Presidents**

*Visit* • 3811 Porter St. NW west side of Wisconsin Ave between Porter and Rodman Sts. Coolidge, Harding, and others played golf here. Only stone wall and the iron mermaids remain today.

## JOHN MARSHALL HOUSE

**Presidents**

*Visit* • 1801 F St NW. Also called Ringgold–Carroll Rooming House. Madison, Monroe, and Van Buren stayed here.

## MASSACHUSETTS AVE, NW

**Hoover**

*Home* • 1701 Massachusetts Ave, NW. Rented. 1917–1918.

*Home* • Massachusetts Ave, NW, 2221 NW. Rented. Now Greek Embassy. 1917.

## MAYFLOWER HOTEL (NOW STOUFFER MAYFLOWER HOTEL)

**Presidents**

*Visit* • 1127 Connecticut Ave, NW, southeast corner of Connecticut Ave and DeSales St. Site of inaugural balls for every president since Coolidge.

## MERIDIAN HILL

### Adams, JQ

*Home* • Sixteenth St between Florida Ave, and Euclid St NW. Also known as the Commodore David Porter House. Upon leaving the White House he rented this house in the country which was about a mile and a half from the White House. 1829.

### Truman

*Visit* • Accepted Netherlands Carillon gift in Meridian Hill Park. 4–4–1952.

## MERIDIAN MANSION

### Coolidge

*Home* • 2400 Sixteenth St NW. 1921–1923.

## METHODIST METROPOLITAN MEMORIAL CHURCH

### Grant

*Church* • Nebraska and New Mexico Aves, NW. The old edifice where he attended at John Marshall Place (southeast corner C St and John Marshall, NW) was torn down. Government building on site. Marker in the church for Grants pew. 1869–.

### McKinley

*Church* • On the arm of a pew midway between and in direct line with two large wall tablets; see silver plate marking the pew occupied by Grant and McKinley. 1897–.

## METROPOLITAN AFRICAN METHODIST EPISCOPAL CHURCH

### Presidents

*Visit* • 1518 M St, NW. Every President since Taft has attended this church. Clinton was the first president to attend inaugural service here. January 20, 1993.

## METROPOLITAN THEATER

### Coolidge

*Church* • 932–936 F St, NW. Services

held here while First Congregational Church was closed for repairs. 1923.

## MUNITIONS BUILDING

### Eisenhower

*Work* • Twentieth and B Sts, NW. 1941–1942.

## N St, NW

### Buchanan

*Home* • 3337 N St, NW. When Senator. 1834–1845.

### Kennedy

*Home* • 3017 N St, NW.

*Home* • 3260 N St, NW. 1952–1953.

*Home* • 3307 N St, NW. 1957–1961.

### Roosevelt, FD

*Home* • 1733 N St NW. 1913.

### Roosevelt, T

*Home* • 1733 N St NW. 1913. 1889–1901.

*Home* • 1810 N St, NW. Now only a entry driveway to a parking lot. 1897–1899.

## NATIONAL ACADEMY OF SCIENCES AND NATIONAL RESEARCH COUNCIL

### Hoover

*Visit* • 2101 Constitution Ave, NW. Honor Madame Marie Curie. 10–30–1929.

## NATIONAL AIR AND SPACE MUSEUM

### Ford

*Visit* • Sixth St and Independence Ave. Dedication. 7–1–1976.

## NATIONAL ARCHIVES

### Hoover

*Visit* • Seventh and Pennsylvania Ave NW. Laid Cornerstone. 2–20–1933.

**Truman**

*Visit* • Dedication of Declaration of Independence. 12–15–1952.

## NATIONAL CATHEDRAL

**Bush**

*Visit* • Massachusetts and Wisconsin Aves, NW. Present for the placing of the final stone. 1992.

**Carter**

*Visit* • 11–15–1979.

**Eisenhower**

*Funeral* • 4–1–1969.

**Roosevelt, FD**

*Visit* • 3–3–1935.

**Roosevelt, T**

*Visit* • Laying of the foundation stone. 1907.

**Wilson**

*Burial* • Bethlehem Chapel (temporarily); final resting place in crypt in upper catacomb, south end of the West side. 1924.

## NATIONAL CATHEDRAL SCHOOL

**Johnson, LB**

*Visit* • Massachusetts and Wisconsin Aves, NW. Commencement speech. 6–1–1965.

## NATIONAL CITY CHRISTIAN CHURCH

**Garfield**

*Church* • Thomas Circle, Fourteenth St at Massachusetts Ave, NW. Was then on Vermont Ave, now on Thomas Circle. Pew bearing his name and dates of birth and death in the entrance to the new church. 1863–1881.

**Johnson, LB**

*Church* • 1931–1969.

*Funeral* • 1–25–1973.

## NATIONAL GUARD ARMORY (OLD)

**Presidents**

*Visit* • Sixth and B (now Independence) Sts. Now site of Air and Space Museum. Eisenhower, Kennedy, LB Johnson, and Truman spoke here.

## NATIONAL HOTEL

**Presidents**

*Visit* • Northeast corner Sixth St and Pennsylvania, NW. Opened in 1827. It was the first building in the US to be designed for hotel purposes. Torn down in the 1930s. Traditional gathering place for southern leaders just as Willard's served the same purpose for northern leaders. Sometimes referred to as Coleman's. Presidents Jackson through Lincoln stayed here.

## NATIONAL LAW ENFORCEMENT OFFICERS MEMORIAL

**Bush**

*Visit* • Judiciary Square, between Fourth and Fifth Sts, NW. Dedication. 10–15–1991.

## NATIONAL PARK STADIUM

**Taft**

*Visit* • W St and Georgia Ave, NW, including the site of Howard University Hospital. Place where first presidential baseball season opened with the president throwing out the first ball. 1910.

## NATIONAL PORTRAIT GALLERY

**Presidents**

*Site* • Eighth and F Sts, NW. The Hall of Presidents includes portrait of Washington saved by Dolley Madison. Lincoln second inaugural reception here. 1865.

## NATIONAL PRESBYTERIAN CHURCH (ST. ANDREW'S PRESBYTERIAN CHURCH)

**Buchanan**

*Church* • Connecticut Ave at Eighteenth and N Sts, NW.

*Church* • It was founded in what was a carpenter shop on what is now White House grounds. Later came to be known as St. Andrew's Presbyterian Church. Torn down and no identifying markers in the area. Ledger shows Buchanan paid pew rent here when president. 1857–.

**Cleveland**

*Church* • Paid rent for pew number 132.

**Eisenhower**

*Church* • Occupied pew number 41. Baptized February 1, 1953. Official member. 1953–1961.

**Grant**

*Church* • Paid pew rent for number 69.

**Harrison, B**

*Church* • (Then known as Church of the Covenant.) Occupied pew number 43. 1889–1893.

**Jackson**

*Church* • See entry above. He paid rent for pew number 6. 1829–1837.

**McKinley**

*Church* • Purchased a pew here.

*Church* • Purchased a pew here.

**Truman**

*Visit* • Visited on the occasion of establishing the church as the national church for all Presbyterians. 10–19–1947.

## NATIONAL PRESS BLDG

**Presidents**

*Visit* • Fourteenth and F NW. Formerly site of Ebbitt House. Most presidents have been card carrying members of the Press Club since the time of Coolidge. Truman played the piano here. 1948.

**Coolidge**

*Visit* • Laid the cornerstone. 1926.

## NAVY DEPARTMENT, BUREAU OF AERONAUTICS

**Nixon**

*Work* • Eighteenth and Constitution Ave, NW. December 1944.

## NAVY YARD SHIP REPAIR FACILITY

**Lincoln**

*Visit* • Ninth and M Sts, SE. Lincoln often visited here during the Civil War. Still in existence and claims the oldest marine railway in the nation.

**Monroe**

*Visit* • Monroe rode the railway back in 1822 when he went to watch the frigate *Potomac* being pulled out of the water and up the rail incline. 1822.

## NEW YORK AVE PRESBYTERIAN CHURCH

**Presidents**

*Church* • 1313 New York Ave, NW, at H St. J Q Adams, Jackson, W H Harrison, Fillmore, Buchanan, and A Johnson attended. Probably most presidents have attended church here either in the old or in the present structure built on the same site.

**Lincoln**

*Church* • He usually attended here during his term of office walking down the center aisle to the eighth pew from the pulpit on the right. (Pew number 14.) The present church was dedicated in 1951 but the pew is in comparatively the same location. Other presidents sit in this pew when attending.

**Truman**

*Visit* • Laid the cornerstone of the present church. 4–3–1951. 1861–1865.

## NINETEENTH ST

**Roosevelt, T**

*Home* • 1215 Nineteenth St, NW. 1891–1895.

*Home* • 1310 Nineteenth St. NW. Lived here while working at Civil Service Commission. Now part of Dupont Circle. 1891–1895.

## NORTH CAPITOL

**Washington**

*Home* • North Capitol St between B and C Sts. He had two houses built here. A stone north of the Capitol and just south of the Union Station shows the location of the two three-story brick houses which he had built as an investment just before he died. 1799.

## OAK VIEW

**Cleveland**

*Home* • 3542 Newark St, NW. Razed in the 1890s. Purchased 1886. Two miles north of Georgetown. Nearby was Woodley property. 1886–1887.

## OBSERVATORY CIRCLE

**Vice Presidents**

*Home* • Massachusetts Ave at Fourth St, NW in the Admiral's House.

## OCTAGON HOUSE

**Madison**

*Home* • 1741 New York Ave, NW, Eighteenth St and New York Ave, NW. Stayed here after the White House was burned. Here he signed the Treaty of Ghent. 1814–1817.

## OFFICE OF NAVY INTELLIGENCE

**Kennedy**

*Work* • Constitution Ave and Eighteenth St NW, Navy Department Building, Room 2064. Building demolished. 1941.

## OFFICE OF PRICE ADMINISTRATION

**Nixon**

*Work* • Independence Ave and Sixth St, SW, in Temporary Building D. New building on site. 1942.

## OLD ADAS ISRAEL SYNAGOGUE

**Grant**

*Church* • G St at Third St NW. Originally built at Sixth and G Sts NW. No longer a synagogue. First synagogue to be attended by a US president. 1869.

## OLD BRICK CAPITOL

**Monroe**

*Work* • First and A Sts, SW to the northeast was the site of the Old Brick Capitol, which was the temporary home for Congress while the Capitol building was being rebuilt following the burning by the British in 1814. Building was used from 1815–1819. Today the Supreme Court stands on this historic ground. Inaugurated here. 1817.

## O'NEAL'S TAVERN

**Jackson**

*Visit* • North side Pennsylvania Ave between Twentieth and Twenty-First Sts, NW. William O'Neal was the proprietor of Franklin Hotel. 1823.

## P ST

**Kennedy**

*Home* • 2808 P St, NW. January–May 1951.

*Home* • 3271 P St, NW. 1953.

*Petersen's House, site of Abraham Lincoln's death.*

## PALISADE LANE

**Bush**
>*Home* • 5161 Palisade Lane. 1969–1977.

## PAN AMERICAN UNION BUILDING

**Presidents**
>*Visit* • Seventeenth St and Constitution Ave, NW. Most presidents since Hoover have spoken here.

## PATENT OFFICE

**Lincoln**
>*Work* • Between F and G Sts NW on the west side of Seventh St. Now houses the National Museum of American Art and the National Portrait Gallery. The south portico is a copy of the Parthenon. Third floor rooms were site of Lincoln's second inaugural ball. March 5, 1865.

## PENNSYLVANIA AVE

**Johnson, A**
>*Home* • 504 Pennsylvania Ave. 1843.

**Polk**
>*Lodging* • 1901 Pennsylvania Ave, NW. 1826.

## PENSION BUILDING

**Presidents**
>*Visit* • Fourth and Fifth Sts between F and G Sts, NW at Judiciary Square. Inaugural balls held here 1885 to 1909 and 1969 to the present. Inaugural balls held here for Arthur, Cleveland, B Harrison, McKinley, T Roosevelt, Taft, Nixon, Carter, Reagan, Bush, and Clinton.

## WILLIAM PETERSEN HOUSE

**Lincoln**
>*Death* • Tenth St, NW. 1865.

## MRS. ANN PEYTON BOARDING HOUSE

**Buchanan**
>*Lodging* • 501 Pennsylvania Ave, NW. Now site of Canadian Embassy. 1821–1831.

**Polk**
>*Lodging* • 1827–1832.

## MRS. PITTMAN'S BOARDING HOUSE

**Pierce**
*Lodging* • 219 Third St, NW. 1837.

## POTOMAC AVE

**Clinton**
*Lodging* • 4513 Potomac Ave, NW, West of Georgetown University campus and south of MacArthur Blvd. While a student at Georgetown University. 1967–1968.

## POWHATAN HOTEL

**Roosevelt, F**
*Lodging* • Eighteenth and H Sts NW at Pennsylvania Ave. 1913.

## Q ST, NW

**Ford**
*Home* • 2500 Q St, NW. Rented apartment. 1949–1951

## R ST

**Grant**
*Home* • R St 3238 R St, NW. Summer home. Lincoln was a frequent visitor, 1861–1865. 1865.

**Roosevelt, FD**
*Home* • 2131 R St, NW. Now Embassy of Mali. 1917–1920.

## RAYBURN HOUSE OFFICE BLDG

**Kennedy**
*Visit* • S. Capitol and Independence Ave, SW. Laid cornerstone. 5–24–1962.

## RHODE ISLAND AVE, NW

**Hoover**
*Home* • 1720 Rhode Island Ave, NW. 1918–1919.

## RIGGS HOUSE

**Harrison, B**
*Home* • Fifteenth and G Sts, NW. Now site of Riggs National Bank. 1887.

## ROCK CREEK CHURCH RD

**Buchanan**
*Lodging* • At Upshur St, NW. 1834.

## ROCK CREEK PARK, CARTER BARRON AMPHITHEATER

**Truman**
*Visit* • Dedication of amphitheater. 5–25–1951.

## ROGERS HOUSE

**Polk**
*Home* • 17 Madison Place, NW. While White House was renovated. Destroyed 1894. 1845.

## FRANKLIN ROOSEVELT MEMORIAL

**Roosevelt, FD**
*Site* • West Potomac Park near the Jefferson Memorial. To be completed 1995. See also: Roosevelt Monument, Ninth St and Pennsylvania Ave, NW, in front of National Archives; Statue on Roosevelt Island.

## ROSEDALE

**Adams**
*Visit* • 3501 Newark St NW. Guest here when he came to view the new capital. 1800.

**Washington**
*Visit* • Dined here. 1790.

## S ST, NW

**Hoover**
*Home* • 2300 S St, NW. 1921–1929

**Roosevelt, FD**
*Visit* • 2244 S St, NW. Uncle's home. 1917–.

**Wilson**
*Death/Funeral* • 2340 S St, NW. Wilson lived here after his retirement until his death. 1921–1924.

## ST. CHARLES HOTEL

**Johnson, A**
*Lodging* • Northwest corner of Third St and Constitution Ave. Later became New Capital Hotel. Razed 1926. Now site of the U.S. Courthouse. 1857–1862. 1869.

## ST. DOMINIC'S CATHOLIC CHURCH

**Johnson, LB**
*Church* • 630 E St, SW. 1950–.

## ST. JOHN'S EPISCOPAL CHURCH

**Presidents**
*Church* • 1525 H St, NW. Lafayette Square near the White House. Every president from Madison to Clinton has attended occasional services here. Building completed in 1816.

**Arthur**
*Church* • Donated a window to the church in his wife's name. She sang in the choir and his children sometimes accompanied him to services. 1881–1885.

**Harrison, WH**
*Church* • Occupied pew 45. 1817–1819. 1841.

**Madison**
*Church* • First to sit in the President's pew when the church was completed. 1816.

## ST. MARK'S EPISCOPAL CHURCH

**Johnson, LB**
*Church* • 301 A St, SE. Attended while vice president. 1963.

## ST. MATTHEW'S CATHEDRAL

**Kennedy**
*Funeral* • 11–25–1963.

## ST. PATRICK'S CATHOLIC

**Adams, JQ**
*Church* • 619 10 St, NW. Attended first Christmas during his presidency. 1825.

**Johnson, A**
*Church* • Attended at times. 1865–1869.

## ST. PETER'S CATHOLIC CHURCH

**Johnson, LB**
*Church* • 313 Second St, SW. Parish founded in 1820. Visited on several occasions.

## ST. REGIS APARTMENTS

**Wilson**
*Visit* • 2219 California St, NW, In–laws of second wife lived here. 1915–.

## ST. THOMAS EPISCOPAL CHURCH

**Roosevelt, FD**
*Church* • 1772 Church St, NW, near Dupont Circle. Burned 1970. The parish garden remains. Roosevelt attended this church regularly. Pew 32 bore a plate. 1913–1928.

## SCOTT–GRANT HOUSE

**Grant**
*Home* • 3228 R St, NW. Used as summer White House.

## SECRETARY OF WAR OFFICE

**Grant**
*Work* • Pennsylvania Ave and Seventeenth St, NW. 1865–1868.

**Monroe**
*Work* • 1814–1815.

## SEDGWICK APARTMENTS

**Truman**

*Home* • 3726 Connecticut Ave, NW. 1935–1936. 1940.

## "SEVEN BUILDINGS"

**Jackson**

*Visit* • 1901–1913 Pennsylvania Ave, NW, corner of Pennsylvania and Nineteenth St, NW. Numbers 4 and 5 of the original seven remain; store is located in the corner building. The corner building served as Department of State when John Marshall was Secretary. Jackson was entertained by Madison here. 1815.

**Madison**

*Home* • 1901 Pennsylvania Ave, NW. Demolished 1958. 1816–1817.

**Van Buren**

*Home* • Fall of 1833 he rented one of the houses from James Kirke Paulding. His home once housed the State Department. 1833.

## SHERATON–CARLTON HOTEL

**Presidents**

*Visit* • 923 Sixteenth St, NW. Most presidents since Truman have met and spoken here. Turman held state receptions here while the White House was undergoing repairs.

## SHERATON PARK HOTEL

**Presidents**

*Visit* • 2660 Woodley Rd, NW. Visited by presidents since Kennedy.

## SHERMAN HOUSE

**Hayes**

*Visit* • 1323 K St, NW. 3–4–1877. 1881.

## SHOREHAM HOTEL

**Presidents**

*Visit* • 2500 Calvert St, NW. The old Shoreham was on the NW corner of Fifteenth and H Sts, NW. Every President since FDR has stayed either in the apartments or the hotel. The present building opened in 1930.

## "SIX BUILDINGS"

**Madison**

*Home* • 2107–2117 Pennsylvania Ave, NW. Stayed two months here during his term as secretary of state. All but 2109 demolished in the 1930s. 1801.

## SIXTEENTH ST

**Adams, JQ**

*Home* • West side of Sixteenth St between I and K Sts, NW. World Center Building now on site. 1829–1834.

**Hoover**

*Lodging* • 1628 Sixteenth Street, NW. For a few months. 1917.

## SMITHSONIAN

**Adams, JQ**

*Work* • The Castle. 1000 Jefferson Dr, SW, at Ninth St. Served as chairman of the special Smithsonian Committees of the House of Representatives. 1838–1848.

**Garfield**

*Visit* • Inaugural Ball. 1881.

**Johnson, LB**

*Visit* • Dedicated Museum of History and Technology. 1–22–1964.

**Nixon**

*Visit* • Dedicated Woodrow Wilson Center. 2–18–1971.

## SOLDIER'S HOME

**Presidents**

*Visit* • Pershing Dr, NW. 3700 block of

North Capitol St, NW. Used as summer home for presidents Pierce to Arthur.

## SPRING VALLEY

**Nixon**
*Home* • 4801 Tilden St, NW. 1951–1953.

## STATLER HOTEL (NOW NEW CAPITAL HILTON)

**Presidents**
*Visit* • 16th and K Sts NW. Used by presidents from Truman to the present.

## STROTHER'S HOTEL

**Jackson**
*Lodging* • Fourteenth St and Pennsylvania Ave, NW. Strother was the proprietor of Mansion Hotel. Jackson stayed here. 1–23–1819.

**Van Buren**
*Lodging* • Settled here in temporary quarters. November 1821.

## SUPREME COURT

**Taft**
*Work* • As Chief Justice he presided in the Senator's old home in the Capitol. 1921–1930.

## SURRATT'S BOARDING HOUSE

**Lincoln**
*Site* • 604 H St, NW. Site of assassination plot. 1865.

## SUTER'S TAVERN

**Adams, J**
*Visit* • High St (now Wisconsin Ave) between Bridge (M St) and Water Sts. It was named Fountain Inn. 1800–1801.

**Washington**
*Visit* • Met here with others to establish federal territory. 3–29–1791.

## ROBERT A. TAFT MEMORIAL BELL TOWER

**Eisenhower**
*Visit* • U.S. Capitol grounds. Dedication. 4–14–1959.

## TANEY HOUSE

**Lincoln**
*Visit* • 318 Indiana Ave, NW. Blagden Row, SE, corner of D and Third Sts, NW. Attended Chief Justice Taney's funeral here. 1864.

## BENJAMIN TAYLOE HOUSE

**Presidents**
*Visit* • 21 Madison Pl, NW, east side of LaFayette Square. Between 1829 and 1868 most presidents were entertained here. McKinley visited so often it became known as the "Little White House." 1897–1901.

## THEODORE ROOSEVELT ISLAND

**Roosevelt, T.**
*Site* • Statue.

## THIRD ST, NW

**Fillmore**
*Home* • 226 Third St, NW. Department of Labor Building on site now. 1837.

## THIRTEENTH ST, NW

**Garfield**
*Home* • 901 Thirteenth St, NW. 1869–1881.

**Hayes**
*Work* • 452 Thirteenth St. NW. While in Congress. 1865–1867.

## THIRTIETH PL, NW

**Johnson, LB**
*Home* • 4921 Thirtieth Pl, NW. 1942–1961.

## THIRTY–FIRST ST, NW

**Kennedy**
*Home* • 1528 Thirty–first St, NW. 1947–1948.

## THIRTY–FOURTH ST, NW

**Kennedy**
*Home* • 1400 Thirty–fourth St, NW. Lived here with sister Eunice and her family. 1949–1950.

## THIRTY–SEVENTH ST, NW

**Kennedy**
*Home* • 37th and O St, NW. 1947.

## TILDEN GARDENS

**Truman**
*Home* • 3000 Tilden St, NW. 1935–1936. 1940.

## TOMBS (RESTAURANT)

**Clinton**
*Visit* • 1226 36th St, NW. Often ate here while a student at Georgetown. 1964–1968.

## TREASURY BUILDING

**Grant**
*Visit* • Fifteenth St and Pennsylvania Ave, NW. Cash Room. inaugural reception. 1869.

**Jackson**
*Visit* • Established location. It is said that when in frustration he stabbed his walking cane in the ground, he declared this spot to be the site of the treasury. 1834.

**Johnson, A**
*Work* • Suite in the west wing, while Mrs. Lincoln was preparing to leave the White House. 1865.

## TUNNICLIFF'S TAVERN

**Adams, J**
*Visit* • SW corner of Ninth St and Penn-

sylvania Ave, SE. Demolished 1932. Gas station on site now. Adams visited several times. 1800.

## TWENTIETH ST, NW

**Wilson**
*Marriage* • 1308 Twentieth St, NW. Demolished in 1960; now the site of apartment building. 12–18–1915.

## TWENTY–FIRST ST, NW

**Harding**
*Home* • 1612 Twenty-First St, NW. Demolished 1960s; now wing of Phillips Gallery. 1915–1916.

## ULINE ARENA

**Eisenhower**
*Visit* • 2–5–1954. 4–4–1960.

## UNION STATION

**Presidents**
*Visit* • Massachusetts Ave at Delaware Ave, NE. Every President from Wilson to Truman arrived by train here.

**Eisenhower**
*Funeral* • Train arrived and departed from this station. 1969.

**McKinley**
*Funeral* • Coffin arrived. September 1901.

**Roosevelt, F**
*Funeral* • Coffin came and left from this station April 1945.

## UNION TAVERN

**Adams, J**
*Visit* • NE corner Bridge and Washington Sts (now M and 30th Sts). Now site of bank. 1800.

## VAN NESS MANSION

**Presidents**
*Visit* • Eighteenth and C Sts, NW. Car-

riage house remains. The Pan American Union now occupies the site. J Q Adams, Madison, Monroe, and Jackson visited.

## VARNUM HOTEL

**Jefferson**
*Lodging* • New Jersey and C Sts, SE, a block south of the Capitol. Was the house of Thomas Law, later converted to the Varnum Hotel. At one time named Congress Hall Hotel. Razed. Now site for part of the Longworth House Office Building. It was row housing at the time Jefferson was living here as vice president. 1800–1801.

**Washington**
*Visit* • Dined with his friend, Thomas Law. 1790s.

## VERMONT AVE, NW

**Harrison, B**
*Home* • 825 Vermont Ave, NW. 1881–1882.

## WALSH–McLEAN HOUSE

**Harding**
*Visit* • 2020 Massachusetts Ave, NW. Now Indonesian Embassy. 1921–1923.

## WALTER REED ARMY HOSPITAL

**Buchanan**
*Visit* • 6825 Sixteenth St, NW. 1849.

**Eisenhower**
*Visit* • Dedication of Armed Forces Institute of Pathology. 5–26–1955.
*Death* • Presidential suite. 3–28–1969.

**Lincoln**
*Visit* • When area was occupied by Fort Stevens. See boulder with plaque commemorating Sharpshooter's tree where Lincoln was under enemy fire. 1864.

## WAR DEPARTMENT

**Eisenhower**
*Work* • Pennsylvania Ave at Seventeenth St, NW, in State, War, and Navy Building. 1926. 1929–1933.

**Taft**
*Work* • Secretary of War. 1904–1908.

## WARDMAN PARK HOTEL (NOW SHERATON–WASHINGTON)

**Eisenhower**
*Home* • 2660 Woodley Rd, NW. 3-room apartment on third floor. 1942. 1944.

## WARDMAN PARK TOWER

**Hoover**
*Home* • 2600 Woodley Rd, NW. While Secretary of Commerce.

**Johnson, LB**
*Home* • 1942.

## WARWICK APARTMENTS

**Truman**
*Home* • 3051 Idaho Ave, NW. 1938.

## WASHINGTON CONVENTION CENTER

**Clinton**
*Visit* • 900 Ninth St NW. Arkansas Inauguration ball held here. 1–20–1993.

## WASHINGTON HOTEL

**Roosevelt, FD**
*Visit* • Fifteenth St, NW, around the corner from the Willard Hotel. Dinner with Vice President Garner. 2–4–1936.

## WASHINGTON MONUMENT

**Arthur**
*Visit* • Dedicated. 2–22–1885.

**McKinley**
> *Visit* • Unveiled. 1899.

**Taylor**
> *Visit* • Laid the cornerstone. 1850.

**Washington**
> *Site* • Center of the Mall at Fifteenth St, NW. See also Washington statue, Washington Circle, Pennsylvania Ave, New Hampshire Ave, and K St, NW; statue, Washington Cathedral, Mount St. Albans, Wisconsin and Cathedral Aves, NW.; statue, National Museum of History and Technology, Smithsonian.

## WESTMORELAND CONGREGATIONAL CHURCH

**Nixon**
> *Church* • Westmoreland Circle, Westmoreland Hills, about a mile from Nixon home on Tilden. 1950–.

## WHITE HOUSE

**Presidents**
> *Home* • 1600 Pennsylvania Ave NW.

**Adams, J**
> *Home* • First to occupy the White House. Arrived by coach from Philadelphia. 1800.

**Cleveland**
> *Marriage* • Blue Room. Only president to be married in the White House. 1886.

**Harrison, WH**
> *Funeral* • Services in the East Room. 1841.

**Kennedy**
> *Funeral* • Lay in state. Novemeber 1963.

**Lincoln**
> *Funeral* • Lay in state in east room. 1865.

**Taylor**
> *Funeral* • Lay in state in the east room. Services conducted here.

*Washington Monument.*

*Maret School.*

**Washington**
> *Visit* • Laid the cornerstone. 10–13–1792.

## WILLARD'S HOTEL (OLD)

**Buchanan**
> *Lodging* • Fourteenth St and Pennsylvania Ave, NW. Prior to inauguration. 1857.

**Fillmore**
> *Home* • 1837–1843. 1849–1850. Mrs. Fillmore died here 3–30–1853.

**Grant**
> *Visit* • Met Lincoln for the first time. March 1864.

**Johnson, A**
> *Home* • 1857–1862.

**Lincoln**
> *Visit* • Prior to inauguration. 1861.

**Pierce**
> *Visit* • Prior to inauguration. 1853.

**Taylor**
> *Visit* • Prior to inauguration. 1849.

**Tyler**
> *Visit* • 1849–1850.

## WILLARD HOTEL (NEW)

**Coolidge**
> *Home* • Pennsylvania Ave and Fourteenth St, NW, suite 328–332. Recently restored. 1921–1923.

**Harding**
> *Visit* • Here to meet Britton. February 1918.
>
> *Visit* • Stayed at the New Willard just before inauguration. 1921.

## WILLIAMSON'S CITY HOTEL

**Monroe**
> *Visit* • Pennsylvania Ave, between Fourteenth and Fifteenth Sts, NW. 1824.

*Home of Warren Harding.*

**Polk**
　　*Lodging* • 1826.

## WILSON BRIDGE WILSON MEMORIAL BRIDGE

**Wilson**
　　*Site* • I–495. Midway on the bridge are two aluminum medallions.

## WOODROW WILSON HOUSE MUSEUM

**Wilson**
　　*Site* • 2340 S St, NW.

## WINDER BUILDING

**Grant**
　　*Work* • 604 Seventeenth St, NW, north-

west corner of Seventeenth and F Sts. Used as Union Army headquarters. 1865.

**Lincoln**
　　*Visit* • 1861–1865.

## WOODLEY ESTATE 3000 CATHEDRAL AVE. NOW OWNED BY MARET SCHOOL.

**Cleveland**
　　*Home* • Leased this house. 1893.

**Van Buren**
　　*Home* • Summer home. 1837–1841.

## WYOMING AVE, NW

**Harding**
　　*Home* • 2314 Wyoming Ave, NW. 1915–1921.

**Taft**
　　*Home* • 2215 Wyoming Ave NW. Now site of Syrian Embassy. This was the first house that they actually owned, with the exception of Sassifern Cottage at Murray Bay. 1921–1930.

　　*Death* • 1930.

## WYOMING APARTMENTS

**Eisenhower**
　　*Home* • 2022 Columbia Rd, NW, at southeast corner Columbia Rd and Connecticut Ave, NW. Apartment 302. 1926–1936.

# FLORIDA

## BARTOW *(Polk County)*

**Taylor**
*Travel* • Marker approximately 2 1/2 miles north of Bartow on US 98. East side of the highway. Fort Fraser site. 1837–1839.

## CAPE CANAVERAL (PORT) *(Brevard County)*

**Presidents**
*Visit* • Carter, Eisenhower, Kennedy, and Nixon.

## CAPE KENNEDY *(Brevard County)*

**Johnson, LB**
*Visit* • Apollo XI launching. 1969.

## CHOCTAWATCHEE RIVER *(Washington County)*

**Jackson**
*Travel* • During military campaign, his horses swam across here. 1818.

## CLERMONT *(Lake County)*

**Presidents**
*Site* • House of Presidents, US 27, 1 mile N of FL 50. Lifesize figures of all U.S. presidents.

## CLEWISTON *(Hendry County)*

**Hoover**
*Visit* • Bishop (now Edwards) House, 325 Del Monte Ave.

*Visit* • Clewiston Inn on US 27 (E Sugarland St). 1961.

*Visit* • Dedication. Herbert Hoover Dike, off San Diego St, near Marina. Marker. 1961.

## DAYTONA BEACH *(Volusia County)*

**Harding**
*Visit* • J. G. Brown's Boarding House with meals at Parkinson House, corner of Ridgewood and Magnolia. 1900.

Florida

10
75
95

5
Tallahasee
Jacksonville

4

3

Miami
2

1

1. Truman home, *Key West*
2. Nixon home, *Key Biscayne*
3. Kennedy home, *Palm Beach*
4. Taylor home, *Tampa*
5. Jackson home, *Pensacola*

## DeBARY *(Volusia County)*

**Cleveland**
*Visit* • Entertained at DeBary mansion, Sunrise Blvd off US 17–92. 1885.

**Grant**
*Visit* • DeBary mansion. See entry above. 1880.

## ENTERPRISE *(Volusia County)*

**Grant**
*Visit* • Brock House three miles from the DeBary Mansion, S Main St off DeBary Ave. Razed. 1–9–1880.

## EVERGLADES CITY *(Collier County)*

**Truman**
*Visit* • Dedication, Everglades National Park. 12–6–1947.

## FORT BASSINGER *(Highlands County)*

**Taylor**
*Travel* • NW of Okeechobee on US 98. Marker just beyond SW corner of the bridge over Kissimmee River. 1837–1839.

## FORT FRASER *(See Bartow)*

## FORT GARDINER *(Osceola County, head of Kissimmee Lake, east of Lake Wales)*

**Taylor**
*Travel* • During Seminole Wars. 1837–1839.

## FORT GATLIN *(See Orlando)*

## FORT GEORGE *(See Pensacola)*

## FORT HEILEMAN *(See Middleburg)*

## FORT JEFFERSON *(See Key West)*

## FORT KING *(See Ocala)*

## FORT MELLON *(See Sanford)*

## FORT MYERS *(Lee County)*

**Hoover**
*Visit* • Edison's estate, 2350 McGregor Blvd. Came for celebration of Edison's birthday. February 1929.

## FORT SAN MARCOS (ST. MARKS)

*(20 miles south of Tallahassee at the junction of the Wakulla and the Apalachee Rivers)*

**Jackson**
*Travel* • Bastion Wall and Museum. 1818.

## FORT SHANNON *(See Palatka)*

## GONZALES *(See Pensacola)*

## GREEN COVE SPRINGS *(Clay County)*

All Presidents visiting came in at the wharf at Green Cove Springs.

**Arthur**
*Visit* • Magnolia Hotel. 2 miles north of Green Cove Springs. Now Magnolia Springs Apts. 1883.

**Cleveland**
*Visit* • He and others came annually to the spa. Union Hotel. 1885–1889.

**Grant**
*Visit* • Old Magnolia Hotel, 2 miles north of Green Cove Springs. Now Magnolia Springs Apts. January 1880.

## JACKSONVILLE *(Duval County)*

**Arthur**
*Visit* • St. James Hotel, west side of Laura St between Duval and Church St facing Henning Park (later site of May-Cohen Department store). 1883.

**Cleveland**
> *Visit* • St. James Hotel. See address above. 2–21–1888 to 27–1888.

**Grant**
> *Visit* • He travelled from here to Orange Park. 1880.

## JUPITER ISLAND *(Martin County)*

**Bush**
> *Church* • Christ Memorial Chapel, 52 South Beach Road (Hobe Sound). 1970–1993.

> *Lodging* • Visited his Mother's winter home SE corner Links Road No. 73 off Gomez (Hobe Sound). 1970–1993.

## KEY BISCAYNE *(Dade County)*

**Kennedy**
> *Visit* • Nixon home, Bay Lane, following election. 1960.

**Nixon**
> *Church* • Key Biscayne Presbyterian Church, 160 Harbor Dr. 1970–.

> *Home* • Bay Lane, off Harbor Drive. Bought two small houses. 1968.

> *Visit* • Key Biscayne Hotel, 750 Ocean Dr. Torn down. 1950.

> *Visit* • Key Biscayne with Charles "Bebe" Rebozo, 500 Bay Lane. 1952–.

## KEY LARGO *(Monroe County)*

**Hoover**
> *Visit* • Usually stayed at Key Largo Anglers Club (Upper Key Largo south of Blackwater Sound and north of Tarpon Basin 105–106 mi. marker). Winters, 1953–1964.

## KEY WEST *(Monroe County)*

**Cleveland**
> *Visit* • Russell House, reception. 3–22–1889.

**Taft**
> *Visit* • Boarded battleship here for trip to Panama. December 1912.

**Truman**
> *Church* • New Naval Chapel. 1945–1953.

> *Lodging* • Navy Base for Winter White House and vacations. 111 Front St. 1945–1953.

> *Visit* • Fort Jefferson National Monument. 1946. 1948.

> *Site* • Key West Little White House Museum. 111 Front St.

## LAKE OKEECHOBEE *(Okeechobee County, south of Okeechobee City near what is known as Taylor's Creek)*

> *Visit* • Old School House, 2 miles north of town on US 98. Now Okeechobee Historical Society Headquarters and Park. 1929.

**Taylor**
> *Travel* • Action in Seminole War. Now site of Zachary Taylor Camp on US 441. Monument now gone. 1837.

## LAKE WALES *(See Mountain Lake)*

## LITTLE PALM ISLAND *(Monroe County)*

**Presidents**
> *Visit* • F D Roosevelt, Truman, and Nixon vacationed here.

## LONG KEY *(Monroe County)*

**Hoover**
> *Visit* • Stayed on the houseboat *Saunterer.* February 1930.

## MAGNOLIA SPRINGS *(See Green Cove Springs)*

## MAITLAND *(Orange County)*

**Arthur**
> *Visit* • Park House at the corner of Cotton

*Kennedy Memorial in Miami.*

Tail Lane and Lake Ave, between Lake Catherine and Park Lake. Razed. 1883.

**Cleveland**
*Visit* • Park House. 1888.

**MARATHON**  *(Monroe County)*

**Presidents**
*Visit* • Eisenhower, Johnson, and Truman.

**MARIANNA**  *(Jackson County)*

**Jackson**
*Travel* • See Jackson line of march in the area including Blue Spring, Lake Jackson, and Oak Grove. 1818.

**MERRITT ISLAND**  *(Brevard County)*

**Harding**
*Visit* • Indianola House. 1895. 1921–1924.

**MIAMI**  *(Dade County)*

**Eisenhower**
*Visit* • Biltmore Hotel, staying in the Tower

Suite when the hotel was used as Pratt General Hospital, 1200 Anastasia Avenue.

**Reagan**
*Visit* • International Airport to meet Pope. Visited Vizcaya Museum. 9–10–87.

**Roosevelt, FD**
*Visit* • Biltmore Hotel. 1200 Anastasia Ave. 1936.

*Visit* • Bayfront Park Amphitheatre, Biscayne Blvd between SE Second St and SE Sixth St. Assassination attempt. February 1933.

*Site* • Gold Coast Railway Museum, 12450 Coral Reef Dr. Pullman car used by Roosevelt, Truman, Eisenhower, and Reagan. Enter at Metrozoo entrance at One hundred twenty-fourth Ave.

**MIAMI BEACH**  *(Dade County)*

**Presidents**
*Visit* • Fountainbleau Hotel, 4441 Collins Ave. Carter, Ford, L B Johnson, and Kennedy.

**Presidents**
*Visit* • Deauville Hotel, Collins Avenue. L B Johnson, Nixon, and Reagan.

**Ford**

> *Visit* • Convention Center, 1881 Washington Ave. RNC. 1968.

**Nixon**

> *Visit* • Convention Center. 1881 Washington Ave. RNC. Stayed penthouse of Hilton-Plaza Hotel. Nominated for president. 8–8–1968. 8–23–1972.

> *Visit* • Miami Heart Institute for treatment. 4701 N Meridian Ave. January 1986.

**Roosevelt, FD**

> *Visit* • Hotel Astor, 956 Washington Ave at Miami Beach. Now under different name. 1934.

## MICANOPY *(Alachua County)*

**Taylor**

> *Travel* • Site of Fort Micanopy in town center. Marker. 1838.

## MIDDLEBURG *(Clay County)*

**Taylor**

> *Travel* • Fort Heileman off FL 21 at Main and Wharf Sts. Marker. 1838.

> *Travel* • Clark-Chalker House, 3889 Main St which was built circa 1835 for headquarters of the U. S. Army for the Second Seminole War. 1838.

## MOUNT DORA *(Lake County)*

**Coolidge**

> *Visit* • Lakeside Inn, 100 N Alexander St. 1929.

## MOUNTAIN LAKE *(Polk County, near Lake Wales)*

**Coolidge**

> *Visit* • Dedication of Bok Memorial Tower, 1151 Tower Blvd (Lake Wales). 1929.

> *Visit* • Bok home for tea. Stucco house connected to the Memorial by a winding rock road. 1929.

## NEGRO FORT *(Franklin County)*

**Jackson**

> *Visit* • 1818.

## OCALA *(Marion County)*

**Grant**

> *Visit* • Silver Springs, 5656 E Silver Springs Blvd. January 1880.

**Taylor**

> *Travel* • Fort King, SE 39 Ave, Fort King Rd. Marker. 1838.

## OKEECHOBEE *(Glades County)*

**Hoover**

> *Visit* • See Lake Okeechobee.

**Taylor**

> *Travel* • Victory over Seminoles under Billy Bowlegs. See south of Okeechobee, near what is known as Taylor's Creek. 1837. See Lake Okeechobee.

## ORANGE PARK *(Duval County)*

**Grant**

> *Visit* • Florida tour. Stopped at the Park View Hotel on Kingsley Ave on the St Johns River. January 1880.

## ORLANDO *(Orange County)*

**Bush**

> *Visit* • EPCOT Center, off I-4 or US 192 south of Orlando. Asbury Hall. 9–30–1991.

> *Visit* • Church Street Station, Church St. 10–3–1992.

**Carter**

> *Visit* • Walt Disney World King Stefan's Banquet Hall and Magic Kingdom Castle, off I-4 or US 192 south of Orlando. 10–1–1978.

*Visit* • Turkey Lake Park. 10–21–1980.

*Visit* • Bookland, 5401 W Oak Ridge Rd to autograph book. 6–10–1989.

**Cleveland**
*Visit* • Tour of Orlando. April 1889.

**Clinton**
*Visit* • Lock Haven Park between Mills and Orange Aves for campaign rally. October 1992.

**Coolidge**
*Visit* • Frederick E. Godfrey House, 335 Ponce de Leon Place. 1–31–1930.

**Johnson, LB**
*Visit* • Cherry Plaza Hotel (now Lakeside Hotel apartments), corner of E Central and Osceola.

*Visit* • Motorcade Orange Ave to Colonial Dr. Colonial Plaza Shopping Center, 2560 E Colonial Dr. 10–26–1964.

**Nixon**
*Visit* • Florida Technological University (Now University of Central Florida), 4000 Central Florida Blvd. 6–8–1973.

*Visit* • Contemporary Resort Hotel in Walt Disney World. 11–17–1973.

**Reagan**
*Visit* • EPCOT Center, Community of Tomorrow. (Sheraton) Twin Towers Hotel, 5780 Major Blvd. 3–8–1983.

**Roosevelt, T**
*Visit* • San Juan Hotel, Orange Ave. 1900s.

**Taylor**
*Travel* • Fort Gatlin. Summerlin St and Gatlin Ave, Edgewood area. 1837–1838.

## PALATKA  *(Putnam County)*

**Grant**
*Visit* • Putnam House (Hotel). Site SW corner Reid and Second Sts. Now occupied by parking lot. January 1880.

**Taylor**
*Travel* • Fort Shannon at FL 100 and FL

20. Marker on Reid St (US 17) between Second and Third Sts. Stationed here. 1837–1838.

*Travel* • Powder magazine at 123 S Second Street. Now site of Presbyterian Church.

## PALM BEACH  *(Palm Beach County)*

**Harding**
*Church* • Royal Poinciana Chapel (near-Fort Worth), 60 Coconut Row next to Whitehall. 1923.

*Visit* • With McLeans. James Clark King House, Clarke Ave. 1922.

**Hoover**
*Visit* • Site of Royal Poinciana Hotel, S Lake Trail between Royal Poinciana Blvd and Cocoanut Walk on Lake Worth. Hotel closed in 1940s. Marker near entrance to Palm Beach Tower. Also attended Poinciana Chapel. January 1933.

**Kennedy**
*Church* • St. Edward's Catholic Church, Sunrise Ave at 165 North County Road. 1934–1963.

*Home* • 1095 North Ocean Dr on the ocean at the north end of the island. SE side opposite entrance to Colonial Lane where N County Rd becomes Ocean Dr. 1934–1963.

*Lodging* • C. Michael Paul villa, 601 N County Rd which was used two years as a holiday White House. Since renovated. 1961–1963.

*Visit* • St. Mary's Hospital, 901 Forty-fifth St. Hospitalized for fever. 1944.

**Truman**
*Visit* • Charles Wrightman House on 513 N County Rd (Ocean Blvd). 1950.

**Wilson**
*Visit* • Cocoanut Row and Whitehall Way at Flagler House Whitehall (Now Flagler Museum). 1900–.

## PENSACOLA *(Escambia County)*

**Bush**

*Visit* • Pensacola Naval Station and Museum, FL 395, Navy Blvd. 3–7–1992.

**Carter**

*Work* • Pensacola Naval Station, FL 395, Navy Blvd. 1946.

**Jackson**

*Home* • SE corner S Palafox and E Intendencia Sts. Bronze marker on building.

*Work* • Government House on the Plaza. July 17 to October 8, 1821. Plaza Ferdinand VII, S Palafox St between E Government and E Zarragossa Sts. Remnants only. Site of surrender now occupied by Chipley Monument. 1821.

*Travel* • Fort George at Palafox and Jackson Sts. His military camp was on the west side of Pensacola at Galvez Springs, Cantonment Clinch, but the attack was made from the east side. 1814, 1821.

*Visit* • Vacaria Baja, home of Don Manuel Gonzalez, Cantonment on Palafox Hwy, US 29. 1821.

*Visit* • Tivoli Theater, SW corner Zaragoza and Barracks St. 1821.

**Roosevelt, T**

*Visit* • Wright St at Tarragona St with Rough Riders. 1898.

## ST. AUGUSTINE *(St. Johns County)*

**Arthur**

*Church* • St. Paul's African Methodist Episcopal on Central Ave. Nothing remains. April 1883.

*Church* • Trinity Episcopal Church, 215 St. George St at the corner of King St. Oldest section is north transcept. Almost completely rebuilt in the early 1900s with the exception of the north transcept and the baptistry. 1883.

*Visit* • Magnolia Hotel on the corner of St. George and Hypolita Sts. Park on site. Burned 1927. April 1883.

*Visit* • St. Francis Barracks/State Arsenal off Marine St. Now headquarters Department of Military Affairs. 1883.

**Cleveland**

*Visit* • Hotel Ponce de Leon. Cordova St between King and Valencia Sts. Now Flagler College. March 1889.

**Grant**

*Visit* • Hotel Ponce de Leon. 1880

**Harding**

*Visit* • Hotel Ponce de Leon. 1918, 1921, 1923. Edward McLean villa. 1922.

**Johnson, LB**

*Visit* • St. Joseph's Academy, corner St George and Bridge Sts, while Vice President. 1963

**Roosevelt, T**

*Church* • Flagler Memorial Presbyterian

*Church* • 36 Sevilla St. October 1905.

*Visit* • Hotel Ponce de Leon. 10–22–1905

*Visit* • Fort San Marcos. San Marco Avenue. 1905.

## ST. PETERSBURG *(Pinellas County)*

**Coolidge**

*Visit* • Vinoy Stouffer Resort Hotel, 501 Fifth Ave NE on Snell Isle on the water front. January 1930.

**Hoover**

*Visit* • Vinoy Stouffer Resort Hotel. 1930–1933.

## SANFORD *(Seminole County)*

**Arthur**

*Church* • Episcopal Church of the Holy Cross, 410 S Magnolia Ave, corner of W Fourth St and Park Ave. 1883.

*Visit* • Hotel Sanford, between Commercial and First St. Now library site. 1883.

**Cleveland**

*Visit* • Hotel Sanford. The city of Sanford hosted the first South Florida Fair which

President and Mrs. Cleveland attended. 1887. 3–21–1889.

### Grant
*Visit* • Inaugurated the South Florida Railroad project. Shovel used by Grant is on display in the Henry Shelton Sanford Library and Museum on First St and Pine Ave. 1–10–1880.

*Visit* • Hotel Sanford.

*Visit* • Railroad station site and original tracks. W Twenty-fifth Street and Old Lake Mary Rd. 1880.

### Taylor
*Travel* • Fort Mellon. Marker Mellonville Ave and E Second St. 1837–1838.

## SILVER SPRINGS *(See Ocala)*

### Presidents
*Visit* • McKinley 1899, Nixon 1970, Carter 1980, and Clinton 1995.

### Carter
*Visit* • Governor's Mansion, 700 N Adams St. 10–9–1980.

*Visit* • State Capitol. Addressed House of Representatives. 10–10–1980.

*Visit* • North Florida Fairgrounds. 10–9–1980.

### Clinton
*Visit* • Governor's Mansion. 3–30–1990. State Capitol. Addressed joint session of legislature. 1995.

### Taylor
*Visit* • Territorial capital. Site of present Capitol. 1838.

## TAMPA *(Hillsborough County)*

### Cleveland
*Visit* • Cherokee Club (El Pasje (now restaurant), 1318 1/2 Ninth Ave, Avenida Republica de Cuba and Ninth Ave. Ybor City section. March 1889.

### Clinton
*Travel* • Performing Arts Center, 1010 N MacInnes Pl. Opening drive to support Universal Health plan. September 1993.

### Johnson, LB
*Visit* • Courthouse, Madison and Pierce Sts. 10–12–1960.

### Kennedy
*Visit* • National Guard Armory, Howard Ave. Spoke. 1963.

*Visit* • Marker in front of Courthouse at Madison and Pierce Streets where he gave an address. 10–8–1963.

### Roosevelt, T
*Visit* • El Pasje Hotel. 1898.

*Visit* • Tampa Bay Hotel, Plant Park between Lafayette and Cass Sts on W Kennedy Blvd. The University of Tampa now occupies the former hotel building. June 1898.

*Visit* • Cherokee Club. 1898.

*Visit* • Crossroads, Seventh Ave and Twenty-second Street, Ybor City section. May and June 1898.

*Work* • National Guard Armory, Howard Ave., Rough Riders encampment. Camp site. 1898.

### Taylor
*Home* • Family quarters. Headquarters. 1837–1838. See marker site of Fort Brooke below.

*Visit* • Old Government Spring, Fifth Ave and Thirteenth St. Brewery. Ybor City section.

*Travel* • Fort Brooke, SW corner Platt and Franklin Sts. Bronze plaque marks the site.

## VERO BEACH *(Indian River County)*

### Nixon
*Visit* • Driftwood Hotel, 3150 Ocean Dr. 1951.

## WINTER PARK *(Orange County)*

### Arthur
*Visit* • Railway Station, Atlantic Coast Line. Site was on Morse Blvd immediately

north of the present station. Tracks ran from the Seminole Hotel on New England Ave through East Park to the station. None of this remains. 1883.

*Visit* • Seminole Hotel. Burned 1902. Site corner of Chase and Osceola Aves on Lake Osceola. 250 Chase Ave NE. Beautiful lawns still exist. April 1883.

*Visit* • Rogers House (later Virginia Inn) on Lake Osceola, corner of what is now Interlachen Ave at SE corner Morse and Interlaken. Now Cloisters Condominium. He was entertained here. Demolished 1966. April 1883.

*Visit* • Lewis Lawrence House at 1300 Summerland Ave. 1883.

### Bush

*Visit* • Thom Rumberger House, 1015 Greentree Dr. 1990–1993.

### Cleveland

*Visit* • Seminole Hotel. 250 Chase Ave NE. 2–24–1889.

### Coolidge

*Visit* • Recreation Hall, Rollins College, 1000 Holt Ave. 1929.

### Roosevelt, FD

*Visit* • Rollins College, Knowles Memorial Chapel, 1000 Holt Ave. 1936.

### Truman

*Visit* • Reception, Rollins College, Knowles Chapel. 3–8–1949.

*Visit* • Dedicated causeway over Lake Estelle on Mills St. Marker. N Mills at Lake Shore. March 1949.

*Visit* • Home of Dr. Holt, President of Rollins College at 208 N Interlaken. Still exists but greatly altered.

# GEORGIA

## AMERICUS *(Sumter County)*

**Carter**

*Education* • Southwestern College, Wheatley St. Administration Bldg. 1941–1942.

*Site* • James Earl Carter Library and Museum. Wheatley St.

## ARCHERY *(Sumter County)*

**Carter**

*Home* • Off US 280 about 3 miles from Plains. 1927–1946.

## ATLANTA *(Dekalb/Fulton Counties)*

**Presidents**

*Visit* • State Capitol, Washington St. B Harrison, McKinley, Nixon, T Roosevelt, and Taft.

*Visit* • Governor's Mansion, SW corner Peachtree and Cain Sts. Demolished 1923 and Henry Grady Hotel placed on site. Now Westin Peachtree Plaza Hotel on site. Cain St is now International Blvd. Cleveland, B Harrison, Hayes, McKinley, T Roosevelt, and Taft. 1870–1921.

*Visit* • Governor's Mansion, fronting on the Prado. Coolidge, Eisenhower, Hoover, L B Johnson, Kennedy, F Roosevelt, and Truman. 1925–1967. Governor's Mansion 39F1 West Paces Ferry Rd. Since 1967.

**Bush**

*Visit* • Martin Luther King, Jr. tomb, Martin Luther King, Jr. Center, 449 Auburn Ave. 1–17–1992.

**Carter**

*Church* • Northside Baptist Church, 3100 Northside Dr NW at intersection with Northside Parkway. 1971–1975.

*Church* • Ebenezer Baptist Church, 407 Auburn Ave NE. 1–14–1979.

*Education* • Georgia Institute of Technology, 225 North Ave, NW. Math classes in D.M. Smith Building (now Ivan Allen College Management Policy and Intnl Affairs). 1942–1943.

*Education* • Room 308 Knowles Dormitory on campus (now site of Bobby Dodd

1. Carter Library, *Americus*
2. Carter home, *Atlanta*
3. Carter home, *Ellijay*
4. Eisenhower home, *Columbus*
5. Carter birthplace, *Plains*
6. Wilson home, *Rome*
7. Roosevelt home, *Warm Springs*

Atlanta

Georgia

*Carter Presidential Center.*

Stadium at Grant Field), Techwood Dr at North Ave. 1942–1943.

**Home** • Governor's mansion West Ferry Paces Rd. 1971–1975.

**Work** • State Capitol, Senate Chamber, Washington St between Hunter and Mitchell Sts. 1963–1967.

**Lodging** • Grady Hotel, 210 Peachtree St NW. 1963–1965.

**Work** • (Senate) Piedmont Hotel, 108 Peachtree St NW. 1965–1967.

**Work** • Governor's office, State Capitol. 1971–1975.

**Work** • Emory University, 1380 S Oxford Rd NE. Carter Center, Emory University, established November 1983. 1982.

**Visit** • State Capitol, Senate Chamber and House Chamber. Unveiled portrait. 2-20-1979.

**Visit** • Governor's Mansion 9–15–80. Ebenezer Baptist church, 407 Auburn Ave. NE. 9–16–80.

**Visit** • Emory University Hospital, 1440 Clifton Rd NE. Surgery. 1984.

**Visit** • Omni Coliseum, 100 Techwood Ave. July 1988. Also here 6–16–1978.

**Visit** • Everybody's Pizza near Emory University, 1040 N Highland Ave NE. 1986–.

**Visit** • Manuel's Tavern, N Highland Ave, 1986–.

**Site** • Carter Memorial Library at N Highland and Cleburne Aves at One Copenhill, two miles east of downtown. Opened 10–1–1986.

**Cleveland**
**Visit** • Kimball House, SW corner Decatur and Pryor Sts on site of old Atlanta Hotel.

Kimball House Restaurant still operating. 10–19–1887.

*Visit* • Piedmont Exposition on Fourteenth St, then called Wilson Ave. Extended from Peachtree Rd at the present Fourteenth St. to the Richmond and Danille Railroad tracks on the east. October 1887.

*Visit* • Porter House, 330 Peachtree St, SW corner of Peachtree and Porter Pl. Sold 1913 and small business on site. October 1887.

*Visit* • Piedmont Driving Club, Piedmont Ave and Tenth St. Today the Club is located at Piedmont and Fifteenth St. October 1887.

### Clinton

*Travel* • Omni, 100 Techwood Ave. 1988.

*Visit* • Carter Memorial Library. 1992. See location under Carter.

### Coolidge

*Visit* • Georgian Terrace Hotel, Northeast corner of Peachtree and Ponce de Leon. See marker near hotel. 1–26–1921.

### Fillmore

*Visit* • Atlanta Hotel, SW corner Decatur and Pryor Sts. Later site of Kimball House. May 1854.

### Grant

*Visit* • On his first and only visit to Atlanta, stayed at a boarding house later known as the Ivy Street Hospital. 1865.

### Jackson

*Travel* • Fort Peachtree on Ridgewood Rd at Ridgewood Circle off Bolton Rd. Marker. War of 1812.

### Johnson, LB

*Visit* • Dinkler Plaza Hotel, 210 Peachtree St NW. 5–8–1964.

### Nixon

*Visit* • Ebenezer Baptist Church, 407 Auburn Avenue NE for funeral Martin Luther King, Jr. 4–9–1968.

### Reagan

*Visit* • Atlanta Hilton, 255 Courtland St. 7–30–1981.

*Visit* • Dedication of Carter Presidential Library, One Copenhill. 10–1–1986.

### Roosevelt, FD

*Visit* • Institute Technology Stadium, Techwood Housing Project, for dedication. Corner North and Techwood. 11–29–1935.

*Funeral* • Funeral train passed through Atlanta en route to Washington. Moved under Peachtree St at Brookwood Station, Peachtree Rd at Deering. 1945.

### Roosevelt, T

*Visit* • Piedmont Park. Arrived at new Terminal Station and was taken to the park for speech. Lunch at the Piedmont Driving Club and a visit to Georgia Tech campus. Wm B Russell Bldg is now on Terminal Station site. 10–20–1905.

### Taft

*Visit* • Arrived on special train at old Union Depot car shed. First time a city guest had been driven by automobile instead of carriage. Union Station now parking lot.

*Visit* • City Auditorium for speech in Taft Hall (now Alumni Hall), Courtland and Washington Sts. between Edgewood and Gilmer. 1–16–1909.

### Wilson

*Church* • First Presbyterian Church, a wooden building at Peachtree and Houston Sts. Present church Peachtree St and Sixteenth St NE. 1882–1883.

*Home* • Mrs. J. Reid Boylston House at 344 Peachtree St. Site now office buildings. While here he often visited William Daniel Grant home, SW corner of Peachtree and Vine Sts. Site now parking lot. 1882–1883.

*Work* • Central Building at the SW corner of East Alabama and Main Sts. SE corner Marietta and Forsyth Sts. Became Alfahhua Bank Bldg and has plaque in the window. 1882–1883.

*Work* • 48 Marietta St., Room 10, second floor back. Opened a law office with Edward I. Renick. May 1882–mid 1883.

## AUGUSTA *(Richmond County)*

**Eisenhower**

*Church* • St. James Methodist Church, 439 Greene St. 1954.

*Visit* • Augusta National Golf Club, NW of city on Berckmans Rd. At first in a cottage belonging to Robert T. Jones. Later in country club house near the tenth tee. While president he had an office near the cottage. 1948–1953. He visited 45 times (last time was October 1967).

**Fillmore**

*Visit* • Received at City Hall and reception at Augusta Hotel. 1854.

**Grant**

*Visit* • 1–1–1880.

**Harding**

*Visit* • Bon Air-Vanderbilt Hotel, corner of Walton Way and Hickman Rd. 1918.

**Hayes**

*Visit* • The Exposition, now site of Paine College, 1235 Fifteenth St. 1891.

**Taft**

*Church* • Tabernacle Baptist Church, 1223 Laney-Walker Blvd. Still there.

*Church* • St. Paul's Episcopal Church, 605 Reynolds St. 1908.

*Church* • St. James Methodist Episcopal Church, 439 Greene St. 1909.

*Church* • Negro Great Bethel Church (Bethel African), 839 Ninth St. 1909. 1910.

*Visit* • Bon Air Hotel, corner of Walton Way and Hickman Rd. Still existing. 1908, 1909.

**Washington**

*Visit* • Richmond Academy. Was a wooden building on Bay Street. Stayed Mrs. Dixon's boarding house near the Richmond Academy. May 1791.

**Wilson**

*Church* • 624 Telfair Street at First Presbyterian Church. 1858–1870.

*Church* • Greene Street Presbyterian Church, 1235 Greene St. 1858–1870.

*Education* • Briefly attended school run by Joseph T. Derry, The Houghton Institute, 69 Greene St. Building burned 1916. 1858.

*Home* • NW corner Telfair and Seventh St. Manse, a large comfortable residence (now private home). See also barn where "Lighthouse Club" met. 1858–1870.

## BAINBRIDGE *(Decatur County)*

**Jackson**

*Travel* • Camp Recovery. See marker at corner Shotwell and Broad opposite First Presbyterian Church.

## CALHOUN *(Gordon County)*

**Carter**

*Visit* • First Baptist Church, 411 College St. 4–10–77. 4–22–79.

## CHICKAMAUGA *(Off US 27 near Ft. Oglethorpe)*

**Eisenhower**

*Work* • Fort Oglethorpe close to the Chattanooga-Chickamauga National Military Park. 1917–1918.

*Lodging* • Bachelor quarters at 14 Barnhardt Circle a few houses up from what is today known as Captain's Quarters. 1917–1918.

**Garfield**

*Work* • Gordon-Lee Mansion, Rosencranz Headquarters, Chickamauga Battlefield. 1863.

**Grant**

*Travel* • 1863.

## COLUMBUS *(Muscogee County)*

**Fillmore**

*Visit* • St. Elmo Mansion, 2810 St. Elmo Dr (Eighteenth St). 1854.

**Polk**

*Visit* • St. Elmo Mansion. On tour of the South upon leaving the White House. 1849.

**Roosevelt, FD**
*Visit* • Springer Opera House at First Ave and Tenth St. 1928.

## CRAWFORD  *(See Lexington)*

## CUMBERLAND ISLAND  *(Camden County, off the mainland)*

**Grant**
*Visit* • Dungeness (ruins), 1–5–1880.

## EBENEZER  *(Effingham County)*

**Washington**
*Visit* • Tavern off FL 21 on FL 275. Marker. 1791.

## ELLIJAY  *(Gilmer County)*

**Carter**
*Home* • Vacation home on Turnip Town Creek. 1982–present.

## FORT BENNING (COLUMBUS)
*(Muscogee County, US 27 on Fort Benning Blvd at Outpost 1.)*

**Eisenhower**
*Home* • 206 Austin Loop. See also marker at entrance to Austin from Vibbert Ave. 1926–1927.

*Work* • Coached the football team. Executive officer of 24th Infantry Regiment. See Doughboy Athletic Field on Vibbert Ave. 1926.

## FORT OGLETHORPE  *(Catoosa County, SE of Chattanooga off US 27)*

**Eisenhower**
*Work* • Teaching officer candidates. 1917.

## FORT SCOTT  *(Decatur County, near Florida border SE of Bainbridge)*

**Jackson**
*Travel* • Took formal command of regu-

lars and Militia fighting the Seminoles. No trace of Fort Scott remains. 1818.

## GAINESVILLE  *(Hall County)*

**Jackson**
*Visit* • Robert Young plantation house near the forks of the old Atlanta Hwy, FL 13 and Hog Mountain Road. Historical marker. Here while fighting the Indians. Travelled Old Federal Road along FL 53 to FL 13. 1818.

**Monroe**
*Visit* • Travelled the Old Federal Road along FL 53 to FL 13. 1819.

**Roosevelt, FD**
*Visit* • Roosevelt Square. Bronze arm supports can be seen in local high school. Dedication, Roosevelt Monument. 3–23–1938.

**Wilson**
*Visit* • House, Broad Street (renamed Jesse Jewell). Torn down and now site of Holiday Inn.

## HEROD  *(Terrell County)*

**Jackson**
*Travel* • Marker County Rd S1526 at junction with FL 55 between Sasser and Herod.

## HOSCHTON  *(Jackson County, near junction of FL 53 and FL 211)*

**Jackson**
*Travel* • During Seminole Wars. On FL 124 near watertower of Jackson County Water Authority (south of I-85). Headquarters. Was a log house. Nothing remains. 1818.

## LEXINGTON  *(Oglethorpe County, on US 78 between Lexington and Crawford)*

**Monroe**
*Visit* • Woodlawn, home of Senator Wm H Crawford. Destroyed by fire 1936. 1819.

## Van Buren

*Visit* • Woodlawn. 1837.

## MACON   *(Bibb County)*

### Fillmore

*Visit* • Hotel Lanier. SE corner Second and Mulberry. Site only. Hotel burned in the 1940s. 1854.

*Visit* • City Hall on Poplar St at intersection with Cotton Ave and First St. Was State Capitol from November 18, 1864, to March 11, 1865. 1854.

## MILNER   *(Lamar County)*

### Presidents

*Visit* • Gachet House, 3 miles west of Barnesville. Visited by Lafayette in 1825.

## MULBERRY GROVE   *(Effingham County, near Rincon)*

### Washington

*Visit* • General Green House. 12 miles NW of Savannah. Sign on highway to Augusta near Monteith station. The plantation house was on the bank of the Savannah River and is now almost impossible to reach. Same plantation where Eli Whitney invented the cotton gin. Burned during the Civil War. Site only (was the settlement of St. Joseph's Town). 1791.

## OXFORD   *(Newton County, near Covington)*

### Fillmore

*Visit* • Orna Villa, home of his friend Dr. Alex Means, 1008 Emory St. Built 1797. On FL 81 N. Now private home.

## PLAINS   *(Sumter County)*

### Carter

*Birthplace* • Hospital Street, Wise Sanitarium (now Convalescent Home).

*Baptism* • Plains Baptist Church, Bond St. Attended. 1924–1981.

*Church* • Marantha Baptist Church, Buena Vista Rd. 1981 to present.

*Education* • Plains High School, Bond St. 1930–1941.

*Marriage* • Plains Methodist Church, Church St. 1946.

*Home* • Church Street (now the Wellon House), upstairs apartment. 1924.

*Home* • Bond Street. Detroyed by fire. 1924–1927.

*Home* • Old Preston Road, Archery. About 3 miles from Plains. 1927–1944.

*Home* • Church Street (Mother's house). Two months. 1953.

*Home* • Olive Street, apartment No. 9. 1953.

*Home* • Old Montgomery House on outskirts of Plains. 1954–1956.

*Home* • Dr. Thad Wise's House on Old Preston Rd near the house where he grew up. ("The Haunted House.") 1956–1961.

*Home* • Woodlawn Dr. 1961–1971. 1957–1977. 1981–.

*Work* • Carter Peanut Warehouse—former business center on Main St. 1953–1971.

*Work* • Depot (off Church Street) campaign headquarters, Hudson and Main Sts. 1976.

*Site* • Carter Family Cemetery, near Archery.

## RINCON   *(See Mulberry Grove)*

## ROME   *(Floyd County)*

### Roosevelt, T

*Visit* • US 27. Martha Berry School for Girls at the white Colonial Administration Building.

*Visit* • Roosevelt Cabin on campus built for his use. Also visited Louisa Hall. 1910.

## Wilson

*Church* • First Presbyterian, 101 E Third St. 1875–1882.

*Lodging* • James W. Bones home, 205 E 10th St. 1875–1882.

*Lodging* • 709 Broad St (Featherstone Place). Citizens Bank now on site. 1875–1882.

*Lodging* • Oak Park SW of the Yancey Place. 1875–1882.

*Lodging* • Brower House. 6 Coral Ave. 1875–1882.

*Lodging* • Manse at 304 E Fourth Ave. 1867–1869.

*Lodging* • Presbyterian Manse, 402 E Third Ave corner of present Fourth St and Third Ave. Torn down. 1875–1882.

*Marriage* • Silver Creek spring (Spring Creek just east of Lindale). Picnic. FL 1E from Rome to Boozeville. South of Boozeville take Booze Mountain Rd. 1882.

*Visit* • Berry College. Administration Building (now Hoge Building), 2277 Martha Berry Blvd. 1910.

## ROSWELL  *(Fulton County)*

### Roosevelt, T

*Visit* • Bulloch mansion at the end of Bulloch Ave. The home of his maternal grandparents. Visited and spoke in Roswell Town Square. 1905.

## ST. SIMON'S ISLAND  *(Glynn County, off shore)*

### Carter

*Visit* • Musgrove Plantation on Lawrence Rd and Fredrika. 1977. 3–18–1978 to 3–20–1978.

## SAPELLO ISLAND  *(McIntosh County, off shore)*

### Carter

*Church* • First African Baptist Church. 1977.

*Visit* • South End House. Vacations. Also stayed at Musgrove Plantation, Grove House cottage. Fishing in the area of St. Simon's Island. 1977–1981.

### Coolidge

*Visit* • South End House (the Spalding home or Coffin Estate).

*Travel* • December 1928.

### Hoover

*Visit* • South End House. Christmas dinner guest of Howard E. Coffin.

## SAVANNAH  *(Chatham County)*

### Presidents

*Visit* • In October 1970, Nixon became the nineteenth president to visit this city. Harding 1920, Coolidge 1926, Hoover 1932, Kennedy 1962, Theodore Roosevelt 1911, and Truman 1962. Others noted below.

### Arthur

*Visit* • Monterey Square on Bull St between Taylor and Gordon Sts at home of Mrs. Henry Botts, 126 W Liberty. Now site of Liberty Inn. 1883.

### Fillmore

*Church* • Independent Presbyterian, Bull St and Oglethorpe Ave. 1854.

*Visit* • Pulaski House, 4 Bryan St at NW corner of Bull St, Johnson Square. House no longer standing. 1854.

### Grant

*Visit* • Screven House, SE corner Bull and Congress Sts. Hotel razed 1880s. Bank now on site.

### McKinley

*Visit* • W. W. Gordon House at northeast corner of Bull St and Oglethorpe Ave. A stuccoed brick dwelling with a small Ionic portico. Juliette Low House. 1896.

*Visit* • Green-Meldrim House on Macon St. Now the parish house St. John's Episcopal Church. SW corner of Lafayette Square. 1896.

### Monroe

*Visit* • Independent Presbyterian at SW corner of Bull St and Oglethorpe Ave. The church built in 1889 was a copy of the one built in 1815 and destroyed by fire in 1889. Monroe dedicated the old church.

*Visit* • William Scarbrough House (now Martin Luther King Blvd), 41 W Broad St which later became a public school building. 1819.

### Nixon

*Visit* • Hunter Army Airfield. Dedicated Ocean Science Center. 10–8–70.

### Polk

*Church* • Independent Presbyterian. Bull St and Oglethorpe Ave. Detroyed by fire 1889. 1849.

*Visit* • Pulaski House. See address above under Fillmore.

### Roosevelt, FD

*Visit* • 200th anniversary celebration. Rode down Broughton St; address at Grayson Stadium.

### Taft

*Visit* • Gordon House. See entry under McKinley. Now National Girl Scout Birthplace shrine. 1909.

### Washington

*Church* • Christ Episcopal, Bull S between E St, Julian, and E Congress. Present structure is third on the site. (John Wesley preached here.) East side of Johnson Square. 1791.

*Visit* • Lachlan-McIntosh House, 110 E Oglethorpe Ave. 1791.

*Visit* • House at St. James Square (now Telfair Place) at NW corner of Barnard and State Sts. 1791.

### Wilson

*Church* • Independent Presbyterian, Bull St and Oglethorpe Ave. 1880s.

*Church* • Anderson Street Presbyterian at NE corner of Anderson and Barnard Sts (Now Hull Memorial Presbyterian at Bull and Thirty-seventh Sts). 1880s.

*Marriage* • Manse next door to the Independent Presbyterian Church, home of the bride's paternal grandfather. The Axson Memorial Building constructed in 1928 on the site of the manse has a reproduction of the manse parlor where the wedding took place. Bull St and Oglethorpe Ave. 1885.

*Visit* • Screven Hotel near the Independent Presbyterian Church. See address above. 1885.

*Visit* • 143 Broad St (Presbyterian Manse and home of his wife's grandparents). 1885.

*Visit* • 164 Hall St with Randolph Axson. Now empty lot. 1891.

## SEA ISLAND *(Glynn County, off shore)*

### Bush

*Honeymoon* • Cloister Hotel, Sea Island Dr. 1945.

### Coolidge

*Visit* • Cloister Hotel on Sea Island Drive. Christmas 1928.

### Eisenhower

*Visit* • Cloister Hotel. 1946.

### Ford

*Visit* • Cloister Hotel. 1974.

## THOMASVILLE *(Thomas County)*

### Eisenhower

*Visit* • Milestone Plantation as a hunting retreat, George M. Humphrey estate. Near Thomasville, 4.8 miles east on Metcalf Rd. 1953–61.

### McKinley

*Visit* • 830 N Dawson St at Hanna-McKinley House where as presidential candidate he met with Republican leaders. 1895.

## TIFTON  *(Tift County)*

**Carter**

*Education* • Georgia Experimental Station. 1953.

## WARM SPRINGS  *(Meriwether County off I-285 or I-85 or FL 85 W on to FL 190.)*

**Roosevelt**

*Home* • Little White House. 1924–1945.

*Church* • Chapel built 1937 on the Foundation Ground opposite Georgia Hall on Oak Rd.

*Visit* • Roosevelt Farm, FL 85W four miles south of Warm Springs at entrance to Pine Mountain Trail west side of highway. See marker.

*Visit* • Marker old Depot site on FL 85W at Alt 27 intersection.

*Visit* • Outdoor Treatment Pool (original treatment center) south side US 27 alt west of FL 85W.

*Death* • Little White House. 1945.

## WASHINGTON  *(Wilks County. First town to be incorporated in Washington's name, 1790.)*

**Wilson**

*Church* • Washington Presbyterian Church 312 E Robert Toombs Ave where his father was often a visiting preacher. 1860s.

*Visit* • 47 Spring St at Barnett-Edwards House. Near the city limits. Visited here as boy when his father preached. Beautifully restored. 1860s.

# HAWAII

**Presidents**

*Visit* • Every President beginning with Franklin Roosevelt has stopped in Hawaii.

## HONOLULU *(Honolulu County)*

**Bush**

*Work* • Pearl Harbor for rest and recreation. 1944.

*Visit* • Pearl Harbor National Cemetery of the Pacific, USS *Arizona* Memorial, Kilo Pier 8, USS *Missouri*. 12–7–1991.

**Ford**

*Visit* • Pearl Harbor, USS *Arizona* Memorial. 12–7–1975.

**Harding**

*Visit* • Beach Hotel. 1915.

**Kennedy**

*Visit* • Hawaiian Village Hotel, 2005 Kalia Rd. 6–8–1963.

**Nixon**

*Visit* • Royal Hawaiian Hotel, 2259 Kalakaua Ave. April 1952.

**Reagan**

*Visit* • St. Andrew's Cathedral. Governor's Mansion. Lodging at Kahala Hilton Hotel, 5000 Kahala Ave. April 1984.

**Roosevelt, FD**

*Visit* • Washington Place for dinner with Governor. Lunch at the Schofield Barracks. Overnight at the Royal Hawaiian Hotel. Dedicated Ala Moana Park. Planted a kukui tree at Iolani Palace. 7–26–1934. Met with MacArthur. 1944.

**Truman**

*Visit* • On the way to meet MacArthur on Wake Island. 1950.

## KILAUEA *(Hilo Island)*

**Eisenhower**

*Travel* • Military camp. 1946.

## OAHU *(Honolulu County)*

**Carter**

*Home* • Nimitz Naval housing, 318 Sixth St. Two-bedroom complex for married officers. 1949–1950.

Honolulu

Hawaii

1. Pearl Harbor

# IDAHO

## BOISE *(Ada County)*

**Presidents**
*Visit* • Every president from Hoover to Bush has visited Boise.

**Carter**
*Visit* • Rodeway Inn, Suite 400, Chinden Blvd and Twenty-ninth St. Garden City. Vacation Camp Indian Creek, Middle Fork Salmon River. 8–21–1978 to 8–24–1978.

**Eisenhower**
*Visit* • State Capitol. Bordered by Jefferson, W State, Sixth and Eighth Sts. 8–19–1952.

**Harrison, B**
*Visit* • First US president to visit. Planted a water oak on grounds and spoke in front of the old Capitol building, which has been torn down. 5–8–1891.

**Roosevelt, FD**
*Visit* • Spoke corner of Capitol Blvd and Bannock, State Capitol. 9–27–1937.

**Roosevelt, T**
*Visit* • Planted a sugar maple on Capitol grounds. Idhana Hotel at NE corner of Main and Tenth Sts. 5–29–1903.

**Taft**
*Visit* • State Capitol. 10–9–1911. Planted an Ohio Buckeye. 1915.

## POCATELLO *(Bannock County)*

**Taft**
*Visit* • Attended dedication of the Oregon Short Line depot. 1915.

## TWIN FALLS *(Twin Falls County)*

**Presidents**
*Visit* • Kennedy, LB Johnson, and Ford before they became president.

**Reagan**
*Visit* • First US president to visit while in office. 10–31–1986.

1. State Capitol, *Boise*

Idaho

1 Boise

Idaho
Falls

84

86

84

# ILLINOIS

## ALTON *(Madison County)*

**Lincoln**
*Site* • Broadway at end of Market St. Last of the Great Debates. Plaque. 10–15–1858.

**Roosevelt, FD**
*Travel* • Railroad platform, 3400 College. 10–14–1936.

## AMBOY *(Lee County)*

**Lincoln**
*Visit* • 106 Main St. Boulder marks site where he spoke. 8–26–1858.

## ANNA *(Union County)*

**Grant**
*Travel* • Camp site here. May 1861.

## BEARDSTOWN *(Cass County)*

**Lincoln**
*Work* • Black Hawk War. Recreation park at north end of Wall St. Plaque on a rock marks spot. 1832.

*Work* • Old City Hall on Public Square, where he practiced law. 1858.

*Site* • City Hall at W Third and State St holds original courtroom where he defended "Duff" Armstrong in a murder trial. 1840s. Debate 1858.

*Visit* • City Square. Granite memorial marks site where he spoke during senatorial campaign.

## BEMENT *(Platt County)*

**Lincoln**
*Site* • Bryant House off IL 105 at 146 E Wilson St. Site where Lincoln and Douglas planned their debates. State memorial. 7–29–1858.

## BERWYN *(Cook County)*

**Lincoln**
*Site* • Statue, *Lincoln, the Friendly Neighbor.* SE corner Cermak Rd and Riverside Dr.

Illinois

Chicago

Springfield

88

55

57

74

72

1. Lincoln home,
   *Charleston*
2. Lincoln home, *Decatur*
3. Lincoln home, *Dixon*
4. Grant home, *Galena*
5. Replica of courthouse
   Lincoln practiced law,
   *Havana*
6. Lincoln home,
   *Springfield*
7. Regan birthplace,
   *Tampico*

## BLOOMINGTON  (McLean County)

**Lincoln**

*Visit* • Majors Hall, where Lincoln made his Lost Speech. S Main and E Front Sts. Tablet. Miller-Davis Houses, 101 N Main, used as temporary office. 1858.

## BUNKER HILL  (Macoupin County)

**Lincoln**

*Site* • Main St. Lincoln statue.

## CAIRO  (Alexandria County)

**Grant**

*Home* • 609 Ohio St. Family lived in rooms on second floor opposite to his head-quarters. 1861.

*Visit* • St. Charles Hotel at Ohio and Sec-ond St. Later known as Halliday House. Burned 1943. 1861.

*Visit* • 1000 E Monroe. Clover Lawn, where he visited his close friend, David Davis. 1881.

*Visit* • Magnolia Manor, Seventh and Washington Ave. Attended reception on re-turn from world tour. Now a museum. 1880.

## CARLINVILLE  (Macoupin County)

**Lincoln**

*Visit* • S Broad and First South St. Bronze boulder marking site of address given. 8–3–1858.

## CARMI  (White County)

**Lincoln**

*Visit* • Ratcliff Inn. 216 E Main St. Now a museum. 1840.

## CARTHAGE  (Hancock County)

**Lincoln**

*Visit* • Courthouse on the Square. Ad-dressed 6000 here. Stone marker south of the courthouse entrance. 10–22–1858.

## CHAMPAIGN-URBANA  (Champaign County)

**Lincoln**

*Work* • County courthouse, Main St and Broadway. Marble tablet on second floor marks the site. 1853–1854.

## CHARLESTON  (Coles County)

**Lincoln**

*Home* • Lived at Goose Neck Prairie (Lin-coln Log Cabin State Park) nine miles south of town. Reconstructed cabin stands on original foundation. See also Shiloh Cemetery NW of park where Thomas and Sarah Lincoln are buried. 1831.

*Visit* • Moore House on S Fourth St, 1 mile north of park. He paid his last visit to his stepmother here. 1861.

*Work* • Courthouse (remodeled) on the town square. He practiced law here. 1837–1861.

*Site* • Site of fourth debate, west side of town on IL 16. Stone at eastern end of fair-grounds marks the spot. 9–18–1858.

## CHICAGO  (Cook County)

**Presidents**

*Visit* • Blackstone Hotel, 636 S Michigan Ave. Theodore Roosevelt through Clinton stayed here.

**Presidents**

*Visit* • Chicago Coliseum, 1513 S Wabash Ave. Theodore Roosevelt, Taft, Harding, and Coolidge were nominated here.

**Presidents**

*Visit* • Conrad Hilton Hotel (Stevens), 729 S Michigan Ave. Truman through Carter stayed here.

**Presidents**

*Visit* • Palmer House, 17 E Monroe at State. Cleveland through Bush stayed here. Sher-man House (Hotel), Clark and Randolph Sts. Now site of the new State of Illinois Center.

Lincoln through Reagan stayed here. Stock-yard Inn, 4178 S Halstead. Every president from Lincoln to Reagan stayed here.

## Arthur

*Visit* • Grand Pacific Hotel, Jackson and LaSalle. Convention held in Exposition Hall, Adams St (now site of Art Institute). June 1880.

## Bush

*Visit* • Hyatt Regency Hotel, 151 E Wacker Dr. 1989–1992

## Cleveland

*Work* • Exposition Hall, Adams St for DNC. Nominated for president. July 1884. Renominated in a specially constructed building. 6–21–1892 to 6–23–1892.

*Visit* • Potter Palmer home, 1350 Lake Shore Dr. 1887.

*Visit* • World's Columbian Exposition. Jackson Park along Lake Michigan between Fifty-sixth and Sixty-seventh. May 1893.

*Visit* • Joy Morton House, 638 Groveland Park. 1893.

## Clinton

*Marriage* • Hillary Rodham home, 236 Wisner Ave, Park Ridge area. Attended First United Methodist Church in Park Ridge. 1973–.

## Coolidge

*Visit* • Drake Hotel, 140 E Walton. 1924.

*Visit* • Coliseum. RNC nominated him for vice president. June 1920.

*Visit* • Electric cross atop Chicago Temple, 77 W Washington St, lit when he pushed the button. Cross gone but temple remains. 12–7–1925.

## Eisenhower

*Visit* • International Amphitheatre, 4220 S Halstead and W Forty-third Sts, adjoins Stock Yards Inn. Nominated for president at RNC. July 1952.

## Ford

*Visit* • Congress Hotel, 520 S Michigan Ave for RNC. 1960.

## Garfield

*Visit* • Grand Pacific Hotel. RNC held in Exposition Hall. See location under Arthur above. 1880.

## Grant

*Site* • Chicago Historical Society, Lincoln Park at Clark St and North Ave. See table on which the Grant-Lee surrender terms were signed.

*Site* • Stephen A. Douglas Monument, 636 E Thirty-fifth St at Lake Shore Dr. Dedication. 1866.

*Site* • Crosby's Opera House site. Washington St west of State. Nominated here for president by RNC. May 1868.

*Site* • Lincoln Park, Stockton and North Ave. Grant statue.

*Visit* • John L. Wilson House, 1145 S Wabash Ave. 1868.

*Visit* • Lyman Trumbull House, 4008 Lake Park Ave.

*Visit* • Charles Farwell House, 120 E Pearson St. 1880s.

*Visit* • Palmer Mansion, 1350 Lake Shore Dr. 1879 and 1880.

*Visit* • Vincennes Ave at Forty-fifth St. Home to attend son's wedding.

## Harding

*Visit* • Exposition Building, Adams St RNC. 1884. Attended again. 1912 and 1916.

*Visit* • World's Columbian Exposition. See location under Cleveland above. 1893.

*Visit* • LaSalle Hotel (demolished), 720 LaSalle. For RNC. 1920.

*Visit* • 6103 Woodlawn Ave to see Ann Britton at her sister's place. 1920.

*Visit* • Chicago Coliseum. RNC nominated him for president. See location under Presidents above. June 1920.

## Harrison, B

*Visit* • Peck House, 1826 S Michigan Ave. 1889.

*Visit* • Civic Auditorium. Michigan Ave at Congress Parkway. Nominated for president. June 1888.

*Visit* • Dedicated statue commemorating the Ft Dearborn massacre at Eighteenth St and Prairie Ave. Now in lobby of Chicago Historical Society. 6–22–1893.

### Hoover

*Visit* • Chicago Stadium, 1800 W Madison. Renominated by RNC for president. June 1932.

*Visit* • International Amphitheater, 4220 S Halstead St, RNC. 7–7–1952 to 7–11–1952. Addressed the RNC. July 25, 1960.

### Johnson, A

*Visit* • Douglas Monument, 636 E Thirty-fifth St and Lake Shore Dr. Dedication. 1866.

### Johnson, LB

*Visit* • International Amphitheater, DNC. 7/21/1952 to 7/26/1952. Again 1956. See location under Eisenhower above.

### Kennedy

*Education* • Tower Hall at Northwestern University, 504 B Lake Shore Dr. July 1942.

*Lodging* • Abbott Hall on Lake Shore Dr on the Chicago campus of Northwestern University. 1942.

### Lincoln

*Church* • St. James Episcopal at Wabash Ave and Huron St. 11–25–1860.

*Visit* • Lodging Tremont House. Site southeast corner Lake and Dearborn Sts. 1860.

*Visit* • Julian S. Rumsey residence, 40 E Huron St, visiting close friends. 1861.

*Visit* • Wigwam, SW corner Lake St and Wacker Dr. Temporary building. Land owned by Garrett Biblical Institute. Nominated for president by RNC. May 1860.

*Site* • Garfield Park, Central Park Ave and Washington Blvd. Statue, *Lincoln, the Rail Splitter.*

*Site* • Grant Park, Randolph and E Fourteenth St. Saint-Gaudens's seated statue of Lincoln.

*Site* • Lincoln Park, Stockton and North Ave. Lincoln monument by Saint-Gaudens.

*Site* • Lincoln Square at Lincoln and Lawrence Ave. Statue, *The Chicago Lincoln.*

*Site* • Oak Woods Cemetery, 1035 E Sixty-seventh St. Statue, *Lincoln, the Orator.*

*Site* • Abraham Lincoln Bookshop, 18 E Chestnut St.

*Site* • Chicago Historical Society in Lincoln Park at Clark St and North Ave. See Lincoln collection.

*Funeral* • Courthouse (which was near the present site of the Daley Center), 66 W Washington.

*Funeral* • Lay in state at City Hall, bounded by Washington, Randolph, Clark, and LaSalle. Destroyed by the Great Fire of 1871.

### McKinley

*Visit* • Auditorium, Michigan Ave at Congress Parkway, RNC. 1884 and 1899.

*Visit* • Memorial Hall of the public library, 78 E Washington St, for banquet and speech. 1899.

*Visit* • Peck House, 1826 S Michigan Ave and Lafayette McWilliams House. 1896.

*Visit* • Borden Mansion, 3949 Lake Park Ave in old Oakland, and Potter Palmer Mansion. 1896.

*Visit* • University of Chicago, Fifty-fifth to Sixty-first Sts, Kent Chemical Laboratory Theatre, to receive honorary doctorate. 10–17–1898.

*Site* • McKinley Park, Thirty-eighth St and Western Ave. McKinley Monument.

### Nixon

*Visit* • Knickerbocker Hotel, 163 E Walton. 1952.

*Visit* • International Amphitheater. See location under Eisenhower above. Nominated for vice president. July 1952. Nominated for president. 7–28–1960.

**Reagan**

*Church* • Hyde Park Church of Christ, Fifty-seventh St and Lexington Ave. 1913–1915.

*Home* • Cottage Way, 832–834 E Fifty-seventh St. Now site of Joseph Regenstein Library. 1913–1915.

**Roosevelt, FD**

*Visit* • Auditorium, Michigan Ave at Congress Parkway. First speech of his campaign for vice president. 1920.

*Visit* • Congress Hotel, 520 S Michigan Ave. 1932.

*Visit* • Chicago Stadium, 1800 W Madison. Nominated at DNC for president. July 1932. 1940. 1944.

*Visit* • Century of Progress, Columbus Dr. Bohemian Cemetery, LaSalle St Station. 10–1–1933.

*Visit* • Union Station and parade, Outer Drive Bridge; lunch Cardinal Mundelin (Stritch residence) at 1555 N State St; LaSalle St Station. 10–5–1937.

*Visit* • Wrigley Field, off Lake Shore Dr at Clark and Addison Sts. 1932.

**Roosevelt, T**

*Visit* • Chicago Coliseum. Renominated for president at RNC. June 1904. Auditorium Theatre, 70 E Congress St. Nominated for president by Bull Moose Convention. 1912.

*Visit* • Mercy Hospital, E 26th St, Stevenson Exprwy at King Dr following assassination attempt. 10–14–1912.

*Visit* • Joseph T. Bowen Mansion, 1430 Astor St. 1904.

*Visit* • Congress Hotel, 520 S Michigan Ave. 1912.

**Taft**

*Visit* • Chicago Coliseum. Nominated for

president, RNC. See location under Presidents. June 1908. June 1912.

*Visit* • Congress Hotel, 520 S Michigan Ave. 1909.

*Visit* • West Side Baseball Park (Lincoln St). 1909.

**Truman**

*Visit* • Drury Lane Theatre (now Drury Lane South) 2500 W Ninety-fourth Pl, Evergreen Park, to see his daughter act.

*Visit* • Chicago Stadium, 1800 W Madison, for DNC. July 1940. Again when he was nominated for vice president. July 1944

*Visit* • Blackstone Hotel, Room 709, for DNC. 1952. 1956.

**Washington**

*Site* • Statue in Washington Park, on Martin Luther King Jr. Dr at Fifty-first St.

**Wilson**

*Visit* • Cyrus McCormick House, 135 Rush St. 1893.

*Visit* • World's Columbian Exposition. 1893.

## CLAYVILLE  *(See Pleasant Plains)*

## CLINTON  *(DeWitt County)*

**Lincoln**

*Visit* • Barnett Hotel, 738 N Grant St (now private and moved from its original site). He often stopped here.

*Site* • Courthouse lawn. A Lincoln statue marks the site where it is said he made the speech containing the words, "You can fool all the people." 1858.

## DANVILLE  *(Vermilion County)*

**Lincoln**

*Work* • Barnum Building stood on NW corner Redden Square, Main and Vermillion Sts. Site of Lincoln-Lamon Law office. 1852.

*Visit* • McCormick Hotel, 103 W Main St,

where he lodged while on circuit. Grier-Lincoln Hotel now on this site. 1837.

*Visit* • William Fithian House (now Vermilion County Museum Society), 116 N Gilbert St. Stayed here while running for senate against Douglas. 1855–.

*Visit* • Hooton House, 207 Buchanan.

*Site* • Statue of Lincoln at the courthouse on the square.

## DECATUR *(Macon County)*

### Lincoln

*Home* • The Lincolns built their first log cabin in Illinois (10 miles west of Decatur, south on US 36), Lincoln Trail Homestead Park. 1830–1831.

*Work* • Macon House. He helped unload and place the first piano to arrive in Central Illinois.

*Work* • Lincoln Square is the site where he practiced law and made his first political speech. Bronze tablet on building at SE corner commemorating arrival of Lincoln family in 1830. See also marked site of the Wigwam, 200 E Main St, where he was endorsed by the State Republican Party for president. 1860.

*Site* • *Lincoln, the Lawyer,* statue at entrance to Macon County Building. One of three statues of Lincoln in Decatur.

*Site* • Millikin University, 110 W Main St. Statue of Lincoln as a young man.

## DIXON *(Lee County)*

### Presidents

*Visit* • Nachusa Hotel, 215 S Galena Ave. Grant, Reagan, T Roosevelt, and Taft. Standing but no longer operating.

### Lincoln

*Visit* • Nachusa House, 215S Galena Ave. 1856.

*Nachusa House in Dixon.*

*Visit* • Courthouse, Second and Ottaway Ave. 1856.

### Lincoln/Taylor

*Site* • Lincoln Monument State Memorial on the west bank of the Rock River is where Jefferson Davis, Zachary Taylor, and Lincoln met during the Black Hawk War. Granite boulder with bronze tablet on Lincoln Statue Dr between Galena and Hennepin Aves on the site of Dixon Blockhouse. Bronze statue of Lincoln. 1856.

### Reagan

*Church* • Christian Church, 123 Hennepin. 1922–1932.

*Church* • Christian Church met in YMCA when Reagans first arrived in Dixon. 1920.

*Education* • Elementary School (South Central Grammar School) at Fifth St and Peoria Ave. 1920–1923.

*Education* • South Dixon High School, Fifth St and Peoria Ave. 1923–1925.

*Education* • North Dixon High School, Morgan and N Ottawa. No longer existing. 1925–1928.

*Ronald Regan's Hennepin home in Dixon.*

*Home* • 816 S Hennepin. 1920–1923. Re-visited for lunch 2–6–1984.

*Home* • 338 W Everett. 1923–1931.

*Home* • 226 Lincolnway. 1931–1932

*Home* • 207 N Galena Ave. 1932.

*Work* • Lowell Park Swimming Pool on Rock River, 3 miles north of Dixon. 1926–1932.

*Visit* • Hazelwood, 3 miles north of town, end of Brinton Ave past the Correctional Center. Now private, drive not open to public. 1941.

## EDWARDSVILLE *(Madison County)*
**Lincoln**
*Visit* • Wabash Hotel (now made into apartments). Douglas also lodged here. 1858.

## EUREKA *(Woodford County)*
**Reagan**
*Education* • Eureka College, 300 East College Ave. Lodging at TEKE House on campus. 1928–1932.

*Visit* • Reagan Physical Education Center, Eureka College. 5–9–1982.

## EVANSTON *(Cook County)*
**Coolidge**
*Visit* • Charles W. Dawes House, 225 Greenwood Ave. Dawes was vice president under Coolidge.

**Kennedy**
*Work* • Midshipmen's school at Northwestern University, Sheridan Rd.

*Work* • Northwestern University, Abbott Hall, facing Lake Michigan. 1942.

*Ulysses S. Grant home in Galena.*

**Lincoln**
   *Visit* • White House, 2009 Dodge. 1806.

## FARMINGTON *(Fulton County)*
**Lincoln**
   *Visit* • Capp's House, SW corner of Fort and Main Sts. 1858.
   *Visit* • Wilkenson House. E Fort St. 1858.

## FORT ARMSTRONG *(On the island of Rock Island near the town of Rock Island)*
**Taylor**
   *Travel* • Military headquarters on Mississippi River. Replica of blockhouse. 1832.

## FORT JOHNSON *(See Warsaw)*

## FREEPORT *(Stephenson County)*
**Lincoln**
   *Visit* • N State Ave and E Douglas St with boulder marking site of second debate. 8–27–1858.

   *Site* • Taylor's Park, one mile east of courthouse on IL 75. Statue, *Lincoln, the Debater.*

**Roosevelt, T**
   *Visit* • Lincoln debate site. 1903.

## GALENA *(Jo Daviess County)*
**President**
   *Visit* • DeSoto House, 230 S Main, played host to nine presidents.

**Grant**
   *Church* • First Methodist Church, 124 South Bench St. Plaque marks his pew. 1860–1861.

   *Home* • 121 High St (area called Cemetery Hill). 1860–1861.

   *Home* • 510 Bouthillier St. Memorial Home. 1865–1867. 1881.

   *Work* • 120 S Main. Marker showing where he worked in father's store. There is a reconstruced Grant Leather store at 211 S Main. Coatsworth-Barrows store is site of his father's store. 1860–1861.

*Work* • Joe Daviess County Courthouse, 312 N Bench St. Volunteered for the army. April 1861.

*Work* • DeSoto House, Main and Green Sts, where he had his campaign headquarters 1868. 1872.

*Visit* • Washburne House, 908 Third St, home of a close friend. where he received the news of his election. 1868.

*Visit* • General Rawlins House, 515 Hill St. Rawlins was a military friend and his secretary of war.

*Visit* • Major General Smith House, 807 S Bench St. He was on Grant's staff.

*Visit* • Illinois Central Railroad Depot, foot of Bouthillier St. Came home to this station. August 1865. Left here to take office as president. 1869.

*Site* • Grant Park, Park Ave and Jackson St. Bronze statue, *Grant, Our Citizen.*

**Lincoln**
*Visit* • DeSoto House, Main and Green St at 230 S Main. Spoke from here. Today a modernized hotel.

**McKinley**
*Visit* • Spoke at Grant Monument. 1899.

**Roosevelt, T.**
*Visit* • Grant Memorial on Bouthillier St. April 1900.

# GALESBURG *(Knox County)*

**Lincoln**
*Site* • E South between Cherry and Cedar on present Knox College campus. Site of fifth debate. Original building preserved. 10–7–1858.

*Site* • Henry M. Seymour Library at Knox College has collection called "Books Lincoln Read."

**McKinley**
*Visit* • 560 N Prairie. 10–7–1899.

*Visit* • Knox College, site of Lincoln Debates. 1899.

**Reagan**
*Church* • Disciples (Christian) on Northwest St. 1915–1918.

*Education* • Silas Willard School, 495 E Fremont St. 1916–1918.

*Home* • 1219 N Kellogg St. 1915.

*Home* • 1260 N Kellogg St. 1915–1918.

# HAVANA *(Mason County)*

**Lincoln**
*Site* • Mason County Courthouse is a replica of the original structure in which Lincoln practiced law.

*Site* • Rockwell Park. Marker on site where Lincoln spoke. August 1858.

# HILLSBORO *(Montgomery County)*

**Lincoln**
*Visit* • Often at Blockburger Inn at Main and Tilson Sts. 1837–.

*Visit* • Corner of Berry and Water Sts at Eccles House. 1837–.

*Visit* • Hillsboro Courthouse, Town Square. Spoke. July 1844. County fairgrounds, now site of Beckemeyer School. Lincoln spoke. September 1858.

# HORSESHOE BEND *(Near Dixon)*

**Taylor**
*Travel* • Battle with the Indians. 1832.

# JACKSONVILLE *(Morgan County)*

**Grant**
*Work* • Fairgounds, W State St. Marker on site where his troops camped en route to Missouri.

**Lincoln**
*Visit* • Duncan Park, 4 Duncan Pl, a fine Georgian house, now a chapter house of the Daughters of the American Revolution.

*Visit* • Illinois College, 1101 W College Ave. Spoke. February 1859.

**Van Buren**
*Visit* • Governor Duncan's home, 4 Duncan Pl. 1842.

## JONESBORO  *(Union County)*

**Lincoln**
*Site* • Fairgrounds N Main St. Site third debate. Commemorating marker on town square. 9–15–1858.

## LAWRENCEVILLE  *(Lawrence County)*

**Lincoln**
*Home* • Trail Monument on US 50 east of town marks the site where the Lincoln family entered Illinois. See bronze figure of Lincoln at west entrance to Lincoln Memorial Bridge. 1830.

## LEWISTOWN  *(Fulton County)*

**Lincoln**
*Visit* • Newton Walker House (private) 1127 N Main St. Guest here of Walker who served with him in the state legislature.

*Visit* • Old courthouse for speech. Courthouse gone but "Lincoln pillars" from the old courthouse are a memorial in the Protestant Cemetery. 1858.

## LINCOLN  *(Logan County)*

**Presidents**
*Site* • Museum of the Presidents. Lincoln College.

**Lincoln**
*Work* • Logan County Courthouse, 914 Fifth St, stands on site of the building where he once practiced law. Here he received his nickname "Honest Abe." Replica of the 1839 structure is the Postville Courthouse Shrine and Museum on Fifth St off US 66.

*Visit* • Old Postville Hotel, Fifth and Madison Sts (formerly Duskin's Inn).

*Visit* • Old Prim Store and Post Office at NE corner Fifth and Washington Sts.

*Visit* • Postville Park, Fifth and Washington, where he pitched horseshoes.

*Site* • Rustic Inn, downtown Lincoln. Site of conspiracy to steal Lincoln's body from its tomb.

*Site* • Lincoln College, Ottawa and Keokuk St. See memorial statue, *Lincoln, the Student.* Also Lincolniana Museum in the McKinstry Memorial Library of the college.

## LOVINGTON  *(Moultrie County)*

**Lincoln**
*Home* • Family camped 2 1/2 miles south of town on IL 32. 1830.

## MATTOON  *(Coles County)*

**Grant**
*Work* • Mustered in here. Marker on Illinois Central Depot. June 1861. See also the Camp Grant flagpole standing in front of the U.S. Grant Motor Inn.

## METAMORA  *(Metamora County)*

**Lincoln**
*Work* • Metamora Couthouse, 113 E Partridge St. Practiced law. Built 1844.

## MONMOUTH  *(Warren County)*

**Lincoln**
*Visit* • Rains obliged him to walk through town. 1858.

**Reagan**
*Church* • Disciples (no address). 1918–1919.

*Education* • Central School. 1918–1919.

*Home* • 218 S Seventh Ave. 1918–1919.

## MOUNT PULASKI *(Logan County)*

**Lincoln**

> *Work* • Courthouse State Historic Site, Town Square. Practiced law. Original structure.

## MOUNT STERLING *(Brown County)*

**Lincoln**

> *Site* • North Grade School campus has a boulder marking the spot where Lincoln spoke. October 1858.

## MOUNT VERNON *(Jefferson County)*

**Lincoln**

> *Work* • Supreme Courthouse, 1400 W Main St, where he won a case.

> *Site* • Lincoln Medallion on courthouse, public square.

## NEW SALEM *(Menard County)*

**Lincoln**

> *Education* • Onstot Cooper Shop is the only original building on the site at Lincoln's New Salem State Park and is where he studied law books. 1831–.

> *Lodging* • Lodged and ate at different homes. Stayed at Offut's store in the back and boarding with Rev. John Cameron. Often at Rutledge Tavern. 1831–1837.

> *Work* • Clerk in store of Denton Offut. 1831.

> *Work* • Joint ownership of store with Berry. Present building is re-creation. 1832.

> *Work* • Postmaster. 1833.

> *Work* • Surveyor here and in surrounding counties. 1833, 1834.

> *Site* • Statue, *The Lincoln from New Salem.*

## NORMAL *(McLean County)*

**Lincoln**

> *Visit* • Jesse Fell House, 502 S Fell Ave

(not original site). Lincoln often visited Fell.

## OTTAWA *(LaSalle County)*

**Lincoln**

> *Site* • Washington Park, Columbus and LaFayette Sts. First debate, marked by boulder. 8–21–1858.

> *Work* • Lincoln Sun Dial at the Ottawa Boat Club by the bridge shows the spot where Lincoln was mustered out following the end of the Black Hawk War.

## PARIS *(Edgar County)*

**Lincoln**

> *Visit* • Alexander House (now office building).

## PEKIN *(Tazewell County)*

**Lincoln**

> *Visit* • Courthouse. Won law case for "Black Nance," an escaped slave.

## PEORIA *(Peoria County)*

**Lincoln**

> *Site* • Courthouse Square, Main and Adams Sts, has a tablet on south portico of the courthouse commemorating the site of his speech. 1854.

**McKinley**

> *Visit* • 324 Courthouse Square to dedicate monument. 1899.

## PERRY *(Scott County)*

**Grant**

> *Work* • Campsite on Perry-Naples Road north of Valley City and east of Perry. Marker.

## PETERSBURG *(Menard County)*

**Lincoln**

> *Visit* • Oakwood Cemetery and grave of Ann Rutledge, edge of town.

*Site* • Lincoln's New Salem State Historic Site. Off IL 97.

## PITTSFIELD *(Pike County)*

**Lincoln**

*Site* • Central Park has boulder marking site of Lincoln speech. 1858.

*Site* • Worthington House, 626 W Washington. Guest there.

## PLEASANT PLAINS *(Sangamon County)*

**Lincoln**

*Visit* • Clayville Tavern on IL 125, 12 miles west of Springfield. Restored. Frequently stayed here attending Whig meetings.

## PONTIAC *(Livingston County)*

**Roosevelt, T**

*Visit* • Dedicated Soldiers and Sailors Monument, courthouse lawn. 1902.

## QUINCY *(Adams County)*

**Lincoln**

*Site* • East side of Washington Park on Washington Square with bronze plaque marking site of sixth debate. 10–3–1858.

**McKinley**

*Visit* • Courthouse Square for speech. 1899.

## ROCKFORD *(Winnebago County)*

**Lincoln**

*Visit* • Courthouse, Main, Second and Third. Debates. 1844.

*Visit* • Rockford Tavern, NE corner Main and Second. Marker on site.

## ROSEMONT *(Christian County)*

**Lincoln**

*Site* • Monument west of town on IL 16.

*First Presbyterian Church has the pew once occupied by the Lincolns.*

## SALEM *(Marion County)*

**Lincoln**

*Visit* • 321 S Franklin. Stayed here while making speeches.

*Visit* • 304 W Schwartz. Stayed here while making speeches. Open to the public.

## SAND RIDGE *(Menard County)*

**Lincoln**

*Home* • Home of Ann Rutledge. 1831–.

## SPRINGFIELD *(Sangamon County)*

**Presidents**

*Visit* • Governor's Mansion. Fourth and Fifth, Jackson and Edwards. Lincoln, Eisenhower, Grant, Hayes, Hoover, T and F Roosevelt, and Taft.

**Carter**

*Visit* • State Capitol House Chamber. Capitol South end of First St west on Capitol. 5–26–1978.

## Eisenhower

*Visit* • Lincoln Tomb, Monument St, to lay a wreath. Oak Ridge Cemetery. 8–19–1954.

## Ford

*Visit* • Lincoln Home Visitor's Center. 426 S Seventh St. 3–5–1976.

## Grant

*Work* • Great campsite (Camp Yates) on the old Jacksonville Rd west of Springfield. Marker. 1861.

*Work* • State Fair Grounds. 1861.

*Visit* • Chenery House and Principle Hotel. Demolished. 1861.

*Visit* • 700 N Fourth St at Benjamin Edwards' house.

## Hayes

*Visit* • Dedicated Lincoln Tomb. 1879.

## Hoover

*Visit* • Rededicated Lincoln tomb. 6–17–1931. Visit to legislature at the state capitol. 11–4–1932.

## Johnson, A

*Visit* • Lincoln Tomb. St. Nicholas Hotel. Fourth St and Jefferson. 1866.

## Lincoln

*Church* • First Presbyterian Church, Seventh and Capitol Ave, has the pew once occupied by the Lincolns. Site of the church they attended was at 302 E Washington St.

*Church* • St. Paul's Episcopal Church (now the Cathedral), 815 S Second St. See church books for record of the Lincoln marriage.

*Marriage* • Ninian Wirt Edwards House. Site Second St, NW corner. Illinois State Historical Society Library on third floor (called Centennial Building). Benjamin Edwards House, 700 N Fourth St. Complete reproduction of original house 406 S Eighth St. 1842.

*Lodging* • Above Joshua Speed store when he first arrived in Springfield. 105 S Fifth St on SW corner Fifth and Washington, where he later had his law office with Herndon. 1856–1861. First lodged here. 1837.

*Tomb of Abraham Lincoln in Springfield.*

*Home* • Globe Tavern. Site 315 E Adams St. On their wedding night. 1842–1843.

*Home* • 214 S Fourth St in a small one-story house. 1843–1844.

*Home* • Eighth and Jackson Sts at NE corner. Lincoln Home National Historic Site. Free admission. 1844–1847. 1849–1861.

*Work* • No. 4 Hoffman's Row (upstairs) 109 N Fifth St in law practice with J.T. Stuart. 1837–1841

*Work* • Lincoln-Logan Law Office, SW corner, Sixth and Adams Sts, third floor. 1841–1844.

*Work* • Lincoln-Herndon law office. 109 N Fifth St. 1844–1847. 1849–1861.

*Work* • State Representative. While capitol was being built, the legislature met in the Second Presbyterian Church, Site 217 S Fourth St. Tablet. 1840s.

*Work* • Moved into the completed capitol in the square bounded by Fifth, Sixth, Washington and Adams Sts.

*Work* • 106 N Fifth St, and a little later to the Tinsley Building at the SW corner of

*Ronald Reagan's Tampico home.*

Sixth and Adams Sts, on third floor. Law practice with Stephen T. Logan. 1841.

*Work* • 105 S Fifth St (now remodeled). A second floor room in the same house is where he roomed in 1837 with Joshua Speed. 1856–1861.

*Visit* • Governor's Mansion at Fourth and Fifth and Edwards. Guest of the governor.

*Visit* • Vachel Lindsay House, 603 S Fifth St, home of his sister-in-law Ann Todd Smith.

*Visit* • C.M. Smith store, 524–528 E Adams St, where the Lincolns traded. Also where he wrote his first inaugural address. 1861. 1852–1861.

*Visit* • Chenery House. 2–6–1861 to 2–11–1861.

*Visit* • 116 N Sixth St. In second floor room of this house he received notice of his nomination for president. 1860.

*Visit* • Lincoln Depot (Great Western Depot), 10th and Monroe Sts where he said

farewell to his fellow citizens. Interior restored. 1861.

*Funeral* • (Old) State Capitol, lay in state. Remains arrived at the Chicago and Alton Railroad Station. Bounded by Fifth, Sixth, Washington and Adams Sts. Opened 1841. Here he gave his "house divided" speech in 1858. U.S. Grant worked here. See also Illinois State Historical Library in the Old State Capitol, Sixth and Adams Sts. Extensive Lincoln collection.

*Burial* • Oak Ridge Cemetery. 5–4–1865. End of Monument Avenue. Lincoln Monument, built 1900.

*Site* • Statue of Lincoln on the state capitol grounds.

*Site* • Lincoln ledger in Springfield Marine Bank, 1 Old Capitol Plaza.

*Site* • Abraham Lincoln Wax Museum, 400 S Ninth St.

**Nixon**

*Visit* • Lincoln home. 9–18–1971.

**Reagan**

*Visit* • State Capitol Building. 11–2–1984.

**Roosevelt, FD**

*Visit* • Lincoln Tomb and Home. Lunch at Executive Mansion. 9–4–1936.

**Roosevelt, T**

*Visit* • Capitol. Lincoln Tomb. 1903.

**Taft**

*Visit* • State Capitol. Lincoln Home and Tomb. 1909. 1911.

## TAMPICO *(Whiteside County)*

**Reagan**

*Birthplace* • 111 Main St. 1911.

*Education* • County School. 1919–1920.

*Home* • Burden Building. 1911–1913.

*Home* • Above Pitney Store. 1919–1920.

## VANDALIA *(Fayette County)*

**Lincoln**

*Lodging* • 615 W Johnson St. 1834–1837.

*Lodging* • Vandalia Hotel, where he shared a room. 1834–1837.

*Work* • Member of state legislature here before capital was moved to Springfield. Vandalia State House, at 315 W Gallatin. 1836–1839.

## WARSAW *(Hancock County)*

**Taylor**

*Travel* • Fort Johnson site which he built. Burned 1814.

## WINCHESTER *(Scott County)*

**Lincoln**

*Visit* • Aiken Tavern. Tablet indicating site of where he stayed in the Scott County Courthoue. 1854.

*Site* • Boulder marking site of Lincoln speech at the Scott County Courthouse.

# INDIANA

## PRESIDENT • LANDMARK TYPE • DESCRIPTION • DATE

### BLOOMINGTON *(Monroe County)*

**Lincoln**
> *Site* • Lilly Library, Indiana University Campus at Seventh St. Lincoln collection.

### BRUCEVILLE *(Knox County)*

**Lincoln**
> *Visit* • Major William Bruce House, corner of Washington and Back Sts. Lincoln spoke and spent the night here. 1844.

### CONNERSVILLE *(Fayette County)*

**Harding**
> *Visit* • McFarlan Hotel, SW corner Sixth and Central and now site of Central State Bank. 1917.

**Harrison, B**
> *Visit* • Elmhurst Mansion opposite the railway station on IN 121. Home of James N. Huston. 1880s.

### CORYDON *(Harrison County)*

**Harrison, WH**
> *Church* • Presbyterian Church, site S

Capitol Ave near Poplar St. Erected 1826 and razed 1912.

> *Site* • Territorial capital. 1813–1816. State capital. 1816–1825. See the Old Capitol Building at Courthouse Square on Old Capitol Ave.

> *Site* • Branham Tavern, N Capitol Ave. He founded the town in 1800 and built this tavern.

### FERRY PARK *(See Troy)*

### FORT HARRISON *(Vigo County)*

**Taylor**
> *Travel* • 1812.

### FORT KNOX II (VINCENNES) *(Knox County)*

**Harrison, WH**
> *Work* • Garrisoned here. 1811–1812.

**Taylor**
> *Travel* • Met WH Harrison here. 1811. Headquarters. 1813–1814. March 1815.

**Indiana**

1 ● Fort Wayne

65

69

2 ● Indianapolis

70

65

4 ●

64

3 ●

1. Lincoln law office
   reconstructed, *Fort
   Wayne*
2. Harrison home,
   *Indianapolis*
3. Lincoln home, *Rockport*
4. Harrison home,
   *Vincennes*

# FORT WAYNE *(Allen County)*

**Harrison, WH**

*Work* • Fort Wayne. 1812. Fort of 1812 replaced by stronger one. 211 S Barr St. Reconstructed. 1803. 1815.

**Lincoln**

*Site* • Louis A. Warren Lincoln Library and Museum, 1300 S Clinton St. Statue of Lincoln as a Hoosier in the plaza. Also reconstructed Springfield law office.

# GENTRYVILLE *(Spencer County)*

**Lincoln**

*Work* • Ferryman across the Ohio River near here. 1826–1830.

# GOSPORT *(Owen County)*

**Harrison, WH**

*Work* • N of town on IN 67, marker commemorating Ft. Wayne treaty. 1803.

# GRANDVIEW *(Spencer County)*

**Lincoln**

*Work* • Lincoln marker downtown in front of library on IN 66. 1820s.

# GRAYSVILLE *(Sullivan County)*

**Harrison, WH**

*Work* • Fort Turman off IN 154 near Graysville. September 1811.

# INDIANAPOLIS *(Marion County)*

**Presidents**

*Visit* • State Capitol, W Washington St. Cleveland, Reagan, T Roosevelt, and Taft.

**Eisenhower**

*Visit* • Butler University, Forty-sixth and Clarendon. 10–15–1954.

**Harding**

*Visit* • Claypool Hotel to see Britton. 8 N Illinois at the NW corner Washington and Illinois Sts. 1917.

*Visit* • Tomlinson Hall and Monument Circle for campaign speeches. 1920.

**Harrison, B**

*Church* • Second Presbyterian Church Pennsylvania and Vermont Sts. Now located at 7700 N Meridian. Former site now city park. 1854–1901.

*Church* • See also Lockerbie Square Methodist Church built 1882, 237 N East St.

*Home* • 600 Block Pennsylvania Ave. Apartment. 1854.

*Home* • Corner of Vermont and New Jersey. Rented 3-room house. 1854–1862.

*Home* • 299 N Alabama. Now site of fire headquarters. 1865–1875.

*Home* • 1230 N Delaware Ave. Museum on the third floor. Entrance fee. 1875–1901.

*Work* • Washington between Meridian and Illinois Sts. Law practice. 1854–1855.

*Work* • 30 1/2 W Washington. Law practice with William Wallace. 1857–1860.

*Work* • Supreme Court of Indiana. Offices in the first statehouse, which was located on the same site as the present. Corner of Senate and Capitol. Reporter. 1860–1862. 1865–1881.

*Work* • Wright's Market Street. Block located at 120 E Market. Law practice with Albert G. Porter and William P. Fishback. 1887–1889. Retirement. 1893–1894.

*Visit* • Columbia Club, 121 Monument Circle. 1900s.

*Visit* • James Whitcomb Riley House, 528 Lockerbie St.

*Visit* • Union Station, 39 Jackson Place. S of Georgia St, between Meridian St and Capitol Ave. Refurbished and still operating. 1888.

*Death* • 1230 Delaware St. 1901.

*Funeral* • Second Presbyterian Church, Pennsylvania and Vermont Sts. Site is now a city park. State Capitol. Body lay in state. Corner of Senate and Capitol. 1901.

*Burial* • 700 W Thirty-eighth St at Crown Hill Cemetery. Entrance at 3402 Boulevard Pl.

*Site* • Statue of Harrison, south entrance to University Park, New York and Vermont Sts.

**Harrison, WH**

*Visit* • Courthouse was used as temporary capitol. He received a hero's welcome here. 1832.

*Visit* • Aquilla Parker's Tavern, east of town. 1840.

**Johnson, A**

*Visit* • State House, speech. 2–26–1863

*Visit* • Bates House. September 1866.

**Johnson, LB**

*Visit* • Soldiers and Sailors Monument, Monument Circle. 10–8–1964. 7–23–1966. Athletic Club, 350 N Meridian. 7–23–1966.

**Lincoln**

*Funeral* • Lay in state in the old State House. Area bounded by Capitol Ave, Washington St, Senate Ave, and Ohio St. 1865.

*Site* • Lincoln Monument, SW corner of University Park, New York and Vermont Sts.

*Site* • Statue on capitol grounds.

**Washington**

*Site* • Statue on capitol grounds.

## JEFFERSONVILLE *(Clark County)*

**Harrison, WH**

*Visit* • Grisamore House, 111–113 W Chestnut St. Visited and delivered speech from front porch. 1840.

## LAFAYETTE *(Tippecanoe County)*

**Grant**

*Visit* • Reynolds House, 622 Main St, visiting his West Point classmate.

**Harrison, WH**

*Work* • Tippecanoe. 7 miles N near IN 43

and I-65. Monument marks site of battle. 1812.

## LEAVENWORTH

**Lincoln**

*Site* • Lincoln Boyhood National Memorial. Off IN 162.

## LINCOLN CITY *(Spencer County)* See Lincoln Boyhood National Memorial on IN 162 containing Lincoln Living Historical Farm and the Cemetery.

**Lincoln**

*Church* • Little Pigeon Church, a mile across the field from the Lincoln home. Near Gentryville on IN 62. 1816–1817.

*Education* • Little Pigeon Creek School. 1817. Went to three different schools in Indiana. At Little Pigeon, he walked 9 miles to and from. About 200 yards east of Little Pigeon Church. 1816.

*Home* • Little Pigeon. See replica near Gentryville. 1816–1830.

## PERRYSVILLE *(Fountain County)*

**Harrison, WH**

*Work* • Harrison's Crossing over Big Vermillion River on march preceeding Battle of Tippecanoe. 1811.

## PLAINFIELD *(Hendricks County)*

**Van Buren**

*Visit* • 205 S East St. Tablet for "Van Buren Elm." 1844.

## ROCKPORT *(Spencer County)*

**Harrison, B**

*Visit* • Brown-Kercheval House, 315 S Second St. 1880s.

**Lincoln**

*Home* • Replicas of his Indiana home in the Lincoln Pioneer Village.

*Grouseland, Vincennes home of William Harrison.*

**Work** • Lower end of Main St. Marker commemorating his first New Orleans flatboat trip. 1828.

**Visit** • Rockport Tavern site, NE corner Main and Second Sts. Small stone marker. 1844.

**Site** • Spencer County Courthouse, block bounded by Walnut, Main, Second, and Third Sts. Fifth on site since 1818. Lincoln spoke here. 10–3–1844.

## SOUTH BEND *(St. Joseph County)*

### Presidents
**Site** • Studebaker Archives Center, 525 S Main St, has carriages belonging to Grant and McKinley and the carriage in which Lincoln rode to Ford's theater.

### Bush
**Visit** • Notre Dame Convocation Center, Notre Dame Ave. 5–17–1992.

**Ford**

*Travel* • University of Notre Dame Athletic and Convocation Center. 3–17–1975.

**Reagan**

*Visit* • Palace Theater (now Morris Civic Auditorium) 211 N Michigan St. Premier "Knute Rockne." 1940.

*Visit* • University of Notre Dame, Joyce Athletic and Convocation Center. 3–9–1988.

**Roosevelt, FD**

*Visit* • Notre Dame University. 12–9–1935.

# TIPPECANOE *(Tippecanoe County)*

**Harrison, WH**

*Work* • Battle of Tippecanoe Monument on the battlefield. 1811.

**Taylor**

*Work* • Expedition. March 1815.

# TROY *(Perry County)*

**Lincoln**

*Work* • Operated a ferry near this point just west of Anderson River. Ferry Park on IN 66 near grounds of a small roadside memorial park. 1820s.

# VERNON *(Jennings County)*

**Nixon**

*Visit* • Courthouse, town center, for dedication of marker. June 1971.

*Visit* • Historical marker commemorating mother's birth, east side of Butlerville on the south side of US 50.

# VINCENNES *(Knox County)*

**Capitol**

*Site* • Original site 217 Main St. Moved to east side of Park St. 1949. The Indiana Territory's first Capitol at First and Harrison Sts. 1800–1813.

**Harrison, WH**

*Home* • 3 West Scott St, Grouseland, NE corner of Park and Scott Sts. Entrance fee. 1802.

*Work* • See capitol above. Contains a table used by WHH. 1800–1812.

*Visit* • Francis Sligo House, off Harrison St. 1801.

**Lincoln**

*Travel* • Lincoln Memorial Bridge over the Wabash River on Vigo St. Near ferry landing where he crossed. 1830. See Lincoln monument on the Illinois side.

*Visit* • Ellis Mansion, 111 N Second St, home of Abner T. Ellis. 1850s.

**Roosevelt, FD**

*Visit* • George Rogers Clark Memorial on Second St. Dedicated June 14, 1936.

# WABASH *(Wabash County)*

**Lincoln**

*Site* • "Lincoln of the People" statue in the courthouse square.

# WEST LAFAYETTE *(Tippecanoe County)*

**Harrison, WH**

*Work* • Tippecanoe Battlefield on Railroad St. See Tippecanoe above.

# WYANDOTTE *(Crawford County)*

**Harrison, WH**

*Visit* • Wyandotte Caves on IN 62, four miles east of new Leavenworth. 1806.

# ZIONSVILLE *(Boone County)*

**Lincoln**

*Visit* • Site of railway station marked by stone monument in Lincoln Park. Lincoln addressed the crowd from a platform here. 1861.

# IOWA

## BOONE *(Boone County)*

**Eisenhower**
*Visit* • Mamie Eisenhower birthplace, 709 Carroll St.

## BURLINGTON *(Des Moines County)*

**Lincoln**
*Visit* • Hudson House at NW corner of Columbia and Fifth St, where he stayed. 1858.

*Visit* • Opera House stood on the northeast corner of Valley and Main St, where he spoke. 1858.

## CENTERVILLE *(Appanoose County)*

**Nixon**
*Visit* • Rathbun Dam, 7 miles north of IA 5. Dedicated. 7–31–1971.

## COUNCIL BLUFFS *(Pottawattamie County)*

**Lincoln**
*Visit* • Oakland Dr and Lafayette Ave. Lincoln Monument commemorates his visit. 9-12-1859 to 9-14-1859.

## DAVENPORT *(Scott County)*

**Reagan**
*Church* • First Christian Church. 510 E Fifteenth St. 1932–1933.

*Lodging* • Room near Palmer Chiropractic School. Meals at the school. 202–220 E Fourth St (now Vale apartment building). 1932–1933.

*Work* • Office on top floor of Chiropractic School. Broadcaster, radio station WOC. 800–110 Brady St between Eleventh and Eighth Sts. 1932–1933.

**Taylor**
*Travel* • Credit Island at the end of Schmidt St. Marker. 1814.

## DES MOINES *(Polk County)*

**Presidents**
*Visit* • Hotel Fort Des Moines, Tenth and Walnut Sts. Bush 1976, 10–15–1990; Coolidge 1922; Ford 10–24–1974,

Iowa

35

80

• Des Moines

1

1. Hoover birthplace, *West Branch*

8–18–1975; Harding 1920; Hoover 10–4–1932; L Johnson 1960; Kennedy 1960; Nixon 3–1–1971; Reagan 1974; Truman 1948; and Wilson 1919.

**Bush**
*Visit* • State Historical Museum, E Sixth and Locust. 10–16–1990.

**Ford**
*Travel* • State Capitol. E Twelfth St between Grand Ave and E Walnut St. 10–24–1974.

*Travel* • Iowa State Fair, E Thirtieth and Grand Ave. 8–18–1975.

**Grant**
*Visit* • Hoyt Sherman House, Woodland Ave at Fifteenth St. Both Grant and McKinley visited. 1870s.

*Visit* • Slavery Hotel, Fourth and Locust. Hotel later called Hotel Kirkwood. Burned 1929. 1875.

**Hoover**
*Travel* • State House Plaza. 10–4–1932.

**Johnson, LB**
*Visit* • State Capitol. 10–7–1964.

*Visit* • Veterans Memorial Auditorium, 833 Fifth Ave. 6–30–1966.

**McKinley**
*Visit* • Woodland Ave. See under Grant above. 1870s.

**Nixon**
*Visit* • State Capitol. 3–1–1971.

**Reagan**
*Church* • Capitol Hill Christian Church, 3322 E Twenty-fifth St. 1933–1937.

*Lodging* • 330 Center St. Now parking lot. 1933–1934.

*Lodging* • 400 Center St. Now parking lot. 1934–1937.

*Work* • 914 Walnut St in Stoner Building on the ground floor at the back. Radio station WHO. Now parking lot. 1933–1937.

*Visit* • State Capitol, E Ninth and Grand Ave. Marriott Hotel, 700 Grand. 2–9–1982. 5–20–1982.

**Roosevelt, FD**
*Visit* • State Capitol. 9–3–1936.

**Roosevelt, T**
*Visit* • The Wellington, 417 Fifth St. 1901.

**Taft**
*Visit* • State Capitol. 1909.

**Wilson**
*Church* • Central Presbyterian Church, 3829 Grand. 9–7–1919.

*Visit* • Coliseum. 1919.

## DUBUQUE *(Dubuque County)*

**Taylor**
*Travel* • Indian agent stationed at Fort Crawford. 1836.

## HUBBARD *(Hardin County)*

**Hoover**
*Home* • Home of his uncle near here.

## KINGSLEY *(Plymouth County)*

**Hoover**
*Education* • Kingsley School on N Main St. 1884–1885.

*Home* • Minthorn Home, south of Methodist Church. 1884–1885.

## OTTUMWA *(Wapello County)*

**Harrison, B**
*Visit* • Coal Palace, 226 W Main, near Union Station. Site now Ballingall Park. Building razed. 10–9–1890.

**McKinley**
*Visit* • Coal Palace (see above entry). In 1891 he was a congressman and he also made a train stop here in 1900. 1891.

*Visit* • Mrs. J. T. Bevin at 226 W Main (Washington and Main).

**Nixon**
*Home* • 232 E Fourth St, Apt 9. 1942–1943.

*Work* • Naval Air Station. 1942–1943.

GEOGRAPHIC GUIDE TO LANDMARKS

**Taft**

*Visit* • Spent the day. 1908. Spoke at the Ball Park. 1912.

## SIOUX CITY *(Woodbury County)*

**Cleveland**

*Visit* • Corn Palace, Fifth and Jackson Sts. September 1887.

**Hoover**

*Home* • Stayed briefly with his Uncle Pennington Minthorn in his pioneer sod house. No exact location. 1881.

## WEST BRANCH *(Cedar County)*

**Hoover**

*Birthplace* • Downey St House. Herbert Hover National Historic Site. Free admission. 1874.

*Church* • Quaker Meeting House, Downey St north of Main St. 1874–1884.

*Education* • West Branch Free School on Downey St between Main and Wetherell Sts. 1879–1885.

*Home* • Downey St at the corner of Penn and Downey. 1874–1878.

*Home* • A block down and across Downey St from the birthplace. Location unclear. 1878–1879.

*Home* • Corner S Downey St and Cedar Sts. 1879–1884.

*Home* • North of West Branch with Uncle Allen and Aunt Millie about a mile north of West Branch. Rt 2. 1884–1885.

*Burial* • Hoover Memorial-Burial site.

*Site* • Presidential Library and Museum.

## WINTERSET *(Madison County)*

**Reagan**

*Visit* • Madison County Courthouse. 11–3–1984.

*Visit* • John Wayne boyhood home, 224 S Second St. 11–3–1984.

# KANSAS

## ABILENE *(Dickinson County)*

**Eisenhower**

*Church* • Church of the River Brethren, Seventh and Buckeye. Now apartments. 1891–1911.

*Education* • Grammar School, Lincoln Elementary, 308 S Buckeye St. Site visitor center. 1898–1902.

*Education* • Garfield, on the north side, 215 N 7th Street. 1902–1904.

*Education* • Abilene High School in the old city hall on the SE corner of Fifth and Broadway. Now site of new city hall. 1904–1906.

*Education* • Abilene High School. Seventh St. Now site of Frontier Apartments. 1906–1909.

*Home* • 112 SE Second St. 1891–1898.

*Home* • 201 SE Fourth St. 1898–1911.

*Work* • Bryan farm, summer work. 1909.

*Work* • Rice-Johntz Lumber Company 306–320 W North Second St. Summer 1909.

*Work* • Belle Springs Creamery (ice plant) off Main St. 1909–1910.

*Visit* • 310 E First (Enterprise) St calling on Gladys Harding. 1911–.

*Burial* • 201 SE Fourth St in chapel at Eisenhower Memorial Center. 1969.

*Site* • Dwight D. Eisenhower Center, Museum and Library, 201 SE Fourth. Eisenhower dedicated museum. Museum entrance fee. 11–11–1954. Groundbreaking for Eisenhower Library and lunch Sunflower Hotel. 9–13–1959. Library free.

## ATCHISON *(Atchison County)*

**Lincoln**

*Visit* • Massasoit House, 210 Main St, where he stayed. Plaque in Courthouse Square, SW corner N Fifth and Parallel Sts. 1859.

## EMPORIA *(Lyon County)*

**Roosevelt, T**

*Visit* • William Allen White House, William Allen White Memorial Drive. 9–21–1912.

Kansas

70

35

Topeka

Wichita

1. Eisenhower home,
   *Abilene*

*Dwight Eisenhower home in Abilene.*

## FORT LEAVENWORTH *(Leavenworth County)*

**Presidents**

*Visit* • Eisenhower, Grant, Lincoln, McKinley, T Roosevelt, Taft, Truman, and Wilson.

**Eisenhower**

*Church* • Memorial Chapel east of the statue of General Grant on Scott Ave. 1917–.

*Home* • Otis Hall, 213 Kearney Ave. Stationed. 1917. 1925–1928.

*Work* • General Staff School. 1915–1926.

*Visit* • Union Pacific Depot, 123 S Esplanade. 1917.

**Grant**

*Site* • Statue at Grant and Kearney Aves.

## FORT RILEY *(Riley County)*

**Truman**

*Visit* • Army reserve camp. 1925–1938.

## FORT SCOTT *(Bourbon County)*

**Taylor**

*Work* • Old Fort on Old Fort Blvd. Restored. 1842–.

## HUTCHINSON *(Reno County)*

**Lincoln**

*Site* • Soldier's Monument with Lincoln statue. First Ave Park, First Ave and Walnut St.

## KANSAS CITY *(Wyandotte County)*

**Presidents**

*Visit* • Arthur, Eisenhower, Harding, FD Roosevelt, and T Roosevelt.

## LAWRENCE *(Douglas County)*

**Arthur**

*Visit* • Free State Hotel (later Eldridge

House) west side of Massachusetts, near Seventh St corner. American House also listed in one source. 1856.

### Hoover

*Education* • Elelventh and Vermont Sts. Quincy Street School, 115 W Quincy. Now Community Center. 1884.

*Home* • 1648 Learnard Ave with Uncle L. J. Miles.

## LEAVENWORTH *(Leavenworth County)*

### Arthur

*Visit* • Planter's House. Site NE corner Shawnee and Main Sts on N Esplanade St. 1856.

### Lincoln

*Visit* • Planter's House. 1859.

*Visit* • Opera House known as Stockton Hall. Site 401 Delaware St. Now occupied by Leavenworth National Bank. 1859.

## LECOMPTON *(Douglas County)*

### Arthur

*Visit* • Old Capitol, in Constitution Hall, N Elmore St. 1856.

*Visit* • Rowena Hotel at the south end of Elmore St. Became dormitories for Lane University.

## RUSSELL *(Russell County)*

### Ford

*Travel* • Met with his vice presidential running mate, Robert Dole. Picnic on grounds of courthouse. 8–20–1976.

## TOPEKA *(Shawnee County)*

### Presidents

*Site* • B Harrison, KcKinley, Taft, each speaking under Old Cottonwood Tree.

### Ford

*Travel* • State Capitol, Park Square bounded by Eighth St to Tenth St and W from Jackson St to Harrison St. Stayed at Ramada Inn, I-70 and E Sixth. 2–11–1975.

### Reagan

*Visit* • Alfred Landon home, 521 SW Westchester Rd. 9–6–1987.

### Roosevelt, T

*Visit* • State Capitol. Governor's Mansion, SW corner Eighth and Buchanan Sts. Occupied. 1901. Cedar Crest and Fairlawn Rd. 5–2–1903.

### Taft

*Visit* • State Capitol. 1911.

## WICHITA *(Sedgwick County)*

### Wilson

*Visit* • AT & SF Railroad station. He collapsed here and was unable to continue his tour. 1919.

# KENTUCKY

PRESIDENT • LANDMARK TYPE • DESCRIPTION • DATE

## ADAIRVILLE  (Logan County)

**Jackson**
> *Visit* • Two miles west of town on US 431 is site of Jackson-Dickinson duel. Marker 100.

## BARDSTOWN  (Nelson County)

**Presidents**
> *Visit* • Old Talbott Tavern, 107 W Stephen Foster Ave. Third oldest building in Kentucky. Jackson, Lincoln, WH Harrison, and Taylor stayed at the Old Talbott.

## BIG HILL  (Madison County)

**Grant**
> *Work* • US 421 and Old Wilderness Rd. A marker notes site where Grant stopped on the way to Knoxville. Marker 514. 1864.

## BIG SANDY VALLEY  (Johnson County)

**Garfield**
> *Work* • War on the Big Sandy, New US 23 and US 460. Marker at site. 1862.

## CARROLLTON  (Carroll County)

**Taylor**
> *Visit* • Stopped on inaugural trip, city center, Courthouse Square, and boat dock. 1849.

## CATLETTSBURG  (Boyd County)

**Garfield**
> *Work* • Marker at Twenty-sixth and Louisa Ave across from Elks Building. Marker at Civil War Army Base on US 23. 1862.

## CLOVERPORT  (Breckenridge County)

**Lincoln**
> *Site* • Lincoln Family trail on US 60. Marker 73. 1816.

## COVINGTON  (Kenton County)

**Grant**
> *Church* • Parents' church, First Methodist Church, corner of Fifth and Greenup Sts. 1854.

> *Lodging* • 520 Greenup St at the home of his parents. His father had a leather goods

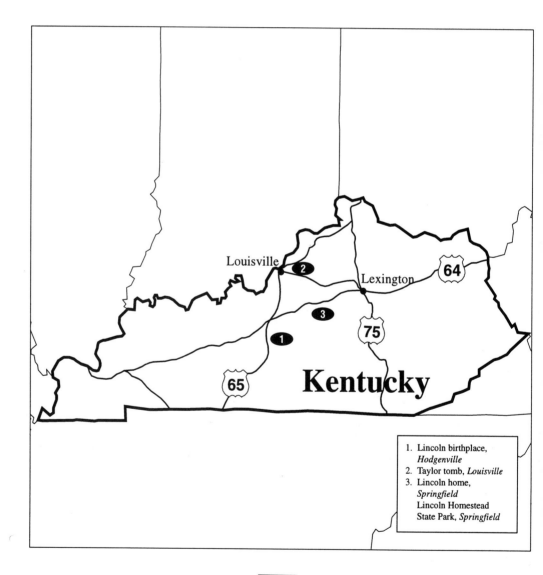

1. Lincoln birthplace,
   *Hodgenville*
2. Taylor tomb, *Louisville*
3. Lincoln home,
   *Springfield*
   Lincoln Homestead
   State Park, *Springfield*

store on Madison Ave. See also Spring Grove Cemetery where elder Grant is buried. 1854.

## ELIZABETHTOWN *(Hardin County)*

**Buchanan**
*Work* • Hardin County Courthouse on City Square. On a law case involving his father. 1812.

*Visit* • Eagle House (Smith Hotel) on City Square. Demolished. 1812.

**Lincoln**
*Home* • Lincoln-Haycraft Memorial Bridge. Site where he crossed the creek on his way to Indiana. Marker 932. 1816.

## FORT ANDERSON *(See Paducah)*

## FORT JEFFERSON *(Ballard County)*

**Grant**
*Work* • US 51, Union supply base used in Civil War. Marker 757. 1861–1862.

## FORT KNOX *(Bullitt, Hardin, and Meade Counties )*

**Eisenhower**
*Visit* • Stood in reviewing stand at Brooks Field, US 31 W and US 60. April 1954.

## FRANKFORT *(Franklin County)*

**Presidents**
*Visit* • Liberty Hall, home of John Brown, 202 Wilkinson St. Jackson, Madison, Monroe, Taylor, and T Roosevelt.

**Lincoln**
*Site* • Capitol. St. Clair and Broadway. Now the Kentucky History Museum. Statue in the Rotunda.

**Taylor**
*Visit* • Crittenden house at Main and Washington Sts. Marker 1154. February 1849.

*Visit* • West Main St. First Presbyterian Church for reception. 1849.

*Visit* • Governor's Mansion, 420 High St. 1849.

## GILBERTSVILLE *(Caldwell County)*

**Truman**
*Visit* • Kentucky Dam dedication, US 62 between Lake City and Grand Rivers. 10–10–1945.

## HARDINSBURG *(Breckinridge County)*

**Lincoln**
*Lodging* • Cabin where Lincolns stayed en route to Indiana. Marker 1003. 1816.

## HARRODSBURG *(Mercer County)*

**Lincoln**
*Site* • Old Fort Harrod State Park, downtown. Mansion museum.

**Roosevelt, FD**
*Visit* • Old Fort Harrod State Park. Dedication of George Rogers Clark Monument. 11–16–1934.

## HAWESVILLE *(Hancock County)*

**Lincoln**
*Work* • Samuel Pate house. KY 334, 3 miles west of town. Won first law case here. Marker 667. 1827.

## HODGENVILLE *(Larue County)*

**Eisenhower**
*Visit* • Lincoln Log Cabin Memorial. 4–23–1954.

**Lincoln**
*Birthplace* • 3 miles south of Hodgenville on US 31E. Granite memorial shrine encloses log cabin that is the traditional birthplace. 1809.

*Church* • Sinking Spring Church, 5 miles north of Knob Creek home. 1811–1816.

*Education* • Knob Creek School, four miles from his home. 1816.

*Home* • Knob Creek Farm on US 31E. Boyhood home and his last home in Kentucky. It has replica of original log cabin. Marker on US 31E. 1811–1816.

*Site* • Lincoln Museum. 66 Lincoln Sq.

## JENNIE'S CREEK *(Johnson County)*

**Garfield**

*Work* • US 23, US 460, 1/2 mile west of junction. Marker 571. 1862.

## LEXINGTON *(Fayette County)*

**Eisenhower**

*Visit* • Transylvania College, Third and Broadway for the 175th anniversary. 4–23–1954.

**Fillmore**

*Visit* • Ashland, Henry Clay's home and tomb. E Main (Richmond Rd) at 120 Sycamore Rd. 1854.

**Harrison, WH**

*Visit* • Phoenix Hotel. Burned 1830s. Another of the same name replaced it 1880, Main and Limestone Sts.

**Lincoln**

*Visit* • 573 West Main at Mary Todd Lincoln House. 1847–.

*Site* • 501 W Short St. Birthplace of Mary Todd. Tablet.

**Van Buren**

*Visit* • Ashland, home of Henry Clay, 1400 Block Richmond Rd. 1842.

## LOUISA *(Lawrence County)*

**Garfield**

*Work* • Occupied town. On US 23 at courthouse yard. Marker 547. 1862.

## LOUISVILLE *(Jefferson County)*

**Presidents**

*Visit* • Galt House, on the river at Fourth and River Sts. Bush, Ford, Grant, and Reagan.

*Visit* • Locust Grove, 561 Blakenbaker Lane. Jackson, Madison, Monroe, and Taylor.

**Arthur**

*Travel* • Opened the Southern Exposition, which was housed in a large building near the river. 1883.

**Grant**

*Visit* • Louisville Hotel. 1866. See A Johnson below.

**Hayes**

*Visit* • Louisville Industrial Exposition. September 1877.

**Hoover**

*Visit* • Memorial Auditorium, Fourth and Kentucky Sts. First time a president in office visited since Wilson.

**Johnson, A**

*Visit* • Louisville Hotel reception, Main and Sixth Sts. He took the steamer from here to Cincinnati. Wharf north end of N Third St. 1866.

**Lincoln**

*Visit* • Farmington, 3033 Bardstown Rd, for two months. 1841.

*Site* • Monument, Fourth St on the west lawn of the library.

**Reagan**

*Visit* • Whitney Hall, Kentucky Center for the Arts, Sixth and Main Sts. Stayed Hyatt Regency Hotel, 328 W Jefferson St. 10–7–1984.

**Taylor**

*Church* • Small house on Second St was the site of services. 1803–.

*Marriage* • Harrods Creek Station on Wolf Pen Rd (in Jefferson County across line from Mercer Co.). Home of bride's sister, Mary Chew. Nothing remains and no marker. 1810.

*Home* • Springfield, 5608 Apache Rd. Now privately owned. 1785–1808.

*Original burial vault of Zachary Taylor.*

---

**Home** • Bear Grass Creek (now downtown Louisville). Farm and early house were wedding gift. 1810.

**Home** • He lived in Louisville as a recruiting officer. No site determined. 1818–1819.

**Home** • East side of First St near Jefferson St when home on extended furlough. 1830.

**Visit** • Soldier's Retreat, 3 miles east of Springfield.

**Burial** • In old vault until 1926 when removed to new site. 1850–1926. See next entry.

**Burial** • 4701 Brownsboro Rd in the National Cemetery. Graves of President and Mrs. Taylor. 1926.

## MAYSVILLE *(Mason County)*

**Grant**
**Education** • Maysville Academy on Fourth St. He lived with an aunt while attending Maysville Academy. Location undetermined. 1836–1837.

**Harrison, WH**
**Visit** • Forrest Retreat on Maysville-Lexington Rd at the junction with Carlisle Pike.

Adjoined the home of Governor Thomas Metcalfe. Stagecoach stop. 1796–.

**Jackson**
**Visit** • See entry above. Also stopped at Cross-Keys Tavern (half-way house) between Lexington and Louisville. Burned 1934. 1796–.

**Taylor**
**Travel** • Headquarters. Site not marked.

## MIDDLE CREEK *(See Prestonsburg)*

## MILL SPRINGS *(See Prestonburg)*

## MUNFORDVILLE *(Hart County)*

**Jackson**
**Visit** • Old Munford Inn, First and Main. Marker 204. 1829.

## PADUCAH *(McCracken County)*

**Grant**
**Church** • Broadway Methodist, NW corner Broadway at Fourth. Destroyed by fire. Marker Broadway at Seventh number 1029 where later church stood. 1861.

**Work** • Fort Anderson, Trimble St between Fourth and Fifth Sts. Fortification site. Grant built. 1861.

**Work** • Supply base in Civil War. N Eighth and Julia Sts. Marker 916. 1861.

**Visit** • Landing at First and Broadway (Broadway at Riverfront). Marker 924. 1861.

**Visit** • General Lew Wallace headquarters. Northwest corner Sixth and Clark. 1861.

## PAINTSVILLE *(Johnson County)*

**Garfield**
**Work** • Site marker in Floyd County Mountain Parkway extension.

## PIKEVILLE *(Pike County)*

**Garfield**
**Work** • Sworn in as Union Brigadier Gen-

GEOGRAPHIC GUIDE TO LANDMARKS

eral. Plaque in the City Park, Hoffman Ave and Main St. 1862.

## PRESTONSBURG  *(Floyd County)*

**Garfield**

*Work* • Headquarters off Main St. Marker 172. 1862. Marker No 85 on KY 114 west of town commemorating victory at Middle Creek Battle. 1–10–1862.

## SINKING SPRING CREEK  *(See*

*Hodgenville.)*

## SMITHLAND  *(Livingston County)*

**Grant**

*Work* • Staging area against Fort Donelson on US 60. 1861.

**Polk/Taylor**

*Visit* • Gower House (luxury inn at the time). See also marker 938.

## SPRINGFIELD  *(Washington County)*

**Lincoln**

*Site* • Lincoln Homestead State Park, 5 1/2 miles north off US 150 on KY 528. Replicas of Lincoln cabins.

## VINE GROVE  *(Hardin County)*

**Lincoln**

*Home* • Route of Lincoln's family travel when migrating from Knob Hill farm to Spencer County, Indiana. KY 144. Marker 858. 1816.

## WASHINGTON  *(Mason County)*

**Taylor**

*Travel* • Inducted into the army. No marker. See Old Washington part of town. 1808.

# LOUISIANA

## BATON ROUGE *(East Baton Rouge Parish)* Capitol

*Site* • Lafayette St and North Bld. Capitol. 1847–1932

*Site* • Built on site of old Louisiana State University 1932. On the edge of University Lake at the north end of Third St extension of Nicholson Dr. Governor's Mansion 502 North Blvd. 1930–1962. Governor's Mansion Capitol Lake Dr. 1962 to present.

**Taylor**

*Church* • Pentagon Barracks used by the Episcopal Church. Adjacent to present Capitol grounds. 1822.

*Church* • Episcopal Church became St. James Church, 208 N Fourth St. 1822–1824.

*Home* • Quarters (now present ground of the state capitol), 727 Lafayette St. See stone marker. Actual site (south of Pentagon buildings on the edge of the bluff near the railroad) a few yards from the Barracks. 1847–1849.

*Travel* • Commanding Officer in the area. Army Headquarters 1840. See Pentagon on Old Louisiana State University Campus. Marker. 1822–1824.

*Visit* • Kleinpeter House, 18 miles south on River Rd, LA 327 at 18666 Perkins Rd. 1826.

## BAYOU ST. JOHN *(Near New Orleans)*

**Jackson**

*Travel* • Schertz Villa, 1300 Moss St. Meeting between Jackson and Jean Lafitte. 1814.

## BAYOU SARA *(Near Francisville )*

**Taylor**

*Home* • Owned a cotton plantation near Bayou Sara. Exact location not determined. 1820s.

*Visit* • Samuel Chew home. Family stayed with his wife's sister, Mrs. Chew, near Bay St. Louis. Nothing remains. 1820.

## CAMP SALUBRITY *(Western Louisiana)*

**Grant**

*Work* • Stationed here. 1845.

1. Taylor home, *Baton Rouge*
2. Locust Grove, *St. Francisville*

Louisiana

61

2

1

Baton Rouge

10

New Orleans

## COTTAGE PLANTATION (BUTLER)

*(West Feliciana Parish)*

**Jackson**
*Visit* • Butler House, US 61, five miles north of St. Francisville. He lodged here en route to Natchez after Battle of New Orleans. 1815.

## COTTAGE PLANTATION (CONRAD)

*(East Baton Rouge Parish).*

**Taylor**
*Visit* • Kleinpeter House. 1826. See Baton Rouge.

## FORT JESSUP *(Sabine Parish)*

**Taylor**
*Travel* • Now Sabine Parish Historical Park. One block off LA 6 in the eastern part of town. Abandoned 1846 and only two stone pillars remain. 1822–1823.

## FORT SELDEN *(Natchitoches Parish)*

**Taylor**
*Travel* • Built fort, 12 miles upstream from Natchitoches at Grand E Core Bluff overlooking Red River. 1821.

## HERMITAGE PLANTATION *(Ascension Parish)*

**Jackson**
*Visit* • Duradou Bringier House. Banquet here after Battle of New Orleans. 1815.

## LAKE PROVIDENCE *(East Carroll Parish)*

**Grant**
*Work* • Grant's Canal on US 50. Markers showing line of his march include: Young's Point, Milliken's Bend, Richmond, Trinidad Plantation, New Carthage, Ione Plantation, Davis Island, Choctaw Bayou, and Hard Times Landing. 1863.

## NEWELLTON *(Tensas Parish)*

**Grant**
*Work* • Winter Quarters, SE of Newellton on LA 608. Winter headquarters. 1863.

*Work* • Dr. Haller Nutt House on road between Milliken's Bend and Hard Times Landing. 1863.

**Roosevelt, T**
*Visit* • Tensas hunting lodge. 1912.

## NEW ORLEANS *(Orleans Parish)*

**Presidents**
*Visit* • Fairmont Hotel (formerly Roosevelt Hotel), 100 Block University Place. Bush, Carter, Coolidge, Ford, and Truman.

**Bush**
*Visit* • Superdome, 1500 block of Poydras St. Nominated for president at RNC. August 1988.

*Travel* • Received Theodore Roosevelt Award. 1986.

**Fillmore**
*Visit* • St. Charles Hotel, 211 St. Charles Ave. 1854.

*Visit* • City Hall, the Cabildo, Jackson Square, 545 St. Charles Ave (building now known as Gallier Hall). 1854.

**Ford**
*Visit* • Edward Hebert Library groundbreaking, Tulane University Convocation at University Fieldhouse, 6823 St. Charles Ave. 4–23–1975.

**Harding**
*Travel* • Reception at City Hall, LaSalle and Poydras, before he boarded the ship for Caribbean tour. 1920.

**Jackson**
*Travel* • 106 Royal St, headquarters. See also Marcarte House on Rodriquet Canal and joining with the Mississippi River south of city. 1814–1815.

*Travel* • Old Mint, 400 Esplanade Ave. Site on which mint stands was the scene of his review of the troops before battle. 1814–1815.

*Travel* • Chalmette National Historical Park at 8606 West St. Bernard Highway. Final battle of the War of 1812. 1814–1815.

*Visit* • Col. Livingston House, 417 Royal Street Patio Royal. 1815.

**McKinley**

*Visit* • Cabildo on Jackson Square, on the uptown side of St. Louis Cathedral. 1901.

*Visit* • Southern University, east end of Robert E. Lee Blvd. Speech and reception. May 1901.

*Site* • Cruise on the Mississippi from Audubon Park, south end Audubon Blvd and east on Mississippi River to Chalmette and return. 1901.

**Polk**

*Visit* • St. Louis Hotel on Charles St near the railroad (now 730 Bienville St). 3–22–1849.

**Roosevelt, T**

*Visit* • St. Charles Hotel, 211 St. Charles Ave. First visit since 1905 (5 hours). 3–11–1912.

*Visit* • Hunting lodge on Tensas Bayou. Expedition said to inspire the popular toy, the "teddy bear." 1907.

*Church* • St. Louis Cathedral on Place d'Armes. 12–3–1847

*Travel* • Place d'Armes honored at a reception. 1847.

*Travel* • City Hall, 545 St. Charles Ave. He was stationed 13 miles south of New Orleans. 1809. New Orleans headquarters. 1827–1829.

*Visit* • St. Charles Hotel, 211 St. Charles Ave. 1847.

*Site* • Had Rodney Plantation 25 miles from New Orleans on the right bank of the river. 1850.

**Taft**

*Visit* • St. Charles Hotel. 211 St. Charles Ave. 1909.

## POINT CLEAR PLANTATION
*(Madison Parish)*

**Grant**

*Work* • Headquarters during Civil War. Original house burned. 1863.

## ST. FRANCISVILLE *(West Feliciana Parish)*

**Grant**

*Work* • Fairview Plantation, overlooking Thompson's Creek. He used as a hospital. 1861.

**Taylor**

*Home* • Locust Grove, off US 61, NE of town. Nothing remains. Cemetery near by has grave of Sarah, his daughter and wife of Jefferson Davis. 1822–1841.

## SHIELD'S SPRING *(See Fort Jessup)*

## TALLULAH *(See Point Clear Plantation)*

# MAINE

## AUGUSTA *(Kennebec County)*

**Presidents**
*Visit* • Augusta House, junction of Green, Grove, Water and Gage Sts. Buchanan 1847, Grant 1865, Polk 1847.

**Presidents**
*Visit* • State House. State and Capitol Sts. Buchanan 1847, Grant 1865, Polk 1847.

**Presidents**
*Visit* • Blaine House (Governor's Mansion). Grant 1873, B Harrison 1889.

**Polk**
*Visit* • Received in Representatives Hall of the State House. 7–2–1847.

## BANGOR *(Penobscot County)*

**Grant**
*Visit* • Hill House. 159 Union St, and Bangor House, SE corner of Main and Union Sts. 1873.

## BRUNSWICK *(Cumberland County)*

**Grant**
*Visit* • Chamberlain Home (now museum) 226 Maine St. 1868. Tontine Hotel. Site corner of School and Maine Sts. 1868 and 1873.

**Pierce**
*Church* • Bowdoin College Chapel. It disappeared long ago. 1820–1824.

*Church* • First Parish Church, 9 Cleaveland St. 1820–1824. Received honorary degree from Bowdoin College. 1868.

*Education* • Attended Bowdoin College, Main, Bath, and College Sts.

*Lodging* • Massachusetts Hall. 1820–1824. Maine Hall, Room 13, later Room 26 at Bowdoin. 1822. Mrs. Grow's Boarding House Cross (now Cleaveland) St. 1820. Benjamin Orr House on Park Row. Probably demolished. 1821.

*Visit* • Stowe House, 63 Federal St. Lodging place of his classmate Henry Wadsworth Longfellow. 1821–1825.

## BUCKSPORT *(Hancock County)*

**Presidents**
*Visit* • Jed Prouty Tavern. Jackson, WH Harrison, and Van Buren.

Maine

Augusta

⬡ 95

Portland

1

1. Bush home,
   *Kennebunkport*

*George Bush's Kennebunkport home.*

## CAPE PORPOISE *(York County)*

**Nixon**
> *Travel* • Weekend in hotel here before entering service. July 1942.

## ISLAND FALLS *(Aroostook County)*

**Roosevelt, T**
> *Visit* • Took camping trips at Island Falls and Lake Katahdin. 1878 and 1879.
>
> *Visit* • Bible Point at Island Falls. 1878.

## KENNEBUNKPORT *(York County)*

**Bush**
> *Baptism* • St. Anne's Episcopal Church, Walker Rd. 9–7–1924.
>
> *Church* • South Congregational, corner Temple and North Sts. 1924–.

> *Home* • Walker's Point. Family vacation home. 1924–.
>
> *Visit* • Shawmut Inn, Turbots Creek Rd. 8–30–1989.

## MOOSEHEAD LAKE
### *(Piscataquis/Somerset Counties)*

**Roosevelt, T**
> *Visit* • Camping. 1872.

## ORONO *(Penobscot County)*

**Kennedy**
> *Visit* • University of Maine, along the Stillwater River. 10–19–1963.

## TOPSHAM *(Sagadahoc County)*

**Johnson, LB**
> *Visit* • Topsham Dairy Queen, Main Street

on ME 24 across the river from Brunswick. 6–23–1967.

# YORK  *(York County)*

**Adams, J**

*Church* • Meeting House built 1774, renovated 1882. 1774.

*Visit* • Woodbridge Tavern (Ritchie's Tavern). 1770.

*Visit* • Excursion to Agamenticus Mountain. 1770.

**Monroe**

*Visit* • Home of Judge David Sewall. June 1817.

# MARYLAND

## ABERDEEN *(Harford County)*

**Truman**
> *Visit* • Aberdeen Proving Ground, MD 22 along Chesapeake Bay. 2–17–1951.

## ANDREWS AIR FORCE BASE *(Camp Springs, near Suitland)*

**Presidents**
> *Travel* • All recent presidents have used this airforce base.

## ANNAPOLIS *(Anne Arundel County)*

**Presidents**
> *Visit* • Reynolds Tavern, Church Circle and Franklin St. Jefferson, Madison, Monroe, and Washington visited.

> *Visit* • Tecumseh Court where dress parades are held. Many presidents have viewed marching cadets at this site.

**Carter**
> *Church* • Naval Academy Chapel, Maryland Ave entrance to the right on Blake Rd. 1943–1946.

> *Education* • Naval Academy, Maryland Ave and Hanover St. Accelerated course. He lived in Bancroft Hall, near Maryland Ave entrance to the Naval Academy. The first home of all midshipmen. 1943–1946.

> *Visit* • Attended Naval Academy Commencement. 6–7–1978.

**Coolidge**
> *Visit* • McDowell Hall when King Williams School was formally turned over to its successor, St. John's College, 60 College Ave. 1928.

**Eisenhower**
> *Visit* • U.S. Naval Academy. 5–17–1953, 6–4–1958. St. John's College, Key Memorial Auditorium dedication, 60 College Ave. 5–22–1959.

**Ford**
> *Education* • Naval Academy. 1942.

**Jefferson**
> *Work* • State Circle, State House. Member of the House of Representatives. 1783–1784.

> *Lodging* • Frances Bryce Boarding House, 18 West St. 1783.

# Maryland

2

1

70 Baltimore 95

3

Annapolis

1. Washington Monument
   State Park, *Middletown*
2. Camp David, Catoctin
   Mountain National Park
3. United States Naval
   Academy, *Annapolis*

*Visit* • Ghiselin Boarding House, 28–30 West St, while attending Continental Congress. 1784.

### Kennedy
*Visit* • Naval Academy graduation. 6–7–1961.

### Madison
*Work* • State House. Member of Constitutional Convention. 1786.

*Visit* • Maryland Inn, Church and Main Sts. Built in the 1770s as an inn by Thomas Hyde. 1780s–. Sign of the Indian King, also called Donald–Stewart House, 10 Francis St, while attending the Constitutional Convention. 1786.

### Monroe
*Work* • State House. Member of House of Representatives. 1782–1784.

*Lodging* • Shared with Jefferson. 1784. See Jefferson above.

### Nixon
*Visit* • U.S. Naval Academy, Navy-Marine Corps Memorial Stadium. 6–5–1974.

### Reagan
*Visit* • U.S. Naval Academy, Marine Corps Stadium. 5–22–1985.

### Truman
*Visit* • Naval Academy. Attended the chapel. 1948.

### Washington
*Work* • State Circle. State House. He resigned his commission in the Old Senate Chamber. 1783.

*Visit* • Lloyd Delaney House, 162 Conduit St. Later became City Hotel. Now Freemason Temple. 1783, 1791.

*Visit* • St. Anne's Church rectory, 215–217 Hanover Street. Often stayed. 1770s.

*Visit* • Governor Robert Eden house. Eden died in the Upton-Scott house at 4 Shipwright St. The mansion was on the site now occupied by Bancroft Hall of the U.S. Naval Academy. 1773–.

*Visit* • Mann's Tavern, formerly Dulany House and later City Hotel and Colonial Theater, 162 Conduit St. 1902.

*Visit* • Governor Ogle house, 247 King George St. 1783.

*Visit* • John Ridout house, 120 Duke of Gloucester St. 1780s–.

*Visit* • Belevedere, home of Governor John Howard, at the head of Calvert St (just south of Chase St). Razed 1876 to make way for extension of Calvert Street. 1790.

## ANTIETAM BATTLEFIELD *(Washington County)*

### Carter
*Visit* • 7–6–1978.

### Hayes
*Work* • 1862.

### McKinley
*Work* • 1862. See McKinley monument on the hill near Burnside Bridge.

## BALTIMORE

### Presidents
*Visit* • Barnum Hotel, corner of Fayette and Calvert Sts. JQ Adams, Buchanan, Fillmore, Jackson, A Johnson, Lincoln, Monroe, Taylor, Washington, and Wilson. Hotel torn down 1889.

### Presidents
*Visit* • Eutaw House, corner Eutaw and Baltimore Sts. Grant, WH Harrison, A Johnson, and Pierce.

### Adams, J
*Church* • Presbyterian Meeting House, standing on a hill just at the back of the town. Now part of the US postal property. Current church at NW corner of Fayette and North Sts. The church he attended was a plain brick building built 1766. 1777–.

*Work* • Congress Hall, corner of Sharpe and Baltimore Sts. Memorial tablet. 1776–1777.

*Visit* • Mrs. Ross Boarding House, probably 9 Market St a few doors below the Fountain Inn. 1777.

*Visit* • Mr. Johnson Public House. February 1777.

**Adams, JQ**

*Funeral* • Merchants Exchange, fronted on Gay Street from Water (Lombard) to Second. Lay in state in the rotunda. Torn down 1902 for the new Customs House. 1848.

**Arthur**

*Visit* • Front Street Theater, NW corner Front and Low Sts. RNC. 6–7–1864 to 6–8–1864.

**Buchanan**

*Visit* • Universalist Church, corner Calvert and Pleasant Sts. Democratic National Committee. May 1848.

**Bush**

*Visit* • Convention Center, 1 W Pratt St. 9–7–1989.

*Visit* • Memorial Stadium, Thirty-third St and Ellerslie Ave. 4–23–1989.

**Carter**

*Visit* • Memorial Stadium. 10–17–1979.

**Clinton**

*Visit* • Memorial Stadium. Threw out first ball. April 1993.

**Eisenhower**

*Visit* • Johns Hopkins University. Charles and Thirty-fourth Sts. 6–10–1958.

*Visit* • Fifth Regiment Armory, Hoffman and Bolton Sts. 10–31–1958.

**Ford**

*Visit* • Fort McHenry Monument, foot of Fort Ave on Whetstone Point. 7–4–1975.

**Grant**

*Visit* • George Small house at Mount Vernon Place. Entertained several times. 1869–1877.

**Jackson**

*Visit* • The Athenaeum, SW corner Lex-

ington and St. Paul Sts, and the Universalist Church. Democratic National Committee. Nomination. May 1832.

**Johnson, A**

*Visit* • Greeted by 100,000 people. August 1865.

**Johnson, LB**

*Visit* • Johns Hopkins, Shriver Hall Auditorium. 10–1–1964, 4–7–1965.

*Visit* • Lyric Theater, 140 Mt Royal Ave. 4–22–1966.

**Lincoln**

*Visit* • 702 Cathedral St where he stayed overnight. 1864.

*Visit* • Front Street Theater, opened September 10, 1829. NW corner Front and Low St. He was renominated and Andrew Johnson nominated as vice president. June 1864.

*Visit* • Speech at the American Institute, Mt Royal Ave and Lanvale St. 4–19–1864.

*Travel* • Passed through on way to 1861 inaugural, Camden Station at Camden and Howard St. President Street Station, at President, Canton, and Aliceanna Sts. Transferred from here to Camden to avert possible assassination attempt. 1861.

*Funeral* • Funeral procession arrived by train. Lay in state at the Merchants Exchange at Gay and Water Sts. 1865.

**Monroe**

*Visit* • Fountain Inn. See location under Washington. 6–1–1817.

*Visit* • Sailed from Baltimore for LeHavre from harbor on Boston St at the foot of Luzerne St. 6–18–1794.

**Pierce**

*Visit* • Maryland Institute Hall, Mt. Royal Ave and Lanvale St. Nominated for president by Democratic National Committee. June 1852.

**Polk**

*Work* • Nominated for President. Odd Fellows Hall. Site Gay and Fayette Sts intersection. May 1844.

**Reagan**
*Visit* • Fort McHenry. 6–14–1985, 10–15–1986.

**Roosevelt, FD**
*Visit* • Munsey Building. Room 214 for Democratic National Committee. 1912.

**Truman**
*Visit* • Friendship Airport, I–95 at Elm St. Dedication 1950.

**Tyler**
*Visit* • Calvert Hall. Site Calvert Street. Nominated for president. May 1844.

**Van Buren**
*Work* • First Presbyterian Church. Site NW corner Light and German Sts. A two-steeple church. Nominated for president. May 1835.

*Visit* • The Athenaeum and the Universalist Church. See under Jackson for locations. Democratic National Committee nomination for vice president. May 1832.

*Visit* • Hall of the Musical Association. Nomination by Democratic National Committee. May 1840.

**Washington**
*Visit* • Congress Hall. Site SW corner Sharpe and Baltimore Sts. Here he was voted full military command. South side of Baltimore between Sharp and Liberty. 1776.

*Visit* • Fountain Inn. Site NE corner Light (now Redwood) and German Sts. He was here 1775, 1789, 1792, and 1797. Site of present Carrolton Hotel.

*Site* • 700 block N Charles St at Mount Vernon Pl. First architectural monument honoring Washington.

**Wilson**
*Church* • First Unitarian Church (Independent church that became Unitarian) at NW corner Charles and Franklin Sts. 1884–1886.

*Church* • Scotch Presbyterian Church, 53 W Fourteenth St. 1884–.

*Education* • Johns Hopkins, Charles and Thirty-fourth St. He lived at 146 Charles St at a boarding house. Moved January 1884 to McCulloh St. 1883–1884. After 1886, 146 became 906. It was one of four houses on the site of the present Walters Art Gallery. September 1883 to May 1886.

*Work* • Johns Hopkins. He delivered his lectures in Hopkins Hall. 1883–1885; 1891.

*Work/Lodging* • While lecturing at Johns Hopkins, he lived at 909 N McCulloh St. 1891; 1893.

*Visit* • 906 McCulloh Street. In 1895 and at other times he stayed here. Lectured each winter. 1888–1897.

*Visit* • Robert C. Hall home, 257 Madison Ave. 1880s.

*Visit* • Fifth Maryland Regiment Armory, Hoffman and Bolton Sts. Democratic National Committee. Nominated. June 1912.

## BETHESDA *(Montgomery County)*

**Presidents**
*Visit* • Bethesda Naval Hospital, 8901 Wisconsin Ave. All presidents since FD Roosevelt have visited. Kennedy's body taken here after flight from Texas. 1963.

**Presidents**
*Visit* • Burning Tree Golf Club, Burdette and River Rds. Most presidents since Harding have played here.

**Nixon**
*Visit* • 7000 Armat Dr, where Julie and David Eisenhower lived in a white brick house. Visited at least twice a week. 1974–.

**Roosevelt, FD**
*Visit* • Naval Hospital Medical Center. Dedication. 8–31–1939.

## BLADENSBURG *(Prince Georges County)*

**Washington**
*Visit* • Indian Queen Tavern, also known

as Washington House. Alt US 1 near
Bladensburg Rd. Used as store and tavern
when he visited. Restored. 1780s.

## BOONSBORO *(Washington County)*

**Washington**

*Site* • Washington Monument State Park
on Alt US 40. First monument to Washington. 7–4–1827.

## BROOKEVILLE *(Montgomery County)*

**Madison**

*Visit* • Caleb Bentley House where he escaped from the British. Two-story white
brick. 1812.

**Monroe**

*Visit* • See entry above. He met Madison
here and drove back to Washington. 1812.

## CAMP DAVID *(Frederick County)*

**Presidents**

*Visit* • National Park is the presidential retreat. Camp David is in the middle of the
park. It is closed to the public, but its entrance and some of the maximum security
fencing can be seen to the right on Park
Central Road for approximately two miles.
Every president since Truman has spent
time here.

**Carter**

*Visit* • Meetings with Anwar al-Sadat and
Mehahem Begin. 9–5–1978.

## CAMP MEADE *(Anne Arundel County)*

**Eisenhower**

*Home* • Bachelor quarters. See only the
oldest part of the post on Taylor Avenue
(right off Mapes Road) including site of
post headquarters during WW II. Nothing
remains of the bachelor quarters or other
buildings which would have been there

during his time except the house mentioned above. 1918.

*Work* • Tank Unit. 1918. See site of US
Army Tank School on Chamberlain Av-
enue. Also site of Tent City for troops  on
Leonard Wood St. 1919–1940.

*Work* • Commander   Tank   Battalion.
1918–1922. Football coach. 1924. See location site on Chamberlain Ave.

## CHARLESTOWN *(Cecil County)*

**Washington**

*Visit* • MD 267 off MD 7. The house next
door to the Indian Queen is thought to be
where he stopped. 1795

## CHESTERTOWN *(Kent County)*

**Eisenhower**

*Visit* • Washington College, Washington
Ave. 6–7–1954.

**Washington**

*Site* • Washington College, Washington
Ave, to which he contributed for its founding.
Received Doctor of Law degree here. 1789.

## COLLEGE PARK *(Prince Georges County)*

**Clinton**

*Travel* • Participated in Democratic primary debate at University of Maryland, off
US 1.

## CUMBERLAND *(Allegany County)*

**Truman**

*Visit* • Fort Cumberland Hotel. Now retirement home, town center. 1928.

**Washington**

*Travel* • Riverside Park at Greene St. Log
cabin moved to the park in 1921 was his
headquarters at the beginning of his military career and during French and Indian
War. The cabin was originally within the

walls of Fort Cumberland on the hill above the park. The Allegheny County Court House now stands on the approximate site. Marker. 1756.

## DEER PARK *(Garrett County)*

**Presidents**
*Visit* • Garfield, Grant, B Harrison, and McKinley.

**Cleveland**
*Honeymoon* • Behind Deer Park Hotel is the Grover Cleveland Cottage with marker. 1886.

**Washington**
*Visit* • Near the park is the site of the old road over which he rode in leading part of Braddock's army. 1748.

## EMMITSBURG *(Frederick County)*

**Eisenhower**
*Visit* • Mount St. Mary's College, on US 15. 6–2–1958.

## FOUNTAIN ROCK *(Washington County)*

**Madison**
*Visit* • Gen. Samuel Ringgold house. College Rd off MD 68. House built by Ringgold 1792. 1801.

**Monroe**
*Visit* • Same as above. 1817.

## FREDERICK *(Frederick County)*

**Harrison, WH**
*Visit* • Dorsey's City Hotel, north side West Patrick between Market and Public Sts. Now Court St. 1841.

**Lincoln**
*Visit* • Ramsey house, 119 Record St, visiting the wounded General George Hartsuff.

## HAGERSTOWN *(Washington County)*

**Harrison, WH**
*Visit* • McIllhenney's Tavern, N Potomac St. 1841.

## HAVRE-DE-GRACE *(Harford County)*

**Washington**
*Visit* • On the Susquehanna. Lafayette House (now a hotel). 1770s.

## LITTLE MEADOW *(Garret County)*

**Washington**
*Visit* • Had frequent camps here. Braddock's Trail built under his direction. 1755.

## MIDDLE RIVER *(Baltimore County)*

**Nixon**
*Home* • Small apartment. Location unknown. 1945.

*Work* • Naval Post. 1945.

## MIDDLETOWN *(Frederick County)*

**Hayes**
*Visit* • Wounded and spent time in a church used as a hospital. July 1863.

**Washington**
*Site* • First Monument to Washington (near Middletown). Washington Monument State Park.

## OAKLAND *(Garrett County)*

**Presidents**
*Church* • St. Matthew's Episcopal, "Church of the Presidents," Second and Liberty Sts. Cleveland, Garfield, Grant, and B Harrison attended while vacationing at Deer Park.

## PERRYVILLE *(Cecil County)*

**Jefferson**
*Visit* • Rodgers Tavern, MD 7.

**Washington**

> *Visit* • Rodgers Tavern, where he stopped many times. 1780s and 1790s.

## PINEY POINT *(St. Mary's County)*

**Presidents**

> *Visit* • Pierce and T Roosevelt.

**Monroe**

> *Visit* • MD 249. Resort served as a summer social center. Monroe stayed here first in the hotel and later in a cottage that in effect became the summer White House. 1817–.

## ROCK HALL *(Kent County)*

**Washington**

> *Visit* • On the shore of the Chesapeake Bay where he crossed many times. Marker. MD 20. Jefferson and Madison also crossed on the ferry here. 1770s.

## ROCKVILLE *(Montgomery County)*

**Hoover**

> *Visit* • Congressional Country Club, River Road. First president to play here. 1924–1933.

## SANDY SPRINGS *(Montgomery County)*

**Hoover**

> *Church* • Friends Meeting House, Meeting House Road. 1928.

## SHARPSBURG *(Washington County)*

**Lincoln**

> *Visit* • Mt. Airy Mansion, MD 34, visiting the Civil War wounded.

## SOUTH MOUNTAIN *(Frederick County)*

**Hayes**

> *Work* • Hayes took part in battle. 9–14–1862.

## WILLIAMSPORT *(Washington County)*

**Washington**

> *Visit* • Spring House, Springfield Lane. Here to consider Williamsport as a possible site for the proposed federal capital. October 1790.

> *Visit* • Otho Holland Williams house on Springfield Lane where he dined while in Williamsport. October 1790.

# MASSACHUSETTS

## AMHERST *(Hampshire County)*

### Coolidge

*Church* • Johnson Chapel on campus, Pleasant St. 1891–1895.

*Education* • Amherst College Pleasant St. Fall of 1891–1895. He lived on South Pleasant St in a brick house. 1891.

*Lodging* • South Pleasant St at Mr. Trott's, first and second year. Boarding places changed many times. 1891–1893. Avery House on Prospect St. 1893–1894.

### Kennedy

*Visit* • Amherst College, field house. Groundbreaking Robert Frost Library, Pleasant St. 10– 26–1963.

## ANDOVER *(Essex County)*

### Bush

*Church* • Academy Chapel. Chapel St. 1937–1942.

*Education* • Phillips Academy, Phillips and Main Sts. 1937–1942.

## ARLINGTON *(Middlesex County)*

### Adams, J

*Church* • Unitarian Church, Pleasant St. 1758.

*Home* • Pleasant St and Massachusetts Ave. Marker on the Green indicates the site of his house. 1758.

## BEVERLY *(Essex County)*

### Taft

*Church* • First Parish Church, 225 Cabot between Hale and Essex. Summers. 1909–.

*Home* • R. D. Evans Cottage, Woodberry Point. Summer home. Now site of Lynch Park at 55 Ober St (Burgess Point). 1909–. Harding visited here. 1910.

*Home* • Green Cottage, Burgess Point. Now site of Lynch Park at 55 Ober St. Summer home. 1910.

*Home* • Peabody College, 70 Corning St. Summer 1911.

*Work* • Board of Trade Building, 244 Cabot. Now Site of Beverly National Bank. 1909.

1. J. Adams home, *Boston*
2. Bush home, *Milton*
3. Coolidge home, *Northampton*
4. J. Adams birthplace, *Quincy*

**Massachusetts**

Boston

# BOSTON *(Suffolk County)*

**Presidents**

*Visit* • Faneuil Hall, Merchants Row. J and JQ Adams, Grant, Kennedy, Monroe, and Washington.

**Presidents**

*Visit* • Revere House. Site Bowdoin Square. Fillmore, Grant, and Pierce.

**Presidents**

*Visit* • State House, Beacon Hill, corner of Beacon and Park. Opened 1798. J and JQ Adams, Fillmore, Jackson, and Taft.

**Presidents**

*Visit* • Tremont House, 275 Tremont. Jackson, Pierce, Tyler, and Van Buren.

**Presidents**

*Visit* • Hotel Vendome, Commonwealth Ave. Originally entrance on Dartmouth but much of that part destroyed by fire, 1975. Cleveland, Grant, B Harrison, and McKinley.

## Adams, J

*Church* • Brattle Square Church. The SW corner of City Hall stands on the site of this church. 1768.

*Church* • King's Chapel, corner of School and Tremont Sts. 1751–1756.

*Church* • Old South Meeting House (1729), 310 Washington St. 1768–.

*Church* • Old North Church (Christ Church), 193 Salem St. Attended after 1768.

*Church* • Unitarian Church, Marlborough and Berkeley Sts. Attended after 1768.

*Church* • Old West Church. Cambridge St.

*Church* • Park Street Church, corner of Park and Tremont Sts. Built 1809.

*Church* • Holy Cross Roman Catholic, 1400 Washington St, which opened 1803.

*Home* • The White House, Mr. Bollan's House, Brattle St, on the corner across from the church and the house of William Cooper less than two blocks from Faneuil Hall. 1767– 1769.

*Home* • Moved to Cold Lane by the Mill Pond when the White House was sold. This street ran northward from Hanover St to the Mill Pond and was indiscrimately called Cold or Cole Lane. 1770.

*Home* • Court St. Returning from Braintree to this house opposite the courthouse (South Queen St, later named Court St). 1771–1774.

*Lodging* • James Cunningham House on Washington St (south end of Boston). 1764.

*Work* • Office in his house on Brattle Square. 1768–1774.

*Work* • King Street study. He also presented cases at town meetings at Faneuil Hall. 1770.

*Work* • Old State House, 206 Washington. Representative to the General Court. 1771–1774; 1775–1777.

*Work* • Law office on Queen St. 1771–1774.

*Visit* • John Hancock Mansion. Site is now occupied by present west wing of State House. 1788.

*Visit* • Green Dragon Tavern, Union St. Marker on site. 1769.

*Visit* • American Coffee House, previously known as British Coffee House. Site is 66 State St on the north side. 1771–.

## Adams, JQ

*Church* • Old South Church, Copley Square. 1786.

*Home* • Entries parallel those of John Adams. 1767–1782.

*Home* • The White House, Brattle St. 1768–1769; 1770–1771.

*Home* • Cold Lane by the Mill Pond. 1769–1770.

*Home* • Court St. 1771–1774.

*Home/Work* • Court St, opposite the courthouse. 1790–1795.

*Home* • No. 39 Hanover St. 1801– 1803.

*Home* • Nassau St (now Tremont) and

Frog Lande (now Boylston St). Site of the present Hotel Touraine. 1806–1809.

**Home** • 57 Mount Vernon St used as a winter house. 1842–.

**Work** • State St. Had his law office under the Centinel Printing shop. 1801–1802.

**Work** • State House, corner Beacon and Park. Member of the Senate. Senate Chamber today is part of original building. 1802.

**Work** • Faneuil Hall, Merchants Row. Nominated for president. 7–4–1817.

**Visit** • Brackett's Tavern (Cromwell's Head). Site on the north side of School St. 1788.

**Visit** • Foster Boarding House, 31 State St.

**Visit** • Mrs. Kilby's Boarding House, State St.

**Funeral** • Lay in state in Faneuil Hall.

## Bush
**Visit** • Boston University, Dickerson Field. 5–21–1989.

## Carter
**Visit** • Dedicated John F. Kennedy Library, Columbia Point on Dorchester Bay. Admission charge. 10–20–1979.

**Visit** • Copley Plaza Hotel, Cafe Plaza, 138 St. James Ave. May 1984.

## Clinton
**Visit** • Boston Park Plaza Hotel and Towers, 64 Arlington St. 1993.

## Coolidge
**Visit** • Adams House. 553 Washington St. While governor he stayed in a room here overlooking the inner court. Razed. 1907–1921.

**Visit** • Touraine Hotel, Tremont and Boylston. 1907–1921.

**Work** • State House in Assembly Chamber. 1907–1908.

**Work** • State House in Senate Chamber. 1912–1915.

**Work** • State House, office of lt. governor. 1916–1918.

**Work** • State House, governor's office. 1919–1920.

## Ford
**Visit** • Old North Church, 193 State St. Remarks at Lantern Service. 4–18–1975.

## Grant
**Visit** • 11 West Newton St at St. James Hotel. When first built this was considered to be one of the most luxurious hotels in the south end. (Now Franklin Square House). 1869.

## Johnson, A
**Visit** • Dedicated Masonic Temple. Site Tremont and Boylston. Fall 1865.

## Kennedy
**Home** • Bellevue Hotel, 10 1/2 Beacon St near the State House. 1946.

**Home** • 122 Bowdoin St. Also used as office. 1946.

**Work** • Columbia Trust Co. Bank in East Boston. July–August 1941.

**Visit** • Ritz-Carlton Hotel, 15 Arlington St during campaign. 1946.

**Visit** • Peter Brent Brigham Hospital, 75 Francis. 1934.

**Visit** • Parker House Hotel, 60 School St. 1941–1960.

**Visit** • Lahey Clinic, 41 Mall Rd, Burlington. 1940.

**Visit** • New England Baptist Hospital, 125 Parker Hill Ave. 1941.

**Visit** • Chelsea Naval Hospital. 1944.

**Visit** • Union Oyster House, 41 Union St. 1941–1960.

**Site** • John F. Kennedy Library, Columbia Point on Dorchester Bay.

## Lincoln
**Site** • Emancipation Statue on Park Square.

## Monroe
**Church** • Old North Church, 193 State St. July 1817.

**Visit** • Harrison Gray Otis House, 45 Beacon St. 1817.

## Roosevelt, T

*Visit* • Brunswick Hotel, Berkeley St, night before his wedding. 10–26–1880.

## Tyler

*Visit* • Bunker Hill Monument, 43 Monument Sq. Dedication. 1843.

## Washington

*Church* • Boston County Building on site where the First Meeting House of Boston was relocated. 1776.

*Church* • Trinity Church, Summer St, faces west on Copley Square.

*Church* • King's Chapel, School and Tremont Sts. 1776, 1789.

*Visit* • Cromwell's Head, 19 School St, was also home of Samuel Brackett with whom he stayed. 1789.

*Visit* • James Bowdoin Mansion, 10 1/2 Beacon St. Bellevue Hotel now stands on the site. 1789.

*Visit* • Soldier's Monument. Dorchester Heights.

## Wilson

*Visit* • Central Congregational Church. April 1896. U.S. Hotel and Young's Hotel. 7-15-1894. Only sites now.

## BOURNE  *(Barnstable County)*

### Cleveland

*Home* • Shore Road, 1 mile from Bourne. Gray Gables Inn was his summer home for several years. 1891– 1904.

## BRAINTREE  *(See Quincy)*

## BROOKLINE  *(Norfolk County)*

### Kennedy

*Birthplace* • 83 Beals St. Admission. 5-29-1917.

*Baptism* • St. Aidan's Catholic Church, 158 Pleasant St. Fount used at baptism still in the church. 1917–1921.

*Education* • Edward Devotion School, 347 Harvard St near the corner of Stedman St. 1923–1924.

*Education* • Dexter School. This school was on Freeman St when Kennedy attended. Building is no longer standing. 1924–1927.

*Home* • 83 Beals St. 1917–1921.

*Home* • Northeast corner of Naples Rd and Abbottsford Rd. Privately owned. 1921–1927.

### Roosevelt, T

*Marriage* • Brookline Unitarian Church, 382 Walnut. 1880.

## CAMBRIDGE  *(Middlesex County)*

### Adams, J

*Church* • First Church, on Watch House Hill southwest of present Lehman Hall. 1751–1755.

*Church* • Holden Chapel in small quadrangle behind Harvard and Hollis Halls. Now used for lectures. 1751–1755.

*Church* • First Parish Church, Massachusetts Ave. 1751–.

*Education* • Harvard University. Three buildings there at the time: Massachusetts Hall, Stoughton College Hall, and Harvard Hall. He lived in Massachusetts Hall and took breakfast in Harvard Hall. 1751–1755.

*Education* • Mrs. Hill's on Charlestown Rd (present Kirkland St) near Cambridge Square. 1751.

*Visit* • Winthrop House at NW corner of present Boylston and Mount Auburn Sts. 1751–1755.

### Adams, JQ

*Church* • First Church. See John Adams above. 1786.

*Education* • Harvard University. See location of buildings under J Adams, including Massachusetts and Wadsworth Halls and Harvard Hall III. 1786.

*Education* • Wigglesworth and Hollis Hall. Wiggleworth House was behind Widener. He had lodging in Hollis Hall. Winter 1786–1787.

## Cleveland

*Visit* • Elliott House. Site north of Dana-Palmer House facing on Quincy St between the Dudley and Eliot Gates. Attended 250th celebration. 1886.

## Hayes

*Education* • Harvard. His classrooms in a building called Dane Law School. Dane Hall was on the Square. Burned. Today site of Matthews Hall. He lived at Mrs. Ford's Rooming House. Nothing remains. 1843–1845.

## Jackson

*Visit* • Received honorary degree from Harvard. 1833.

## Kennedy

*Education* • Harvard. 1936–1940.

*Education* • Roomed 32 Weld Hall in the Yard with Torbet MacDonald. Weld is at the south boundary of the Old Yard. Fall 1936. Winthrop (Gore). 1937–1938. Gore Hall F-14. 1939–1940.

*Visit* • Hasty Pudding Club, corner of Massachusetts Ave and Holme's Pl. 1936–1940.

*Visit* • Spee Club at corner of Mt. Auburn and Holyoke Sts. 1937–.

## Monroe

*Visit* • Received honorary degree from Harvard. 1817.

## Pierce

*Visit* • Brattle House, 105 Brattle St, just after nomination. 1852.

## Roosevelt, FD

*Church* • Harvard, at Holden Chapel, Peabody St. 1900–1904.

*Education* • Harvard. 1900–1904.

*Education* • He lived at Westmorly Court. 1900–1904.

*Education* • Great Hall of Memorial Hall used as dining hall. 1900–1904.

*Site* • Gray's Hall. Facing south end of the Old Yard. Signet Club upstairs. FDR was a member. 1900–1904.

## Roosevelt, T

*Church* • Christ Church, Farwell Place, Zero Garden St. 1876–.

*Education* • Harvard. 1876–1880.

*Education* • Arrived and took a room on the second floor of a boarding house at 16 Winthrop St on the SW corner of Holyoke two blocks south of Massachusetts Ave near Harvard's indoor Athletic Building. Plaque on NE corner of the indoor Athletic Bldg. 1876.

*Education* • Great Hall of Memorial Hall used as dining hall. 1876–.

*Education* • Gray's Hall facing south end of Old Yard. Signet Club upstairs. Member. 1876–.

*Education* • Fly Club. 2 Holyoke Place. 1876–.

*Visit* • 101 Brattle St. 1905.

## Washington

*Church* • Christ Church, Farwell Place. 1775.

*Visit* • Longfellow-Craigie House, 105 Brattle St. 1775.

*Visit* • Vassal Mansion, 94 Brattle St, residence and headquarters. 7–15–1775 to 4–4–1776.

# CONCORD *(Middlesex County)*

## Ford

*Visit* • Patriot Day ceremony. 4–19–1975.

# EAST GLOUCESTER *(Essex County)*

## Wilson

*Visit* • "The Flying Jib" cottage. 1896.

## GROTON  (*Middlesex County*)

**Grant**

*Visit* • Governor Boutwell House opposite the Town Hall. 279 Main St. Built 1851. 1869.

**Roosevelt, FD**

*Church* • Groton Chapel, off MA 111. 1896–1900.

*Education* • Groton School. 1896–1900.

## HAVERHILL  (*Essex County*)

**Adams, JQ**

*Church* • First Parish Church. Site Main St adjacent to city library. Uncle John Shaw was minister. 1785–1786.

*Education* • Lodged with his uncle at the parsonage while preparing for Harvard. Main St on the site now adjacent to public library. 1785–1786.

**Washington**

*Visit* • Mason's Arms (Harrods) standing on what later became the town hall. 1791.

## HYANNIS PORT  (*Barnstable County*)

**Johnson, LB**

*Visit* • Kennedy summer home. July 1960.

**Kennedy**

*Church* • Church of St. Francis Xavier, 347 South St. 1929–1963.

*Home* • Summer home on Cape Cod. 1929–1963.

*Site* • Kennedy Memorial, Ocean St on MA 28. 1966.

## LEXINGTON  (*Middlesex County*)

**Ford**

*Visit* • Lexington Green for Patriot's Day. 4–19–1975.

**Washington**

*Visit* • Munroe Tavern, 1332 Massachusetts Ave. Hat rack he used is preserved. 11–5–1789.

## LOWELL  (*Middlesex County*)

**Presidents**

*Visit* • Merrimack House, 310 Merrimack St. Buchanan, Jackson, Polk, Tyler, and Van Buren.

**Adams, JQ**

*Visit* • Old Town Hall, Shattuck and Merrimac Sts. 1830.

**Lincoln**

*Visit* • Old Town Hall, Shattuck and Merrimac Sts. 1848.

*Visit* • Overnight at Child-Barlett House, Kirk and French Sts. 1848.

## LYNN  (*Essex County*)

**Coolidge**

*Work* • Summer executive offices here 3 miles from White Court. Seventh floor Security Trust Co. Building on Central Square. 1925.

**Taft**

*Church* • First Unitarian, Corner of Summer and Main. 1909–.

## MAGNOLIA  (*Essex County*)

**Wilson**

*Visit* • Next to Colonel House at Coolidge Point on the North Shore (near Manchester). Mid– August 1910, 1913.

## MARBLEHEAD  (*Essex County*)

**Adams, J**

*Visit* • Azor Orne House, 18 Orne St, to meet with revolutionary Committee of Safety. Old Town Hall on Washington St.

## MARION  (*Plymouth County*)

**Cleveland**

*Visit* • Captain Hadley House. Summer 1887.

*Visit* • Perry Brown House, Front St. Summer 1888.

*Visit* • Heller cottage on Front St. Summer 1889.

*Visit* • Old Kelly House on Water St. Summer 1890.

## MARTHA'S VINEYARD   *(Dukes County)*

**Clinton**

*Travel* • Vacation on the island. August 1993.

## MILLBURY   *(Worcester County)*

**Taft**

*Church* • Congregational Church with Grandfather Torrey. Main and Church Sts. 1864.

*Education* • At village school. 1864.

## MILTON   *(Norfolk County)*

**Bush**

*Birthplace* • 173 Adams St. Private.

*Church* • St. Michael's Episcopal Church, 112 Randolph Ave.

*Home* • 173 Adams St. 1924.

*Home* • Centre St. 1925.

## NAHANT   *(Essex County)*

**Roosevelt, T**

*Visit* • Henry Cabot Lodge estate at East Point. Demolished. 1884, 1885, 1902.

## NEWBURYPORT   *(Essex County)*

**Adams, JQ**

*Church* • Church of the First Religious Society (Unitarian), Pleasant St. 1787–1790.

*Education* • Theophilus Parson's law office, 98 High St. He lodged with Mrs. Martha Leathers, on State St, a block from Parson's law office.

*Visit* • Cushing House, corner of Fruit St. 1837.

## NORTHAMPTON   *(Hampshire County)*

**Coolidge**

*Church* • Edwards      Congregational

Church, at the corner of South and Main Sts (original burned). 1905–1933.

*Education* • Law office John C. Hammond and Henry P. Field. Site on Main St. Building demolished. 1895–1897.

*Home* • Lyman House, 63 Center St. No longer standing. 1895.

*Home* • 40 Round Hill in house of Robert Weir. Meals at Rahar's Inn. 1895–1898.

*Home* • 162 King St. Now business site. 1898–1905.

*Home* • Baker Hall of Clarke Institute. 1904.

*Home* • Norwood Hotel, Bridge St. 1905.

*Home* • 5 Crescent St at the corner of Prospect St., in a small furnished house owned by J.E. Brady. October 1905 to August 1906.

*Home* • 21 Massasoit St. Summer 1906 rented half of a two-family house. 1906–1930.

*Home* • The Beeches, an estate at the end of Munroe St. 1930–1933.

*Work* • Law office, Main St. Two rooms on the second floor of the new Masonic Building. 1898–1933.

*Work* • City Council Office, City Hall, Main St. 1898.

*Work* • City Solicitor Office, City Hall, Main St. 1900–1902.

*Work* • Clerk of Court Office, Courthouse, Main St. 1903.

*Work* • Mayor's Office. City Hall, Main St. 1910–1912.

*Work* • Smith College, Allen Field, Elm St. Received official notification of his nomination as vice president. 1920.

*Visit* • Rahar's Inn, a three-story building off Main St. 1895.

*Death* • The Beeches. 1933.

*Funeral* • Edwards      Congregational Church. Church site is near City Hall.

*Site* • Forbes Library with Coolidge Memorial Room. 20 West St. Free.

**Hoover**

*Visit* • Edwards Congregational Church. 1933.

**Pierce**

*Education* • Studied law with Samuel Howe. 1826.

## PALMER *(Hampden County)*

**Presidents**

*Visit* • Scott's Tavern, marker near parking lot of K-Mart. J. and JQ Adams, and Washington.

## PROVINCETON *(Barnstable County)*

**Carter**

*Work* • Naval Base. 1951–1952.

## QUINCY (BRAINTREE) *(Norfolk County)*

**Adams, J**

*Birthplace* • 133 Franklin St. Free. 1735.

*Baptism* • First Parish Church, 1306 Hancock St. Replaced church at 1266 Hancock. 1735.

*Church* • Same as above. 1735–1826.

*Education* • Dame Belcher's school, across the Coast Road. 1741–1743.

*Education* • Free Latin School, near Meeting House about 1 mile from home. 1743–1750.

*Education* • Marsh's School, Franklin St, about two doors from the Adams House. Razed. 1750–1751.

*Honeymoon* • 141 Franklin St.

*Home* • 133 Franklin St. 1735–1764.

*Home* • 141 Franklin St. 1764–1788.

*Home* • Old House, Peacefield, 135 Adams St. Admission charge. 1788–1826.

*Death* • Old House, Peacefield, 135 Adams St. 7–4–1826.

*Funeral* • First Parish Church, 1306 Hancock St. 1826.

*Burial* • 1266 Hancock St in the churchyard. Adjacent to City Hall (built 1844). 1826.

*Burial* • 1306 Hancock St. Removed from churchyard and later placed in the granite crypt beneath the church portal. 1829.

*Site* • Monument of Adams and Son on Hancock St at the edge of Merrymount Park near the corner of Fenno St.

**Adams, JQ**

*Birthplace* • 141 Franklin St. Free. 1767.

*Baptism* • First Parish Church. See J Adams above. 1867; 1867–1848.

*Education* • At home, 141 Franklin St. 1767–1778.

*Home* • 141 Franklin St. 1767–1768.

*Home* • Old House, 135 Adams St. Entrance fee.

*Burial* • First Parish Church, 1306 Hancock St in the Crypt. 1848.

*Site* • Abigail Adams Cairn, Franklin

*Site* • St. Penn's Hill at Faxon Park. Marks the place where 7-year-old John Quincy watched the Battle of Bunker Hill. 353 Franklin St.

**Monroe**

*Visit* • 135 Adams St. Dined here with J Adams. July 1817.

*Visit* • Josiah Quincy House, 20 Muirhead St. 1817.

**Truman**

*Visit* • First Parish Church, 1306 Hancock St. 10–28–1948.

## SALEM *(Essex County)*

**Adams, J**

*Work* • Old Courthouse, Town House Square. 1769.

**Adams, JQ**

*Visit* • East India Marine Hall, 173 Essex St. Dedicated by Adams. 10–14–1825.

**Arthur**

*Visit* • Essex Institute and Peabody Museum, 132 Essex St. 9–8–1882.

**Coolidge**

*Church* • Congregational Tabernacle, Washington and Federal Sts, while at Swampcott summer White House. 1925.

**Monroe**

*Visit* • Almshouse on the Neck from lower Essex St. Town Hall opening and reception. Restored. 7–8–1817.

*Visit* • Nathaniel Silsbee House, 94 Washington Square East. Now Knights of Columbus Club. 1817.

**Pierce**

*Visit* • George B. Loring House, 328 Essex St. 1853–.

**Taft**

*Visit* • Essex Institute, 132 Essex St. Unveiled tablet. Delivered address in Ames Memorial Hall.

**Washington**

*Visit* • Joshua Ward House, 148 Washington St. Today called Hotel Washington. 10–29–1789.

## SHREWSBURY *(Worcester County)*

**Adams**

*Visit* • Farrar's Tavern (Pease). Junction of the "Great Road" with the road to Westboro about a mile from Northboro line. 1774.

**Washington**

*Visit* • Farrar's Tavern. See location above. 1787.

## SPRINGFIELD *(Hampden County)*

**Adams, J**

*Visit* • Zenas Parsons Tavern. See Washington below. 1770s.

**Monroe**

*Visit* • Zenas Parsons Tavern. See Washington below. 1817.

**Roosevelt, T**

*Honeymoon* • Massasoit House, Main and Lyman Sts, near railroad for first night of honeymoon. 1880.

**Washington**

*Visit* • Zenas Parsons Tavern. SE corner Court St (now Court Square), near Water St. 1789.

## SWAMPSCOTT *(Essex County)*

**Coolidge**

*Visit* • White Court, next door to Red Gables on Puritan Road at 35 Little's Point. Now Marian Court Junior College. Was vacation site and summer White House. 1924.

## UXBRIDGE *(Worcester County)*

**Washington**

*Visit* • Taft Tavern on Sutton and Sylvan corner. 1791.

## WATERTOWN *(Middlesex County)*

**Washington**

*Visit* • Marshall Fowle House, 28 Marshall St. 1791.

## WEYMOUTH *(Norfolk County)*

**Adams, J**

*Church* • First Church (Weymouth Meeting House, sometimes called the North Parish). Abigail's father was pastor here for 49 years.

*Marriage* • Smith House, then at the corner of North and East Sts. Married by the bride's father. 1764.

*Lodging* • Abigail's birthplace at the corner of North and East Sts beside the Old North Cemetery. A large section of the house was torn down but the ell of the gambrel-roofed house was moved to 450 Bridge

St in 1838. In 1947 the ell was moved for the last time to the junction of Norton and North Sts. Entrance fee. 1744.

### Adams, JQ

*Church* • See John Adams above. First Church.

*Lodging* • Stayed with Smith grandparents while the manse was at the corner of North and East Sts. 1767–.

## WEST BROOKFIELD *(Worcester County)*

### Adams, J

*Visit* • Same as next entry.

### Washington

*Visit* • Hitchcock's Tavern. Still standing in the center of the village and in use. 1789.

## WILLIAMSTOWN *(Berkshire County)*

### Garfield

*Education* • Williams College. West College building (1790) now a dormitory. 1854–1856.

## WINTHROP *(Suffolk County)*

### Kennedy

*Lodging* • 165 Webster St to visit his grandparents (P.J. Kennedy). 1917–.

## WORCESTER *(Worcester County)*

### Presidents

*Visit* • Mechanics Hall, 321 Main. McKinley, Taft, T Roosevelt, and Wilson.

### Adams, J

*Church* • Congregational Meeting House. (Old South Church). The City Hall stands on the site. 1755–1758.

*Education* • Dr. Nahum Willard law office, across from Franklin (originally South St) on Main St. Site now occupied by the Boston Store. 1755–1756.

*Lodging* • He stayed at the James Putnam House across the Green where the Park Building stands today. 1756–1758.

*Lodging* • Dr. Nahum Willard on Franklin St (originally South St). 1756–1758.

*Lodging* • Major Nathaniel Green House midway between Walnut and Sudbury Sts on the site of the present Day Building. 1755.

*Work* • Taught school here. One-room log house school. Marker in front of the courthouse on edge of the sidewalk. 1755.

### Grant

*Visit* • Bay Street Hotel, Bay St. 1869.

### Hayes

*Visit* • Bay Street Hotel, Bay St. 1877.

### Johnson, LB

*Visit* • Holy Cross College. 6–10–1964.

### Lincoln

*Visit* • 49 Elm St. Lincoln Mansion where he dined in 1848.

### Roosevelt, T

*Visit* • Rockwood Hoar House, 16 Hammond St. 1905.

1. Ford Library, *Ann Arbor*
2. Ford home, *Grand Rapids*
3. Bush home, *Trenton*

**Michigan**

96

Lansing

Detroit

94

1

3

2

# MICHIGAN

## ANN ARBOR *(Washtenaw County)*

**Bush**

*Visit* • University of Michigan Stadium, Main St. 5–4–91.

**Ford**

*Education* • University of Michigan. Entrance facing Regents Square. 1931–1933; 1937.

*Education* • Deke House. 611 1/2 E. William St. 1932–1935.

*Site* • Gerald Ford Library. 1000 Beal St on north campus of University of Michigan. Dedication 1983.

**Johnson, LB**

*Visit* • University of Michigan commencement. 5–22–1964.

## BATTLE CREEK *(Calhoun County)*

**Harding**

*Visit* • Battle Creek Sanitarium. North Washington Ave and Champion St. 1889.

## DETROIT *(Wayne County)*

**Bush**

*Visit* • Pontchartrain Hotel, 2 Washington Building. Attended RNC where he learned of his nomination as vice president. Also stayed at Plaza Hotel, Renaissance Center. 1980.

*Visit* • Joe Louis Arena, 600 Civic Center Dr (Griswold and E Jefferson). RNC. July 1980.

**Cleveland**

*Visit* • University of Michigan. 2–21– 1892.

**Fillmore**

*Visit* • 1841 and 9–27–1849.

**Garfield**

*Visit* • 1863–1866.

*Visit* • Christian Church on SW corner Jefferson Ave and Beaubien St. 1864, 1866.

*Visit* • Merrill Block, NE corner Jefferson and Woodward Aves. 1866.

**Grant**

*Church* • St. Paul's Episcopal, Larned and Woodward Aves. First organized 1824. Church now located at 4800 Woodward Ave. 1849–1851. 1866.

*Church* • First Methodist, NE corner Woodward Ave and Congress St. 1850. In 1851 moved to corner of Woodward Ave and State St. 1835–1850.

*Home* • 253 Fort St East in a rented cottage. Now a parking lot.

*Home* • 1369 Fort St. Site now commercial area. House moved to State Fair Grounds. North side West State Fair off Woodward (MI 1) at Ralston. 1849–1850.

*Lodging* • W. A. Bacon House. Site NE corner Russell St and Jefferson Ave. Sold and moved. 1850–1851.

*Lodging* • National Hotel. Site at corner of Michigan, Grand, and Woodward Aves. Later site of First National Bank. 1848–1849.

*Visit* • Exchange Hotel, SW corner Jefferson Ave and Shelby. Attended weekly balls. 1849–1851.

*Visit* • Senator Zacharia Chandler house at Second and Fort (144 Fort) site of Detroit News Building. Attended a hero's reception at the Biddle House (subsequently American House) on Jefferson Ave. 1865.

*Work* • Fort Wayne at the foot of Livernois Ave. Take W Fort St to I-75 S. Exit 44 to Jefferson Ave. North on Jefferson to Fort Wayne in Springwells Township. Closed to the public. 1848–1851.

*Work* • Military barracks located on south side of Gratiot Ave centering about Russell St. Commandant. 1851.

### Harrison, WH

*Visit* • Marker at Capitol Square. As Governor 5–10–1803. Again 9–29–1813 and 9–8–1815.

*Work* • Captured fort. Stayed at May's Farm just west of Fort Shelby. 1813.

*Work* • Hull House, SW corner Jefferson Ave and Randoph St (1st brick house in Detroit), headquarters. 1813.

### Hayes

*Visit* • Ex-Governor Baldwin house, 110

Fort St West. Now occupied by office bldg. 9–18–1879.

### Hoover

*Visit* • Detroit City Hall, Woodward Ave and Griswold St. Visit Independence Hall (replica)in Greenfield Village. 10–21–1929.

### Johnson, A

*Visit* • Biddle House Hotel. Site on Jefferson Ave. 1866.

*Visit* • Michigan Central RR Station, SE corner of Michigan Ave and Griswold St. 1866.

### Monroe

*Church* • Indian Council House. Now occupied by Fireman's Hall. SE corner Jefferson Ave and Randolph St. Later site of Woodworth Hotel. 1817.

*Visit* • Fort Shelby at the foot of Shelby St between Wayne and Griswold Sts. 8–13–1817.

*Visit* • Government Wharf at the foot of Randolph St. 1817.

*Visit* • Governor Cass residence on Larned St. 1817.

*Visit* • Woodworth's Steamboat Hotel at NW corner Woodbridge and Randolph Sts. Now site of Renaissance Center. 1817.

### Nixon

*Visit* • Pontchartrain Hotel, 2 Washington Blvd. RNC. 1980.

### Pierce

*Visit* • Lodged Russell House. Site NE corner Woodward Ave and Cadillac Sq. Site later occupied by First National Bank Building. 1861.

### Taylor

*Travel* • Joined Third Infantry here.

*Visit* • Fort Wayne at the foot of Livernois Ave with his brother Captain Joseph Taylor stationed in Detroit. 1845.

### Truman

*Visit* • Cadillac Square. "Give 'em Hell" campaign speech. Labor Day 1948.

**Van Buren**

*Church* • Methodist Church, Woodward Ave and Congress St in the morning. St. Paul's Episcopal at Larned and Woodward in the afternoon. 1842.

*Visit* • American House. Site south side of Jefferson Ave just east of Randolph St. 1842.

**Washington**

*Site* • Statue at E Jefferson and Randolph west of Renaissance Center entrance.

## EAST GRAND RAPIDS *(See Grand Rapids)*

## EAST LANSING *(See Lansing)*

## FARMINGTON *(Oakland County)*

**Lincoln**

*Visit* • Botsford Inn, Eight Mile Rd and MI 16. Has writing desk said to have been used by him.

## FORT MACKINAC *(Mackinac County)*

**Taylor**

*Travel* • Stationed here. 1818–1819.

## GRAND RAPIDS *(Kent County)*

**Bush**

*Visit* • Gerald Ford Museum, 303 Pearl St NW, for dedication. 9–18–1981. Again 10–29–1992.

**Ford**

*Church* • Grace Episcopal Church, built 1814. Hall SE, corner of Plymouth and Hall. 1922–1951.

*Education* • Madison Elementary School NE, corner Madison Ave and Franklin (now 747 Madison SE). Only steps remain. 1919–1927.

*Education* • Grand Rapids High School (South High School), 421 Fountain St NE. 1927–1931.

*Marriage* • Grace Episcopal Church, 1815 Hall SE. 1948.

*Marriage* • Reception at Peninsular Club, 120 Ottawa NW at the corner of Fountain and Ottawa. Now Grand Rapids Office Supply Company. 1948.

*Home* • 457 Lafayette Ave, SE, near Garfield Park with his mother's parents (Gardner). 1914–1916.

*Home* • 716 Madison Ave. Now occupied by Paul I. Phillips Recreation Center. 1916–1921.

*Home* • 630 Rosewood Ave. 1922–1923.

*Home* • 649 Union Ave SE. 1923–1929.

*Home* • 2163 Lake Dr SE. 1929–1933.

*Home* • 1011 Santa Cruz Dr. Vice President Nixon was a guest here. 1933–1948.

*Work* • Ford Paint and Varnish Co, 601 Crosby NW. Now Standard Detroit Paint Co. 1930–1933.

*Work* • Ford and Buchen law firm. 620 Michigan Trust Building, 40-50 Pearl NW. 1941–1942.

*Work* • Butterfield, Keeney and Amberg law firm. Suite 500 Michigan Trust Building. 40–50 Pearl NW. 1946–1948.

*Visit* • 330 Washington SE. Apartment of Betty Ford. 1948.

*Visit* • 636 Fountain St. Home of Betty Ford's parents. 1948.

*Visit* • Butterworth Hospital, 100 Michigan NE. Treatment. 1918.

*Travel* • Calder Plaza for Republican party rally. Remarks at Calvin College Knollcrest Fieldhouse, 3201 Burton SE. 10–29–1974.

*Site* • Gerald Ford Museum, 303 Pearl St. 1981. Hosted symposium on humor and the presidency. 1986.

**Reagan**

*Visit* • Gerald Ford Museum. 9–18–1981.

## KALAMAZOO *(Kalamazoo County)*

**Lincoln**

*Vist* • Bronson Park, South St. Tablet marks spot where Lincoln spoke. 1856.

## LANSING *(Ingham County)*

**Bush**

*Visit* • Wharton Center for the Performing Arts at Michigan State University for presidential debate with Clinton; Lansing Civic Center. 10–19–1992

**Clinton**

*Visit* • Campus of Michigan State University, presidential debate: Bush, Clinton, and Perot. October 1992.

**Taft**

*Visit* • Capitol Ave between Allegan and Ottawa Sts. Capitol. 1919.

## MUSKEGON *(Muskegon County)*

**Lincoln**

*Site* • Soldiers' and Sailors' Monument, W Clay Ave between Third and Fourth Sts. Lincoln statue.

**McKinley**

*Site* • McKinley Monument. Webster Ave between Third and Fourth Sts.

## OTTAWA BEACH *(Ottawa County)*

**Ford**

*Lodging* • Summer cabin near Bitely on Little South Branch of the Pere Marquette River 30 miles from Grand Rapids, 1910.

## SAGINAW CITY *(Saginaw County)*

**Roosevelt, T**

*Visit* • City Auditorium, Washington and James Aves. Bull Moose Campaign. 10–8–1912.

**Taft**

*Visit* • City Auditorium. Campaign. Stayed Hotel Bancroft. 1911.

## TRENTON *(Wayne County)*

**Bush**

*Church* • St. Thomas Episcopal Church, Nichols Dr and Andover Rd. Original church burned. 1945.

*Home* • 2920 Parkwood. 1945.

# MINNESOTA

## CAMP RIPLEY *(Morrison County)*

**Truman**
*Work* • Summer camp for national guard 1932 –.

## FORT SNELLING *(Ramsey County)*

**Taylor**
*Home* • Quarters inside the fortress at Fort Snelling south of the center of Minneapolis. 1828–1829.

## MINNEAPOLIS *(Hennepin County)*

**Cleveland**
*Visit* • West Hotel, Hennepin Ave and Fifth St. 1887.

**Lincoln**
*Visit* • Nicollet House. Site Washington Ave between Hennepin and Nicollete Aves. Now occupied by modern Nicollet Hotel.

*Site* • Lincoln Statue, Victory Memorial Drive.

**McKinley**
*Visit* • Exposition Building for RNC. 1888 and 1899.

**Taft**
*Church* • Westminister Presbyterian Church, Nicolett Mall at Twelfth St. 1909.

*Visit* • Minneapolis Club, 729 Second Ave South. 1909.

## REDWOOD FALLS *(Redwood County)*

**Eisenhower**
*Visit* • Hiawatha Bridge, Intersection Main and Broad Sts. Dedication. 10–18–1960.

## ROCHESTER *(Olmstead County)*

**Johnson, LB**
*Visit* • Mayo Clinic, 102-110 Second Ave SW. 1948; 1955.

**Kennedy**
*Visit* • Mayo Clinic. 1944.

**Reagan**
*Visit* • Mayo Clinic. 1989.

Minnesota

94

Minneapolis

1

35

1. Taylor home, *Fort Snelling*

# ST. PAUL *(Ramsey County)*

## Arthur

*Visit* • Northern Pacific East-West hook up. Fourth and Sibley Sts. 1883.

## Carter

*Travel* • House of Hope Presbyterian Church, 797 Summit Ave, for Hubert Humphrey funeral. 1–16–1978.

*Visit* • Landmark Center. Lambert Landing. 8–17–1979.

## Cleveland

*Travel* • Capitol, Wabasha, and Tenth Sts. Stayed at Ryan Hotel. September 1887.

## Harding

*Visit* • State Fair, Bounded by N Snelling, W Como, and Larpenteur Aves. Spoke in the Fine Arts Building. State Capitol for reception and dinner Senator Kellogg home, Third St (Kellogg Blvd). 1920.

## McKinley

*Visit* • JJ Hill House, 240 Summit Ave. Speech at the Auditorium, 145 W Fourth St. 1899.

## Roosevelt, T

*Visit* • Capitol; Nicollet Hotel. 1903.

## Wilson

*Visit* • Capitol. Armory, 600 Cedar St. Auditorium. 1919.

Mississippi

55

20 Jackson

1. Grant home, *Holly Springs*

# MISSISSIPPI

## BAYOU PIERRE *(Jefferson County)*

**Jackson**
*Home* • In a log cabin 30 miles above Natchez at the meeting of Bayou Pierre and the Mississippi River near Springfield Plantation. 1791.

## BAY ST. LOUIS *(Hancock County)*

**Taylor**
*Home* • Army barracks. 1820.

## BIG BLACK RIVER *(Webster County)*

**Grant**
*Work* • Battle. West of Jackson. May 1863.

## BRUINSBURG *(Claiborne County)*

**Grant**
*Work* • Marker in Port Gibson for Bruinsburg road where Grant landed his forces. 4–30–1863. Ten historical markers on the line of Grant's march, Port Gibson to Bruinsburg.

## CHAMPION'S HILL *(Hinds County)*

**Grant**
*Work* • Marching route, on old Edwards-Bolton Highway. Battle. 5–16–1863.

## CLINTON *(Hinds County )*

**Jackson**
*Visit* • Moss House (ruins), off Raymond Rd. 1818.

## CORINTH *(Alcorn County)*

**Garfield**
*Work* • Civil War site. 1861.

**Grant**
*Visit* • Elgin House, 615 Jackson St (private). Headquarters. Marker. 1862.

## FOXWORTH *(Marion County)*

**Jackson**
*Visit* • John Ford House, off SR 24. 1814.

## GRAND GULF (Claiborne County)

**Grant**

> *Work* • Temporary base. See Grand Gulf Military Park, 8 miles west of SR 61. 1863.

## GULFPORT (Harrison County)

**Wilson**

> *Church* • Lutheran Church, Thirty-first Ave facing Thirteenth St. The church was formerly Presbyterian. A bronze plate marks the pew where he sat. 12–28–1913.

## HICKORY (Newton County)

**Jackson**

> *Travel* • South of town on banks of Pottoxchitto Creek. 1815.

## HOLLY SPRINGS (Marshall County)

**Grant**

> *Church* • Methodist Church, 175 E Van Dorn Ave and Spring St. Grant kept his mules in the basement but first removed the stained glass window for safekeeping. 1862.

> *Home* • 331 W Chulahoma Ave. Walter Place. 1862.

> *Visit* • 330 Salem Ave. Coxe-Dean House. Marker. 1862.

## IUKA (Tishomingo County)

**Grant**

> *Visit* • Brinkley House, Eastport St. Served as headquarters. 1862.

## JACKSON (Hinds County)

**Carter**

> *Visit* • Governor's Mansion. Capitol St between N Congress and N West Sts. 10–31–1980.

**Jackson**

> *Visit* • Hero's welcome at the Capitol, corner of President and Capitol Sts. Building

no longer extant. Tablet on side of the Baptist book store. 1828.

**Taft**

> *Visit* • State Capitol. 1909.

## NATCHEZ (Adams County)

**Grant**

> *Visit* • Rosalie, foot of Broadway corner of Canal and Orleans Sts. Lodged here with his family. 1863.

**Jackson**

> *Marriage* • Springfield, where Hwy 553 crosses the Trace, turn off and take a side trip (about a mile east of Richland Plantation). Between Fayette and Church Hill. Still a working plantation. 1791.

> *Honeymoon* • Near the ruins of Windsor mansion is an historical marker for the Bruinsburg Rd relating that Jackson had a trading post here and also honeymooned here. 1791.

> *Visit* • See Abner Green Mansion 23 miles north of Natchez. 1791.

> *Visit* • Elms Court, south of Natchez on US 61.

> *Visit* • Mercer House, NW corner S Wall and State Sts (private). January 1840.

## OXFORD (Lafayette County)

**Grant**

> *Work* • Headquarters. 1862.

## PASS CHRISTIAN (Harrison County)

**Wilson**

> *Visit* • Dixie White House, a cottage fronting on the Gulf of Mexico at 767 E Beach Blvd. 1913–1914.

## PORT GIBSON (Claiborne County)

**Grant**

> *Visit* • L. P. Williams House NW corner Church and Walnut Sts. 1863. See also

Grand Gulf Military Monument Park near Port Gibson.

## RAYMOND   *(Hinds County)*

**Grant**

*Work* • Civil War Battle. Victory for Grant. 5–12–1863.

## RODNEY   *(Adams County)*

**Taylor**

*Visit* • Cypress Grove Plantation on the Mississippi River north of Natchez. 1841–1849.

## SPRINGFIELD   *(See Natchez)*

## VICKSBURG   *(Warren County)*

**Grant**

*Visit* • Vicksburg National Park, I-20 and 3201 Clay St. Entrance east end at Memorial Arch.

*Work* • Courthouse (now museum), 1008 Cherry St. Here on July 4, 1863, he had the Union flag flown. McKinley and T Roosevelt were also here.

*Visit* • Balfour House, 1002 Crawford St, on the Heights of Vicksburg during the siege. 1863.

**McKinley**

*Visit* • Vicksburg National Cemetery, Grant-Pemberton Monument. Entrance at Connecting and Union Aves. May 1901.

**Taft**

*Travel* • Visited on tour. 1909.

## YAZOO CITY   *(Yazoo County)*

**Carter**

*Travel* • Yazoo City High School Museum, Dr. Martin Luther King, Jr. Drive. Dedication. 7–21–1977.

1. Truman home, *Clinton*
2. Harry S Truman Library, *Independence*
3. Truman home, *Kansas City*
4. Truman birthplace, *Lamar*
5. Grant home, *St. Louis*

**35**

Kansas City
**3**
**2**

**70**

St. Louis **5**

**1**

**44**

**4**

**Missouri**

# MISSOURI

## BELMONT *(Mississippi County)*

**Grant**
> *Work* • Belmont Battlefield, MO 77. Captured Confederate Camp. November 1861.

## BELTON *(Cass County)*

**Truman**
> *Visit* • Masonic Home of Missouri, Western Unit, 12101 E Banniser Rd. Initiated into Masonic Lodge. 1909.

## BOLIVAR *(Polk County)*

**Truman**
> *Visit* • Bolivar Statue, Town Square. Dedication. 7–5–1948.

## BROOKFIELD *(Linn County)*

**Grant**
> *Work* • Salt River Railroad Bridge. 1861.

## CAPE GIRARDEAU *(Cape Girardeau County)*

**Grant**
> *Work* • Fort A, east end of Bellevue St.

Command of SW district of Missouri. 1861.

## CLINTON *(Henry County)*

**Truman**
> *Home* • Father traded house on Park Ave, Kansas City, for equity in 80 acres in Henry County. 506 E Bodine St. 1904.

## COLUMBIA *(Boone County)*

**Jefferson**
> *Site* • University of Missouri. Original Jefferson tombstone is on the quadrangle.

## FULTON *(Callaway County)*

**Truman**
> *Visit* • Westminster College gymnasium, 501 Westminster Ave. With Churchill. 1946.

## GRANDVIEW *(Jackson County)*

**Truman**
> *Church* • Grandview Baptist Church, 2400 Grandview Blvd. Member. 1887– 1972.

*Home* • Grandfather Young's house, 12301 Blue Ridge Blvd. 1887–1890; 1906–1917.

*Work* • Family farm. 12301 Blue Ridge Rd. 1906–1917.

*Work* • Appointed Postmaster. Post Office on the grounds of the old farm, 12301 Blue Ridge Rd. 1914.

## HANNIBAL *(Marion County)*

### Carter

*Travel* • Toured while taking the Delta Queen down the Mississippi. Mark Twain's boyhood home, 208 Hill St. Becky Thatcher Book Store. Mark Twain Cave, MO 79 south. Town Square. 8–23–1979.

### Hoover

*Visit* • Mark Twain boyhood home, 208 Hill St. 1935.

### Roosevelt, FD

*Visit* • Mark Twain Memorial Bridge over the Mississippi River. Dedication. 9–4–1936.

## HARRISON *(Cass County)*

### Truman

*Home* • Twice his family moved to different houses in Harrison. 1885.

## INDEPENDENCE *(Jackson County)*

### Carter

*Visit* • Truman High School gym. Truman Library and grave site. Truman home. 9–2–1980.

### Ford

*Visit* • Truman statue at courthouse. 5–8–1976.

### Johnson, LB

*Visit* • Truman home. 10–11–1968.

*Site* • Truman Library. 1964. Signed Medicare Bill in presence of Truman. 7–30–1965.

### Kennedy

*Visit* • Truman home. July 1960.

### Nixon

*Visit* • Truman Library and home. 3–21–1969. Funeral. 12–27–1972.

### Reagan

*Visit* • Jackson County Courthouse. 9–2–1985.

### Truman

*Church* • First Presbyterian Church, Lexington and Pleasant Sts. 1890.

*Church* • First Baptist Church, 500 W Truman Rd. 1896–1902.

*Education* • Noland School, 533 S Liberty St. New school on site. 1890–1893.

*Education* • Columbian School. Torn down. 320 or 340 S River Blvd (near Walnut). 1893–1897.

*Education* • Ott High School, 624 N Liberty St. Now parking lot. 1897–1901.

*Education* • Independence (Central) High School. Now site of Palmer Junior High. 1901.

*Marriage* • Trinity Episcopal Church, 409 N Liberty. 1919.

*Home* • 619 South Crysler St. 1890–1896.

*Home* • 909 Waldo St. 1896–1902.

*Home* • 902 North Liberty. 1902.

*Home* • 219 North Delaware St. 1919–1935. Summer White House. 1945–1953. Retirement. 1953–1972. Free under 16 and over 62.

*Work* • Clinton Drugstore, 100 W Walnut. 1896.

*Work* • Jackson County Court House, Independence Square. See restored office he used. 1922– 1924.

*Visit* • Missouri Pacific Railroad Station, Pacific at Grand Ave. 1930.

*Visit* • Doe and Butch Tavern, Main St.

*Visit* • Auditorium World Headquarts Building, Church of Latter Day Saints, 517 W Walnut. 11–6–1950.

*Visit* • Memorial Hall, on Maples Ave, where he voted. November 1948.

*Funeral* • Carson Funeral Home, Lexington Ave and Fuller St.

*Burial* • Courtyard behind the library. 1972.

*Site* • Harry S Truman Library, Delaware St and US 24.

## KANSAS CITY *(Jackson County)*

### Presidents
*Visit* • Muehlbach Hotel, Twelfth St, SW corner Baltimore Ave. Most presidents from Harding to Carter stayed here.

### Cleveland
*Visit* • Coates House, 1003 Broadway. 1887.

### Eisenhower
*Visit* • Baltimore Hotel, Baltimore Ave from Eleventh to Twenfth Sts. Building razed 1939. 1915.

### Ford
*Visit* • Crown Center Hotel, 2345 McGee. Convention Headquarters. 1976.

*Visit* • Kemper Sports Arena, 1800 Genessee St. Nominated for president at RNC. 8–19–1976 to 8–20–1976.

### Hoover
*Visit* • Civic Auditorium. Nominated for president Republican National Committee. June 1928.

### Reagan
*Visit* • Alameda Plaza Hotel (now Ritz-Carlton), Warnall Rd at Ward Parkway, for Republican National Committee. 1976.

### Truman
*Church* • Benton Boulevard Baptist Church. 1902–1904.

*Education* • Spalding Commercial College, New York Life Building, NE corner Ninth St and Baltimore Ave. 1901–1902.

*Education* • Kansas City Law School, Nonquitt Building (now gone) 1013 –1015 Grand Ave. Now site of United Missouri Bank Building. 1923–1925.

*Lodging* • 2650 E Twenty-ninth St. Building razed. 1905.

*Home* • 2108 Park Ave. 1902–1905.

*Lodging* • 1314 Troost Ave. 1905–1906.

*Lodging* • 214 E Thirty-fifth St. Roomed for a time with Arthur Eisenhower. 1904–1906.

*Home* • 3404 Karnes Blvd. Owned but never lived in. 1921.

*Work* • Santa Fe RR with L. J. Smith construction outfit. 4515 Kansas Ave. 1901.

*Work* • Kansas City Star, mailroom clerk. 1729 Grand Ave. 1902.

*Work* • Tenth and Walnut Sts in basement of National Bank of Commerce. 1903–1905.

*Work* • Grand Theater as an usher. 704 Walnut. Building razed. 1903.

*Work* • Ninth and Main and Delaware just north of C & A office Union National Bank as bookkeeper. 1905–1906.

*Work* • Convention Hall. He drilled his men in the hall. 1917.

*Work* • Morgan and Co. Oil Investments, 703 Ridge Arcade. 1919.

*Work* • Haberdashery, 104 W Twelfth. Now Union Bank site. 1919–1922.

*Work* • Courthouse, Twelfth to Thirteenth Sts and Oak to Locust Sts, second floor. Judge of Jackson Co. 1922–1924. Presiding judge. 1926–1934.

*Work* • Kansas City Automobile Club, Twenty-seventh and Main. 1924–1926.

*Work* • Retirement. Federal Reserve Bank Bldg. (1107) at Tenth and Grand. 1953–1957. After 1957 offices in the Truman Library.

*Visit* • Union Station, 2400 Main St. Dedicated 1914. He came in here many times. 1914–1953.

*Visit* • Savoy Grill of Savoy Hotel on Ninth St. 1919.

*Visit* • Phillips Hotel (now Radisson Suite Hotel), Baltimore and Wyndotte at Twelth St. 1930.

*Visit* • Research Hospital (surgery), 2316 E Meyer Blvd. 1954; 1963.

*Visit* • Jackson statue in front of new courthouse. Dedicated. 1934.

*Death* • Research Hospital, 2316 E Meyer Blvd. 1972.

*Site* • Forest Hill Cemetery. Young and Truman family plots.

### Washington

*Site* • Equestrian statue on Washington Square at Pershing Rd.

## LAMAR *(Barton County)*

### Truman

*Birthplace* • 1009 Truman Ave. 1884.

*Church* • First Baptist, 1108 Gulf St. Name on cradle roll. 1884.

## MEXICO *(Audrain County)*

### Grant

*Work* • Stationed here. Summer 1861.

## MONROE CITY *(Marion County)*

### Grant

*Work* • Monroe Seminary Building, Third St.

## ST. GENEVIEVE *(St. Genevieve County)*

### Harrison, WH

*Visit* • Francois Valle House, 167 S Gabouri St. 1804.

## ST. JOSEPH *(Buchanan County)*

### Lincoln

*Visit* • Edgar House, 101 Francis St. Now occupied by paper box company. 1859.

## ST. LOUIS

### Bush

*Visit* • St. Francis de Sales Roman Catholic Church, 2653 Ohio. 9–28–1992.

*Visit* • Washington University Field House. Debate with Clinton. 10–11–1992.

### Cleveland

*Church* • Presbyterian Church, SW corner Washington and Compton Aves. 1887.

*Visit* • St. Louis Exposition. Dedication. 1903.

*Visit* • Exposition Building. Nominated for president DNC. June 1888.

### Clinton

*Travel* • First of famous bus tours with Al Gore ended in St. Louis. July 1992. Second campaign bus tour began here going to St. Paul, Minnesota. August 1992.

*Travel* • Washington University gymnasium, 1635 Washington Ave. For presidential debate with Bush and Perot. 10–11–1992.

### Eisenhower

*Work* • Jefferson Barracks, Grant Rd and Kingston. Army physical exam. 1911.

*Visit* • Hotel Statler. 9–20–1952.

### Grant

*Church* • Methodist Church. Current site 801 First Capitol Dr. 1848.

*Marriage* • Fourth and Cerre Sts at the Dent home. Lived here immediately after wedding. 1848.

*Home* • White Haven on Gavois Rd. 1854–1855; 1857–1858.

*Home* • Jefferson Barracks Historical Park. See his farm Grantwood, sometimes called Wish-ton-wish, one and one half miles south of White Haven. 1855–1856.

*Home* • Hardscrabble, 10501 Gravois Rd. 1856–1858.

*Home* • Seventh and Lynch near the river. Lot owned by Grant. 1858–1867.

*Home* • House in town, 209 S Fifteenth St. 1858–1860.

*Lodging* • 209 S Fifteenth St (Harry Boggs house) during the week; returned to White Haven every weekend. 1858–1860.

*Work* • Old Courthouse, Fourth St to Market to Chestnut Sts, where he freed his only slave. 1859.

*Work* • McLellan, Hillyer and Moody law firm, Pine St. 1858–1859.

*Work* • U.S. Customs House. Site SE corner Third and Olive Sts. 1859.

*Work* • Jefferson Barracks, on Alt 67 and Bypass 50 SE of Kirkwood. 1844. 1861.

*Visit* • Campbell House, Fifteenth and Locust Sts.

*Visit* • Washington University, Forest Park Parkway. 1864.

## Harding

*Visit* • World's Fair. 1904.

*Visit* • Coliseum, 2608 Washington Ave. 1920.

*Visit* • Union Station, south side of Market St and Eighteenth-Twentieth Sts. 1920.

## Harrison, WH

*Visit* • Auguste Choteau House on Main St. Bounded by Market, Walnut and Second Sts. 1804.

## Jefferson

*Site* • Jefferson National Expansion Memorial.

## Johnson, A

*Visit* • Lindell Hotel, Washington Ave. Banquet at Southern Hotel. 1866.

## Johnson, LB

*Visit* • St. Louis University, 221 N Grand Blvd. Chase-Park Plaza Hotel dinner. Bicentennial of city. 2–14–1964.

## Lincoln

*Visit* • Scott's Hotel, SW corner Third and Market Sts. 1847.

*Visit* • Old National Hotel, SE corner of Third and Market. Building razed. Marker on site. 1847.

## McKinley

*Work* • Nominated president. June 1896.

## Roosevelt, FD

*Visit* • Soldier's Monument opposite City Hall. Dedication. 10–14–1936.

## Roosevelt, T

*Visit* • St. Louis Exposition, Forest Park at Lindall Blvd and Oakland Ave; Kingshighway to Skinker Blvd. 1903.

*Visit* • 4421 Maryland Ave. 1903, 1904.

*Visit* • Planter's Hotel, 401 Fourth St, Chestnut to Pine. 1906, 1916.

*Church* • Second Presbyterian, 2608 Washington Ave. November 1904.

## Taylor

*Travel* • Headquarters. 1820. 1821. Commander Missouri Territory. Old National Hotel SE corner Third and Market Sts. Replaced 1847. 1814.

## Wilson

*Visit* • Coliseum, DNC nominated him for president. June 1916. He spoke here. 9–5–1919.

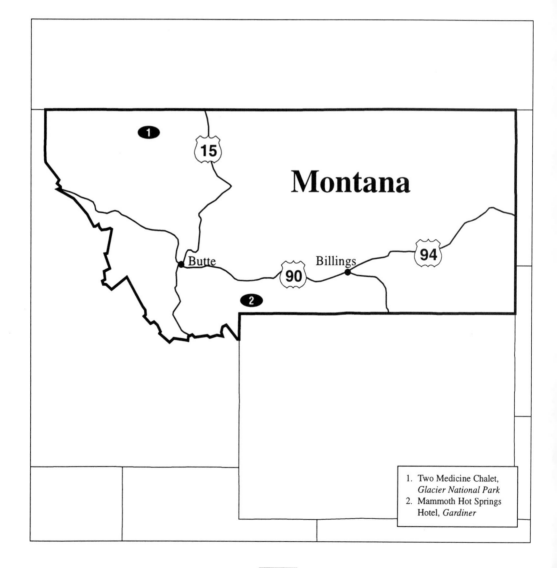

1. Two Medicine Chalet, *Glacier National Park*
2. Mammoth Hot Springs Hotel, *Gardiner*

# MONTANA

## BILLINGS *(Yellowstone County)*

**Wilson**
*Visit* • Auditorium, Fair Grounds. 1919.

## BUTTE *(Silver Bow County)*

**Harding**
*Visit* • Butte mine. Boarded train at the Great Northern Station. 1923.

**Taft**
*Visit* • Leonard Copper Mine, off US 91 at Noble St. 1909.

*Visit* • Courthouse, Corner of Montana and Broadway. 1909.

## GARDINER *(South Park County)*

**Harding**
*Travel* • Visited on Western tour 1923. From here visited Yellowstone National Park and Old Faithful. In Gardiner he stayed at Mammoth Hot Springs Hotel. 1923.

**Roosevelt, T**
*Visit* • Arch at the entrance to the park on US 89. Dedicated. 1903.

## GLACIER NATIONAL PARK *(NW Montana)*

**Roosevelt, FD**
*Visit* • Two Medicine Chalet on US 2. Crossed Great Divide, US 2 near Idaho line. Summit in Marias Pass in center of highway is a shaft monument honoring him. 8–5–1934.

## HELENA *(Lewis and Clark County )* Capitol

*Site* • Governor's Mansion Chessman House, 304 N Ewing. 1913–1959.

**Roosevelt, T**
*Visit* • State Capitol. Sixth Ave between S Montana and S Roberts Sts. 1903.

**Taft**
*Visit* • State Fair Grounds. 1909.

*Visit* • State Capitol. Sixth Ave between S Montana and S Roberts Sts. 1909.

**Wilson**
*Visit* • State Capitol. 1919.

## LIBBY *(Lincoln County)*

**Ford**
> *Visit* • Libby Dam, MT 35. Dedicated. 8–24–1975.

## MISSOULA *(Missoula County)*

**Carter**
> *Visit* • University of Montana, University Ave. Mansfield lecture series. 1986.

## THOMPSON FALLS *(Sanders County)*

**Roosevelt, T**
> *Travel* • Hunting trip, including Clark

Fork on the Columbia River near the Idaho line. 1886.

## YELLOWSTONE *(Yellowstone County)*

**Arthur**
> *Travel* • August 1883.

**Harrison**
> *Visit* • Marshall's Hotel (later Firehouse Hotel) on the confluence of Nez Perce Creek and the Firehole River. Removed in 1892. Harrison stayed here while a senator. 1881.

# NEBRASKA

## LINCOLN *(Lancaster County)*

**Lincoln**

*Site* • Monument. West side of Capitol lawn.

*Site* • O St. Columns between which Lincoln stood to review the Civil War troops, moved from Washington, DC.

**Roosevelt, FD**

*Visit* • State Capitol. 10–10–1936.

**Roosevelt, T**

*Visit* • State Capitol and Governor's Mansion. 1903.

**Taft**

*Visit* • State Capitol. 1911.

## OMAHA *(Douglas County)*

**Ford**

*Birthplace* • 3203 Woolworth Ave. 1913–1915.

**Harding**

*Visit* • Fontanelle Hotel, Howard St between Fourteenth and Fifteenth Sts. 1920.

**Lincoln**

*Site* • Union Pacific Headquarters, Fifteenth and Dodge Sts. Replica of Lincoln funeral car.

**Truman**

*Travel* • Spoke at Ak-Sar-Ben Auditorium. Dedicated War Memorial. Visit Boys Town, One hundred-thirty-second and W Dodge Rd. 6–5–1948.

**Nebraska**

🛡️ **80**

Omaha ⬤**1**

| 1. Ford home, *Omaha* |

# NEVADA

## BOULDER (HOOVER) DAM *(Clara County)*

**Hoover**
*Visit* • Off US 93. 11–12–1932.

## CARSON CITY *(Ormsby County )*

**Eisenhower**
*Visit* • Capitol. North Carson St. 1913.

**Grant**
*Visit* • Capitol. North Carson St. 1879.

*Visit* • Crystal Bar, NW corner C and Taylor. See International Hotel register with photo of Grant. 1879.

**Roosevelt, T**
*Visit* • Capitol. North Carson St. May 1903.

**Nevada**

80

1 Carson City

Las Vegas

1. Crystal Bar, *Carson City*

# NEW HAMPSHIRE

## AMHERST *(Hillsboro County)*

**Pierce**

*Church* • Methodist Chapel, Middle St. 1827–.

*Church* • Congregational Church, Church St near the Boston Post Rd. 1827–.

*Education* • Parker House, 12 Main St. Law study with Edmund Parker. 1827.

*Marriage* • 1 Pierce Lane. Means mansion. 1834.

## CONCORD *(Merrimack County)*

**Presidents**

*Visit* • State Capitol. Arthur, Bush, Eisenhower, Ford, Grant, B and WH Harrison, Hayes, Jackson, Monroe, Polk, Reagan, Taft, and Van Buren.

**Harrison, WH**

*Visit* • Eagle Hotel, Eagle Square, 205 N Main. 1841.

**Hayes**

*Visit* • Eagle Hotel. St. Paul's School. September 1877.

**Jackson**

*Church* • First Congregational Meeting House (Old North Church), 177 N Main St. 1833.

*Church* • Unitarian Church, 274 Pleasant St. 1833.

*Church* • Baptist Church, State St. 1833.

*Visit* • Eagle Hotel, Eagle Square. Summer 1833.

*Visit* • State prison. 1833.

**Monroe**

*Church* • Old North Church. 7–20–1817.

*Visit* • Barker's Tavern, Main St. Nothing remains. July 1817.

**Pierce**

*Baptism* • St. Paul's Episcopal Church, 18 Park St. Attended. 1863–1869.

*Church* • South Congregational Church, 27 Pleasant St. 1842–1863.

*Home* • Moved to present site at 14 Penacook St. 1842–1848.

*Home* • 52 S Main St. Only steps remain. 1849–1860.

93

89

Concord

● 1

2

**New Hampshire**

1. Pierce home, *Concord*
2. Pierce home, *Hillsborough*

*Franklin Pierce was baptized here at St. Paul's Episcopal Church.*

**Lodging** • John George's house near the North Church. 1829–.

**Lodging** • Eagle Hotel, Eagle Square. 1830s. His old boarding house with Mr. Williams. 1858–.

**Work** • State Capitol, North State St. State Legislature. 1829–1833.

**Work** • Merrimack Bank Law Office, Main St. 1838–1845. 1848–1853.

**Work** • Merrimack County Courthouse and Merrimack Bank. 1842–1845.

**Work** • Ayre's Block over the Franklin Book Shop, Main St near the Capitol. Law office. 1845–1857.

**Work** • President, State Constitutional Convention. Marker on Main St. 1850.

**Death** • 52 S Main St in his room in the southeast corner. 1869.

**Funeral** • St. Paul's Episcopal Church, 18 Park St.

**Funeral** • State Capitol, Main St. Lay in state here.

**Burial** • Old North Cemetery on N State St near downtown.

**Site** • Statue on The Plaza of the Capitol.

## CORNISH *(Sullivan County)*
**Wilson**

**Church** • South Congregational Church, Center Rd. Now United Church of Cornish. 1913–1916.

## DOVER *(Strafford County)*
**Lincoln**

**Visit** • Lincoln House, 107 Locust St. 1860.

**Visit** • Old City Hall, Central St. 1860.

**Monroe**

**Visit** • William Hale House, 5 Hale St (now 192 Central St), and the Episcopal Church. 1806.

**Washington**

**Visit** • Folsom Tavern, 21 Spring St. Now vacant lot. No marker. 11–4–1789.

## EXETER *(Rockingham County)*
**Lincoln**

**Visit** • Robert Lincoln boarding place, corner of High and Pleasant Sts. Lincoln's son attended the academy in Exeter.

## FRANCESTOWN *(Hillsborough County)*
**Pierce**

**Church** • Old Meeting House on the village common. Built 1820.

**Education** • Francestown Academy on the village common. Marker on Francestown turnpike. 1820.

**Lodging** • Peter Woodbury house on corner near Francestown Academy. 1820.

## FRANCONIA *(Grafton County)*
**Eisenhower**

**Visit** • Old Man of the Mountain. 6–24–1955.

*Franklin Pierce home in Concord.*

## GOFFSTOWN  *(Hillsboro County)*

**Clinton**

    *Visit* • Democratic presidential primary debate. 1992.

## HANCOCK  *(Hillsborough County)*

**Pierce**

    *Church* • Meeting House, Main St on NH 123. Built 1820, remodeled and moved 1851. 1820.

    *Education* • Hancock Academy, second floor of the Vestry. First building east of the church on NH 123. 1818–1820.

    *Education* • Academy boarding house across the street from the bandstand. 1820.

## HANOVER  *(Grafton County)*

**Eisenhower**

    *Education* • Dartmouth College, north end of the Green. Commencement. 6–14–1953.

## HILLSBOROUGH  *(Hillsborough County )*

**Pierce**

    *Birthplace* • Log house on branch of the Contoocook River. Now underwater. 1804.

    *Church* • South Congregational Church, Town Center. 1804–1829.

    *Education* • Hillsboro Center schoolhouse. Nothing remains. 1807–1818.

    *Education* • John Burnham house. Main St, studying law. 1824.

    *Home* • Junction of NH 9 and NH 31. Built 1804. Entrance fee. 1804–1833.

    *Home* • NH 31 and Old Turnpike. 1834–1842.

    *Work* • Postmaster. 1824. Practicing attorney. 1827–1829.

*Boyhood home of Franklin Pierce.*

## ISLE OF SHOALS *(OFF COAST OF ROCKINGHAM COUNTY)*

**Harding**

*Visit* • 1902. Later visited Taft at his summer home. See Taft under Little Boar's Head. 1910.

## JEFFERSON *(Coos County)*

**Garfield**

*Visit* • Cheshire House built 1837. SE corner of Central Square between Roxbury and Church Sts. 10–20–1871.

*Visit* • Soldier's Monument. Dedication. October 1871.

**Monroe**

*Visit* • William A. Kent house, Pleasant St. 7–19–1817.

## LANCASTER *(Coos County)*

**Harding**

*Visit* • Mount Prospect, home of John W. Weeks. Vacation. 1922.

## LITTLE BOAR'S HEAD *(Rockingham County)*

**Arthur**

*Visit* • Bachelder's Hotel. Was on the coast between Rye Beach and Little Boar's Head. 1880s.

**Garfield**

*Visit* • John Bachelder place and at Bachelder's Hotel. Hotel torn down 1928. 1880s.

**Pierce**

*Home* • On the old Brown farm. General area on the coastal highway. 1865–1869.

**Taft**
> *Visit* • Hollister, summer home, the second house north of Atlantic Ave on Ocean Blvd. 1884. 1909.

## MANCHESTER *(Hillsborough County)*

**Bush**
> *Visit* • TV-WMUR station for presidential debate. 1–20–1992.

**Clinton**
> *Visit* • See Bush entry above.

**Hayes**
> *Visit* • Maplewood House. May 1877.

## MOUNT WASHINGTON

**Hayes**
> *Visit* • Tip Top House. May 1877.

## NASHUA *(Hillsborough County)*

**Reagan**
> *Travel* • Nashua High School. Site of debate with Bush. 1980.

## NORTH CONWAY *(Carroll County)*

**Hayes**
> *Visit* • Wiley House. May 1877.

## NORTH HAMPTON *(Rockingham County)*

**Pierce**
> *Education* • Studied law under John Burnham. 1824.

## PLYMOUTH *(Grafton County)*

**Hayes**
> *Visit* • Kearsarge House. May 1877.

## PORTSMOUTH *(Rockingham County)*

**Pierce**
> *Education* • Levi Woodbury law office. 1825.

**Washington**
> *Church* • Queen's Chapel, Chapel St. St. John's Church now on site. 1789.
>
> *Church* • North Church. 1789.
>
> *Visit* • Governor John Langdon House, 143 Pleasant St. 1789 and 1791.
>
> *Visit* • Chase House on Court. 1789.
>
> *Visit* • Old State House. 1789.
>
> *Visit* • Governor Goodwin Mansion on Hancock St.
>
> *Visit* • Governor John Wentworth House, 346 Pleasant St.

## RYE BEACH *(Rockingham County)*

**Pierce**
> *Visit* • Ocean House. Vacation. 1852–.
>
> *Home* • Little Boar's Head by the sea. See Little Boar's Head above.

## TAMWORTH *(Carroll County)*

**Cleveland**
> *Home* • Near Tamworth. Summer home, "Intermont." 1904–1908.

# NEW JERSEY

## ASBURY PARK *(Monmouth County)*

**Wilson**
*Visit* • Mid-Atlantic National Bank Building, 601 Mattison Ave. 1916.

## ATLANTIC CITY *(Atlantic County)*

**Johnson, LB**
*Visit* • Convention Hall, 2301 Boardwalk between Georgia and Mississippi Aves. From Pageant Motel he went to DNC to accept presidential nomination. 8–26–1964.

## BASKING RIDGE *(Somerset County)*

**Monroe**
*Visit* • Lord (Wm Alexander) Stirling House, 96 Lord Stirling Rd. 1778.

## BEDMINSTER *(Morris County)*

**Washington**
*Visit* • Vanderweer House site. Gen. Knox's headquarters. US 202 and US 206 below Dutch Reformed Cemetery. Moved to E Jersey Olde Towne near Piscataway. 1778–1779.

## BOUND BROOK *(See Raritan)*

## BURLINGTON *(Burlington County)*

**Grant**
*Home* • General Grant House, 305 Wood St. 1862–1865.

## CALDWELL *(Essex County)*

**Cleveland**
*Birthplace* • Manse, 207 Bloomfield Ave. 1837.

*Baptism* • Presbyterian Church, 814 Madison Ave. 1837–1841.

*Home* • 207 Bloomfield Ave. 1837–1841.

## CAMDEN *(Camden County)*

**Clinton**
*Travel* • Started here on first of campaign bus tours with Al Gore. Ended in St. Louis. 7–17–1992.

**Coolidge**
*Visit* • Delaware River Bridge (now Benjamin Franklin Bridge). Dedication. 1926.

80

287

78

2

Newark

4

3

Trenton

1

New Jersey

1. Grant home, *Burlington*
2. Cleveland birthplace, *Caldwell*
3. Cleveland home, *Princeton*
4. Washington home, *Somerville*

## CAMP DIX   *(See Fort Dix)*

## CAMP MERRITT   *(Bergen County)*

### Truman
*Visit* • Soldiers Monument, Madison Ave (near Cresskill). 1918.

## CAPE MAY POINT   *(Cape May County)*

### Harrison, B
*Visit* • John Wanamaker's cottage, corner Cape and Yale. Now Christian Family Retreat. June 1889.

*Home* • Summer residence. New cottage built especially for Mrs. Harrison during final illness. 1890, 1891, 1890.

## CRESSKILL   *(Bergen County)*

### Truman
*Visit* • Camp Merritt.

## ELBERON   *(Monmouth County)*

### Arthur
*Visit* • MacVeagh's cottage where he came to pay tribute to Garfield's memory. 9-2-1881.

### Garfield
*Visit* • Charles Francklyn Cottage on Elberon Hotel grounds, corner Ocean and Lincoln Aves. 1881.

*Death* • Transferred here. 9-6-1881. Died 9-19-1881 at 10:35 p.m. Hotel and cottage where he died have been demolished.

*Site* • Garfield statue at Broadway.

### Grant
*Church* • St. James Episcopal Chapel, known as "Church of the Presidents," Ocean Ave. Also attended by Arthur, Garfield, and Wilson. Now a museum.

*Visit* • Howard Potter Cottage, 991 Ocean Ave (Long Branch). Wrecked by vandals and razed. 1867.

*Visit* • Thomas Murphy Cottage. NW corner Park and Ocean Aves. 1874.

### Harrison, B
*Visit* • Rode up and down Ocean Ave in electric cars. 1889.

*Visit* • Elberon Hotel, corner Ocean and Lincoln Aves. 1889.

### Hayes
*Visit* • Owned a summer cottage. Also stayed Elberon Hotel, Ocean and Lincoln Aves. 1877.

*Visit* • Normanhurst. Site Cedar and Norwood Aves in W Long Branch visiting Vice President Hobart. Guggenheim Library now on site. 1897.

### Wilson
*Home* • Shadow Lawn was his summer home. 1916. Burned down 1927. Replaced by a building now part of Monmouth College. Here he woke up in 1916 to learn he had been reelected. Wilson Hall now on the site at Cedar and Norwood Aves, West Long Branch. 1911–1916.

## ELIZABETH   *(Union County)*

### Monroe
*Visit* • Here late summer, a site chosen as brigade headquarters. 1778. See also Basking Ridge.

### Washington
*Visit* • Boxwood Hall, 1073 East Jersey St. 4-23-1789.

*Visit* • Belcher-Ogden Mansion, 1046 E Jersey St. 1778.

## ENGLEWOOD   *(Bergen County)*

### Arthur
*Visit* • Son Wm Lewis Herndon Arthur died here July 8, 1863.

## ENGLISHTOWN   *(Monmouth County)*

### Washington
*Travel* • Hulse Memorial (now funeral parlor), Main St. Headquarters night before

Battle of Monmouth. See also the Washington Elm behind the house. Plaque on front door. 1778.

*Visit* • Village Inn. Main St at corner of Water St. 1778.

## ERSKINE (RINGWOOD) *(Passaic County)*

**Washington**
*Visit* • Ringwood Manor State Park near Erskine, off County Rd 511. 1781.

## FORT DIX *(Burlington/Ocean Counties)*

**Eisenhower**
*Work* • Stationed here with tank unit. December 1918.

*Site* • Fort Dix Military Museum, Pennsylvania Ave.

## FORT LEE *(Bergen County)*

**Roosevelt, FD**
*Visit* • George Washington Bridge across Hudson River near Fort Lee. Opened while governor of New York. 1931.

## FREEHOLD *(See Monmouth)*

## GLASSBORO *(Gloucester County)*

**Johnson, LB**
*Visit* • Hollybush, Glassboro State College, Heston Rd. Site of conference with Soviet President Kosygin. 6–23–1967. Here for commencement. 6–4–1968.

## HACKENSACK *(Bergen County)*

**Roosevelt, FD**
*Visit* • George Washington Bridge on I-95. See Fort Lee above.

**Washington**
*Visit* • Washington Mansion House, Main St on the Courthouse Sq. NE room 19 on second floor. Bronze tablet on the house. 1770s.

## HOHOKUS *(Bergen County)*

**Washington**
*Visit* • Hermitage, 335 N Franklin Turnpike (now museum). 1778.

## JERSEY CITY *(Hudson County)*

**Washington**
*Visit* • Van Wagenen House, 298 Academy St. Was part of Apple Tree House where he dined. 1779.

## LAKEWOOD *(Ocean County)*

**Cleveland**
*Home* • Little White House (Straus House), a short distance north of the Lakewood Hotel. 1893–1908.

*Home* • Laurel House on the north side of Main St, west of Lexington Ave. 1889–1890.

*Home* • Lakewood Hotel facing Seventh St between Clifton and Lexington Aves. 1891–1892; 1908.

**Grant**
*Visit* • Bricksburg House (later called Laurel House). See location under Cleveland above. 1869.

## LAMBERTVILLE *(Hunterdon County)*

**Washington**
*Visit* • John Holcombe House, north end of Main St on the right. He was quartered here. Marker on the street. Private. July 1777 and June 1778.

## LONG BRANCH *(Monmouth County)*

**Presidents**
*Site* • Seven Presidents Oceanfront Park, Ocean and Joline Ave. NJ 35.

## McKONKEY FERRY HOUSE *(Mercer County)*

**Washington**
*Visit* • Washington Crossing State Park where he stopped Christmas night before going to Trenton. 1776.

## MADISON *(Morris County)*

**Roosevelt, T**
*Visit* • Loantaka, the Roosevelt place where he spent four summer seasons. Western side of Kitchell Rd between Madison Ave south to Woodland Ave. 1863–1866.

**Washington**
*Visit* • Sayre Mansion, 31 Ridgedale Ave. 1777

## MIDDLEBROOK *(Somerset County)*

**Washington**
*Travel* • Winter headquarters. 1778–1779.

*Travel* • See Chimney Rock and also Washington Rock, south of N Plainfield in State Park. 1777.

## MILLSTONE *(Somerset County)*

**Washington**
*Travel* • John Van Doren House where he stayed after the Battle of Princeton. 1777. NF.

## MONMOUTH (FREEHOLD) *(Monmouth County)*

**Monroe**
*Visit* • Monmouth Battlefield State Park, off NJ 33. Last battle in which he participated. Monument north of courthouse, Main and Court Sts. 6–28–1778.

## MONTCLAIR *(Essex County)*

**Washington**
*Travel* • Headquarters. Site Valley Rd and Claremont Ave. Marked by boulder. 1780.

## MORRISTOWN *(Morris County)*

**Washington**
*Travel* • Ford House, 230 Morris St. Headquarters. Great storehouse relics. 1776–1777. 1779–1780. See Morristown National Historical Park, Washington Place.

*Travel* • Arnold Tavern. Site NW side Morristown Green, Park Square at junction NJ 24 and US 202. Headquarters. Burned. Marker. 1777.

*Site* • Bronze statue, intersection Morris and Washington Aves across from Ford House.

## MORVEN *(See Princeton)*

## NEWARK *(Essex County)*

**Lincoln**
*Site* • Essex County Courthouse, Springfield Ave and Market St. Bronze statue in the plaza.

**Roosevelt, T**
*Site* • Dedicated Lincoln statue, at Essex County Courthouse. 1911.

**Washington**
*Site* • Statue. Washington Park, Broad St. Washington Place and Washington St at the south end of the park.

## NEW BRUNSWICK *(Middlesex County)*

**Adams, J**
*Visit* • White Hart Tavern. See Washington below.

**Ford**
*Travel* • Rutgers University, College Ave, to deliver lecture at Eagleton Institute of Politics. April 1983.

**Washington**
*Visit* • NE corner Albany and Neilson Sts is site of the White Hart Tavern (later Duff's Inn). He was host to his staff in the

tavern after the Battle of Monmouth. Marker across street from Hyatt. 1778.

## NEW FREEHOLD *(Monmouth County)*

**Washington**

*Travel* • Battle of Monmouth Courthouse, Court St, which ended as a draw. (Molly Pitcher). 1778.

## NEWTON *(Sussex County)*

**Washington**

*Visit* • Cochran House (now greatly altered) near Courthouse Square. 7–26–1782.

## PARK RIDGE *(Bergen County)*

**Nixon**

*Home* • Bears Nest Condominium, 239 Spring Valley Rd. 1990–1994.

## PATERSON *(Passaic County)*

**Ford**

*Visit* • Great Falls National Historic site. 65 McBride Ave. Dedicated. 6–6–1976.

## PERTH AMBOY *(Middlesex County)*

**Adams, J**

*Visit* • Perth Amboy Inn. He stopped here on the way to Staten Island. Nothing remains. 1776.

**Washington**

*Site* • Statue in park in front of City Hall, City Hall Square.

## PLAINFIELD *(Union County)*

**Washington**

*Visit* • Drake House, 602 Front St. He spent time here at the time of the Battle for the Watchungs, also known as the Battle of the Short Hills. 6–25–1777 to 6–27–1777.

*Travel* • Washington's Rock in N Plainfield. See Middlebrook.

## POMPTON LAKES *(Passaic County)*

**Washington**

*Visit* • Near NJ 208 and Pompton Lakes. Small house with a large marker. Used when he and his troops moved to Smith Cove, NY, from Morristown.

## PRINCETON *(Mercer County)*

**Cleveland**

*Church* • First Presbyterian Church, 61 Nassau St. Plaque on pew he occupied. 1896–1908.

*Home* • Westland, 58 Bayard Lane (now 15 Hodges Rd). Private. 1896–1908. Also purchased a farm about 3 miles from town as a convenient stopping place when hunting.

*Work* • Princeton, 185 Nassau St. 1899.

*Death* • Westland. 1908.

*Funeral* • Westland. President Theodore Roosevelt attended.

*Burial* • Princeton Cemetery, 28 Greenview Ave. 1908.

*Site* • Cleveland Memorial Tower in Graduate School area, College Rd.

**Jefferson**

*Work* • Princeton University. Congress met in Nassau Hall on University campus. June 1783.

*Visit* • Morven, 55 Stockton St. 11–4–1783.

**Johnson, LB**

*Visit* • Wilson School Public and International Affairs, Prospect Ave. Dedication. 5–11–1966.

**Kennedy**

*Church* • St. Paul's Roman Catholic, 214 Nassau St. 1935.

*Education* • Princeton University, 185 Nassau St. 1935.

*Education* • He stayed in S Reunion Hall (torn down 1965). Bricks from the fireplace in Hall's living room frame a bronze plaque honoring him (south entry of the class of 1939 dormitory). 1935.

## Madison

*Church* • Trinity, Stockton St. 1769–1772.

*Education* • College of New Jersey (Princeton). Lodged in Nassau Hall, 185 Nassau St. 1769–1772.

*Work* • Nassau Hall. Congress met here. June 1783.

*Visit* • American Whig Society in upper chamber of Nassau Hall. Society moved to new Whig Hall. 1838. Located off University Place north of McCormich Hall. Many presidents beginning with Andrew Jackson were honorary members. 1769–1772.

## Monroe

*Work* • Nassau Hall. Congress met here. June 1783.

## Roosevelt, T

*Visit* • Cleveland home, 58 Bayard Lane. 1908.

## Truman

*Visit* • Nassau Hall. 6–17–1947.

## Washington

*Visit* • Morven, 55 Stockton St on the edge of Princeton towards Trenton. While Continental Congress met in Princeton he stayed here. 1783.

*Visit* • Thomas Olden House, on US 206 at 344 Stockton St. 1776, 1791.

*Visit* • Nassau Hall, Princeton University, where Battle of Princeton ended. 1777.

*Travel* • Princeton Battlefield State Park, 500 Mercer Rd.

*Site* • Monument stone on campus.

*Travel* • Washington-Rochambeau route to Yorktown. Marker on grounds of Trinity Church. 1781.

## Wilson

*Church* • First Presbyterian Church, 61 Nassau St. Pew No. 57. 1890–1897.

*Church* • Second Presbyterian Church, 26 Nassau St. Now Nassau Christian Center. 1897–1913.

*Church* • Princeton Memorial Chapel on campus. Old Marquand Chapel burned 1920. New University chapel 1928. 1875–1879; 1891– 1913.

*Church* • Trinity Episcopal Church, Stockton St. 1876.

*Education* • Princeton University. 1875–1879. Princeton University, Whig Hall, where he attended the Whig Society. New Whig Hall Hall built 1893 on the same site. 1890.

*Lodging* • Wright Bower rooming house SE corner of Washington and Nassau Sts. Torn down and new building on site. 1875.

*Lodging* • Witherspoon Hall, off University Place. Dormitory on campus. 1876.

*Lodging* • Witherspoon Hall, Princeton University. Accustomed to meet after prayer meeting in No. 9 East Witherspoon.

*Lodging* • University Hotel. September 1876.

*Home* • 72 Library Pl. Private. 1890–1896.

*Home* • 82 Library Pl. 1896–1902.

*Home* • Prospect. President's house on campus. Now used for special events. 1902–1911.

*Home* • 25 Cleveland Lane. 1913.

*Lodging* • Nassau Hotel. While Ellen visited family, he stayed here. Palmer Square. Now gone. Reproduction of colonial style inn on site. 1890, 1892.

*Lodging* • Princeton Inn opposite Trinity Church on Stockton St next to the current police station. Demolished. 1911–1913.

*Work* • Witherspoon Hall. His study office was 12 West Witherspoon Hall. 1890–1902.

*Work* • Nassau Hall, Room 1. President of Princeton. 1902–1910.

**Washington**

*Visit* • Merchants and Drovers Tavern (restored), junction of Westfield and Grand Aves. On his inaugural journey. 1789. Also 1791.

## RARITAN *(Somerset County)*

**Harding**

*Church* • Third Reformed Church, 10 West Somerset St. 1920.

*Visit* • Freylinghuysen House, between Raritan and Morristown on NJ E 28. Now site of Toys-R-Us. Site Knox-Porter resolution. 1921.

## RIDGEWOOD *(Bergen County)*

**Washington**

*Visit* • Paramus School House, 650 E Glen Ave. 1778.

## ROCKINGHAM *(See Rocky Hill)*

## ROCKY HILL *(Somerset County)*

**Washington**

*Visit* • Berrien House at Rocky Hill, 3 miles east of Princeton NJ 318. In the Blue Room he wrote his farewell address to the army. Fall 1783.

## SADDLE RIVER *(Bergen County)*

**Nixon**

*Home* • 1981–1989.

*Work* • Office in Porillo Tours Plaza Building, 557 Chestnut Ridge Rd.

## SEABRIGHT *(Monmouth County)*

**Taft**

*Honeymoon* • Albemarle Hotel. For a few days before sailing for Europe. Demolished. 1886.

## SEA GIRT *(Monmouth County)*

**Wilson**

*Lodging* • Summer mansion near the ocean. Demolished. 1911–1913.

## SOMERVILLE *(Somerset County)*

**Washington**

*Home* • Wallace House, 38 Washington Pl. Occupied by him and Martha. 1778 and 1779.

*Visit* • Dutch Parsonage, 65 Washington Place. 1778. 1779.

## SOUTH ORANGE *(Essex County)*

**Reagan**

*Visit* • Seton Hall University. 5–21–1983.

**Washington**

*Visit* • Timothy Ball House, 425 Ridgewood Ave. See walnut tree to which he tied his horse. 1770s.

*Travel* • Washington Rock. Crest Dr beyond Ridgewood Ave. 1780.

## SPRING LAKE *(Monmouth County)*

**Wilson**

*Church* • East Orange Presybterian Church. 1911.

## TRENTON *(Mercer County)*

**Lincoln**

*Visit* • State Capitol. 121 West State St. Spoke to the two houses of the legislature 2–21–1861.

**Monroe**

*Work* • Jacob Bergen's French Arms was meeting place of Congress. See plaque on West State St between Chancery Ln and Warren. October 1784.

*Lodging* • Stayed at Rising Sun Hotel. 1794. 1817.

**Washington**

*Work* • State Capitol. Federal Government met. 1794.

*Travel* • Old Barracks Museum, Barrack St. Site of famous day-after-Christmas Battle of Revolutionary War. 1776. See the old barracks, South Willow St. 1886.

*Visit* • Douglass House, 193 S Broad St. Original location in 1777. Brought to Memorial Drive 1823 and the exterior restored. In the extreme easterly part of Mahlon Stacy Park. Meeting place with his officers. 1777.

*Site* • Battle Monument surmounted by his statue. Intersection N Warren St and N Broad St.

### Wilson

*Work* • Governor's office in State House, 121 W State St. Office located on the first floor, first office on the right. 1911–1913.

*Visit* • Site of Government House used as governor's mansion. 1798–1845. Wilson here. 1912. Marker on W State St between Chancery Lane and Warren.

*Site* • Taylor Opera House where he accepted Democratic nomination for governor. 1910.

## WASHINGTON CROSSING STATE PARK *(Mercer County)*

### Washington

*Visit* • Johnson House, popularly known as the McKonkey Ferry House, a few hun-dred feet north of intersection of NJ 29 and County Rd 546. Restored. 1776.

*Travel* • See island in the middle of the Delaware where he had boats hidden for crossing. 1776.

*Travel* • See stone monument just across the river on Pennsylavnia side commemo-rating the event on Christmas Eve. 1776.

## WAYNE *(Passaic County)*

### Washington

*Visit* • Dey Mansion, 199 Totowa Rd (Preakness Valley Rd). One of his many headquarters. July, October, and November 1779.

## WHITE HORSE *(Mercer County)*

### Washington

*Visit* • Site of White Horse Tavern on US 206 at junction with I-95. Named for white horse Washington was riding. Torn down 1972 and now site of Sizzler Restaurant.

## WOODSTOWN *(Salem County)*

### Carter

*Church* • First Baptist Church, 117 S Main St. 1981.

GEOGRAPHIC GUIDE TO LANDMARKS

New Mexico

Santa Fe

Albuquerque

**40**

**25**

**New Mexico**

# NEW MEXICO

## ALBUQUERQUE *(Bernalillo County)*

**Roosevelt, T**
*Visit* • Alvarado Hotel, Gold Ave and First St. Hotel demolished and new hotel on site. May 1903.

**Taft**
*Visit* • Alvarado Hotel. 1909.

## SANTA FE *(Santa Fe County)*

**Hayes**
*Visit* • Capitol. Palace Ave. 1880.

**Roosevelt, T**
*Visit* • Governor's Palace. 1903.

*Visit* • State Capitol, Galisteo St at Montezuma. 1903.

**Taft**
*Visit* • State Capitol. Galisteo St at Montezuma. 1909.

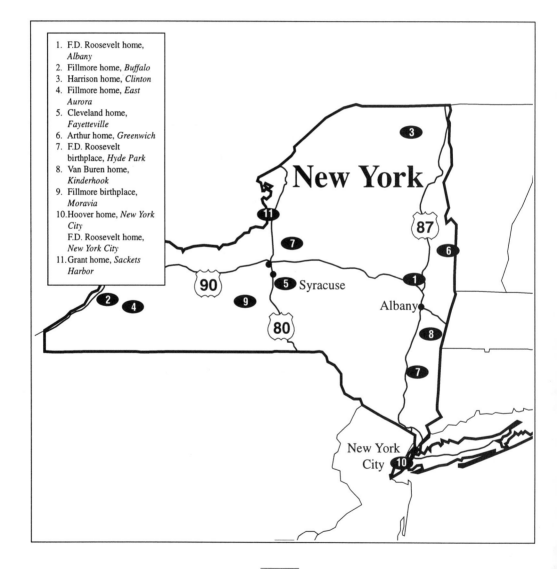

1. F.D. Roosevelt home,
   *Albany*
2. Fillmore home, *Buffalo*
3. Harrison home, *Clinton*
4. Fillmore home, *East
   Aurora*
5. Cleveland home,
   *Fayetteville*
6. Arthur home, *Greenwich*
7. F.D. Roosevelt
   birthplace, *Hyde Park*
8. Van Buren home,
   *Kinderhook*
9. Fillmore birthplace,
   *Moravia*
10. Hoover home, *New York
    City*
    F.D. Roosevelt home,
    *New York City*
11. Grant home, *Sackets
    Harbor*

**New York**

87

90

80

Syracuse

Albany

New York
City

# NEW YORK

## ADIRONDACK MOUNTAINS

*(Franklin County)*

### Cleveland

*Visit* • Derby's Prospect House on the Upper Saranac. 1884. Again on Saranac Lake. 1885.

### Harrison, B

*Lodging* • Leased a cottage in the Adirondacks, near Loon Lake. July-September 1892. Built Berkeley Lodge, one of the finest cottages on the second Lake Fulton chain, which he used until his death. President's Cottage is still standing. It was part of Lake Loon Hotel. At Camp Doud. 1895.

### Roosevelt, T

*Visit* • Camping trips here, including Lake George and Lake Placid. 1871 and 1877.

*Visit* • Wilson St. Hubert's on the Au Sable River. June 1909.

## ALBANY *(Albany County)*

### Presidents

*Visit* • Delwan House. Site corner Broadway and Steuben. Arthur 1881, Fillmore 1829–1831, Lincoln 1861, A Johnson 1866, and T Roosevelt 1882.

### Arthur

*Burial* • Albany Rural Cemetery. Cemetery Ave off Broadway at Menands. 1886.

### Cleveland

*Home* • Governor's Mansion, 138 Eagle St. First governor to occupy this mansion. 1883–1885.

*Home* • The Towers, a small house near the governor's mansion. 1885.

*Work* • State Capitol, the governor's office. State St. 1883–1884.

*Visit* • Pruyn House, 19 Elk St. 1883.

### Fillmore

*Marriage* • Schuyler Mansion, SW corner Clinton and Catharine Sts. 1858.

*Home* • Delwan House. Site corner of Broadway and Steuben. 1829–1831.

*Work* • Old Capitol Building in the State Legislature. 1829–1831.

### Grant

*Visit* • Old Capitol. State St. 1865.

*Funeral* • New Capitol. State St. Lay in state here for two days. 1885.

### Harrison, WH
*Visit* • Van Rensselar House. Cherry Hill between McCarty and First Aves. Property extended from Broadway to the river. 1832, 1841.

### Johnson, A
*Visit* • State Capitol and Executive Chambers. 1866. Lodged Delwan House. 1866.

### Lincoln
*Visit* • Old Capitol. 1861.

*Funeral* • Old Capitol. Lay in state in Assembly Chamber. 1865.

### McKinley
*Education* • Albany Law School, SW corner of New Scotland and Holland Aves. Present building built in 1928. 1866–1867.

### Roosevelt, FD
*Home* • 248 State St. 1910–1912.

*Home* • Governor's Mansion, 138 Eagle St. 1929–1933.

*Lodging* • Hotel Ten Eyck, State and Pearl Sts. Later site of Albany Hilton. 1913.

*Work* • Albany City Hall. Senate had to meet here after a fire in the capitol. 1911.

*Work* • Capitol in the State Senate. 1911–1913.

*Work* • Governor's office in the old capitol on State St. 1929–1933.

### Roosevelt, T
*Church* • First Dutch Reformed Church, SW corner of North Pearl and Orange Sts. Box pew used while governor is marked with a bronze tablet. 1881–1900.

*Home* • Governor's Mansion, 138 Eagle St. 1898–1900.

*Lodging* • Delvan House. Also stayed in a residential hotel corner of State and Eagle Sts.

*Work* • State Capitol in State Legislature. 1881.

*Work* • Old St. James Hotel for some legislative sessions. 1882–1884.

*Work* • Governor's office. First to take the oath of office in the new capitol and to occupy the new executive office. 1898–1900.

### Taft
*Visit* • Union RR station, 547 Broadway, for speech. 1909. 1911.

### Van Buren
*Church* • Dutch Reformed Church at Clinton Sq (56 Orange St). Oldest pulpit in America (1656). 1815–1833.

*Home* • State St, opposite Mrs. Jones's boarding house at 120 State. Rented house while attorney general. Also used as law office. 1815–1827.

*Home* • 92 State St (Stevenson House) now occupied by National Savings Bank. 1828–1829.

*Lodging* • Ladies' parlor at Bements on State St. 1833.

*Lodging* • Congress Hall, took rooms here on Capitol Hill. Site between Capitol and Washington Ave. Demolished 1878. 1831.

*Work* • Old Capitol, second floor. Senate Chambers. 1813–1820.

*Work* • Governor's office in old capitol. 1829.

### Washington
*Visit* • Schuyler Mansion, 32 Catherine St, SE corner of Clinton and Catherine Sts. Now museum. 1783.

*Visit* • Pruyn House, 19 Elk St (207 Old Niskayuna Rd). 1783.

## AUBURN *(Cayuga County)*
### Johnson, A
*Visit* • 33 South St. Private. August 1866.

## AUSABLE CHASM *(Clinton County)*
### McKinley
*Visit* • On NY 373 south of Plattsburgh. 9–10–1897.

## BALLSTON SPA *(Saratoga County)*

**Presidents**

*Visit* • Sans Souci Hotel, Main St. Jackson, Van Buren, Pierce. The hotel destroyed in 1887. Of all the hotels existing in the heyday of presidential visits, only the Medbery still exists. Brookside (Aldridge House) is now an historical museum.

**Arthur**

*Education* • State and National Law School for a few months. Also taught school in the Sans Souci Hotel on Broadway (Main St). 1849.

## BARRYTOWN-ON-HUDSON

*(Dutchess County)*

**Roosevelt, T**

*Lodging* • John Aspinwall House. Summer 1867.

## BRONXVILLE

**Kennedy**

*Home* • 294 Pondfield Rd. New house on site. 1930–1941.

## BUFFALO *(Erie County)*

**Cleveland**

*Church* • Breckenridge Church, corner of Breckenridge and Mason at 50 Breckenridge. 1855–.

**Cleveland**

*Education* • Spaulding's Exchange training at the law firm of Henry W. Rogers, Dennis Bowen, and Sherman. 1855.

*Home* • Lewis F. Allen House, Niagara St. Also with his uncle on Grand Island. 1855–.

*Lodging* • Southern Hotel, corner Seneca and Michigan. 1856–1873.

*Home* • 284 Main and Swan Sts, Room F in Weed Block. 1873–1883.

*Work* • Lewis F. Allen on Niagara St. 1855–1862.

*Work* • County Courthouse, Erie County. Assistant D.A. Offices in the old courthouse, Lafayette Sq. Buffalo Library now on this site. 1862–1865.

*Work* • Law firm partnership with Vandefpoel. Old Post Office Building, corner of Pearl and Swan. 1865–1868.

*Work* • Lanning and Folsom law firm, corner of West Seneca and Pearl Sts. 1868.

*Work* • County Courthouse as sheriff of Erie County. 1871–1873.

*Work* • Bass and Bissell law firm, 284 Main St, second floor, where name is still on the door. 1872–1888.

*Work* • City Hall, Church and Franklin Sts. Mayor. Site of old Erie County Hall which was city/county hall combined. 1882.

*Visit* • Iroquois Hotel on a trip to Buffalo. One M & T Plaza. Now site of new M & T Bank and Tower. 1891.

**Fillmore**

*Church* • Unitarian Church, 695 Elmwood (near Erie Co. courthouse). 1831–1865. Lincoln with him in February 1861.

*Church* • Baptist Church, 965 Delaware Ave. 1865, 1874.

*Church* • Episcopal Church, Shelton Square W. Occasionally attended by the Fillmores. 1865–1874.

*Education* • Asa Rice and Joseph Clary law office on Main St. 1821–1823.

*Home* • 114 (now 180) Franklin St. 1830–1848.

*Home* • W Genesee St and Delaware Ave. Bronze tablet marks site. 1858–1874.

*Work* • Joseph Clary law partnership, Main St between Eagle and Court. Second floor of American block. 1830–1832.

*Work* • Nathan K. Hall law partnership. See office in above entry. Future President Cleveland was a student in the firm. 1832–1837, 1843–1848. 1853–.

*Work* • University of Buffalo, Main St, entrance opposite Niagara Falls Blvd. He was first chancellor. 1856–1874.

*Site* • Niagara Square, Buffalo City Hall, statues of Fillmore and Cleveland.

*Death* • W Genesee St and Delaware Ave. 1874.

*Burial* • Forest Lawn Cemetery, 1411 Delaware Ave between his two wives. 1874.

**Garfield**

*Travel* • After nomination, left Mentor, Ohio, for New York City on August 3 and was greeted in Buffalo by 50,000, including two future presidents: B Harrison and McKinley. Arthur joined him in Albany for the trip to New York City. 1880.

**Johnson, A**

*Visit* • Niagara Square speech. Introduced by Fillmore. 1866.

**McKinley**

*Death* • Middle of Fordham Dr between Elmwood Ave and Lincoln Parkway. Site of assassination is marked by a bronze tablet embedded in a low boulder set in a grass plot. It was at the Temple of Music on the Exposition grounds. 1901.

*Death* • Milburn House, 1168 Delaware Ave. House no longer exists. 9–14–1901.

**Roosevelt, FD**

*Visit* • McKinley Monument, Niagara Square. 10–16–1936.

**Roosevelt, T**

*Work* • Theodore Roosevelt Inaugural National Historic Site (Wilcox Mansion). 641 Delaware Ave. 9–14–1901.

## CAMP TAHAWUS *(Essex County)*

**Roosevelt, T**

*Visit* • While lunching on the edge of Lake Tear-in-the-Clouds, he received word that McKinley was dying. 7–13–1901.

## CATSKILL *(Greene County)*

**Van Buren**

*Marriage* • Home of the bride's sister,

Christina Cantine, W Main St off W Bridge St. Also Samuel Wilson, "Uncle Sam," the official symbol of the U.S., lived here 1817–1823. Now offices. 1807.

## CHESTER *(Orange County)*

**Ford**

*Visit* • Glenmere Country Club. Name entered in the Hall of Fashion Fame. 1975.

## CLINTON *(Oneida County)*

**Cleveland**

*Church* • First Presbyterian Church, at South Park Row, where his father was pastor. 1850–1852.

*Education* • Clinton Grammar School, foot of College Hill. 1850–1851.

*Home* • 26 Utica St. 1850–1852.

**Taft**

*Visit* • Hamilton College, NY 412. 1913.

## COHOES *(Albany County)*

**Arthur**

*Work* • Principal of academy. High Department of District School. Lived at the academy. 1852–1853.

## DOBBS FERRY *(Westchester Coonty)*

**Roosevelt, T**

*Lodging* • Summer vacations. 1871, 1872.

**Washington**

*Visit* • Livingston House, corner Broadway and Livingston Aves. Planned Yorktown campaign. Stone marker. 1781. Here again 5–6–1783.

## EAST AURORA (FORMERLY AURORA) *(Erie County)*

**Fillmore**

*Home* • Main St. 1821–1826.

*Home* • 24 Shearer Ave. Millard Fillmore Museum. Restored home. 1826–1830.

*Work* • 686 Main St. Office burned. 1826–1830.

## EAST PARK  *(Dutchess County)*

**Roosevelt, FD**

*Home* • Dream Cottage, south of East Park between Hudson and Poughkeepsie on NY 9G. Built 1938 as a retreat. 1938–1945.

## FAYETTEVILLE  *(Onondaga County)*

**Cleveland**

*Church* • Presbyterian Church (now the United Church Building), Genessee St. 1841–1850.

*Education* • His schooling began in the little red frame district schoolhouse. 1841–1848.

*Education* • Fayetteville Academy, across the road from the manse, where the Twitchell House is now. 402 Elm St. 1848–1850.

*Education* • Town academy at the foot of College Hill called the Clinton Liberal Institute. 1851–1852.

*Home* • 109 Academy St. First house on the road entering from Montclair. He swam in Limestone Creek and Chittenango River and fished in Green Lake. 1841–1850.

*Lodging* • John McVicar Store, Genessee St near Limestone Creek. 1852–.

*Work* • John McVicar Store. Still exists. 1852–.

## FISHKILL  *(Dutchess County)*

**Washington**

*Visit* • Headquarters. Now Van Wyck Homestead Museum, NY 9 and I-84. Restored. 1781.

## FOLSOMDALE  *(Wyoming County)*

**Cleveland**

*Visit* • Courted Frances Folsom in old Folsom mansion, near Cowlesville off NY 239. 1885–1886.

## GARRISON  *(Putnam County)*

**Grant**

*Visit* • Glenclyffe, Hamilton Fishhouse. 1869–1877.

*Grover Cleveland boyhood home in Fayetteville.*

**Washington**

*Travel* • Beverly House, at foot of Sugar Loaf Hill across from West Point. 1780.

## GREENWICH  *(Washington County)*

**Arthur**

*Education* • James I Lowrie School, Academy St. 1839–1844.

*Home* • Parsonage, 24 Woodlawn Ave. Moved from another street. 1839–1844.

## HARMON  *(Westchester County)*

**Washington**

*Visit* • Van Cortlandt Manor House near Croton Point Park a mile from Croton. 1780–1789.

## HEMPSTEAD  *(Nassau County)*

**Ford**

*Visit* • Hofstra University. 5–6–1981.

## HOLLAND PATENT  *(Oneida County)*

**Cleveland**

*Church* • Presbyterian Church. 1853–1855.

*Home* • Main and Elm Sts in the Presbyterian manse. 1853–1855.

## HOOSICK *(Rensselaer County)*

**Arthur**

*Church* • Baptist. Father was pastor here. 1849–1853.

## HUDSON *(Columbia County)*

**Van Buren**

*Home* • 309 Warren St. Buildings standing but not marked in any way. Law office the same address. 1808–1813.

## HYDE PARK *(Dutchess County)*

**Roosevelt, FD**

*Birthplace* • Rt 9, two miles south of the town of Hyde Park. Entrance fee. 1882–1905.

*Baptism* • Hyde Park Episcopal Chapel.

*Church* • St. James' Church on US 9 about a mile from Hyde Park.

*Education* • His mother gave him his first schooling at home. At 6 he went to a kind of kindergarten at the home of family friends nearby.

*Funeral* • After services in East Room of White House, his body was brought to Hyde Park.

*Burial* • Hyde Park rose garden. 1945.

*Visit* • Laid cornerstone for library. 11–19–1939. Dedication. 6–30–1941.

**Truman**

*Visit* • Dedication as National Shrine. 4–12–1946.

## JORDANVILLE *(Montgomery County)*

**Roosevelt, T**

*Visit* • Jordanville Library dedication. 8–26–1908.

## KINDERHOOK *(Columbia County)*

**Van Buren**

*Birthplace* • Kinderhook Tavern some 3 miles from Lindenwald. It stood at the bottom of a hill upon a slight knoll on the present Hudson St opposite Williams St. Torn down. 1782.

*Baptism* • Dutch Reformed Church, Main St. 12–15–1782. Attended 1782–1862.

*Education* • Common School up the road from the tavern. 1790.

*Education* • Kinderhook academy at age 12. 1794–1796.

*Education* • Articled to Francis Sylvester (lawyer) at age 14. 1796–.

*Home* • Tavern. See birthplace in above entry. 1782.

*Home* • Present 46 Hudson St. 1782–1796.

*Lodging* • Cornelius Sylvester store. 1796–.

*Home* • When work began on Lindenwald, he moved to the village of Kinderhook where he engaged rooms for two months. 1841.

*Home* • Lindenwald, NY 9 H south of Kinderhook. Entrance fee. 1841–1862.

*Work* • Cornelius Sylvester store, Main St. 1796.

*Work* • James I Van Allen law office, town center. 1803–1808.

*Death* • Lindenwald. 1862.

*Funeral* • Little Dutch Reformed Church. 1862.

*Burial* • Kinderhook Cemetery. 1862.

## KINGSTON *(Ulster County)*

**Arthur**

*Church* • First Reformed Church, Main St between Wall and Fair Sts. 1884.

*Hyde Park, birthplace of Franklin Roosevelt.*

*Visit* • General Sharpe House, Albany Ave, corner of Clinton Ave. 1884.

## LAKE MOHONK *(Ulster County)*

**Hayes**
*Visit* • Attended conference and spent time at family graveyards. Located in the Shawangunk Mountains, 5 miles west of New Palz. 1889.

## LAKE PLACID *(Essex County)*

**Cleveland**
*Visit* • Stevens House. 1886.

**Roosevelt, FD**
*Visit* • Olympic Stadium. 9–13–1935.

## LAKE TEAR-OF-THE CLOUDS *(Essex County)*

**Roosevelt, T**
*Visit* • Received word here McKinley was

dying. Stayed Tahawus House (Club) in the Keene Valley. 1877.

## LETCHWORTH STATE PARK
*(Wyoming County)*

**Fillmore**
*Visit* • Seneca council. See museum on NY 19A. 1872.

## LINDENWALD *(See Kinderhook)*

## LOON LAKE *(Franklin County)*

**Harrison, B**
*Lodging* • Leased a cottage in the Adirondacks. He had a summer camp on Second Lake near Old Forge. July–September 1892.

**Taft**
*Visit* • Fenton's was a small rustic resort in the Adirondacks where the Collins side of Nellie Taft's family had lived for years. 1885.

## MASSENA *(St. Lawrence County)*

**Nixon**
*Visit* • Eisenhower Lock on St. Lawrence Seaway. 6–27–1969.

## MONTVILLE *(Cayuga County)*

**Fillmore**
*Education* • Law office of County Judge Walter Wood, Main St. Marker. 1819–1821.

## MORAVIA *(Cayuga County)*

**Fillmore**
*Birthplace* • Off NY 90, E on Skinner Rd to Summer Hill. Replica of log cabin at Fillmore Glen State Park. Replica. 1800.

*Marriage* • Powers House. Moved from Church St to Smith St. Now private. A tablet at St. Matthew's Episcopal Church,

Smith St, commemorates the event. 1826.

## MOUNT MCGREGOR *(Saratoga County)*

**Grant**
*Lodging* • Grant Cottage off I-87, exit 16 west on Ballard Rd. 1885.

*Death* • Grant Cottage. 1885.

## NEWBURGH *(Orange County)*

**Washington**
*Visit* • Liberty and Washington Sts was his headquarters. Stone house (Hasbrouch House) used as headquarters for many of his commanding officers. 1782–1783.

## NEWCOMB *(Essex County)*

**Roosevelt, T**
*Work* • Monument indicating site where he became president, NY 28N (Roosevelt-Marcy Memorial Highway). 1901.

## NEW HOPE *(Cayuga County)*

**Fillmore**
*Education* • Academy where his teacher was his future wife—Abigail Powers. 1819.

*Work* • Father sent him to clothmakers Zaccheus Cheney and Alvan Kellogg where he remained for several years. Old Salt Rd at Kellogsville. 1815–1819.

## NEWPORT *(Herkimer County)*

**Presidents**
*Visit* • Both Tyler and Arthur vacationed here. No further details available.

## NEW WINDSOR *(Putnam County)*

**Washington**
*Work* • Temple Hill Rd 1 mile north of Vails Gate. Last encampment of his Revolutionary Army. Headquarters. 1780–1781.

*Replica of Millard Fillmore birthplace.*

## NEW YORK CITY (SITES ARE LISTED ALPHABETICALLY)

### ALBEMARLE HOTEL

**Taft**

*Honeymoon* • First night. On Madison Ave at Fifth Ave and Twenty-fourth St. New building on site. 1886.

### AMERICANA HOTEL

**Presidents**

*Visit* • 801 Seventh Ave. All presidents from Kennedy to Carter.

### AMERICAN HOUSE

**Harrison, WH**

*Visit* • 135 Fulton St. 1841.

### ARTHUR LAW FIRM

**Arthur**

*Work* • Arthur, Phelps, Knevals and Ransom, 155 Broadway. 1878–1881.

### ASTOR HOUSE

**Presidents**

*Visit* • Lower Manhattan, 225 Broadway. West side Broadway between Vesey and Barclay Sts. Transportation Building now on site. Old address was 1 Great George St which was the extension of Broadway beginning at St. Paul's Chapel and ending at Broome St. Buchanan, Fillmore, Grant, Lincoln, Pierce, and Wilson visited.

### JOHN JACOB ASTOR HOUSE

**Hayes**

*Visit* • 338 Fifth Ave. May 1877.

**Roosevelt, T**
*Visit* • May 1877.

## BANCROFT HOUSE

**Arthur**
*Lodging* • 904 Broadway. Midtown Manhattan. 1856–1859.

## BENJAMIN BUTLER HOUSE

**Van Buren**
*Visit* • Greene St and Waverly Place near Gramercy Park when he left for home as ex-president. 1841.

## BRADY STUDIO

**Lincoln**
*Site* • 643 Broadway. Photography of Civil War period.

## BROAD ST

**Cleveland**
*Work* • 15 Broad St. Worked with law firm of Bangs, Stetson, Tracy and McVeagh. Bank of New York now on site. Later office moved to 45 William St. 1889–1893.

**Nixon**
*Work* • 20 Broad St. With law firm of Mudge, Duque, and Hazeltine which became Nixon, Mudge, Rose, Buthrie, and Alexander. Now site of visitor's entrance to the Stock Exchange. 1963–1969.

## BROADWAY

**Adams, J**
*Visit* • 133 Broadway. Site of John Jay House. April 1789.

**Arthur**
*Work* • With Culver & Parker law firm. 289 Broadway. Site now occupied by a shoe store. 1852–1856.

*Work* • 155 Broadway. Law firm. Business buildings on site. 1878–1886.

**Monroe**
*Lodging* • 90 Broadway. Home of Lawrence Kortwright. 1786.

**Roosevelt, FD**
*Work* • 120 Broadway. Law firm with Basil O'Connor, the Equitable Building. Began practicing law with him in 1924.

**Van Buren**
*Lodging* • 237 Broadway. Mechanics Hall. 1822.

**Washington**
*Home* • 39 Broadway. Rented a house just below Trinity churchyard, McComb mansion. Marker. Now site of Lamston's Building. He moved here from No. 3 Cherry St. 1790.

## BROOKLYN BRIDGE

**Arthur**
*Visit* • Dedicated. 1883.

**Cleveland**
*Visit* • Was present at dedication as governor. 1883.

## BRYANT PARK

**Pierce**
*Visit* • Fronts on Sixth Ave. Opened first World's Fair in America at the Crystal Palace on this site. 1853.

## CALVARY BAPTIST

**Clinton**
*Church* • W Fifty-seventh St. Attended at beginning of DNC. 7–12–1993.

## CALVARY EPISCOPAL CHURCH

**Arthur**
*Church* • Fourth Ave and Twenty-first St. 1859–1880.

*Marriage* • First marriage. 1859.

## CAPE'S TAVERN

**JQ Adams**

> *Visit* • 18 Broadway. Demolished 1793. Later site of City Hall. First Nationwide Bank now on site. 7–17–1785 to 7–20–1785.

**Washington**

> *Visit* • 12–2–1783.

## CARLYLE HOTEL

**Kennedy**

> *Lodging* • 35 E Seventy-sixth St and NE corner of Madison. Resident's entrance on opposite side at 50 E Seventy-seventh St. During campaign and when visiting NYC. Duplex suite. 1960s.

**Truman**

> *Visit* • Usually stayed here when in NYC. 1953–1972.

## CARNEGIE HALL

**Hoover**

> *Visit* • 881 Seventh Ave. 10–31–1932.

## CARTER, LEDYARD, AND MILBURN

**Roosevelt, FD**

> *Work* • 54 Wall St. Joined 1907; 1905 clerkship at this old law firm. 1907–1911.

## CASTLE CLINTON

**Presidents**

> *Visit* • Lower Manhattan at the Battery (later known as Castle Garden). Jefferson, Jackson, Tyler, Polk, and Pierce visited.

## CATHERINE LANE

**Van Buren**

> *Lodging* • Now an umimpressive alley near 346 Broadway. Had quarters in boarding house on this street. 1802.

## CEMETERY ONE-HUNDRED

**Grant**

> *Burial* • The Heights/Harlem Twenty-second St. Originally placed in vault here. 1885.

## CENTRAL PARK

**Hayes**

> *Site* • Unveiled the Halleck statue. May 1877.

## CENTRE ST

**Roosevelt, T**

> *Work* • 240 Centre St. Police Headquarters. Now luxury apartments. 1895–1897.

## CHRIST EPISCOPAL CHURCH

**Roosevelt, T**

> *Church* • Oyster Bay, Long Island. 61 East Main. 1884–1909.

> *Funeral* • 1909.

## CHURCH OF ANNUNCIATION

**Monroe**

> *Funeral* • W Fourteenth St. Memorial when body transferred to Richmond, VA. 1858.

## CHURCH OF THE ASCENSION

**Tyler**

> *Marriage* • 36-38 Fifth Ave on the northwest corner of Tenth St. Second marriage. 6–26–1844.

## CHURCH OF THE HEAVENLY REST

**Arthur**

> *Church* • 551 Fifth Ave (near 45th St). Now site of camera store. 1880s.

> *Funeral* • Wife's funeral here previously. Cleveland and Hayes attended. 1886.

**Wilson**
> *Church* • 1884–.

## CHURCH ST

**Nixon**
> *Work* • 1945.

## CITY HALL

**Carter**
> *Visit* • Between Broadway and Park Row. Governor's Room. 8-8-1978.

**Grant**
> *Funeral* • Lay in state. 1885.

**Hayes**
> *Visit* • Governor's Room. Grant also attended. May 1877.

**Johnson, A**
> *Visit* • City Hall, Executive Chambers. 1865.

**Lincoln**
> *Funeral* • Lay in state in the rotunda. A large catafalque was built at the top of the grand staircase. 1865.

**Monroe**
> *Funeral* • Lay in state. 1831.

**Washington**
> *Site* • Contains the writing desk used during his first inauguration. 1789.

## CITY HOTEL

**Van Buren**
> *Lodging* • 115 Broadway. Built on site of old City Tavern in 1793. Torn down 1850. Recently site of Boreel Building. Had a suite here. August 1833, March 1829, and after retirement during the cold months. 1848–.

## CITY TAVERN

**Adams, J**
> *Visit* • Site west side of Broadway (No. 18) between Thames and Little Queen (Cedar) Sts. Demolished 1793. 1789.

## CLARENDON HOTEL

**Pierce**
> *Visit* • 137 Riverside Dr at Eighty-sixth St (entrance on Eighty-sixth St) 1859–1860.

## COBBLE HILL

**Washington**
> *Travel* • Extension of Brooklyn Heights. Used Cobble Hill as an observation post during the Battle of Long Island. See also No. 197 Amity St where mother of Sir Winston Churchill was born. 1776.

## COLLEGIATE CHURCH OF ST. NICHOLAS

**Roosevelt, T**
> *Church* • NW corner of Forty-eighth St in Fifth Ave shopping district. Member of this church. His pew is marked by a tablet. Oldest congregation in Manhattan. 1858–.

## COLONNADE ROW ASTOR PLACE (ALSO KNOWN AS LAGRANGE TERRACE)

**Tyler**
> *Visit* • On the west side of Lafayette St. Numbers 428–434, called Colonnade Row. Home of second wife. Remains of house belonging to David Gardiner whose daughter married Tyler. 1844–.

## COLUMBIA UNIVERSITY

**Eisenhower**
> *Work* • President's office. Morningside Heights. W One hundred fourteenth to One hundred twentieth Sts between Broadway and Amsterdam Aves. 1948–1952.

**Truman**
> *Visit* • Lectures. 1959.

## COLUMBIA UNIVERSITY LAW SCHOOL

**Roosevelt, FD**

*Education* • Morningside Heights at 435 W One hundred sixteenth St and Broadway (main campus of Columbia). 1904–1907.

**Roosevelt, T**

*Education* • Entered 1880, dropped out in 1881. Law school was located 8 Great Jones St on NW corner of Lafayette Place. 1880.

## COMMODORE HOTEL

**Eisenhower**

*Work* • 125 E Forty-second St, NW corner Lexington Ave. Now Grand Hyatt Hotel. Campaign headquarters 1952–1953.

**Nixon**

*Visit* • Met Whittaker Chambers. 8–17–1948.

## CONTINENTAL HOTEL

**Arthur**

*Lodging* • Near Union Square at Broadway and Fourteenth St. Arthur lived here during his bachelor days. 1853–1855.

## COOPER UNION

**Lincoln**

*Work* • Union Auditorium. Bounded by Astor, Third Ave, Seventh St, and Fourth Ave. Opened 1859. He made the speech which is credited with winning him the nomination for the presidency. 1860.

**Tyler**

*Marriage* • Wedding party gave them a sendoff on the ferry boat. 1844.

**Van Buren**

*Lodging* • 1803–.

## CUSTOMS HOUSE

**Arthur**

*Work* • 55 Wall St. 1872–1878.

## EAST HAMPTON

**Tyler**

*Marriage* • On Lafayette Square. Wedding reception at the Gardiner residence. 1844.

## EAST COAST MEMORIAL PARK (BATTERY PARK)

**Kennedy**

*Visit* • Dedication. 5–23–1963.

## ELM ST

**Arthur**

*Work* • 346 Broadway between Catherine Lane and Leonard St east side of Lafayette St (originally 346 Elm St). Now occupied by NY Life Insurance Building. Office when Assistant Quartermaster General. 1861.

## FEDERAL HALL

**Washington**

*Visit* • Site of original 28 Wall St, NE corner Wall and Nassau Sts. Inauguration. 4–30–1789. Inauguration marked by a statue of Washington. The west wall contains some of the original Holland bricks. The actual stone on which he stood is preserved in a glass case within the building. Senate Chamber for second inaugural. 1793. The first building on this site was New York's City Hall, but in 1789 it became the seat of federal government and Congress met here for its first session. This is not the building one sees today. After the government moved to Philadelphia, it fell into disrepair and was sold for salvage. Today's structure

*Federal Hall in the financial district.*

was built in 1842 to be the U.S. Customs House and in 1955 it became a national memorial.

## FEDERAL PLAZA

**Nixon**
*Work* • Law firm. Broadway and Worth (28 Federal Plaza) on Foley Square. 1988–1994.

## FIFTH AVE

**Hoover**
*Home* • Between Fifty-ninth and Sixtieth Sts. Now site of Sheray Netherland building. 1903–1904.

**Nixon**
*Home* • 810 Sixty-second and Fifth Ave. 10-room cooperative with view of Central Park and the Plaza Hotel. 1963–1969.

*Work* • 521 Fifth Ave. Nixon campaign headquarters. 1968.

## FIFTH AVE HOTEL

**Presidents**
*Visit* • East side of the block between Twenty-third and Twenty-fourth Sts. Was the headquarters of the Republican Party. Arthur, Garfield, Grant, B Harrison, and Hayes visited.

## FIFTH AVE PRESBYTERIAN CHURCH

**Carter**
*Church* • 705 Fifth Ave, NW corner W Fifty-fifth St. Attended after DNC. 1976.

**Roosevelt, T**
*Church* • Funeral held here for mother and first wife. 1884.

## Wilson

*Church* • 1916–.

## FIFTY-FIRST ST

### Cleveland

*Home* • 12 W Fifty-first St. Site occupied by Amtrak Travel Center. 1892.

## FIFTY-SEVENTH ST

### Roosevelt, T

*Home* • 6 W Fifty-seventh St. In 1873 he changed to this house close to Central Park from 28 E Twentieth St. First winter after marriage spent here. Stayed here while going to Columbia Law School. Now Arista Building. Also 1882.

## FIRST PRESBYTERIAN CHURCH

### Buchanan

*Church* • 48 Fifth Ave between Eleventh and Twelfth, one block above Church of the Ascension. 1856–.

## FLATBUSH DUTCH REFORMED CHURCH

### Presidents

*Church* • Brooklyn. 866 Flatbush Ave at Church Ave. Original bell donated in 1796 was brought to Flatbush in time to toll the death of Washington in 1799. It has tolled at the death of each succeeding president.

## FLUSHING MEADOWS

### Kennedy

*Visit* • Groundbreaking, U.S. Pavilion. 12–14–1962.

## FORDHAM UNIVERSITY

### Truman

*Visit* • Fordham Road and Third Ave. Kealing Hall. 5–11–1946.

## FORTY-FIFTH ST

### Roosevelt, FD

*Home* • 40 W Forty-fifth St. He and his bride had an apartment here. Now site of Webster Condos. 1905.

### Roosevelt, T

*Home* • 55 W Forty-fifth St. Rented this house. Now site of lunch place. 1882.

## FRANKLIN HOUSE

### Washington

*Home* • No. 3 Cherry St, several doors east of present Franklin Square. One of the piers of the Brooklyn Bridge on the Manhattan approach covers the site of the house. Official mansion when he became the first president. He went from here to his first inaugural. April 1789–1790.

## FRAUNCES TAVERN

### Washington

*Work* • SE corner of Pearl and Broad Sts at 54 Pearl St. Formerly DeLancey House. Reconstructed. Bade farewell to his officers in the Long Room upstairs, which remains and looks much as it did. 1783.

## GARDEN CITY HOTEL

### Taft

*Visit* • 45 Seventh St, Garden City, Long Island. 1913.

## GOTHAM HOTEL

### Hoover

*Visit* • 2 W Fifty-fifth St. 1914–1917.

## GOUVERNEUR RESIDENCE

### Monroe

*Home* • 63 Prince St. 1830–1831.

*Death* • 7–4–1831.

*Funeral* • Procession from Samuel L. Gouveneur's residence to City Hall. 1831.

## GOVERNOR CLINTON HOTEL

**Truman**
> *Visit* • Seventh and Thirty-first Sts. 1934.

## GOVERNOR'S ISLAND

**Grant**
> *Work* • It was called Fort Columbus. June 1852.

**Reagan**
> *Visit* • Admiral House. 7–4–1986.

## GRACIE MANSION

**Presidents**
> *Visit* • Facing the river near the north end of Carl Schurz Park (now official residence of the mayor). East End Ave and Eighty-eighth St. JQ Adams, Carter, Reagan, Truman, and Washington visited.

## GRAMERCY PARK HOTEL

**Kennedy**
> *Home* • 2 Lexington Ave at Gramercy Park North. Lived on second floor of the hotel in the 1920s as a young boy. Often played in Gramercy Park.

## GRAND CENTRAL STATION

**Presidents**
> *Visit* • Forty-second St between Lexington and Vanderbilt Aves. Most presidents from Grant to Eisenhower.

## GRANT STATUE

**Grant**
> *Site* • Grant Square at Dean St and Bedford Ave.

## GRANT'S TOMB

**Grant**
> *Burial* • Vault near Riverside Dr. Temporary tomb. Tomb is built on the site of the

Claremont Hotel. Cleveland and ex-presidents Hayes and Arthur at funeral. A memorial tree marks the site at the back of the present tomb. August 1885.
> *Site* • Riverside Park Memorial Tomb. 1897.

**Harrison, B**
> *Visit* • Laid cornerstone. April 1892.

**McKinley**
> *Visit* • Formally dedicated the tomb. 1897.

## GREENWOOD CEMETERY

**Roosevelt, T**
> *Visit* • 1 Harrison Place. Brooklyn. First wife buried here. 1884.

## HARLEM (BATTLE OF HARLEM HEIGHTS)

**Washington**
> *Work* • Wall plaque on the east side of Broadway between One hundred sixteenth and One hundred seventeenth Sts. 1776.

## HILTON HOTEL

**Presidents**
> *Visit* • 1335 Ave of the Americas. Carter, Ford, LB Johnson, Kennedy, and Reagan (who announced his presidential candidacy here) visited.

## IDLEWILD INTERNATIONAL AIRPORT

**Truman**
> *Visit* • Dedicated. 7–31–1948.

## IMPERIAL HOTEL

**Harding**
> *Visit* • Broadway and Thirty-second St. Now apartments. 1917.

*Tomb of Ulysses Grant.*

## JULIAN'S HOTEL

**Van Buren**

*Lodging* • Washington Square. Suite of rooms overlooking Washington Square while he was working on a manuscript. Winter 1848.

## KENNEDY HOUSE

**Washington**

*Work* • 1 Broadway near Bowling Green. Headquarters early days of the Revolution. 1776.

## LEXINGTON AVE

**Arthur**

*Home* • 123 Lexington Ave. On Gramercy Park north of E Twenty-eighth St. Principal home. Later home of Wm Randolph Hearst. Plaque on site. 1865–1886.

*Work* • 1863–1871. Sworn in as president here. 1881.

*Death* • 1886.

## LONG ISLAND

**Monroe**

*Honeymoon* • Across East River from Manhattan Island.

**Roosevelt, T**

*Visit* • Lloyd's Neck, Old Oak Tree. Family picnic site. Memorial established 1926. 1886–.

**Washington**

*Travel* • Battle of Brooklyn Heights. 1776.

## McALPIN HOTEL

**Truman**

*Visit* • Broadway at Thirty-fourth St. 1918.

## McCOMB (MACOMB) MANSION

**Washington**

*Home* • Now 39 Broadway. Moved here from Franklin House. February 1790.

## MADISON AVE

**Cleveland**

*Home* • 816 Madison Ave. 1889–1892.

**Roosevelt, FD**

*Home* • 200 Madison Ave. Lived here while attending Columbia Law School. 1904.

**Roosevelt, T**

*Home* • 422 Madison Ave. Following Alice's death in 1884 he always stayed with his sister, Bamie, when he was East. Lived here 1895–1897.

*Home* • 689 Madison Ave. Rented Bamu House. 1886–.

## MADISON SQUARE GARDEN

**Presidents**

*Visit* • Includes visits at both old and new site of the Gardens. Eisenhower, Hoover, L B Johnson, Kennedy, FD Roosevelt, and Truman.

**Carter**

*Visit* • Between Seventh and Eighth Aves and Thirty-first and Thirty-third Sts. DNC. Nominated for president. July 1976.

*Visit* • DNC. Renominated for president. 8–14–1980.

**Clinton**

*Visit* • DNC. Accepted nomination. 1992.

## MADISON SQUARE PARK

**Arthur**

*Site* • Statue. NE corner of the park. 1899.

## MADISON SQUARE PRESBYTERIAN CHURCH

**Roosevelt, T**

*Baptism* • 432 Third Ave NW corner E Thirtieth St. Torn down for apartments. Also member. 1860s.

GEOGRAPHIC GUIDE TO LANDMARKS

## Wilson
*Church* • 1880s.

## MAIDEN LANE

### Jefferson
*Visit* • 57 Maiden Ln. Took house here when Secretary of State. Olympic-York Building now on site. 1790–1793.

### Madison
*Visit* • 19 Maiden Ln. Boarding house of Mrs. Dorothy Elsworth. Atlantic Bank occupies site. 1787–1789.

## MANHATTAN HOTEL

### Harding
*Visit* • Forty-third St. 1917.

## MARBLE COLLEGIATE CHURCH

### Nixon
*Church* • Fifth Ave and W Twenty-ninth St. Norman Vincent Peale's Marble Collegiate Church. 1961–1969. Scene of daughter Julie's wedding. 1968.

## MECHANICS HALL

### Van Buren
*Visit* • 237 Broadway. Site of Woolworth Building. Quarters here for November session of State Supreme Court. 1822.

## METROPOLITAN MUSEUM

### Hayes
*Visit* • Central Park. Opened the museum. 1880.

## MORGAN HOUSE

### Hayes
*Visit* • 411 Fifth Ave. May 1877.

## MORNINGSIDE DR

### Eisenhower
*Home* • 60 Morningside Dr at W One hundred sixth St. While president of Columbia University. 1948–1951.

## MORRIS-JUMEL MANSION

### Washington
*Home* • Jumel Terrace between One hundred sixtieth and One hundred sixty second Sts (Edgecombe Ave). Headquarters until defeat at Fort Washington and the Laurel Hill redoubt. 1770s.

## MORTIER HOUSE

### Washington
*Travel* • On Varick St continuation of 7th Ave at the corner of Charlton St, lower Manhattan, Greenwich Village. One of his headquarters during the Revolution. Razed 1849. One of his bodyguards hanged who fed him a dish of poisoned peas. 1776.

## MULBERRY ST

### Roosevelt, T
*Work* • No. 300. Also listed 240 Centre St. Between Grande and Broome Sts and Centre Market St. Now turned into luxury apartments. Site of Police Headquarters. 1895–1897.

## MURRAY'S WHARF

### Washington
*Work* • 120 Wall St. Wall and South Sts. Bronze plaque identifies the site where he landed on way to his inauguration. 1789.

## MUTUAL LIFE BUILDING

### Arthur
*Work* • Nassau St at Cedar and Liberty Sts. Office here following retirement. 1885–.

## NASSAU ST

### Arthur
*Work* • 82 Nassau St. Law firm of Ran-

som, Phelps, and Arthur. Variety store on site now. 1871.

*Work* • 117 Nassau St. Law partnership with Henry D. Gardiner. 1856–1861; 1863–1872.

## NATIONAL ARTS CLUB

**Roosevelt, T**

*Visit* • 15 Gramercy Park South (formerly Governor Tilden's residence). Used the club for daily luncheon conference. 1900s–.

## NEW YORK HOSPITAL

**Nixon**

*Visit* • Cornell Medical Center, 525 E Sixty-eighth St. 4–18–1994.

*Death* • 4–22–1994.

## NEW YORK INSTITUTE FOR THE BLIND

**Cleveland**

*Work* • Between Eighth and Ninth Aves and Thirty-third and Thirty-fourth Sts. Assistant teacher in the literary department of the institute. At night he and his brother were in charge of the boy's dormitory. 1853–1854.

## NEW YORK WORLD'S FAIR (FLUSHING MEADOWS)

**Roosevelt, FD**

*Visit* • Cornerstone Federal Building. 6–30–1938. Dedication opening. 4–30–1939.

## OLD BEEKMAN

**Grant**

*Visit* • Northeast corner of Beekman and Gold Sts in City Hall district. 1869–.

## OMNI PARK CENTRAL HOTEL

**Clinton**

*Visit* • 870 Seventh Ave between Fifty-fifth and Fifty-sixth Sts. 1992.

**Arthur**

*Visit* • 1882.

## OYSTER BAY (LONG ISLAND)

**Eisenhower**

*Visit* • Dedication Roosevelt home. 6–14–1953.

**Roosevelt, T**

*Church* • Christ Episcopal Church, 61 E Main St. 1884–1919.

*Honeymoon* • Tranquillity, near site of present Sagamore Hill on Cove Neck Road. Demolished. 1880.

*Home* • Same as above. 1880s. Home Sagamore Hill (was called Leeholm). 1884–1919. On Cove Neck Road. National Historcal site. 1874 established summer home here. Retired to Sagamore. 1909–1919.

*Death* • Sagamore Hill. 1–6–1919.

*Funeral* • Christ Episcopal Church, 61 E Main St. Harding and Taft attended. 1919.

*Burial* • Young Memorial Cemetery, Main St. 1919.

## PARK AVE

**Hoover**

*Home* • 876 Park Ave. 1920.

*Home* • 950 Park Ave. 1920.

*Home* • 993 Park Ave. 1920.

## THE PLAYERS

**Cleveland**

*Visit* • 16 Gramercy Park. He frequently lunched here later in his life. 1890–.

## PLAZA HOTEL

**Presidents**

*Visit* • Fifth Ave at Fifty-ninth St. Carter and Nixon visited.

## PLYMOUTH CONGREGATIONAL CHURCH

**Presidents**

*Visit* • Cranberry and Orange Sts, in West Central Brooklyn. Now Our Lady of Lebanon. Cleveland, Lincoln, and Wilson visited.

## PRESBYTERIAN HOSPITAL

**Roosevelt, FD**

*Visit* • 622 W One hundred sixty-eighth St. Treated. 1921.

*Visit* • 6–30–1938.

## RICHMOND HILL MANSION

**Adams, J**

*Home* • SE corner of Charlton and Varick Sts. Lived here when he was vice president. 1789–1790. In 1817 the property was sold to John Jacob Astor who cut down the hill and rolled the mansion down to this site. Demolished in 1849. See Charlton-King-Vandam historic district for houses of the time.

**Washington**

*Home* • Headquarters during the war. 1775.

## ROOSEVELT HOSPITAL

**Roosevelt, T**

*Visit* • 56 E Ninety-third St (now alco-holism center). Treatment. 1918.

## ROOSEVELT MEMORIAL

**Roosevelt, T**

*Site* • Central Park West between Seventy-seventh and Eighty-first Sts.

## ST. BARTHOLEMEW'S EPISCOPAL CHURCH

**Hoover**

*Church* • Madison Ave and Forty-fourth St (109 E 50th) Park Ave and Fiftieth to Fifty-first Sts. 1933–1964.

*Funeral* • 1964.

## ST. NICHOLAS HOTEL

**Fillmore**

*Visit* • 521–523 Broadway at Washington Place and Mercer St. May and June 1854.

**Van Buren**

*Visit* • 1840s.

## ST. PATRICK'S CATHEDRAL

**Johnson, LB**

*Visit* • Fifth Ave (460 Madison Ave). Installation of Archbishop. 4– 4–1968.

*Visit* • Robert Kennedy funeral. June 1968.

**Nixon**

*Visit* • Robert Kennedy funeral. 1968.

## ST. PAUL'S CHAPEL

**Presidents**

*Visit* • Facing Broadway between Fulton, Church, and Vesey Sts in City Hall district. Still stands. J Adams, JQ Adams, Madison, and Monroe visited.

**Monroe**

*Funeral* • 1831.

**Washington**

*Church* • Canopied pew set apart for his use. 1789.

## ST. THOMAS EPISCOPAL CHURCH

**Harrison, B**

*Marriage* • Fifth Ave at Fifty-third St. Second marriage. Destroyed by fire 1907. New church on site opened 1914. 1896.

## ST. VINCENT'S HOSPITAL

**Cleveland**
  *Visit* • 152 W Eleventh St, NE corner Seventh Ave. Patient. 1891.

## SECOND ST CEMETERY

**Monroe**
  *Burial* • Astor Place. 52-74 E Second St (NYC Marble Cemetery) between Second and First Aves, north side. Fronts on Second St. 1836. Removed 1858.

## SEVENTY-SIXTH ST

**Roosevelt, FD**
  *Marriage* • 8 E Seventy-sixth St. Townhouse of Eleanor's aunt, Mrs. Livingston Ludlow. President T Roosevelt was there to give away the bride. 3–17–1905.

## SHERATON CENTRE HOTEL

**Presidents**
  *Visit* • 811 Seventh Ave and Fifty-second St. Carter and Nixon visited.

## SIXTIETH ST

**Hoover**
  *Home* • 14 E Sixtieth St. Winters. 1909–1911.

## SIXTY-FIRST ST

**Adams, J**
  *Visit* • 421 E Sixty-first St. Abigail Adams Smith House. Now headquarters Colonial Dames of America. 1798.

## SIXTY-FIFTH ST

**Roosevelt, FD**
  *Home* • 47 E Sixty-fifth St, between Madison and Park Aves. Next to his mother's house at 49. Now belongs to Hunter College. Lived here off and on. 1908–1943.

## SIXTY-FIFTH ST

**Nixon**
  *Home* • 142 E Sixty-fifth St. 1980–1981.

## SIXTY-SIXTH

**Grant**
  *Home* • 3 E Sixty-sixth. 1880–1885.

## STATEN ISLAND

**Adams, J**
  *Work* • Met Gen. Howe at the Christopher Billopp House in Tottenville. Also called Conference House. September 1776.

**Roosevelt, T**
  *Lodging* • Left side of Signs Road, not far from Richmond Ave, New Springville. Belonged to his grandfather. House no longer extant. Now New Springville Park. 1858–.

**Tyler**
  *Lodging* • Gardiner-Tyler House, 27 Tyler Ave between Broadway and N Burgher Ave in West New Brighton. It belonged to his wife's people. Still standing.
  *Visit* • 27 Tyler St, Brighton. 1857.

## STATUE OF LIBERTY (LIBERTY ISLAND)

**Cleveland**
  *Visit* • Dedicated. 10–28–1886.

**Ford**
  *Visit* • Anniversary. 7–4–1976.

**Johnson, LB**
  *Visit* • 1964.

**Reagan**
  *Visit* • Lighted Torch. 7–3–1986.

**Roosevelt, FD**
  *Visit* • Dedication. Fiftieth anniversary. 10–28–1936.

## TOBIAS STOUTENBURGH HOUSE

**Adams, J**
  *Visit* • Corner of Nassau St near City Hall. 1774.

## CHARLES TAFT HOUSE

**Taft**
*Visit* • 480 Clinton Ave (Brooklyn). Brother's home.

## HENRY W. TAFT HOUSE

**Taft**
*Visit* • Pelham Manor. Brother's house. Was also at 45 William.

## TAMMANY HALL

**Johnson, A**
*Visit* • Seventeenth St and Fourth Ave, NE corner. DNC. 5–20–1868 to 9–21–1868.

## TENTH ST

**Wilson**
*Visit* • 12 W Tenth St. Visited future wife. House still exists. 1915.

## THIRTY-SIXTH ST

**Roosevelt, FD**
*Home* • 125 E Thirty-sixth St. Between Park and Lexington Aves. Had a house here. After his marriage his mother finished building two adjoining houses on Sixty-fifth St to which they moved. No marker. 1905–1907.

## TRINITY CHURCH

**Madison**
*Church* • At the head of Wall St. 1789–1790.

**Monroe**
*Marriage* • 1786. Attended 1830–1831.

**Washington**
*Church* • Often attended the old church. The current structure was finished 1846 but the churchyard dates from 1681.

## TWENTIETH ST

**Roosevelt, T**
*Birth* • 28 E Twentieth St. Upstairs front bedroom. Home. Entrance fee. 1858–1873.

## TWENTY-FIRST ST

**Arthur**
*Home* • 34 W Twenty-first St. His wife's home and his residence until outbreak of Civil War. Now empty lot. Used for storage. 1859–1861.

## TWENTY-SECOND ST

**Arthur**
*Home* • Twenty-second St and Broadway Lived in family hotel. 1861–1865.

## TWENTY-SIXTH ST

**Arthur**
*Home* • Took furnished house here. 1864.

**Roosevelt, T**
*Visit* • 26 W Twenty-sixth St. Aunt Annie (Mrs. James K. Gracie) home. 1881.

## UNION SQUARE

**Lincoln**
*Site* • Fourth Ave near Seventeenth St. Statue.

## UNITED NATIONS

**Presidents**
*Visit* • Every president, beginning with Truman, has addressed the UN.

**Bush**
*Work* • Forty-fifth St. Eleventh floor of the US Mission directly across First Ave from UN Headquarters. Ambassador to the UN. 1971– 1973.

## VAN COURTLANDT HOUSE

**Washington**

*Home* • North Riverdale (Bronx). Broadway and Two hundred forty-second St on a high bluff overlooking lake. Occupied after the Revolution. Mansion stands in the south part of the park, not far from Broadway. 1781, 1783.

## VANDERBILT HOTEL

**Coolidge**

*Visit* • 4 Park Ave betweem E Thirty-third and E Thirty-fourth Sts, west side (now offices). 1932.

## WILLIAM VAN NESS HOUSE

**Van Buren**

*Work* • 30 Broad St. 1801. 4 Wall St, 1802–1803.

## VAN PELT MANOR HOUSE

**Washington**

*Visit* • Eighty-second St and Eighteenth Ave. Used during the Revolution. House built 1686.

## VICTORIA HOTEL

**Cleveland**

*Home* • 4 W Twenty-seventh St. After leaving White House first stayed here then went to 816 Madison Ave. 1889–1892.

*Visit* • Conferences held for selecting cabinet members. February 1885.

## VINCENT-HALSEY HOUSE

**Adams, J**

*Home* • 3701 Provost Ave and E Two hundred thirty-third St, The Bronx. Served for two months as the nation's executive mansion when he left Philadelphia to escape yellow fever epidemic.

## WALDORF ASTORIA HOTEL

**Presidents**

*Visit* • 315 Park (Waldorf Towers) Ave and Fiftieth St. Every president since Hoover has visited.

**Bush**

*Home* • Official residence of US Ambassador to UN, overlooking the East River, Suite 42-A.

**Hoover**

*Home* • Thirty-first floor, suite 31-A. 1933–1964.

*Death* • 1964.

**Kennedy**

*Honeymoon* • First night. 9–12–1953.

**Nixon**

*Home* • Stayed here while looking for an apartment. 1963. Had a suite on the thirty-fifth floor. November 1968.

## WALKER ST

**Arthur**

*Work* • 51 Walker St. Now parking lot. Office while quartermaster. 1862.

## WALL ST

**Arthur**

*Work* • Old Merchant's Exchange Building. Later site National City Bank Building. 1871–1878.

**Grant**

*Work* • 2 Wall St at the corner of Broadway. President of Mexican Southern Railroad. Banco Portugues do Atlantico Building on site. 1881.

**Jefferson**

*Work* • At Capitol as Secretary of State. Federal Hall. 1790–1793.

**Madison**

*Work* • At Capitol as member of House of Representatives. Federal Hall. 1789–1790.

**Monroe**

*Work* • At Capitol as member of Virginia delegation. 1785.

*Visit* • 15 Wall St. House of Mrs. Daubigny where some congressmen boarded. 1785–1786.

**Roosevelt, FD**

*Work* • 52 Wall St. Law firm of Marvin, Hooker and Roosevelt. Morgan Guarantee Trust Building on site. 1915–.

*Work* • 54 Wall St. Law firm. Morgan Guarantee Trust Building on site. 1908–.

**Roosevelt, T**

*Work* • 44 Wall St. Roosevelt and Kobbe law firm. 1909–1919.

**Van Buren**

*Education* • Studied law. 1813.

*Visit* • 1 Wall St at Mrs. Rosa Keese's boarding house. Banco Portugues do Atlantico Building on site. 1813.

## WASHINGTON ARCH

**Washington**

*Site* • At the foot of Fifth Ave in the heart of Greenwich Village. The wooden arch built in 1889 to commemorate the centennial of his inauguration was later replaced by the arch that stands today.

## WASHINGTON HOTEL

**Van Buren**

*Lodging* • Broadway and Chambers. 1837–1841.

## WASHINGTON SQUARE

**Roosevelt, FD**

*Home* • 29 Washington Square. 1942–.

## WAVE HILL

**Roosevelt, T**

*Home* • Riverdale. 675 W Two hundred fifty-second St at Sycamore Ave. Entrance on Independence Ave at W Two hundred forty-ninth St, west side. Late 1800s.

## WORLD'S FAIR 1853 (BRYANT PARK)

**Pierce**

*Visit* • Sixth Ave. 1853.

## YMCA SLOAN HOUSE

**Nixon**

*Visit* • 356 W Thirty-fourth St. 1936.

## NIAGARA FALLS  *(Niagara County)*

**Presidents**

*Visit* • Carter, Cleveland, A Johnson, Lincoln, McKinley, FD Roosevelt, Taylor, and Tyler.

## NILES  *(Cayuga County)*

**Fillmore**

*Home* • Grew up on a farm in the Finger Lake region at present-day Niles, near Lake Skaneateles. 1802–1819.

## OWASCO  *(Cayuga County)*

**Van Buren**

*Church* • Dutch Reformed Church in town center. 1858.

## OYSTER BAY  *(See New York City)*

## PERRY  *(Wyoming County)*

**Arthur**

*Church* • First Baptist Church. 1835–1837.

*Home* • His father became pastor of First Baptist Church when Arthur was 4 years old. Parsonage stood in the rear of the W. T. Oline House on Elm St. 1835.

## PLATTSBURG *(Clinton County)*

**Coolidge**
*Visit* • Witherill Hotel, 25 Margaret St. 1924.

**Harding**
*Visit* • Witherill Hotel, 25 Margaret St. 1917.

**McKinley**
*Church* • Methodist Episcopal Church, 19 Oak St. Burned 1956. 1897.

*Church* • First Presbyterian, 34 Brickerhoff St. Still standing. 1897.

*Church* • Bluff Point Trinity Episcopal Church, Trinity Square. Still standing. 1897.

*Visit* • Champlain Hotel, three miles from Bluff Point Trinity Church. 1897.

## POCANTICO HILL (NORTH TARRYTOWN) *(Westchester County)*

**Ford**
*Visit* • Union Church, 555 Bedford Rd with Nelson Rockefeller. 11–21–1976.

**Nixon**
*Visit* • Rockefeller Estate. Bedford Rd. Private. 10–23–1972.

**Reagan**
*Visit* • Rockefeller Estate. 7–3–1986 to 7–4–1986.

## POESTENKILL *(Rensselaer County)*

**Garfield**
*Visit* • 1854.

## RIVERDALE *(The Bronx)*

**Kennedy**
*Education* • Riverdale County Day School, Fieldstone Rd. 1926–1928.

*Home* • 5040 Independence at SE corner of Two hundred fifty-second St. New house on site. 1928–1930.

## ROCHESTER *(Monroe County)*

**Van Buren**
*Church* • First Presbyterian Church. 1827.

## RYE *(Westchester County)*

**Bush**
*Marriage* • First Presbyterian Church, Boston Post Rd, NW. 1945.

*Visit* • Marvin Pierce House, 25 Onondaga St (Indian Village). Private. 1945–.

## SACKETS HARBOR *(Jefferson County)*

**Grant**
*Church* • Sackets Harbor Presbyterian Church. 1843–.

*Lodging* • Madison Barracks, Pike St. The former Union Hotel where he often lodged is now a visitor center with an orientation show. 1848–.

## SARANAC LAKE *(Franklin-Essex Counties)*

**Arthur**
*Visit* • Former Blagden Cottage, also called Camp Alpha or Camp Sunrise. Vacation here. 1881–.

**Cleveland**
*Visit* • Upper end of Saranac Lake at the north of Saranac Inn. Past Lake Clear, junction NY 86. Former Blagden Cottage, also called Camp Alpha or Camp Sunrise. 1884, 1885.

**Coolidge**
*Church* • Saranac Lake Presbyterian Church, 23 Church St. 1926.

*Visit* • White Pines Camp in an estate close to the lake. 1926.

**McKinley**
*Visit* • Hotel Champlain, 2 miles south of Plattsburgh. 1897.

## SARATOGA SPRINGS *(Saratoga County)*

**Presidents**

*Visit* • Washington, Madison, JQ Adams, Jackson, Van Buren, Tyler, Fillmore, Pierce, Buchanan, Grant, Hayes, Garfield, Arthur, Cleveland, B Harrison, T Roosevelt, Taft, and FD Roosevelt visited.

**Adams, JQ**

*Visit* • Walworth House, Pine Grove, on N Broadway. Other presidents: Jackson, Tyler, Fillmore, and Buchanan. Razed in 1955.

**Arthur**

*Visit* • United States Hotel. Site Broadway and Division Sts. Arthur proposed to his wife on the porch of the hotel. 1831.

*Visit* • Moon's Lake House with George Crum, the potato chip creator. Western side of Lake Saratoga. 1881–.

**Cleveland**

*Visit* • Moon's Lake House. 1880s.

**Grant**

*Visit* • Guest of honor for opening of Leland Opera House, part of Grand Union Hotel grounds. Demolished 1952. 7–4–1865.

**Harrison**

*Visit* • Thompson House, Union Ave, with his daughter, Mrs. Robert McKee, who rented the house. 1891.

*Visit* • Grand Union Hotel, Broadway. 1891.

**Taft**

*Visit* • Congress Hotel, Broadway and Spring Sts. 1909–1913.

**Tyler**

*Visit* • Avoided posh hotels. On one occasion stayed at Mrs. Sylvia S. Roger's house. 1844–.

**Van Buren**

*Visit* • Congress Hotel. Now site of Public Library. 1831–.

*Visit* • United States Hotel. 1831–.

**Wilson**

*Visit* • Congress Hall Hotel. 1894.

## SCHAGHITCOKE *(Rensselaer County)*

**Arthur**

*Work* • District School No. 14 during winter vacations. 1846–1848.

## SCHENECTADY *(Schenectady County)*

**Arthur**

*Church* • First Baptist Church. Torn down. 1845–1848.

*Church* • Chapel at Union College. 1845–1848.

*Education* • Lyceum at Union and Yale Sts. 1844–1845.

*Education* • Union College on Union St opposite Terrace. 1845–1848.

**Carter**

*Church* • Union College Chapel. 1951.

*Education* • Union College. Studied nuclear physics. 1951.

**Grant**

*Visit* • Union College. 1865.

## SCOTT *(Cortland County)*

**Fillmore**

*Work* • Schoolmaster and practiced law here. 1819.

## SCHUYLERVILLE *(Saratoga County)*

**Washington**

*Visit* • Gen. Philip S. Schuyler country residence just outside village limits near Saratoga Monument. After 1777.

## SPARTA *(Livingston County)*

**Fillmore**

*Work* • Apprenticed to clothmaker. Left after 4 months. 1814.

## Spuyten Duyvil (Formerly a Village on Hudson River)

**Roosevelt, T**
*Home* • Summer home. 1870.

## Summer Hill (Cayuga County)

**Fillmore**
*Birthplace* • Log cabin in Locke township. Skinner Hill Rd south of Moravia.

## Syracuse (Onondaga County)

**Johnson, LB**
*Visit* • University of Syracuse. Dedicated journalism building. 8–5–1964.

## Tappan (Rockland County)

**Washington**
*Travel* • Headquarters for trial of Major Andre at the De Wint Mansion. 1780; 1783.

## Tarrytown (Westchester County)

**Pierce**
*Visit* • Sunnyside, on Sunnyside Lane. Washington Irving home.

## Ticonderoga (Essex County)

**Adams, J**
*Site* • Replica of John Hancock Mansion in Boston houses the NY State Historical Association, NW corner of Montcalm St and Moses Circle.

## Tottenville (Richmond County)

**Adams, J**
*Visit* • Billipp House, Hylan Blvd. 1776.

## Union Village (Now Greenwich) (Washington County)

**Arthur**
*Church* • Bottskill Baptist Church, 32 Church St. 1839–1844.

*Education* • James I Lowrie School. 1839–1844.

## Valatie (Columbia County)

**Van Buren**
*Work* • Made his first official court appearance in the local tavern. 1798–1801.

## Verplanck's Point (Westchester County)

**Washington**
*Travel* • Headquarters. 1782.

## West Point (Orange County)

**Presidents**
*Visit* • Almost every president since Franklin Roosevelt has spoken at graduation.

**Eisenhower**
*Church* • West Point Chapel. 1911–1915.

*Education* • Military Academy. 1911–1915

*Education* • He lived on the fourth floor of the Beast Barracks.

**Grant**
*Church* • Old Episcopal chapel when attendance was required. 1839–1843.

*Education* • Military Academy. 1839–1843.

*Visit* • Library. 1865.

**Johnson, A**
*Visit* • Reviewed the cadets. Met with officials in the library. 1865.

**Monroe**
*Travel* • 1817.

**Washington**
*Visit* • Established headquarters here 7–8–1778.

*Site* • Military Beverly House, south of Garrison and near West Point. 1780.

*Site* • Recommended West Point as early as 1783 as place for a military academy.

## WEST TROY (FORMERLY WATERLIET) *(Albany County)*

**Arthur**
*Church* • First Baptist Church, corner of Canal and Ohio. 1853–1855.

## WEVERTOWN *(Warren County)*

**Roosevelt, T**
*Site* • NY 28 to Boreas Bridge State Campsite. On the ridge above the Boreas Valley a bronze plaque on a granite boulder marks the approximate spot where T Roosevelt was when he automatically became the 26th president. 1901.

## WHITE FACE MOUNTAIN HIGHWAY *(Essex County)*

**Roosevelt, FD**
*Visit* • Dedication. 9–13–1935.

## WHITE PLAINS *(Westchester County)*

**Washington**
*Travel* • Virginia Rd north of White Plains. Washington headquarters. 1776.

## WILLIAMSBURG *(Kings County)*

**Arthur**
*Home* • Moved from here to New York. Exact location unknown. 1856–1857.

## YORK *(Livingston County)*

**Arthur**
*Home* • Baptist parsonage. 1837–1839.

GEOGRAPHIC GUIDE TO LANDMARKS

# North Carolina

Raleigh

**40** **85** **95**

Charlotte

1. Polk birthplace,
   *Mecklenburg County*
2. A. Johnson birthplace,
   *Raleigh*

# NORTH CAROLINA

## ASHEVILLE  *(Buncombe County)*

**Presidents**

*Visit* • Grove Park Inn, 290 Macon Ave. Coolidge, Hoover, FD Roosevelt, and Taft visited.

**McKinley**

*Visit* • Glen Rock Hotel. 400 Depot St. 1897.

**Wilson**

*Visit* • Swannanoa Hotel, 49 Biltmore Ave. Now site of parking lot. 1880s.

*Marriage* • Eagle Hotel. Site corner of Eagle and Biltmore Sts about two blocks from the square. 1883.

## BODIE ISLAND  *(Dare County)*

**Cleveland**

*Visit* • Hunting trip. 1894.

## CARTHAGE  *(Moore County)*

**Johnson, A**

*Home* • Shack used as home and taylor shop. There is a marker on the lawn of the courthouse. 1824–1825.

## CHAPEL HILL  *(Orange County)*

**Buchanan**

*Visit* • University of North Carolina at Chapel Hill. Spoke at the University. 1860.

**Bush**

*Education* • Pre-flight training. 1942.

**Ford**

*Work* • Pre-flight training. 1942.

**Johnson, A**

*Visit* • University of North Carolina at Chapel Hill. May 1867.

**Kennedy**

*Visit* • University. 10–12–1961.

**Polk**

*Church* • Old Chapel in Old East Hall on the campus. 1816–1818.

*Education* • University of North Carolina. See Old East Hall. Lodged on third floor of New College with Wm D. Moseley, later governor of Florida. Called South Hall. 1816–1818.

*Visit* • Hilliard's Hotel, later The Eagle and still later Chapel Hill Hotel, fronting on

Franklin St. Gerard Hall for reception. 1847.

## CHARLOTTE *(Mecklenburg County)*

**Jackson**

*Education* • Queen's College, 301 Tryon. Marker SE corner of Third and S Tryon Sts. Now occupied by First Union bank. 1783–1784.

**Nixon**

*Visit* • Coliseum, 100 Paul Buck Rd. Billy Graham Day. 10–15–1971.

## CHESTERFIELD *(Burke County)*

**Wilson**

*Visit* • Hamilton Erwin House, Maplewood, NC 18 just north of Piedmont Rd east side. Set back from highway. 1885.

## DAVIDSON *(Mecklenburg County)*

**Wilson**

*Church* • Chapel. Davidson College. Now site of Fine Arts Bldg. 1873–1874.

*Education* • Davidson College. Chambers Hall. Site where present Chambers Hall is located in campus center. 1873–1874.

*Visit* • Eumenean Literary Society Building west side of campus. Gave his first public speech here. 1873–1874.

*Education* • 9 ground floor north wing of Old Chambers, used as the main building of the college. 1921 burned. 1873–1874.

*Lodging* • Mary Scofield boarding house, Depot and Main next to Carolina Inn where computer center now stands. 1873–1874.

## DURHAM *(Durham County)*

**Nixion**

*Church* • Duke University Chapel, Chapel Dr off Duke U Dr, West Campus. 1934–1937.

*Church* • Friends Meeting House, 404 Alexander Ave. 1934–1937.

*Education* • Duke University Law School. 1934–1937.

*Lodging* • He lived at 814 Sixth St (now Clarendon St). 1934–1935. Also lived at Duke Forest in a shack nicknamed Whipporwill Manor. Now part of a golf course. 1935–1937.

*Work* • University library. 1934–1937.

## EDENTON *(Chowan County)*

**Monroe**

*Visit* • Chowan County Courthouse, E King St. 1819.

## FAIRVIEW *(Buncome County)*

**Presidents**

*Visit* • Sherrill's Inn, on US 74 east from Asheville, 3.1 miles east of Fairview Post Office on Ferguson's Peak. Now private. Fillmore and Jackson also stayed here.

## FLAT ROCK *(Henderson County)*

**Wilson**

*Visit* • Farmer's Hotel (now Woodfield Inn), south side of Flat Rock on US 25. 1883.

## GEORGETOWN *(Union County)*

**Jackson**

*Home* • He made his home with McKemey on the east side of the road from Crawford, so it was in North Carolina instead of South Carolina. 1782–1784.

*Home* • Later stayed with Joseph White nearby. 1784.

*Work* • Taught school, Waxhaw County. 1784–1785.

## HIGH POINT *(Guilford County)*

**Carter**

*Visit* • High Point University, 833 Montlieu Ave. Auditorium. Campaign speech. 1976.

**Roosevelt, T**
*Travel* • October 1905.

## HOPEWELL *(Mecklenberg County)*

**Polk**
*Church* • Hopewell Presbyterian Church. First building 1765, current building 1831. Family church of the Knox family. Beatties Ford Rd. 1795–1806.

## HORSE COVE *(Macon County)*

**Wilson**
*Visit* • Stayed in one of Thompson's frame houses. 1879.

## JOHNSONVILLE *(Harnett County)*

**Jackson**
*Work* • Law practice on circuit. 1787.

## MCLEANSVILLE *(Guilford County)*

**Jackson**
*Work* • Law practice on circuit. 1787.

## MARTINSVILLE (ALSO KNOWN AS GUILFORD) *(Guilford County)*

**Jackson**
*Work* • Helping friend in store. 1787.

## MORGANTON *(Burke County)*

**Jackson**
*Work* • Courthouse. New courthouse (1837) on site. On circuit here. 1787.

## NEW BERN *(Craven County)*

**Monroe**
*Visit* • Coor-Bishop House, 501 E Front St. 1819.

**Truman**
*Church* • First Baptist, Middle St between S Front and Pollock Sts. 1948.

*North Carolina's marker claiming birthplace of Andrew Jackson.*

**Washington**
*Church* • Episcopal Church, Main St. Original burned. Marker. 1791.

*Visit* • Stanly House, 307 George St. 1791.

*Visit* • Tryon Palace, 613 Pollock St.

## NORTH CAROLINA STATE LINE

**Jackson**
*Birthplace* • Marker claiming site of birth by North Carolina. On Old Charlotte Rd from Waxhaw. Turn east at Union County/NC State line signs. 1767.

## PINEHURST *(Moore County)*

**Ford**
*Visit* • World Golf Hall of Fame, SR 2 junction US 15/501 and SR 211. Dedicated. 9–11–1974.

## PINEVILLE *(Mecklenburg County)*

**Polk**
*Birthplace* • Near Pineville off US 521, 12 miles south of Charlotte. Replica of log house in which he was born. 1795.

*Replica of log house in which James Polk was born.*

---

*Education* • School along present US 521. Before 1806.

## PROVIDENCE *(Mecklenburg County)*

**Polk**

*Church* • Providence Presbyterian Church, SR 16 south of Charlotte toward Waxhaw. Present church built, 1858 site of original. Aborted baptism. 1795–1806.

## RALEIGH *(Wake County)*

**Buchanan**

*Visit* • 1868.

**Grant**

*Visit* • Haywood House, 127 E Edenton St. Grant came for secret meeting with Sherman.

**Johnson, A**

*Birthplace* • House stood near the corner of Fayetteville and Morgan Sts. Marker on site. Building has been moved to Mordecai Historic Park, 1 Mimosa St. 1808.

*Church* • Statehouse was used for public services by travelling ministers from every denomination. Probably Johnson's parents attended here and he may have been baptized here. This building was destroyed by fire in 1810. 1794–1810.

*Site* • City Cemetery at the corner of S East and E Hargett Sts. See grave site of his father, marked simply J.J., just inside the gate. Difficult to see when covered by leaves. Andrew Johnson visited. 6–4–1867.

**Roosevelt, T**

*Visit* • Capitol. Union Square, facing Morgan St and bounded by Wilmington, Edenton, and Salisbury Sts. October 1905.

**Truman**

*Visit* • Attended dedication of Three Pres-

*Statue of North Carolina's presidents, James Polk, Andrew Jackson, and Andrew Johnson.*

idents Statue, Jackson, Polk, and A Johnson. 10–19–1948.

**Van Buren**
*Visit* • 1827.

**Washington**
*Site* • Statues in the Capitol Rotunda and
on the south lawn.

## ROCKFORD *(Surry County)*

**Jackson**
*Work* • Law practice right after he finished his law studies in Salisbury. 1786.

## SALEM *(Forsyth County)*

**Washington**
*Visit* • Salem Tavern, 800 South Main St.
1791.

*Church* • Salem Church in Salem Village.

## SALISBURY *(Rowan County)*

**Jackson**
*Church* • Third Presbyterian Church (near
Salisbury) between Iredell and Thyatira.
After 1781.

*Education* • Law office at 200 W Fisher St.

*Lodging* • He lived at Rowan House (formerly the Hughes Hotel). Security Bank
now occupies the site. 201 S Main St.
1785.

*Work* • Jackson St is the site of the Spruce
McKay law office where he worked. Also
see old well nearby which was there in his
day. 1784–1786.

**Washington**
*Visit* • Captain Edward Yarbobo House, E
Main St, a few doors east of the Public
Square. 1791.

*Visit* • Hughes' Hotel. See location under
Jackson above. 1791.

*Visit* • See steps from which he spoke on
library lot. 1791.

## SKYLAND

**Wilson**
*Honeymoon* • Small summer resort off
US 25 across from the Western Steer
about a mile north of Skyland. Stayed in
cottage next to Arden Park Hotel. Now
industrial park. 1885.

## SUMMERFIELD *(Guilford County)*

**Jackson**
*Visit* • McNairy House near Lake Brandt.
1786.

## WADESBORO *(Anson County)*

**Jackson**
*Lodging* • Ingram House, 11 miles from
Lilesville, north off US 74 and off County
Rd 1703. Open field where house once
stood. Marker in woods nearby. 1785.

*Work* • Courthouse where he practiced has
been destroyed. 1785–1786.

## WILMINGTON *(New Hanover County)*

**Taft**
*Visit* • Edward B. Dudley House, Front
and Nun Sts. 11–9–1909.

**Washington**
*Visit* • Burgwin-Wright House, 224 Market St on road from New Bern. Marker. Restored. 1791.

*Visit* • House, corner Front and Dock Sts.
Marker. 4–25–1791.

*Visit* • Market St on road from New
Bern. Marker commemorating his visit.
1791.

**Wilson**
*Church* • First Presbyterian Church, corner of Third and Orange. The church he attended burned in 1925. 1874–1885.

*Church* • Second Presbyterian Church on occasion. 1874–1885.

*Home* • C. H. Robinson House, Front and Nun Sts temporarily while manse was being readied. 1874.

*Home* • Manse, corner Fourth and Orange Sts. Church playground on the site now. 1874–1885.

## WINSTON-SALEM *(Forsythe County)*

**Bush**

*Travel* • Wait Chapel, Wake Forest University, Silas Creek Rd, for first debate with Michael Dukasis. 1988.

**Carter**

*Visit* • Wake Forest, Wait Chapel. 3–17–1978.

# North Dakota

1 Bismarck

94

1. T. Roosevelt home,
   *Bismarck*

# NORTH DAKOTA

## BISMARCK *(Burleigh County)*

**Grant**
*Visit* • Territorial Capitol. Laying of the cornerstone. 9–5–1883.

**Roosevelt, FD**
*Visit* • Old State Capitol. 1920.

**Roosevelt, T**
*Home* • East of Memorial Building on Capitol grounds is the Roosevelt Cabin, which was removed from Medora.

*Visit* • Old State Capitol. 4–7–1903.

*Visit* • Governor's Mansion, 320 Avenue B. 1903.

**Wilson**
*Visit* • Old State Capitol. 1919.

## DICKINSON *(Stark County)*

**Roosevelt, T**
*Visit* • Attended first Fourth of July celebration held here and was the chief orator. 1886.

## ELKHORN *(Billings County)*

**Roosevelt, T**
*Home* • Ranch House site, NW corner of Billings County. Only a few foundation stones show where the cabin stood in the 1880s. He often used this place for hunting expeditions. 1883–.

## FARGO *(Cass County)*

**McKinley**
*Visit* • Speech. 1899.

## GRAND FORKS *(Grand Forks County)*

**Kennedy**
*Visit* • University of North Dakota field house. 9–25–1963.

## LITTLE MISSOURI *(Billings County)*

**Roosevelt, T**
*Site* • Theodore Roosevelt National Memorial Park.

*Visit* • Pyramid Park Hotel. Demolished. 1883.

## MARMARTH  *(Slope County)*

**Roosevelt, T**
   *Visit* • 1883–1889.


## MEDORA  *(Billings County)*

**Roosevelt, T**
   *Home* • Maltese Cross Cabin. Cabin has
   been removed to the state capitol grounds,
   Bismarck. Also known as Chimney Butte
   Ranch. Site is about 7 miles from Medora.
   1883–1887.

   *Visit* • Rough Riders Hotel, Main St.
   1883–1889, 1900, 1903.

   *Visit* • DeMores Chateau. Now ruins.
   1883–.

*Interior of Maltese Cross Cabin, Theodore Roosevelt's Medora home.*

# OHIO

## ADENA *(Jefferson County)*

**Monroe**

*Visit* • Worthington Mansion, Adena Rd, off Pleasant Valley Rd. 1819.

## BETHEL *(Clermont County)*

**Grant**

*Home* • Grant's family arrived June 1840. Corner of Plane and N Charity. Now site of laundry. 1840–1854.

## BLOOMING GROVE (CORSICA)

*(Morrow County)*

**Harding**

*Birthplace* • OH 97. Marker and flag indicate the spot. 1865.

*Baptism/Church* • Blooming Grove Methodist Church on the south edge of town. 1865–1873.

*Education* • One room schoolhouse outskirts of town. No marker. 1865–1873.

*Education* • Buckhorn Tavern School. No remains or marker. 1865–1873.

*Home* • OH 97 east edge of town. A marker next to birth marker indicates site of Harding homestead. 1865–1873.

## CALEDONIA *(Marion County)*

**Harding**

*Church* • Caledonia Methodist Church, 201 S Main St and South St. 1873–1880.

*Education* • School across from the Methodist Church. 1873–1880.

*Home* • 139 S Main St, a few doors from the town square in a yellow-brown frame structure. 1873–1880.

*Home* • Highway 309 north side two miles east of Caledonia to a 40-acre farm just over the county line. No marker. Sits 200 feet back from the road just east of another house nearby. 1880–1882.

*Work* • Argus News office, Main St. No site marker. 1875.

1. McKinley home, *Canton*
2. Garfield birthplace,
   *Chagrin Falls*
3. Garfield Park, *Cincinnati*
   Harrison home, *Cincinnati*
   Taft birthplace, *Cincinnati*
4. Hayes home, *Columbus*
5. Hayes Museum, *Fremont*
6. Grant home, *Georgetown*
7. Garfield home, *Hiram*
8. Harding Museum, *Marion*
9. Garfield home, *Mentor*
10. Grant birthplace, *Point
    Pleasant*

**Ohio**

Columbus

Cincinnati

*William McKinley home in Canton.*

## CANTON *(Stark County)*

### McKinley

*Church* • First Methodist, SW corner W Tuscarawas St and Cleveland Ave. Pew marked with silver plate. Now called Church of the Savior. See also McKinley memorial windows given by Mrs. McKinley. 1867–1877.

*Marriage* • First Presbyterian Church, now known as Christ Presbyterian Church, 530 W Tuscarawas St. 1871.

*Home* • William McKinley, Sr., 101 Tuscarawas St W. Number changed after 1887 to 131 Tuscarawas St W. 1867–1871.

*Visit* • Saxton homestead, 331 Market Ave. Mrs. McKinley's girlhood home. 1871–1901.

*Work* • Law office, second floor, First Na-tional Bank, SW corner Market and Tuscawaras Sts. 1867–1877.

*Work* • Courthouse on Public Square. Stark County Prosecutor. 1869–1871.

*Work* • Board of Directors, Harder Bank, 7 East Tuscawaras. 1870–1877.

*Funeral* • Courthouse, Public Square, where he lay in state. 1901.

*Funeral* • First Methodist Church. The church has the American flag that draped the casket. See address above. 1901.

*Burial* • Westlawn Cemetery, Seventh St NW, in a temporary vault to the left of Seventh St entrance. 1901.

*Burial* • Westlawn Cemetery, McKinley Memorial. McKinley Monument Dr NW off Seventh St NW. 1907.

### Roosevelt, T

*Visit* • Westlawn Cemetery. 5–27–1907.

*Statue of William McKinley in front of monument where he and his wife are entombed.*

## CATAWBA ISLAND

**Hayes**

*Home* • Summer home used by relatives until recently when house burned. 1881–1893.

## CHAGRIN FALLS  *(Cuyhoga County)*

**Garfield**

*Birthplace* • One mile and a half south of Orange Center, 3 miles from town of Chagrin Falls. See Moreland Hills. Site marked by row of wooden benches. 1831.

*Baptism* • Chagrin River. Possibly at Miles Road. 3–3–1850.

*Church* • Disciples Church. Located near junction of two branches of Chagrin River one mile west of what is now Chagrin Falls about three miles from his home. Because he served in so many churches in this area and because the area has been highly developed, places and dates cannot be set with complete accuracy. Nothing on site. 1831–1833.

*Church* • Disciples Church, 24 Walnut St, which he helped construct. Torn down 1932. This is the parent church of the current Federated Church United Church of Christ, 76 Bell St. 1852–1858.

*Education* • Various sites but mainly at Griffith School House in town. 1833–1852.

*Education* • One room district school. See also River Road School under Moreland Hills. It is also difficult to identify specific locations of his schools. 1848–1850.

*Lodging* • 23 Walnut St while working on the nearby church. Front part is original.

*Work* • Preaching at Disciples Church. See possible locations under Chagrin Falls, Solon, and Chesterland. 1858–.

*Work* • Town Hall on Main St. Center of his campaign for president. Burned 1944. Rebuilt on site. 1880.

## CHESTERLAND  *(Geauga County)*

**Garfield**

*Church* • Site Presbyterian Church associated with Garfield, SW corner Sherman and Chillicothe. Built 1830; dedicated 1835.

*Church* • Site Free Will Baptist. Originally on east side of Chillicothe south of Sherman Rd. 1840–1870.

*Church* • Disciples Church. Built on Township Park 250 feet north of Mayfield Rd facing Chillicothe Rd. Dedicated 1853.

*Education* • Geauga Academy. The old Chester High School building is on the site. Lodged with local family at 12570 Chillicothe. Now Remembrance Shop. 1848–1850.

*Work* • Site of ashery, south side of Mayfield Rd just west of Heath Rd corner. 1847.

## CHILLICOTHE  *(Ross County)*

**Hayes**

*Site* • Lucy Webb Hayes's birthplace. 90 W Sixth. Built 1825.

**Wilson**

*Lodging* • Reeves-Woodrow-Butler House. 62 S Paint at W Fourth St (uncle's home). 1865–.

*Work* • Law office (uncle), 4 E Second, Room 4 and later at 4 Carlisle Block (corner) N Paint and W Main Sts. 1865.

## CINCINNATI  *(Hamilton County)*

**Garfield**

*Site* • Cincinnati Historical Society, Garfield Park at Garfield Place between Vine and Elm Sts. See also bronze statue of WH Harrison.

**Adams, JQ**

*Church* • Wesley Chapel Methodist Church, 322 E Fifth St, north side between Sycamore and Broadway. 1843.

*Site* • Dedicated observatory on Mt. Ida. Changed to Mt. Adams in his honor. See observatory on Avery Lane at Observatory Place. 11–9–1843.

**Arthur**

*Visit* • Exposition Hall, Elm St between Twelfth and Fourteenth Sts. Attended RNC. Lodged Grand Hotel, SW corner Fourth and Central Ave. 1876.

**Buchanan**

*Site* • Smith and Nixon's Hall. DNC nomination for president. June 1856.

**Garfield**

*Work* • Garfield Place between Vine and Elm Sts. Law office. No marker. 1860–1861.

*Funeral* • Monumental Park. Lay in state. 1881.

*Site* • Monument in Garfield Park. Garfield Place between Vine and Elm Sts.

**Grant**

*Work* • Union Army Headquarters, SW corner Arch St and Broadway.

*Work* • 739 W Eighth St, headquarters. Moved to Burnett House for larger quarters. 1861.

*Visit* • Burnett House, NW corner Third and Vine. Met with Sherman in Parlor A to plan Sherman's invasion. 1861. Here with President A Johnson. 1866.

*Visit* • Spencer House, NW corner Front and Broadway.

**Harrison, B**

*Church* • First Presbyterian Church, between Fourth and Fifth and Walnut and Main. Built 1851 and demolished in 1936. 1851–.

*Education* • Farmer's College, 5553 Belmont Ave. Became Belmont College in 1880 and Ohio Military Institute in 1890. In those days College Hill was known as Pleasant Hill and Belmont Ave was the original Colerain Rd. 1847–1850.

*Lodging* • Home of married sister Betsy

Eaton while a law apprentice. 323 W Third St. 1852–1853.

*Home* • The Point. See North Bend. 1853–1854.

*Work* • Storer and Gwynne Law Office, Hart's Building on E Fourth St. 1852–1854.

**Harrison, WH**

*Church* • Daniel Drake House, 429 E Third St, used as a church. Site is now occupied by St. Anthony Syrian Maronite Church. See also Christ Episcopal Church below. 1791–1798.

*Church* • Christ Episcopal Church, 318 E Fourth St, north side between Sycamore and Broadway. 1817–1841.

*Honeymoon* • Fort Washington, corner of Third St, east of Broadway near intersection with Ludlow St. Monument marker for Fort Washington. 1795.

*Home* • Rented a house on Broadway just below Fourth St. 1812–1814.

*Work* • Ferry Landing log office. Also Land Officer Register the same year. No remains or marker. 1798.

*Work* • First Territorial House (no remains). Secretary of the Northwest Territory. 1798–1799.

*Visit* • Main St Hotel while clerk of court. 1835–1840.

*Visit* • Henri House on W Main between Court and Canal. 1841.

*Visit* • Gen. James Findlay House, 38 N Front St. 1812–.

*Funeral* • Wesley Chapel Methodist Church, 322 E Fifth St. This church has been in continuous use since 1831. 1841.

**Hayes**

*Church* • Presbyterian Church, north side of E Fourth St near Main St. Demolished. 1849–1852.

*Church* • St. John's Episcopal, SE corner Seventh and Plum. Now a parking lot. 1849–1852.

*Church* • St. Paul's Methodist, Seventh and Smith. Built 1879.

*Marriage* • Cincinnati Wesleyan Female College where he courted Lucy. 1847.

*Marriage* • Webb House, 141 Sixth St. Area became the site of the Clarion Hotel. 1852.

*Lodging* • New Law Building (sleeping quarters), 127 E Third St. 1849–1852.

*Lodging* • Mrs. Fulton's Boarding House, Fourth and Vine Sts. 1849–1852.

*Home* • 141 Sixth St. Nothing remains. 1852–1853.

*Home* • 383 Sixth St. Nothing remains. 1853–1872.

*Lodging* • Carlisle House, NW corner of Sixth and Mound Sts. Temporarily. 1872–1873.

*Work* • Law office, 127 E Third St. 1850s. New Law Building, room 6 on 3rd floor between Main and Sycamore Sts. 1849–1861. Also at Number 8 Selves' Building at Sixth and Walnut. This building was demolished.

*Work* • Old City Hall, corner W Eighth St and Plum. City solicitor. New city hall built here 1888. 1858–1861.

*Work* • Exposition Hall, Elm St btween Twelfth and Fourteenth Sts. RNC nomination for president. June 1876.

*Visit* • Fountain Square on Fifth St between Vine and Walnut. He spoke at the unveiling of the fountain. 1871.

*Site* • Spring Grove Cemetery, burial site of 18-month old Joseph, Spring Grove Ave. 1863.

## Hoover

*Visit* • Monument, Eden Park Hill, off US 22 (Gilbert Ave). 10–22–1929.

## Johnson, A

*Visit* • Spencer House, NW corner Front and Broadway. 1866. Burnett House, NW corner Third and Vine Sts.

(now site of Union Central annex). 1861, 1863.

## Lincoln

*Visit* • Burnett House. Stopped en route to inaugural. 1861. See location under A Johnson.

*Site* • Lytle Park, 421 E Fourth St. Bronze statue (without beard).

## Taft

*Birthplace* • Mount Auburn, 2038 Auburn Ave. Restored. Free admission. 1857.

*Church* • First Congregational Unitarian Church, SE corner Fourth and Race Sts. 1857–1900. Christ Episcopal, 318 E Fourth St on occasion. 1886–1900.

*Church* • St. John's Unitarian, NW corner Twelfth and Elm Sts. 1886–1900.

*Education* • Sixteenth District School in Mount Auburn section, Southern Ave facing Young St (now William H. Taft School). Bronze plaque on building says he attended school in a 4-room brick structure on this site. 1862–1870.

*Education* • Woodward High School, E Thirteenth, Woodward and Sycamore Sts and Broadway. 1870–1874.

*Education* • Cincinnati Law School, 414 Walnut St. 1878–1880.

*Marriage* • 69 Pike St (Herron House). Site is now under interstate highway. 1886.

*Home* • 2038 Auburn Ave. 1857–1886.

*Home* • 60 Auburn Ave E Walnut Hills, upon return from honeymoon. 1886.

*Home* • E McMillan St. Nothing remains. 1887–1890.

*Home* • 118 E Third St where Mrs. Taft lived with the children. NE corner of Third and Lawrence. 1892–1898.

*Home* • Madison Rd east of Annwood Ave in East Walnut Hills. 1898–1900.

*Lodging* • 316 Pike St (now the Taft House Museum). On its four columned portico he was formally notified of his nomination for the presidency. It was the home of his brother, Charles. 1908.

**Work** • Lloyd Law firm, 56 Johnston Building. Worked part time. 1878–1880. 1883–1887.

**Work** • Halstead's newspaper as a reporter. NE corner of Fourth and Race Sts at the *Cincinnati Commercial News*. 1880.

**Work** • Hamilton County Courthouse, bounded by E Central Parkway, Main, E Court, and Sycamore Sts. Completed 1919. It is fourth courthouse on this site. Assistant prosecutor in the old building. 1880–1882.

**Work** • Collector, Internal Revenue Federal Building on Government Square. New government buildings on site. 1882–1883.

**Work** • Superior Court of Cincinnati. See Hamilton County Courthouse. 1887–1890.

**Work** • City Hall on Government Square as US Circuit Judge. New building on site. 1892–1900.

**Work** • Cincinnati Law School, 414 Walnut St. Dean and professor. 1896.

**Visit** • Grand Hotel, SW corner 4th and Central Ave for welcome for Grant upon his return from around-the-world tour. 1879.

**Taylor**
**Visit** • Pearl St House (Hotel). No marker. 1849.

## CLEVELAND *(Cuyahoga County)*

**Adams, JQ**
**Visit** • Congregational Church, north side Public Square. 1843.

**Carter**
**Visit** • Convention Center, 3100 Tower City Center, Music Hall. Presidential debate with Reagan. Stayed Bond Court Hotel. 10–28–1980.

**Coolidge**
**Visit** • Municipal Auditorium, NW corner

E Sixth and St. Clair. RNC where he was nominated vice president. 1924.

**Garfield**
**Church** • Eighteenth Ward Disciples Church, Circle and Franklin Sts. 1857–1858.

**Church** • Miles Ave Church of Christ. 1850s.

**Work** • Barge work. Exact location not determined. 1848.

**Funeral** • Lay in state in Public Square. Funeral in Pavilion. Grant and Hayes attended. 1881.

**Burial** • Lake View Cemetery, 12316 Euclid Ave in temporary vault located at the edge of the cemetery. 1881.

**Burial** • Lake View Cemetery, 12316 Euclid Ave. James A. Garfield Monument. 1893.

**Grant**
**Visit** • Stadium Hotel. See A Johnson below.

**Harding**
**Site** • Dinner, Hotel Hollenden. Corner E Sixth and Superior Ave. 1920.

**Visit** • Gray's Armory, 1234 Bolivar Rd for campaign speech. 1920.

**Harrison, B**
**Visit** • Garfield Monument, Euclid Ave. Dedication. 1890.

**Visit** • Stillman Hotel, northside of Euclid Ave just east of Erie (E Ninth St). Later used for Stillman Theater. Razed 1901. 1890.

**Hayes**
**Church** • First Methodist. Site SW corner Erie and Euclid. 1880–.

**Visit** • Linus Austin House, 3625 Prospect St. Son lived here. 1892.

**Death** • Cleveland Railway Station. See Union Station at the foot of Water (W Ninth) and Bank (W Sixth). Heart attack. January 1893.

*James Garfield statue inside the monument to the president.*

**Jefferson**
> *Site* • Statue in front of Cuyahoga County Courthouse, W Lakeside and Ontario.

**Johnson, A**
> *Visit* • Stadium Hotel, at SE corner of W Sixth St and St. Clair Ave (formerly Angier House and later the Kennard House). Came in at Lake Shore Depot. 1866.

**Lincoln**
> *Visit* • Weddell House, SW corner of Sixth St and Superior Ave. From second floor balcony Lincoln addressed the street crowd. Plaque at the site. Now occupied by Rockefeller Building. 1861.
> *Funeral* • Public Square. Lay in state. East of the monument on Superior Ave and Ontario. 1865.
> *Site* • Lincoln statue facing the Mall in front of the Board of Education Building, 1385 E Sixth St (west entrance). 1932.

**McKinley**
> *Visit* • Hollenden Hotel. See Harding. 1899.

**Roosevelt, T**
> *Church* • St. Paul's, E Fourtieth and Euclid Ave. Attended Ruth Hanna wedding. June 1903.

**Van Buren**
> *Visit* • American House on Superior Ave. 1842.

## COSHOCTON *(Coshocton County)*

**Garfield**
> *Site* • See mule-drawn canal barge, Monticello II, on the Ohio-Erie Canal. Similar to one on which Garfield worked. 1848.

## COLUMBIANA *(Columbiana County)*

**McKinley**
> *Visit* • Camp McKinley just west of town. Now main office of Columbiana Council of Boy Scouts. Was the home of his grandfather. 1840s.

## COLUMBUS *(Franklin County)*

**Presidents**
> *Visit* • Neil House, 41 S High St. Arthur, Cleveland, Garfield, Grant, Harding, B and WH Harrison, Hayes, Jackson, A Johnson, Lincoln, McKinley, T Roosevelt, Taft, Van Buren, and Wilson.

**Fillmore**
> *Visit* • State Capitol, Broad and High Sts. 1854.

**Ford**

*Visit* • State Fairgrounds, E Eleventh Ave. State Capitol, Governor's Cabinet Room. Neil House Hotel, 41 S High St. 5–26–1976.

*Visit* • State Capitol. Fort Hayes Career Center. 11–1–1976.

**Garfield**

*Work* • Capitol, in senate chambers as senator. At the time it was meeting in Ambrose Hall. 1859–1861.

*Lodging* • 193 S Third St. Now site of Marshall Fields. 1859–1861.

**Grant**

*Site* • My Jewels Monument near NW corner of capitol. Includes Grant, Hayes, Garfield.

*Site* • Group sculpture, State Capitol, at the head of the stairs.

**Harding**

*Church* • Baptist, Rich and Third. Now a parking lot site. 1901–1904.

*Lodging* • Great Southern Hotel, 310 S High St across from the statehouse. 1901.

*Work* • Capitol, in Senate Chambers. 1901–1904.

*Work* • Capitol, in lt. governor's office. 1904–1906.

**Harrison WH**

*Work* • Site of former courthouse of Franklinton. 55 S Hague just south of Broadway. Building used as schoolhouse. Site now occupied by low cost housing. He was a member of state senate meeting here when Capitol burned. 1819–1821.

**Hayes**

*Church* • First Methodist Church. Current site 3000 Euclid. 1867– 1871.

*Education* • Thomas Sparrow law office boarding with Dr. P. Sisson on the east side of High St near Rich St. No number. 1842–1843.

*Honeymoon* • With sister and brother-in-law, Fanny and William Platt. High St near Spring St. 1852.

*Home* • East side of High St near Rich St, home of sister and her husband. 1842–1843.

*Home* • 51 E State. 1868–1869.

*Home* • 96 S Grant. 1869–1870.

*Home* • Seventh St near the Capitol. 1870.

*Home* • 60 E Broad St, duplex. Household bank later on site. 1876–1877.

*Work* • Ohio Supreme Court. At the time in the State Capitol (Courthouse) in Franklinton. 1852.

*Work* • Capitol, in the governor's office. 1871–1872.

**Hoover**

*Visit* • State Capitol. 6–17–1931.

**Johnson, A**

*Visit* • State Capitol. 1863, 1866.

**Lincoln**

*Funeral* • Lay in state in the Capitol rotunda. 1865.

*Site* • Lincoln Memorial (bust) in the Capitol at head of stairs.

**McKinley**

*Home* • Chittenden Hotel, NW corner of Highland and Spring Sts when governor. When it burned, he moved to Neil House. 1892–1894. Neil House. 1894–1896.

*Site* • McKinley Memorial at west entrance to the Capitol grounds facing High St.

*Work* • Camp Chase near Columbus where he enlisted. 1861.

*Work* • Capitol in governor's office. 1892–1896.

**Monroe**

*Visit* • Stopped on return from Detroit. August 1817.

**Roosevelt, T**

*Visit* • Capitol. 1912.

## CRESTLINE *(Crawford County)*

**Harding**

*Work* • Hardware store. All four stores existing at time have been destroyed. 1882.

## DAYTON *(Montgomery County)*

**Eisenhower**

*Site* • US Air Force Museum. 4 1/2 miles north of Dayton on Springfield Pike at Old Wright Field. B-70 aircraft used by Truman and Eisenhower.

**McKinley**

*Site* • Dayton Library, 215 Third St. Cooper Park, E Third and St. Clair Sts. McKinley Monument.

**Truman**

*Site* • U.S. Air Force Museum. B-70 aircraft used by Truman and Eisenhower.

## DEFIANCE *(Defiance County)*

**Harrison, WH**

*Work* • Fort Winchester built 1812.

## DELAWARE *(Delaware County)*

**Hayes**

*Birthplace* • 51 E William St between Sandusky and Union Sts. House is gone. Small stone monument marks the spot. An oil company service station stands on the site. 1822.

*Baptism* • Presbyterian Meeting House. Services held in Old Courthouse in city center. 1823.

*Church* • First Presbyterian Church. New church on the site at 73 W Winter St. 1823–1842.

*Education* • Private school, corner of Franklin and Winter Sts. 1833–1835.

*Education* • Private school. Mrs. Murray's home at 15 N Franklin St. 1835–.

*Marriage* • Courted Lucy at the Sulphur Springs on campus of Ohio Wesleyan University, South Sandusky St. 1847.

*Home* • 51 E Williams St (see birthplace above). 1822–1842.

*Visit* • The Mansion House, now Elliott Hall, on the campus of Ohio Wesleyan. A student meeting place where he met with young people. 1847.

*Site* • Ohio Wesleyan University, South Sandusky St. Bronze marker on the campus commemorates his living in Delaware.

## FALLEN TIMBERS *(Lucas County)*

**Harrison, WH**

*Work* • Battle fought 1794. 1813.

## FORT AMANDA *(Auglaize County)*

**Harrison, WH**

*Work* • Site of fort used in 1812.

## FORT FAYETTE *(Fulton County)*

**Harrison, WH**

*Work* • Encamped here on way to Legionville. 1792.

## FORT GREENVILLE *(Darke County)*

**Harrison, WH**

*Work* • Winter headquarters. 1793.

## FORT HAMILTON *(Butler County)*

**Harrison, WH**

*Work* • Monument on OH 177, 25 miles north of Cincinnati. 1791.

## FORT JEFFERSON *(Darke County)*

**Harrison, WH**

*Work* • Outpost. 1791.

## FORT MEIGS *(Lucas County)*

**Harrison, WH**

*Work* • Historic site near Fallen Timbers.

During War of 1812 under his command. National Monument and stockade. 1813.

## FORT RECOVERY   *(Mercer County)*

**Harrison, WH**

*Work* • Reconstructed fort. 1793.

## FORT ST. CLAIR   *(Preble County)*

**Harrison, WH**

*Work* • Site of fort. 1792.

## FREMONT   *(Sandusky County)*

**Harding**

*Visit* • Spiegel Grove. See Hayes. 1920.

**Hayes**

*Church* • St. Paul's Episcopal Church, NW corner of Park and Court Sts (built 1842). 1872–. Methodist Episcopal Church (Hayes Memorial Church), NW corner of Park and Birchard Aves. Now occupied by First Brethern Church. 1872–1898.

*Home* • Vallet House. Lodged with uncle. 1829 Buckland Ave. Before 1852.

*Home* • 1337 Hayes Ave. Museum, library, and home, called Spiegel Grove. Entrance fee. 1873–1893.

*Lodging* • Thompson House, south of junction of E State St and Ohio Ave. Now Uniroyal store, 323 E State. 1845–.

*Work* • J.S. Tyler Building, second floor, law practice. Site NW corner of Front and Croghan Sts. 1845–1849.

*Death* • 1337 Hayes Ave. 1893.

*Funeral* • 1337 Hayes Ave. President-elect Cleveland attended. 1893.

*Burial* • Oakwood Cemetery, 1225 Oakwood Rd, one-half mile south of Fremont. Later removed to Spiegel Grove. See family circle plot. Section on the right side coming from Buckland Ave. 1893.

*Burial* • Removed from Oakwood and buried on the grounds of Spiegel Grove,

junction of Hayes and Buckland Aves. 1915.

**McKinley**

*Visit* • Spiegel Grove. 1897.

## GAMBIER   *(Knox County)*

**Hayes**

*Education* • Kenyon College. Rosse Hall was originally the chapel. 1838–1842.

*Education* • Kenyon College. Rosse Hall existed during his time. Old Kenyon built in 1824 burned 1949 but the exterior is an exact duplicate. 1838–1842.

## GEORGETOWN   *(Brown County)*

**Grant**

*Church* • Methodist Church, Grant Ave, across the street from his home. 1823–1839.

*Education* • Thomas Upham's village school, corner N Apple and Grant Ave. 1825–1827.

*Education* • 5 Water St at Second and S Water St. 1827–1839.

*Home* • 219 Grant Ave. 1823–1839.

*Work* • Grant Ave at his father's tannery across the street from their home. 1830s.

## HIRAM   *(Portage County)*

**Garfield**

*Church* • Hiram Christian Church. 6868 Wakefield Rd. Corner Wakefield and Garfield Rd on OH 82. 1851–1861.

*Education* • Hiram Eclectic School. Original building off Hinsdale demolished 1969. 1851–1854.

*Lodging* • He lived in basement of original college building. Site just behind present Henry Hall. Demolished 1969. 1851–1854.

*Lodging* • He boarded at 11221 on OH 700 about 1 mile SW of the college site. 1858–1861.

*Marriage* • Lucretia Rudolph's parents' home, north side of OH 305, east of Hiram Center. Now demolished. 1858.

*Home* • Zeb Rudolph House, north side OH 305 east of Hiram. 1856–1859.

*Home* • Northrup House, 11221 on OH 700. 1859–1861.

*Home* • 6825 Hinsdale St which he had bought during the war and sold to Hinsdale 1872. 1861– 1872.

*Site* • See cemetery at Hiram Hill where his last born son was buried next to his first born. Fairview Cemetery, corner of OH 82 and Ryder Rd, west of Hiram. 1874.

*Work* • Eclectic School, teaching. 1851, 1854, 1856, 1857. President. 1857–1861.

*Work* • Preached at churches in the Hiram area. 1854–1861.

# IBERIA COLLEGE (NEAR CALEDONIA) *(Morrow County)*

**Harding**

*Church* • Methodist church, 3607 County Rd 30. Church stands on former site of the college. Marker. 1880–1882.

*Education* • Ohio Central College. Site 7 miles east of Blooming Grove. Then called Iberia College. Bronze marker. 1880–1882.

*Lodging* • He boarded with others at Professor A. C. Crist's. 1880–1882.

# KINGSTON *(Ross County)*

**Hayes**

*Lodging* • Elmwood, home of Lucy's aunts. OH 361 north of town on west side of highway north of viaduct. Now Boggs Farm Mailbox number 5769 near Circleville.

# LEBANON *(Warren County)*

**Presidents**

*Visit* • Golden Lamb, 27 S Broadway,

built 1816. The following were among the guests: WH Harrison, Hayes, and McKinley. Host to seven other presidents.

# MARION *(Marion County)*

**Harding**

*Church* • Seventh Day Adventist (church of his mother). 550 Windsor Ave is the current address. At first met in City Hall and later in a new church at SW corner of center and Mill. Attended before 1882.

*Church* • Trinity Baptist, 1330 N Main. 1865–1901. Following 1901 at 220 S Main St. He was a member 1882–1923.

*Marriage* • 380 Mt. Vernon Ave in the front hall of the house. 1891.

*Home* • N East St (now N Prospect St) opposite the old interurban station, second door south of county jail. 1882–1891.

*Home* • 380 Mt. Vernon Ave. Restored turn of the century. Both Taft and Coolidge visited him here in 1920. Museum is in a bungalow behind the house. 1891–1924.

*Lodging* • 498 E Center St where he often visited his father. His father's doctor's office was at 193 1/2 E Center. 1889–1923.

*Work* • Taught in one-room school known as the White School House, SE corner Main and Williamsport. Now site of WMRN Radio Station. 1882.

*Work* • Marion Mirror in the printing office on Miller Block. 1884–1885.

*Work* • Fite Block at the corner of East and Center Sts opposite the Methodist Church, second floor, 195 E Center, next to present Episcopal Church. Building gone and no marker. 1885–1890.

*Work* • South side E Center St and next to the Episcopal Church and almost opposite

*Tomb of Warren Harding in Marion.*

the county jail. *Marion Star* in the lower half of the building. 229 E Center. Now parking lot. 1890–1915.

*Visit* • Carrie Fulton Phillips House, 417 S Main St on Gospel Hill. Now an empty lot. 1905–1920.

*Visit* • Ann Britton home, 733 E Center St. 1905–.

*Funeral* • 498 E Center St (father's home). Coolidge and Taft attended. 1924.

*Burial* • Marion Memorial Cemetery off OH 423. Buried here temporarily. Section across Vernon Heights Blvd from present tomb. Main entrance on Delaware just before Vernon Heights intersection. 1923–1927.

*Burial* • Tomb on OH 423, south edge of Marion. Full scale Greek Temple style memorial and tomb on Vernon Heights Blvd. President Hoover and Coolidge here for dedication. 1927.

**Hoover**
*Visit* • Harding Memorial Dedication. 6–16–1931.

**Taft**
*Visit* • Harding home, 380 Mt. Vernon Ave. 12–24–1920.

## MENTOR *(Lake County)*

**Garfield**
*Church* • Disciples Church, Main St. 1876–1881.

*Home* • Lawnfield, 1059 Mentor Ave, OH 615 south from OH 2 and follow signs. Entrance fee. 1876–1881.

*Work* • Campaign office behind Lawnfield. 1880.

**Grant**
*Visit* • Garfield home, 1059 Mentor Ave. 1880.

## MIDDLE BASS ISLAND *(Ottawa County)*

**Harrison, WH**
*Work* • Meeting with Commodore Perry. See 352-foot granite column on South Bass Island. 1813.

**Hayes**
*Visit* • Retreat. Also Cleveland, B Harrison, and Taft.

## MINERVA *(Stark County)*

**McKinley**
*Visit* • McKinley farm two miles east of town on Lincoln (US 30) highway. Boyhood years.

## MORELAND HILLS *(Cuyahoga County)*

**Garfield**
*Birthplace* • Log cabin in Orange Township on the end of a ravine sloping down to the Chagrin River. Today the community of Moreland Hills. Located on SOM Center Rd (OH 91). Follow foot

*Lawnfield, home of James Garfield in Mentor.*

trail into woods at the Town Hall and see area of cabin outlined by wooden benches. 1831.

*Education* • Rude one-room district school where he spent his childhood. Take SOM Center Rd between Solon and Moreland Hills to corner of River Rd to site of River Rd School. 1841–1847.

*Home* • See marker on the grounds of the Town Hall. See location of birthplace above. See area of Garfield farm on SOM

Center Rd south of Amos Boynton Farm. 1831–1842; 1843–1856. Amos Boynton (uncle) farm site on W Juniper Rd at SOM Center Dr (OH 91) north of Garfield farm.

## MOSCOW  *(Clermont County)*

### Grant

*Church* • Grant Memorial Church is a modest building of rough native stone. See also Grant House Museum. Adjacent to the park is Point Pleasant. 1824.

*Home* • Grant Memorial State Park has the original homestead of the Grant family.

## MUSKINGUM COUNTY

**Garfield**

*Lodging* • Henry Ballou House. 1851.

*Work* • He taught here in the old school house which still exists. Spring 1851.

## NAVARRE *(Stark County)*

**McKinley**

*Work* • Brick store building NE corner Market and Canal Sts.

## NILES *(Trumbull County)*

**McKinley**

*Birthplace* • 36 S Main St. House burned 1935. Dollar Bank now occupies the site. A plaque is located on the left side of the building. House moved at one time to Riverside Park area but destroyed by vandals. 1843–1853.

*Church* • Niles Methodist Episcopal Church. Burned. 1843– 1852.

*Education* • Fundamentals at Niles public school. Later site of marble and granite company on the main street of town. 1843–1852.

*Site* • National McKinley Birthplace Memorial, 40 N Main at Church St (OH 46). See also statue of McKinley in the courtyard.

**Taft**

*Visit* • McKinley Memorial, 40 N Main St. Dedication. 1917.

## NORTH BEND *(Hamilton County)*

**Harrison, B**

*Birthplace* • North Bend/Cleves, SE cor-

*Memorial to William Harrison in North Bend.*

ner of Symmes and Washington Aves, site. Marker. 1833.

*Church* • North Bend Presbyterian Church, 25 E State Rd (Cleves). 1833–1854.

*Education* • One-room log school house near home for the basics. 1838–1847.

*Honeymoon* • The Point. See below. 1853.

*Home* • The Point, 5 miles below North Bend on the Ohio River at its intersection with the Miami. The two-story brick structure near site of Fort Finney was his boy-hood home. Razed. 1833–1854.

### Harrison, WH

*Marriage* • Home of Dr. Stephen Wood, tennant of Colonel Symmes, 116 Nebo St. 1795.

*Home* • Farm on Ohio River. Farm house burned 1858. 1796–1801, 1814–1817, 1819–1825, 1836–1841.

*Home* • SE corner of Symmes and Washington Aves (Cleves). Demolished 1858. Marker.

*Burial* • Off Cliff Rd one mile east of the intersection of US 50 and OH 128 on Loop Ave south of Harrison Ave in the William Henry Harrison State Park. 1841.

## NORWALK  *(Huron County)*

### Hayes

*Church* • Norwalk Academy Chapel on E Seminary St. 1836.

*Education* • Norwalk Academy, near 80 E Main. Now site of Norwalk High School. 1836–1837.

## ORANGE TOWNSHIP  *(Cuyahoga County)*

### Garfield

*Church* • In childhood walked three miles through the woods to church. 1831–.

*Education* • Rude one-room district school. See also Moreland Hills. Before 1847.

*Work* • Perry Mapes Ashery. 1845–1847.

## OXFORD  *(Butler County)*

### Harrison, B

*Church* • High St. Chapel was located in Old Main replaced by a new Harrison Hall.

*Education* • Oxford College, now Miami University. At the west end, High St passes the attractive faded brick building that for 79 years housed Oxford College. It is now

a women's dormitory. Harrison Hall is the site of Old Main where he held debates. Two dormitories remain that were there when he was a student. 1850–1852.

*Lodging* • He lodged at Mansion House at SW corner of Main and High Sts. 1849.

*Marriage* • 121 High St at home of Caroline Scott (Harrison). House built about 1827. An oil service station is now on site. 1853.

## PEPPER PIKE

### Garfield

*Church* • Garfield Memorial United Methodist Church, Lander Circle at Lander and Chagrin Blvd (OH 87). 1848–1850.

## PIQUA  *(Miami County)*

### Harrison, WH

*Work* • 9845 N Hardin Rd 3 1/2 miles NW of Piqua on OH 66. Marching point. 1812.

## POINT PLEASANT  *(Clermont County)*

### Grant

*Birthplace* • Two-room cabin on the Ohio River, 25 miles east of Cincinnati at the intersection of OH 232 and US 52. 1822.

*Home* • Same as birthplace. 1822–1824.

### Harding

*Visit* • Grant birthplace. 1922.

## POLAND  *(Mahoning County)*

### McKinley

*Church* • Poland Methodist Episcopal Church. The church he attended is now site of Bank One. Present church, built 1903, to which Mrs. McKinley contributed in memory of her husband, is at 1940 Boardman-Poland Rd at US 224. See McKinley Memorial window in the vestibule. 1852–1867.

*Education* • Local public school on the village green later moved to Main St north of the now Withers Apartments. Now called US 224. 1852–1855. See also The Little Red School House, Poland Township. 4515 Center Rd. 1858.

*Education* • Poland Seminary (Methodist), 47 College St off S Main. Now site of Jr. High School. Plaque. 1855–1860.

*Education* • Law School, 24 College St. Previously Lee's Academy for girls. 1855–1860.

*Education* • Law office of Judge Charles E. Glidden, junction of Boardman and Youngstown Sts. 1865–1866.

*Home* • 214 S Main St. Site now parking lot. 1852–1855.

*Home* • 111 S Main St. Site now parking lot. 1855–1867.

*Home* • 21 Riverside Dr. Still standing. 1867–.

*Work* • Kerr District School about four miles from Poland. Exact location unknown. 1860. Later clerked in the town post office on S Main St. Post Office was in the same building as the Case tailor shop, 221 S Main.

*Visit* • 301 S Main, home of his sister. Built about 1845.

*Visit* • Swimming hole on Yellow Creek, identified by a black oak, at the end of Main St. 1850s.

*Visit* • Poland Commons playing ball. Site of Poland Village Town Hall on S Main. 1850s.

*Visit* • Fowler Tavern, site where he enlisted. Old Stone Tavern, 121 Main St. Built 1804. 1861.

*Site* • Soldiers Monument in Riverside Cemetery on Riverside Rd. Dedicated. 1887.

## PUT-IN-BAY *(Ottawa County)*

**Harrison, WH**
   *Work* • 1813.

## RICHWOOD *(Union County)*

**Harding**
   *Visit* • Globe Hotel, Main St. 1899.

## RIPLEY *(Brown County)*

**Grant**
   *Education* • Presbyterian Academy (Ripley College of John Rankin) at Third and Mulberry. 1836–1839.

## SOLON *(Cuyahoga County)*

**Garfield**
   *Church* • Disciples Chapel, Bainbridge Rd at OH 91 (SOM Center Rd). Also houses Historical Society. 1848–1850.

   *Work* • Taught and did carpentry work. 1849.

## SUNBURY *(Delaware County)*

**Presidents**
   *Visit* • Sunbury Tavern (now Hopkins House). B Harrison and Hayes.

## TOLEDO *(Lucas County)*

**Harrison, WH**
   *Work* • 1812–1813.

**Johnson, A**
   *Visit* • Island House. 1866.

## WARRENSVILLE TOWNSHIP
*(Cuyahoga County)*

**Garfield**
   *Work* • Taught here and at Blue Rock. 1850.

## YOUNGSTOWN *(Mahoning County)*

**Presidents**
   *Site* • The Butler Institute of American Art has a collection of miniatures of American Presidents. 524 Wick Ave.

## McKinley

*Visit* • Dr. John Deetrick House, 220 N Phelps St. 1899.

*Visit* • Platform at B & O railroad station for last speech of his tour. Mahoning Ave. 1899.

## ZANESVILLE  *(Muskingum County)*

### Garfield

*Visit* • Black's Music Hall (now the second floor of Eckerd Drug Store) where he gave a campaign speech. 1873.

Oklahoma

Oklahoma
City

40

1

1. Kennedy Monument,
   *Big Cedar*

# OKLAHOMA

## BIG CEDAR *(LeFlore County)*

**Johnson, LB**
> *Visit* • Dedicated Kennedy Monument, OK 103 Ouachita National Forest. 9–25–1964.

**Kennedy**
> *Site* • Kennedy Monument. Site where he made his only speech in Oklahoma. Camp Doniphan (adjoining Fort Sill) Comanche County near Lawton. 10–29–1961.

**Truman**
> *Visit* • Military site. 1917–1919.

## EUFALA *(McIntosh County)*

**Johnson, LB**
> *Visit* • Eufala Dam dedication. 9–25–1964.

## FORT GIBSON *(Wagoner County)*

**Taylor**
> *Travel* • OK 10. Commander of the post. 1841.

## FORT TOWSON *(Choctaw County)*

**Taylor**
> *Travel* • US 70. Superintended the post. 1841.

## FORT WASHITA *(Johnston/Marshall Counties)*

**Taylor**
> *Travel* • OK 22. Built the fort. 1842.

## OKLAHOMA CITY *(Oklahoma County)*

**Harding**
> *Visit* • State Fair Grounds in stock pavilion for a major campaign speech, NW Tenth St and May Ave. 1920.

**Reagan**
> *Visit* • State Capitol, Lincoln Blvd between Twenty-first and Twenty-third Sts. Skirvin Hotel. 3–16–1982.

*Fort Washita, constructed under the command of Zachary Taylor.*

## PAWHUSKA *(Osage County, Osage Indian Reservation)*

**Hoover**
> *Lodging* • Uncle Laban Miles home, 621 Granview St. 1882–1883.

## POTEAU *(LeFlore County)*

**Presidents**
> *Visit* • Kerr Country Mansion, 1507 S McKenna, 6 miles south of Poteau. Kennedy and LB Johnson visited.

## STILLWATER *(Payne County)*

**Nixon**
> *Visit* • Oklahoma State University, Lewis Field. 5–11–1974.

# OREGON

## ASHLAND *(Jackson County)*

**Lincoln**
> *Site* • Lithia Park. Marble statue.

## NEWBERG *(Yamhill County)*

**Hoover**
> *Church* • Meeting House, 414 N Meridian. Friends Pacific Academy. 1885–1888.

> *Education* • Pacific Academy (now George Fox College), run by the Society of Friends. 414 N Meridian. He shared a room with his brother in one of the newly constructed buildings. 1885–1887.

> *Home* • 115 S River Rd and E Second St. 1885–1888.

## PORTLAND *(Multnomah County)*

**Presidents**
> *Visit* • Benson Hotel, 309 SW Broadway. Carter, Ford, and Nixon.

> *Visit* • Portland Hotel, SW Sixth St between Yamhill and Morrison Sts. T Roosevelt 1903, Taft 1909, and Wilson 1919.

**Ford**
> *Visit* • Lewis and Clark College, Pumplin Sports Center, 0615 SW Palatine Hills Rd. 5–22–1976.

**Harding**
> *Visit* • Multnomah Hotel, 319 SW Pine. 1923.

**Hayes**
> *Visit* • Esmond Hotel at Front and Morrison Sts. 1880.

**Lincoln**
> *Site* • Statue of Lincoln on square, SW Main and Madison Sts.

**Nixon**
> *Church* • First Friends Church. 9–21–1952.

**Taft**
> *Church* • First Unitarian Church, 1011 SW Twelfth. 1909.

> *Church* • Laid cornerstone of First Universalist Church (East Portland). 1909.

**Wilson**
> *Visit* • Spoke at the auditorium. Admission was given to those who received tick-

1. Hoover home, *Newberg*
2. Hoover home, *Salem*

ets in a state-wide lottery. 1919. Also here 1911.

## SALEM *(Marion County)*

**Hoover**

*Church* • Highland Ave Friends Church, South Highland Ave. 1889–1890.

*Education* • Capitol Business College, Chemeketa, SW corner Commercial. 1889–1890.

*Home* • Hazel and Highland Aves, NW corner of Highland. 1888–1891.

*Work* • Oregon Land Company, 325 Commercial St. 1888–1891.

**Nixon**

*Travel* • State Capitol. September 1952.

**Roosevelt, T**

*Visit* • State Capitol. 5–21–1903.

**Taft**

*Visit* • Carroll College, Benton Ave. 1909.

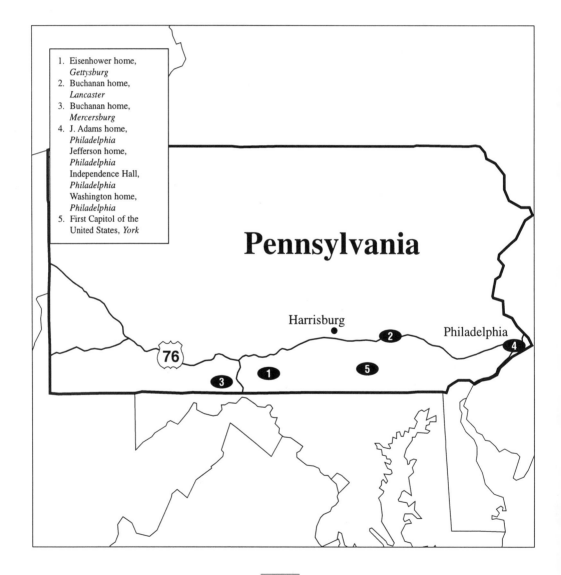

1. Eisenhower home,
   *Gettysburg*
2. Buchanan home,
   *Lancaster*
3. Buchanan home,
   *Mercersburg*
4. J. Adams home,
   *Philadelphia*
   Jefferson home,
   *Philadelphia*
   Independence Hall,
   *Philadelphia*
   Washington home,
   *Philadelphia*
5. First Capitol of the
   United States, *York*

# Pennsylvania

Harrisburg

Philadelphia

76

# PENNSYLVANIA

## BEDFORD SPRINGS  *(Bedford County)*

**Presidents**
   *Visit* • Epsy House. B Harrison, Polk, Taylor, and Tyler.

**Buchanan**
   *Lodging* • Bedford Springs Hotel, about four miles south of Bedford on old US 220. 1816–.

**Washington**
   *Visit* • Espy House, 123 E Pitt St. Headquarters. 1794.

## BETHLEHEM  *(Lehigh County)*

**Presidents**
   *Visit* • Sun Inn (still stands as a modern hotel). 560-564 Main St. J Adams, Buchanan, and Washington.

## BRYN MAWR  *(Montgomery County)*

**Wilson**
   *Church* • Bryn Mawr Baptist Church on Gulph Road near baptist manse at 905 Gulph Rd. 1885–1888.

*Home* • Wildgoss Boarding House. Address unknown. 1885.

*Home* • Betweenery on the edge of Bryn Mawr's campus. 1885–1887.

*Home* • 905 Gulph Rd. 1887.

*Work* • Bryn Mawr College, Taylor Hall. 1885–1888.

## CARLISLE  *(Cumberland County)*

**Buchanan**
   *Education* • Dickinson College, W High St. 1807–1809.

   *Lodging* • He lived with Professor James McCormick. 1807–1809.

**Washington**
   *Church* • First Presbyterian, NW corner of Public Square at intersetion of Hanover and High Sts. 1794.

   *Visit* • Blaine House (private), 4 N Hanover St. Marker. 1794.

   *Visit* • Carlisle Barracks, .5 mile NE Carlisle on US 11. He reviewed the troops here. Second oldest army post in the US. 1794.

   *Visit* • Courthouse, City Square. 1794.

## CHADDS FORD *(Delaware County)*

**Washington**

*Visit* • Battle of Brandywine. Used Benjamin Ring House as his headquarters. House reconstructed. 9–11–1777.

## CHESTER *(Delaware County)*

**Washington**

*Visit* • Mary Withy's Inn or Washington House (also Pennsylvania Arms), Market St between Fourth and Fifth Sts. 1777.

## CHEYNEY *(Delaware County)*

**Carter**

*Visit* • Cheyney State College. 5–20–1979.

## CHURCH HILL (NEAR MERCERSBURG) *(Franklin County)*

**Buchanan**

*Church* • The Presbyterian Church of the Upper West Conococheague, County Rd 3009. 1791.

## CONEMAUGH *(Cambria County)*

**Grant**

*Travel* • RR station. 1866.

## COVE GAP *(Franklin County)*

**Buchanan**

*Birthplace* • On SR 16. Marked by a stone pyramid in the James Buchanan State Forest. 1791.

*Home* • Same as birthplace. 1791–1794.

## CRAFTON *(Allegheny County)*

**Jackson**

*Visit* • Obey House, Steuben and Obey Sts. 1820s.

## CRESSON SPRINGS *(Cambria County)*

**Harrison, B**

*Church* • Mountain House. 1890–.

*Lodging* • Lived in a Queen Anne cottage here in the mountains west of Altoona. 1890.

*Visit* • Carnegie House. 12 Third St. 1890s.

## DUNWOODIE FARM (NEAR MERCERSBURG) *(Franklin County)*

**Buchanan**

*Home* • About 5 miles east of the Gap and 2 miles east of Mercersburg on the West Conococheague Creek. 1794–1796.

## EPHRATA *(Lancaster County)*

**Buchanan**

*Visit* • 1860s.

**Jefferson**

*Visit* • The Cloisters. 1780s.

**Lincoln**

*Visit* • Mountain Spring Hotel (Camp Silver Bell), Main and Garden Sts. Buchanan also guest. 1861.

**Washington**

*Visit* • Visited at times in Johann Peter Miller's House, The Cloisters, at the western boundary of town. 1780s.

## FORT DUQUESNE *(Allegheny County, County Rd 837)*

**Washington**

*Work* • Engaged in fighting here in the French/Indian War. 1758.

## FORT LE BOEUF (NEAR NOW WATERFORD) *(Erie County, off US 19)*

**Washington**

*Work* • Delivered message here during French Indian War. 1753.

*Memorial to site where Abraham Lincoln made the Gettysburg address.*

## FORT NECESSITY  *(Fayette County, 10 miles east of present Uniontown, off US 40)*

**Washington**

*Work* • Erected fortification. Great Meadows with stockade. Later bought the Great Meadows clearing. Replica of original fort. 1754.

*Work* • See also Washington Tavern which is built on a 234-acre tract which he owned. 1769 to 1799.

## FRANKLIN  *(Venango County)*

**Washington**

*Work* • Fort Machault at Sixth and Elk. French fort reconnoitered.

*Work* • Fort Venango at Eighth and Elk. French fort reconnoitered.

## GERMANTOWN  *(NW section of Philadelphia)*

**Jefferson**

*Visit* • Stenton House. See Washington below.

**Washington**

*Travel* • Stenton House. Stopped here before the Battle of Brandywine. Eighteenth and Courtland Sts. 1777.

## GETTYSBURG  *(Adams County)*

**Carter**

*Travel* • Gettysburg National Park. Mamie Eisenhower home. 7–6–1978.

**Eisenhower**

*Home* • Rented a house for himself and his family on the Gettysburg College campus, Spring Ave. 1918.

*Home* • Former Tau Omega home on North Washington St. 1918.

*Home* • Adjacent to the southwest boundary Gettysburg National Military Park. 1954, 1961–1969.

*Work* • Commander of tank Training School at Camp Colt. 1917–1918.

*Work* • 300 Carlisle St on the Gettysburg College Campus where he had an office. 1961–1969.

### Lincoln
*Visit* • Lincoln Room, Wills House, Center Square. Room where he wrote the Gettysburg Address has been preserved. 1863.

*Site* • Gettysbury National Military Park, US 15, 30. The site where Lincoln made the Gettysburg Address is marked by the Lincoln Address Memorial, near the west entrance to the cemetery.

### Nixon
*Visit* • Eisenhower home. October 1967.

### Roosevelt, FD
*Visit* • Battlefield speech. 5–30–1934.

## HARRISBURG *(Dauphin County)*

### Buchanan
*Lodging* • Golden Eagle on Market Square while at the Assembly. 1814–1816.

*Work* • Capitol. Member House of Representatives. The courthouse then serving as the state capitol stood at the head of the square about three blocks from the river. The Dauphin County courtroom on the first floor served as the chamber of the assembly with the Senate on the second floor. 1814–1816.

### Harrison, WH
*Work* • Zion Lutheran Church. Nominated for president. December 1839.

### Johnson, A
*Visit* • Bolton House. 1866.

### Roosevelt, FD
*Visit* • State Capitol. 10–29–1936.

### Roosevelt, T
*Church* • Zion Lutheran Church. 4–2–1903.

*Visit* • Dedicated new Capitol, Capitol Hill at Third and State Sts. 10–4–1906.

### Tyler
*Work* • Delegate to Whig National Convention where he was nominated for vice president. Zion Lutheran Church. December 1839.

## JOHNSTOWN *(Cambria County)*

### Johnson, A
*Travel* • RR station at Walnut St. Renovated. September 1866.

## JUMONVILLE *(Fayette County)*

### Washington
*Work* • Half King's Rocks where he met with Delaware Indian Chief Tanacharison at the Jumonville victory.

## KUTZTOWN *(Berks County)*

### Adams, J
*Visit* • Old Kemp House (now called Whispering Springs), US 222. 1777.

### Washington
*Visit* • See above entry. 1782.

## LANCASTER *(Lancaster County)*

### Adams, J
*Visit* • Courthouse on Centre Square on way to new capital in Washington, DC. 5–29–1800. Also here 9–27–1777.

### Buchanan
*Church* • English Presbyterian Church, 140 E Orange St where he rented pew 23. 1812–1868.

*Education* • Studied law under James Hopkins, corner of E King and Duke Sts. 1809–1812.

*Home* • 42 E King St where he purchased a small tavern for living quarters. He

*Wheatlands, home of James Buchanan.*

bought several buildings in the SW corner of the square as an investment. 1813–1821.

***Home*** • 52 E King St. 1833–1848.

***Home*** • 1120 Marietta Ave (Wheatland Estate). 1840–1857; 1861–1868.

***Lodging*** • Widow Dutchman's Inn across the street from Hopkin's mansion at the corner of E King and Duke Sts. 1809–1821.

***Lodging*** • White Swan Hotel on the town square where he took meals. Site only. 1809–1821.

***Work*** • Law Practice at 42 E King St. 1812–1814. 1817–1821. 1849–1853.

***Visit*** • Masonic Lodge 43, Heritage Center. Joined 1816. 1823.

***Death*** • 1120 Marietta Ave. 1868.

***Funeral*** • 1120 Marietta Ave. 1868.

***Burial*** • Woodward Hill Cemetery, 511 S Queen St. 1868.

**Taylor**

***Visit*** • White Swan Hotel, Town Square. 1849.

**Washington**

***Visit*** • Salisbury White Horse, Cross Keys and West King St, one block west of Center Square. Site only. 1777.

***Visit*** • Courthouse on Centre Square. 7–4–1791.

## LEBANON *(Lebanon County)*

**Harrison, WH**

***Visit*** • Buck Hotel, corner of Eighth and Cumberland (now a drug store on the ground floor). 1841.

## LOCK HAVEN *(Clinton County)*

**Carter**
> *Visit* • Fallon Hotel, 131 E Water St. 1968.

## LUMBERVILLE *(Bucks County)*

**Washington**
> *Visit* • Black Bass Hotel. One place he did not sleep since proprietor refused. 1777.

## McCONNELLSBURG *(Fulton County)*

**Presidents**
> *Visit* • Fulton House, 110-112 Lincoln Way East. Still operating. John Adams (occupied front room to right of stairs on second floor), Buchanan, WH Harrison, and Taylor.

## McKEESPORT *(Allegheny County)*

**Nixon**
> *Visit* • Penn McKee Hotel, 124-132 Fifth Ave. 1947.

## MEADVILLE *(Crawford County)*

**McKinley**
> *Education* • Allegheny College. See Bentley Hall between Park Ave and N Main St. 1860.

> *Lodging* • He had a room in a house north of the college campus. Building still stands, became a home for orphans of Odd Fellows. 1860.

**Washington**
> *Work* • Bicentennial Oak near NE corner Main and Randolph Sts. Reported to have stopped here on the way to Fort Le Beouf. 1753.

## MERCERSBURG *(Franklin County)*

**Buchanan**
> *Birthplace* • Log cabin moved to the campus of Mercersburg Academy from Cove Gap. 1791.

> *Church* • Presbyterian Church at the corner of Seminary and Park Sts. 1796–1809.

> *Education* • Old Stone Academy (and the common schools), 43 W California St where the Presbyterian parsonage now stands. 1797–1807.

> *Home* • North Main St. Now the James Buchanan Hotel. There is a marker across the street for birthplace of his niece who was his hostess in the White House. He spent his childhood here after age of five. 1796–1809.

**Carter**
> *Visit* • Buchanan birthplace. 7–6–1978.

## MILFORD *(Pike County)*

**Kennedy**
> *Visit* • Pinchot Institute (Pinchot Grey Towers estate), off US 66. Dedication. 9–24–1963.

## OHIOPYLE *(Fayette County)*

**Washington**
> *Work* • Ohiopyle Falls on the Youghiogheny River is the site which he reconnoitered on his first military expedition. SR 381. May 1754.

## PERRYOPOLIS *(Fayette County)*

**Washington**
> *Site* • Grist mill built for and owned by him on East Independence St. 1774–1789.

## PHILADELPHIA *(Philadelphia County)*

**Presidents**
> *Visit* • Bellevue-Stratford Hotel, Broad and Walnut Sts. Ford, Nixon, Reagan, and Truman.

**Presidents**
> *Visit* • Carpenters Hall, 320 Chestnut St.

**Presidents**
> *Visit* • Congress Hall, SE corner Sixth and Chestnut Sts.

*Family home of James Buchanan in Mercersburg.*

**Presidents**

*Visit* • Continental Hotel, SE corner Ninth St and Chestnut Sts. Grant, Hayes, A Johnson, and Lincoln.

**Presidents**

*Visit* • Convention Hall, Thirty-fourth and Vine Sts (Civic Center Blvd). Eisenhower, Hoover, LB Johnson, Kennedy, FD Roosevelt, and Truman.

**Presidents**

*Visit* • Independence Hall, Chestnut between Fifth and Sixth Sts. Capital Pennsylvania. 1683–1799. Capitol of the United States. 1790–1800.

**Adams, J**

*Church* • Presbyterian Meeting House. Site at corner of High (Market) St and White Horse Alley (now Bank St). 1774–1800.

*Church* • St. Peter's, Third and Pine Sts. 1774–1800.

*Church* • Christ Church, Second St above Market St. 1774–1800.

*Church* • Baptist Meeting House, Lagrange Place just north of Christ Church. 1774–1800.

*Church* • Second Presbyterian Church, NW corner of Third and Arch Sts. (church now at Twenty-second and Walnut). 1774.

*Church* • Third St Presbyterian Church (also called Pine St Church). 1774–1800.

*Church* • St. Mary's Roman Catholic Church, 224-250 S Fourth St. Marker. Built 1763. 1774.

*Church* • Zion Lutheran. Fourth and Cherry Sts. 1799.

*Home* • House two miles out of city with view of the Schuykill River off Vine St. at northern boundary of city. Bush Hill area. 1790.

*Home* • He took over the Washington dwelling at the corner of Sixth and Market Sts–an ample brick mansion–the President's House. He preferred to stay in another house between Fifth and Sixth on Market. 1797–1800.

*Lodging* • Slate House SE, corner Norris' Alley and Second St. Demolished. 1868.

*Lodging* • At the Stone House opposite the City Tavern held by Mrs. Yard on Arch St. 1774.

*Lodging* • Walnut St (southside) between Second and Third Sts, at the house of Mr. Duncan. Now office buildings, no marker. 1777.

*Lodging* • Moved to Rev. Mr. Sprout on Third St. 1777.

*Lodging* • As vice president lodged at Francis' 11-13 S Fourth St. No marker. 1790s.

*Work* • Carpenters Hall. 1774.

*Work* • Independence Hall. 1774–1776.

*Work* • Presided over the Senate as vice president. West annex of Independence Hall on second floor just above the House of Representatives. 1790–1797.

*Work* • President's office. 1797–1800. Inauguration, Congress Hall, in the House of Representatives chamber. 1797.

*Visit* • City Tavern, west side Second St between Walnut and Chestnut. 1790–1800.

*Visit* • The Indian Queen, east side of Fourth St below Market. No marker. 1790–1800.

*Visit* • Oeller's Hotel across the street from Congress Hall at Sixth and Chestnut. Monroe also here. No marker. 1797.

### Buchanan

*Visit* • 518 Walnut St. 1834–.

*Visit* • Merchant's Exchange Hotel, 40-48 N Fourth St below Arch. 1856–.

### Carter

*Education* • Radar School for 3 weeks. 1946.

*Visit* • Walnut Street Theater, Walnut and Ninth. First debate with Ford. 9–24–1976.

*Visit* • Independence Hall to receive Liberty Medal. 7–4–1990.

### Ford

*Visit* • Independence Hall. 9–6–1974. 7–4–1976.

*Visit* • University of Pennsylvania, bounded by Chestnut, Pine, Thirty-second and Fortieth Sts. Commencement. 5–18–1975.

### Grant

*Visit* • Home of George W. Childs, 2128 Walnut St. 1870–1880.

*Site* • Academy of Music, SW corner Broad and Locust. RNC. Renomination. June 1872.

### Harrison, W

*Education* • University of Pennsylvania Medical School. Studied with Benjamin Rush. 1791.

*Visit* • Marshall House, College of Physicians and Surgeons, 19 S Twenty-second St. 1791.

*Work* • Delegate. Met in Congress Hall. 1799.

### Hayes

*Visit* • Fairmont Park. Benjamin Franklin Parkway for Centennial. Exhibition Building. July 1876. May 1877.

*Visit* • US Mint, SE corner Seventeenth and Spring Garden Sts. Reception at Independence Hall. 1878.

### Jackson

*Work* • US House of Representatives, Congress Hall. 1796–1797.

*Work* • US Senator, Congress Hall, second floor. 1797–1798.

*Visit* • 1795. On Presidential tour. 1796. 1797. 1833.

### Jefferson

*Church* • St. Peter's Episcopal, Third and Pine. Also attended Christ Church at times. 1776–.

*Home* • House located near Gray's Ferry on the Schuykill River, then a few miles outside Philadelphia. 1790–1793.

*Home* • 5275 Germantown Ave at the Clarkson-Watson House. 1793.

*Home* • 806 Market St across from the State Department. 1797–1800.

*Lodging* • Benjamin Randolph House on Chestnut St between Third and Fourth Sts. 1775.

*Lodging* • City Tavern, west side of Second St at the corner of Gold St and Bank Alley (between Chestnut and Walnut). 1775–.

*Lodging* • Hilzheimer House (later Gratz store), SE corner of Market and Seventh Sts. Wrote Declaration of Independence here. 1776.

*Lodging* • Indian Queen, east side of Fourth St below Market. Razed.

*Lodging* • With Madison and others at the home of Mrs. House and her daughter, Mrs. Elizabeth Trist at Fifth and Market. 1780–1783.

*Lodging* • Francis Hotel, 11-13 S Fourth St while he was vice president. 1797–1800.

*Work* • Pennsylvania State House, now known as Independence Hall, as delegate to Continental Congress. 1775–1776.

*Work* • Congress Hall, as member of Congress from Virginia. 1783–1784.

*Work* • 13 High (Market) St with office as Secretary of State. Later on Arch St, two doors east of Sixth St. The Duponceau House on Sixth St near Chestnut was the first office of Foreign Affairs of the US. 1790–1793.

*Work* • Vice president presiding over Senate, second floor of Congress Hall. 1797–1801.

*Visit* • American Philosophical Society, 104 South Fifth St. He served as president. At least 12 American presidents have been members. 1801–1809.

*Visit* • Bartram's Gardens, Elmwood Ave west of Fifty- fourth St. 1790–1793.

*Visit* • Shippen House, SE corner Fourth and Locust Sts. Sometime meeting place of the Philosophical Society.

*Visit* • Benjamin Franklin in Franklin Court. Museum now on site. 1790–1793.

*Visit* • Strawberry Mansion in Fairmont Park near Dauphin St entrance. 1790–1793.

*Visit* • Lemon Hill in Fairmont Park, East River Dr. 1790–1793.

*Visit* • Woodford Mansion in Fairmont Park, Thirty-third and Dauphin Sts.

**Kennedy**
*Visit* • Independence Hall. 7–4–1962.

**Lincoln**
*Visit* • Delegate to the National Convention of the Whig Party. Held in Chinese Museum, Ninth and Samson. June 1848.

*Visit* • Independence Hall. 2–21–1861.

*Funeral* • Lay in state in Independence Hall. 4–4–1865.

*Site* • Lincoln Monument on Lemon Hill in Fairmont Park.

**McKinley**
*Visit* • Hotel Walton, Broad and Locust Sts for Veteran celebration. 1899.

*Site* • Exposition Auditorium. Renomination. June 1900.

**Madison**
*Church* • St. Peter's Episcopal Church, Third and Pine Sts. 1780–.

*Lodging* • In a house belonging to James Monroe on Spruce St. 1794.

*Lodging* • In a large fashionable dwelling on Spruce St. 1796.

*Lodging* • With Mrs. Mary House at Fifth and Market Sts, a block from the Pennsylvania State House (Independence Hall).

*Work* • Independence Hall. Delegate to the Continental Congress. 1780–1783. 1787–1788. Member of Congress of the

Confederation. Later member of the House of Representatives when the capital moved to Philadelphia. 1790–1797.

*Visit* • Dolly Payne lived with her mother at Fouth and Walnut. 1780–1793.

## Monroe

*Lodging* • Settled into lodgings arranged by Jefferson. 1791.

*Work* • Congress Hall. End of the second floor when he took his seat in the Senate. 1790–1794.

## Pierce

*Lodging* • McKibben's Merchant Hotel, 40-48 N Fourth St on his way to inauguration. 1853.

## Roosevelt, FD

*Visit* • Convention Hall. 6–27–1936.

## Roosevelt, T

*Visit* • Hotel Walton. 1900.

*Visit* • Exposition Hall. Nomination as vice president. 1900.

## Truman

*Visit* • Convention Hall, for his acceptance speech. Stayed at the Hotel Majestic. 7–15–1948.

*Visit* • Chapel of the Four Chaplains, Russell H. Conwell Memorial Church, Broad and Berks Sts. 2–27–1951.

## Tyler

*Honeymoon* • Wedding trip to Philadelphia with his second wife. 1844.

## Van Buren

*Visit* • Washington Hotel (later Merchant's Hotel) regarded as unequaled in the country. Site 40-48 N Fourth St. 1839.

## Washington

*Church* • St. Peter's, Third and Pine Sts, pew no. 41. 1790–1797.

*Church* • Christ Church, Second St above Market St. 1790–1797.

*Church* • Market Square Church directly across from Morris House at 5441 Garmantown Ave. Market Square Presbyterian Church built on site of original. 1793.

*Church* • Zion German Lutheran Church, until 1870 at Fourth and Cherry Sts. Memorial service, "First in War..." 1799.

*Home* • President's House, 528-530 Market St, one door east from the SE corner of Sixth St. Marker. This street was the site of many famous houses. 1793–1797.

*Home* • 5441 Germantown Ave at Deshler-Morris House. 1793.

*Work* • Carpenters Hall for First Continental Congress. 1774.

*Work* • Independence Hall for Continental Congress. Presided over Convention. 1774, 1775, 1787. In the east room, now known as the Declaration Chamber, he accepted his appointment as General and Commander-in-Chief of the Continental Army. 7–16–1775.

*Work* • Congress Hall. In the House of Representatives, for second inauguration. This and John Adams's inauguration (1797) were the only inaugurations held here. This was originally the County building. 1793.

*Work* • Congress Hall. From here he delivered his Farewell Address.

*Visit* • Old slate-roof house, Second St between Walnut and Chestnut where he lodged at times after 1774. William Penn lived here. 1699–1701.

*Visit* • West side of Second St above Walnut. He probably stayed with Dr. Wm Shippen, Jr., Locust and Fourth Sts. He often ate at the New Tavern (or City Tavern). 1774.

*Visit* • North Third St. His lodging during the First Continental Congress is uncertain but seems it was at Wm Carson's, a tavern called the Harp and Crown, on N Third St just below Arch St. 1774.

*Visit* • Chestnut St between Third and Fourth Sts. Lodged with Mrs. Randolph. 1775.

*Visit* • Benjamin Chew's home on S Third St (No. 110) between Walnut and Spruce. November 1779 to March 1780.

*Visit* • Watson House, 5275-5277 Germantown Ave. Spent several nights here. 1790. 1793.

*Visit* • 9 N Eighth St. Lodged with Mrs. Rosannah White for a month. 1798.

*Visit* • Half Moon Tavern (formerly State House Inn) directly across Chestnut St from State House (Independence Hall). No markers. 1790s.

*Visit* • Powell House, 244 S Third St.

*Visit* • Gilbert Stuart studio, 5140 Germantown. 1796–.

*Visit* • Stuart studio in house at the SE corner of Fifth and Chestnut Sts where he sat for at least two portraits.

*Visit* • Old City Hall at SW corner Fifth and Chestnut. Built 1791.

*Visit* • Strawberry Mansion just beyond the Woodford Mansion at Thirty-third and Dauphin Sts.

*Visit* • Lemon Hill Mansion, Fairmont Park.

*Travel* • Stenton Mansion, Eighteenth and Courtland Sts. Used as headquarters during the Revolutionary War.

*Site* • Washington Monument on the Ben Franklin Parkway and Spring Garden St in front of the Philadelphia Museum of Art.

## PITTSBURGH  *(Allegheny County)*

**Harrison, B**
*Visit* • Carnegie Library, 4400 Forbes Ave. Dedication. 2–13–1890.

**Harrison, WH**
*Work* • Fort Pitt. Point State Park at confluence of Allegheny, Monongahela, and Ohio Rivers. 1791.

*Visit* • Tannehill's Tavern, Water St. 1792.

*Visit* • Pittsburgh House. January 1841.

**Johnson, A**
*Travel* • St. Charles Hotel. 1866.

**McKinley**
*Church* • Christ Methodist Episcopal Church, corner of Penn and Eighth Sts. 8–28–1899.

**Washington**
*Work* • See Fort Duquesne. Fort Pitt at Point Park. See also blockhouse, 25 Penn Ave. 1753. 1758.

*Work* • Washington Crossing Bridge, Fortieth St at Allegheny River. 1753.

*Site* • Arbuckle Coffee Building between Wood St, Strawberry Alley, and 808 Liberty Ave. See busts of Washington and Lincoln on exterior wall.

## POTTSTOWN  *(Montgomery County)*

**Washington**
*Visit* • The Trappe about 9 miles from Pottsgrove. Headquarters. 9–21–1794 to 9–26–1794.

## SCENERY HILL  *(Washington County)*

**Jackson**
*Visit* • Century Inn near center of town, US 40. 1825. On the way to inauguration. 2–2–1829.

## SCRANTON  *(Lackawanna County)*

**Clinton**
*Travel* • Court St Methodist Church for funeral of Hugh Rodham. 1993.

## SMITHLAND  *(Clarion County)*

**Buchanan**
*Visit* • Smithland Hotel, south of SR 861 past Leatherwood Presbyterian Church. June 1843.

## SOMERFIELD  *(Sommerset County)*

**Monroe**
*Visit* • Great Crossings Bridge. Dedicated. Visible only during dry season. July 4, 1818.

## Washington

*Travel* • See marker near Great Crossings Bridge indicating he crossed 1/2 mile above on military expedition. 11–18–1753.

## STATE COLLEGE  *(Centre County)*

**Eisenhower**

*Visit* • Pennsylvania State University. Off Bus US 322. 6–11–1955.

## SWARTHMORE

**Johnson, LB**

*Visit* • Swarthmore College, Chester Rd (SR 320). 6–8–1964

## TAWAMENCIN  *(Chester County)*

**Washington**

*Travel* • Was at the Frederick Wampole farmhouse during the winter sojourn at Valley Forge.

## UPLAND  *(Elk County)*

**Grant**

*Visit* • Wilcox-Kane-Clay House on Wilcox-Clermont Rd north of Wilcox. 1868.

**Roosevelt, T.**

*Visit* • Clay Mansion on Wilcox-Clermont Rd north of Wilcox. 1906.

## VALLEY FORGE  *(Chester County. I-76 and US 422)*

**Ford**

*Visit* • Valley Forge State Park. 7–4–1976

**Hoover**

*Visit* • 5–30–1931.

**Monroe**

*Work* • 1777. See Stirling headquarters where he often stayed.

**Washington**

*Travel* • Winter headquarters. Peter Wentz Homestead served as headquarters. 1777–1778. See also battlefield.

## WASHINGTON  *(Washington County)*

**Presidents**

*Visit* • Sign of General Jackson Tavern on the corner of S Main and West Strawberry Sts. Torn down 1889. W Harrison, Jackson, Monroe, Polk, and Taylor.

**Grant**

*Visit* • Laid cornerstone of the town hall. 1868.

**Taylor**

*Visit* • At the Old Globe Inn, W corner of S Main St and W Strawberry Alley. 1849.

**Washington**

*Visit* • Current First Presbyterian Church (1868) built on one of two lots presented to him. SE corner Wheeling and College Sts.

## WASHINGTON CROSSING

*(Washington Crossing State Park at the north side of bridge on Route 532.)*

**Washington**

*Visit* • Old Ferry Inn. Christmas 1776.

## WATERFORD  *(Erie County)*

**Taylor**

*Lodging* • Eagle Hotel on US 19 at corner of High and First Sts. Restored. 1848.

**Washington**

*Work* • Washington Sentinel Tree. Legend he climbed to reconnoiter the French Fort LeBoeuf. On US 19 1/2 mile from Eagle Hotel. On private property behind supermarket. 1753.

*Work* • Washington Monument (only memorial of him in British uniform). High and First Sts. 1753.

## WOMELSDORF  *(Lebanon County)*

**Washington**

*Visit* • Seltzer House, Tulpehocken Rd. 1793.

# YORK  *(York County)*

## Adams, J

*Work* • James Smith law office at corner of S George St amd Mason Alley while presiding over Board of War. 1777.

*Work* • Courthouse. Main entrance was on S George St. Here on second floor for Continental Congress. 1777.

*Visit* • General Daniel Roberdeau house, formerly Globe Inn. S George St on Centre Square next to Colonial Hotel and opposite Christ Lutheran Church. 1777.

*Visit* • Golden Plough Tavern on West Market St. 1777.

*Visit* • Wright's Ferry over Susquehanna River. Crossed here to join Continental Congress in York. 1777.

## Buchanan

*Visit* • dined Henry Welsh House on W Market St. 3–6–1861.

*Visit* • Courthouse on Centre Square. 7–1–1848.

*Visit* • Golden Horse Inn, corner Market and Water Sts. 1840.

## Garfield

*Visit* • Jeremiah Black House, Brockie, 2 miles SW of York. 1880s.

## Grant

*Visit* • Accompanying Johnson; see below.

*Visit* • Home of Erastus H. Wesier to see some fine horses. April 1865.

## Harrison, WH

*Church* • First Presbyterian was on north side of E Market and east side of Queen St. Demolished 1860. 10–8–1836.

## Jackson

*Visit* • Hammersly Hotel, then Ziegle and renamed Sign of General Jackson and later site of Hartman Building. SE corner Centre Square and George St. 1819.

## Johnson, A

*Visit* • Washington House on E Market St and Centre Square near Duke. Was Spangler Inn, later known as Sign of General Washington and then Washington House. Demolished 1885. More important public men entertained here than at any other place in York. April 1865.

## Taylor

*Visit* • Washington House. See Johnson above. 8–10–1849.

## Van Buren

*Visit* • White Hall Hotel (later National House), NE corner Beaver and Market Sts. 6–21–1839.

*Visit* • Washington House on E Market and Centre Square. 1840.

## Washington

*Church* • First Zion Reformed Church, W. Market St. Burned. 4–3–1791.

*Church* • See First Presbyterian Church at the NE corner of Market and Queen Sts.

*Visit* • Baltzer Spangler's Tavern on Market St. Later called Washington House.

*Visit* • Thomas Hartley House on E Market in front of Trinity United Church of Christ. Marker. July 1791.

*Visit* • Courthouse. 4–2–1791.

*Visit* • Wright's Ferry over Susquehanna River. Crossed. 1791. 1794.

GEOGRAPHIC GUIDE TO LANDMARKS

Woonsocket ●

# Rhode Island

Providence ●

⬡ 95

Newport
1

1. St. Mary's Church,
   *Newport*

# RHODE ISLAND

## BRISTOL *(Bristol County)*

**Presidents**

*Visit* • Linden Pl 500 Hope St. Arthur, Jackson, and Monroe.

**Washington**

*Visit* • Mt Hope Farm at 250 Metacon Ave. Home of Governor Braddock. March 1781.

## CHARLESTOWN *(Washington County)*

**Bush**

*Education* • Naval Air Station for training. 1943–1944.

## MELVILLE

**Kennedy**

*Work* • PT Melville Training School, Narragansett Bay. Promoted to lieutenant junior grade. October to December 1942.

## NEWPORT *(Newport County)*

**Arthur**

*Visit* • Stone Villa. 1884.

**Cleveland**

*Visit* • Chateau Nooga, corner of Bellevue and Narragansett. 1889. 1893.

**Eisenhower**

*Visit* • US Naval Base. Old Colony House, Washington Square. 9–4–1957 to 9–30–1957. 7–11–1960.

*Visit* • Commandant's Residence, Quarters No. 1 on Fort Adams, Harrison Ave. Used as Summer White House, staying in an admiral's quarters on Coaster's Harbor Island in Narragansett Bay. 1958.

*Visit* • Eisenhower Park. Dedication. 7–2–1960.

**Kennedy**

*Marriage* • St. Mary's Church, 250 Spring St. 9–12–1953.

*Visit* • Hammersmith Farm, Harrison Ave (Ocean Drive), home of Auchincloss family. Site of wedding reception. 1953 Used as Summer White House while he was president. 1961–1963.

*Visit* • The Breakers, Ochre Pt Ave. 1962.

**Pierce**
> *Visit* • Bellevue House and Fort Adams on Harrison Ave. 1852.

**Roosevelt, T**
> *Visit* • Beaulieu, between Marble House on Bellevue Ave and Clarendon Court. 1907.
>
> *Visit* • Cliff Lawn, corner of Cliff Walk and Bath Rd. 1902.

**Washington**
> *Church* • Trinity Church, Queen Anne Square at Spring and Church Sts, Pew 81. 1789.
>
> *Visit* • Old Colony House, Washington Square. The nation's second oldest capitol building. Washington, Jefferson, and Eisenhower were all entertained here. 1789.
>
> *Visit* • Vernon House, Rochambeau headquarters. 1789.
>
> *Visit* • Benton House (delapidated) behind the Thames St shops. 1789.

## PROVIDENCE  *(Providence County)*

**Presidents**
> *Visit* • Golden Ball Inn, opposite Old State House. Name changed to Roger Williams House, City Mansion, and finally Mansion House. J Q Adams, Monroe, and Washington. Still exists.

**Adams, JQ**
> *Visit* • John Brown House, 52 Power St, which he described as "the most magnificent and elegant mansion that I have ever seen on this continent." 1825.

**Hayes**
> *Visit* • Hopkins Mansion, corner of Benefit and Hopkins Sts. May 1877.
>
> *Visit* • Governor's Mansion, 83 John St. 1877.

**Jackson**
> *Visit* • Old State House, 150 Benefit St. 1833.

**Johnson, LB**
> *Visit* • Brown University, Meehan Auditorium, Prospect and College Sts. 9–28–1964.

**Lincoln**
> *Visit* • Federal Building east end of Exchange Place has a plaque honoring the occasion when he gave a preelection speech here. 2–28–1860.

**Pierce**
> *Visit* • City Hotel. 1852.

**Roosevelt, FD**
> *Visit* • State Capitol. 10–21–1936.

**Washington**
> *Visit* • Stephen Hopkins House, 10 Hopkins St at the corner of Benefit and Hopkins. He visited here twice. 1790.

## QUONSET POINT

**Nixon**
> *Work* • Naval Training School. 1942. See Naval Education and Training Center on Narragansett Bay just north of Newport.

## WOONSOCKET  *(Providence County)*

**Lincoln**
> *Visit* • City Hall, 169 Main St. Plaque commemorating speech he made here. 5–8–1860.

# South Carolina

## AIKEN *(Aiken County)*

**Bush**

*Church* • St. Thaddeus Episcopal Church, 125 Pendleton St. Church of his grandfather. 1924–1925.

*Lodging* • Barnard Villa on Magnolia St. Now site of Whitehall mansion which was built for Robert McCormick. Previously home of grandfather. Burned 1925. 1924–1925.

*Visit* • Old Langley Depot, SC 421 Langley. Arrived here to visit grandparents. 1924–1925.

**Eisenhower**

*Visit* • Uncle John's Cabin, 467 Easy St, which he used as a guest house when he came to Aiken.

**Kennedy**

*Visit* • CaneBrake, 531 Coker Springs Rd (at Easy St and Whiskey Rd intersection. Coker Springs Rd is between the two). 1942.

**Taft**

*Visit* • Beech Island Agricultural Club. County Rd 125 and north of SC 302. 1908.

## ARCADIA *(Georgetown County)*

**Monroe**

*Visit* • Prospect Hill, mansion on Waccamaw River. Marker. US 17, north side near entrance to Hobcaw-Barony. Stayed here. Prospect Hill was renamed Arcadia in 1906. 4–21–1819.

**Washington**

*Visit* • Clifton Plantation. Burned. 4–29–1791.

## BARNWELL *(Barnwell County)*

**Bush**

*Church* • Church of the Holy Apostles, junction of Burr and Hagood. Church of his grandfather, George Herbert Walker. 1925–.

*Lodging* • Duncannon, Home of George Bush's Walker grandparents. Off SC 64 about 3 miles from Barnwell City limits towards Snelling. Now private. 1924–.

1. Kennedy home, *Charleston*
2. Wilson home, *Columbia*
3. Jackson birthplace, *Waxham*

## BRANCHVILLE *(Orangeburg County)*

### Presidents
*Visit* • Branchville depot dining room. McKinley, T Roosevelt, and Taft ate here.

## CAMDEN *(Kershaw County)*

### Jackson
*Work* • Stockade jail, 600 Block of S Broad St. Watched the battle of Camden. Roadside marker. The remains rebuilt into a church. 1781.

### Washington
*Visit* • Adam Fowler Mansion, SE corner Fair and York Sts. House burned. 1791.

*Visit* • Washington House, 1413 Mill St. Moved to new location, corner of King and Fair Sts. 1791.

## CHARLESTON *(Charleston County)*

### Jackson
*Visit* • Dock Street Theater. 135 Church St, SW corner of Church and Queen Sts. Planter's Hotel later on this site.

*Visit* • Quarter House Tavern, at fork of the Broad Path, 6 miles north of city. 1783.

*Visit* • McCrady's Tavern on Meeting St. On Unity Alley, off Bay St. Now site of present Restaurant Million. 1783.

### Kennedy
*Church* • Catholic Cathedral on Broad St. 1942.

*Home* • 40 Murray Rd. January 1942.

*Home* • House on Sullivan's Island near the beach. 1942.

*Work* • Sixth Naval District Headquarters. ONI office in Charleston. 1941–1942.

*Visit* • Francis Marion Hotel. 1942.

*Visit* • Fort Sumter Hotel. 1942.

*Visit* • Charleston Naval Hospital for treatment. 1942.

### Roosevelt, FD
*Visit* • Citadel; Sgt. Jasper Monument. 10–23–1935.

*Visit* • Bernard Baruch estate, Hobcaw Barony, north of Charleston on US 17. 1944.

### Roosevelt, T
*Visit* • Mills House Hotel on the corner of Meeting and Queen Sts. 1905. Villa Marguerita, 4 S Battery St. 1905.

### Taft
*Church* • Unitarian Church, 4 Archdale St. January 1909.

*Visit* • Charleston Hotel, Meeting St. Razed. 1909.

### Van Buren
*Visit* • Poinsett House, 110 Broad St. 1827.

### Washington
*Church* • St. Michael's Church, Broad and Meeting Sts, Pew 43. 1791.

*Visit* • Thomas Heyward Jr. House, 87 Church St. 1791.

*Visit* • Old Exchange, 122 E Bay St at end of Broad St. 1791.

## COLUMBIA *(Richland County)*

### Presidents
*Visit* • State Capitol, Gervais St between Assembly and Sumter Sts. L Johnson, Nixon, Polk (old Capitol), and FD Roosevelt. 1855 to present.

### Presidents
*Visit* • Governor's Mansion, Richland St between Lincoln and Gadsden Sts. Carter, Ford, and FD Roosevelt. 1868 to present.

### Taft
*Visit* • Pendleton St on the Quadrangle of the University of South Carolina. Spoke from President's house, DeDaussure College, fronting the old university campus. Sumter St. House demolished in 1939. 1909. 3–20–1910.

*Childhood home of Woodrow Wilson on Hampton Street in Columbia.*

**Van Buren**

    *Visit* • State House before becoming president. 1827.

**Washington**

    *Visit* • Unfinished State House. 1791.

    *Site* • Statue front entrance to the Capitol.

**Wilson**

    *Church* • First Presbyterian Church, NE corner Marion and Lady Sts (1324 Marion St). 1870–1874.

*Church* • Columbia Theological Seminary. Marker on Blanding St between Henderson and Pickens. 1870–1874.

*Education* • Classical School of Charles H. Barnwell. Corner Hampton and Henderson Sts. 1870.

*Honeymoon* • 1531 Blanding St. First week spent in sister's home. 1882.

*Home* • Pryor House, corner Pickens and Blandings Sts. 1870.

*Home* • Manse, 1531 Blanding St. No longer standing. 1870–1871.

*Home* • 1705 Hampton St, corner of Hampton and Henderson Sts. 1871–1876.

*Lodging* • 1301 Washington St with aunt (Mrs. James Woodrow). 1870–.

## GEORGETOWN *(Georgetown County)*

**Taft**

*Visit* • 1894.

**Washington**

*Visit* • Hampton Plantation, off US 17 south of Georgetown. 1791. See also Washington Oak on the lawn of Hampton Plantation.

*Visit* • Pyatt House, Front St between Wood and King Sts. 1791.

*Visit* • Winyah Indigo Society Hall, corner Prince and Cannon Sts. 1791.

## GREENFIELD *(Georgetown County)*

**Van Buren**

*Visit* • Poinsett home, White House, east of Georgetown on Black River. 1827.

## HANGING ROCK BATTLEFIELD

*(Lancaster County)*

**Jackson**

*Work* • SC 58, south of Heath Springs. Assisted here in defeat of the British in Revolutionary War battle. 1780.

## HEATH SPRINGS *(Lancaster County)*

**Washington**

*Visit* • James Ingram home site, about 2.8 miles south of Heath Springs. Destroyed by Sherman's Army. 5–26–1791.

## HORLBECK CREEK *(Charleston County)*

**Washington**

*Visit* • Snee Farm. Marker off US 17. 1791.

## LANCASTER *(Lancaster County)*

**Washington**

*Visit* • Barr's Tavern. Site east of US 521 at northern city limits. Roadside marker. 5–27–1791.

*Visit* • Major Crawford's house, SC 5, west of intersection SC 5 with US 521. 5–27–1791.

## LAURENS *(Laurens County)*

**Johnson, A**

*Church* • Methodist Church. 1825.

*Work* • Tailor shop stood on the north side of the courthouse square. Marker. 1825.

*Visit* • Sarah Wood House on S Harper St. (Fowler Childress home). Quilt made by Johnson and Sarah is in South Carolina Museum. 1825.

## PLANTERSVILLE *(Georgetown County)*

**Van Buren**

*Visit* • Poinsett Plantation on the old Conway-Georgetown Rd, on the Peedee River. Site of White House or Casa Blanca. 1842.

## WAXHAW *(Lancaster County)*

**Jackson**

*Birthplace* • James Crawford House. Marker on the site of the Crawford Homestead, US 521. Site approximately 8 miles north of Lancaster. 1767.

*Baptism* • Waxhaw Presbyterian Church. See next entry. 1767.

*Church* • Waxhaw Presbyterian Church off US 521 6 miles north of Lancaster. Latest of several that replaced the log cabin erected in 1755. 1767–1784.

*Education* • Academy, at the Waxhaw Church, run by Wm Humphries and later by James Stephenson. 1772–1778.

*Education* • See model of school of his time in the Jackson State Park off US 521.

*Marker claiming birthplace of Andrew Jackson in South Carolina.*

***Education*** • Francis Cummin's Classical School in the New Acquisition; name given to the territory across the Catawba which SC received from NC to settle the Waxhaw boundary. 1778–1780.

***Home*** • James Crawford House. See birthplace above. 1767–1782.

***Home*** • George McCamie's house, west side of road (in North Carolina). Also Joseph White's house. No markers. 1782–1784.

***Work*** • Saddle shop of his relative Joseph White. 1783.

***Work*** • Taught in country school. 1784.

# SOUTH DAKOTA

## BLACK HILLS *(Pennington County)*

**Coolidge**
*Visit* • South Dakota State Game Lodge, 32 miles from Rapid City. Vacation. Summer 1925 and 1927.

## HERMOSA *(Custer County)*

**Coolidge**
*Church* • Timber chapel. 1927.

## MADISON *(Lake County)*

**Nixon**
*Visit* • General Beadle State College, Mundt Library. 6–3–1969.

## MOUNT RUSHMORE *(Pennington County)*

**Presidents**
*Site* • Faces of Washington, Lincoln, Jefferson, and T Roosevelt carved in the stone.

**Eisenhower**
*Visit* • 6–11–1953.

## Roosevelt, FD
*Visit* • Dedication of Jefferson Memorial. 8–30–1936.

## PIERRE *(Hughes County)*

**Kennedy**
*Visit* • Oahe Dam dedication. 8–17–1962.

## RAPID CITY *(Pennington County)*

**Coolidge**
*Lodging* • Rapid City High School where he had his summer office and made his announcement "I do not choose to run." 1927.

**Eisenhower**
*Visit* • Ellsworth AFB dedication. 6–13–1953.

**Roosevelt, FD**
*Visit* • Emmanuel Episcopal Church. 8–30–1936

## SIOUX FALLS *(Minnehaha County)*

**Clinton**
*Visit* • Howard Johnson Hotel. Democratic primary debate. 2–23–1992.

# South Dakota

• Pierre

• Rapid City

**1**

⬭ **90**

Sioux Falls •

| 1. Mount Rushmore |
|---|

*Mount Rushmore, faces of George Washington, Thomas Jefferson, Theodore Roosevelt, and Abraham Lincoln were carved on a peak in the Black Hills between 1927 and 41.*

**Roosevelt, T**

*Church* • Livingston Memorial Reformed Church (now East Side Presbyterian), corner Fairfax Ave and 6th St.

*Church* • German Lutheran, 214 S Walts St. 1903.

*Visit* • Cataract Hotel, Ninth St at Phillips Ave. April 1903.

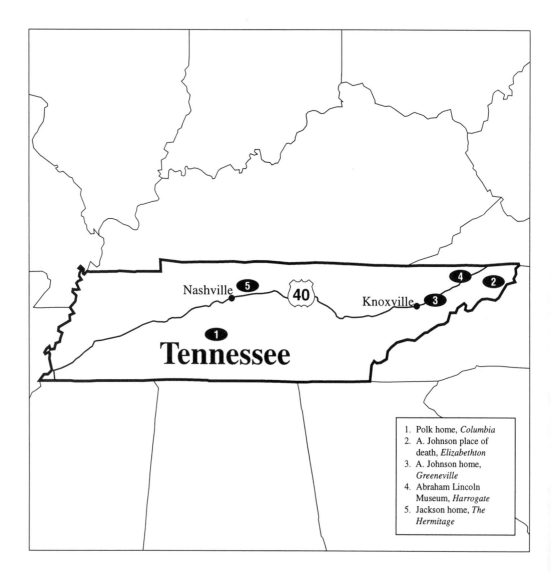

1. Polk home, *Columbia*
2. A. Johnson place of death, *Elizabethton*
3. A. Johnson home, *Greeneville*
4. Abraham Lincoln Museum, *Harrogate*
5. Jackson home, *The Hermitage*

# TENNESSEE

## BOLIVAR *(Hardeman County)*

**Grant**
*Work* • Magnolia Manor, 418 N Main St. Headquarters. 1862.

## CARTER STATION *(Carter County)*

**Johnson, A**
*Lodging* • Stover Farm. House has been moved to the outskirts of Elizabethton. It was on the Watauga River near the Isaac Lincoln House. 1875.

## CHATTANOOGA *(Hamilton County)*

**Cleveland**
*Visit* • Civil War sites. 10–17–1887.

**Garfield**
*Work* • NE corner of Fourth and Walnut Sts. Headquarters. 1862.

**Grant**
*Work* • Brabson House, 407 E Fifth. Headquarters for Federal officers. 1863.

*Work* • Lookout Mountain at Point Park. 1863. See also Cravens House used as headquarters.

*Work* • Missionary Ridge. 1863.

*Work* • Orchard Knob at McCallie Ave and E Third St. 1863.

*Work* • Moccasin Bend and Brown's Ferry on Brown's Ferry Rd. 1863.

**Harding**
*Visit* • Missionary Ridge and other Civil War battle sites. 1920.

*Visit* • Patten Hotel. Billy Sunday Tabernacle for major campaign speech. 1920.

**Hayes**
*Visit* • Staunton House for banquet and lodging. Civil War sites. September 1877.

## CLARKSVILLE *(Montgomery County)*

**Wilson**
*Visit* • Site 304 S Second St visiting his father. 1885–1893.

## CLOVER BOTTOM *(Davidson County)*

**Jackson**
*Home* • Stone's River bottom land. US 70 N, west of Stone's River. Marker 170-2. After 1788.

**Visit** • Clover Bottom Mansion, 2930 Lebanon Rd. Marker 157-2. After 1792.

**Work** • Burr's Landing where Lebanon Rd crosses the bridge at Stone's Landing. Jackson built boats here. 1791–.

## COLUMBIA  *(Maury County)*

**Jackson**

*Visit* • 301 W Seventh St visiting in Polk's home. 8–23–1836.

**Johnson, A**

*Home* • Site is present 207 W Sixth St. 1825.

*Work* • James Shelton tailor shop, NE corner of the Public Square. 1825.

**Johnson, LB**

*Visit* • Columbia City College (now Columbia State Community College), Hampshire Ave west of Columbia. Ground breaking ceremony. 3–15–1967.

**Polk**

*Church* • Old Zion Presbyterian, 6.3 miles west of Columbia and 1 mile south of Hwy 99. 1806–1816.

*Church* • First Presbyterian Church, corner of N Garden and W Sixth. Burned 1847. Now site of Middle Tennessee Bank. 1816–1825. 1841–1845.

*Church* • First United Methodist on W Seventh St, west of site of Polk's law office. Memorial window in the church for Polk. On site of old Methodist Church. 1816–1825.

*Education* • Zion Academy. 1813–1814. See Polk above.

*Home* • 301 W Seventh St. Entrance fee. 1816–1824. 1841–1845.

*Home* • Moved into a house of their own across the street from Sam Polk on W Seventh St north side at Walker St next to Dunnington-Carmack House and now site of parking lot for Oakes and Nichols Funeral Home. Only steps remain. 1825.

**Lodging** • Next door to 301 W Seventh visiting Aunt Marie Polk Walker (Mrs. James Walker). 1812–.

*Lodging* • Site across the street from 301 W Seventh Current Presbyterian Church is on the site of his sister's house.

*Lodging* • Rattle and Snap on a hill-top 7 1/2 miles west of Columbia on US 43. Home of his cousin, George Polk. 1812–1849.

*Lodging* • Hamilton Place adjacent to Rattle and Snap (above entry). Cousin's home. 1812–1849.

*Lodging* • Rally Hill, 319 W Eighth at end of Walker. Home of his sister, Jane Marie, and her husband, James Walker. 1812–1849.

*Lodging* • Athenaeum Rectory, 808 Athenaeum St. Home of nephew, Samuel Polk Walker. 1812–1849.

*Work* • Store clerk briefly. See original store fronts on the Public Square. 1812.

*Work* • Law practice, NW corner Seventh and Garden Sts. See brass plaque on the front of the Nations Bank. 1820–1825. 1841–1845.

*Work* • Courthouse, Public Square. Present courthouse on same site. 1820–1845.

*Visit* • Patrick Maguire House. Site on W Seventh St just west of Courthouse. Here on last visit to Columbia. 1812–1849.

**Van Buren**

*Travel* • Visited Polk and greeted crowds in the Public Square. 1842.

## DANDRIDGE  *(Jefferson County)*

**Jackson**

*Visit* • Shepard's Inn, 136 E Main St. Polk and A Johnson also here at one time. After 1790.

## DOVER  *(Stewart County)*

**Grant**

*Work* • Dover Hotel, Petty St. Surrender

*Grant was present at the Dover Hotel for the Confederate surrender.*

site. Original structure still exists. Near Fort Donelson. 1862.

## DUCK RIVER VALLEY  *(Maury County)*
**Polk**
  *Home* • Marker on side of the road on US 31 just north of Columbia. 1806–1816.

## ELIZABETHTON  *(Carter County)*
**Johnson, A**
  *Death* • W Elk Ave at Fudd Town on the outskirts of Elizabethton. House in which he died has been moved here from Carter Station. 1875.

## FORT DONELSON  *(Stewart County)*
**Grant**
  *Work* • Fort Donelson National Military Park. Site of first decisive Union victory of Civil War. 1862.

*Work* • Fort was captured. February 1862.

## FRANKLIN  *(Williamson County)*
**Jackson**
  *Visit* • Masonic Hall on Second Ave South where he came to meet Chickasaw Indian Chiefs. 1830.
  *Visit* • Eaton House, 125 N Third Ave. After 1800.
  *Visit* • Carnton, off US 431, 1 mile SE of Franklin. After 1800.
**Polk**
  *Visit* • Carnton. See above. 1812–.

## GALLATIN  *(Sumner County)*
**Jackson**
  *Visit* • Cragfont Mansion, near Castalian Springs on TN 25, 7 miles east of Gallatin. After 1800.
  *Visit* • Wynnewood Tavern, TN 25, 8 1/2 miles east of Gallatin. 1800.

*Visit* • Mrs. John Donelson House. Marker 552-10, west of Two-Mile Pike junction with Gallatin Rd. After 1790s.

## GREENEVILLE    *(Greene County)*

**Jackson**

*Visit* • Organized Masonic Lodge. Site of present courthouse. 1801.

*Visit* • Dickson-Williams Mansion, Church and Irish Sts. Once used as a hospital. Now being restored. 1790–.

**Johnson, A**

*Church* • Asbury Methodist Church, corner of Main and Summer Sts across from North Greene Museum. After 1827.

*Church* • Cumberland Presbyterian, N Main and Church. Marker. After 1827.

*Church* • First Presbyterian, 100 Block W Main. Established in 1789; current church built in 1848.

*Education* • Greeneville College. Site 4 miles south of town on old road to Asheville. Attended debates. 1839–.

*Education* • Tusculum College, TN 107 about 3 miles east of Greeneville. Attended debates here. See Samuel Doak House occupied until 1829 at the west end of the campus. 1827–1829.

*Honeymoon* • McArdle House (wife's home). Tradition has the house on Main St near present Greene County Courthouse but exact location is unknown. 1827.

*Home* • Main St. Two-room house. See marker. 1827–1830.

*Home* • Water St (College and Depot Sts). 1830–1851.

*Home* • Main St. Behind the house was the Gum Spring where he camped when he first came to town. His daughter moved into a house across the street. Entrance fee. 1852–1875.

*Home* • Camped near Gum Spring, Main

*Andrew Johnson Tomb.*

St. (Off College St behind the Andrew Johnson House). Autumn 1826.

*Work* • With store keeper Armitage. 1826.

*Work* • NW corner of Depot and College Sts. Inside Visitor Center. 1827.

*Work* • Town Council. There was no city hall at the time and the city fathers often met in his tailor shop. 1829–1831.

*Work* • Mayor. Used his tailor shop as his office. 1831–1833.

*Visit* • Valentine Sevier House on S Main, home of his daughter.

*Funeral* • Courthouse, corner Main and Depot Sts. Present courthouse on same site. 1875.

*Burial* • Andrew Johnson Cemetery, Monument Ave. 1875.

*Site* • Tusculum College, Andrew Johnson Presidential Library. He was a college trustee. 1870–1875.

**Polk**

*Visit* • Dickson-Williams Mansion, Church and Irish Sts. Built 1815–1821.

## HARROGATE *(Clairborne County)*

**Lincoln**

*Site* • Abraham Lincoln Museum on the campus of Lincoln Memorial University.

## THE HERMITAGE *(Outside Nashville)*

**Jackson**

*Church* • Presbyterian Church. See little chapel on grounds of Tulip Grove estate. 1823–1845.

*Home* • Donelson's blockhouse. To reach it he had to ferry the river and take the Kentucky road northward 6 or 7 miles then branch off on a poor trail for 3 or 4 miles more. 1789–1790.

*Home* • Casper Mansker Blockhouse. Retain. 1790–1791.

*Home* • Poplar Grove (Poplar Flat or Old Hickory) in Jones River bend located on east side of Cumberland River near present Old Hickory Dam. 1791–1797.

*Home* • Hunter's Hill on present Saundersville Rd. No remains of the original house. There is a marker on US 70 near Lebanon off Shute Lane. Marker 178-2. Original house built in 1819. Log houses built in 1804–1819. Entrance fee. One of the small log cabins still stands. The larger house is built from logs taken from the original house and is on the original site. 1796–1804.

*Work* • Operated his first store at his Hunter's Hill house, present Saundersville Rd. Nothing remains. 1792–.

*Work* • Moved store to Clover Bottom. No exact site determined. 1792–.

*Visit* • Tulip Grove near the Hermitage originally called Poplar Grove but renamed at the suggestion of visiting Van Buren. Home of Jackson's nephew and namesake. 4–20–1842.

*Death* • The Hermitage. 1845.

*Funeral* • The Hermitage on the front verandah. 1845.

*Burial* • The Hermitage garden. Near the house are the tombs of Andrew and Rachel. 1845.

## HUNTSVILLE *(Scott County)*

**Reagan**

*Church* • First Presbyterian Church at Helenwood near Huntsville. 1982.

## JACKSON *(Madison County)*

**Grant**

*Work* • James Lyon House, 512 E Main St. Site of command post. Marker on the building. 1862.

## JEFFERSON *(Rutherford County)*

**Jackson**

*Work* • Brick courthouse in middle of the Public Square. Conducted legal business. 1804–1811.

## JOHNSON CITY *(Washington County)*

**Nixon**

*Visit* • East Tennessee State University. 10–20–1970.

## JONESBOROUGH *(Washington County)*

**Presidents**

*Visit* • Broylesville Inn (near Jonesborough), Gravel Hill Rd and McQueen Rd off old TN 34. Jackson, Polk, and A Johnson. Built 1797.

*Visit* • Chester Inn, 106 W Main St, corner of Main and Cherokee Sts on the Great State Route from Washington, DC. Jackson, A Johnson, and Polk. Built 1797.

*Visit* • Washington House (Hotel). Site behind Courthouse near railway station. Jackson, A Johnson, Polk, and Van Buren. After 1788.

### Jackson

*Church* • First Presbyterian Church, 128 W Main St between Washington Dr and Second Ave. 1788–1790.

*Work* • Courthouse, 100 E Main St. Admitted to bar here. Current courthouse built on site of the old; dedicated 1913. 1788–1790.

*Visit* • Christopher Taylor House two miles west of town. See site TN 353 and marker TN 81 and 353. Moved to 124 on N Main St by historical society. 1788–1790.

*Visit* • Dueling site, Duncan's Meadow, now the recreation park on Boone St. 1788–.

*Visit* • Dueling site, south of town, probably where Cellafoam Co. now stands, off S Britt Ave and W. Main St. 1788–.

*Visit* • Broyles House off First St between Woodrow and Main, 119 W Main. Built about 1840.

*Visit* • Old Masonic Building, 129 E Main. Masonic lodge charter signed by Jackson. Possibly A Johnson visited here as a member of the Masonic Lodge. 1788–.

*Visit* • Mansion House (May House), 204 W Main St.

### Johnson, A

*Church* • Methodist, 211 W Main St. Built 1847 on the site of the old church.

*Visit* • Buckhorn, 613 E Main St. Built as an inn in 1800.

*Visit* • The Mansion House (May House).

See Jackson above. 1860s.

*Visit* • Gresham House. 1860s.

*Visit* • Blair House, 115 College St.

*Visit* • Blair House, 210 W. Main St. Gosnell House-Gresham Hotel, 127 W Main St. See also Blair house, SE corner of Cherokee and E College. Gresham-Landstrom House, 200 S Cherokee St.

### Polk

*Visit* • Campaign speech in field above the town. 1841. Again near the Presbyterian church. 1843.

### Van Buren

*Visit* • Nathan Gammon House, Main St, almost opposite the courthouse, and William Gammon House, Main St. 1836. Gammon-Stirling House, 204 E Main, SE corner E. Main and Spring. 1836.


## KINGSPORT *(Sullivan County)*

### Presidents

*Visit* • Netherland Inn, 2144 Netherland Inn Rd, just west of Kingsport, while travelling the Great Stage Rd to and from Washington, D.C. Jackson, A Johnson, and Polk.


## KNOXVILLE *(Knox County)*

### Jackson

*Visit* • Blount Mansion, 200 W Hill Ave. See marker behind the Visitor Center for Blount Mansion. 1794–. See also Governor's office located behind Blount Mansion.

*Visit* • Chisholm Tavern, corner Gay and West Hill. See also Governor's office located behind Blount Mansion.

*Work* • Member of First Constitutional Convention, SW corner of Gay and Church Sts. 1794.

### Nixon

*Visit* • University of Tennessee, Neyland Stadium. 5–28–1970.

## Reagan
*Visit* • World's Fair. Site Henley St. 5–2–1982.

## LEESBURG *(Washington County)*

### Presidents
*Visit* • DeVault Tavern off TN 81, NE of Jonesborough. Jackson, A Johnson, and Polk.

## LIMESTONE *(Washington County)*

### Presidents
*Visit* • Broylesville Inn. Jackson and A Johnson.

## MEMPHIS *(Shelby County)*

### Ford
*Travel* • Commerce Square Fountain dedication. Holiday Inn, Rivermont. 5–14–1976.

### Grant
*Church* • Beale St Baptist Church, Beale St. 1880.

*Work* • Hunt-Phelan House, 533 Beale St. Used as headquarters.

*Visit* • Gayoso House. Headquarters. E side Front St between McCall and Gayoso Aves. A Johnson and T Roosevelt also here. Hotel rebuilt three times. 1862.

### Jackson
*Visit* • Bell Tavern (demolished 1920s), west side of Front St between Overton and N Parkway. 1819.

### McKinley
*Visit* • Court Square, Adams Ave and Second St, Peabody Hotel, 149 Union Ave. 1901.

### Taylor
*Travel* • Fort Pickering Site. 1809. Commandant here before 1813. North side of Crump Blvd near eastern end Memphis-Arkansas Bridge. Also in Memphis on inaugural tour. 1849.

## Truman
*Visit* • Hotel Peabody, 149 Union Ave. 1941.

## MISSIONARY RIDGE *(See Chattanooga)*

## MURFREESBORO *(Rutherford County)*

### Garfield
*Church* • Church of Christ, E Main St. He conducted services here during the Civil War. Church torn down and replaced. See plaque on building. 1863.

*Visit* • Robert Wendell House, E College St. Headquarters. 1863.

### Jackson
*Work* • Presbyterian Church. Attended legislative sessions.

*Visit* • Oakland, 900 N Maney Ave, where he visited his physician, Dr. Mentlo. See medical office adjacent. 1800–.

*Visit* • Major Bradley's farm, Hurricane Hill, near Murfreesboro. 1800–.

### Polk
*Education* • Samuel P. Black Institution. Site NE of Bradley School on South Academy St. 1814–1816.

*Marriage* • Childress Place on E Main. Following wedding, parties held for a week in homes of Ruckers, Lytles, and Wendells. 1824.

*Work* • Clerk of the State Senate. Senate met in the Maury County Courthouse on the square which burned 1822. Present building on same site. 1819–1822.

*Work* • Member of the State Legislature. Met in the Presbyterian Church, 300 block of E Vine St. Marker. 1823–1825.

*Visit* • Childress place visiting his future wife. Described in land books as 60 poles west of the west fork of Stone's River. Plantation several miles outside town. Joel Childress was father-in-law. Childress owned land on the Bradyville Pike near the Black Fox Springs area. 1822–.

## Van Buren

*Visit* • Colonel Charles Ready, Jr, east corner of the public square at the site of the present day Commerce Union Bank park area. After 1837.

## NASHVILLE *(Davidson County)*

### Presidents

*Visit* • Maxwell House, NW corner Fourth and Church Sts. Cleveland, Hayes, Jackson, A Johnson, McKinley, T Roosevelt, Taft, and Wilson.

*Visit* • Nashville Inn. Site Public Square and Market St (Second Ave). Fillmore, Jackson, A Johnson, Monroe, and Van Buren.

### Carter

*Visit* • Legislative Plaza, Hyatt Regency Hotel. 10–26–1978.

### Cleveland

*Visit* • Belle Mead Plantation, 110 Leake Ave off US 70-S. Home of General W.H. Jackson. Arrived at the little RR station at Belle Meade from Memphis. Visited State Capitol. 1887.

### Garfield

*Visit* • Cunningham House on High St. Headquarters.

### Hayes

*Visit* • Arrived at Louisville RR station. Lodged Hotel Hermitage, SW corner Sixth Ave and Union St. 1877.

*Visit* • Customs House, corner of S. Eighth St and Broadway. Laid cornerstone. 1877.

*Visit* • State Capitol. 1877.

*Visit* • Mrs. Polk at Polk Place, SW corner Union St and N. Seventh Ave. 1877.

### Jackson

*Church* • First Presbyterian Church (now Downtown Presbyterian Church), Fifth Ave and Church St (154 Fifth Ave N). Mrs. Jackson was a member. 1791–1823.

*Work* • Law office site, 333 Union St. 1789–1796.

*Work* • Tennessee District Attorney. Site of Courthouse same as current courthouse. 1791–1796.

*Work* • Member of Tennessee Superior Court. Served in original courthouse. 1798–1804.

*Visit* • City Hall. Site of present courthouse on Public Square. Site of shooting match. 1788.

*Visit* • City Hotel on Town Square which was the scene of the fight between Jackson and Coffee on one side and Jesse and Thomas Benton on the other. 1813. Was first known as Talbot Tavern (1804) and later as City Hotel. Marker 28-1. Now site of business buildings. 1796–.

*Visit* • Travellers' Rest, 636 Farrell Parkway, 6.7 miles SW Nashville center. 1800–.

*Visit* • Belle Meade Mansion, 110 Leake Ave off US 70-S. Current mansion completed 1853. 1807–.

*Visit* • Fort Nashborough, First Ave N. Replica of original fort. Jackson lodged in a blockhouse some 10 miles away. 1788–.

*Visit* • Vauxhall Gardens (with dining room and ballroom), Marker 266-4. Demonbreun St near S. 9th Ave.

*Visit* • Governor Neil S Brown home, Idlewild, Main St near Neil Ave. Marker 535-10.

*Visit* • Nashville Female Academy. Corner of Church and McLemore. Founded 1819. Jackson visited.

*Site* • Jackson Monument on Capitol grounds. Bust of Jackson on Executive Level of Capitol.

### Johnson, A

*Church* • McKendree Methodist Church, 523 Church St. Johnson inaugurated governor here. 1853–.

*Home* • Confiscated Lizinka Campbell Brown House, Charlotte Ave, directly in front of the Capitol. Marker 68-1. Bronze tablet on Legislative Plaza near top of steps in front of War Memorial Building. 1862–1864.

*Work* • Capitol. Lower house of Tennessee legislature, First Masonic Hall, Church St between Fourth and Fifth Ave. 1835–1838. 1839–1841.

*Work* • Capitol, Charlotte Ave as member of State Senate. Capitol after 1843 when cornerstone laid. 1841–1843.

*Work* • Capitol in Governor's office on the first floor. Charlotte Ave. 1853–1857.

*Work* • Capitol as Military Governor. Charlotte Ave. 1862–1864.

*Visit* • He roomed with John Netherland. 1835–.

*Home* • Nashville Inn, Market St and Public Square. 1853–1856.

*Visit* • Verandah Hotel, Market St. Moved here when the Nashville Inn burned. 1856.

*Visit* • St. Cloud Hotel, corner of Spring and Summer (now Church & Fifth). 1862–1865.

*Visit* • Boarded with Mrs. Anna M. Roach. 1862. See also Neill S. Brown House where Mrs. Lincoln visited him in October 1862.

*Site* • Bust on the Executive Level of the Capitol.

## Johnson, LB

*Visit* • State Capitol. 3–15–1967.

## Kennedy

*Visit* • Vanderbilt University, Dudley Field. Marker 408-7. 5–18–1963.

## McKinley

*Visit* • Union Station, Broadway at SW corner of Tenth Ave. 1880.

*Visit* • Parthenon, Centennial Park, West End. For opening. 1880.

*Site* • Marker for Nashville Centennial south side of Broadway between entrance to US. Courthouse and Eighth Ave South.

*Visit* • Nashville Female Academy, corner of Church and McLemore. Marker 3 A 43. 9–12–1819.

*Grave of James Polk.*

## Nixon

*Visit* • Grand Ole Opry House. 3–16–1974.

## Polk

*Church* • First Presbyterian Church (now Downtown Presbyterian Church), Fifth Ave North and Church St. Marker. Current church dates from 1851. 1839–1845.

*Church* • McKendree United Methodist, 523 Church St. 1849.

*Education* • Felix Grundy office in Grundy House, SW corner Union and Vine at Seventh Ave. 1818–1820.

*Home* • First rented a spacious brick house on one of Nashville's better streets. 1839–1841.

*Home* • Polk Place near the Capitol. SW corner Union St and Seventh Ave N. Marker on the side. Now site of motel. 1849.

*Work* • State Capitol as governor. The building where he had his office was replaced in 1843. He took the oath of office at the McKendree Methodist Church 523 Church St. 1839–1841.

*Death* • Polk Place. See above. 1849.

*Funeral* • McKendree Methodist Church,

523 Church St. Current church is fourth structure on this site. 1849.

***Burial*** • Old City Cemetery near S Fourth Ave. Within the cemetery, plot is located between Central and Poplar next to Masonic Lot. 1849.

***Burial*** • Buried in the garden at Polk Place, Union St and Seventh Ave North. May 1850.

***Burial*** • Capitol grounds, Charlotte Ave. See tomb and monument. 1893.

***Site*** • Bust of Polk on the Executive Level of Capitol.

**Reagan**

***Visit*** • Capitol Building and Radisson Plaza. 3–15–1982.

**Roosevelt, FD**

***Visit*** • Union Station on Broadway, State Capitol and Polk's Tomb, Andrew Jackson school, Ward Belmont School for Girls, George Peabody School, Vanderbilt University, and Fisk University. 11–17–1934.

***Visit*** • Parthenon, Centennial Park, West End. 11–17–1934.

***Visit*** • The Hermitage. 11–17–1934.

**Roosevelt, T**

***Visit*** • Stayed with Mrs. Campbell Brown of Spring Hill.

***Visit*** • Ryman Auditorium, Fifth Ave. 1907.

***Visit*** • Peabody College, Twenty-first Ave S and Edgehill Ave. 1907.

**Taft**

***Visit*** • Belle Meade Mansion. 1909. See Cleveland for location.

***Visit*** • Hermitage Hotel, 231 Sixth Ave North, has hosted several presidents. It is now a Park Suite. 10–28–1911.

***Visit*** • Union Station on Broadway. 1911.

***Visit*** • Ryman Auditorium, Fifth Ave. 1911.

**Van Buren**

***Visit*** • Nashville Female Academy. 1842. See Jackson for location.

**Wilson**

***Visit*** • Joseph R. Wilson (brother) home, 1012 Fifteenth Ave South. 1905. 1907. 1912.

***Visit*** • Hotel Hermitage, SW corner Sixth Ave and Union St. 1912.

## READYVILLE *(Rutherford-Cannon Counties)*

**Jackson**

***Visit*** • Charles Ready House, The Corners. Line separating the counties is drawn through the center of the house. 1829–1837.

## ROGERSVILLE *(Hawkins County)*

**Presidents**

***Visit*** • Hale Springs Inn, 110 W Main. Also called McKinney Tavern. Still operating. Jackson, A Johnson, and Polk. 1790–.

**Jackson**

***Visit*** • Rogers Tavern, 205 S Rogers. Built in 1786.

## RUTLEDGE *(Grainger County)*

**Johnson, A**

***Work*** • Tailor shop. Marker at SW corner of the courthouse. 1826–1827.

## SAVANNAH *(Hardin County)*

**Grant**

***Visit*** • William H Cherry mansion used as headquarters. March 1862.

## SHILOH *(Hardin County)*

**Grant**

***Work*** • Shiloh National Military Park (Pittsburg Landing). Compelled Confederate withdrawal. About 50 miles south of I-40 near Savannah on TN 22. 1862.

## WARRENSBURG *(Greene County)*

**Johnson, T**

***Marriage*** • Office of justice of the peace, Mordecai Lincoln, 1827. No visible site.

# TEXAS

## AUSTIN *(Travis County)*

**Presidents**

*Visit* • Guest Governor's Mansion. 1010 Colorado St, between W Tenth and W Eleventh Sts. Bush, Clinton, LB Johnson, and Reagan.

**Presidents**

*Visit* • Driskill Hotel, 117 E Seventh St. Once it was said the Texas legislature had three houses—the Senate, the House of Representatives, and the Driskill Hotel.

**Clinton**

*Visit* • State Capitol. January 1992.

**Johnson, LB**

*Church* • Central Christian Church, 1110 Guadalupe. 1935–1943.

*Home* • 4 Happy Hollow Ln. 1935.

*Home* • 1901A Dillman St. 1943–.

*Lodging* • Driskill Hotel, 112 E. Sixth St. Memorabilia of his suite still remain. 1934–1948.

*Lodging* • Stephen Austin Hotel, 701 Congress Ave. 1935–1937.

*Work* • Office, Director of the National Youth Administration in Texas, Sixth floor Littlefield Building at Congress and Sixth Sts. 1935–1937.

*Work* • KTCB radio station office, 119 E Tenth St. 1943–.

*Visit* • Seton Hospital, 1201 W Thirty-eighth St. 1937.

*Visit* • State Capitol. Unveiled portrait, Senate Chamber. 5–28–1965.

*Visit* • Agudas Achim Synagogue, 4300 Bull Creek Rd. Dedication. 12–30–1963.

*Visit* • University of Texas, bounded by W Ninteenth, Guadalupe, and Red River Sts. 5–30–1964. Gregory Gym. 2–27–1968.

*Site* • Johnson Presidential Library, University of Texas campus, 2313 Red River St.

**McKinley**

*Visit* • Capitol. May 1901.

*Visit* • Governor's mansion, 1010 Colorado St. 1901.

**Nixon**

*Visit* • Dedicated Johnson Presidential Library. 5–22–1971.

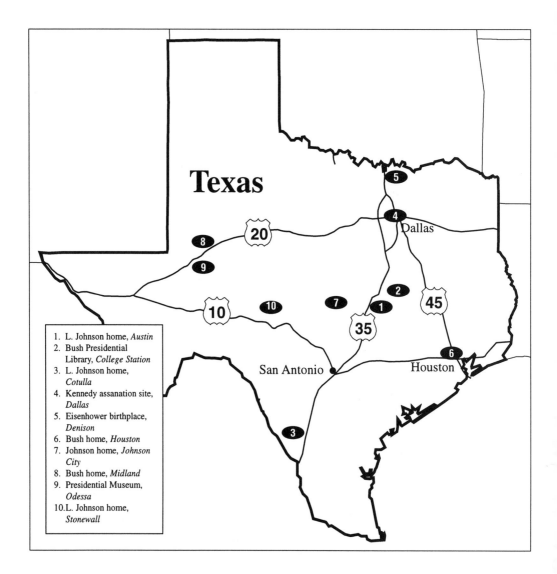

**Texas**

1. L. Johnson home, *Austin*
2. Bush Presidential Library, *College Station*
3. L. Johnson home, *Cotulla*
4. Kennedy assanation site, *Dallas*
5. Eisenhower birthplace, *Denison*
6. Bush home, *Houston*
7. Johnson home, *Johnson City*
8. Bush home, *Midland*
9. Presidential Museum, *Odessa*
10. L. Johnson home, *Stonewall*

Dallas

San Antonio

Houston

## BEAUMONT *(Jefferson County)*

**Carter**

*Visit* • Jack Brooks Federal Building, Broadway. Dedication. 6–24–1978.

## BERCLAIR *(Goliad County)*

**Bush**

*Lodging* • Lazy F Ranch of William Parish. Visiting for more than 20 years.

## BONHAM *(Fannin County)*

**Presidents**

*Visit* • Sam Rayburn Museum on US Hwy 82 West. Rayburn funeral. First Baptist Church, 710 N Center. Eisenhower, LB Johnson, Kennedy, and Truman. November 1961.

**Truman**

*Visit* • Sam Rayburn home, on US 82 W Bonham. High School Stadium, 1901 Broad. 9–27–1948.

## BROWNSVILLE *(Cameron County)*

**Grant**

*Work* • At Fort Brown with Taylor. Foot of Taylor Ave. Now on Southwest Texas University campus. 1846.

**Harding**

*Visit* • Toured battlefields of Mexican War. 1920.

**Taylor**

*Travel* • Fort Brown Reservation at the foot of Taylor Ave. Taylor established the fort in 1846. Original fort destroyed by hurricane 1867 and a new permanent fort built. 1867–1869.

## CAMP POLK *(Near San Antonio)*

**Eisenhower**

*Lodging* • Quartered in Barracks. 1941.

## COLLEGE STATION *(Brazos County)*

**Bush**

*Site* • Bush Library on campus of Texas A & M University. 12–15–1992.

**Johnson, LB**

*Visit* • Texas A & M with Eisenhower. 1937.

## CORPUS CHRISTI *(Nueces County)*

**Bush**

*Work* • U.S. Naval Air Station southside on Ocean Dr, Ward Island. Began his navy training. 1942.

**Taylor**

*Travel* • General Taylor's Camp, Mesquite St. Site where the drawbridge crosses the ship channel. Future Presidents Pierce and Grant were also here in Mexican War. 1845– 1846.

*Travel* • Artesian Park, 800 Chaparral St. A granite shaft marks the site of his headquarters. 1845–1846.

## COTULLA *(La Salle County)*

**Johnson, LB**

*Church* • Church of Christ, Medina and North Kerr. 1928–1929.

*Home* • 202 S Neal St. 1928–1929.

*Work* • Welhausen Elementary School, 804 Lane. 1928–1929.

## DALLAS *(Dallas County)*

**Bush**

*Visit* • Dallas Convention Center, 605 S Griffin St. Renominated for vice president. August 1984.

**Coolidge**

*Visit* • Union RR Station, 400 S Houston St. Walked from station to Jackson St. Renovated. March 1930.

**Ford**

*Visit* • Alamo and night at Fairmont Hotel, 1717 N Akard. 4–9–1976.

*Dealey Plaza in Dallas.*

*Visit* • Texas Fairgounds, Hall of States Building. US 67/80. Visited Apparel Mart. 10–9–1976.

**Johnson, LB**

*Work* • Love Field on US Air Force One where he was administered the oath of office as president. Seven miles northwest of downtown. 1963.

*Visit* • Adolphus Hotel, 1321 Commerce St. Assaulted here. 1960.

**Kennedy**

*Death* • Dealey Plaza, Houston and Elm Sts; sixth floor of the Texas School Book Depository Building. Site of assassination. 1963.

*Death* • Parkland Memorial Hospital, 5201 Harry Hines Blvd. 1963.

*Death* • Marker, Houston St near Elm St, on spot where Kennedy was assassinated. 11–22–1963.

*Funeral* • Vernon O'Neal Funeral Home, Oak Lawn. 1963.

*Site* • Cenotaph and Memorial Park at Main and Market Place dedicated to him.

**Reagan**

*Visit* • Convention Center, 650 S Griffin. Renominated for president. 8–23–1984.

**Roosevelt, FD**

*Visit* • Robert E. Lee Park, Hall St and Turtle Creek Blvd. Dedicated the Lee statue. 6–12–1936.

**Truman**

*Visit* • Adolphus Hotel, 1321 Commerce St. 1915. 1941.

**DENISON** *(Grayson County)*

**Eisenhower**

*Birthplace* • 208 E Day St. Two-story white frame house. Restored. Now stands in a two-acre state park, 100 E Shepherd and 600 S Lamar Ave. Entrance fee. 1890.

*Home* • 208 E Day St. 1890–1891.

*Visit* • 600 S Lamar Ave. 4–20–1946.

## EL PASO *(El Paso County)*

**Harrison, B**

*Visit* • Courthouse for speech. RR station, San Francisco and S Davis Sts. 1891.

**McKinley**

*Church* • Station St Methodist Church. May 1901.

*Visit* • San Jacinto Plaza, bordered by Oregon, Main, Mesa, and Mills Sts. May 1901.

*Visit* • Texas end of International Bridge, US 54 (Patriot Freeway). 1901.

**Taft**

*Visit* • La Aduana Fronteriza (Custom House), SE corner Calle 16 de Septiembre and Ave. Juarez for a state dinner on the Mexican side of the border. 1909.

## FORT HOOD *(Coryell and Bell Counties)*

**Carter**

*Visit* • Blackwell Mountain. 6–24–1978.

## FORT WORTH *(Tarrant County)*

**Bush**

*Visit* • Radisson Plaza, 815 Main St. Formerly Hotel Texas and then New Hyatt Regency Hotel. 1981.

**Johnson, LB**

*Visit* • Blackstone Hotel. 9–14–1948.

*Visit* • Hotel Texas, 815 Main St. Now called Radisson Plaza. November 1963.

**Kennedy**

*Visit* • Radisson Plaza, Commerce and Eighth Sts, 815 Main St. He spent the night of before going to Dallas. 11–21–1963.

**Roosevelt, T**

*Visit* • White Elephant Saloon, 106 E Exchange Ave. Said to be his "watering hole"

when he scoured these parts for rough riders. 1898.

## FREDERICKSBURG *(Gillespie County)*

**Johnson, LB**

*Church* • St. Barnabas Episcopal Church, 605 W Creek St. 1908–.

*Visit* • St. Mary's Roman Catholic Church, 306 W San Antonio. 11–22–1964.

## HOUSTON *(Texas County)*

**Presidents**

*Visit* • Hyatt Regency Hotel, 1200 Louisiana. Bush, Carter, Ford, Nixon, and Reagan.

**Bush**

*Church* • St. Martin's Episcopal Church, 717 Sage Rd. 1960–.

*Home* • 5525 Briar Dr. Only the flagpole remains after the house was removed to make room for five new houses. 1960–1967.

*Home* • 5838 Indian Trail St. 1977–1980.

*Home* • 710 North Post Rd. 1980–1981.

*Home* • Hotel suite (legal residence), 111 North Post Oak Lane, in the Houstonian which is a hotel and condominium complex. Room 271. 1989–1992. 1985.

*Home* • 11-A SW Oak St. Temporarily while permanent home was being built. 1993.

*Home* • 9 SW Oak. Retirement home. 1993–present.

*Work* • President of Zapata Petroleum. Offices in Houston Club Building. 1960–1967.

*Work* • Park Laureate Building. 1000 Memorial Dr. Office. 1992– present.

*Visit* • Molinas Mexican Restaurant, 7933 Westheimer. A favorite with Bush.

*Visit* • Otto Bar-B-Que, 5502 Memorial Drive. 1977–1989.

*Visit* • Astrodome, between Kirby and Fannin Drs north of the South Loop Freeway. Renominated for president. 8–17–1992.

*Visit* • University of Houston, N Main. Later accepted nomination at the Astrodome. 8–20– 1992.

**Ford**

*Visit* • Battleship Texas, 3527 Battleground Rd. 4–22–1976.

*Visit* • Astrodome, Kirby and Fannin. RNC. 8–20–1992.

**Johnson, LB**

*Home* • 435 Hawthorne St with his Uncle George. 1930–1931.

*Work* • Houston High School, 1304 Capitol St. 1930–1931.

**Kennedy**

*Visit* • Rice Hotel, Crystal Ballroom, corner Texas Ave and Main St for major speech to Greater Houston Ministerial Association. 9–12–1960.

*Visit* • Rice University Coliseum, 810 Bagby. 11–21–1963.

**McKinley**

*Visit* • Auditorium for a speech. 1901.

# INTERNATIONAL BRIDGE (ANCUNA) *(Val Verde County)*

**Eisenhower**

*Visit* • Met Mexican president. 10–24–1960.

# JEFFERSON *(Marion County)*

**Presidents**

*Visit* • Excelsior House, 211 W Austin St. Grant and Hayes.

# JOHNSON CITY *(Blanco County)*

**Johnson, LB**

*Baptism* • Dallahite baptizing hole at Flat Creek between Stonewall and Johnson City. Area possibly flooded. 1923.

*Church* • First Christian Church, 401 E Sixth St. 1908–1973.

*Education* • Johnson City High School, Sixth St and Ave D. 1921–1924.

*Home* • Ninth St. Free admission. 1913–1924. 1926.

*Home* • 507 E Seventh St with his Aunt Kitty and Uncle Tom. 1921.

*Visit* • Blanco County Courthouse where he voted. Town Square. 1908–.

# KARNACK *(Harrison County)*

**Johnson, LB**

*Marriage* • Plantation home of Lady Bird Johnson, The Brick House, on SR 43, 2.7 miles SW of Karnack. State marker. 1934–.

# KINGSLAND *(Llano County)*

**Johnson, LB**

*Lodging* • Formerly the Haywood Ranch. Located on south bank of the Llano River arm of Lake Lyndon B. Johnson near Kingsland community. 1961.

# KINGSVILLE *(Kleberg County)*

**Taft**

*Visit* • H.M. King ranch (1,200,000 acres). Immediately west of town on SR 141. Marker. 1909.

# LAREDO *(Webb County)*

**Taylor**

*Travel* • Headquarters. 1846.

# MIDLAND *(Midland County)*

**Bush**

*Church* • First Presbyterian Church, 800 W Texas St. 1950–1960.

*Home* • 405 E Maple St. Called Easter Egg Row. 1950–1953.

*Home* • 1412 W Ohio Ave. 1953–1955.

*Home* • 2703 Sentinel Dr. 1955–1960.

*Work* • Bush-Overby Oil Development Company, 732 McClintic Building, 300 W Texas. 1951–1953.

*Work* • Zapata Petroleum Company as partner, Midland National Bank Building, 401 W Texas. 1953–1960.

## ODESSA *(Ector County)*

### Presidents
*Site* • Presidential Museum, 622 N Lee St on the lower level of the Ector County Library.

### Bush
*Home* • E Seventh St. Now vacant lot. 1947–1948.

*Work* • Ideco, an oil company, as an apprentice. 1948–1950.

## PALO ALTO *(Cameron County)*

### Grant
*Work* • Battle of Palo Alto. Battlefield 5 1/2 miles NE of Brownsville. One of only two battles fought on American soil during the war with Mexico. 1846.

### Taylor
*Travel* • First battle of the Mexican War. 5–8–1846.

## PEARSALL *(Frio County)*

### Johnson, LB
*Church* • Christian Church, 402 S Ash St. 1930.

*Home* • 120 S Oak. 1930.

*Work* • Pearsall High School, S Alabama St as principal. 1930.

## PORT ARANSAS *(Mustang Island)*

### Roosevelt, FD
*Visit* • Tarpon Inn (seafood restaurant) on the main street.

## PRAIRIE VIEW *(Waller County)*

### McKinley
*Visit* • Prairie View A & M University, for a speech. 1901.

## RESACA DE LA PALMA *(Cameron County)*

### Taylor
*Travel* • Battlefield marker, Paredes Line Rd (FM 1847) between Price Rd and Coffee Port Rd. 5–9–1846.

## ROBSTOWN *(Nueces County)*

### Johnson, LB
*Work* • Roeder and Koether Gin Co. Nothing remains. 1924.

## ROCKPORT *(Aransas County)*

### Taylor
*Travel* • Camped here for a time near the center of town. Taylor Oak, Pearl, and Bay Sts is said to be where he pitched his tent. 1846.

## ST. JOSEPH'S ISLAND *(Aransas County)*

### Taylor
*Travel* • Temporary camp. 7–25–1845.

## SAN ANTONIO *(Bexar County)*

### Presidents
*Visit* • The Alamo, Alamo Plaza. McKinley to the present have visited and many have spoken at the Alamo.

### Bush
*Visit* • Plaza San Antonio Hotel, 555 S Alamo St. 10–7–1992.

### Eisenhower
*Home* • Fort Sam Houston, Bachelor Quarters (BOQ). 906 Easley, building 688, apartment E near entrance to the Infantry Post. 1915–1916.

*Home* • 177 Artillery Post Rd. 1941.

*Home* • 179 Artillery Post Rd. 1941–1942.

*Work* • Fort Sam Houston Gates on New Braunfels Ave at Grayson in NE San Antonio between I-35 and Harry Wurzbach Hwy. On the site is a building of gray limestone with loopholes like a fort which is the Quadrangle. 1915–1917. 1941.

*Marriage* • Menger Hotel, Alamo Plaza. 1915–1916.

*Marriage* • Garden of Allah restaurant on Alamo Place where the engagement was announced. 1916.

### Grant

*Visit* • Menger Hotel, 204 Alamo Plaza, NE corner of Alamo Plaza and Blum St. 1870.

### Harrison, B

*Visit* • Menger Hotel, 204 Alamo Plaza. Grand Opera House, site Alamo Plaza. 4–20–1891.

*Visit* • Fort Sam Houston. New Braunfels Ave. 1891.

### Johnson, LB

*Marriage* • St. Mark's Episcopal Church, 315 E. Pecan St on NW corner Jefferson and Pecan Sts. 1934.

*Marriage* • St. Anthony Hotel, 300 E Travis at Navarro across from the Plaza Hotel, for wedding reception. 1934.

*Honeymoon* • Plaza Hotel, Travis St. 11–17–1934.

*Visit* • Victory Plaza. 4–8–1966.

### Roosevelt, T

*Visit* • Menger Hotel, 104 Alamo Plaza. He recruited his Rough Riders here. 1898.

*Visit* • Roosevelt Park, off Mission Rd at the old Fairgrounds where he trained the Rough Riders. Roosevelt Ave and Simpson St. 1898.

*Visit* • Riverside Park, 9315 Nelson Rd.

His regiment encamped here. After drill he treated the troops to beer at the saloon at the entrance to the park. 1898.

*Visit* • Fort Sam Houston. New Braunfels Ave. 1898.

### Taft

*Visit* • Menger Hotel, 204 Alamo Plaza. 1909.

*Visit* • Fort Sam Houston, New Braunfels Ave. Laid the Chapel cornerstone. Lodged at St. Anthony Hotel, 300 E Travis. 1909.

### Truman

*Visit* • St. Anthony Hotel, 300 E Travis. 1939.

*Visit* • Gunter Hotel, 205 E Houston St. 9–26–1948.

## SAN MARCOS *(Hays County)*

### Johnson, LB

*Education* • San Marcos Normal School. Summer 1922.

*Education* • Southwest Texas State Teachers College, Austin St. 1927– 1930.

*Lodging* • He roomed in the Pirtle House, 609 N Austin. 1927. Mrs. Miller's rooming house, N Commanche St. 1929.

*Lodging* • With Alfred Johnson over Dr. Evan's garage. Site 222 Talbot. 1928–1929. Mrs. Hooper's rooming house, W Hopkins St. 1929–1930.

*Visit* • Southwest Texas State College. Strahan Gym, Aquarena Springs Dr. 11–8–1965. Again 8–24–1968 in football stadium for summer commencement. 10–20–1964.

## STONEWALL *(Gillespie County)*

### Johnson, LB

*Birthplace* • Lyndon Baines Johnson National Historical Park. Original building gone but rebuilt from original planking. 1908. Free admission.

***Church*** • St. Francis Xavier Catholic Church. 1960s.

***Education*** • One-room Junction School (the little country schoolhouse) located in the historical park. 1913–1920.

***Education*** • Stonewall and Albert Schools. 1920–1921.

***Home*** • LBJ Ranch. 1969–1973.

***Death*** • Died on US 290 en route from Stonewall to the hospital in Austin. 1973.

***Funeral*** • Lay in state at the Ranch. 1973.

***Burial*** • In the family graveyard on the Ranch. (Now part of the LBJ Historical Park.) 1973.

**Kennedy**
***Visit*** • Overnight. 1960.

**UVALDE** *(Uvalde County)*

**Johnson, LB**
***Visit*** • Ex-Vice President Garner home, 333 North Park. 1952. 1958.

**Roosevelt, FD**
***Visit*** • RR station to visit Garner. 9–27–1942.

**Truman**
***Visit*** • Garner home. 1944. 9–26–1948. 1958.

**WACO** *(McLennan County)*

**Presidents**
***Visit*** • Baylor University, Dutton and Speight, S Fifth and Seventh Sts. Eisenhower 5–25–1956, Ford (Waco Hall) 4–29–1976, L B Johnson (Heart O' Texas Coliseum) 5–28–1965, and Truman 3–6–1947.

1. Hotel Utah, *Salt Lake City*

# UTAH

PRESIDENT • LANDMARK TYPE • DESCRIPTION • DATE

## SALT LAKE CITY *(Salt Lake County)*

**Presidents**

*Visit* • Mormon Tabernacle, Temple Square. Grant, B Harrison, Hayes, and almost every president since Theodore Roosevelt.

**Grant**

*Visit* • Walker House. Site. Main St. 10–3–1879.

*Visit* • State Capitol. Old Courthouse (burned). 1879.

**Hayes**

*Visit* • Walker House. 9–5–1880.

**Kennedy**

*Visit* • Hotel Utah, 15 E South Temple.

**Reagan**

*Visit* • Little America Hotel, Main St. 9–4–1984.

**Roosevelt, T**

*Visit* • County Building, used as capitol, 4th S and S State Sts. 5–29–1903.

**Taft**

*Church* • Unitarian Church, 569 S 1300 E. 9–24–1909.

**Truman**

*Visit* • Hotel Utah, 15 East S Temple. 6–26–1945.

**Vermont**

● Burlington

● Montpelier

🛡 **89**

| 1. Arthur birthplace, *Fairfield* |
| 2. Coolidge birthplace, *Plymouth* |

# VERMONT

## BENNINGTON *(Bennington County)*

**Coolidge**
*Visit* • Battle Monument on Monument Ave. 1891.

**Harrison, B**
*Visit* • Battle Monument on Monument Ave. 1891.

**Hayes**
*Visit* • Banquet in a tent pavilion. 1877.

## BRATTLEBORO *(Windham County)*

**Hayes**
*Visit* • Hotel Brooks, Main St. August 1877.

*Visit* • Bigelow House. Was originally Hayes Tavern of his ancestors. 1889.

## BURLINGTON *(Chittenden County)*

**Coolidge**
*Marriage* • Maple Street. 10–4–1905.

**Taft**
*Visit* • For celebration of tercentenary of discovery of Lake Champlain. 1912.

## DUMMERSTON *(Windham County)*

**Hayes**
*Visit* • Knight homestead. President Hayes' family lived here. 1889.

## FAIRFIELD *(Franklin County)*

**Arthur**
*Birthplace* • Replica of the house off VT 108 near Fairfield. 1829.

## HINESBURGH *(Chittenden County)*

**Arthur**
*Church* • Baptist Church.

*Home* • Main St on Route 116, two doors from the public library. 1834–1835.

## ISLE LA MOTTE *(Grand Isle County)*

**Roosevelt, T**
*Visit* • Camping. Here he recieved the news McKinley had been shot. 1901.

## LUDLOW *(Windsor County)*

**Coolidge**

*Church* • Black River Academy Chapel, High St. 1886–1890.

*Education* • 14 High St. Black River Academy. Now a museum near the village center. 1886–1890.

*Home* • Lodged Charles Parker House on Main St. Also with Mrs. Sherwin. 1887–1888.

## MANCHESTER *(Bennington County)*

**Grant**

*Visit* • Equinox House, Main St, on historic US 7. Still standing and operating. 1869–1877.

**Lincoln**

*Visit* • Hildene, summer home of son Robert. VHS marker is located on the front of the estate, 1.5 miles south of Manchester on VT 7A. 1861–1865.

**Roosevelt, T**

*Visit* • Equinox House, Main St on US 7. September 1912.

**Taft**

*Visit* • Hildene. A bedroom there is known as the Taft bedroom. Music Hall, Town Center. Still standing. 10–9–1912.

## MIDDLEBURY *(Addison County)*

**Monroe**

*Visit* • Middlebury College to receive honorary degree. See the surrey he used near the Sheldon Art Museum on Park St. June 1817.

## MONTPELIER *(Washington County)*

**Presidents**

*Visit* • State Capitol. State Street. Most presidents from the time of Coolidge have visited here. 1857–present.

**Harrison, B**

*Visit* • State Capitol. 1891.

## Lincoln

*Site* • State Capitol. Bust of Lincoln.

**Taft**

*Visit* • State Legislature. 10–8–1912.

## NORTH FAIRFIELD *(Franklin County)*

**Arthur**

*Church* • Baptist Church.

*Home* • Baptist parsonage. 1829–1832.

## NORTH POWNAL *(Bennington County)*

**Arthur**

*Work* • Old Oak Seminary, Main St. 1851–1852.

**Garfield**

*Work* • Taught school in the old Oak Seminary, Main St. 1854–1855.

## ORWELL *(Addison County)*

**McKinley**

*Visit* • Fort Ethan Allen, 3 miles off VT 22-A near Orwell. 7–4–1897.

## PLYMOUTH NOTCH *(Windsor County)*

**Coolidge**

*Birthplace* • Family home on VT 100 A. Entrance fee. 7–4–1872.

*Church* • Near family home. 1872–1933.

*Education* • Small stone building only steps away from his doorstep. District School No. 9. 1877–1886.

*Work* • Took the oath of office in family home. 1923.

*Burial* • Plymouth Cemetery, about .9 miles southwest of Plymouth Notch off VT 100A. 1933.

**Hoover**

*Visit* • Coolidge homestead and gravesite. 1933.

## PROCTOR *(Rutland County)*

**McKinley**

*Visit* • Home of Redfield Proctor. July 1897.

*Birthplace of Calvin Coolidge.*

## RUTLAND  *(Rutland County)*

**Hayes**

*Visit* • Main St at Sycamore Lodge. Private house. 1877.

## ST. JOHNSBURY  *(Caledonia County)*

**Coolidge**

*Church* • North Congregational Church at corner of Main and Church Sts. 1890–1891.

*Education* • St. Johnsbury Academy, southern end of Main St. Bronze tablet commemorates Coolidge visit. 1890–1891.

*Lodging* • He lived in the L. W. Roswell home at 4 Main St, opposite the Academy. 1890–1891.

## WILLISTON  *(Chittenden County)*

**Arthur**

*Church* • Trinity Baptist Church. Current site 19 Mountain View Rd. 1832–1834.

*Home* • Baptist parsonage, Mountain View Rd (not proven). 1832–1834.

1. Ford home, *Alexandria*
   Washington home,
   *Alexandria*
2. National Cemetery,
   *Arlington*
3. Harrison birthplace,
   *Charles City County*
   Tyler birthplace, *Charles
   City County*
4. Jefferson archives,
   *Charlottesville*
   Monroe home,
   *Charlottesville*
5. Kennedy home, *McLean*
6. Jefferson home,
   *Monticello*
7. Madison home,
   *Montpelier*
8. Washington tomb,
   *Mount Vernon*
9. Taylor birthplace,
   *Orange*
10. Jefferson home, *Poplar
    Forest*
11. Monroe tomb, *Richmond*
12. Wilson birthplace,
    *Staunton*
13. Washington home,
    *Westmoreland County*

Richmond

Virginia

# VIRGINIA

## ALBEMARLE *(Albemarle County)*

**Presidents**

*Visit* • Mitchie Tavern on VA 53 exit 24 off I-64. Originally 17 miles NW of present site but dismantled and reconstruced here in 1927. Jefferson, Madison, and Monroe visited. Entrance fee.

**Jefferson**

*Education* • James Maury School. Marker on VA 231 west of Gordonsville. 1757–1759.

## ALEXANDRIA

**Presidents**

*Visit* • Christ Church, 118 N Washington. Coolidge, Hoover, Reagan, F D Roosevelt with Winston Churchill, and Wilson with David Lloyd George.

**Adams, JQ**

*Visit* • Lyceum, Washington St. He was one of the early lecturers here.

**Ford**

*Church* • Immanuel Episcopal Church-on-the-Hill, off Seminary Road. This chapel is on the grounds of the Virginia Theological Seminary. His pew was second row from the back on the right facing the pulpit. 1955–1974.

*Home* • 3426 Gunston Rd, Parkfairfax Apartment. 1948–1949.

*Home* • 3538 Gunston Road, Parkfairfax Apartment. 1948–1951.

*Home* • 1521 Mount Eagle Place, Parkfairfax Apartment. 1951–1955.

*Home* • 514 Crown Dr. 1955–1974.

*Visit* • George Washington Masonic National Memorial, Shorters Hill. 1975.

**Nixon**

*Home* • Beverly Park Apartments near Four-Mile Run, 3819 Old Dominion Rd, Apt. 12. January 1942.

*Home* • 3426 Gunston Road, Parkfairfax Apartment. 1947–1948.

*Home* • 3538 Gunston Road, Parkfairfax Apartment. 1948–1951.

**Truman**

*Visit* • Washington National Masonic Memorial, Shorters Hill. 2–22–1950.

## Washington

*Church* • Christ Church, 118 N Washington St. See chandelier and Pew No. 69. 1773–1799.

*Church* • Round Hill, SW of Alexandria. Also referred to as Tetotum Church. 1732–.

*Home* • Townhouse. Corner of Pitt and Cameron Sts. 1771–1789.

*Work* • City Hall, Cameron St between Royal and Fairfax Sts. 1758–1799.

*Visit* • Lee-Fendall House, home of Lee family, 614 Irinoco Street. 1748–1799.

*Visit* • Washington's River Farm, 8301 E Boulevard Dr.

*Visit* • River Farm Park, 7931 E Boulevard Dr is part of the estate once owned by him.

*Visit* • Gadsbys Tavern, 134 N Royal St, SE corner of Royal and Cameron Sts. Here he recruited for his Revolutionary army. It was called Wise's Fountain Tavern in his day. Now a museum. 1770s.

*Visit* • Carlyle House, 121 N Fairfax St. Entrance fee. Received commission 1755. Plans made for campaigns of French and Indian War. Conferences. 1785.

*Site* • George Washington Grist Mill Historical State Park, 5514 Mount Vernon Memorial Hwy. Has a replica of one of his mills.

*Visit* • Cornerstone of original DC. South of Alexandria at the mouth of Great Hunting Creek on Jones Point. Marker. 4–15–1791.

*Funeral* • Old Presbyterian Meeting House at 321 S Fairfax Street. Free. 1799.

## Wilson

*Site* • Woodrow Wilson Memorial Bridge. Route I-495. Medallion on bridge.

## APPOMATTOX *(Appomattox County)*

### Grant

*Work* • Courthouse. See markers on VA 24 indicating site of Grant headquarters and his camp site the night before the surrender.

1865.

*Work* • McLean's House, near the Courthouse, where Lee's surrender to Grant took place in the parlor. 1865.

## ARLINGTON *(Arlington County)*

### Presidents

*Visit* • Washington Golf and Country Club. Presidents since Taft have played on the links of this course on N Glebe Rd. Present Club building erected 1958. Taft, Wilson, and Harding were early members.

### Bush

*Visit* • U.S. Marine Corps War Memorial (Iwo Jima Memorial), US 1, for speech against flag burning. 1989.

### Ford

*Visit* • Pentagon. Marshall Memorial Corridor. 4–20–1976.

### Johnson, LB

*Home* • Buckingham Apartments. 222 N George Mason Dr. 1942.

### Reagan

*Visit* • Pentagon. Dedicated MacArthur corridor. 9–10–1981.

### Washington

*Visit* • Abingdon north of Four Mile Run fronting the Potomac River opposite mouth of Anacostia River. Home of his stepson, John Parke Custis. Ruins next to parking lot of Washington International Airport.

## ARLINGTON NATIONAL CEMETERY

### Presidents

*Visit* • All presidents since 1921 have attended ceremonies at the Tomb of the Unknown Soldier. Final service for Unkown Soldier 11–11–1921. Harding, Coolidge, Taft, and Wilson attended.

### Bush

*Visit* • Marine Corps War Memorial. 8–7–1992.

### Clinton

*Visit* • Kennedy grave. January 1993.

*Mclean's House, were Robert E. Lee surrendered to Ulysses Grant.*

## Kennedy
*Visit* • Dedication. Paderewski's grave marker. 5–8–1963.

*Burial* • Below Lee Mansion. 1963.

## McKinley
*Visit* • Maine Monument. Here for dedication. 12–28–1899.

## Taft
*Burial* • Arlington National Cemetery, Section 30. 1930.

## Truman
*Visit* • Unveiling Memorial Carillon. 12–21–1949.

*Visit* • Unveiling statue of John Dill. 11–1–1950.

# ASH LAWN

## Monroe
*Home* • Near Charlottesville, off US 250 and VA 239. See also statue in the garden. Entrance fee. 1799–1819.

# BARBOURVILLE  *(Orange County)*

## Taylor
*Birthplace* • Marker on highway at Montebello. There is also some evidence he might have been born at Hare Forest in Orange County about 4 miles from the Courthouse. Site only. 1784.

# BELMONT  *(Loudon County)*

## Adams, JQ
*Visit* • Ludwell Lee's House.

## Monroe
*Visit* • Ludwell Lee's House. JQ Adams and Monroe were quartered in the same bedchamber. He and Adams came for farewell dinner honoring LaFayette. 1817.

# BELVOIR  *(Fairfax County)*

## Washington
*Visit* • Often visited Fairfax family. 1732–1799.

## BLENHEIM *(Albemarle County)*

**Jefferson**
> *Honeymoon* • Now called Honeymoon Lodge. 1772.

## BLOOMSBURY *(Orange County)*

**Presidents**
> *Visit* • Family home of Madison and Taylor ancestors. Now private. Marker. 1784–.

## BRANDON *(Prince George County)*

**Harrison, WH**
> *Church* • Brandon Episcopal Church on Morning Star Rd, VA 10 and County Rd 1201. 1773. 1791.
>
> *Education* • Attended school in a building at Lower Brandon. 1786–1787.

**Polk**
> *Visit* • Entertained while President by a member of Harrison family. See also Brandon Church which is in Plantation Parish and has been in existence since 1616. 1845–.

## BRANDY STATION *(Culpepper County)*

**Clinton**
> *Travel* • Followed route of Jefferson on way to inauguration on US 29. January 1993.

**Jefferson**
> *Visit* • Fleetwood, home of friend, John Strobe. Site only where the Civil War Battle of Brandy Station took place. On route US 29 east of Culpepper. November 1800.

## BURROWSVILLE *(Prince George County)*

**Grant**
> *Travel* • VA 10. Flowerdew Hundred Bridge where his army crossed the James River. June 1864.

## CARMEL CHURCH *(Caroline County)*

**Grant**
> *Work* • Headquarters when his troops took Confederate territory.
>
> *Work* • Long Creek. May 1864.

## CARTER'S GROVE

**Presidents**
> *Visit* • Jefferson, Reagan, FD Roosevelt, and Washington.

## CASTLE HILL *(Albemarle County)*

**Presidents**
> *Visit* • Between Charlottesville and Gordonsville on VA 231. Marker. Private. Buchanan, Jackson, Jefferson, Madison, Monroe, Tyler, Van Buren, and Washington.

## CEDAR CREEK BATTLEFIELD
*(Shenandoah County)*

**Hayes**
> *Work* • Civil War battle, also known as Battle of Winchester. South of Middletown on US 11. Belle Grove is in the center of the battlefield. Promoted to Brig. Gen. 10–19–1864.

## CENTREVILLE *(Fairfax County)*

**Clinton**
> *Travel* • Followed same route as Jefferson's inaugural. January 1993.

**Jefferson**
> *Visit* • Brown's Tavern, Newmarket, near Centreville. November 1899.
>
> *Visit* • Breakfast Newgate Tavern on way to inauguration. 1800.

## CHANCELLORSVILLE *(Spotsylvania County)*

**Lincoln**
> *Visit* • Battlefield site. On VA 3 off VA 20, 14 miles from I-95. Marker. April 1863.

## CHANTILLY *(Fairfax County)*

**Kennedy**
> *Visit* • Dulles Airport, US 50. Dedication. 11–17–1962.

## CHARLES CITY COUNTY *(Charles City County)*

**Presidents**
> *Visit* • Shirley Plantation west of Berkeley on VA 5. Jefferson, FD Roosevelt, T Roosevelt, Tyler, and Washington. Admission fee.

**Grant**
> *Work* • His army passed Charles City Courthouse on its way to the James River and crossed at Weyanoke. Marker V-12. Part of the army crossed at Wilcox's Wharf a mile south of Westover Church. VA 5 and County Rd 619. June 1864.

**Harrison, B**
> *Visit* • While president he came to visit his ancestral home, Berkeley. 1889–.

**Harrison, WH**
> *Birthplace* • Berkeley Plantation off VA 5 between Richmond and Williamsburg. Restored. V-7 Marker. Entrance fee. 1773.
>
> *Church* • Westover Episcopal Church. Perhaps baptism. Off Virginia VA 5. 1773–1795.
>
> *Education* • Tutored at Berkeley Plantation in an attached building. 1773–1786.
>
> *Visit* • North Bend, home of Sarah Minge, Harrison's sister. Off VA 5. Now bed and breakfast.

**Jefferson**
> *Marriage* • The Forest. Marker V-15. 15.1 miles SE of Richmond near County Rd 607. Two miles SE of Malvern Hills. Site only. Marker. 1772.

**Lincoln**
> *Visit* • He met with General McClellan at Berkeley Plantation during the war. 1865.

**Tyler**
> *Birthplace* • Greenway, five miles east of

Westover Church on VA 5. Being restored. Marker V-10. 1790.
> *Church* • Westover Church. East of Berkeley off VA 5. The old church was near Westover and right on the river. Later the church was moved, brick by brick, and rebuilt not far from the present VA 5 on what is called Old Indian Trail. Marker V-14. 1790–1862.
>
> *Education* • Little school on the grounds of Greenway. 1795–1802.
>
> *Education* • Samuel Tyler home West Berry on west side of VA 156 near B Harrison Memorial Bridge and VA 5. 1807–1809.
>
> *Honeymoon* • Mons Sacer on the NW corner of Greenway. 1813.
>
> *Home* • Greenway. See birthplace. 1790–1813. 1821–1829.
>
> *Home* • Mons Sacer, on the northwest corner of Greenway. 1813–1815.
>
> *Home* • Woodburn, adjoining Mons Sacer. 1815–1821.
>
> *Home* • Sherwood Forest, off VA 5 and a few miles east of Berkeley. Previously known as Walnut Park. Private house recently opened. Marker V-21. Entrance fee. 1842–1862.
>
> *Visit* • About .5 mile from Greenway. Historic courthouse building near current county offices. Marker V-11. 1790–1862.

## CHARLOTTESVILLE *(Albemarle County)*

**Bush**
> *Visit* • University of Virginia for Commencement Address. 1981. Governor's Conference. 1989. Second presidential debate with Clinton. 1992.

**Clinton**
> *Visit* • University of Virginia for Governor's Conference. 1989. Second debate with Bush. 1992.

**Jefferson**
> *Site* • Albemarle County Courthouse at

*Greenway, birthplace of John Tyler.*

NW corner Jefferson and Park Sts. Archives contain some of his correspondence.

***Church*** • NW wing of the Ablemarle County Courthouse used at first as a church, "the common temple." 1770–1826.

***Work*** • Founder of the University of Virginia and chief designer. Also Chancellor. 1819.

***Visit*** • Colonial Hotel, Court Square. He had a room and often stayed here in the 1820s. Monroe also stayed here. Nothing remains and no marker.

***Visit*** • Eagle Tavern on the Court Square. Now gone but is the site of Monticello Hotel which kept the old Eagle Register. Jefferson, Madison, Monroe, T Roosevelt, and Wilson registered.

***Visit*** • Swan Tavern, Courthouse Square on Park St. 1800–.

***Visit*** • Levi Opera House on the Court

Square. Jefferson, Madison, and Monroe all saw performances here.

**Madison**
***Church*** • Services held at Albemarle County Courthouse. NW corner of Jefferson and Park Sts. 1751–.

**Monroe**
***Church*** • Services held at Albemarle County Courthouse. 1790–1799.

***Home*** • See marker on the NE corner of Fifth and Market Sts. 1789–1790.

***Home*** • Monroe House on the crest of Monroe Hill, University of Virginia Campus. Imposing white house still exists. 1790–1794. 1796–1799.

***Home*** • Carrsgrove on Stribling Ave. Monroe owned for 13 years.

***Work*** • Law offices in the outbuildings of Monroe House. Now a part of the University of Virginia. 1790–1811.

**Pierce**

*Visit* • Tavish House. 1855.

**Roosevelt, T**

*Visit* • University of Virginia, Cabell Hall. 1903.

**Truman**

*Visit* • Stanley Woodward House 5 miles from Charlottesville toward Shadwell off VA 53. From VA 729 south to second stop sign; left and immediately left again on Colle Ln. Estate called Colle. 9–10–1947.

**Washington**

*Site* • Statue on the University of Virginia campus in front of Rotunda.

**Wilson**

*Education* • University of Virginia Law School. Old Law College building. 1879. Reentered 1880.

*Lodging* • At the University of Virginia, he lived in Dawson Row, Room 158 in House F. West end of lawns, 1879–1880, and room 31 in West Range, Dawson Row. Plaque on wall. 1880.

*Visit* • Jefferson Hall, University of Virginia, where he was a member of Jefferson Society. 1879–1880.

## CHATHAM MANOR *(East of Fredericksburg on VA 3)*

**Lincoln**

*Visit* • Came here to confer with his military commanders who had headquarters here. Manor and marker. 1862.

**Washington**

*Visit* • Here in his early years. 1732.

## COLD HARBOR *(Hanover County)*

**Grant**

*Work* • Richmond National Battlefield Park. Main visitor center, Chimborazo Park, 3215 E Broad St, Richmond. Here Grant suffered his worst repulse. 6–3–1864.

## COLONIAL BEACH (MONROVIA) *(Westmoreland County)*

**Monroe**

*Birthplace* • Ancestral Westmoreland home. Now long vanished. Marker. VA 205. 1758.

*Home* • 1758–1780.

## CULPEPER *(Culpeper County)*

**Clinton**

*Church* • First Baptist Church, corner West and Scanlon Sts. Attended on way to inaugural. 1–17–1993.

**Grant**

*Lodging* • Virginia Hotel, corner of N Main and W Cameron. Now business location but upper part is original. April 1864.

## DARBYTOWN *(Henrico County)*

**Grant**

*Work* • Deep Bottom Battle. He succeeded in drawing the Confederate forces from the besieged Petersburg. 7–27–1864.

## DUBLIN *(Pulaski County)*

**Hayes**

*Work* • Battle of Cloyd's Mountain. Union victory. 5–9–1864.

## EDGEHILL *(Albemarle County)*

**Jefferson**

*Home* • Wife's inheritance. Married daughter lived here. Both original and later house on the grounds. About a mile east of Shadwell on VA 22. Marker on the highway. 1774–.

## ELK HILL AND ELK ISLAND *(Goochland County)*

**Jefferson**

*Home* • Estate inherited from his father-in-law. Junction of VA 6 and County Rd 608, near Columbia. 1774–.

## ELTHAM

### Harrison, WH

*Visit* • Eltham plantation, birthplace of his mother. VA 249 east of New Kent Courthouse and north on VA 30. 1773–.

### Washington

*Visit* • Often stopped here where his wife's mother lived. The house, destroyed by fire. 1875. 1758–1781. Attended his stepson's funeral here. 1781.

## ENNISCORTHY

### Presidents

*Lodging* • Jefferson, Madison, and Monroe. Jefferson's family took refuge here when the British raided Charlottesville during the war. County Rd 627 SW of Charlottesville off VA 20 west. Original house burned in 1839 or 1940.

## FAIRFAX COUNTY

### Truman

*Church* • New Pohick, US 1, 10 miles south of Alexandria. 9301 Richmond Hwy (on US 1 at Telegraph and Old Colchester Rds.) April 1947.

### Washington

*Church* • Old Pohick Church. Site NE of new Pohick Church. Demolished. 1732–1745.

*Church* • New Pohick Church. See his pew number 28. 1745–1773.

## FAIR OAKS   *(Henrico County)*

### Grant

*Work* • Battle. 1865.

## FALLS CHURCH   *(Fairfax County)*

### Clinton

*Travel* • Followed Jefferson's route to inauguration. January 1993.

### Eisenhower

*Lodging* • Tallwood, 708 E Broad St with his brother Milton. Private. 1934. 1942–.

### Jefferson

*Travel* • Wren's station, site 312 Broad St (Leesburg Pike). Horses fed on his trip to inaugural. November 1800. Ravensworth, near junction of County Rd 649 and County Rd 620. Between Monticello and Washington he stayed with William Henry Fitzhugh. Little remains. 1801–1809.

### Madison

*Visit* • Wren's Tavern, Rokeby, Wiley's Tavern, Minor home and to Salona while escaping the burning of the capital. 1814.

### Van Buren

*Visit* • Ravensworth. Christmas 1822. See Jefferson.

### Washington

*Church* • Falls Church, corner of South Washington and Fairfax Sts. 1745–1773.

## FALMOUTH   *(Stafford County)*

### Washington

*Church* • Brunswick Parish Church. US 17 and US 1. 1732–1745.

*Education* • Hobby's School, next to Brunswick Parish Church. 1739–1743.

## FARMVILLE   *(Prince Edward County)*

### Grant

*Work* • Clifton home. 4–8–1865.

*Work* • Prince Edward Hotel. Room marked. 1865.

## FISHER'S HILL   *(Shenandoah County)*

### Hayes

*Work* • Civil War battle October 1864. Fisher's Hill marker. Union Army victory and timely for Lincoln's reelection campaign.

*Brunswick Parish Church, George Washington's church in Falmouth.*

**McKinley**

    *Work* • Same as above.

## "FLOWERDEW HUNDRED" *(Prince George County)*

**Grant**

    *Work* • Mansion on the banks of James River. VA 10. Marker near the site where Grant's army crossed the river. 1864.

## FORT BLACKWATER *(Franklin County)*

**Washington**

    *Work* • French and Indian War. Terry's Fort. NW US 220 near Rocky Mount. 1752–1758.

## FORT FREDERICK *(Montgomery County)*

**Washington**

    *Work* • West bank of New River at Ingles Ferry. 1752–1758.

## FORT LEWIS *(Bath County)*

**Wilson**

    *Visit* • Green Valley at Fultz House, formerly Lewis family home, County Rd 629 7.2 miles from Warm Springs. 1880.

## FORT MAYO *(Patrick County)*

**Washington**

    *Work* • On Mayo River just above the North Carolina line in Virginia. French and Indian War. Marker on US 58 west of Spencer. 1752–1758.

## FORT MONROE *(Elizabeth City County)*

**Grant**

    *Visit* • Grant was here in April 1864. Inside the moat. Home occupied by commanding general.

**Jackson**

    *Visit* • Quarters of Captain House at No. 47 the Fort. Same house but other wing from that later occupied by Robert E. Lee. Across street from Casement Museum. From I-64 take either VA 143 or 169 and follow signs to Fort Monroe. 1829.

    *Church* • Episcopal Church. 7–8–1829.

**Lincoln**

    *Visit* • Lincoln in Quarters No. 1. May 1862.

**Wilson**

    *Church* • Chapel of the Centurion. Attended several times when visiting Fort.

*Visit* • Casement. One time prison of Jefferson Davis.

# FORT MYER

### Eisenhower
*Home* • In senior officers quarters. On the edge of Arlington National Cemetery with entrance on US 50 NE of Arlington Blvd and Pershing Dr. 1942. Quarters 1. 1945–1948.

### Truman
*Visit* • Chapel for George Marshall funeral. 1959.

# FORT NORFOLK *(Norfolk County)*

### Lincoln
*Visit* • West end of Front St. Meeting with generals to plan assault. Impressive remains. 1862.

# FORT WOOL (RIP RAPS)

### Jackson
*Travel* • Spent vacations here. Man-made island in the middle of Hampton Roads channel. This abandoned army base is not open to the public. Can be seen from walls of moat at Fort Monroe. 1831. 1832. 1835.

### Lincoln
*Visit* • Watched barrage from its ramparts. 1865.

# FREDERICKSBURG *(Spotsylvania County)*

### Arthur
*Visit* • Homes of Dr. Brodie Herndon and Hansbrough families at The Chimneys, 623 Caroline St. Now LaFayette restaurant. 1858–.

### Cleveland
*Visit* • Mary Washington Monument at Washington Ave and Pitt St, near her grave. Dedication. 1894.

### Coolidge
*Visit* • Spotsylvania Battlefield Park. 10–19–1928.

### Eisenhower
*Visit* • Mary Washington Monument. Laid a wreath on Mother's Day. 5–9–1954.

### Grant
*Work* • Civil War Battlefields of Wilderness, Chancellorsville, and Spotsylvania Courthouse. 5–8–1864 to 5–21–1864.

### Harding
*Visit* • Camp near town for reenactment of the Battle of Chancellorsville. 10–1–1921.

### Jefferson
*Visit* • Rising Sun Tavern, Caroline St. He met with others as he outlined the bill for religious liberty. 1777.

### Monroe
*Church* • St. George Church, NE corner Princess Anne and George Sts. 1786–1789.

*Home* • 301 Caroline St. Private. 1786–1789.

*Work* • Law office, 908 Charles St between George and William Sts. 1786–1789.

### Roosevelt, FD
*Visit* • James Monroe office, 900 Charles St.

### Washington
*Church* • St. George Episcopal Church, NE corner Princess Anne and George Sts. 1745–.

*Education* • John Marye's School. Site NW corner of Princess Anne and Charlotte Sts. Not confirmed. 1740–.

*Home* • Ferry Farm on King's Highway 1 about 1.6 miles from town. Nothing remains of the house where he lived from age 6-11. Site of Cherry Tree myth. Plans underway for reconstruction. 1738–1748.

*Home* • Rappahannock River, Traditional site of dollar throw. 1738–.

*Lodging* • Martha Washington home,

1200 Charles St, NW corner of Lewis and Charles Sts. 1772–1789.

**Lodging** • Kenmore on Washington Ave between Lewis and Farquier Sts. Home of his sister, Betty Lewis. 1772–.

**Visit** • Lodge where he was admitted to the Order of Masons, NE corner of Princess Anne and Hanover Sts. 1772–.

**Visit** • The Rising Sun Tavern, Caroline St between Fauquier and Hawke Sts. 1770s.

## GLOUCESTER COUNTY

**Jefferson**
   **Visit** • Roswell, home of his friend, John Page. Near Carter's Creek and Capahosic. East bank of the York. Only ruins. 1770s–.

**Monroe**
   **Home** • Farm on York River. 1780–.

**Tyler**
   **Home** • 638-acre farm on the north side of the York River. Exact location not found. 1829–1835. 1844.

## GORDONSVILLE *(Orange County)*

**Clinton**
   **Travel** • Followed Jefferson's route on way to inauguration. 1993.

**Jefferson**
   **Visit** • Exchange Hotel off Main St (US 33 on eastern edge of town). Others who lodged here were Madison and Monroe. Entrance fee. 1760–.

   **Visit** • Walker's Mill, SW of Gordonsville on VA 231. On way to inauguration. November 1800.

## GREAT FALLS PARK

**Washington**
   **Visit** • Patowmack Canal. Canal venture which failed. County Rd 604 near Langley. Site of ruins. 1785.

## GUNSTON HALL *(Fairfax County)*

**Jefferson**
   **Visit** • Gunston Hall. US 1 and turn east on VA 242. Twenty miles south of Washington and near Lorton. Entrance fee. 1774–.

**Washington**
   **Visit** • Gunston Hall. 1735–.

## HAMPDEN SYDNEY *(Prince Edward County)*

**Harrison, WH**
   **Church** • Chapel on campus. 1787.

   **Education** • Hampden Sydney College. Only building remaining from his time is the Birthplace on Via Sacra. It was built in the 1750s as a law office on the Slate Hill Plantation of Nathaniel Venable, where plans were adopted to establish the college in 1775. 1787.

## HAMPTON *(Elizabeth City County)*

**Bush**
   **Visit** • Hampton University, Armstrong Field. 5–12–1991.

**Tyler**
   **Home** • Villa Margaret, near Old Point Comfort. Family summer place. Site Queen St. Villa razed early 1900s. Site is now occupied by girl's dormitory of Hampton University. 1850s.

## HANOVER *(Hanover County)*

**Jefferson**
   **Visit** • Taylor's Ordinary. There are two inns by that name in Hanover, one at Taylorsville and the other near Fork Church.

**Washington**
   **Visit** • Taylor's Ordinary. He rested at the second of the two on US 301, across from the Hanover Courthouse. 1754–.

*Appomattox Manor, Ulysses Grant's headquarters during the siege of Petersburg in 1865.*

## HATCHER'S RUN  *(Dinwiddie County)*
**Grant**
> *Work* • Battle. 1865.

## HICKORY HILL  *(Fairfax County)*
**Kennedy**
> *Home* • 1953–1956.

## HOPEWELL (FORMERLY CITY POINT)  *(Prince George County)*
**Grant**
> *Work* • Appomattox Manor at the end of Cedar Lane on the shore of the river. Headquarters during the siege of Petersburg. Free. 1865.

**Lincoln**
> *Visit* • Met with Grant here. April 1865.

## HOT SPRINGS  *(Bath County)*
**Presidents**
> *Visit* • Homestead Hotel, right off US 220. L B Johnson, McKinley, and Truman visited.

### Harrison, WH
> *Travel* • Hotels of period. Burned. 1836.

### Taft
> *Church* • St. Luke's Episcopal Church. 1908.
>
> *Visit* • He stayed at a bungalow on a hill above the Bon Air Hotel where he rested before his inauguration. 1908.

### Wilson
> *Honeymoon* • Homestead Hotel for second honeymoon. Suites 1, 2, 3 in the new wing. 1915.

## JAMESTOWN  *(James County)*
### Harding
> *Visit* • Hampton Roads and Jamestown Exposition grounds and Naval Station; Billy Sunday Tabernacle. 1920.

### Roosevelt, FD
> *Visit* • Area sites include church ruins. 7-5-1936.

### Roosevelt, T
> *Visit* • Jamestown Tercentennial Celebration at Sewall Point. Today the grounds are occupied by the Naval Training Station. 1907.

## KENWOOD   (*Albemarle County*)

**Roosevelt, FD**

> *Travel* • Once a year he took a short vacation here. 1940–1945.

## KERNSTOWN   (*Frederick County*)

**Hayes**

> *Work* • Battle of Frederick County. US 11 just south of Winchester. 7–24–1864.

**McKinley**

> *Work* • Battle. 7–24–1864.

## KING GEORGE COUNTY

**Madison**

> *Baptism* • Strother's Church. Site mile upstream and north of Emmanuel Church off US 301. 3–31–1751.

> *Church* • Hanover Parish Church, 9415 King's Highway. 1751–.

**Monroe**

> *Work* • Completed his law studies and stayed on small estate he owned. Exact location undetermined. 1780–1781.

## LACEY SPRINGS   (*Rockingham County*)

**Polk**

> *Visit* • Lincoln Inn on US 11. Burned 1898. Marker. 1848.

**Van Buren**

> *Visit* • Lincoln Inn on US 11. Rumor that Lincoln also stopped here. Burned 1898. Marker. 1848.

## LANGLEY   (*Fairfax County*)

**Bush**

> *Work* • Director of CIA with offices on the Seventh floor. VA 193, George Washington Memorial Parkway. 1976–1977.

**Eisenhower**

> *Visit* • Cornerstone laying CIA Building. 11–3–1959.

**Ford**

> *Visit* • Central Intelligence Agency. Swearing in George Bush. 1–30–1976.

## LEESBURG   (*Loudoun County*)

**Adams, JQ**

> *Visit* • Oak Hill, on US 15 near junction with US 50. 1825.

**Monroe**

> *Church* • St. James' Episcopal Church, 14 Cornwall St NW. 1808–1830.

> *Home* • Oak Hill, on US 15 near junction with US 50. 1808–1830.

## LEXINGTON   (*Rockbridge County*)

**Johnson, LB**

> *Visit* • George C. Marshall Research Library dedication. 5–23–1964.

## LIMESTONE FARM   (*Albemarle County*)

**Monroe**

> *Home* • He owned this farm. US 250 east of Charlottesville/Shadwell. About 1800 to 1828.

## LOVINGSTON   (*Nelson County*)

**Jefferson**

> *Visit* • Union Hill, County Rd 647 about 2 miles from Lovingston, home of William Cabell. Site only. Original house moved to Hanover County. 1779.

## LYNCHBURG   (*Campbell County*)

**Garfield**

> *Work* • Sandusky, about 4 miles from Lynchburg off County Rd 676 in a two-story L-shaped house. Quartered here. 1864.

**Hayes**

> *Work* • Fort Early at NE corner Fort and Vermont Aves on US 29. Business.

> *Work* • Sandusky, about 4 miles from Lynchburg off County Rd 676 in a two-

GEOGRAPHIC GUIDE TO LANDMARKS

story L-shaped house. While an officer on the staff during the Civil War he was quartered here. 1864.

**Jackson**
*Visit* • Dr. John W. Cabell House on NE side of Main St between Fifth and Sixth. Demolished. 1815.

**Jefferson**
*Visit* • Joseph Nichols Tavern, SE corner Fifth and Madison. 1700s and 1800s. Miller-Clayton House, Riverside Park at Ash St entrance. 1800–1809.

**McKinley**
*Work* • Sandusky. See Hayes above. McKinley and Hayes roomed together here. 1864.

# McLean  *(Fairfax County)*

**Kennedy**
*Home* • Merrywood, 700 Chain Bridge Rd. 1953.

*Home* • Hickory Hill, 1147 Chain Bridge Rd. Private. 1953–1956.

# Manikan  *(Goochland County)*

**Jefferson**
*Church* • Dover Church, just east of Manikan on River Rd. No longer exists and exact location unknown. 1752–1757.

# Markham  *(Fauquier County)*

**Wilson**
*Visit* • Robert Stribling House. I-66 east of Front Royal, Markham exit, 1/2 mile south on County Rd 688, right turn and cross RR tracks. First house on left. 1897.

# Massaponax Church  *(Spotsylvania County)*

**Grant**
*Work* • Wilderness campaign. South of Fredericksburg at intersection of US 1 and VA 208. Go 3.6 miles south on US 1. 1864.

# Middleburg  *(Orange County)*

**Kennedy**
*Home* • South of the village of Midddleburg off Route 58. Take County Rd 776 south to first crossroads right to first estate on left to Glen Ora. Leased as weekend retreat. 1961–1962.

*Church* • Attended mass at the Middleburg Community Center, 300 W Washington St. 1961–1962.

# Middletown  *(Frederick County)*

**Hayes**
*Work* • South Mountain campaign. September 1862.

*Work* • Battle of Cedar Creek just west of Middletown. 10–19–1864.

**Madison**
*Honeymoon* • Belle Grove Plantation on US 11 about a mile south of town. 1794.

# Monticello (near Charlottesville)  *(Albemarle County)*

**Jefferson**
*Home* • VA 53, 3 miles south of town. Entrance fee. 1770–1826.

*Death* • 1826.

*Funeral* • 1826.

*Burial* • On the grounds. 1826.

# Montpelier  *(Orange County)*

**Madison**
*Home* • Modest wooden structure which later became the mansion it is today. VA 20 4 miles south of Orange. Entrance fee. 1751–1836.

*Death* • 1836.

*Funeral* • 1836.

*Burial* • Madison Cemetery, off County Rd 639. 1836.

*Belle Grove Plantation, honeymoon site of Dolley and James Madison.*

**Monroe**
> *Visit* • Often visited Madison. 1775–.

## MOUNT VERNON *(Fairfax County)*

**Washington**
> *Home* • 8 miles south of Alexandria. Originally called Hunting Creek. Entrance fee. 1735–1738. 1748–1799.
> *Death* • 12–14–1799.
> *Burial* • First buried in old vault at Mount Vernon. 1799.
> *Burial* • Present tomb. 1831.

## NATURAL BRIDGE *(Rockbridge County)*

**Jefferson**
> *Visit* • Once owned the land on which it is found. US 11 south of Lexington.

**Washington**
> *Visit* • Surveyed the area. See where he carved his initials in the rock. 1750s.

## NEW KENT COUNTY

**Tyler**
> *Marriage* • Cedar Grove Plantation, on

VA 106, No. 5900 about a mile north of US 60 on west side of road behind trees. 1813.

> *Visit* • New Kent Cemetery. Behind the dwelling of Cedar Grove is the brick-walled cemetery where Letitia Christian Tyler is buried. 1842.

> *Visit* • New Kent Courthouse, VA 249. Burned 1862 and repaired.

**Washington**
> *Marriage* • St. Peter's Church near White House, SW of the New Kent Courthouse. County Rd 609/642 off VA 249. 1759.

> *Marriage* • White House on VA 614 off VA 608 on Pamunkey River. Burned June 1862. 1759.

> *Honeymoon* • According to some sources the couple spent their honeymoon at the White House, VA 614. 1759.

> *Honeymoon* • Another source says that they spent part of honeymoon in the honeymoon cottage at Rockahock, NE side of Chickahominy River or south side of York River. Also site of Fort Royal and near Walker's Station.

> *Visit* • Chestnut Grove Plantation off VA 33 at junction with County Rd 623 between the White House and Elthan. Burned 1927. 1758–.

> *Visit* • Poplar Grove Mansion on the Pamunkey River where he first met Martha Dandridge Custis. 1758. Exact site undetermined. Between road to Cousic and the present VA 249 which leads from New Kent courthouse to West Point. 1758–.

> *Visit* • Claremont, home of the Allen family said to be visited by every President from Washington to Buchanan. Across the River from Green Springs, just before the James River turns north again. 1750s–.

> *Visit* • New Kent Courthouse (1691–1775), on VA 249. 1758–.

> *Visit* • Old Tavern next to the Courthouse. 1758–.

## NEWPORT NEWS *(Warwick County)*

**Jackson**

*Visit* • Dry Dock Company on Washington Ave between Thirty-fifth and forty-ninth Sts. See also Norfolk below. 1833.

## NEWTOWN *(Caroline County)*

**Madison**

*Education* • Donald Robertson Academy. The site is near the junction of County Rd 625 and 628. 1762–1767.

*Lodging* • With his grandparents who lived nearby. No remains or marker. 1762–1767.

## NORFOLK *(Norfolk County)*

**Bush**

*Visit* • Naval Air Station, Hampton Blvd and Ninety-ninth St. 4–21–1989.

**Carter**

*Home* • 1009 Buckingham Ave, Apt 236 on Bolling Square. 1946–1947.

*Work* • U.S. Navy Station, Hampton Blvd and Ninety-ninth St. 1946–1948.

*Visit* • Botanical Gardens, Airport Rd, for the commissioning of the USS *Mississippi* at Pier 12. 9–7–1976.

**Jackson**

*Visit* • Gosport Navy Yard (now Norfolk Naval Shipyard). Arrived here by steamboat at the Stone dry dock for inspection. On this trip he was back and forth between Norfolk and Portsmouth and Fort Monroe. 7–7–1829.

*Visit* • Arrived off new Naval Hospital, Old Number One, and received a 24-gun salute from battery on Town Point Wharf, Gosport Navy Yard. 7–8–1829.

*Visit* • 6225 Powhatan Ave, Edgewater. Moved from Tazewell St. 1829.

**Monroe**

*Visit* • Moses Myers House, corner of Bank and Freemason Sts. 1817.

## NORTH ANNA RIVER *(Hanover County)*

**Grant**

*Work* • Operations in the Civil War. None of the battlefield is preserved today. North Anna Battlefield, 5 miles south of Carmel Church (see above) on US 1. 5–23–1864 to 5–26–1864.

## NOTTOWAY *(Nottoway County)*

**Grant**

*Work* • Nottoway Courthouse, US 460. Passed here in pursuit of Lee. April 1865.

## OAK GROVE (NEAR WAKEFIELD) *(Westmoreland County)*

**Washington**

*Church* • Pope Episcopal Church east of Oak Grove, VA 3. Marker. 1744.

*Education* • School. Marker. Junction VA 3 and VA 205 south of Colonial Beach west of junction. 1774–1776.

## OAK HILL *(Loudoun County)*

**Monroe**

*Home* • On US 15 about a mile north of junction with US 50. 1808–1830.

## OLD POINT COMFORT *(Elizabeth City County)*

**Tyler**

*Honeymoon* • With second bride in a cottage here. Owned a cottage near Fort Monroe where they often vacationed. See Hampton. 1844.

## OPEQUON *(East of Winchester)*

**Hayes**

*Work* • Battle of Opequon. 9–19–1864.

## ORANGE *(Orange County)*

**Madison**

*Church* • Orange County Courthouse used as church. 103 W Main St. 1751–.

*Church* • Anglican Brick Church about six or seven miles from Montpelier, off County Rd 639. 1751–1836.

*Lodging* • Meadow Farm, plantation of his uncle, along the old road towards Fredericksburg from Orange off VA 20.

*Visit* • Woodley Plantation, a short drive from Montpelier to home of his brother and niece. On Gordonsville Rd. House is restored. Private. 1751–.

*Visit* • Family farm, north of Orange on County Rd 612 (Monrovia Rd). Working farm still in Taylor-Madison family. Marker at entry. A new house was built on the site in 1855. 1751–.

*Burial* • Cemetery at Anglican Brick Church. Left off County Rd 639 to secondary road. 1836.

*Site* • Museum, 129 Caroline Street.

**Taylor**

*Birthplace* • Possibly Hare Forest near Orange. Off Rapidan Rd (out E Main) County Rd 615. Turn on County Rd 700 and go 1.4 miles. Restored. Privately owned. One of three places in Virginia that may have been his birthplace. 1784.

*Baptism* • Possibly St. Thomas Parish, 119 Caroline St. 1784. Not certain. There was also a brick Anglican church on the property at Meadow Farm at the time of Taylor.

## PEARISBURG *(Giles County)*

**Hayes**

*Work* • Giles Courthouse Battle. Received concussion. 5–10–1862.

## PETERSBURG *(Dinwiddie County)*

**Grant**

*Work* • In nearby Hopewell, the City Point Unit of Petersburg National Battlefied Park

offers guided tours of Grant's headquarters (cabin) on the lower lawn of Appomattox Manor. 6–18–1864.

*Work* • Wallace-Seward House, 204 S Market St. Headquarters. 1865.

**Lincoln**

*Visit* • Centre Hill Mansion on a court on the North side of Franklin St between Jefferson and Adams Sts. Now the headquarters of National Park Service. April 1865.

**Taft**

*Visit* • Centre Hill Mansion. 1909.

**Tyler**

*Visit* • Centre Hill Mansion.

**Washington**

*Visit* • Golden Ball Tavern, SE corner Grove Ave and North Market St. 1791.

## POINT COMFORT *(Elizabeth City County)*

**Lincoln**

*Visit* • For an informal peace conference. 1865.

## POPLAR FOREST (NEAR LYNCHBURG) *(Bedford County )*

**Jefferson**

*Home* • Vacation retreat. Off US 460 west of Lynchburg, right to VA 661 and follow signs. Restored. Entrance fee. 1806–1819.

## PORT CONWAY *(King George County)*

**Madison**

*Birthplace* • Belle Grove Plantation of his maternal grandmother (Catlett Moore), VA 207 on north bank of the Rappahannock River. Marker. 1751.

*Baptism* • Strother's Church, 1 mile NE of birthplace. Disappeared. 1751.

## PORTSMOUTH  (Norfolk County)

**Presidents**

*Visit* • Crawford House, NW corner High and Crawford. Fillmore, Tyler, and Van Buren. Marker.

**Carter**

*Visit* • Naval Hospital, Effingham St north of Crawford. His eldest son was born here. 1947.

**Jackson**

*Visit* • John W. Murdaugh House, NW corner Crawford and London. Now Psychiatric Association, Ltd. July 1829.

*Visit* • Ball-Nivison House, 417 Middle St just north of London St. 1833.

## POUND GAP  (Wise County)

**Garfield**

*Work* • Here during the Civil War. 1861–1863.

## QUANTICO  (Prince William County)

**Truman**

*Visit* • Harry Lee Hall, U.S. Marine Corps Base, US 1 off I-95. 6–15–1950.

## RAPIDAN  (Madison County)

**Carter**

*Visit* • From US 29 take VA 231 west from Madison to Banco, County Rd 670 through Criglersville. 10–25–1978. 5–13–1979.

**Hoover**

*Lodging* • See Presidential cabin. Free. Limited access. 1929–1933.

*Visit* • Outdoor fireplace used as a backdrop where most official photos were made.

## RICHMOND  (Henrico County)

**Presidents**

*Church* • St. John's Episcopal Church, 2401 E Broad St between N Twenty-fourth and N Twenty-fifth Sts. Jefferson, Madison,

Monroe, Tyler, and Washington attended. Patrick Henry gave his famous speech here.

*Visit* • Jefferson Hotel, 100 W Franklin St. B Harrison, McKinley, Wilson, Coolidge, Taft, FD Roosevelt, T Roosevelt, Truman, Reagan, and Carter have stayed here.

*Visit* • Powhattan House SE corner of Broad and Eleventh. Fillmore, W Harrison, and Tyler visited.

*Visit* • Swan Inn, north side of Broad St, midway between Eighth and Ninth Sts. Destroyed. Jefferson, Tyler, and Washington visited.

*Work* • Quesnay Academy, Academy Square. Convention meetings. Madison, Monroe, and Washington attended. 1788.

**Carter**

*Visit* • John Marshall Hotel. 4–7–1979.

**Eisenhower**

*Visit* • St. Paul's Episcopal, 815 E Grace St. Mother's Day. 5–9–1954.

*Visit* • Virginia House. South side of Sulgrave Rd in Windsor Farms. Lunch to honor 165th anniversary Richmond Light Infantry Blues. May 1954.

**Ford**

*Visit* • Capitol. Capitol Square bounded by Bank, N Ninth, Capitol, and Governor Sts. 10–23–1976.

**Grant**

*Visit* • City Hall Broad St. 1867.

*Work* • Richmond National Battlefield. 3215 E Broad St. 1854.

**Harrison, WH**

*Education* • Dr. Andrew Leiper home/office. Eighteenth and Franklin Sts. Apprenticed to Dr. Leiper. 1790.

*Home* • Governor's Mansion. With his father, Governor Benjamin Harrison. 1790–1813.

**Hayes**

*Visit* • Capitol. Capitol Square bounded by Bank, N Ninth, Capitol, and Governor Sts. 10–30–1877.

*Visit* • Exchange Hotel, Franklin and Fourteenth Sts. Demolished 1920. 10–30–1877.

### Jefferson

*Home* • Governor's Mansion. Moved into a rented house and the state assembly convened in temporary quarters. He lived in a house owned by his uncle by marriage, Thomas Turpin, while Governor, center of Shockoe Hill. Site near Twelfth and Franklin.

*Visit* • Ampthill Plantation, south end of Ampthill Rd off Cary St.

*Visit* • Formicola's Tavern Between Fifteenth and Seventeenth Sts on south side of Main. 1780.

*Visit* • John Marshall House, NW corner N Ninth and E Marshall Sts (818 E. Marshall).

*Visit* • Wilton Plantation. South end Wilton Rd off Cary St. House moved to this site in 1935 and was restored. Home of William Randolph. Jefferson also courted Ann Randolph here unsuccessfully. Six miles below Richmond. 1754–.

*Work* • Governor. Capitol (old). Foot of Council Hill on Pearl St at the NW corner of what is now Cary St and Fourteenth St. 1779–1881.

*Work* • Hogg's Tavern Fifteenth and Main (southwest corner). Met here with others to plan for the new Capitol. 1770–.

*Site* • Jefferson Hotel 100 W Franklin St. See statue in upper lobby over a pool which was once the home of live alligators. It narrowly escaped destruction in the 1901 fire and while being carried out was dropped and the head knocked off. The original sculptor repaired it, and it now stands facing entrance.

### Johnson, A

*Visit* • Spottswood House, Main and Eighth Sts. One of the few hotels open in 1865. 1865. 1867.

*Visit* • City Hall, Broad St. 1867.

*Church* • St. Paul's Episcopal, 815 E Grace St. 1867.

### Lincoln

*Visit* • Confederate White House. 1201 E Clay St. Georgia Room where Lincoln conferred with Gen Weitzel. Entrance fee. 4–3–1865.

### Madison

*Visit* • George Wythe House. 503 E Grace St. 1776–.

*Visit* • Home of his cousin John Marshall. 1770–.

*Work* • First African Baptist Church. Broad and College Sts. First Baptist Church built 1802 (later First African Baptist). Demolished 1876. State constitutional convention. 1829–1830.

*Work* • House of Delegates. Site NW corner Cary and Fourteenth Sts. Capitol was a former warehouse. 1784–1786. The Academy is located on what is now Twelfth St between Broad and Marshall Sts. Plaque on Twelfth street. Virginia Ratification Assembly. Site now occupied by West Hospital. 6–2–1788. Virginia Assembly. 1799–1800. Hall of Delegates for state constitutional convention. First met here and then shifted to First African Baptist Church. 1829.

### Monroe

*Home* • Governor's Mansion. While he was governor the mansion was being repaired. His place of residence not determined. 1799.

*Visit* • Formicola's Tavern between Fifteenth and Seventeenth Sts on south side of Main. 1782–1783.

*Visit* • John Marshall House, NW corner N Ninth and E Marshall Sts (818 E. Marshall). 1784.

*Work* • First African Baptist Church Broad and College Sts. First Baptist Church built 1802 (later First African Baptist). Demolished 1876. State constitutional convention. 1829–1830.

*Work* • Virginia Assembly. Capitol (old). Foot of Council Hill on Pearl St at the NW corner of what is now Cary St and Fourteenth St. 1782.

*Work* • House of Delegates. 1786–1788. State Legislature. 1788–1790. Governor. 1799–1802. 1811. Hall of Delegates. 1829.

*Burial* • Hollywood Cemetery. Entrance SW corner of Cherry and Albemarle Sts. Body removed from original cemetery in New York City and brought here. Wife buried in same plot. 1858.

## Polk

*Visit* • Capitol. Capitol Square bounded by Bank, N Ninth, Capitol, and Governor Sts. 5–28–1847. 3–5–1849.

## Reagan

*Visit* • John Marshall Hotel. 10–27–1981.

## Taylor

*Visit* • Union Hotel, Ninth and Main. Reception on occasion of laying the cornerstone of the Washington Monument. Fillmore and Tyler attended. 2–22–1850.

*Visit* • Washington Monument State Capitol Grounds. To lay cornerstone. Fillmore and Tyler attended. 2–22–1850.

## Tyler

*Church* • Capitol Square bounded by Bank, N Ninth, Capitol, and Governor Sts. Church services held in the Hall of Delegates. 1823–1827.

*Church* • St. Paul's Episcopal. 815 E Grace St. 1845–1862.

*Education* • Edmund Randolph House, 1002 Capitol St. Studied here. 1809–1811.

*Home* • Governor's Mansion. Corner of Capitol and Governor Sts with his father who was governor. 1809–1811. After 1813 on the same site as the first mansion. 1825–1827.

*Work* • First African Baptist Church. Broad and College Sts. First Baptist Church built 1802 (later First African Baptist). State constitutional convention. Demolished 1876. 1829–1830.

*Work* • State Legislature. 1811–1816. House of Delegates 1823–1825. Governor. 1825–1827. State Legislature. Speaker of lower house. 1838–1840. Member of Congress of Confederate States. 1862.

*Death* • Exchange Hotel. Franklin and Fourteenth Sts. Demolished 1920. 1–18–1862.

*Funeral* • Lay in state when it was site of Confederate Congress. 1862.

*Burial* • Hollywood Cemetery. Entrance SW corner of Cherry and Albemarle Sts. Near Monroe's grave. His second wife is buried in the same plot, and his first wife is buried in the family plot at Cedar Grove. 1862.

## Washington

*Visit* • Bell Tavern. After 1846 called City Hotel and finally St. Charles Hotel. Across Shockoe Creek on E Main St in Shockoe. It replaced Bowler's Tavern which stood on north side of Main St in Shockoe just below Fifteenth. The St. Charles was demolished in 1903. 1784.

*Visit* • Ampthill Plantation, south end Ampthill Rd off Cary St. Here attending Virginia Ratification Convention. 1775.

*Visit* • Eagle Tavern. South side of Main St between Twelfth and Thirteenth Sts. Entertained here. Building burned. 3–26–1791.

*Visit* • Masonic Lodge Franklin Street between Eighteenth and Nineteenth Streets. 3–26–1791.

*Visit* • Pump House. Lock Park Pumphouse Rd, just north of the Boulevard Bridge. 1791.

*Visit* • Wilton Plantation. South end of Wilton Rd off Cary St. 1770–.

# ROANOKE *(Roanoke County)*

## Roosevelt, FD

*Visit* • Dedication of Veteran's Facility Hospital. 10–19–1934.

*Grave of John Tyler.*

**Roosevelt, T**
 *Visit* • RR Station, Shenandoah Ave and Randolph St. 10–22–1907.

## ROOSEVELT ISLAND *(See District of Columbia)*

## ROSEWELL

**Jefferson**
 *Visit* • Near Carter's Creek off the York River and near Capehosic Ferry. East side

of York River. Now a ruin. Stayed here. 1770s.

## ROUND HILL *(King George County)*

**Monroe**
 *Church* • Possibly baptism. SW of Alexandria. Near Franconia and Keene Mill Rds. 1758–1786.

**Washington**
 *Church* • Little remains but a few bricks. 1732–.

## SALONA *(Fairfax County)*

**Madison**
 *Visit* • Smoot House, 1214 Buchanan St off VA 9 near Falls Church from which he watched the fire which gutted the White House. 1814.

## SCOTTSVILLE *(Albemarle County)*

**Roosevelt, T**
 *Church* • Christ Church, VA 20 and turn east of Glendower. 1903–.

 *Visit* • Pine Knot, vacation home for several summers. Now in disrepair. Off VA 20, turn right on first road past Christ Church. 1905

## SHADWELL *(Albemarle County)*

**Jefferson**
 *Birthplace* • Marker on VA 20. See also marker on immediate outskirts of Shadwell. South of marker is a representation of the house in which he was born. No such representation exists but going south and walking a few hundred feet to the right up a hill there is a stone marker at the actual site of the birthplace. 1743.

 *Visit* • Marker VA 20. Edgehill site. See Edgehill above.

 *Home* • House burned 1770. 1752–1770.

*Church* • St. Paul's Church where many of his relatives were baptized. No marker or remains. 1743–.

*Visit* • Pantops, adjacent to Shadwell. Later home of his daughter.

## SPOTSLYVANIA  *(Spotsylvania County)*

### Grant

*Work* • Battle site. In Spotsylvania at the T intersection turn on County Rd 613. May 1864.

## STAUNTON  *(Augusta County)*

### Presidents

*Visit* • Fillmore, Jefferson, and Madison said to have their names on the register of The Washington Tavern which was formerly on the site of the Virginia Hotel.

### Coolidge

*Church* • First Presbyterian Church, Coalter St. 12–2–1928.

### Eisenhower

*Visit* • Mary Baldwin College, Frederick St between New and Market St. 10–27–1960.

### Pierce

*Visit* • Virginia Hotel, S New St at railroad tracks. 8–16–1854. 1855.

### Roosevelt, FD

*Visit* • First Presbyterian Church. Dedicated restoration of Wilson birthplace. 5–4–1941.

### Wilson

*Birthplace* • The Manse, 24 N Coalter St. Father pastor at the First Presbyterian Church. Entrance fee. 1856.

*Baptism* • First Presbyterian Church Coalter St. Site is now the Administration Building of Mary Baldwin College at N New and E Frederick Sts. 1856.

*Site* • Museum. Corner Beverly and Coalter Sts.

## STEVENSBURG  *(Culpeper County)*

### Clinton

*Travel* • Followed Jefferson's route to inauguration. 1–17–1993.

### Jefferson

*Visit* • Zimmerman's Cross Keys Tavern (now Walker House). On the way to inauguration. November 1800.

## STRATFORD HALL

### Eisenhower

*Visit* • VA 3 south of Wakefield. Entrance fee. 5–4–1958.

## SUMMER HILL  *(Hanover County)*

### Grant

*Visit* • Here at various times occupying the house which still belongs to the Newton family. Visitors welcomed. One mile south of Hanover on US 301, turn east on County Rd 605 and go 7 miles. A sign points to Summer Hill. 1863–.

## TUCKAHOE

### Jefferson

*Home* • Tuckahoe Plantation off River Rd. West of W Richmond on VA 649 and River Rd. Entrance fee. 1745–1752.

*Education* • Small building on the grounds. Taught here by Reverend William Douglas. 1745–1752.

## VIRGINIA BEACH  *(Princess Anne County)*

### Bush

*Home* • Home here when he was reassigned to Norfolk. 1945.

### Harrison, B

*Visit* • Princess Anne Hotel, Sixteenth Street and Oceanfront. February 1892.

## WAKEFIELD (ALSO KNOWN AS POPE'S CREEK) *(Westmoreland County)*

**Coolidge**
*Visit* • 1924.

**Washington**
*Birthplace* • Original house burned. VA 3, north on VA 204. 1732–1745.

*Visit* • Blenheim on Pope Creek. See Westmoreland County.

## WARM SPRINGS *(Bath County)*

**Harrison, WH**
*Visit* • Warm Springs Inn at northern end of town. 1836.

**Monroe**
*Visit* • Warm Springs Inn at northern end of town. No longer standing. August 1815.

## WARRENTON *(Fauquier County)*

**Monroe**
*Visit* • Warren Green Hotel (just behind the Courthouse), built on site of old Norris Tavern where he stayed. 1825.

**Pierce**
*Visit* • Warren Green Hotel. 1856.

## WASHINGTON *(Rappahannock County)*

**Washington**
*Visit* • Town laid out by Washington. A building he visited still stands. 1749.

## WAYNESBORO *(Augusta County)*

**Presidents**
*Visit* • On the grounds on the site of the Old Mountain Top Tavern three ex-presidents joined with others to decide the location of the University of Virginia in 1818: Jefferson, Madison, and Monroe. Site I-64 at junction of Skyline Drive and Blue Ridge Pkwy next to Howard Johnson's to the right of service station. 1818.

**Coolidge**
*Visit* • Swannanoa Country Club, junction of the Blue Ridge Parkway and US 250. Stayed at the Swannanoa Palace. The Country Club is on hard surface road 1 mile past entrance to the Palace. 1929.

## WESTMORELAND COUNTY

**Harrison, W**
*Church* • Baptism, Westover Episcopal Church. No records. 1773.

**Monroe**

*Education* • Campbellton, home of Archibald (Alexander) Campbell, near Wirtland-Johnsville at the Washington Parish church. Now in King George County. 1769–1774.

*Home* • Monroe family lived in this area on Monroe's Creek within 1 1/2 miles of the Potomac River. Property under control of Westmoreland Historical Preservation Corporation. 1758–1780.

**Tyler**
*Church* • Baptism, Westover Episcopal Church. No record. 1790.

**Washington**
*Baptism* • Yeocomico Church, 8.1 miles NW of Callao on VA 3 near Hague. VA 3. Marker. 1732.

*Church* • Nominy Church, 3.7 miles east of Templemans Cross Roads on VA 3. Marker JT-2. 1745–.

*Home* • Blenheim. Family home. Used after Wakefield burned (on the same estate as Wakefield). Renovated and on National Register of Historic Places. 1780 to 1787.

*Visit* • The Glebe in the Northern Neck 4.4 miles east of Templemans Cross Road on VA 3. Marker JT-3. At the edge of the Glebe Country Club. Private. 1771.

*Visit* • Bushfield, home of one of his half-brothers, John. Near The Glebe. Marker JT-5. Private. 1732–.

## WILDERNESS BATTLEFIELD *(Orange and Spotsylvania Counties)*

**Grant**

*Work* • VA 20 and 20 miles east of Orange. Battle launched 5–4–1864. Campaign markers. Only pieces of the battlefield survive today. 1864.

## WILLIAMSBURG *(York County)*

**Presidents**

*Church* • Bruton Parish Church. At the corner of the Palace Green and the Duke of Gloucester St. Jefferson, Madison, Monroe, T Roosevelt, Tyler, and Washington. Jefferson sat near the pulpit in the half of the south gallery which was assigned to students of the college.

**Carter**

*Visit* • William and Mary College. Debate at the College Phi Beta Kappa Memorial Hall. 10–22–1976.

**Eisenhower**

*Visit* • House of Burgesses. Building has been reproduced in exact replica on the original foundation. 5–15–1953.

**Ford**

*Visit* • House of Burgesses. Building has been reproduced in exact replica on the original foundation. 1–31–1976.

*Visit* • William and Mary College. Debate at the College Phi Beta Kappa Memorial Hall. 10–22–1976.

**Jefferson**

*Education* • William and Mary College. Received his B.A. The Main Building was called the College. There was also the Bafferton. 1760–1762.

*Education* • George Wythe House. On the Palace Green leading to the Governor's Palace at the corner of Prince and George. Studied law with George Wythe. 1762–1767. Stayed with Wythe on the Palace Green with his wife. 1776.

*Home* • Governor's Palace North at the end of the Palace Green. 1779–1780.

*Lodging* • Edward Charlton. His two-story frame house stood almost directly across Duke of Gloucester St from the Raleigh Tavern. 1768–1800.

*Visit* • Raleigh Tavern. Duke of Gloucester St. Tavern burned in 1857 but recently restored. 1760–.

*Work* • House of Burgesses. Building has been reproduced in exact replica on the original foundation. Attended sessions. 1769–. The House of Burgesses convened in the Raleigh Tavern. Spring of 1775. Governor. 1779–1781.

*Work* • Member of the Virginia Legislature. Wren Building East end of Gloucester St at William and Mary College. Legislature convened here until Capitol was built. 1769–1774. 1776–1779.

**Johnson, LB**

*Visit* • Conference Center, 50 Kingsmill Rd. 10–8–1967.

**Madison**

*Education* • William and Mary College. 1774–1775. Dropped out in 1775 to participate in the Revolution. 1780. Reading law.

*Home* • President's Home, William and Mary College. Lived with his cousin who was president of the College. 1776–1779.

*Work* • House of Burgesses. Building has been reproduced in exact replica on the original foundation. Delegate to Virginia Convention. 1776–1777. Council of State. 1778–1779.

**Nixon**

*Visit* • Conference Center, 50 Kingsmill Rd. 3–11–1971.

**Reagan**

*Visit* • Williamsburg Lodge S England St. 10–18–1981.

*Visit* • Governor's Palace. North at the end of the Palace Green. Dinner with French president Mitterand. 10–19–1981.

*Visit* • Providence Hall. 5–27–1983 to 5–30–1983.

**Roosevelt, FD**

*Visit* • Wren Building. East end of Gloucester St at William and Mary College. 10–20–1934.

**Truman**

*Visit* • Wren Building. East end of Gloucester St at William and Mary College. 1948.

**Tyler**

*Education* • William and Mary College. 1802–1807.

*Lodging* • Bassett Hall. SE old town. Williamsburg off Francis near intersection with Waller St. Martha Washington's sister's home where Tyler was living when notified of Harrison's death. 1836–1841.

*Lodging* • Judge James Semple home. Francis St near the intersection with Waller St. Boarded with his brother-in-law, Judge Semple. 1802–. 1836–1838.

*Visit* • Raleigh Tavern. Duke of Gloucester St. Tavern burned in 1857 but was recently restored. Attended a banquet in his honor.

*Work* • Law office still standing. At the corner of Francis and South England Sts. 1836–1838.

**Washington**

*Education* • Wren Building. East end of Gloucester St at William and Mary College. Short surveyor course here. Received his surveyor's commission here. 1748.

*Work* • Wren Building. East end of Gloucester St at William and Mary College. Assembly convened in this building in the Great Hall until the Capitol was built.

*Visit* • George Wythe House. On the Palace Green leading to the Governor's Palace at the corner of Prince and George. Headquarters here before the siege of Yorktown. 1781. Also here 1772–.

*Visit* • Wetherburn's Tavern. 1770–1774.

*Visit* • Custis House. See site at the corner of Nassau and Francis St near western edge of old town. No markers. Martha's 6-chimney house where he courted her. 1758–1759. Honeymoon possibly spent here. 1759.

*Visit* • John Carter Store, next to Raleigh Tavern, Duke of Gloucester St. Not restored. 1758–1771.

*Visit* • Mrs. Campbell's Coffee House (Tavern) on Duke of Gloucester next to the Capitol. 1758–1771.

*Visit* • Raleigh Tavern. Duke of Gloucester St. Tavern burned in 1857 but was recently restored. 1758–1771.

*Work* • House of Burgesses. Building has been reproduced in exact replica on the original foundation. Attended sessions. 1758–1774.

# WINCHESTER *(Frederick County)*

**Hayes**

*Work* • Battle of Winchester or Kerntown. Visit to Old Taylor Hotel, 225 N Loudoun St. 7–23–1863.

**McKinley**

*Work* • Same as above.

**Washington**

*Church* • St. George's Episcopal Church, near Harewood. Ruins. 1748–1752.

*Lodging* • 204 S Loudoun St, while he built Fort Loudoun. 1755–1756.

*Work* • Surveyor's office, NE corner Cork and Braddock Sts. 1755–1756.

*Work* • Fort Loudoun. Site between Clark and Peyton Sts. Part of SW bastion is all that is left of the redoubt built in 1756–1757.

*Visit* • Red Lion Tavern, SE corner of Cork and Loudoun St. 1748–.

*Visit* • Lots owned by Washington, corner Fairfax Ln and Braddock. Marker.

*Visit* • Near Winchester is a spot known as Washington's Cave where meetings of the Mystic Tie (Masonic) were held. 1748–.

# WOODLAWN

**Washington**

*Visit* • Home of adopted daughter. 9000 Richmond Highway. Entrance fee. 1745–1799.

# YEOCOMICO (OLD) *(Westmoreland County)*

**Washington**

*Baptism* • Church near Wakefield. VA 3 SW of Tucker Hill on Rte 66. Located on NW side of the Yeocomico River. Marker JT 7. 1732. See also Westmoreland.

# YORKTOWN *(York County)*

**Hoover**

*Visit* • Yorktown Battlefield. 10–19–1931.

**Reagan**

*Visit* • Battlefield for bicentennial. 10–19–1981.

**Washington**

*Visit* • Moore House on VA 170 is where terms of surrender were arranged. 1781.

*Visit* • Shield House (Thomas Sessions House) on Nelson St across the road from the Nelson House. Private. 1781.

*Visit* • Swan Tavern (replica), corner of Main and Ballard. 1781.

*Site* • Yorktown Victory Center, Old VA 238 and The Colonial National Historical Park to see tent used by Washington.

*Travel* • Washington-Rochambeau route to Yorktown. Marker on VA 238.

*Visit* • Marker on site of old Courthouse and new Courthouse in colonial style on same site.

*Visit* • See Battlefield site on York River.

*Site* • Yorktown Victory Monument at corner of Main St and Zweybruken Rd.

# WASHINGTON

## FORT LEWIS *(Pierce County)*

**Eisenhower**

*Home* • House on the base. 1940–1941.

*Work* • Chief of Staff. Buildings were temporary and none remain. 1940–1941.

## FORT VANCOUVER *(Clark County)*

**Grant**

*Home* • 1106 E Evergreen Blvd. Now maintained as Ulysses S. Grant Museum. 1852–1853.

## OLYMPIA *(Thurston County)*

**Roosevelt, T**

*Visit* • Old State Capitol. 600 S Washington St. Old Thurston County Courthouse now called Old Capitol Bldg. May 1903.

## PASCO *(Franklin County)*

**Wilson**

*Visit* • September 1919.

## PLYMOUTH *(Benton County)*

**Eisenhower**

*Visit* • McNary Dam, US 82. Dedication. 9–23–1954.

## SEATTLE *(King County)*

**Presidents**

*Visit* • Four Seasons Olympic Hotel, 411 University St. Carter, Eisenhower, Ford, LB Johnson, and Truman.

*Church* • Seattle Opera House, Seattle Center near Elliott Bay. Site.

**Wilson**

*Church* • First Presbyterian Church, 7th and Spring Sts. 1919.

*Visit* • Arena, Mercer St at 3rd Ave N. 1919.

## SPOKANE *(Spokane County)*

**Carter**

*Visit* • Riverfront Park, NW of city limits. Spokane Convention Center, 334 W Spokane Falls Blvd. 5–5–1978.

## TACOMA *(Pierce County)*

**Roosevelt, T**

*Visit* • Tacoma Hotel. (Sheraton Tacoma). 1320 Broadway Pl. May 1903.

Washington

Seattle

Olympia

90

5

1

1. Ulysses S. Grant
   Museum, *Fort Vancouver*

# WEST VIRGINIA

## BECKLEY (FORMERLY RALEIGH)
*(Raleigh County)*

**Hayes**
*Work* • Headquarters. Mrs. Martha Davis House. Nothing remains. Winter 1862.

## BERKELEY SPRINGS *(Morgan County)*

**Madison**
*Marriage* • Harewood. Today the residence of Dr. and Mrs. John A. Washington. Off WV 51.

**Washington**
*Site* • Berkeley Springs State Park, 121 Washington St. Original Washington bath.

## BETHANY *(Brooke County)*

**Garfield**
*Visit* • Alexander Campbell Mansion, 3/4 mile east of Bethany on WV 331.

## CAMP REYNOLDS (FORMERLY CAMP HASKELL) *(Nicholas County)*

**Hayes**
*Home* • Here with family in a double log cabin. November 1862–1863.

## CAMP TOMPKINS *(Fayette County)*

**Hayes**
*Work* • On US 60 east of Gauley Bridge. Now site of Hawk's Nest Golf Club. Military headquarters. 1861–1862.

## CAMP WHITE *(Kanawha County)*

**Hayes**
*Work* • March 1863–1864.

## CAPON SPRINGS *(Hampshire County)*

**Pierce**
*Visit* • Hotel Mountain House. Hotel burned 1911. 1853, 1854.

## CARNIFEX FERRY *(Nicholas County)*

**Hayes**
*Work* • Battlefield State Park, WV 129, 5 miles off US 19. September 1861.

**McKinley**
*Work* • Had his first action here. Also took part in engagements at Clark's Hollow and Princeton, West Virginia. 1862.

**West Virginia**

79

Charleston

64

77

1. Harpers Ferry
2. McLure House,
   *Wheeling*

## CHARLESTON *(Kanawha County)*

**Carter**

*Travel* • Governor's mansion. 1716 Kanawha Blvd. 3–17–1977.

*Travel* • Charleston Civic Ctr, 200 Civic Center Dr. 5–27–1978.

**Jackson**

*Visit* • Hollygrove, 1710 Kanawha Blvd. Private. 1829.

**Kennedy**

*Visit* • Kanawha Hotel at the corner of Summers and Virginia Sts. 1960, 1963.

*Visit* • State Capitol. 6–20–1963.

**Lincoln**

*Site* • Statue. 1900 E Washington St.

**Roosevelt, T**

*Visit* • Old Capitol. Site only. 1900.

## CLIFFTOP *(Fayette County)*

**Presidents**

*Visit* • Old Stone House (Tyree Tavern), 2 miles south of junction US 60 and WV 41 near Clifftop. Hayes, Jackson, and McKinley.

## CONRAD STATION *(Lewis County)*

**McKinley**

*Work* • Served in Union forces near here. 1861.

## FAYETTEVILLE *(Fayette County)*

**Hayes**

*Work* • On WV 16. Headquarters. Winter 1861–1862.

## FLAT TOP MOUNTAIN *(Mercer County)*

**Hayes**

*Work* • Flat Top, off US 19. June 1862.

## FORT ASHBY *(Mineral County)*

**Washington**

*Work* • One of 69 forts built at the direction of Col. Washington and the only one restored. It is near the intersection of WV 28 and WV 46. 1752–1758.

## GAULEY BRIDGE *(Fayette County)*

**Hayes**

*Work* • Miller Tavern, Main St, northeast of railway crossing, was headquarters of Union Army officers. 1861.

*Work* • Service West Virginia. 1861–1865. South Mountain and Cedar Creek. 1865.

**McKinley**

*Work* • Headquarters Miller Tavern. See Hayes above. 1861.

## HARPERS FERRY *(Jefferson County)*

**Adams, JQ**

*Visit* • 1843.

**Carter**

*Visit* • 7–6–1978.

**Jefferson**

*Visit* • See Jefferson's Rock, a scenic overlook that he described in 1783 as "stupendous" and "worth a trip across the Atlantic to view." October 1784.

**Wilson**

*Visit* • Bolivar. Hilltop House, Ridge Rd, was once his retreat.

## PARKERSBURG *(Wood County)*

**Hayes**

*Work* • Swan House Hotel. Demolished. 7–12–1863.

## PRINCETON *(Mercer County)*

**Hayes**

*Work* • Battle area, WV 10. 5–1–1862.

## ROMNEY *(Hampshire County)*

### Lincoln

*Site* • Nancy Hanks's birthplace. She was born on the eastern slope of Saddle Mountain. Site is accessible from US 50 on County Rd 6/2 near Antioch, west of Romney. A stonemarker shows the cabin's location and a replica is nearby.

## SWEET SPRINGS *(Monroe County)*

### Presidents

*Visit* • On WV 311. Hotels of the era destroyed. WH Harrison, Monroe, Pierce, and Tyler.

## UNION *(Monroe County)*

### Van Buren

*Visit* • Salt Sulphur Springs, south off US 219. Private. 1837.

## WESTON *(Lewis County)*

### Hayes

*Work* • US 19. Stationed here. July–August 1861.

## WHEELING *(Ohio County)*

### Presidents

*Visit* • McLure House, 1200 Market St. First opened 1852. Arthur, Eisenhower, Garfield, Grant, B Harrison, Kennedy, McKinley, Nixon, T Roosevelt, Taft, and Truman.

## WHITE SULPHUR SPRINGS

*(Greenbrier County)*

### Presidents

*Visit* • Cottage on the grounds of the world-famous Greenbrier Resort. The two-story colonnaded cottage has been turned into a museum. It was summer White House for Van Buren, Tyler, and Fillmore. The White Sulphur Springs Hotel was famous as Old White but was torn down in 1913 to make way for the Green Brier Hotel.

*Visit* • Old White. Buchanan, Fillmore, WH Harrison, Monroe, Pierce, Tyler, and Van Buren.

*Visit* • Green Brier. Coolidge, Eisenhower, Ford, Kennedy, Nixon, and Wilson.

### Eisenhower

*Visit* • Ashford General Hospital. 1944.

### Tyler

*Honeymoon* • President's Cottage. 1844.

# WISCONSIN

## BAD AXE *(Vernon County)*

**Taylor**
*Travel* • Battle of Bad Axe. 1832.

## BOSCOBEL *(Grant County)*

**Kennedy**
*Visit* • Hotel Boscobel (birthplace of Gideon Bible). Room 19. 1960.

## BRULE *(Douglas County)*

**Coolidge**
*Church* • Congregational Church about 0.2 mile from Brule on County Rd H. 1928.

*Visit* • Vacation at Cedar Island Lodge on Bois Brule River off US 2 west of Iron River. 1928.

**Eisenhower**
*Visit* • Bois Brule River off US 2. September 1947.

**Hoover**
*Visit* • Visit with Coolidge. See above.

## FORT CRAWFORD *(Crawford County)*

Crawford Medical Museum (Prairie du Chien), 717 S Beaumont Rd.

**Taylor**
*Travel* • Built fort and was stationed here off and on. 1821–1837.

## FORT HOWARD *(Outagamie County)*

**Taylor**
*Travel* • See historical museum, 407 Merchants Ave. 1816–1818.

## GREEN BAY *(Brown County)*

**Ford**
*Travel* • Green Bay Packers Hall of Fame Building. Also Brown County Veterans Memorial Arena. Both located 1901 S Oneida St. 4–3–1976.

## JANESVILLE *(Rock County)*

**Lincoln**
*Visit* • Tallman Mansion, 440 N Jackson St. 1859.

**Wisconsin**

90

Madison

17

94

Milwaukee

1

1. Fort Crawford,
   *Crawford County*

## LaCrosse  (LaCrosse County)

**Taft**

*Visit* • YMCA building dedication. 1909.

## Madison  (Dane County)

**Presidents**

*Visit* • Arthur, Bush, Carter, Cleveland, Coolidge, Ford, Garfield, Grant, Hayes, Hoover, Kennedy, McKinley, Nixon, Reagan, T Roosevelt, Taft, Truman, and Wilson.

**Cleveland**

*Visit* • Vilas home, 521 N Henry St. September 1887.

**McKinley**

*Visit* • Old State Capitol. 1899.

**Roosevelt, T**

*Visit* • LaFollette home, 314 S Broom St. 1893.

*Visit* • State Capitol. 1903. 1911.

**Taft**

*Visit* • Executive Mansion, 130 E Gilman St. 1917.

*Visit* • 1908. 1915. 1916. 1918.

## Milwaukee  (Milwaukee County)

**Ford**

*Visit* • Pfister Hotel, 424 E Wisconsin Ave, room 621. 8–25–1975.

**McKinley**

*Visit* • Pfister Hotel. September 1899.

**Roosevelt, T**

*Visit* • Hotel Gilpatrick. He was shot by a would-be assassin. Hotel demolished. 1912.

*Visit* • Plankinton House. SE corner of Second and Wisconsin. Leveled in 1915 to make way for the present Plankinton Arcade. 4–2–1903.

**Taft**

*Visit* • Northwest Depot, 433 West St. Paul Ave. 9–24–1909.

## Portage  (Columbia County)

**Taylor**

*Travel* • Site of Fort Winnebago. Only the Surgeon's Quarters remains. East on SR 33 at the Fox River. 1833–1835.

## Prairie du Chien  (Crawford County)

**Taylor**

*Home* • Had a house for his family just outside Fort Crawford. 1832–1839. See Fort Crawford above.

## Superior  (Douglas County)

**Coolidge**

*Lodging* • Summer White House in Superior Central High School, 1015 Belknap St. 1928.

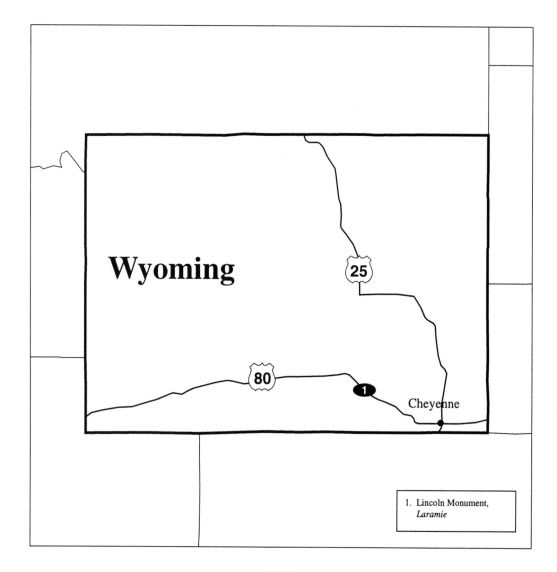

**Wyoming**

25

80

1

Cheyenne

| 1. Lincoln Monument, |
| *Laramie* |

# Wyoming

## CHEYENNE *(Laramie County)*

**Bush**

> *Visit* • State Capitol. Capitol Ave between Carey and Twenty-fourth and Twenty-fifth Sts. Afterwards went to fish on Middle Crow Creek. 1989.

**Nixon**

> *Visit* • State Capitol. June 1956.

**Roosevelt, FD**

> *Visit* • Fort Francis. E. Warren, entrance at end of Randall Ave. St. Mark's Episcopal Church, 1908 Central Ave. 10–11–1936.

**Roosevelt, T**

> *Church* • First Methodist Church, Eighteenth and Central Ave. 1903.

> *Church* • First Congregational Church, 3501 Forest Dr. 1910.

> *Visit* • State Capitol. May 1903.

> *Visit* • Frontier Days Celebration in front of Capitol. 1910.

**Truman**

> *Visit* • Governor's Mansion. 6–6–1948.

## FORT WASHAKIE *(Fremont County)*

**Arthur**

> *Travel* • On US 287. He entered Montana territory at Cinnabar riding a horse. The first president to visit while in office. August 1883.

## FORT YELLOWSTONE *(See Yellowstone below)*

## GRAND TETON NATIONAL PARK JACKSON LAKE

**Carter**

> *Visit* • Brinkerhoff Lodge, Park Dr and US 287. 8–24–1978 to 8–31–1978.

**Nixon**

> *Visit* • 8–19–1971.

## LARAMIE *(Albany County)*

**Lincoln**

> *Site* • Lincoln Monument on US 30, 10 miles SW of Laramie on the Lincoln Highway. World's largest bronze head.

## YELLOWSTONE *(NW corner of Wyoming)*

**Arthur**

*Visit* • Wind River Valley. Stayed Mammoth Hot Springs Hotel, US 89. August 1883.

**Carter**

*Visit* • Hebgen Lake. 1981.

**Coolidge**

*Visit* • June-September 1929.

**Ford**

*Work* • Ranger. Summer 1936.

*Travel* • Old Faithful Lodge, between West Thumb and Madison junctions. 8–29–1976.

**Harding**

*Honeymoon* • 1921.

**Roosevelt, FD**

*Visit* • Mammoth Hot Springs, US 89, W. M. Nichols cottage. 9–24-1937 to 9–26–1937.

**Roosevelt, T**

*Visit* • Campsites near mouth of Blacktail Creek, Cottonwood Creek, Calcite Springs Overlook. April 1903. Mammoth Hot Springs Hotel. Laid cornerstone of Roosevelt Arch at Wyoming/Montana boundary. 4–11–1903.

**Taft**

*Visit* • Old Faithful Inn. See location under Ford. 1907.

# PICTURE CREDITS

Photographs and ilustrations appearing in Landmark of American Presidents were received from the following sources:

**AP/Worldwide:** pp. 27, 44, 78, 143, 255, 395, 406, 418, 421, 459, 508, 555, 577, 657; **Bettman Archive:** pp. 86, 252, 298. **Courtesy of Maeola and Dean Brown:** p. 377; **Courtesy of Peggy Daniels:** 431; **Courtesy of Jeff Dewey:** p. 735; **Kathy Edgar:** p. 680; **Susan Edgar:** p. 731; **Courtesy of John F. Kennedy Library:** p. 353; **Courtesy of Library of Congress:** p. 3, 23, 52, 62, 74, 94, 103, 110, 118, 127, 135, 151, 168, 178, 194, 203, 212, 222, 232, 240, 249, 262, 273, 286, 296, 306, 315, 317, 326, 338, 365, 375, 387; **Courtesy of Kathy Marcaccio:** pp. 8, 154, 158, 165, 181, 264, 344, 361, 495, 523, 675, 684, 689, 696, 709, 711, 713, 726; **Courtesy of Terry Peck:** p. 89; Carl Wheeless: pp. 6, 12, 38, 39, 42, 44, 47, 50, 51, 55, 56, 61, 67, 72, 84, 86, 89, 93, 97, 102, 105, 106, 107, 114, 121, 125, 133, 138, 141, 145, 149, 166, 170, 173, 180, 183, 184, 185, 197, 198, 202, 205, 207, 210, 215, 220, 224, 226, 231, 235, 238, 241, 247, 254, 257, 272, 275, 281, 288, 290, 295, 299, 305, 308, 325, 337, 340, 351, 356, 358, 368, 369, 374, 380, 386, 389, 390, 396, 398, 399, 409, 410, 419, 422, 433, 450, 493, 494, 501, 509, 515, 541, 542, 543, 547, 548, 549, 563, 569, 625, 626, 627, 645, 647, 649, 654, 673, 674, 683, 694, 695, 702, 711, 728, 746, 757, 761, 764, 767, 770, 773, 779; **Courtesy of the White House:** p. 429. **Courtesy of the White House Collection:** p. 34; **UPI/Bettmann News photos:** pp. 363, 400.

# INDEX